The
POLITICS
of
AMERICAN
GOVERNMENT

COMPLETE EDITION

The
POLITICS
of
AMERICAN
GOVERNMENT

Foundations, Participation, Institutions, and Policy

COMPLETE EDITION

Stephen J. Wayne
Georgetown University

G. Calvin Mackenzie
Colby College

David M. O'Brien
University of Virginia

Richard L. Cole
University of Texas at Arlington

St. Martin's Press, New York

Executive editor: Don Reisman

Development: St. Martin's staff

Project editor: Douglas Bell

Production supervisor: Alan Fischer

Text design: Robin Hessel Hoffmann

Graphics: Precision Graphics

Photo research: Ibid. Editorial, Inc.; Corbett Gordon Associates

Cover and interior display photography: Preston Lyon

Library of Congress Catalog Card Number: 92-62741

Manufactured in the United States of America.

9 8 7 6 5
f e d c b a

For information, write:
St. Martin's Press, Inc.
175 Fifth Avenue
New York, NY 10010

ISBN: 0-312-06751-8

Dedication

These pages bear the fruits of our country's proud
political tradition. Enjoy them. Improve them. Live them.
And give them to your children.

To
Jonathan C. Cole
Mary Ashley Cole
Andrew C. Mackenzie
Peter W. Mackenzie
Rebecca M. Knight
Benjamin M. O'Brien
Sara A. O'Brien
Talia M. O'Brien
Jared B. Wayne
Jeremy B. Wayne

Brief

Contents

List of Features

Table of Contents

Preface

As our title indicates, this is a book about politics. We chose to emphasize politics because we believe it is the lifeblood of government—its dynamic, living quality. We view politics as the process or struggle among people to better themselves, to pursue their own interests within society. That pursuit, of course, cannot go completely unrestrained. It is the job of government to condition and constrain political activities. It is the responsibility of government to try to resolve the issues that underlie and energize people in their pursuit of economic, social, and personal goals. Thus politics and government are closely and inevitably interrelated. This book is the story about that interrelationship: how politics influences government—and how government influences politics.

In placing the focus of the book on the drama of American political life, we do not argue that politics is good or bad, but rather that it is an important—necessary—means for the expression of needs and desires, both of individuals and of groups. In emphasizing politics, we have tried to maintain a perspective that is realistic but not cynical. We hope that our description of how politics affects people in their daily lives will lead students to see that they should become politically active, for their own sakes as well as for the sake of their country.

One objective of our book is to address legitimate concerns that all of us have as citizens: to live in a peaceful society, to be secure in our homes and communities, to enjoy the blessings of liberty and the protection of our basic rights, to have a secure economic future, and, above all, to be able to shape our own destinies by influencing the decisions and actions of government. Another goal is to make the study of politics and government lively and accessible to everyone, particularly to those who may not see what difference the political system makes to them. The decisions of government have a direct or indirect impact on all of us, whether or not we choose to participate in the process which affects those decisions.

In making its decisions and in determining public policy, government may not have an answer to all or even most of the problems of society, but it still has an important role to play in determining whether conditions get better or worse. The way government handles conflicts among contending groups will help determine whether discord in society will be exacerbated or ameliorated.

For this reason, we take a careful look at the outputs of government—its authoritative decisions and actions and their consequences for society. Who gains, and who loses? Are the same people benefited or disadvantaged most of the time? The anwers to these questions affect the equity of the system, its capacity to be fair and just to everyone. Equity is a critical issue for a democratic political system, for a system that is based on political equality.

Our interest in equity also applies in our examination of the input to government, input that different political actors have through elections and their access to policy makers. That input is not equal. Some groups seem to exercise more influence than others by virtue of their reputations, resources, and leadership capabilities. Identifying such influential groups, understanding their sources of power, and evaluating their motivations and strategies for affecting public policy will enable us to determine how fairly and responsively the democratic process is working in the United States. Our interest in equity includes those who have long played a major role in the American political process as well as those who are approaching the system from the perspective and experience of outsiders.

Although the pursuit of economic interests within the political process is an important subject, we must be just as concerned with identifying the ideas and ideals that individuals and groups bring to the rough-and-tumble of politics. Economic, social, and political beliefs, ideas, and interests often intertwine and reinforce each other. Conflict within the political system often centers on whose moral and social values should prevail in society at large. We see this with issues concerning the environment or health care, where disagreement involves ethical and moral judgments, as well as, possibly, the profits and losses of the participants. Thus, we need to examine the impact that ideas, ideology, traditions, and values have on the politics of American government.

In short, we examine the broad range of interests that underlie the activities of those who participate in the American political process. We discuss outsiders and insiders, average citizens and political leaders. We examine their activities as they try to influence government officials and affect policy decisions. We examine those decisions in terms of their impact on contemporary society as well as on the continuing saga of American politics.

Pedagogy

To bring its subject into sharp focus, each chapter begins with an engaging, real-life story about politics. Throughout the text, other general-interest boxes reinforce our politics theme. Four other kinds of boxes appear in most chapters:

- *Becoming Political* boxes provide students with resources and data they can use to get information about federal, state, and local government and become more involved in issues that are important in their lives.
- *People in Politics* essays provide brief biographies of people who have made a difference in American political life—people who span the political spectrum from Ruth Bader Ginsburg to Colin Powell, from Ralph Nader to John Dingell, from LaDonna Harris to Anne Richards.
- *Constitutional Conflict* essays examine the core constitutional issues that are involved in contemporary debates in American government.

■ *Case Studies* analyze current issues, pose questions for discussion, and highlight our focus on the drama of politics.

The Ancillary Package

We are proud to have assembled a complete and purposeful ancillary program. Each piece in our program is designed to make teaching more effective and to heighten students' interest in American government and, particularly, their American government course.

The largest work in our program is the *Instructor's Resource Manual*. This looseleaf binder contains a *Teacher's Guide*, written by an experienced teacher and text publisher, Herbert M. Levine. For each chapter of our book, the guide includes an outline and overview, learning objectives, key terms and concepts, recommended assignments, and discussion exercises. Following the *Teacher's Guide* are *Lecture Outlines and Lectures*, written by Paul Benson of Tarrant County Junior College. The outlines list topics that follow the major headings of each chapter of the textbook; they also suggest a range of supplementary topics and issues that relate to, but do not repeat, material in the text. The lectures provide topical narratives of two to three pages that can be expanded into 50-minute lectures. These outlines and lectures are also available on floppy disks, for both IBM-compatible and Macintosh computers. The disks let instructors rearrange, delete, add, and print material at will.

The *Instructor's Resource Manual* also includes a section called *Documents*. These primary sources include excerpts from *The Federalist*, Supreme Court cases, and political speeches. The documents can be copied and given to students either for homework assignments or for advance preparation for classroom discussion. In addition, the Manual offers a *Student Survey of Political Attitudes*, which has been adapted for use in introductory American government classes by Clyde Wilcox of Georgetown University and Elizabeth Adell Cook of American University. The survey can be used at the beginning of the course or in conjunction with Chapter 7, Public Opinion. The survey results allow students to explore the relationship between their political identification and their perspectives on contemporary issues. Students can compare their political attitudes with the attitudes of classmates or of various national samples. Survey responses can be tabulated and analyzed with or without a computer— we provide complete instructions for both methods.

Available as a separate bound book is a *Test Item File*, which contains over 1,200 multiple-choice, fill-in, essay, and true-false questions. In addition, we offer, free to adopters, a *State and Local Government Supplement*, authored by Richard L. Cole, and a set of over fifty color transparencies, which are enlarged versions of illustrations included in the text.

A unique print ancillary for our book is *Ralph Nader Presents, Practicing Democracy: A Guide to Student Action*. This resource, authored by Katherine Isaac of the Center for the Study of Responsive Law, provides students with the basic tools for citizen participation, detailing the ways in which students can lobby, use the initiative and referendum processes, boycott, and educate the public to produce change. The supplement gives students a history of how citizens have used such techniques to advance their causes. Introductory essays by Paul Wellstone and Richard Bond provide personal accounts of two individuals who left private life to become active participants in the political system, one as a Democratic senator from Minnesota, the other as a campaign manager for George Bush and later as chair of the Republican National Committee.

Our software ancillaries include the aforementioned lecture outlines and lectures on disk, which is titled *Teaching The Politics of American Government: Outlines and Lectures on Disk*. Our *Computerized Test Item File* contains over 1,200 questions in a format that allows full randomization and authoring capabilities, as well as the selection of test questions according to low, moderate, or high difficulty. A useful adjunct to this testing software is *Micrograde*, a program for record keeping and tracking student grades. Adopters of our book may also send for *Presidential Campaign*, by David Garson of North Carolina State University. This software program allows a student to run a simulated presidential campaign from April to November, as a challenger or an incumbent, and as a Republican, a Democrat, or an Independent.

Additionally, we offer four videos that St. Martin's Press has developed for use in college classrooms. These include four separate works: "Women and Politics," "Interest Groups in America," "Presidential Leadership," and "The Selection and Confirmation of Supreme Court Justices." Each video runs for approximately 25 minutes and can be used in a single class section, with time for instructors to include their own prefatory and concluding remarks—and to stop the tape for comment. An accompanying *Video Guide* includes, for each video, a summary of the text, a copy of the narrator's script, test and discussion questions, and a list of supplemental classroom activities.

Finally, a *Study Guide* is available for sale to students. This includes introductory essays about how to study and how to do a research paper on American government. Each chapter includes an interactive review section (chapter overview, learning objectives, outline, and matching exercises for key terms); practice tests (multiple-choice, true-false, and essay questions); and an in-depth assignment.

For information about these ancillaries—and about special packages and discounts for those who want to use *The Politics of American Government* with other readers and topical books published by St. Martin's Press—please contact your local St. Martin's sales representative, or call or write to St. Martin's Press, College Desk, 175 Fifth Avenue, New York, NY 10010 (phone: 1-800-221-7945).

Acknowledgments

We wish to acknowledge and thank some of the many people who contributed to this book. Bert Lummus conceived of the text, initially contracted for it, and encouraged us with good humor, patience, and support. We are most appreciative, Bert, of your continuing faith in us and the project.

Don Reisman, Executive Editor, has orchestrated the project at St. Martin's from beginning to end. He has done so with skill and imagination, never losing sight of our basic objective and his—to excite and educate students about American politics, to show them how they can make a difference. A big, big job—well done, Don.

Caroline Smith, the first developmental editor at St. Martin's to tackle our prose and organization, was truly a remarkable "wordsmith." We greatly appreciate her efforts as well as her continuing interest in the project even after she changed jobs. Cheryl Kupper, who became the principal developmental editor for the project, converted our manuscript into the form you are about to read. Cheryl, a true professional, improved the book on almost every page. We are indebted to her for her skill, dedication, and hard work. Doug Bell completed the editorial phase of this project, met the elusive deadlines, and made improvements and updates throughout. We particularly thank Doug for his consideration of our wishes and his tremendous efforts to bring the project to its conclusion.

Thanks also to Joanne Daniels, Barbara Heinssen, Rochelle Diogenes, Bob Weber, Frances Jones, Mary Hugh Lester, Kenny Nassau, Janice Wiggins, and others at St. Martin's Press who have contributed so much to the editing, production, and marketing of this book.

We would also like to acknowledge the friendship, generosity, and contributions of one of the author's closest friends, who allowed us to photograph his fabulous collection of political buttons and trinkets and provided the commentary for the description that accompanies them. We are grateful that he was willing to share his collection with us and our readers.

We want to thank our assistants who helped us with research and graphics: Lisa Prenaveau Andrzejewski, Geertruida C. Degoede, Mark Drozdowski, Caroline Jesky, Cathy Naff, Janet Newcity, Eric Pages, Fengyan Shi, and Molly Sonner.

We cannot close without saying how much we have appreciated the sacrifices and adjustments our families have made as we worked on this book. Our children especially have patiently endured our weekend writing. We have dedicated this book to them, not only because of their patience but also because they (and their peers who will read this book) embody the hopes and hold the keys to the strength, endurance, and vitality of our political system.

Finally, we thank the many faculty members who answered questionnaires and submitted reviews to St. Martin's Press, as well as those who helped the authors with their individual chapters at their respective universities:

Alan I. Abramowitz, Emory University
Douglas J. Amy, Mount Holyoke College
Donald G. Balmer, Lewis and Clark College
Ryan J. Barilleaux, Miami University
Leroy W. Beattie, Gillette Community College
William Borges, Southwest State University
John M. Bowen, Sr., Towson State University
James Brent, Ohio State University
Gary Bryner, Brigham Young University
Barbara C. Burrell, University of Wisconsin, Madison
David T. Canon, University of Wisconsin, Madison
Christopher P. Carney, University of Wyoming
Michael X. Delli Carpini, Barnard College
Allan J. Cigler, University of Kansas
Kristina K. Cline, Riverside Community College
Clarke E. Cochran, Texas Tech University
Ann H. Cohen, Illinois State University
Phillip J. Cooper, University of Kansas

W. Douglas Costain, University of Colorado, Boulder
Ann N. Crigler, University of Southern California
Paige Cubbison, Miami Dade Community College
Burnet V. Davis, Alma College
Dorothy Dodge, Macalester College
William Merrill Downer, Thiel College
Diana Dwyre, Syracuse University
Patrick L. Eagan, John Carroll University
Stephen Frank, St. Cloud State University
James M. Gerhardt, Southern Methodist University
Paul A. Gough, Northern State University
John C. Green, University of Akron
Kenneth P. Hayes, University of Maine, Orono
James F. Herndon, Virginia Polytechnic Institute/State University
Samuel B. Hoff, Delaware State College
Paul Stephen Hudson, Oglethorpe University
Charles Scott Keeter, Virginia Commonwealth University
Barbara Kellerman, Fairleigh Dickinson University
Matthew R. Kerbel, Villanova University
Robert W. Langran, Villanova University
James F. Lea, University of Southern Mississippi
Tracy L. R. Lightorp, LaGrange College
Charles Longley, Bucknell University
Joseph Losco, Ball State University
Joseph Marbach, Temple University
James R. McKee, Christian Brothers University
Lauri McNown, University of Colorado, Boulder
Lorraine Murray, Oakton Community College
Charles Noble, California State University, Long Beach
Diana M. Owen, Georgetown University
B. Guy Peters, University of Pittsburgh
James P. Pfiffner, George Mason University
Raymond Pomerleau, San Francisco State University
John R. Pottenger, University of Alabama, Huntsville
Charles Prysby, University of North Carolina, Greensboro
James W. Riddlesperger, Jr., Texas Christian University
David Robinson, University of Houston, Downtown
Michael J. Robinson, Georgetown University
David H. Rosenbloom, American University
Mark Rothman, CW Post Campus of Long Island University
Diane Ellen Schmidt, Southern Illinois University, Carbondale
Joseph F. Schuster, Eastern Washington University
Bradbury Seasholes, Tufts University
Jeffrey L. Sedgwick, University of Massachusetts, Amherst
James R. Simmons, University of Wisconsin, Oshkosh
Steven S. Smith, University of Minnesota, Twin Cities Campus
Allan Spitz, University of Alabama, Huntsville
Harold W. Stanley, University of Rochester
Willard Brewer Stouffer, Jr., Southwest Texas State University
C. Neal Tate, University of North Texas
Edward Thompson, California State University, San Marcos

Joseph K. Unekis, Kansas State University
Lois T. Vietri, University of Maryland, College Park
Walter E. Volkomer, Hunter College
Thomas G. Walker, Emory University
Shirley A. Warshaw, Gettysburg College
David R. Weaver, Saginaw Valley State University
Clyde Wilcox, Georgetown University
Raymond B. Wrabley, University of Pittsburgh, Johnstown

Stephen J. Wayne
G. Calvin Mackenzie
David M. O'Brien
Richard L. Cole

About the Authors

STEPHEN J. WAYNE (Ph.D., Columbia University) is a professor and the head of the American government section at Georgetown University. Besides being a veteran instructor of American government, he has been a Washington insider specializing in presidential politics for over twenty-five years. He has authored numerous articles and published several books about the presidency, including *The Road to the White House* and *Presidential Leadership* (with George C. Edwards III). Invited frequently to testify before Congress and to lecture to senior federal executives, Wayne also has shaped public opinion about the presidency and electoral politics as a commentator for radio, television, and newspapers.

G. CALVIN MACKENZIE (Ph.D., Harvard University) is the Distinguished Presidential Professor of American Government and chair of the government department at Colby College. With expertise in presidential appointments, Congress, and public policy, Mackenzie is among the foremost American scholars and commentators on the staffing of national administrations. He is a former congressional staff member and has worked in or advised executive-branch agencies, including the departments of Defense and Treasury. *The Politics of Presidential Appointments* and *The House at Work* are among his many books; he also has contributed to a wide range of academic and popular journals and is interviewed often on television and radio.

DAVID M. O'BRIEN (Ph.D., University of California, Santa Barbara) is a professor in the Woodrow Wilson Department of Government and Foreign Affairs at the University of Virginia, where he also helps edit the series "Constitutionalism and Democracy" for the university press. A former Judicial Fellow at the Supreme Court and Fulbright Scholar in Great Britain and Japan, O'Brien is one of the most prominent political scientists studying the Supreme Court. His several books about the judiciary include *Storm Center: The Supreme Court in American Politics*, which in 1987 received the American Bar Association's Silver Gavel Award. O'Brien writes frequently for major newspapers and contributes often to the op-ed page of the *Los Angeles Times*.

RICHARD L. COLE (Ph.D., Purdue University) is dean of the School of Urban and Public Affairs at the University of Texas, Arlington, where he is also a professor specializing in political science methodology, urban politics, and public policy. He is a former president of the Southwest Political Science Association and former president of the North Texas chapter of the American Society for Public Administration. In addition to dozens of monographs, journal articles, and book reviews, Cole's recent books include *Texas Politics and Public Policy* and *An Introduction to Political Inquiry*. He will soon publish a new book about political science methodology with St. Martin's Press.

The
POLITICS
of
AMERICAN
GOVERNMENT

The American Political Environment

- Three concepts: *politics*, *government*, and *public policy*

- Politics and power: personal freedom and social welfare; concentrated power and distributed power; majority rule and minority rights; individual liberty and the common good; authority and the rule of law; beneficiaries of government action

- The American political culture: the "American ethos"; subcultures and diversity; consensus, conflict, and apathy

The 1992 presidential election became a three-way battle among 1988 victors Bush-Quayle, third-party candidates Perot-Stockdale (see page 278), and ultimate winners Bill Clinton and Al Gore. The political items pictured at left are a small sample of the more than one thousand buttons produced for the 1992 campaign. These highlight labor's traditional support of the Democratic party *(top left)*, Clinton's avocation as a saxophone player *(top right)*, and the Republican party's elephant symbol *(top middle)*. Also see page 238, which shows 1908 Republican winners Taft-Sherman on one of the most famous political items, "Elephant Ears." The phrase *Mother of* to denote great size is highlighted on the Republican button at bottom right.

Here's the problem Bill Clinton faced when he entered office. Millions of Americans lacked adequate health care. Millions of others feared that their health insurance would not cover a catastrophic illness. With medical costs exploding, most Americans believed that the health-care system needed repair. Ironically a majority was also satisfied with the quality of the health care they were receiving.[1]

The delivery and cost of health care is one of the most complicated and contentious issues to perplex contemporary policy makers. During his presidential campaign, Bill Clinton promised to extend health-care coverage to all Americans. From the moment he began to formulate a proposal to reform the system and control costs, however, he faced a chorus of dissenting voices and a furious debate among conflicting interests over how the problem should be resolved.

Is health care a right or a privilege? If it is a right, then everyone should be covered regardless of ability to pay. Yet millions of Americans had no coverage, or inadequate coverage, because they could not afford it or could not obtain it, or did not choose to buy it. Who should pay for their care—providers, other consumers, employers, or unions?

Should the employed be required to buy it? And what about the unemployed?

Even for those with health insurance, medical costs have been spiraling at the rate of 10 percent per year. Americans now spend about $900 billion a year on health care. If unchecked, these expenditures would exceed $1 trillion by the year 2000.

What should the government do? Interest groups representing people of all ages, health-care professionals, and health-care insurers, lawyers, and manufacturers have hurriedly supplied sophisticated studies in hopes of influencing the public debate. Washington lobbyists, working for groups with a stake in the outcome, have had a field day organizing grass-roots efforts to influence policy. Professional associations in the health-care industry also contributed large sums to candidates running for office in 1992, and they have continued to contribute long after the election was over.[2]

Nor did the Clinton administration sit on the sidelines. Hillary Rodham Clinton was given the job of organizing a task force, assisted by over five hundred experts, to develop a new health-care plan. The task force heard from over six hundred different interests and received written testimony from many more. Even the courts got involved. When some objected to the task force holding closed hearings and private meetings, the court required it to work in full public view.

Once the president sent his proposal to Congress, the lobbying shifted to the committee rooms and legislative chambers of Capitol Hill. Pressure from groups that would be affected by the legislation became so intense that President Clinton referred to it in his State of the Union Address on January 25, 1994: "For sixty years this country has tried to reform health care. President Roosevelt tried, President Truman tried, President Nixon tried, President Carter tried. Every time, the special interests were powerful enough to defeat them. But not this time."

Following the president's address, the administration mounted its own massive public relations effort. A special team directed by Deputy Chief of Staff Harold Ickes responded to media requests for information. The president, the vice president, Mrs. Clinton, and members of the Cabinet barnstormed the country. Special White House representatives were assigned to influence health industry groups, businesses, labor unions, and others.[3]

Positions in Congress began to solidify. Most Republicans opposed programs that raised taxes, burdened small businesses, limited individual choice, or jeopardized the private practice of medicine, while most Democrats urged universal extended coverage, cost containment, and caps on payments to those whom the new system would benefit most. Congress struggled throughout 1994 to resolve these issues.

Nor would the fight end in Congress. How health care would be administered by the Department of Health and Human Services, what regulations the agency would issue, and how those regulations were to be enforced also would be subject to public argument and outside pressures. Litigation would also undoubtedly result, as aggrieved parties seek to acquire by judicial judgment what they cannot obtain by legislation or administrative decision.

The contentious issue of health care illustrates the politics of American government: who participates, how influence is exerted, and what impact that influence has on public policy. Such controversies reveal how politics affects government, how government makes policy, and how that policy affects society and sets up new political activity.

DISAGREEMENT IS NORMAL. In a nation of a quarter of a billion people, many with different ethnic, religious, and racial identities, spread across thousands of miles of varied terrain, involved in tens of thousands of competing economic enterprises, disagreement is inevitable.

Some Americans believe that government should keep its hands off the economy; others believe that it should actively shape and regulate economic life. Some Americans think that government's first priority should be a strong national defense; others think that a decent standard of living for everyone should come first. Some argue that abortion is a private matter beyond the proper reach of government; others argue that government should prohibit abortion on the same grounds that it prohibits people from killing each other.

In every dimension and on every plane of American life, disagreement abounds. It is a way of life. If we had no place to resolve our differences, they would tear the country apart. But we do have such a place. In *government* we have a set of institutions and procedures through which we may express and seek to resolve our disagreements.

Although we disagree about many things, government is possible because we do not disagree about all things—about the need for government, for example. On other fundamental principles and values, and even on some important matters of public policy, there is also broad consensus. That consensus has allowed us to create institutions, laws, and procedures that most Americans regard as proper and legitimate. None of us agrees with all the decisions Congress makes, but most of us agree that a representative legislature like Congress is the proper place for those decisions to be made. Consensus, then, allows us to resolve our disagreements, and it provides the basis for governing.

Yet in spite of this consensus, differences of opinion persist over what government should do, how it should do it, and for whose benefit (and at whose cost) it should be done. These disagreements about what we believe and where

Reuters/Bettmann

© Bob Daemmrich/Stock, Boston

For most hot-button issues, both opposition and support are very well organized. (Left) *Hillary Rodham Clinton spoke to a wary audience at the 1993 AMA convention about spiraling health-care costs.* (Right) *A rally against gun control legislation takes place outside the Texas state capitol in Austin. The gun lobby had succeeded in blocking significant gun controls at the federal level until passage of the Brady bill in 1993.*

our interests lie are what fuel politics. *Politics* is the means by which we pursue our various and often conflicting needs. *Politics* also provides the basis on which government takes action. In other words, **politics** embodies the substance *and* the form of conflict and consensus.

The goal of most political confrontation is power. To gain the power we need to assert our preferences over, or to protect ourselves from, those with whom we disagree and join with others with whom we do agree. Those who have power control the institutions of government. And those who control the institutions of government determine what government does and what its policy is. That is why power is so important to politics.

This book is about both *American politics*—that is, battles for power—and *American government*—how those battles are structured and resolved. We believe that government can be best understood when it is viewed through the lens of politics because practically everything government does, and every action it takes, is the result of political activity of one kind or another. That is why politics is the framework for this book and government, the principal subject.

ONE BASIC CONCEPT: POLITICS

Today the word "politics" is often used disparagingly. Political candidates who accuse their opponents of "playing politics" mean to imply that the other candidate has been somehow unethical, or at least underhanded. In the 1992 presidential campaign, independent candidate H. Ross Perot appealed to many Americans precisely because of his contempt for "traditional politics." Bill Clinton's equivocation in answering questions about his past and his changing positions on some key issues made him vulnerable to the charge that he was a "typical" politician.

Originally, however, the term "politics" had a positive meaning. The modern term derives from the Greek word *polis*, roughly translated as "city-state." Throughout the ancient world, the polis, an independent city and the land that surrounded it, was the basic unit of political organization. Early Greek philosophers, such as Plato and Aristotle, believed that loyalty to a polis was part and parcel of being human. Aristotle, in fact, referred to the citizens of a city-state as "political animals." In these small communities, "government" meant face-to-face discussions of community issues among all citizens.

In the ancient world, politics was the process by which the community determined how its will would be implemented. Politics is that same process today. Contemporary society has become much more diverse and complex, of course, and so has politics. But it is still the means through which who gets what, when, and how is determined, and it is still fundamental to the operation of government. In a world where values and beliefs conflict, where resources are limited and desires virtually limitless, and where ego and ambition seem to be insatiable, the quest for political gain is inevitable.

Although politics sometimes leads to excesses and abuses, in itself it is neither bad nor dangerous. Insofar as it facilitates the expression of disagreement and the building of consensus, it is critical to the health of a democratic society. Without politics, there would be no mechanism other than force to resolve disagreements.

People get politically involved in various ways. (Top left) *Rock the Vote aimed to register voters between the ages of 18 and 25 at rock concerts across the country.* (Bottom left) *The women chained themselves to concrete blocks inside a truck in front of the White House to protest a toxic waste incinerator in Liverpool, Ohio, in 1993.* (Above) *In a more conventional mode, a citizen testifies at a local hearing.*

Politics is an end as well as a means, however. It is an *end* because it is an activity that has value in and of itself. It links citizens to their government and guides that government as it goes about its principal tasks of formulating, implementing, and adjudicating public policy. It is a *means* to other ends because it gives people the opportunity and the tools to advance their own interests by influencing who gets into office and what actions those officeholders take while they are in government.

TWO OTHER CONCEPTS: GOVERNMENT AND PUBLIC POLICY

The term **government** refers to the *formal institutions* within which decisions about public policy are made and to the *processes and procedures* of decision making. The California State Assembly, the Federal Trade Commission, and the Supreme Court, for example, are government institutions. They and

Associated Press

Government's job is to make and enforce public policy, sometimes with harsh consequences. In the summer of 1993, a police boat rescued survivors from the freighter Golden Venture *which ran aground off the coast of New York City. The ship was packed with Chinese immigrants trying to enter the United States illegally. Ten died in this accident. Immigration laws limit the number of aliens who may come in. Those caught entering illegally are entitled to a hearing, for which they may wait months, even years.*

all other government institutions exercise their authority by means of various processes and procedures that permit policy making, policy implementation, and adjudication. The ratification of treaties by the U.S. Senate, the vetoing of legislation by the president, the inspection of meat-processing plants by the Department of Agriculture, and the conduct of criminal trials in the federal district courts all exemplify the exercise of formal government power.

Public policy is what governments make. The federal government and some state governments impose and collect taxes on personal incomes. The personal income tax, therefore, is public policy. The federal government does not ban the ownership of handguns. The freedom to own handguns, therefore, is public policy in the United States, although, inasmuch as some states and many cities ban the possession of handguns, it may not be public policy at the state or local level.

Policies are not necessarily the same as laws, and how laws are implemented has a lot to do with what public policies really are. If the law says that the speed limit is 55 miles per hour on a particular highway in Illinois, but the Illinois State Police never stop any drivers unless their speed exceeds 65 miles per hour, then public policy is really 65 miles per hour because no penalty is imposed as long as drivers stay under that speed. Those who implement a policy, the state police in this instance, often have a large discretionary role in defining what that policy really is.

POLITICS AND POWER: A CRITICAL RELATIONSHIP

For political activity to succeed, it must be accompanied by the exercise of power. **Power**, in this sense, is the ability to get someone to do something that he or she would not otherwise do. Power may be wielded through persuasive skills, legal authority backed by force, threats, or even rewards.

Power is exerted by and within all institutions of government. Presidents exercise power when they persuade reluctant legislators to support their policy positions, as President Clinton did in 1993, when he convinced a majority of the members of Congress to support his deficit reduction plan despite their many misgivings. Congress exercises power when it initiates policy and obtains reluctant presidential support, as the Democratic majority did in 1990 when it persuaded then-President George Bush to generate new deficit-reducing revenues through taxes despite his campaign promise not to raise taxes. Interest groups exercise power when they convince political leaders to reverse their positions on policy matters, as senior citizens' groups did in 1989 when they virtually forced Congress to withdraw a tax to finance the catastrophic health-care plan enacted in the previous year, and as they continued to do in 1993 and 1994, when they participated in the debate over the content of President Clinton's health-care proposals.

Clearly, power is a normal, everyday component of politics, and there could be no politics without power.

Personal Freedom and Social Welfare

The exercise of power often affects individuals and the community in very different ways. One person's liberty, after all, may be another's constraint. For example, many Americans cherish their right to possess and use firearms. Yet we all know that firearms are dangerous, and their use can cause harm. Therefore, we must have laws, that is, public policy, to protect society from the undesirable effects of firearms. The political issue is how to write public policy that satisfies both those who want to own guns and use them legally and those who believe that the very availability of guns contributes significantly to violence in our society. The intensity of feeling on both sides explains why Congress has had such difficulty enacting gun control, even given the concern about crime and the desire for government to act.

Library of Congress

Strongly held beliefs about individual initiative and opportunity lie at the core of American democracy. In the last century, the westward expansion of the United States was justified by the doctrine of "manifest destiny," which held it the right and duty of Americans to settle the entire continent. The popular 1872 painting, America's Progress, by John Gast, symbolizes the taking of the West. Thousands of prints of this image hung on living-room walls during the 1890s.

Punishing objectionable speech is always difficult in a society that prides itself on its citizens' individual freedom. The remarks of Professor Leonard Jeffries about Jews at the Empire State Black Arts and Culture Festival in July of 1991 outraged many people and led to his dismissal as head of the black studies department at the City College of New York. A federal judge subsequently ruled that his firing by the Board of Regents violated his First Amendment rights of free speech. Jeffries was reinstated and awarded $400,000 in damages.

To take another example, free speech is a basic individual right. Without it, a democracy could not exist. But speech also can be harmful. Words are not as lethal as bullets, but they can cause psychological injury and they can precipitate violence. Should speech, then, be as limited as the possession of firearms? Should it be limited at all, and if so, under what conditions? Should a society be able to outlaw obscene or abusive language, or appeals that urge people to break the law?

These questions pit the rights of individuals to say and do what they like, and to protest policies and laws that they believe to be unjust, against the obligation of society to protect the health and well-being of its members, which includes maintaining laws that the majority in the community supports.

How can the freedom of an individual be protected while the rights of others are simultaneously preserved? Should people be allowed to protest abortion by blocking entrances to clinics? Should they be allowed to defend animal rights by destroying medical laboratories or by sabotaging the traps of hunters? Should those who preach hatred and advocate violence be allowed to do so in public places such as schools and churches? Does the same answer apply, say, if the Ku Klux Klan holds a rally in a community where its actions are likely to produce violent reactions?

Drawing the line between personal liberty and the needs of the community is a difficult political task, but one that government must perform. In accomplishing this, government makes policy judgments that are naturally shaped and conditioned by the political climate in which they occur. In short, *politics influences government, which in turn influences politics.*

Concentrated Power and Distributed Power

How power is distributed within the government affects not only which public policies are made but also who benefits the most from them. When power is concentrated in the hands of a few individuals or groups, decision making is more efficient, and government can act more quickly and decisively. But those with the power are likely to make decisions that advance their own goals and benefit their own interests, often at the expense of others.

When power is widely distributed, there is less opportunity for a few people to dominate decision making and determine policy outcomes. But arriving at a consensus, much less agreeing on the details of public policy, is a far harder undertaking. This is the problem faced by the U.S. Congress and other legislative bodies when they try to draft public policy into law. Both the membership of Congress and the disposition of power within Congress are designed to reflect the pluralism of American society. This makes it difficult, and sometimes impossible, to enact strong legislation that solves the nation's problems. This may be one reason why contemporary Congresses have been held in such low esteem by many within the country.

Obviously, then, there are tradeoffs between concentrated and distributed power: the efficiency of government is greater with concentrated power, but the representative character of government is greater with distributed power. These tradeoffs in turn can have a profound effect on politics and policy making. Generally speaking, widely distributed power can impede the functioning of government and perpetuate the status quo. On the other hand, the more power is distributed, the more influential minorities are likely to become and the better able they are to protect their rights and interests, even against the majority.

Majority Rule and Minority Rights

The tension between minorities and majorities, especially when it pertains to the exercise of personal freedom and the establishment of community standards, is one of the principal ongoing problems in the American political system. It is inherent in any democracy, although different societies try to resolve it in different ways. What is a democracy, and why does it inevitably produce this clash between the majority and various minorities?

A **democracy** is a form of government in which citizens have a right to control their own destiny. Democracy works on the principle of popular consent. The term itself comes from the Greek words *demos*, meaning "people," and *kratos*, meaning "authority." The people have authority; they have the right to make or influence decisions that affect their everyday lives.

Thus, in a democracy every citizen should have an equal opportunity to influence public policy through equal representation in government. Rule by the people, or "popular rule," is accomplished through the predominance of the majority in decisions that affect the whole society. If the wishes of the majority are *not* reflected in public policy decisions, the system itself is not democratic, even though public officials may have been selected democratically.

Majority rule is vital for a democracy, even though it has its dangers. Those in the majority can—and sometimes do—dominate those in the minority, disregard their needs, threaten their interests, and deny them their basic rights. That is why the principle of majority rule has to be modified in practice. As limits are placed on individual behavior, so too must they be placed on group behavior, *even if the group constitutes a majority.*

The United States Constitution was designed to do just that—to create a government that people of all opinions could influence but that no single group, including the majority, could easily control. James Madison, one of the architects of the Constitution, argued that this was a major strength of the new system. But it has also been perceived by some as a weakness. The very difficulty that people have in manipulating the system to their own advantage makes that system resistant to change. This resistance is a source of constant frustration to those who want quick, efficient, and popular solutions to problems.

Library of Congress

Sometimes the imposition of "community standards," the norms of the majority, violates the rights of a minority. Old Jim Crow laws in the South discriminated against African Americans by segregating them in many basic daily activities, from attending school or the movies to sleeping, eating, drinking, and using rest rooms. The "Colored Only" drinking fountain was only one of these many separate facilities.

Individual Liberty and the Common Good

Government exists to protect the lives and liberties of the people who live within its jurisdiction, and to provide for their well-being and happiness. These lofty ideals sometimes clash with one another, however. Which is more important—protecting the liberty of individuals or providing for the well-being of society? The competing priorities of government are well illustrated by comparing the goals articulated in the Declaration of Independence with those in the United States Constitution.

The authors of the Declaration talked about "life, liberty, and the pursuit of happiness." If securing these rights is the purpose of government, and if the British system failed to secure them, then these American revolutionaries believed that the colonies had good reason to declare independence and establish a government that would protect their rights.

The Declaration of Independence is important not only for its statement of the purpose of government but also for its identification of the foundation on which government rests. The second paragraph sets forth the assumptions and logic of a government based on popular consent:

We hold these truths to be self-evident, that all men are created equal, that they are endowed by their Creator with certain unalienable Rights, that among these are Life, Liberty, and the pursuit of Happiness. That, to secure these rights, Governments are instituted among Men, deriving their just powers from the consent of the governed, That whenever any Form of Government becomes destructive of these ends, it is the Right of the People to alter or abolish it, and to institute new Government, laying its foundation on such principles and organizing its powers in such form, as to them shall seem most likely to effect their Safety and Happiness.

In 1776 the signers of the Declaration needed to justify the Revolution in terms of a fundamental goal of government to protect and preserve individual human rights such as liberty, equality, and popular sovereignty. By 1787, however, the delegates to the Constitutional Convention that met in Philadelphia to restructure the new government defined their needs differently. After nearly a decade of living in a loose confederation of states with little effective central authority, they perceived the need for greater economic, social, and political stability. Their objective was thus to improve the national government's capacity to make and implement public policy.

In the preamble to their new constitution, the framers enunciated a set of values different from those articulated by the signers of the Declaration. They wanted "to form a more perfect Union, establish Justice, insure domestic Tranquility, provide for the common defence, promote the general Welfare, and secure the Blessings of Liberty."

Do these two eloquent statements of the purpose of American government conflict? Perhaps not, but their emphasis is certainly different. The Declaration of Independence stresses *individual* liberties while the Constitution emphasizes *social* goals. And as we have noted earlier, the unavoidable tension between individual liberties and broad social goals has been evident throughout American history. The duty of government is to defuse situations in which that tension occurs and try to resolve them by establishing public policy.

When a government makes public policy, it does so on the basis of its **authority**, that is, its lawful power. In a democratic society that authority is derived, directly or indirectly, from the people. In most cases, voters do not make policy decisions themselves, but they have a voice in selecting those who do. Voters choose policy makers to represent them, and then they try to influence the decisions their representatives make. Thus we frequently hear the terms *representative democracy* or *representative government* to describe the American political system and to distinguish it from *direct democracy* in which every citizen has an opportunity to participate in the formulation of public policy decisions, such as in town meetings.

The authority of the government is embodied in *law*. The Constitution is the supreme law of the United States, but it is not the only law. Treaties, statutes, executive orders, and judicial opinions are also part of the body of rules that must be observed by all members of the society, including those in government.

None of the rules—from laws, to policies, to the procedures by which government operates—are neutral in their effects. As with policy itself, the rules by which decisions are made benefit some and hurt others. Thus they can impinge both on the principle of majority rule and on the rights of individuals and groups in the minority. For example, the power of the Supreme Court to determine the constitutionality of both local and national laws restricts the ability of those in the majority to determine public policy because no legislature can take any action that violates the Constitution. In the case of abortion, for instance, the Supreme Court's recent interpretation of the Constitution has

The interests of the community often conflict with the rights of individuals. (Left) ordinances that prohibit smoking in office buildings constrain one's rights to smoke, and (right) rules requiring students to begin the school day with a prayer limit their right to act on other beliefs. Government's overarching purpose is to settle such issues and be fair to all sides.

© Matthew Neal McVay/Stock, Boston

© Emily Stong/The Picture Cube

No public official is above the law. When President Nixon concealed suspected criminal activities of members of his administration in violation of the law, Congress threatened to impeach him. Nixon chose to resign instead. He was wrought with emotion as he spoke to his staff in his final hours as president. His wife, Patricia, stood by his side.

Laffont/SYGMA

prevented states from banning abortion, although it still permits them to place certain restrictions on it.

Procedural rules shape policy outcomes, and therefore political struggles often go on over the rules themselves. This occurred during the Constitutional Convention when delegates from the large and small states clashed over representation in Congress. It occurred in 1876 when Democrats and Republicans disputed the electoral returns in five states. It occurred in the mid 1970s when newly elected members of Congress sought to make committee chairs more responsive to majority influence. In each of these cases, politics affected rule making, and rule making affected the disposition of the issue.

The divisions of authority mandated by the Constitution have also contributed to the politics of the governing process. By separating institutions of government and assigning each a primary sphere of authority, then imposing elaborate internal checks and balances on the exercise of that authority, the Constitution builds competition into the system. The president cannot appoint officials to the executive departments and agencies without Senate approval. Congress cannot appropriate money unless the president approves; however, Congress can override presidential disapproval of its legislation by a two-thirds vote in each of its legislative bodies. The Supreme Court cannot enforce its own rulings; only the president has that power. Congress cannot determine the constitutionality of its own legislation; the Supreme Court has assumed that prerogative. The federal system too, with its divisions of authority between the national government and the states, often plays off competing interests, needs, and policy goals against each other. In short, politics—the competition among conflicting interests—is built into the design and operation of the system.

Over the years, the dispersion of authority among the branches and levels of government has given well-organized and well-funded groups more opportunities to exert influence on public officials than have those with fewer resources at their disposal. This influence is often used to prevent policies that adversely affect the interests of powerful groups from becoming law.

The dispersion of authority also leads to the dilution of policy decisions. To make policies acceptable to as many as possible, policy makers find they must alter or remove objectionable items. This practice diminishes opposition, but it also diminishes a policy's scope or impact. It may even change its character. Take President Bush's 1988 campaign pledge to clean up the environment. The environmental proposals submitted by his administration included new and tougher standards for automobile emissions and industrial energy consumption. Before these proposals were made final, however, the administration consulted with industry leaders, labor representatives, conservation groups, health experts, and others. They also consulted those congressional leaders sensitive to the interests and concerns of these groups. Ultimately, Bush did not get what he originally wanted, and the resulting legislation established policy that was weaker than environmentalists wanted but stronger than business and labor wanted. Had the president not compromised, however, his proposals would have had little chance of getting through Congress. Even after environmental legislation was enacted in 1990, the battles continued over how the law would be implemented. The Clinton administration has directed the Environmental Protection Agency (EPA) to be more aggressive in identifying and penalizing companies that pollute the environment.

AP/Wide World Photos

In times of crisis, the power of government expands, while the rights of individuals shrink. At the outset of World War II, Congress authorized the detention of Americans of Japanese ancestry for "security reasons." Over 100,000 men, women, and children were forced to spend the war years in government-run camps. The 237 residents of Bainbridge Island in Washington State, for example, were evacuated under armed guard and sent to camps in California. In 1988 Congress apologized to the Japanese-American community and offered each family $20,000.

In normal times, then, politics usually produces small, incremental changes in public policy. In deciding what those changes will be, the advantage clearly goes to those with the resources to influence both the selection of the people in power and the subsequent decisions they make. Those with greater resources are also likely to be benefiting from government policy already, and thus they are reluctant to support changes that might undercut their existing advantage. For this reason, government officials tend to tinker with the distribution of resources rather than to redistribute them on a larger scale.

Certain crises, however, seem to require larger changes in the status quo. In the 1930s, for example, President Franklin Roosevelt proposed and Congress promptly enacted legislation to help small farmers, unemployed laborers, and older citizens who were especially hurt by the Great Depression. In the early 1980s, confronting a stagnant economy with high unemployment and inflation, President Ronald Reagan got Congress to legislate both a large reduction in taxes and a major reorientation of spending from domestic to national security concerns to stimulate the economy. During critical times, public officials have greater incentive and freedom to make more comprehensive policy changes.

THE AMERICAN POLITICAL CULTURE

Underlying the political system of any nation are the dominant values, beliefs, and attitudes its citizens hold about their governance, their nation's unique history, and their rights and responsibilities in society. Together, these values, beliefs, and attitudes constitute the unique **political culture** of a people. That culture, in turn, largely determines the structure and rules of a political system and the bounds of acceptable behavior within it.

The political culture of the United States, for example, has been unusually hospitable to a republican form of government (as opposed to a monarchy) and to democratic rules of participation (rather than authoritarian modes of decision making). Indeed, over time, both republicanism and the democratic process have become enshrined in America's public institutions. The culture shapes the political system, and the system, in turn, affects the culture.

American political life is not guided by a single, cohesive theory like monarchism or communism, however. In fact, in many ways political development in the United States has been more practical than theoretical. Even the American Revolution lacked the kind of guiding idea that has inspired other national revolutions. Most of the American revolutionaries seemed to mean it when they said that they wanted protection of their rights as Englishmen, even as that desire led them to the conclusion that they could no longer endure British rule. It was not the charm of a new or more appealing philosophy that lured them away from their British citizenship; it was a practical need to run their own affairs in a way they thought would best suit their interests.

Throughout the nation's history, practical needs, not philosophical concerns, have produced the major political issues that the country has had to address. How to broaden political participation; how to resolve the conflict between states that permitted slaveholding and states that prohibited it; how to meet the challenges of industrialization and immigration; how to cope with the Great Depression; how to protect American interests abroad in the face of foreign wars; how to adjust to new realities wrought by technological sophis-

The debate over reforming health care has been complex, confrontational, and often contradictory, pitting people's desires for broad coverage and maximum choice against their reluctance to pay more for expanded benefits. (TOLES copyright The Buffalo News. Reprinted with permission of UNIVERSAL PRESS SYNDICATE. All rights reserved.)

tication and the existence of weapons of mass destruction—these have been the central concerns of American politics. In each instance, Americans have relied not on the tenets of a political philosophy but on the politics of the situation to arrive at policy solutions.

The "American Ethos"

Although the American political culture is a composite of pragmatic attitudes, values, and traditions, two beliefs lie at its core: (1) the commitment to democracy, a political system that stresses liberty and equality, and (2) the commitment to capitalism, an economic system based on free enterprise that encourages individuals to seek financial self-interest. These ideas are the basis of the **American ethos.**

Democracy   In democratic America, many people believe that one of the government's primary responsibilities is to protect individual liberty. This belief, articulated in the Declaration of Independence, was reaffirmed in the Bill of Rights, which includes the first ten amendments. In the words of the late political scientist Clinton Rossiter:

We have always been a nation obsessed with liberty. Liberty over authority, freedom over responsibility, rights over duties—these are our historic preferences. . . . Not the good man, but the free man . . . ; not national glory but individual liberty has been the object of political authority and the test of its worth.[4]

To preserve liberty, Americans believe that political processes must be open and responsive to the needs and opinions of individual citizens. As former Senator J. William Fulbright noted, "The values of democracy are in large part the processes of democracy—the way in which we pass laws, the way in which we administer justice, the way in which government deals with individuals."⁵ The best way to protect one's liberty, so the thinking goes, is to be able to speak on one's own behalf in the councils of power, to be present—or at least represented—in the places where public policy decisions are made.

But people must have more than mere *access* to government. They must also be *equal* in its eyes. In general, the American belief system enshrines equality in two different forms: political equality and equality of opportunity.

In application, *political equality* is the belief that every vote counts the same, that all citizens have the same rights and obligations, that they are the same before the law and entitled by government to the same treatment. Americans have consistently supported this kind of equality.

They have differed, however, over *equality of opportunity*. Although Americans widely endorse the principle of equal opportunity for all, they disagree over its applications. If equality of opportunity does not already exist, how should it be achieved? What should government do about it, and specifically, what compensatory actions should government take to improve opportunities for those who start out behind or become "less equal," even if they do so by reason of their own shortcomings? Americans disagree, often violently, on their answers to these questions (see Tables 1-1, 1-2, and 1-3).

Why the disagreements? Intrinsic tensions between equality and liberty are to blame, as they have been for much of the conflict in American political history. The contemporary debate over affirmative action is a good example. Some people believe that the achievement of genuine equality of opportunity requires policies designed to make up for previous practices of discrimination. They feel that extraordinary measures are necessary to offset previously limited opportunities for disadvantaged groups. Corporations, for example, may undertake vigorous recruitment programs that encourage female or minority job

Changing attitudes and the rules that reflect them is difficult and often controversial. When President Clinton proposed that the military admit acknowledged homosexuals, he drew considerable criticism, particularly from those in uniform. Colin Powell, then chairman of the Joint Chiefs of Staff, was outspoken in his opposition. Powell had already been chosen the 1993 Harvard commencement speaker, and the invitation was not withdrawn. He was greeted by "lift-the-ban" signs from some of the degree recipients, and by the appearance of hundreds of pink balloons.

AP/Wide World Photos

TABLE 1-1

Changes in Public Attitudes toward Political Equality

STATEMENT	THOSE WHO AGREE (PERCENT)	
	1984	1992
1. Our society should do whatever is necessary to make sure that everyone has an equal opportunity to succeed.	94	95
2. We have gone too far in pushing equal rights in this country.	51	53
3. One of the big problems in this country is that we don't give everyone an equal chance.	54	71
4. It is not really that big a problem if some people have more of a chance in life than others.	43	38
5. The country would be better off if we worried less about how equal people are.	60	54
6. If people were treated more equally in this country, we would have many fewer problems.	73	84

SOURCE: Based on data from the American National Election Studies, conducted by the University of Michigan, Center for Political Studies, and provided by the Inter-University Consortium for Political and Social Research, Ann Arbor, Michigan.

TABLE 1-2

Changes in Public Attitudes toward Government Efforts to Improve Equality of Opportunity

STATEMENT	THOSE WHO AGREE (PERCENT)		
	1984	1991	1993
1. Government should do something to reduce income differences between rich and poor.	60	64	67
	1982	1991	1993
2. Are we spending too much, too little, or about the right amount of money on improving the conditions of African Americans?			
Too little	42	37	39
Too much	18	16	17
About right	40	47	44
3. Are we spending too much, too little, or about the right amount of money on welfare?			
Too little	28	24	17
Too much	44	40	57
About right	28	37	26

SOURCE: Based on cumulative data from the General Social Surveys, University of Chicago. National Opinion Research Center.

TABLE 1-3

Changes in Public Attitudes toward the Role of Government (percent)

STATEMENT	1972	1982	1984	1992
1. There is much concern about the rapid rise in medical and hospital costs. Some feel there should be a government insurance plan that would cover all medical and hospital expenses. Others feel that medical expenses should be paid by individuals and through private insurance. What is your position? **Government insurance plan**	53	—	48	65
2. Some people feel that the government should see to it that every person has a job and a good standard of living. Others think the government should just let each person get ahead on his or her own. What is your position? **Government should see to a job and good standard of living**	41	38	43	39
3. Some people feel that the government should make every possible effort to improve the social and economic positions of African Americans. Others feel that the government should not make any special effort to help them because they should help themselves. What is your position? **Government should help African Americans**	45	35	46	31
4. Some people think the government should provide fewer services, even in areas such as health and education, in order to reduce spending. Others feel that it is important for the government to provide many more services, even if it means an increase in spending. What is your posiiton? **Government should decrease services and spending**	—	57	49	46

SOURCE: Based on data from the 1972, 1982, 1984, and 1992 American National Election Studies, conducted by the University of Michigan, Center for Political Studies, Ann Arbor, Michigan. Data provided by the Inter-University Consortium for Political and Social Research, Ann Arbor, Michigan.

applicants. If all applicants are equally qualified on all established criteria, the woman or the minority person will be hired in order to offset the effects of past discrimination in employment. These and other affirmative action programs load the dice in favor of those who have been denied opportunities in the past.

But is "increased equality" truly "equality"? Critics argue that preferential affirmative action policies put members of historically advantaged groups—generally whites, males, and heterosexuals, who are in the middle and upper classes—at a *disadvantage*, depriving them of a fair shake, when they compete with members of the groups targeted by affirmative action programs for jobs, college admissions, loans, scholarships, and housing. Further, these programs curtail individual liberties because they limit the freedom of employers, college administrations, banks, and landlords to choose whomever they wish.

Affirmative action is not the only kind of policy that helps some at the expense of others and exacerbates the natural tensions between liberty and equality. In fact, it is difficult to think of any policy decision that does not. The challenge for any democratic government, then, is how to respond to the interests of the majority without impinging on the rights of any minorities.

Capitalism   Americans believe not only in political liberty but also in economic liberty. The American economy is run as a **free-enterprise system**. The "free" in "free enterprise" means that individuals are encouraged to pursue their financial interests on their own, without government planning, help, or interference, creating products and services that they can sell for a profit.

The essence of free enterprise is competition, and, theoretically at least, the marketplace alone determines which ventures succeed and which fail. Americans believe that businesses thrive in a free-enterprise system because economic freedom encourages individual initiative and stimulates the creativity that leads to success. Freedom thus fuels the engine of economic progress.

Capitalism is a form of economic organization based on private ownership and private control of the means of production and distribution. Its roots lie in a commitment to individualism, which helps explain the disinterest with which collectivist theories like communism and socialism have usually been greeted in the United States.[6] Americans have never believed that government, or any designated planning agency, could generate as much economic growth or as high a standard of living as a free market in which individual entrepreneurs operate in the service of the profit motive. This belief in the social benefit of individual initiative is another component of the American ethos.

© George Mars Cassidy/The Picture Cube

A free-enterprise system allows those with initiative to prosper. But when things go wrong, it provides no safety net for the losers. In the late 1980s, the U.S. economy was buffeted by high interest rates, bank foreclosures, and the collapse of many savings-and-loan institutions. Well into the 1990s, the sound of the auctioneer's gavel rang throughout the land.

Subcultures and Diversity

The United States has a dominant political culture, but it also has many sub-cultures, as most large countries do. The Cajuns of Louisiana, the Yankees of New England, the Amish of Pennsylvania, the Cubanos of Miami, the Mexicans of San Antonio, the Hasidic Jews of Brooklyn—these and many other groups have distinctive traditions, perceptions, interests, and values that sometimes differ markedly from those of the dominant political culture.

The diversity of American society has shaped the character of American politics. The indigenous population of North America was supplanted by set-tlers primarily from Europe who came to America in search of greater economic opportunity, social equality, and religious and political freedom. Over the years the United States has continued to attract refugees and immigrants from all over the world. It has been considered a strength of American culture that the United States contains so many diverse ethnic, racial, and religious groups. But this very diversity (see Table 1-4) is what gives rise to tension within the society.

Racial and ethnic groups For many years, the United States was viewed as a huge melting pot, a place where Old World cultures were gradually dissolved and transmuted into the culture of the newer American nation. Today, how-ever, the melting-pot image is not as accurate or as powerful as it used to be. New immigrants feel less pressure to assimilate, and second- and third-generation descendants of immigrants have become increasingly conscious of and interested in rediscovering their ancestral heritages.

One consequence of the revived interest in Old World origins and the heightened awareness of and pride in historic and cultural roots is the prolif-eration of organizations whose aim is to promote, preserve, and in some cases exalt various ethnic identities. Many of these groups, such as the Japanese American Foundation, the American Latvian Association, and the American Israel Public Affairs Committee, have gotten involved in the political process. They are concerned primarily with aid to and trade with their homelands, for-eign policy toward those countries, immigration, and certain domestic meas-ures, such as bilingual education, which are intended to help their members prosper in American society without necessarily disappearing into it.

The increasing self-awareness of these racial and ethnic groups generates conflict among them, as well as between them and groups that are closer to the majority culture. Much of the conflict stems from perceptions of inequality: in income and living standards, in education and employment opportunities, and in political influence.

In the past three decades, government officials have been unable to escape the economic, social, and political consequences of this inequality. Congress has debated civil rights legislation, Native American treaty rights, public hous-ing programs, a variety of welfare measures, numerous job bills, and immigra-tion laws. The Supreme Court has considered cases involving school desegre-gation, inequalities in public accommodations, racial quotas, affirmative action, and reverse discrimination. Presidents have been under increasing pres-sure to appoint members of minority groups to public office, to award contracts to minority-owned firms, and to develop programs that benefit the less fortu-nate who are disproportionately represented in certain minority groups.

Members of racial and ethnic communities have formed effective interest groups that have been clearly heard in the political arena. The Urban League,

TABLE 1-4

Immigrants to the United States by Country of Birth, 1971 to 1991 (in thousands)

	1971–1980	1981–1990	1991		1971–1980	1981–1990	1991
ALL COUNTRIES	4,493.3	7,338.1	1,827.2	NORTH AMERICA[1]	1,645.0	3,125.0	1,211.0
EUROPE[1]	801.3	705.6	135.2	Canada	114.8	119.2	13.5
France	17.8	23.1	2.5	Mexico	637.2	1,653.3	946.2
Germany	66.0	70.1	6.5	Caribbean[1]	759.8	892.7	140.1
Greece	93.7	29.1	4.8	Barbados	20.9	17.4	1.5
Ireland	14.1	32.8	4.8	Cuba	276.8	159.2	10.3
Italy	130.1	32.9	2.6	Dominican Republic	148.0	251.8	41.4
Netherlands	10.7	11.9	1.3	Haiti	58.7	140.2	47.5
Poland	43.6	97.4	19.2	Jamaica	142.0	213.8	23.8
Portugal	104.5	40.0	4.5	Trinidad, Tobago	61.8	39.5	8.4
Romania	17.5	34.3	4.6				
Soviet Union	43.2	84.0	57.0	CENTRAL AMERICA[1]	132.4	458.7	111.1
Spain	30.0	15.8	1.8	Belize	—	18.1	2.4
United Kingdom	123.5	142.1	13.9	Costa Rica	12.1	15.5	2.3
Yugoslavia	42.1	19.2	2.7	El Salvador	34.4	214.6	47.4
ASIA[1]	1,633.8	2,817.4	358.5	Guatemala	25.6	87.9	25.5
Afghanistan	2.0	26.6	2.9	Honduras	17.2	49.5	11.5
Bangladesh	—	15.2	10.7	Nicaragua	13.0	44.1	17.8
Cambodia	8.4	116.6	3.3	Panama	22.7	29.0	4.2
China: Mainland	202.5[2]	388.8[2]	33.0				
Taiwan	—	—	13.3	SOUTH AMERICA[1]	284.4	455.9	79.9
Hong Kong	47.5	63.0	10.4	Argentina	25.1	25.7	3.9
India	176.8	261.9	45.1	Brazil	13.7	23.7	8.1
Indonesia	—	14.3	2.2	Chile	17.6	23.4	2.8
Iran	46.2	154.8	19.6	Colombia	77.6	124.4	19.7
Iraq	23.4	19.6	1.5	Ecuador	50.2	56.0	10.0
Israel	26.6	35.3	4.2	Guyana	47.5	95.4	11.7
Japan	47.9	43.2	5.0	Peru	29.1	64.4	16.2
Jordan	29.6	32.6	4.3	Venezuela	7.1	17.9	2.6
Korea	272.0	338.8	26.5	AFRICA[1]	91.5	192.3	36.2
Laos	22.6	145.6	10.0	Egypt	25.5	31.4	5.6
Lebanon	33.8	41.6	6.0	Ethiopia	—	27.2	5.1
Pakistan	31.2	61.3	20.4	Ghana	8.8	14.9	3.3
Philippines	360.2	495.3	63.6	Nigeria	8.8	35.3	7.9
Syria	13.3	20.6	2.8	South Africa	11.5	15.7	1.9
Thailand	44.1	64.4	7.4	OTHER COUNTRIES[3]	37.3	41.9	6.3
Turkey	18.6	20.9	2.5				
Vietnam	179.7	401.4	55.3				

[1] Includes countries not shown separately.

[2] Includes data for Taiwan.

[3] Includes data for Australia, New Zealand, and unknown countries.

SOURCE: U.S. Immigration and Naturalization Service, *Statistical Yearbook*, annual; and releases. As printed in the *Statistical Abstract of the United States, 1993*. Washington, D.C.: Bureau of the Census, 1993, table 8, 11.

Some groups seek to create traditions that set them apart, while others never give up old ones. (Left) A Chicago family celebrates Kwanza, a new holiday that coincides with Christmas and focuses on the African heritage of African Americans. (Right) Hasidic Jews stop to pray on the way to New York's Catskill mountains. So many people parked beside the Thruway and flagged down others that it jeopardized highway safety. Finally, officials created a special "Mincha area" for the afternoon prayer.

the Congress of Racial Equality (CORE), the Southern Christian Leadership Conference (SCLC), and many other African-American groups have organized to promote racial equality. Rev. Jesse Jackson mobilized minority groups in the "rainbow coalition," which supported his candidacy for the Democratic presidential nomination in 1984 and 1988. Spanish-American groups such as the National Council of La Raza and the Mexican American Legal Defense and Education Fund are active in states with large Hispanic populations—Florida, Texas, New Mexico, Arizona, and California. Asian Americans are well organized in California and other Pacific Coast states. These groups have commanded recognition within the political parties and Congress. Special presidential aides also provide liaisons to these and other ethnic groups, as well as to senior citizens, religious organizations, and many interest groups.

Borne up by an alliance of diverse ethnic and racial groups that he called "the Rainbow Coalition," Rev. Jesse Jackson campaigned for the Democratic presidential nomination in 1984 and 1988. He and his family acknowledged a standing ovation after he addressed the 1988 Democratic convention.

In sum, the increased self-awareness of racial and ethnic groups is having a profound effect on the politics of American government. It is producing a more complex pluralistic society in which more groups are making more demands and exercising more influence on government. The result has been to increase the level of conflict and to extend political struggles to more people over more issues.

The women's movement   Women, too, have experienced inequality in various forms, and the women's movement has had a profound impact on politics. In the first half of this century, men were more active politically than women. They voted with greater regularity—American women were not universally guaranteed the right to vote until 1920—and they determined the issues that went on the public policy agenda. Even after women obtained suffrage, their beliefs and voting behavior did not differ much from men's for many years, a fact that some attributed to the stratification of roles in the society.

Times have changed, however. In the late 1960s and the 1970s, women swarmed into the marketplace and approached the political arena. In both, they found many things not to their liking, and they became intensely concerned with many issues that affected them directly: abortion and other women's health concerns, maternity leave and child-care policies, equal pay and equal job opportunities, marital rights, and divorce laws.

Consistent with their developing awareness of their economic needs were their political attitudes and opinions, which began to differ from those of men. Women became more sympathetic than men to a larger government role within the economic and social spheres and less supportive of a foreign policy based on military force. As the political parties began to deviate on these issues, a gender gap emerged with women more likely to vote for Democratic candidates and men more inclined to support Republicans.

In addition, women began to form their own interest groups, such as the National Organization for Women (NOW) and the Women's Political Caucus, and through them, began to join feminist causes and support feminist issues

The women's movement has brought a variety of family issues into the public arena. When it came out that President Clinton's choice for attorney general, Zoë Baird, had hired illegal aliens to care for her children and had not paid their social security taxes, Mrs. Baird (left) *withdrew. Clinton's second choice also had a "Zoë Baird problem." Finally, Clinton chose Janet Reno* (right), *who has no children.*

© Dennis Brack/Black Star

© Dennis Brack/Black Star

more successfully. More women also began to seek and win elective office, both at the state and at the federal levels.

These developments introduced a new dimension into American politics, and the ever-increasing political activity of women continues to have a powerful impact on the American political scene.

Other sources of diversity   Other kinds of differences within the American population have produced conflicting policy goals and have generated political strife. Geographic differences among and within states, as well as emerging regional identities, have created competition for tax dollars, government services, and special programs. The movement of the population to the South and Southwest has turned states in the Sunbelt against those in the Frostbelt, the Midwest, and the Northeast; it has pitted new high-technology industries (silicone chips, robotics, pharmaceuticals, and biogenetic engineering), which promote free trade and new markets, against older "smokestack" businesses (steel, automobiles, rubber, aluminum), which want protection against foreign competition.

Population movements from rural to metropolitan areas, and from metropolitan to suburban areas and back again, have set the stage for increasing public concern with issues such as homelessness, street crime, drug abuse, subsidized mass transit, medical and welfare programs, and environmental and energy policies. The aging of the population has intensified demands for policies that benefit older citizens, such as Social Security, Medicare, catastrophic health insurance, and an end to mandatory retirement.

The list goes on. Many different religious groups speak out on political issues ranging from abortion to prayers in schools to vouchers and tax subsidies for religious education to state laws on health and employment. Advocates of gay rights work to change public policy on issues such as military service, fair

Dewey Stokes, president of the Fraternal Order of Police, displays a National Rifle Association ad opposing the "Brady bill," which forces states to impose a waiting period for the purchase of handguns. The bill is named for Ronald Reagan's former press secretary, James Brady (at right). Brady suffered massive brain damage when he was shot during the assassination attempt on Reagan. Many police groups support the waiting period, as did President Clinton, who signed it into law on November 30, 1993.

Reuters/Bettmann

housing and employment practices, and health care. Occupational associations, economic groups, and even leisure-time organizations have also become better organized and more involved in the political process. Across the board, interest groups from the Pharmaceutical Manufacturers Association, to the National Education Association, to the American Association of Retired Persons have become more adept at influencing not only the selection of public officials but also the decisions of lawmakers already in office.

Consensus, Conflict, and Apathy in American Democracy

Both consensus and conflict grow from the soil of the American culture, and both shape American politics and government. The consensus, which emerges from shared fundamental beliefs and values, embraces the need for government, the rules of the game, and the general nature of public policy. The conflict, which springs from the diversity of the population and from the different needs, interests, and goals that flow from that diversity, usually swirls around the specific content of the public policies themselves and generates *most* of the political activity.

Consensus builds support for the government and the policies that the government produces. For the most part, the American people have been willing to abide by the constitutional system established in 1787 and modified over the years. The system has demonstrated sufficient flexibility to adjust to changing times, it has been amenable to popular influence, and it has worked in the opinion of most Americans.

The wide diversity of interests is what produces the political battles over issues. Most of these contests occur among those groups, whether large or small, that are directly affected by a particular issue. The general public is likely to get involved only when the policy goes into effect or the cost of that policy

Abortion has become one of the nation's most confrontational issues. (Left) The National Organization for Women holds a vigil in Pensacola, Florida, on March 11, 1993, after the murder of Dr. David Gunn outside his clinic by an opponent of abortion. (Right) That same spring, Operation Rescue protested abortion outside the Aware Women's Clinic for Choice in Melbourne, Florida.

© Cindy Karp/Black Star

© Cindy Karp/Black Star

A Sampling of Public Opinion in the Early 1990s

STATEMENT	POSITIVE RESPONSE (IN %)
A. The less government the better.	35
B. There are more things government should be doing.	65
A. We need a strong government to handle today's complex economic problems.	74
B. The free market can handle our complex economic problems without government being involved.	26
A. The main reason government has become bigger over the years is that it has gotten involved in things that people should do for themselves.	40
B. Government has become bigger because the problems we face have become bigger.	60
C. How important is it in making people true Americans that they try to get ahead on their own efforts?	
Extremely important	35
Very important	45
Somewhat important	14
Not at all important	5
D. How important is it in making people true Americans that they treat people of all races and backgrounds equally?	
Extremely important	54
Very important	39
Somewhat important	6
Not at all important	2

SOURCE: Based on data from the 1992 American National Election Study, conducted by the University of Michigan, Center for Political Studies, Ann Arbor, Michigan. Data provided by the Inter-University Consortium for Political and Social Research, Ann Arbor, Michigan.

must be paid for. Most of the time, only a small portion of the population knows or cares much about public policies, and an even smaller portion gets involved and tries to influence the content of those policies.

Is a democratic society in which only a small portion of the population gets politically involved unhealthy and unsafe? Perhaps. Apathy increases the likelihood that a well-organized, well-financed minority can get its way. The plight of industrial workers in the United States in the late nineteenth and early twentieth centuries and the plight of consumers before the 1960s illustrate what can happen to a majority of the people if they are unorganized or underinvolved. A silent or even an inattentive majority does pose a threat to the democratic process.

However, if most issues aroused most people most of the time, society would be in a state of constant turmoil. Compromise would be even more difficult than it already is, and decision makers would be pushed and pulled in every direction and, perhaps, unable to act. In all likelihood, support for the government and its policies would be weakened because people who felt strongly and did not get their way would be discontented.

A vibrant and stable democracy needs both consensus and conflict. Some of the people must be well informed and actively involved—preferably not the same ones on every issue—and most of the people must generally support the system and the decisions of its policy makers, although they may not perceive the effects of those decisions on their daily lives.

The strength of the American system is that it permits those who are interested to participate in politics and have an effect on policy outcomes. It also gives the general citizenry regular opportunities to participate as well, by voting in elections and by freely expressing their opinions about the issues that concern them in various ways. Thus, periodic elections, a free and critical press, and abundant opportunities for citizens to petition and protest keep public officials responsive to the whole society, even though many people within that society choose not to involve themselves in political activities all, or even most, of the time.

SUMMARY

In a culture where disagreement and self-interest are the norm, where individual liberty and the common good are often mutually exclusive, and where rewards are limited while desires are virtually insatiable, the quest for political gain is bound to be a preoccupation. It is certainly so in the United States. Somewhere, some group is always perceiving itself to have less of the pie. Somewhere, some group is always struggling to achieve parity with some other group, and preferably advantage. The resolution of these policy issues inevitably results in benefits to some and costs to others. This is the essence of politics.

If *politics* is the ongoing contest among individuals and groups to influence the values, beliefs, and policy goals of the society in their favor, *government* is the institutional mechanism for determining the rules of that contest and who wins it over time. Government is the authority that determines who gets what and when by formulating policy decisions that distribute resources, allocate costs, and make and enforce rules.

When government makes decisions, it exercises authority. It is the task of government to do so in a way that reflects the desires of the majority but does not violate the rights of the minority. This is a difficult task. The Constitution provides general guidelines, but each generation must decide for itself how to interpret them, that is, it must decide where to draw the line between majority rule and minority rights.

How government makes decisions may be controversial as well. The rules by which any political system operates are not neutral. They benefit some at the expense of others. Those who understand the rules are best able to benefit from them. And those who understand and can most effectively manipulate the rules to their advantage have tended to be the best-organized, best-funded, and best-led groups. This is why the political system in the United States seems to advantage the advantaged. It is also why government tends to maintain the status quo, and why policy changes are more often incremental than innovative.

That Americans accept the political system and the rules by which it functions even though they do not always benefit from the policy it establishes is testimony to the consensus underlying the basic values and beliefs of American culture. Most Americans believe that *democracy* is the best form of government and that *capitalism* is the best economic system. Both systems are predicated on the concept of individual liberty, the idea that people should be free to pursue their own interests so long as that pursuit does not impinge on the general welfare of the society. When it does, law may impose restraints. Americans also believe in political equality, that all citizens have equal rights and responsibilities under law. These shared beliefs in individual liberty and political equality provide the foundation on which the political system rests, and the political system in turn provides the mechanisms for the debate and resolution of disagreements.

Society in the United States consists of many different ethnic, racial, and religious groups. This diversity has contributed to the strength and vitality of American society and its political system. But it has also led to continuous battles over *public policy* issues, battles that pit different individuals and groups against one another as they pursue their own interests, values, and beliefs. These battles are the essence of contemporary politics, the fuel that fires the engines of government and keeps them running.

This chapter thus ends where it began: with the contention that although politics and government are different, they are inseparable. Politics motivates and drives the institutions of government, which in turn, influence society and its politics.

KEY TERMS AND CONCEPTS

politics
government
public policy
power

democracy
authority
political culture

American ethos
free-enterprise system
capitalism

LEARNING MORE ABOUT POLITICS

Scholarly studies

Dahl, Robert A. *A Preface to Democratic Theory*. Chicago: University of Chicago Press, 1963. An extended discussion of the concept of democracy and its many meanings.

Dionne, E. J. *Why Americans Hate Politics*. New York: Simon and Schuster, 1992. A leading journalist's account of why so many Americans have been turned off by contemporary politics and politicians and what can be done about it.

Greider, William. *Who Will Tell the People: The Betrayal of American Democracy*. New York: Simon and Schuster, 1993. A thoughtful critique of what is wrong with our democratic system and how it can be fixed.

Lasswell, Harold. *Politics: Who Gets What, When, How*. New York: Meridian Books, 1958. A classic study of the politics of influence by a scholar who helped shape the discipline of political science.

Lipset, Seymour Martin. *The First New Nation: The United States in Historical and Comparative Perspective*. New York: Norton, 1979. An inquiry into the economic, historical, and sociological factors that shaped the American character.

Tocqueville, Alexis de. *Democracy in America*. Edited by J. P. Mayer. New York: HarperCollins, 1988. A study of American democracy as seen through the eyes of a French traveler in the United States in the 1830s.

Leisure reading

Orwell, George. *Animal Farm*. New York: Knopf, 1993. A satire about a revolution that went bad. It should be read in conjunction with study of the American struggle for independence.

Orwell, George. *1984*. New York: Knopf, 1992. A powerful fictional description of a totalitarian society.

Smith, Hedrick. *The Power Game: How Washington Works*. New York: Random House, 1989. A contemporary account of Washington politics by a journalist who has covered the scene for many years.

Primary sources

Safire, William. *Safire's New Political Dictionary*. New York: Random House, 1993. A former presidential speechwriter, now a journalist, explores the language of politics.

Stanley, Harold W., and Richard G. Niemi. *Vital Statistics on American Politics*. Washington, D.C.: Congressional Quarterly, annual. Contains a wealth of statistical data on various aspects of American politics.

Statistical Abstract of the United States. Washington, D.C.: Bureau of the Census, annual. A basic source of information on United States politics, economics, and society collected and updated by the Census Bureau and the Department of Commerce.

Organizations

Center for Democracy, 1101 15th Street, N.W., Suite 505, Washington, DC 20005; (202) 429-9141. Promotes democratic values and practices abroad.

Common Cause, 2030 M Street, N.W., Suite 300, Washington, DC 20036; (202) 833-1200. A citizens' lobby. Interested in the operation of government and its responsiveness to the people.

National Academy of Public Administration, 1120 G Street, N.W., Suite 850, Washington, DC 20005; (202) 347-3190. Devoted to the study and improvement of the administration of government. Members are former or current public officials or distinguished students of government.

Public Citizen, 2000 P Street, N.W., Suite 700, Washington, DC 20036; (202) 833-3000. A part of activist Ralph Nader's organization. This group promotes democratic practices and tries to coordinate citizen action campaigns.

P A R T

Constitutional Politics

CHAPTER

2

The
Constitutional
Basis of
American
Politics

- The founders' Constitution—revolutionary or reactionary? The Articles of Confederation and the Continental Congress, the Constitutional Convention, ratification

- Enduring ideas and essential tensions: popular sovereignty, limited government, unalienable rights, separation of powers, federalism, judicial review

- The living Constitution: operations of government, formal amendment, judicial review

The items pictured at left represent the political campaigns of the 1860s. The four candidates in perhaps the most important of all United States elections—in 1860—are seen at the bottom (in "tintypes," an early photographic technology). Republican Abraham Lincoln's strongest rival in the general election was not the Northern Democrat Stephen Douglas but the Southern Democrat John Breckinridge of Kentucky. The Constitutional Union party nominated former House Speaker John Bell. Lincoln won handily, capturing a plurality of the popular vote but a majority of the electoral vote.

In 1864, Lincoln and Andrew Johnson defeated former Union Army commander George McClellan. Lincoln believed he would lose, but generals Sherman and Grant won key war victories, and Lincoln swamped McClellan 10 to 1 in electoral votes. In 1868, the major issue was Reconstruction, and General Grant won easily over Democrat Horatio Seymour. Interestingly, the Republicans depended on the African American vote to help them win.

Alexia Morrison was an independent counsel appointed in 1983 to investigate allegations that a former assistant attorney general, Theodore Olson, had lied before a congressional subcommittee about the withholding of certain Environmental Protection Agency documents from Congress. Morrison soon became the focus of a larger conflict between Congress and the president over the constitutionality of the appointment of special prosecutors. That controversy eventually led to a landmark ruling in Morrison v. Olson *(1988).*

Morrison was appointed under the Ethics in Government Act of 1978. That act provides for the appointment of independent counsel to investigate government wrongdoing if the attorney general, after a preliminary review, determines that an investigation is warranted. The attorney general must request the appointment of counsel from a special division of the United States Court of Appeals for the District of Columbia. Once appointed, counsel may be removed only for reasons related to performance as specified in the act.

The concept of independent counsels is highly controversial. Presidents Richard Nixon and

33

Ronald Reagan both contended that independent counsels, and the limitations imposed by Congress on their removal, intrude on the president's powers and violate the principle of separation of powers. Article II of the Constitution states that the president "shall nominate, and by and with the advice and consent of the Senate, shall appoint ambassadors, other public ministers and consuls, judges of the Supreme Court, and all other officers of the United States, whose appointments are not herein otherwise provided for, and which shall be established by law."

The Constitution says nothing about the power to remove presidential appointees and other government officials, however. It provides for only one method of removing nonelected government officials: impeachment. The House of Representatives is authorized to pass articles of impeachment and the Senate to try individuals charged with "treason, high crimes, and misdemeanors." Yet in the past two hundred years, few officials and federal judges have been impeached. As a result, competing views of who has the power to remove executive officials for other-than-impeachable offenses have developed. Presidents have contended that they alone have the sole power of removal, but Congress has not always accepted this view of the Constitution.

When Congress and the president disagree on a constitutional issue, the Supreme Court may have to interpret the Constitution and try to resolve the controversy. Before the Morrison case, the Court had handed down two other major rulings on the removal power. In 1926 it upheld President Woodrow Wilson's firing of a postmaster. But in 1935 it ruled that a member of the Federal Trade Commission could not be removed by President Franklin Roosevelt simply because the president disagreed with the commissioner's decisions. Alexia Morrison's investigation of Theodore Olson provided the Court with a third opportunity for interpreting the constitutional status of the removal power.

As soon as Morrison began her investigation, Olson challenged her appointment in the United States Court of Appeals for the District of Columbia on the ground that the appointment violated the principle of separation of powers. The court of appeals agreed with this argument. Morrison promptly appealed that ruling to the Supreme Court. In the spring of 1988, with only one justice dissenting, the Supreme Court held that the appointment of independent counsel does not violate the Constitution.

Three months after that ruling, Morrison concluded her two-year investigation, deciding that there was not enough evidence to seek an indictment of Olson. But in the process an important principle of constitutional law had been established: the appointment and removal of special prosecutors, and other "inferior officers" in the federal government, is a power shared by Congress and the president. In December 1992, the statute providing for the appointment of special prosecutors expired, but the 103rd Congress expressed strong interest in reenacting a provision for their appointment.

35

....

The

Constitutional

Basis of

American

Politics

MORRISON V. OLSON ILLUSTRATES HOW THE CONSTITUTION can be both a prescription for political struggle and a framework for resolving political conflict. Politics involves contests over competing interests and powers. The dispute between Morrison and Olson was a conflict between the executive and legislative branches of government. Because the Constitution says nothing about whether the president or Congress has the sole power of removal, it invites political struggles between these two branches of government. But the Constitution also provides that the Supreme Court may review and decide such cases and controversies. The Constitution thus is as much a framework for government as a blueprint for a dynamic political process.

This chapter examines the basic principles and structure of the Constitution. We discuss the historical context in which the document was drafted and ratified, the original Constitution of 1787, and how the Constitution has changed over the years, as well as the ways in which constitutional change may occur. Politics in America differs from politics in other countries because of the nature of the Constitution. The United States Constitution, the oldest written constitution in the world, is unique because it combines the idea of the rule of law with the notion that government is based on the consent of the governed.

THE FOUNDERS' CONSTITUTION

The founders' Constitution, as the historian Max Farrand observed, was a "bundle of compromises."[1] It was forged by a group of pragmatic statesmen who had to overlook, if not reconcile, their conflicting views about the politics of government. How did the Constitution come about? (Key events surrounding the creation of the Constitution are listed in the box on page 36.)

The Revolutionary Background

In 1774 twelve of the original thirteen colonies sent delegates to the First Continental Congress. This gathering had no official status; rather it was convened by delegates representing each of the colonies in order to pass resolutions denouncing the English Parliament and Crown. The colonies had unsuccessfully demanded representation in Parliament. They argued that only by having their own representatives in Parliament could they defend their economic interests. The demand for political representation intensified when Britain imposed taxes on goods imported into the colonies, and the slogan "No taxation without representation" became a popular rallying cry. In addition, colonists opposed the use of judges appointed by King George III to enforce laws they deemed unconstitutional.

In response to growing opposition to the English Crown, the First Continental Congress recommended economic sanctions against Britain and boycotts of its goods. It also declared some acts of Parliament unconstitutional and urged colonists to arm themselves and form their own militias. The colonies and Britain were headed for war.

Fighting broke out between colonial and British troops in April of 1775. In May the Second Continental Congress passed a resolution putting the colonies in a state of defense. Hostilities spread, and pressure grew for complete separation from Britain. In the spring of 1776 a committee of the Continental

Key Events in the Creation of the Constitution

April 1775	American Revolution begins in Massachusetts, at Lexington and Concord.
July 1776	Declaration of Independence is proclaimed.
November 1777	Articles of Confederation are adopted by the Continental Congress.
March 1781	Articles of Confederation are ratified by the states.
September 1783	Treaty of Paris ending the Revolutionary War is signed in Paris.
April 1784	Congress ratifies the Treaty of Paris.
August 1786–February 1787	Shays's Rebellion takes place.
May–September 1787	Constitutional Convention drafts and adopts the Constitution of the United States.
June 1788	Constitution of the United States is ratified.
March 1789	Congress meets for the first time, in New York.
April 1789	George Washington is inaugurated as president, in New York.
September 1789	John Jay becomes the first chief justice of the Supreme Court.
September 1789	Congress proposes the Bill of Rights.
December 1791	The Bill of Rights is ratified.

The 1771 Battle of Lexington was no battle at all. Rather, it was a piece of colonial folklore. In fact, British troops marching through Lexington encountered a group of colonial militiamen and ordered them to lay down their arms. The "embattled farmers" obeyed, but a musket accidentally went off. The British fired into the crowd, killing eight. The Minutemen still went quietly, as shown by eyewitness Amos Doolittle, a Connecticut Minuteman, but the event became enshrined as "the shot heard 'round the world."

The Signing of the Declaration of Independence *was painted by John Trumbull, whose father was a colonial governor of Connecticut and supported the Revolution. The Declaration offered legal justification for independence from Great Britain.*

Congress began work on a resolution proclaiming the colonies free and independent. Committee members decided that Thomas Jefferson would draft the resolution—the Declaration of Independence. Drawing on the philosophy that individuals have unalienable rights to "life, liberty and the pursuit of happiness," Jefferson compiled a long list of the despotic "abuses and usurpations" of power by King George III. On July 1, 1776, the Continental Congress began debating Jefferson's draft and making changes in the wording. Three days later, on July 4, it approved the Declaration of Independence.

Later in 1776, the Continental Congress also considered a proposed set of "Articles of Confederation and Perpetual Union." The **Articles of Confederation,** the United States' first constitution, was approved in 1777 but was not ratified by all thirteen of the former colonies until 1781.

The Articles of Confederation

Under the Articles of Confederation, the unicameral, or one-house, legislature known as the Continental Congress was composed of delegates from the states.

But this Congress had no effective power to regulate commerce or collect taxes. Tariffs, weights and measures, and currency varied from state to state. There was no separate executive or national judiciary; neither was there a national army. Instead, each of the original thirteen colonies was an independent and sovereign state that could conduct its own foreign policy without reference to the policies of other states.

This presented grave problems. When several of the states refused to repay debts they had incurred during the Revolutionary War, for example, the Continental Congress had no power to compel them to do so. Nor did it have any enforcement powers in any area. It could only ask each state to comply with and enforce its laws and policies voluntarily.

The economic problems facing the country and tensions between creditors and debtors were also a growing concern. In the aftermath of the Revolutionary War, imports and exports declined sharply, wages fell by as much as 20 percent, and money was in short supply. In 1786 and 1787 tensions came to a head in economically depressed western Massachusetts when the legislature refused to respond to petitions from debt-ridden farmers demanding the issuance of paper money and legislation to stop banks from foreclosing on their homes and farms. The angry farmers, led by Daniel Shays, formerly a captain in the Revolutionary army but now a destitute farmer, rebelled against the government of Massachusetts and eventually marched on the federal arsenal at Springfield. It took the Massachusetts state militia a year to put down Shays's Rebellion. (The box on page 39 describes this uprising in more detail.)

Shays's Rebellion dramatically underscored the weakness of the national government under the Articles of Confederation. It also coincided with the states' selection of delegates to the Constitutional Convention, which opened in Philadelphia in May 1787. And it was fresh in the minds of convention delegates, who planned to revise the Articles of Confederation but ended up drafting a new constitution, one that greatly strengthened the powers of the national government.[2]

The Constitutional Convention

Despite their opposing interests and conflicting views of government, delegates to the Constitutional Convention agreed that the Articles of Confederation were defective. The Continental Congress lacked three important powers: to regulate commerce, to raise funds to support a national army, and to compel compliance by the states. Within five days after the convention convened, on May 25, 1787, delegates had decided that "a *national* Government ought to be established consisting of a supreme legislative, executive and judiciary."[3]

Though agreeing that government must rest on the consent of the governed, the delegates shared a distrust of direct democracy. They feared a tyranny of the majority as much as they feared the tyranny of a minority—the concentration of power in too few hands. From the outset, the convention was inclined toward creating a **republic**, or representative form of government. Such a government would have the power to make and enforce laws but would derive its authority directly or indirectly from the citizens through popular elections. The objective, in the words of James Madison, a delegate from Virginia, was a "mixed" form of government, one that combined democratic and representative elements so as to minimize the possibility of tyranny by either the majority or a minority.[4]

For information about the makeup of the Constitutional Convention, see the box on page 40.

The Great Compromise The delegates were sharply divided over the form the new republic should take. Conflicts between large states and small states over

On July 8, 1786, the Massachusetts state legislature adjourned without responding to petitions from debt-ridden farmers angered by high taxes and the scarcity of money. The farmers demanded the issuance of paper money and legislation to stop banks from foreclosing on their homes and farms because of nonpayment of taxes.

Later that summer, at town meetings and at a convention of representatives of some fifty Massachusetts towns, protesters condemned the state legislature for its inaction and for levying high taxes and denounced state judges for enforcing the foreclosures. By August 31, 1786, discontent had turned to violence. Mobs in Northampton, Concord, Worcester, and elsewhere disrupted courts and prevented the judges from hearing cases. In response, the governor of Massachusetts sent six hundred of the militia to protect the state supreme court in Springfield. On September 26 a destitute farmer named Daniel Shays, a former Revolutionary War captain, led a rebellion against the Massachusetts government. Along with some five hundred insurgents, he confronted the state militia in Springfield and forced the state supreme court to adjourn.

Shays's uprising in Springfield, the site of a federal arsenal, prompted Congress to authorize General Henry Knox to raise an army of 1,340 to put down the insurrection. But Knox's federal forces never saw any fighting because state troops put down the insurgents in eastern Massachusetts. In the meantime, though, Shays's insurgents moved to the western part of the state and gathered a force of close to 1,200 in Worcester. On December 26 Shays's new forces began marching west toward Springfield. Now the governor called for 4,400 of the militia to be enlisted for one month, and ordered them to assemble in both Boston and Springfield.

Bettmann

Debt-ridden farmers and townspeople attack a local official who has come to foreclose on a property. Such uprisings grew increasingly common in western Massachusetts after the Revolution and eventually led to the "rebellion" of Captain Daniel Shays in 1787.

On January 25, 1787, Shays's insurgents reached Springfield. As they approached the arsenal, the state militia greeted them with artillery fire. Four insurgents were killed, and the rest broke ranks and fled. Two days later the state militia pursued Shays's forces eastward through the state. Then, in a surprise attack on the morning of February 4, the militia captured 150 insurgents and sent Shays fleeing into Vermont. By the end of the month Shays's Rebellion had been crushed, and the weakness of the Articles of Confederation and the need for a stronger national government had become dramatically clear, at least to some.

their representation in Congress, and between states in the North and states in the South over taxation and representation, proved to be the major problems.

During the first few weeks debate focused on the **Virginia Plan,** which was drafted by James Madison and presented by Edmund Randolph, Virginia's governor. It called for a strong central government with a *bicameral legisla-*

State legislatures and governors appointed 74 men to go to the Constitutional Convention, but 19 of the appointees declined to attend. Rhode Island was not represented at all. Of the 55 who attended, 14 left before the convention closed, 39 signed the final draft of the Constitution (that number includes the signature of one absentee that was added later), and 3 refused to sign the document. Of the 55 men who attended the convention

46 had been members of colonial or state legislatures

7 had been governors

42 had been delegates to the Continental Congress

8 had signed the Declaration of Independence

47 had been born in America

31 had attended college—some in Britain; some in America: Princeton (10), William and Mary (4), Yale (3), Harvard (2), Columbia (2)

21 had seen military service—18 as officers in the Continental Army

34 had studied law

13 were in business

10 were planters

21 were younger than 40 years old (the youngest was 26)

14 were over 50 years old (Benjamin Franklin, the oldest, was 81; the average age was 43)

ture—a legislature with two houses. Representatives in the lower house would be elected by voters in the states. Representatives in the upper house would be chosen by those in the lower house from nominees submitted by the state legislatures. The representation of states in the national legislature would be based on wealth and population; thus, the large states—Virginia, Massachusetts, and Pennsylvania—would dominate. In addition, the Virginia Plan called for an executive chosen by the legislature and for a judiciary with considerable power.

Junius Brutus Stearns painted Washington Addressing the Constitutional Convention *in 1856. This was one of five paintings from which a set of colored lithographs was struck and offered for popular sale. But whether or not the painter knew much about what the Convention and its participants looked like is a matter of speculation.*

James Madison: Constructing the Constitution

The American Constitution is what it is primarily through the efforts of James Madison. Born into the Virginia planter aristocracy in 1751, Madison entered Princeton University at the age of 15. After taking a four-year course in two years, he returned to Montpelier, the family plantation, and prepared for public life. From then on, Madison advocated religious freedom and independence from Britain.

At age 25, Madison went to the Virginia Constitutional Convention and later served in the Virginia House of Burgesses. At the Continental Congress in 1781 he voted to ratify the Articles of Confederation. His big chance to shape the future country came at the Constitutional Convention of 1787. When the Convention threw out the Articles of Confederation, they took as their working document the Virginia Plan, a series of resolutions drafted largely by Madison. The Virginia Plan proposed a federal government divided into legislative, executive, and judicial branches, and that framework was eventually adopted for the Constitution.

Madison then collaborated with two other proponents of the new Constitution, Alexander Hamilton and John Jay, on a series of 85 articles in favor of ratification. The *Federalist* essays were published serially in the New York papers under the name "Publius" from October 1787 to August 1788. Madison has been identified as being the author of essay 29.

Neither the Virginia Plan nor the Constitution had a bill of rights, and Madison, along with others, believed that the separation of powers within the federal government made guarantees of specific liberties unnecessary. Opponents of ratification, however, claimed that the absence of such guarantees made federal power dangerous, and the Federalists pledged their support of a formal bill of rights

© White House Historical Assoc./National Geographic Society

Nearing the end of his presidency at the age of 65, James Madison sat for this portrait by John Vanderlyn.

once ratification was achieved. On this basis, Virginia became the tenth state to ratify the Constitution in 1788.

Seated in the new House of Representatives, Madison began work on the additions to the Constitution. He studied similar bills passed by state governments, particularly Virginia's Declaration of Rights composed by George Mason in 1776. The new amendments were presented for approval in September 1789, and in late 1791, ratification by Virginia made Madison's Bill of Rights part of the Constitution.

Delegates from small states opposed this plan and supported the **New Jersey Plan,** proposed by William Paterson of New Jersey. It gave considerable regulatory and taxing power to Congress and called for a unicameral (single-house) legislature. All states would be represented equally, and the plural executive would not have veto power.

By the end of June the convention was at an impasse. A committee, known as the Committee of Eleven, was given the task of hammering out a compromise. On July 5 it presented the solution that became known as the **Great Compromise.** The compromise was the creation of a bicameral legislature in which representation in the lower house (the House of Representatives) would be based on population and representation in the upper house (the Senate) would be equal for every state regardless of its size. Members of the House were to be chosen by popular election. Senators were to be chosen by state legislatures.

The three-fifths compromise   Slavery was another divisive issue. Delegates from southern states wanted slaves to be counted as part of a state's population, which would increase the South's representation in the House of Representatives, but they opposed the idea of giving slaves the right to vote. Delegates from northern states insisted on the principle of equal representation of all citizens, which discounted slaves because they were not considered citizens in the South and thus could have no impact on the number of representatives that a state elected to the House of Representatives. Delegates realized that the Constitution was certain to be defeated if any restriction was imposed on the power of states to determine who could vote. But delegates from the northern and southern states remained divided over whether and how to count slaves.

The delegates finally agreed to the **three-fifths compromise,** which stated that "three-fifths of all other Persons" (that is, slaves) would be counted for purposes of taxation and representation. As a concession to the southern states, the larger issue of slavery and trading in slaves was put off for two decades by Article I, Section 9, which prevented Congress from outlawing the slave trade until 1808.

The convention continued for more than a month debating issues involving Congress's powers and the powers of the president. But the major conflicts over state representation and the structure of government had been resolved. On September 17, 1787, thirty-nine of the remaining delegates signed the document; only three refused to do so.[5]

The Signing of the Constitution, *painted in 1987 by Louis S. Glanzman, was based on authenticated portraits of those who were at the convention and on architectural records of the time. The Delaware, Pennsylvania, and New Jersey societies of the Daughters of the American Revolution commissioned the painting to celebrate the bicentennial of the Constitution.*

Although the delegates approved the Constitution, they still had to secure its ratification by the states. To outmaneuver the opposition, they recommended (in Article VII) a novel method of ratification. Amendments to the Articles of Confederation were supposed to be ratified by *all* state legislatures. But instead of submitting the Constitution to the state legislatures, the Constitutional Convention recommended that the Congress of the Confederation send the document to the states for ratification by special conventions of the people. According to this plan, the Constitution would be ratified if at least *nine* of the thirteen states gave their approval. Congress and the thirteen states agreed to this.

Ratification by special state conventions of the people was politically significant. In James Madison's words, it meant that the Constitution was not a mere treaty "among the Governments and Independent States" but the expression of "the supreme authority of the people themselves."[6] Ratification by only nine of the states was also a defensive strategy, because it was far from certain that all thirteen states would ratify the new constitution.

The erosion of the states' power and the repudiation of the states' sovereignty did not escape the attention of those who were opposed to the new constitution. Known as the Anti-Federalists, they were opposed to the Constitution because it concentrated so much power in a national government and retained too little authority for the states, both individually and collectively. In the words of Patrick Henry of Virginia, "what right had they [the delegates] to say, *We, the People?* . . . Who authorized them to speak the language of, *We, the People,* instead of *We, the States?* States are the characteristics, and the soul of the confederation. If the States are not the agents of this compact, it must be one great consolidated National Government of the people of all the States."[7] But Henry lost, not only in Virginia but in all the other states.

Peter F. Rothermel painted this romantic view of Patrick Henry Before the House of Burgesses *in 1851. The restored interior of the Hanover County Courthouse where Henry actually argued cases and defended First Amendment rights is more austere.*

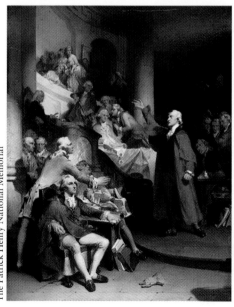

The Patrick Henry National Memorial

Photo courtesy of Lois W. Wickham

Delaware ratified the Constitution on December 7, 1787. Within weeks, Pennsylvania, New Jersey, Georgia, and Connecticut gave their approval. Massachusetts followed in February 1788, but with a closely divided vote of 187 to 168. In the spring of 1788, Maryland and South Carolina gave their overwhelming endorsements. Then, in June, close votes in New Hampshire and Virginia secured the required nine states needed for ratification. But the battle was not over. New York's ratification convention was bitterly divided. Opponents feared that the national government was granted too much power and that representatives from small states might conspire in Congress against New York's commercial interests. New York's approval, however, was crucial for the success of the union because this large commercial state separated New England from the states in the South. It was largely owing to the leadership of Alexander Hamilton that New York finally voted in favor of ratification.[8]

The price of ratification in several states—notably Massachusetts, New York, and Virginia—was agreement that the First Congress would adopt a bill of rights that specifically guaranteed individuals' civil rights and liberties. (North Carolina did not ratify until November 1789, and Rhode Island held out until May 1790.) In 1789 the First Congress adopted twelve amendments to the Constitution and promptly submitted them to the states. Ten of the amendments, known as the **Bill of Rights,** were ratified by the states on December 15, 1791. The protections contained in the Bill of Rights are listed below.

With the ratification of the Constitution and the Bill of Rights, the framework for a dynamic political process was in place. It remained for succeeding generations to work out the details of government. As Maryland delegate John Mercer observed toward the end of the Constitutional Convention, "It is a great mistake to suppose that the paper we are to propose will govern the United States. It is the men whom it will bring into the government and interest in

---

The Bill of Rights

Amendment	1	The rights of religion, speech, press, and assembly.
Amendment	2	The right to bear arms.
Amendment	3	Protection against the quartering of soldiers in one's home.
Amendment	4	The right to be secure against unreasonable searches and seizures.
Amendment	5	The right to "due process of law," protection against double jeopardy, and the privilege against self-incrimination.
Amendment	6	The right to counsel for one's defense and to a speedy and public trial by an impartial jury.
Amendment	7	The right to a jury trial in civil law cases.
Amendment	8	Prohibition of excessive bail, fines, and "cruel and unusual punishment."
Amendment	9	The retention by the people of rights that are not enumerated in the Constitution.
Amendment	10	The retention by the states or by the people of powers not delegated to the national government.

maintaining it that is to govern them. The paper will only mark out the mode and the form. Men are the substance and must do the business."[9]

The Constitution: Revolutionary or Reactionary?

During much of the nineteenth century, the founders and the constitution they created were revered. But early in the twentieth century Charles A. Beard, and other progressive historians, advanced an economic interpretation of the Constitution as reactionary and antidemocratic. They contended that the founders thwarted majority rule and created a strong national government in order to protect the proprietary interests of an economic elite.[10] Recently, however, the progressives' evidence and interpretation of the founding period have been disputed. Bernard Bailyn, Forrest McDonald, and Gordon S. Wood claim that the real struggle was not over economic interests but differing political views of government power.[11] They point out that in late-eighteenth-century America there was no great mass of people without property and that all the founders had an interest in promoting economic prosperity. The deeper political conflict was over republicanism and how to promote civic order while preserving individual liberty.

Political scientist Martin Diamond argues that the Constitution, far from being reactionary, was revolutionary.[12] It carried forth the revolutionary principles of the Declaration of Independence, respecting individuals' equal freedoms and popular sovereignty as the basis of government. Thus, by creating a system of ordered liberty and limited government based on the consent of the governed, the Constitution brought to completion the revolution begun with the Declaration of Independence.

This hand-colored engraving by Amos Doolittle celebrates the inaugural of George Washington.

Courtesy of John Carter Brown Library/Brown University

Private collection

This brass breeches button, also from the 1780s, uses the same imagery to commemorate the inauguration. Each circle bears the initial of an original state. "GW" occupies the center, ringed by the legend "Long Live the President." In the engraving (left), the circles carry the state seals, with the state's name, its number of inhabitants, and the count of its senators and representatives. People bought these mementos to learn something about the new nation.

In certain respects the Constitution was both reactionary and revolutionary: reactionary in addressing the defects of the Articles of Confederation; revolutionary in creating a strong central and representative government. The Constitution and the Bill of Rights reflected the political struggles of the founding period and laid the basis for a dynamic political process.

ENDURING IDEAS AND ESSENTIAL TENSIONS

In just forty-three hundred words the Constitution provides a blueprint for self-government. It is a model for free-government-in-the-making, as James Wilson, one of its drafters, observed:

A free government has often been compared to a pyramid. This allusion is made with peculiar propriety in the system before you; it is laid on the broad basis of the people; its powers gradually rise, while they are confined, in proportion as they ascend, until they end in the most permanent of all forms. When you examine all its parts, they will invariably be found to preserve that essential mark of free governments—a chain of connection with the people.[13]

The Constitution provides for both continuity and change because of the interplay of certain enduring ideas: the principles of popular sovereignty, limited government, and individual unalienable natural rights. These ideas led the founders to establish a system of checks and balances by distributing power among the branches of the national government, dividing power between the national and state governments, and creating the basis for judicial review.

Popular Sovereignty

"A government of our own is our natural right," exclaimed Thomas Paine, the well-known pamphleteer of the American Revolution.[14] The Revolutionary War was fought, as the Declaration of Independence stated, because of a "long train of abuses" by the English Crown. The colonists charged that King George III, among other things, taxed them but denied them representation and made judges dependent on his will.

In rejecting the British aristocratic model of government, in which sovereignty rested with the Crown, the colonists proposed the revolutionary idea of **popular sovereignty,** the idea that government is based on the consent of the people and is accountable to the people for its actions.[15] Although the framers of the Constitution were not inclined to support direct popular involvement in government, they did subscribe to the principle that government authority is based on the consent of the governed. This principle is expressed in the opening lines of the Preamble to the Constitution: "We, the People of the United States, . . . do ordain and establish this Constitution for the United States of America."

Limited Government

The idea of **limited government** follows from the notion of popular sovereignty. Fearful that the only alternative to constitutionally limited government was political tyranny, the founders sought to ensure that the authority of government—its ability to make and enforce laws that limit individual freedom—would be restricted to **express powers,** powers specified and delegated to the national government by the Constitution.[16] These express powers are listed in the first three articles of the document: Article I details the legislative powers of Congress; Article II describes the executive powers of the president; Article III indicates the powers of the federal judiciary.

47

....

The

Constitutional

Basis of

American

Politics

The constitutional provisions granting powers to the government have given rise to ongoing political struggles. For in addition to the express powers, the Constitution confers on Congress **implied powers,** powers that might be inferred from those that are expressly delegated. The "necessary and proper" clause (Article I, Section 8) is a basis for Congress's implied powers. This clause gives Congress the power "to make all laws which shall be necessary and proper for carrying into execution the foregoing powers, and all other powers vested by this Constitution in the government of the United States." Because this clause gives Congress wide-ranging authority to carry out its other powers by enacting legislation "necessary and proper" to its execution of those powers, it is often referred to as the "elastic clause."

How far Congress may go in exercising its implied powers has often been a matter of controversy. Indeed, the scope of Congress's legislative powers became the focus of an enduring struggle almost immediately after ratification of the Constitution. In December 1790, Secretary of the Treasury Alexander Hamilton proposed that Congress charter a national bank. The ensuing debate about the constitutionality of Congress creating a national bank pitted Hamilton and the Federalists (who favored a strong national government) against Madison and Jefferson over fundamental principles of constitutional interpretation and politics.

Hamilton contended that a national bank would strengthen the national government by aiding in tax collection, administering public finances, and securing loans to the government. The Senate, half of whose members had been delegates to the Constitutional Convention, unanimously endorsed Hamilton's

National Gallery of Art

Alexander Hamilton, portrayed here by John Trumbull, had been General Washington's private secretary during the Revolutionary War. An ardent advocate of a strong central government, Hamilton wrote over half of The Federalist *papers and worked hard for ratification of the Constitution. As the first Secretary of the Treasury, he pursued policies that were sharply opposed by Jeffersonian Republicans. Yet in 1800, when Jefferson and Aaron Burr were tied in electoral votes and the presidential election went into the House, Hamilton supported Jefferson. Burr later challenged him to a duel and shot to kill. Hamilton died the next day, July 11, 1804.*

proposal. By contrast, in the House of Representatives Madison maintained that creation of the bank was beyond the scope of Congress's delegated powers. But despite Madison's opposition, the House adopted a bill chartering the bank. On February 25, 1791, President George Washington signed the act incorporating the first Bank of the United States and granting it a twenty-year charter.

When the bank's charter expired in 1811, its renewal was defeated in Congress by just one vote, and four years later, Congress established the second Bank of the United States with another twenty-year charter. Economic hardship brought by the War of 1812 and the national government's reliance on state banks for loans were the overriding considerations in Congress. Opposition to a national bank remained strong in the states, however, and eventually it led to the Supreme Court's landmark decision in *McCulloch v. Maryland* (1819). In his decision, Chief Justice John Marshall upheld the constitutionality of the national bank with a broad reading of congressional powers: "Let the end be legitimate, let it be within the scope of the constitution, and all means which are appropriate, which are plainly adapted to that end, which are not prohibited, but consistent with the letter and spirit of the constitution, are constitutional."[17]

Although Madison agreed with the *McCulloch* decision, he continued to bristle at the expansive interpretation of the power of Congress advanced by the Supreme Court. Opposition persisted, and support for the bank gradually diminished. In 1832, Congress passed another bill extending the bank's charter, but President Andrew Jackson vetoed the bill and again challenged the Court's interpretation of and authority over the Constitution. Nevertheless, the Court had successfully established the basis for a broad interpretation of Congress's implied powers.

In addition to express and implied powers, in the conduct of foreign affairs the national government has **inherent powers,** powers that are not specifically enumerated in the Constitution. The states may make no claims in this area. But political contests between Congress and the president occasionally arise over claims of inherent powers, particularly in times of international crisis. These disputes force presidents to defend their actions in terms of the Constitution and to be accountable to Congress and the people.

Unalienable Rights

One of the founders' main objectives in constraining the powers of government was to ensure the **unalienable rights** of individuals. According to the social theory of the English philosopher John Locke, people are born with certain rights granted to them in advance by "nature." Among these, as the Declaration of Independence proclaims, are "Life, Liberty, and the Pursuit of Happiness." Because these rights precede the creation of government, they are not granted by government and therefore cannot be taken away by government. Instead, so this thinking goes, it is the duty of government to protect its citizens against any encroachment on those rights.[18]

By limiting government power to that which is specifically granted in the Constitution, the founders hoped to safeguard individuals' unalienable rights. That was one of the arguments used by James Madison, Alexander Hamilton, and other defenders of the Constitution to win its ratification by the states. In *The Federalist, No. 84*, one of a series of newspaper essays defending the new Constitution, Alexander Hamilton wrote: "The Constitution itself, in every rational sense, and to every useful purpose, is a bill of rights." By this he meant that a government with limited and delegated powers would not expand to usurp individuals' rights and those rights would be secure.

Those who opposed the Constitution were unpersuaded, however. Fearful that the national government's power would be too great and would expand at the expense of the states and the people, they urged the creation of a separate bill of rights, which was ratified in December 1791.

Separation of Powers

Because the founders were wary of the concentration of government power, they distributed power among the three branches of the national government (see Figure 2-1). This **separation of powers** was designed to create a delicate balance in which the legislative, executive, and judicial branches would check and balance each other in various ways. "Ambition must be made to counteract ambition," Madison argued in *The Federalist, No. 51.*

The principle of separation of powers is embodied in the Constitution's grant of legislative power to Congress, executive and other powers to the president, and judicial power to the Supreme Court and the federal courts. Yet these powers are not entirely or completely separate; the three branches are actually separate institutions that share political power. Congress, for instance, passes legislation that the president must approve or veto; a two-thirds vote by both the House of Representatives and the Senate may override a presidential veto. The president makes treaties with foreign governments and appoints members of the federal judiciary, but presidential treaty making and judicial appointments are subject to ratification or confirmation by the Senate. (The Constitutional Conflict on page 51 describes an area where the separation of powers is not clear.)

Congress, the president, and the judiciary share various other powers. As a result, they check and balance each other both directly and indirectly. This division and sharing of powers makes political change difficult and slow. In the words of Justice Louis D. Brandeis, "The doctrine of the separation of powers was adopted by the Convention of 1787, not to promote efficiency but to preclude the exercise of arbitrary power. The purpose was not to avoid friction, but, by means of the inevitable friction incident to the distribution of the governmental powers among three departments, to save the people from having one institution dominate the government."[19]

The effects of power sharing by separate institutions are evident in the operation of constitutional checks and balances through the years. The president has vetoed congressional acts more than 2,400 times. Congress has overridden about 95 of those vetoes. The Supreme Court has ruled more than 180 congressional acts or parts of acts unconstitutional. The Senate has refused to confirm 29 nominees to the Supreme Court (out of 142 nominations) and has rejected at least 9 cabinet nominations as well as many subcabinet appointees. Congress has impeached 14 federal judges and convicted 7. Congress has passed, and the states have ratified, 4 amendments to the Constitution overturning decisions of the Supreme Court. In short, separation of powers is often a prescription for political struggle. The conflict is reflected in President Andrew Jackson's irate response to a Supreme Court decision with which he disagreed: "John Marshall has made his decision, now let him enforce it." Each branch of government at different times and in various ways checks and thwarts the actions of another.

POWERS

President:
• Commander-in-chief of the military
• Makes treaties with other countries
• Appoints ambassadors, federal judges, Supreme Court justices, other federal officials
• Administers U.S. laws
• Acts as head of state

Congress:
• Passes federal laws
• Raises taxes
• Regulates foreign and interstate commerce
• Declares war
• Raises and funds the military
• May borrow money by issuing bonds for sale

Supreme Court:
• Reviews lower federal court rulings and appeals from state courts that involve federal law or constitutional issues
• Hears cases involving foreign ambassadors as first and final court
• Rules on disputes between states

CHECKING POWERS

President:
• Vetoes laws
• Orders special sessions
• Exerts political pressures
• Appeals directly to citizens

Supreme Court:
• Rules on constitutionality and legality of laws passed by Congress and signed by the president

Congress:
• Overrides veto
• Approves or rejects president's budget
• Ratifies treaties (Senate)
• Approves or rejects president's cabinet nominees, ambassadors, and others
• Investigates and reorganizes executive departments
• May impeach the president

Congress:
• Proposes constitutional amendments to override rulings
• Changes size of Supreme Court and numbers of lower federal courts
• Approves or rejects Supreme Court nominees
• May impeach federal judges

President:
• Nominates Supreme Court justices and federal judges
• Pardons those convicted under federal laws
• May refuse to enforce federal court orders

Supreme Court:
• May rule the actions of the president or others in the executive branch unconstitutional or illegal
• Interprets treaties signed by president

Figure 2-1 *Separate institutions sharing power.* SOURCE: *Adapted from* Scholastic Update, *vol. 119, no. 1 (September 8, 1986).*

Power sharing, however, also encourages cooperation and compromise. Congress and the president must work together to enact legislation and appropriate funds for the operation of government. The Supreme Court sometimes depends on the other two branches to enforce its rulings. When the Supreme Court handed down its landmark rulings mandating school desegregation, in *Brown v. Board of Education* (1954 and 1955), both presidential action and congressional action were required to overcome opposition in the South.

Terminating Treaties

Who has the power to *terminate* treaties: The president? The Senate? The president with the agreement of the Senate? In Article II, Section 2, the Constitution says: "The President . . . shall have power, by and with the advice and consent of the Senate, to make treaties." But the Constitution is silent about the power to terminate treaties, and that silence, on at least one occasion, has given rise to a conflict between the president and the Senate.

In 1979 Republican senator Barry Goldwater and several other senators sued Democratic president Jimmy Carter because he unilaterally terminated a mutual defense treaty with Taiwan without the Senate's approval. Carter claimed that as president he had the inherent power to terminate treaties. But Goldwater and other senators countered that because treaties are made with the Senate's consent, the president must secure the Senate's consent to terminate them.

The Supreme Court was unable to resolve the dispute. In *Goldwater v. Carter* (1979), in a brief unsigned opinion, the Court dismissed the suit and suggested that the case presented a "political question" for the president and the Senate to decide. In a separate opinion, Justice Lewis F. Powell, Jr., contended that the case was not ripe for judicial resolution because the full Senate had not passed a resolution barring Carter from terminating the treaty with Taiwan. In another opinion, Justice William H. Rehnquist argued that regardless of whether a few senators sued the president or whether the full Senate and the president were at odds over the suspension of a treaty, the Court should not decide the conflict but leave it to be resolved by the president and the Senate. In a dissenting opinion, Justice William J. Brennan, Jr., claimed that the president has the constitutional authority to unilaterally terminate a treaty.

Federalism

The Constitution divided power not only among the branches of the national government but also between the national and state governments. The result is **federalism,** a system of government in which power and authority are divided among and shared by the national government and the state governments.[20]

The framers of the Constitution had no real alternative to establishing a federal system. They could not abolish the thirteen original states or deny them their governing powers. What they could do was establish a national government with its own independent powers and leave intact the powers of the states that were not otherwise delegated to the new national government. Thus, each state retained its own executive branch, legislature, and judicial system. Individuals were to be subject to both state and national laws. This division has made the politics of government decentralized, and flexible and responsive to the heterogeneous population of the United States.

The Constitution reserves to the states all powers that are not granted to the national government and not expressly denied to the states; these are known as **reserved powers.** Powers that are not given exclusively to the national government may be exercised by the states; these are known as **concurrent powers.** Concurrent powers exercised by the national government and the states include the power to tax, to regulate commerce, and to make and enforce criminal laws. The distribution of power between the national government and the states is shown in Table 2-1.

TABLE 2-1

Distribution of Power between the National Government and the States

POWERS RESERVED TO THE NATIONAL GOVERNMENT	POWERS RESERVED TO THE STATES	CONCURRENT POWERS
Coining money and currency	Establishing local governments	Taxing
Conducting foreign relations	Regulating trade within the state	Borrowing money
Making treaties	Conducting elections	Establishing courts
Regulating foreign and interstate commerce	Ratifying amendments to the Constitution	Chartering banks
Providing an army and navy	Exercising powers not granted to the national government or denied to the states	Spending for the general welfare
Declaring war		
Establishing post offices		
Protecting patents and copyrights		
Regulating weights and measures		
Admitting new states		
Making laws necessary and proper to carrying out specifically delegated powers		

Because the national and state governments share certain powers, conflicts may arise between them. The Constitution requires that federal law prevail in such conflicts. The **supremacy clause** in Article VI stipulates that "This Constitution, and the laws of the United States which shall be made in pursuance thereof; and all treaties made . . . under the authority of the United States, shall be the supreme law of the land; and the judges in every State shall be bound thereby; anything in the Constitution or laws of any State to the contrary notwithstanding." Every government official, state and national, is bound to support the Constitution.

Rarely do state laws directly contradict federal law. More frequent—and more troubling—are cases involving the concurrent powers of the national and state governments, such as the powers to tax and regulate commerce. Conflicts between the national and state governments are ultimately decided by the Supreme Court. When state and federal laws governing, for instance, highway safety or telecommunications come into conflict, the Court must decide whether Congress has preempted state regulation or whether the existence of a variety of different state laws interferes with the need for national and uniform regulations.

Throughout the nation's history the Court has generally supported the authority of the national government to regulate interstate commerce and has interpreted that authority more and more broadly. But the Court has also upheld state regulations when they do not "unduly burden" the national government or its regulation of interstate commerce.

Judicial Review

Article III, Section 1, of the Constitution says, "The judicial Power of the United States shall be vested in one Supreme Court, and in such inferior courts as the Congress may from time to time ordain and establish." Nowhere does the

Constitution give the Supreme Court the power to strike down any congressional or state legislation or any other official government action that violates a provision of the Constitution. Yet the federal judiciary has assumed this power of **judicial review,** a power that makes courts the final arbitrator of major political conflicts. The courts, by exercising judicial review, have taken on the role of guardian of the Constitution.[21]

Both Alexander Hamilton and James Madison argued that judges would exercise some checking power over state legislatures, but they did not agree on whether the Supreme Court would have the power to strike down acts of Congress and the president. Hamilton contended in *The Federalist, No. 78,* that "independent judges" would prove "an essential safeguard against the effects of occasional ill humors in society." Also in *The Federalist, No. 51,* Madison called the judicial power an "auxiliary precaution" against the possible dominance of one branch of government over another. Yet during a debate in the First Congress, he observed: "Nothing has been offered to invalidate the [view] that the meaning of the Constitution may as well be ascertained by the legislative as by the judicial authority."[22]

Despite the absence of a specific constitutional provision, the supremacy of the Supreme Court's interpretation of the Constitution over the interpretations of other branches is a logical implication of the Constitution. The Constitution is the supreme law of the land, and judges take an oath to uphold it— that was the argument made by Chief Justice Marshall in *Marbury v. Madison* (1803).

The case of *Marbury v. Madison* grew out of one of the great episodes of early American politics. Shortly after the ratification of the Constitution, two rival political parties emerged with widely different views of the Constitution and government power. The Federalists supported a strong national government in which the federal courts would have the power to interpret the Constitution. Their opponents, the Anti-Federalists and later the Jeffersonian Republicans, favored the states and state courts.

The struggle came to a head with the election of Thomas Jefferson as president in 1800. In that election the Jeffersonian Republicans defeated the

Rembrandt Peale painted both these two great Virginians, who were political enemies. (Left) John Marshall, "the greatest Chief Justice," served on the Supreme Court from 1801 until 1835. Under him, the Court expanded federal powers. His opinion in Marbury v. Madison *gave particular pain to President Jefferson. (Right) Thomas Jefferson, who distrusted federal power, was the third president of the United States. He wrote the Declaration of Independence, and he died on July 4, 1826, its fiftieth anniversary.*

Federalists, who had held office since the creation of the republic. Fearful of what the Jeffersonian Republicans might do once they assumed office in March 1801, President John Adams and the Federalist-dominated Congress in January created a number of new judgeships and appointed Federalists to fill them all. Appointed chief justice was Adams's secretary of state John Marshall. Marshall, continuing to work as secretary of state, delivered commissions for the new judgeships in the final days of Adams's term but failed to deliver them all before Adams's term expired. Some were left for his successor, Jefferson's secretary of state, James Madison, to deliver.

The Federalists' attempt to "pack" the courts with Federalist judges infuriated the Jeffersonian Republicans. President Jefferson instructed Madison not to deliver the rest of the commissions.

William Marbury was one of the newly appointed judges whose commission was not delivered. He decided to sue to force Madison to give him his commission. In his suit he sought a *writ of mandamus,* a court order directing a government official (Madison) to perform a certain act (hand over the commission). Marbury argued that Section 13 of the Judiciary Act of 1789 authorized the Supreme Court to issue such writs. He saw this strategy not only as a way of getting his commission but also as a means by which the Court could take a stand against the Jeffersonians.

The Supreme Court faced a major dilemma. On the one hand, if it ordered Madison to deliver Marbury's commission, it was likely that President Jefferson would refuse to let Madison comply, because he opposed the Federalists' attempt to pack the federal courts with their supporters. The Court would then be powerless, perhaps permanently. On the other hand, if it refused to issue the writ, it could appear weak, thereby confirming the Jeffersonian argument that the courts had no power to intrude on the executive branch.

Chief Justice Marshall handed down the Court's decision on February 24, 1803. Marbury had a right to his commission, Marshall observed. But, he went on to say, the Court had no power to issue the writ of mandamus. The Judiciary Act's authorization of the Court to issue such a writ was unconstitutional because it expanded the Court's original jurisdiction beyond that provided in the Constitution.

Article III of the Constitution, according to Marshall, granted the Court original jurisdiction *only* in cases involving ambassadors, foreign ministers, and states. William Marbury, however, was none of these. Thus, the Court declared Section 13 of the Judiciary Act unconstitutional and simultaneously established the Court's power to declare acts of Congress unconstitutional.

Chief Justice Marshall's brilliant opinion not only asserted the power of judicial review but defused the political controversy surrounding the case. It gave President Jefferson no opportunity to retaliate. The Jeffersonians fervently disagreed with the reasoning behind the Court's decision, but there was little they could do about it.

During the first half of the nineteenth century, the Court struck down a number of state laws, thereby reaffirming the power of the national government over the states. But it was not until 1857, in *Dred Scott v. Sanford,* that the Court declared another act of Congress unconstitutional. In that case the Court struck down the Missouri Compromise, which had excluded slavery from the nation's territories. The decision badly damaged the Court's reputation and helped to precipitate the Civil War. However, it confirmed the precedent and practice of judicial review established in *Marbury v. Madison* and reaffirmed the Supreme Court's position as a coequal branch of government having considerable influence on the politics of government and the direction of public policy.

THE LIVING CONSTITUTION

The Constitution is a flexible document. Indeed, the major conflicts of American politics—between the national government and the states and between majority rule and individual and minority rights—are fueled by conflicting interpretations of the meaning of the Constitution.

During the past two hundred years, constitutional change has been in the direction of making the Constitution a more democratic document than it was in 1787, and expanding its protection of the civil liberties and rights of individuals. Change has occurred through applications of the Constitution to the day-to-day operation of government, through formal amendments, and by means of judicial review.

Day-to-Day Operation of Government

The Constitution sets out only a broad framework for the governing process. Within that framework, politics determines the day-to-day workings of government and the outcome of public policies.

As the nation's population has increased from barely 4 million in 1787 to over 250 million today, government institutions have changed profoundly. The size of Congress, for instance, has expanded from the 22 senators and 54 representatives elected in 1789 to the 100 senators and 435 representatives, assisted by a staff of more than 25,000, serving today. The power vested in the president now resides in a large executive branch with more than 3 million employees. The federal judiciary has likewise grown, from 19 to more than 1,000 judges, plus more than 15,000 supporting personnel—law clerks, magistrates, and secretaries, among others. In addition, new kinds of government agencies, corporations, and regulatory agencies have powers that cut across and combine the authority of Congress, the executive branch, and the judiciary.

As America's governing institutions have changed, so have government practices, and all those changes have established precedents for the future. Not only is the presidency a larger, more central part of government than it was in the century following ratification of the Constitution, but its powers are greater because past presidents vigorously asserted their constitutional authority.

Advances in science and technology—in nuclear energy, telecommunications, biomedical technology, and other areas—have created new political conflicts and required numerous adjustments in the workings of government. For example, in the age of sailing ships, when the ocean protected the United States against hostile nations, there was ample time for Congress to establish war policy. Now, the existence of nuclear weapons and missiles calls for rapid decision making and action. The result is a shift of power from Congress to the president—in effect, a modification of the Constitution.

Social forces, rising expectations, and decreasing resources have resulted in other modifications. Interest groups and broad political coalitions forged to promote equal civil rights and liberties have pressured the government to enact

The Library of Congress was begun in 1800 as a legislative library for use by members of Congress. The moving spirit behind the new library was Thomas Jefferson, who believed that legislators needed free access to the ideas of the world in order to do their job. The original collection of the Library was destroyed when the British burned Washington in 1814. After the fire Jefferson sold the nation his treasured personal library of six thousand volumes. Growth has been steady ever since. Today the Library of Congress occupies three buildings near the Capitol—the magnificent Thomas Jefferson Building of 1897, the handsome John Adams Building of 1938, and the contemporary James Madison Memorial Building of 1980. The collection today numbers over 97 million items.

The Library of Congress is a reference and research library. Its twenty-one general reading rooms are open at no charge to all members of the public for research and study. Millions of readers and tourists visit the Library annually. Handicapped individuals across the nation are aided by the National Library Service for the Blind and Physically Handicapped.

Another important function of the Library of Congress is registering copyrights (for a nominal fee) for American authors. One copy of any formally copyrighted work published in the United States must be deposited with the Library.

The National Archives of the United States is the central depository for the nation's permanently valuable records. Housed in a massive neoclassic building boasting seventy-two Corinthian columns (completed in 1937), the National Archives is the home of the most cherished documents in America—the Declaration of Independence, the Constitution, and the Bill of Rights. Sealed in special helium-filled cases and guarded around the clock, the documents are displayed to the public daily at the Archives building. At night and in times of emergency, the cases containing the documents sink into a sealed underground vault.

The records of the National Archives span two centuries and total billions of pages of textual material, 6 million photographs, 5 million maps and charts, 100,000 films, and 80,000 sound recordings. Although researchers from across the nation and around the world routinely use the National Archives to research virtually every aspect of American history, government, and policy, the most popular subject by far is genealogical research. The National Archives holds the records of all the agencies ever involved with immigration, as well as pension and census records dating back many decades. Any member of the public aged 16 and over may conduct research at the National Archives at no charge.

In addition to the main archives in Washington, D.C., the National Archives operates presidential libraries containing the papers of Herbert Hoover, Franklin Roosevelt, Harry Truman, Dwight Eisenhower, John Kennedy, and Lyndon Johnson. Records of primarily regional interest are deposited in the Archives Branches of the fifteen Federal Archives and Record Centers found across the country.

---

new laws and to amend the Constitution. As a result, the Constitution has become more democratic than it was originally. And although social and political changes have generated many new issues, most of them have been resolved within the constitutional framework.

Formal Amendment

The Constitution has been amended only twenty-six times in two hundred years. The amendment process (spelled out in Article V) was designed to be difficult. Two-thirds of the members of Congress (or a national constitutional

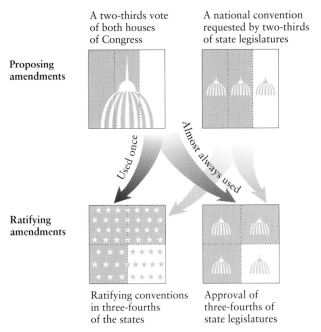

A two-thirds vote
of both houses
of Congress

A national convention
requested by two-thirds
of state legislatures

**Proposing
amendments**

Used once

Almost always used

**Ratifying
amendments**

Ratifying conventions
in three-fourths
of the states

Approval of
three-fourths of
state legislatures

Figure 2-2   *The amendment process.*

convention called for by two-thirds of the states) must pass an amendment and
then three-fourths of the states must ratify it (see Figure 2-2). To date, only
Congress has initiated amendments. The idea of a national constitutional convention worries many political observers, who fear that such a gathering might
become a convention to revise the Constitution much as the Constitutional
Convention of 1787 "revised" the Articles of Confederation.

Tens of thousands of proposed amendments have been introduced in
Congress, but only a few have been passed and ratified by the states. Among
recent proposals that have failed to win approval were a proposal to grant
home rule (self-government) and Senate representation to residents of the District of Columbia and the Equal Rights Amendment, which would have outlawed discrimination on the basis of gender.

The first ten amendments, the Bill of Rights, were ratified just four years
after the adoption of the Constitution. They were necessary to quell fears about
the coercive power of the national government and to secure the rights of individuals. Five later amendments overturned rulings by the Supreme Court—a
remarkably small number, given the thousands of decisions handed down by
the Court. The Eleventh Amendment (1798) granted the states sovereign immunity from suits by citizens of other states. The Thirteenth (1865) and Fourteenth (1868) Amendments (known as the Civil War Amendments) abolished
slavery and made African Americans citizens of the United States. The Sixteenth
Amendment (1913) gave Congress the power to enact a federal income tax.
The Twenty-sixth Amendment (1971) extended the right to vote in all federal
and state elections to citizens who are age 18 and older.

The majority of the remaining amendments to the Constitution have
made government processes more democratic. The Seventeenth Amendment
(1913) provided for the popular election of senators. Voting rights were extended to African Americans by the Fifteenth Amendment (1870), to women

Supporters of women's suffrage parade in front of the Capitol in 1913. Another seven years would pass before the Nineteenth Amendment was ratified, on August 19, 1920, declaring that the right to vote "shall not be denied or abridged . . . on account of sex."

Library of Congress

by the Nineteenth Amendment (1920), to residents of the District of Columbia by the Twenty-third Amendment (1961), and to indigents (through the ban on poll taxes) by the Twenty-fourth Amendment (1964). These constitutional amendments, together with the Supreme Court's rulings promoting the principle of *one person, one vote* (that is, all electoral districts within the same state must be approximately equal in population), have made the Constitution a more democratic document and the political process more open, accessible, and responsive to the people.

Judicial Review

The Supreme Court's role in interpreting the Constitution has long been controversial. As Chief Justice Charles Evans Hughes once declared, "We are under a Constitution, but the Constitution is what the judges say it is."[23] Through judicial review, the Court gives authoritative meaning to the Constitution in light of new claims and changing conditions. And it does so by bringing new claims, such as a right to privacy, within the language, structure, and spirit of the Constitution.

The Supreme Court legitimates and occasionally initiates constitutional change through its interpretation of the Constitution. In the nineteenth century, for example, it expanded the power of Congress to regulate a broad range of social and economic activity. It has sanctioned presidents' claims of inherent power in foreign affairs and of *executive privilege*—the power to withhold some White House communications in the interest of national security. In this century the Court has enforced the Bill of Rights against the states. Previously it had interpreted those amendments as applying only to the national government.

Given the enormous power wielded by the Court in interpreting and applying the Constitution, *how* it should interpret that document remains highly controversial. The controversy has embroiled both liberals and conservatives at different times. In the late nineteenth and early twentieth centuries liberals attacked the Court for becoming a "superlegislature" because it overturned progressive economic legislation. In the last few decades conservatives have cried "judicial imperialism" when criticizing the Court's decisions in the areas of civil liberties and civil rights.

The Watergate controversy (see the Case Study on page 60) illustrates the power of the Court to restrain the other branches of government through its interpretation of the Constitution.[24] In its unanimous ruling in *United States v. Nixon* (1974), the Court held that President Richard Nixon had to release tapes of conversations between the president and his aides that had been recorded in the White House and that contained evidence that the participants had engaged in criminal activities.

Even the justices disagree on how they should interpret the Constitution. Some argue for what is known as **strict construction,** interpretation that is confined to a literal reading of constitutional text, supplemented by historical precedent and what can be learned about the historical context of specific provisions. Others urge a **broad reading** of the text, structure, and spirit of the Constitution, an approach that may require judges to formulate a broad principle that is applicable to different cases in light of changing circumstances.

The debate over how to interpret the Constitution is almost as old as the document itself and is likely to continue as long as the American system of constitutional politics survives. As Justice Felix Frankfurter wisely observed, "Constitutional law is not at all a science, but applied politics."[25]

Constitutional interpretation evolves with the Court and the country. Constitutional law is best viewed as a constantly evolving dialog between the Supreme Court and the American people. By deciding only immediate cases, the Court infuses constitutional meaning into the resolution of the surrounding political controversies. In *Marbury v. Madison,* for example, Chief Justice Marshall resolved the dispute at hand but by no means laid to rest the larger controversy over judicial review and the Court's power to strike down congressional legislation.

Yet the Court by itself cannot lay political controversies to rest. Its power turns on the cooperation of other political institutions and, in the end, on the public's acceptance of its rulings. In the words of Chief Justice Edward White, the Court's power to interpret the Constitution "rests solely on the approval of a free people."[26] In sum, the major confrontations that the Court attempts to resolve, such as controversies over school desegregation, school prayer, and abortion, are determined as much by the possibility of developing consensus in a pluralistic society as by what the Court says about the meaning of the Constitution.

On the night of June 17, 1972, five men broke into the headquarters of the Democratic National Committee, housed in the Watergate complex in Washington, D.C. Their purpose was to plant bugging devices so that they could monitor the Democratic party's campaign plans for the fall presidential election. The "plumbers," as they were called, were caught by some off-duty policeofficers. The next day it was learned that one of them, E. Howard Hunt, a former agent for the Central Intelligence Agency, worked for President Nixon's reelection committee.

Nixon and his associates managed to cover up their involvement in the break-in and won reelection in November 1972. But reporters and congressional committees continued to search for links between the break-in and the White House. Judge John Sirica, who presided over the trial of the five burglars, pressed for a full disclosure of White House involvement. These investigations led to further cover-ups.

In the spring of 1973 the Senate Select Committee on Presidential Activities of 1972, chaired by Senator Sam Ervin of North Carolina, began its investigation. The proceedings were carried on national television. Nixon's former counsel, John Dean, became the star witness, revealing much of the president's involvement in the cover-up. Another aide disclosed that Nixon had installed devices to tape conversations in the Oval Office. The possibility that the tapes contained evidence of Nixon's involvement in the cover-up escalated the crisis.

The Senate Select Committee and a special prosecutor appointed to investigate illegal activities of the White House, Archibald Cox, immediately

Attorney General Elliot Richardson resigned (and so did the assistant attorney general), rather than follow President Nixon's order to fire Archibald Cox, the special prosecutor (left). The third-ranking Justice official, Robert H. Bork, did it.

sought a small number of the tapes. Nixon refused to relinquish them, claiming an executive privilege to withhold information that might damage national security interests.

The special prosecutor then subpoenaed Nixon's attorneys to turn over the tapes. When Nixon again refused, Judge Sirica ordered the release of the tapes. But Nixon still did not comply. Cox appealed to the United States Court of Appeals for the District of Columbia, which urged that an attempt be made

SUMMARY

The First Continental Congress met in 1774 to pass resolutions denouncing the English Parliament and Crown. In 1776 the Second Continental Congress drafted a resolution—the Declaration of Independence—that proclaimed the American colonies to be free and independent states. In 1777 it approved the *Articles of Confederation*, the nation's first constitution. Under the Articles, Congress lacked the power to regulate commerce, collect taxes, or enforce its legislation. After the Revolutionary War, the nation's economic problems worsened, coming to a head with Shays's Rebellion, a revolt by debt-ridden farmers against the government of Massachusetts.

to reach a compromise. When that failed, the court ruled that Nixon had to hand over the tapes.

After the court of appeals ruling, Nixon announced his own compromise. On Friday, October 19, 1973, he offered to provide summaries of relevant conversations. Cox found the deal unacceptable. Nixon then ordered Cox dismissed, thereby unleashing a wave of public anger. Within four days Nixon was forced to tell Sirica that nine tapes would be forthcoming.

The public outcry against Nixon did not subside, nor did the release of the nine tapes end the controversy. It was soon discovered that an 18½-minute segment of the first conversation between Nixon and his chief of staff after the break-in had been erased. That and other revelations prodded the House of Representatives to establish a committee to investigate the possibility of impeachment of the president. Three months later, in February 1974, the House directed its Judiciary Committee to begin hearings on impeachment. Nixon continued to refuse to give additional tapes to the Judiciary Committee and to Leon Jaworski, who had replaced Cox as special prosecutor.

After a federal grand jury investigating Watergate indicted top White House aides and secretly named Nixon as an unindicted co-conspirator, the House Judiciary Committee subpoenaed the release of all documents and tapes related to the Watergate break-in. Nixon remained adamant about his right to decide what to release. This confrontation between the special prosecutor and the president set the stage for the case of *United States v. Nixon.*

The Supreme Court heard oral arguments for the case on July 8, 1974. The fundamental issue, the special prosecutor contended, was "Who is to be the arbiter of what the Constitution says?" Nixon's claim of executive privilege in withholding the tapes, the prosecutor insisted, was an attempt to place the president above the law.

In contrast, Nixon's attorney, James St. Clair, asserted that the case should be dismissed because there was a "fusion" between the criminal prosecution of Nixon's aides and the impeachment proceedings against the president. He argued that this "fusion" violated the principle of separation of powers and that the president should decide what would be made available to the House Judiciary Committee. The dispute, he insisted, was essentially a political one, one that the Supreme Court should avoid.

The Court disagreed. Just sixteen days after hearing oral arguments, it unanimously rejected Nixon's claim of executive privilege as inconsistent with "the fundamental demands of due process of law in the fair administration of justice."

Discussion questions
1. How does *United States v. Nixon* illustrate the political struggles that arise over the meaning of the Constitution?
2. What role does the Supreme Court play in resolving political conflicts?
3. Why did President Nixon comply with the ruling in *United States v. Nixon* even though he disagreed with the Court's interpretation of the Constitution, and what is the significance of his doing so?

In 1787 delegates from the states met in Philadelphia to revise the Articles of Confederation but quickly decided to establish a national government with legislative, executive, and judiciary branches. The new government would be a *republic;* it would have the power to make and enforce laws but would derive its authority from the citizens through popular elections.

Two plans for the new government were proposed to the convention. The *Virginia Plan* called for a bicameral legislature in which the representation of states would be based on wealth and population. The *New Jersey Plan,* in contrast, called for a single-house legislature in which all states would have equal representation. A committee was formed to arrive at a compromise between the two plans. Its solution, the *Great Compromise,* was to create a bicameral legislature in which representation in the lower house (the House of Representatives) would be based on population but all states would be represented equally in the upper house (the Senate).

Slavery was another divisive issue. Delegates from the southern states wanted slaves to be counted as part of the population for purposes of representation. Delegates from the northern states insisted on equal representation of all citizens, thereby excluding slaves. The delegates finally agreed to the *three-fifths compromise:* three-fifths of a state's slave population would be counted for purposes of taxation and representation.

The Constitutional Convention recommended that the new constitution be sent to the states for ratification by special conventions. The constitution would be ratified if nine of the thirteen states gave their approval. In some states—especially New York, Virginia, and Massachusetts—the Constitution met with opposition from those who were concerned that it gave the national government too much power. Their approval was finally obtained when it was agreed that the First Congress would adopt a bill of rights that guaranteed the civil rights and liberties of individuals. The first ten amendments compose the *Bill of Rights.*

Central to the Constitution is the idea of *popular sovereignty,* the idea that government is based on the consent of the people and is accountable to the people for its actions. From this notion follows the idea of *limited government,* the restriction of government authority to *express powers,* which are powers specified and delegated to the national government by the Constitution. The government also has certain *implied powers,* which can be inferred from its express powers, as well as *inherent powers* in the area of foreign affairs.

One of the main reasons for limiting the powers of government is to safeguard the *unalienable rights* of individuals. These natural rights were ensured not only through the passage of the Bill of Rights but also through the distribution of power among the three branches of the national govern-

ment. The *separation of powers* is designed to create a delicate balance in which the three branches check and balance each other in various ways. In reality, the powers of the government are not truly separate but are shared.

The Constitution also distributes power between the national and state governments, in a system known as *federalism.* All powers that are not granted to the national government and are not expressly denied the states are known as *reserved powers.* In addition, the national government and the states share some powers, which are known as *concurrent powers.* When conflicts arise between the national government and the states, the *supremacy clause* in Article VI of the Constitution requires that federal law prevail.

Although the Constitution does not give the judiciary the power of *judicial review*—the power to strike down any legislation or other government action that violates constitutional provisions—the federal courts have assumed this power because the Constitution is the supreme law of the land and judges take an oath to uphold it. The Supreme Court claimed this power in *Marbury v. Madison* (1803).

During the last two hundred years, constitutional change has occurred in three ways: through the applications of the Constitution to the day-to-day operation of government, through formal amendments, and through judicial review. Changes in government institutions, scientific and technological advances, and social forces have brought about modifications of the constitutional structure of government. In addition, the Constitution has been amended twenty-seven times, and the Supreme Court has occasionally initiated change through its interpretation of the Constitution. The Court's role in constitutional change has been controversial. Some justices and scholars have argued for a *strict construction,* or literal reading of constitutional text. Others have urged a *broad reading* of the text, structure, and spirit of the Constitution.

Articles of Confederation
republic
Virginia Plan
New Jersey Plan
Great Compromise
three-fifths compromise
Bill of Rights

popular sovereignty
limited government
express powers
implied powers
inherent powers
unalienable rights
separation of powers

federalism
reserved powers
concurrent powers
supremacy clause
judicial review
strict construction
broad reading

LEARNING MORE ABOUT THE CONSTITUTION

Scholarly studies

Farrand, Max. *The Framing of the Constitution.* New Haven, Conn.: Yale University Press, 1913 (paperback ed., 1962). A classic introduction to the creation of the Constitution by the editor of the definitive collection of papers and proceedings of the Constitutional Convention.

McDonald, Forrest. *Novus Ordo Seclorum: The Intellectual Origins of the Constitution.* Lawrence: University of Kansas Press, 1985. One of the best contemporary studies of the intellectual background and forces that contributed to the drafting and ratification of the Constitution.

Wood, Gordon S. *The Creation of the American Republic, 1776–1787.* New York: Norton, 1993. A widely acclaimed and pathbreaking study of the intellectual trends and political conflicts that led to the creation of the Constitution.

Leisure reading

Kammen, Michael. *The Machine That Would Go by Itself.* New York: Knopf, 1987. One of numerous books that appeared during the Constitution's bicentennial year, but one that stands out in showing how the Constitution has survived amid the myriad changes that have taken place in the country over the past two hundred years.

Primary sources

Farrand, Max, ed. *The Records of the Federal Convention of 1787.* 4 vols. New Haven, Conn.: Yale University Press, 1913 (paperback ed., 1986). The definitive collection of the debates at the Constitutional Convention. In 1987 a fifth volume based on additional documents was added to the set.

Hamilton, Alexander, John Jay, and James Madison. *The Federalist Papers.* This collection of 85 essays, written to help win support of the Constitution by the New York ratifying convention, contains some of the most illuminating arguments about the nature of the Constitution. It has gone through many editions and many editors; the edition by Clinton Rossiter contains a fine introduction (New American Library, 1961).

Kurland, Philip, and Ralph Lerner. *The Founders' Constitution.* 5 vols. Chicago: University of Chicago Press, 1987. An easy-to-use guide to what the framers said about each part of the Constitution. It contains most of their statements and arranges them according to each provision in the Constitution.

Storing, Herbert J. *The Complete Anti-Federalist.* 7 vols. Chicago: University of Chicago Press, 1981. A collection of the arguments made against the Constitution and for the addition of a bill of rights by the opponents of ratification.

CHAPTER 3

Federalism in Theory and Practice

- Federalism as a political issue

- The changing nature of American federalism

- Federal-state-local relations: national regulation of states and localities; grants-in-aid, conditions, politics, distribution criteria, and regional controversies; state and local influence on national policy making

- Federalism in action: the minimum age for alcohol consumption; control and management of water resources

At left are the candidates of 1872, 1876, and 1880. Democrat Horace Greeley was no competition for Ulysses S. Grant in 1872, even though many considered Grant a drunkard and a crook after his first administration. (Suffragette Susan B. Anthony was one active Republican supporter.) Soon after the election, Greeley required psychiatric hospitalization.

The centennial campaign of 1876 pitted Rutherford B. Hayes, Republican governor of Ohio, against Democrat Samuel J. Tilden, New York's district attorney. A dispute over electoral votes led Congress to establish an electoral commission, which awarded all disputed votes to Hayes and gave the Republicans a one-vote victory in the Electoral College.

In 1880, Republican Congressman James Garfield of Ohio defeated General Winfield Hancock. An economic depression had receded, and almost 80 percent of the electorate turned out—to vote mostly for Republicans. When Garfield was assassinated by a rejected office seeker just months after the election, Vice President Chester Arthur succeeded him.

On April 21, 1993, President Clinton unveiled his education reform package, formally called "Goals 2000: Educate America Act." Among other things, the president proposed a National Education Standards and Improvement Council which would develop and certify standards for schools to meet in order to achieve a number of goals. Among those goals: at least 90 percent of students should finish high school; students should demonstrate competence in English, math, science, foreign languages, the arts, history, and geography; the United States should be first in the world in math and science; every adult American should be literate; and every school should be free of drugs and violence. The Clinton plan did not require schools to meet nationally set standards. It did, however, talk about standards for academic and occupational subjects, national tests to check whether students are learning the required skills, and financial rewards to states that revamp their school curricula along broadly set federal guidelines.

As expected, the school reform proposal generated immediate controversy and debate. Some worried that national standards would stifle teacher creativity; some felt that the proposal left too little room for parent involvement; and some felt that the bill did too little to equalize expenditures on education among different school districts.

But, as frequently is the case in American politics, the most heated argument over the proposal centered not on the merits of the plan or of the specific educational goals. Rather, it focused on the proper roles of various levels of governments—state, local, and national—in setting education standards and getting students to meet them.

Speaking on behalf of a more active role in education reform for the national government, Education Secretary Richard Riley emphasized the voluntary nature of the plan. "This bill," he said, "will help to establish internationally competitive standards so communities and states can, if they wish, gauge their curriculum and instruction against those that are world-class." Concerned about the role of states in setting education policy, Republican Representative Steve Gunderson of Wisconsin expressed his reservations, exclaiming that "the bill

has the potential to go beyond [voluntary state and local compliance]. The traditional federal role is guidelines, not standards—voluntary or mandatory."

Governors, too, were concerned that a federal role in setting school standards intruded on state prerogatives. Patricia Sullivan, lobbyist for the National Governors' Association, made it clear that the nation's governors were "frustrated that folks at the state level would be given a checklist by the federal government." Further, she warned, "This is a pretty substantial shift in relations between the federal government and education. It's always been a state game." Colorado Governor Roy Romer and South Carolina Governor Carrol Campbell summed up the states' view when they wrote to Secretary Riley, "Some governors believe that it is inappropriate for . . . a federally appointed entity to certify either state content standards or opportunity to learn standards. Even on a voluntary basis, some of the governors believe that this is an example of federal intrusion into an area that has historically been a responsibility of the states."[1]

THE BATTLE OVER PRESIDENT CLINTON'S EDUCATION REFORM proposal illustrates one of the principal lessons of politics and policy making in the American federal system. Deciding which *level* of government should be responsible for a particular policy is often as important and as hotly debated as the policy itself. Which level of government, for example, should be responsible for setting education standards, for establishing abortion laws, for setting environmental rules and regulations, for regulating businesses and professions, for establishing welfare policies? Which level should set minimum wage rates for public and private sector employees, determine the appropriate age for alcohol consumption, set speed limits on roads and highways? Should these activities be the responsibility of the national government, or should they be the responsibility of the states and their local subdivisions?

FEDERALISM AS A POLITICAL ISSUE

In nonfederal countries such as Great Britain, political debate ordinarily is limited to whether government *should* get involved in some activity. In the United States, the debate is about not only *whether* government should be involved but *which level* of government should be responsible for a particular activity.

Early in his administration President Clinton expressed the view that "the real genius of the federal system" is the flexibility it gives to states in carrying out policy initiatives. The national government should establish "general principles," the president said, but we should "honor the Founding Fathers by encouraging experimentation in the states."[2] Throughout the nation's history the debate over what the "Founding Fathers" actually intended when they created a federal form of government has been fueled by the ambiguous language of the Constitution. They provided no clear definition of the precise relationships between the various levels of government. But the debate continues for other reasons as well. National legislators are elected from local districts and are responsible to local constituents, and many Americans prefer a large measure of local self-control. For those reasons, even more than constitutional vagueness, federalism is likely to remain an intensely political issue. How much (or how little) trust Americans have in the ability of the federal, state, and local governments to handle homelessness, air pollution, and other public problems is shown in Figure 3-1.

Debates over the "true" meaning of federalism have been at the heart of some of the most important political battles in United States history, including slavery, the regulation of business and industry, the civil rights movement, and environmental protection. The legalistic and scholarly terms in which constitutional debates over the proper roles of government are couched often disguise other, more political concerns. When interest groups, political parties, and individuals advocate more or less control by Washington or by the states, they frequently do so to achieve specific policy goals. People who believe state and local governments are likely to support their views on an issue—be it welfare, gun control, abortion, or prayer in public schools—will argue that the Constitution "clearly" reserves authority for such decisions to the states and

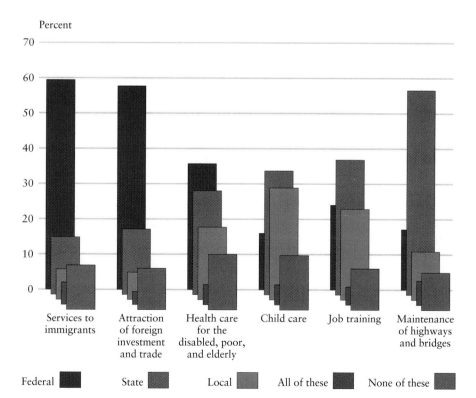

Figure 3-1 *People's trust and confidence in the ability of three levels of government to handle public problems most effectively.* SOURCE: *Adapted from survey conducted by the Advisory Commission on Intergovernmental Relations, published in* Changing Public Attitudes on Governments and Taxes *(Washington, D.C.: ACIR, 1990), 8.*

communities. The federal system will suffer, they say, if such decisions are "nationalized." People who believe the national government is likely to be supportive of their views will make the opposite argument. The Constitution, they say, "obviously" delegates responsibility in these areas to the national government.

In this chapter we examine the political aspects of federalism. We trace the evolution of the American federal experience and look at power and influence in the federal system, focusing especially on the ways in which the national government and the states and localities attempt to regulate and influence each other's behavior.

THE CHANGING NATURE OF AMERICAN FEDERALISM

Since the nation's founding, advocates for the national, state, and local governments have sparred over the meaning of federalism and over the proper division of power and responsibility in the American political system. In 1860, these debates erupted in the Civil War. In the 1960s, civil rights issues raised the question of the proper role of the states and the national government in the American federal system. In the 1980s, issues of federalism were again at the forefront of public debate as President Ronald Reagan attempted to get the national government "off the back of the American people." In the 1990s, health care, abortion, education reform, and the environment continue to raise questions about the balance of national, state, and local responsibility.

Not surprisingly, the founders did not foresee all the issues that would confront subsequent generations. A certain vagueness, however, has contributed to the adaptability of the Constitution and it has ultimately strengthened the federal system. It has permitted states to experiment with differing policies and government arrangements, but it has kept those experiments within acceptable bounds. It has permitted—even encouraged—political struggles, and these struggles, in turn, have redefined federalism and made it relevant to contemporary needs.

The concept of federalism has been evolving since 1787, and it will go on evolving as the nation faces new issues and continues to debate how best to deal with old ones. In short, federalism is, as some people say, "unfinished business."

National Supremacy Versus States' Rights, 1787–1865

In the period from the ratification of the Constitution to the end of the Civil War, the constitutional debate continued over the proper role of governments in the American system. Those seeking more power and responsibility for the national government vied for power with those seeking to protect and enhance the rights of the individual states.

Those who maintained a *nation-centered* view—the Federalists—believed that the Constitution emanated from and was applicable to the American people as a whole. They did not see the Constitution simply as a pact among the states. From the Federalist perspective, the national government had a legitimate interest in protecting and promoting the health, safety, and welfare of the people themselves; its interests and obligations did not end just with its dealings with state governments. As Chief Justice John Marshall stated in the

John Marshall: Defining Federal Power

At the Virginia ratifying convention in 1788, John Marshall, a successful lawyer and close friend of George Washington, was an influential speaker in favor of the new Constitution. After ratification, however, Marshall declined the several different positions he was offered in the new federal government. From 1797 to 1798, he did serve as Minister to France, and from 1799 to 1800 he was member for Virginia in the House of Representatives. A staunch Federalist, in 1800 Marshall accepted the post of Secretary of State in the troubled administration of President John Adams.

When Chief Justice Oliver Ellsworth resigned unexpectedly from the Supreme Court later in 1800, Adams offered the post to Marshall. He accepted, becoming the fourth Chief Justice. From this exalted position, Marshall set forth interpretations of the Constitution that have become the foundations for American constitutional law.

Marshall believed that the Constitution was essentially a flexible document open to judicial interpretation in the light of individual cases and changing times. He also believed strongly in federal supremacy over the states. Most important, Marshall believed that the institutions of government could gain the respect of the people only by being effective. His opinions helped establish not only the basic principles of constitutional law but also the prestige and independence of the Supreme Court.

Marshall's most famous opinion is undoubtedly the 1803 case of *Marbury v. Madison*, in which he established the Court's power to declare a law unconstitutional and therefore void. Marshall's enunciation of the principle of judicial review firmly established the Supreme Court, not Congress, as the final arbiter of the Constitution.

In *Dartmouth College v. Woodward* in 1819, Marshall's opinion established the sanctity of the contracts clause of the Constitution. (This case was also notable for the emotional plea of Daniel Webster, arguing for the defense, who said, "It is, sir, as I have said, a small college, and yet there are those who love it.")

In the complicated case of *McCulloch v.*

Library of Congress

The decisions of John Marshall, the fourth chief justice of the Supreme Court, greatly enhanced the powers of the national government and of the Court itself.

Maryland, the issue was whether the state of Maryland had the right to tax the Baltimore branch of the Bank of the United States. In his opinion, Marshall held that the "necessary and proper" clause of the Constitution gave the federal government the right to grant corporate charters. He further held that Maryland's attempt to tax the bank clashed with the sovereignty of the Constitution and was thus unconstitutional. Marshall's opinion established the primacy of the federal government over state governments, and his words gave authority to "loose construction" of the Constitution. As he wrote, "Let the end be legitimate, let it be within the scope of the Constitution, and all means which are appropriate, which are plainly adapted to that end, which are not prohibited, but consist with the letter and spirit of the Constitution, are constitutional."

In *Gibbins v. Ogden* in 1824, Marshall ruled that states cannot interfere with interstate commerce, which is solely in the domain of the federal government under the commerce clause of the Constitution. Today's vast body of regulation on interstate commerce owes its origin to this crucial decision.

69

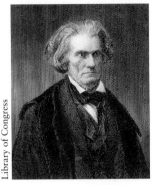

Senator John C. Calhoun (S.C.) championed states' rights and the idea that states could nullify federal rulings if, in their judgment, the national government had exceeded its authority. When slavery became the dominant national issue, Calhoun's positions became the central planks in the platform of proslavery advocates.

Dred Scott was a slave in Missouri but a free man when his owner took him to the Minnesota Territory. The controversy over his status led to the Supreme Court decision that the federal government "had no right to interfere for any purpose but that of protecting the rights of the owner, leaving it altogether to the states to deal with this race." With this pivotal decision, parties and platforms fragmented, and the Civil War became inevitable.

1819 case of *McCulloch v. Maryland,* the national government "is the government of all; its powers are delegated by all; it represents all, and acts for all."[3]

Marshall and other Federalists saw the Constitution as a document of and for national unity. They believed that the national government could draw on a rich array of delegated *and* implied powers to promote the general welfare of the country. As Secretary of the Treasury Alexander Hamilton put it, the test for determining whether an act of Congress is constitutional is the end, or goal, that it addresses:

If the *end* be clearly comprehended within any of the specified powers, and if the measure have an obvious relation to that *end,* and is not forbidden by any particular provision of the Constitution, it may safely be deemed to come within the compass of the national authority.[4]

Those who held a *state-centered* view—the Anti-Federalists—had a different perspective. They believed that the Constitution was a compact among the states and that the states themselves were the legitimate center of power and authority in the federal system. This position was eloquently advanced in 1798 in the Virginia and Kentucky Resolutions, which were drawn up by James Madison and Thomas Jefferson in opposition to the Alien and Sedition Acts of 1798 and were passed by the legislatures in both Virginia and Kentucky.[5] The resolutions implied that the national government did not have *all* government power; that its powers were limited by the language of the Constitution; that some rights were reserved for the states; and that states could protect their rights.[6]

This position was taken to its extreme in the 1820s and 1830s by many advocates of states' rights, especially by John C. Calhoun, senator from South Carolina. His **doctrine of nullification** argued that *sovereignty*—ultimate government power—could not be divided among levels of government but instead resided with the states. The Constitution, he thought, was an agreement made by sovereign states that had established a central government to perform certain tasks for them. Calhoun viewed the central government as an agent of the states. He argued that whenever a state found an act of Congress to be in violation of the Constitution, that state could declare the congressional act null and void within its own borders. This position was clearly at odds with the views of those advocating a nation-centered form of government.

By the 1840s slavery had become the dominant issue dividing advocates of the nation-centered and the state-centered notions of federalism. As always, both groups pointed to the Constitution for support. Opponents of slavery referred to the due process clause of the Fifth Amendment, which states that "No person . . . shall be . . . deprived of life, liberty, or property, without due process of law." They further argued that since Congress had full sovereignty over the territories by virtue of its treaty and war powers, Congress could limit or abolish slavery in the territories as it wished.

Relying on positions similar to those advanced by Calhoun, proponents of slavery argued that since the national government was merely an agent of the states, it could not administer the territories against the interest of any of the states. They argued that slaveholders had a constitutional right to bring slaves into any territory without legal hindrance. They also relied on the Fifth Amendment, arguing that since slaves were property, legislation abolishing slavery would be a destruction of property without compensation and therefore a violation of the amendment's due process protections. This argument was accepted by Chief Justice Roger Taney in the *Dred Scott* case.

Scott, a slave, had moved with his owner from the slave state of Missouri to the free state of Illinois and later to free territory under the Missouri Compromise. When his owner died, Scott sued for his freedom, claiming that the years he had spent in Illinois and the free territory had ended his bondage. The case made its way through the courts in Missouri, moved into federal court, and in 1857 was decided by the Supreme Court.

The Supreme Court ruled against Scott, stating that he could not sue because as a Negro and as a slave he was not a citizen of the United States. The Court went on to consider the issue of sovereignty over the territories. The federal government, Chief Justice Taney stated, had no general sovereignty over the territories at all. Congress had only the powers associated with the right to acquire territories and prepare them for statehood; it could not exercise internal police powers. This meant that Congress could not prevent slavery in the territories and that the Missouri Compromise, which had excluded slavery from the territories, was unconstitutional.

The *Dred Scott* decision greatly intensified the crisis that ultimately led to the Civil War. It is often said that while *Dred Scott* did not "cause" the Civil War, it was the straw that broke the nation's back.

Redefining State and National Roles, 1865–1933

The Civil War permanently altered federal-state relations. Nullification theory was discredited by the outcome of the strife, and the Union was preserved. Since that time, few Americans have seriously proposed that a state can declare an act of Congress null and void or can secede from the Union. But from the perspective of defining federalism, little else was settled.

Between 1865 and 1933, a new relationship known as **dual federalism** emerged. It recognized separate and distinct spheres of authority for the national and state governments. The staunchest advocates of dual federalism viewed the distribution of power between the levels of government as fixed and unchangeable. The states were judged to be on an equal plane with the national government, and the Tenth Amendment was cited as the constitutional evidence of an area of authority reserved for the states.[7]

This philosophy can be seen in *Texas v. White* (1869), which tested whether Texas was responsible for bonds issued by its confederate government during the Civil War. Chief Justice Salmon P. Chase stated:

Under the Constitution, though the powers of the States were much restricted, still all the powers not delegated to the United States, nor prohibited to the States, are reserved to the States, respectively, or to the people. . . . Not only . . . can there be no loss of separate and independent autonomy to the States, through their union under the Constitution, but it may be not unreasonably said that the preservation of the States, and the maintenance of their governments, are as much within the design and care of the Constitution as the preservation of the Union and the maintenance of the National Government. The Constitution, in all its provisions, looks to an indestructible Union, composed of indestructible States.[8]

During this period the United States was rapidly industrializing, and the public began looking to government at all levels for greater social and economic regulation. State attempts to curb industrial excesses and business monopolies proved largely ineffective, however, so it fell to Congress to regulate economic practices and the social effects of big railroads and other industrial giants. Much

Senator Stephen A. Douglas (Ill.) was one of four presidential candidates in the 1860 election. The Democrats had split into northern and southern factions over the issues of slavery, states' rights, and congressional sovereignty over the territories, virtually ensuring their defeat. When no candidate captured a majority of the popular vote, the Electoral College selected Republican Abraham Lincoln. Just seven days after Lincoln's inauguration, the southern states seceded, and by April the nation was plunged into civil war.

of the debate over proper federal-state relations centered on the interpretation of the interstate commerce clause of the Constitution (Article I, Section 8) and on the proper role of Congress in regulating the nation's commerce.

Attempting to distinguish between *inter*state commerce, which Congress could regulate, and *intra*state commerce, which was under the authority of the states, the Supreme Court invalidated a number of regulatory actions by Congress on the ground that they usurped state authority. In 1895 the Court significantly weakened the effects of the Sherman Anti-Trust Act of 1890 (a federal act attempting to prevent unlawful monopolies) by declaring that monopolistic manufacturing activities were not within the scope of national regulatory influence because manufacturing is not commerce.[9] During the 1890s the Court also severely curtailed the powers of the Interstate Commerce Commission, which had been created in 1887 to regulate commerce, particularly the railroads.

The case of *Hammer v. Dagenhart* (1918) presents most forcefully the doctrine of dual federalism. In that case the Supreme Court invalidated the federal Child Labor Act of 1916—which barred from interstate commerce commodities produced by manufacturers employing children—on the ground that the act invaded an area reserved for state activity. Justice William R. Day wrote the following:

In interpreting the Constitution it must never be forgotten that the nation is made up of states to which are entrusted the powers of local government. And to them and to the people the powers not expressly delegated to the national government are reserved. . . . The power of the states to regulate their purely internal affairs by such laws as seem wise to the local authority is inherent and has never been surrendered to the general government.[10]

Justice Day's use of "expressly" in the *Dagenhart* decision altered the meaning of the Tenth Amendment. Almost 130 years earlier, the framers had very deliberately rejected the term there.

During the Great Depression of the 1930s President Franklin Roosevelt proposed a number of actions to speed the nation's economic recovery. One of these, the National Industrial Recovery Act of 1933 (NIRA), created a massive public works program and also attempted to establish uniform codes and regulations for much of the nation's business and industry. Reflecting the philosophy of dual federalism, the Court struck down the National Industrial Recovery Act in 1935 in the case of *Schechter Poultry Corporation v. United States*. The Court said that "the authority of the federal government may not be pushed to such an extreme as to destroy the distinction . . . between 'commerce among the several states' and the internal commerce of a state."[11] Nullification of the NIRA proved to be the last significant Court decision supporting the concept of dual federalism.

Expansion of the Federal Government, 1933–1968

The Great Depression ended an era and ushered in **cooperative federalism,** which stressed a partnership and a sharing of functions, responsibilities, and programs between the states and the national government. Since the late 1930s, the courts have generally interpreted the Constitution so as to extend the national government's control and regulation of business and commerce. In the case of *United States v. Darby Lumber Company* (1941), for example, the Supreme Court upheld the Fair Labor Standards Act of 1938, which, among other provisions, prohibited the shipment in interstate commerce of goods produced by child labor and thus effectively overturned the *Hammer v. Dagenhart* decision. Actions by Congress and the courts have greatly enlarged the role of the national government in such areas as education, housing, transportation, civil rights, environmental protection, and social services.

The period from 1933 to 1968 was marked by increased use of **grants-in-aid,** which are programs through which the national government shares its fiscal resources with state and local governments (they are described in detail later in the chapter). By 1930, fifteen grant programs were allocating about $120 million to the states annually. Between 1930 and 1960, the number of grant-in-aid programs increased dramatically. In the period sometimes called the "First New Deal"—about 1933 to 1935—new grant programs were enacted for the distribution of surplus farm products to the needy, free school lunches, emergency highway expenditures, emergency relief work, general relief, administration of employment security, and assistance in meeting local government costs. In the "Second New Deal"—about 1935 to 1939—additional grant programs were created for child welfare, mothers' and children's health, services for crippled children, old-age assistance, aid to dependent children, aid to the blind, general health services, fire control, wildlife conservation, public housing, emergency road and bridge construction, and venereal disease and tuberculosis control.

By 1960, some 132 grant programs existed, allocating almost $7 billion annually. Most of the grants made available during this period went to state governments; a few went directly to cities. Also, most of the grants were for

During the Great Depression of the 1930s, the Works Progress Administration put nearly nine million people to work on roads, bridges, parks, and projects in the arts. (Left) WPA workers in Lawrence County, Tennessee, are building a road to link farmers with markets in Memphis. (Right) In the 1960s, Head Start, one victory in the War on Poverty, provided food, medical care, and early education to prepare disadvantaged children for school.

Dirck Halstead/UPI/Bettmann

UPI/Bettmann

specific purposes or programs defined by Congress. The regulatory role of the national government, in the form of rules and regulations that had to be met in order for grants to be awarded, increased significantly. So did national reliance on the grant-in-aid system for achieving a range of objectives, especially in social welfare, housing, and transportation.[12]

During the 1960s the number of federal grants available to state and local governments exploded. In 1965 and 1966, Congress enacted 130 new grant programs. Under President Lyndon B. Johnson's Great Society program, grants were used to expand the range of federal activity. By 1968, almost $19 billion was allocated through the grant programs, many of which provided money directly to cities, bypassing the state governments.

Grants-in-Aid to Mandates and Regulations, 1968 to the Present

When the Republicans gained control of the White House in 1968, a new chapter in the history of federalism was written. Calling his approach the **new federalism,** President Richard M. Nixon deemphasized the use of grants for specific purposes and focused instead on large grants to local governments in general policy areas. In theory, such grants gave the recipient governments greater discretion in the expenditure of funds, and they also removed from the national government a degree of control over how the funds were spent. Throughout Nixon's presidency and Jimmy Carter's as well, the amount of money allocated through grant-in-aid programs continued to grow. By 1980, the national government was annually allocating $91.5 billion to states and localities.

In 1980 President Reagan announced a program called New Federalism, but his approach differed from Nixon's. Reagan called for a significant slowdown in the rate of increase in the funding of grant programs, and in both 1982 and 1987 the amount of money made available actually declined. In addition, the number of programs declined significantly, as did the proportion of state and local budgets funded by grants. In 1980 grants-in-aid accounted for 25.8 percent of total state and local spending, but by the end of the decade the percentage had dropped to about 17 percent. This turned around somewhat in the 1990s. More than eighty new grant programs were enacted from 1989 to 1992, and spending on all grants increased by 46 percent. In 1992 grants represented about 22 percent of state and local spending and almost 13 percent of the federal budget. But most of these increases occurred in grants targeted for individuals, not in grants going to local governments for general purposes.

The Reagan administration placed considerably less emphasis on grants-in-aid as a tool for national policy making, but a higher proportion of grants went to state governments than to local governments, and states had greater authority over the funds. This policy continued in the Bush administration, contributing to what some observers believed to be a revitalization of state governments. But it also left local governments with considerably less revenue to deal with the myriad problems facing America's cities. Early in his presidency, Bill Clinton proposed a few modest assistance programs for distressed cities and neighborhoods, but his focus on deficit reduction precluded any major new spending on grants-in-aid. Throughout this period, the federal government—through various mechanisms discussed later in this chapter—greatly increased its *monitoring and regulation* of state and local activities. From 1970

During the years of Ronald Reagan's New Federalism, many federal grants were reduced, leaving local governments with significantly larger financial burdens. (Left) In New York the Motta family lives in a welfare hotel; their food stamp allowance was cut from $152 to $61 per month. (Right) In West Philadelphia, a housing project stands broken, empty, and bankrupt.

to 1990, for example, it issued over two hundred "preemptive statutes" that displaced or replaced state and local laws. This was twice as many such statutes as had been passed in the *entire history* of the United States until then.

Is Federalism Dead?

The Tenth Amendment made explicit the concept of powers reserved to the states: "The powers not delegated to the United States by the Constitution, nor prohibited by it to the States, are reserved to the States respectively, or the people." The interpretation of the Tenth Amendment in order to identify and define appropriate spheres of state and national government activity has been a subject of intense and continuing political debate. In an important court case in 1976, *National League of Cities v. Usery*, the Supreme Court held that some areas of state activity—in this instance the setting of minimum wages for municipal employees—are exempt from national-level encroachment. The Tenth Amendment, the Court ruled, provides absolute protection for at least some areas of state (and municipal) government functions. As it said, "There are attributes of sovereignty attaching to every state government which may not be impaired by Congress . . . because the Constitution prohibits [Congress] from exercising [its] authority in that manner."[13]

To some observers the *National League of Cities* ruling seemed to imply that the Supreme Court might actively champion states' rights. Soon, however, the Court began issuing decisions that served to erode severely the principle of state sovereignty established in the case.[14] In *Garcia v. San Antonio Metropolitan Transit Authority* (1985), the Court ruled that local governments have to adhere to minimum-wage standards set by Congress (at a cost to local governments of about $1.75 billion annually).[15] In this 5-to-4 decision the Court ruled that except in rare situations the Constitution does not limit the national government's power to interfere in state affairs. The notion of state functions beyond the control of Congress, the Court said, is "both impracticable and doctrinally barren."[16]

In the equally important case of *South Carolina v. Baker* (1988), the Supreme Court ruled that income earned from tax-exempt state and local bonds can be subject to federal taxation if Congress chooses to apply such a tax. The doctrine of intergovernmental tax immunity, established in *McCulloch v. Maryland* (1819) but considerably reduced in scope in this century, would no longer necessarily be supported. And, in a case decided in 1990, the Court agreed that a federal judge could order a local legislative body to raise revenues to provide for more equitable school financing.[17]

To some, these recent cases seem virtually to have eliminated any vestige of protected state or local sovereignty. As Justice Sandra Day O'Connor commented in her dissenting opinion in the *Garcia* case, "The States as States retain no status apart from that which Congress chooses to let them retain." Together, the cases seem to imply that officials of the national government are the sole judges of the limits of national power and that, in fact, there is almost no arena of state activity that is beyond the regulatory authority of the national government if the national government chooses to exercise control in that area.

Although state and local governments have "won" a few significant federalism decisions in recent years,[18] the present situation is one that some scholars term "permissive federalism." This expression alludes to the fact that there continues to be some sharing of power and authority by the national and state governments, but the state and local share of power and authority depends on the permissiveness of the national government.[19] Federalism, then, is not dead but is in a significantly weakened condition.

FEDERAL-STATE-LOCAL RELATIONS: POWER AND POLITICS

The federal system of the United States poses particular challenges for the national government, as it attempts to influence and regulate local governments, and for local governments, as they in turn attempt to affect activities at the national level. The national government, in its attempts to regulate states and localities, may issue direct orders and it may preempt state and local activities. Also, through grants-in-aid, and the *conditions* attached to these grants, the national government may encourage certain state and local activities and discourage others. (The Constitutional Conflict on page 77 describes one such attempt.)

National Regulation of States and Localities

Direct orders Occasionally the national government issues direct orders that local governments must comply with or else face civil or criminal penalties. The Equal Employment Opportunity Act of 1972 bars job discrimination by state and local governments on the basis of race, color, religion, sex, and national origin. As a result of this law, some localities have been required to reinstate, promote, or pay individuals who have been discriminated against in violation of the act. The 1977 Marine Protection Research and Sanctuaries Act Amendments prohibit cities from dumping sewage sludge in the ocean. The Americans with Disabilities Act of 1990 requires local governments to see to it that all fixed-rate public transportation systems be made accessible to the handicapped,

The Limits of the Federal Government's Coercive Authority over State and Local Governments

The Tenth Amendment says that state and local governments retain powers that are "not delegated to the [national government] by the Constitution." But what are these powers? Throughout American history the answer to that question has been debated.

As recently as 1992, in the case of *New York v. United States*, the Supreme Court ruled that the national government could not force a state to take legal responsibility for disposing of all the low-level radioactive waste produced within its borders. At issue was a 1980 federal law that had made states responsible for disposing of low-level radioactive waste generated within their borders by private and public producers. In 1985, the law had been amended to require states that were unable to dispose of such waste by 1996 to take possession of the waste and to be held liable in court for any damages caused by their failure to do so.

The state of New York and two of its counties sued the federal government, arguing that the law violated the Tenth Amendment. While upholding some parts of the law, the Supreme Court did find the portion that required states to take possession of the waste material by 1996 to be in violation of the states' political autonomy provided by the Tenth Amendment. Writing for the majority in the 6-to-3 decision, Justice Sandra Day O'Connor stated that "In this [take possession] provision, Congress has crossed the line distinguishing encouragement from coercion."

A continuing source of constitutional controversy in the area of federalism will be the determination of what areas of state activity—if any—are permanently beyond the regulatory control of the national government.

© Frances M. Roberts

The Americans with Disabilities Act (1990) prohibits discrimination in public services and requires ready access to all public facilities. The costs are high, however. Modifications to accommodate a single disabled student at Veterans' Memorial High School, in Warwick, Rhode Island, ran to $51,850.

(Left) *New York City's infamous landfill at Fresh Kills, Staten Island, belches odors and leaches the soil. Worse, it is almost full.* (Right) *After weeks of wandering at sea, unable to get permission to dump its 3,000 tons of garbage and medical waste into the waters off anyone's coast, this Long Island garbage barge rests with its tugboat at a drilling platform in Louisiana. It finally came home still full, and trucks carted the cargo away.*

that all new buses and transit facilities be equipped with wheelchair lifts, and that transit services be provided to people who are unable to use public transit facilities. In 1991 the Environmental Protection Agency issued a ruling requiring all municipal landfills to meet certain conditions designed to prevent contamination of soil and underground water supplies—at a cost to local governments of about $330 million per year—thereby establishing the first comprehensive federal standards for city dumps. The box on page 79 lists major federal statutes that regulate state and local governments.

Preemption   Early in the nation's history, Congress assumed the authority to *preempt*, or remove from state activity, policy areas having broad national implications. The Copyright Act of 1790 and the Bankruptcy Act of 1898, for example, stipulated that all regulatory activity in these fields would be exercised exclusively by the national government. More recently, in 1984 Congress preempted the power of local governments to regulate cable television rates. In such situations national-level authority expands to occupy a field previously administered by state and local governments.

A process known as **partial preemption** occurs when the national government establishes minimum standards in certain areas and authorizes state and local governments to exercise primary responsibility for the function *as long as* they maintain standards at least as high as those set by the national government. States may impose stricter standards, but if a state or locality fails to enact the base-level standard set by Congress, the national government assumes responsibility for doing so.

Age Discrimination in Employment Act Amendments of 1986 Outlaws mandatory retirement at age 70; 7-year delay for police, firefighters, and professors.

Americans with Disabilities Act (1990) Sets national standards to prohibit discrimination in public facilities and to promote handicapped access.

Asbestos Hazard Emergency Response Act of 1986 Directs school districts to inspect for asbestos hazards, develop response plans, and take protective actions necessary; requires state review and approval.

Cash Management Improvement Act of 1990 Creates new procedures for disbursing federal aid to states; reduces interest states earn on federal funds.

Child Abuse Amendments of 1984* Authorizes "Baby Doe" regulations protecting seriously ill newborns.

Civil Rights Restoration Act of 1987* Expands prohibitions against racial, gender, handicapped, and age discrimination by institutions that receive federal assistance.

Clean Air Act Amendments of 1990 Imposes stricter standards for urban smog, municipal incinerators, and toxic emissions and for controlling acid rain.

Commerical Motor Vehicle Safety Act of 1986 Establishes national standards for commercial and school bus drivers.

Consolidated Omnibus Budget Reconciliation Act of 1985 Extends Medicare hospital insurance taxes and coverage to new state and local government employees.

Drug-Free Workplace Act of 1988 Requires federal grantees and contractors to certify a drug-free workplace and to create awareness, sanction, and treatment programs.

Education of the Handicapped Act Amendments of 1986 Expands coverage and services for preschool children, ages 3–5.

Education of the Handicapped Act Amendments of 1990* Allows parents to seek tuition reimbursement under the *Handicapped Education Act*.

Emergency Planning and Community Right-to-Know Act of 1986 Promulgates new hazardous waste cleanup standards; establishes community right-to-know program; expands local emergency response planning.

Fair Housing Act Amendments of 1988 Extends *Civil Rights Act of 1968* to cover the handicapped and families with children.

Hazardous and Solid Waste Amendments of 1984 Reauthorizes and strengthens the *Resource Conservation and Recovery Act of 1976*; regulates underground storage tanks for petroleum and hazardous substances and requires annual EPA inspections of hazardous waste sites.

Highway Safety Amendments of 1984 Sets uniform national minimum legal drinking age of 21.

Lead Contamination Control Act of 1988 Requires states to assist schools with testing and remedying lead problems in drinking coolers.

National Voter Registration Act of 1993 Requires states to establish procedures for voters to register at local welfare and unemployment compensation offices or when applying for a driver's license by mail.

Ocean Dumping Ban Act (1988) Outlaws remaining ocean dumping of municipal sewage sludge.

Older Workers Benefit Protection Act of 1990* Broadens the *Age Discrimination in Employment Act*'s prohibitions against discrimination in employee benefit plans.

Safe Drinking Water Act Amendments of 1986 Promulgates new national drinking water standards; establishes enforcement and penalties for non-compliance.

Social Security Amendments of 1983 Prohibits state and local governments from withdrawing from Social Security coverage; accelerates increases in payroll taxes.

Social Security: Fiscal 1991 Budget Reconciliation Act Extends Social Security coverage to state and local government employees not covered by a public employee retirement system.

Surface Transportation Assistance Act of 1982 Enacts uniform size and weight requirements for trucks on interstate highways.

Voting Accessibility for the Elderly and Handicapped Act (1984) Requires states and political subdivisions to ensure accessible polling places for federal elections and a reasonable number of accessible registration sites.

Voting Rights Act Amendments of 1982 Extends the 1965 *Voting Rights Act* for 25 years and expands its coverage of disabled voters and those needing language assistance; prohibits any voting practice that results in discrimination, regardless of intent.*

Water Quality Act of 1987 Sets up new grant programs and requirements for states to control nonpoint pollution; promulgates new requirements for municipal storm sewer discharges; directs EPA to develop regulations of toxic wastes in sewage sludge; reduces and restructures funding for waste treatment plants.

*   Indicates reversal of a Supreme Court decision.

SOURCE: U.S. Advisory Commission on Intergovernmental Relations, *Intergovernmental Perspective*, Fall 1993.

Partial preemption occurred, for example, when Congress passed the Water Quality Act of 1965. The law gave states one year to set acceptable standards of quality for interstate waters within their boundaries. After that year passed, the secretary of health, education, and welfare (and, more recently, the head of the Environmental Protection Agency) was authorized to enforce federal standards in any state that failed to do so. Similarly, the Clean Air Act of 1970 set air quality standards throughout the nation and required the states to develop effective plans for their implementation. In 1990 amendments to this act established strict regulations that cities will have to meet in reducing urban smog and required state agencies to prepare new studies of pollution in cities.

Since the ratification of the Constitution, more than 350 preemption statutes have been passed by Congress. However, only a handful of them were passed prior to 1900, and more than half of them have been adopted in the past two decades. This concentration reflects the growing complexity of contemporary policy issues and the real need for uniform national standards in many areas. But the increased use of preemptive legislation reflects political considerations as well. In the 1930s, liberals championed the use of preemptive tactics as a means of overcoming the reluctance of many states to pass progressive economic and labor legislation. In the 1960s, liberals again relied on preemptive legislation as a key weapon in implementing policies in the areas of civil rights, fair housing, age discrimination, and voting rights.

President Ronald Reagan consistently voiced opposition to the extended use of preemptive tactics. "In the absence of clear constitutional authority," he declared, "the presumption of sovereignty should rest with individual states."[20] Yet as many preemptive statutes were passed in the Reagan and Bush years as had been passed during the liberal Democratic administrations. In the Reagan and Bush years, business and industry groups (especially in banking, communications, and transportation) repeatedly sought federal preemption as protection from more aggressive state regulations. For example, the Bus Regulatory Reform Act, signed by Reagan in 1982, nullified the authority of states to engage in economic regulation of the busing industry. The 1990 Nutritional Labeling and Education Act, which was signed into law by President Bush, preempted state nutritional-labeling requirements.

Grants-in-aid   The use of grants-in-aid is an even more common, and in many instances more effective, way for the national government to see that its objectives are carried out at the state and local levels. The Sixteenth Amendment, ratified in 1913, gave Congress the power to impose an income tax. The revenues to be obtained by this means would enable the national government to share its extensive resources with the states. This sharing took the form of grants-in-aid.

The volume of grants-in-aid has exploded since the 1960s. Today over $200 billion annually is allocated by the federal government through these programs. Through grants-in-aid the national government has been able to encourage state and local governments to pursue objectives that otherwise might have been politically difficult or impossible. Grants-in-aid have been used to fund projects in mass transportation, urban renewal, housing, drug rehabilitation, crime reduction, health care, low-income home energy assistance, pollution, nuclear-waste disposal, solid-waste disposal, highway beautification, and aid to homeless youth, as well as in many other areas. In any given year,

Congress enacts new grant programs to provide support in such areas as drug abuse and education relating to youth gangs, education for homeless children, living arrangements for runaway youths, prevention of abuse of the aging, lead poisoning prevention, and care services for homebound people with AIDS.

State and local governments have benefited from federal monies in all these areas. They too are able to engage in many activities that would not be possible—or at least would be much more costly and difficult—in the absence of federal aid.

Conditions of Aid

The many conditions and requirements that recipients must satisfy to receive federal grants can influence state and local policies. These conditions are of two types: crosscutting requirements and crossover sanctions.

Crosscutting requirements pertain to nondiscrimination, environmental protection, planning and coordination, labor standards, and public access to government information and decision making and are attached to almost all federal grants. As an example, the 1964 Civil Rights Act guarantees nondiscrimination in all federally assisted programs. Today there are approximately sixty such requirements.

Crossover sanctions impose national sanctions or penalties in one area to influence state or local policy in another area. The Intermodal Surface Transportation Act of 1991, for example, contained over a dozen crossover sanctions, including one requiring states to adopt mandatory motorcycle helmet and seat belt laws by 1994. States that fail to do so must spend up to 3 percent of their highway funds on highway safety activities. The same strategy was used in 1984, when Congress passed a law that required the withholding of a portion of federal highway funds from any state that did not set its minimum drinking age at 21 or higher.

Such requirements almost always reflect worthy objectives. Nevertheless, local officials frequently claim that they fail to take local conditions into account, that they are unnecessary and duplicative, and that they are too costly. It is estimated that compliance with the Americans with Disabilities Act of 1990, for example, will cost local governments between $35 and $45 million annually for the purchase and maintenance of lift-equipped buses and several hundred million dollars to modify subways and other transit facilities.

In 1980 Edward Koch, then mayor of New York, estimated that the total cost to his city of complying with federal mandates over a four-year period would be $711 million in capital expenditures, $6.25 billion in expense budget dollars, and $1.66 billion in lost revenues.[21] Mayor Koch described what he called "the most graphic example of a mandate gone haywire," the federal government's prohibition on ocean dumping. "Every way the City turns with its sludge," he complained, "it encounters another federal regulation." Disposing of city waste on land, he said, will "create an end product laden with heavy metals [which will] permanently rob the landfill of future agricultural use and endanger the area's watertable." Compliance, the mayor estimated, would cost $250 million in capital investment and $35 million in annual operating costs, much of which would have to be paid directly by the city.[22]

Ronald Reagan came to office in 1981 promising to eliminate or reduce grant-related regulations. Just two days after his inauguration Reagan appointed a task force (chaired by Vice President Bush) to identify regulations that could be dropped. In August, 1983, the task force issued its report, claiming "substantial improvements in federal regulatory policies [which would result in] savings of more than $150 billion to consumers, businesses, universities, and state and local governments over the next ten years."[23]

As it turned out, however, Reagan's presidency was associated with a net increase in federal regulations in several policy areas. Political considerations won out over the president's stated philosophy. At the urging of the trucking industry, for example, the administration supported a transportation bill that denied federal highway funds to states that did not approve the use of larger trucks carrying more weight than many states permitted at the time.

Figure 3-2 shows the growth of the major forms of federal regulation of state and local governments between 1931 and 1990.

Grants-in-Aid: A Typology

There are three types of grants: categorical grants, block grants, and general revenue sharing. **Categorical grants** are made for specific purposes defined by Congress, such as library construction, child welfare, adoption assistance, and bridge and road construction. Categorical grants can be used only for the purposes stated in the legislation that creates and funds the program. State and local decision makers thus have little discretion in how the grant money is spent. As of 1991 there were 543 categorical grants. Among the more recently approved are the Drug Abuse Prevention and Education Relating to Youth Gangs

Figure 3-2 *Major forms of national regulation of state and local governments, 1931–1990.* SOURCE: *Adapted from Timothy J. Conlan, "And the Beat Goes On: Intergovernmental Mandates and Preemption in an Era of Deregulation,"* Publius: The Journal of Federalism 21 *(Summer 1991): 51.*

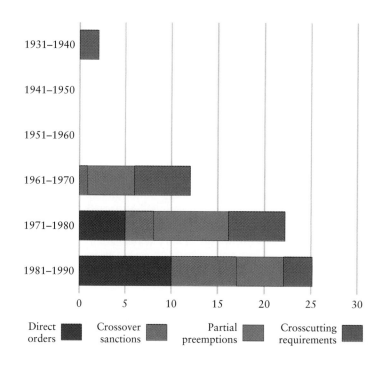

program (approximately $12 million per year), the Emergency Community Services for the Homeless program (about $19 million per year), and the AIDS Education program (about $14 million per year).

Block grants allow appropriated funds to be used in broad policy areas such as job training, health, and public housing. Congress establishes the areas in which the funds are to be used, and state and local officials determine how the money is actually spent. Today there are fourteen block grants in the areas of education, health and human services, housing, criminal justice, job training, and transportation. More block grants were approved during the Reagan administration than during any previous administration. As president, George Bush continued the trend with his proposal for the creation of a $20 billion block grant by consolidating a number of existing grant programs. President Clinton has also maintained this trend, as revealed in the 1993 report "The National Performance Review." Designed to streamline the federal government, the report recommended consolidating fifty-five categorical grants (disbursing $12.9 billion annually) into six block grant programs.

General revenue sharing (GRS), created by the State and Local Fiscal Assistance Act of 1972, distributed approximately $6 billion annually to state and local governments until 1980 and about $4 billion annually to local governments thereafter until the program was terminated in 1986. These monies were allocated to nearly thirty-nine thousand local governments with almost no "strings" attached. The recipient governments could use GRS money for any purpose as long as they did not spend it in a discriminatory manner.

General revenue sharing was the centerpiece of President Nixon's domestic program. In GRS Nixon saw opportunities for managerial as well as political reform. From a management perspective, GRS countered the complex and largely unregulated growth of federal grants. Politically, by giving state and local governments maximum flexibility in spending the funds, GRS shifted power away from Congress, the national bureaucracy, and Washington-centered interest groups, all of which Nixon viewed as loyal principally to the Democrats and Democratic constituents. The successful passage of GRS also demonstrated the growing political influence of a new interest group: the intergovernmental lobby, which consists of organizations representing state and local governments. As one observer noted at the time:

The passage of general revenue sharing is the most successful grassroots lobbying effort undertaken thus far. In spring 1971, delegations of mayors, governors, and county officials swarmed over Capitol Hill demanding congressional passage of this program. . . . The Democratic leadership and Chairman [Wilbur] Mills eventually capitulated to this outpouring of favorable support.[24]

General revenue sharing expired in 1986 as a result of President Reagan's budget reduction efforts and congressional and presidential concern about large federal deficits.

Politics of Grants-in-Aid

In general, block grants are popular among conservatives and advocates of states' rights. Presidents Nixon and Reagan were supportive of these grants in part because they knew full well that most local electorates and local officials would not support social programs, especially those designed to sharply redistribute resources from upper- to lower-income populations. Block grants tend also to be popular among state and local officials, because they allow greater discretion in spending the funds.

Categorical grants are more appealing to liberals, particularly those who believe the national government should be actively involved in addressing pressing social and urban problems. Congress, too, generally prefers categorical grants, because they allow greater congressional influence in determining and monitoring how the money is spent.

Categorical grants frequently are supported by private interest groups pressuring Congress to approve programs to address their particular needs. Thus, each categorical grant tends to build a constituency of people whose programs or projects are funded largely by that grant program. These people naturally become very protective of "their" grants and feel threatened when the grants are considered for termination or conversion to other types of grants. Consider the 1971 congressional testimony by the director of a neighborhood center in East Akron, Ohio, who feared that Nixon's proposed general revenue sharing program would mean the elimination of the community action grant program:

But I am saying to this committee and to everybody in Washington: How could they even think about passing a revenue-sharing bill that is going to say, "you take the money, to State or city or anywhere else, and do what you want with it."

What will happen to poor people? In the city where I live they may as well jump over into the river right now, because that is what will happen. . . .

I have heard all kinds of people with big degrees talk about it [general revenue sharing]. But let me tell you something: Who did anything for the poor before the Federal Government came in? Who helped us? We had States and cities all along. . . . What did the poor people get? Nothing. You went year after year, day after day, begging, and you received nothing.[25]

Table 3-1 compares the outlays of various types of grants-in-aid between 1972 and 1992. In particular notice the increasing proportion of outlays distributed as categorical grants.

TABLE 3-1			
Billions of Dollars Distributed through Grants-in-Aid, 1972–1992 (in current dollars)			
TYPE OF GRANT	1972	1980	1992
Categorical grants	$31.0	$72.5	$154.5
Block grants	2.9	10.3	14.1
General revenue sharing	—	6.8	—
Other general purpose grants	1.0	1.8	2.4
Total	$34.9	$91.4	$171.0

SOURCES: Congressional Budget Office, *The Federal Government in a Federal System: Current Intergovernmental Programs and Options for Change* (Washington, D.C.: U.S. Government Printing Office, 1983), 25; and Office of Management and Budget.

Distribution Criteria

Grants may be categorized as formula grants or as project grants, depending on the criteria used for distribution of the money.

Formula grants are distributed according to a formula that is applied proportionally to all eligible recipients. A grant program to aid education, for example, might allocate a certain amount of money to all school districts, depending on the number of pupils whose families' incomes are below a certain level. By simply calculating the number of pupils who fall into this category, all school districts across the country will immediately know how much they are entitled to receive.

The political controversies surrounding formula grants concern the elements to be included in the formula and the weighting of those elements. The Case Study on page 87 examines the struggle over the formula for community development block grants. Another bitter fight broke out in 1988, when Congress considered changing the formula for distributing money through the Alcohol, Drug Abuse, and Mental Health (ADAMH) block grant. The original formula included a factor that benefited states receiving funds under the older categorical grants that had been eliminated when the ADAMH block grant was approved. Critics argued that that element of the formula gave too much of the ADAMH money to northern states and too little to southern and western states. As an aide to Representative Henry Waxman of California said, "You won't find anyone with a dispassionate interest who would not say the existing formula is an outrage." The deputy director for government and community relations at the New York State Division of Substance Abuse Services did not find the existing formula unfair, however. Commenting on the proposed change, which would yield fewer ADAMH dollars to northern states, he said, "I don't see anything equitable in a proposal which would entail closing down drug treatment programs in high-risk areas like New York."[26]

Project grants are grants for which potential recipients must apply directly to the agency responsible for administering the grant. That agency reviews the proposals and determines which ones are to be funded and at what level. There is not enough money to fund every potential project, so competition for the funds may be keen.

Federal agencies and departments maintain greater control and authority over project grants. These grants, which proliferated in the 1960s, have been used for policy areas that might not receive sufficient attention from state and local decision makers in the absence of national funding—areas such as education for handicapped youth, programs for the aging, AIDS research, drug rehabilitation, and bilingual education.

Project grants are often a focus of much political controversy. Those whose applications are not approved may attribute their failure to obtain funds to federal bureaucrats who make poor decisions or are out of touch with local problems. They argue that project grants place too much control at the national level, ignore the specialized needs of local areas, and give an advantage to jurisdictions that are large and wealthy enough to hire staffs with the skills required for drafting federal grant proposals.

The box on the following page describes the unbelievable events that occurred when the town of Sidney, Nebraska, applied for what it thought would be a simple project grant.

Sidney, Nebraska (population 6,300), needed a new snowplow for its airport. The snowplow in use was a 1936 truck equipped with a front-end scraper. Said City Manager Merle Strause, "It's an old Civil Defense vehicle that we bought in 1954 for $50 and it's seen the last of its days."

The city approached the Federal Aviation Administration (FAA), which grants funds for airport improvement, to obtain partial funding for the snowplow. The FAA said that Sidney could go ahead with plans to purchase a snowplow, but not the $3,500 dump truck with a blade on it that the town wanted. Instead, it said, Sidney needed a plow costing $83,000. Before purchasing the snowplow, however, the town would need a building costing about $106,000 to house the plow. And, because a construction project was involved, it would also have to make an airport layout plan costing about $25,000.

The state Aeronautics Department became involved. It agreed to pick up some of the town's expense. The consultant whom the town was forced to hire to prepare the information requested by the state and federal governments stressed that all the town wanted was a snowplow. The compromise plan agreed to by the FAA and state officials called for a $45,000 snowplow, a $22,000 layout, and a $66,000 building for the plow. That was as low as Sidney could get the FAA to go.

After a year of frustration, Sidney found a way out. The town finally withdrew its request for a snowplow and filed a new request, which was shortly filled—for a dump truck with a blade on the front end.

SOURCE: *Washington Post*, September 12, 1978, A3; October 22, 1978, A13.

The Regional Controversy over Grant Distribution

Not surprisingly, given the huge amounts of money allocated through the grant-in-aid system, controversies and conflicts sometimes arise over the regional distribution of the funds. Some states and regions receive considerably higher per person allocations than do others. Table 3-2 shows the per person distribution of federal grants-in-aid to the top and bottom five states as of 1991.

State and local officials in the Frostbelt (states in the Midwest and Northeast) often express the opinion that their industrial and economic problems justify higher proportions of federal grant assistance. Officials in the Sunbelt (states in the South and Southwest) argue that rapid population growth in their sections of the country brings unique problems calling for increased federal aid for their areas. The dispute has led to clashes between coalitions of legislators, mayors, and governors over distribution formulas, a rivalry that has been described as a "regional war."[27] In the summer of 1991, for example, senators from the South and senators from the Midwest and Northeast sparred over proposed changes in formulas for funding the Community Development Block Grant (CDBG) program. Senator Phil Gramm of Texas argued that "Texas gets cheated by the current formula" and proposed an amendment that would eliminate the age of housing from the formula. Gramm's proposal, which would have greatly increased Texas's proportion of CDBG money, was countered by Senator Alan Dixon of Illinois, who said:

There are not many places left where the poor, old Northeast-Midwest part of this country with its great cities gets a little help once in a while, not many. The CDBG

The Struggle over the CDBG Formula

The Community Development Block Grant (CDBG) program allocates billions of dollars to local governments for housing, neighborhood revitalization, and community services. When the program was established in 1974, the formula for distributing the money was based on three factors: poverty, overcrowded housing, and population. Cities in the Sunbelt, which were experiencing rapid population increases, benefited from the formula. Cities in the Frostbelt, which were losing population, suffered under the original formula.

When the program was considered for renewal in 1977, a number of groups sought changes in the formula so as to benefit older cities in the North and Midwest. The Northeast-Midwest Congressional Coalition in the House of Representatives proposed a formula that would give 20 percent weight to the degree of population *loss*, 30 percent weight to the poverty rate, and 50 percent weight to the age of a community's housing stock. This formula would have given maximum benefit to Frostbelt cities.

A bitter dispute broke out between Frostbelt and Sunbelt interests over the proposed new formula. Southern interests criticized the proposed formula and its inclusion of a factor measuring the age of housing stock as not really measuring need. David Peterson, director of the Southern Growth Policies Board, charged that Frostbelt advocates "wanted to shift the money to the Northeast and they couldn't find any better measure." Sunbelt cities argued that rapid population increases created special needs and that population growth should be factored into the distribution formula. Ann Lower, administrative assistant to a Texas representative, commented: "We have to realize there are two types of urban problems. We've got to separate federal aid into two packages, one to aid the Detroits and one for the Sunbelt cities." Representatives from California introduced legislation retaining the old formula, which benefited their districts.

At first one section of the country seemed destined to lose funds if the other section was to get what it wanted. Southern and western cities stood to lose millions of dollars annually in federal aid if the efforts of Frostbelt advocates succeeded.

In May 1977 the House passed legislation that included a formula that would dramatically increase the proportion of CDBG funds received by older northern cities. For the legislation to get through Congress, several political compromises had to be reached. An additional billion dollars was added to the program so that increases to the Frostbelt cities would not mean a reduction to Sunbelt cities. In addition, a "dual formula" was agreed upon: a city could select either the original (1974) formula or the new formula, depending on which one treated that city best in the allocation process. Finally, in 1977 Congress passed the Urban Development Action Grants program, which was designed to supplement CDBG funds and would distribute funds to distressed cities.

As a result of the political bargaining and compromises that surrounded the new CDBG formula, cities in the Northeast received a 77 percent increase over the amount of money they would have received under the 1974 formula. Cities in the Midwest received a 66 percent increase. Cities in the South and Midwest lost no money and, in fact, realized increases of 8 percent and 14 percent, respectively.

Discussion questions

1. Why can the controversies surrounding formulas for distribution of funds be just as intense and bitter as the controversies surrounding program goals and objectives?
2. In the resolution of the CDBG controversy, no region lost funds; in fact, all regions received increases. What does this outcome say about the politics of policy making, especially when large amounts of money are to be distributed among numerous groups?
3. Do you believe that regional controversies over the allocation of federal funds will diminish or increase in the next several years? Why?

SOURCES: Rochelle Stanfield, "Government Seeks the Right Formula for Community Development Funds," *National Journal*, February 12, 1977, 237–243; Rochelle Stanfield, "Pockets of Poverty—The Other Side of Houston," *National Journal*, March 24, 1979, 476–479; Dennis R. Judd, *The Politics of American Cities* (Glenview, Ill.: Scott, Foresman, 1988), 351–352.

TABLE 3-2	
Per Person Federal Aid Received by Selected States in Fiscal Year 1991	
TOP 5 RECIPIENTS	PER PERSON GRANTS TO STATE AND LOCAL GOVERNMENTS
Alaska	$1,303
Wyoming	1,253
New York	876
Montana	865
North Dakota	847
BOTTOM 5 RECIPIENTS	PER PERSON GRANTS TO STATE AND LOCAL GOVERNMENTS
Florida	$409
Virginia	434
Nevada	444
New Hampshire	460
Arizona	480

SOURCE: Advisory Commission on Intergovernmental Relations, *Significant Features of Fiscal Federalism, 1993 Edition*, vol. 2 (Washington, D.C.: ACIR, 1993), 195.

grants are one. . . . Now, my friend from Texas wants to take this pittance, this pittance for the poor in the inner cities of America. . . . I think this is an unacceptable, greedy attitude to take.

Regional policy research centers have sprung up in Washington, D.C., whose sole purpose is to identify and promote public policies that would benefit the various regions. These so-called think tanks often engage in small skirmishes among themselves. In the late 1980s the Sunbelt Institute (representing the eleven states of the old Confederacy and five border states) issued reports asserting that southern states, on average, send more than $1.50 to the national government in taxes for every dollar returned in federal aid while some northern states receive far more in federal aid than they contribute to the federal treasury. The Northeast-Midwest Institute (representing eighteen northeastern and midwestern states) immediately issued its own report, critical of the Sunbelt Institute's report. Congressional representatives from each region were drawn into the debate. To the Sunbelt Institute's report, New York senator Daniel Patrick Moynihan curtly replied that "everybody is entitled to their own opinions, but not their own facts."[28]

Competition for federal funds has been growing as the proportion of dollars distributed by the federal government through grant-in-aid programs has been declining. So regional clashes over federal aid are likely to continue and increase in intensity.

State and Local Influence on National Policy Making

State and local governments use certain tools of their own in an attempt to influence national policy making, including the allocation and distribution of grants. All national legislators are elected from states or local districts and ultimately are responsible to voters at the local level. Thus, members of Congress are sure to give some attention to the concerns of their constituents. Also, state and local governments can go to court to challenge the actions of the national government and may, at least temporarily, halt or delay national initiatives. Two additional tools that local officials may use to influence national policies are grantsmanship and the intergovernmental lobby.

Grantsmanship The efforts of local officials to maximize the amount of federal grants they receive and to have grant rules interpreted so as to achieve the best funding distribution for their areas are termed **grantsmanship**. Cities and states that are most capable of exploiting the various options and opportunities provided by the grant program are able to garner far more than their "fair" share of federal grants. Consider the comments of John Chafee, governor of Rhode Island:

> Let us take the case of a 1-year-old boy on aid to dependent children who has a hearing problem that can be corrected. There is the temptation—and I must say this is a very real one—to refer such a patient, not to the program which is best organized to meet his particular need, but to the program in which the State obtains the best financial advantage. The Federal government will pay 50 percent of the cost when the care is provided by the Crippled Children's Division; it will pay 56 percent under Title XIX since he is on aid to dependent children; and, if he is cared for by vocational rehabilitation, the Federal government will soon pay 75 percent of the bill. Each of these programs has some variation in standards for eligibility but nonetheless the differences in Federal reimbursement seem extremely puzzling.[29]

Grantsmanship is frequently criticized by those who believe that federal grants should go to local areas because of demonstrated problems or needs, not because of officials' skills in obtaining grants. Moreover, officials at the national level seek to prevent what they consider to be "manipulation" of the grant programs. In 1991 the Bush administration issued rules preventing states from using money collected from donations or from special taxes paid by hospitals as matching money to qualify for federal Medicaid payments. That ruling, it is estimated, will cost state governments between $3 and $5 billion per year.

The intergovernmental lobby One of the most effective strategies used by state and local governments in recent years has been to organize the **intergovernmental lobby**. Following the explosion of grants-in-aid in the 1960s, representatives of state and local governments began organizing themselves into lobby groups and organizations to press for more federal aid for states and communities, to see that grants are designed to meet state and local needs, and to keep abreast of new rules and regulations affecting grants. Unlike other private lobbies, the intergovernmental lobby is funded almost exclusively with public money—state and local funds and even federal grants.

The most important organizations in the intergovernmental lobby are listed in Table 3-3. But the organizations identified in the table are just a few of the dozens of groups that represent state and local interests. Other members of the growing intergovernmental lobby include the American Association of State Highway and Transportation Officials, the Association of State and Interstate Water Pollution Control Officers, the National Association of Attorneys General, the American Association of School Administrators, the National

TABLE 3-3

The Intergovernmental Lobby

ORGANIZATION	EMPLOYEES	BUDGET (APPROX.)	PORTION OF BUDGET FROM FEDERAL GOVERNMENT (PERCENT)	MAJOR ISSUES
National Conference of State Legislatures 40,000 (approx.) legislators and staff of 50 U.S. states, commonwealths, and territories	140	$13 million	20	1. Health care 2. Crime 3. Welfare reform
National League of Cities 20,000 (approx.)	75	$8 million	20	1. Unfunded federal mandates 2. Health care 3. Environmental legislation
United States Conference of Mayors U.S. cities with over 30,000 population (approx. 1,000)	50	$8 million	33	1. Unfunded federal mandates 2. Crime and violence 3. Hunger and homelessness
National Association of Counties 2,000 counties	75	$11 million	24	1. Health care 2. Unfunded federal mandates 3. Welfare reform, job training
National Governors' Association 55 state and territorial governors	100	$10 million	35	1. Health care 2. Welfare reform 3. Children and violence
National Association of Towns and Townships Local governments in small and rural areas mostly with populations of 25,000 or less (13,000 approx.)	10	$1 million	20	1. Regulatory flexibility 2. Clean water 3. Environment

SOURCE: Authors' interviews with officials of each organization, 1994.

Association of State Budget Officers, the National Association of State Mental Health Program Directors, the Council of State Community Development Agencies, the National Association of State Units on Aging, and the National Association of State Alcohol and Drug-Abuse Directors.

Many states and cities believe that the national organizations cannot adequately represent their particular interests and thus have opened their own offices in Washington. Thirty states, about one hundred cities, and a dozen or so counties have offices in Washington. California has the largest presence in Washington of all the states: separate offices represent the state, twenty-three cities, and seven counties. Sometimes all this lobbying activity can lead to awk-

In 1992, mayors and other politicians from across the nation lobbied Washington for more urban aid. (Front row: Rep. Maxine Waters, D-Calif.; Atlanta Mayor Maynard Jackson; Jesse Jackson; New York Mayor David Dinkins; Osborne Elliot, co-chair of the march; Jerry Brown, Democratic presidential candidate; and Boston Mayor Raymond Flynn.) In 1993 Sharon Pratt Dixon, mayor of Washington, pleaded for another kind of federal help: National Guard troops to help control lawlessness in her city's streets. The president bumped her request to the Congress.

ward and seemingly contradictory situations. The state of New York, for example, has separate lobbyists serving the interests of the governor, the state assembly, and the state senate. In the debate over President Reagan's block grant proposals, lobbyists for the Democratic-controlled New York state assembly opposed the block grants and lobbyists for the Republican-controlled state senate supported them.

The 1960s and 1970s were in many ways a golden age for the intergovernmental lobby. Federal aid to states and cities rose steadily, reaching $91.5 billion by 1980, just over 25 percent of total state and local fiscal outlays. The passage of the general revenue sharing program in 1972 was perhaps the crowning achievement of these organizations.

By contrast, the Reagan-Bush years were a time of declining political influence. During this period the intergovernmental lobby was not able to prevent the elimination of the $4.6 billion general revenue sharing program, the termination of urban development action grants, and a slowdown in federal funds for housing, transportation, and many social programs.

With the election in 1992 of former Arkansas governor Bill Clinton to the presidency, the intergovernmental lobby hoped for more productive relationships. Indeed, the cabinet appointments of former governors Richard Riley (South Carolina) and Bruce Babbitt (Arizona) and former mayors Federico Peña (Denver) and Henry Cisneros (San Antonio) were seen as hopeful signs. But Clinton's early focus on cutting the budget deficit and on reforming health care made it clear that expansive new programs to assist state and local governments would not be priorities of his presidency. The realities of budget constraints make it appear certain that the intergovernmental lobby will not soon achieve the level of influence that it enjoyed in the 1970s.

FEDERALISM IN ACTION

Two contemporary issues provide excellent examples of federalism in action and illustrate many of the concepts discussed in this chapter: minimum allowable age for alcohol consumption and the proper role of governments in water control and management.

Setting the Minimum Age for Alcohol Consumption

For most of the nation's history, individual states have assumed the authority to set rules and regulations concerning the sale and use of beer, wine, and liquor—including the minimum age required for purchase and consumption.[30] Before 1984, twenty-eight states had established minimum ages below 21 for the purchase of some or all categories of alcohol.

Until 1984, setting rules and regulations for alcohol purchase and consumption was considered a responsibility of state governments. The national government had provided grants to states for the purpose of developing programs to reduce drunk driving but had not formulated policy in this area. However, as drunk driving began to arouse public concern and as grassroots organizations like MADD (Mothers Against Drunk Driving) were formed, national officials became more interested in the problem. In 1982 President Reagan appointed a commission to examine the drunk-driving issue. In its report, released in 1983, the commission recommended that each state establish 21 as the minimum age for the possession of all alcohol *and* that federal grants for road and construction projects be denied to states that did not comply with the age recommendation. The latter recommendation, the threat of withholding federal funds from noncompliant states, proved controversial and eventually became the means by which the national government exerted authority in an area previously reserved to the states.

Grassroots organizations like Mothers Against Drunk Driving helped bring national attention to the issues of driving while intoxicated. MADD lobbied for stricter laws and harsher penalties, and eventually the federal government threatened to withhold highway monies from states that did not raise the minimum drinking age to twenty-one. President Reagan had "no misgivings about this judicious use of federal power."

Photo courtesy of MADD

Congressional opposition centered on the issue of states' rights. New Hampshire senator Gordon Humphrey asked, "Who are we, the national legislature, who have done a perfectly abysmal job of managing our own business, to tell the state legislatures . . . how to conduct their business?"[31] In a similar vein, Montana senator Max Baucus said, "The real issue is whether the Federal Government should intrude into an area that has traditionally and appropriately been left to the States and force them into accepting its solution to the problem of drunk driving."[32]

However, the majority of the members of Congress did not share this view, and in 1984 the National Minimum Drinking-Age Act was enacted into law. It established 21 as the minimum age required for the purchase and consumption of alcohol and provided for the withholding of portions of federal highway trust funds from any state that failed to establish this minimum age. Reflecting on the act's possible usurpation of state authority, President Reagan commented that "the problem [of drunk driving] is bigger than the individual States. It's a grave national problem, and it touches all our lives. With the problem so clear-cut and the proven solution at hand, we have no misgivings about this judicious use of federal power."[33]

The National Minimum Drinking-Age Act specified that higher proportions of highway funds would be denied to states the longer they delayed in establishing the required minimum age. The effectiveness of this provision is illustrated by the fact that as of 1993 all states had raised to 21 the minimum age for buying liquor.

Federal regulatory activities of this type are *crossover sanctions*: the federal government threatens to withhold funds in one program area (in this case, highway monies) to achieve policy objectives in another area (here, the minimum age required for alcohol purchase and consumption). The growth of federal grant programs in recent years and the increased reliance of state and local governments on these grants has made crossover sanctions a potent policy tool. The national government has used it successfully to achieve uniform state policies in areas such as highway beautification and energy conservation as well as in establishing a uniform minimum drinking age.

The Control and Management of Water Resources

Water is the nation's most precious natural resource, and its management provides an excellent example of the politics of policy making in a federal system. For decades the national, state, and local governments have debated their proper roles in managing the nation's water supplies. As one long-time observer of water policies put it: "Two of the most difficult problems with which people in the United States must live [are] water [and] federalism."[34]

Prior to 1900, many western states sought assistance from the national government in developing a regional policy of sound water conservation and management. At first the national government responded to their request by ceding federally owned land to the states, which sold the land and used the proceeds to develop their own water policy programs. But although millions of acres of federal land were turned over to the states, a viable, comprehensive policy for water resource management never emerged.

Responding to increased needs, Congress passed the Reclamation Act of 1902, which created a fund from the sale of public lands to be used to build irrigation projects. Participating farmers were to repay the cost of the projects in interest-free installments; this money would then be used to fund more projects. A central issue in the passage of the Reclamation Act was the involvement of the national government in water policy, an area previously left to the states. Some observers believed that the national government was overstepping the bounds of its legitimate authority. A speaker addressing the National Irrigation Congress in 1906 set forth this position:

Any plan or scheme that seeks to transfer the control and administration of irrigation affairs, from the several States to the general government at Washington, is regarded as an encroachment upon the rights of the State and an interference with individual prerogative acquired under local custom and law, and meets with more or less hostility on the part of those largely interested in irrigation affairs.[35]

In this century much of the debate over water issues has centered on water management: the authority to store, use, and transport water. Initially, states exercised almost exclusive authority in this area. However, there were those who believed that the national government *should* be involved in water policy and should assume *greater* responsibility. Representative George Ray of New York complained that the Reclamation Act "surrenders all control" and amounts to a "robbery or looting of the Treasury of the United States."[36] The vote in favor of the bill reflected strong regional differences. Western states favored it; northern states opposed it.

In the twentieth century a number of court decisions have strengthened the role of the national government. In 1908 the Supreme Court ruled that traditional state control over water policy was mitigated by treaties and agreements made at the national level. In 1963 it added that national interests in water policy extended to federal establishments such as national recreational areas and national forests. Thirteen years later the Court extended the sphere of national influence to include groundwater withdrawals that affect water levels on federal lands and, still more recently, groundwater on nonfederal lands.

In pursuing water-related projects, the national government has spent billions of dollars on dams, ports and harbors, reservoirs, irrigation efforts, and hydroelectric power plants. These projects provide significant "pork-barrel" opportunities for members of Congress, but they may also seem to be very important to the economic health and vitality of particular areas, especially back home. Therefore, attempts to end or cut back on such projects frequently meet intense political opposition.

President Jimmy Carter experienced such opposition in 1977 when he tried to change the direction of national water policy to focus less on the construction of massive projects and more on the less costly policies of conservation and water resource management. Carter's proposals encountered considerable hostility in regions that depended on large-scale federally funded construction projects. Governor Allen Olson of North Dakota argued that failure to fund expanded water projects in his state would result in "irreparable harm to the state of North Dakota," and Wyoming governor Ed Herschler called the Carter proposal a "complete strangulation of the western states."[37]

President Reagan was more supportive of traditional water construction projects, despite the considerable budget pressures he faced while in office. In

Virtually every state and city, as well as many counties and other municipalities, publishes an annual handbook that provides information about legislative members, describes all the government offices and agencies, lists every officeholder and agency head, and provides information about the judicial system. Variously called "blue" or "red" books (from the color of the volume's cover), legislative manuals or registers, directories, and yearbooks, these volumes contain detailed information and helpful addresses. Typical features of a state handbook include photographs, brief biographies, and the addresses of the governor, the lieutenant governor, all members of the state legislature and judiciary, department and agency heads, and county and city legislators and officials; detailed information on the state's congressional delegation; the state constitution; names of state party officials; names of press

corps members; and lists of state birds, insects, songs, and the like.

Most handbooks are authorized publications. The official *New York State Red Book*, for example, has been published annually since 1892. It is authorized by concurrent resolutions of the state senate and assembly. The *Illinois Blue Book* and the *Connecticut Register* and *Manual* are the responsibility of each state's secretary of state. The *Directory of Oklahoma* is published by the Oklahoma Department of Libraries, and the *Nebraska Blue Book* is compiled by the clerk of the legislature.

Any college or university library is likely to have the handbook for its own state and municipality. Larger libraries usually have the handbooks for their own states and municipalities and often have them for neighboring states. Business and reference libraries often have handbooks for most of the states.

1986, with strong presidential support, Congress passed a water resource bill authorizing the expenditure of $16 billion in water projects. For the first time, however, state and local governments were required to pay significant portions of the cost of constructing new projects (in some cases an amount equal to almost half of the total cost). As Lloyd Bentsen, then senator from Texas, put it, "Unless [local governments] are willing to put up their share of the costs, the project will not be built."[38] Reagan's influence in supporting the 1986 water projects bill was enhanced by Republican control of the Senate, which "helped create significant differences between the Senate and House versions of all the . . . bills introduced. . . . In every case the Senate version provided less federal money and more water policy reforms."[39]

The nation's evolving water management policy illustrates some of the lasting tensions between the national government and state and local governments in the American federal system. The national government was slow to become involved in an area that was viewed as an exclusive concern of state and local governments. But over the years, often responding to regional demands, the national government has become a more influential player.

The issue of water policy also illustrates the influence exerted by the federal budget on government relations in a federal system. Once the national government becomes involved in a policy area and billions of federal dollars are committed to projects in various states and regions, it may be difficult for the national government to retreat from its involvement—even when the initiative for reduced involvement comes from the national government itself.

Throughout the nation's history there have been conflicts over the meaning of federalism and the proper division of power and responsibility among federal, state, and local governments. During the period following the ratification of the Constitution, those who favored more power and responsibility for the national government were opposed by those who sought to protect and enhance the rights of individual states. Those with a nation-centered view believed that the Constitution was applicable to the American people as a whole. Those with a state-centered view believed that the Constitution was a compact among the states and that the states were the legitimate center of power and authority. Advocates of states' rights argued that if the national government overstepped its legitimate boundaries, its acts should be null and void; this position is known as the *doctrine of nullification.*

The conflict over national supremacy versus states' rights intensified along with opposition to slavery, finally culminating in the Civil War. After the war, nullification theory was discredited, and a new relationship known as *dual federalism* emerged. It recognized separate and distinct spheres of authority for the national and state governments. During this period much of the debate over federal-state relations centered on the proper role of Congress in regulating the nation's commerce. The Supreme Court invalidated a number of regulatory actions by Congress on the ground that they usurped state authority.

The Great Depression of the 1930s ushered in a period of *cooperative federalism*, which stressed a partnership and a sharing of functions, responsibilities, and programs between the states and the national government. This era was marked by increased use of *grants-in-aid*, programs through which the national government shared its fiscal resources with state and local governments. By 1960 there were about 132 grant programs, with most of the grants made for specific purposes defined by Congress.

President Nixon's *new federalism* deemphasized the use of grants for specific purposes and focused instead on large grants in general policy areas. These gave the recipient governments greater discretion in the expenditure of funds, but they also decreased the national government's control over how the funds were spent. During the Reagan adminis-

tration there was a slowdown in the rate of increase in the funding of grant programs.

Recent Supreme Court rulings are seen by many as having eliminated, or at least significantly reduced, all traces of state and local sovereignty. There continues to be some sharing of power and authority between the national and state governments, but the state and local share depends largely on the permissiveness of the national government.

In its attempts to regulate states and localities, the national government may issue direct orders, preempt state and local activities, or use grants-in-aid to encourage certain activities and discourage others. Occasionally the national government issues direct orders that local governments must comply with or else face civil or criminal penalties. *Partial preemption* occurs when the national government establishes policies and delegates the responsibility for implementing them to state and local governments, provided that they meet certain conditions or standards. A more common approach is the use of grants-in-aid. Grants have been used to fund projects and efforts in a wide variety of areas, ranging from mass transportation to nutrition programs for the elderly.

Grants can also be used to influence the administration of state and local policies; this is accomplished through the conditions and requirements that recipients must satisfy in order to receive the aid. *Crosscutting requirements* apply across the board and deal with issues such as environmental protection and labor standards. *Crossover sanctions* impose national sanctions in one area to influence state or local policy in another.

There are three types of grants. *Categorical grants* are made for specific purposes defined by Congress and give the recipient states and localities little discretion in terms of how the money is to be spent. *Block grants* allow appropriated funds to be used in broad policy areas, with state and local officials determining how the money is actually spent. *General revenue sharing* is a system in which federal funds are allocated to state and local governments to be used for virtually any purpose, provided that the money is not spent in a discriminatory manner.

Grants may also be categorized by their criteria for distribution. *Formula grants* are distributed according to a formula that is applied proportionally to all eligible recipients. *Project grants* are those for which potential recipients must apply directly to the agency responsible for administering the grant; the agency determines which proposals are to be funded and at what level.

Some states and regions receive considerably higher per person allocations of grant monies than others do. As a result, controversies and conflicts sometimes arise over the regional distribution of grant funds. Officials in Frostbelt states and in Sunbelt states often clash over the formulas for the distribution of federal funds.

State and local governments naturally attempt to influence the adoption and distribution of federal grants. The term *grantsmanship* refers to efforts by local officials to maximize federal grants received and to influence the interpretation of grant rules in ways favorable to their locality. State and local governments have also organized an *intergovernmental lobby* to press for more federal aid, see that grants are designed to meet their needs, and keep abreast of new rules and regulations.

KEY TERMS AND CONCEPTS

doctrine of nullification
dual federalism
cooperative federalism
grant-in-aid
new federalism

partial preemption
crosscutting requirements
crossover sanctions
categorical grant
block grant

general revenue sharing
formula grant
project grant
grantsmanship
intergovernmental lobby

LEARNING MORE ABOUT THE FEDERAL SYSTEM

Scholarly studies

Conlan, Timothy. *New Federalism: Intergovernmental Reform from Nixon to Reagan.* Washington, D.C.: Brookings Institution, 1988. A thorough account of events in American federal relations focusing especially on the presidencies of Richard Nixon and Ronald Reagan. The author presents an especially interesting analysis of the "politics" of intergovernmental relations during those years.

Hamilton, Christopher, and Donald T. Wells. *Federalism, Power, and Political Economy.* Englewood Cliffs, N.J.: Prentice-Hall, 1990. A contemporary overview of federalism, suggesting that federal conflicts are central to an understanding of politics and economics in America.

Kincaid, John, ed. *American Federalism: The Third Century.* Annals of the American Academy of Political and Social Science. Newbury Park, Calif.: Sage, 1990. A collection of essays by scholars examining various aspects of federalism in the 1990s, including fiscal roles, finance, regulation, and court decisions.

Nice, David C. *Federalism: The Politics of Intergovernmental Relations.* New York: St. Martin's Press, 1986. A good textbook on federalism, with a useful look at various models of federal systems as well as a discussion of interstate relations.

Peterson, Paul E., Barry G. Rabe, and Kenneth K. Wong. *When Federalism Works.* Washington, D.C.: Brookings Institution, 1987. An examination of the operation of nine federal programs in education, health, and housing. The study attempts to assess why some federally sponsored programs work well and others do not.

Riker, William H. *The Development of American Federalism.* Boston: Kluwer Academic Publishers, 1987. A collection of essays dealing with various aspects of federal relations. The book presents an especially interesting look at institutions such as Congress, the presidency, and the military in a federal context.

Swartz, Thomas R., and John E. Peck. *The Changing Face of Fiscal Federalism.* Armonk, N.Y.: M. E. Sharpe, 1990. A collection of essays examining federalism from a fiscal perspective, focusing primarily on the Carter, Reagan, and Bush presidencies. The book focuses especially on the "winners" and "losers" in the changing system of federal finance.

Walker, David B. *Toward a Functioning Federalism.* New York: HarperCollins, 1987. An excellent brief overview of the most important aspects of American federalism. The book presents an especially insightful look at the various stages of development of the United States federal system.

Leisure reading

Caro, Robert. *The Power Broker: Robert Moses and the Fall of New York*. New York: Vintage Books, 1975. A biography of Robert Moses, master planner and builder of New York City in the 1930s and 1940s, with a special focus on his use of the intergovernmental grant system to supplement the city's budget in accomplishing his goals.

Moynihan, Daniel P. *Maximum Feasible Misunderstanding*. New York: Free Press, 1970. A critical look at the implementation of the community action programs of the 1960s. Moynihan explores particularly the problems of implementing and evaluating programs whose objectives are unclear and contradictory.

Stanford, Terry. *Storm over the States*. New York: McGraw-Hill, 1967. Presents the perspective of a state governor operating in the American federal system.

Wills, Garry. *Explaining America: The Federalist*. New York: Penguin Books, 1981. An interesting look at the political philosophies of Alexander Hamilton and James Madison with particular attention to their ideas on federalism.

Primary sources

The Budget of the United States. Washington, D.C.: U.S. Government Printing Office, annual. Provides budgetary information on intergovernmental programs and changes in the system.

Statistical Abstract of the United States. Washington, D.C.: Bureau of the Census, annual. Provides detailed statistics, often on a state-by-state basis, in a range of government and policy areas.

Organizations

Advisory Commission on Intergovernmental Relations, 800 K Street, N.W., Washington, DC 20575; (202) 653-5540. A government commission that publishes useful studies and reports on various aspects of American federalism. Especially useful is its annual report, *Significant Features of Fiscal Federalism*, which presents detailed fiscal information on numerous intergovernmental programs and issues.

American Society for Public Administration, 1120 G Street, N.W., Washington, DC 20005-2885; (202) 393-7878. A scholarly organization focusing on many aspects of American federalism. Especially useful is its journal *Public Administration Review*, which contains articles dealing with the funding, administration, implementation, and evaluation of intergovernmental programs.

Center for the Study of Federalism, 1616 Walnut Street, Temple University, Philadelphia, PA 19103; (215) 787-1480. An interdisciplinary educational and research institute located at Temple University. Its publication, *Publius: The Journal of Federalism*, is an excellent source of scholarly research dealing with federal issues.

PART II

The Politics of Liberty and Equality

Civil Rights and Liberties

- Rights, liberties, and constitutional politics: the nationalization of the Bill of Rights

- Civil rights and criminal justice: due process; unreasonable searches and seizures; government interrogations and the right to counsel; the right to a fair trial; prohibition against cruel and unusual punishment

- Rights and liberties versus economic interests

The memorabilia at left evoke the campaigns of 1884, 1888, and 1892. Grover Cleveland, New York's governor, was the Democratic candidate in all three elections, winning in 1884 and 1892. He defeated Republican James Blaine in 1884, despite the issue of having fathered a son out of wedlock. His victory was the first for Democrats since 1856, when James Buchanan captured the presidency.

In 1888, the key issue was the tariff, and Republican Benjamin Harrison defeated Cleveland by denouncing free trade and promising to protect American industries. In 1892, however, the result was reversed. Cleveland won decisively over Harrison, and the Democrats carried Congress.

When the Supreme Court handed down its watershed ruling on abortion, in Roe v. Wade *(1973), the issue of abortion was elevated to the national political agenda.[1] Most Supreme Court cases have a political dimension. They involve people or institutions that are in conflict with one another or with the government. When that conflict enters the judicial arena, it concerns rules of law and how those rules are interpreted. The law may be the Constitution, statutes, or prior rulings known as precedents. In any case, it is for the courts to resolve the legal issue. Their judgments often have widespread implications, affecting not only the individuals in the specific case but the society as a whole. In this sense, courts interact with and affect the political environment.*

After the Court handed down its decision in Roe, *states could no longer outlaw abortions or impose criminal penalties on doctors who perform medically safe abortions. The Court declared that during the first trimester (about three months) of a pregnancy women have the right to decide whether to continue or terminate the pregnancy. States may regulate abortions during the second trimester, but only to safeguard the health of women and the unborn. In the third trimester, states' interests in preserving the life of the unborn become compelling, and they may limit, even ban, abortions except when necessary to save a woman's life.*

Until the mid-nineteenth century, most states had permitted abortions before the quickening, or first movement, of the fetus, and an abortion at a later stage of pregnancy was usually considered only a minor offense. After the Civil War, however, states gradually began to toughen their laws. By 1910 every state except Kentucky had made abortion a felony. After the sexual revolution of the 1960s, however, fourteen states had liberalized their laws to permit abortions when the woman's health was in danger, when fetal abnormality was likely, and when the woman was a victim of rape or incest. Four states had also repealed all criminal penalties for abortions done in early pregnancy. Thus, the legal status of abortion had returned to about where it had been a century earlier.

Roe *left numerous questions unanswered and afforded ample opportunities for noncompliance, however. While most states adopted new laws in conformity with* Roe, *many others sought to limit the availability of abortion by such means as withholding funds for abortion and denying the use of public hospitals for the performance of abortion. Likewise, Congress passed several laws restricting the availability of abortion and barring the use of federal funds for programs in which abortion is included as a method of family planning.*

By the 1980s the Court's ruling on abortion was an issue in presidential politics as well. All four Republican platforms endorsed by Ronald Reagan and George Bush supported a constitutional amendment "to restore protection of the right to life for unborn children." Moreover, the Reagan and Bush administrations appointed only judges who were opposed to abortion to the federal judiciary, including the Supreme Court. They also encouraged and joined in litigation that might undercut and ultimately lead to the reversal of Roe.

As the Court's composition changed in the 1980s, speculation mounted that Roe *would be overturned. However, despite six appointments to the Court by presidents Reagan and Bush, a bare majority of the justices upheld the "essence of* Roe" *in* Planned Parenthood of Southeastern Pennsylvania v. Casey *(1992). In a surprising and extraordinary majority opinion, justices Sandra O'Connor, Anthony Kennedy, and David Souter were joined in part by justices Harry Blackmun and John Stevens. In their dissent, Chief Justice William Rehnquist and justices Clarence Thomas, Antonin Scalia, and Byron White argued that* Roe *should be completely overturned.*

Although not overruling Roe, *the majority in* Casey *did uphold most of Pennsylvania's restrictions on access to abortions. Women must be informed by doctors about fetal development, give their consent (minors must obtain parental consent), and wait at least 24 hours after giving their consent before obtaining an abortion. The majority also imposed certain reporting and public disclosure requirements on doctors who perform abortions. It also struck down as an "undue burden" a requirement that married women notify their spouses of their desire to obtain an abortion, because that requirement potentially exposed women to spousal abuse, violence, and economic duress.*

In sum, a bare majority reaffirmed Roe *while rejecting much of the analysis on which it was based. States may not completely ban abortions, but the Court signaled that it would uphold restrictions that do not "unduly burden" women seeking abortions.*

THE ABORTION CONTROVERSY ILLUSTRATES HOW civil rights and civil liberties are linked to larger political struggles. In *Roe*, the Court elevated the abortion controversy to the national political agenda. Interest groups on both sides of the controversy were mobilized, and state legislatures and Congress passed legislation aimed at limiting the Court's ruling. The Reagan and Bush administrations urged the Court to reconsider *Roe*, and they appointed to the Court justices who they thought would overrule the decision. The Court is a political institution, and its rulings may invite larger political struggles. But civil rights and liberties ultimately depend not only on the Court's rulings but also on the achievement of political consensus.

Wide World Photos, Inc.

A 1989 pro-choice march on the U.S. Capitol brought together many Hollywood stars and feminist leaders, including Molly Yard, Eleanor Smeal, Marlo Thomas, Whoopi Goldberg, and Cybill Shepard. At the time, supporters of choice feared that the Supreme Court would overrule Roe v. Wade *when it decided* Webster v. Reproductive Health Services *(1989).*

Reuters/Bettmann

Even after a bare majority of the Court declined to overrule Roe v. Wade *expressly in* Planned Parenthood of Southeastern Pennsylvania v. Casey *(1992), pro-choice forces continued to rally. Antiabortion activists had stepped up their demonstrations at abortion clinics, and had even bombed some. Access to these clinics became a high priority. Patricia Ireland, president of NOW, addressed a more somber crowd on the Capitol steps on March 12, 1993, after the fatal shooting of Dr. David Gunn outside his Florida abortion clinic.*

One of the great ongoing struggles in American politics involves the protection of civil rights and civil liberties. **Civil rights** are rights that government may not categorically deny or infringe on because of an individual's race, gender, or ethnicity. **Civil liberties** are freedoms that government must respect, such as the freedom to think, communicate, and express oneself in a manner that conforms to one's beliefs and values.

The government has not always respected every individual's civil rights and liberties. Women, along with African Americans and other minority groups, have been discriminated against, and for much of American history so-called subversive political ideas and speech have been punished. As a result, American politics has been animated by political struggles aimed at guaranteeing equal civil rights and liberties for all people.

Political struggles over civil rights and liberties stem from the competing demands for majority rule and for individual or minority rights. We have seen already how difficult it is to have a government based on majority rule that also respects the rights of individuals and minorities. Conflicts between the majority and minority often arise over such issues as free speech, school prayer, the rights of the accused, abortion, and the rights of homosexuals. Resolving those disagreements is crucial to the stability and vitality of the political system.

Conflicts over civil rights and liberties trace back to the development of guarantees for individual rights in England. The Magna Carta (1215), the Petition of Right (1628), and the English Bill of Rights (1689) recognized the equality of individuals before the law and placed certain limitations on government power. Those basic charters, together with the philosophical tradition of unalienable natural rights, inspired America's founders when they drafted the Declaration of Independence, the Constitution, and the Bill of Rights. The core idea of these documents is that all people enjoy certain rights and liberties that are essential to their personal freedom and well-being and to their equality before the law.

The Constitution itself was viewed by some as a bill of rights. Alexander Hamilton argued that individuals' rights and liberties would remain secure because the powers of the national government were limited to those expressly granted to it in the Constitution. In addition, the states would continue to safeguard civil rights and liberties because the states were closer to the people and directly accountable to them. But the Anti-Federalists, who feared that the national government would not only usurp the powers of the states but deny individuals their rights and liberties, did not agree. They forced the addition of the first ten amendments, the **Bill of Rights**, to the Constitution more or less as a condition for ratification in Massachusetts, Virginia, and New York.

The Anti-Federalists were probably correct. The 1787 Constitution contained only five provisions that directly protected civil liberties. Because these provisions were not thought sufficient to protect individual rights and liberties, the states ratified the Bill of Rights in 1791. James Madison, the principal drafter of the Bill of Rights, had also sought protection for individuals' "rights of conscience" and limitations on the powers of the states to deny civil rights and liberties, but Congress rejected those proposals.

Initially, the guarantees of the Bill of Rights were viewed as limitations only on the federal government, not on the states. Congress assumed that the states would ensure individuals' civil rights and liberties under their own constitutions. Yet the state constitutions varied widely in their safeguards of individual rights and liberties and in how diligently they protected them. As a result of these differences, the Supreme Court finally *nationalized* the Bill of Rights. The Court made the guarantees of the Bill of Rights applicable to the states as well as to the federal government by construing them to be included in the Fourteenth Amendment's guarantee of "due process of law." Not only did the nationalization of the Bill of Rights involve the Court in political controversy, because it expanded the judiciary's supervision over state legislation, but the Court became a powerful arbitrator in the struggle for civil rights and liberties.

We now turn to the functions of the Supreme Court as an arbitrator of civil rights and liberties. How has it sought to balance individual rights against societal interests? In particular, how has it interpreted the constitutional guarantees of the rights of the accused? And what about other rights, such as the right of privacy, that are not explicitly mentioned in the Constitution? (In the next chapter we take up issues of political freedom—the freedoms of speech, press, and religion—along with the quest for equality and the elimination of racial and nonracial discrimination.)

THE NATIONALIZATION OF THE BILL OF RIGHTS

The guarantees in the Bill of Rights are stated in broad terms. The First Amendment is the only one that specifically singles out Congress and excludes the states from its prohibitions on passing laws respecting the establishment of religion and denying the free exercise of religion and the freedoms of speech, press, and assembly. Nevertheless, in the twentieth century the Supreme Court applied the guarantees in the Bill of Rights to the states.

The prevailing view in the nineteenth century was that the first ten amendments limited the powers of the national government only. This view was well stated in Chief Justice John Marshall's ruling in *Barron v. Baltimore* (1833). Marshall held that Barron could not sue the city of Baltimore for depriving him of his property without just compensation and due process of law, as stated in the Fifth Amendment. The city had graded streets and diverted some streams, and the resulting soil deposits made Barron's wharf unusable. But Barron could not sue for damages unless the Fifth Amendment applied to states and localities, not just to the federal government. In ruling that it did not, Chief Justice Marshall pointed out that the language of the First Amendment and the history of the adoption of the Bill of Rights demonstrated that the purpose of the Bill of Rights was to guard against, as he put it, "encroachments of the general government—not against those of the local governments."[2]

But with the adoption of the Fourteenth Amendment in 1868 there was a new basis for applying the Bill of Rights to the states. Indeed, one of the motives of Congress at the time was to overturn Chief Justice Marshall's decision in *Barron*.[3] Like the Fifth Amendment, the Fourteenth contains a due process clause, but that clause specifically limits the power of the states: "No State shall make or enforce any law which shall abridge the privileges or immunities of citizens of the United States; nor shall any State deprive any person of life, liberty, or property, without due process of law; nor deny to any person within its jurisdiction the equal protection of the laws."

Immediately after the adoption of the Fourteenth Amendment, lawyers tried to convince the Supreme Court that the Fourteenth Amendment "incorporated" or "absorbed" the guarantees of the Bill of Rights and applied them to the states. Yet, with one exception during the last century, the Court refused to go along with that argument. The exception came in 1897, when the Court held that the concept of eminent domain, which is contained in the Fifth Amendment's guarantee that private property shall be taken "without just compensation," also applies to the states.

In 1925, however, the Court ruled in *Gitlow v. New York* that a major provision of the First Amendment (the guarantee of the freedoms of speech and press) applied to the states. In this revolutionary decision Justice Edward T. Stanford simply announced that "for present purposes we may and do assume that freedom of speech and press, which are protected by the First Amendment from abridgement by Congress, are among the fundamental personal rights and 'liberties' protected by the due process clause of the Fourteenth Amendment from impairment by the States."[4]

In the 1930s and 1940s the Court applied the remaining guarantees of the First Amendment—those dealing with religion and the right of assembly—to the states on a case-by-case basis. But the Court remained reluctant to apply to the states the rest of the Bill of Rights, particularly the rights of the accused contained in the Fourth through Eighth Amendments.

During the 1960s, when the Court was headed by a liberal chief justice (Earl Warren), it selectively incorporated the other principal guarantees of the Bill of Rights into the Fourteenth Amendment's due process clause and made them applicable to the states (see Table 4-1).[5] In addition, in 1965 it found a "right of privacy" (which is not specifically mentioned in the Constitution) and applied it to the states under the Fourteenth Amendment.

By the 1970s all of the major provisions of the Bill of Rights had been held to apply to the states. The only ones that do not apply are the right to keep and bear arms (Second Amendment); the provision against the quartering of troops in private homes (Third); the provision for grand jury indictments (Fifth); the right of a jury trial in civil cases (Seventh); the provision that the other enumerated rights "shall not be construed to deny or disparage others retained by the people" (Ninth); and the provision that "the powers not delegated to the United States by the Constitution, nor prohibited by it to the States, are reserved to the States respectively, or to the people" (Tenth).

The Court's nationalization of the Bill of Rights, particularly the guarantees pertaining to criminal justice and the rights of the accused, sparked a major and continuing controversy in American politics. In 1968 Richard M. Nixon based his successful presidential campaign on attacking the Court's rulings on criminal justice and calling for a "return to law and order in the country." And throughout the 1980s the Justice Department pressed, often unsuccessfully, for the Court to overturn some of the most controversial rulings on the rights of the accused that had been handed down in the 1960s. The Reagan administration, for example, asked the Court to overturn its earlier rulings upholding the use of the exclusionary rule under the Fourth Amendment. The **exclusionary rule** requires that evidence illegally obtained by police in violation of the Fourth Amendment's requirements for searches and seizures be excluded at trial. Critics of the rule argue that it is costly because it often allows guilty people to go free and does not deter police misconduct. Although

	TABLE 4-1	
	The Nationalization of the Guarantees of the Bill of Rights	
YEAR	GUARANTEE AND AMENDMENT	CASE
1897	Eminent domain (V)	*Chicago, Burlington & Quincy Railroad v. Chicago*
1925	Freedom of speech (I)	*Gitlow v. New York*
1931	Freedom of press (I)	*Near v. Minnesota*
1932	Right to counsel in *capital* cases (VI)	*Powell v. Alabama*
1934	Free exercise of religion (I)	*Hamilton v. Regents of the University of California*
1937	Assembly and petition (I)	*DeJonge v. Oregon*
1947	Establishment of church and state (I)	*Everson v. Board of Education of Ewing Township*
1948	Public trial (VI)	*In re Oliver*
1949	Unreasonable searches and seizures (IV)	*Wolf v. Colorado*
1961	Exclusionary rule (IV)	*Mapp v. Ohio*
1962	Cruel and unusual punishment (VIII)	*Robinson v. California*
1963	Counsel in all criminal cases (VI)	*Gideon v. Wainwright*
1964	Compulsory self-incrimination (V)	*Malloy v. Hogan*
1965	Confrontation of witnesses (VI)	*Pointer v. Texas*
1965	Right of privacy*	*Griswold v. Connecticut*
1966	Trial by impartial jury (VI)	*Parker v. Gladden*
1967	Right to a speedy trial (VI)	*Klopfer v. North Carolina*
1968	Jury trial in nonpetty criminal cases (VI)	*Duncan v. Louisiana*
1969	Double jeopardy (V)	*Benton v. Maryland*
1972	Right to counsel in all cases involving a jail term (VI)	*Argersinger v. Hamlin*

* The right of privacy is not enumerated in the Bill of Rights, but the Supreme Court found it in the "penumbras" or "shadows" of the provisions of the First, Third, Fourth, and Fifth amendments.

the Court made exceptions to the application of the exclusionary rule, it nevertheless refused to abandon the rule in all criminal cases. (This controversy is the subject of the Case Study on page 108.)

The controversy over rulings upholding the rights of the accused stemmed not only from the Court's enforcing individual rights over social interests in law enforcement and crime control but also from its involvement in matters that had traditionally been the responsibility of the states. State court judges, police, and prosecutors resented the Supreme Court's supervision of their decisions and the imposition of the requirements contained in the Bill of Rights on their criminal-justice procedures. Indeed, in 1958 thirty-six state chief justices issued a report protesting the Court's "erosion of the federal system."[6]

The intensity of the opposition partially explains why guarantees of the Bill of Rights were *selectively* applied on a case-by-case basis, rather than being

To ensure police compliance with the requirements of the Fourth Amendment, the Supreme Court, in *Weeks v. United States* (1914), created the controversial exclusionary rule. The exclusionary rule forbids the use of evidence obtained illegally by police as a result of actions that do not comply with the requirements of the amendment. In 1961 the Court held that this rule applies to state as well as to federal law enforcement officials.

The exclusionary rule has engendered considerable debate and political controversy. Critics argue that its price is too high—that criminals can and do go free as a result of mistakes or misconduct by the police. They contend that instead of forbidding the use of illegally obtained evidence at trial, the courts should hold police liable and award damages for illegal searches. Defenders of the exclusionary rule counter that few police officers are prosecuted and most could not afford to pay civil damages. In addition, they point out that the only way to protect personal autonomy and privacy, the core values of the Fourth Amendment, is to deter police misconduct by enforcing the rule.

In two 1984 rulings, *United States v. Leon* and *Massachusetts v. Sheppard*, the Court cut back on, but stopped short of overturning, the exclusionary rule. The case involving Alberto Leon began in August 1981, when a confidential informant told a police officer in Burbank, California, that two persons whom he knew as "Armando" and "Patsy" were selling cocaine and methaqualone at their home. The informant gave the police their address but also claimed that they generally kept only small quantities of drugs there, storing the rest at another location. The police began an investigation, staking out

Courtesy of Priscilla Machado

Dollree Mapp was booked by Cleveland police on May 27, 1957. Ms. Mapp's lawsuit against the department for making an illegal search and seizure in her house led to the Supreme Court's landmark—and controversial—ruling in Mapp v. Ohio *(1961). There the Court held that the Fourth Amendment's exclusionary rule applies to cases in state as well as federal courts. As a result, evidence illegally obtained by police may not be used at trial against a defendant.*

the residence of Armando Sanchez, who had previously been arrested for possessing marijuana, and Patsy Stewart, who had no prior criminal record.

In the course of the investigation, the officers saw a car belonging to Ricardo Del Castillo, who had previously been arrested for possessing fifty pounds of marijuana, arriving at Sanchez's house. The driver entered the house and left shortly thereafter with a small paper bag. A check of Del Casti-

extended all at once as some justices wished. Members of the Supreme Court disagreed over the extent to which they should defer to state courts and how and which guarantees of the Bill of Rights should be applied to the states.

Although controversy continues, the Supreme Court is unlikely to overturn its rulings applying the Bill of Rights to the states. However, under its last two chief justices, Warren Burger and William Rehnquist, the Court has increasingly given greater weight to states' law enforcement interests when balancing competing individual and societal interests in the area of criminal justice.

llo's probation records led the police to Alberto Leon. Leon had been arrested in 1980 on drug charges, and one of his companions informed the police that he was heavily involved in the importation of drugs into the United States.

One day during their surveillance of Sanchez and Stewart, police officers saw them boarding separate flights to Miami, Florida; they later returned to Los Angeles together. They were stopped at the airport and agreed to a search of their luggage. A small amount of marijuana was discovered, but they were allowed to leave the airport.

On the basis of this and other investigations, the police applied for a warrant to search the residences of Sanchez, Stewart, and Leon for a long list of items related to drug trafficking. The search produced a large quantity of drugs, and all three were subsequently indicted by a grand jury and charged with conspiracy to possess and distribute cocaine and other drugs.

Leon's attorney filed a motion to suppress the evidence seized pursuant to the warrant on the ground that the police failed to fully establish probable cause for the issuance of a warrant as required under the Fourth Amendment. A district court judge granted the motion, and a federal appellate court subsequently affirmed that ruling. The Reagan administration appealed the appellate court's ruling and asked the Supreme Court to decide "whether the Fourth Amendment exclusionary rule should be modified so as not to bar the admission of evidence seized in reasonable, good-faith reliance on a search warrant that is subsequently held to be defective."*

* *United States v. Leon*, 468 U.S. 897 (1984).

The Supreme Court granted review in the *Leon* case along with another, *Massachusetts v. Sheppard* (1984). In the *Massachusetts* case, police had made an arrest using a warrant that is usually issued for searches for controlled substances, instead of an arrest warrant. A judge had signed the wrong warrant after finding that the police had established probable cause in their application for the warrant, even though they had used the wrong application form because it was a Sunday and their office had run out of the correct forms. In both cases the Supreme Court held that the police had acted in "good faith," that their warrants were valid, and that, therefore, the evidence discovered by their searches could be used at trial.

The debate over the exclusionary rule is certain to continue, and the rule may eventually be abandoned. The Court has become more sympathetic to society's interests in law enforcement and in not penalizing police for good-faith mistakes. It has, for instance, recognized "good-faith exceptions" to the rule in situations in which police conducted a search in good faith using a warrant that was later found to be defective.

Discussion questions
1. What are the arguments for and against the Supreme Court's enforcement of the exclusionary rule under the Fourth Amendment?
2. Should the Supreme Court balance the rights of the accused against victims' rights and law enforcement interests? If so, on what basis does the Bill of Rights authorize the Court to balance competing interests such as these?

CIVIL RIGHTS AND CRIMINAL JUSTICE

Americans enjoy a great number of civil rights and liberties that limit the coercive powers of government. Some are a result of the Supreme Court's interpretation of the Constitution and congressional legislation designed to ensure equal access to justice and equality before the law. Others are contained in state constitutions and bills of rights. Many, such as due process of law and freedom from unreasonable searches and seizures, are rooted in principles that origi-

Individuals' Rights and Safeguards in Criminal Prosecutions

The Bill of Rights guarantees certain limitations on the power of government in criminal procedures and law enforcement.

1. The right to be secure in one's person, house, papers, and effects against unreasonable searches and seizures. (Fourth Amendment)
2. The issuance of a search or an arrest warrant only with probable cause, supported by oath or affirmation, and particularly describing the place to be searched and the person or things to be seized. (Fourth Amendment)
3. Indictment by a grand jury for a capital or an otherwise infamous crime. (Fifth Amendment)
4. No double jeopardy. (Fifth Amendment)
5. Immunity against compulsory self-incrimination. (Fifth Amendment)
6. The right to be informed of the nature and cause of an accusation. (Sixth Amendment)
7. The right to a speedy and public trial, by an impartial jury. (Sixth Amendment)
8. The right of accused people to confront witnesses for and against them. (Sixth Amendment)
9. The right to be represented by counsel in criminal cases. (Sixth Amendment)
10. The prohibition of excessive bail, excessive fines, and cruel and unusual punishment. (Eighth Amendment)

nated in the English common law and are embodied in the guarantees of the Bill of Rights. The provisions of the Bill of Rights that limit the powers of state and federal governments in criminal procedures and law enforcement are examined in this section and listed in the box above. The major stages in the criminal-justice process are presented in Figure 4-1.

Due Process of Law

Under the due process clauses of the Fifth and Fourteenth Amendments, no person shall be deprived of "life, liberty, or property, without due process of law." But what is **due process?** What "process" is "due"?

Those are vexing questions, for the concept of due process is broad and elusive. The concept can be traced to the English Petition of Right (1628) and then to the Magna Carta (1215), where it originally meant simply "the law of the land." Due process, as Justice Felix Frankfurter once explained, "is compounded of history, reason, the past course of decisions, and stout confidence in the strength of the democratic faith which we profess. Due process is not a mechanical instrument. It is not a yardstick. It is a delicate process of adjustment inescapably involving the exercise of judgment by those whom the Constitution entrusted with the unfolding of the process."[7]

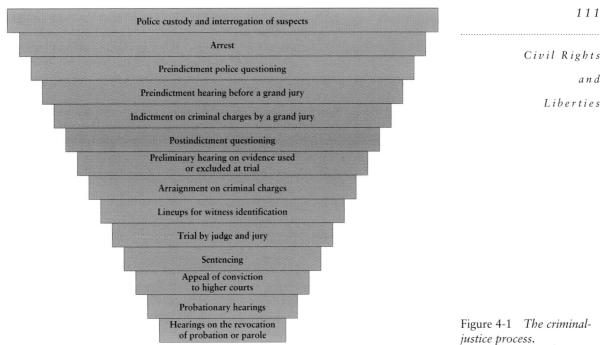

Figure 4-1   *The criminal-justice process.*

There are basically two kinds of due process: procedural and substantive.

Procedural due process   **Procedural due process** is concerned with *how* the law is carried out, whether by police, judges, legislatures, or administrative agencies. Procedural due process pertains to the specific rights and procedural guarantees mentioned in the Bill of Rights. The Court has also sought to enforce a more general standard of fairness in criminal procedures and law enforcement. In *Rochin v. California* (1952), for example, the Court reversed the conviction of Antonio Richard Rochin for selling and possessing narcotics. Police with no arrest or search warrant had broken into Rochin's home and found him in bed. Rochin immediately swallowed two morphine capsules that were on a table next to the bed. The police tried to make him cough up the evidence, repeatedly kicking him and trying to make him gag. Finally they took him to a hospital and ordered a doctor to pump his stomach. At Rochin's trial the prosecution introduced the regurgitated morphine as evidence. In an opinion for the Supreme Court overturning Rochin's conviction, Justice Frankfurter observed that the conduct of the police "shocks the conscience. . . . Due process of law [means that] convictions cannot be brought about by methods that offend 'a sense of justice.' "[8]

The Court has held that some laws are unconstitutional because they are overly broad or *void for vagueness.* Laws that made it a crime to treat the American flag "contemptuously," for instance, have been struck down because individuals may not know exactly what is permitted and what is prohibited. In general, the Court holds that "[a] statute which either forbids or requires the doing of an act in terms so vague that men of common intelligence must necessarily guess at its meaning and differ as to its application, violates the first essential of due process."[9]

During the 1960s and 1970s, the Supreme Court greatly expanded the requirements of procedural due process by applying them to administrative agencies and other government institutions. For example, it held that individuals must be given some kind of hearing or opportunity to challenge the termination of welfare benefits; student suspensions from school; and the disconnecting of electric, gas, and water services by public utilities.[10] However, in the 1980s and 1990s the Supreme Court became more conservative and more sensitive to societal interests as opposed to the interests of individuals demanding a fair hearing. It now resists further expansions of the concept of procedural due process. It has also let certain criminal convictions stand even though the accused's rights were not fully honored because some "harmless error" was made by the prosecution at the trial.[11]

Substantive due process **Substantive due process** is concerned with the subject matter of a law, regulation, or executive order. Substantive due process places limitations on *what* government may do. The Court looks at the substance of the law itself, why it was enacted, and whether it is "unreasonable," "irrational," or "arbitrary" in light of the concept of due process and other constitutional guarantees. Because the Court may overturn laws, substantive due process is highly controversial. As Justice Oliver Wendell Holmes once observed, the Court becomes a "superlegislature" by imposing its own view of the reasonableness of a law and overturning the will of elected legislators.

Justices Oliver Wendell Holmes (left) *and Louis D. Brandeis* (right), *the two "great dissenters," were among the Court's most respected justices. Holmes had fought in the Civil War and served on the Court from 1902 to 1932. Brandeis was the first Jewish justice and served on the Court from 1916 to 1939. Both were progressive legal thinkers, and when they were on the Court together, they frequently dissented together.*

In the late nineteenth and early twentieth centuries, the Court employed substantive due process to strike down government regulation of economic relations that governed the prices of goods, child labor, and the wages and hours of workers. It did so on the basis of a "liberty of contract," which, though not specifically mentioned in the Constitution, is implicit in the concept of due process, according to the Court. During the period when the Court was employing the concept of substantive due process to enforce the liberty of contract, it was dominated by conservatives who opposed virtually all progressive social welfare legislation. Between 1897 and 1937, over two hundred state and federal laws were overturned as unreasonable and infringing on the liberty of contract.

The Court's use of substantive due process to promote the interests of business created a major political battle, particularly when it invalidated much of the early New Deal economic legislation. In 1937 President Franklin Roosevelt retaliated. He proposed that the number of justices be increased from nine to fifteen so that he would be able to appoint new justices and thereby secure a majority willing to uphold his New Deal program. His opponents claimed that he was simply trying to "pack" the Court. But the Court then handed down a series of decisions—which humorists called "the-switch-in-time-that-saved-nine"—abandoning its use of substantive due process and liberty of contract. Since 1937, no economic regulation has been struck down on the grounds of substantive due process.

The Court has also employed substantive due process to overturn laws infringing on individuals' civil liberties rather than their economic liberties. Notably, in the 1965 case of *Griswold v. Connecticut,*[12] the Court invoked the right of privacy under the Fourteenth Amendment's due process clause to overturn a law prohibiting the use of contraceptives. In its highly controversial 1973 ruling in *Roe v. Wade,* the Court went even further by striking down most laws

© Dennis Brack/Black Star

Norma McCorvey (left), *the "Jane Roe" of the controversial abortion case* Roe v. Wade, *with Los Angeles attorney Gloria Allred. The two met to hear oral arguments in* Webster v. Reproductive Health Services, *in which the Reagan administration unsuccessfully asked the Supreme Court to overturn* Roe v. Wade.

The Freedom of Information Act (FOIA) was enacted in 1966. The act requires agencies and departments of the executive branch of the United States government to provide the fullest possible disclosure of information to the public.

The Privacy Act of 1974, a companion to FOIA, provides safeguards against an invasion of privacy through the misuse of records by federal agencies. The Privacy Act allows most individuals to gain access to federal agency records about themselves and to seek amendment of any incorrect or incomplete information.

Both laws make federal agencies accountable for information disclosure policies and practices. Although neither law grants an absolute right to examine government documents, both laws establish the right to request records and to receive a response to the request. If a record cannot be released, the requester is entitled to be told the reason for the denial and has the right to appeal the denial and, if necessary, challenge it in court.

As a result of the rights granted by the FOIA and the Privacy Act, federal agencies may not keep secret records. Disclosure of federal government information cannot be controlled by arbitrary or unreviewable actions.

The FOIA does not apply to elected officials of the federal government, including the president, vice president, senators, and representatives. It does not apply to the federal judiciary, to private companies, to persons who receive federal contracts or grants, to tax-exempt organizations, or to state or local governments (all states and some localities, however, have passed laws similar to the FOIA).

Often the most difficult part of obtaining information under the provisions of the FOIA and the Privacy Act is determining which agency has the records. There is no central government records office that handles all FOIA requests; there is no central index of federal government records about individuals. To find the correct agency, consult a government directory such as the *United States Government Manual* or a commercially produced directory such as *Information USA*. Both are found in virtually every library.

The next step is to write a simple letter to the agency's head or to its FOIA or Privacy Act officer. The letter should contain three important elements. First, state that the request is being made under the FOIA or Privacy Act (or both). Second, identify as clearly as possible the records that are being sought. Finally, include the name, address, and signature of the requester. There is no need to explain the reason for the request. Anyone can write a request letter; there is no need for a lawyer.

Federal agencies are required to respond to FOIA requests within ten working days, with actual disclosure of the requested information to follow promptly thereafter. There is no fixed response time for Privacy Act responses, but most are answered within thirty working days. In practice, however, the deadlines are not always met. Patience and a follow-up phone call are sometimes required.

Agencies may charge fees for processing some requests, particularly if the requester will use the information for commercial purposes. The fees are often reduced or waived for small requests made by individuals seeking information for personal or scholarly use.

Under the FOIA, an agency can withhold some or all of the following types of records: documents classified for national security, internal personnel rules and practices, information exempt under other laws, confidential business information, internal government communications, documents that affect personal privacy, and documents relating to law enforcement, financial institutions, and certain geological information. Under the Privacy Act, all records held by the Central Intelligence Agency and some records of agencies involved with criminal law enforcement may be withheld.

For detailed information and sample request letters, see the fourth report by the House Committee on Government Operations, entitled "A Citizen's Guide on Using the Freedom of Information Act and the Privacy Act of 1974 to Request Government Records." This inexpensive guide, one of the most widely read congressional committee reports in history, is easily available in most libraries and from the U.S. Government Printing Office.

forbidding abortion. It did so on the basis of the right of privacy and a balancing of the interests of women against the interests of the state.

The contemporary Supreme Court, however, has been reluctant to rely on substantive due process to protect or extend benefits to individuals. Indeed, the two dissenters in *Roe,* justices Rehnquist and White, protested that the Court was reviving substantive due process when it struck down Texas's abortion law as a violation of a woman's fundamental right of privacy. Although Rehnquist's view did not prevail in *Roe,* in 1988 he commanded a bare majority of the justices to hold (in *DeShaney v. Winnebago County Department of Social Services*[13]) that social workers were not accountable for violating a 4-year-old boy's constitutional rights. The social workers had failed to protect the child from repeated beatings by his father that left him brain damaged, even though on occasion they had taken him into custody as a precaution against his father's abuse. In his opinion on the case, Chief Justice Rehnquist wrote that the Fourteenth Amendment's due process clause does not guarantee a child a substantive right that requires social workers to ensure his safety. This ruling underscores the Court's refusal to further expand substantive due process.

Thurgood Marshall: A Liberal Voice for the People

The first African American to sit on the Supreme Court, Thurgood Marshall was nominated to the high bench by President Lyndon B. Johnson in 1967. His appointment symbolized the politics of the times. A Democratic president and a Democratic Congress had pushed through the first major civil rights legislation in more than a century, striking down barriers and expanding opportunities for minorities and women. Marshall's career stands as a larger-than-life metaphor for that controversial period in American politics.

No single issue touched Marshall's life more than racial discrimination. Born in 1909, he grew up in Baltimore, the son of a waiter and a schoolteacher. After attending Lincoln University and Howard University Law School, he led the National Association for the Advancement of Colored People Legal Defense and Education Fund in the 1940s and 1950s. As an NAACP lawyer, he argued before the Supreme Court—and won—the watershed 1954 school desegregation case, *Brown v. Board of Education of Topeka, Kansas*, along with twenty-eight other cases that extended protection to individuals and minorities.

During his twenty-four years on the Court, Marshall sat through a 180-degree turn in the Court's direction. He had come aboard at the height of a liberal-egalitarian revolution in constitutional law forged by the Warren Court. Between 1961 and 1969, over 76 percent of its rulings each term went in a liberal direction. During the next seventeen years under Chief Justice Burger, the Court's rulings were liberal less than 50 percent of the time.

Republican President Ronald Reagan's choice of three conservative justices to the bench, Anthony Kennedy, Sandra Day O'Connor, and Antonin Scalia, as well as the elevation of William Rehnquist to be Chief Justice, consolidated the counterrevolution on the Court. In 1990, virtually every ruling on the rights of individuals under the Fourth and Fifth amendments went the government's way. Marshall warned that the country's "war on drugs," for example, must not come at the sacrifice of basic liberties. He implored the Court to take the burden of *Brown* seriously in the face of failed efforts to achieve integration in many schools across the country.

Reuters/Bettmann

As he announced his resignation, Justice Marshall sat under a portrait of the first Chief Justice, John Jay. Asked why he was retiring, the 82-year-old Justice replied: "I'm old! I'm old and I'm falling apart!"

Yet by the late 1980s, a critical mass on the bench was no longer sympathetic. Justice Marshall became increasingly isolated in defending the Court's role as a guardian of civil liberties and civil rights. When the old warrior retired in 1991, the Rehnquist Court seemed poised to overturn landmark decisions on abortion, affirmative action, and religious freedom. The Senate confirmation of Bush nominee Clarence Thomas to fill the "black seat" on the Court did little to hearten Marshall.

The Supreme Court's last uncompromising champion of liberalism died on January 24, 1993, the end of an era in constitutional law and politics.

SOURCE: Based on "The Triumph of the Right" by David M. O'Brien, *Los Angeles Times*, June 30, 1991, M1.

In sum, whereas liberals attacked the pre-1937 Court for imposing its economic vision under the doctrine of substantive due process and "liberty of contract," conservatives criticized the post-1937 Court for doing precisely the same thing—imposing its moral perspective through its application of the "right of privacy." The use of substantive due process will always be hotly contested because it pits the Court against the forces of the majority. Any time the Court sides with the individual or with a minority against the state or society, its decisions are likely to be controversial.

Freedom from Unreasonable Searches and Seizures

Like many other rights, the freedom from "unreasonable searches and seizures" provided for in the Fourth Amendment is rooted in the history of the English common law and the American colonial experience. The principle that people should be "secure in their persons, houses, papers, and effects" was well expressed in a speech by William Pitt the Elder:

The poorest man may in his cottage bid defiance to all the force of the Crown. It may be frail; its roof may shake; the wind may blow through it; the storms may enter, the rain may enter,—but the King of England cannot enter; all his forces dare not cross the threshold of the ruined tenement.[14]

Yet during the colonial period, royalist judges issued *writs of assistance* or *general warrants*, which allowed the British to search and ransack homes. The purpose of the Fourth Amendment was to prevent such intrusion—to forbid police from conducting "arbitrary," "unreasonable," and "general" searches and seizures.

The key to this protection is the requirement that a magistrate issue a warrant before a search or an arrest can be made. The exceptions may occur when the arrest is made in a public place or the police are in "hot pursuit" of a suspect or someone's life is in danger. Even when the police arrest or "seize" a person in a public place, they must still have *probable cause* to believe or a *reasonable suspicion* that the person committed or was about to commit a crime. In *California v. Hodari D.* (1991), however, the Rehnquist Court held that police may chase a person even though they do not have probable cause or a reasonable suspicion that that person is engaged in criminal activities.[15] Hodari D., a teenager standing with others on a street corner at night, ran away at the sight of an undercover police car. The police then chased him and recovered a piece of crack cocaine that he had thrown away, and the crack was used at trial against him. Even though the police did not have a basis for questioning or detaining Hodari D., the Court held that, for the purposes of the Fourth Amendment, he had not been "seized." When the police arrest a person, moreover, they may search him or her as well as whatever area and items are in "plain view."

To obtain a warrant, the police must swear under oath that they have "probable cause" for its issuance. The warrant must describe the specific places that will be searched and the particular things to be seized. When these conditions are met, a search and seizure is considered reasonable, and the police are barred from conducting more wide-ranging searches.

The provisions of the Fourth Amendment apply not only to people's houses but also to their apartments, their offices, and (under some circumstances) their cars and other personal effects such as clothing and luggage. In general, the Court has held that the amendment "protects people, not places" and applies in cases in which the Court deems someone to have a "reasonable expectation of privacy."

In response to the growth of government and the rise of the administrative state, in which government agencies regulate virtually every kind of activity, the Court has ruled that in some circumstances administrative officials, such as housing inspectors and agents of the Occupational Safety and Health Administration, must obtain a warrant before searching a home or business without the owner's consent. However, the Court has also held that individuals have no reasonable expectations of privacy in papers or records held by third parties such as banks, accountants, and lawyers. And in 1985 the Court upheld a school principal's warrantless search of a student's purse and locker. Two years later it also upheld the warrantless search of an employee's office by her supervisor. In *National Treasury Employees Union v. Von Raab* (1989)[16] and *Skinner v. Railway Labor Executives' Association* (1989),[17] the Court upheld, respectively, drug testing of employees and alcohol testing of employees involved in serious accidents. The Court has also ruled that individuals do not have reasonable expectations of privacy and Fourth Amendment protection against warrantless searches of garbage in trash cans or of the interior and contents of their cars; nor does the Fourth Amendment protect them against police helicopters flying over their property in search of marijuana plants.

Other threats to personal privacy posed by new technologies and changing law enforcement techniques have been addressed by the Court as well. The threat to personal privacy posed by the use of wiretaps, electronic eavesdropping devices, and secret television cameras could not, of course, have been foreseen by the drafters of the Fourth Amendment. When initially confronted by the issue of whether wiretapping constituted an "unreasonable search and seizure," in the 1925 case of *Olmstead v. United States,* a bare majority of the Court said no.[18] Chief Justice William Howard Taft reasoned that the Fourth Amendment protects individuals only against the seizure of physical objects and actual physical entry into their premises; it does not protect them against the tapping of telephone wires. But forty years later, in *Katz v. United States* (1967), the Court reversed itself. It held that police must obtain a search warrant before conducting wiretaps—even wiretaps placed in public telephone booths—because the amendment safeguards individuals' "reasonable" and "legitimate expectations of privacy."[19] Subsequently, in the Crime Control and Safe Streets Act of 1968, Congress established federal guidelines for the use of electronic surveillance by law enforcement officials and forbade any unauthorized person from tapping telephones and using other kinds of electronic listening devices.

Government Interrogations and the Right to Counsel

Individuals enjoy a number of rights under the Fifth and Sixth Amendments, which bar the government from coercing confessions and forcing the disclosure of incriminating evidence. One of these, known as the privilege against **self-incrimination,** may be traced back to the seventeenth century, when ecclesiastical courts in England forced confessions from religious dissenters through torture. In response to criticism of this practice by English judges, the privilege against self-incrimination was incorporated into the English common law.

The privilege, or right, against self-incrimination is a fundamental principle of an **adversary** (or **accusatory**) **system** of justice. People may not be forced to testify against themselves or to prove their innocence. In the American adversary system, the government has the burden of proof and may not coerce an individual to testify. In contrast, with the **inquisitorial system** used in France and other European countries, the accused person is presumed guilty, interrogated by magistrates, and denied many of the other rights afforded under an adversary system.

Although the Fifth Amendment protection against self-incrimination literally applies only during criminal trials, it has been extended to protect individuals who are summoned to appear before other government institutions and agencies. It may be invoked in the proceedings of grand juries, congressional and state investigatory committees, and some administrative agencies. Nor may individuals lose their government employment because they claimed the privilege before a disciplinary board. But individuals may invoke the privilege only when their disclosures would in fact prove incriminating, not merely embarrassing.

The privilege against self-incrimination may be waived by an individual who is offered a **grant of immunity** by a prosecutor, grand jury, or congressional investigatory committee; such a grant must be approved by a judge. Grants of immunity are offered when the government is more interested in obtaining information about some criminal activity, such as drug trafficking, than in prosecuting a particular individual. In exchange for immunity from subsequent prosecution (which would be based directly on the incriminating testimony), the witness may no longer claim the Fifth Amendment or refuse to testify.

The Supreme Court has also sanctioned the practice of **plea bargaining,** in which an accused person, in order to obtain probation or a reduced sentence, pleads guilty to a lesser offense than the one with which he or she was originally charged. In exchange for the lighter sentence, defendants who plea-bargain must surrender their constitutional rights against self-incrimination, as well as their right to a speedy and public jury trial and to confront witnesses against them. Plea bargaining is advantageous for the government as well as for the accused, because it eliminates the time and cost of going to trial. Approximately 90 percent of all guilty pleas result from plea bargains that are struck between the accused and the prosecution.

The most controversial extension of the protection against self-incrimination is the Supreme Court's use of it to limit police interrogations of criminal suspects. For years the Court reversed convictions that were based on coerced confessions and police brutality. But this practice meant that the Court had to examine all the circumstances in each case to determine whether the accused's rights had been violated, and it provided little guidance for the police and added to the Court's workload by increasing the number of criminal appeals.

To safeguard the rights of the accused, the Court handed down several landmark rulings that had wide-ranging consequences for the criminal-justice system. In *Escobedo v. Illinois* (1964), it held that whenever a person becomes the primary suspect in a criminal investigation he or she has the right to request the assistance of counsel.[20] A year earlier, in *Gideon v. Wainwright* (1963), it ruled that any individual accused of a criminal offense but too poor to hire a lawyer has the right to a court-appointed attorney.[21] Both cases acknowledged that without the assistance of counsel individuals may not fully understand their rights and may be intimidated by police and by the judicial process.

Subsequently, in *Miranda v. Arizona* (1966), Chief Justice Earl Warren sought to establish objective standards for determining whether confessions were coerced.[22] Ernesto Miranda, a 23-year-old indigent with a ninth-grade education, had been arrested and charged with kidnapping and raping an 18-year-old girl on the outskirts of Phoenix, Arizona. At the police station the rape victim identified Miranda in a police lineup; two officers then took him into a separate room for interrogation. At first denying his guilt, Miranda eventually confessed and wrote out and signed a brief statement admitting and describing the crime. After his trial and conviction, Miranda's attorneys appealed, contending that the use of the confession obtained during police interrogations, in the absence of an attorney, violated Miranda's Fifth Amendment right to remain silent. The Court agreed, holding that confessions cannot be introduced at trial unless the police informed the suspect of his or her constitutional rights. This procedural safeguard is known as the **Miranda warnings.**

The *Miranda* decision, like the rulings on the exclusionary rule, has been widely criticized for "handcuffing" the police and making law enforcement more difficult. The Court has become more sensitive to these concerns and, although it is unlikely to overturn the *Miranda* decision, has recognized certain exceptions and modified its enforcement of the *Miranda* warnings. For example, in 1989 the Court, by a bare majority, stated that police no longer have to use the precise language of the *Miranda* warnings (see the box below) when informing suspects of their rights under the Fifth Amendment.[23]

These and other rulings were crucial to ensuring individuals' Sixth Amendment right to counsel and to achieving equality before the law for rich and poor citizens. Subsequent decisions held that the right to counsel applies

---

Miranda Rights

1. You have the right to remain silent and refuse to answer questions. Do you understand?
2. Anything you do say may be used against you in a court of law. Do you understand?
3. You have the right to consult an attorney before speaking to the police and to have an attorney present during any questioning now or in the future. Do you understand?
4. If you do not have an attorney available, you have the right to remain silent until you have had an opportunity to consult with one. Do you understand?
5. If you cannot afford an attorney, you have the right to have one appointed for you. Do you understand?
6. Now that I have advised you of your rights, are you willing to answer questions without an attorney present?

to virtually every stage of the criminal-justice process—from initial police interrogations and preliminary hearings, through trials and sentencing, to the first appeals of convictions and sentences. Only when individuals confront the possibility of fines or do not actually face imprisonment has the Court held that they have no right to a court-appointed attorney.

Still, the Court's rulings protecting the rights of the accused remain controversial. For one thing, law enforcement officials resent the Court's second-guessing their operations. For another, the Court's decisions may make law enforcement efforts more costly and difficult, because police must follow the Court's guidelines. Moreover, guilty individuals are sometimes allowed to go free as a result of the Court's decisions. Finally, many people have little sympathy for those who are *accused* of crimes, even though they may be innocent, and it is sometimes hard to see that the Supreme Court's rulings are designed to safeguard the presumption of innocence.

The Right to a Fair Trial

When a criminal case goes to trial, a number of other safeguards come into play to ensure that the accused gets a fair trial. In addition to being guaranteed the assistance of counsel, accused individuals are guaranteed the *right to be informed of the nature and cause of the accusation* against them. It is the responsibility of the prosecutor, the attorney representing the government and the public, to bring the charges. Usually this is done through an indictment by a grand jury. A **grand jury** is composed of twelve or more citizens who hear the government's charges against a suspect on the basis of a preliminary presentation of the evidence and then may approve an **indictment,** a written statement of the charges or offenses for which the accused will stand trial. Not all states require grand jury indictments, however. About half permit the prosecution to present a **bill of information,** a document specifying the charges and evidence against an accused, to a judge at a preliminary hearing. The accused's attorney may now counter and seek to exclude evidence that may later be used at the defendant's trial. The defendant then gets time to prepare a defense.

At trial, the prosecution presents the evidence against the defendant and the latter's attorney presents evidence in his or her defense. In criminal cases, defendants have the right to be tried by a **petit jury,** traditionally consisting of twelve persons selected by the judge and the prosecution and defense attorneys from members of the community. The jury determines the guilt or innocence of the accused. In some jurisdictions the jury determines the penalty or sentence to be imposed on a person who has been convicted of a crime. In other jurisdictions the judge does this.

During the trial the defendant has the *right to confront witnesses*. The defendant (or the defense attorney) may call and question witnesses about their understanding of the facts in the case in order to try to persuade the judge and jury that their testimony is unreliable. At the same time, the prosecution introduces witnesses and questioning designed to prove the defendant's guilt. This confrontation—or "fight"—between advocates is the essence of an adversary system of justice. It is derived from the Anglo-Saxon substitution of trials for private out-of-court battles. Judge Jerome Frank, a sharp critic of the "fight theory" and abuses of the adversary process, provides a classic description of why that confrontation remains crucial to ensuring a fair trial:

In this typical courtroom, the jury listens intently as the judge interrupts a witness and opposing attorneys wait to resume their arguments. The adversary system is time-consuming and costly, but it is the heartbeat of the judicial system. It also gives citizens the opportunity to participate by serving on juries.

Many lawyers maintain . . . that the best way for a court to discover the facts in a suit is to have each side strive as hard as it can, in a keenly partisan spirit, to bring to the court's attention the evidence favorable to that side. . . . We obtain the fairest decision "when two men argue, as unfairly as possible, on opposite sides," for then "it is certain that no important consideration will altogether escape notice."[24]

A particularly vexing issue for the Court in recent years has involved the right of defendants to confront their accusers in cases of alleged rape and sexual abuse of children (see the Constitutional Conflict on page 123). In *Michigan v. Lucas* (1991) the Court upheld a state "rape shield" law requiring that evidence of sexual conduct be barred at trial unless the defendant is given notice of its introduction at least ten days prior to the trial.[25] In two earlier cases the Court ruled that defendants on trial for sexually abusing children do not have an absolute right to confront their accusers and that states may shield alleged victims from face-to-face confrontations with defendants by introducing the children's testimony through the use of videotaped statements or closed-circuit television. Then, in *White v. Illinois* (1992), the Court unanimously held that in trials involving child sexual abuse the Sixth Amendment permits the introduction of the victim's testimony made to police and doctors, and the Court rejected the claim that an accused has a right to confront the witness at trial.[26]

Criminal suspects may not be subject to **double jeopardy**—that is, after an acquittal they may not be retried for the same offense in the same court, whether state or federal. However, they may be tried in both state and federal courts for an offense that violates both state and federal laws.

Confronting Child Accusers

The Sixth Amendment says that "In all criminal prosecutions, the accused shall enjoy the right . . . to be confronted with the witnesses against him." But in criminal cases involving alleged sexual abuse of children, should the accused confront the victim?

By a 5-to-4 vote, the Supreme Court held that defendants on trial for allegedly abusing children do not have an absolute right under the Sixth Amendment to confront their accusers. In *Maryland v. Craig* (1990) and *Idaho v. Wright* (1990), the Court held that states may shield victims from face-to-face confrontations with defendants by introducing the children's testimony through videotaped statements or closed-circuit television. Subsequently, in *White v. Illinois* (1992), the Court unanimously held that prosecutors may introduce as evidence children's statements to doctors and police, along with the results of medical examinations, without giving the defendant's attorney an opportunity to cross-examine the victim.

The Sixth Amendment requires the federal government to give the accused *a speedy and public trial before an impartial jury.* The Seventh Amendment guarantees people a jury trial in civil cases involving controversies over amounts exceeding $20. These provisions for jury trials are based on the English common law principle that a trial by a jury of one's peers is the surest way to safeguard against arbitrary and vindictive prosecutions. They may temper the enforcement of unpopular and outdated laws, and they serve as a hedge against a corrupt or overzealous prosecutor and a biased or eccentric judge.

The Sixth Amendment does not explain what constitutes a speedy trial, but Congress has done so. Under the Speedy Trial Act of 1974, a person who is arrested must be charged with a specific crime within thirty days, arraigned ten days later, and tried by a jury within two months of arraignment. In major metropolitan areas, those requirements are not always met because of the large number of criminal cases, procedural delays requested by defendants, and the frequency of plea bargaining.

Although trials have historically been public, widespread newspaper and television coverage of sensational trials may create a conflict between the defendant's right to a fair trial and the claims of reporters to freedom of the press under the First Amendment. Defendants, for instance, often claim that pretrial and trial publicity prejudices judges and juries, thereby denying them their right to a fair trial. Reporters counter that closed judicial proceedings deny them their rights under the First Amendment. Today fair trial/free press controversies, with few exceptions, are resolved in favor of open trials. Only in extraordinary circumstances may pretrial hearings and trials be closed to the press and the public. In 1981 the Supreme Court approved the use of cameras in the courtroom as long as they are not disruptive.[27] Television coverage of criminal trials is regulated by each of the states, and a few federal courts have experimented with cameras in the courtroom. The Supreme Court, however, refuses to allow television coverage of its own proceedings.

Judges may employ a number of safeguards and remedies to protect the rights of the accused against the effects of prejudicial publicity. If pretrial publicity reasonably threatens the chances of obtaining an impartial jury, the de-

(Left) *In a Simi Valley courtroom, Officer Theodore Briseno described events on the night that four white Los Angeles police officers beat motorist Rodney King. As the evidence against the officers, a home videotape, was being shown, Officer Briseno said that he had "thought the whole thing was out of control." When a jury acquitted all four, riots erupted throughout Los Angeles County.* (Right) *Rodney King appeared at a press conference just after the riots and pleaded, "Can't we all just get along?"*

fendant may ask for a change of venue—that is, for the trial to be moved to another locality where there has been less publicity. When jurors are selected, the defendant's attorney may question them about the publicity and their views of the defendant. On the basis of that questioning, the attorney may ask the judge to bar potential jurors from hearing the case. During the trial, jurors may be sequestered and forbidden to read or watch news coverage of the trial. Only in extraordinary cases may the judge issue a gag order forbidding the prosecution, defendant's counsel, and witnesses from talking with reporters about the trial.[28] Finally, a judge may declare a mistrial, and a defendant always retains the right to appeal a conviction on the ground that prejudicial publicity prevented a fair trial.

Juries must be not only impartial but representative of a fair cross-section of the community. This does not mean, however, that defendants are entitled to a jury that includes members of their own race, gender, religion, and national origin or is representative of the proportions of such individuals in the community. Rather, the defendant's rights and those of potential jurors are denied only if members of a particular group are denied the opportunity to be selected for jury service.[29]

Traditionally, juries were made up of twelve members who had to agree unanimously that the defendant's guilt was "beyond a reasonable doubt." The standard of "proof beyond a reasonable doubt" applies for all criminal cases tried in federal courts and in state criminal cases. But some states have adopted smaller juries than the traditional twelve-member jury and permit nonunanimous verdicts in order to reduce the costs of conducting jury trials. The Supreme Court has upheld juries with as few as six persons in civil and criminal cases—except cases involving the death penalty—in state courts.[30] And it continues to require a unanimous verdict by six-member juries, although nonunanimous verdicts have been approved for juries with more than six members.[31]

Reuters/Bettmann

Who is this man? People east of the Hudson River know him as the "Teflon Don," the virtually unconvictable John Gotti, reputed boss of the Gambino crime family. Most jurors avoided his many trials, and some who did not allegedly regretted serving. Here he raises his fist in victory after another acquittal in 1990. He was not so lucky in 1992, and now serves a life sentence without possibility of parole.

The Prohibition against Cruel and Unusual Punishment

After trial and conviction, the accused is sentenced. In federal and most state courts, judges and juries have some discretion in sentencing within the rules that set terms of imprisonment for various offenses. Some states, however, have systems of **determinate sentencing** in which a mandatory length of imprisonment is specified for each offense.

The only limitation on sentencing and punishment provided in the Constitution is the Eighth Amendment, which forbids the levying of "excessive fines" and the inflicting of "cruel and unusual punishment." Fines are subject to the standard of reasonableness and are set primarily by legislative guidelines. According to the Supreme Court, the ban on cruel and unusual punishment limits the imposition of punishment in two ways. First, it prohibits barbaric forms of punishment, such as torture and unnecessary infliction of pain. Second, it forbids punishment that is grossly disproportionate to the crime committed. In 1910, for instance, the Court struck down a law providing for twelve years of hard labor for anyone convicted of falsifying a government document. But in *Rummell v. Estelle* (1980) it upheld a life sentence imposed on an individual for three thefts that totaled $289.[32] Rummell had refused to plea-bargain, and because he insisted on a trial, the prosecution charged him under the state's criminal-rehabilitation statute, which imposed a mandatory life sentence on anyone convicted of three felonies. Subsequently, though, the Court found that a life sentence without the possibility of parole was excessive for a person convicted of writing a $100 bad check.[33]

In the past few decades a major controversy has centered on whether the death penalty is a cruel and unusual punishment and hence unconstitutional. Justice William J. Brennan, Jr., maintained that it is, arguing that whenever the state takes a life, it violates the fundamental principle of respect for human dignity embedded in the Constitution. Chief Justice Rehnquist counters that capital punishment was permissible when the Constitution was drafted and that state legislatures, not the Court, should decide whether the death penalty should be imposed.

In an important ruling in *Furman v. Georgia* (1972), a bitterly divided Court held that the death penalty is not cruel and unusual punishment but that there must be precise standards for imposing it in order to minimize the potential for injustice and ensure the equal protection of the law.[34] Without standards for guiding a jury's discretion in imposing death sentences, individuals convicted on the basis of dissimilar facts and offenses could be unfairly sentenced and executed. *Furman* in effect invalidated most of the capital punishment laws at that time. Within the next decade, thirty-six states redrafted their laws and reintroduced the death penalty.

When reviewing challenges to these new laws, the Court ruled that capital punishment may be imposed only in cases involving murder and not in cases involving rape or other crimes unrelated to murder.[35] It also overturned laws requiring mandatory death sentences for certain crimes, including the killing of police officers. States are required to specify the circumstances, such as the age or role of the accused and the circumstances of a murder, that allow a judge and jury to sentence the accused to death row rather than to life imprisonment. Moreover, juries must be allowed to consider all mitigating factors when deciding whether to impose the death penalty. In 1989 the Court also held that states may execute minors age 16 or older and convicted murderers who are mentally disturbed or retarded. Under Chief Justice Rehnquist, the more conservative Supreme Court has become less willing to overturn death sentences, and the number of executions is expected to increase dramatically in the 1990s. Figure 4-2 summarizes public opinion on the death penalty.

Outside the Florida prison where serial killer Ted Bundy was about to be executed, supporters of capital punishment waited, half hoping to see the lights dim as the current was delivered to Bundy in the electric chair. There was a moratorium on executions in the late 1960s and early 1970s, but the number of executions steadily increased in the late 1980s. The United States is one of the few industrialized nations that still imposes death penalties.

© Dennis Hamilton/Gamma-Liaison

RIGHTS AND LIBERTIES VERSUS
ECONOMIC INTERESTS

127

Civil Rights

and

Liberties

The Supreme Court assumed the role of "guardian of civil rights and liberties" after 1937. Before then, it was preoccupied with protecting economic and property interests. With the gradual nationalization of the Bill of Rights, the Court began devoting more attention to cases involving civil rights and liberties and the equal protection of the law, abandoning its role as a champion of economic interests. As a result, a **judicial double standard** evolved. Since 1937, the Court has upheld, under the Fourteenth Amendment's due process clause, virtually all legislation regulating economic interests. But it has given greater scrutiny to, and has often invalidated, legislation that impinges on individuals' civil rights and liberties.

The Court's role as a guardian of individual rights is illustrated by the attention given to the special problems of indigents in the criminal-justice system. Beginning with the ruling in *Gideon v. Wainwright* (1963), in which the Court stated that people have the right to a court-appointed attorney if they are too poor to hire their own, the Court has sought to ensure equal access to justice in several areas. Defendants who are too poor to hire lawyers must be given transcripts of their trials so that they can prepare appeals.[36] If sanity is an issue in the defense, states must provide access to a psychiatrist.[37] Prison officials must also provide an "adequate law library" so that prisoners may make a "meaningful appeal."[38] And indigents may not be held beyond the maximum term or imprisoned solely because they cannot pay fines.[39]

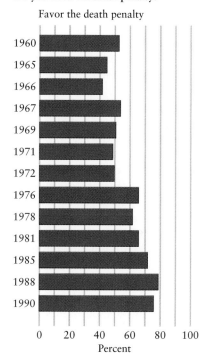

Do you favor the death penalty?

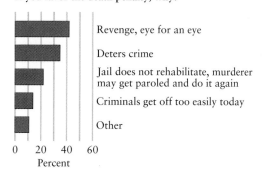

If you favor the death penalty, why?

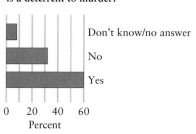

Do you think that the death penalty is a deterrent to murder?

Figure 4-2 *Public opinion on capital punishment.* SOURCE: *Surveys by the Gallup Organization, 1960–1988; by CBS News/* New York Times, *August 16–19, 1990; and by ABC News/*Washington Post, *May 18–20, 1981.*

In addition to enforcing the guarantees of the Bill of Rights, the Court has struck down numerous laws that infringe on rights and liberties not specifically mentioned in the Constitution. The Court's application of the *right of privacy* in overturning laws forbidding contraceptives and abortions remains perhaps the most controversial of these actions. But the right of privacy actually embraces a broader concept, "the right to be left alone." As Justice Louis Brandeis put it:

The makers of our Constitution undertook to secure conditions favorable to the pursuit of happiness. They recognized the significance of man's spiritual nature, of his feelings and of his intellect. . . . They conferred, as against the Government, the right to be left alone—the most comprehensive of rights and the right most valued by civilized men.[40]

Accordingly, the Court has sought to ensure various other constitutionally protected privacy interests, such as the right of *associational privacy*—that is, the right to form and join groups and organizations of one's own choosing.[41] The Court has also defended privacy interests in a person's home, papers, property, and effects as protected by the Fourth Amendment's guarantee against "unreasonable searches and seizures," as well as privacy interests under the Fifth Amendment's privilege against self-incrimination. It has not, however, extended the right of privacy to cover all matters of personal autonomy. In *Bowers v. Hardwick* (1986), for instance, it rejected the claims of a homosexual that laws prohibiting sodomy between consenting adults violate the constitutional right to privacy.[42]

The Court has enforced other rights that are not specifically mentioned in the Constitution as well. In 1969, for instance, it struck down a one-year residency requirement for the recipients of state welfare benefits. It did so on the ground that individuals have a fundamental *right to travel* from one state to another, while acknowledging that the federal Department of State may regulate their international travel.

The Court's exercise of its supervisory powers over civil rights and liberties is likely to remain controversial. Its post-1937 double standard of protecting civil rights while not scrutinizing laws that infringe on economic interests is widely criticized. Still, the Bill of Rights contains explicit language that guarantees a variety of civil rights and liberties; only the Fifth Amendment mentions economic interests in providing that a person may not be deprived of "life, liberty, or property" without the due process of law and that private property may not be taken "for public use without just compensation." The Court has shown no willingness to expand protection of economic interests under the due process clause or to return to its pre-1937 defense of property rights and economic liberty.[43] It has been more willing, however, to scrutinize land use laws and environmental regulations under the "taking clause" of the Fifth Amendment, which prohibits governments from taking private property for public use without providing just compensation. In *Nollan v. California Coastal Commission* (1987), for example, it struck down regulations that required owners of beachfront property to provide public access across their land as a condition of obtaining building permits, holding that such regulations violate the Fifth Amendment's taking clause.[44]

The Court's enforcement of those enumerated guarantees, in James Madison's words, is "an auxilliary precaution" against the tyranny of the majority. As Justice Robert H. Jackson eloquently observed:

The very purpose of a Bill of Rights was to withdraw certain subjects from the vicissitudes of political controversy, to place them beyond the reach of majorities and officials and to establish them as legal principles to be applied by the courts. One's right to life, liberty, and property, to free speech, a free press, freedom of worship and assembly, and other fundamental rights may not be submitted to vote; they depend on the outcome of no elections.[45]

Because the Court has the task of enforcing the guarantees of the Bill of Rights, it often thwarts the will of the majority and becomes the center of political controversy. Yet the Court accomplishes little unless its rulings have the support of other branches of government and, ultimately, command a national consensus. In Chief Justice Edward White's words, "The Court's power rests solely on the approval of a free people."[46]

SUMMARY

Civil rights are rights that government may not categorically deny or infringe on because of an individual's race, gender, or ethnicity. *Civil liberties* are freedoms that government must respect, such as the freedom to think, communicate, and behave in a manner that conforms to one's beliefs and values. Political struggles over civil rights and liberties stem from the competing demands for majority rule and for individual or minority rights.

The Federalists argued that the Constitution would protect individuals' rights and liberties because the powers of the national government were limited to the powers expressly granted to it. The Anti-Federalists believed that this protection was not sufficient. Their concerns resulted in the passage of the *Bill of Rights*, the first ten amendments to the Constitution.

Initially the guarantees contained in the Bill of Rights were viewed as limitations only on the federal government, not on the states. But because the state constitutions varied widely in their protection of individual rights and liberties, the Supreme Court eventually nationalized the Bill of Rights—that is, made its guarantees applicable to the states as well as to the federal government.

The due process clause of the Fourteenth Amendment specifically limits the power of the states. The Supreme Court did not use this clause to apply the guarantees of the Bill of Rights to the states until the middle decades of the twentieth century, however. By the 1970s, all the major provisions of the Bill of Rights had been held to apply to the states.

The nationalization of the Bill of Rights was highly controversial. The guarantees pertaining to criminal justice, such as the *exclusionary rule* (which excludes evidence obtained in violation of the Fourth Amendment), were subjected to especially severe criticism.

Under the due process clauses of the Fifth and Fourteenth Amendments, no person shall be deprived of "life, liberty, or property, without due process of law." There are two kinds of *due process*. *Procedural due process* is concerned with how law is carried out. *Substantive due process* is concerned with the subject matter of a law, regulation, or executive order.

One area where the Supreme Court has been particularly active is the Fourth Amendment freedom from "unreasonable searches and seizures." Holding that the amendment "protects people, not places," the Court has extended its provisions to cover not only people's houses and apartments but also their offices, cars, and personal effects. It has also addressed the threat to personal privacy posed by new technologies, ruling that the police must obtain a warrant before conducting wiretaps.

Individuals enjoy a number of rights under the Fifth and Sixth Amendments, which bar the government from coercing confessions and forcing the disclosure of incriminating evidence (*self-incrimination*). The privilege against self-incrimination is a fundamental principle of an *adversary* (or *accusatory*) *system* of justice, in which the government must prove that an accused person is guilty. In contrast, in an *inquisitorial system*, an accused person is presumed guilty. An individual who is offered a *grant of immunity* may waive the privilege against self-incrimination. The Supreme Court has sanctioned the practice of *plea bargaining*, in which the accused, in order to obtain probation or a reduced sentence, pleads guilty to a lesser offense than the one with which he or she was originally charged.

The most controversial aspect of the protection against self-incrimination is its use to limit police interrogations of criminal suspects. In 1966 the Supreme Court ruled that confessions cannot be introduced at trial unless the suspect has been informed of his or her constitutional rights by the police. This procedural safeguard is known as the *Miranda warnings*. Related Court rulings require that suspects be allowed to request the assistance of counsel and that criminal suspects who cannot afford counsel be assisted by court-appointed attorneys.

Accused individuals are guaranteed the right to be informed of the nature and cause of the accusation against them. Usually this is done through an *indictment* by a *grand jury*, but in some states the prosecution may present a *bill of information* to a judge at a preliminary hearing. In criminal cases, defendants have the right to be tried by a *petit jury*; during the trial, the defendant has the right to confront witnesses. The Sixth Amendment also requires the federal government to give the accused a speedy and public trial.

Widespread newspaper and television coverage of sensational trials may create a conflict between the defendant's right to a fair trial and the claims of reporters to freedom of the press. In such cases the defendant may ask for a change of venue. Jurors may be sequestered during the trial. In extreme cases the judge may issue a gag order forbidding the prosecution, counsel, and witnesses from talking to reporters about the trial.

Criminal suspects who have been acquitted may not be subject to *double jeopardy* in the same court. However, they may be tried in both federal and state courts for an offense that violates both federal and state laws.

In federal and most state courts, judges and juries have some discretion in sentencing; however, some states have systems of *determinate sentencing* that specify a mandatory length of imprisonment for each offense. The Eighth Amendment forbids "cruel and unusual punishments" as well as punishment that is grossly disproportionate to the crime. A major controversy of the last few decades centers on whether the death penalty constitutes cruel and unusual punishment.

Since 1937 a *judicial double standard* has evolved in which the Supreme Court has upheld virtually all legislation regulating economic interests but has invalidated legislation impinging on individuals' civil rights and liberties. In addition to enforcing the guarantees of the Bill of Rights, the Court has struck down laws that infringe on rights and liberties not specifically mentioned in the Constitution, such as the right of privacy.

KEY TERMS AND CONCEPTS

civil rights	self-incrimination	indictment
civil liberties	adversary (accusatory) system	bill of information
Bill of Rights	inquisitorial system	petit jury
exclusionary rule	grant of immunity	double jeopardy
due process	plea bargaining	determinate sentencing
procedural due process	*Miranda* warnings	judicial double standard
substantive due process	grand jury	

Scholarly studies

Abraham, Henry J. *Freedom and the Court.* 5th ed. New York: Oxford University Press, 1988. A highly readable and enjoyable survey of the Supreme Court's rulings in the areas of civil liberties and civil rights.

Berns, Walter. *The Death Penalty: Cruel and Unusual Punishment.* New York: Basic Books, 1979. A provocative argument for the imposition of capital punishment based on society's moral outrage at heinous crimes.

Black, Charles L., Jr. *Capital Punishment: The Inevitability of Caprice and Mistake.* New York: Norton, 1974 (revised ed., 1982). A classic and provocative condemnation of the imposition of the death penalty based on the inevitability of discretionary injustice.

Cortner, Richard C. *The Supreme Court and the Second Bill of Rights: The Fourteenth Amendment and the Nationalization of Civil Liberties.* Madison: University of Wisconsin Press, 1981. A wonderfully detailed discussion of the cases in which the Supreme Court applied the guarantees of the Bill of Rights to the states.

Craig, Barbara, and David M. O'Brien. *Abortion and American Politics.* Chatham: Chatham House, 1993. A case study of the controversy over abortion and how it has played out in the courts, the states, Congress, the executive branch, public opinion polls, and in the activities of pro-life and pro-choice interest groups.

Kalven, Harry, Jr., and Hans Zeisel. *The American Jury.* Chicago: University of Chicago Press, 1986. A comprehensive study of the history of the jury system and its impact on American law.

Schwartz, Herman, ed. *The Burger Court Years.* New York: Viking, 1987. A fascinating collection of essays assessing the Burger Court years and their legacy for civil rights and liberties in a number of important areas.

Leisure reading

Baker, Liva. *Miranda: Crime, Law and Politics.* New York: Atheneum, 1983. A detailed history of the watershed ruling in *Miranda v. Arizona* and of the subsequent controversy and debate sparked by that ruling.

Irons, Peter. *The Courage of Their Convictions.* New York: Penguin Books, 1990. Tells the stories of several individuals who took their cases all the way to the Supreme Court and describes the impact of the Court's rulings on their lives and on the course of constitutional law.

Lewis, Anthony. *Gideon's Trumpet.* New York: Random House, 1989. An excellent introduction to the judicial process in a case study of the landmark ruling that extended the Sixth Amendment's right to counsel to state courts.

Primary sources

Schwartz, Bernard, ed. *Roots of the Bill of Rights: An Illustrated Source Book of American Freedom.* 5 vols. New York: Chelsea House, 1981. A comprehensive collection of primary documents bearing on civil rights and liberties.

Organizations

United States Civil Rights Commission, 1121 Vermont Avenue, N.W., Washington, DC 20425; (202) 376-8312. A government agency authorized by Congress to study and recommend changes in laws bearing on civil rights and liberties.

CHAPTER

5

Issues of

Freedom and

Equality

- Freedom of religion: separation of church and state; freedom of religious exercise

- Freedom of speech and press: protected, unprotected, and symbolic speech; speech-plus-conduct; freedom of association

- The quest for equality: the extension of voting rights; reapportionment and equal representation; ending racial discrimination; nonracial discrimination; affirmative action and reverse discrimination

The election of 1896 was the first to feature celluloid buttons as a major form of campaigning. The chief political issue was the gold-versus-silver standard. Democrats supported coining silver at a ratio of 16:1 over gold, and the button for their candidate, William J. Bryan, represented this by a clock with its time set at 16 minutes to 1. Meanwhile, Ohio's Republican governor, William McKinley, stumped for "The Full Dinner Pail." Popular campaign items included bugs of gold or silver, and bicycle clubs were active in supporting their favorite candidates. McKinley and the Republicans defeated the "Great Commoner" Bryan, but Bryan would reappear as the Democratic candidate in the elections of 1900 and 1908.

Outside the 1984 Republican National Convention in Dallas, Texas, Gregory "Joey" Johnson and other members of the Revolutionary Communist Youth Brigade held a rally in protest of the Reagan administration's policies toward Latin America and its support of the contras in Nicaragua. After a march through the streets, Johnson set fire to an American flag while the crowd chanted, "America, the red, white, and blue, we spit on you." Police officers moved in and arrested Johnson.

During Johnson's trial his attorney argued that, like the Vietnam War protestors of the 1960s and 1970s, Johnson had burned the American flag as a form of political protest and that his form of political expression is protected by the First Amendment guarantee of freedom of speech. Nevertheless, Johnson was convicted of flag desecration in violation of a Texas law forbidding abuse and destruction of the American flag.

Johnson appealed to the Texas Court of Criminal Appeals, which reversed his conviction on the ground that his flag burning was politically expressive conduct protected by the First Amendment. That ruling was then appealed to the Supreme

Court by Texas's attorney general in Texas v. Johnson *(1989).*

The American flag is one of the most potent political symbols, for protest as well as for patriotism, in the United States. The Supreme Court has often been involved in controversies over the flag. One of the issues that has come before the Court is the authority of government to require participation in symbolic acts honoring the flag. Another is the legitimacy of punishing those who abuse the flag as a way of expressing their political views. In 1943, for example, the Court struck down a law requiring children in public schools to salute the American flag at the beginning of each schoolday. In this case the Court upheld the claim of a Jehovah's Witness who challenged the constitutionality of the mandatory flag-salute statute on the ground that it violated his First Amendment rights by forcing his children to worship a graven image in violation of their religious beliefs. Subsequently the Court also overturned the conviction of a protester who had burned the American flag in violation of a law making it a crime to do so; reversed the conviction of an individual for wearing a small American flag on the seat of his pants; and sided with a student who had hung the American flag upside down with a peace symbol attached to it from the window of his dormitory room.

Despite the more conservative composition of the Court in the late 1980s, it again upheld the First Amendment protection of political expression in Texas v. Johnson. *The Court struck down the Texas law as well as laws in forty-seven other states that made it a crime to desecrate the American flag. In the opinion announcing the majority's decision, Justice William J. Brennan wrote, "if there is a bedrock principle underlying the First Amendment, it is that the Government may not prohibit the expression of an idea simply because society finds the idea itself offensive or disagreeable."[1]*

Former President George Bush immediately denounced the Court's ruling and called for a constitutional amendment that would overturn it. "Flag burning is wrong—dead wrong," exclaimed Bush, continuing to sound a theme of his 1988 campaign.[2] In the aftermath of the Court's ruling, numerous congressional leaders in both parties joined Bush in calling for a constitutional amendment to reverse the Court's judgment. Instead, Congress passed the Federal Flag Protection Act of 1989, which authorized the prosecution of individuals who desecrate the American flag. That law was immediately challenged and overturned by the Court in United States v. Eichman *(1990).[3] Following that ruling, another attempt to overturn the Court's ruling by means of a constitutional amendment failed. The House of Representatives voted 254 to 177 against the amendment—34 votes short of the required two-thirds needed to propose a constitutional amendment. The proposed amendment also fell 9 votes short of the required two-thirds majority needed in the Senate.*

FLAG DESECRATION TOUCHES THE PULSE OF American politics. Most Americans agree that it is wrong, and few actually burn the flag. But the ruling in *Texas v. Johnson* illustrates the difficult role the Supreme Court plays in safeguarding the rights of minorities and those who express unpopular views. It also illustrates the controversy and opposition the Court is likely to generate when it takes a position that supports those who speak or behave in a manner that the majority finds objectionable. Finally, it demonstrates that the Court

A compromise: "It shall be an offense to attack, damage, deface, burn, kick or step on an American flag except one that a politician has wrapped himself in."

cannot avoid political issues as it fulfills its judicial role as an interpreter of the Constitution.

Among the political freedoms that are essential to free government are those that James Madison called "the equal rights of conscience"—the freedom of religion and the freedoms of speech and press. Under the First Amendment, individuals are equally free to worship or not to worship according to their own conscience and to express their opinions as they please. But these basic freedoms are not (and cannot be) absolute. Individual and societal interests often collide—for example, in disputes over prayer in public schools and the advocacy of unpopular ideas like revolution. As in other areas of public policy where the interests of the majority and a minority clash, the Supreme Court must draw lines between permissible and impermissible restrictions on individual freedoms. In drawing lines that define those freedoms, the Court has historically sought to ensure that those freedoms are enjoyed equally by all citizens.

We focus in this chapter on religious freedom and the freedom of expression. How has the Supreme Court defined the boundaries of those freedoms in response to major political controversies and shifts in public opinion? And what has been the Court's special role in applying the Fourteenth Amendment to eliminate racial and nonracial discrimination and achieve equal voting rights and greater access to the political process for all people?

FREEDOM OF RELIGION

Many of the people who settled in the American colonies were escaping from religious persecution and state churches in England and on the European continent. Although some colonists professed support for religious freedom, the colonies were far from tolerant of religious diversity. Most had an established religion and required holders of public office to adhere to it. Catholics, Jews, atheists, and those who held no religious beliefs were excluded from office.

By the time the Constitution was ratified in 1789, religious freedom and tolerance had become more accepted. Four of the original thirteen colonies never had established churches. Three abandoned their establishment practices during the American Revolution. The remaining six gradually accepted religious diversity and evolved from sponsoring particular churches to providing state support for all Protestant or Christian faiths.

Article VI of the Constitution indicates that freedom of religion was deemed a fundamental political freedom. It provides that "no religious test shall ever be required as a qualification to any office or public trust under the United States." The First Amendment is broader and more explicit: "Congress shall make no law respecting an establishment of religion, or prohibiting the free exercise thereof."

The First Amendment provides a dual protection for religious freedom. First, the **establishment clause** expressly forbids the creation of a national religion; it separates church and state. Second, the **free exercise clause** guarantees that individuals may worship as they please.

These two provisions raise more vexing questions than they settle about the scope of religious freedom. Does the amendment forbid the establishment of a national church but allow the states to sponsor particular religions? Does all state aid to religious schools constitute an establishment of religion or do only certain forms of aid? Religious *beliefs* are protected, but how far may states go in prohibiting certain religious *practices*, such as the use of poisonous snakes in religious services? And, how can the provisions for separation of church and state and free exercise of religion be reconciled when they conflict?

Preston Kelly of Canton, North Carolina, handles a poisonous snake during a religious service of the Holy Ghost Followers, a Pentecostal sect. The Supreme Court has upheld laws forbidding the use of poisonous snakes in religious ceremonies as a valid exercise of state police power and has rejected claims that the practice is protected under the First Amendment's guarantee of the free exercise of religion. Despite state laws and the Court's rulings, however, some Pentecostals still use poisonous snakes in their religious rituals.

UPI/Bettmann

According to James Madison and Thomas Jefferson, the establishment clause embodies "a high wall of separation" between church and state. This was the view taken by the Supreme Court in *Everson v. Board of Education of Ewing Township* (1947), in which it ruled that the principle of separation applies to the states no less than to the national government. In this case the Court held that a state must be "*neutral* in its relations with groups of religious believers and nonbelievers" but religious organizations may benefit from government programs that have a clearly secular purpose. The Court approved the state's providing free bus rides to schoolchildren regardless of whether they were attending public schools or private religious schools. As Justice Hugo Black explained:

The "establishment of religion" clause of the First Amendment means at least this: Neither a state nor the federal government can set up a church. Neither can pass laws which aid one religion, aid all religions, or prefer one religion over another. Neither can force nor influence a person to go or remain away from church against his will or force him to profess a belief or disbelief in any religion. No person can be punished for entertaining or professing religious beliefs or disbeliefs, for church attendance or non-attendance. No tax in any amount, large or small, can be levied to support any religious activities or institutions, whatever they may be called, or whatever form they may adopt to teach or practice religion. . . . In the words of Jefferson, the clause against establishment of religion by law was intended to erect a "wall of separation" between Church and State.[4]

Critics of the wall-of-separation theory argue, however, that the Court has gone too far in its emphasis on strict neutrality, particularly in its rulings forbidding school prayer. They contend that this neutrality has actually led to state hostility toward religion. In their view, the government is forbidden not from aiding religion but only from showing *favoritism* toward any particular religion.[5] In contrast, supporters of the Court's interpretation claim that religious services or aid of any type of established religion is in violation of the establishment clause.

The controversy over religious establishment came to a head in 1948 in a case involving school prayer. The issue was a "released-time" program for religious education in which children in public schools could attend one-hour classes of Protestant, Catholic, or Jewish instruction during school hours and in the school building. The Court held that this program violated the wall-of-separation doctrine that organized religion in the public schools establishes religion over nonreligion. But in a second "released-time" case a few years later, the Court allowed children to have the option of attending classes in religious instruction held *off* the school grounds.

Despite the Court's decisions, and its distinction between prayers held in public schools or away from them, many schools chose to interpret the ruling narrowly, arguing that it applies only to formal instruction in a religion and not to prayer itself. This argument was used to defend a practice that had become customary in many schools: requiring schoolchildren to begin the schoolday with a prayer. This practice was challenged in the landmark cases of *Engel v. Vitale* (1962) and *Abington School District v. Schempp* (1963).[6] In *Engel*, the New York State Board of Regents recommended the daily recital in the public schools of a twenty-two-word nonsectarian prayer: "Almighty God, we acknowledge our dependence upon Thee, and we beg Thy blessings upon us, our parents, our teachers, and our country." *Schempp* involved a challenge to the required recital of the Lord's Prayer in schools in Pennsylvania and Maryland. In both cases the Court found that the "high wall of separation" had been breached by these religious activities.

The Court's rulings were widely criticized at both the state and the national levels. Numerous constitutional amendments designed to overturn them were introduced in Congress. Although those attempts failed, state and local governments found ways of evading the decisions. By 1983 almost half of the states had enacted laws permitting voluntary moments of silence or prayer in public schools. Those laws were being attacked by people who claimed that children were subjected to peer pressure to conform and that children's rights under the free exercise clause were being violated. In 1985 the Court overturned Alabama's law because it required a "moment of silent meditation or *prayer*" and did not have a clear secular purpose. But some of the written opinions in this case seemed to indicate that a majority of the justices might be willing to uphold laws that do not mention prayer but merely allow for moments of silent meditation and religious reflection.[7] Nonetheless, in *Lee v. Weisman* (1992) the Court held that prayers during a high school graduation ceremony run afoul of the First Amendment's establishment clause.

In recent years the Court has moved somewhat away from enforcement of a "high wall of separation" and has adopted instead an "accommodationist" or "preferentialist" approach to church-state relations. Chief justices Warren Burger and William Rehnquist, among others, have championed this interpretation of the First Amendment. Unlike the high-wall theory, this approach holds that government may aid or extend benefits to religion as long as it does not prefer one religion over another. In advancing this view of the First Amendment, the Court has evolved a three-part test. If a law or program is to avoid violating the establishment clause, (1) it must have a *secular legislative purpose*, (2) its *primary effect* must neither advance nor inhibit religion, and (3) it must *avoid excessive government entanglement with religion*.

Given the Court's current "accommodationist" approach toward church-state controversies, it must draw some very fine lines in determining what the establishment clause forbids and permits. In 1984, for example, the Court split 5 to 4 in upholding the display of a crèche during the Christmas holiday season by the city of Pawtucket, Rhode Island. Chief Justice Burger's opinion for the majority interpreted the crèche as a secular, not a religious, symbol and found no excessive government entanglement with religion.[8] However, in 1989 the Court reconsidered the circumstances under which local governments may display a crèche and a Jewish menorah. Again splitting 5 to 4, the justices held that the display of a crèche *inside* a city office building violates the establishment clause, but they upheld the display of a menorah next to a Christmas tree *outside* a city or county office building. The crucial difference between the displays, in the view of the majority, was that the display of the crèche inside a public building suggested that the government was endorsing a particular religion, but the exterior display suggested that the government was promoting peace and religious freedom.[9]

The Court thus has taken an ambivalent position. On the one hand, it holds that the First Amendment forbids state-sponsored school prayer, the posting of the Ten Commandments in classrooms, and laws banning the teaching of evolution or requiring instruction in "creation science." On the other hand,

When the city of Pawtucket, Rhode Island, put up this crèche as part of a Christmas display in the heart of the city's shopping district, it was sued for advancing religion in violation of the First Amendment's guarantee against the establishment of religion. But a bare majority of the Supreme Court in Lynch v. Donnelly *(1984) upheld the city's display, because it deemed the crèche to be a secular symbol and because the expenses of the display were paid for by merchants, not the city.*

it permits the study of the Bible and religion as part of secular education in public schools.[10] And in some circumstances it has approved loans of books and other services from public schools to private religious schools, exemption from real estate taxes on property owned by religious schools, and tax deductions for parents who send their children to parochial schools.

In general, the Court tries to distinguish between legitimate state aid to students, even those in sectarian schools, and illegitimate state sponsorship of religion. In *Witters v. Washington Department of Services for the Blind* (1986), for example, it approved a state's giving higher-education grants to the blind even though one recipient, Larry Witters, chose to study at a Christian college. According to Justice Thurgood Marshall, the state's grant program did not violate the establishment clause because it had a secular purpose, and denying a grant to Witters would violate his right of free exercise under the First Amendment.[11]

Freedom of Religious Exercise

The free exercise clause embodies the principle of state neutrality with respect to the religious convictions held by individuals. Religious *beliefs* may not be prescribed or coerced by the state. People, therefore, may not be required to take an oath that they believe in God as a condition of government employment. But in some circumstances the government may regulate, and even ban, religious *actions* or *practices*.

Basing its decisions on the distinction between religious beliefs and practices, the Supreme Court has sought to ensure religious freedom by enforcing a **secular regulation rule**. This rule requires that all laws must have a reasonable secular purpose and that they do not discriminate on the basis of religion. But the rule also means that people may not claim exemption from permissible

Wide World Photos, Inc.

As members of the press crowded around him, Emerson Jackson, a Native American Church holyman, performed a "cedar ceremony" on the lawn outside the Supreme Court the day the Court heard oral arguments in Employment Division, Department of Resources of Oregon v. Smith *(1990). In that case, two Native Americans had claimed that Oregon violated the First Amendment guarantee of religious freedom in denying unemployment compensation after firing them as drug counselors because they used peyote during religious services of the Native American Church. The Supreme Court rejected their arguments by a bare majority.*

government regulations on religious grounds, because that would amount to religious favoritism and would violate the establishment rules. In *Reynolds v. United States* (1879), for instance, laws forbidding polygamy were upheld over the objections of Mormons, even though the practice was part of Mormon religious beliefs.[12] Subsequently the Court ruled that states may require school-children to have smallpox vaccinations, denying claims for exemption by Christian Scientists.

The Court has also upheld laws restricting the sale of pamphlets and books in public buildings over the objections of the Hare Krishna, who contend that such sales are part of their religious rituals. It has ruled that the Amish may be required to pay Social Security taxes even though doing so is contrary to their faith. And it has upheld so-called blue laws requiring businesses to close on Sundays, despite the claims that Sunday closing could cause economic hardship to religious groups that observe their Sabbath on Saturday, such as Orthodox Jews. In all of these cases the Court has argued that the state, because of its obligation to protect the health and well-being of all citizens, may limit practices that adversely affect society. Clearly, such decisions can create tensions.

The Supreme Court has not always sided with the state. It has ruled, for instance, that parents have the right to send their children to religious schools instead of to public schools, as long as those schools are certified by the state. Nor may children in public schools be forced to salute the American flag if doing so violates their religious convictions (as it does Jehovah's Witnesses'). In *Wisconsin v. Yoder* (1972) the Court even ruled that the Amish may not be required to attend school beyond the eighth grade because such a requirement would contradict their religious beliefs and cultural practices.[13] Because society needs to provide all children with a minimum level of education, however, it may require education up through the eighth grade.

Animal Sacrifices

May governments ban animal sacrifices in religious ceremonies without violating individuals' freedom of religious exercise? The First Amendment says that "Congress shall make no law . . . prohibiting the free exercise [of religion]."

At issue in *Church of Lukumi Babalu Aye v. City of Hialeah* (1992) was the constitutionality of a city ordinance prohibiting animal sacrifices in religious ceremonies. Attorneys for the church challenged the constitutionality of the ordinance, claiming that it violated the First Amendment and effectively barred the practice of Santeria. Practiced in the Caribbean and in parts of the United States by Cuban refugees, Santeria involves the sacrifice of animals at birth, marriage, and death rites, as well as in ceremonies to cure the sick and to initiate new members. An estimated 50,000 to 60,000 followers of Santeria live in southern Florida. In challenging the ordinance, the attorneys argued that, because the state of Florida does not bar the killing of animals, Hialeah was discriminating against a religious minority. Florida allows hunting, fishing, and trapping, medical research that results in the death of animals, the sale of lobsters to be boiled alive, and the practice of feeding live rats to pet snakes.

In this case the Supreme Court held that states and localities, while permitting other forms of killing

Reuters/Bettmann Newsphotos

A follower of Santeria, a mix of African ritual, Voodoo, and Catholicism, waits at the Iglesia Lukumi Babalu Aye in Hialeah, the first public place of worship in Florida where animals are sacrificed during services. The city passed an ordinance against ritual sacrifice, but the church claimed this violated its religious freedom.

of animals, may not then ban sacrifices or ritual killings. Such laws, the Court ruled, lack a compelling state interest and abridge the freedom of religion.

Recently the Court has signaled that it may no longer exempt religious minorities from generally applicable laws. In *Employment Division, Department of Human Resources of Oregon v. Smith* (1990), the Court abandoned its balancing test, which weighed the free exercise claims of individuals against the regulatory interests of states, when rejecting two Native Americans' claims that in denying them unemployment compensation, Oregon had violated the free exercise clause.[14] Both were fired from their jobs because they took peyote (an intoxicating drug produced from mescal cacti) during religious ceremonies of the Native American Church. They did not contest their being fired. They did argue that the Court's prior rulings forbade the state from denying them unemployment compensation because they had been fired because of their religious beliefs and practices. The Court overturned prior rulings and held that religious minorities are not exempt from otherwise generally applicable laws.

In these and other cases (see the Constitutional Conflict above), the Court has avoided trying to define religion. The First Amendment does not protect

Although the Supreme Court exempted the Amish from sending their children to school after the eighth grade because of their unique religious and cultural beliefs, in Minnesota v. Hershberger *(1990), it held them responsible for complying with highway safety and other generally applicable laws.*

only traditional or orthodox religions. Rather, it guarantees the right of each person to define his or her own religious beliefs. And that is the greatest guarantee of religious freedom. For as Justice Robert H. Jackson so eloquently put it, "If there is any fixed star in our constitutional constellation it is that no official, high or petty, can prescribe what shall be orthodox in politics, nationalism, or religion, or other matters of opinion, or force citizens to confess by word or act their faith therein."[15]

FREEDOM OF SPEECH AND PRESS

The freedom of speech and press is often called the "preferred freedom" because it is integral to the politics of a constitutional democracy. Campaigns, elections, and government accountability to the people would have little value without free and uncensored exchanges of opinion. The First Amendment, in Justice William J. Brennan's words, registers "a profound national commitment to the principle that debate on public issues should be uninhibited, robust, and wide-open, and that it may well include vehement, caustic, and sometimes unpleasantly sharp attacks on government and public officials."[16]

The broad protection accorded freedom of speech and press today is a product of Supreme Court rulings in only the past fifty years. Prior to *Gitlow v. New York* (1925),[17] the First Amendment did not apply to the states, and censorship of unpopular and subversive ideas was common. Before the Civil War, abolitionist literature was censored and burned in both the North and the South. Thereafter, many states passed laws forbidding obscene and indecent publications, including some works by outstanding English and American authors, such as James Joyce's *Ulysses*, Henry Miller's *Tropic of Cancer*, and Theodore Dreiser's *An American Tragedy*. In the late nineteenth and early twentieth centuries, fears of the spread of subversive ideas and doctrines—anarchism, socialism, communism—led to a rash of prosecutions during World War I and again during World War II.

The prevailing view of the First Amendment throughout the nineteenth century was that it incorporated freedoms inherited under the English common law. In this view, the First Amendment required only that there be *no prior restraint* on publications. This meant that censorship *before* publication was prohibited. Although that remains an important guarantee, individuals had no protection against *subsequent punishment* for what they said; books could be banned and newspapers closed. Moreover, under English law, individuals could be prosecuted for **seditious libel**—that is, for defaming or criticizing the government or its officials.

Most of the founders' generation accepted this view of freedom of speech and press. Indeed, the Federalist Congress passed the Sedition Act of 1798, making it a crime to "utter false, scandalous and malicious" statements about the government. It did so in order to silence its Jeffersonian critics. But when prosecutions were brought under the act, there was a violent public reaction, and after his election in 1800 President Jefferson pardoned those who had been convicted under the act; the act expired in 1801.

James Madison, the author of the First Amendment, insisted that the amendment embodied greater protection than the mere requirement of no prior restraint. But not until after World War I did the Supreme Court begin to articulate the constitutional principles and rules that ensure freedom of speech and press today.

Protected Speech

The First Amendment guarantee of free speech and press is not self-interpreting. The Court must give it meaning by developing tests or standards that define the scope of protected speech and press. The **clear and present danger formula**, perhaps the Court's best-known test in this area, was formulated by Justice Oliver Wendell Holmes in *Schenck v. United States* (1919). In that case the Court upheld the conviction of Charles T. Schenck under the Espionage Act of 1917 for urging resistance to the draft and distributing antidraft leaflets during World War I. Schenck's antidraft advocacy at a time of war constituted, in the Court's view, "a clear and present danger" to the country. In Justice Oliver Wendell Holmes's familiar words:

The character of every act depends upon the circumstances in which it was done. . . . The most stringent protection of free speech would not protect a man in falsely shouting fire in a theater and causing a panic. . . . The question in every case is whether the words used are used in such circumstances and are of such a nature as to create a clear and present danger that they will bring about the substantive evils that Congress has a right to prevent. It is a question of proximity and degree.[18]

Despite the Court's ruling against Schenck, the clear and present danger test was formulated as a broad measure to protect individuals against prosecution for unpopular ideas. Majorities may be tempted to suppress minority views, but "the theory of our Constitution," Holmes contended, is that government has no power to say what is true or false. Each individual has the right to express his or her own beliefs.

Justice Oliver Wendell Holmes.

In the 1920s, however, the Court was unwilling to go along with Holmes's position affording protection for unpopular speech. Instead, it relied on the common law "bad tendency" doctrine. Under this doctrine the test used by the Court was whether speech tends to corrupt public morals, incite crime, and disturb the public peace. In 1925, when upholding the conviction of Benjamin Gitlow under New York's criminal anarchy statute—Gitlow had published a book calling for a Russian-type revolution in New York—the Court maintained that as long as the law against it was reasonable, **subversive speech** could be punished.

Once the World War I hysteria over subversive political speech subsided, however, the Court greatly expanded the protection of free speech, acknowledging it as a "preferred freedom." Basically, this meant that the Court gave special scrutiny to laws limiting freedom of speech and took on the task of assuring the rights of those who, in Justice Hugo Black's words, "are helpless, weak, outnumbered, or . . . are nonconformist victims of prejudice and public excitement."

In the aftermath of World War II, the perceived threat of international communism ushered in the Cold War and led to further censorship of views that were considered subversive. The Court again cut back on the protection accorded free speech; it upheld the Alien Registration Act of 1940 (the Smith Act), the first federal legislation restraining political speech since the ill-fated Sedition Act of 1798.

In *Dennis v. United States* (1951) the Court upheld the convictions of eleven leaders of the American Communist party for advocating the overthrow of government, even though they had not done anything illegal other than teach and advocate communism. In this decision a majority of the justices reinterpreted the clear and present danger test. The question in every case, stated Chief Justice Fred Vinson, was always "whether the gravity of the 'evil,' discounted by its improbability, justifies such invasion of free speech as is necessary to avoid the danger."[19] Vinson left no doubt that the threat of *international* political events warranted the convictions under the Smith Act.

The two dissenters in the *Dennis* ruling, justices William O. Douglas and Hugo L. Black, vehemently protested the Court's recasting of the clear and present danger test into a test that upheld the suppression of speech. Douglas pointed out that the convictions were for the *mere advocacy* of communist doctrines; there was no evidence that the Communist party was in fact conspiring to overthrow the government violently, and books advocating communism could be found in public libraries. For his part, Justice Black championed an "absolutist interpretation" of the First Amendment. He summarized his position as follows:

I read "no law abridging" to mean *no law abridging*. The First Amendment, which is the supreme law of the land, has thus fixed its own value on freedom of speech and press by putting these freedoms wholly "beyond the reach" of *federal* power to abridge. . . . Consequently, I do not believe that any federal agencies, including Congress and this Court, have power or authority to subordinate speech and press to what they think are "more important interests."[20]

Although Justice Black was unable to persuade his fellow justices to accept this absolutist position, the Court gradually expanded the First Amendment protections in a series of rulings beginning in the late 1950s.[21] By 1969, in the case

Justice Hugo Black

© William R. Sallaz/Gamma-Liaison

As a result of the political struggles over "subversive speech" and government attempts to forbid "hate speech," the Supreme Court has held that the First Amendment gives broad protection to individual self-expression. Thus, rallies by almost any group, such as this recent Ku Klux Klan gathering in Denver, are permitted. The government may not censor or regulate the content of speech that does not fall into the categories of obscenity, libel, fighting words, or commercial speech.

of *Brandenburg v. Ohio*, it took the position that only the advocacy of immediate, violent, and illegal action may be subject to criminal prosecution.

The *Brandenburg* decision illustrates the premium now placed on First Amendment values and how far the Court is willing to go in protecting freedom of speech. Charles Brandenburg, the leader of a Ku Klux Klan group, was arrested, tried, and convicted under Ohio's criminal syndicalism statute for "advocat[ing] . . . the duty, necessity, or propriety of crime, sabotage, violence, or unlawful methods of terrorism as a means of accomplishing industrial or political reform" and for "voluntarily assembl[ing] with any society, group, or assemblage or persons formed to teach or advocate the doctrines of criminal syndicalism."

Standing before a burning cross, Brandenburg had addressed a small rally of hooded men, some of whom carried firearms, declaring, among other things, that if the president, Congress, and the Supreme Court continued "to suppress the white, Caucasian race, it's possible that there might have to be revengenance taken."[22] The major evidence introduced against Brandenburg during his trial was two films of his speeches at rallies. Brandenburg unsuccessfully appealed his conviction to a state appellate court and then to the state supreme court, which denied review. When he appealed to the United States Supreme Court, however, the justices unanimously voted to overturn his conviction and to strike down Ohio's law as an unconstitutional violation of the First Amendment.

Speech that has **social redeeming value**, because it addresses matters of public concern, is now fully protected. The government may neither exercise prior restraint nor subsequently punish individuals for speech or publications that touch on political, scientific, literary, or artistic matters. Even speech that might threaten national security is protected. In 1971, at the height of the

Vietnam War, the Court maintained that the government "carries a heavy burden" of justifying its attempts at censorship. In this watershed ruling, the Court rejected the Nixon administration's attempt to prevent the *New York Times* and the *Washington Post* from publishing excerpts from the *Pentagon Papers*, a 47-volume history of America's involvement in the Vietnam War that had been classified as top secret.[23]

Determining what speech has social redeeming value, however, is often politically controversial. The interests of communities in discouraging certain types of speech conflict with those of individuals who claim that the First Amendment protects their right of self-expression. In the late 1980s and the 1990s, for example, more than thirty states, as well as numerous localities, colleges, and universities, enacted "hate-crime" and "hate-speech" laws. St. Paul, Minnesota, for instance, made it a crime to place on public or private property a burning cross, swastika, or other symbol likely to arouse "anger, alarm, or resentment in others on the basis of race, color, creed, religion, or gender." But the constitutionality of that ordinance was challenged by Robert A. Vicktora, a white teenager, who along with several other white youths burned a cross after midnight on the lawn of the only African-American family in his neighborhood. In *R.A.V. v. City of St. Paul, Minnesota* (1992), the Supreme Court ruled that the ordinance violated the First Amendment because it punished certain kinds of speech based on their content. Writing for the Court, Justice Antonin Scalia observed that "the First Amendment does not permit St. Paul to impose special prohibitions on those speakers who express views on disfavored subjects."[24] In *Wisconsin v. Mitchell* (1993), however, the Court upheld laws that give defendants longer prison terms if they commit crimes that are motivated by racial, religious, or gender bias. In that case, an African American who said "go get that white boy" and was convicted of assaulting the individual received a four-year prison sentence instead of a two-year sentence under Wisconsin's prison-enhancement statute for so-called hate crimes.

Unprotected Speech

The broad protection afforded the freedoms of speech and press is not absolute. Speech that lacks social redeeming value is outside the scope of First Amendment protection. In *Chaplinsky v. New Hampshire* (1942), which upheld the conviction of Chaplinsky for calling a police officer "a goddamned racketeer," Justice Frank Murphy explained the Court's rationale for defining some categories of speech as unprotected and outside the scope of the First Amendment:

There are certain well-defined and narrowly limited classes of speech, the prevention and punishment of which has never been thought to raise any Constitutional problem. These include the lewd and the obscene, the profane, the libelous, and the insulting or "fighting" words—those which by their very utterance inflict injury or tend to incite an immediate breach of the peace. It has been well observed that such utterances are no essential part of any exposition of ideas, and are of such slight social value as a step to truth that any benefit that may be derived from them is clearly outweighed by the social interest in order and morality.[25]

There are only four categories of unprotected speech: obscenity, libel and slander, fighting words, and commercial speech. Yet defining standards for each category has proven extraordinarily vexing.

Obscenity   Obscenity has been subject to government censorship for centuries, but defining what is obscene has been a persistent problem. Prior to *Roth v. United States* (1957), federal courts permitted state and local governments to ban major literary works. They did so under an English common law rule set forth in 1868. Known as the Hicklin rule, it permitted the banning of books on the basis of isolated passages that might tend to "deprave and corrupt those whose minds are open to such immoral influences." This was a very broad standard and, as Justice Felix Frankfurter put it, would eliminate virtually all literature "except that only fit for children."

In the *Roth* decision the Court held that obscenity is "not within the area of constitutionally protected speech." But it also rejected the Hicklin rule for determining what is obscene. Justice Brennan, in his opinion for the Court in *Roth*, announced a new test: "whether to the average person, applying contemporary community standards, the dominant theme of the material taken as a whole appeals to prurient interests."[26] Basically, the *Roth* test meant that only hard-core pornography was outside the scope of First Amendment protection. But the justices remained unable to agree on how to define obscenity. That problem led Justice Potter Stewart to confess that, although he could not define it, "I know it when I see it."

The *Roth* ruling ignited political controversy. It appeared to open the floodgates for purveyors of pornographic materials. Presidential commissions studied the problem, and state and local law enforcement agencies sought tougher standards. Under pressure to overturn *Roth*, the more conservative Court of the 1970s redefined the basis for determining whether material is obscene. In *Miller v. California* (1973), the Court stipulated three tests for judging allegedly obscene material: (1) whether the average person, applying local community standards, would find that a work, taken as a whole, appeals to a prurient interest; (2) whether the work depicts in a patently offensive way sexual conduct specifically defined as "obscene" in law; and (3) whether the work, taken as a whole, lacks "serious literary, artistic, political, or scientific value."[27]

Although many law enforcement agencies thought the *Miller* decision gave them broader power to prosecute purveyors of obscenity, the Court subsequently reaffirmed that only hard-core pornography lies outside the First Amendment's protection. The use or public display of "four-letter words" may not be banned.[28] However, students in public schools may be disciplined for the use of indecent as well as obscene language.[29]

Under the Court's current approach, states may forbid the sale of pornographic materials to individuals under the age of 18, completely ban child pornography,[30] and prohibit sexually explicit live entertainment and films in bars.[31] In addition, municipalities may use exclusionary zoning to regulate the location of adult bookstores and theaters.[32]

The Federal Communications Commission (FCC), which regulates the broadcast media, also has the power to prohibit indecent and obscene language on the airwaves. The FCC was given this power in 1934 because radio, television, and other electronic media were considered a scarce public resource that should be licensed and regulated in the public interest. In 1978, in a case initiated by the FCC, the Court ruled that comedian George Carlin's monolog "Filthy Words," on seven dirty words that cannot be said on radio or television, could be banned because children and unsuspecting listeners otherwise could not be completely protected from "patently offensive, indecent material presented over the airwaves."[33] However, eleven years later the Court struck down a congressional statute authorizing the FCC to ban telephone "dial-a-porn" services and held that only hard-core obscene messages may be so outlawed.

Libel and slander **Libel** is false statement of fact or defamation of character by print or by visual portrayal on television. **Slander** is defamation of character by speech. Both damage an individual's reputation by holding the person up to contempt, ridicule, and scorn. Both also may be subject to criminal or civil prosecution.

Criminal convictions for seditious libel under the Sedition Act of 1798 carried a maximum sentence of five years' imprisonment. But there was widespread public outcry over the prosecutions under the act, and in *New York Times Co. v. Sullivan* (1964) the Court expressly noted that the act was inconsistent with the values of the First Amendment.[34]

Today libel suits are primarily civil—that is, for compensatory and punitive damages (monetary awards). Compensatory damages are based on an individual's actual financial losses as a result of being libeled, such as loss of employment or income. Punitive damages aim to punish wrongdoers by making them pay for their victims' mental suffering and for the damage done to their victims' reputations. Because awards for punitive damages are based on a jury's subjective view of the injury, they may be very large. A former beauty contest winner who sued *Penthouse* magazine, for example, received $1.5 million in compensatory damages and $12.5 million in punitive damages.

The landmark ruling in *New York Times v. Sullivan* established the standards for determining when public officials and public figures may recover damages. Such individuals must prove "actual malice"; they must show that statements about them were made with knowledge of their falsity or with reckless disregard of their truth or falsity. This standard makes winning libel awards exceedingly difficult for public figures. Private individuals, those who neither hold public office nor have well-known reputations and have not been thrust into the limelight, may recover damages on a lesser standard. They simply must show that the statements were false and that the publisher was negligent in its reporting.

The Court's standards make it relatively easy for individuals to bring libel suits to trial. When juries rule in their favor, they tend to make large awards. But in about two-thirds of the cases the awards are later reduced or overturned by appellate courts. Some critics contend that the Supreme Court has made it too difficult for public officials and public figures to win libel cases. Publishers, however, claim that the law of libel has a chilling effect on freedom of the press. They frequently face high court costs in defending their publications, and reporters and editors may be questioned at trial about their editorial processes.

The Court, nevertheless, has tried to maintain a line that will ensure robust exchanges, sharp public criticism, and freedom of the press. In 1988 it reaffirmed the principles established in the *Sullivan* case, holding that they apply to satires and cartoons as well as to stories and reporting. *Hustler Magazine v. Falwell* (1988) reversed a lower court's $200,000 award to the Reverend Jerry Falwell for "emotional distress" caused by a parody portraying him as having committed incest with his mother in an outhouse.[35] It did so because the characterization was not presented as factual truth and thus actual malice could not be shown.

Fighting words Fighting words (described by Justice Murphy in the *Chaplinsky* case, page 146) have been held to be unprotected speech because they are likely to incite violence or lead to a breach of the peace and public order. In recent years, however, the Court has reversed every conviction for controversial or "fighting" words. So it is uncertain that any prosecution under this category of unprotected speech would be upheld.

Commercial speech Commercial speech, or advertising, was for many years deemed to be outside the scope of First Amendment protection. Ostensibly, commercial speech (such as ads for prescription drugs and lawyers' services) does not receive First Amendment protection because it does not bear on political matters. In addition, governments have important interests in regulating some kinds of advertising. The Court, therefore, upholds regulations aimed at ensuring truth in advertising. But it also recognizes that in some cases the public's interests in obtaining information may justify extending First Amendment protection to commercial speech. Accordingly, it has overturned state and local laws forbidding the advertising of the price of prescription drugs, routine legal services, the availability of abortion services, and some other kinds of professional services. In addition, the Court has ruled that corporations' advertisements, newsletters, and mailings are protected under the First Amendment.[36]

Symbolic Speech, Speech-plus-Conduct, and Freedom of Association

Besides extending First Amendment protection to virtually all forms of *pure speech*, the Supreme Court has ruled that certain other kinds of expression are protected by the First Amendment because they involve the communication of ideas. These include symbolic speech, speech-plus-conduct, and the freedom of association.

Conduct that involves the communication of political ideas, often as a protest, is known as **symbolic speech**. The Court has held, for example, that wearing a black armband in school,[37] displaying a red flag,[38] and turning the American flag into a peace symbol in order to protest the Vietnam War[39] are protected forms of expression under the First Amendment.

Speech-plus-conduct also involves the communication of ideas, but the ideas are conveyed through marching, picketing, and sit-ins on sidewalks and streets and in other public areas. Protection for these kinds of expression is rooted not only in the First Amendment's guarantee of free speech but also in its provision for freedom of association and "the right of the people peaceably to assemble, and to petition the government for a redress of grievances."

In public places like streets and parks, individuals have the right to engage in political activities subject only to *reasonable time, place,* and *manner* restrictions. Thus, cities may limit the hours that parks may be used or the times sound trucks may travel the city streets. In 1989, for example, the Court upheld a New York City ordinance requiring the use of the city's sound system and city engineer for all concerts held in Central Park. Time, place, and manner restrictions must apply equally and not discriminate against particular kinds of political expression.

In February of 1960, a group of African American students from North Carolina A&T College, who had been refused service at a lunch counter reserved for white customers, staged a sit-down protest at Woolworth's in Greensboro, N.C. These three stayed seated throughout the day. (The woman at the left came to the counter for lunch, but decided not to sit down.) Civil rights activists often used such protests, and the litigation they sparked, to desegregate public accommodations.

UPI/Bettmann

The protection accorded to the **freedom of association** is broader than the freedom to organize rallies and peaceful protests. It also includes the right to join political parties and religious, economic, and other kinds of organizations. The disclosure of an organization's membership list cannot be compelled by election officials[40] or by legislative investigating committees.[41] Nor may individuals be dismissed from employment because of their political association[42] or be required to disclose their associations in order to gain admission to the bar.[43]

This demonstration took place on the streets of Miami Beach during the 1973 Republican national convention that nominated Richard M. Nixon for a second term as president. Such protests expressed increasing public anger at Nixon's conduct of the war in Vietnam. "Stop the mad bomber" refers to his order to expand the war by bombing supply routes in Cambodia. This escalation greatly increased casualties and contributed to the destabilization of Southeast Asia.

J.P. Laffont/SYGMA

However, the Court has ruled that the freedom of association may be limited in certain ways when there are overriding societal interests in doing so. It has upheld the Hatch Act of 1940, which forbids federal employees from actively campaigning in elections and assuming leadership positions in political parties.[44] Such federal and state laws have been found to be a reasonable way of ensuring a neutral civil service. The Court has also held that the First Amendment right of association of members of an all-male club was outweighed by a state law prohibiting gender discrimination in public and private organizations.

Ironically, the Supreme Court provokes controversy by protecting the rights of protesters to express their political views through marches, pickets, and other kinds of demonstrations. Along with its rulings extending First Amendment protection to pure speech and symbolic speech, the Court has defended the rights of individuals and minorities to engage in these activities. In doing so, it has challenged the views of the majority and invited more political controversy. Yet in defending the right to express unpopular views, the Court ensures the freedom of public discussion and debate that is essential to democratic self-governance and a free society.

THE QUEST FOR EQUALITY

The concept of equality and equal freedoms for all citizens is mentioned neither in the Constitution nor in the Bill of Rights. Nevertheless, it is the bedrock of a political system based on the consent of the governed. The Declaration of Independence was emphatic about equality of political freedoms: "We hold these truths to be self-evident: That all men are created equal; that they are endowed by their Creator with certain unalienable Rights." But not until 1868, with the ratification of the Fourteenth Amendment, did the Constitution expressly provide that no person shall be deprived of "the equal protection of the laws." Achieving that equality in practice has proven to be extraordinarily difficult. Just how difficult is indicated in the box on page 157. There remains no greater struggle in American politics than the struggle to guarantee all citizens their basic civil rights without discrimination due to their race, religion, national origin, or sex. That struggle reflects the impact of social movements and the increasing diversity of American society on the politics of government (see Figure 5-1, page 152).

The Extension of Voting Rights

The narrow victory of General Ulysses S. Grant in the 1868 presidential election convinced the Republican party that to maintain its control of Congress it needed the votes of African Americans. So it proposed the Fifteenth Amendment (ratified in 1870), which guaranteed the voting rights of African Americans by forbidding the abridgment of any citizen's right to vote "on account of race, color, or previous condition of servitude." The amendment did not mention discrimination on the basis of gender.

Despite their continued disenfranchisement, some women hoped that they might win **suffrage**, the right to vote, in federal elections by claiming that this right was guaranteed by the Fourteenth Amendment's privileges and immunities clause. Susan B. Anthony gave this as her defense when she was prosecuted

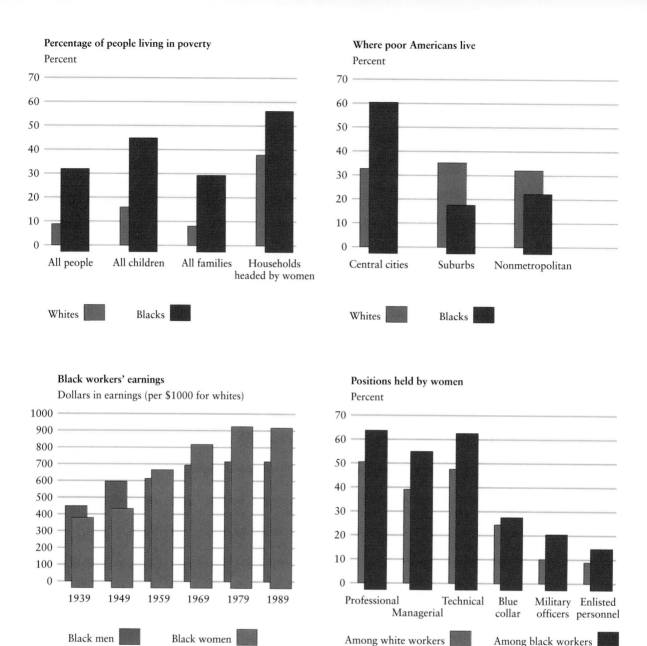

Percentage of people living in poverty

Percent

Whites   Blacks

Where poor Americans live

Percent

Whites   Blacks

Black workers' earnings

Dollars in earnings (per $1000 for whites)

Black men   Black women

Positions held by women

Percent

Among white workers   Among black workers

Figure 5-1 *Some measures of comparative socio-economic status in the United States.* SOURCE: *Andrew Hacker,* Two Nations: Black and White, Separate, Hostile, Unequal *(New York: Scribner's, 1992), 100–102. Reprinted with permission of Charles Scribner's Sons, an imprint of Macmillan Publishing Company, and the author's agent, Robin Straus Agency. Copyright © 1992 Andrew Hacker.*

for casting a ballot in a federal election in 1872, but the argument was rejected by a federal court. In 1875 the Supreme Court dashed the hopes of a woman who sought to vote in a Missouri election when it held that "the Constitution of the United States does not confer the right of suffrage upon anyone."[45] By 1913, only nine states allowed women to vote. Political pressure in support of women's suffrage mounted during World War I as large numbers of women entered the work force and contributed to the war effort. In 1918 President Woodrow Wilson endorsed women's suffrage, and during the next year Congress submitted to the states a constitutional amendment granting women the right to vote. The Nineteenth Amendment was ratified in 1920.

(Left) *The founder of the women's movement, Elizabeth Cady Stanton* (seated), *held the first convention on women's rights in Seneca Falls, N.Y., in 1848. Susan B. Anthony, however, was probably the most famous and active feminist of the late nineteenth century. Women had fought to end slavery, but when African Americans got the vote after the Civil War, they did not. After 1890, they focused on one goal: suffrage.* (Right) *In 1870, Mrs. D. S. Sonnesberger was the first woman voter in Jackson County, Wyoming. Women found it easier winning suffrage in the West, partly because the more voters a territory had, the sooner it could become a state.*

Although African Americans were guaranteed the right to vote by the Fourteenth and Fifteenth Amendments and many were elected to office in the South during Reconstruction, white-dominated state governments and party organizations soon erected barriers such as poll taxes and literacy tests. By the turn of the century, African Americans were effectively disenfranchised.

In 1937 the Supreme Court ruled that poll taxes did not violate the Fourteenth and Fifteenth Amendments. That decision sparked a campaign to get the states and Congress to abolish poll taxes. The campaign had considerable success in the states; by 1960, only Alabama, Arkansas, Mississippi, Texas, and Virginia retained poll taxes. Congress finally banned poll taxes in federal elections with the Twenty-fourth Amendment, ratified in 1964, and two years later the Court decided that the Fourteenth Amendment's equal protection clause forbids poll taxes in state elections.

Among the goals of the civil rights movement of the 1950s and 1960s was the elimination of all barriers to voting rights for African Americans (see the box on page 154 for a chronology of the civil rights movement in those decades). Rev. Martin Luther King, Jr., launched voter registration drives in the South, where there was widespread resistance and often violence. Congress had passed civil rights acts in 1957 and 1960, but they had proven ineffective in ending the discriminatory practices that discouraged African Americans from voting. Not until Congress passed the Voting Rights Act of 1965 was suffrage for African Americans effectively guaranteed.

Chronology of the Civil Rights Movement

May 1954	The Supreme Court hands down its decision in *Brown v. Board of Education*, declaring racial segregation in public schools unconstitutional. This was a major victory for the National Association for the Advancement of Colored People (NAACP), which had been challenging the constitutionality of racial segregation in the courts for almost twenty years.
December 1955	African Americans boycott the bus company in Montgomery, Alabama, to protest racial segregation. Rev. Martin Luther King, Jr., is a leader of this boycott and subsequent protests.
February 1960	African American college students stage the first sit-in at a luncheonette counter in Greensboro, North Carolina, to protest against racial segregation in public accommodations.
May 1961	African Americans begin "freedom rides" by attempting to sit in the sections of interstate buses reserved for "whites only." There is widespread violence, buses are burned, and U.S. marshals must restore order in some parts of the South.
September 1962	The effort to enroll James Meredith as the first African American to attend the University of Mississippi leads to violence.
April 1963	Police retaliate against African Americans who attempt to hold a public demonstration in Birmingham, Alabama.
June 1963	Medgar Evers, state chairman of the NAACP in Mississippi, is murdered in Jackson.
August 1963	Civil rights leaders organize a major march in Washington to push for passage of civil rights legislation as committees of the Senate and House were debating what eventually would emerge as the Civil Rights Act of 1964.
September 1963	African Americans begin to boycott public schools in northern cities in order to protest de facto racial segregation.
June 1964	Three white civil rights workers are murdered in Neshoba County, Mississippi.
July 1964	The first of many ghetto riots by African Americans starts in Harlem, New York City. During the summer, riots erupt in other major cities around the country.
January 1965	Rev. King starts the first of a series of protest marches in Selma, Alabama. In February and March, marchers are attacked by police.
August 1965	Inner-city riots erupt in Los Angeles and Chicago.
June 1966	James Meredith is shot during a protest march in Mississippi.
Summers, 1966 and 1967	Ghetto riots erupt in Chicago, Cleveland, New York, and more than sixty-five other cities.
April 1968	Rev. King is murdered in Memphis, Tennessee.

(Left) *The march from Selma, Alabama, to the state capitol in Montgomery on March 7, 1965, marked a turning point in the civil rights movement. At issue were discriminatory voter registration practices in the South. After marchers had twice been beaten back by mounted police, and two white civil rights workers had been murdered, the Reverend Martin Luther King, Jr., led about 25,000 on the final march. As King shifted his tactics from passive resistance to confrontation, he emerged as the single most important leader in the movement.* (Right) *The events in Selma helped Democratic President Lyndon B. Johnson push the Voting Rights Act of 1965 through Congress, and Rev. King was among those invited to watch him sign the act into law.*

The Voting Rights Act bans the use of literacy tests, tests for educational achievement and understanding, proofs of "good moral character," and certificates verifying the qualifications of registered voters in any state or subdivision where less than 50 percent of the citizens of voting age were registered on November 1, 1964, or voted in an election that November. Moreover, it authorizes the United States Civil Service Commission to appoint federal examiners to register voters where the attorney general deems this to be necessary for the enforcement of the Fifteenth Amendment.

The Voting Rights Act remained controversial because it limited the powers of the states to determine the qualifications for voting. However, the Supreme Court affirmed its constitutionality in 1966, and the act has been extended several times since then. It was last extended by Congress in 1982 and is not scheduled to lapse until 2007. The major provisions of voting and other civil rights legislation are shown in the box on page 156.

Reapportionment and Equal Representation

Besides striking down poll taxes and other barriers to exercising voting rights, the Supreme Court has become involved in **reapportionment,** the reallocation of legislative seats on the basis of population, geography, or some combination of the two. Traditionally, the courts avoided reapportionment issues on the ground that they involve political questions that must be resolved by legislative bodies. However, in a landmark decision (*Baker v. Carr*, 1962),[46] the Court ruled that such controversies contain issues of fairness and justice that open them to judicial review as well.

Major Provisions of Civil Rights Legislation

1957   The Civil Rights Commission is created, and trying to prevent a person from voting in federal elections is made a crime.

1960   The Department of Justice is authorized to appoint federal referees to investigate allegations of the denial of African Americans' voting rights, and using interstate commerce to threaten or carry out a bombing is made a criminal offense.

1964   Legislation bars certain devices and literacy tests that were used to deny voting rights to African Americans; forbids discrimination on the basis of race, color, religion, and national origin in public accommodations such as restaurants, motels, lunch counters, gas stations, theaters, stadiums, and boardinghouses with more than five rooms for rent; authorizes the Department of Justice to bring lawsuits to compel the desegregation of public schools; forbids discrimination in employment on the grounds of race, color, religion, or national origin in all businesses employing twenty-five workers or more; authorizes the cutting of federal funds from any program that discriminates on the basis of race, color, religion, or national origin.

1965   Legislation authorizes the appointment of voting examiners to supervise federal, state, and local elections in areas where discrimination is determined to have been practiced or where less than half of the voting-age residents were registered in the 1964 presidential election.

1968   Legislation bans discrimination in the sale and rental of most housing, except by private owners who sell or rent their homes without the use of a real estate agent.

The issues of fairness and justice to which the Court referred pertain to the relationship between population and representation. In a democracy all voters must be equal. One person's vote cannot count for more than another's. Yet representation is decidedly unequal when members of the House of Representatives or members of state legislatures represent districts with different numbers of residents, a condition that was prevalent in many states after the Civil War. In most cases, rural districts enjoyed equal or even greater representation than urban areas, even though their populations were smaller. For example, the Court's ruling in *Baker v. Carr* involved a challenge to the apportionment of Tennessee's state legislature. Despite growing urbanization and population changes over a sixty-year period, Tennessee had not reapportioned its voting districts since 1901. As a result, the population ratio for urban and rural districts in the state was more than 19 to 1. Charles Baker and several other citizens and urban residents claimed that urban residents were being denied the equal protection of the law under the Fourteenth Amendment and asked the Court to order state officials to hold either an at-large election or an election in which legislators would be selected from constituencies in accordance with the 1960 federal census.

Born into poverty in rural Mississippi in the 1940s, Anne Moody was deeply affected by her experiences as a black child in a segregated society. The corrosive conditions under which she was forced to live gradually drew her into an increasingly active role in the civil rights movement of the 1960s. In her autobiography she describes an event—the murder by arson of an entire black family by the white citizens of her community—that sharpened her consciousness and the anger that drove her activism:

Soon people started walking back down the road. The screams and hollering had stopped. People were almost whispering now. They were all Negroes, although I was almost sure I had seen some whites pass before. "I guess not," I thought, sitting there sick inside. Some of the ladies passing the car had tears running down their faces, as they whispered to each other.

"Didn't you smell that gasoline?" I heard a lady who lived in the quarters say.

"That house didn't just catch on fire. And just think them bastards burned up a whole family," another lady said. Then they were quiet again. . . .

We sat in the car for about an hour, silently looking at this debris and the ashes that covered the nine charcoal-burned bodies. A hundred or more also stood around—Negroes from the neighborhood in their pajamas, night-gowns, and housecoats and even a few whites with their eyes fixed on that dreadful scene. I shall never forget the expressions on the faces of the Negroes. There was almost unanimous hopelessness in them. The still, sad faces watched the smoke rising from the remains until the smoke died down to practically nothing. There was something strange about that smoke. It was the thickest and blackest smoke I had ever seen.

Raymond finally drove away, but it was impossible for him to take me away from that nightmare. Those screams, those faces, that smoke, would never leave me.

SOURCE: Anne Moody, *Coming of Age in Mississippi* (New York: Dell, 1968), 134–136.

When the Supreme Court granted review in *Baker v. Carr,* it faced two central issues: (1) whether the malapportionment of a state legislature is a "political question" for which courts have no remedy and (2) the merits of Baker's claim that individuals have a right to equal votes and equal representation. With potentially broad political consequences, the case divided the Court. On one side were the justices who believed that the case presented a nonjusticiable political question—that is, a question not subject to judicial resolution. On the other side were those who thought that the issue was justiciable, and they were prepared to address the merits of the case. One justice considered the issue justiciable but did not want to address the merits of the case. As a consequence, the Court's majority opinion was limited to the jurisdictional question: Was apportionment an issue that courts could decide? The Court's answer was yes.

In two subsequent cases in the 1960s, the Court applied the principle of **one person, one vote** to congressional legislative districts and to state legislative districts. The principle of one person, one vote requires that the weight of votes cast in different election districts must be roughly equal. In the 1970s and 1980s the Court extended the rule to virtually all local elections as well.

The Court's rulings meant that district lines for congressional, state, and local elections must be redrawn every ten years to ensure equal (though not proportional) representation. This reapportionment requirement has made the American electoral process at all levels more open, accessible, and democratic. It has also made reapportionment a perennial partisan issue that reemerges every ten years, after the national census.

Ending Racial Discrimination

Despite the Reconstruction Amendments to the Constitution, new barriers to equality emerged in the form of so-called **Jim Crow laws,** which separated the races in public transportation and accommodations and discriminated against African Americans in other ways. In the late nineteenth century, segregation persisted in housing, education, and employment and was permitted by the Supreme Court. In 1883 the Court struck down as unconstitutional the Civil Rights Act of 1875, which had forbidden discrimination in public accommodations such as hotels, theaters, and railroad carriages. According to the Court, Congress had exceeded its power under the Fourteenth Amendment by prohibiting *private* individuals from discriminating. The amendment, in the Court's view, forbade only *state* discrimination.

Subsequently, in the case of *Plessy v. Ferguson* (1896), the Court affirmed the **separate but equal doctrine** by upholding Louisiana's law requiring separate but equal facilities for the races in railroad cars.[47] Although it struck down laws specifically denying or limiting the right of nonwhites to acquire property, it upheld until 1948 the enforcement of **restrictive covenants,** contracts in which property owners agree not to sell or lease their property to members of certain racial or religious groups.

Beginning in the 1930s, individuals and organizations like the National Association for the Advancement of Colored People (NAACP) began filing lawsuits to force the end of racial segregation in housing, education, and employment. Like the other branches of government, the Court was slow to respond. Not until 1954 did it step firmly and unequivocally into the racial discrimination controversy with its landmark decision in *Brown v. Board of Education of Topeka* (1954).[48] In that case the Court finally rejected the separate but equal doctrine, holding that racially segregated public schools violated the equal protection clause of the Fourteenth Amendment.

Even when handing down *Brown*'s mandate for ending segregated schools, the Court was reluctant to press too hard too quickly for desegregation; the justices knew how much political controversy their ruling would stir. It was another year before the Court handed down its remedial decree stating that school boards must proceed with "all deliberate speed to desegregate public schools at the earliest practical date."[49] The decree of "all deliberate speed" was a compromise between requiring precise deadlines for school desegregation (which was certain to provoke massive resistance) and simply allowing states and localities to comply with *Brown*'s mandate at their own discretion.

As it turned out, the justices were right. The *Brown* decision and its enforcement decree met with massive resistance, school closings, occasional violence, and widespread evasion. The vagueness of the phrase "with all deliberate speed" actually served to justify noncompliance. Progress toward achieving integrated schools was deliberately slow and uneven. In addition, President Dwight Eisenhower refused to use the power of the executive branch to ensure compliance until he was forced to send the National Guard to quell resistance to the desegregation of Central High School in Little Rock, Arkansas. Eisenhower sent the troops not because he favored the Court's ruling but because it was the law of the land.

The Department of Justice had no authority to force desegregation until the passage of the Civil Rights Act of 1964. As a result, in the decade following the *Brown* decision, less than 2 percent of all African-American students in the

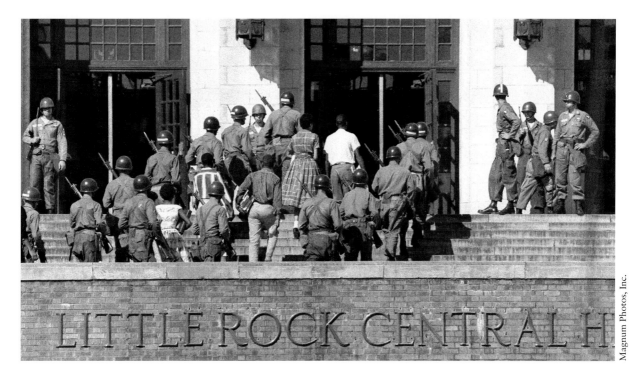

LITTLE ROCK CENTRAL H

In 1957, when Arkansas governor Orval Faubus defied a court order to integrate the state's public schools and refused to guarantee any student's safety, Republican President Dwight D. Eisenhower sent Army troops to Little Rock Central High School to ensure order. Brown v. Board of Education of Topeka *(1955) had mandated desegregation "with all deliberate speed." In* Cooper v. Aaton *(1958), the Supreme Court unanimously rebuffed Little Rock's efforts to evade compliance with* Brown.

South attended desegregated schools, and there was virtually no effort to achieve desegregation in the North and West.

The major advance in ending racial segregation, not only in education but in housing and employment, came after the passage of the Civil Rights Act of 1964. Title VI of this act forbids schools from discriminating "on the ground of race, color, or national origin in any program or activity receiving federal assistance." Subsequent amendments extended the act to forbid discrimination based on gender and age, as well as discrimination against the handicapped and Vietnam veterans. Besides authorizing the withholding of federal funds from schools that discriminate, the Department of Justice was authorized to enforce the act and the mandate of *Brown*. Title II of the act forbids discrimination in public accommodations—inns, hotels, restaurants, theaters, and the like. Title VII makes it illegal for employers in any business or industry with fifteen or more employees to discriminate on the basis of race, color, national origin, religion, or sex.

By the late 1960s the Supreme Court also made it clear that it would no longer abide delays in complying with *Brown*'s mandate. In proclaiming that "continued operation of racially segregated schools under the standard of 'all deliberate speed' was no longer permissible," the Court stated that school districts had to "terminate immediately dual school systems based on race and operate only unitary school systems."[50]

During the 1970s, 1980s, and early 1990s, the issue of bringing an end to segregated schools was replaced by the issue of achieving integrated schools. This was a particularly troublesome question in the North and West, where schools were segregated as a result of housing patterns (**de facto segregation**) not because of laws and official policies (**de jure segregation**). One device for overcoming de facto segregation is busing children to schools they would not ordinarily attend. Although busing can be a means of achieving integrated schools, it violates the tradition of neighborhood schools, creates lengthy travel for some students, and sometimes increases racial tensions within schools.

The Court's position on busing is clear. It has upheld the power of federal judges to order busing as a remedy for segregated schools *within* school districts but not *between* them. In *Milliken v. Bradley* (1974), for instance, the Court held that lower federal courts could not order the busing of schoolchildren to and from Detroit's overwhelmingly black inner-city school district and fifty-one neighboring, suburban, predominantly white school districts.[51] Given the racial composition of many school districts, this position has not enabled proponents of integration to achieve integrated public schools. It may, however, have contributed to the movement of white families from the cities to suburban neighborhoods to escape busing.

Forty years after the landmark ruling in *Brown v. Board of Education*, approximately 500 school desegregation cases remain in the lower federal courts around the country. Most involve the issue of whether school systems have eliminated vestiges of past discrimination, even though many districts are heavily populated by whites, African Americans, Hispanics, or Asians.

In *Freeman v. Pitts* (1992) the Supreme Court held that lower federal courts may withdraw from their supervision of desegregation efforts once school districts have complied with desegregation orders even though schools

In June of 1963, Alabama Governor George C. Wallace physically barred the way when John F. Kennedy's deputy attorney general, Nicholas Katzenbach, accompanied two African American students in to register at the University of Alabama. Wallace had promised to fight integration "even to the point of standing in the schoolhouse door," and he staged this event to gain national attention. He did indeed win what he sought, and he later ran three times (unsuccessfully) for the presidency.

Library of Congress

remain racially imbalanced due to housing patterns and other socioeconomic factors.[52] At the same time, in *United States v. Fordice* (1992) the Court held that Mississippi's admission policies and funding for its state colleges and universities perpetuated racial segregation and had failed to achieve a system of racially integrated higher education.[53] Together, these decisions recognized both the importance of equal opportunities in education and the limitations of what courts and local school boards can do in areas that remain or are becoming more racially segregated due to housing patterns and population changes.

Nonracial Discrimination

All legislation and government policy, by its very nature, discriminates because it confers burdens or benefits on some groups and not on others. For example, states regulate drivers' licenses, and most states also require that drivers be at least 16 years old and pass a driving test. From the standpoint of civil rights, the question is whether laws and regulations are reasonable and do not unfairly discriminate against particular groups.

When considering challenges to law and policy under the Fourteenth Amendment's equal protection clause, the Supreme Court must decide whether the discrimination is invidious and unconstitutional. During the mid-1950s and the 1960s, the Court evolved a two-tier approach to applying the equal protection clause. When reviewing challenges to legislation that deals solely with economic matters, it uses a **minimal scrutiny test.** The Court simply looks to see whether the legislation in question has a rational basis. Using this test, the Court has not struck down any federal or state economic legislation under the equal protection clause since 1937.

When legislation is based on a "suspect classification" or denies individuals their "fundamental rights," the Court uses a **strict scrutiny test** for determining its constitutionality. The strict scrutiny test puts the burden of proof on the state, which must demonstrate a "compelling interest" to justify the law or

On September 13, 1974, helmeted police lined the streets of South Boston as school buses, escorted by motorcycle police, carried African American students to South Boston High School. Many communities that were under court orders to achieve integrated schools in the 1970s experienced widespread boycotts and sporadic violence. In the 1990s, about five hundred public school districts remain under federal judicial supervision as they try to achieve and maintain integrated schools.

UPI/Bettmann Newsphotos

Ruth Bader Ginsburg: Judicial-Restraint Liberal

Appointed to the Supreme Court of the United States in 1993 by President Bill Clinton, Justice Ruth Bader Ginsburg is the second female, sixth Jewish, and 107th member of the Court. When announcing her nomination, President Clinton called her "the Thurgood Marshall of the women's movement," and "neither liberal nor conservative" but instead a moderate and well respected jurist who would be a "force for consensus building" on the Court.

Prior to her appointment to the Court, Justice Ginsburg served for thirteen years on the Court of Appeals for the District of Columbia Circuit. Before that she taught at Columbia Law School and Rutgers University Law School, and she served as general counsel for the American Civil Liberties Union.

In the 1970s Ginsburg was at the forefront of the women's movement in law. She not only wrote frequently on women's rights, she argued six gender discrimination cases before the Supreme Court and won five of them. During one case, Justice William Rehnquist asked her why women were not content now that Susan B. Anthony's face was on a coin. Ginsburg passed up the bait but what she almost said, she says, was, "No, your Honor, tokens won't do."

Justice Ginsburg has been one of the most articulate advocates of the view that the equal protection clause of the Fourteenth Amendment forbids gender-based discrimination. As she told Senator Arlen Specter during her confirmation hearings,

The framers of the Fourteenth Amendment meant no change . . . at all in the status of women before the law, but in 1920, when women achieved the vote, they became full citizens. And you have to read this document as a whole—changed, as Thurgood Marshall said, over the years by constitutional amendment and by judicial construction. . . . I remain an advocate of the equal rights amendment, I will tell you, for this reason: because I have a daughter and a grand-daughter, and I would like the legislature of this country and of all the states to stand up and say, 'We know what that history was in the nineteenth century, and we want to make a clarion call that women and men are equal before the law, just as every modern human rights document in the world does since 1970.' I'd like to see that statement made just that way in the Constitution.

Wide World Photos, Inc.

Bill Clinton and Ruth Bader Ginsburg walked along the colonnades at the White House as they headed for a news conference where the president nominated Ginsburg to the Supreme Court. Confirmed by the Senate 96 to 3, Ginsburg finds the workload at the Court "staggering."

Born in Brooklyn, New York, in 1933, Justice Ginsburg received her BA from Cornell University and attended Harvard and Columbia law schools, where she received her LLB and JD degrees. She then clerked for a federal district court judge. But even after her clerkship year in 1961, no law firm in New York would hire her—because she was a woman, a Jew, and a mother. As a result Ginsburg spent a couple of years doing legal research before assuming a teaching position at Rutgers.

Justice Ginsburg is married to a Washington lawyer and law professor, Martin David Ginsburg. She is the mother of two children and is also a grandmother.

SOURCE: Quotations from David Margolick, "Trial by Adversity Shapes Jurist's Outlook," *New York Times*, June 25, 1993, A19; and "Excerpts from Senate Hearing," *New York Times*, July 22, 1993, A20.

policy in question. Suspect categories include race, nationality, and alien status. Laws that make distinctions based on these characteristics are generally considered suspect or invidious forms of discrimination because those characteristics are immutable. Individuals cannot choose or change their race or nationality, and laws that impose burdens or deny benefits on the basis of these categories invariably fail to pass the Court's strict scrutiny test.

In the past two decades, the Court has confronted an increasingly broad range of claims of nonracial discrimination, including claims of discrimination based on gender, age, and wealth. In response to these new challenges, the Court has created a third, intermediate test—the **strict rationality test**, also known as the **exacting scrutiny test**. It has done so primarily because a majority of the justices have refused to consider gender a "suspect classification" under the Fourteenth Amendment, even though gender is an immutable characteristic.

Under the strict rationality, or exacting scrutiny, test, legislation must in a reasonable way further some legitimate government policy. This means that not all laws discriminating on the basis of gender, age, or wealth, for example, will be found to unconstitutionally or invidiously discriminate. Rather, laws that discriminate on the basis of these characteristics must have a legitimate goal that is advanced in a reasonable way by legislation or a government policy.

Gender-based discrimination has been approved by the Court in cases challenging an all-male military draft,[54] the enforcement of statutory rape laws against males but not females,[55] the assignment of female guards in prisons,[56] and the denial of health benefits to women who miss work because of pregnancy leaves.[57] On the other hand, the Court has struck down laws discriminating against women in cases involving the denial of benefits for dependents of female (but not male) military personnel;[58] the sale of 3.2 beer;[59] and the denial of seniority status to women who take pregnancy leaves from work.[60] Moreover, in 1986 the Court unanimously agreed that female employees could sue employers for sexual harassment under the Civil Rights Act. Finally, in 1991 the Court overturned a fetal protection policy of Johnson Controls, a Milwaukee-based manufacturer of automobile batteries. Under Johnson Controls' policy, fertile female employees were barred from certain jobs that exposed them to high levels of lead, which can pose severe health risks to developing fetuses. The Court struck down that discriminatory policy as a violation of the rights of women under the Civil Rights Act of 1964 and the Pregnancy Discrimination Act of 1978.[61] The case study on page 164 discusses the battle over the Equal Rights Amendment.

Age discrimination in employment is another area in which the Court has encountered claims of invidious discrimination. Congress responded to the pressures brought by groups of senior citizens and to demographic changes in the American population by prohibiting age discrimination under the Age Discrimination in Employment Act of 1967, which was amended in 1975 and 1978. The Supreme Court has upheld several claims under this legislation. However, the Court has found no constitutional objection to a state law requiring police officers to retire at the age of 50. Nor did the Court find any constitutional violation on the basis of age when, in *Gregory v. Ashcroft* (1991), it upheld a Missouri law requiring state judges to retire at 70.[62]

In other areas of nonracial discrimination, where benefits for illegitimate children or welfare benefits, for example, are at issue, the Court also applies its exacting scrutiny test, taking each case on its own merits. Basically, the Court tries to balance the interests of government against the claims of individuals to equal protection of the law, and the results are sometimes unpredictable.

The Battle over the Equal Rights Amendment

After the turn of the century, political pressure began to mount for the adoption of a constitutional amendment to guarantee equal rights for women. Indeed, each year for almost fifty years—from 1923 to 1972—Congress considered a proposal for an equal rights amendment. Finally, in response to the resurgence of the women's movement and lobbying by women's organizations, in 1972 Congress passed the proposed Equal Rights Amendment (ERA). The proposed amendment read:

Section 1. Equality of rights under the law shall not be denied or abridged by the United States or by any State on account of sex.

Section 2. The Congress shall have the power to enforce, by appropriate legislation, the provisions of this article.

Section 3. The Amendment shall take effect two years after the date of ratification.

Within a year after the proposal of the ERA, twenty-two states had ratified the amendment. But by 1978, one year before the deadline for ratification by three-fourths of the states, only thirty-five states had voted for ratification—three short of the number needed. Opposition to the amendment intensified as the National Council of Catholic Women, Mormon and other religious groups, the Eagle Forum led by Phyllis Schlafly, and other organizations mobilized to defeat the ERA. Three states voted to rescind their earlier support and, faced with the prospect of defeat of the amendment in 1979, Congress voted to extend the ratification deadline for three years. In 1982 the ERA was defeated; fifteen states refused to ratify, and five that had supported the amendment rescinded their votes.

The ERA divided rather than united women both politically and culturally. Some women's groups argued that the amendment would not in fact ensure equality in higher education and employment. Others believed that the ERA would do away with protective legislation safeguarding the rights of women in the workplace, requiring marital and child support from divorced husbands, and exempting women from compulsory military registration and service. Still others claimed that the amendment was

© Charles Steiner/SYGMA

Far from uniting women, the battles to win state ratification of the Equal Rights Amendment produced bitter political and cultural divisions. Women formed groups to fight for and against ratification, and after a decade of wrangling, the ERA was finally defeated.

only symbolic. But some of the ERA's supporters maintained that even a symbolic affirmation of the constitutional equality of women was important.

By the late 1970s, many gender-based classifications that the ERA was originally intended to outlaw had been rendered illegal by Congress, executive orders, and rulings of the Supreme Court that applied the equal protection clause, the Civil Rights Act of 1964, and other federal legislation.

Discussion questions
1. What is your view of the Equal Rights Amendment? Should it have been passed? What is the significance of the states' failure to ratify the amendment?
2. What does the defeat of the Equal Rights Amendment reveal about American politics?

Affirmative Action and Reverse Discrimination

Affirmative action in education and employment has been especially controversial. **Affirmative action**, which originated with Lyndon Johnson's Democratic administration in 1964–1965, is a policy designed to help women and
members of minority groups advance in education, employment, and other
areas in which they have been discriminated against. Affirmative action programs give preference to women and minorities over white males in, for example, admission to college and promotion in the workplace. These programs
have been attacked for practicing **reverse discrimination**—that is, for penalizing
white males in violation of their rights under the Fourteenth Amendment's
equal protection clause.

During Jimmy Carter's presidency, affirmative action programs were promoted and defended. During Ronald Reagan's presidency, the Department of
Justice challenged the constitutionality of such programs. Regardless of which
party has controlled the executive branch, affirmative action programs adopted
at the state and local levels have been bitterly contested in the courts.

Defenders of affirmative action argue that the policy legitimately aims at
compensating blacks, women, and others for the disadvantages they have suffered as a result of past discrimination. Because members of these groups were
previously denied equal opportunities in education and employment, proponents of affirmative action contend, they frequently do not have the education,
training, or seniority necessary for some jobs and promotions, and judging
them by the criteria used to judge white males will perpetuate their disadvantage. What affirmative action does is move beyond **equality of opportunity** to
equality of result in education and employment.

Critics, however, claim that affirmative action programs go too far in the
pursuit of greater equality. They maintain that such programs constitute reverse
discrimination, infringing on the liberty of whites and denying them equal opportunities. To support this position, critics often rely on the words of Justice
John Marshall Harlan in his dissenting opinion in *Plessy v. Ferguson* (1896):
"Our Constitution is color-blind and neither knows nor tolerates class among
citizens."[63]

When confronted with challenges to affirmative action programs, the Supreme Court initially was as sharply divided as the rest of the country. One of
the most important cases was *Regents of the University of California v. Bakke*
(1978).[64] Alan Bakke, a white male, was denied admission to the medical
school at the University of California at Davis. He contended that his application had been rejected because the school set aside 16 out of 100 admissions
for African Americans, Chicanos, Asians, and Native Americans—groups that
had previously been underrepresented in the student body. He claimed that this
policy violated his rights under the Civil Rights Act and the Fourteenth Amendment because some of the minority students admitted under the school's affirmative action program had grade-point averages and test scores lower than his.

The Court agreed in part with Bakke. The majority opinion stated that
quota systems (programs that set aside a precise number of openings for minorities) like the one at the University of California are unconstitutional. At
the same time, however, the Court upheld the constitutionality of affirmative
action programs. Those that do not guarantee a specific number of slots for
minorities but consider race as one among many factors in student admissions,
the Court said, are permissible.

Cases pending before the Supreme Court are analyzed in *Preview of United States Supreme Court Cases*, published regularly during each Court term by the Public Education Division of the American Bar Association. Each discussion summarizes the issues, facts, background, significance, arguments (for and against), and amicus briefs (for and against) for each case. *Preview* is an excellent source for clearly written descriptions of the cases awaiting decision; it can be found in law and research libraries.

Once a case has been decided, the justices issue their opinion. The final draft is given to the reporter of decisions, the Court official responsible for overseeing the publication of opinions. The reporter adds a headnote at the beginning summarizing the decision and adds a list at the end of how each justice voted. When a decision is announced, 275 copies, called "bench opinions," are made. They are distributed to the news media and other interested parties. One copy is immediately sent to the Government Printing Office, which then prints several thousand copies, called "slip opinions," for immediate distribution, primarily to federal and state courts and agencies and to the public. Finally, the decision, along with any corrections from the slip-opinion version, is incorporated by the Government Printing Office into the formal record of Supreme Court decisions, *United States Reports*.

When a Supreme Court decision is referred to, or cited, in a formal text, a specific format is followed. Court citations always begin with the names of the parties to the case, starting with the appellant (the person bringing the case), followed by *v.* (meaning "versus," or "against"), followed by the name of the appellee (the person responding)—all usually underscored or italicized. Next comes the volume of *United States Reports* in which the decision appears, followed by the page number on which the decision begins. Next, if a specific quotation from the decision is being cited, the word *at* and the page number of the quote appear. In parentheses following the page number is the year in which the decision was made. For example, the case *McCulloch v. Maryland*, 17 U.S. 316 at 317 (1819), is found in volume 17 of *United States Reports* starting on page 316, with the particular quote cited appearing on page 317; the decision was made in 1819.

Information about Supreme Court decisions can also be found in commercial publications such as *Supreme Court Reporter*, *United States Law Week*, and *United States Supreme Court Reports, Lawyer's Edition*. In addition, computerized legal databases such as LEXIS contain Supreme Court decisions. Sources like these are found in all law libraries and in many research libraries.

Affirmative action programs in employment have proven even more divisive. In 1979 the Court ruled that employers and labor unions may agree to adopt private affirmative action programs despite the objections of white members of the union. The following year it upheld Congress's power to set aside 10 percent of its funds for public works projects to be used to pay for supplies and services provided by minority-owned businesses. As a consequence, the Court's decisions provided little clear guidance for policy makers. In every case the justices split 5 to 4 or 6 to 3, with those in the majority often disagreeing on why they should uphold or strike down affirmative action programs. Still, in three out of four rulings during the 1980s, the Court upheld the constitutionality of affirmative action programs, basing its decisions on its exacting scrutiny test. Programs aimed at promoting African Americans and other minorities and women over white employees with more seniority have proven particularly troublesome. The Court was unable to establish a principle for judging the constitutionality of such programs. From 1984 to 1987 it upheld some programs and struck down others.

By 1989, however, changes in the composition of the Court resulted in a conservative majority inclined to oppose most affirmative action programs. In *City of Richmond v. J. A. Croson* (1989), the Court struck down an affirmative action program in Richmond, Virginia, that required nonminority building contractors to subcontract 30 percent of all city-awarded projects to minority-owned businesses.[65] This set-aside quota was as much a remedy for past discrimination as a way to help black construction companies penetrate the local building industry. Half of Richmond's population was black, but minority-owned firms had won less than 0.6 percent of the $25 million awarded in city contracts in the preceding five years.

In announcing the Court's ruling, Justice Sandra Day O'Connor noted that Richmond's affirmative action program was not narrowly targeted to the city's African Americans, because minority-owned businesses from all over the country were eligible to bid on projects. The ruling also held that state and local governments may no longer adopt affirmative action programs unless they are designed as remedies for past discrimination in specifically denying opportunities for African Americans and other minorities.

J. A. Croson was a major break with prior rulings because the Court abandoned its use of the exacting scrutiny test for upholding affirmative action programs. It signaled that henceforth the tougher strict scrutiny test would be employed in determining the permissibility of affirmative action programs. Under this test, states and localities must have a "compelling interest" in adopting any program that discriminates on the basis of race, regardless of whether that discrimination is for the purpose of conferring benefits, rather than burdens, on racial minorities and women. This decision thus threw into question the constitutionality of hundreds of state and local affirmative action programs and has forced city governments and state legislatures to redraft their laws in anticipation of further challenges to the constitutionality of those programs.

One year after *J. A. Croson*, however, a bare majority of the justices upheld affirmative action programs adopted by the *federal* government and approved by Congress. In *Metro Broadcasting, Inc. v. Federal Communications Commission* (1990), the Court upheld the FCC's policy of giving preferences to minority owners of broadcast companies when awarding licenses to operate television stations.[66] The FCC had adopted its affirmative action policy to promote the public's interests in broadcast diversity, and the Court ruled that Congress could authorize the FCC to do so on the basis of its powers as the national legislature. More generally, the Court held that Congress may enact affirmative action programs on the basis of its constitutional powers to "provide for the general welfare" and to enforce the equal protection guarantee of the Fourteenth Amendment.

Although the Court's rulings in *J. A. Croson* and *Metro Broadcasting, Inc.* might appear to contradict each other, they achieved a political compromise by making it difficult for state and local governments to adopt affirmative action programs while upholding the power of Congress to do so. But those rulings did not end the controversy over affirmative action and reverse discrimination. Along with *J. A. Croson* the Court handed down several other decisions that made it much more difficult for women and minorities to prove discrimination in the workplace and, at the same time, made it easier for white males to attack affirmative action programs in the courts. Those rulings touched off a bitter debate in Congress and between Congress and the administration of George Bush over whether and how to override the Court.

After a two-year battle, Congress passed and President Bush signed into law the Civil Rights Act of 1991, which overturned twelve Supreme Court rulings. The major provision that was returned to employers who were sued for discrimination is the burden of proving that their hiring practices are "job-related to the position in question and consistent with business necessity."[67] Congress also expanded the coverage of the 1866 Civil Rights Act to bar discrimination in all phases of employment, not just in hiring practices.[68] It also extended protection against discrimination based on race, religion, gender, and national origin to employees of United States companies who are stationed abroad.[69] In addition, Congress reversed four other rulings that had made it more difficult for African Americans and women to prove discrimination in employment[70] and had made it easier for whites to challenge court-ordered affirmative action programs.[71]

The Civil Rights Act of 1991 also, for the first time, allows women, members of religious groups, and the disabled, along with racial minorities, to sue for monetary damages for intentional discrimination. However, Congress had to compromise to win passage of the law. For example, it put a cap of $300,000 on the amount of damages that women and members of nonracial minority groups may win in discrimination suits, whereas there is no limit on the amount of awards that members of racial and ethnic minority groups may receive if they prove discrimination in the workplace.

As the controversy over affirmative action programs shows, political struggles over civil rights and liberties usually involve more than a conflict between an individual and the state. They often reflect deeper divisions in society and competing interests that must be reconciled over time.

SUMMARY

The First Amendment provides a dual protection for religious freedom. The *establishment clause* forbids the creation of a national religion, and the *free exercise clause* guarantees that individuals may worship as they please. In 1947 the Supreme Court took the view that the establishment clause embodies "a high wall of separation" between church and state; it ruled that the government must maintain strict neutrality on matters involving religion. Critics claimed that this neutrality amounted to state hostility toward religion, and in recent years the Court has moved toward an "accommodationist" approach. This approach involves a three-part test. If a law or program is to avoid violating the establishment clause, (1) it must have a secular legislative purpose, (2) its primary effect must neither advance nor inhibit religion, and (3) it must avoid excessive government entanglement with religion.

Under the free exercise clause, religious beliefs may not be prescribed or coerced by the state, but in some circumstances the government may regulate or ban religious practices. The Court's *secular regulation rule* requires that all laws must have a reasonable secular purpose and do not discriminate on the basis of religion. But individuals may not claim exemption from permissible government regulations on religious grounds.

The First Amendment also guarantees freedom of speech and press. Before 1925, however, the First Amendment was viewed as requiring only that there be no prior restraint on publications; individuals had no protection against subsequent punishment for what they said or wrote. In particular, they could be prosecuted for *seditious libel*—defaming or criticizing the government. After World War I, the Supreme Court began expanding the protection accorded freedom of speech and press. Under the Court's *clear and present danger formula*, speech is not protected if it creates a danger of serious consequences. At first this doctrine was applied to *subversive speech* such as advocating the overthrow of government, but gradually the Court modified the doctrine so that only the advocacy of immediate, violent, and illegal action may be subject to criminal prosecution. Speech that touches on political matters or has *social redeeming value* because it addresses matters of public concern is now fully protected.

There are four categories of unprotected speech: obscenity, libel and slander, fighting words, and commercial speech. Identifying *obscenity* has been a persistent problem for the Supreme Court. In *Miller v. California* (1973) it stipulated three tests for judging allegedly obscene material: (1) whether the average person, applying local community standards, would find that a work, taken as a whole, appeals to a prurient interest; (2) whether the work depicts in a patently offensive way sexual conduct specifically defined as "obscene" in law; and (3) whether the work, taken as a whole, lacks "serious literary, artistic, political, or scientific value."

Libel is false statement of fact or defamation of character by print or by visual portrayal on television. *Slander* is defamation of character by speech. *Fighting words* are unprotected speech because they are likely to lead to a breach of the peace and public order. *Commercial speech* (advertising) was until recently deemed to be outside the scope of First Amendment protection, but the Court has overturned laws forbidding advertising of certain kinds of professional services.

The Court has ruled that certain other kinds of expression are protected by the First Amendment. These include *symbolic speech*, or conduct that involves the communication of political ideas; *speech-plus-conduct*, in which ideas are conveyed through marching, picketing, and the like; and *freedom of association*, which includes the right to join political parties and religious, economic, and other kinds of organizations.

With the ratification of the Fourteenth Amendment in 1868, the Constitution expressly provided that no person shall be deprived of "the equal protection of the laws." However, it has been extremely difficult to achieve that equality in practice. *Suffrage* was extended to African Americans with the ratification of the Fifteenth Amendment in 1870, but women did not gain the right to vote until the ratification of the Nineteenth Amendment in 1920. Obstacles to voting by African Americans, such as poll taxes and literacy tests, were removed in the early decades of the twentieth century, but not until the enactment of the Voting Rights Act of 1965 was suffrage for African Americans effectively guaranteed.

Another area involving the equal protection of the laws is *reapportionment*, the reallocation of legislative seats on the basis of population, geography, or some combination of the two. Under the principle of *one person, one vote*, the weight of votes cast in different election districts must be roughly equal; therefore, district lines must be redrawn every ten years on the basis of census results.

Other barriers to equal protection of the laws take the form of racial and nonracial discrimination. Racial segregation by *Jim Crow laws* was commonplace in the decades following the Civil War. In *Plessy v. Ferguson* (1896), the Supreme Court upheld the *separate but equal doctrine*, and until 1948 it upheld the enforcement of *restrictive covenants*. The separate but equal doctrine was overturned in *Brown v. Board of Education of Topeka* (1954), but not until the passage of the Civil Rights Act of 1964 was there a sustainable effort to effectively enforce desegregation.

During the 1970s, 1980s, and early 1990s, efforts were made to overcome school segregation caused by housing patterns (*de facto segregation*), not by law (*de jure segregation*). Efforts to integrate the public schools through such devices as busing have had limited success.

When considering issues of discrimination, the Court uses a *minimal scrutiny test* to review legislation dealing with economic matters, but it uses a *strict scrutiny test* to review matters involving individuals' fundamental rights. When considering claims of nonracial discrimination, it uses a *strict rationality*, or *exacting scrutiny, test*. Under this test, legislation that discriminates on the basis of gender, age, or wealth is unconstitutional unless it furthers some legitimate government policy in a reasonable way.

Affirmative action is a policy designed to help women and minority groups advance themselves in areas in which they have been discriminated against. The goal of affirmative action programs is to move beyond *equality of opportunity* to *equality of result*. Critics claim that such programs are a form of *reverse discrimination*. During the 1980s the Supreme Court tended to uphold the constitutionality of affirmative action programs. In the early 1990s, however, it handed down several decisions that made it harder for women and minorities to prove discrimination in the workplace and easier for white males to attack affirmative action programs in the courts. The Civil Rights Act of 1991 overturned some of those rulings and required employers to prove that their hiring practices are not discriminatory.

establishment clause
free exercise clause
secular regulation rule
seditious libel
clear and present danger formula
subversive speech
social redeeming value
obscenity
libel
slander
fighting words

commercial speech
symbolic speech
speech-plus-conduct
freedom of association
suffrage
reapportionment
one person, one vote
Jim Crow laws
separate but equal doctrine
restrictive covenants

de facto segregation
de jure segregation
minimal scrutiny test
strict scrutiny test
strict rationality, or exacting
   scrutiny, test
affirmative action
reverse discrimination
equality of opportunity
equality of result

LEARNING MORE ABOUT ISSUES OF FREEDOM AND EQUALITY

Scholarly studies

Edsall, Thomas, and Mary Edsall. *Chain Reaction: The Impact of Race, Rights, and Taxes on American Politics.* New York: Norton, 1992. A provocative study of how the civil rights era has affected American politics in the 1990s.

Graham, Hugh Davis. *The Civil Rights Era: Origins and Development of National Policy, 1960–1972.* New York: Oxford University Press, 1992. A fine historical analysis of the civil rights movement and its impact on American politics.

Levy, Leonard W. *Emergence of a Free Press.* New York: Oxford University Press, 1985. A rich account of freedom of speech and press during the founding period.

Lewis, Anthony. *Make No Law: The Sullivan Case and the First Amendment.* New York: Random House, 1992. An insightful analysis of the Supreme Court's landmark ruling on libel and subsequent decisions in the area.

Peltason, Jack W. *Fifty-eight Lonely Men: Southern Federal Judges and School Desegregation.* Urbana: University of Illinois Press, 1971. An insightful study of the efforts of federal district court judges to enforce the ruling in *Brown v. Board of Education* in southern states.

Leisure reading

Friendly, Fred W. *Minnesota Rag: The Dramatic Story of the Landmark Supreme Court Case That Gave New Meaning to Freedom of the Press.* New York: Random House, 1982. A wonderful account of *Near v. Minnesota* (1931), the ruling prohibiting prior restraints on newspapers.

Kluger, Richard. *Simple Justice.* New York: Knopf, 1976. A definitive and readable story of the Court's school desegregation decision in *Brown v. Board of Education* (1954).

Rembar, Charles. *The End of Obscenity.* New York: HarperCollins, 1986. The story of the struggle to persuade the Supreme Court to broaden First Amendment protection, told from the perspective of a lawyer involved in several of the leading obscenity cases in the 1960s.

Primary sources

O'Brien, David M. *Constitutional Law and Politics: Civil Rights and Civil Liberties.* New York: W. W. Norton, 1991. A comprehensive collection of the Supreme Court's most important rulings on civil rights and liberties. The collection also contains introductory essays on the history and politics of the Court's interpretive decisions regarding the Bill of Rights and the Fourteenth Amendment.

Schwartz, Bernard, ed. *Statutory History of the United States: Civil Rights.* 2 vols. New York: Chelsea House, 1970. A useful and comprehensive collection of the federal laws and other congressional materials and documents related to civil rights and liberties.

Organizations

United States Civil Rights Commission, 1121 Vermont Avenue, N.W., Washington, DC 20425; (202) 376-8312. A government agency authorized by Congress to study and recommend changes in laws bearing on civil rights and liberties.

The Politics
of Participation

CHAPTER

6

Political Socialization and Participation

- Political socialization: changes over the life cycle; party affiliation; major political events; agents of political socialization; attitudes and behavior

- Political participation: ways of participating; who participates; political participation and public policy

The campaign of 1900 was similar to that of 1896 (see page 133), in that Republican William McKinley again defeated William J. Bryan, and major issues were again "The Full Dinner Pail" and free silver. The Democrats' 16:1 theme was represented this time on the horn-of-plenty pin for Bryan-Stevenson. But also note the famous McKinley factory pin and the two eclipse pins: The populace was excited by a solar eclipse in 1900, and at least seven different eclipse pins were produced. The major new issue in 1900 was imperialism, and Bryan's anti-imperialist stance proved unpopular.

McKinley's running mate was Theodore Roosevelt, the governor of New York who had become famous during the Spanish-American War for helping to found the volunteer cavalry regiment known as the Rough Riders. Roosevelt was as energetic as McKinley was laid back. In September, 1901, when McKinley was assassinated, Teddy Roosevelt became president at age forty-two.

Lyndon B. Johnson's father, Sam Ealy Johnson, served several terms in the Texas legislature, and he often took young Lyndon with him on his campaign trips and to the legislature. Here is how Johnson's biographer Doris Kearns describes the impact of that experience:

After the war in 1918, when Lyndon was ten, Sam began another stint in the legislature, which lasted until 1924. The war had bred an ugly intolerance in the country, and Texas was no exception. In the spring of 1918, under the sway of strong anti-German sentiment, a loyalty bill was passed in the legislature. . . . "My father stood right up against that situation," Johnson later said. "He got up on the floor of the House of Representatives and made a wonderful speech pleading for tolerance and common sense. He was a great civil libertarian . . . he fought the Ku Klux Klan and defended civil liberties on all levels."

"I loved going with my father to the legislature. I would sit in the gallery for hours watching all the activity on the floor and

then would wander around the halls trying to figure out what was going on. The only thing I loved more was going with him on the trail during his campaigns for reelection. We drove in the Model T Ford from farm to farm, up and down the valley, stopping at every door. My father would do most of the talking. He would bring the neighbors up to date on local gossip, talk about the crops and about the bills he'd introduced in the legislature. . . . I'd never seen him happier. Families all along the way opened their homes to us. If it was hot outside, we were invited in for big servings of homemade ice cream. If it was cold, we were given hot tea. Christ, sometimes I wished it could go on forever."[1]

AMERICANS PARTICIPATE IN POLITICS IN DIFFERENT ways and for different reasons. No one is born political—at least not in the sense that understanding of the political system and interest in public affairs are genetic traits. Our interest in politics is inspired by our family, our friends, and our life experiences; when that interest has been established, we must learn how to function politically.

This chapter explores the processes by which Americans become political. It looks at how we orient ourselves to the American political culture and political system and then examines how we participate in politics and government. The chapter concludes by describing the impacts of the constraints Americans encounter and the choices we make as participants in politics.

POLITICAL SOCIALIZATION

Political socialization is an ongoing process in which individuals acquire the information, beliefs, attitudes, and values that help them comprehend the workings of a political system and orient themselves within it. Through political

In the August heat, Speaker of the House Sam Rayburn and Senate Majority Leader Lyndon Johnson left the 1956 Democratic national convention and rushed back to Washington to meet with President Eisenhower about the Suez Canal crisis. Both Texans who lived and breathed politics, they each rose from modest circumstances to wield enormous power in Congress during the 1950s and 1960s.

UPI/Bettmann

socialization, people learn to be **citizens**, or members of a political society. The study of political socialization casts light on citizens' feelings and concerns about their government and the politics of their country. It also reveals how attitudes and beliefs condition individuals' participation in the political process. That participation is not uniform. A Native American girl coming of age on a reservation in Oklahoma is likely to perceive the political world and orient herself to it quite differently than a prep school girl growing up in Westchester County, a wealthy enclave north of New York City. Some people are indifferent and do not bother to vote. Others get indignant over certain government actions or politics and lead petition drives or run for office. Still others are inspired by a candidate or by a cause to volunteer their time or contribute funds.

Studying political participation helps us comprehend broad patterns of behavior within a political system. Just as a chemist would find it essential to identify the characteristics of molecules before explaining chemical elements, so it is important to explore the characteristics of American citizens before we try to describe and explain the politics of American government. In later chapters we look at group and mass political behavior; here our focus is on individuals and the way they become citizens.

We start with a warning, however. Political socialization and political participation are among the most complex areas to analyze.[2] Human motives are difficult enough to penetrate and explain. Furthermore, much of the research on political socialization focuses on children and how they learn about the political universe and develop a sense of their own place within it. But children lack the cognitive and expressive skills necessary to permit sophisticated inquiry into their socialization processes. As a result, research on individual political behavior is still shot through with large areas of uncertainty. Although consensus has emerged on some aspects of how socialization occurs and participation patterns unfold, many issues remain controversial.

Changes over the Life Cycle

Political socialization is an endless process. People keep learning as their life experiences accumulate and their circumstances change. The values and skills they acquire early in life may not be adequate for their needs later in life. Thus, they refine their attitudes and values throughout their lives in response to the new needs they develop and the new information they acquire.

No one is sure exactly how early political socialization begins, but we know that many children in the second grade already possess some knowledge and ideas about the political system in which they live (see the box on page 176). Most of them are aware of the existence of a government and are able to identify two important authority figures: the president of the United States and the police officer. They may also be familiar with political symbols like the flag, the national anthem, and George Washington. Most American children, for example, learn to recite the Pledge of Allegiance before they have any idea what its words mean.

The majority of American children in the preadolescent period develop positive feelings about their nation's government and its leaders, and most have a benign view of the police officer as a helper and protector. They see the president as a good and wise person who is interested primarily in the welfare of the nation. Many children in this age group compare the president to their father and place the president near the top of their list of favorite people.

This positive view is not universal, however. To some extent, a child's view of the incumbent president may be affected by important personal characteristics like race or parental occupation. In 1971, for instance, studies of preadolescent African-American and Mexican-American children found much higher negative perceptions of President Richard Nixon than were common among white children in the same community.[3] In 1973, children of military families expressed more positive attitudes toward Nixon than did children of civilian families. Thus, although most preadolescent American children express positive attitudes toward the political system and its leaders, there are variations in that pattern.

The positive character of most children's early perceptions of the American political system is an important development. It facilitates the bonding between citizen and government that is essential to the legitimacy of a govern-

Children Encounter the World of Politics

Researchers study children and their views and understanding of the political world to learn about the foundations of political attitudes and behavior. The following comments are typical of what they hear.

"Tommy, what is the government?"

"The government is like the President, but he isn't actually a President. The builders, the street makers, and all these people work for the government. The sidewalks and streets are the government's property, and he lets people walk in them.

"He has a moneymaking machine, and he makes lots of money. But he doesn't use it. . . . Maybe he makes the laws of the country. Maybe he tells the numbers on the license plates.

"He's the judge of the wildlife service. I sent him that letter about banding birds and he told the wildlife service to send me that pamphlet.

"I've got it! The government is the boss of all the governors, probably. Like the President is boss of all the senators. Senators are people from all different states.

"I heard on the radio that he's in charge of the income tax. He can higher it or lower it." [Age 7]

"George, have you ever heard of a political party?"

"I've heard about parties, but not political parties."

"When have you heard about parties?"

"When it's somebody's birthday."

"Well, have you heard about the Democrats and the Republicans?"

"Well, yeah, they are some sort of organization. . . ."

"What comes to your mind about these organizations?"

"Kennedy. . . ."

"What is that?"

"Well, he was a Democrat." [Age 10]

"What can you tell me about the President?"

"Well, the President has quite a direct handling of the country. First, any bill—he can veto just about any bill. I don't really know too much about this. From what I've heard it's correct. He can veto any bill and he has the power—I mean he can make bills. I mean not all of them, but, well, they pass, and he has something to do with it. And if he can get the people's support in him—well, that will help the country a lot." [Age 11]

SOURCE: Robert D. Hess and Judith V. Torney, *The Development of Political Attitudes in Children* (Chicago: Aldine, 1967), 1–4.

ment's right to rule. If citizens do not believe that a government is legitimate, they are unlikely to participate faithfully in its processes or support its decisions. In the United States there is widespread acceptance of the legitimacy of the government. Most children become patriotic before they have acquired enough information to explain the loyalty they feel. Although these strongly positive feelings tend to be modified as children grow older, they play an important role in the maintenance and stability of the American political system by securing the support of most of its citizens early in their lives.

There is evidence of important differences in the political socialization of male and female children, although these differences appear to be narrowing. In most families in which both parents are present, children of both sexes perceive their father as the more relevant political role model and as the more knowledgeable parent on political matters. Even though the mother is the more frequent conversation partner with children on such matters as sex, religion, and study, the father has the advantage when the topic is politics. In addition, the early socialization of children has long emphasized the public roles of males and the private roles of females.[4] This reinforcement of the association between men and politics helps explain why men typically have higher participation levels than women.

As children move into adolescence, their perceptions of the political world tend to become more sophisticated. They begin to recognize that there is more to government than presidents and police officers. They become aware of Congress, courts, and cabinet members, and the distinctions among various levels of government.

Wide World Photos, Inc.

Before he had been in office for two months, President Clinton hosted a special for young people televised by ABC from the White House. For 90 minutes the president answered questions from forty children. During a commercial break, he returned the school yearbook of a California girl, which she had highlighted to show which classmates' fathers might lose jobs in the timber industry because of concern over the spotted owl.

A sense of the conflict that pervades politics also emerges at this point. Children begin to recognize that individuals may take sides in disagreements among candidates, political parties, and interest groups on controversial issues. They are confronted by the need to choose a side, to position themselves within the political universe. This is a critical stage in the process of political socialization, because it shapes the lifelong attitudes of many Americans.

Party affiliation   The most important of these choices is that of an affiliation with a political party. In the United States, citizens do not join a party in the way that they join a club or a church. They make no formal profession of membership, they receive no membership card, and they are not required to pay dues. What they tend to do instead is simply to identify with a particular political party (or, in many cases, to identify themselves as independents). Party identification is an important concept in American political analysis because the political party identification that begins for many children in elementary school structures their orientation to politics throughout their lifetimes.

Many children have a notion of the existence of Republicans and Democrats and can identify themselves with one party or the other in the early elementary grades. Several studies done in the 1960s found that more than half of the fifth-graders questioned had a party preference. By the twelfth grade, according to another study, almost two-thirds of a national sample had a party preference. More recent research has indicated that larger numbers of children than was the case in the 1950s and 1960s are identifying themselves as "independents" or adopting no partisan preference.[5]

Most of these early partisan attachments are based on very little substantive knowledge. Children identify themselves with a political party or as an independent without being able to express an ideological or issue-based ex-

Political attitudes take root early, and even schoolchildren often identify with a particular party. But they have little understanding of ideological differences until adolescence. After that, their political attitudes and patterns of participation may last a lifetime.

planation for their choice. In some cases they can cite a prominent political personage as a referent for their party choice. They have identified with Republicans, for instance, because they admire President Ronald Reagan or President George Bush or because they dislike something they hear about President Bill Clinton. Few, however, are able to go beyond a superficial knowledge of individual political figures in explaining their preference for a particular party. Awareness of substantive differences between the parties rarely comes before the last years of elementary school, and even then less than 10 percent of children can make distinctions based on issues or ideology.[6] Not until high school do most people acquire an understanding of the substantive differences between political parties.[7]

Political cynicism   Along with the increase in knowledge about politics and partisanship that occurs in the adolescent years comes a modification of the positive attitudes held in earlier years. Teenagers' political views become more realistic, and teens begin to perceive political figures in less heroic terms as they begin to understand the complexities and controversies of politics. It is also during the teenage years that most people begin to perceive government as a constraint on personal behavior by means of local curfews, minimum ages for driving and drinking, and school attendance requirements.

Cynicism in political attitudes tends to develop in early adulthood and to increase, in varying degrees, throughout the remainder of the life cycle. This delayed development is not surprising, for children and adolescents are not asked to participate in American politics. With adulthood comes broader exposure to the daily realities of politics, government, and public policy. The first significant opportunities to participate in politics also emerge at this time. Some adults remain unaffected, but for many this new perspective on the political world yields diminishing faith in the effectiveness of political institutions and decreasing trust in political leaders and their motives.

Major political events   The acquisition of political attitudes and attachments is further complicated by the major political events that occur during a person's lifetime. Each generation of Americans is exposed to a different set of stimuli because each lives through a different period of history.

Major events, especially those occurring during the formative years, may have a lifelong impact on the generation that experiences them. The generation of southern white citizens who came of age during and immediately after the Civil War learned to view Republicans as the villains of that war and as "carpetbaggers" who rode roughshod over the South during Reconstruction. Their allegiance to the Democratic party was tightly forged as a result. Similarly, the generation of Americans who reached adulthood during the Great Depression of the 1930s found many reasons to blame the Depression on Herbert Hoover and the Republicans and to attach their loyalties to the Democrats. In both cases, Democratic party loyalties remained in place long after the passing of the events that created them. The New Deal generation of Democrats, for instance, remained a core component of the Democratic party for many decades after Franklin Roosevelt's first election to the presidency in 1932.

Younger people who have come of age politically during the 1970s and 1980s have been affected less by any single major events than by the general movement away from strong political party orientations that has been characteristic of this period. The combined effect of Vietnam, Watergate, the Iran-contra affair, and other political scandals and failures has been to create a trend toward disaffection in American politics. At the same time, the organization of political campaigns has shifted away from the political parties. Even though some young people have found themselves attracted to charismatic political figures like Ronald Reagan in the 1980s and Bill Clinton in the 1990s, that attraction has not appeared to translate into deep and abiding loyalty to a particular political party. The large number of young adults who now think of themselves as political independents is not surprising, since they came of age at a time when political parties may have appeared irrelevant in shaping their political interests.[8]

Recent studies have discovered significant increases in political alienation in the past few decades.[9] This is especially notable in the attitudes of young people. The 75 million members of the baby boom generation (people born between 1947 and 1964) now compose nearly one-third of the American people and 60 percent of eligible voters. Having come of age at a time of scandals, assassinations, and an unpopular war, many baby boomers never developed

During the 1960s and early 1970s, student protest, long a tradition in Latin America and Europe, came of age in the United States, along with more than half of today's voters. This photograph, taken at the peace march on Washington in late 1967, epitomized the conflicts and hopes of the period. "Flower power" was only one of the more positive responses by baby boomers to the Vietnam War. For some, distrust of authority and political alienation became enduring attitudes.

comfortable attachments to political parties or to other aspects of mainstream politics. Their political socialization has been significantly different from that of preceding generations. And because there are so many of them, their alienation from traditional politics has had a major effect on public life in America (see the Case Study on page 182).

Agents of Political Socialization

How do young Americans acquire their information and attitudes about politics? Two theories have been proposed.[10] One theory suggests that individuals are taught most of what they come to know about politics by people and institutions with an active interest in influencing their beliefs. These are **agents of political socialization,** groups and individuals from whom citizens acquire political information and learn political attitudes and values. The other theory suggests that individuals themselves have considerable autonomy in acquiring the political information they find useful and the political attitudes they find comfortable.

The two theories are not necessarily at odds. In American society there are agents that attempt to socialize young people to accept and adapt to the prevailing political culture. But there are also ample opportunities for young people to shape their own political socialization through independent acquisition and evaluation of political information.

The family   The family is the dominant agent of political socialization in the early years. At least until children begin school, they spend most of their waking hours in contact with one or more members of their family. Even during the

© Aneal Vohra/The Picture Cube

The family that demonstrates together is more likely than not to keep demonstrating together. Children are most apt to absorb the family's political attitudes when they are young and when those attitudes are expressed clearly and frequently.

The Politics of a Generation: The Baby Boom

The year 1947 saw the beginning of a demographic development that will deeply influence American life and politics well into the twenty-first century. Although it was not much noticed at the time, Americans began to have babies by the millions.

In 1940 the median age at first marriage was 24.3 for men and 21.5 for women. By 1947 the medians had dropped to 23.7 and 20.5, and in 1956 they bottomed out at 22.5 and 20.1. With the marriages—and increasingly without them—came babies. In 1940, 2.6 million babies were born in the United States. In 1945, there were 2.9 million. By 1947 the number of births had grown to 3.8 million, and it stayed over 3.6 million until 1967. From 1953 through 1963, on average, 4.2 million babies were born every year in the United States.

This was the baby boom, and it produced the largest population cohort in American history. The effect on public life was dramatic. As the baby boomers began to reach school age in the early 1950s, an unprecedented wave of new school construction began, with major impacts on public budgets and tax rates. By 1965 the pressure of local school budgets had grown so great that the federal government began to provide aid to education for the first time. By 1979 a new cabinet-level Department of Education had been created to supervise the myriad programs that had grown up in the wake of that initial decision.

As family size grew in the 1950s and 1960s, the demand for more and larger houses grew as well, accelerating the move to the suburbs and the end of the tradition of the multigenerational nuclear family living under one roof. Not only were there a lot of baby boomers, but they had access to more disposable income than any previous generation. Those with products to sell took notice. As the baby boomers reached puberty and early adulthood, they quickly became the favorite target of mass marketers, inspiring fads like Hula-Hoops and coonskin caps and trends like rock-'n'-roll music, informal dress, and a preference for television over books.

As the baby boomers passed through the crime-prone years of early adulthood, crime rates shot up. As they finished high school in record num-

bers, they inspired unprecedented demands for college education. As they reached working age, they required more new jobs than the economy had ever before produced. As their incomes grew to the highest levels in history, they created a vast new market for consumer electronics, luxury cars, pricey restaurants, and other amenities of the good life. And as they age, they will blaze yet another trail into the golden years. By the year 2035 almost one-fourth of the United States population will be over 65—more than double the current figure. Demand for retirement housing, medical care, and a cure for Alzheimer's disease will grow apace.

In 1968 the first of the baby boomers became eligible to vote. (The voting age was still 21.) Baby boomers represented less than 10 percent of the potential electorate in that election. By 1972, however, with the voting age lowered to 18, baby boomers composed more than 20 percent of the potential electorate. By 1976 their percentage had grown to more than one-third, by 1984 to half, and by 1992 to almost 60 percent.

By virtue merely of their strength in numbers, baby boomers have had the potential to be the controlling force in American politics. But they haven't become so because they have resisted traditional forms of political organization, especially strong loyalty to a political party. To date, baby boomers have been less likely than members of other generations to vote and less likely to identify strongly with either major political party. This generation, notes political scientist Paul Light, has been less a kingmaker than a heartbreaker, a reliable source of support for no party or candidate or broad-based political movement.

To an extent rarely encountered before in American politics, the baby boomers went their own way. Probably it is not surprising that a generation so large would have so many diverse impulses. This was not only America's largest generation but also its freest: free from the pressure to conform that had characterized the generations of the two world wars, free—because of the invention of the birth control pill and the availability of abortion—from the inevitability of unwanted children, free from the im-

Bill and Hillary Rodham Clinton are the first baby boomers in the White House.
(TOLES copyright The Buffalo News. Reprinted with permission of UNIVERSAL PRESS SYNDICATE. All rights reserved.)

perative felt by earlier generations to help support financially marginal family members, and free from the need to participate in politics in order to get what they wanted. The baby boomers forged their own identities. Some fought in the Vietnam War; others protested against it. Some joined the civil rights movement; others rioted in urban ghettos. Some were the first in their families to go to top colleges or work in top firms or start their own companies. Others became homemakers, farmers, or factory workers, as their parents had been.

Whatever the baby boomers were, they were not a cultural or an economic monolith. More than any previous generation, they had the power, the means, and the opportunity to make their own life choices. And they made them. They were not a political monolith either, for the same reasons. Their political diversity reflected their cultural and economic diversity. And they became a great frustration to national and local political leaders even as they-

themselves became those leaders. There was no herding, and often no leading, the baby boomers. They resisted traditional calls to political action and political loyalty. They turned inward to their own cultural, racial, and economic groups and found little reason to work hard at bridging the differences—and sometimes the hostilities—among those groups. When the baby boomers came of political age, the United States became more difficult to govern than it had been at any time in this century.

Discussion questions
1. How would you characterize the political attitudes and opinions of baby boomers you know, perhaps including your parents?
2. Did any single political event, on the order of the Great Depression or the Civil War, affect the political party loyalties of the baby boomers?
3. Do you think the baby boom generation will pass on its own complex pattern of political socialization and participation to its children?

TABLE 6-1

Student and Parent Reports of Party Identifications (in percent)

STUDENTS LABEL THEMSELVES	PARENTS LABEL THEMSELVES						
	STRONG DEM.	WEAK DEM.	IND. DEM.	IND.	IND. REP.	WEAK REP.	STRONG REP.
Democrat	89	71	53	33	17	14	8
Independent	8	18	37	51	37	13	9
Republican	3	11	10	16	46	73	84
Total	100	100	100	100	100	100	100

SOURCE: Richard G. Niemi, *How Family Members Perceive Each Other* (New Haven, Conn.: Yale University Press, 1974), 59. Copyright © 1974. Reprinted with permission of the publisher.

years that children do attend school, the family remains an important reference point for most children.

There is strong reason, therefore, to suspect that the family is a powerful influence on the attitudes and values that children acquire to help them understand and cope with the political world. But that is not always so. Although parents are in an unusually good position to influence their children's political attitudes, they do not always make their influence felt. Many families simply don't talk about politics very often. Studies of the impact of family on a child's acquisition of political attitudes have indicated that the potential for family influence is likely to be realized only when three conditions are met: (1) a close relationship among family members, (2) significant agreement among adults in the family on political values and attitudes, and (3) frequent communication of those values and attitudes to the child. Thus, if both parents are active Republicans or Democrats who are very interested in politics and discuss politics frequently at home, it is much more likely that their son or daughter will adopt their views and their partisan preferences than if they were not interested in politics or disagreed with each other on fundamental political matters.

Most studies have found that the development of party identification is the area in which the family has the greatest influence. There is close but not perfect congruence between the party identification of children and that of their parents, especially if the parents' party identification is strongly held.[11] Table 6-1 indicates some of the dimensions of this relationship. It shows, for example, that among students whose parents were strong Democrats, 89 percent think of themselves as Democrats. Conversely, for those whose parents were strong Republicans, 84 percent said that they too were Republicans.

In the past several decades, old notions about the role of the family as a socializing agent have become increasingly suspect as American families have undergone dramatic changes. Most of the research on this subject was carried out before the large-scale entry of women into the work force and the explosive increase in the divorce rate among younger couples. Fewer young Americans than ever before grow up in families in which the parents remain married and

Most children first come into contact with the political world through patriotic rituals in school, like the Pledge of Allegiance to the flag and the observance of national holidays. But schools have less impact on political socialization than one might expect.

the mother does not work outside the home. Recent projections suggest, for example, that more than half of all children born in the early 1980s will become part of a single-parent family before they reach the age of 18.[12] A consequence is that the family is a less potent source of political attitudes and orientations than it was when children spent more time with both of their parents than they often do now.

Schools Schools have many of the same advantages that families have as potential influences on the political socialization of children. They occupy a good many of the child's waking hours, and they are expressly designed as instruments of instruction. Moreover, much of the content of educational curricula is aimed at teaching children about the American political system and guiding them to become good citizens. Because schools provide children with many kinds of socializing experiences, one would expect them to play a significant role in political socialization as well. But most of the evidence indicates that they do not.

Studies of the impact of school civics courses have consistently shown how little impact such courses have on either the knowledge or the attitudes of the students exposed to them.[13] Nor is there significant evidence that teachers are likely to have much independent impact on the political attitudes of their students.[14] A lot of ritualistic patriotic activity takes place in schools: saluting the flag, recognizing national holidays, singing patriotic songs, and so on. During the Persian Gulf War, for example, students in public schools wrote letters and sent food to American soldiers, festooned their buildings with yellow ribbons, and joined vigorously in the patriotic fervor of the moment. These activities may reinforce support for the political system among children, but they do not appear to have a lasting impact on adult attitudes or political behavior.

Schools seem to have little independent impact on political socialization. Instead, they tend to complement other, more important socializing forces in a child's life. Since public education in the United States is locally controlled, teachers and curricula tend to reflect, within certain broad limits, the prevailing values of the community in which a school is located. For many decades after the Civil War, for example, southern schoolteachers often referred to that conflict as the War of Northern Aggression. Today, in school districts close to military bases or defense manufacturing facilities, patriotism is usually given greater emphasis in the curriculum than it receives in districts where military influence is absent. It would be unusual indeed to find local public schools fostering values that were at odds with popular beliefs in their communities. This congruence of values helps explain why schools rarely have much independent effect on the political socialization of a community's children.

In a more indirect way, however, schools have traditionally influenced political socialization. Schools equip people to comprehend and participate in the political world. The more formal education people obtain, the better informed they are likely to be about politics, the greater their interest in politics is likely to be, and the more likely they are to take part in political activities.[15] This is not to suggest that schools have an independent impact on individual political socialization, only that people who are well educated may be better equipped to direct their own political socialization than those who are not well educated.

But even this generalization has become increasingly suspect. One of the most remarkable developments in the United States after World War II was a spectacular increase in citizens' education levels. Between 1948 and 1970, the median number of school years completed by Americans jumped from a little over nine to more than twelve. The 1980 census was the first ever to report that a majority of adults in every state were high school graduates. In 1970, only about one adult in five had ever been to college; by 1982, one person in three had had at least one year of college. Half of all baby boomers started college, and nearly one-fourth of them finished. In sum, since World War II, more Americans have more education than ever before.

Since higher education levels have historically induced greater political interest, knowledge, and participation, it was anticipated that a better-educated American citizenry would become more involved in public affairs. But no such trend materialized. Voting turnout declined after World War II; interest in politics did not increase noticeably. One study of political apathy found that "at every level of education interest was down. . . . Moreover, apathy had risen among precisely those of whom it would have been least expected: people with college experience."[16]

Peers Peer groups share some of the advantages of families and schools in influencing the political socialization of individuals. In some ways, in fact, their advantages are even greater. Interaction with a peer group tends to persist into adulthood as exposure to family and school declines. Most people are members of peer groups throughout their lives (although the composition and character of those groups may change) and tend to be receptive to communications received from peer groups. In fact, people are often much more attentive and accommodating to members of peer groups than they are to those in their schools or families.

When peer groups actively engage in political discussions or activities, they are likely to be very influential in shaping the political orientations of their members. A classic study of this phenomenon was conducted at Bennington College in the 1930s.[17] The results showed that a substantial majority of the students in the study had become politically liberal during their college years, despite the fact that many of them came from families with quite different ideological views. The study indicated that interaction with peers was the major source of the attitudes acquired by the Bennington students. When most of them were reinterviewed twenty years later, the overwhelming finding was that the effects of peer interaction during their college years had persisted over time—that is, their ideological liberalism had remained intact. More recent studies of schoolchildren in Detroit and in high schools across the country have reiterated the significance of peer groups in the formation and solidification of some political attitudes.[18]

The mass media Anyone who has grown up in the contemporary United States would naturally expect the communications media, especially television, to have a significant impact on the way citizens come to perceive their political environment. The reason is obvious: Americans spend a great deal of time watching television—an average of twenty-eight hours a week for adults[19] and twenty-six hours a week for children.[20] Adults also pay some attention to the print media. Two-thirds of all American households receive at least one newspaper a day,[21] and many adults scan or peruse several magazines each week.

The frequency with which Americans are exposed to the mass media invites the assumption that the media play a significant role as socializing agents. The evidence, however, is mixed. The media play an important role in setting the boundaries of political debate and in identifying important issues. Most studies have shown that they are an important source of political information, that citizens' familiarity with issues comes primarily from the communications media. The spread of AIDS, overworked air traffic control systems, the demise of communism in eastern Europe—people learn about issues like these principally from the print and broadcast media. But there is little evidence to suggest that the media have much independent effect on political attitudes. In other words, most people's opinions and political behavior are not altered significantly by their exposure to the mass media.

One explanation for the absence of a strong relationship between media exposure and political attitudes is that much of what people pay attention to on television or in newspapers and magazines has little to do with politics. Most people use the media primarily for entertainment. Viewing or reading communications with specific political content consumes only a small portion of the time that most people spend with their television set or daily newspaper. A significant number of Americans have little more than a peripheral interest in politics, and this is clearly reflected in the way they use the communications media.

A second reason the media appear to have so little effect on political attitudes or behavior is that most people watch or read programs or articles that support their existing political views and partisan preferences. Psychologists refer to this phenomenon as **selective perception**. A conservative citizen, for instance, is much more likely to read newspaper columns by conservatives William F. Buckley, Jr., and George Will than to read columns written by liberals Michael Kinsley and Mary McGrory. Doing so is comfortable, rein-forces one's opinions, and helps convince one that those opinions are correct.

Thus, for most people the mass media serve to reinforce the political socialization process. For some they are important sources of political infor-mation, but for most they have little independent effect on political beliefs and behavior. Americans tend to use information acquired from the mass media not as a basis for constant reexamination of their attitudes or as fuel for political activity but as fortification for values and perceptions already formed.

Some recent studies have suggested that the cumulative effect of television watching may be to increase disaffection and cynicism among Americans. The lengthening of election campaigns combined with extensive television coverage often leads to boredom rather than to heightened interest.[22] Intensive scrutiny of political scandals and the private lives of public officials inevitably makes American leaders seem less heroic than they often appeared in the days before television. During the 1992 primary campaign in New Hampshire, for example, no single story received more coverage than Gennifer Flowers's allegations of Bill Clinton's marital infidelity. The accumulation of such stories tends to re-duce support for the political system and esteem for its leaders.

In the political socialization of younger Americans, increasing reliance on television now often substitutes for the role that parental communications once played. Political scientist Paul Light has written, for example, that "television became a new social parent. . . . Recall the question of why parents did not pass on their party loyalty to their children. Perhaps one answer is that TV got in the way."[23]

Secondary groups   Americans start joining organizations in early childhood and continue to do so throughout their lives. Sociologists refer to groups that people join voluntarily as **secondary groups,** in contrast to the primary groups, such as the family or cliques at school, in which there is close person-to-person interaction. Typical of the secondary groups to which Americans belong are professional associations, social or service clubs, labor unions, and political action organizations.

Membership in a group may have some effect on an individual's political socialization if three important conditions are met: (1) the individual identifies closely with the group's values or objectives; (2) those values or objectives relate directly to some aspect of politics; and (3) the group engages in promotional activities designed to inspire specific political attitudes or actions on the part of its members. In recent years, for instance, the Catholic church and some fundamentalist Protestant sects have made aggressive efforts to get the federal and state governments to prohibit abortion. The efforts of these church groups have had an impact on both the attitudes and the political activity of some of their members, stimulating or solidifying their personal opposition to abortion and inspiring them to engage in political action designed to change public policy on the abortion issue.

When the necessary conditions are satisfied, secondary groups can have an impact on individual political socialization. But that does not often happen. A good many of the secondary groups that Americans join—the bridge club, the bowling league, the volunteer fire company—do not engage in political activity and provide little inspiration for their members to do so. Even groups with specific political objectives, such as the National Conservative Political Action Committee or the liberal People for the American Way, can rarely take

Cheap off-shore labor and a lingering national recession have thinned the ranks of organized labor, which once commanded many millions of Americans. Fears that the North American Free Trade Agreement would move many manufacturing jobs south of the border drew labor supporters into the streets once again in the fall of 1993. But even as Lane Kirkland, president of the AFL-CIO, spoke against NAFTA in San Francisco's Union Square, half the crowd came not from unions but from an odd bedfellow, the Sierra Club.

credit for affecting the political socialization of their members. They tend to attract members who already share the group's objectives and values—indeed, who join for precisely that reason. Usually a secondary group does not cause a change in the attitudes or activity of an individual so much as it provides an outlet for personal beliefs already well formed.

Traditionally, a major impact of secondary groups has been to support and strengthen party affiliation. If an individual was inclined by parental influence and other forces to identify with the Democratic party and then joined a labor union that was closely linked with the Democrats, membership in the union would tend to tighten the individual's bond with the party. But the solidarity and appeal of many of the large groups that once served as building blocks of American politics is in decline. As a leading political reporter, E. J. Dionne, has noted,

the party system of the New Deal was relatively stable because definable groups voted together and largely held together, even in bad times. Now, almost everything conspires against group solidarity. Unions are in trouble. . . . New jobs in the service industry promote individualism. The decline of the small town and the old urban ethnic enclaves . . . further weaken social solidarity.[24]

An important consequence is that secondary groups no longer reinforce party identification the way they once did.

Attitudes and Behavior

As noted earlier, political socialization is a dynamic process, one that continues throughout the life cycle. Important aspects of belief systems and political attitudes begin to take shape before adulthood. These are not immutable, but

Gloria Steinem: Thoroughly Modern Feminist

Political activist and writer Gloria Steinem first came to notice as a voice for the newly emerging women's movement in 1963 with the publication of her exposé article, "I Was a Playboy Bunny." From that beginning Steinem rose to national prominence as a political feminist. In 1971, along with Betty Friedan, Bella Abzug, and Shirley Chisholm, Steinem founded the National Women's Political Caucus (NWPC), an organization dedicated to encouraging women to run for public office.

In 1972, Steinem became the founding editor of *Ms.* magazine. Within a year, *Ms.* had attained a circulation of 500,000. Many of today's most significant women's issues—equal pay, reproductive freedom, maternity leave, date rape, sexual harassment—were first identified and discussed in the pages of that publication. In a very real sense, *Ms.* raised the consciousness of an entire generation of women. But because advertisers were reluctant to appear in a "radical" magazine, Steinem spent most of her time on the road, speaking on campuses and in towns and cities around the country to raise money. She still found time to write trenchant articles and books, most notably a collection of essays called *Outrageous Acts and Everyday Rebellions,* first published in 1983.

Steinem remains an editorial consultant to *Ms.* She is also very active as a lecturer, organizer, and spokesperson for the feminist movement and issues of equality. Over the years, she has helped to found the *Ms.* Foundation for Women, Voters for Choice, the Women's Action Alliance, and the Coalition of Labor Union Women.

Recently Steinem has come to take a wider view of feminism, tying it to larger questions of self-esteem and self-knowledge for both women and men. "Progress for women," she says, "lies in becoming more assertive, more ambitious, more able to deal with conflict. Progress for men will lie in becoming more empathetic, more compassionate, more comfortable working inside the home."[1] Her

Brad Markel/Gamma-Liaison

Gloria Steinem, long-time activist and leader in the women's movement, expanded her definition of politics to include the Washington Mall and the shopping mall. "Politics also may be who's doing the dishes," she says.

1992 book, *Revolution from Within: A Book of Self-Esteem,* explores these issues.

Although she has now slowed the pace of her public appearances, Steinem has hardly given up on organized feminism. She frequently points out that the issues first raised by feminists in the early 1970s are still in the news today—but as national, not feminist, issues. We will know progress has been made, says Steinem, "when young men on campuses get up and ask as much as young women do, 'How can I combine a career and family?'"[2]

[1] Interview in *Esquire,* quoted in *Current Biography* entry.

[2] *USA Today* magazine interview, August, 1989.

In *Outrageous Acts and Everyday Rebellions*, Gloria Steinem describes how certain important political realities became clear to her in July of 1969:

Now there is a meeting under way to discuss [Senator George] McGovern's own potential campaign [in 1972]. He phoned to invite me to join the group being put together by [Senator Abraham] Ribicoff, and asked that each of us give a little advance thought to our advice.

The truth is that I haven't thought about politics, at least not in the conventional sense that I would have five or six months ago, since I woke up to the fact that my own position, and the position of women in general, was political in the deepest sense. I'm told that it's called the Feminist Realization.

I thought about it as I hung up the phone. Six months ago, I would have been honored by McGovern's invitation to a "serious" (i.e., male and therefore grown-up) political meeting, but full of doubt about whether I could contribute in a "serious" (male) way. I had raised as much money and done as much political work as anyone in McGovern's last brief presidential effort [in 1968] and still had been treated like a frivolous pariah by much of McGovern's Senate staff, but I had refused to admit even to myself that this was so. In fact, one of his chief aides only stopped saying "get her out of here" when he discovered that I had brought in the single biggest contributor. . . . Nonetheless, the aide didn't like women in politics, and he said he feared someone would think I was having an affair with the candidate.

Even in South Dakota, where many of us had gone to help McGovern get reelected to the Senate in spite of his conservative constituents' belief that "George became a hippie" in Chicago, I was made to feel that I had to dress dowdily (I actually went out and bought covered-up, mud-colored clothes) and lurk around corners.

Those events were echoes of every political campaign I had ever worked in as a volunteer, from Students for Stevenson in 1952 to McGovern. Like other women, I had either stayed at the edges doing menial jobs or been hidden away in some backroom because (a) it might be counterproductive to admit that a female was working on speeches or policy decisions, and (b) if she was under sixty and didn't have terminal acne, someone might think she was having an affair with the candidate.

Not only had I suppressed all those years of anger, just assuming that I was lucky to be allowed to volunteer for a campaign at all, but I also had defined politics very narrowly; the faraway events in Washington or Saigon or city hall. I couldn't admit that any power relationship in life is political: therefore politics also may be who's doing the dishes, or who's getting paid half the wages that a man would get for the same job, or who's expected to take the roles of service and support everywhere, including in political campaigns.

It's a realization I owe to those brave women whose meetings I started covering last winter. A lot of them were younger than I. Most had come out of the peace or civil rights movements, where they had figured out that even if those admirable and idealistic groups relegated women to doing mimeographing and making coffee, a woman-run movement against sexism was a necessity. They changed my life. It will never be the same.

neither do they change easily. Alteration of political attitudes formed in the preadult years requires exposure to potent stimuli in adulthood. And because those stimuli appear only infrequently, attitudes formed early in life usually remain at the core of a person's belief system.

Involvement in political activities, however, is another story. The evidence examined here suggests strongly that preadult experiences have a much greater impact on adult political attitudes (what we think) than on political behavior (how we act). To a certain extent, of course, childhood learning will contribute to an adult's predisposition to engage actively in political forms of behavior, but so too will the situations and problems that people encounter in their adult lives. Even those with little predisposition to engage in political activity and with little confidence in their own political skills may become deeply involved in issues that affect them directly and inspire them to active political involvement: the discovery of a toxic contaminant in their water supply, the desire to improve the quality of their children's schools, a neighborhood effort to prevent the construction of a new highway. The important point here is that early socialization is likely to have a much greater impact on the formation of political attitudes and values than on adult political activity.

POLITICAL PARTICIPATION

Political participation is a critical ingredient in a successful democracy. Government cannot be "for the people" if it is not also "of the people and by the people." Public participation in policy making must be sufficient to ensure an accurate reflection of both the intensity and the direction of popular concerns. But participating in politics and government is not easy. It takes time and energy; it requires knowledge of political and government processes; and it requires that people feel that their political activity will make a difference.

    Participation is a variable, not a constant. Some people participate; others do not. Some people participate extensively, others only minimally. Why? Part of the answer comes from variations in the socialization patterns discussed earlier. Part also results from differences in opportunities or incentives to participate, from external factors that have a direct effect on people's lives. Three important aspects of political participation are (1) the ways in which Americans most commonly participate in political life, (2) the characteristics of those who participate and those who do not, and (3) the impact of participation on public policy.

Ways of Participating

Political participation encompasses a variety of activities. Some, like running for political office, are very demanding. Others, like voting, require only minimal amounts of time and knowledge. Between these extremes is a wide range of other activities.

Campaign activity   Participation in political campaigns is an obvious way in which individuals attempt to influence public policy. Securing the election of people who share one's views is probably the most direct way to get those views embedded in public policy, and participating in a campaign is not difficult if a person has the desire to do so. The vast majority of campaign workers are volunteers, and political candidates are always glad to get help. Campaign activity may consume a lot of time, but the amount of time invested is usually up to the volunteer. Although broad experience in politics may be useful in a campaign, it is not a prerequisite. Much campaign work still requires only the ability and the willingness to stuff envelopes, make phone calls, or distribute campaign literature.[25]

TYPE OF ACTIVITY	1968	1972	1976	1980	1984	1988	1992
Voted*	76	73	72	71	74	70	75
Worked for party or candidate	6	5	4	4	4	3	3
Attended rallies or meetings	9	9	6	8	8	7	8
Tried to persuade others how to vote	33	32	37	36	32	29	38
Wore campaign button, displayed bumper sticker	15	14	8	7	9	9	11
Contributed money to campaign	9	10	16	8	13	9	6

TABLE 6-2
American Citizens Active in Various Forms of Political Participation, 1968–1992 (in percent)

* These are self-identified voters. This figure generally exceeds the percent of eligible adults who participate in any single national election.

SOURCE: Data for 1968–1980 are adapted from David B. Hill and Norman R. Luttbeg, *Trends in American Electoral Behavior* (Itasca, Ill.: Peacock, 1983), 99. Data for 1984–1992 are adapted from the National Election Studies.

What campaign activity does require is political interest. The participant must care about the outcome of the race and believe that one candidate is better than the others. That so many Americans have never participated in campaign activities (see Table 6-2) suggests that even this level of interest is not very common.

Indeed, much current research suggests that levels of political interest are in decline in the United States, especially among the young.[26] Because of their mobility and willingness to do the menial work of politics, young people normally constitute the core of campaigns. But in recent decades disaffection with conventional politics has kept many young people away from campaigning. This helps explain why campaign activity is a relatively rare form of political participation.

Voting   Voting is widely regarded as the simplest form of political activity. Not surprisingly, therefore, it is also the form that is engaged in most frequently. Voting is the only political activity in which many Americans participate regularly. Nevertheless, despite its relative ease, a substantial number of Americans do not vote regularly. As Table 6-2 indicates, more than one-fourth of the American people do not even identify themselves as regular voters.

Why do people not vote? Some say that they lack time, interest, or motivation. Registration requirements in many states (discussed in Chapter 10) may also be an impediment. Much is made of the relatively low percentage of eligible Americans who vote, but we need to remember that there are other ways to affect the political process. And even nonvoters may engage in these other forms of political participation.[27]

Personal contacting Some citizens directly contact a political figure or a public agency for the purpose of altering public policy. The issue at stake may relate to the welfare of the community or the nation, but it is more likely to involve a personal concern or problem: the woman who frequently appears at city council meetings to plead for better care of the gardens in a public park; the parents of a handicapped child who contact state welfare agencies to get public support for their child's training; the couple who contact local officials for assistance in getting a traffic light placed at a busy intersection where their child was hit by a car. A growing number of Americans now contact their local, state, and national representatives to try to influence those officials' votes on policy issues.

One of the interesting things about individuals who engage in personal contacting is that they often do not think of themselves as politically active. Many of them, in fact, are not very interested in politics, especially partisan politics. The fact that they are active in the kinds of direct ways described here does not necessarily imply that they will also participate in other ways. Personal contacting may be their principal, perhaps their sole, mode of political participation. However, because it requires considerable initiative as well as some knowledge and persistence on the part of the contacter, it is a form of political participation in which few Americans engage. In the United States most political participation beyond the act of voting takes the form of collective, rather than individual, action.

Cooperative activity An American citizen who wants to influence public policy and who thinks about effective strategies for doing so is likely to calculate that his or her message will have more impact if it comes from an organized group rather than from a single voice. This belief is nothing more than the old law of politics that says there is strength in numbers. The greater the number of people who support a particular course of action, the greater is the likelihood that such a course will be pursued by public officials.

The emphasis on cooperative forms of political participation is evident at both the local and the national levels. In most communities, policy decisions are frequently influenced by the efforts of organized groups of citizens: the PTA working for increases in school budgets, the chamber of commerce trying to hold down the tax rate in order to attract new business investment, the city employees' union supporting candidates for local office who will vote for increases in salaries or benefits. Similarly, at the national level, organized interest groups are a major factor in politics and in public policy making. Few significant interests in American public life are not now organized as groups with their own lobbyists in Washington. There are thousands of such organizations, reflecting interests as diverse as those of autoworkers, milk producers, the mentally retarded, summer camps, and importers of exotic animals. Interest groups are a commanding presence in contemporary American politics, and we look at their role more closely in Chapter 8.

Cooperative activity requires more initiative than voting but less than personal contacting. Those who engage in it may have significant levels of information, at least about the issues that concern the groups in which they participate, but a high level of information is not a requirement for this sort of participation. One can be part of a group without being an expert on the issues with which it is concerned. In fact, for many people high interest but low information is a motivation to join a group and participate in its cooperative

At its national convention in San Antonio, the American Association of Retired Persons (AARP), the country's second-largest lobbying group, sponsored a "fun run." Then the delegates sat down to hammer out what legislation they would support or oppose in the coming year. Senior citizens, many of whom have the time, interest, and resources to do much more than vote, are still growing in number and political influence.

activities. In general, the number who do so is smaller than the number who vote but larger than the number who engage in personal contacting.[28]

Unconventional participation   Each democratic political system establishes certain regular channels for citizen participation; of these, elections are the most common. Open legislative and administrative hearings are another such channel. Not all efforts at public participation follow these conventional channels, however. Some circumvent them and, therefore, may be termed **unconventional participation.** They include such activities as protest demonstrations, sit-ins, rent strikes, riots, assassinations, and revolutions.

Unconventional activities most often occur when individuals or groups of citizens do not know how to follow conventional participation channels or do not believe that they will be able to influence public policy by going through those channels. Unconventional participation is often engaged in by those who are frustrated or believe themselves powerless to compete effectively in conventional politics. A good example is student activism against the Vietnam War in the 1960s. Under the laws in effect at the time, most students could not vote. They did not have the money or the organizational skills necessary to establish effective national interest groups, nor did their individual contacts with government officials seem to produce much change in the conduct of the war. Consequently, many students chose to express their opposition to the war outside of the routine channels of political participation: in street demonstrations, mass marches, sit-ins, and other kinds of organized protest.

Participation in unconventional activities often precedes participation in more conventional forms of politics. The initial political participation of John Kerry, later a Democratic senator from Massachusetts, was as a young Vietnam veteran protesting that war. John Lewis, later a Democratic representative from Georgia, first gained public attention when he was clubbed by state troopers in a voting rights demonstration in Alabama in 1965. Like Kerry and Lewis,

During the Vietnam War, unconventional political strategies, some with tragic outcomes, were the only ones available to those who lacked the power to influence policy. On May 4, 1970, National Guardsmen fired tear gas into a crowd of war protesters at Kent State University. In the confusion that followed, the Guard panicked and fired live bullets at the students, killing four.

many current mayors, city councillors, and state legislators entered politics only after using unconventional tactics. Thus, protesting against the political system does not prevent later participation—even leadership—in the system.

Social scientists have little reliable data on the number of people who participate in unconventional political activities. Most analysts believe that it is not very large, perhaps 1 or 2 percent of the population. Among certain population groups, however, the percentage may be substantially higher. One study in upstate New York found that less than 3 percent of white citizens had ever taken part in a street demonstration but 11 percent of African-American citizens had done so.[29]

Unconventional forms of participation may have a greater effect on public policy than one would anticipate from the small percentages of people who are typically involved in them. The primary reason is their intensity and, in the age of television, their visibility. During the civil rights movement of the 1950s and 1960s, only a small percentage of the American people, even of African Americans, participated personally in public protest activities, but those who did captured national attention and became important symbols of the issues involved. In the summer of 1963, African-American citizens in Birmingham, Alabama, sat stoically on a sidewalk in nonviolent protest of the racial discrimination then embedded in the laws of that city and state. Public officials responded by assaulting them with police dogs, cattle prods, and water from fire hoses. The number of people directly involved on either side was not large, but

In the summer of 1963, people around the world saw clearly, many for the first time, how the South, as exemplified by the Birmingham police, treated African Americans who were deemed to be out of line. As television viewers saw live pictures of police dogs being set on peaceful protesters, their understanding of segregation, of civil rights, and of civil disobedience changed forever.

Americans all over the country watched these events on television. The vividness of the pictures concentrated national attention on the civil rights issue and helped solidify support for the significant pieces of national civil rights legislation that were enacted in 1964 and 1965.

Nonparticipation   A sizable number of Americans do not participate in political activities at all. They do not vote regularly; they engage in no direct contacts with public officials; they are not members of any group involved in political action; and they do not participate in unconventional forms of political activity. They are politically inactive.

Among these inactive citizens we find several different types of people: those who are elderly and infirm, mentally incompetent, or incarcerated in prisons or other confining institutions; those who live lives of poverty and desperation and lack the skills, confidence, or energy necessary to take part in political life; and those who believe that political life is inherently corrupt or unfair and inequitable. Still others are inactive because they are basically satisfied with their own lives and with the state of national affairs and see no reason to invest any time or effort in political activities directed at change.

Whatever their reasons, approximately one-fifth of American adults are politically inactive.[30] What does it say about democracy in the United States if one-fifth of its citizens take no active part in choosing their leaders or in shaping the public policies that regulate their lives? Does this much nonparticipation threaten the vitality of the democratic process?

Many believe that government cannot rest on the consent of the governed if so many people are uninvolved. Others, however, contend that as long as participation is possible and encouraged, the system meets democratic criteria. A democracy could become unstable, unworkable, and highly volatile if everyone participated extensively at all levels and on most issues. Thus, some level of nonparticipation may be necessary for stability and efficiency in public life.

Who Participates?

Answers to the question of who participates must be given with caution. Participation patterns are complex, and no simple formulation can adequately describe or accurately predict the participation level of all individuals. Citizens from all types of backgrounds are found among the most active segments of the population, but they are also found among the least active. The same is true of every category in between. Nevertheless, some regular patterns of political participation do exist, and examining these may shed light on the role of political participation in shaping American politics and public policy. Keep in mind, however, that these are broad patterns to which there are numerous exceptions.

The impact of socioeconomic status   One of the most consistent findings of studies of American political participation is that participation correlates closely with an individual's **socioeconomic status (SES),** an analytic measure of one's relative social and economic standing. The higher one's SES, the greater is the likelihood that one will participate actively in politics. Most active participants are citizens with high levels of education and income. Among the inactives and those whose only activity is voting are a disproportionate number of citizens with low levels of educational attainment and income.

Two political scientists who have studied political participation extensively, Sidney Verba and Norman Nie, created an index of socioeconomic status and an index of political participation that allowed them to identify the relationship between status and participation. That relationship is indicated in Figure 6-1. The figure shows six categories of political participants, ranging from "lowest" (least active) to "highest" (most active). Identified in each category are the percentages of upper-, middle-, and lower-SES individuals. As the level of political participation increases, the percentage of upper-SES individuals increases and the percentage of lower-SES individuals decreases.

Figure 6-1 *Socioeconomic status at varying levels of participation.* SOURCE: *Sidney Verba and Norman H. Nie,* Participation in America: Political Democracy and Social Equality *(New York: Harper and Row, 1972), 131. Reprinted by permission.*

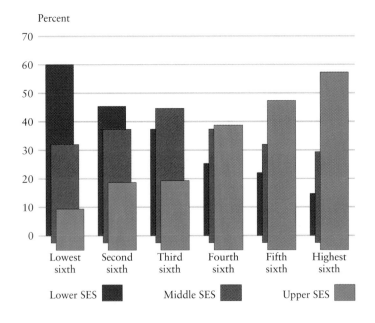

This relationship is not very surprising when one thinks about the advantages that higher-SES individuals have as political participants. Because they are well educated, they are likely to have acquired more knowledge about the workings of the political system. They are also more likely to follow political issues on television and in the press. Their higher levels of income may indicate that they have a substantial financial interest in many public policy decisions (taxes and investment regulations, for example). Most important, studies of political participation suggest that people of high socioeconomic status tend to have higher levels of political efficacy.

Political efficacy is an individual's feeling that he or she can bring about a desired political outcome. Citizens with a high level of political efficacy usually feel that their participation in politics makes a difference, that engaging in political activity is likely to produce results. In contrast, those with low levels of efficacy have little confidence that their political participation will have any significant impact. They may feel that they are insignificant and that politicians are not going to pay any attention to them no matter what they do.

Other demographic correlates No other demographic characteristic matches the impact of socioeconomic status on participation, but several others appear to affect participation levels. Age is one. In general, young adults, particularly those under age 30, and people over age 65 are less likely to be active participants than are those in between. Verba and Nie found, as Figure 6-2 indicates, that participation levels tend to increase as one gets older, level off in middle age, and then drop as one moves into the traditional retirement years.

Race, gender, religion, and community size are also factors in participation. African Americans, for example, are less likely than whites to be politically active, in part because they are overrepresented in the lower socioeconomic status groups. Women are less likely to be active than men, although the gap between the sexes has been narrowing in recent years and has disappeared in

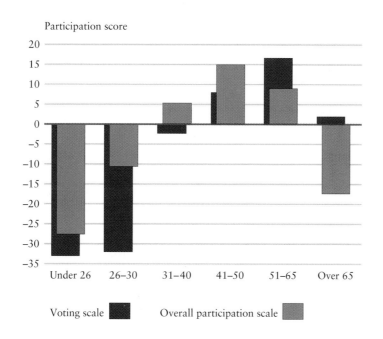

Figure 6-2 *Political participation over the life cycle. The participation score (vertical axis) indicates how much more or less each age group is apt to participate than the average citizen. Zero is the mean for the entire population. Scores above zero indicate above-average participation; scores below zero, less than average.* SOURCE: *Sidney Verba and Norman H. Nie,* Participation in America: Political Democracy and Social Equality *(New York: Harper and Row, 1972), 139. Reprinted by permission.*

*Americans participate in policy making in many ways, at least on the local level.
(Left)* At town meetings on Nantucket Island, every citizen discusses and votes on
every issue in an almost pure democracy. *(Right)* Native American tribes have sovereignty in their own territories and make policy decisions at tribal councils like this
Navaho "summit meeting" in New Mexico, which included neighboring tribal leaders, business executives, and politicians from nearby states.

voting participation.[31] Catholics are somewhat more likely to be politically
active than Protestants. And people who live in small towns are slightly less
active than those who live in cities.

Political Participation and Public Policy

Two important pieces of information emerge from this material on political
participation: (1) the American people vary in the way they participate in political life; (2) socioeconomic status is the principal determinant of that variation. Where does that leave us?

Some have argued that the critical issue is whether everyone has the opportunity to participate. As long as the opportunity to participate is widespread, they say, individuals are free to choose whether they will participate or
not. And if policy decisions are made primarily by those who participate actively, that is all right as long as all citizens can participate when they choose.

Not everyone supports this view, however. Those who question it point
out that there is an important difference between the legal right to participate
in politics and actual possession of the skills and incentives necessary to do so.
They argue that nonparticipation is rarely just the exercise of free choice, because those who participate less are usually disadvantaged in terms of information, political skills, and political efficacy.

Variations in participation levels would be less a matter of concern were
it not for their close correlation with socioeconomic status. If participants and
nonparticipants were scattered randomly throughout the population, the actual
level of participation might not make much difference in terms of public policy.
The participants would be a representative sample of the whole population,
and presumably public officials would respond just as they would if everyone
participated. But participation patterns are not random, and the political views
of those who do participate are often quite different from the political views

of those who do not.[32] To the extent that policy decisions are a response to what public officials hear from the public, that response is skewed toward the views of those who are most likely to make themselves heard: the active participants. Thus, the haves tend to speak with a louder, steadier, and more influential voice than the have-nots, and they can perpetuate their advantage.

The policies of government result from the processes of politics. When some people participate and others do not, both process and policy are affected. The question of who participates and who does not directly and deeply affects the politics of American government.

SUMMARY

Political socialization is an ongoing process in which individuals acquire the information, beliefs, attitudes, and values that help them comprehend the workings of a political system and orient themselves within it. Through political socialization, people learn to be *citizens,* or members of a political society.

Political socialization continues throughout the life cycle. The process begins early—many second-graders already possess some knowledge about the political system. During the preadolescent period, the majority of American children develop positive feelings about their government and its leaders, feelings that play an important role in the maintenance and stability of the political system.

During adolescence, children's perceptions of the political world tend to become more sophisticated. Adolescents begin to recognize that individuals may take sides in disagreements among candidates, political parties, and interest groups. They are confronted by the need to make choices, of which the most important is the choice of a party affiliation. By the twelfth grade a majority of American adolescents have a party preference, although in recent years an increasing number have identified themselves as "independents."

Cynicism in political attitudes tends to develop in early adulthood and to increase throughout the remainder of the life cycle. The acquisition of political attitudes is further complicated by the major political events that occur during a person's lifetime.

Agents of political socialization are groups and individuals from whom citizens acquire political information and learn political attitudes and values. The family is the dominant agent of political socialization in the early years. The potential for family influence is likely to be realized only when there is a close relationship among family members, significant agreement among adults in the family on political values and attitudes, and frequent communication of those values and attitudes to the child. The development of party identification is the area in which the family has the greatest influence. With the increase in single-parent families, however, the family is becoming a less potent source of political attitudes.

Although much of a child's time is spent in school, schools do not play a significant role in political socialization. Teachers and curricula tend to reflect the prevailing values of the community in which a school is located.

When peer groups actively engage in political discussions or activities, they are likely to be very influential in shaping the political orientations of their members. The mass media, in contrast, provide political information but do not have a significant effect on political attitudes. Most people watch programs or read articles that support their existing political views, a phenomenon known as *selective perception.* Thus, for most people the mass media serve to reinforce political socialization.

Secondary groups such as professional associations and labor unions may affect an individual's political socialization if three conditions are met: (1) the individual identifies closely with the group's values; (2) those values relate directly to some aspect of politics; and (3) the group engages in promotional activities designed to inspire specific political attitudes or actions on the part of its members. Traditionally, a major impact of secondary groups has been to support and strengthen party affiliation, but this is less true today.

People vary greatly in the extent to which they participate in politics and in the types of activities in which they engage. The most common forms of political participation are campaign activity, voting, personal contacting, and cooperative activity.

Participation in political campaigns does not require skill or experience, but it does require political interest. Levels of political interest have been declining in the United States and campaign activity is a relatively rare form of political participation.

The most frequent form of political activity is voting. It is the only political activity in which many Americans participate regularly. Many people, however, do not vote, saying that they lack time, interest, or motivation or that registration requirements create an impediment.

Some citizens directly contact a political figure or public agency for the purpose of altering public policy; this may be their sole mode of political participation. Because personal contacting requires considerable knowledge and initiative, few Americans participate in this way. Citizens are much more likely to engage in cooperative activity designed to influence public policy, and organized groups are active at all levels of government.

Unconventional participation includes such activities as protest demonstrations and riots. These activities occur most often when individuals or groups do not know how to participate in conventional ways or do not believe that they will be able to influence public policy by going through conventional channels. Unconventional forms of participation may have a significant effect on public policy because of their intensity and visibility.

About one-fifth of American adults do not participate in political activities at all. Among them are the elderly, mentally incapacitated, or incarcerated; the poor; and those who believe that political life is corrupt or unfair.

Participation correlates closely with an individual's *socioeconomic status (SES),* or relative social and economic standing. The higher one's SES, the greater is the likelihood that one will participate actively in politics. People with a high level of *political efficacy*—the belief that one has the capacity to bring about a desired political result—are also more likely to participate. Other demographic factors that affect participation levels are age, race, gender, religion, and community size.

KEY TERMS AND CONCEPTS

political socialization
citizen
agents of political socialization

selective perception
secondary group
unconventional participation

socioeconomic status
political efficacy

LEARNING MORE ABOUT POLITICAL SOCIALIZATION AND PARTICIPATION

Scholarly studies

Abramson, Paul R. *Political Attitudes in America: Formation and Change.* San Francisco: Freeman, 1983. A comprehensive examination of what Americans believe and the factors that shape and alter those beliefs.

Conway, M. Margaret. *Political Participation in the United States.* 2nd ed. Washington, D.C.: Congressional Quarterly, 1991. A recent survey of scholarship on many elements of political participation.

Graber, Doris A. *Media Power in Politics.* 4th ed. Washington, D.C.: Congressional Quarterly, 1992. An overview of the character of the American mass media and their impact on political behavior and attitudes.

Greenstein, Fred I. *Children and Politics.* New Haven, Conn.: Yale University Press, 1965. An original and imaginative exploration of the ways in which children come to know and relate to the political world.

Jennings, M. Kent, and Richard G. Niemi. *The Political Character of Adolescence.* Princeton, N.J.: Princeton University Press, 1974. A richly detailed study of the critical period between childhood and adulthood when adolescents begin to develop political attitudes and skills of their own.

Newcomb, Theodore M. *Persistence and Change: Bennington College and Its Students After Twenty-five Years.* New York: Wiley, 1967. A detailed longitudinal study of attitudinal development in a single group of students both during college and in subsequent years.

Sigel, Roberta S., ed. *Political Learning in Adulthood: A Sourcebook of Theory and Research.* Chicago: University of Chicago Press, 1989. A compilation of some of the best recent research on political socialization.

Verba, Sidney, and Norman H. Nie. *Participation in America: Political Democracy and Social Equality.* Chicago: University of Chicago Press, 1987. A comparative study of impressive scope, analyzing participation patterns in the United States and abroad.

Leisure reading

Moody, Anne. *Coming of Age in Mississippi.* New York: Dell, 1992. Autobiographical writings of an African-American girl growing up in segregationist Mississippi.

Morris, Roger. *Richard Nixon: The Rise of an American Politician.* New York: Holt, 1991. A biography of the early life and initial political experiences of one of the dominant American figures of the second half of the twentieth century.

Wills, Garry. *Reagan's America.* New York: Viking Penguin, 1988. The impact of friends and events on the political development of the nation's fortieth president, which includes a chapter on the legacy of the Reagan era.

Primary sources

Greenstein, Fred I., and Nelson Polsby, eds. *Handbook of Political Science.* Reading, Mass.: Addison-Wesley, 1975. Readings on topics in political science, with excellent essays on both political socialization and political participation.

Renshon, Stanley Allen, ed. *Handbook of Political Socialization.* New York: Free Press, 1977. A set of important articles about the study and substance of political socialization.

Organizations

Committee for the Study of the American Electorate, 421 New Jersey Avenue, N.E., Washington, DC 20003; (202) 546-3221. A nonpartisan research group that studies issues involving low and declining voter turnout.

League of Women Voters of the United States, 1730 M Street, N.W., Washington, DC 20036; (202) 429-1965. A nonpartisan organization that works to increase participation in government.

Partnership for Democracy, 2335 18th Street, N.W., Washington, DC 20009; (202) 483-0030. A foundation that provides technical and financial assistance to grassroots citizen and community organizations concerned with public policy issues.

CHAPTER 7

Public

Opinion

- The nature of public opinion: characteristics and the distribution of differing opinions
- Discovering public opinion: election polls; sampling theory; dangers of polling
- Public knowledge and opinions: characteristics of public knowledge; political ideologies; democratic beliefs
- Public opinion and governance

Norma McCorvey, Gregory Lee Johnson, and Magic Johnson have aroused public opinion. Norma McCorvey and Gregory Johnson are not well known, although McCorvey might be recognized by her pseudonym, Jane Roe. Magic Johnson was a professional basketball player. Yet each of them has gained a degree of notoriety and, in doing so, affected public policy. Their actions, the events they triggered, and the public's reaction to those events illustrate many of the characteristics of American public opinion today.

McCorvey challenged Texas's restrictive abortion law in 1970. In 1973, in Roe v. Wade, *the Supreme Court invalidated that law and established standards for states that wished to limit access to abortion. Since then the American public has been divided over an issue that has had a profound impact on American politics.*

Upset with the policies of the Reagan administration and American corporations, Gregory Johnson burned an American flag in public. For this political protest, Johnson was arrested, charged, and convicted under a Texas law that made desecration of the flag a crime. When the Supreme Court reversed Johnson's conviction on the ground

In 1904, enormously popular Republican Teddy Roosevelt easily defeated Judge Alton Parker. As a hero in the battle of San Juan Hill during the Spanish-American War, Roosevelt campaigned for the Square Deal and Equality; when he urged the country to "stand pat," voters supported him. Parker chose an 82-year-old millionaire as his running mate, in an election in which nobody could have triumphed over T.R. The Equality issue was spawned when Roosevelt had dinner with Booker T. Washington, the African American educator. Also note the "rebus" pin *(bottom right)*; the candidate was so popular and famous that his name could be conveyed by a picture of a rose and the letters *VELT*.

that his actions were "expressive conduct" protected by the First Amendment, President George Bush urged Congress to initiate a constitutional amendment that would remove desecration of the flag from the protection of the First Amendment. In a poll taken after Bush made his proposal, 70 percent of Americans indicated that they favored such an amendment.[1]

Magic Johnson has AIDS. The announcement of his condition, which stunned not only the sporting world but also the general public throughout the country, focused attention on this disease, the risks of getting it, and the methods for avoiding it. Johnson's willingness to tell the public about

his infection, and the subsequent death of tennis star Arthur Ashe, who had contracted the disease through a blood transfusion, raised the public's awareness of the devastation caused by AIDS. An internationally known basketball star and the idol of many fans, Johnson was appointed by George Bush to the Presidential Commission on AIDS. His angry resignation from that commission during the 1992 presidential campaign to protest inadequate government funding to fight the disease heightened public debate over whether the government was doing enough to find causes and cures for this contemporary plague.

TOGETHER, THESE THREE CASES REVEAL A LOT about the breadth, depth, and consistency of American public opinion. Some issues, such as abortion, generate ongoing widespread interest and are extremely divisive. Others, like respect for the flag, are also emotional but generate overwhelming consensus. Still others, like AIDS, produce increasing concern as more and more people see that they too could be infected with the disease. Such concern puts pressure on the government to do more about finding a solution.

Being a public figure often involves great sacrifice. Tennis star Arthur Ashe, who acquired the AIDS virus from blood transfusions and who had been seriously ill for some time, considered his condition a private matter. When USA Today *was about to reveal his illness, however, he acknowledged having the disease and defended his right to privacy. Unlike Magic Johnson, Ashe did not become a spokesperson for AIDS prevention, but his death is a stark reminder that all are vulnerable.*

Novovitch/Liaison

In some respects these three issues are exceptional, however, precisely because they arouse such strong emotions. Most issues do not. The dominant public mood is one of apathy. As a rule, people become concerned only when an issue "hits home"—*their* home.

The extent of the public's interest and awareness, the depth of its feelings, and the level of agreement and disagreement are important for a government based on popular consent. Elected officials need to be concerned about public opinion not only for their own political survival but for the survival of the system as well. As public servants, government officials are expected to be sensitive to the needs and desires of the population and to take these needs and desires into account when making and implementing policy decisions.

Public opinion incorporates the basic values and beliefs on which the government system is predicated as well as specific preferences that get translated into public policy decisions. In this sense, public opinion is a critical component in determining what should be done, when, and how. It also provides a means of evaluating how the system is working and how government officials are performing.

What are the values, attitudes, and opinions of the American people? What policy issues do they consider most important, and how strongly do they feel about them? How can these opinions be determined? Those are the questions that need to be answered if public officials are to make responsive policy decisions.

In this chapter we examine the characteristics of public opinion and its distribution within society. We discuss how to determine public opinion through polling, what levels of information and range of attitudes and opinions people have, which aspects of public opinion are most critical to the operation of a democracy, and what impact these opinions have on the operation of politics and government.

THE NATURE OF PUBLIC OPINION

Public opinion consists of **opinions,** judgments on current issues; **attitudes,** broad orientations toward policy areas; and **values,** basic ideals and beliefs. Figure 7-1 shows this configuration for the issue of abortion. Of the three

Figure 7-1 *Public opinion on abortion.*

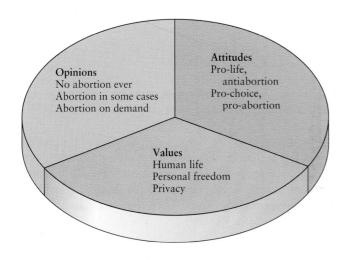

Perceptions shape reality. Images of burning oil wells, SCUD missiles against the night sky, and American soldiers in the hot desert gave Americans their picture of the Persian Gulf War. These images underscored both the vital interest of the United States in the area—oil—and the extremely harsh conditions to which ground forces were subjected.

components, opinions change most readily and values are the most stable. Values and attitudes help shape opinions. They provide a conceptual and perceptual lens through which to observe events and make judgments, and they help determine the **salience,** or importance, of issues.

Naturally, issues that touch on personal security, political equality, national security, and other core values elicit a stronger response than issues that do not. Similarly, issues that have the most direct and immediate impact tend to be more salient than issues whose effect is indirect or potential. To illustrate, in the 1980s United States policy toward Iraq was not of primary interest or concern to the American public even though the United States had tilted toward Iraq in the war between Iraq and Iran. However, after the Iraqi invasion of Kuwait in August 1991, United States policy toward Iraq became a salient issue. The perception that vital American interests were involved, the commitment of American troops to the Persian Gulf, and the outbreak of war brought the issue home to millions of Americans.

Characteristics

Policy makers commonly assess three characteristics of public opinion: direction, stability/fluidity, and intensity. **Direction** refers to the proportion of the population that holds a particular view. Evaluations of direction over time indicate the **stability** and **fluidity** of public opinion. Over the last two decades, for example, the Gallup poll has included the question "Do you think abortions should be legal under any circumstances, legal only under certain circumstances, or illegal in all circumstances?" The responses have changed very little, showing remarkable stability (see Figure 7-2A). There has been much more fluidity in the public's evaluation of the performance of individual presidents in their first year in office (see Figure 7-2B).

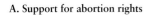

A. Support for abortion rights

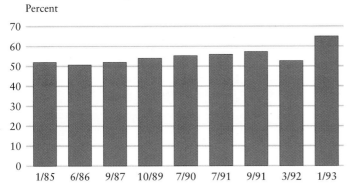

B. Approval of presidential performance

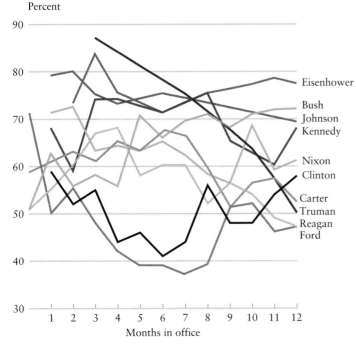

Figure 7-2   *Stability and fluidity of public opinion.* SOURCE: *For Part A:* Washington Post, *January 22, 1993, A16. © 1993 The Washington Post. Reprinted with permission. For Part B:* Public Opinion *(January–February 1989): 36; update for Gallup polls by authors. Reprinted with the permission of The American Enterprise Institute for Public Policy Research, Washington, D.C.*

Intensity refers to the depth of feelings. Since opinions are easy to express, even without much information, intensity is a good indicator of whether people will act on the basis of their opinions. Naturally, the more intense people feel about an issue, the more likely they are to do something about it. A good illustration of the impact of strong public opinion on public policy is the success experienced by opponents of gun control legislation. Despite evidence that the general public favors restrictions, opponents have blocked limits on the sale and possession of firearms. However, as proponents of gun control began to organize and reveal their strong feelings on the issue, the influence of the gun control opponents has been reduced.

Intensity is measured by asking people how strongly they feel about particular issues. Table 7-1 illustrates one response to a question designed to measure the intensity of feelings about contracting AIDS.

TABLE 7-1

Intensity of Public Opinion on AIDS *(percentage responding)*

HOW CONCERNED ARE YOU THAT YOU, YOURSELF, WILL GET AIDS?

RESPONSES	ALL AGE GROUPS	18–29 ONLY	50–64 ONLY
Very concerned?	19	28	19
A little concerned?	19	20	19
Not very concerned?	26	29	21
Not at all concerned?	36	23	41

SOURCE: Poll conducted November 16–19, 1989 by Gallup. *The Gallup Report*, November 1989, 3.

Distribution

On any issue, people with different backgrounds usually have different opinions. Table 7-2 indicates how various population groups differ on the issue of abortion. It should come as no surprise that women tend to be more supportive of the legal right to obtain an abortion in all cases than men, although it is also interesting to note that a slightly larger proportion of women also oppose legalized abortion than men. What may be more surprising in this survey is the pro-choice orientation of Catholics, in view of the church's strong opposition to abortion.

In assessing public opinion, pollsters divide the population into three broad groups based on the relative level of information that people possess: the mass public, the attentive public, and opinion makers (see Figure 7-3). The **mass public** is the largest (approximately 75 to 80 percent of the population), the least informed, and the most apathetic group most of the time.[2] It is subject to the greatest swings in mood and shifts in opinion and thus is the most easily manipulated of the three groups—at least for the short periods when its attention can be directed toward public policy issues.

The second group is the **attentive public** (approximately 15 to 20 percent of the population). Better informed and more interested than the mass public, the attentive public comprises people who have a general awareness of issues, candidates and officials, and politically relevant events. The attentive public tends to have well-developed and consistent opinions on many issues and may participate in political debates about them. Members of this group, however, tend to refrain from most political activities other than voting.

The third group consists of **opinion makers** (less than 5 percent of the population). They inform and shape the views of others. Their interest level, knowledge, and political activities set them apart. Included in this smallest group are party leaders, elected and appointed government officials, business executives, labor leaders, some members of the media, educational and religious institutions, and other active groups. The opinion makers tend to hold the most consistent political beliefs.

The opinion makers, the attentive public, and the mass public differ not only in level of information but in political attitude. Political scientist Herbert

Figure 7-3   *Distribution of public opinion.*

TABLE 7-2			

How Groups Differ on Abortion (percentage responding)

WHICH COMES CLOSEST TO YOUR POSITION? ABORTION SHOULD BE . . .

	LEGAL IN ALL CASES	LEGAL IN MOST CASES	ILLEGAL IN MOST CASES	ILLEGAL IN ALL CASES
All voters	34	30	23	9
Said it was important to their vote	34	11	27	26
Men	31	32	25	8
Women	37	28	22	10
Non-H.S. grad.	26	22	27	15
H.S. grad.	27	30	26	12
Some college	36	30	23	8
College grad.	35	31	23	7
Postgrad.[1]	43	29	20	6
White	34	30	24	9
Black	38	29	17	9
Hispanic	31	26	25	16
Asian	22	30	27	13
Married	30	30	26	10
Single	43	29	18	7
Protestant	30	31	26	9
Catholic	30	29	26	10
Jewish	62	31	5	1
Born again	13	19	41	24
Attend church weekly[2]	19	25	35	17
Democrat	40	31	17	7
Republican[3]	25	28	32	12
Independent	37	30	22	8
18–29 years[4]	41	27	21	8
30–44	34	32	23	8
45–59	31	31	26	9
60+	30	27	24	11

[1] Fifty-one percent of women with a postgraduate education compared to 36 percent of men with the same level of education said abortion should be legal in all cases.

[2] Sixty percent of those with no religion said abortion should be legal in all cases.

[3] Twenty-eight percent of GOP women compared to 23 percent of GOP men said abortion should be legal in all cases.

[4] Women in every age category under 60 were more likely than men to say abortion should be legal in all cases. Forty-four percent of 18–29-year-old women said abortion should always be legal; thirty-seven percent of 18–29-year-old men did.

SOURCE: Survey conducted on November 3, 1992, by Voter Research and Surveys for a consortium of the major news networks as appears in *American Enterprise*, Vol. 4, No. 1, January/February 1993, 103. Copyright © 1993, The American Enterprise. Distributed by The New York Times/Special Features.

McClosky found significant differences between elite and mass attitudes toward the principles and practices of democracy. Although most people value freedom of speech in the abstract, they differ about how that freedom should be applied. The elite (most of the opinion makers and some of the attentive public) express more support for individual civil liberties than the masses do.[3]

The attentive and mass publics determine the direction and intensity of public opinion on a particular issue. The opinion makers define the alternatives, the specific policies that are considered. They also affect the content of public debate. That debate, in turn, can affect the attention that issues receive and the extent to which the mass public gets involved. For example, public concern over the escalating costs of health care created a salient issue for the 1992 presidential campaign. The debate over how to control these costs, however, was structured by President Clinton's comprehensive health plan, which he introduced to Congress in the fall of 1993.

DISCOVERING PUBLIC OPINION

How do policy makers discover what people think about an issue? They observe their behavior, they monitor their communications, and they ask them questions. However, some individuals in every group are more demonstrative and outspoken than others, perhaps because of the intensity of their opinions or because of their personalities and their need to express themselves. Since it is important to determine the opinions of a range of people, not just those who are vocal, most policy makers survey the population as a whole. The most efficient way to do this is through **public opinion polls.**

Polls indicate the direction, the stability, and to some extent the intensity of public opinion prevailing at the time the poll is taken. They report which groups of people are most likely to support certain policies, be concerned about certain issues, and vote for particular candidates. Polls can also indicate which issues do not generate much public interest or awareness and thus may not have to be resolved by public officials. During an election campaign, polls provide feedback to candidates about voters' concerns, their political attitudes, and their reactions to the symbols, issues, and images that the candidates are using. Indeed, this information is now available so quickly that candidates are able to assess the damage caused by an opponent's charges almost immediately and respond to them quickly. The failure to do so can be fatal, as Democrat Michael Dukakis found out in 1988 when he failed to answer George Bush's charge that he was soft on crime, weak on defense, and out of step with basic American values. In 1992, effective polling enabled Democrat Bill Clinton to reply to his opponents' charges within 24 hours.

Polls, however, cannot predict what opinions people will hold in the future. That is why polls taken several days before an election may not accurately forecast the results of the election if a large number of voters make up or change their minds after the poll is completed. Voter preferences for Harry Truman in 1948 and Ronald Reagan in 1980 crystallized in the week before the election, confounding pollsters who had sampled opinion earlier.

Even if polls do accurately reflect public opinion, they may not measure its intensity or the extent to which people might act on the basis of it. More often than not, polls are a snapshot that policy makers may consider, rather than a detailed guide for action.

Speculating on electoral winners is an American pastime as old as elections themselves. Formal attempts to forecast elections have a shorter history. In 1824 the Harrisburg *Pennsylvanian* conducted the first "straw" poll, asking its reporters to assess public support for the four candidates seeking the presidency. The equivalent of tossing a piece of straw into the air to gauge the direction of political winds, polls survey a small group of people to determine the attitudes of the electorate as a whole.

The first prediction based on a national sample was made in 1892, when the *New York Herald* tallied polls collected by newspaper editors across the nation.[5] The largest and most comprehensive of the early national surveys were the polls conducted by *Literary Digest,* a popular monthly magazine. The *Digest* mailed millions of ballots and questionnaires to people whose names appeared on lists of automobile owners and in telephone directories. In 1924, 1928, and 1932, the *Literary Digest* poll correctly predicted the winner of the presidential election; in 1936, however, it did not. That year the poll forecast a huge victory for Republican candidate Alf Landon. Instead, Democratic incumbent Franklin Roosevelt won over 60 percent of the popular vote and swept all but two states.

What went wrong? The major flaw was that those who returned the ballots and questionnaires did not represent the electorate at large. In 1936 automobile owners and telephone subscribers simply were not typical voters. Cars and phones were upper-class luxuries during the Depression, and the upper class was decidedly more Republican than the electorate as a whole.

While the *Digest* was tabulating its 2 million responses and predicting a Landon victory, a number of other pollsters were conducting more scientific surveys and correctly forecasting Roosevelt's reelection. The national polls of George Gallup and Elmo Roper differed from the *Digest* poll in two principal respects: they were considerably smaller, and they tried to approximate the characteristics of the entire population in their **sample**—that is, the portion of the population whose opinions were assessed.

As Gallup, Roper, and other pollsters refined their sampling techniques and established a record for accuracy, public confidence in election polling began to grow. That confidence was shattered in 1948, however, when the major pollsters forecast a victory for Republican candidate Thomas Dewey over Democratic incumbent Harry Truman. With Dewey leading by a substantial margin, the pollsters stopped conducting surveys several weeks before the election. Undecided voters, the pollsters reasoned, would cast their votes along the same lines as those who had already decided. In fact, of the late deciders, who made up 14 percent of the electorate, three-fourths voted for Truman.[6]

Pollsters were surprised again in 1980, when they correctly forecast a win for Republican Ronald Reagan but vastly underestimated the size of his victory. With their final surveys completed four days before the election, most national polling organizations did not detect a late surge of support for Reagan. By interviewing until the eve of the election, pollsters working for both Republican and Democratic candidates discovered the Reagan surge and therefore provided a more accurate forecast of the magnitude of his win.

The forecasting errors of 1948 and the underestimates of 1980 emphasize a principal limitation of polls mentioned earlier: they reflect opinion at the time the survey is taken but cannot anticipate future opinions. The closer to election

George Gallup: Polling Public Opinion

The modern science of opinion polling reaches back to the 1920s and the pioneering work of George Gallup (1901–1984). In 1928, Gallup earned a Ph.D. at the University of Iowa. In his doctoral dissertation, he designed a method of gauging public opinion using scientifically selected samples. Gallup showed that many polls then in existence inadvertently introduced distortions and bias by the way they selected respondents. He argued, however, that accurate, unbiased samples were possible using statistical analysis. In other words, the responses of a few thousand randomly chosen respondents would accurately represent the views of the entire population. Putting theory into practice, Gallup founded the American Institute of Public Opinion in 1935 to provide polls commercially.

At first, Gallup's work was viewed with considerable skepticism even after he predicted the results of the 1934 congressional elections to within one percentage point. Two years later, Gallup correctly predicted the results of the 1936 presidential election between Republican Alf Landon and Democrat Franklin Roosevelt, while those who conducted larger but less scientific surveys did not. Gallup's success demonstrated the value of surveys that randomly select their respondents.

The results of the 1936 election gave scientific polling techniques far greater credibility. Soon politicians were regularly commissioning polls to gauge public opinion on the issues and the candidates. Business also began to rely on polls as the basic framework of the new science of market research.

The hard-won acceptance of opinion polling suffered a major setback in the presidential election of 1948 when Gallup, along with most other pollsters, incorrectly predicted that Republican Thomas E. Dewey, who was leading in the polls, would be elected. By concluding their polls ten days before the election, they failed to detect the late surge for Democrat Harry Truman, who eventually won a decisive victory. For months following this embarrassing faux pas, Gallup received letters addressed to "Mr. Wrong." But he and others recovered from their

Library of Congress

George Gallup was an early successful practitioner of polling, the art now so potent that it shapes policy agendas for presidents. Early surveys took days to tally, with responses punched on cards which were then machine-sorted. Today samples are chosen and responses are analyzed almost instantaneously. A president can discover what the public thought of his speech the previous night while he drinks his morning coffee.

mistake and have enjoyed an excellent record ever since. Today, polling is so widely used and apparently so accurate that it sometimes seems to substitute for the elections themselves.

Fifty years of polling millions of Americans taught George Gallup three lessons, he said: (1) the collective judgment of the American people is sound; (2) the public will make great sacrifices for the national good in times of crisis; and (3) the will of the people sooner or later becomes law.

SOURCES: *The Gallup Report*, 241, October 1985; *New York Times*, obituary, July 28, 1984; Richard Reeves, "George Gallup's Nation of Numbers," *Esquire*, December 1983.

St. Louis Mercantile Library

The night of the 1948 election, early returns from the Northeast showed Republican Thomas E. Dewey in the lead. The polls had forecast a Dewey victory, and the Chicago Tribune, *which had endorsed Dewey, published its first edition under the headline that he had won. The morning after the election, President Truman happily showed off the* Tribune's *mistake during his victory speech.*

day a poll is taken, the more accurate it is likely to be. However, the weakening of voters' ties to political parties and the inability to correctly predict who will actually vote have also impeded the accuracy of election forecasts. A good example of this problem occurred in 1992 when one poll conducted for Cable News Network (CNN) and *U.S.A. Today* indicated that the election would be a toss-up; most others showed a substantial Clinton lead. The discrepancy resulted from differing judgments over who would vote.

Pollsters have responded to the challenge of voter indecision and volatility with improved surveying techniques that produce more consistently accurate results. Between 1936 and 1950, for example, the average error of the final Gallup poll was 3.6 percent. Between 1952 and 1960 the average error fell to 1.7 percent; between 1962 and 1970 it declined to 1.6 percent; and between 1972 and 1992 it decreased even further, to 1.4 percent.[7] How have these improvements in accuracy been achieved?

Sampling Theory

The main reason that polls have become increasingly accurate is improvements in the methods used to choose the sample. Since the objective of surveying is to generalize from a small number of people to the population as a whole, it is essential that the people interviewed be representative of that population. The odds of the sample being representative can be estimated when the sample is chosen through random selection techniques.

Random selection simply means that every element in the population (in this case, the eligible electorate) has an equal chance of being included in the sample, and the choice of any one element would not preclude the choice of any other. The *Literary Digest* sample of 1936 was not random. There was no way to determine whether the people interviewed were typical, and as it turned out they were not.

Since sampling is based on a mathematical theory of probability, the odds of being right or of being wrong can be calculated. In a random sample, these odds are determined primarily by the size of the sample, not by the size of the population being sampled. Naturally, the more the sample approximates the size of the population, the more likely it is to be accurate and the more confidence can be placed in the results of the survey. The way to increase the accuracy of a sample, therefore, is to enlarge it. However, enlarging it adds to the costs of the survey. At some point a law of diminishing returns sets in: the gain in accuracy is small, but the increase in costs is considerable.

In assessing the results of a random sample, two factors must be considered: sampling error and level of confidence. **Sampling error** refers to the degree to which the sample could deviate from the population as a whole. Thus, if a poll with a sampling error of ± 3 reported that 50 percent of those surveyed thought the president was doing a good job, poll takers could generalize that anywhere from 47 to 53 percent of the whole population held that opinion.

Even within the range of sampling error, however, there is always a chance that the results of the sample could be incorrect; the smaller that chance, the greater is the confidence that one would have in the results. Most national surveys are based on a **level of confidence** of 95 percent, meaning that nineteen times out of twenty the results of the sample are probably within the range of its sampling error.

Dangers of Polling

Public opinion polls can provide a wealth of information—information that has immense value for candidates and public officials as well as for private groups that wish to influence government policy. Anyone who bases decisions on the results of polls, however, should be aware of their limitations. In addition to the possibility of making incorrect assumptions or having a sampling error, polls are timebound and opinions can change. Polls may also present an inaccurate picture because of the way their questions are worded, the way surveys are constructed, or the way responses are interpreted.

Bias can be introduced by using emotional or controversial words. For example, terms such as *pro-choice, baby-killing, rape,* or *incest* in a question about abortion affect the response. So do phrases like "don't you believe?," "isn't it true?," and "most people believe, don't you?" In surveys conducted during the Persian Gulf War, for example, slight changes in wording produced large differences in responses. Take the two questions in Table 7-3, which were asked in national surveys during the same time period. The insertion of the words "President Bush's decision" plus a few minor changes in terminology seemed to affect over 10 percent of the responses.

There are other dangers. Questions of the agree/disagree variety may be biased toward the "agree" response. The choice of closed- or open-ended questions also may affect the kinds of responses obtained. **Closed-ended questions** force a person to choose among a list of responses. **Open-ended questions** have no predetermined answer. Responses to closed-ended questions can be categorized and analyzed more easily than open-ended responses. Such questions, however, lead people to express opinions on issues about which they have little

T A B L E 7 - 3			
Approval of the Deployment of United States Troops to Saudi Arabia (percentage responding)			
	APPROVE	DISAPPROVE	DON'T KNOW
Do you approve or disapprove of the United States sending troops to Saudi Arabia to protect Saudi Arabia from Iraq? (*New York Times*, August 9–10, 1990)	66	28	6
Do you approve or disapprove of President Bush's decision to send troops to help defend Saudi Arabia? (Gallup, August 9–12, 1990)	78	17	6

or no information, or do not feel strongly about, or they may force responses into categories that do not accurately reflect people's opinion.

The order in which questions are asked also can affect the responses people give. Information included in the early questions may be used to answer later questions. Similarly, answers to the initial questions might affect answers to later questions, particularly if people try to be consistent in their answers. For example, both the Gallup poll and the *New York Times*/CBS News poll wanted to determine how voters perceived George Bush and Bill Clinton in the summer of 1992 (see Table 7-4). Gallup asked people simply if their opinion of each of these candidates was favorable or unfavorable; the *New York Times*/CBS News poll gave people two additional options; the poll allowed them to indicate whether they were undecided or hadn't heard enough about the candidates to make a judgment. The favorable rating of the candidates differed significantly in these two polls, which were conducted at approximately the same time. That difference can be attributed, in large part, to the format of the questions.

T A B L E 7 - 4				
Two Surveys of Voter Perceptions (percentage responding)				
GALLUP POLL			*NEW YORK TIMES*/CBS NEWS	
BUSH	CLINTON		BUSH	CLINTON
		RESPONSES		
40	63	Favorable	27	36
53	25	Unfavorable	49	24
—	—	Undecided	22	31
—	—	Haven't heard enough	2	9
7	12	Don't know	—	—
—	—	No answer	1	1

SOURCE: "Some Pitfalls in Polling," *New York Times*, August 9, 1992, E5. Copyright © 1992 by The New York Times Company. Reprinted by permission.

The interview itself can affect the response. An interviewer who develops rapport with the *respondent* (the person being interviewed) may be able to elicit more information than can be obtained from an impersonal questionnaire. But personal interviews also tend to generate socially desirable responses. A good illustration of this tendency can be seen in the poll taken at the voting precincts during the 1989 Virginia gubernatorial election. The number of people who told pollsters that they had cast their ballots for Democrat Douglas Wilder, an African American, was much higher than the number who said that they had voted for his white Republican opponent, Marshall Coleman. When the results of the election were tallied, however, the vote was much closer than the poll indicated it would be. The same phenomenon occurred during the nonpartisan primary in Louisiana in 1991. The number of people who voted for David Duke, a former Grand Dragon of the Ku Klux Klan and supporter of Nazi ideology, was much higher than the number who indicated they would do so in polls taken before the election.

There are other examples of this tendency. More people regularly tell pollsters that they have voted than actually have; more say that they have voted for the winner than actually have. To achieve a more accurate forecast of votes or more accurate information about other personal matters (such as income), pollsters usually use written ballots or questionnaires, which people are asked to complete and deposit in a closed container. Under these conditions, even the interviewer does not know their response.

Error can also be introduced by the way survey results are interpreted. In the early preelection polls in which respondents are asked to indicate their

Michael P. Smith/SYGMA

Social and political acceptability are essential for election to office. David Duke transformed himself from Nazi sympathizer (left) and Grand Dragon of the Ku Klux Klan to candidate for governor of Louisiana in 1991 (right). Yet his past continues to haunt him: he did not receive enough votes to make the run-off election for governor.

© Lee Corkran/SYGMA

preferences for candidates, the people who tend to do best in these surveys are those who are best known, not necessarily those who are the most electable. Senator Gary Hart led all other Democratic presidential candidates in the December 1987 preelection poll in Iowa, even though he had only recently reentered the race after withdrawing in May following allegations of adultery. In the caucus election one month later, he finished in fifth place. The Hart example suggests that the interpretation of polls, and the prognoses that often follow from them, must be made with great care.

People should keep the following guidelines in mind when interpreting poll results:

1. Check the sampling error. If the margin for error exceeds the margin separating two responses, one response cannot be interpreted as more probable than the other. For example, if the random sampling error is ±4 percent and candidate A leads candidate B by 2 percent (say, 51 to 49), the contest is too close to call.

2. Determine whether the group sponsoring or conducting the poll has a vested interest in the results. Treat skeptically any findings disclosed by candidates, their organizations, and their supporters.

3. Examine the survey questions. Do the questions measure what the pollsters claim they do? Remember that the wording of the questions, their placement in the survey, and the responses permitted can all affect the results. Be sensitive to any positively or negatively valued buzzwords, symbols, goals, or names of individuals that may influence responses.

4. Check the time frame during which the poll was conducted. Have any events that might change respondents' opinions occurred between the time the poll was taken and the day the results were published? A new candidate entering a campaign, for example, can affect the distribution of support among the other candidates.

5. Remember that random selection is the key to sampling accuracy. The results of surveys that do not use a random sample may be interesting or provocative, but they cannot be considered representative of the population as a whole. With this in mind, discount polls, popular with some local media, that require respondents to telephone or mail in their responses. Such surveys usually only measure the preferences of people who are concerned enough to take the time and initiative to respond.

PUBLIC KNOWLEDGE AND OPINIONS: WHO KNOWS WHAT?

The political opinions of the majority of the public rest on an extremely limited information base. Why are some people more informed, interested, and involved in political life than others? Why do some have more consistent political beliefs, look to government for solutions to problems, and show greater tolerance of minority rights? The answer has a lot to do with their education, their ideology, and their understanding of democracy.

Characteristics of Public Knowledge

Lack of information   Survey after survey conducted during the past thirty years has shown that the public is poorly informed about government officials and political issues. Not only do Americans know little about specific issues, but most people would be hard-pressed to name their representatives in the national and state legislatures, much less recall their representatives' performance in office unless they have been involved in a scandal or have abused their position. Knowledge about characters in popular television series tends to be greater than knowledge about most public officials, even high-ranking ones.

To illustrate this point, the *Washington Post* conducted a survey at the end of the 1988–1989 Supreme Court term, one of the most contentious in recent history. The results of the survey indicated that more people knew the name of the judge on a popular soap opera than the name of the chief justice of the Supreme Court. Is it any wonder that name recognition is usually the first and most important objective of candidates at the beginning of an election campaign?

Education seems to be the key variable in determining which people are informed and how much information they possess. Those with higher levels of formal education tend to be better informed. The educational process develops the intellectual tools with which to perceive and judge information about political issues. Also, the more education people have, the more likely they are to have absorbed the values of intellectual curiosity associated with education, as well as the motivation to increase their knowledge.

Not only higher levels of education but also higher income is associated with greater political information. The relationship between income and information can be attributed in part to the demands of a professional or business life, which requires that one be aware of what is going on in the political arena. The relationship may also be due to efforts to protect one's income or profession from those who might threaten it. In addition, education and income tend to be associated with each other. Better-educated people tend to make more money, and those who make more money tend to be the better educated.

Age is also strongly associated with a person's level of information on political issues. As people get older, as they develop greater stakes in their community and profession, they become more aware of the effects of political decisions on their lives and well-being. As the number of government policies affecting senior citizens increases, older people have an incentive to remain informed and involved.

What implications does the low level of information have for the politics of government? It gives government leaders more initial discretion in making policy decisions. With less direction from the public, they have more flexibility to fashion a solution. This is particularly evident in foreign affairs and in complex technological issues such as nuclear energy, information technology, and biomedical research.

Although political leaders tend to have more flexibility when the public is less informed, they do not have a blank check. Policies that lie outside the range of what is considered acceptable, policies that clash with the values, mores, or basic beliefs of the society, and policies that cannot be supported by government revenues cannot be pursued. For example, few have considered a national health system run by the government, often referred to as "socialized medicine," to be a viable solution to the health-care problems in the United

States, even though it has been utilized in other Western democracies such as Canada, Sweden, and Great Britain.

Another consequence of limited public knowledge is that it tends to encourage short-term solutions. Not understanding the complexity of issues and impatient to see results, the public expects and demands results here and now. These demands are quickly converted into political pressure on government officials for quick fixes rather than longer-term solutions.

A third implication of the low level of public information is that it seems to increase the power of interest groups and their leaders. When many people are uninformed and uninterested, opinion leaders, particularly those who represent large and powerful groups, exercise more clout. A poorly informed public is easier to manipulate.

Ambivalence The consistency with which beliefs and opinions are held varies. People are often ambivalent about issues—they seem to talk out of both sides of their mouths. Surveys of public opinion indicate that Americans want to protect and preserve their interests around the world but shy away from involving United States forces in that effort; they want to help those who cannot help themselves but are opposed to most government-run welfare programs at home or extensive foreign aid abroad; they believe in the sanctity of human life as well as the right of individual choice.

This ambivalence stems in part from clashing values. Americans cherish numerous values such as liberty, equality, and opportunity. Unless they are able to order these values in terms of their relative importance, conflicts are likely to develop and persist.

One way to resolve such conflicts is to adopt a **belief system**, a set of related ideas that helps people understand and cope with the world around them and that also provides guidelines for behavior. A religion, such as Christianity, Islam, or Judaism, is one example of a belief system. An ideology, such as communism or capitalism, is another.

Frequently, however, people do not accept all the tenets of a belief system, and they may adhere to religious, political, and economic belief systems that are not logically congruent, that do not easily mesh with one another. That is why public opinion frequently lacks consistency.

Education is a key variable in determining the consistency of someone's beliefs. People with more education tend to be more consistent in the political positions they take and the political beliefs they hold and express. Education not only increases their awareness of issues but gives them the skills to think logically and spot inconsistencies in their beliefs.

Diversity In addition to low levels of information and ambiguous attitudes, public opinion in the United States is also diverse. That diversity reflects the heterogeneity of the population—its various subcultures, races, and education and income levels. Table 7-5 illustrates these differences in opinion on a number of contemporary issues. The table, which indicates the percentage of people who agree with each statement, reveals both similarities and differences in the opinions of those in the five demographic groups being examined. Notice that education and income often vary directly with each other, and that significant generational differences exist between those in the youngest and oldest age groups on several issues. It is also interesting that opinion differences between the races tend to be greater than differences between the genders, although the latter do seem to be increasing.

Diversity of Public Opinion, 1992 (percentage agreeing)

ISSUES*	GENDER		RACE		AGE			
	MALE	FEMALE	WHITE	NONWHITE	18–29	30–49	50–64	65 +
1. Women and men should have equal roles.	75	75	75	73	83	79	69	62
2. The Gulf War was worth it.	65	47	59	36	49	58	58	53
3. The death penalty should be abolished.	14	24	16	38	20	20	17	18
4. Government should see to it that people have good jobs and an acceptable standard of living.	26	34	26	50	40	30	25	25
5. Government should improve the social and economic conditions of African Americans.	21	24	19	40	27	23	22	18
6. Government should provide fewer services to reduce government spending.	38	26	33	18	24	33	34	33

* The questions put for each issue were these:

1. Recently there has been a lot of talk about women's rights. Some people feel that women should have an equal role with men in running business, industry, and government. . . . Others feel that a woman's place is in the home. . . . Where would you place yourself on this scale (1 . . . 7) or haven't you thought much about this?

2. All things considered, do you think that the [Gulf] War [in 1991] was worth the cost or not?

3. Do you favor or oppose the death penalty for persons convicted of murder?

4. Some people feel the government in Washington should see to it that every person has a job and a good standard of living. Others think the government should just let each person get ahead on his or her own. Where would you place yourself on this scale (1 . . . 7) or haven't you thought much about it?

The ambivalence and contradictions in people's attitudes and opinions can be very frustrating for policy makers who look to public opinion for guidance. What should public officials do when people demand a balanced budget and more government services but oppose the taxes that are necessary to pay for this level of government activity? Inconsistent public attitudes, however, do give public officials considerable discretion in designing the specifics of policy decisions.

Political Ideologies

To illustrate the power of belief systems, we turn to the subject of political ideologies. A **political ideology** is a set of interrelated attitudes that shape judgments about and reactions to political issues. Ideologies provide a general orientation toward the political system, a perceptual lens with which to view and evaluate events.

ISSUES*	EDUCATION				INCOME			
	DROP-OUT	HIGH SCHOOL	SOME COLLEGE	COLLEGE GRAD.	UNDER $15,000	$15,000–$25,000	$25,000–$49,000	$50,000+
1. Women and men should have equal roles.	62	74	82	83	69	75	75	81
2. The Gulf War was worth it.	48	55	57	61	43	52	62	64
3. The death penalty should be abolished.	23	17	16	25	26	21	17	14
4. Government should see to it that people have good jobs and an acceptable standard of living.	43	29	26	27	40	33	30	18
5. Government should improve the social and economic conditions of African Americans.	25	13	20	31	29	18	22	20
6. Government should provide fewer services to reduce government spending.	25	28	26	42	22	27	33	40

5. Some people feel that the government in Washington should make every effort to improve the social and economic position of African Americans. Others feel that the government should not make any special effort to help African Americans because they should help themselves. Where would you place yourself on this scale (1 . . . 7), or haven't you thought much about this?

6. Do you think government should provide child-care assistance to low- and middle-income working parents, or isn't it the government's business?

SOURCE: The American National Election Studies, conducted by the University of Michigan, Center for Political Studies, Ann Arbor, Michigan. Data provided by the Inter-University Consortium for Political and Social Research, located at the University of Michigan, Center for Political Studies, Ann Arbor, Michigan.

In the United States the two dominant political ideologies are **liberalism** and **conservatism.** Perhaps no two words in the English language have been used more often, and with less consistency in meaning, than *liberal* and *conservative*. What do these terms mean today?

During the Great Depression of the 1930s, when Franklin Roosevelt's administration decided to use the government as a massive force to restore the health of the economy, deep divisions between those who supported and opposed the president's proposals emerged within American society. The term *liberal* came to refer to those who favored the substance of Roosevelt's New Deal program: government intervention in the economy, government programs to aid the poor, and government support for the rights of workers to unionize and to better their economic conditions. More recently, liberals have also supported government intervention to protect civil rights and promote equal opportunity for minorities who have not been afforded the same privileges and opportunities as the majority. Liberals have tended to oppose government actions that threaten to deprive individuals of basic personal and political freedoms, particularly the freedom to deviate from social norms and to oppose government policies.

In general, liberals have subscribed to a literal reading of the First Amendment, which states that Congress shall pass no law (and, by implication, the executive shall issue no regulation) that abridges freedom of speech, press, and religion and the right of people to assemble peaceably and "petition the government for a redress of grievances." Liberals' desire for greater social equality and personal freedom extends to foreign policy as well. Liberals tend to favor policies of accommodation, reject war as an instrument of diplomacy, and support programs designed to help the economically and politically deprived.

Conservatives have tended to fear government involvement *more* in the economic sphere, particularly where such involvement places restrictions on the free-enterprise system, and *less* in the social realm, particularly in matters of law and order where individual behavior is constrained. Conservatives have usually voiced opposition to increased taxation, especially as a device to redistribute wealth. As proponents of private enterprise, conservatives prefer to keep capital in the hands of individuals and nongovernment groups, to be spent and invested as they see fit. They contend that a vigorous economy will generate solutions to many of the country's social ills.

Conservatives accept the notion of individual liberties, although they are less likely than liberals to permit behavior that deviates from social norms and community standards. They see the need for an ordered and stable society in which property is protected and entrepreneurship encouraged, and they contend that the government has a major responsibility for providing that protection as well as protection against external threats to the national interests and security of the United States. Since World War II, conservatives have generally supported a foreign policy based on military strength and the extension of aid, primarily military, to governments that are politically allied with the United States and in a position to strengthen American geopolitical interests.

Compared to liberals, conservatives seem to be more satisfied with the status quo, more willing to accept economic and social inequalities as natural consequences of the human condition, and more resistant to large-scale social change. Liberals, in contrast, believe that the government can and should be used as a powerful force in achieving greater social and political equality and greater economic opportunity for all.

Do people actually think along these ideological lines? Do they use liberalism and conservatism as a basis for formulating opinions and making decisions? The evidence suggests that they do. It also suggests that the more information people have, the more likely they are to maintain views on policy issues that are consistent with their ideological orientation.

Although that orientation does not dictate issue positions for most people, it is a useful device for self-identification and for explaining and even rationalizing policy positions and candidate preferences. But whether ideology is the principal reason for forming an opinion, taking a position, or arriving at a political judgment remains difficult to say. Studies conducted during the 1950s found little data to support the proposition that ideology affects voting for most Americans.[8] Studies conducted during the 1960s found some support for this proposition, with more than twice as many people explaining their voting choices in ideological terms in 1964 and 1968 than in 1956.[9] Ideological awareness has continued to grow. In recent presidential elections there has been a strong association between ideological self-identification and voting, although there is little evidence that ideology itself causes people to vote as they do.[10] Figure 7-4 identifies patterns of ideological self-identification from 1972 to 1993. Note the impact of the early Reagan years in which the proportion of conservatives increased and that of liberals declined. The gap between conservatives and liberals has declined substantially in recent years.

Who are the liberals and conservatives in the American electorate? Political scientists assembled an array of demographic statistics to describe individuals who fit into these categories in 1982 and 1992 (see Table 7-6). The data indicate that men are more conservative than women, nonwhites are more conservative than whites, and older Americans are more conservative than younger people. Other research has found that the higher the education level, the greater the tendency, and probably the ability, to think in ideological terms.[11]

The ideological orientation of the American electorate has had an impact on partisan politics. As Table 7-6 indicates, conservatives tend to ally themselves with the Republican party and liberals with the Democratic party. Ideology has also affected policy making. Problems that are defined in ideological terms tend to be more difficult to resolve. Ideologues are not good compromisers.

Although there was some shifting in the ideological orientation of the American polity in the 1980s, there was no ideological revolution. The proportion of conservatives grew, but the dominant orientation remained moderate. The American people continue to display considerable latitude in the application of their political views to the issues of the day. That is why American politics is characterized more by pragmatism than by ideology.

Associated with shifting patterns in ideological identification have been changes in public attitudes on some major economic and social issues. During the early 1980s the public showed less support for large-scale government programs than it had during the previous two decades. Cynicism toward big government, and particularly toward government-run services such as the postal service, the internal revenue service, and the immigration service, has continued, as have persistent complaints about endless government regulations and paperwork. Within the social sphere, Americans, particularly young Americans,

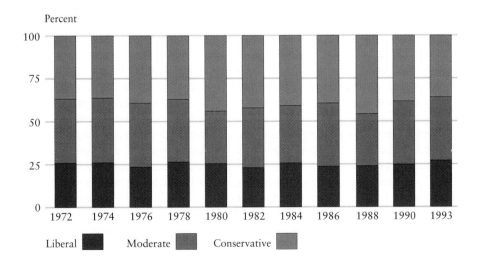

Figure 7-4 *Percentage of Americans identifying themselves as liberal, moderate, or conservative, 1972–1993.* SOURCE: *Analysis based on data from the American National Election Studies, conducted by the University of Michigan, Center for Political Studies, Ann Arbor, Michigan. Data provided by the Inter-University Consortium for Political and Social Research, located at the University of Michigan, Center for Political Studies, Ann Arbor, Michigan; and National Opinion Research Center, general social surveys, for 1993.*

	TABLE 7-6					
	Political Ideologies: Who Has Them? (percentage agreeing)					
	LIBERAL		MODERATE		CONSERVATIVE	
	1982	1992	1982	1992	1982	1992
Sex						
Male	30	26	37	29	33	45
Female	29	30	42	34	29	37
Age						
18–29	31	32	43	35	26	33
30–49	35	32	36	26	29	43
50–64	23	21	44	33	33	46
65 and up	24	19	38	40	38	41
Race						
White	42	27	35	31	23	43
Nonwhite	25	36	42	37	34	28
Party						
Democrat	35	44	40	32	25	24
Republican	17	8	37	27	46	66
Independent	31	28	49	35	20	38

SOURCE: The American National Election Studies, conducted by the University of Michigan, Center for Political Studies, Ann Arbor, Michigan. Data provided by the Inter-University Consortium for Political and Social Research, located at the University of Michigan, Center for Political Studies, Ann Arbor, Michigan.

have become more tolerant of certain kinds of behavior, such as personal living styles, than they were in the past. But they are also more supportive of harsh penalties, the death penalty, for example, for those who commit heinous crimes.

Democratic Beliefs

In addition to their varying levels of knowledge and differing ideological perspectives, Americans hold a range of attitudes toward government, society, and the interaction between the two. These attitudes condition the kinds of issues public officials must consider and the range of options they can employ in dealing with them. Those attitudes have an impact in five areas that are critical to the operation of a democracy: the role of government, trust in public officials, political efficacy, support for democratic processes, and tolerance of others.

The role of government What do the American people see as the proper role of government? In the economic realm, support for government intervention to promote employment, control inflation, and foster growth has remained fairly consistent since the Great Depression. However, there has been disagreement over how much the government should be involved in the economy, and what its legitimate functions should be. This disagreement is often couched in partisan and ideological terms, with Democrats and liberals supporting a larger government role than Republicans and conservatives.

In the realm of social issues, attitudes do not fit neatly into partisan categories, although they do divide along ideological lines. Liberals in general, and racial and ethnic minorities in particular, favor a more vigorous government role—promoting racial integration, voting rights, and affirmative action programs—than do conservatives and majority racial and ethnic groups. On issues where moral judgments come into play—pornography, obscenity, homosexual behavior, abortion—there also tends to be a liberal-conservative cleavage, with conservatives inclining toward more government intervention than liberals.

Abortion is a particularly divisive social issue (see the Case Study, page 228). Recent surveys indicate that age, education, and religion are the most important factors in explaining public attitudes on abortion. As a general rule, young people and those with more formal education favor the pro-choice position of legalized abortion in all cases more than do older people and those with lower educational levels. Jews are more sympathetic to abortion than Catholics, although Catholics tend to support the pro-choice position of legal abortion in all or most cases almost as often as Protestants do. Among all age groups, those with higher educational levels are more likely to support the legal right to have an abortion (see Table 7-2, page 211).

Trust in public officials The question of what the government should do in certain policy areas becomes meaningless unless citizens can trust public officials to mean what they say, say what they mean, and do what they promise. Without trust, no government can operate successfully; without trust, the motives of public officials will always be suspect and their actions subject to misunderstanding and misinterpretation.

In the early 1970s, President Richard Nixon lost the trust of the American people when he attempted to cover up the involvement of his White House staff in the burglary of the Democratic National Committee at the Watergate office building. As a result, his power declined, and he lost the ability to govern effectively.

Watergate was one of a series of events, including the Vietnam War, that resulted in a steady decline of trust in the United States government in the 1960s and 1970s. As the economy improved in the early 1980s, trust in government

J.P. Laffonte/SYGMA

Trust in government has declined significantly since the 1960s. Public dissatisfaction with the Vietnam War and with the Watergate cover-up prevented President Johnson from running for reelection in 1968 and forced President Nixon from office. Here Nixon waves good-bye to his staff after resigning under threat of impeachment in 1973. Nixon's legacy of suspicion and distrust in the presidency has been difficult for his successors to overcome.

In recent years no issue has galvanized the American public more than abortion. Two groups, described as pro-life and pro-choice, have been pictured as locked in mortal combat for the hearts and minds of the American people. These groups have in fact struggled, but the cleavage between them is far greater than the divisions among the population as a whole.

The surprising fact about the distribution of opinions on the abortion issue is that it is not much different from the distribution of opinions on most other issues. The majority of people have opinions on the issue that are somewhere between making abortion legal in all cases or illegal in all cases. They favor legal abortion under some conditions but not others. And the conditions vary. Surveys taken by the *Washington Post* in March of 1992 and January of 1993 reveal the range of opinions. The surveys indicate the percentage of people who believe abortion should be legal:

	3/31/92	1/17/93
When the woman's life is endangered	87	91
When the pregnancy is a result of rape or incest	79	86
When there is a chance the baby will be born deformed	63	73
When the woman may suffer severe physical health damage	80	86
When the woman's mental health is endangered	70	79
If the parents don't want another child	32	45
If the family can not afford to have the child	39	49

Given the results of these and other national surveys, why has the issue been presented in such stark terms as pro-choice or pro-life? Part of the answer may have to do with the polls themselves. Polls that have room for only one question on an issue and permit only two or three responses to it are not likely to measure gradations in public attitudes and opinions. By forcing people to choose between sides, they present the issue as a struggle between extremes.

Discussion questions

1. Do surveys on the abortion issue suggest that most Americans hold moderate or extreme positions on this issue?
2. Do most surveys, including the one that appears in this case study, measure how strongly people feel about issues?
3. What kind of guidance (if any) do these surveys provide to those charged with making public policy decisions?
4. What are some of the hazards in using surveys to gauge public opinion and make public policy?

SOURCE: Survey data from the *Washington Post*–ABC News Poll, as reported in *The Washington Post*, January 22, 1993, A16. © 1993 The Washington Post. Reprinted with permission.

increased, but as Figure 7-5 shows, it leveled off by the middle of the decade and by the 1990s (with the exception of the period immediately following the Persian Gulf War) was on the decline once again as the economy fell into a recession in 1991 and 1992. A series of incidents involving members of Congress and executive branch officials abusing the perquisites of their office further eroded Americans' trust of those in power.

People tend to be less willing to give government officials leeway in developing policy if they have little trust in the ability of those officials to find acceptable solutions. A decline in trust also shortens the length of time the public is willing to wait for results. It increases cynicism and discourages the participation in the political process that is so important in a democracy.

Levels of trust are not uniform throughout the population. Young people traditionally exhibit more trust in government than their elders do. Although political trust among young people declined during the late 1960s and early 1970s, by the mid-1970s young people were again the most trusting of any age group, and they have remained so since that time. Political trust is also generally greater among people with higher education. White college graduates have generally been more trusting than whites with lower levels of education. In contrast, African-American college graduates have been less trusting than African Americans who do not have a college education.

Trust also varies among racial groups, largely in response to their ability to identify with a particular president and his policies. For example, trust in government among African Americans rose during the early 1960s but declined after Nixon became president in 1969. Conversely, when Jimmy Carter became president, African Americans' trust in government increased while levels of trust among whites continued to decline. Political trust among whites declined steadily from 1958 until 1980, rose slightly during the Reagan presidency, and has declined since 1991.

Political efficacy For civic responsibility to be taken seriously, citizens must believe that they can make a difference, that they can bring about a desired political outcome. This belief is known as **political efficacy** (see Chapter 6). Like trust, political efficacy has declined. Evidence of this trend can be seen in decreasing levels of voter turnout through the 1980s.[12] In the 1960s, a little over 60 percent of the eligible population voted; in the 1970s and 1980s, that percentage declined. Barely more than half of the electorate voted in the 1988

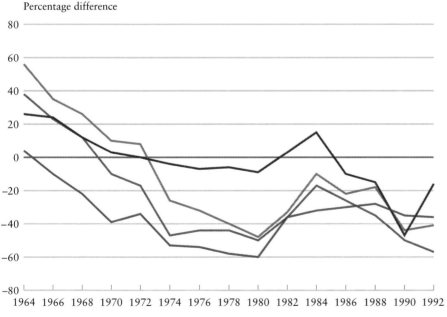

Percentage difference

Government benefits all —— Can trust government ——
Politicians care —— Tax money wasted ——

Figure 7-5 *Trust in government, 1964–1992.* SOURCE: *Analysis based on data from the American National Election Studies, conducted by the University of Michigan, Center for Political Studies, Ann Arbor, Michigan. Data provided by the Inter-University Consortium for Political and Social Research, located at the University of Michigan, Center for Political Studies, Ann Arbor, Michigan.*

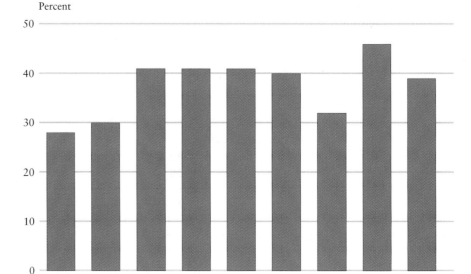

Percent

Figure 7-6 *Political effi-cacy.* SOURCE: *Data from the American National Election Studies, conducted by the University of Michigan, Center for Political Studies, Ann Arbor, Michigan. Data provided by the Inter-University Consortium for Political and Social Research, located at the University of Michigan, Center for Political Studies, Ann Arbor, Michigan.*

presidential election, although turnout did increase to 55 percent in 1992. Even so, a sizable proportion of American voters still apparently believes that their vote does not really matter (see Figure 7-6).

Differences in political efficacy are evident among different groups within the population. African Americans and Hispanics have a lower sense of efficacy than whites do. Education explains much of the difference. Studies conducted regularly since the 1950s have consistently found that education is correlated with higher levels of political efficacy. Yet the increase in educational levels in the general public has not resulted in an overall increase in political efficacy, nor has it led to an increase in the portion of the population that votes. Among the factors that contribute to lower efficacy today are the weakening of party loyalties, the attention given to conflicts of interest and unethical behavior by public officials, and the size and complexity of modern government and the average citizen's difficulties in dealing with that government.

Trust and efficacy are related. People who trust government tend to feel that they can affect its decisions. People who lack trust often feel helpless; they can become alienated, and their alienation can create conditions that undermine democratic political processes.[13]

Support for democratic processes   For a democratic government to function effectively, the people must value the rules of the game—the principles and processes of the system. If one group perceives the rules as unfair, members of that group are unlikely to be content with electoral or policy decisions made in accordance with those rules, and they may choose not to abide by those decisions.

Evidence suggests that most Americans do value the fundamental norms that underlie their political system.[14] Democratic principles are predicated on the concept of majority rule, but they also include the protection of minority rights. In the abstract, the American public supports both majority rule and minority rights. In practice, however, certain types of groups (atheists, racists, communists, and Nazis, for example) and certain forms of speech (obscenity and inflammatory words) and behavior (desecration of patriotic symbols) are not readily tolerated. Nevertheless, surveys conducted during the last two decades have found an increasing level of tolerance for diverse lifestyles and behaviors. In theory at least, people seem more willing today than they were in the past to tolerate homosexual behavior, accept dual careers for women and men, and vote for minority and women candidates for office. Is the level of tolerance changing? Some data suggest that it may be.

Tolerance of others   Tolerance is a learned behavior. It is influenced by family, school, community, and the many associations people have in the course of their daily lives. Once again, level of education seems to be the most important factor. The more education a person has, the more likely it is that he or she will be tolerant of others.

Take free speech, for example. Most Americans are taught that freedom of speech is a central element of their belief system and that it is protected by the First Amendment to the Constitution. Yet how tolerant are people of speech that contains objectionable ideas, fighting words, or racial or religious slurs? In the late 1980s some colleges and universities created codes that punished those whose speech and actions denigrated others, particularly women and certain minority groups. Critics of these codes contended that they established language and behavior that was **politically correct** and thereby limited individual rights protected by the First Amendment. Proponents, however, contend that some words can lead to behavior that violates people's rights, behavior that society has a right to prevent. Several such codes have subsequently been declared unconstitutionally vague by federal courts.

How tolerant are the American people? Figure 7-7 gives some indication of people's willingness to let others express their beliefs. Obviously, the American people have a way to go before they accept in practice what they preach in theory. Nevertheless, Americans seem to be more tolerant than in the past.[15] Whether that tolerance would continue to increase in the light of major economic, social, or political upheavals is difficult to say. The case of Germany during the 1930s and 1940s, when the Nazis gained control and eliminated minority groups, provides a thought-provoking example in view of the relatively high levels of education prevailing in that country at the time.

A considerable amount of research has focused on differences in beliefs and behavior between **elites**, people in leadership positions, and the **masses**, those who are generally described as followers.[16] The key finding of this research, which should come as no surprise, is that elites tend to be more supportive of political rights for individuals than the masses are (see Table 7-7).

Does the fact that elites are more tolerant than the masses and more supportive of the norms and practices of democracy threaten the democratic character of the system? According to a group of scholars known as **democratic elitists**, the answer is no. As long as those in power make decisions and take actions in accordance with democratic principles, they argue, the character of the system is not threatened (although, obviously, public support of basic democratic values is still essential).[17]

Another factor that affects tolerance is personality. The need for a more structured and ordered existence makes some people less able to accept behavior that violates the norms of society than others who can function in a looser, less structured environment. The term **authoritarian personality** is often used

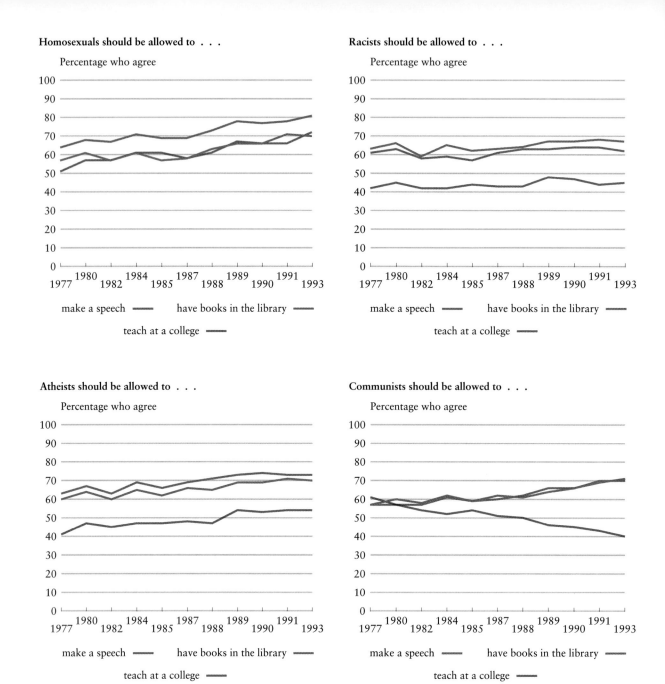

Figure 7-7 *Tolerance of homosexuals, racists, atheists, and communists.* SOURCE: *General social surveys, National Opinion Research Center, University of Chicago.*

	ELITE	MASS
TABLE 7-7		
Two Views of Freedom (percentage agreeing)		
Books that preach the overthrow of the government should be banned from the library	13	51
It is a good idea for the government to keep a list of people who take part in demonstrations	17	50
When the country is at war, people suspected of disloyalty should be watched closely or kept in custody	22	54
A teacher who refuses to salute the flag at a school assembly should be suspended or dismissed	17	47

SOURCE: Data from Herbert McClosky and Alida Brill, *Dimensions of Tolerance* (New York: Russell Sage, 1983), 71, 109, 121, 153. Reprinted by permission of the publisher.

to describe people who are prone to doctrinaire views and willing to follow those who preach them. Their behavior pattern of dominance and submission is thought to compensate for deeply held feelings of insecurity.[18]

The impact of personality on tolerance is difficult to measure, although it is frequently used to explain behavior. In general, the less real and direct a perceived threat is, the more tolerant people are likely to be, regardless of their personality. When an issue hits home, when it becomes personal, when one's job, or property, or lifestyle is put in jeopardy, then it is more difficult for people to be tolerant.

PUBLIC OPINION AND GOVERNANCE

Regardless of what different groups of Americans believe about issues that are vital to democratic government, the general public does not dictate policy. It cannot. Relatively few people have the time, interest, or motivation to contact government representatives directly. Moreover, policy issues do not seem to have a significant influence on the voting behavior of the American public.

What is the role of public opinion in the determination of policy? Public opinion helps establish the salience of issues and, to some extent, identifies acceptable and unacceptable policy alternatives. Take the drug problem as an example. Policy options range from educational campaigns in schools to methadone treatment centers for addicts to criminal prosecution for those who sell illegal drugs. To date, however, the legalization of "hard" drugs has not been seen as a viable option because it conflicts with the strongly held view that these drugs are dangerous and their use should be discouraged.

A high level of interest and concern indicates that an issue is important and, usually, that something must be done about it. If there is a dominant mood or opinion, public officials tend to follow it. Scholars who have studied opinion change and policy outcomes have found a correlation between the two;[19] they have also found that opinion change precedes rather than follows policy change, a pattern that we would expect in a democracy.[20]

For most issues, however, there is not a single dominant opinion but a variety of opinions. These opinions are developed, publicized, and communicated by the opinion makers and the elites, who have the skills, contacts, and motivation to try to convert them into policy decisions. Specific courses of action are more likely to be influenced by the interchange between opinion makers and government officials than by the general public. On most issues the majority does not rule; in fact, the dominant mood is often one of apathy. But the values and beliefs of the majority are still important because they set the limits within which policy debate occurs and policy decisions are made.

Do officials respond to the public's opinions, or do they try to shape them? The answer is that they try to do both. At the national level, government officials regularly make use of public opinion polls to discern the contours of political attitudes and the prevalent opinions of the day. In 1979 Jimmy Carter cited the results of a national survey conducted by his pollster, Pat Caddell,

Listening to America

How do American presidents know what people want them to do? How do they know what people do *not* want them to do? Increasingly, the president frames policy based less on principles and promises and more on polls that take the daily temperature of the populace.

In late December of 1993, a panel of presidential pollsters discussed their art at the American Enterprise Institute. There Stanley Greenberg, whose firm works for the Democratic National Committee, pointed out some notable connections between the policies of the Clinton administration and the data from the firm's polls.

Early in the construction of the health-care package, for example, a value-added tax was proposed as a way to finance it. When polls revealed that "the public wasn't ready for a VAT," however, the White House backed off and moved on. And when the polls showed that the public wanted Vice President Gore to take on Ross Perot in a debate over the North American Free Trade Agreement, the White House overcame its misgivings and sent Gore out to do battle. The polls were right. Gore was convincing, and the NAFTA became law soon after.

Greenberg's frankness alarmed his listeners.

"You cannot make decisions simply driven by polls," said Richard Wirthlin, President Reagan's pollster, who acknowledged that he had met personally with Reagan twenty-six times during his first year in office. "When I listen to you speak," said Patrick Caddell, President Carter's pollster, "it sounds like you all are running a campaign there."

"The presidency is not a campaign," Greenberg replied. Yet polling data seem to be vital to the Clinton administration. Greenberg's routine included meeting with the President himself at least once a week to discuss the latest poll results, and meetings almost every day with others at the White House.

What is wrong with poll-driven policies? Wirthlin made one point clearly. You should make policy, he said, based on "what the President believes, what he thinks, and what he wants to accomplish." That is leadership. No one asked the clearest question, however: what happens if the public mood changes? Should policy change as well?

SOURCE: Based on, and quotations taken from, Richard L. Berke, "Clinton Aide Says Polls Had Role in Health Plan," *New York Times*, December 9, 1993, A20.

One of the most poignant symbolic expressions of public opinion—and feeling—is the AIDS quilt. Begun in June of 1987 in San Francisco as a memorial to those who had died of the disease, the quilt grows larger every day. On the mall in Washington in 1993, it contained over twenty-four thousand panels and covered the equivalent of fifteen football fields.

Hardly a single celebrity makes an appearance without a red ribbon, the symbol of concern over AIDS. Here Anjelica Houston wears hers on her hip. But when one soap-opera star accepted an award without a ribbon, she was pilloried in the media.

when he described the public mood as a malaise that needed to be cured. Throughout their presidencies, Ronald Reagan, George Bush, and Bill Clinton also used surveys conducted for them or their parties to assess and react to the public mood.

Each of these presidents, as well as others who preceded them, was accused of trying to manipulate public opinion. But such accusations do not take account of the fine line between leading and following. A good leader gets out in front, but not too far. Although Americans may fault their political leaders for failing to heed public opinion or to lead public opinion—or sometimes even for trying too hard to lead, with the result that they manipulate public opinion—in reality public officials make most of their decisions without knowing exactly how the public will react. Moreover, effective policy may demand that officials do what they think is right and what will benefit the public most in the long run, regardless of the public mood and the short-run consequences of a decision. But there is a danger here. American history is filled with examples of policies that failed or had to be curtailed because of lack of public support. Prohibition is one outstanding example; the Vietnam War is another.

Finally, what is the impact of public opinion on the politics of American government? The public's values and beliefs constitute the intellectual foundation on which the political system rests; the public's opinions frame the policy debate and affect the government's decisions. Those decisions, in turn, are continuously subject to public evaluation and reevaluation. Public opinion therefore is a critical component of democratic politics.

Public opinion consists of *opinions* (judgments on current issues), *attitudes* (broad orientations toward policy areas), and *values* (basic ideals and beliefs). Values and attitudes shape opinion and determine the *salience*, or importance, of issues. Public opinion is described in terms of *direction* (the proportion of the population that holds a certain view), *stability* or *fluidity* (whether or not a view changes over time), and *intensity* (how strongly a view is held).

The population falls into three broad groups based on the amount of information each has. The *mass public* is the least informed, most apathetic, most easily manipulated, and the largest. The *attentive public* is better informed and more interested, but it takes little political action beyond voting. These two groups determine how far people may be willing to go on an issue. *Opinion makers* are set apart by their interest, knowledge, and political activities. They shape specific policies, influence others, and inform public debate.

The most efficient way to discover public opinion is by *public opinion polls*, or surveys. Such polls ask questions of a *sample* that represents the population under study. Samples are *randomly selected*, that is, every element of the population under study has an equal chance of being included. In assessing the accuracy of a sample, poll takers consider two factors: *sampling error*, or the degree to which the sample could deviate from the population as a whole, and *level of confidence*, or the extent to which the results could be incorrect by chance.

Polls may be inaccurate because of how questions are worded, how surveys are constructed, or how responses are interpreted. Emotional or controversial words may introduce bias. *Closed-ended questions* (which force a choice from a list of items) or *open-ended questions* (which have no predetermined answer) may also influence responses, as may the order of the questions. The way an interview is conducted also affects the response.

Most Americans are poorly informed about government officials and political issues. Education seems to be the key variable here. Those with more formal education tend to be better informed. Above-average income also correlates with higher levels of political information. And as people age, they become more aware of how political decisions affect them. Yet a poorly informed public lets government leaders be too flexible in making policy decisions, it encourages short-term solutions, and it gives added power to interest groups.

To take a stand on complex issues, people often adopt a *belief system*, a set of simplified ideas that helps them understand and cope with the world. A *political ideology* is a belief system that shapes responses to policy issues and positions. The two dominant political ideologies in the United States are *liberalism* and *conservatism*.

Liberals tend to support government intervention in social and economic programs, especially to protect civil rights and promote equal opportunity, and to oppose government action that might deprive individuals of basic freedoms. Conservatives tend to oppose government involvement, especially in the economic sphere, contending that a free market produces the prosperity that solves many of the country's social ills. Conservatives lean toward the Republican party, while liberals lean toward the Democrats.

Most Americans agree that government should promote employment, control inflation, and foster growth. They disagree over how extensive such intervention should be. Thus, attitudes toward the role of government vary widely, as do levels of trust in public officials and levels of belief in *political efficacy*, the idea that political participation can make a difference.

The American public supports the principles of majority rule and minority rights in theory. In practice, however, certain groups and certain forms of speech and behavior are not readily tolerated. On many college campuses, for example, the requirements of *political correctness* may or may not impinge on tolerance and freedom of speech.

Tolerance seems to vary with age and education. Research also shows that *elites* (those who lead) support political rights for individuals more than do the *masses* (those who follow). *Democratic elitists* say that as long as those in power honor democratic principles, the system is not threatened. People with *authoritarian personalities* are very intolerant.

Public opinion does not dictate policy. It does establish the salience of issues and set limits on acceptable policy alternatives. A high level of public interest indicates that an issue is important and requires action. But in most cases, no single opinion dominates. When many different opinions exist, policy is more apt to be produced by negotiations between opinion makers and government officials than by the general public.

public opinion
opinions
attitudes
values
salience
direction *which way opinion swings*
stability *won't change opinions*
fluidity *always change*
intensity *how strong opinions*
mass public

attentive public
opinion makers
public opinion poll
sample
random selection
sampling error
level of confidence
closed-ended question
open-ended question
belief system

political ideology
liberalism
conservatism
political efficacy
political correctness
elites
masses
democratic elitists
authoritarian personality

LEARNING MORE ABOUT PUBLIC OPINION

Scholarly studies

Abramson, Paul R. *Political Attitudes in America*. Rev. ed. San Francisco: Freeman, 1986. A comprehensive survey of attitudes toward politics and government.

Cantril, Albert H. *The Opinion Connection: Polling, Politics, and the Press*. Washington, D.C.: Congressional Quarterly, 1991. An introduction to the merits and pitfalls of polling and the application of polling to the political process.

Cook, Elizabeth A., Ted G. Jelen, and Clyde Wilcox. *Between Two Absolutes: Public Opinions and the Politics of Abortion*. Boulder, Colo.: Westview Press, 1992. Uses extensive survey data to analyze public opinion on this divisive and highly emotional issue.

Erikson, Robert S., Norman R. Luttbeg, and Kent L. Tedin. *American Public Opinion: Its Origins, Content, and Impact*. 4th ed. New York: Macmillan, 1991. An excellent summary of the literature on political opinion by three political scientists.

Lipset, Seymour Martin, and William Schneider. *The Confidence Gap*. Baltimore, Md.: Johns Hopkins University Press, 1987. Two well-known students of public opinion and political behavior assess Americans' declining level of confidence in their economic, political, and social institutions.

McClosky, Herbert, and Alida Brill. *Dimensions of Tolerance: What Americans Believe About Civil Liberties*. New York: Russell Sage, 1983. A study of political beliefs that argues that tolerance is a learned behavior reinforced by group associations.

Sapiro, Virginia. *The Political Integration of Women*. Urbana: University of Illinois Press, 1984. An excellent analysis of the development of women's political consciousness in the 1980s.

Smith, Robert C., and Richard Seltzer. *Race, Class, and Culture: A Study in Afro-American Mass Opinion*. Albany: State University of New York Press, 1992. Examines racial attitudes and opinions within the African-American community and between that community and white American society.

Stimson, James A. *Public Opinion in America: Moods, Cycles, and Swings*. Boulder, Colo.: Westview Press, 1991. Presents a theory of how the public moods change and the impact of those changes on politics and elections.

Leisure reading

Edsall, Thomas B., with Mary D. Edsall. *Chain Reaction: The Impact of Race, Rights, and Taxes on American Politics*. New York: Norton, 1992. A study of three divisive issues and their impact on contemporary American politics.

Harris, Louis. *Inside America*. New York: Vintage Books, 1987. A summary of a well-known pollster's findings about attitudes and beliefs in America, written in a lucid, tongue-in-cheek style.

Hoffer, Eric. *The True Believer*. San Bernardino, Calif.: Borgo Press, 1991. A provocative analysis of the psychological and social needs that underlie mass movements.

Primary sources and organizations

The Gallup Poll, 53 Bank Street, Princeton, NJ 08540; (609) 924-9600.

Inter-University Consortium for Political and Social Research, Institute for Social Research, University of Michigan, Ann Arbor, MI 48106; (313) 764-5494.

Roper Center for Public Opinion Research, User Services Department, P.O. Box 440, Storrs, CT 06268; (203) 486-4440.

CHAPTER

8

Political

Interest

Groups

- Individuals, groups, and society

- Political interest groups and democratic theory

- The origins and development of political groups: theories of group formation and the evolution of political interest groups

- Sources of group influence on public policy

- Electoral activity by political action groups: types and targets of lobbying

- Consequences of the group struggle

The fight over clean-air laws was a classic confrontation between those who wanted to clean up the environment and those who wished to make money and preserve jobs. It was a fight that was fought in 1970, when the first Clean Air Act was passed; in 1977, when amendments were added; in 1986, when the issue resurfaced; and again in 1990, when a new bill was enacted into law. The conflict pitted two broad coalitions of overlapping and conflicting interests against each other. On one side were the environmentalists and their allies from state and local governments, public interest groups, and concerned members of the scientific community. On the other were energy producers, energy consumers, and other groups that depend on oil and soft coal, such as utilities, manufacturers, and the labor unions of workers in these industries.

Within each coalition there was considerable diversity and some disagreement. Industries, located primarily in the East and Midwest, that used high-sulfur soft coal took a much tougher stand against restrictions on emissions into the atmosphere than did industries, located largely in the West, that

Republican William Howard Taft was groomed to run for the presidency in 1908 by Teddy Roosevelt, as reflected in the "You and I Ted" campaign pin *(above right)*. Taft handily defeated the populist Democrat William Jennings Bryan, who lost his third presidential election. Although Taft had been Roosevelt's secretary of war as well as his close friend, his administration was less energetic and less progressive—so much so, that Roosevelt decided to run again in 1912, first for the Republican nomination and, when he failed to receive it, as the Progressive, or "Bull Moose," candidate. Since Taft weighed more than three hundred pounds in 1908, it seems fair to consider him that election's "heavy" favorite.

were less dependent on high-sulfur coal. Similar geographic lines were drawn between eastern and western utilities and between state officials in these two regions. Governors from rural states clashed with their counterparts in the industrial states over the extent of the regulations and the time frame needed to meet them.

Each coalition worked with its own allies on Capitol Hill. In 1986 and again in 1990 the environmentalists turned to Henry A. Waxman, a Democratic representative from the smog-ridden Los Angeles area, who chaired the House health and environment subcommittee, and George Mitchell, a Democratic senator from Maine and the Senate majority leader. The energy coalition worked with John D. Dingell, a Democratic representative from Detroit, who chaired the House Energy and Commerce Committee under whose jurisdiction the bill fell, and Robert Byrd, a Democratic senator from coal-producing West Virginia and the president pro tempore of the Senate.

Each coalition developed a similar strategy. The environmental group used studies conducted by nationally recognized and politically neutral institutions like the National Academy of Science to identify the causes and consequences of pollution. The energy coalition hired a research firm to challenge the data, particularly the contention that the principal problems were caused by human activities, especially industry. Pointing to the high cost of controlling pollution, the energy proponents emphasized the dire economic consequences that would result from the additional burdens placed on producers and consumers in the United States.

In 1986 the forces opposing clean-air legislation had been successful. With the backing of the Reagan administration, they prevailed on their congressional allies to block the legislation in

committee. But defeat is rarely final as long as an issue remains alive. The battle, lost by the environmentalists in 1986, was resumed in subsequent Congresses. By the end of the 1980s, growing environmental concern had generated sufficient political pressure to make the adoption of some clean-air legislation more likely. The country had suffered through a drought, hot summers, and a major oil spill off the coast of Alaska. These pressures forced President Bush to be far more sympathetic to environmental matters than President Reagan had been. Changes in congressional leadership also contributed to a more favorable climate for enacting environmental legislation.

During the first year of his administration, President Bush delivered a major speech on the environment. He later proposed legislation that would tighten controls on utilities that burned soft coal and would institute new, tougher auto emission standards. His proposals, praised at first by environmentalists and criticized by energy producers and users, became the focus of a new debate and provided the basis for the compromise legislation enacted in the fall of 1990, amendments to the Clean Air Act.

Defeat, however, is rarely final. This time American business took the lead and urged the Bush administration to avoid issuing stringent rules to implement the new law. In 1992, facing enormous political pressure from organized interests that had supported the administration, as well as a tough reelection campaign, the Bush administration relented and failed to promulgate regulations that would vigorously enforce the act. It was left to the Clinton administration to issue regulations by which the 1990 legislation was to be effectively implemented and then to make certain that those regulations were vigorously enforced.

THE EBB AND FLOW OF INTEREST GROUP activity in the continuing struggle over environmental issues illustrates the politics of American government. Interest group activity occurs within a political system that encourages people to organize to pursue their objectives and protects them as they do so, but constrains them by keeping their activity within bounds defined by law. Such activity is consistent with a democratic process. In fact, it invigorates that process by encouraging people to express their desires and beliefs and by providing government officials with information they need to make responsive policy judgments.

But group activity is not without its dangers. The exertion of influence is not always fair and just and the results are not always equitable. Some organized groups, by virtue of their money, connections, or skills, can get what they want more easily than others can. Does this unequal representation of people and this unequal power that interest groups exercise undercut the democratic process? Is this consistent with the principle of majority rule that requires the wishes of each member of society to be weighted equally? Do the resulting policies serve the country's short- and long-term interests?

To address these questions, we examine three aspects of group activity: the composition of interest groups and the functions they serve for their members and for society as a whole; the methods used by these groups and the ways in which they affect the political process; and the policy outcomes that result from this activity—that is, who gains and who loses.

Lobbyists are a common sight lined up outside the door of the House Ways and Means Committee room as they wait to buttonhole key legislators and plead in their clients' interests. Success in shaping legislation to their clients' liking enhances the prestige and profits of their firms. This corridor is known as "Gucci gulch," so named for the expensive Italian shoes that lobbyists favor.

Jose R. Lopez/NYT Pictures

People join and participate in groups from birth to death. The family is the first and most basic social unit. As people get older, they associate with others by virtue of where they live, what they believe, and what they like to do. Neighborhood, religious, and recreational groups form the basis of these early associations. As a presidential candidate, Jimmy Carter referred to his various associations in describing himself to the American public: "I am a Southerner and an American. I am a farmer, an engineer, and father and husband, a politician and former governor, a planner, a businessman, a nuclear physicist, a naval officer, a canoeist, and, among other things, a lover of Bob Dylan's songs and Dylan Thomas's poetry."[1] Groups provide a sense of community and security. They contribute to a person's social identity and self-enhancement. They help people reinforce their values, clarify their goals, and identify their achievements.

Belonging to a group can also be a source of economic benefit. Labor unions, business groups, and professional organizations regularly seek to promote the financial interests of their members. Groups can enhance their supporters' political influence as well by mobilizing their membership and others who are sympathetic to their cause to affect government—who gets elected, what decisions public officials make, and when those decisions are made. In short, in a democracy numbers count.

Finally, groups can promote values and ideas. They provide an incentive for like-minded people to get together and a vehicle for debating, extending, and practicing their beliefs. Ideological groups such as the National Conservative Political Action Committee and the liberal American Civil Liberties Union and religious institutions such as the Catholic church and the National Council of Churches are examples of groups that organize around a distinct set of beliefs.

Groups that attempt to influence the personnel and policies of government are known as **political interest groups.** They have three primary characteristics: (1) shared interests and goals, (2) an organizational structure, and (3) a desire to influence public policy. A group is not a political interest group unless it becomes involved in the political process and tries to influence public policy. The local bridge club is a group, but it is not a political interest group. The American Farm Bureau Federation, the Teamsters Union, the National Rifle Association, and the American Political Science Association are political interest groups. Institutions such as universities and corporations also get involved in political activities and are often referred to as *organized interests.* They may join together in associations such as the American Association for Higher Education or the National Association of Manufacturers to become political interest groups.

Political interest groups differ from political parties. They tend to have a narrower membership base than parties, especially the major parties—the Democrats and the Republicans. In addition, political interest groups are more focused on policy issues than are political parties, which are concerned primarily with elections and, if they are successful, with the organization of government. And whereas parties take positions on a wide range of issues, most political interest groups focus their political involvement on those issues that are directly related to their interests and about which their members feel strongly. The National Rifle Association is concerned with the possession of

The steps of the Capitol make a magnificent stage set for every imaginable group that seeks a forum and media attention. Different groups appear daily, including Act Up demanding AIDS funding, the Gray Panthers demanding Medicare funding, and the Ku Klux Klan demanding recognition.

firearms but not with farm subsidies, tax increases, or abortion. The Republican party, however, has taken positions on all three issues.

In many ways political interest groups supplement the role of political parties in the government process by representing and promoting interests on a wide range of public policy issues. Political interest groups broaden and strengthen the ties between representatives and their constituents. However, they also heighten and enlarge the political struggle. Many diverse, overlapping, and conflicting groups compete for access and influence within government, within the parties, within the electorate, and, increasingly, within the electoral arena. Some believe that this competition is beneficial to a democratic society, that interest groups perform a useful and necessary function. Others are not so sure, fearing that groups promote their own interests at the public's expense. The automobile industry's objections to high emission standards, the National Rifle Association's campaign to protect the rights of gun owners, and the tobacco lobby's attempt to head off restrictive laws on smoking are three illustrations of interest group positions and activities that some would regard as harmful to the general public. Does group activity aid or hurt the democratic process? The answer is that it can do both, depending on how well groups represent the population as a whole, how effectively they exercise influence, and how much of that influence shapes public policy.

POLITICAL INTEREST GROUPS AND DEMOCRATIC THEORY

Group activity is consistent with democratic theory. On the one hand, it can strengthen democracy. Political interest groups can educate people about their civic responsibilities. By increasing public awareness, providing an outlet for public expression, and encouraging participation in the political process, interest groups energize the political system, extend democracy, and channel self-

With the tobacco industry in turmoil, workers from North Carolina came to Capitol Hill to lobby against increasing cigarette taxes to pay for the Clintons' health-care package. (Far right) R.J. Reynolds conducts meetings around the country to teach smokers how to get involved politically and protect their rights. Tobacco companies have also mounted a public relations offensive to dispute the evidence that smoking increases the likelihood of cancer.

interested behavior into legitimate and productive political activity. On the other hand, group activity can weaken democracy if the competition between groups is unbalanced—that is, if certain groups by virtue of their size, status, access to government, or skills in influencing government become dominant. For example, for years the American Medical Association (AMA) was the most powerful health-care group, effectively preventing the development of programs that the AMA viewed as a threat to private medical practice in the United States. But as other health-care professionals and citizen activists organized and lobbied for new policies and a larger government role in health care, the AMA's influence began to erode, and eventually the organization was forced to temper its opposition to a large government role in health care.

Domination by political interest groups is precisely what James Madison feared and why he defended the Constitution in *The Federalist, No. 10*. He argued that people naturally pursue their own interests. If given the freedom to do so, they form *factions* (Madison's term for political interest groups) that have the potential to gain power, control the government, and make policy in their own interests. The dilemma for Madison was to maintain freedom for individuals to join groups and for groups to pursue their own interests while at the same time controlling the harmful effects of their behavior on society.

Madison saw the structure designed by the framers of the Constitution as an effective way to resolve this dilemma. The representational character of the system refined and distilled public passions, and separate institutions checking and balancing one another decreased the likelihood that a single group, even if it were in the majority, could dominate the government and thereby threaten to reduce or eliminate the rights of others, particularly those in the minority. That is why Madison lauded and defended the republican form of government created by the Constitution as infinitely better than a direct democracy. He also believed that the large size of the country would act as a hedge against a large faction gaining control.

Another problem, one that Madison did not address, results from the interaction of groups and from their impact on government. Group struggles

244

tend to encourage compromises in policy. Though necessary in a large, plural-istic society like that of the United States, compromises entail risks. They can produce wishy-washy policies that do not alienate powerful groups but do not solve difficult problems either. The 1990 amendments to the Clean Air Act are an example of the kind of compromises that democratic governments make when trying to devise solutions to social and economic problems.

In short, the actions of political interest groups in a democratic system cut two ways. Political interest groups add a dimension to representation or detract from representation, depending on how well they reflect the interests and needs of the general public. Similarly, they can make governing easier or more difficult, depending on how well their interests and needs are transformed into policies.

We look at the consequences of interest group activities for American politics and government later in the chapter. First, however, we need to examine the interest group phenomenon itself: why groups have developed and how they have evolved in the United States, what resources are available to them, and the ways in which they have sought to affect public policy.

THE ORIGINS AND DEVELOPMENT OF POLITICAL GROUPS

In the last several decades, there has been a surge in the activity of political interest groups. Why? What causes these groups to be created? Why have some flourished and others faded quickly from the scene?

Theories of Group Formation

One of the first political scientists to address those questions was David Tru-man.[2] Writing in the 1950s, Truman postulated that major disturbances within the political environment produce conditions that encourage group activity.[3] He reasoned that people whose interests are adversely affected by these con-ditions will band together to improve their lot. In the process, he suggested, they will frequently turn to the government for help.

Truman went on to argue that the creation and activity of political interest groups spurs other people to organize to promote their interests. The process of competitive mobilization that is initiated generates additional group for-mation and activity. At some point a balance among groups is achieved, and the activity stabilizes. The equilibrium lasts until a new disturbance reactivates the cycle.[4]

Truman's **disturbance theory** assumes the existence of an active and in-formed citizenry that has the will and the capacity to organize and pursue its interests and redress its grievances. A problem not addressed by disturbance theory is that people do not all have the same will and capability to organize themselves. Some have greater incentive to do so than others. The differences in people's incentives led economist Mancur Olson to suggest that the principal incentives for joining a group are the **selective benefits** that people receive from being members.[5] If the benefits of membership were generally available to peo-ple who did not join, there would be little incentive to join. Olson's logic is the reason that the American Association of Retired Persons, the U.S. Chamber of

Commerce, and many other groups offer their members specific benefits in addition to working for the collective good of members and nonmembers alike.

A problem with Olson's theory of selective benefits, however, is that it does not appear to be equally applicable to all types of groups. People who join economic groups tend to be motivated more by direct economic benefits than are those who join issue-oriented or ideological groups. Thus, a prospective member of an economic group such as a labor union or a business association is inclined to judge the advantages and disadvantages of belonging on the basis of financial gain. The motive for joining a pro-life or pro-choice group is very different and probably depends on how strongly a person feels about the merits of the issue.

Another political scientist, Robert Salisbury, used the analogy of the marketplace to explain why some groups prosper and others do not. A group that has a valuable product and is able to promote it, he suggested, will probably be successful in creating and maintaining its organization. Salisbury saw the group's leaders, or entrepreneurs, as he called them, as holding the key to this success.[6]

Of course, the resources available to the founders of various groups are not equal. In another influential study of interest groups, Jack Walker argued that group formation and activity, particularly in contemporary times, are tied closely to the nature of a group's financial base. Start-up funds need to be sufficient to begin the group and support its operations. At least initially, Walker notes, these funds need to be obtained from outside the membership base, although over time the membership may be able to sustain itself.[7]

Government actions can figure prominently in generating group activity. Groups form as a consequence of new legislation and regulations. As Walker pointed out, more than half of the groups representing senior citizens were organized after the passage of the Medicare legislation and the Older Americans Act in 1965.[8] Thus, not only do groups try to influence what the government does, but the government itself also stimulates group mobilization and activities.[9]

When we put all these theories together, we do not wind up with a single reason that explains why groups develop. Rather, various factors seem to be conducive to the origination and maintenance of group activity. These include a discernible interest by the public, an interest that is affected by conditions in the social and economic environment; an incentive for joining and a benefit (not necessarily an economic one) for remaining a member; and leaders who are able to articulate and communicate this benefit to those who desire it (the communication task often requires a strong financial base). When these conditions are present, groups are likely to be created and sustained.

We now turn from theory to practice and look at the evolution of political interest groups in the United States.

The Evolution of Political Interest Groups

Although political interest groups have existed throughout the nation's history, their development has occurred in waves (lending support to Truman's disturbance theory). The first of these waves occurred prior to the Civil War, from 1830 to 1860. During this period a number of significant political interest groups, ranging from the anti-immigration, anti-Catholic Know-Nothings of the 1830s and 1840s to the anti-slavery abolitionists of the 1850s, appeared.

The second wave of group activity occurred during the 1880s, when industrialization and unsettled labor conditions brought about the formation of unions like the American Federation of Labor and the Knights of Labor. Another spurt in the creation and growth of political interest groups took place from 1900 to 1920. This period saw the expansion of national business and trade associations like the U.S. Chamber of Commerce, the National Association of Manufacturers, the American Medical Association, and the American Farm Bureau Federation. Such large groups were made possible by a technological revolution that facilitated rapid, nationwide communications.

Activity by political interest groups continued to increase, but the next major period of growth was not until the 1960s. This new surge continued through the 1980s. In addition to the proliferation and professionalization of groups formed to pursue economic interests, such as business, labor, and trade associations, this period also saw the rapid rise of idea and issue groups focusing on basic beliefs and values (the main categories of political interest groups are listed in Table 8-1 on page 248). Idea and issue groups include public interest groups such as Common Cause and Public Citizen (one of citizen-activist Ralph Nader's organizations); civil rights groups such as the Congress of Racial Equality and La Raza; and environmental, education, and other issue advocacy organizations.

The idea and issue groups differ from economic interest groups in that material benefit is not their primary goal. Rather, they are organized and motivated by a belief or an ideal about how society and government should be structured or what public policy is most desirable. Ideological groups fit into this broad category of idea and issue organizations, as do such organizations as the National Gay Rights Organization, the National Organization for Women, and the various pro-life and pro-choice groups. Most of these groups are organized around social or political issues. They are expressive groups; they reach out to the general public through the mass media.

Why have political interest groups become so numerous since 1960? The growth of federal programs and regulatory activities prior to and during this period encouraged individuals and groups whose economic interests were affected by government actions to become more involved in the political process. In most cases they have tried to protect and expand programs that benefit them. Farmers want to maintain and enlarge their crop subsidies; laborers want to preserve and increase minimum wages and improve working conditions; senior citizens want to make sure that Social Security payments will continue and will be adjusted for inflation. The list of groups wishing to protect their piece of the action has expanded in tandem with the expansion of government in the domestic sphere.

The political movements of the 1960s and 1970s also contributed to the increase in group activity. The civil rights struggles and the protests against the Vietnam War demonstrated that organized political activity could have an impact on public policy. These movements became models for those who felt that government was not responsive to their needs and desires, such as environmentalists and consumers, and those who were adversely affected by changes in public policy. Business groups expanded their efforts to resist policies that increased their costs or restricted their freedom to do business. Conservative

TABLE 8-1	
Political Interest Groups	
BASIC TYPE	SPECIFIC GROUPS
Economic	
Business	American Newspaper Publishers Association
	U.S. Chamber of Commerce
	National Association of Manufacturers
	National Federation of Independent Businesses
	Tobacco Institute
	United Ship Owners of America
Labor	AFL-CIO
	American Federation of Teachers
	International Brotherhood of Teamsters
	International Longshoremen's Association
	NFL Players Association
	National Association of Government Employees
Agriculture	American Farm Bureau Federation
	American Feed Industry Association
	National Corn Growers Association
	National Grange
	National Milk Producers Federation
	National Turkey Federation
Other professional associations	Institute of Electrical and Electronic Engineers
	National Association of Professional Insurance Agents
	National Health Lawyers Association
	National Society of Fund Raising Executives
	Reserve Officers Association
Noneconomic	
Public interest	Common Cause
	Congress Watch
	Friends of the Earth
	League of Women Voters
	March of Dimes
	Public Citizen
	United States Public Interest Research Group

groups became more active, influential, and successful in opposing the government's increasing economic intervention and social welfare programs.

Instant and cheap systems of national communication such as WATS lines, fax machines, and computerized mailing lists have made it possible for organizations to reach out and broaden their membership by promoting issues, raising money, and mobilizing grassroots activities on behalf of their interests. Moreover, the potential membership base of many of these public interest, citizen, and consumer advocacy groups was greatly enlarged after World War II by the increasing proportion of the population with some college education.

BASIC TYPE	SPECIFIC GROUPS
Noneconomic	
Single-issue	American Civil Liberties Union
	American Rifle Association
	National Abortion Rights League
	National Coalition to Ban Handguns
	National Committee to Preserve Social Security and Medicare
	National Organization for the Reform of Marijuana Laws
	National Right to Life Committee
Ideological	Americans for Democratic Action
	The Conservative Caucus
	Liberty Lobby
	People for the American Way
	National Center for Policy Alternatives
Civil rights	American Arab Anti-Discrimination Committee
	Anti-Defamation League of B'nai B'rith
	Association for Retarded Citizens of the United States
	National Association for the Advancement of Colored People
	National Council of La Raza
	National Organization for Women
Religious	American Jewish Conference
	Moral Majority
	National Conference of Catholic Bishops
	National Council of Churches
Government	Council of Large Public Housing Authorities
	National Association of Counties
	National Association of State Boards of Education
	National League of Cities
	National Governors Association

College graduates tend to be more aware and concerned about the policy issues that affect them and their environment than are people with less education.

Changes in the political system—notably, the fragmentation and weakening of political parties, the candidate orientation of elections, laws regulating contributions and expenditures, and the opening of the legislative process to public scrutiny—also contributed to this outpouring of group activity. These changes have made candidates for office more solicitous of group support and public officials more responsive to organized interests.

All of these changes have affected the politics of American government.

Ralph Nader: In the Public Interest

In 1964, Ralph Nader, a young attorney on the staff of the Department of Labor, produced an exhaustively detailed legislative report on highway safety. The next year, that report was expanded into a book, *Unsafe at Any Speed*, a scathing indictment of the design practices of the American automobile industry. In his book, Nader alleged that dangerous design flaws, not poor road conditions or bad judgments by drivers, were responsible for many serious highway accidents.

Nader's treatise generated strong public support for passage of the Traffic and Motor Vehicle Safety Act of 1966. During hearings on the bill, the president of General Motors admitted that private detectives had been hired to investigate and discredit Ralph Nader. The revelation transformed Nader into a folk hero.

Nader quickly became the leader of a growing national consumer-rights movement. He recruited hundreds of young lawyers and activists to his new research organization, the Center for the Study of Responsive Law. "Nader's Raiders," as they soon came to be called, investigated a wide range of public interest issues. Investigations by Nader and his organization helped lead to mandatory automobile safety features such as seat belts and shatterproof glass, the creation of the Environmental Protection Agency in 1970 and the Occupational Safety and Health Administration (OSHA) in 1976, and passage of the Freedom of Information Act in 1974. More recently, the placement of air bags in automobiles was also a consequence of his efforts.

Today Nader-inspired organizations such as Public Citizen, Congress Watch, Public Interest Research Groups in twenty-six states, the Disability Rights Center, the Center for Auto Safety, the Freedom of Information Clearinghouse, and the Equal

Sipa Press

For thirty years, consumer advocate Ralph Nader has spearheaded efforts to make government more responsive, citizens more active, and products more safe. He has fought tirelessly against government of, by, and for the corporations.

Justice Foundation carry on the fight for consumer rights, corporate and government accountability, and citizen activism. Although Nader's critics contend that his work has provided a bonanza for liability lawyers and that some of his organizations' activities have been funded by these very same lawyers, his supporters point to the money and lives that he has saved for the average citizen and to the increased levels of participation he has generated.

Known for his ascetic lifestyle, Ralph Nader continues to crisscross the country, speaking on the need for citizen empowerment and responsive government, testifying before Congress, lobbying the president and the executive branch, and all the while staying at the center of controversy.

At some point, almost every group with a cause goes to Washington to "petition the Government for a redress of grievances." One of the most impressive gatherings took place on August 28, 1963, when Martin Luther King, Jr., led a march to promote civil rights. With the Lincoln Memorial as a backdrop, King intoned the speech that installed the phrase "I have a dream . . ." in the American consciousness.

They have made it more pluralistic and more responsive to outside pressures. They have turned the nation's capital into a city of lobbyists and representatives. The number of Washington-based groups, government relations offices of major corporations, and lobbyists, lawyers, and others involved in public relations has mushroomed in recent years. Take trade associations, for example. In 1971, 19 percent of them were headquartered in Washington; twenty years later roughly one out of three was located in the nation's capital.[10] Ten years ago there were approximately 10,500 people working for organizations in Washington whose principal objective was to influence the government's decisions on public policy; today there are approximately 14,000.[11] These include 4,500 officers of trade and professional associations and labor unions, 1,500 corporate representatives, 2,200 advocates of special causes, 2,800 lawyers representing clients in legal or regulatory matters or registered as lobbyists or foreign agents, 2,500 public relations consultants and lobbyists, 200 officials of political action committees, and 250 policy experts associated with think tanks.[12] In the Senate, where lobbyists are supposed to register with the Office of Public Records, 3,065 were lobbyists registered in 1976, and 8,531 were registered in 1992; the number has doubled every ten years.[13] Today there are so many lobbyists that they have even formed their own associations, such as the American League of Lobbyists and the National Association of Business Political Action Committees. These two organizations were extremely active in opposing President Clinton's proposal to limit their tax deductions for business expenses, such as taking public officials to lunch or inviting them to attend conferences at the lobbyist's expense.

The objective of all these groups is to influence government decisions that protect or promote their own or their clients' interests. To do this, they need to know what is happening, how it affects them, and what they can do about it. The need for information is a principal reason for the vastly increased Washington presence of so many organized interest groups. Much staff activity is directed toward simply finding out what is going on or is likely to occur. This monitoring function is as important as lobbying itself because groups may not even be aware that they have an interest that requires their involvement until a congressional committee holds a hearing on an issue or an agency proposes a new regulation to implement legislation.[14] Edward Laumann and David Knoke report the case of a lobbyist for a trade association reading the *Federal Register*, which publishes new government regulations, and discovering, much to his dismay, that the Federal Aviation Administration (FAA) was about to issue a rule requiring detailed flight plans from noncommercial pilots:

> The trade association director muttered, "We've got a problem," and spent a frantic morning on the phone alerting his group's membership to apply pressure on the FAA to set aside the regulation. The executive realized that once detailed flight plans were on record with the FAA, the open-disclosure provisions of the Freedom of Information Act would allow anyone to learn where his member companies' planes were flying on their aerial explorations for oil, gas, and minerals. The alert director's quick mobilization of collective response saved the corporations potentially millions of dollars' worth of secret data that might have fallen into the laps of their competitors.[15]

Once organizations determine that they have a discernible interest in an actual or a projected government decision, they try to affect that decision. What are their sources of influence? Why are some successful and others not?

SOURCES OF GROUP INFLUENCE ON PUBLIC POLICY

All groups are not equally influential. Their power varies with a number of factors: their size, the composition of their membership, their unity and sense of purpose, their leadership, and the resources they have at their disposal. Their goals are also a factor in determining whether or to what extent they are apt to be successful. Goals that are grandiose, or lie outside the mainstream of public norms, values, or beliefs—the legalization of narcotics, for example, or the establishment of socialized medicine—are not likely to be achieved. Among unequal interest groups, then, some begin with a considerable advantage.

Take size, for example. Groups with a large membership—such as the American Association of Retired Persons, with 32 million members, or the American Automobile Association, with 31 million—exercise influence by virtue of their numbers. However, large groups are sometimes plagued by divisiveness. Issues that are salient to some of the members are less important to others. Dissension may dissipate the group's impact or even discourage the group from taking a position. Large labor unions like the AFL-CIO, business federations like the U.S. Chamber of Commerce, and women's groups like the National Organization for Women fall into this category. They are interested in a large number of public policies, but their members are united on only a few issues. For business and labor, unifying issues are bread-and-butter economic issues such as the minimum wage, health benefits, job security, and favorable working conditions. For women's groups, the issues that are most likely to produce a consensus include equal employment opportunity and equal pay, reproductive rights, and child care. Smaller organizations, such as the Milk and Ice Cream Association, the National Association of Home Builders, and the National Bankers Association, have a narrower membership base and fewer policy interests, but there is greater consensus among the members about which issues are salient. Unity brings strength to the smaller interest groups.

Library of Congress

The Equal Rights Amendment to the Constitution, a guarantee of equal rights under law regardless of sex, sat around Congress for nearly fifty years before both houses passed it in 1972. When the ERA went out for ratification, many women saw it as a second emancipation proclamation. Others, like those in Phyllis Schlafly's Eagle Forum, found it a threat to family values and to business. Senator Orrin Hatch (R-Utah) joined in criticizing the ERA. When three-quarters of the states still had not approved it in 1982, the ERA went back on the shelf.

A related factor is emotional intensity. To some extent, depth of feeling can compensate for lack of numbers. Consider the success of ethnic organizations, such as the American Jewish Congress and the National Association of Arab Americans, in maintaining a high level of support for their respective sides in the Arab-Israeli dispute. Emotions have also intensified the struggle over the rights of homosexuals and whether or not sexual orientation can be considered a relevant factor in hiring, adoption, and military service or for family health-care benefits. Groups on both sides of these complex issues have members who feel very strongly and hold extreme positions, as President Clinton discovered

T. Michael Kaza/U.S. Chamber of Commerce

Another issue that engendered strong emotions was the family leave bill, which became law on February 5, 1993. The law requires employers to grant workers up to twelve weeks of unpaid leave for the birth or adoption of a child or the illness of a close family member, and it was strongly opposed by business groups. After meeting with Richard Lesher, president of the Chamber of Commerce (lectern, right), Senator Orrin Hatch (lectern, left) and Rep. Charles Stenholm (D-Texas) criticized the bill when Congress first considered it in 1991.

when he raised the issue of whether homosexuals should be permitted to serve openly in the United States military.

Membership distribution affects a group's influence. On one hand, groups that are geographically concentrated, such as federal government workers, may exercise a great deal of local power but tend to have much less national influence. On the other hand, large groups with a dispersed membership, such as the National Education Association (NEA) and the American Bar Association (ABA), can be influential on many levels of government. In addition, the social and professional status of a group's membership has an impact on the group's ability to shape public policy. Organizations like the NEA and the ABA have benefited from their members' prestige, experience, and status within the community.

Financial resources are also very important, not only for staffing an organization and keeping the members informed but also for lobbying (discussed later in the chapter) and supporting like-minded candidates when they campaign for public office. The Planned Parenthood Federation of America, a pro-choice group that has been active in the abortion controversy, had a budget of over $330 million in the early 1990s. The American Heart Association, a major combatant against smoking, had a budget of almost $290 million—of which a third was spent on public education.[16] Extensive resources enable organizations to engage in a variety of political activities.

Many large political interest groups have both an elected leadership to establish policy and an administrative staff to carry on the work of the organization. Often, however, the administrative staff, with its professional expertise and day-to-day involvement, assumes de facto leadership. The staff defines the group's positions on issues and works to get them adopted by Congress and government agencies.

For organizations with staffs in Washington, an important source of influence is contacts with people in government. Washington is full of former members of Congress and former executive branch officials, including senior White House staff, who represent organized interests. Former service secretaries and top-level military and civilian Department of Defense officials may be found working for major government contractors or even for foreign governments. Federal regulatory agencies are often composed of people who have worked in the industries they are charged with regulating. Thus, personal contacts within the relevant government agencies enhance an interest group's ability to influence those agencies.

Some political interest groups have benefited from a lack of effective opposition. Traditionally, producers, such as automobile manufacturers, pharmaceutical companies, and dairy farmers, have been better represented and more successful than the consumers of their products. Other groups have gained or lost credibility as their claims, interests, and objectives coincided or conflicted with public moods, attitudes, and beliefs. The tobacco industry is a good example. It was able to exert considerable influence when most adult Americans smoked. Research findings indicating a strong relationship between smoking and heart disease and lung cancer have put the tobacco industry on the defensive, and it has become much less able to influence public policy decisions than it was a decade ago. In contrast, groups like the American Heart Association and the American Cancer Society have had a major impact on food processing, product labeling, and smoking.

Both Michael Deaver (below), *deputy chief of staff for President Reagan, and Lyn Nofziger* (bottom), *head of the political office, used their White House contacts after leaving government and were accused of violating ethics rules. Deaver was convicted of lying to Congress about his lobbying efforts; Nofziger, also convicted of improper activities, won acquittal on appeal.*

© Michael Evans/SYGMA

© Randy Taylor/SYGMA

ELECTORAL ACTIVITY BY
POLITICAL ACTION GROUPS

How do political interest groups influence the politics of American government? A group that is interested in influencing public policy has two options: it can support specific candidates in an effort to affect who the policy makers will be, and it can try after the election to influence the decisions they make. Let us now examine the first option, electoral activity.

Political interest groups have always been interested in who is elected to office and have always been active in political campaigns. Before the 1970s, they channeled most of their activity through the Democratic and Republican party organizations, which exercised more control over nominations and general election campaigns than they now do. Indeed, federal legislation prevented corporations and labor unions from making direct contributions to political campaigns, so they had to work within the party system to exert influence. They did, of course, find many ways to make their help indispensable.

Today, the nomination process is less subject to the dictates of party leaders and more a product of campaign activities initiated by candidates and regulated by government. Laws that limit private contributions, subsidize presidential elections, and require candidates to report revenue and expenditures govern the financial environment in which elections occur.

The vehicles for reaching voters have evolved as well. Radio and television have become the principal media through which elections are observed, perceptions formed, and candidates judged. Computerized mailings have assumed considerable importance. They are used for soliciting financial appeals, shaping candidates' images, and generating popular support. Together these changes have revolutionized the electoral process and have generated much activity outside the rubric of the parties and their organizations. They have provided incentives and opportunities for political interest groups to have an impact on nominations, to influence the positions of candidates and parties, and to affect the results of elections.

Pro-choice and pro-life groups endorse candidates, run commercials, and mobilize supporters. In certain areas of the country, environmental groups compete with economic interests—loggers in the Northwest, fishermen on both coasts, utilities in the Midwest—to influence the selection of candidates, their positions on key issues, and their success or failure. Today, very few political issues lack an electoral component, and very few political interest groups avoid electoral politics.

The Federal Election Campaign Act of 1972 and later amendments encourage the participation of nonparty groups by allowing them to contribute more money to candidates than individuals are allowed to contribute. Known as **political action committees (PACs)**, these groups solicit voluntary contributions and use the money to influence political campaigns and policy outcomes. PACs can contribute money to candidates,[17] spend money in support of or in opposition to candidates,[18] and mobilize and register voters on behalf of candidates. PACs can also contribute to state and local political parties in an effort to turn out a large vote. The opportunity to affect who wins and who loses provides a powerful incentive for PACs to organize and participate in the electoral process, and they have done so in a big way.

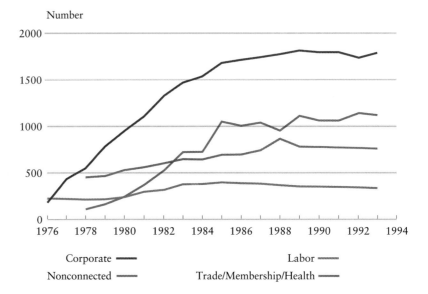

Figure 8-1 *The growth of PACs, 1976-1993.* SOURCE: *Federal Election Commission,"FEC Releases Year-end Federal PAC Count," February 11, 1994.*

Types of PACs

PACs are composed of people who have connections to established organizations—corporate employees, union members, trade association members—or those who are unconnected to such organizations but share the same interests in public policy issues. The Xerox Corporation PAC, the AFL-CIO PAC, and the National Association of Realtors PAC are known as *connected* PACs. *Nonconnected* PACs include ideological groups, such as the National Conservative Political Action Committee and Citizens for the American Way, as well as issue groups, such as the PAC for the National Rifle Association or for the Sierra Club.

Of these types of PACs, those representing businesses and those falling into the nonconnected category have grown most rapidly in recent years (see Figure 8-1). They have also tended to raise and spend the most money. Figure 8-2 graphs expenditures by type of PAC. Table 8-2 indicates which individual PACs spent the most in 1992.

TABLE 8-2	
Top Political Action Committees in 1992	
POLITICAL ACTION COMMITTEE	TOTAL CONTRIBUTIONS TO FEDERAL CANDIDATES
National Association of Realtors	$2,950,138
American Medical Association	2,936,086
International Brotherhood of Teamsters	2,442,552
Association of Trial Lawyers of America	2,336,135
National Education Association	2,323,122

SOURCE: Federal Election Commission, 1993.

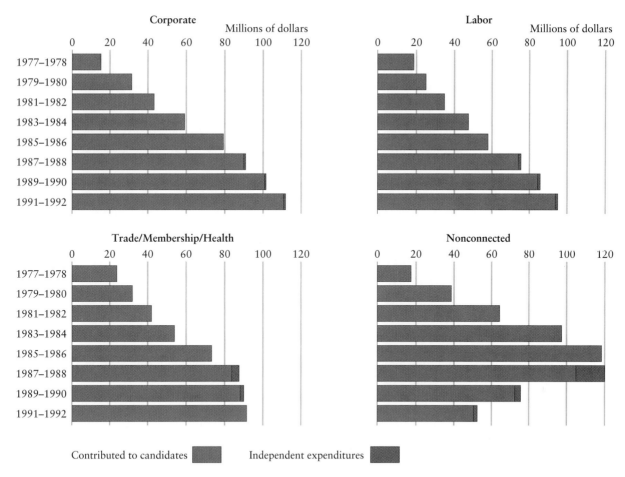

Figure 8-2   *PAC support of candidates during the 1978–1992 election cycles.*
SOURCE: *Federal Election Commission, "Record," July 1993, vol. 19, no. 7.*

Spending by PACs

Where does the money go? That question is fairly easy to answer because PACs are required to report their receipts and expenditures to the Federal Election Commission, a government agency. Most of the money spent at the national level goes to incumbents.

PACs play a more important role in congressional politics than in presidential politics. Within Congress, PACs are more important to members of the House of Representatives than to members of the Senate. Ninety-four members of the House in the 103rd Congress (1992–1994) have received over $1 million from PACs during the ten-year period from January 1, 1983, through December 21, 1992.[19] Democrats have been the principal beneficiaries primarily because they have outnumbered Republican representatives in recent years. During the 1991–1992 election cycle, House Democrats received 45 percent of their contributions from PACs; Senate Democrats received 26 percent.[20]

At the presidential level, PAC contributions are not as critical. They usually account for less than 5 percent of the total contributions candidates receive in their quest for their party's nomination. No PAC contributions are permitted in presidential elections, but the grassroots activities and voluntary efforts of PACs can be a vital supplement to a candidate's campaign. Corporate and trade association PACs have given a larger proportion of their campaign funds to incumbents than have labor and nonconnected PACs. One explanation for this pattern may be that corporate and trade PACs want to help people who are in the best position to help them, but labor and nonconnected PACs want to get people who share their views into position to help them. The first might be called a pragmatic electoral strategy, the second an ideological one.

What is the impact of PAC money? The answer to that question is not very clear. There is little tangible evidence to support the proposition that campaign contributions or activities "buy" legislators' votes. But there does seem to be a relationship between legislative support for a PAC and campaign contributions from a PAC. Not surprisingly, PACs are inclined to support legislators who are sympathetic to their interests.

PACs: Pro and Con

The increasing involvement of PACs in the electoral process has generated considerable criticism and proposals for reform. That criticism has stemmed in part from the pressure that has been on people to make "voluntary" contributions, pressure that can be seen in the following memo sent by a corporate executive to his company's managers in 1992:

It is very important for us to have our views heard by congressmen, senators, and staffers within the government. Without the chance to tell our story on a wide range of issues, we cannot influence the decisions made. We have a broad range of customers: Air Force, DOD, NASA, DOE, etc., so there are many committees and people that need to hear our story.

Access to these people is not theoretically bought, but if you want to see them in a timely manner, it is expected for us to make a contribution to their campaign funds. . . .

Corporations cannot provide these funds by law, but their employees can. The PAC is merely a bank account funded by salaried employees that provides these "access" funds. . . .

Contribute! Consider it a premium on an insurance policy on our business.[21]

In addition to the pressure on donors, critics of PACs contend that they exercise undue influence on public officials. Since PACs contribute overwhelmingly to incumbents, it is natural to infer that they do so to obtain the sympathetic ear of those already in power. This practice raises the suspicion that PACs expect something in return for their contributions and that the more money a candidate receives from a particular PAC, the more difficult it will be for that person to make independent decisions once in office.

Not only does PAC money go to incumbents, but it goes disproportionately to party leaders and the chairs of committees and subcommittees. (Table 8-3 indicates the twenty-five top PAC recipients in the House.) It goes to these individuals because PACs want to gain access to them. This distribution of funds would not elicit so much objection if all segments of society were equally represented by PACs, but they are not. Corporate and trade associations are more numerous and raise and spend more money than their chief adversary,

TABLE 8-3		
Top PAC Recipients in the House of Representatives, 1983–1992		
HOUSE REPRESENTATIVE	PARTY—STATE	PAC RECEIPTS
Majority Leader Richard Gephardt	D—MO	$3,049,977
Democratic Caucus Vice-Chair Vic Fazio	D—CA	2,645,384
Energy and Commerce Chair John Dingell	D—MI	2,486,597
Minority Leader Robert Michel	R—IL	2,473,727
Majority Whip David Bonior	D—MI	2,295,290
Ways and Means Chair Dan Rostenkowski	D—IL	2,222,189
Speaker Thomas Foley	D—WA	1,995,083
Representative Robert Matsui	D—CA	1,969,509
Representative Charles Wilson	D—TX	1,942,898
Representative Bob Carr	D—MI	1,892,567
Representative Martin Frost	D—TX	1,867,853
Representative Sam Gibbons	D—FL	1,823,451
Representative John Murtha	D—PA	1,821,922
Representative Philip Sharp	D—IN	1,808,284
Representative John Bryant	D—TX	1,797,546
Representative Butler Derrick	D—SC	1,751,699
Judiciary Chair Jack Brooks	D—TX	1,739,944
Democratic Caucus Chair Steny Hoyer	D—MD	1,737,322
Minority Whip Newt Gingrich	R—GA	1,713,634
Science, Space, and Technology Chair George Brown	D—CA	1,711,176
Representative Al Swift	D—WA	1,706,555
Representative James Quillen	R—TN	1,696,038
Representative Stephen Neal	D—NC	1,675,384
Representative Jack Fields	R—TX	1,675,113
Public Works and Transportation Chair Norman Mineta	D—CA	1,652,031

SOURCE: Common Cause, "News Release," March 12, 1993, 1–2. Reprinted with permission.

labor unions, and all three groups raise and spend much more than consumer groups. Similarly, nonconnected, ideologically conservative groups have been more active and more successful fundraisers than their liberal opponents.

Critics of PACs believe that because certain types of organizations are especially well represented by PACs, they are in a stronger position to exercise influence and shape public policy than are organizations not represented by PACs. Although this criticism may be true, it must be said that it is very difficult to know for certain why legislators behave as they do. Potential influences on legislators range from their own partisan and ideological orientations to their personal views to the pressures exerted by constituents and political interest groups (including PACs). Nevertheless, groups that can gain better access and make a more compelling case have an advantage over others. One expert, Frank Sorauf, argues that this advantage is greatest "in the narrower, less salient issues that escape party, presidential, or popular attention."[22]

Other political scientists have also found a relationship between money and influence. Richard L. Hall and Frank W. Wayman studied the participation of members of the House of Representatives on three committees (Agriculture, Education and Labor, and Energy and Commerce) in three issue areas (milk price supports, job training, and natural gas deregulation). They found that committee members tended to devote more time and effort to issues that concerned organized interests within their constituencies than to issues that did not. They also found a relationship between PAC contributions and the level of committee activity: the greater the contributions, the greater the activity. This finding led Hall and Wayman to conclude that although PAC money may not have bought votes, "it apparently did buy the marginal time, energy, and legislative resources that committee participation requires."[23] In other words, the contributions had an impact; they were an incentive for members of Congress to work harder to achieve the goals of the contributing groups. And as Table 8-4 shows, health-care interest groups certainly believe this to be the case.

Another issue concerning PACs is their effect on political parties. Most political scientists believe that PACs hurt parties. They siphon funds away from them; they encourage policy-oriented candidates who may not have a history of party involvement or allegiance; and they promote their own agendas. These activities detract from the ability of the parties to take consistent positions on policy issues, to attract candidates who support those positions and are willing to toe the party line, and to assume responsibility for how the candidates they favor perform once they gain office.

Proponents of PACs, in contrast, note that PACs help finance the cost of elections, thereby reducing the burden on taxpayers and the general public; they increase public knowledge of the issues; and they encourage people to participate in the electoral process and to vote. These activities contribute to the functioning of a democratic society. Moreover, by supporting candidates who are sympathetic to their points of view and are in a position to help them achieve their policy objectives, PACs link the public with its representatives—another important objective of democracy. Finally, they point out that PAC election activity is a right protected by the First Amendment to the United States Constitution.

Nonetheless, there have been frequent proposals to reform the system and limit the influence of PACs. Recent proposals have included imposing spending limits on congressional candidates, lowering or eliminating the amount of money PACs are allowed to contribute, or even providing public funding as is done in presidential elections.

LOBBYING

Once an election is over, what can a group do to ensure that its point of view is forcefully presented when issues of concern arise on Capitol Hill or in a state legislature? It can use **lobbying**, a term that describes the behavior of people who accost their elected representatives in the lobbies of legislatures and other government buildings and try to persuade them how to vote on an issue. The word also unfortunately suggests some of the seamy sides of representation, and it is often associated with unethical behavior in politics.

TABLE 8-4			
Leading Health-Care Lobbyists, 1979–1993			
PAC	1979–1993	1991*	1993*
American Medical Association	$15,016,193	$245,240	$282,597
National Association of Life Underwriters	7,702,144	242,950	272,200
American Hospital Association	2,525,957	148,211	233,600
Independent Insurance Agents of America	4,370,458	249,217	181,673
American Dental Association	6,002,861	165,585	174,175

* Data are for the first ten months of these nonelection years.

SOURCE: Federal Election Commission.

Lobbyists do congregate in and around legislative bodies, but they do much more than that. Their principal function is to provide public officials with information to influence their opinions and positions. Although lobbyists can use a variety of positive and negative inducements in this effort, they must be careful not to exceed the bounds of proper conduct or make permanent enemies. Because lobbyists typically deal with the same officials again and again, they take care to see that the information they provide is correct. Lobbyists believe that their ability to persuade is directly related to their credibility. They fear that if they mislead, purposely or accidentally, their information and arguments will always be viewed skeptically by those they are trying to influence.[24]

Types of Lobbying

Lobbying can take many forms: a memo or statement to a public official indicating a group's position; an organization's sending influential constituents to Washington to plead its case; or a public relations campaign in which millions of people participate and millions of dollars are spent.

Lobbying may be direct or indirect (see Figure 8-3). In direct lobbying, group representatives themselves contact public officials; with indirect lobbying, they stimulate others to do so. Whether direct or indirect, the aim of the lobbying activity is still the same: to influence the decisions of public officials and affect public policy in a manner that accords with the group's interests.

Lobbyists attempt to influence the policy process directly by testifying at public hearings and by providing detailed policy statements and supporting material to public officials and their staffs. They even draft proposed bills or regulations for use by a committee considering legislation or an agency attempting to implement it. Even when lobbyists do not testify or prepare position papers, they make a point of attending hearings when proposals in which they are interested are being considered.

Examples of interest groups using these direct methods to affect policy deliberations abound at the national and state levels. Following the Supreme Court's *Webster* decision in 1989, which opened the door to legislative consid-

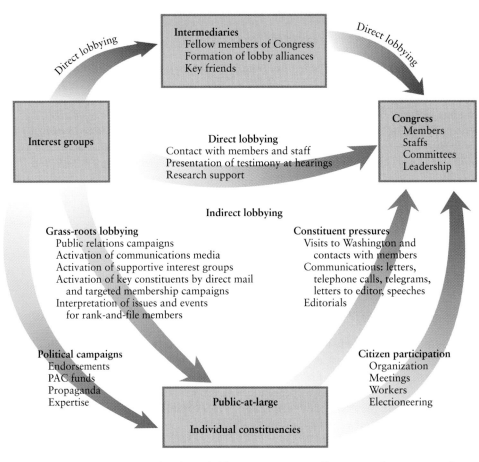

Figure 8-3 *Direct and indirect lobbying.* SOURCE: *William J. Keefe, Henry J. Abraham, William H. Flanigan, Charles O. Jones, Morris S. Ogul, and John W. Spanier, American Democracy: Institutions, Politics, and Policies, 2nd ed. (Chicago: Dorsey Press, 1986), 259, modified by the author. Copyright © 1986 Dorsey Press. Reprinted with permission.*

eration of the abortion issue at the state level, pro-choice groups drafted bills that would protect the reproductive rights of women, and pro-life organizations proposed legislation that would prohibit abortion after the twentieth week of pregnancy. Both sides issued public statements, wrote speeches for their sympathizers, and provided officials at all levels of government with research and data to support their positions.

These same groups have been active within the public arena as well, instituting grassroots lobbying campaigns to build support for a particular position within the general public, particularly among people who feel strongly about the issue and are likely to communicate their feeling to those in government. A good example of this type of indirect lobbying is the successful effort by the banking industry to prevent a provision of the 1982 tax bill from taking effect. The provision would have required banks to withhold 10 percent of depositors' interest for taxes, much as businesses withhold a part of employees' salaries. The banking industry generated 22 million letters to members of Congress, which resulted in the removal of the withholding provision.[25]

Many political interest groups also use so-called legislative and policy

The Federal Election Commission (FEC) maintains records of campaign finance reports. The reports, which are open to the public, include detailed information about the sources of a candidate's funds and how the money is being spent. The FEC reports how much money a candidate has raised and spent in a current campaign, who has given or loaned money to a candidate, and when those contributions were received during the election cycle. It also reports on the financial activity of PACs, broken down by types, and national party committees. The FEC also monitors independent spending during elections.

These reports, all available to the public, are published in monthly FEC newsletters, occasional press releases, and election pamphlets beginning with the 1977–1978 election cycle and continuing to the present. They are also available on computerized indices and, for a fee, may be accessed directly from the FEC's computerized files.

To get campaign finance information from the Federal Election Commission, contact the Public Records Office, 999 E Street, N.W., Washington, DC 20463; (800) 424-9530. Researchers can also get information from the record offices that the FEC maintains in each state. Call the toll-free number for an up-to-date directory of these offices.

---

alerts to energize their members to write, telephone, or telegraph the president and members of Congress in support of the group's position. This tactic of arousing concerned people can be used by practically anyone who has a following and access to the mass media. Conservative radio talk-show hosts and Christian fundamentalist ministers used this device to mobilize their listeners and supporters against President Clinton's proposal to permit homosexuals in the military. Telephone calls to the White House averaged 50,000 a day, ten times their normal volume, during the brief period when the issue was a prime focus of public attention. At the height of the controversy, members of Congress received over a half a million letters in a single day.

Two other tactics used in grassroots lobbying are the *direct-mail approach*, used very successfully by conservative groups in the late 1970s and early 1980s, and *targeted membership campaigns*, used by the U.S. Chamber of Commerce, the National Rifle Association, and various other groups. Direct mail, particularly as used by fundraiser Richard Viguerie, has been the major reason for the financial success of conservative groups in the past twenty years. Viguerie put together over three hundred mailing lists with the names of more than 25 million contributors to various conservative causes. Not only were these individuals likely targets for fundraising drives, but they also constituted a large number of potential activists for various conservative causes. According to Viguerie: "Raising money is only one of several purposes of direct-mail advertising letters. A letter may ask you to vote for a candidate, volunteer for campaign work, circulate a petition among your neighbors, write letters and post cards to your Senators and Congressmen, urging them to pass or defeat legislation and also ask you for money to pay for the direct-mail advertising campaign."[26]

Computer technology makes it possible to target the people who are most likely to be influenced by a particular campaign. Targeted membership campaigns minimize the waste of mass mailings and are less visible than direct mail to opposition groups—until their impact hits home. The U.S. Chamber of Com-

During 1993, opposition to the North American Free Trade Agreement brought together such strange partners as Ross Perot, Doris Day, and the AFL-CIO. In the fall a coalition of environmentalists, consumer groups, and humane societies took out full-page newspaper ads to generate grass-roots opposition to the legislation. The ads claimed that NAFTA would cost tens of thousands of jobs, kill dolphins and wild songbirds, permit importation of foods soaked in carcinogenic pesticides, devastate the landscape, create a "toxic hell," and suppress democracy. The ad was loaded with clip-out/send-in coupons (below). All this threatened the Clinton administration, but the bill passed comfortably.

Hon._____

(Your local representative)

U.S. House of Representatives
Washington, D.C. 20515

I am strongly opposed to NAFTA. It will harm the natural environment here, in Canada and in Mexico, and it will cost the U.S. thousands of jobs. I urge you to vote "no" on NAFTA. Please inform me of your position.

NAME _____

ADDRESS _____

SOURCE: *8 Fatal Flaws of NAFTA, advertisement by Public Citizen,* New York Times, *September 22, 1993, A17.*

5. RAVAGING NATURAL RESOURCES

If the name of NAFTA is not changed to the Corporate Aid Agreement, it should become the Natural Resources Raiding Agreement, because many laws that try to restrict corporate trade in resources will be illegal under NAFTA. Efforts to conserve resources for the future are a no-no. Two examples:

➤ In the U.S. there are now laws which prevent exports of raw unprocessed logs from certain public lands (see caption above). A similar law exists in Canada for softwoods. The laws are for conservation purposes–to protect scarce resources, and to encourage *local use* of whatever logs are cut down, i.e. for labor intensive work like building, or furniture-making. Under NAFTA, if a country banned the export of such logs, it could face sanctions.

➤ NAFTA could devastate the resources of *all three* NAFTA countries. *That is its intention:* To help corporations seize resources, wherever they hide. Under NAFTA, a member country cannot adopt a conservation restriction if it *reduces the percent of a resource that is exported to another member country.* For example, Canada now exports 40% of its natural gas to the U.S. If Canada tries to slow the flow, to conserve for the future, NAFTA could make that illegal.

8. NAFTA'S BIG BUCKS BACKERS

If NAFTA succeeds, multinational corporations stand to reap huge windfall profits. *That is why the agreement was created in the first place.* The lobbying is underway. Eastman Kodak and American Express have spearheaded a pro-NAFTA coalition of 2,000 of the largest corporations in the country, including such stellar environmentalists as Exxon, Dupont, General Electric, Dow Chemical, and Union Carbide. And now, using your tax dollars, Mr. Clinton has appointed a "NAFTA Czar" to blitz the public and push the deal.

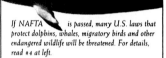

If NAFTA   is passed, many U.S. laws that protect dolphins, whales, migratory birds and other endangered wildlife will be threatened. For details, read #4 at left.

With the side agreements sadly revealed as window dressing and the new line up of giant corporate backers, the question still remains: *Why is the Clinton-Gore administration pushing so hard for an agreement that undermines many of the social and environmental goals for which it was elected?* In any case, it is now clearly up to citizens to block this scheme, and we can. NAFTA still must get through Congress. The message is simple: *As currently written, NAFTA is not fixable and will cause disaster.* Help us fight against it. Use the coupons below. Thank you.

merce has used computer-based technology to mobilize its constituents (local chambers, firms, business-related trade associations) on legislative issues that affect them; and it is able to do so on a district-by-district basis. In claiming credit for getting four sympathetic House members onto a crucial conference committee on legislation affecting accounting practices, a Chamber official noted that his organization had urged members in four congressional districts to contact House Ways and Means Committee chair Dan Rostenkowski (D-Illinois) and request that he appoint their representatives as conferees. Rostenkowski may not have been aware of the Chamber's involvement, however, because all the communications came directly from local businesspeople. Similarly, the National Rifle Association mailed more than 10 million letters and spent over $1.7 million in 1988 in an effort to prevent the enactment of a bill that required a seven-day waiting period for the purchase of a handgun.[27] Yet the legislation, known as the Brady Bill, became law in 1994.

Targets of Lobbying

Most Americans tend to equate lobbying with efforts to influence the legislative process. Any experienced lobbyist knows, however, that the legislative process is only one part of the government system and that it is not always the most important or most pertinent part for a particular group on a particular issue.

At the national level, Congress looks to the presidency for much of its agenda each year, and the executive agencies have a great deal of discretion in the administration of the laws. The courts, moreover, have the power to interpret and, in some cases, to invalidate laws passed by Congress. At the state level, similar patterns of interaction and spheres of influence are evident. What determines the best place for a group to lobby, and what kinds of activities are most successful in different branches or levels of government?

Legislatures Sometimes getting legislation passed is vital to a group's interests. This was the case in 1979 when the Chrysler Corporation asked the federal government to guarantee the repayment of loans that the corporation wished to obtain from banks, loans that it needed to stay in business. No federal agency had the power to grant such guarantees without a legislative mandate. Congressional action is also required when industries seek import tariffs to protect domestic manufacturers against foreign competition or when public interest groups seek laws requiring government proceedings and documents to be open to public inspection (so-called sunshine laws). And when the banking industry seeks to modify regulations on how much capital they must hold or the conditions under which they may engage in interstate banking, specific provisions must be written into new legislation. Right after the 1992 elections, the American Bankers Association hired two well-connected Washington attorneys with close ties to the Democratic party and the Clinton administration, Charles Manatt (former chair of the Democratic National Committee) and Thomas Boggs (a former law partner of Commerce Secretary Ron Brown) to pursue these and other policy objectives.

Legislators are relatively easy to lobby. They are open and accessible, and as elected representatives they have to be sensitive to outside pressures, particularly when those pressures come from their constituencies. Lobbyists can also provide things that legislators need and want as they carry out their legislative responsibilities: information about how legislation will affect their constituents, political support for the legislator or for the legislation, and financial support in the next election. For these reasons lobbyists are generally welcome or at least tolerated in the halls of legislatures and in lawmakers' offices.

How successful lobbyists are is another question. The main challenge facing lobbyists who hope to influence legislative bodies is the relatively large size of most legislatures and the large number of members that must be contacted and persuaded. A second problem, particularly at the national level, stems from the degree of activity and number of groups interested in any particular issue. Legislators deal with a variety of issues and must be receptive to a range of special pleaders. Lobbyists are rarely alone in presenting their position or unified in the advice they give. Normally, they can expect opposition within legislatures and by other groups.

The proliferation of lobbying has resulted in coalition building among diverse groups. The formation of alliances in support of and in opposition to clean-air laws, described at the beginning of the chapter, illustrates the coalition building that regularly occurs among groups with similar interests and objectives. To cite another example, even before President Clinton proposed his health-care reform package to the nation, health-care groups began to form alliances in support of or opposition to his plan.

A third limitation on the ability of lobbyists to get their way is the fact that legislators frequently behave as if they do not owe lobbyists anything. They may use the professional and personal services provided by lobbyists—legislative research, political support, financial contributions, electoral endorsements, grassroots activity—without promising anything in return. They may also avail themselves of limited benefits such as invitations to speak (and relax) at conventions held in plush resorts or even small gifts (less than $200 for House members and $300 for senators)—again without promising the lobbyists anything in return.[28] In short, legislators are able to manipulate the lobbyists who attempt to manipulate them, thereby undercutting the lobbyists' influence on legislative outcomes.

The executive branch   Chief executives—the president and the state governors—and their administrative agencies have also become a major focus of lobbying activities. As in the legislature, lobbying in the executive branch is viewed as legitimate and is usually not discouraged. Lobbyists and executive-branch officials tend to have mutual needs and interests. Whereas interest groups desire access, visibility, and support for their objective, chief executives and their administrations require political allies. Particularly at the national level, where political parties are weak, interest groups can be mobilized to build support for the president's programs. Even before President Clinton proposed his deficit-reduction plan to Congress, for example, he had assembled business leaders at the White House and asked them to back his proposal to increase their corporate taxes.

The use of outside groups to generate political support for the president is not a recent phenomenon. In 1978 an office was created in the White House (known as the public liaison office) to do just that—to orchestrate the activity of interest groups behind the administration's key priorities as well as to serve these groups' political, policy, and membership needs.

In addition to trying to influence policy making in the executive branch, interest groups try to shape the content and application of rules governing policy implementation. Indeed, most executive agencies are required to publish draft regulations and hold public hearings to solicit input from interested individuals and organizations.

The judiciary   The judicial arena is also a focus of group activity. Political interest groups that have little or no hope of achieving their ends through the legislative and executive processes often turn to the courts for help. For those who wish to prevent a hostile majority from depriving them of what they consider their basic rights, the courts are a last resort. Business groups, for instance, have regularly appealed to the courts to invalidate government attempts to regulate their operations. In the early part of this century, they successfully challenged state and national laws that limited the hours employees could work and established the minimum wage they could be paid. Today, they continue to contest regulations that affect how they do business—regulations on health, safety, the environment, even personnel practices such as hiring and promotion.

How does one go about lobbying the judicial branch of government? The first thing any interested group can do is to try to influence the selection of judges. Although the judicial selection process, particularly at the national level, is often portrayed as nonpolitical, political considerations are involved in the nomination process and frequently in the confirmation process as well. The vast majority of judicial appointees are members of the president's party. Most of them are confirmed by the Senate without much challenge, but occasionally a nominee provokes considerable controversy. This was the case when federal judges Robert Bork (1987) and Clarence Thomas (1991) were nominated to fill vacancies on the Supreme Court (the conflict over the Bork nomination is described in Chapter 15).

Attempts to influence the judiciary do not stop with the judicial selection process. Political interest groups often try to obtain through litigation what they cannot achieve through legislative or executive action. The area of civil rights provides many illustrations. The school desegregation case of *Brown v. Board of Education* (1954) was started in the absence of legislation because a law making segregation illegal was unlikely to be enacted by Congress or southern state legislatures in the 1950s. Similarly, civil rights groups have gone to court to try to force executive agencies to obey legislative mandates and judicial decisions. Other groups, in contrast, have used the judiciary to try to reverse administrative rulings such as those regulating the environment.

In addition to filing court cases themselves, interest groups may file **amicus curiae** ("friend of the court") **briefs** in support of positions in pending cases. Over one hundred different groups filed briefs with the Supreme Court in connection with *Regents of the University of California v. Bakke*, a 1978 case dealing with whether state or federal government could require affirmative action programs to make up for past discrimination. "Friends of the court" in this matter included such diverse organizations as the American Federation of Teachers, the American Indian Bar Association, the American Jewish Congress, the NAACP Legal and Educational Fund, the United Farm Workers, and the United Mine Workers. Eleven years later, the Court received seventy-eight briefs in the case of *Webster v. Reproductive Health Services*. Of these, forty-six favored the Missouri abortion law and thirty-two opposed it. Similarly, over one hundred organizations and groups filed amicus curiae briefs in the case of *Planned Parenthood of Southeastern Pennsylvania v. Casey*, which was decided by the Supreme Court in 1992. These briefs debated issues ranging from when life begins to the legislative history of abortion in America to the constitutionality of the *Roe v. Wade* decision.

Efforts to influence the justices by means of legal arguments have been supplemented by more visible demonstrations of public support. One pro-choice group organized a campaign to send a million postcards to the Supreme Court. Both sides on the abortion issue have engaged in extensive media campaigns, including full-page advertisements in newspapers that the justices were likely to read, such as the *Washington Post* and the *New York Times*. There have even been demonstrations outside the Supreme Court building when the major abortion cases were argued and when the decisions were announced.

Whether public rallies, private correspondence, or legal briefs have any impact on Supreme Court decisions is unclear, although they obviously serve the political interest groups' needs for visibility and public education and, indirectly, for their own fundraising. But the Court is not oblivious to the outside world. In their 1989 and 1990 opinions stating that burning the American flag is a form of protest protected by the First Amendment to the Constitution, the justices went to great lengths to explain their decisions in anticipation of adverse public reaction. The Court, however, is not expected to follow or conform to popular opinion when interpreting the law.

The Limits of Protest

Sipa Press

Protests that elicit police response are often staged to gain public support for a cause. After Wichita mounted police forcibly broke up demonstrators blockading a family planning clinic in 1991, Operation Rescue replicated this scene nationwide.

The Constitution protects the right of association and the right to protest government policies and actions. But how far can that protest go? If it involves illegal activity, such as forcibly interfering with a military or police operation, it can obviously be stopped or prevented.

But what about nonviolent protest such as Operation Rescue, a pro-life group that has opposed abortion by blocking off clinics in which abortions are performed? Whose rights are protected by the Constitution, those who do the blocking or those who are impeded or even prevented from entering because the clinic is blocked?

These issues, generated by the abortion controversy, were prevalent in the case of *Bray v. Alexandria Women's Health Clinic*, first argued before the Supreme Court during October 1991 and then reargued a year later after Justice Clarence Thomas joined the Court. Technically, the case was not about abortion or even the limits of abortion protest. Both issues, however, contributed to the specific question before the justices, whether or not a 1971 federal law prohibiting conspiracies to deny people their civil rights could be used against protestors who block abortion clinics. In January 1993, a divided Supreme Court indicated that it could not. Then, in January 1994, the Court held that a federal racketeering law could be used to prosecute those who denied access to clinics.

This clash between the rights of protestors and those whose rights may be restricted by the protest reflects the tension that is inevitable in a democratic society. The issue for the society is how to deal with that tension in a way that preserves the rule of law and ensures that the law itself is equitable. Frequently this becomes a question of how to protect minority rights in a political system that is predicated on the principle of majority rule.

On the larger question, can a democratic government insure that majority interests will prevail while minority rights are also protected? And which government institution is ultimately responsible for achieving this, the legislative, the executive, or the judiciary?

Changes in Lobbying and Lobbyists

As American society grows more pluralistic and as government grows larger and more decentralized, many new groups are seeking to influence government, and lobbying activity has increased manyfold in Washington, D.C., and in most state capitals. Foreign interests have also found new ways to be represented. Before the 1980s most foreign companies used the commercial sections of their embassies to promote their interests in the United States. Embassies still provide their nationals with diplomatic and consular services, but foreign companies— and countries—have increasingly turned to American firms to represent them in Washington. Not only do they hire American citizens, they also pay them huge fees, especially if they happen to be former government officials. A 1992 report by the General Accounting Office found that eighty-two executive officials, legislators, and senior congressional staff members who had left their posts between 1986 and 1992 were working as lobbyists or representatives for foreign interests.[29] This practice became a campaign issue in the 1992 presidential election when third-party candidate H. Ross Perot spoke derisively of "high-priced Washington lobbyists in their $1,000 suits and alligator shoes" selling their expertise to the highest bidders.

Foreign representation by Americans in Washington is extensive. Between 1988 and 1992, Japanese interests used more than 125 public relations specialists, lobbyists, lawyers, and political and economic consultants to represent them. In 1992 alone they spent over $60 million on American representation. Canada spent $22.7 million, while Germany, France, Mexico, and Hong Kong each spent over $10 million buying information and influence in Washington.[30] Such large expenditures by foreign governments and companies raise serious political, economic, and national security concerns.

The lobbying business has also become more specialized. Lawyers and law firms are still major players, but public relations firms, issues management firms, and accounting firms are increasingly active. Some of the largest offer a wide variety of services, ranging from lobbying to coalition building, grassroots development, media consultation, fundraising, events planning, issue research, and public opinion polling. Environmental groups, energy producers and consumers, and banks regularly use these firms in addition to their own public relations professionals. Lobbying, in short, has become a more public activity.

There have been legal changes as well. Sunshine laws mandating that congressional committee meetings and executive agency deliberations be open to the public have forced lobbyists and decision makers to operate in public view and occasionally in the public spotlight. New ethics and finance laws and rules which presidents have issued to their staffs have imposed more stringent requirements on public officials who interact with lobbyists. The media also report on more improprieties. In one highly publicized incident during the 102nd Congress (1990–1992), five senators were accused of using their influence to obtain special favors for the Lincoln Savings and Loan Bank of California owned by Charles H. Keating, Jr. (see the Case Study on page 270).

Charles Keating and the Keating Five

Charles H. Keating, Jr., first came to the attention of federal bank regulators in February of 1984 when his real estate development company, American Continental Corp., purchased the California-based Lincoln Savings and Loan Association. Prior to 1984, Lincoln was a small thrift institution that had enjoyed stable but moderate growth. Despite an agreement with the Federal Savings and Loan Insurance Corporation (FSLIC) to pursue slow growth, Keating almost immediately began a major expansion effort. Much of this expansion was based on risky and otherwise questionable loans, often to Keating's business associates. These activities eventually led to action by Federal Home Loan Bank Board (FHLBB) officials. Their investigation found numerous violations of banking laws, and the regulators recommended severe restrictions on Lincoln's activities. The cost to the taxpayers of bailing out Lincoln Savings and Loan to protect the money that people had deposited in it was $2.6 billion.

In an effort to block further FHLBB action, Keating enlisted the assistance of several senators who sat on key committees or who represented areas served by Lincoln. On several occasions, the "Keating Five" senators or members of their staffs met with or contacted FSLIC and FHLBB officials on Lincoln's behalf.

By itself, this intervention by the senators was not illegal or even unusual. Most senators and representatives do try to help their constituents with government-related problems. What was questionable, however, was that the "Keating Five" senators had received a total of $1.5 million in political contributions from Keating and his associates. The Senate found none of these contributions improper. The issue by implication, then, was whether these senators helped Charles Keating more than they would have helped any other constituent, and whether they helped him because of the large contributions they had received from him for their campaigns.

On February 27, 1991, the Senate Ethics Committee issued findings which many observers believe did little to clarify what is and is not permissible behavior for senators acting on behalf of their constituents. The committee determined that four of the senators, Dennis DeConcini (D-AZ), John Glenn (D-OH), John McCain (R-AZ), and Donald Riegle (D-MI) were guilty of poor judgment and that DeConcini and Riegle gave the appearance of impropriety. Senator Alan Cranston (D-CA) received a harsher judgment: the committee rebuked him on the floor of the Senate.

Senator Cranston was unrepentant in his reply. Speaking to his colleagues on the Senate floor, he denied allegations of impropriety. Then, turning to the senators who were present, he asked: "How many of you, after really thinking about it, could rise and declare that you have never, ever helped—or agreed to help—a contributor close in time to the solicitation or receipt of a contribution? I don't believe any of you could say 'never' "

The scandal damaged everyone involved. Glenn, the space hero, and McCain, the war hero, survived with their reputations somewhat tarnished but with their Senate seats intact. The others did not. Cranston, who was suffering from prostate cancer, did not seek reelection in 1992, and DeConcini and Riegel both decided to retire in 1993 rather than face tough reelection battles and the possibility of defeat.

Charles Keating was found guilty of securities fraud, sentenced to ten years in prison, and fined $250,000 by a California Superior Court. He was also found guilty in United States District Court on broader federal fraud and racketeering charges. If that were not enough, he is a defendant in a variety of civil suits filed by bondholders, the Securities and Exchange Commission, the Office of Thrift Supervision, and other state agencies.

SOURCES: John R. Cranford with Janet Hook and Phil Kuntz, "Decision in Keating Five Case Settles Little for Senate," *Congressional Quarterly*, vol. 49 (March 2, 1991), 517–523; and Richard L. Berke, "Cranston Rebuked by Ethics Panel," *New York Times*, November 21, 1991, A1, D21.

The "Keating Five" as they sat at the Senate hearings. (Clockwise from top center): senators Alan Cranston, Donald Riegle, Jr., John McCain, John Glenn, and Dennis DeConcini. In the center is Charles Keating as he was led back and forth to court.

Discussion questions

1. How far should members of Congress be able to go in representing the interests of their constituents? Should the standard be different for constituents who have made large campaign contributions than for those who have not?

2. What criteria should be used to determine when members of Congress have stepped over the bounds of propriety? Is the "appearance" of impropriety enough to warrant sanctions? Explain why or why not.

3. Does the unwillingness of the Senate Ethics Committee to impose harsher sanctions on the "Keating Five" indicate that the Senate is politically incapable of policing the activities of its own members? Explain why or why not.

4. In spite of the scandal, senators McCain and Glenn won reelection in 1992. Why, then, do you suppose senators DeConcini and Riegle announced their retirements in 1993 rather than face bruising Senate campaigns in 1994?

Foxes guarding the fox den

Regulation of Lobbying

Some lobbying activities seem inconsistent with the operation of a political system in which the influence of the wealthy should be no greater than that of the poor. These practices range from illegal activities, such as providing money, gifts, and vacations in exchange for favorable policy decisions, to legal but questionable actions, such as offering honoraria for speeches (now unacceptable for executive-branch officials and members of Congress), making contributions to fundraisers, and extending social invitations. Elected officials and their respective political parties often encourage these exchanges by holding fundraisers or retreats where individuals plan legislative strategy and build their resources for upcoming elections. For example, in February 1993 Republican House members invited lobbyists to their retreat and charged each $6,000 for the privilege of attending. Not to be outdone, the Democrats invited many of the same lobbyists, and others who would pay, to purchase tables or seats at their presidential dinner. For a little extra money, lobbyists could attend one of the small receptions where they could mingle with the president, vice-president, cabinet members, and congressional leadership. Such solicitations obviously raise important political and ethical issues for a democratic government.

Over the years there have been numerous attempts to control lobbying activities. The Federal Regulation of Lobbying Act, enacted in 1946, required that anyone hired by someone else for the principal purpose of lobbying Congress must register and file a financial report. This law was later challenged as placing undue restrictions on constitutionally protected activity. The Supreme Court upheld the law but interpreted the registration provision very narrowly. Since then, while most lobbyists who represent American groups do not register with the government, those representing foreign governments must do so.

More recent legislation directed at campaign activities and lobbying includes the Federal Election Campaign Finance Act of 1971 and its 1974, 1976, and 1979 amendments and the Ethics in Government Act of 1978 (see Table 8-5, page 274). The latter aims at conflicts of interest that may impair the ability of government officials to act in the public interest. For example, former mid- and high-level officials are prohibited from lobbying an agency they have just left on "any particular matter" of "direct and substantial interest" to that agency for one year. President Clinton's appointees were asked to extend these limits to five years and to restrict their representation of foreign interests. And former executive-branch officials may never represent anyone on any issue they were directly involved with while in government. These restrictions are intended to slow the revolving door between government and the private sector.

There is considerable controversy over the effectiveness of laws and regulations governing ethical conduct in and after public office. Proponents argue that because the careers of public officials often begin and end in the private sector, there is a need for rules that prevent private gain at public expense. Others fear that the requirements for financial disclosure, the limits placed on private employment after government service, and the restriction of foreign representation may keep some of the best people out of government.

CONSEQUENCES OF THE GROUP STRUGGLE

What are the consequences of the American system of interest group representation? Does it have an impact on national policy? Does it diminish government's ability to pursue nationwide policies and long-term interests in favor of those with narrower, more immediate and direct appeal?

When resources are limited, it is almost inevitable that some people will benefit more than others. In 1960 E. E. Schattschneider suggested that the beneficiaries of the struggle among political interest groups are people in higher socioeconomic brackets, those with the most money, the best organizations, and the greatest influence.[31] Most citizens can never be adequately represented—and if they were, Schattschneider believed, the system would become hopelessly stalemated.[32]

Today, more than three decades later, there are many more organized interests, but the system still favors the "haves" in the sense that it is resistant to innovative change. Moreover, corporations, educational institutions, and local governments still outnumber public interest and consumer groups and have a larger and more pronounced presence in Washington. They have more resources to hire high-powered lawyers, lobbyists, and public relations firms, which they believe give them greater ability to influence government's decisions.

How effective are political interest groups in actually affecting policy outcomes? Much depends on how much competition there is among groups within a particular policy sphere and on who will benefit from and who will pay for a new policy. In general, if there is little competition, an interest group seeking change will be more likely to get what it wants than if there is much competition among groups with comparable resources. A good example of a noncompetitive situation is "pork-barrel" legislation—price supports for agriculture, subsidies for medical research, or public works projects—in which the benefits are concentrated but the costs are widely dispersed. Here those who will gain a lot

Ethical Restrictions on Legislative and Executive Employees

	LEGISLATIVE	EXECUTIVE
Honoraria	House members and their staffs may not personally accept honoraria, but they can donate individual fees up to $200 to charity. Senate members may accept honoraria up to a certain percent of their salaries; honoraria to be phased out dollar for dollar as the cost-of-living allowance increases.	Presidential appointees may not accept honoraria. Civil servants cannot accept honoraria from prohibited sources. (These are yet to be defined.)
Other outside income	House members cannot practice another profession while in Congress, nor can they serve for pay on boards of directors. Their total outside income is limited to 15 percent of the salary for executive level II. The Senate does not limit outside income.	Presidential appointees may not earn outside income. Civil servants cannot accept earned outside income from prohibited sources involving prohibited activities.
Gifts	House and Senate members cannot accept gifts over a certain value ($200 in the House, $300 in the Senate). They may accept meals, but not in connection with overnight trips.	No member of the executive can accept gifts from prohibited sources. Presidential appointees may not accept a free meal. Civil servants may accept a meal of under $20.
Travel	Limitations placed on the length of travel (number of days and nights) paid for by outside groups, including lobbyists.	
Conflict of interest	Employees cannot personally participate in contacts with executive or judicial agencies in which they have a financial interest.	
Financial disclosure	Required, although blind trusts are permitted.	All presidential appointees and most senior career executives must make annual public disclosures of their sources and amounts of income.
Postemployment restrictions	Lifetime ban on lobbying on particular matters in which an employee was personally and substantially involved. Two-year ban on other matters under an employee's official responsibility. Members of Congress cannot lobby anywhere in the legislative branch for one year after leaving office. The one-year ban also applies to former congressional staff lobbying the staffs and members with whom they were most directly related.	Lifetime ban on lobbying on particular matters in which an employee was personally and substantially involved. One-year ban on lobbying at a former agency by all federal employees and military officers of grade-level GS-17 and above, with some exceptions if lobbying for nonprofits. Top officials cannot lobby anywhere in the government for one year after leaving office. Top Clinton appointees pledged not to lobby their former agencies for five years. They may never represent a foreign entity after leaving office, nor may they engage in trade negotiations or represent a foreign country for five years after leaving government service.

from the legislation have much more incentive to organize and try to influence policy than do those who will have to pay for the new policy.

But if there is competition between groups—like that over pollution standards between environmental groups and industries that burn soft coal, or that over oil import tariffs between producers and consumers of oil—there may be a standoff until the competitors can make a deal or until one side wins. Either way, the basic orientation is toward the status quo because in American government it is easier to prevent the passage of laws than to enact new laws and easier to continue policy than to change it.

Change *is* possible, but it is usually incremental, and it is often the product of strong presidential leadership. In the 1960s, presidents Kennedy and Johnson changed things with their New Frontier and Great Society programs designed to help low socio-economic groups. In the 1980s, President Reagan changed things back despite pressure from powerful interest groups that had benefitted from those programs and had organized to protect their benefits. He did so by appealing to the general public and by working with institutions in the executive branch, such as the Office of Management and Budget, and with committees in Congress, such as the House and Senate budget committees, that were less sensitive to pressure from single-issue interest groups. In the 1990s, President Clinton followed Reagan's example, working simultaneously outside and inside government to build support for his proposals to reduce the deficit, provide affordable health care for all Americans, and reform the welfare system.

In short, organized interests try to influence what government does, but those interests may be offset or deflected by fragmented interests, public moods, or skilled political leadership, particularly presidential leadership. Thus, although political interest groups usually do not dictate policy, under a system designed to respond to public pressures, they do influence it.

SUMMARY

Americans live in a highly organized society. They pursue their common economic and social interests and beliefs by joining and participating in *political interest groups*, which attempt to influence the personnel and policies of government. These groups have a narrower membership base than political parties and are more focused on policy issues, particularly those issues about which their members feel very strongly.

Political interest groups can strengthen democracy by educating people about their civic responsibilities, increasing public awareness, providing an outlet for public expression, and encouraging participation in the political process. However, their behavior does not necessarily promote the rights and interests of others. If certain groups come to dominate decision making, they will shape policy in their interests. If they do not, if struggles among competing groups persist, the result may be compromises that are necessary in a pluralistic society, but that

sometimes also result in less than ideal solutions to the problems at hand.

Although political interest groups have existed throughout the nation's history, they have undergone their greatest development since the middle of the twentieth century. The rapid increase in the number of interest groups after 1950 was spurred by the growth of government programs and regulatory activity and by the political movements of the 1960s and 1970s. Changes in the political system, especially in the nature of parties and elections, also contributed to the increase in group activity.

Several factors affect the ability of interest groups to shape public policy: size, unity, and emotional intensity. Additionally, groups that are geographically concentrated tend to exercise more power locally than nationally. Organizations of professionals derive influence from their members' prestige. Financial resources are another source of power. A group's influence is also affected by its leadership and by the contacts that group leaders develop with people in government.

Before the 1970s, much of the electoral activity of political interest groups was funneled through the Democratic and Republican party organizations. Today the nomination process is less subject to the influence of party leaders, and interest groups have incentives and opportunities to impact nominations, influence the positions of candidates and parties, and affect election outcomes.

Nonparty groups, known as *political action committees (PACs)*, solicit contributions from their members and make donations to candidates. They also engage independently in other campaign activities to support or oppose particular candidates.

The amount of money spent by PACs has led some observers to conclude that public officials are bound to be influenced by their contributions. They point out that most PAC money goes to incumbents, especially party leaders and committee chairs. Another criticism of PACs is that they weaken the political parties by siphoning funds away from them and encouraging policy-oriented candidates who may lack party allegiance. Proponents of PACs respond that they help finance elections, increase public knowledge of the issues, and encourage voting.

Lobbying is the practice of providing public officials with information designed to influence their opinions and positions on current issues. Lobbyists can influence the legislative process directly by testifying at public hearings, providing policy statements to members of the legislature, and drafting proposed bills. They can also launch public relations campaigns in the media or by direct mail to urge their members and sympathizers to contact government officials who must be sensitive to public opinion and outside pressures.

The relatively large size of legislatures and the number of members who must be contacted create difficulties for lobbyists. Another problem is the level of activity and the number of political interest groups involved on any given issue. These conditions have resulted in coalition building among diverse groups.

Lobbyists' targets include not only legislatures but also the executive branch and the judiciary. Interest groups lobby executive officials and agencies to gain access, visibility, and support for their interests. In exchange they offer their members' political support for the administration and its politics. In addition to attempting to influence the formulation of policy, groups try to shape the content and application of rules governing its implementation.

The judicial arena has also become a focus of group activity. Political interest groups try to influence the selection of judges and may bring lawsuits if they are unable to achieve their ends through the legislative and executive processes. Sometimes groups file *amicus curiae briefs* in support of positions in pending cases.

In recent years there have been a number of changes in the nature of lobbying. The amount of lobbying activity in Washington, D.C., and in state capitals has increased dramatically. Foreign companies and governments increasingly hire American firms to represent them. The lobbying business has become more specialized, with law firms joined by public relations, issues management, and accounting firms. Sunshine laws force lobbyists to operate in public view, and new ethics and finance laws and regulations have imposed stringent requirements on public officials who interact with lobbyists or become lobbyists after they leave office. The intent of these rules is to slow the revolving door between government and the private sector.

The extent to which political interest groups actually affect policy outcomes is largely determined by the degree of competition among groups in a particular area and by the distribution of benefits and costs. If there is little competition, a concerned group is in a better position to get what it wants, particularly if costs are distributed among the general population. If there is competition between groups, either the groups with the most influence will gain incrementally or there may be a standoff. In either case, the basic orientation is toward the maintenance of the status quo unless and until the president provides strong leadership on one side or the other.

political interest group	theory of selective benefits	lobbying
disturbance theory	political action committee	amicus curiae brief

Scholarly studies

Berry, Jeffrey M. *The Interest Group Society*. 2nd ed. Glenview, Ill.: Scott, Foresman/Little, Brown, 1989. An easy-to-read text that effectively synthesizes information on political interest groups and how they affect government.

Clawson, Dan, Alan Neustadtl, and Denise Scott. *Money Talks: Corporate PACs and Political Influence*. New York: Basic Books, 1992. A contemporary account of corporate political action committees and their impact on American politics.

Lowi, Theodore. *The End of Liberalism: Ideology, Policy, and the Crisis of Public Authority*. 2nd ed. New York: Norton, 1979. A classic analysis and criticism of interest group politics in America.

McFarland, Andrew S. *Common Cause*. Chatham, N.J.: Chatham House, 1984. An excellent study of the organization, operation, and leadership of the largest citizens' lobbying group, Common Cause.

Petracca, Mark, P., ed. *The Politics of Interests*. Boulder, Colo.: Westview Press, 1992. An up-to-date collection of case studies and research on interest groups and their impact on the American system.

Schlozman, Kay L., and John T. Tierney. *Organized Interests and American Democracy*. New York: HarperCollins, 1990. A comprehensive text on interest groups and their impact on the American system, based in part on interviews with 175 Washington representatives of major organizations.

Leisure reading

Birnbaum, Jeffrey H., and Alan S. Murray. *Showdown at Gucci Gulch*. New York: Vintage, 1987. Two journalists describe how lobbyists tried to influence the Tax Reform Act of 1986.

Luker, Kristin. *Abortion and the Politics of Motherhood*. Berkeley: University of California Press, 1984. A balanced and lucid study of the abortion issue based on over two hundred interviews with pro-life and pro-choice activists.

Wolpe, Bruce C. *Lobbying Congress: How the System Works*. Washington D.C.: Congressional Quarterly, 1990. A "how-to" guide with case studies.

Primary sources

The Capital Source: The Who's Who, What, Where in Washington. Washington, D.C.: The National Journal, semiannual publication. A reference book, published twice a year, that lists people, positions, addresses, and telephone numbers for government officials, media correspondents, interest groups, think tanks, and others doing policy research, consultation, and lobbying.

Encyclopedia of Associations. 3 vols. Detroit: Gale Research, Inc., annual. A comprehensive listing of organizations by type and geographic area.

The Washington Representatives. Washington, D.C.: Columbia Books, Inc., annual. A listing of Washington representatives, clients, and their areas of principal legislative and regulatory concerns.

Organizations

Common Cause, 2030 M Street, N.W., Washington, DC 20036; (202) 833-1200. The citizens' lobby, Common Cause is concerned with issues of governance such as the availability of government information, contributions to candidates, and salaries for public officials.

Federal Election Commission, 999 E Street, N.W., Washington, DC 20463; (202) 219-3420 (information services); (800) 424-9530 (public records). This commission collects, analyzes, and sends out information on election laws, contributions, and other campaign activities. It releases annual reports as well as election summaries.

National Abortion Rights Action League, 1156 15th Street, N.W., Suite 700, Washington, DC 20005; (202) 973-3000. A pro-choice group that lobbies legislatures, brings court cases, and mounts public relations efforts.

National Right to Life Committee, Inc., 419 7th Street, N.W., Suite 500, Washington, DC 20004; (202) 626-8800. A pro-life group that lobbies legislatures, brings court cases, and mounts public relations efforts.

Office of Public Liaison, The White House, 1600 Pennsylvania Avenue, N.W., Washington, DC 20500; (202) 456-2930. This White House office handles relations with organized political interest groups. It services their needs, keeps track of their positions, and tries to mobilize them behind key presidential initiatives.

CHAPTER 9

Political Parties

- Parties and partisans

- A brief history of the two-party system: development and regionalization of national parties; the Civil War and its aftermath; the Republican era and the Roosevelt realignment

- The nature of American parties: major and minor parties

- Party organization at the national, state, and local levels

- Parties and elections: the electoral process and the electorate

- Parties and governance: determining party positions and converting positions into public policy; partisan influence on the legislature, executive, and judiciary

Third-party candidates are featured in the political display on the left. Socialist Eugene V. Debs ran five times from 1900 to 1920 and was actually in jail during his last campaign. In 1948, Democrat Harry Truman and Republican Thomas Dewey faced two third-party challengers: Henry Wallace of the Progressive party and Dixiecrat segregationist Strom Thurmond of the States' Rights party. Progressive Robert LaFollette was a factor in the 1924 campaign, and in 1968 American Independent Party candidate George Wallace took aim at Republican Richard Nixon and Democrat Hubert Humphrey. Of all the third-party contenders, however, no one captured more popular votes than Ross Perot did in 1992.

All political parties claim to support policies that are in the interests of the country. They differ, however, over which policies should be pursued, at what cost, and to whom. Republicans and Democrats have tended to approach the problems of cost and benefits in different ways.

The Republicans see the free enterprise system with its internal competition and private ownership as key to the country's economic and social well-being and political vitality. They are leery of any policy that takes money out of the private sector, such as increased taxes, or that competes with it, such as public assistance programs, or that limits competition, such as new government regulations. The Republican constituency, made up of middle-class and upper middle-class voters, white-collar workers, and business entrepreneurs and executives, has been largely sympathetic to this view, and it has been critical of big government, particularly the government in Washington. In their campaign rhetoric, their party platforms, and their elected officials' positions since the early 1980s, the Republicans have opposed most new domestic spending programs and any increase in federal

279

taxes to pay for them. "Read my lips!" said George Bush in his 1988 presidential campaign. "No new taxes!"

The Democrats have taken a different tack. Since the New Deal era of Franklin Roosevelt, they and their political constituency of middle- and lower middle-class voters, organized labor, and ethnic and religious minorities have been more receptive to large government programs that provide services directly to people—subsidies to farmers, welfare to the needy, and pensions and healthcare benefits for workers. They have also supported a progressive tax system to pay for them, a system in which the wealthy pay comparably more.

With each party pursuing its own policy and controlling a different part of the government—the Republicans, the White House, the Democrats, one or both of the houses of Congress—the problem of budget deficits got worse, and the national debt tripled during the 1980s.

President George Bush and the Democratic leadership in Congress decided to tackle the problem in 1990. Both sides compromised, Bush agreeing to tax increases while the Democrats supported spending cuts. The agreement became law; Bush was severely criticized by conservative members of his party; and the deficit continued to rise.

In the campaign of 1992, the Republicans reverted to their antitax/antispending position of the past. Bush confessed that the 1990 tax increase was a mistake and promised that it would not happen again if he were reelected. The Democrats, who blamed the deficit on twelve years of misguided Republican policies, nominated a presidential candidate, Bill Clinton, who promised to reduce the deficit by half in four years with tax increases for the rich, tax cuts for the middle class, and reduced government spending. His initial proposals, introduced during his first two months in office, engendered considerable opposition.

During the spring and summer of 1993, Republicans and some conservative Democrats complained that the president's proposal contained too much new spending, too many new taxes, and too few cuts in existing programs. President Clinton, who had already backed off his campaign promise to lower taxes on the middle class, agreed to cut more and spend less. Even with these modifications, however, the president had difficulty obtaining unified support from his party and any support from the Republicans. Congress finally agreed on a deficit reduction plan, but one that reduced his tax increases even further and enlarged the spending cuts he had proposed. The president had to make compromises with his own party to achieve even his basic objectives.

DIFFERENCES OVER WHAT GOVERNMENT should do, how much it should spend, and who should pay reveal much about the character of political parties in the United States: their differing constituencies, philosophies, and orientations of policies. They also reveal similarities in their internal composition, pragmatism, and propensity to take the politically expedient course. Successful political parties must be sensitive to the continuities and changes in the opinions of their partisans as well as to those of the general population. And even when they are, they have great difficulty imposing policy positions on their candidates and on elected officials. Individualism and diversity characterize American politics today.

Political parties reflect the society in which they operate. Just as that society is diverse in its thinking and beliefs, so is each of the major parties. The parties respond to their diverse constituencies by reflecting and transmitting their constituents' needs and desires into electoral support and issue positions.

If politics is a struggle for position, power, and policy, parties are the vehicle by which the struggle is carried out. Parties help focus citizens' demands and convert them into public policy decisions through the electoral and governing processes. These functions are critical in a representative democracy. Citizens need help in choosing among competing candidates and policy positions. Candidates need help in running for office. Public officials need help in representing their constituents and deciding which policies to pursue. Political parties provide this help. In this way they enhance the accountability of those in office and allow the public to hold them responsible for the successes or failures of their elected and appointed officials.

In this chapter we explain how political parties influence the political environment in which they operate. We trace the history of the two-party system in the United States and then focus on the major and minor parties, examining the organization of the major parties at the national, state, and local levels. Finally, we discuss the interaction of parties and the electorate and how contemporary parties affect election results and decision making in government.

PARTIES AND PARTISANS

A **political party** is an organization whose goal is to win elective office in order to influence the policies of government. It is composed of three interacting groups of supporters, or **partisans**: professionals, candidates and elected officials, and rank-and-file voters (see Figure 9-1).

Professionals are the smallest group. They are employed by the party. For them, the party is an organization to which loyalty is owed, for which work is performed, and from which compensation is received. That work includes raising money, mobilizing sympathizers, developing positions, projecting images, making appeals, and maintaining traditions. In performing these functions, party professionals compile and maintain lists of rank-and-file supporters, provide liaison to elected party leaders at all levels of government, coordinate party activities, and handle the administrative chores of running a large organization.

For members of the second group of partisans—candidates for public office and elected officials—the party is a source of funds and services. Simply running as a Republican or a Democrat activates the support of a sizable portion of the electorate. Most candidates need that support to win office, and a party needs to have its partisans in office if it is to influence public policy.

Both professionals and candidates carry the party's banner. The rank-and-file supporters are more difficult to identify. In the United States these partisans rarely carry membership cards or attend political meetings. They may not even vote. In most cases, all they have to do is think of themselves as partisans or state that they are partisans, although some states do require formal registration as a condition for participating in a party's primary election.

Partisanship is a lens through which political events can be judged and electoral choices made. The more strongly people feel about a party, the more likely they are to support that party's candidates and its policy positions.

A BRIEF HISTORY OF THE TWO-PARTY SYSTEM

Political parties have evolved significantly over the years. That evolution has been influenced not only by the federal character of the political system in the United States but also by major events such as the Civil War, the recession of the early to mid 1890s, and the Great Depression of the 1930s. How the parties

Figure 9-1   *The composition of political parties.* SOURCE: *Adapted from Frank J. Sorauf and Paul Allen Beck,* Party Politics in America, *7th ed. (New York: Harper-Collins, 1992), 11. Copyright © 1992 by Frank J. Sorauf and Paul Allen Beck. Reprinted by permission of HarperCollins Publishers.*

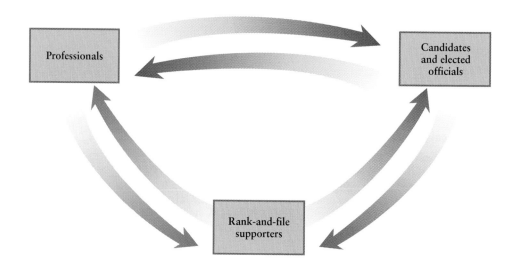

reacted to these conditions, how they proposed to deal with the attendant economic and social problems, and who they appealed to for support have all affected the composition of the parties and their success or failure in winning elections and governing the country. Here we trace the history of American political parties from the beginning of the Republic to the contemporary period. The five stages during which the composition of the parties shifted and new partisan majorities emerged are illustrated in Figure 9-2.

Figure 9-2 *The evolution of American political parties.* SOURCE: *Data on minor parties primarily from Congressional Quarterly,* Guide to Elections, *2nd ed. (Washington, D.C.: Congressional Quarterly, 1985); amended and updated by the authors. Reprinted by permission of Congressional Quarterly, Inc.*

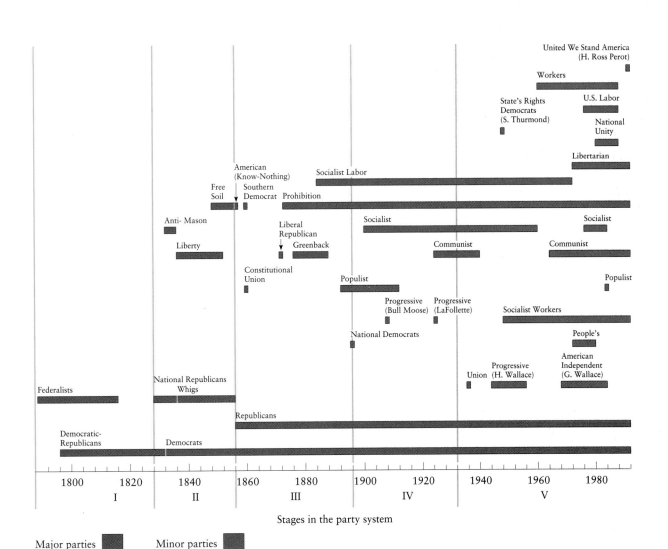

The Development of National Parties, 1789–1824

Parties are not mentioned in the Constitution and did not exist prior to the presidency of George Washington. They came into being largely to support or oppose this first administration's policies: the assumption by national government of the Revolutionary War debt, the taxation of imported goods to protect domestic industry, and the establishment of a national bank to regulate currency. Commercial interests—merchants, manufacturers, bankers, creditors, and speculators—supported Washington. Farmers, laborers, debtors, and other less advantaged members of society opposed him. Those who saw their interests adversely affected by Washington's policies turned to Thomas Jefferson, who had resigned from his cabinet position to lead the loyal opposition.

The political groupings that emerged during this period also differed in their foreign policy orientations. Those who backed the administration—the **Federalists**—tended to be more pro-British in sentiment than those who opposed it. They supported the treaty that Ambassador John Jay had negotiated with the British to end the official state of hostilities. Jefferson's supporters, known as **Democratic-Republicans**, or simply **Republicans**, opposed.[1] Although the Jay Treaty was ratified, it engendered a partisan debate and vote— the first party vote in Congress.

Partisanship was evident in the elections of 1796 and 1800. In fact, so unified were the Republicans in the presidential election of 1800 that all of their electors voted for the two Republican candidates, Jefferson and Aaron Burr. The result was a tie that forced the House of Representatives, still controlled by the party of the previous administration, the Federalists, to choose between Republicans Jefferson and Burr.[2] By 1800 these two parties were competing within most states and at the national level.[3]

Neither the Republicans nor the Federalists enjoyed much popular backing; their most active supporters were primarily elected officials and people who desired public office. Of the two parties, the Federalists had the narrower base. Concentrated in the Northeast, Federalists tended to be people with property, high social status, and considerable political influence. Unable and seemingly unwilling to broaden their appeal, the Federalist party declined rapidly as a competitive force. Their demise was accelerated by the War of 1812, in which some of their New England supporters allegedly undermined the United States' war effort and expressed sympathy for the British.

The Republicans professed more confidence than the Federalists in the common people. Blessed with a succession of prestigious presidential candidates—the so-called Virginia dynasty of Jefferson, Madison, and Monroe— they were able to expand their base of support. They became the majority party by 1800 and the only national party by 1820. The last Federalist candidate for president ran in 1816 and received only a handful of electoral votes.

The early party system contributed to the nation's evolving political tradition in several important respects. It channeled the debate about how the nation should develop, what role the government should play in that development, and which national policies should be pursued. It provided a mechanism for resolving differences of opinion about public issues. It created an institutional means for recruiting public officials and for influencing their policy judgments. Finally, it forced candidates to be sensitive to public opinion and public officials to represent their constituents' interests.

By the mid 1820s, the Republicans had become victims of their own success. Without a rival party, they split into feuding factions. In the presidential election of 1824, five Republican candidates campaigned for the presidency. Two dominant groups emerged: one, the National Republicans, supported John Quincy Adams; the other, the Democratic-Republicans, backed Andrew Jackson. After Jackson failed to win a majority of votes in the Electoral College and was defeated by a vote in the House of Representatives in 1824, he organized a broad-based political coalition and engaged in grassroots campaigning that led to his election four years later.

The 1828 election was the first in which people in a majority of the states chose the electors. Jackson's victory marked the beginning of the movement toward popular election of the president. It also spurred the shift of power from the national government to the states. The congressional party caucus, which had been used to nominate presidential and vice presidential candidates between 1800 and 1824, was replaced by national nominating conventions controlled by state party leaders. Increasingly, members of Congress owed their nomination and election to the state party and its leadership.

Jackson's new electoral coalition changed the landscape of American politics. His principal backing came from economically disadvantaged groups: small farmers and newly enfranchised voters in the West and South, Catholics and new immigrants in the East. Jackson's following, known as the **Democrats**, soon dominated the Democratic-Republican party, which dropped the word "Republican" from its name.

A new party known as the **Whigs** emerged in opposition to Jackson. A diverse group composed of prosperous farmers in the South and West, com-

North Wind Picture Archives

THE GREAT CHEESE LEVEE.

When Andrew Jackson won the presidency, his supporters took it as a victory for the common people. They thronged to his inaugural in Washington and followed him back to the White House, where they celebrated for three days. It was a raucous party. This drawing shows a similar event on February 22, 1837, shortly before Jackson left the White House. His supporters hacked off huge chunks of a 1400-pound cheese that was kept in the vestibule. By one contemporary account, "the air was redolent with cheese, the carpet was slippery with cheese."

mercial interests in the East, and antislavery advocates in the Northeast and Appalachia, the Whigs held themselves together in national campaigns by running military heroes as candidates.

The policies of these new parties reflected their bases of support. Jackson's Democrats advocated a rural agrarian society in which the national government had a limited role, church and state were separate, and greater economic opportunities were available for common people. In contrast, the Whigs, like their Federalist predecessors, envisioned a more industrial society in which a strong central government promoted policies that were designed to stimulate economic development.

By 1840 the Democrats and Whigs were competitive national parties. For the first time, there was two-party competition in the South and West, and there were no regions of one-party domination as there had been in prior decades and would be again.[4] With heated competition, voter participation soared, reaching a high of 80 percent of eligible voters in the 1840 presidential election, nearly double the highest rate attained earlier.[5]

Three minor parties emerged during this period: The Anti-Masons (a protectionist party that favored internal improvements), the Liberty party (a party that opposed the existence of slavery), and the Free Soil party (a party that opposed the extension of slavery into the western territories and the influx of new immigrants into the country). Although none of these parties could generate much popular support or staying power, together they revealed growing discontent within the two major parties. This discontent was to lead to the breakup of the two-party system during the prelude to the Civil War and to its eventual restructuring during and after the war.

The Civil War and Its Aftermath, 1856–1892

The new **Republican** party was organized in 1854. Composed of disillusioned Whigs, who feared and opposed new immigrants, Anti-Masons, Free Soilers, and others opposed to slavery (abolitionists) or its expansion (white laborers, small farmers, and some entrepreneurs), the Republicans ran their first presidential candidate, John C. Frémont, in 1856. Frémont did surprisingly well. Even though he was not elected, he received 40 percent of the vote.

By 1860 the Democrats had split over slavery, dividing into northern and southern factions with each running its own presidential candidate. The Whigs, controlled by antislavery forces, lost their support in the South and suffered defections in the North over the immigration issue. With the Democrats divided and the Whigs no longer a viable political force, the Republican candidate, Abraham Lincoln, won the 1860 election with only 39.8 percent of the popular vote, the smallest winning percentage in history.

Out of the chaos of the Civil War, the turmoil of Reconstruction, and the issues created by the Industrial Revolution, new partisan coalitions evolved. During this period, industrialization expanded rapidly. The Republicans evolved from their beginnings as a party of small business, labor, and farmers into a party that was increasingly dominated by big business. Banking and commercial interests also influenced the northern wing of the Democratic party, but its southern wing remained controlled by the white supremacists who sought to reimpose the pre–Civil War social and economic structure in the

The first presidential candidate put up by the new Republican party in 1856, John C. Frémont (above) did well, but lost. Abraham Lincoln (right), who lost the Senate race in Illinois in 1858, won the presidency for the Republicans in 1860 with under 40 percent of the popular vote but a majority in the Electoral College. Created out of various factions opposed to slavery and its expansion in the territories, the Republican party stood for national unity during the Civil War; it emerged from the war as the dominant party.

This first integrated jury ever empaneled in the South was to hear the treason trial of Jefferson Davis in 1867. But the trial was postponed, and the charges were dropped.

287

South. African Americans were effectively disenfranchised in the South following the withdrawal of federal troops in 1876.

Minor parties, such as the agricultural Greenback party and the urban Socialist Labor party, organized to appeal to farmers and workers whose grievances had not been adequately addressed by the major parties. In addition, new parties opposed to the consumption of alcohol (the Prohibition party) and favoring more participation by the people in government (the Populist party) emerged. The Prohibitionist party, which still exists—its presidential candidate in 1992, Earl Dodge, received 935 votes—is the oldest third party in the United States. The Populist party, which later became the Progressive party, supported Theodore Roosevelt's Bull Moose candidacy against Republican William Howard Taft and Democrat Woodrow Wilson in 1912. Roosevelt received more votes in that election (27.4 percent) than any other third party candidate in American history.

The Republican Era, 1896–1928

A recession in 1893, during the Democratic administration of Grover Cleveland, led to a shifting of political forces which ultimately culminated in a realignment of the major parties' electoral coalitions. At the turn of the century, the Republicans emerged as the majority party. They gained adherents in the Northeast and Midwest, while the Democrats lost them. In the grain-producing states of the prairies and the silver-mining states of the Rockies, the Democrats picked up support, largely on the basis of a policy advocated by William Jennings Bryan, their unsuccessful candidate for the presidency in 1896, 1900, and 1908. Bryan's "free silver" policy would have required the government to buy and coin an unlimited amount of silver. The South remained staunchly Democratic. Thus, partisan conflict during this period took on a regional coloration.

William Jennings Bryan electrified the 1896 Democratic National Convention with his famous "cross of gold" speech. The gold standard had divided the party and the country, as farmers and laborers, unable to pay their debts in gold, urged the free and unlimited coinage of silver. Bryan trumpeted their cause at the convention, imploring delegates "not to press down upon the brow of labor this crown of thorns." His speech so moved the delegates that they nominated him for president in 1896, in 1900, and in 1908. Each time, however, he lost.

Library of Congress

There were also divisions along ethnic and religious lines, with the newer wave of immigrants, largely Catholics and primarily from southern and eastern Europe, affiliating with the Democratic party while those who had immigrated earlier, largely Protestants from northern Europe, turned to the Republicans. Parties that appealed to the plight of industrial workers in the cities, such as the Socialists and Communists, also gained a foothold during this period.

The Republican party and its white, Anglo-Saxon, Protestant constituency dominated national politics for the next three decades. During this period the Democrats controlled Congress for only six years and the White House for only eight. In the 1920s, however, the flow of new immigrants, combined with unpopular Republican policies, particularly Prohibition, led the urban ethnic groups to return to the Democratic party. In 1928, for the first time, the Democrats won a majority in the large cities.

The Roosevelt Realignment, 1932–1968

In the 1932 election, which occurred during the greatest economic depression in the nation's history, the Republicans suffered, and the Democrats expanded their support among white southerners and Catholics and gained support from organized labor. By 1936 African Americans had abandoned the party of Lincoln for the party of economic recovery, the Democrats. Jewish voters, attracted by President Franklin Roosevelt's liberalism and his anti-Nazi foreign policy, also shifted their allegiance to the Democratic party. Although the Republicans retained their hold on northern Protestants, the Democrats made inroads among them as well, particularly those in the lower socioeconomic groups. The electorate thus was divided along economic class lines: less prosperous voters were likely to be Democratic, and more prosperous voters were likely to be Republican. The exception was the South, where voters, regardless of their socioeconomic status, maintained their Democratic loyalties.

The economic division between the parties became evident in the policy perspectives they adopted. Since the New Deal, the Democrats have generally believed that the government should play an important role in solving the nation's economic and social problems, and the Republicans have been more leery of government involvement, particularly national efforts to regulate private industry and expand social services. The Republicans have tended to look to private enterprise for economic and even social solutions.

It is difficult to know precisely when the Roosevelt realignment was completed. But after World War II, new issues, such as civil rights, American military involvement in Korea and then Vietnam, the deterioration of the nation's cities, and the associated urban problems of crime, poverty, and drugs, divided the country and strained the Democrats' electoral coalition. These issues weakened the loyalties of some of the party's traditional supporters and allowed the Republicans to attract new voters and to encourage older ones to split their ticket and vote for more Republicans, particularly at the national level.

The discontent generated within the Democratic party, combined with the relative homogeneity of the Republican party, created a fluid political environment in which minor parties with new policies, ideologies, and candidates emerged to challenge the major parties. Since 1948 there have been twelve new or newly reconstituted minor parties. None of them, however, has commanded the allegiances and electoral support of a significant portion of the electorate, and only two presidential candidates of a minority party, George Wallace in 1968 and H. Ross Perot in 1992, received a sizable vote. Wallace won 13.5 percent of the popular vote and 46 electoral votes, and Perot received 18.5 percent of the popular vote but no electoral votes.

The Democrats lost their dominance at the presidential level in 1968, and their status as the majority party eroded even further after that. No longer did over half of the electorate consider itself Democratic. Although Democrats still commanded the allegiance of a plurality of voters, the gap between the parties narrowed. By the end of the 1980s, the major parties were at or near parity with the Democrats clinging to a slight advantage.

The coalitions that comprise the parties have shifted as well.[6] Before we discuss these contemporary coalitions, however, we turn to the character and organization of today's political parties in the United States.

THE NATURE OF AMERICAN PARTIES

The United States has a two-party tradition in which one of two major parties has usually held the support of a majority of the electorate. Third parties have never played as significant a role in American political life.

Major Parties

The two major American parties share characteristics that distinguish them from the major parties in other democratic political systems. They are diversified in composition, decentralized in structure, and pragmatic in their approach to policy making.

Why is this? Part of the answer lies in the federal character of the American system. The Constitution vests substantial powers and responsibilities in the states, including the conduct of elections for all federal and state officials. In fact, except for the election of the president and vice president, all elections in the United States are for state or local officials or for state representatives to Congress. The party system reflects this decentralized federal structure. Candidates are recruited at the state or local level and are responsive primarily to their own constituencies. Many of the issues they address have important consequences for their state or locality. This parochialism affects the policy positions they take and, if elected, the decisions they make. It also influences the structure, outlook, and operation of the major political parties.

At the national level, the major parties consist of representatives of the fifty state parties. At the state level, they consist of local party representatives. Political parties in the United States, unlike many European parties, have not been strong, cohesive, centralized, national organizations throughout most of their existence. The American electoral system has encouraged the major parties to be large and heterogeneous, to take moderate positions, and to be pragmatic. Most candidates are chosen in a district in which one person is elected (known as a **single-member district**). There is no prize for coming in second. As a result, candidates must appeal to the majority of voters within their districts, and the parties must be receptive to a variety of candidates from different districts.

In other countries and in some states and cities in the United States, there are electoral systems in which several candidates are elected from the same district (known as a **multimember district**) on the basis of the proportion of the votes they or their party receives. In elections decided by proportional voting there is an incentive for candidates to reaffirm their party's positions, downplay their own personal beliefs, and appeal to their party's rank and file for support. As a consequence, candidates selected in multimember districts tend to be more loyal to their party and its ideological perspective than are those chosen in single-member districts.

Since the United States encompasses a large geographic area with a highly diverse population, its major parties must be broad-based and adopt positions that are acceptable to as much of the electorate as possible. Hence, parties' policy positions tend to be in the mainstream of public attitudes and opinions. Competition between the parties also discourages elected officials from taking extreme stands for fear of alienating a significant portion of the electorate. Republican conservative Barry Goldwater's presidential campaign in 1964 and Democratic liberal George McGovern's presidential campaign in 1972 both resulted in high rates of defection by party supporters, who voted for the candidate of the other party.[7]

Another related reason for the pragmatic, moderate, nonideological approach of the major parties is the consensus that exists among the electorate about basic political values. This consensus about the goals of government and the objectives of public policy is shared by the leaders and the rank and file of both parties; where they disagree is on the means to achieve these goals, that is, the specific policy solutions. Thus, for example, the major parties in the United States are divided not over whether there should be equal opportunity but over how best to achieve that goal.

Minor Parties

Minor parties have been a part of the American political landscape since 1831 when a small party, known as the Anti-Masons, held a national convention to nominate candidates and propose a set of governing principles. Minor parties have come and gone quickly since then. But some of the shortest-lived have exerted the greatest influence by getting one or both of the major parties to address their concerns.

In general there have been two basic types of minor parties: ideological parties and issue/splinter parties (see Tables 9-1 and 9-2). Of the two, **ideological parties** have had greater longevity but less political impact. Oriented toward

TABLE 9-1		
Ideological Parties		
	LIFE SPAN	PLATFORM
Socialist party	1901–	Replacement of much private enterprise with a worker-run state
Libertarian party	1971–	Opposition to most government regulation and, particularly, to state-sponsored social programs

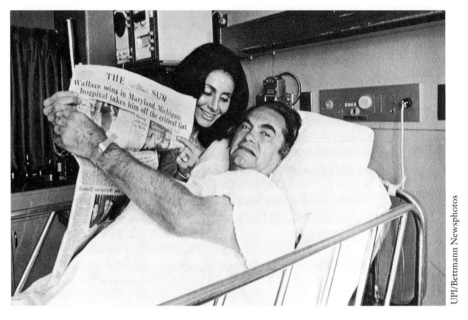

UPI/Bettmann Newsphotos

"Segregation now, segregation tomorrow, segregation forever," George Corley Wallace promised Alabamians in 1963. Yet when he ran for president on the American Independent Party ticket in 1968 (there wasn't "a dime's worth of difference" between Democrats and Republicans, he said), he got almost 10 million popular votes (and 45 electoral votes) promoting states' rights rather than overt segregation. In 1972, two days after he was shot campaigning outside a shopping center in Maryland, he won the Democratic primaries in Michigan and Maryland. But he was paralyzed below the waist and did not try again to win the presidency.

a set of ideas that differ significantly from those of the major parties, ideological parties, such as the Socialists, the Communists, and the Libertarians, advocate a new way of thinking about the relationship between government and society. Because their beliefs lie outside those of mainstream America, however, their followings are loyal but not large.

The other type of minor party, the **issue/splinter party**, has had more political success. Created out of dissatisfaction with one or both of the major parties when they ignore an important issue, take an unpopular stand, or nominate an unattractive candidate, these parties seek to get the major parties to change their ways. They do this largely by attracting support for their own candidates, thus reducing the electoral coalitions of the major parties.

Although splinter parties have not been able to get their candidates elected, they have drawn attention to their interests, reduced the vote going to the major parties, and forced one or the other to take the actions or support the positions that prompted their protest in the first place. In 1892, for example, the Populist party supported farmers, miners, and small ranchers who favored the free coinage of silver and government regulation of commerce when both major parties rejected these positions. The Democrats subsequently adopted a free-silver policy.

Another splinter party was the Progressive (Bull Moose) party. Unhappy with President William Howard Taft and hoping to reform the electoral process, a group of Republicans split from their party and nominated former Republican president Theodore Roosevelt. The split within the Republicans

TABLE 9-2		
Splinter Parties		
	LIFE SPAN	PLATFORM
Protest parties		
Greenback party	1876–1884	Inflationary paper money to raise the prices of farm products
Populist party	1892–1908	Inflationary monetary policy through the free coinage of silver; government ownership of railroads; direct election of senators; graduated income tax
Promotion parties		
Free Soil party	1848–1852	Opposition to the extension of slavery to new territories
Know-Nothing party	1854–1856	Opposition to immigration
Personality parties		
Progressive party: Theodore Roosevelt	1912	Antitrust laws; direct primary; unemployment insurance
American Independent party: George Wallace	1968	Opposition to civil rights legislation; hawkish stance on Vietnam
National Unity party: John Anderson	1980	Independent, nonideological, moderate leadership
United We Stand America: H. Ross Perot	1992–	Deficit reduction; end to government stalemate; citizen activism

enabled Democrat Woodrow Wilson to win the presidency with only 42 percent of the total vote.

Eighty years later another group of voters, this time dissidents from both parties, supported the candidacy of H. Ross Perot and his agenda of reducing the budget deficit, reenergizing the government, and reforming the political system. Perot's efforts and the sizable vote he received focused attention on these issues after the election. Other issues that have attracted the attention of minor parties include immigration, taxation, and civil rights.

One way in which minor parties can achieve their objectives is by persuading supporters of a major party of the merits of their policy positions. Infiltration is another. By running candidates for elective and party office, protest groups may win through the ballot box what they are unable to obtain from the major party's leadership. Reform movements in the Democratic party used this tactic to challenge and defeat entrenched political bosses in New York City in 1961 and in Chicago in 1979. More recently, in 1986, two followers of political extremist Lyndon LaRouche ran for the offices of lieutenant governor and secretary of state in the Illinois Democratic primary. The state party organization completely disregarded their challenge and barely campaigned for

Reuters/Bettmann

*When independent presidential candidate H. Ross Perot addressed the American
Newspaper Publishers Convention in May of 1992, polls showed him running neck
and neck with George Bush and Bill Clinton. Perot dropped out of the race two
months later, when some of his activities, particularly his penchant for investigating
those with whom he disagreed, were publicized. Under the banner of United We
Stand, America, he got back in the race in October of 1993.*

its own nominees. With a low voter turnout and little information available,
obscure LaRouche candidates with the American-sounding names of Fairchild
and Hart defeated Democratic nominees with the ethnic-sounding names of
Pucinski and Sangmeister. The victory by LaRouche's followers sent a clear
message to every party organization: Don't take voters for granted! (The
LaRouche candidates went on to lose in the general election.)

Minor parties have been an outlet for dissent, allowing voters to voice
their unhappiness with the major parties while affirming their support for democratic electoral politics. They have been a source of policy innovation. Wom-
en's suffrage, the direct election of senators, the graduated income tax, and the
minimum wage are among the policies first proposed by minor parties. In raising these and other issues, ideological and splinter parties have affected political
debate and the distribution of electoral support even though they have not had
much direct impact on government or staying power of their own.

PARTY ORGANIZATION

In the decentralized organization of the major political parties, power is dispersed (see Figure 9-3). Separate structures at the national, state, and local levels
operate largely independently. Each exercises autonomy over its nominations
and campaigns as well as over the election of its own officials.

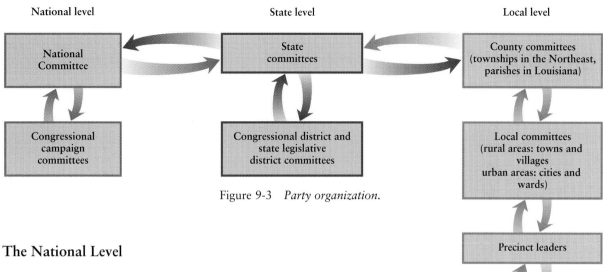

National level   State level   Local level

Figure 9-3 *Party organization.*

The National Level

At the national level, parties have traditionally been weak. Even when the parties first emerged and power was centralized in Congress, there was no effective party organization beyond the informal congressional caucuses that met to decide whom their electors should vote for in the Electoral College. Only after national conventions replaced the congressional caucuses did the parties establish national committees to make arrangements for the conventions and coordinate national campaigns more effectively. The Democratic National Committee was organized in 1848, the Republican National Committee in 1856. Initially each was composed of an equal number of representatives from their state parties. The Republicans have maintained this principle of equal representation, but the Democrats have not. In addition, each party has increased the size of its national committee to include state party chairs and, in the case of the Democrats, other elected and appointed party leaders.

Both national committees used to operate more like confederations of state parties than like independent entities. The Democrats no longer do so. They now provide representation to the states on the basis of their population and their support for Democratic candidates. This has given larger states like California, New York, and Texas much more influence on the national committee.

Both parties have also increased their national administrative apparatus. Prior to World War I, neither party had a headquarters, a staff, and a full-time paid chairperson.[8] Today both have all three, and their large staffs and budgets in the millions of dollars expand even further during election years.

Generally speaking, the national parties direct the bulk of their energies to presidential campaigns. They raise and dispense funds, identify and target voters, survey and communicate with the public, develop policy positions, and generate partisan appeals. They also provide assistance directly to candidates as well as to state and local party organizations.

The Republicans have led the Democrats in those activities. During the 1970s they aggressively expanded their fundraising and technical services while the Democrats, saddled with a divided party and a sizable debt from the 1968 presidential campaign, were unable to do so. In the 1980s the Democrats began to emulate the Republicans in providing some of these benefits for their candidates, but they still lag in fundraising and campaign support. During the

Washington lawyer and lobbyist Ron Brown was chairman of the Democratic National Committee from 1989 to 1993. He engineered the party's recovery from its defeats in the 1980s, raising money and repositioning the party for its victory in 1992. For his efforts, President Clinton named him secretary of the Commerce Department. Brown was not the first African American in the cabinet, but he was the first to chair a major political party.

295

Rich Bond: Loyal Optimist

Photo courtesy of Rich Bond

As chairman of the Republican National Committee, Rich Bond brought down the gavel and opened the party's convention in 1992.

My fascination with politics began when I was ten years old. On a blustery fall afternoon, I stood for hours to catch a glimpse of John Kennedy as his motorcade passed through my home town. Thirty years later, I gavelled open the Republican National Convention as chairman of the party. During the twelve years of the Reagan and Bush presidencies, I rode in numerous motorcades and watched people straining to glimpse the nation's leader—much as I had done as a boy.

As I got older, I was motivated by more serious purposes. I realized that government is the primary agent of change in America and that political involvement gives your voice weight on issues you care about—from education and the environment to the economy and foreign affairs. And so I decided to become involved.

In high school I rang doorbells and put up yard signs for local candidates. In college I debated the issues of the Vietnam War, and I went door to door for Mayor John Lindsay of New York. After college I worked in the Nassau County government, and I met George Bush, who was then the Republican party's national chairman.

At the time, Mr. Bush was speaking at our annual fund raiser, and the Watergate scandal was in full force. In his speech Bush had the difficult job of defending President Nixon while distancing the Republican party from the scandal. His forceful performance made a lasting impression. He presented the Republican party as a worthy cause, dedicated to the proposition that the government which governs least governs best. I wanted to help change the system and make national leaders more responsive to the concerns of taxpaying citizens.

I began to work on political campaigns and for nineteen years I held a series of related jobs: campaign manager, field operative for the Republican National Committee, congressional press secretary, presidential campaign political director, and White House aide. Then I succeeded George Bush as chairman of the Republican National Committee.

Ironically, it was President Bush who now needed defending. His popularity had plummeted, the media were hostile, and Democrats (including Bill Clinton) had lined up to run against him. Even many Republicans were drifting away from his banner. So it happened that the president whom I was to defend was the former party chairman who had inspired me to pursue a career in politics.

Despite Bush's defeat, the Republican party emerged intact, gaining seats in the House and breaking even in the Senate, and making gains on the state level. As is customary in the face of a presidential defeat, I stepped down as party leader, my love for politics intact, and with an eye toward reclaiming the White House.

My personal odyssey from a grassroots volunteer as a high school student to the leader of one of our nation's major political parties is testimony to the virtue of involvement. Politics asks only that you walk through the door and volunteer your time, and make your voice heard. After that, your imagination will be your only boundary.

1991–1992 election cycle the Republican National Committee raised $83.4 million, compared to $65.3 million for the Democratic National Committee.[9]

Republican fundraising advantages have been reinforced by the success of their congressional campaign committees. Both parties in both houses of Congress have established committees to raise money for the reelection of their legislators and for the recruitment and training of challengers to take on the incumbents of the other party. During 1991–1992, the Republican congressional committees raised a total of $103.8 million compared to $37.3 million for the Democrats.[10] These committees also provide campaign services. Congressional campaign committees have become a powerful political force, reducing the dependence of congressional candidates on state and national party organizations and increasing the independence of members of Congress.[11]

Another development that has strengthened the national Democratic party has been that party's rules for the selection of delegates to nominate its presidential and vice presidential candidates. Beginning in the 1970s and continuing into the 1990s, a series of party commissions have reformed the delegate selection process and, with the approval of the national committee, imposed these reforms on the state parties. The new rules deal with who can participate in the primaries and caucuses, when these contests can be held, how the delegates are to be apportioned, and for whom they can vote at the national convention.

Both the Democrats' nationalization of party rules and the centralization of fundraising and campaign services by both parties have significantly increased the influence that national party organizations have on their state and local affiliates. Still, the national organization does not control the selection of the party's nominees, the platforms on which nominees run, or the conduct of political campaigns.[12]

As the national party organizations have become more important, groups within the parties have become more active. Caucuses representing women, ethnic minorities, gay activists, and others have striven for greater visibility within the parties as well as for more influence on "their" issues. Pro-life and pro-choice proponents have been active within both major parties. More broadly based policy groups have also tried to affect the general orientation of their parties' programs. One such group, the Democratic Leadership Council, created in the mid 1980s to advocate a more moderate agenda than that which has been articulated in recent years by most Democratic presidential candidates and congressional leaders, received considerable notoriety and became more influential when one of its organizers and early chairs, Bill Clinton, was elected president in 1992.

The State Level

Some of the developments that have affected national party organizations have also affected state party organizations. The organizational structure of many of them has been strengthened, and their operations have been institutionalized. Most state parties now have a permanent staff. Their fundraising capabilities have been substantially improved, their operating budgets have increased, and their ability to train and assist candidates in the general election has been enhanced.[13] In general, state Republican parties have done a better job of organizing and raising money than have their Democratic counterparts.[14]

The strengthening of state party organizations has not been easy. The growth of primary elections, which make it easier for candidates to get on the ballot and encourage candidates to mount their own campaigns and make their own appeals to voters, has made it more difficult for state party leaders to exercise control over the nomination process. Similarly, the growth of the civil service system at all levels of government has reduced the patronage powers of party leaders and elected officials. The influence of television as a vehicle for communicating to the electorate has also weakened the capacity of parties at all levels to present their candidates to the voters.

State party structures are decentralized. In most states, there is a party committee composed of representatives from different geographic subdivisions, usually counties. State party committees vary in size, composition, and function. Some elect their members in primary elections, others in local caucuses, and still others at state conventions. Because most state party committees meet infrequently, the chairperson has considerable discretion in the conduct of party affairs. In only a few states, however, is the position of chairperson a full-time paid job. Turnover is therefore high: state chairs average less than three years in office.[15]

State chairpersons play a variety of roles. Some serve as the principal link between a high-ranking elected official, such as the governor, and the state party organization. Others exercise influence on their own in the absence of a governor or powerful big-city mayor. In addition, chairs often serve as spokespersons for their party.

Electing candidates to state and national office remains the primary goal of state parties, although they get involved in a variety of activities, ranging from taking official positions on salient issues to holding meetings and conventions to conducting fundraising and membership drives. State parties recruit potential nominees and help them with their campaigns. Like the national parties, state parties in recent years have improved their own capacity to raise money, compile lists of voters, and provide organizational support to candidates. In fact, national party fundraising activities have benefited state party organizations by giving them the task of distributing a substantial portion of these funds to candidates within their states. State legislative campaign committees often supplement the efforts of the state party in providing campaign support. All these developments have strengthened the state parties and increased their electoral impact. They have not, however, eliminated the need for candidates to obtain funds on their own, build their own grassroots organizations, or hire their own campaign consultants.[16]

The Local Level

Local parties also have their own organizations. They too are built around geographic subdivisions, usually counties or cities. The county organization is made up of representatives from still smaller units—wards or precincts. The chair of the county committee or the mayor of the town or city is usually the key figure in directing the party's efforts, assisted by precinct captains and ward leaders.

It was primarily at the local level, particularly in cities, that political organizations, referred to as *machines* because of the effectiveness of their operation, and party leaders, referred to as *bosses* because of their near-total control over party affairs, flourished during the second half of the nineteenth century and the first half of the twentieth. These local organizations provided benefits for their members, many of whom were newly arrived immigrants who needed help securing jobs, obtaining housing, learning English, and in general becoming integrated into the life of American cities. In exchange for this help the machine got their votes.

The machines weakened and eventually lost their hold over city politics as a result of several factors. Not only did immigrants become assimilated into society, but urban governments expanded their social and economic services. Also, a civil service system based on merit gradually replaced a political appointment system based on partisanship. Other political reforms, such as the direct primary, reduced the power of party leaders to control nominations. Today only a few strong party machines remain, such as the Cook County Democratic organization in Chicago and the Nassau County Republican organization on Long Island, New York, which still operate much as the old-style machines did, using patronage to maintain the loyalty of a cadre of workers and political supporters.

Local party organizations tend to be loosely structured. Most of their leaders and workers are volunteers; there may be no paid staff. Most of their activities, like those of the state parties, are organized around election campaigns: arranging fundraising events, contributing money to candidates, and publicizing themselves and their candidates through media advertising, press releases, telephone campaigns, and the distribution of campaign literature. The local organization also maintains lists of registered voters and organizes get-out-the-vote campaigns.

Local campaign activity has increased in recent years. Some of that increase seems to be the result of greater competition between the parties at the local level. In areas where such competition is weak, there is less incentive for the parties to mount a strong campaign. For years, local party organizations in the South were less active than those in the Northeast, the Midwest, or the Pacific Coast, because they had less competition. But Republican gains in the

Library of Congress

UPI/Bettmann

Boss William Marcy Tweed (cartoon), *the legendary chief of the Tammany Hall Democratic club in New York City, built the first modern political machine during the 1860s. Chicago Mayor Richard Daley* (right) *built what may have been the last great urban machine. It ruled the town until Daley died in 1976. When Sen. Abraham Ribicoff spoke of the "Gestapo tactics" the Chicago police used to quell disturbances during the 1968 Democratic convention, Daley shouted obscenities at him from the convention floor.*

South over the last three decades have forced Democratic party organizations to take their membership-building and campaign activities more seriously.[17]

In recent years the power of racial minorities has grown substantially in urban areas. Beginning in the 1970s and continuing into the 1990s, African Americans, Hispanics, and Asian Americans have won mayoral contests in most of the nation's largest cities. The gains of these groups mirror those of European immigrants a half-century earlier, particularly the Irish and Italians. Women too have seen increased electoral success at all levels of government.

PARTIES AND ELECTIONS

If parties are election oriented, then their principal function must be to get their candidates into office. To do this they need to influence the electoral process, the electorate, and the election results. Today, the parties exercise less influence over the conduct of elections, the nomination of candidates, the structure of the campaign, and the actual vote itself than they did three or four decades ago. They still remain an important factor, but only one among many.

Parties and the Electoral Process

Getting out the vote   For the first one hundred years of American history, the methods used by parties to get out the vote were often dishonest and sneaky. Parties printed and distributed the ballots, listing only their own candidates, and paid people to take time off from work to vote. Because voting was open and public, enormous pressure was exerted on people to vote for the party's ticket. Allegations of fraud against the parties for registering ineligible voters, stuffing ballot boxes, and miscounting the results were frequent.

Fraudulent activity was reduced toward the end of the nineteenth century by the passage of state laws that governed the conduct of elections. Uniform procedures for voting were established. Standard ballots, designed by state officials, were introduced, as was the requirement for secret voting. Today, punch cards and voting machines have replaced paper ballots, reducing fraud and making it possible to determine the outcome of the election quickly and accurately. States have also enacted laws for the registration of voters, the oversight of the vote, and the designation of the official results. Boards of elections monitor these activities and provide information to the public. These laws have forced the parties and their candidates to compete more honestly. They have not eliminated questionable activities, however. In the 1993 gubernatorial race in New Jersey, for example, Ed Rollins, a well-known Republican campaign consultant, boasted that his team had spent many millions in "street money" to discourage minorities from voting, a claim he later denied. (The box on page 301 details some of the "dirty tricks" attempted during the 1972 presidential campaign.)

Primary elections   Party organizations have been affected by other changes in the electoral process as well. Chief among these has been the evolution of the nomination process.

The congressional caucus system for nominating presidential and vice presidential candidates began to break down in the 1820s. It was replaced by

During the 1972 presidential campaign, White House chief of staff H. R. Haldeman asked an old school friend, Donald Segretti, to join the Committee to Reelect the President. Segretti's job was to gather intelligence, play pranks, and in other ways sabotage Democratic candidates. Segretti enthusiastically set about his tasks. The "tricks" that his unit in the Nixon campaign organization and others affiliated with the White House performed ran the gamut from sophomoric pranks to illegal breaking and entering. They included:

Placing phony orders for food, liquor, and limousines and charging them to Democratic candidates.

Paying $20 to a University of Florida woman to run naked in front of Democratic presidential candidate Edmund Muskie's hotel screaming, "Senator Muskie, I love you!"

Writing a letter on "Citizens for Muskie" stationery, accusing Senator Henry Jackson (D-Washington) of being a homosexual and Senator Hubert Humphrey (D-Minnesota) of cavorting with prostitutes at the expense of lobbyists.

Implying in a letter sent to the *Manchester Union Leader* that Senator Muskie was biased against French Canadians because he allegedly laughed at an aide's use of the ethnic slur "Canuck."

It was not Segretti but G. Gordon Liddy, however, who orchestrated the break-in at the Watergate office complex in order to bug the phone of Democratic National Committee Chairman Larry O'Brien. The Watergate break-in led two young

AP/Wide World Photos

Donald Segretti (right) *distributed a fake letter from Edmund Muskie accusing his rivals of sexual misconduct right before the 1972 Florida primary. He also gave out cards at a Wallace rally reading: "If you like Hitler, you'll love Wallace. Vote for Muskie." Segretti was sentenced to a year in jail.*

Washington Post reporters, Carl Bernstein and Bob Woodward, to investigate. Their stories eventually prompted a full-scale Senate investigation of the illegal campaign activities undertaken by the Nixon organization.

SOURCES: Based on Carl Bernstein and Bob Woodward, *All the President's Men* (New York: Simon and Schuster, 1974), 112–139, 141–149; and John Dean, *Lost Honor* (New York: HarperCollins, 1982), 81–83, 332–334.

state and national party conventions that were usually controlled by party leaders. Local precincts chose delegates to county conventions, which in turn chose delegates to state conventions, which in their turn chose nominees for state office and delegates to the national nominating conventions. This system was not as representative or as receptive to popular control as it appeared to be, however. Party leaders could use their clout to affect the choice of delegates and influence their behavior at the conventions. Not only did the nomination process minimize the impact of the party's rank and file, but in areas of one-party dominance it effectively denied a voice to supporters of the minority party. The nomination was, in effect, the election.

The capacity of the system to be manipulated by party leaders, combined with the selection of unpopular, unimaginative, and in some cases unethical candidates, led to demands for reform. At the beginning of the twentieth century, the Progressive movement responded to these demands by urging a direct primary in which the rank-and-file supporters of a party would choose the party's nominees.

In 1904 Florida became the first state to hold such an election. Others followed suit. By 1916 twenty states had some type of primary; by the mid 1950s most of them did. Indiana was the last state to adopt this method of nominating candidates for state office; it did so in 1976.

Primaries are more democratic than multistaged delegate selection processes because they allow more people to participate. However, even in primaries those who participate may not be an accurate reflection of the general electorate or even the party. The better-educated, higher-income, more professional supporters of the party tend to be overrepresented.

Primaries have not only improved participation; they have also affected representation. In areas in which the parties are competitive, primaries have generally improved representation and have often heightened competition between parties. In areas dominated by a single party, however, primaries have had the opposite effect, decreasing competition and working to perpetuate the dominance of the majority party.[18] In such areas ambitious politicians generally seek nomination by the majority party, for winning its primary is tantamount to winning the general election. The incentive to stay within the party gives that party the power to exclude certain individuals and groups by denying them the opportunity to run for office. Thus, in the South before 1965, African Americans were effectively prevented from running by state party leaders and were barred from voting by registration and voting laws as well as by social pressure from the majority white community.

Primaries have also encouraged a different type of candidate, one who can appeal to the party's rank and file, not simply to its leadership. They have encouraged factions built on personal followings. They have also made it more difficult for parties to maintain consistent policy positions, because the parties can no longer control who is nominated or what appeals those nominees make.

Modern campaigns Campaigns affect who wins and who loses. Without a strong campaign, it is difficult for a challenger to gain sufficient recognition to defeat an incumbent; without a strong campaign, it is difficult for candidates from the minority party to overcome their partisan disadvantage; without a strong campaign, it is difficult to win an open seat or a nonpartisan election.

The growth of the mass media, particularly television, has reduced the traditional role of parties as the principal link between candidates and voters. The use of sophisticated techniques, such as polling and fundraising by candidates seeking office, has led to the rise of a new group of professionals who have rivaled and in many instances replaced party pros as campaign strategists and technical advisers. Changes in the campaign finance law have increased the influence of PACs and encouraged candidates to seek money and organizational support from a variety of sources. Thus many outside figures now compete with the party for influence in the campaign of the party's own candidates, and they continue to vie for influence with the candidates they helped after the election is over.

Parties and the Electorate

Parties need a coalition of supporters to win elections. They count on their partisans to provide the core of this coalition, but they must try to attract other factions to win an election. These electoral coalitions are stable, but they are not static. They shift with the issues, the candidates, and events. The Democratic coalition, built during Franklin Roosevelt's presidency, for example, has undergone major changes since that period.

One of the most significant and enduring of these changes has been the defection of southern white Protestants, who had supported the party since the Civil War. The seeds of this defection were sown in 1948, when the Democratic National Convention adopted a strong civil rights plank in its party platform and some southern delegates walked out (they later supported J. Strom Thurmund's splinter-party candidacy). The defection of this group from their party was accelerated in the 1960s by the advocacy of civil rights legislation and other social programs by presidents John F. Kennedy and Lyndon Johnson. In the 1970s the party's nomination of liberal presidential candidates and its adoption of liberal campaign platforms continued to alienate white southerners. Even moderate southern Democrats like Jimmy Carter and Bill Clinton were unable to win a majority of the white vote in the South, although with the help of African Americans, Carter did win a majority of the total southern vote in 1976. Clinton did not in 1992.

The exodus of white southerners from the Democratic party continued through the 1980s. In 1952, 85 percent of this group considered themselves Democrats; by 1978, that proportion had shrunk to 51 percent; by 1990, it was down to 33 percent, while 37 percent of white southerners identified with the party of Abraham Lincoln, the Republicans.[19]

The Democrats have also suffered declining support from several other key groups of their New Deal coalition. Organized labor, for example, remains Democratic, but the decreasing proportion of blue-collar workers (especially union members) in the population has made labor a smaller and hence less important component of the electorate. Catholic identification with the Democratic party has also weakened. Through the Carter administration, a majority of Catholics considered themselves Democrats; by the end of the Reagan administration, only a bare plurality did.

Although the Democrats have seen the allegiance of some of their key New Deal groups weaken, they have benefited from increased support from racial minority groups, notably African Americans and Hispanics (with the exception of those of Cuban descent, who vote Republican). African Americans and Hispanics continue to think of themselves as Democrats and have voted overwhelmingly for Democratic candidates at all levels of government. Relatively low socioeconomic status has worked to reinforce the Democratic inclinations of many of these minority voters, but it has also lowered their turnout at the polls. Demographic differences in the parties are revealed in Table 9-3.

Since 1980 discernible differences have developed in the partisan identities and voting patterns of men and women. Women are more likely than men to

As part of the inaugural festivities, the Clintons sang "We Are the World" on the steps of the Lincoln Memorial with a large chorus, among them Tipper, Al, and Albert Arnold Gore III, Ashford and Simpson, Stevie Wonder, Michael Jackson, Diana Ross, and Kenny Rogers. Such well-scripted, media-oriented events not only celebrated Clinton's victory; they also enhanced his image, a task deemed necessary for someone who was plagued by character issues during the campaign.

identify with the Democratic party, and men are more likely to prefer the Republican party. This split has produced a "gender gap" in the range of 4 to 8 percent. It is larger among whites than among nonwhites, larger among people in higher socioeconomic brackets than among less advantaged groups, and larger among people with more formal education than among those with less.[20]

Another important shift in the electoral coalitions has been the movement of new voters, particularly youth. After being more Democratic than their elders, younger voters (ages 18 to 29) began to change their political allegiances and modify their ideological orientations in the 1980s. They became more conservative than the general public on a host of economic and social issues and more Republican in their voting behavior, supporting Ronald Reagan in 1980 and 1984 and George Bush in 1988. During this decade a majority of the younger voters entering the electorate identified with the Republican party. However, in 1992 the 18-to-29-year-old voters returned to the Democratic fold, voting for Bill Clinton at approximately the national average.

In light of these shifts, how can the Democratic party's electoral coalition be described today? The Democrats have become the party of ethnic and racial minorities. They still receive overwhelming support from minority racial groups, people with the lowest incomes, and people who live in central cities. However, the relatively small size of the last two groups compared with the general population, and their lower turnout at the polls, make them less important components of the total electorate than they were in the past. Similarly, some of the traditional Democratic-oriented groups, such as union members and Catholics, also provide less support, while a majority of southern whites seem to have deserted the party altogether at the presidential level. Clearly, the Democratic New Deal coalition has eroded and to some extent aged.

In the last three decades the Republicans have gained adherents, probably more from new voters than from a wholesale shift of existing ones. These changes have narrowed but not eliminated the differences in partisan support which exist between the two major parties. As an electoral coalition, Republicans have become more white, more middle-class, and more suburban. They have gained support in the South and Southwest. They have maintained the

TABLE 9-3

Demography of Democrats and Republicans in the 1990s (percent)

	REPUBLICAN	DEMOCRAT	INDEPENDENT	NO. OF INTERVIEWS
National	**29**	**38**	**33**	**4929**
Sex				
Male	30	36	34	2476
Female	28	40	32	2453
Age				
18–29 years	29	33	38	871
30–49 years	29	37	34	2014
50–64 years	28	42	30	993
65 & older	33	43	24	1029
Boomer (26–46)	29	36	35	2133
Region				
East	24	41	35	1197
Midwest	30	32	38	1368
South	32	40	28	1510
West	32	39	29	854
Race				
White	32	34	34	4319
Nonwhite	11	65	24	610
Black	9	71	20	457
Hispanic	23	52	25	367
Education				
College grads.	36	32	32	1185
College inc./tech.	33	34	33	1295
H.S. grads.	28	38	34	1575
Less than H.S. grad.	21	50	29	844
Income				
$40,000 & over	35	32	33	1474
$25,000–39,999	32	34	34	1233
$15,000–24,999	26	41	33	902
Under $15,000	23	51	26	1013
Religion				
Protestant	34	36	30	2695
Catholic	26	42	32	1428

SOURCE: *The Gallup Poll Monthly*, July, 1992, 49. Reprinted with permission of Gallup Poll News Service.

traditional loyalties of Protestants and gained support from Christian fundamentalists who backed Democratic candidates through 1976. George Bush received 81 percent of the votes of this group in 1988 and 61 percent in 1992. The contemporary Republican party thus consists of members of racial and religious majorities and higher socioeconomic groups.

Christian fundamentalists have exercised increasing influence on Republican party politics. Although they supported George Bush in 1992, they forced him and other Republicans to take very conservative positions, especially on social issues like abortion, school prayer, and "family values." They are also playing a larger role in supporting Republican candidates at the state and local levels. George Allen's large victory as governor of Virginia in 1993 was due in part to the support he received from Christian groups.

© Paul S. Conklin

What conclusions can be drawn about the parties today? The old electoral coalitions have changed and, in the Democrats' case, weakened (see Figure 9-4). The Democratic party has lost much of its partisan advantage. What is less clear is whether the Democrats will remain the party of a plurality of the electorate.

It is clear that a partisan **dealignment** has been occurring over the last thirty years. A *dealignment* is a weakening of the attachment that people feel toward political parties. This dealignment has led more people to think of themselves as independents and vote more for the candidate and less for that candidate's partisan affiliation. It is not clear, however, whether a **realignment** is occurring. A *realignment* is a shifting in the partisan attitude of the electorate. It normally occurs over a series of elections and is characterized by changes in the allegiances of some existing voters and the development of partisan preferences among many new voters from the majority party to the minority party.

These shifts in partisan attitudes have produced a more volatile electorate, one on which neither party can depend as confidently. They have also contributed to the decline in the party's influence over its candidates, the electorate, and elected officials.

PARTIES AND GOVERNANCE

Despite its emphasis on elections, the party's ultimate objective is to control the machinery of government so as to influence the formulation of public policy in accordance with the interests and needs of its supporters. These interests and needs are articulated by the party in its quadrennial platform, by its candidates during the campaign, and by party leaders and elected officials during non-election periods.

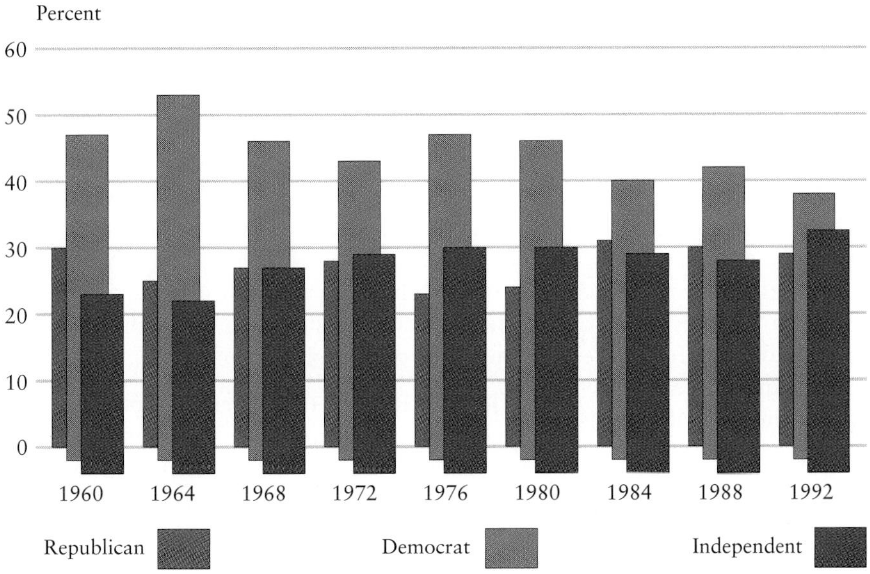

Figure 9-4   *Party affiliation.* SOURCE: *The Gallup Poll Monthly,* July, 1992, 49.
Reprinted with permission of Gallup Poll News Service.

Determining the Party's Positions

A **party platform** is a formal statement of beliefs, opinions, and policy stands
tied together by a set of underlying principles based on the party's ideological
orientation. (See Becoming Political on page 308.) Over the years the platforms
of the two major parties have differed significantly despite the common allegation that there is not a dime's worth of difference between them. Between
1944 and 1976, for example, 69 percent of the pledges made in one party's
platform were not made in the other's.[21] The sharpest distinctions between
Democrats and Republicans have been evident in issues relating to stimulating
and regulating the economy, providing social welfare, and, to a lesser extent,
subsidizing agriculture and other domestic industries. Democrats have supported greater government involvement, and Republicans have been more inclined to look to the private sector for policy solutions. Foreign affairs and civil
rights have not produced as many clear-cut or consistent differences between
the two parties.

Differences between party platforms are important because elected officials do attempt to redeem the promises they and their parties make. One study
of party platforms and campaign promises made during presidential election
campaigns between 1960 and 1984 found that presidents "submitted legislation or signed executive orders that are broadly consistent with about two-
thirds of their campaign pledges."[22] Of these, a substantial percentage were
enacted into law, ranging from a high of 89 percent of those proposed during
the Johnson administration to a low of 61 percent of those proposed during
the Nixon years.[23]

Every four years at their national nominating conventions, the two major parties articulate their philosophy, goals, and positions on the issues of the day in their platform. In developing these platforms, both parties follow a similar procedure. They appoint a platform committee, composed of representatives of the candidates who are seeking the party's nomination and other party leaders and officials, to draft a document for approval at the nominating convention.

This committee usually holds public hearings across the country in the spring of the presidential election year. Representatives of powerful groups and policy experts are invited to testify at these hearings, and their recommendations serve as the basis for an initial draft usually written by a small subcommittee and the party professionals who work for it. This draft is then presented to the full committee when it convenes, approximately one week before the convention begins.

To some extent the full platform committee repeats the same exercise. Subcommittees, organized on the basis of policy areas, hold hearings, revise the initial draft, and present it to the full committee for approval. After the committee has adopted a completed platform, it reports that platform to the convention, which can accept it in its entirety or with modifications.

Platforms are important despite the conventional wisdom that they are forgotten once the convention is over and the campaign is concluded. Elected officials do have a relatively good record of meeting their pledges. While approximately three-fourths of a party platform consists of high-sounding rhetoric, about one-fourth of it contains fairly specific promises that successful congressional and presidential candidates try to redeem.

Here are some of the domestic policy positions adopted by the Democrats in 1992. How many of them have already become national policy?

Jobs Rebuild America through investment in infrastructure, defense conversion, and a national information network.

Deficit Reduce the deficit by spending cuts (eliminate nonproductive programs, achieve defense savings, reform entitlement programs, cut government administrative costs, and apply a strict "pay-as-you-go" rule for new non-investment spending) by generating new revenues from a growing economy and increased taxes on the rich.

Education Expand Head Start and student health and nutrition programs; make college education affordable to all qualified students by revamping the student loan program and instituting a program of national service by which loans could be partially or fully paid off; support public school choice but not vouchers for private schools.

Health care Reform the health-care system to control costs and make health care affordable and accessible to all Americans.

Abortion Stand behind the right of every woman to choose, consistent with *Roe v. Wade*, regardless of ability to pay; support a national law to protect that right.

Party platforms are available from national committee headquarters: Republican National Committee, 310 1st Street, S.E., Washington, DC 20003, (202) 863-8500; Democratic National Committee, 430 S. Capitol Street, S.E., Washington, DC 20003, (202) 863-8000.

Party platforms set the tone of a campaign. They also provide an agenda for governing and criteria by which to judge the new administration. The most powerful candidate usually controls the party platform committee and influences its deliberations. In 1992, Clinton did that, but Bush could not. Conservative Republican delegates pushed their own agenda and forced President Bush to adhere to it. Some believe it contributed to Bush's defeat.

Converting Positions into Public Policy

The successful conversion of a partisan agenda into legislative enactments and executive actions is an important measure of responsible party government. The agenda, which consists of the party platform and the promises made by party candidates, provides a standard by which elected officials can be held accountable for their decisions and actions.[24] Officials who consistently abandon their party's positions may jeopardize their status with the electorate and the benefits they receive from their party's leaders—benefits such as legislative committee assignments and presidential support.

The task of influencing government is not easy. A party organization has limited leverage over public officials, regardless of their partisan affiliation. The heterogeneous nature of the major parties and their decentralized structures result in policy positions that are not equally attractive and salient to all candidates and officeholders. Moreover, platforms become dated over time.[25] Although legislators of both parties maintain committees and caucuses to define partisan policy positions, during nonelection years the parties have difficulty articulating and promoting stands on issues. Finally, in the United States' system of separate institutions sharing power, there may not be one controlling party. The executive branch can be controlled by one party and the legislative branch by another, or congressional control can be divided. In either situation, credit or blame is difficult to assess. Thus, party is but one influence among many on public policy.

Partisan Influence on the Legislature

Parties shape the structure and operation of most legislatures. The majority party controls committees, recruits most of the staff, and influences rule making, personnel, and policy matters. The vote on legislative leadership generally occurs along party lines. The Speaker of the House and the Senate majority leader are chosen on straight party votes.

Although the effect of partisanship on substantive matters varies with the issue, it tends to be greater than any other factor in affecting the outcome of voting at the final stage of deliberation.[26] For example, from the beginning of the Carter administration through the Bush administration a majority of Republicans opposed a majority of Democrats on approximately 48 percent and 45 percent of the roll-call votes in the House and in the Senate, respectively.[27] On partisan issues, Democratic members of Congress tend to vote with their party about 75 percent of the time and Republicans, 73 percent. In recent years these percentages are even higher.[28]

A continuing difficulty for the parties, however, is that they have few sanctions that they can impose on members who refuse to support the party's position. Party leaders cannot control or in some cases even influence the nomination, campaign, and election of those who wear the party label. Hence, the ability of the leadership to affect legislative decision making rests primarily on persuasion. In situations where constituency, executive, or other strong pressures push against the party's position, however, persuasion may be difficult.

Partisan Influence on the Executive and Judiciary

Traditionally, chief executives perform a number of functions that may be subject to party influences. They set the agenda for public debate, choosing which initiatives they wish to emphasize. They nominate certain people to high ex-

Politics is the art of wheeling and dealing. Legislative leaders have few sanctions they can invoke against those who do not toe the party line, and so they must make deals. During the redrafting of Clinton's first deficit-reducing budget in the summer of 1993, House Ways and Means Committee chairman Dan Rostenkowski (D-Ill.) and Charles Rangel (D-N.Y.), an influential member of the black caucus, stepped outside for a talk. Rangel opposed spending cuts that conservative Democrats supported. To reach agreement, Rostenkowski had to discover what Rangel really wanted.

Jose R. Lopez/NYT Pictures

ecutive positions and, in the federal government, to judicial positions as well. They even exercise some discretion over the performance of government services. In each of these activities they are affected by partisan considerations, but they also influence those considerations.

Even if a president, governor, or mayor does not hold a formal position within a party, he or she is considered to be the party's leader at the national, state, or local level. As such, a chief executive can make policy decisions and personnel choices (including the choice of national committee chair) and also have an impact on a party's financial and electoral support. Some choose not to do so, however. Presidents in particular have neglected their parties in recent years because of the time and energy that partisan activities take. They must also take a bipartisan approach in foreign affairs and, when their party does not control the legislature, in domestic affairs as well. Vice presidents are often asked to perform these partisan tasks, which range from lobbying legislators to courting party leaders to speaking before various party groups.

Presidents and other chief executives who disregard their party once they are in office can pay a high price for their neglect. They may not need their party's support to get elected, but they do need it to govern effectively.

Legislators are likely to support a chief executive of their own party because they and the chief executive share similar goals and objectives. Their political fates are also usually bound together. A good example was the support many Democratic members of Congress gave President Clinton on his deficit-reduction plan even though that plan contained tax increases and spending cuts opposed by some of their constituents. In this case, Democrats saw Clinton's popularity and programmatic success as tied to their own. Moreover, chief executives usually have desirable rewards that can be bestowed on partisan supporters, such as patronage appointments, campaign resources, and media exposure. On the other hand, an unpopular president or governor hurts the party and can affect the success of legislators running on the same ticket in the next election.

The electoral fates of the legislature and executive are not as closely linked as they once were, however. Presidential "coattails," to which candidates of the president's party may cling during presidential elections, have gotten shorter.[29] And chief executives have even less influence over the election of fellow partisans during nonpresidential elections and practically no influence over their nomination. In 1986 a popular president, Ronald Reagan, campaigned actively for the reelection of eight Republican senators. Although he helped them raise money and may have increased the size of their vote, six of them lost. Reagan's experience indicates the very limited ability of contemporary presidents to share their popularity with their party's candidates for Congress.

Partisanship is an important consideration in the appointment of federal court judges and some state judges, and partisan divisions are evident even in states where judges are selected on the basis of merit alone.[30] However, the influence of party on judicial decision making is more difficult to discern. Although studies have found that Republican and Democratic judges differ on certain types of issues, these studies have not been able to determine whether the differences are a result of partisanship or differing values, ideology, and judicial philosophy.[31]

Moreover, the mores of judicial decision making require judges to make their decisions on the basis of law, not politics, although personal and partisan factors may intrude on these decisions. The sentence given to a person convicted of a heinous crime could affect a state judge's reelection; the determination whether a reapportionment plan accords with federal guidelines could affect a party's chances in the next election. Nonetheless, partisan considerations do not affect the judiciary in the same way they affect the legislative or executive branches.

The political party is thus an instrument for governance although it does not control government. What it does, however, is link institutions and promote cooperation. Parties help produce an agenda and contribute to consensus building within institutions and among the general public. In theory this linkage between politics and government also contributes to public accountability, although weak party discipline and separate institutions that may be controlled by different parties make that accountability harder to achieve in practice. Nevertheless, the performance of party members in government affects the election prospects of others who run on the same party label.

The crucial relationship between party and government puts a premium on building and maintaining party unity. Only by converting public choices into coherent partisan positions can the parties minimize internal struggles and thereby maximize their chances of winning. Party unity also facilitates governance. It promotes accountability by making it easier for the public to allocate responsibility for the government's decisions and actions. That is why political parties are an important component of a democratic system and why partisan politics are essential to its operation.

SUMMARY

A *political party* is an organization whose goal is to win elective office in order to influence the policies of government. It is composed of three groups of supporters, or *partisans:* professionals, who are employed by the party; candidates and elected officials; and rank-and-file voters.

Parties are not mentioned in the Constitution, but they began to take shape during the administration of George Washington. Two political groupings emerged, one supporting and the other opposing the administration's policies. They became known as the *Federalists* and the *Democratic-Republicans* (or Republicans). In the mid 1820s the Republicans split into feuding factions. One of them formed the coalition that succeeded in getting Andrew Jackson elected in 1828. Jackson's followers became known as the *Democrats* and were opposed by a new party known as the *Whigs*.

In 1854 the *Republican* party was organized. When the Democrats split over the slavery issue in 1860 and the Whig party collapsed, Republican candidate Abraham Lincoln was elected president. Originally composed of small-business owners, laborers, and farmers, the Republican party increasingly became influenced by big business. At the turn of the century, when economic conflict between rural and urban interests culminated in a partisan *realignment*, the Republicans dominated national politics for the next three decades, until the election of Franklin Roosevelt in 1932.

During the Great Depression of the 1930s the electorate divided along economic class lines: less prosperous voters were likely to be Democratic, and more prosperous voters were likely to be Republican. The Democrats expanded their support among white southerners and racial and religious minorities. Since the end of the 1960s, the Democratic New Deal coalition has frayed but not disintegrated. No longer does that party comprise a majority of the electorate, although it still constitutes a plurality.

The Republicans have gained adherents, and the proportion of voters considering themselves independent has also increased.

In the United States the major parties are diversified in composition, decentralized in structure, and pragmatic in their approach to policy making. One reason for these characteristics is the federal character of the American system: most elections are for state or local officials or state representatives to Congress. Another reason is that candidates must appeal to the majority of the voters in *single-member districts*. In *multimember districts*, where elections are decided by proportional voting, there is greater incentive for party loyalty and partisan appeal.

Issue/splinter parties are created when dissidents split off from a major party. They often succeed in drawing attention to their concerns, reducing the electoral success of the party they left, and encouraging one major party or the other to support the action or position that prompted their protest. In contrast, *ideological parties* subscribe to beliefs that lie outside the mainstream of society. They have not had as much impact on the politics, policy, or government as have splinter parties.

At the national level, the parties direct the bulk of their energies to presidential campaigns. They raise funds, target voters, communicate with the public, develop policy positions, generate partisan appeals, and provide assistance to candidates. National party organizations have become more important in recent years with the development of their fundraising capabilities and the Democrats' nationalization of party rules for the presidential nomination. The centralization of fundraising has also strengthened state party organizations, particularly during campaigns. These trends have begun to offset the decline in influence that state party organizations suffered with the growth of primaries in the twentieth century.

State parties focus on electing candidates to state and national office; they also raise funds, take official positions on salient issues, and recruit potential nominees. At the local (county or city) level, parties are active primarily during election campaigns, especially when there is real competition between the parties.

The advent of primaries was not the only factor that reduced the influence of parties. The growth of the mass media has also affected the traditional role of parties as the link between candidates and voters, and the use of sophisticated techniques, such as polling, has led to the rise of a new group of professionals who compete with party professionals to influence campaign strategy. Campaign finance laws have permitted the growth of PACs, which provide additional funding sources. These changes have weakened the ability of the parties to control the electoral process.

Their hold on the voters has also been reduced. Partisan loyalties have become less intense. More people identify themselves as independent. The gap between the parties has also narrowed. Democrats have lost their status as the majority party although they still command the allegiance of a plurality of voters.

There have also been changes within the major parties' electoral coalitions. The Democrats have been hurt by the defection of southern, white Protestants, primarily at the national level, by the decline in the proportion of Catholics who regularly support Democratic candidates, and by the reduction in the blue-collar labor vote. They have retained the support of African Americans and most Hispanic groups. Republicans have profited from the growth of white-collar workers within the electorate and from the increased support they have received from Christian fundamentalist groups and from younger voters in the 1980s. In recent years a gender gap has also appeared. Women are more oriented toward the Democratic party and its candidates, while men are more inclined to vote Republican.

Parties want to influence the electoral process and maintain the loyalty of as much of the electorate as possible in order to get their candidates into office. Their ultimate goal is to affect public policy in accordance with the principles, beliefs, and interests of their partisans. Every four years they draft a *platform* that articulates their philosophy and policy positions on the important issues of the day. These platforms and the campaign promises that party candidates make are important because elected officials do try to redeem them once in office.

Parties shape the structure and operation of most legislatures, and partisanship carries more weight than any other factor in affecting the outcome of voting. However, the parties have few sanctions that they can impose on elected officials who do not support their positions. As a result, the party's ability to affect legislative decision making rests primarily on persuasion and consensus building.

Chief executives are considered to be their party's leaders and are expected to make policy decisions and personnel judgments that reflect the party's positions. Executives who disregard their party once in office have difficulty governing effectively. Partisanship is a major factor in the appointment of the federal judiciary and some state judges, but it has a less direct impact on judicial decision making than it has on decision making in legislative and executive branches. The political party contributes to government by promoting cooperation and enhancing the accountability of government to the people.

political party
partisan
Federalists
Democratic-Republicans
    (Republicans)

Democrats
Whigs
Republicans
single-member district
multimember district

ideological party
issue/splinter party
dealignment
realignment
party platform

LEARNING MORE ABOUT POLITICAL PARTIES

Scholarly studies

Beck, Paul Allen, and Frank J. Sorauf. *Party Politics in America.* 7th ed. New York: HarperCollins, 1992. A recent revision of a highly regarded text on political parties.

Black, Earl, and Merle Black. *Politics and Society in the South.* Cambridge, Mass.: Harvard University Press, 1987. An excellent study of contemporary southern politics.

Ceaser, James W. "Political Parties—Declining, Stabilizing, or Resurging?" In *The New American Political System,* 2nd version, edited by Anthony King, 87–137. Washington, D.C.: American Enterprise Institute, 1990. A reflective, concise essay on contemporary parties.

Cotter, Cornelius P., James L. Gibson, John F. Bibby, and Robert Huckshorn. *Party Organizations in American Politics.* Pittsburgh: University of Pittsburgh Press, 1989. A comprehensive study of party organizations in the states.

Herrnson, Paul S. *Party Campaigning in the 1980s.* Cambridge, Mass.: Harvard University Press, 1988. Provides evidence of the strengthening of national party influence on electoral campaigns.

Key, V. O., Jr. *Southern Politics.* Knoxville, Tenn.: University of Tennessee Press, 1984. The classic study of southern politics from the end of the Civil War until the middle of the twentieth century.

Maisel, L. Sandy. *Parties and Elections in America,* 2nd ed. New York: McGraw-Hill, 1992. A basic parties text with an election orientation. The author is a political scientist who has himself run for public office and has been active in party politics.

Leisure reading

O'Connor, Edwin. *The Last Hurrah.* Boston: Little, Brown, 1985. One of the best novels on urban politics. It tells the story of an old-style Irish politician's final attempt to win reelection against a modern media candidate.

Warren, Robert Penn. *All the King's Men.* New York: HarBraceJ, 1990. A fictionalized account of southern politics, Louisiana style, based on the story of Huey Long's reign as Democratic party boss.

Williams, T. Harry. *Huey Long.* New York: Vintage, 1981. A wonderfully written biography of the life and times of Louisiana's most influential and colorful political leader.

Primary sources

Kinnell, Susan, ed. *The Democratic and Republican Parties in America: A Historical Bibliography.* Santa Barbara, Calif.: ABC-CLIO Information Services, 1983. An annotated bibliography of articles from scholarly journals published between 1973 and 1982 on the history and operation of the Democratic and Republican parties.

Johnson, Donald Bruce, ed. *National Party Platforms.* Vols. I, II. Urbana: University of Illinois Press, 1978. A collection of the platforms of the major and minor parties from 1840 to 1976.

Organizations

Democratic Congressional Campaign Committee and Democratic Senatorial Campaign Committee, 430 S. Capitol Street, S.E., Washington, DC 20003; (202) 863-1500, (202) 224-2447. These committees raise and distribute funds for Democrats who seek election or reelection to the House of Representatives and the Senate.

Democratic National Committee, 430 S. Capitol Street, S.E., Washington, DC 20003; (202) 863-8000. This committee, supported by a large staff, makes and implements policy and personnel decisions for the Democratic party.

National Republican Congressional Committee, 320 1st Street, S.E., Washington, DC 20003; (202) 479-7000. National Republican Senatorial Committee, 425 2nd Street, N.E., Washington, DC 20002; (202) 675-6000. These committees raise and distribute funds for Republicans who seek election or reelection to the House of Representatives and the Senate.

Republican National Committee, 310 1st Street, S.E., Washington, DC 20003; (202) 863-8500. This committee, supported by a large staff, makes and implements policy and personnel decisions for the Republican party.

Senate Democratic Policy Committee, S-118 Capitol Building, Washington, DC 20510; (202) 224-5551. This committee establishes policy for the Democratic party in the Senate.

Senate Republican Policy Committee, 347 Russell Office Building, Washington, DC 20510; (202) 224-2946. This committee establishes policy for the Republican party in the Senate.

Elections

- Elections and democracy: suffrage, meaningful choice, and political equality

- The American voter: turnout and voting behavior

- The election campaign: presidential and nonpresidential nomination and election processes; campaign organization and strategy

- Analyzing election results

- Elections and governance

In 1912 and 1916, the Democrats nominated New Jersey's governor, Woodrow Wilson. A former politics professor and president of Princeton University, Wilson won in 1912 because Republicans, who constituted the majority, split their vote between William Howard Taft and former president Theodore Roosevelt. The latter had thrown his "hat in the ring" and subsequently joined the Progressive ticket with Hiram Johnson of California as his running mate.

In 1916, when foreign policy was the major issue, Teddy Roosevelt supported the Republican candidate, former Supreme Court Justice Charles Evans Hughes. Wilson, who ran on the slogan "He kept us out of war," was reelected by a small margin.

It was March 6, 1991. President Bush had just delivered an address to Congress in which he declared that the United States and its coalition had been victorious in the Persian Gulf War. The first public opinion poll following Bush's speech revealed that almost 90 percent of the American people approved of the job that he was doing as president. He looked like a sure bet to win reelection, so sure, in fact, that no prominent Democrat wanted to run against him. Only a little-known former senator, Paul Tsongas of Massachusetts, declared his candidacy in March of that year.

Six months later the political climate in the United States began to darken. A deepening economic recession, a pervasive public pessimism, and a growing anger and frustration with government at the national level encouraged challengers to George Bush, even within his own party. Although Bush easily defeated Republican Pat Buchanan to secure his party's nomination, the 22 percent of the vote that Buchanan received indicated that Bush was in serious trouble. Public opinion polls throughout 1992 confirmed the precipitous decline in the president's popularity.

Of the principal Democratic candidates, Governor Bill Clinton of Arkansas was the best organized and financed. But three weeks before the first Democratic primary in New Hampshire, a woman who claimed she had had a twelve-year relationship with him accused him of marital infidelity. Two weeks later another negative story charged that he had dodged the draft during the Vietnam War and participated in anti war protests. Despite these charges—he denied the first while admitting to marital problems, and explained the second as opposition to the war—Clinton survived the New Hampshire primary. He came in second and went on to win the southern regional Democratic primaries, his party's nomination, and ultimately, the presidency.

How could a governor from a small state with little national experience or exposure, a candidate with considerable personal vulnerabilities, defeat an incumbent president who had successfully prosecuted one war and presided over the end of another, the Cold War, a president who was the most popular in recent history? The answer involves the rules under which the nominations and general election are conducted, the environment in which those elections occurred, the candidates and their campaigns, and the judgment of the electorate about what was and was not relevant.

During the nomination period, the rules and procedures prescribed by the political parties favor those candidates with the best organization and the most money. In 1992, these were George Bush and Bill Clinton. Their ability to mount effective campaigns in the many states that hold primaries and caucuses at the beginning of the nomination process gave them the potential to collect a large number of delegates and, at the same time, to withstand losses or embarrassments in a few states. In the general election, the electoral college system

also favors the major party candidate who can win the most large states and puts others, especially independent candidates, at a disadvantage.

The political environment was another key factor. As the public mood shifted from euphoria over victory in the Gulf war, to pessimism over the economy and the future, to anger over alleged abuses by public officials in Congress and the executive branch and frustration over everyone's inability to address pressing national issues, people became more discontent with the current leadership and more eager for change. These attitudes hurt the incumbent and helped his challengers.

The candidates tried to ride this wave of public discontent. Clinton focused on the economy and other domestic issues. Emphasizing the need for change and moderate policy solutions, he directed his appeal to those unhappy with the status quo, particularly Democrats and Independents. Bush first minimized the economic problems, then acknowledged them and blamed them on the inaction of the Democratic Congress. He stressed his character and experience, calling Clinton "slick" and Independent H. Ross Perot "authoritarian" by contrast. Perot lashed out at the whole Washington crowd, lobbyists and policy makers alike, claiming that his success as a businessman gave him the skills to get government working again. Perot's criticism, particularly during the presidential debates, seemed to reinforce Clinton's contention that the president had failed to provide strong leadership. Both Perot and Clinton hit a responsive chord in those who wanted change and believed that new leadership was necessary to get it.

Being a Democrat was an advantage for Clinton. He was seen as more electable than Perot and more likely to get along with Congress. On election day, a plurality of voters overrode their misgivings and voted for him.

THE 1992 PRESIDENTIAL ELECTION IS A PRIME example of a dynamic political process at work, of a candidate who defied initial odds and an electorate that reconsidered its early impressions and judgments, of effective versus ineffective campaigns, and of the powerful impact of economic conditions on voting behavior. These are some of the key features of the American electoral system.

In the United States all legislators, most chief executives (presidents, governors, and mayors), and many state judges are chosen in elections for fixed terms of office. Elections resolve conflicts, at least temporarily. They decide among competing people, policies, and parties. Society's willingness to accept the results of the vote ensures the primacy of the rule of law and enhances the stability of the political system.

This chapter discusses the political aspects of the electoral process. It first looks at the relationship between elections and democracy and then focuses on the American voter, on who votes and why. Finally, it examines the stages of the electoral process, campaign strategy and tactics, election returns, and the implications of the election for governance.

ELECTIONS AND DEMOCRACY

Elections are a mechanism for making important political choices. They frame policy debate, select public officials, and influence the decisions of public officials. These functions are essential for a democratic government because they establish and reaffirm popular control.

If elections are to link the people to their representatives, they must meet three criteria: universal suffrage, meaningful choice, and majority rule. **Universal suffrage** means that all citizens who are responsible for their own actions are permitted to vote in order to protect and promote their own interests.[1] If

Wide World Photos, Inc.

For the electoral process to work, candidates for office must communicate with the public. In presidential elections, the televised "debate" has become the principal forum in which the major contenders try to put themselves and their ideas forward. After many arguments over times, places, and formats, Bush, Clinton, and Perot met at three such media events. Although candidates tend to respond in set patterns to reporters' questions rather than debating each other, these debates are important because more people watch them than any other campaign event.

some people are denied the right to vote, their ability to influence the decisions of public officials will be reduced. Effective representation and electoral power go hand in hand.

Meaningful choice implies that there is some opportunity to select among different options. This criterion requires a minimum of two candidates whose views are not identical and who have sufficient resources to present their beliefs to the public. It also implies that the voters have an opportunity to make that choice, that elections are structured in such a way that people can easily and effectively choose among competing candidates. In rendering this judgment, the votes of all those who choose to participate in the election should be equal. The application of this principle of **political equality** requires that the majority rule, that the candidate with the most votes win.

Why do the losers accept such a result? The answer is that the democratic system protects the losers as well. It does so by obligating the winners to govern by the rule of law. The law contains provisions and safeguards that protect all members of society against arbitrary and capricious actions by those in power. One of the most important of these safeguards is the electoral system itself.

Each of these democratic criteria seems logical, straightforward, and non-controversial; yet each has generated considerable conflict. In the United States much of the conflict has focused on suffrage—the question of who may vote. A second problem is how to structure the election so as to ensure meaningful choice. Rules governing voter registration, ballot access, vote challenges and recounts, even the hours and places for voting, all shape how well elections convert public opinion into choices that reflect that opinion. A third controversy, in recent years, has referred to the principle of equality. Some argue that individual candidates have the right to spend their own money and utilize their own resources during a campaign. Others argue that this is not democratic, that no person or group should exercise greater influence in an election simply on the basis of wealth.

Suffrage: Who Can Vote?

The framers of the Constitution struggled with the problems of participation and representation. In theory, they favored a government of, by, and for the people. In practice, they feared that the self-interested behavior of the general public could lead to what James Madison referred to as a "tyranny of the majority."

One way to prevent such a tyranny was to restrict suffrage—that is, to limit the right to vote. Such restrictions, however, would not be consistent with the political rights articulated in the Declaration of Independence or with the preamble to the Constitution. Moreover, they would have jeopardized the ratification of the Constitution. So the framers took another tack. They designed a system to represent three different constituencies: (1) the nation (president and vice president), (2) the states (Senate), and (3) the people (House of Representatives). They avoided the potentially divisive issue of who would be eligible to vote by making the states responsible for resolving that question, retaining for Congress the power to legislate on these matters if it chose to.

Initially most states required property ownership as a condition of voting. Since most property was owned by white men, this requirement effectively disenfranchised women and racial minorities. Some states imposed an additional requirement: belief in a Christian God.

In the early nineteenth century, pressure developed to expand the franchise—to enable more people to vote. By the middle of the 1830s, property ownership and religious beliefs had been dropped as qualifications for voting in most states. However, gender, race, and age barriers remained. It took the enactment of three constitutional amendments to remove them. The Fifteenth Amendment, ratified in 1870, abolished race, color, and national origin as qualifications for voting, at least in theory. In practice, formal and informal restrictions effectively prevented large-scale voting by African Americans in the South for another hundred years. The Nineteenth Amendment, ratified in 1920, prevented states from denying women the right to vote. The Twenty-sixth Amendment, ratified in 1971, established a uniform minimum voting age of 18. Each of these amendments was passed as a result of successful struggles in the public arena—that is, political struggles—by those who favored the expansion of

For many decades, the extension of suffrage to women met considerable resistance. After the Civil War, women who demanded voting rights were depicted as mannish, even lewd. In this Currier and Ives print, The Age of Brass (1869), women wear men's hats, smoke cigars, expose their legs, and look downright nasty. The one man on the scene holds a baby, a sign of frightful role reversals to come if women should get the same rights as men.

This ominous prediction was not borne out, at least when women received the right to vote 51 years later. In 1920, the year the Nineteenth Amendment was ratified and became part of the Constitution, these Philadelphia voters were pictured as modest if purposeful, and barely showed an ankle.

The 18-Year-Old Vote

We take it for granted today that any citizen who is 18 years of age and older should have the right to vote. But thirty years ago that was not the case. States used to set their own minimum age for voting, and most required that their citizens be 21 or over to vote.

There was not much support to establish a national minimum voting age of 18 until the development of massive opposition to the Vietnam War. Then "conscription without representation" became an issue. If men were old enough to be drafted into the armed services and sent to fight in Vietnam, putting their lives on the line in the process, then, it was argued, they should be old enough to choose the public officials responsible for this policy. Besides, increasing educational levels for younger people combined with the desirability of expanding the electorate in a democracy were other reasons offered for allowing citizens who had reached the age of 18 to vote.

Nonetheless, considerable opposition to lowering the voting age remained. Proponents of states' rights, particularly those in the South, contended that the establishment of national qualifications denied the states their constitutional right to set the voting age. Others believed that these younger Americans were not sufficiently mature, responsible, or informed to vote. Some even felt that allowing 18-year-olds to vote could adversely affect public policy. It might, for example, create pressure to lower the drinking age (which also varied from state to state) or encourage candidates to make unrealistic promises as a means of gaining votes in school board elections.

The good news is that these fears have not been realized—since the Twenty-sixth Amendment, which established a uniform voting age of 18, has been in effect since July 1, 1971. The bad news is that relatively few 18–21-year-olds actually vote (see Figure 10-1, page 329). The youngest age group has had the lowest percentage of voter registration and turnout of any other age group within the population. This fact alone leads to a number of serious questions about our youngest voters:

Discussion questions
1. In retrospect, were the principal arguments put forth by the proponents of the Twenty-sixth Amendment valid?
2. Why do you think people between the ages of 18 and 21 do not exercise their right to vote with nearly the same regularity as do those in other age groups?
3. Does the lower voter participation of those between 18 and 21 years old confirm the allegation that younger people are less informed, interested, and responsible? Are they turned off to democracy?

suffrage against those who wanted to maintain the status quo. (The debate over lowering the voting age to 18 is described in the Case Study above.)

The restrictions on suffrage, which prevented the United States from achieving the goal of political equality, benefited those in power, generally the most well-to-do members of society. By undercutting challenges to those in power, these restrictions had fostered considerable resistance to change, especially at the state and local levels. As suffrage was gradually extended, however, these consequences were also gradually reversed. Women and minority groups increased their representation in government. Policies that benefited the newest members of the electorate were enacted and implemented. The party system became more competitive at all levels of government, and within the parties there were more opportunities for the rank and file to be heard and to influence the selection of nominees.

In the early days of the republic, the states had complete authority to determine the conduct of federal elections. Subsequently, constitutional amendments and congressional statutes limited that discretion, particularly the right to set qualifications for voting. Nevertheless, state laws that establish registration regulations, ballot access, electoral challenges, and even the procedures for the time, place, and manner of voting continue to have an important impact on the electoral process.

Take voter registration, for example. Originally designed as a reform to prevent illegal voting (such as voting more than once), voter registration requirements have been used by states to discourage voting. Some states imposed residence requirements of up to two years, reducing the number of voters by effectively preventing anyone who had recently moved into the state from casting a ballot. Perhaps this explains why the proportion of the electorate that votes in the United States has been lower than the proportion voting in most other Western democracies.[2]

It has required federal law to change these arcane rules and ease voter registration. Today states cannot require residence of more than 30 days to vote in national elections. Moreover, a recently enacted "motor voter" bill that will take effect in 1995 requires states to allow residents to register to vote by mail or when they apply for or renew their driver's license. State offices that serve the disabled will also have to have voter registration material available, as will military recruitment offices and welfare assistance offices. Approximately half the states already have instituted these or similar laws.

Easing registration requirements is likely to increase voter turnout. Estimates of the size of this increase have ranged from 5 to 9 percent.[3]

Electoral choice is also affected by the rules for getting on the ballot. States can make it tough or easy to run for office. They can impose residence requirements on the candidates, make them pay a filing fee, and require them to obtain the signatures of a certain number or percentage of registered voters before their names can be placed on the ballot. The more rigorous these requirements are, the fewer the candidates and the greater the party's control over its nominees. H. Ross Perot encountered this difficulty in his 1992 presidential campaign. His organization spent considerable time and money collecting signatures simply to get his name on the ballot in all fifty states.

The authority of the states to conduct general elections extends to primaries as well. The type of primary, the date for holding it, and the rules for determining the winner are all established by state law. In some cases these laws have elicited considerable controversy, particularly when they conflict with national party rules.

In two landmark decisions, *Cousins v. Wigoda* (1975) and *Democratic Party of the U.S. v. La Follette* (1981), the Supreme Court held that the parties may determine their own rules for delegate selection and refuse to seat delegates at their national conventions who are not chosen in accordance with those rules. Despite these rulings, however, increased popular participation in the nomination process has weakened the ability of party leaders and organizations to select candidates for office. As a result, the responsiveness of many elected officials to the constituencies that elected them has increased, but in a way that fragments rather than concentrates political power. This may produce a more democratic political system but also a more divided government.

Voter Registration

The Twenty-fourth Amendment to the Constitution, adopted in 1964, banned the payment of poll taxes and other taxes as a prerequisite for voting in federal elections. The Twenty-sixth Amendment, adopted in 1971, lowered the national voting age to 18. Federal law sets the date of presidential and congressional elections and forbids voting discrimination based on race. Beginning in 1995 the new federal "motor voter law" requires states to permit voter registration by mail or when people apply for a driver's license. Until 1995 procedures for registering to vote continue to differ from state to state, however.

In Minnesota, for example, citizens are able to register by mail throughout the year or in person on Election Day. A state agency encourages and oversees voter registration, and voter registration forms are provided as a service by the motor vehicle department when people apply for a driver's license. When registering in Minnesota, individuals are asked only for their date of birth, their citizenship status (only United States citizens can vote), and whether they have registered in the state before.

In contrast, Virginia has had no mail registration, no Election Day registration (the registration books close thirty days before the election), no state voter registration agency, and no "motor voter" program; deputized registrars are appointed at the discretion of local officials. When registering in Virginia, individuals are asked for their date of birth, place of birth, age, sex, Social Security number, citizenship status, whether they have registered in the state before, and whether they have any criminal convictions or disqualifying mental conditions.

Have the differences in voting registration practices made a difference in voter turnout? In the 1988 presidential election, 65.5 percent of eligible voters in Minnesota cast a ballot, compared to 48 percent in Virginia. The national voter turnout in 1988 was 50.15 percent. In the 1992 elections, the turnout in Minnesota was 74 percent; in Virginia it was 61 percent. On the national scene, voter turnout for the presidential elections was 33 percent in 1988 and 55.9 percent in 1992.

Political Equality: What Limits on Campaign Contributions?

The third democratic criterion, making sure that all citizens have an equal voice and vote in the electoral process, has generated a decade-long debate over campaign finance, specifically, whether the American tradition of unrestricted private funding of political campaigns undercuts the democratic process. Before the mid 1970s, campaigns were financed entirely by individual contributions. Both parties depended on a small number of wealthy donors for much of their funding.[4] As campaign expenditures increased, primarily as a result of rising media costs, questions began to be raised about the connection between giving and governing. Did the wealthy exercise disproportionate influence? What did they get for their money? Could elected officials be responsive to large donors and to the general public at the same time? Did the high costs of running discourage qualified individuals from seeking office?

UPI/Bettmann

Discrimination in registration and voting practices persisted long after ratification of the Fifteenth and Nineteenth amendments. African Americans had little recourse in one-party states where segregationists controlled the dominant Democratic party. In protest, Fannie Lou Hamer and others founded the Mississippi Freedom Democratic party and tried to get seated in place of the regular delegation at the 1964 Democratic convention in Atlantic City. At first they were denied admission, but after a struggle, Ms. Hamer took one of the two at-large seats they were given. After Congress enacted the voting rights bill in 1965, the federal government was required to intervene in counties where large numbers of citizens were not registered.

Congress debated these issues, and in 1971 and again in 1974 it enacted legislation to limit campaign spending and provide government support for presidential nominations and election campaigns. The Federal Election Campaign Act (FECA) required public disclosure of all contributions and expenditures above a certain amount and created the Federal Election Commission to monitor activities and oversee compliance.

Parts of this legislation were highly controversial. In particular, the limits on contributions generated considerable opposition. Some saw the limits as a restraint on freedom of speech; others viewed them as a proper concern of government. In *Buckley v. Valeo* (1976) the Supreme Court took a middle position. Arguing that personal expenditures can be a form of expression but campaign finance can be regulated, the Court upheld the right of Congress to restrict the amount of money people could contribute to candidates for office in any federal election, but not the amount people could spend *independently* on behalf of those candidates.

How Far Can a Legislator Go in Soliciting Financial Support?

Political campaigning in the United States has traditionally been funded by private individuals and groups. Only the presidential nominations and elections receive outright government subsidies. Soliciting contributions is an activity protected by the First Amendment to the Constitution, which guarantees freedom of speech so long as the contribution is voluntary. It cannot be obtained as a condition for holding a government job, getting a contract, or receiving a special favor. Sometimes, however, the line between a personal appeal for money and an implicit promise to help the person or the group that gives the money can be thin or nonexistent.

Take the case of *McCormick v. United States* (1991). Robert McCormick, a state legislator in West Virginia, asked a group of foreign doctors who had failed to qualify for licenses and wished special legislation to practice medicine in that state to con-

tribute to his primary reelection campaign. Five of them did, giving McCormick a total of $5,250. Their contributions exceeded the legal limits for individuals in West Virginia. To make matters worse, McCormick neither reported the contributions as required by state law nor declared the money as revenue on his taxes.

Convicted of extortion, a federal crime, McCormick appealed on the grounds that the contributions per se did not constitute evidence that he had "sold his vote" for money. A majority of the United States Supreme Court agreed, arguing that elected officials regularly state their positions on pending legislation and also ask their supporters for contributions. To prove extortion, the Court contended, prosecutors must show that the money was given *only* because of an explicit promise to do something.

Even after the Supreme Court decision, however, the legislation remained controversial (see Constitutional Conflict above). Republicans were generally opposed to it for practical as well as philosophical reasons. They believed that limits on individual contributions denied their party its traditional financial advantage. Some Republicans also objected to the very idea of government subsidies, arguing that the government should not support semipublic political organizations. Democrats, in contrast, contended that such support for parties and their nominees was a legitimate function of government and that equalizing the amount of money candidates had available to them would produce a more democratic result. This partisan debate has continued.

The campaign finance legislation did correct some problems it was designed to address. The wealthy can no longer exercise disproportionate influence on an individual election contest unless they happen to be candidates themselves: there are no effective limits on what a person can contribute to his or her own campaign (unless the person is running for the presidency).[5] The size of a contribution and the name of the candidate who receives it are now part of the public record, and newspapers regularly report this information. Finally, at the presidential level there is greater opportunity for candidates of both parties, even those who lack national recognition, to obtain the necessary financial support with the help of government matching funds and grants.

The legislation has had several unintended consequences, however. The law has contributed to factionalism within the parties and has reduced the parties' influence over the campaigns of their own candidates. Most federal funds and many private contributions go directly to the candidates, not to the party. As a result, candidates are forced to create and use their own campaign organizations rather than relying on the party's.

Another problem for the parties has been the growth of political action committees (PACs), which the legislation not only permits but encourages (see Chapter 8). The Supreme Court decision that allows PACs to spend an unlimited amount on their own also reduces the parties' influence over the electoral process. In 1979 Congress reacted to the parties' plight, as well as to the decline in voter turnout, by amending the law to permit state and local parties to spend unlimited funds on efforts to encourage people to register and to vote. These so-called soft-money expenditures have skyrocketed in recent years. In 1992 they were reported by the national parties to the Federal Election Commission at $51.4 million for the Republicans and $36.3 million for the Democrats.[6]

In short, who votes, what choices they have, and how much influence they exert over election outcomes are all critical issues. Elections that maximize voter participation, voter choice, and voter influence reaffirm the principle of popular control of government and the practice of holding public officials accountable for their actions and decisions.

THE AMERICAN VOTER

The expansion of suffrage has made the United States political system more democratic—at least in theory. In practice, however, there has always been a gap between eligible voters and actual voters. This gap has traditionally been widest for newly enfranchised voters. Table 10-1 indicates the magnitude of this gap.

What explains the gap in turnout, particularly among newly eligible voters? Part of the answer may have to do with the time required for these people to develop the interest, knowledge, and incentive to vote. Women, for example, received the right to vote in 1920 but voted at a lower rate than men until 1986. Similarly, African Americans living in the southern states effectively

Extending suffrage to women offered the potential of reforming the electoral process and of making public officials more attentive to the needs of all people. It took considerable time, however, for the potential to be realized.

		TABLE 10-1	
		Suffrage and Turnout	
YEAR	TOTAL ADULT POPULATION (INCLUDING ALIENS)*	TOTAL PRESIDENTIAL VOTE	PERCENTAGE OF ADULT POPULATION VOTING
1824	3,964,000	363,017	9
1840	7,381,000	2,412,698	33
1860	14,676,000	4,692,710	32
1880	25,012,000	9,219,467	37
1900	40,753,000	13,974,188	35
1920	60,581,000	26,768,613	44
1932	75,768,000	39,732,000	52.4
1940	84,728,000	49,900,000	58.9
1952	99,929,000	61,551,000	61.6
1960	109,672,000	68,838,000	62.8
1964	114,090,000	70,645,000	61.9
1968	120,285,000	73,212,000	60.9
1972	140,777,000	77,719,000	55.5
1976	152,308,000	81,556,000	53.5
1980	164,595,000	86,515,000	52.6
1984	174,447,000	92,653,000	53.1
1988	182,600,000	91,602,291	50.2
1992	187,033,000	104,552,736	55.9

* Restrictions based on sex, age, race, religion, and property ownership prevented a significant portion of the adult population from voting in the nineteenth and early twentieth centuries. Of those who were eligible, however, the percentage casting ballots was often quite high, particularly during the last half of the nineteenth century.

SOURCE: Population figures for 1824 to 1920 are based on estimates and early census figures that appear in Neal R. Pierce, *The People's President* (New Haven, Conn.: Yale University Press, 1979). Copyright © 1979. Reprinted with the permission of the publisher. Population figures from 1932 to 1988 are from the U.S. Department of Commerce, Bureau of the Census, *Statistical Abstract of the United States* (Washington, D.C., 1987), 250. Figures for 1988 and 1992 were compiled from official election returns published by the Federal Election Commission.

gained the ability to vote in the mid 1960s, but their rate of participation still lags behind that of whites.

Turnout

The motivations for voting are complex. They have to do with interest in the campaign, concern about the outcome, feelings of civic responsibility, and a sense of political efficacy.[7] Generally speaking, people who identify with a political party are more strongly motivated to vote than those who do not. They tend to have more interest in the campaign, more knowledge about the candidates and issues, and more concern about the outcome of the election.[8]

Demographic characteristics and socioeconomic status also contribute to political involvement. Of these, the most important is education. The more educated a person is, the more likely he or she is to vote (see Table 10-2).[9] Education enhances one's ability to understand the issues, to follow the cam-

TABLE 10-2						
Education and Voting Turnouts, 1968–1992						
YEARS OF EDUCATION	1968	1972	1976	1980	1984	1988	1992
Less than high school	64%	59%	60%	57%	57%	50%	51%
High school diploma	83	75	70	61	66	62	76
Some college	82	81	80	77	78	78	83
B.A. and advanced degree	89	90	88	91	91	92	93

SOURCE: Data from American National Election Studies, conducted by the University of Michigan, Center for Political Studies, Ann Arbor, Michigan. Data provided by the Inter-University Consortium for Political and Social Research, located at the University of Michigan, Center for Political Studies, Ann Arbor, Michigan.

paign, and to discern the difference between candidates' positions. It also goes hand in hand with higher income, which, in turn, may increase a person's perceived stake in the outcome of an election.[10]

Given the effect of education on voting, it is surprising that from 1960 to 1990 electoral turnout decreased even though educational levels for the population increased. To explain why this has occurred, it is necessary to look at other factors that affect the vote.

One of these factors is age. Studies have shown that the youngest group of eligible voters, those under the age of 30, vote less regularly than people in the middle age groups (see Figure 10-1). Older people—those over age 70—also are less likely to vote. Greater mobility, weaker partisanship, and a less developed sense of community contribute to lower rates of participation among the young. Poor health and decreased interest are the major reasons for lower turnout by senior citizens. Demographic trends, which have resulted in larger proportions of younger and older voters, have undoubtedly helped to reduce voting turnout during this thirty-year period, but these trends do not fully explain the decline because all age groups have experienced lower turnout.

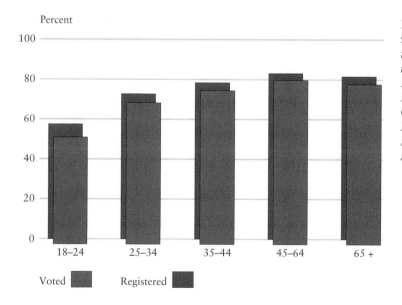

Figure 10-1 *Age and voting, 1992.* SOURCE: *Data from the American National Election Studies, conducted by the University of Michigan, Center for Political Studies, Ann Arbor, Michigan. Data provided by the Inter-University Consortium for Political and Social Research, located at the University of Michigan, Center for Political Studies, Ann Arbor, Michigan.*

Another contributing factor has been the public's increasingly negative feelings about the performance of those in government. These feelings have led to greater apathy, more cynicism, and lower efficacy (see Chapter 6). A recent study of voting behavior by three political scientists, Paul R. Abramson, John H. Aldrich, and David W. Rohde, found that 62 percent of the decline in turnout can be attributed to the combined effects of weaker partisan affiliation and feelings of less political effectiveness.[11] Negative political advertising may have produced a similar effect, reducing the appeal of candidates running for office and thus decreasing the motivation to vote for them.

This discussion of voter motivation may suggest why turnout declined from 1960 to 1990. But does it explain why voter turnout increased in 1992? Only in part. Factors unique to the 1992 election appear to be more directly responsible for the 5-percent increase in turnout.

The environment, the candidates, and the campaign contributed to the larger proportion who voted. People seemed to be more aware of the issues and more concerned about them in 1992 than they were in some previous elections, particularly in 1984 and in 1988. That concern, undoubtedly aroused by the recession, generated a higher than normal vote. The candidates, primarily H. Ross Perot, may also have provided greater incentive. Perot's independent candidacy seemed to energize those who were most angry and frustrated with the major parties and their nominees. Had Perot not run, many of the 19.7 million people who voted for him would probably have stayed at home. The percentage of Democrats who voted was also slightly larger than in previous years, although the percentage of Republicans who voted declined.[12] Finally, there was the campaign itself, especially the candidates' use of television talk shows to reach and motivate a portion of the electorate usually little affected by traditional campaign events. Whether or not turnout continues to rise, however, will depend on longer-term trends of citizen satisfaction with government, feelings of efficacy, and ease in registering and voting.

Who votes is as important a question to a democracy as who is eligible to vote. The answer not only indicates the extent to which the ideal of equal participation and influence is being achieved but also reveals levels of satisfaction and dissatisfaction among the population. It forecasts how representative the government is likely to be and which segments of the society are likely to benefit the most.

Turnout has partisan implications as well. The Republican party, composed of a larger proportion of well-educated, high-income, white-collar workers, usually gets a greater percentage of its adherents to vote than does the Democratic party. The higher Republican turnout has helped that party counter the Democrats' advantage in number of registered voters. In contrast, since the beginning of the 1980s, lower turnout among younger voters has hurt the Republicans more than it has hurt the Democrats because newer voters identified with the Republicans more than with the Democrats during this period. In 1992 turnout among Republican voters (82 percent) was only marginally higher than among Democratic voters (80 percent), according to data from the American National Election Studies.

Would the results of recent presidential elections be different if everyone voted? Political scientist Ruy A. Teixeira contends that they would not be. He argues that nonvoters typically have much weaker partisan ties than do voters and therefore would be more likely to be influenced by general perceptions of the candidates than by partisan inclinations. He speculates that their vote

Television talk shows have become popular venues for candidates. "Larry King Live" on CNN certainly helped H. Ross Perot's presidential bid. When Perot announced that he might run if enough people wanted him, the CNN switchboard was flooded with favorable calls—and Perot ran. Talk-show campaigning probably enhances voter turnout and affects voting behavior because it reaches many people who might otherwise pay little attention to the campaign.

would probably reflect the vote of the electorate as a whole, and he supports his argument with surveys of nonvoters that have been taken after elections.[13]

Voting Behavior

Who votes obviously influences the outcome of the election. But so do the political attitudes and social groupings of the electorate. Most voters do not come to an election with a completely open mind. They come with preexisting beliefs and attitudes. Of these, the most important is partisan identification.[14] A majority of the electorate still identifies with a political party, a commitment that is relatively stable and has both direct and indirect influences on voting.

As we saw in Chapter 6, people develop political attitudes early in life and generally maintain and strengthen them as they get older. Although partisan attitudes can change, they are less likely to vary than positions on issues and perceptions of candidates. Moreover, when people do drop their partisan identity, they are more likely to think of themselves as independents than as supporters of another party, and they are still more likely to vote for candidates of their former party than for those of other parties. Actually, two-thirds of those who claim to be independent lean toward one party or the other. These *independent leaners* often vote in a more partisan fashion than do people who continue to claim a weak partisan allegiance.[15] Thus, partisan predispositions directly affect the vote of those who feel strongly about their party and its candidates, and they indirectly affect the vote of those who feel less strongly but still tend to view their party's nominees more favorably than they view the opposition.[16]

Party identification is important because it provides a framework for analysis; it offers cues for evaluating the candidates and their stands. In general, the less that is known about the candidates, particularly those who are running for state or local office, the greater is the influence of party because it becomes the primary factor that people use in deciding how to vote. In contrast, at the presidential level more information might be available to voters, such as experience, character, leadership potential, and issue positions, which can affect their vote.

Today about two-thirds of American voters consider themselves either Democrats or Republicans. This percentage is less than the three-fourths who identified with one of the two major parties in 1952. The decline in party identification has resulted in more **split-ticket voting,** that is, voting for candidates of both parties, more emphasis on candidates' characteristics and less on their party affiliation, and a greater tendency to make voting decisions later in the campaign.

Group orientations can also influence voting. Most people see themselves as members of groups. To the extent that groups believe their interests are best served by particular parties, candidates, or issues, they will tell their members how to vote in a given election.

Group associations generate pressures that find expression in the political process. These pressures may reinforce partisan inclinations, or they may undermine them by creating cross pressures that give mixed signals to voters.[17] Take white blue-collar workers in the 1980s, for example. Their partisan identities oriented them toward the Democrats and that party's stands on economic issues. Yet their dissatisfaction with the Democratic party's positions on welfare, law and order, and defense and national security issues, combined with their unhappiness with the presidency of Jimmy Carter, led many to support Ronald Reagan in 1980 and 1984. They did, however, return to the Democratic fold in 1992.[18]

Cross pressures delay voting decisions. Voters who feel these pressures will tend to decide later in the campaign whether to vote and, if so, for whom. To minimize the impact of cross pressures, parties and candidates go to great lengths to coordinate their messages and target them to specific electoral constituencies.

The candidates themselves and the issues of the day also affect how people vote. Voters' perception of candidates have become more important in recent years, largely because of the greater use of television, which tends to emphasize personality and leadership at the expense of issues. The specific issues that affect voting behavior vary with the election, the constituency, and the candidates. Whether issues—be they jobs, crime, education, environment, health, or na-

Large events that take on great emotional and symbolic impact can affect voting behavior. Jimmy Carter's defeat in 1980 was due in part to the crisis that followed the capture of a group of American diplomats in Teheran. Carter's inability to free the hostages became a metaphor for his weak leadership and a failed presidency.

tional security—are salient depends on four factors: (1) how much attention they receive from the media, (2) how directly they affect voters, (3) how much the candidates differ on them, and (4) voters' awareness of candidates' differences.[19] Thus, important public concerns, particularly those that relate to fundamental values and needs—individual well-being, personal safety, economic prosperity—may not be campaign issues unless the public perceives that the candidates and their parties approach them in different ways.

The more concrete the issue, the more likely it is to have a discernible electoral impact. In the 1980s the recurring budget deficit was a theoretical concern for most Americans, one which had a minimal electoral impact. However, increasing taxes to reduce the deficit was a very real issue, one that had discernible electoral consequences. Walter Mondale's promise to raise taxes to help reduce the deficit hurt his candidacy in 1984, while George Bush's promise not to do so helped his in 1988. However, by 1992 the deficit, along with an economy in recession, had become a real issue, and opposition to tax increases to cope with it had declined somewhat.

In short, in every election there are multiple influences on voting. Because these influences, either singly or together, can affect the outcome of the election, candidates and parties try to shape them by designing a campaign strategy that puts their best case to the voters, one that emphasizes their own strengths and their opponents' weaknesses. Campaigns do matter. A single campaign may be too short a period to change attitudes or alter associations, but it is long enough to affect perceptions and influence voting. At least this is what the candidates and their campaign managers believe as they prepare for the election.

How do people weigh various factors in arriving at their decisions, and what questions do they try to answer? Political scientists have proposed two models of voting: retrospective voting and prospective voting. **Retrospective voting** is based on an assessment of the past performance of the parties and their elected officials in the light of the promises they made, political events that have occurred, and the conditions that currently exist.[20] Voters base their judgment on their accumulated political experience. They ask, "Am I better off now than I was when the other party and leaders were in power?" In contrast, **prospective voting** anticipates the actions of candidates once they assume office. Voters compare their own values, beliefs, and opinions to those of the candi-

Wide World Photos, Inc.

Just as the hostage crisis was Carter's Achilles' heel, the recession of the early 1990s was George Bush's. During this period, when a new hotel in Chicago announced that it was hiring for service jobs, over two thousand people stood in freezing weather for a chance at a job, any job. The President's inability even to say the "R" word cost him his second term in office.

dates and parties; then they base their judgment on their sense of which party and which candidates are likely to benefit them the most after the election.

The retrospective and prospective models are theoretical formulations of the thought processes that voters go through when they decide how to vote. In practice, they undoubtedly do both look backward and forward, to arrive at their judgments on election day. They evaluate the candidates and their parties and how well they have done largely on the basis of how good or bad conditions seem to be. If the economy is strong, society harmonious, and the nation apparently secure, people assume that their leaders, particularly the president, must be doing a good job. If conditions are not favorable, they tend to blame those in power, particularly the president. This is part of the voting decision, but not the only part. Voters also anticipate which of the candidates and parties, given the record of the past, is likely to do better in the future. Thus, both retrospective and prospective analyses help people arrive at the rationales they use for their voting decisions.

THE ELECTION CAMPAIGN

Every candidate's objective is to win, to convince voters that she or he is the most qualified and will do the best job. The campaign is the mechanism candidates use to achieve this objective. Frequently, they have to conduct two campaigns: one to gain their party's nomination and another to compete in the general election. Because they are conducted at a different time under different rules, appeal to different electorates, and often emphasize different issues, positions, and leadership traits, these campaigns are quite different.

Of the two, the campaign for a party's nomination has changed the most in the twentieth century. Formerly an internal matter decided by party leaders, the quest for nomination today occurs within the public arena, usually in primary races among self-declared volunteers for office. Candidates are selected on the basis of their appeal to these primary voters. If successful, they must run again in the general election, refocusing their campaign and broadening their appeal to the entire electorate. This frequently requires them to soften their partisan rhetoric, to reposition themselves toward the center of the political spectrum, and to stress those issues and personal traits that will attract the support of independents, members of the other party, and members of their own party who did not vote for them in the primaries.

The quest for office is also conditioned by the rules that govern the election, by the environment in which the election occurs, and the electorate to which the candidates must appeal. Of these, the economic and social environment is the most variable factor, changing from election to election. The rules are more predictable, but they too have changed, particularly those that pertain to the presidential nomination process. The electorate is stable but not static, as we noted in Chapter 9.

The Presidential Nomination Process

In theory, national nominating conventions still designate the major parties' nominees for president and vice president and formulate the platforms on which they will run. In practice, party activists have the greatest influence on those judgments. The movement toward increased popular control of the nomination process came during the 1970s, when the Democratic party revised its rules to encourage greater public participation and more representative delegates at its nominating conventions.

These changes made primary elections the preferred mode of delegate selection. Today approximately three-fourths of the delegates to both the Democratic and the Republican national conventions come from states that hold some form of primary. The remaining delegates come from states that utilize a multistage party **caucus**. The Democrats choose additional delegates, known as **superdelegates**, from among the party's elected and appointed leaders.

Another major objective of the rule changes was to more accurately reflect popular preferences in the selection of delegates. That is why the Democrats adopted the principle of **proportional voting**, in which delegates are awarded to each candidate in proportion to the number of popular votes the candidate receives. To be eligible for delegates, however, a candidate must receive a minimum percentage of the total vote, or *threshold*, usually 15 percent.

Initially the Democratic party also established quotas in order to achieve more equal representation at its nominating conventions. The quotas specified that minorities and women had to be represented on the state delegations in proportion to their numbers within the state. Protests over the quotas, which were deemed inconsistent with the principle of personal choice, led the Democrats to eliminate them and adopt affirmative action guidelines for designated minority groups while continuing to require that the delegates be equally divided between men and women.

The Republicans have not imposed similar national rules on their state parties. Nevertheless, state Republican parties operate under rules that have increased rank-and-file participation and have broadened representation at their conventions. The chief difference is that the Republicans permit states to have **winner-take-all voting**. In a winner-take-all system, the candidate or the delegates (if they run separately) with the most votes win and the losers get nothing. Such a system benefits front-running candidates and puts them in a position to lock up the nomination earlier than Democratic candidates usually can. Both Ronald Reagan in 1980 and George Bush in 1988 benefited by winner-take-all voting.

The changes in the way the parties select their delegates have resulted in greater public involvement in the nomination process. In 1968, before the reforms, only 12 million people participated. Four years later that number rose to 22 million. By 1988, with two contested nominations, it was almost 37 million, the highest primary turnout in history.

Turnout declined in 1992. Approximately 20 million people voted in the 40 Democratic primaries compared to 23 million who had voted in 37 primaries four years earlier. On the Republican side, turnout in the early contests when President Bush was challenged by Pat Buchanan was similar to 1988; turnout in the later primaries, however, after Bush had effectively wrapped up the nomination, dropped sharply. In all, about 13 million people voted in the 1992 Republican primaries.[21]

Although a larger portion of the electorate is now involved in the nomination process, primary voters are not equally distributed among all segments of society. Generally speaking, better-educated, higher-income, older party

TABLE 10-3
The Democratic Electorate, 1992

		VOTED FOR		
PERCENT OF				
TOTAL VOTE		CLINTON	BROWN	TSONGAS
100	Total, 29 states	50%	21%	20%
	Gender			
47	Men	50	22	20
53	Women	51	20	21
	Race			
80	Whites	47	23	25
14	Blacks	70	15	8
4	Hispanics	51	30	15
	Age			
12	18–29 years	47	24	19
33	30–44 years	45	26	22
25	45–59 years	51	19	20
30	60 and older	59	15	18
	Religious affiliation			
50	Protestant	55	14	21
30	Catholic	44	24	24
6	Jewish	45	15	33
	Education			
8	Without a high school diploma	67	14	10
27	High school graduate	61	17	15
27	Some college	48	23	18
20	College graduate	42	24	26
18	Some postgraduate education	38	23	28
	Family income			
15	Less than $15,000	62	17	13
25	$15,000 to $29,999	55	19	18
30	$30,000 to $49,999	48	23	21
18	$50,000 to $74,999	45	23	25
11	$75,000 and over	38	23	29
	Those who identify themselves as			
67	Democrats	57	19	17
29	Independents	36	25	27
4	Republicans	34	18	32
35	Liberals	47	26	20
45	Moderates	54	18	19
20	Conservatives	48	17	23
	Those whose say their family's financial situation is			
14	Better today than four years ago	44	24	22
39	Same today as four years ago	50	20	20
45	Worse today than four years ago	53	20	18

SOURCE: This table constructs a Democratic primary electorate from exit polls conducted in twenty-nine Democratic primary states from February to June by Voter Research and Surveys. *New York Times*, July 12, 1992, 18. Copyright © 1992 by The New York Times Company. Reprinted by permission.

TABLE 10-4

The Demography of National Convention Delegates, 1968–1992

	1968		1972		1976		1980		1984		1988		1992	
	DEM.	REP.	DEM.	REP.	DEM.	REP.	DEM.	REP.	DEM.	REP.	DEM.	REP.	DEM.	REP.
Women	13%	16%	40%	29%	33%	31%	49%	29%	50%	44%	48%	33%	48	43
African Americans	5	2	15	4	11	—	15	3	18	4	23	4	16	4
Under thirty	3	4	22	8	15	7	11	5	8	4	4	3	—	3
Median age (years)	(49)	(49)	(42)	—	(43)	(48)	(44)	(49)	(43)	(51)	(46)	(51)	—	—
Lawyers	28	22	12	—	16	15	13	15	17	14	16	17	—	6
Teachers	8	2	11	—	—	4	15	4	16	6	14	5	—	4
Union members	—	—	16	—	21	3	27	4	25	4	25	3	—	—
Attended first convention	67	66	83	78	80	78	87	84	74	61	65	68	45	—
College graduate	19	—	21	—	21	27	20	26	20	28	21	32	20	35
Postgraduate*	44	34	36	—	43	38	45	39	51	35	52	34	52	33
Protestant	—	—	42	—	47	73	47	72	49	71	50	69	47	71
Catholic	—	—	26	—	34	18	37	22	29	22	30	22	30	27
Jewish	—	—	9	—	9	3	8	3	8	2	7	2	10	2

* Includes those in the category of college graduates.

SOURCE: CBS News Delegate Surveys, 1968 through 1980. Characteristics of the public are average values from seven CBS News/ *New York Times* polls, 1980. Warren J. Mitofsky and Martin Plissner, "The Making of the Delegates, 1968–1980," *Public Opinion* (December–January 1980): 43. Data reprinted with permission of CBS, Inc. and The American Enterprise Institute for Public Policy Research, Washington, D.C. 1984 and 1988 data for delegates and public supplied by CBS News from its delegate surveys and reprinted with permission of CBS News. 1992 data in the *New York Times*, July 13, 1992, B6, the *Washington Post*, August 16, 1992, A19, and survey data supplied by the Republican National Committee.

members participate more frequently than younger people with less education and lower incomes. Racial minorities in particular have tended to be poorly represented among those who vote in primary elections, although Jesse Jackson's campaigns for the Democratic nomination in 1984 and 1988 generated a higher turnout of African Americans than in previous campaigns. Table 10-3 presents a demographic profile of the 1992 Democratic voters.

Representation at the nominating convention has also improved for various groups within the parties. The percentage of women and minorities who attend conventions has increased significantly since 1968 (see Table 10-4). But even though conventions are demographically more representative of the American electorate, they are not necessarily ideologically more representative. In fact, the delegates who attended conventions in the past twenty years were usually much more aware of issues than was the average voter. The delegates also tended to be more ideological in their thinking than were most other partisan supporters. Studies of recent convention goers have found Republican delegates to be more conservative and Democratic delegates more liberal than their party's rank-and-file members (see Table 10-5).[22] The stronger ideological position of the delegates may explain why recent party platforms contained unequivocal stands on controversial issues such as abortion, taxes, capital punishment, and the Balanced Budget and Equal Rights amendments,[23] positions that many of the party's rank and file did not accept.

The Ideology of National Convention Delegates

IDEOLOGY	1976		1980		1984		1988		1992		GENERAL POPULATION IN 1992
	DEM.	REP.	DEM.	REP.	DEM.	REP.	DEM.	REP.	DEM.	REP.	
Liberal	40	3	46	2	48	1	43	0	47	01	27
Moderate	47	45	42	36	42	35	43	35	44	28	38
Conservative	8	48	6	58	4	60	5	58	5	70	32

SOURCE: CBS News Delegate Surveys, 1976 through 1980. Characteristics of the public are average values from seven CBS News/ *New York Times* polls, 1980. Warren J. Mitofsky and Martin Plissner, "The Making of the Delegates, 1968–1980," *Public Opinion* (December–January 1980): 43. Data reprinted with permission of CBS, Inc. and The American Enterprise Institute for Public Policy Research, Washington, D.C. 1984 and 1988 data for delegates and public supplied by CBS News from its delegate surveys and re-printed with permission of CBS News. 1992 data published in the *New York Times*, July 13, 1992, B6, and the *Washington Post*, August 16, 1992, A19.

The changes in rules have affected party leaders as well. They have re-duced the leaders' ability to choose delegates and influence delegates' behavior at the convention. The greater openness of the nominating process and in-creased participation by the rank and file have encouraged people who have not been party regulars in the past to become involved. They have also forced candidates and the delegates who support them to depend less on the party apparatus and more on their own organizing skills.

On balance, the rules for delegate selection have led to an increase in the number of candidates and to the creation of separate candidate organizations. Even incumbents face opposition, as did George Bush in 1992, Jimmy Carter in 1980, and Gerald Ford in 1976.

The trend toward greater popular control of the nomination process has taken its toll on the parties. It has encouraged interests within the parties to organize, make demands, and exert influence on the selection process, the plat-form, and elected officials. It has made it harder for the party to project a unified appeal to the voters. For those in power, these changes have made governing more difficult and have spurred the development of new strategies and tactics for those seeking the nomination.

Preconvention strategy and tactics   In the past, entering primaries was optional for leading candidates and necessary only for those who lacked party support. Today everyone must do it. No longer can an acknowledged political leader sit on the sidelines and wait to be drafted by party leaders and rank-and-file sup-porters as William Jennings Bryan was in 1896 by the Democrats and Wendell Wilkie was in 1940 and General Dwight Eisenhower was in 1952 by the Re-publicans. Aspirants now have to generate a movement on their own behalf. They have to mount their own campaigns, raise their own money, build their own organizations, hire their own consultants, and actively campaign for many months, even years, to obtain the nomination.

Campaigns usually start well before the first caucuses and primaries are held because candidates need to do well in these early tests of their appeal to

UPI/Bettmann

The presidential nominating process was never the same again after the 1968 Demo-
cratic convention in Chicago. Vice President Hubert H. Humphrey had not entered a
single presidential primary, yet with the endorsement of Lyndon Johnson, the estab-
lished party leaders who controlled the convention gave him the nomination. Sup-
porters of Eugene McCarthy and Robert Kennedy felt cheated and demanded
changes. After Humphrey's defeat, the party established a commission that reformed
the nomination process and forced candidates to appeal to the rank and file for votes.

voters. George McGovern began his successful quest for the 1972 Democratic
nomination in January of 1971; twenty years later fellow Democrat Paul
Tsongas launched an unsuccessful bid for his party's nomination in March of
1991. The first contests have assumed great importance because of the attention
they attract and the momentum they can generate.

For all candidates, the key to doing well is doing better than expected.
For example, Eugene McCarthy's surprising challenge to President Lyndon
Johnson in the 1968 New Hampshire primary, George McGovern's surprisingly close second-place finish to Edmund Muskie in New Hampshire in 1972,
Jimmy Carter's surprising victories in Iowa and New Hampshire in 1976, and
Gary Hart's surprising second-place win over John Glenn in Iowa and his defeat
of Walter Mondale in New Hampshire in 1984 converted those little-known
candidates into major challengers or even front-runners overnight. It also subjected them to greater scrutiny and higher expectations. In Hart's case, both
the scrutiny and the expectations proved to be more harmful than beneficial.
He was forced to withdraw from the 1988 presidential race when newspapers
published reports of his alleged marital infidelity.

One reason for beginning so far ahead of the nomination is the time it
takes to raise the money needed for a serious campaign. Millions of dollars are
necessary to build an organization, pay its expenses, move around the country,
and project an appeal. Financial pressures have forced most candidates to devote much of their time to fundraising.

Moreover, the increasing use of the mass media, particularly television,

UPI/Bettmann

A politician's private life seems to become public business when it becomes public knowledge. Senator Gary Hart learned this lesson in March of 1988 when he had to withdraw from the Democratic presidential primary race with his wife, Lee, and his son, John, looking on. In answering questions about rumored womanizing, Hart had challenged reporters to catch him in the act. Two weeks later, a reporter spied candidate Hart entering a Washington townhouse with an unidentified woman and waited in the bushes until they emerged the next morning. When the tabloids ran photographs of Hart aboard the yacht Monkey Business *with a model named Donna Rice on his knee, he was finished as a presidential candidate.*

by aspirants for their party's nomination has upped the financial ante. Television time is not cheap. In New Hampshire in 1992, the cost of a single 30-second commercial on a major station in Manchester was $1,000 during prime time. Design and production expenses also have to be factored into the total cost of an advertisement. Yet candidates feel that they have no choice but to take to the airwaves, since more and more people obtain their information about the campaign from the mass media. Besides, an increasing number of states have scheduled their caucuses or primary election toward the front end of the nomination periods, which usually begins in early March and ends in early June.[24] In 1988 and again in 1992 almost one-third of the elected delegates to both parties' national conventions were chosen by the end of the first week in which all states were permitted to hold their nomination contests. To reach the millions of people who will vote during this early period, candidates must engage in multimedia, multistate campaigning.

In addition to the costs of media, candidates have to contend with the expense of building an organization and conducting public opinion polls. An effective organization is essential. No longer can candidates depend solely on state party leaders and their organizations to generate support and deliver the vote. However, the activities of state leaders can be important and often crucial. Candidates who are in a position to obtain this support usually have an advantage over others. George Bush was in such a position in 1988, as was Walter Mondale four years earlier. Having occupied the vice presidency, both had dispensed political, financial, and symbolic support to other party leaders. So when these vice presidents became presidential candidates, they could turn to those whom they had helped in the past for help in their own campaigns.

With intentions clear, money in hand, and an organization in place, it is necessary to ascertain public sentiment, appeal to it, and, if need be, manipulate it. Public opinion polling is necessary for assessing the public mood, designing and targeting messages, and monitoring the campaign. Another device that is frequently used to explore the public mood is the focus group—a collection of individuals who are brought together and are asked to discuss and respond to a variety of real and hypothetical situations involving candidates, issues, and ideology. Information gleaned from focus groups is often extremely helpful in creating and adjusting a campaign appeal. Focus groups were used extensively by candidate Bill Clinton in 1992 to gauge voter reaction to the allegations about his character and to his response to those allegations. Candidates who cannot afford to conduct polls or survey focus groups often find themselves at a competitive disadvantage. They are forced to guess at what is on the voters' minds and whether their appeals are being well received.

In building an electoral coalition, it is necessary to tailor messages to specific groups within the party. For example, in the 1992 Democratic contest Senator Tom Harkin adopted policy positions designed to appeal to his party's liberal constituency, specifically organized labor and economically disadvantaged groups; Governor Bill Clinton and Senator Bob Kerrey fashioned their positions with the party's middle-class constituents in mind. Former senator Paul Tsongas took a different tack, urging the party faithful to discard their traditional beliefs about the government's role in the economy in favor a more business-oriented approach. Former governor Edmund "Jerry" Brown, Jr., spoke about the need for radical restructuring of the political system.

Polls can track public reactions and help guide candidate appeals, but they are not a substitute for mounting an effective campaign. Even with the most accurate polls in hand, candidates still need to make critical tactical decisions about how and where to use their resources. If they are not well known, their initial goal must be to gain recognition. To do this, candidates have no choice but to compete in the early contests. Doing well in those races will provide them with opportunities they would not otherwise have. Doing poorly, however, will terminate their candidacy.

One major change in the presidential selection process is that outsiders, even if unknown, can win (as Bill Clinton proved). Debates help hopeful nominees to become known, but they must distinguish themselves from each other while looking and acting presidential. The 1992 Democratic candidates looked as much alike in dress and manner as they had in 1988, when they were dubbed the "seven dwarfs."

Candidates who are better known have greater flexibility. They are also in a better position to take advantage of their reputation and political influence to build a strong organizational and financial base and use it to buttress their status as a leading candidate. This is what George Bush did in 1988. He built what his campaign manager referred to as a "firewall" in the South by raising more money, collecting more endorsements, creating larger state organizations, and running more television advertisements than any of his Republican opponents. The "firewall" was intended to cement his initial advantage, preventing his campaign from collapsing if he lost one or more of the early contests (he did lose in Iowa) and putting him in an almost unassailable position if he won them. Bill Clinton pursued much the same strategy in 1992, helped by his superior organizational support and fundraising capabilities.

Leading candidates must be careful to avoid raising expectations too high because they will then have too far to fall. The media are certain to highlight any stumbles that candidates make, as they did in 1984, when Jesse Jackson referred to New York as "Hymie Town"; in 1988, when Senator Robert Dole accused George Bush of lying about his program; and in 1992, when H. Ross Perot addressed a largely African-American audience as "you people." Each of these remarks not only offended the group at which it was aimed, it also reflected unfavorably on the character of the person who made it.

National nominating conventions   After the delegates have been selected, the national nominating conventions are held. The conventions decide on the party's rules, choose its presidential and vice presidential nominees, and write the party platform. Despite all the debate and voting that take place at the conventions, the conventions actually decide little that has not been preordained by the delegate selection process. Nevertheless, they have several important purposes. They reward the party faithful—activists who were involved in the nomination, regulars who have toiled for the party, and elected officials, party leaders, and other prominent individuals who desire public recognition and political support. They unify groups that have been divided by the nomination process, stimulating them to pull together during the election campaign. Finally, the national conventions constitute a massive public appeal by the party on behalf of its candidates in the general election.

Satisfying the first of these purposes has not been too difficult. Conventions are large public events, and party leaders and activists regard them as the place to be. Cities compete vigorously to host them, even though it is a logistical nightmare to seat, feed, house, transport, and protect so many people. In 1992, approximately 25,000 delegates, alternates, media representatives, and invited guests and visitors attended the Democratic convention in New York, and about 20,000 attended the Republican convention in Houston.

Conventions can be divisive before they become unifying. During a long nominating process, policy disagreements are voiced and personal animosities aired. If the nomination is in doubt, these divisions are exacerbated, and the front-runner must try to generate a **bandwagon effect** that induces uncommitted delegates and those pledged to other candidates to get on board. To create this effect, the front-runner's organization must defeat any motion on any issue that raises doubts about who the eventual winner will be. No concessions can be made until the nomination is secured.

In 1976 President Gerald Ford, challenged by Ronald Reagan, successfully employed the bandwagon strategy. His organization pressured Republican

© Lisa Quinones/Black Star

Convention speakers can create impressions that unify or divide their parties. At the Democratic convention in 1988 (left), Jesse Jackson delivered a message of inclusion; but at the Republican convention in 1992 (right), Pat Buchanan's message was one of exclusion. Buchanan's speech pleased the delegates, but it alienated potential Republican voters.

delegates to defeat a change in party rules that would have required presidential nominees to disclose their choice for vice president before the convention voted for the presidential candidate. Ford's victory on this key procedural vote indicated that he had the necessary votes to win the nomination.

If the nomination is a foregone conclusion, as it has been in recent years, there are incentives for all participants to accommodate one another. The winner needs a unified party and support in the general election. The losers need to save face, maintain their influence, and position themselves for the next election or for appointment to high public office if the party's nominees win the election. The losers are usually willing to get behind the successful candidate in exchange for something—for example, a chance to be heard during prime viewing hours, to have their most cherished positions included in the platform, or to obtain changes in the rules for the next go-round. Thus, in the last three Democratic conventions, Jesse Jackson, a prominent African-American leader and an unsuccessful candidate for the Democratic nomination in 1984 and 1988, was permitted to address the delegates during prime time. In 1992, two defeated candidates, Jerry Brown for the Democrats and Pat Buchanan for the Republicans, were given time to speak to their respective conventions in the hope that they and their followers would support the party's nominees.[25]

The third purpose of conventions, to enhance the party's public image and improve its chances in the election, is often the most difficult to achieve. The interests of the party and those of the media may be in conflict. Both seek to entertain as well as inform. But while the party is trying to present a unified front by scripting the convention proceedings to make them appear interesting and favorable to the party's image—in effect, to conduct a huge pep rally— the media emphasize dramatic, newsworthy events, focusing on disagreements and potential problems for the party and its nominees. The media often devote less attention to the official proceedings than to unofficial activities both inside and outside the convention hall.[26]

Conventions are one of many stimuli voters receive during the election campaign. They occur at the midpoint of the process—at the end of the nomination period but at the beginning of the general election campaign—months before the actual vote. Although they generate more concentrated coverage than any other event, frequently consuming more television time than the rest of the campaign, their impact tends to be diffuse and distant.

In the short run, conventions almost always boost the popularity of the party's nominees and decrease the popularity of the party's opponents. In 1992 Democratic candidate Bill Clinton went up a startling 16 percent in the polls following his party's convention, the largest "bounce" since the Gallup Poll has been measuring this phenomenon, compared to only 5 percent for Republican George Bush, which was much closer to the average 6 percent gain for those boosts. The increase in popularity may be short-lived, however. Several months later the impact of the convention may be harder to discern.

Political scientists have suggested three major effects of conventions on voters. They heighten interest, thereby potentially increasing turnout. They arouse latent feelings, thereby raising political awareness. They color perceptions, thereby affecting the electorate's judgments about the candidates, the parties, and the issues.[27] Studies have also found that convention watchers tend to make their voting decisions early in the campaign. About one in five says that she or he does so at the time of the convention.[28]

The Presidential Election

Whereas the nomination process has undergone many changes in recent decades, the general election process has not. The presidential election still occurs within the context of the Electoral College system.

When the framers of the Constitution fashioned the system for choosing the president and vice president, they rejected the idea of a direct popular vote, preferring instead an indirect method in which a group of **electors** would choose the president. Their plan was to have states choose electors in any manner they desired. The electors, equal in number to the senators and representatives from a state, would meet as the **Electoral College** and exercise their own judgment in selecting the president and vice president. It was expected that they would select the most qualified candidate, not necessarily the most popular one.

Today, electors are no longer chosen directly by state legislatures; they are chosen by the electorate of each state. When that electorate votes for president, it actually selects electors who are pledged to a particular presidential candidate. Moreover, the electors who are chosen no longer make an independent judgment. They cast their votes for the candidate of their party.

In all but two states (Maine and Nebraska), the candidate who wins the popular vote receives *all* of the state's electoral votes.[29] A candidate needs only a plurality of the popular vote to carry the whole state in the Electoral College. This winner-take-all method of voting in the Electoral College is known as the **general ticket system.**

A majority of the votes in the Electoral College, 270 out of 538, is needed to win. It is possible for a candidate to win a majority in the Electoral College and not win a majority or even a plurality of the total popular vote. This situation has occurred twice: in 1876 and 1888 (see the box on page 346). If no candidate wins a majority in the Electoral College, the House of Representatives, voting by state delegations with one vote to a state, selects the president. It is thus possible for the candidate with the most votes in the Electoral College to lose the presidency in the House. That is what happened to Andrew Jackson in 1824. Jackson led in both popular and electoral votes in a four-way race but did not have a majority of electoral votes. Thus, it was left to the House of Representatives to decide who the president would be.

According to the Twelfth Amendment, when the House selects the president, it must choose from among the three candidates with the most electoral votes. This limitation eliminated Henry Clay, the Speaker of the House at the time of the 1824 election, who had come in fourth. Clay threw his support to John Quincy Adams, who won in the House of Representatives even though he had received nearly 45,000 fewer popular votes than Andrew Jackson. It was alleged at the time that Clay backed Adams in exchange for a promise of appointment as secretary of state. Although Clay vigorously denied the charge, Adams did appoint him to that position.

The Constitution puts the responsibility for choosing a vice president on the Senate if no one vice presidential candidate receives a majority in the Electoral College. The Senate has chosen a vice president in this manner only once. In 1837, because of a personal scandal, Richard Johnson, Martin Van Buren's running mate, fell one vote short of a majority in the Electoral College. The Senate elected him anyway.

The structure and operation of the Electoral College benefit the largest states because they have the most electoral votes and cast those votes as a bloc. By giving an advantage to the large states, the Electoral College benefits groups that are concentrated in those states and tend to vote cohesively. These include such groups as Jews, Hispanics, and African Americans living in urban areas. The Electoral College also aids the very smallest states, those with four electoral votes or less; these states gain more influence than they otherwise would have from the two votes given to every state by virtue of its two senators.

Nonpresidential Nominations

Some of the changes that have affected presidential selection have affected the election campaigns for other offices as well. The nomination process, especially, has changed. There are now more contested nominations within the parties, and more people are likely to vote in them, particularly when they occur in presidential election years. Fundraising has become a necessity for most candidates; media advertising has become the principal instrument for reaching large numbers of voters.

Presidential candidates who received the most popular votes were defeated in the Electoral College in 1876 and 1888.

The election of 1876 was marred by illegal voting and ballot fraud, especially in many of the southern states. Separate slates of electors claiming to have been duly elected were filed from Florida (4), Louisiana (8), and South Carolina (7). Charges of fraud and voting irregularities were made by both parties. The Republicans, who controlled the three state legislatures, contended that Democrats had forcibly prevented newly freed men from voting. The Democrats alleged that many nonresidents and nonregistered people had voted. In Oregon, one Republican elector was challenged on the ground that he held another federal position at the time and hence was ineligible to be an elector.

Three days before the Electoral College vote was to be officially counted, Congress established a commission to examine and try to resolve the disputes about the electors. The commission was to consist of fifteen members: ten from Congress (five Republicans and five Democrats) and five from the Supreme Court. Four Supreme Court justices were designated commission members by the congressional act (two Republicans and two Democrats), and they were to choose a fifth justice. It was expected that they would select David Davis, a political independent; but on the day the commission was created, Davis was appointed to the United States Senate by the Illinois legislature. The Supreme Court justices thus chose Joseph Bradley, an independent Republican. Bradley sided with his party on every issue. By a strictly partisan vote, the commission validated all of the Republican electors, thereby giving Rutherford B. Hayes a one-vote margin of victory in the Electoral College. Hayes, with nearly a quarter of a million fewer votes than Samuel J. Tilden, the Democratic candidate, was elected president.

Rutherford B. Hayes (R)

Samuel J. Tilden (D)

Benjamin Harrison (R)

Grover Cleveland (D)

The other election in which the winner of the popular vote lost in the Electoral College occurred in 1888. Benjamin Harrison, the Republican candidate, had 95,096 fewer popular votes than Grover Cleveland, the Democratic candidate. Cleveland, however, had only 168 electoral votes compared to Harrison's 233, so Harrison was elected president. Cleveland's loss of Indiana by about 3,000 votes and New York by about 15,000 led to his defeat.

SOURCE: Stephen J. Wayne, *The Road to the White House, 1992* (New York: St. Martin's Press, 1992), 17. Photos courtesy of the Library of Congress.

The level of competition varies, however. There tends to be more competition within the majority party than within the minority party, more competition where the two parties are evenly matched than where they are not, more competition for open seats than for seats held by an incumbent who is seeking reelection, and more competition where the party organization is not supporting a particular candidate than where it is.[30]

The competition, in turn, affects voter turnout.[31] Contested primaries naturally attract more voters than uncontested ones do. Even so, only a minority of the electorate (about 30 percent) regularly participates in these nomination contests. The smaller the turnout, the greater the impact a strong party organization has because it can identify and mobilize electoral support for its preferred nominees.

The strategy and tactics for nomination campaigns are similar for national, state, and local offices. The principal differences in these contests involve the cost of the campaigns, the use of media, and the ability to employ sophisticated campaign technology, including public opinion polling. Most money tends to be spent in statewide elections for governors and senators. These nomination campaigns are also likely to depend more on visual media, primarily television advertising, to convey a message. Because of the cost of buying television time, candidates for other state and local offices have to rely more on radio and print journalism and try to generate more coverage on local news. Similarly, public opinion surveys, a staple for presidential, senatorial, and gubernatorial candidates, are too expensive for most other candidates, who must depend more on their own impressions, instincts, and skills.

Nonpresidential Elections

All elections except for the presidential election are conducted by the states according to state law.

The legal environment: redistricting   The Constitution requires that representation in the House of Representatives be reapportioned every ten years on the basis of the national census. States that lose or gain seats have to redraw their congressional boundaries. This practice is known as **redistricting.**

Initially states enjoyed complete discretion in redistricting. Beginning in the 1960s, however, a series of judicial decisions set limits on that discretion. One limitation concerns the size of the population within a legislative district. In the case of *Wesberry v. Sanders* (1964) the Supreme Court held that all districts within a state must be approximately equal in population so that no individual voter will be overrepresented or underrepresented. To do otherwise, the Court said, would be inconsistent with the principle of **one person, one vote.** Today the populations of the various districts within a state usually cannot vary in size by more than 1.5 percent. However, from one state to another, the populations of districts can vary considerably. Montana, for example, has one at-large district with over 800,000 people; Wyoming has one district with 456,000 people.

Another legal limitation has to do with minorities. In redistricting, states cannot discriminate against a particular group, nor can they dilute minority voting strength. Since 1965, the Voting Rights Acts have required the states to maximize minority representation and have given the Justice Department the

Ann W. Richards: Star of the Lone Star State

Democrat Ann W. Richards was elected the forty-fifth governor of Texas in 1990—the first woman to hold that post in over half a century. (Texas's only other woman governor was Miriam A. "Ma" Ferguson, who served in 1925–1927 and 1933–1935, largely as a stand-in for her husband, James E. "Pa" Ferguson, who had been impeached while serving as governor in 1917.)

Ann Richards's political career began in 1976, when she was elected commissioner of Travis County; she was reelected in 1980. Then two years later she was elected Texas state treasurer and in 1986 was reelected without opposition. As treasurer, Richards updated Texas's accounting procedures and found new sources of state revenue.

In 1988 Richards delivered the keynote address to the Democratic National Convention. Her spirited speech, in which she accused George Bush of being born with a "silver foot in his mouth," received wide attention, making her better known nationally than she was in her own state. In 1992 she chaired the Democratic National Convention.

Richards's run for the governorship in 1990 began with a closely contested primary race among the Democrats. The campaign was marred by allegations that Richards, a recovered alcoholic, had also used drugs. In the primary, Richards led the voting with 39 percent, but her closest opponent, Attorney General Jim Mattox, came in second with 37 percent. In the runoff primary, Richards won 57 percent of the vote, much of it provided by women in Texas cities. In the general election, she beat Republican candidate Clayton Williams with 51 percent of the vote. Again, the crucial edge was provided by women in the metropolitan regions.

Under the Texas Constitution, the governor has very limited powers. But Richards has effectively used the appointment power to place a record number of women and minorities on state boards and commissions. She has been outspoken on a number of issues, but politically cautious on many others. She has taken strong public stands on measures such as a state lottery, insurance rate reform, stricter ethics standards, tougher environmental laws, and

Bob Daemmrich/SYGMA

In the spring of 1993, Governor Richards uses her watch to show President Clinton that he is late, as usual. He had come to boost her choice for the Senate, Bob Kreuger—but to no avail. Kreuger lost badly in the special election to fill Lloyd Bentsen's Senate seat.

prison expansion. Although she has been unyielding against restrictions on abortion rights, she has accepted versions of ethics and environmental laws that proponents found significantly diluted.

Governor Richards has skillfully used the media to focus public attention on important issues. Her reputation, however, has been tarnished by public criticism of two high-profile appointees, Lena Guerrero (to the Texas Railroad Commission) and Bob Krueger (to the U.S. Senate). Guerrero's forced resignation and Krueger's defeat by Republican Kay Bailey Hutchison suggest that Richards has difficulty extending her personal popularity to others.

responsibility and authority to make sure that they do so.[32] This discretion was utilized during the Bush administration to force states to create minority districts. The purpose was twofold: to demonstrate the administration's concern for civil and voting rights and to concentrate Democratic voters, who were more apt to support Hispanic and African American candidates, in order to give Republicans a better chance to win in nonminority districts.

Although Congress and the judiciary have acted to prevent racial discrimination, they have been less successful in eliminating the practice of **gerrymandering,** or drawing district boundaries in such a way as to give one party an advantage. The term *gerrymander* was coined in 1812 or 1813 to describe the shape of a particular legislative district in Massachusetts during the governorship of Elbridge Gerry. The district, which looked a little like a salamander and was dubbed a "Gerry-Mander," is shown in Figure 10-2.

To gain an advantage from gerrymandering, parties attempt to draw legislative districts in such a way that their partisans constitute a stable but not overwhelming majority in as many districts as possible and their opponents constitute a majority in as few of them as possible. Gerrymandering is thus a powerful political tool for the party in power.[33] In states where one party is clearly dominant and refuses to change the district borders, the only way the party out of power can effect a change is to gain control of the legislature. But because of the way the districts are drawn, it cannot gain control of the legislature without a large influx of new voters who favor its candidates and positions. Populations do change, but changes in the partisan composition of an electorate are slow to be reflected in the composition of its government.

Figure 10-2 *The first gerrymandered congressional district* (left), *and one of the most recent* (right). SOURCE: *Data for North Carolina from* New York Times, *July 29, 1993, A12.*

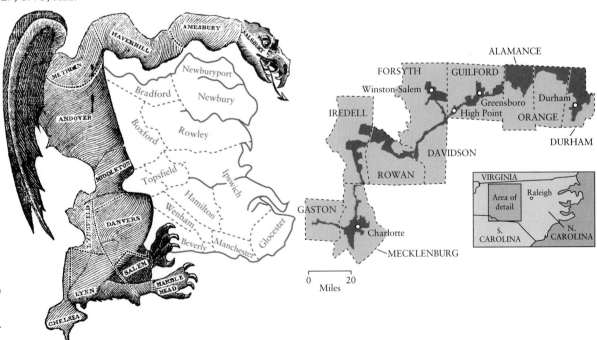

Until recently, the Democrats have been the principal beneficiaries of gerrymandering. They have used it not only to preserve their dominance of the state legislatures but to maintain their control of the House of Representatives. Since 1932, they have enjoyed a majority in the House in all but four years. A good example of the successful use of partisan gerrymandering occurred in California after the 1980 census gave that state additional House seats. The Democratic state legislature blatantly redrew the districts to their party's advantage, and the Democratic governor, Jerry Brown, signed the legislation into law. The Republicans protested, but to no avail.

In the state of Indiana, a Republican legislature and executive turned the tables on the Democrats and gained congressional seats as a result of redistricting. The Democrats took the issue to court and lost, but in the process the Supreme Court ruled in the case of *Davis v. Bandemer* (1986) that partisan gerrymanders are justiciable issues—that is, they are subject to adjudication by the courts. This decision thrust the courts into the politics of reapportionment.

After the 1990 census, federal judges played an active role in resolving redistricting disputes. At that time a majority of the federal judiciary had been appointed by presidents Reagan and Bush, so the judges' decisions tended to be more favorable to Republican redistricting plans than to those designed by Democratic-controlled legislatures.[34]

Another new wrinkle was added to reapportionment controversies in the 1990s. The census, which is the basis on which seats in the House of Representatives are reapportioned, was itself subject to challenge. Several cities, states, and citizen groups alleged that several million people, primarily living in the inner cities, were undercounted, but they were unable either to convince the Census Bureau to adjust its 1990 population count statistically or to force that agency to do so through legal action. In a decision in April 1993 a U.S. District Court judge ruled that former Commerce Secretary Robert A. Mosbacher, who made the decision to use the actual census count and not the adjusted figures, did not act in an arbitrary and capricious manner and that therefore his decision could not be overruled by the court. The judge did go on to say, however, that had he made the decision on which census data to use, he would have used the adjusted figures.

The stakes are high in redistricting. Apportionment is a major factor that affects partisan control of legislatures. Once districts are redrawn and representatives are elected from them, those representatives are difficult to defeat. The partisan composition of legislatures for the next decade is likely to be decided on the basis of the redistricting that occurs after the census.

The institutional environment: incumbency Partisan gains from redistricting are preserved in large part by incumbency. In most elections, incumbents have an advantage. Incumbency provides recognition, which, in turn, generates support. The electorate is more likely to vote for candidates who are known than for those who are not, and challengers are usually not nearly so well known.

Incumbents can also use the perquisites of their office to help themselves get reelected. But they must be careful. It is against federal law for United States government employees, such as congressional staffs, to engage in campaign activities in the course of their official duties. To circumvent this rule, candidates may have their staff members take a leave of absence during the campaign. The employees are not supposed to be given extra compensation for this campaign activity when they return to the public payroll.

The availability of staff, travel funds, and free mailings gives incumbents a head start and at the same time discourages qualified people from challenging them. Incumbents also have a fundraising advantage. Potential contributors see incumbents as better able to help them because of their established position in government. The ability of incumbents to raise money, combined with the high costs of running, particularly for statewide office, also discourages would-be opponents. Thus, those who oppose incumbents are often placed in a catch-22 situation: they cannot obtain sufficient funds, coverage, or voluntary support because their chances are not viewed as promising, and they cannot improve their chances without the necessary funds, coverage, and voluntary support. One by-product of this predicament is an increase in the number of challenges by wealthy individuals with little political experience.

The advantages of incumbency vary with the position. In general, the more visible and less service oriented the office, the more vulnerable is the incumbent. United States senators and governors fit into this category. Their prestigious office is likely to attract strong challengers. Moreover, their decisions and policies are apt to receive public attention and generate controversy. In contrast, members of the House of Representatives tend to be more secure. They enjoy relatively high name recognition in their districts, but their role in the legislative process generally receives little scrutiny. Moreover, they can use their offices to perform constituency services, which enhance their personal reputations while downplaying their ideological convictions.

The extent of the incumbency advantage is indicated by the data in Table 10-6. From 1980 to 1990, over 90 percent of incumbents in the House of Representatives were renominated and reelected, compared with almost 80 percent of those in the Senate. In 1992, however, public frustration with government combined with the decennial redistricting to reduce the power of incumbency for those who chose to run. Of those who stood for reelection, nineteen were not renominated, and twenty-four were defeated in the general election. Others chose to retire rather than face possible defeat.

TABLE 10-6					
Congressional Incumbency and Reelection, 1980–1992					
	INCUMBENTS RUNNING IN GENERAL ELECTION		INCUMBENTS DEFEATED IN GENERAL ELECTION		PERCENT SUCCESSFUL	
YEAR	HOUSE	SENATE	HOUSE	SENATE	HOUSE	SENATE
1980	398	29	31	9	90.7	55.2
1982	393	30	29	2	90.1	93.3
1984	409	29	16	3	95.4	89.6
1986	393	28	6	7	98.0	75.0
1988	408	27	6	4	98.3	85.2
1990	406	32	15	1	96.0	96.9
1992	348	27	24	4	93.1	85.2

SOURCE: Norman J. Ornstein, Thomas E. Mann, and Michael J. Malbin, *Vital Statistics on Congress, 1991–1992* (Washington, D.C.: Congressional Quarterly, 1992), 58–59; updated by the authors. Reprinted by permission of Congressional Quarterly, Inc.

Normally the incumbency advantage extends to the presidency as well. Of the fourteen presidents who have sought reelection in the twentieth century, nine have won. Franklin D. Roosevelt was reelected three times. Today the Twenty-second Amendment prevents an individual from being elected to the presidency more than twice.

Organization and Strategy

Although candidates run on their own, they tend to use similar campaign organizations and strategies (see Figure 10-3). The components of a campaign organization are dictated by the functions that have to be performed: raising and spending money, traveling and giving speeches, monitoring opinion and creating an image, formulating and targeting a message, and meeting with the media and mounting efforts to get out the vote.

In developing and implementing a strategy, candidates must design and project a basic appeal. The appeal indicates the reasons why people should vote for them. Partisanship plays a major role in the appeal, especially for the candidate of the dominant party.

In articulating partisan themes, candidates normally stress issues that conjure up positive associations with their party and have the most direct impact on constituents, such as jobs, taxes, and crime and other social issues. They assume that people will be most concerned about the pocketbook issues that affect them personally—income, inflation, and jobs. Negative images of the opposition party are also part of most campaign appeals. Democratic candidates refer to the Republicans as the party of the rich, the party of big business, the party that is insensitive to the plight of the less fortunate. Republicans, in turn, picture the Democrats as the party of big government, big spending, and big taxes.

Traditionally, foreign affairs have not played as large a role as domestic affairs in most campaigns. However, in recent elections the impact of foreign policy on the economy, on international politics, and on leadership itself has been sufficient to force candidates for national office to address international matters such as United States military and economic aid, covert intelligence operations, open markets and fair trade, and even issues such as human rights, in addition to pressing domestic concerns. In 1980 the presence of American hostages in Iran was a major issue. In 1984 the arms race and funding for the Reagan administration's Strategic Defense Initiative ("Star Wars") were of concern. In 1988 attention shifted to arms control. The end of the Cold War and concern about a range of domestic issues muted the impact of foreign policy in 1992.

How do candidates demonstrate their qualifications for the positions they seek? Incumbents point to their experience, their record, and their performance in office. Challengers describe their own potential and criticize their opponent's record. In an election in which none of the candidates is an incumbent, experience in other public offices or, occasionally, other types of work may be cited as qualifications. Increasingly, neophyte candidates for major positions such as senator or governor engage in extensive media advertising to gain public recognition, exploit their strengths and their opponents' weaknesses, and build support for their candidacy.

In the end, the object is to amass a winning coalition. Beginning with a

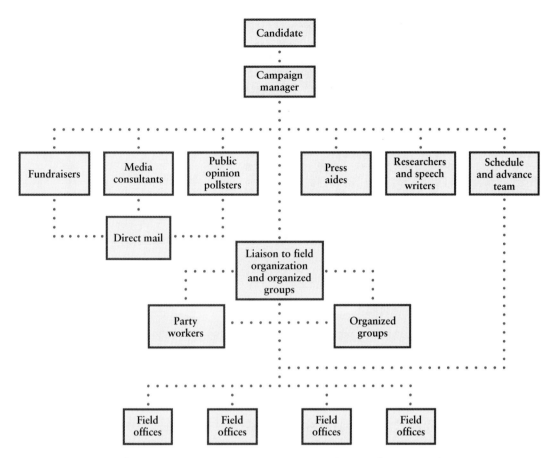

Figure 10-3 *Typical campaign organization*. SOURCE: *L. Sandy Maisel,* Parties and Elections in America, *2nd ed. (New York: McGraw-Hill, 1993), 190. Copyright © 1993 McGraw-Hill. Reproduced with the permission of McGraw-Hill.*

core of strong party identifiers, candidates need to hold on to their weaker partisan supporters, attract independents, and gain some support among members of the opposition party. This is why candidates of the dominant party emphasize their partisan affiliation and those of the minority party stress their leadership abilities and issue positions when appealing to independent voters and weak party identifiers. In nonpartisan elections, issue positions and candidate images are more pronounced than in partisan appeals.

In designing a winning coalition, presidential candidates must keep the Electoral College in mind. Their object is to build a winning *geographic* coalition by concentrating their campaign in areas where it is likely to do them the most good—the large states plus other states that appear to be most competitive. It is not wise to devote many resources to areas where the candidate is considered extremely strong or extremely weak. Thus, in recent presidential campaigns Republicans have tended to rely on the South and West and focus their resources on several of the key industrial states in the Midwest, which the Democrats had to win if they were to secure a majority in the Electoral College (see Figure 10-4). The Democrats, in turn, had much less flexibility, concentrating their resources on all the large industrial states and a few other small states that inclined toward their party. This strategic emphasis was reversed in

With the odds against him, Walter Mondale, Democratic candidate in 1984, undertook a bold strategy. He gambled that a female running mate, who was also an Italian, a Catholic, and from the East, might attract women, Catholics, and others who might vote for Ronald Reagan. His choice of Geraldine Ferraro, here with the candidate and New York Governor Mario Cuomo, seemed good until her taxes, her past campaigns for Congress, and her husband's business associates came under media scrutiny.

© Tannenbaum/SYGMA

Figure 10-4   *The Electoral College vote, 1980–1992.* SOURCES: *Data for 1980, 1984, and 1988 adapted from "America at the Polls 2: The Vote for President, 1968–1984,"* Congressional Quarterly Almanac, *as it appeared in the* New York Times, *November 4, 1992, B13. Data for 1992 adapted from* Congressional Quarterly, *November 7, 1992, 3549. Reprinted by permission of Congressional Quarterly, Inc.*

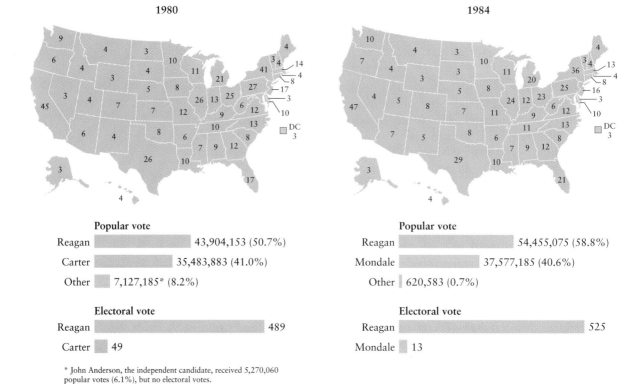

1980

1984

Popular vote

Reagan   43,904,153 (50.7%)
Carter   35,483,883 (41.0%)
Other   7,127,185* (8.2%)

Electoral vote

Reagan   489
Carter   49

Popular vote

Reagan   54,455,075 (58.8%)
Mondale   37,577,185 (40.6%)
Other   620,583 (0.7%)

Electoral vote

Reagan   525
Mondale   13

* John Anderson, the independent candidate, received 5,270,060 popular votes (6.1%), but no electoral votes.

1992. With two moderate southern candidates on their ticket in 1992, the Democrats emphasized that region, an area of strength prior to 1964. By refocusing their attention on the South, the Democrats forced the Republicans, who could no longer take that region of the country for granted, to do the same. The result was an election campaign fought in the South and in the largest, most competitive states.

Prior to 1992 the Republicans were thought to have an advantage in the Electoral College because more states consistently voted for Republican candidates than for Democratic candidates. The results of the 1992 election cast doubt on this theory of Republican advantage.

ANALYZING THE ELECTION RESULTS

When the campaigns are over and the voters have made their decisions, political pundits, media analysts, party officials, and the winning and losing candidates dissect and evaluate the election returns to find their meaning. This analysis is important for several reasons. It helps the winners define and claim their electoral mandate—what the people want them to do. It helps the losers know why they lost, and equally important, what they might do to win the next time around. For other observers, it helps to clarify the meaning of the election, obviously important for a government based on popular consent.

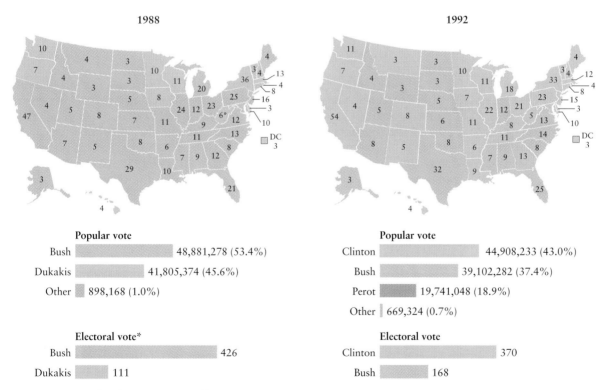

1988

1992

Popular vote

Bush 48,881,278 (53.4%)

Dukakis 41,805,374 (45.6%)

Other 898,168 (1.0%)

Popular vote

Clinton 44,908,233 (43.0%)

Bush 39,102,282 (37.4%)

Perot 19,741,048 (18.9%)

Other 669,324 (0.7%)

Electoral vote*

Bush 426

Dukakis 111

Electoral vote

Clinton 370

Bush 168

* One Democratic elector from West Virginia voted for
Senator Lloyd Bentsen, the Democratic candidate for vice president.

Most interpretations of elections focus on the presidency, and use more data than simply the actual vote count. To discover who voted for whom and why, researchers conduct surveys that ask voters to identify the principal reasons for their choices and how they feel about the candidates and issues. The two most frequently cited surveys of this sort are the large exit poll conducted for the major news networks, newspapers, and wire services on election day (see Table 10-7) and a smaller but more comprehensive pre- and post-election survey conducted by the National Election Center at the University of Michigan for scholars across the country.

Interpretations of these data usually produce mixed messages, but they do suggest the dominant issues, images, and inclinations toward or away from political parties that seem to have shaped the retrospective and, to a lesser extent, the prospective judgments of the electorate.

In 1976, it was the Watergate scandal, President Ford's pardon of Richard Nixon, and a shaky economy that contributed to challenger Jimmy Carter's victory. That Carter himself was a southern Democrat, a moderate, and an outsider at a time when Washington insiders were viewed with some suspicion helped him defeat the incumbent Republican president.

However, when Carter sought reelection four years later, being a Democrat, a Southerner, a moderate, and an incumbent was not enough. Poor performance ratings overcame the advantage that partisanship and incumbency normally bring to the president of the dominant party. Carter was judged on the basis of his potential for office the first time, but he was judged on his actual performance in office the second time. That judgment was very harsh. The vote for Carter fell below his 1976 totals in every single state.

Ronald Reagan was the beneficiary of the judgment that Carter did not deserve another four years as president. By 1980, it was Reagan, not Carter, who voters believed had the greater *potential* for leadership. That potential was the primary reason he won, not his ideology, policy positions, or personal appeal.

Four years later it was a different story. Then Reagan's personal appeal, policy successes, and strong presidential leadership contributed to his victory. Voters rewarded him for what they considered a job well done. Although they had voted *against* Carter in the previous election, they voted *for* Reagan in 1984.

This trend of retrospective voting continued in 1988. George Bush won because the electorate evaluated the Reagan administration positively, associated Bush with that administration, and concluded that he, not his Democratic opponent, Michael Dukakis, would be better able and more likely to maintain the good economic times and the policies and leadership that produced them. Bush's favorable image and Dukakis's negative one seemed to reinforce this judgment.

The analysis of the 1992 election also suggests that it was a retrospective vote, but one that worked to the president's disadvantage. An unhappy electorate turned Bush out of office because they were disgruntled about his leadership, his economic policies, and a myriad of other domestic problems. A survey conducted for the Republican National Committee found a majority of voters believed that Bush would not behave any differently the next time around.

Although people had serious reservations about Bill Clinton's character and lack of experience, they still saw him as more likely to effect change, par-

Persona is critically important to a candidate's success. Ronald Reagan, an actor by profession, was a natural president. Whether throwing out the first baseball, speaking on the Normandy beach about the Allied invasion of Europe, or simply addressing Congress, he wore the role easily. George Bush did not. He appeared awkward and never quite seemed natural as president, even when he loosened his tie and rolled up his sleeves.

ticularly with respect to the economy. Since 51 percent of the electorate felt the economy was the most important issue and only 10 percent believed it was character and trust, Clinton won despite his personal vulnerabilities.

The mood of the country also provided the climate that permitted the independent candidacy of H. Ross Perot to get off the ground and acquire a base of support. Tapping the anger and frustration of the voters, Perot promised to do something about the problems of the deficit, the faltering economy, and a deadlocked and out-of-touch government. His straight talk and unconventional campaign, targeted to those who were "sick and tired" of the way things were, those who had lost confidence in the major parties and their candidates, won him almost as many votes among independents as Clinton and Bush got. (See Table 10-7, page 358.) However, Perot failed to persuade enough Republican and Democratic partisans to support his candidacy. His failure to do so attests to the difficulty that independent candidates face with the American electorate and in the Electoral College. Perot won no states and received no electoral votes despite the fact that he received 19 million popular votes.

TABLE 10-7

Portrait of the American Electorate, 1984–1992

	PERCENT OF 1992 TOTAL	1984		1988		1992		
		REAGAN	MONDALE	BUSH	DUKAKIS	CLINTON	BUSH	PEROT
Total vote:		59	40	53	45	43	38	19
Men	46	62	37	57	41	41	38	21
Women	54	56	44	50	49	46	37	17
Whites	87	64	35	59	40	39	41	20
Blacks	8	9	90	12	86	82	11	7
Hispanics	3	37	62	30	69	62	25	14
Asians	1	—	—	—	—	29	55	16
Married	65	62	38	57	42	40	40	20
Unmarried	35	52	47	46	53	49	33	18
18–29 years old	22	59	40	52	47	44	34	22
30–44 years old	38	57	42	54	45	42	38	20
45–59 years old	24	60	40	57	42	41	40	19
60 and older	16	60	40	50	49	50	38	12
Not high school graduate	6	50	50	43	56	55	28	17
High school graduate	25	60	39	50	49	43	36	20
Some college education	29	61	38	57	42	42	37	21
College graduate	24	—	—	62	37	40	41	19
College graduate or more	40	58	41	56	43	44	39	18
Postgraduate education	16	—	—	50	48	49	36	15
White Protestant	49	72	27	66	33	33	46	21
Catholic	27	54	45	52	47	44	36	20
Jewish	4	31	67	35	64	78	12	10
White born-again Christian	17	78	22	81	18	23	61	15
Union household	19	46	53	42	57	55	24	21
Family income under $15,000	14	45	55	37	62	59	23	18
$15,000–$29,999	24	57	42	49	50	45	35	20
$30,000–$49,999	30	59	40	56	44	41	38	21
$50,000–$74,999	20	66	33	56	42	40	42	18
$75,000 and over	13	69	30	62	37	36	48	16

ELECTIONS AND GOVERNANCE

In addition to determining who is elected, elections influence what government will do. That is why understanding the meaning of the election is so important. Contrary to popular belief, campaign promises and party platforms do get translated into public policy. Media scrutiny, frequent elections, and the desire

TABLE 10-7

Portrait of the American Electorate, 1984–1992 (continued)

	PERCENT OF 1992 TOTAL	1984		1988		1992		
		REAGAN	MONDALE	BUSH	DUKAKIS	CLINTON	BUSH	PEROT
Family's financial situation is:								
Better today	25	86	14	—	—	24	62	14
Same today	41	50	50	—	—	41	41	18
Worse today	34	15	85	—	—	61	14	25
From the East	24	53	47	50	49	47	35	18
From the Midwest	27	58	41	52	47	42	37	21
From the South	30	64	36	58	41	42	43	16
From the West	20	61	38	52	46	44	34	22
Republicans	35	92	7	91	8	10	73	17
Independents	27	63	36	55	43	38	32	30
Democrats	38	25	74	17	82	77	10	13
Liberals	21	28	70	18	81	68	14	18
Moderates	49	53	47	49	50	48	31	21
Conservatives	29	82	17	80	19	18	65	17
Employed	68	60	39	56	43	42	38	20
Full-time student	5	52	47	44	54	50	35	15
Unemployed	6	32	67	37	62	56	24	20
Homemaker	8	62	38	58	41	36	45	19
Retired	13	60	40	50	49	51	36	13
First-time voters	11	61	38	51	47	48	30	22

NOTES: 1992 data were collected by Voter Research and Surveys based on questionnaires completed by 15,490 voters leaving 300 polling places around the nation on election day. Data based on surveys of voters conducted by the *New York Times* and CBS News: 9,174 in 1984; and 11,645 in 1988. Those who gave no answer are not shown. Dashes indicate that a question was not asked or a category was not provided in a particular year. Family income categories in 1984: under $12,500, $12,500–$24,999, $25,000–$34,999, $35,000–$50,000, and over $50,000. In 1988: under $12,500, $12,500–$24,999, $25,000–$34,999, $35,000–$49,999, $50,000 and over. "Born-again Christian" was labeled "born-again Christian/fundamentalist" in 1992 and "fundamentalist and evangelical Christian" in 1988. Male and female college graduates include those with postgraduate degrees in 1976 and 1980; "occupation" refers to head of the household. Family financial situation is compared to four years ago in 1984 and 1988; 1984 numbers from NBC News.

SOURCE: Voter Research and Surveys as printed in the *New York Times*, November 5, 1992, B9. Copyright © 1992 by The New York Times Company. Reprinted by permission.

to be reelected provide incentives for redeeming campaign promises and staying responsive to the electorate.

Elections, however, are rarely clear mandates, even though public officials, particularly the president, may claim them. People vote for the same candidate for different reasons, and they vote for different candidates for the same reason. Because many elections for many positions are conducted on the same day, the judgment of the electorate is likely to be mixed and may produce seemingly contradictory results, such as a legislature controlled by one party and an executive controlled by the other. At the national level, divided partisan control was the rule, not the exception, between 1968 and 1992. This made governing more difficult, because the parties proposed different and often competing priorities and policy agendas.

Elections reflect popular sentiment—but they do so imperfectly. For the most part, they force voters to decide between people rather than between policy positions. Moreover, differing national, state, and local constituencies often provide outcomes that mirror the decentralized character of the political system more than they reflect a national perspective. Finally, the length of the electoral process and the promises made by candidates to obtain and retain office have enlarged public expectations of government performance and, at the same time, made those expectations harder to live up to. Today's successful candidates owe less to their party leaders and organizations and more to themselves, their campaign organizations, and their constituencies. Once in office, they tend to behave independently, influenced the most by the people who elected them. At the national level, especially, the result is more people who wish to lead and fewer who are willing to follow, which in turn has increased the difficulty of obtaining a consensus on public policy.

SUMMARY

Elections are essential for a democratic society. They frame policy debate, select public officials, and influence the decisions of public officials. To perform these functions, elections must meet three criteria. There must be *universal suffrage*; all citizens who are responsible for their own actions must be permitted to vote. There must be a *meaningful choice*—that is, an opportunity to select among different options that are clearly presented to the voters. There must be *political equality*. Everyone's vote must count equally, with no one individual or group exercising undue influence.

In the early years of the nation, suffrage was extremely limited. In the 1830s, property requirements for voting were dropped, but gender, race, and age barriers remained in many states. The Fifteenth Amendment extended suffrage to citizens regardless of their race, color, and national origin. The Nineteenth Amendment prevented states from denying women the right to vote. The Twenty-sixth Amendment established a uniform voting age of 18.

The expansion of suffrage has increased the number of eligible voters, but the percentage of citizens who actually vote has declined. Among the reasons for lower turnout are decreased party iden-

tification, mobility among younger voters, and the growing number of older people with poor health and less interest in politics. Government scandals have also contributed to the increased apathy and cynicism of the electorate. In 1992, turnout increased for the first time in over thirty years because of concern about the recession, the appeal of H. Ross Perot, and the use of television talk and entertainment shows to reach additional voters.

States establish the rules and procedures for the conduct of elections. The more rigorous these requirements are, the lower voter turnout is likely to be. State laws also govern primary elections. These laws sometimes conflict with party rules. In cases of conflict the Supreme Court has held that parties may determine and enforce their own rules for delegate selection.

In recent years the equity issue has focused on the use of money and other resources in support of candidates running for office. Congress sought to regulate contributions and expenditures by the enactment of campaign finance legislation. That legislation has placed limits on campaign spending, provided government support for presidential nomination and election campaigns, and required public disclosure of contributions and expenditures over a certain amount. These laws have reduced but not eliminated the disproportionate influence of the wealthy on the electoral process, but they have also contributed to factionalism within the parties and have reduced the parties' influence on candidates.

Elections are critical for a democracy, but so is the participation of the electorate. Turnout varies with demographic and attitudinal factors. The principal demographic characteristics that contribute to voting are education, socioeconomic status, and age, all of which correlate with one another. Older, more educated, higher-income professionals tend to vote more often and thus are in a better position to influence policy makers than those who are younger, less educated, with lower incomes, people with greater needs that government could address. Voting also varies with partisanship, interest in the election, concern over the outcome, a sense of civic responsibility, trust in government, and political efficacy. People who identify strongly with a political party, follow the election, and care who wins will vote more often than those who lack these motivations for voting.

Some of the attitudes that affect whether people vote also affect how they vote. Party identification is the single most important influence. It provides a framework for analysis and offers cues for assessing the candidates and their stands. Group associations influence voting because they generate cross pressures that find expression in the political process—pressures that may reinforce or undermine partisan inclinations. The candidates and the issues also affect how people vote. Some voters base their vote on what the candidate has achieved in the past; this is known as *retrospective voting*. Others base their vote on the anticipated actions of the candidate; this is termed *prospective voting*.

Candidates and parties contrive their campaigns to affect the electorate's judgment. There are usually two campaigns: one is to gain their party's nomination and, if successful, the other is to win the general election. Of the two, the quest for the nomination has changed the most in the twentieth century, particularly at the presidential level. Since 1972, presidential nominess have been chosen by party activists and sympathizers when they participate in the primaries and caucuses and not primarily by party leaders at the national convention. Today, about three-fourths of the delegates to the national nominating conventions are chosen in state primary

elections. The remainder are chosen in party *caucuses*. The Democrats select additional *superdelegates* from the party's elected and appointed leaders. The Democrats have also adopted the principle of *proportional voting*: delegates are awarded to each candidate in proportion to the number of popular votes the candidate receives. The Republicans still permit *winner-take-all voting*. The percentage of women and minorities who attend conventions has increased significantly, but it is not clear whether convention delegates better represent the beliefs and attitudes of party supporters than they used to.

Modern presidential campaigns usually start well before the first caucuses and primaries are held. One reason for this is the time it takes to raise the money needed for a serious campaign. Millions of dollars are needed to build an organization, pay for television time, conduct public opinion polls, and develop voter appeals. Another reason for competing in the early contests, especially for candidates who are not well known, is to gain voter recognition.

The national nominating convention decides the party's rules, choose its presidential and vice presidential nominees, and write the party platform. Usually the nominees have been preordained by the delegate selection process. In cases in which the nomination is in doubt, the front-runner tries to generate a *bandwagon effect*, inducing uncommitted delegates and delegates pledged to other candidates to join the winning team. An important function of the convention is to unify groups that have been divided by the nomination process and launch the general election campaign with a broad national appeal.

The presidential election occurs within the context of the Electoral College system. A group of *electors*, meeting as the *Electoral College*, chooses the president. The voters in each state select the electors, who are equal in number to a state's senators and representatives. Under the *general ticket system*, the candidate who wins the popular vote in a given state receives all of the state's electoral votes. This system benefits the largest states.

Some of the changes that have affected the presidential selection process have affected nonpresidential selection as well. Primaries have become the route to nomination at most levels of government. These primaries have led to more competition within the parties and have left them more factionalized.

To win the nomination, candidates must build their own organization, raise their own money, design their own strategy, and mount a campaign that appeals to those partisans who are most likely to participate. The techniques they use and the appeals they make carry over to the general election. The principal difference, however, is that the appeal must be broadened in the general election and targeted not only to party identifiers but also to independents and members of the opposite party.

The laws governing the general election have also changed, particularly as they apply to reapportionment. When seats in the House of Representatives are reapportioned every ten years on the basis of the national census, a practice known as *redistricting*, boundaries must be drawn in such a way that they are approximately equal in population and give adequate representation to minorities within the state. However, *gerrymandering*, the practice of drawing district boundaries to favor the party in power, is still common.

Partisan gains from redistricting are preserved by incumbency. Incumbency leads to recognition, which in turn generates electoral support and enables incumbents to raise more money than most of their challengers. The advantages of office also help incumbents when they seek reelection.

Candidates and parties are naturally interested in who wins, but they also need to assess the meaning of the election. In describing the long- and short-term factors that explain the results, analysts focus on the partisan disposition of the election, current issues, and candidate images. They believe that these factors, singularly and together, influence the retrospective judgment of the electorate about the performance of those in power and the prospective judgment of who will be most likely to pursue and achieve desirable policies. In 1992 it was the accumulation of domestic problems and the perceived failure of President Bush to deal adequately with them that resulted in his defeat. Bill Clinton was seen as the candidate most likely to effect the kind of change people wanted.

The election naturally has important implications for governance. It provides an agenda of priorities as well as a potential coalition of supporters. It is up to those in power, especially the president, to convert that agenda into a series of proposals and mobilize a coalition to support them. Claiming an election mandate at the beginning of their administration is a device presidents frequently use to achieve their policy objectives.

KEY TERMS AND CONCEPTS

universal suffrage	caucus	Electoral College
meaningful choice	superdelegate	general ticket system
political equality	proportional voting	redistricting
split-ticket voting	winner-take-all voting	one person, one vote
retrospective voting	bandwagon effect	gerrymandering
prospective voting	elector	

LEARNING MORE ABOUT ELECTIONS

Scholarly studies

Abramson, Paul R., John H. Aldrich, and David W. Rohde. *Change and Continuity in the 1988 Elections.* Washington, D.C.: Congressional Quarterly, 1991, and volumes for previous elections. A thorough analysis of the vote in presidential elections.

Campbell, Angus, Philip E. Converse, Warren E. Miller, and Donald E. Stokes. *The American Voter.* Chicago: University of Chicago Press, 1980. A classic study that postulates a theory of voting behavior that is still applicable. Not easy reading but worth the effort.

Fishel, Jeff. *Presidents and Promises.* Washington, D.C.: Congressional Quarterly, 1985. An examination of the campaign promises of presidential candidates from 1960 to 1980 and the extent to which they have been carried out.

Jacobson, Gary C. *The Politics of Congressional Elections.* 3rd ed. New York: HarperCollins, 1991. A thorough analysis of the impact of party, incumbency, money, and other factors on the outcome of congressional elections.

Nie, Norman H., Sidney Verba, and John R. Petrocik. *The Changing American Voter*. Cambridge, Mass.: Harvard University Press, 1980. A skillful examination of voting patterns.

Sorauf, Frank J. *Money in American Elections*. New York: HarperCollins, 1988. A good source of information about campaign finance, from the sources of money to the expenditures of the candidates to proposals for reform.

Wattenberg, Martin P. *The Rise of Candidate-Centered Politics*. Cambridge, Mass.: Harvard University Press, 1991. An examination of presidential elections during the 1980s and their increasing candidate orientation.

Wayne, Stephen J. *The Road to the White House, 1992*. New York: St. Martin's Press, 1992. A nuts-and-bolts description of the arduous quest for the nomination and the general election.

Wolfinger, Raymond E., and Steven J. Rosenstone. *Who Votes?* New Haven, Conn.: Yale University Press, 1980. An attempt to answer the questions of who votes and why by examining the impact of socioeconomic status, age and sex, political culture, and state laws on voter turnout.

Leisure reading

Cramer, Richard Ben. *What It Takes: The Way to the White House*. New York: Random House, 1992. A highly readable journalistic account of the candidates in 1988, with emphasis on their motivation and drive for the presidency.

Crouse, Timothy. *The Boys on the Bus*. New York: Ballantine, 1986. A not-so-flattering account of the press corps's coverage of the 1972 presidential campaign.

Troy, Gil. *See How They Ran*. New York: Free Press, 1991. A historical account of presidential campaigns from their beginning through the 1980s.

White, Theodore H. *The Making of the President, 1960*. New York: Atheneum House, 1989. A classic description of the Kennedy-Nixon election by a journalist who observed the campaign and the candidates up close.

Primary sources

Guide to U.S. Elections. 2nd ed. Washington, D.C.: Congressional Quarterly, 1985. A collection of statistical data on elections for Congress, the presidency, and governorships as well as information on parties.

Scammon, Richard, ed. *American Votes*. Washington, D.C.: Congressional Quarterly, 1955–present. Official election statistics compiled on a state-by-state basis for every election since 1954.

Organizations

Committee on House Administration, H-326 Capitol Building, Washington, DC 20515; (202) 225-2061. Holds and publishes transcripts of hearings on legislation dealing with the electoral process; oversees the Federal Election Commission.

Federal Election Commission, 999 E Street, N.W., Washington, DC 20463; (800) 424-9530. Issues a monthly newsletter, press releases, and various other reports in addition to its public computer file on campaign expenditures for all national campaigns.

Inter-University Consortium for Political and Social Research, University of Michigan, Ann Arbor, MI 48104; (313) 763-5010 (data archives). Has conducted national surveys during presidential and congressional elections since 1952 and disseminates data to scholars for analyses of voting behavior.

League of Women Voters, 1730 M Street, N.W., Suite 1000, Washington, DC 20036; (202) 429-1965. Provides information to voters on election rules and procedures at the national, state, and local levels; also provides information on candidates' positions.

Senate Committee on Rules and Administration, 305 Russell Office Building, Washington, DC 20510; (202) 224-6352. Holds and publishes transcripts of hearings and legislation dealing with the electoral process; oversees the Federal Election Commission.

CHAPTER **11**

Politics

and the

News Media

- News media in a democratic society

- Freedom of the press: the rights of individuals; regulation of radio and TV; economics

- History of the media: newspapers, electronic media, and technical change

- The media slant; manipulation by candidates; campaign advertising; the impact of the media on politics

- Media coverage of the president, the Congress, and the judiciary

- The impact of the media on public policy

In 1920, the Democrats endorsed the League of Nations and nominated James M. Cox, Ohio's governor. Cox chose New Yorker Franklin D. Roosevelt as his running mate. The victors, however, were Republicans Warren G. Harding and Calvin Coolidge. Harding's campaign theme was "Back to Normalcy," and his election was considered a defeat for Woodrow Wilson's policies. The Harding administration was plagued with scandals, however, and the president didn't survive his term, dying in office in 1923. "Silent Cal" Coolidge succeeded him and won reelection in 1924, using the slogan "Keep Cool with Coolidge."

As Washington Post *reporter Walter Pincus looked through a public works appropriation bill, he noticed a line item requesting funds for the production of an "enhanced radiation warhead." The weapon, designated for use on the United States' Lance missiles, was to be based in Europe. Having served on the staff of the Senate Foreign Relations Committee and conducted research on tactical nuclear weapons, Pincus recognized the importance of this single line buried deep in the nuclear weapons appropriation section of the bill.*

Pincus's article in the Washington Post *identified the "enhanced radiation warhead" as a neutron bomb. The story explained that the United States was "about to begin production of its first nuclear battlefield weapon specifically designed to kill people through the release of neutrons rather than to destroy military installations through heat and blast."[1] More important,* Post *editors gave the story a shocking headline: "Neutron Killer Warhead Buried in ERDA Budget." In Pincus's article the neutron bomb was described as a terrible, secret new weapon that "leaves buildings and tanks standing . . . but [kills] people." He went on to list* the effects of the neutron bomb in gruesome detail: "A heavy dose of neutrons attacks the central nervous system" and results in "almost immediate incapacitation with convulsions, intermittent stupor, and a lack of muscle coordination," followed by death "in a few hours to several days."[2]

The story immediately focused attention on the neutron bomb as a political issue. Senator Mark Hatfield (R-Oregon) moved to block funds for the weapon. President Jimmy Carter, whose administration had supported development of the neutron warhead, came under pressure to postpone production of the weapon. With public concern and opposition growing, Carter refused to make an immediate commitment on whether or not to produce the bomb and deploy it in Europe as had originally been planned.

The publicity surrounding the issue embarrassed some of America's allies. In West Germany, the Netherlands, and Belgium, public opposition to deployment of the weapon developed quickly. Meanwhile the Soviet Union, a Cold War adversary, initiated a propaganda campaign of its own, emphasizing the "evilness" of the weapon and the danger to Europe if it was deployed. Faced by these conflicting pressures, President Carter decided to defer production of the bomb. Carter's about-face caused red faces among leaders who had gone out on a limb to support him on this issue.

THIS EPISODE DEMONSTRATES THE IMPACT the news media can have on public policy. The knowledge, experience, and investigative skills of a single reporter culminated in a wave of public reactions that deferred an entire weapons system and weakened a presidential administration. The news media are not always this influential, but their potential to alert and inform the public can and does have a powerful effect on what democratic governments say and do.

NEWS MEDIA IN A DEMOCRATIC SOCIETY

Newspapers, radio, and television are essential for a democracy. They are the critical link between the people and their government. They provide information and analysis about policy issues, and they also sensitize policy makers to public opinion—which enables them to respond to the needs and desires of the population. Finally, the media play a critical role in reporting and evaluating the decisions of government. Only if the news media perform such a role can the people exercise judgment and hold those in government accountable for their actions.

To perform those functions adequately, the news media need to be able to operate freely—that is, to investigate and report without restrictions on the collection and dissemination of information. Poet John Milton, philosopher John Stuart Mill, and politician Thomas Jefferson wrote eloquently about the need for free inquiry and a free press. In a treatise entitled *Areopagitica* (1644), Milton reasoned that free inquiry is necessary for discovering truth: "Let her [Truth] and Falsehood grapple; whoever knew Truth put to the worse in a free and open encounter."[3] John Stuart Mill echoed this thought in his essay *On Liberty* (1859). Without a free marketplace of ideas, he asserted, "if the opinion is right, [people] are deprived of the opportunity of exchanging error for truth; if wrong, they lose, what is almost as great a benefit, the clearer perception and livelier impression of truth produced by its collision with error."[4] In a letter to a friend, Jefferson wrote, "Were it left to me to decide whether we should have a government without newspapers or newspapers without government, I should not hesitate a moment to prefer the latter."[5] Milton, Mill, and Jefferson believed that the most important role of the press is to provide a "marketplace of ideas," a forum in which the truth will emerge. In a government based on the consent of the governed, such a forum is essential not only for discerning truth but for evaluating the performance of public officials.

In authoritarian political systems, news media have a different function. Far from criticizing the government, they are its biggest booster, buttressing those in power by transmitting their messages to the people. Even entertainment programming contains information that government wishes to convey.

In a democracy, those in power also wish to make known their achievements and publicize their successes, and the job of the media is to report what they say and do. But the news media also function as watchdogs, presenting other information and perspectives. The watchdog role of spotlighting and criticizing government policy and activity results in an interdependent but often adversarial relationship between the news media and those in positions of authority. The tension generated by this relationship is essential to the maintenance of a free and democratic political system in which the government and the governed are permanently linked through open discussion and public criticism.[6]

How the media perform their informational and educational roles affects the politics of American government. The media have the power to influence opinion, to shape attitudes and beliefs, and to motivate activity. In exercising this power, they generate tension among those within the public arena whose interests, needs, or values might be affected directly or indirectly by the subject being reported.

SYGMA

The value of a free press for a democracy lies in its revelation of truth. But the media can also create perceptions of problems when none may exist. Take the incident in January 1992, when George Bush vomited and nearly fainted at a state dinner in Japan. The problem was a stomach virus, but rumors that the president was more seriously ill persisted. Were the media performing a critical public service by giving this event such detailed coverage?

The source of this tension varies with the issue. Sometimes it is a constitutional or legal question—freedom of the press versus the rights of individuals, groups, and government. Sometimes tension arises from a clash between a candidate's attempt to shape his or her own image and the media's desire to uncover "truth" about the candidate. Sometimes tension arises from the mixed messages given by the administration's presentation of its major achievements and media coverage of the administration's principal failures. Tension is also evident in government itself—in the give-and-take between people's right to know and the government's need to protect confidentiality and maintain national security. Even the attention given to issues versus the attention given to personalities has sparked debate about how well informed the citizenry actually is or can be and how well the media are doing their job and meeting their public responsibilities. We explore these issues in this chapter, looking at the impact of the news media on politics and government in the United States.

FREEDOM OF THE PRESS

The First Amendment to the Constitution guarantees freedom of the press, but the Supreme Court has *not* held that freedom to be absolute. The Court has ruled that freedom of the press must be balanced by the rights and needs of others in society—individuals, groups, even the government. For the media, the basic rights are to obtain information, to structure and analyze it, and to print or air it. For others, the basic rights include the rights to privacy, truthfulness, and fairness.

A Free Press Versus the Rights of Individuals

Where should the line be drawn between freedom of the press and protection for individuals and society as a whole? The media have a right to collect, evaluate, and disseminate information about public officials so long as that information is truthful, but they may not knowingly publish or broadcast information that is false. The information reported can be personal so long as it relates to the conduct of public affairs. The media have no right to invade the privacy of nonpublic figures, however. The media may also obtain and transmit information about national security, but they have no right to violate laws that prevent the dissemination of material that is harmful to that security. Each of these areas gives rise to potential conflicts that may have to be adjudicated within the legal system.

Libel By what standard should the press be held liable for falsehoods, printed or broadcast, that cause a person harm? The courts have ruled that two standards should be employed, one for private individuals and another for public figures. Private individuals need prove only that a publisher or broadcaster did not exercise reasonable care in determining the truth; this lack of care is termed *negligence*. Public figures must prove that a publisher or broadcaster knew prior to publication or airing that a statement was false and showed reckless disregard for the truth by publishing or airing it; this behavior is termed *actual malice*.

The distinction between negligence and actual malice was made to protect debate on controversial issues and keep public officials accountable. If falsity alone were the principal standard, publishers or broadcasters might be reluctant to print or air anything that was the least bit controversial. They would play it safe, and this policy would work to the advantage of those in power by shielding them from outside scrutiny.

Fair trial   A criminal act is news. But how the news is presented can affect the impartiality of a jury. Jurors need to have open minds and must base their decision only on the evidence and testimony presented during the trial. When there is a lot of publicity before or during a trial, as was the case with the Watergate defendants, those involved in the Iran-contra affair, or in local matters in which heinous crimes are committed, obtaining a fair trial may be difficult.[7]

Before judges can impose restrictions on the press, however, they must try to ensure a fair trial by other means. These include insulating witnesses from the media; issuing gag orders prohibiting out-of-court statements by witnesses, lawyers, or court officials; moving the trial away from the area in which the crime occurred if the crime received extensive pretrial coverage; and sequestering the jury, that is, isolating the jury from information presented outside the courtroom. According to the Supreme Court, restricting press coverage is the least tolerable method of ensuring a fair trial. As more states permit live television coverage of criminal and civil trials—at least one cable channel now provides an endless diet of live and taped courtroom trials—the issue of coverage versus defendants' rights will become an even greater concern.

Confidentiality of news sources   Should journalists be forced to disclose information or identify sources that may be needed in a criminal trial or other judicial proceeding? Journalists often claim that the First Amendment exempts them from revealing confidential sources so as to ensure that they are able to obtain critical information. Those in the media fear that if the identity of sources who request anonymity is not protected, sources will be reluctant to provide information that could be used against them.

The Supreme Court, however, has ruled that journalists are not privileged, that they must respond like other citizens when they are subpoenaed for information. (See the Constitutional Conflict on page 370.) To counter the effects of this ruling, many states have passed **shield laws** that give journalists some protection against forced disclosure, similar to protections enjoyed by doctors, lawyers, and clergy.

The executive branch has tried to restrict what the media report. During the Persian Gulf War in 1991, access to the battle area was limited, and information about operations was not released until it could no longer threaten the success of the operation or the lives of those involved. Even in peacetime the government uses a classification system that restricts access to information that, if it became public, could damage national security. Since government officials may classify more material than necessary, the media as well as scholars and other students of government face an ongoing problem of obtaining information that they believe they need to know and have a right to know.

Congress addressed this problem in 1966, when it enacted the Freedom of Information Act. This law, designed to facilitate access to government doc-

Frequently, the news media report activities that violate law, activities which the government has the right and the responsibility to prevent. Information about illegal activities may be obtained from sources who wish to remain anonymous for fear of reprisal or punishment. Protecting the confidentiality of their sources is a traditional and necessary obligation of reporters. Without such protection, they believe, people would be reluctant to blow the whistle on others.

Reporters are not the only ones who claim a privilege of confidentiality. Doctors, lawyers, and clergy also make similar claims. But how far should a privilege of confidentiality extend? Should those with knowledge of potentially harmful or illegal actions be required to inform authorities who have the responsibility to investigate, prevent, or punish such activity? Should reporters, for example, be exempt from grand jury inquiries?

The Supreme Court answered this question in the case of *Branzburg v. Hayes* in 1972. In this case, a reporter who had written about the illegal manufacture and use of drugs in a local community was summoned before a grand jury. He appeared in court but refused to reveal the identities of those involved. The state court ordered him to do so, and the Supreme Court by a narrow margin sustained the state court's ruling. The Court majority argued that freedom of the press did not exempt reporters from the normal obligations of citizenry, and these include responding truthfully to grand jury inquiries about alleged criminal activities.

In reaction to this and subsequent decisions affirming the government's right to require media to reveal their confidential sources, some states enacted shield laws to protect the anonymity of news sources. The Supreme Court has acknowledged that Congress also has the power to enact a shield law.

uments, places on the government the burden of showing why a document must remain classified. (Some ways to use the Act were described on page 114.) The media have not used this law very much, however, because of the long time it takes to process the requests and because "leaks" by people within the government are usually easier, quicker, and cheaper sources of information.

In 1976 Congress enacted legislation which requires that the meetings of many federal agencies and congressional committees be open to the public. There are exceptions, of course, and the legislation has not been uniformly obeyed. Supreme Court deliberations, for example, are conducted in complete secrecy. All the state governments have passed open meeting and record laws, but states too vary in the degree of public access that is permitted.

President Ronald Reagan issued directives to stop leaks of classified information but backed away from controversial proposals such as requiring lie detector tests. CIA agents and many Defense Department employees must agree to government review of any material they have written prior to its publication. The courts have upheld the validity of such agreements as a legitimate requirement of the job.

The government occasionally uses another technique to try to prevent certain information from becoming public. It goes to the judiciary to obtain restraining orders to prevent the publication or broadcasting of information that it believes would be harmful to the national security. This action is known as **prior restraint**. Although the Supreme Court has upheld the concept of prior restraint, it has been reluctant to approve it in practice. For example, in 1971

President Nixon tried to prevent the *New York Times*, the *Washington Post*, and other newspapers from releasing portions of a classified history of United States policy in the Vietnam War (the *Pentagon Papers*). By a 6-to-3 vote the Supreme Court ruled against the administration. In the case of *New York Times v. United States*, it held that the government's effort to prevent publication amounted to an unconstitutional prior restraint.

Regulation of Radio and Television

Regulation of the electronic media is more extensive than regulation of the print media. The reason for the difference is that the airwaves are considered to be in the public domain. Broadcasters are given licenses to use the airwaves only if they agree to operate in the "public interest, convenience, or necessity."

The agency responsible for regulating the electronic media is the Federal Communications Commission (FCC). It licenses stations, oversees their technical operations, and investigates citizens' complaints. The FCC rarely decides to revoke a broadcaster's license; rather, it imposes fines and warnings on broadcasters that do not serve the public interest.

The FCC has enforced three rules that affect the coverage of politics: the fairness doctrine, the equal time rule, and the right of rebuttal. The **fairness doctrine** required that discussions of important public issues be aired and that conflicting sides of an issue be presented. Under this rule, when the president gave a political address on radio and television, a representative of the party out of power was permitted to give a response, usually for the same amount of time.

In 1987, concerned that a conservative FCC might abolish or fail to enforce the fairness doctrine, Congress enacted a bill that would have given it the force of law. President Reagan vetoed the bill, however, and Congress failed to override the veto. A short time later the FCC suspended the use of the fairness doctrine.

The second regulation that has had an impact on politics is the **equal time rule**. It requires a broadcaster that allows a candidate for public office to appear on the station or carries advertising for that candidate to provide other candidates for the same office with similar opportunities. Prior to 1983 this rule applied to all candidates, including those of minor parties. The FCC subsequently allowed radio and television stations some flexibility in staging debates (which are considered news events) and determining which candidates to invite. News shows and coverage of news events have been exempt from the equal time rule. The application of this regulation in 1980 and 1984 meant that Ronald Reagan's old movies could not be shown on television because his opponents could have demanded and received equal time.

The third rule, the **right of rebuttal**, was established by the Supreme Court in the landmark case of *Red Lion Broadcasting Co. v. FCC* (1969). In this case a liberal author whose book on Senator Barry Goldwater was criticized by a conservative preacher asked for equal and free time to reply to his critic. The Court agreed, ruling that individuals or groups whose honesty, integrity, or character has been attacked during a broadcast, or a candidate whose opponent has been endorsed by a station, has a right of rebuttal.

The fairness doctrine, the equal time rule, and the right of rebuttal can be justified on grounds of equity. From the perspective of the media, however, the regulations are restrictive and costly to broadcasters. Because they require that more time be devoted to public programming, they may lead to a reduction in revenue from advertising, a serious problem for businesses that seek to make a profit. As a consequence, the fairness doctrine has resulted in bland news coverage; the equal time rule, in little or no time to any candidate (because of the requirement to provide time to *all* candidates); and the right of rebuttal, in avoidance of critical commentary.

The Economics of a Free Press

The vast majority of media in the United States are and always have been privately owned and operated.[8] This is not surprising in view of the strength of the free-enterprise system and the suspicion with which Americans have traditionally viewed government-owned and -operated media. Although some public support is provided to the Corporation for Public Broadcasting, a government corporation—the only national government media—radio stations and a television network run by the United States Information Agency are forbidden to broadcast or even distribute their programs within the country.

Not only are the news media private, but they are big business. Approximately sixteen hundred papers are published daily in the United States.[9] Most of the large ones, those with circulations over 100,000, are part of newspaper chains like Gannett, Knight-Ridder, and Times Mirror. The ten biggest chains account for approximately half of the daily circulation in the United States.[10] These chains maintain their own news bureaus, which distribute reports, features, and news analyses to member papers. The editors of the member papers determine what material provided by the bureau gets published, and they usually do not obtain national news from other sources, such as the national news services offered by Associated Press, United Press International, Reuters, the *New York Times*, and the *Washington Post*.

A similar concentration of news organizations is evident in the television news industry. The three commercial networks, ABC, CBS, and NBC, and the cable news network, CNN, dominate national news. There are independent local stations and a few small independent networks, but their resources for obtaining and evaluating national news are extremely limited. They have relatively few reporters, camera crews, and producers and are forced to follow the lead of the major networks for national news. Not surprisingly, there is a tendency toward "pack journalism," as reporters from many stations focus on the same story.

Another trend in contemporary media communications is the development of giant conglomerates, companies that own and operate a combination of newspapers and radio and television stations. Since 1975, the FCC has barred such companies from acquiring more than one outlet in any single market, such as a city or metropolitan area. However, outlets acquired prior to that date are not affected by the regulation, and some corporations, such as the New York Times and Capital Cities/ABC, continue to own multiple communications outlets across the country. Exceptions are also made. In 1993, the FCC approved Rupert Murdoch's ownership of both a major newspaper and a television station in the metropolitan New York market, largely because Murdoch had offered to save the once-again-dying *New York Post*, a paper he had owned several years before.

One reason for the concern about concentrated ownership relates to the lack of diversity in the news. Another pertains to bias, that is, news that is unfair and prejudicial. A large and growing portion of the public (almost 70 percent) believes that the news media do not deal fairly with all sides, that they favor some groups over others. And that percentage has been growing.[11]

Some critics place the blame for this perceived bias on the news industry itself.[12] They contend that the news giants do not put as many resources into investigating and reporting wrongdoing by companies with which they do business as they do into investigating and reporting problems that these companies may encounter with the government. They also claim that the media have a tendency to give more favorable treatment to those who are sympathetic to their business orientation than to those who are not.[13] Another frequently heard criticism of the news media, particularly at the state and local levels, is that they are conservative and pro-business and that during election campaigns they give more and better coverage to candidates whose views match their own.

Whether or not these charges are correct, they do raise the issue of how the profit-making orientation of the media affects their capacity to report the news fairly, accurately, and critically. To put it simply, profit-making media must capture and maintain as large an audience as possible. That is how they make money. To attract and maintain such an audience, they must provide a product that people desire; they must please their audience or face the risk of losing their readers, listeners, or viewers. The dilemma they face is how to meet market demands by satisfying their audience and simultaneously fulfill their role in a democracy, particularly if the majority of people do not desire much information about, or critical evaluation of, politics and government.

For the most part, the news media have attempted to resolve this dilemma by making the news entertaining. They emphasize action rather than ideas, politics rather than policy, people rather than institutions. They focus on conflict, drama, and the human dimension because these aspects of the news spark public interest. Moreover, in the interests of saving time and money, valuable commodities in a private-enterprise system, they may become overly dependent on a few sources and fail to devote sufficient resources to verifying the information they receive, much less providing alternate perspectives. These practices, conditioned by economic pressures, may undercut the democratic process, making the news media imperfect instruments for performing their critical educational and informational roles.

A BRIEF HISTORY OF THE NEWS MEDIA

The tension between the media's democratic goals and economic needs is apparent in the history of the news media in the United States—a history marked by professional change, economic competition, and technological advances.

Newspapers

In 1690 Benjamin Harris of Boston published what many experts consider the first newspaper in North America: *Publick Occurrences, Both Foreign and Domestick*. Only one issue was printed, however. The paper contained news that colonial authorities viewed as offensive, so Harris was barred from publishing it again. The next newspaper, the *Boston News-Letter*, was a little more successful. Its content was cleared by the colonial government but was dull and inoffensive. Several newspapers that followed the *News-Letter* also contained "safe" news. James Franklin changed all this in 1721, when he began the *New England Courant*. Printed without government approval, Franklin's paper was critical of the colonial authorities. They responded to the negative publicity by obtaining a court order forbidding James Franklin from publishing the *Courant* without their approval. To evade the order, he named his younger brother Benjamin as the paper's official publisher. In 1729 Benjamin Franklin left Boston, moved to Philadelphia, and took over the *Pennsylvania Gazette*, which became the best and most profitable newspaper in the colonies.

During the Revolutionary War, newspapers became more numerous and politically polarized. Most supported the revolution and became important sources of propaganda, reprinting many revolutionary treatises such as the Declaration of Independence and Thomas Paine's *Common Sense* and *Crisis* papers. The politicization of the press did not end with the war. The debate between the Federalists and the Anti-Federalists was carried on in newspapers. The most eloquent defense of the Constitution, *The Federalist Papers*, was written for publication in newspapers, as were opposing pieces.

The press of this period was not only highly partisan but also shrill, subjective, and argumentative. The primary objective was to convince readers of the merits of a particular position or action, not to report the news objectively. In 1798 a Federalist Congress passed the Sedition Act, which made "false, scandalous, or malicious" articles about the government a crime. Directed at critics of John Adams's administration, the law engendered considerable criticism and was allowed to lapse in 1801 after Thomas Jefferson's Democratic-Republican party gained control of the executive and legislative branches.

Newspapers in the eighteenth century were not aimed at the masses; they were written for the upper class, and their content was primarily business and political news. Their audience and content began to change in the 1830s, when technological improvements, growth in literacy, and the movement toward greater public involvement in the democratic process all contributed to the development of the penny press—newspapers that sold for a penny. These papers were oriented toward the less prosperous members of society. Benjamin Day began the first of them, the *New York Sun*, in 1833. The *Sun* provided readers with interesting and lively content: local news, human interest stories, crime and violence. It quickly won a large audience and thus was successful in attracting advertisers. Imitators were soon being published.

Not all the newspapers aimed at the general public were sensational. In 1841 Horace Greeley founded the *New York Tribune*. Greeley appealed to the intellect; he also used his paper to promote various causes and crusades. In 1851 Henry Raymond founded a similar paper, the *New York Times*.

The penny press revolutionized American journalism. Newspapers began to rely on advertising rather than on subscription revenue as their primary source of income. To attract advertisers, they had to attract a large number of readers. To attract readers, the content had to be different and eye-catching. As a result, there was a change in what was reported and how it was reported.

Prior to the development of the penny press, news was rarely "new"; many stories were weeks old before they appeared in most newspapers and were simply rewritten or reprinted from other newspapers. With more newspapers aimed at a general readership, a higher premium was put on gathering

Ida Tarbell: Respectable Muckraker

Between 1902 and 1912, a new breed of educated, socially conscious journalists—which Theodore Roosevelt called "muckrakers"—were busy exposing business abuses and government corruption. Among them was a tall, spare woman named Ida Minerva Tarbell.

Born in 1857, Ida Tarbell grew up in the midst of America's first oil boom near her home in northwestern Pennsylvania. Her father, Franklin, did well selling huge wooden oil-storage barrels, and with the money he made, he went into the oil-drilling business for himself.

With the crash of 1872, Tarbell's fortunes declined. The railroads raised their shipping rates sharply to the independent producers, while granting huge rebates to the South Improvement Company, a front for John D. Rockefeller's notorious Standard Oil Company. The financial crunch forced many independent producers to sell out or face ruin. Quickly, Standard Oil gained a near monopoly over oil production in the state.

Ida Tarbell graduated from Allegheny College, the only woman in her class, in 1880. By 1883 she was writing for a popular magazine, *The Chatauquan*. Her articles were noted by S. S. McClure, who was starting a new magazine; he solicited contributions and later gave her a job. After publishing a series of articles on the life of Abraham Lincoln, Tarbell turned her attention to the oil industry. She discovered and exposed secret agreements between the railroads and Standard Oil that resulted in the failure of many independent producers, including her father.

Her exposé appeared in November of 1902

Ida M. Tarbell Collection/ Pelletier Library

and ran for twenty-four months. (When an executive of a Rockefeller-controlled bank had threatened to ruin *McClure's* if she persisted, Tarbell had replied, "Well, I am sorry, but of course that makes no difference to me.")

Public reaction to Tarbell's work forced President Roosevelt to renew his trust-busting efforts. In 1906, the government sued Standard Oil under the Sherman Antitrust Act of 1890. Standard lost in court, lost again on appeal, and lost for good in the Supreme Court in 1911. The oil trust was finally dismantled, but Tarbell's work did not help her ruined family. Her father died in 1905, and her brother later collapsed mentally and physically.

In 1906 Tarbell joined another muckraker, Lincoln Steffens, at the reformist *American Magazine*, and she became a freelance journalist after 1915. She died in 1944.

news quickly and reporting it in an exciting, easy-to-read manner. The invention of the telegraph helped, making it possible for an emerging Washington press corps to communicate news about government to the entire country.

During the Civil War, military censorship was first introduced. In areas under Union control, information potentially helpful to the Confederacy was restricted. The Civil War also resulted in a change in journalistic style. The "inverted pyramid" form of reporting was introduced. A story was quickly summarized in the lead paragraph, and details were presented in the following paragraphs; so if the telegraph lines went dead, the most important information (who, what, where, when, why, and how) still got through.

A FEW THINGS THE VERSATILE YELLOW KID MIGHT DO FOR A LIVING.

The term yellow journalism *comes from the comic strip "The Yellow Kid," which first appeared in Pulitzer's* New York World *in 1986. As shown here, the Kid's night-shirt was colored yellow. His adventures in rough streets and back alleys made the comic strip an instant hit—which sparked a bidding war between Pulitzer and his rival, William Randolph Hearst. The comic strip's popularity lasted a few years, while the competition among newspapers continues to be waged.*

Between 1850 and 1900, as the population grew, the number of daily newspapers grew from 254 to 2,226, and circulation rose from 758,000 to 15,102,000. Sensationalism and aggressive crusading began to dominate the news, giving rise to **yellow journalism**, a term that had its origin in a battle for the rights to a popular comic strip, "The Yellow Kid."

Joseph Pulitzer, who bought the *New York World* in 1883 and built its circulation into the largest in America, profited from yellow journalism. Pulitzer's main audience was the large immigrant class in New York. His paper's

"Extra" editions of Hearst's New York Journal *carried banner headlines about the sinking of the battleship* Maine. *The paper sensationalized the story and even offered a reward of $50,000 for the identity of the perpetrators. Publicity generated by this so-called yellow journalism helped lead to the Spanish-American War and to greater United States influence in the hemisphere.*

stories on crime and sex, stunts like sending a reporter around the world, and crusades against the horrible conditions of sweatshops and tenements became the prototype for other large-circulation dailies such as William Randolph Hearst's *New York Journal*. Hearst and the *Journal* are most famous for their involvement in the Spanish-American War. Before the start of the hostilities, Hearst deliberately stirred up public sentiment in support of the war; once the war broke out, he covered it aggressively and sensationally.

One of the byproducts of this era was an expansion of other types of

This cartoon by Leon Barritt depicts Pulitzer and Hearst's rivalry over "The Yellow Kid" and even war. Although they are seen grappling over children's blocks, the fight was real. One result of such competition among the media is that they pander to the interests of the largest audience, rather than engaging readers in informative discussions of important issues.

THE BIG TYPE WAR OF THE YELLOW KIDS.

Largest Circulation Daily Newspapers*	
Wall Street Journal	1,795,206
USA Today	1,506,708
Los Angeles Times	1,146,631
New York Times	1,145,890
Washington Post	802,059
Newsday (N.Y.)	777,129
New York Daily News	758,358
Chicago Tribune	724,257
Detroit Free Press	580,372
San Francisco Chronicle	556,765

* Circulation as of September 1992.

SOURCE: *Editor and Publisher's International Yearbook*, 1993.

crusading journalism. Magazines were especially active in publishing articles aimed at reforming big business and other enemies of the masses. Ida Tarbell exposed the unfair business practices of John D. Rockefeller and the Standard Oil Company, and Lincoln Steffens revealed corruption in several city and state governments. Theodore Roosevelt called such writers "muckrakers" and used this reform movement to advance his own political ambitions.

This period also saw the rise of the *New York Times* as a paper of record. Operating on the view that news is not entertainment but valuable public information, the *Times* adopted the motto "All the news that's fit to print." Its coverage of World War I demonstrated the paper's strengths. It published the entire texts of important speeches and documents as well as detailed military news.

In the early 1900s the number of daily newspapers started to decline. The economics of publishing, which made it essential to achieve lower unit costs and higher advertising revenues by increasing circulation, caused many newspapers to fold or merge with competitors. The result has been less competition and more consolidation along with the growth of newspaper chains. Only four daily newspapers today have circulations over 1 million. (See the box above listing the dailies with the largest circulation.)

One recent development has been the growth of national newspapers such as the *Wall Street Journal* and *U.S.A. Today* and the national and regional distribution of such large metropolitan dailies as the *New York Times*, *Los Angeles Times*, *Washington Post*, and *Miami Herald*. These newspapers feature a larger amount of national and international news than do most other local, city-oriented papers. They also bring more in-depth discussion of policy issues to those who want it.

Electronic Media

Radio The electronic media have developed steadily during the twentieth century. Radio was the principal electronic medium from the 1920s to the 1950s.

In his famous fireside chats on radio, President Franklin Roosevelt reached millions of listeners and built support for his policies and programs. A president's role as "Communicator-in-Chief" has become critical, as more and more citizens get their information from electronic media rather than from the printed press.

Dominated by the major networks, it broadcast entertainment and news programs to a national audience. The first radio station began operating in 1920. Radio stations did not provide regular news coverage, but they excelled at covering special events as they were happening. The 1924 presidential election was the first to be reported on radio; the conventions, major speeches, and election returns were broadcast live that year. During the 1928 election, both presidential candidates (Herbert Hoover and Alfred E. Smith) spent campaign funds on radio advertising.

Radio soon became the most important medium for reporting fast-breaking news stories. The speed with which newspapers could bring current events to readers was limited by the need to print and deliver papers. A radio station could have a story on the air in a matter of minutes. Politicians soon became aware of the power of radio to transmit ideas. Franklin Roosevelt was the first to use radio to appeal directly to the people and mobilize support for a political agenda. His "fireside chats" fostered a personal relationship between the president and the public, and his technique became the model for future presidents.

Radio also became extremely effective at reporting foreign news. In addition to being faster than print journalism, radio had the advantage of being able to convey the excitement and color of the scene. Correspondents like H. V. Kaltenborn and Edward R. Murrow provided excellent coverage of the events that led to World War II. They and other correspondents reported regularly from battlefields in Europe and Asia.

Radio lost its national audience to television in the 1950s but did not fade away. Instead, stations broadcast specialized programming aimed at smaller, local audiences. Today there are more radio stations operating than there were in radio's "glory days" in the 1940s,[14] and radio remains a favorite communications medium of candidates seeking public office. Relatively cheap and accessible, it enables them to target their messages to the smaller but homogeneous audiences that listen to different types of radio stations. President Reagan used radio effectively to deliver policy statements on Saturday, a generally slow news day. Presidents Bush and Clinton have continued this practice. Radio is also useful for keeping commuters informed of fast-breaking events and national news.

Television   After World War II, television transformed the American public into a large viewing audience. The percentage of homes with television sets in the United States rose quickly. In 1950, 9 percent of the households in the United States had televisions; ten years later, that percentage had grown to 87; by 1980, it had reached 98 percent. Today almost 80 percent of American households have at least *two* television sets. Similarly, the average length of time that the television set is turned on each day has risen from approximately 4½ hours in 1950 to about 7 hours today (see Figure 11-1).

As television dominated the American media, three networks—ABC, CBS, and NBC—dominated television. During this formative stage, most of the commercial stations in the United States were affiliated with one of these three networks. The networks provided them with the bulk of their entertainment programming and national news.

Television featured daily newscasts almost from the outset, but its impact was initially felt more strongly through its coverage of special events. For example, televised coverage of the Senate hearings on organized crime in 1950–1951 had a dramatic impact. Public awareness of organized crime increased, and the chairman of the committee that conducted the inquiry, Senator Estes Kefauver of Tennessee, became a national hero and a presidential candidate as a result of his television exposure. Kefauver's rise to prominence demonstrated the potential of television as a vehicle for increasing name recognition and enhancing personal image. It soon became a major medium through which campaigns were directed and elections observed.

Figure 11-1   *Households with radios, televisions, cable television, and VCRs, 1930–1992.* SOURCE: *Samuel Kernell,* Going Public, *2nd ed. (Washington, D.C.: Congressional Quarterly, 1993), 108; updated by authors. Reprinted by permission of Congressional Quarterly, Inc. Data for 1991 and 1992 from* Statistical Abstract of the United States *(Washington, D.C., 1993), 561.*

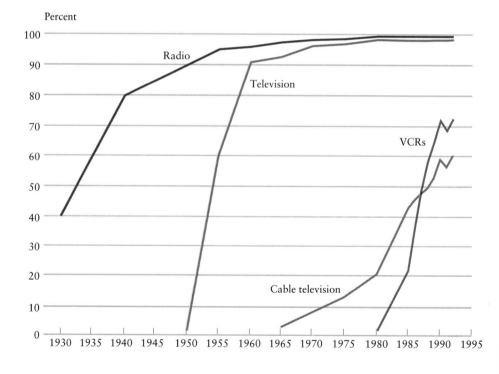

The effect of television was felt as early as the 1952 presidential election. The most important news event of that campaign was a speech by General Dwight Eisenhower's running mate, Richard Nixon. Accused of obtaining secret campaign funds in exchange for political favors, Nixon defended himself in a television address. He denied accepting contributions for personal use, accused the Democratic administration of being soft on communism, criticized his campaign opponents, and vowed that he would never force his children to give up their dog, Checkers, who had been given to the Nixons by political supporters. The emotion of the speech, and particularly the reference to Checkers, generated a favorable public reaction, ended discussion of the campaign funds, and kept Nixon on the Republican ticket.

Paid television advertising by the political parties also first appeared in the 1952 election. The televised marketing of candidates was to revolutionize the electoral process, particularly the strategy and tactics of the campaign and the informal qualifications for candidacy. It enabled candidates to craft their own image and challenge their opponents'.

In the next several years television's power to convey images was demonstrated repeatedly. In 1954 it contributed greatly to the downfall of Senator Joseph McCarthy, who had made a name for himself by charging that communists had infiltrated the government. During eight weeks of televised hearings by McCarthy's committee into possible communist influence in the Army, the public was able to view and evaluate the senator's unsubstantiated charges and browbeating of witnesses and others who denied his allegations.

Another example of the power of television came during the four presidential debates held in 1960 between Senator John F. Kennedy and Vice President Richard M. Nixon, particularly the first debate. In that confrontation, the vice president appeared pallid; the color of his suit blended into the background; he seemed to need a shave; and he shifted uneasily in his seat. He did

In the first televised presidential debate, Senator John Kennedy (left) *took the offensive, gesturing, speaking quickly, spouting statistics, and pledging to "get the country moving again." The camera caught the qualities that people sought in a president— strength, knowledge, and determination; in contrast, it revealed a cold, distant, nervous Richard Nixon* (right). *The debates vastly improved Kennedy's public image and contributed to his victory in 1960.*

Stanley Tretick/SYGMA

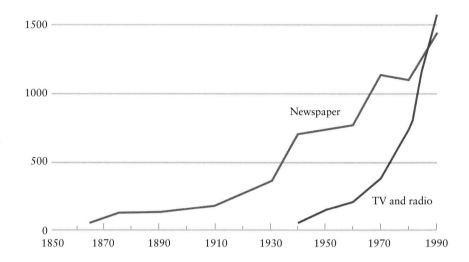

Number

Figure 11-2 *Growth of Washington press corps, 1864–1990.* SOURCE: *Samuel Kernell,* Going Public, *2nd ed. (Washington, D.C.: Congressional Quarterly, 1993), 69. Reprinted by permission of Congressional Quarterly, Inc.*

not look nearly as good as he sounded. Senator Kennedy, in contrast, appeared fresh; his clothes made him stand out; and his facial expressions and gestures came across well on television. Those who heard the debate but did not see it judged Nixon the winner. Those who saw the debate were more impressed by Kennedy. This television exposure—of both candidates—clearly contributed to Kennedy's victory.

The visual medium also increased support for the civil rights movement. The 1963 protest staged in Birmingham, Alabama, by Dr. Martin Luther King, Jr., and the reaction to it by the white police—attack dogs, water cannons, and cattle prods—created unforgettable images for television viewers. For much of the public, television provided the evidence that justified the struggle of the civil rights advocates.

The decade of the 1960s also saw the increasing importance of television network news and the growth of a large Washington press corps (see Figure 11-2). In 1948, NBC and CBS began airing 15-minute newscasts. By 1963, the national news was extended to a half-hour. Since that year, the majority of Americans have cited television as their principal and most believable source of news and have depended on it heavily for information on politics and government news (see Table 11-1).[15]

The Vietnam War demonstrated the impact of television news. It was the first "living-room war." Nightly pictures of the pain and suffering of the victims of the war, including American military casualties, and persistent, critical evaluations of the progress of the war by correspondents in the field of operations had a powerful effect on the public's conscience and helped turn national sentiment against the war.

Television affected the print media as well. Since television reports news at or close to the time it happens, newspapers and magazines had to supplement

TABLE 11-1

Use and Trustworthiness of Media, 1963–1994 (percent)

	1963	1976	1978	1982	1986	1988	1990	1992	1993	1994
Source of most news*										
Television	55	64	67	64	66	65	69	69	67	64
Newspapers	53	49	49	44	36	42	43	43	41	42
Radio	29	19	20	18	14	14	15	16	20	19
Magazines	6	7	5	6	4	4	3	4	3	4
People	4	5	5	4	4	5	7	6	3	3
Most believable†										
Television	36	51	47	53	55	49	54	56	69‡	—
Newspapers	24	22	23	22	21	26	22	22	26	—
Radio	12	7	9	6	6	7	7	7	—	—
Magazines	10	9	9	8	7	5	4	4	—	—
Don't know/no answer	18	11	12	11	12	13	13	12	—	—

* Question: "First, I'd like to ask you where you usually get most of your news about what's going on in the world today—from the newspapers or radio or television or magazines or talking to people or where?" (More than one answer permitted.)

† Question: "If you got conflicting or different reports of the same news story from radio, television, the magazines, and the newspapers, which of the four versions would you be most inclined to believe—the one on the radio or television or magazines or newspapers?" (Only one answer permitted.)

‡ Question: "How much do you feel you can trust the news media?" Percentages indicate respondents who trust the media a great deal.

SOURCE: "America's Watching: Public Attitudes Toward Television 1993" (New York: The Network Television Association and the National Association of Broadcasters, 1993), 29, 31. Reprinted from Harold W. Stanley and Richard G. Niemi, *Vital Statistics on American Politics* (Washington, D.C.: Congressional Quarterly, 1994), 74. Reprinted by permission of Congressional Quarterly, Inc. Updated by authors with data from Times-Mirror Center for People and the Press, June 1993 and January 1994.

their reporting with additional coverage and commentary in order to provide a product that people would want to buy. They also had to find news by investigating activities and events. The *Washington Post*'s reporting of the Watergate scandals during 1972 and 1973 is a good example of the power and profitability of the investigative journalism that grew out of changing media roles—and of the increasing attempt by officials to manipulate news media and the increasing dependence of media on government for information.

The *Post* reported that White House aides had broken into the Democratic National Committee headquarters at the Watergate complex and that President Nixon had participated in a cover-up of the attempted burglary. Attacked by high officials including the president and the vice president, the *Post* did not abandon the story. Its revelations eventually prompted a congressional investigation, the hiring of a special prosecutor, and ultimately the resignation of President Nixon. *Post* reporters Bob Woodward and Carl Bernstein helped usher in a new era of investigative reporting.

The Vietnam War and Watergate were turning points in the relationship among the press, the government, and the public. The government accused the press of helping the enemy with its critical coverage. The press accused the government of withholding and falsifying information in order to maintain support for the war and demonstrate that it was being won. The credibility gap

AP/Wide World Photos

The war in Vietnam was the first one brought into the living rooms of most Americans. Media coverage of the war—especially the televised images of death, destruction, and incredible human suffering—helped turn public opinion against United States involvement in Vietnam. Here is one of the most famous photographs of any war, captioned "Terror of War" (June 8, 1972): Children flee in panic from an air strike in which napalm bombs were dropped. The girl in the center of the picture runs naked, having ripped off her burning clothes.

between news media and government reached its height during the late 1960s and early 1970s.

Since that time the media and government have continued to be accused of deceiving the American people. Government has been accused of covering up wrongdoing, releasing only favorable news, and manipulating events by scripting and orchestrating presidential activities such as trips and speeches. The media have been accused of being overly negative, biased, and trivial, of being obsessed with personalities at the expense of policies, and of entertaining more than informing.

In fact, some observers allege that a national media elite has evolved at the major networks, news services, and newspapers. A study conducted in 1979 and 1980 by S. Robert Lichter, Stanley Rothman, and Linda Lichter found that a media elite can be clearly distinguished from mainstream America. The researchers described that elite in the following way:

The media elite are a homogeneous and cosmopolitan group, who were raised at some distance from the social and cultural traditions of small-town middle America. Drawn mainly from big cities in the northeast and north central states, their parents tended to be well off, highly educated members of the upper middle class. Most have moved away from any religious heritage, and very few are regular churchgoers. In short, the typical leading journalist is the very model of the modern eastern urbanite.[16]

Moreover, they found the elite to be liberal in ideological perspective and Democratic in partisan allegiance and voting behavior. They concluded that this

R. Mims/SYGMA

The power and impact of the media were clearly illustrated during the Watergate affair. Two young reporters for the Washington Post, *Carl Bernstein* (left) *and Bob Woodward, revealed the White House involvement in the burglary of the Democratic National Committee, the coverup of that involvement, and the dirty tricks and illegal activities perpetrated by workers for the 1972 Committee to Re-Elect the President, which they and others abbreviated as CREEP.*

liberal orientation could not help but shape the perspectives of those who report the news.[17]

How liberal members of the media elite actually are, however, is open to question. Journalists who were interviewed for the study just described were not representative of all or even most reporters and correspondents in the United States. But even if they had been—even if most reporters were liberal and Democratic and most owners and editors were conservative and Republican—that would not prove that the news itself is ideological and partisan, much less which ideological and partisan perspectives it favors.

Despite these conflicting views, the vast majority of Americans still believe what they read and see in the media. Moreover, they still regard most media sources favorably but give television the highest marks (see Table 11-2).[18]

Technological Change

Communication satellites, laser fiber optics, and integrated circuits for high-speed transmission of digital images and data have opened up additional channels for communicating the news quickly. The Clinton administration has proposed the development of a communications "superhighway," a voice, video, and data network that can transmit information in a matter of seconds across the country, enabling subscribers to access hundreds of stations and data banks. In several cities there have been experiments with interactive television, which allows viewers to react to what they see and to indicate their opinions by pressing keys on a device attached to the television set.

Technology in the newsroom has changed as well. Video display terminals have replaced typewriters; computerized databases are used to supplement the reporting of conditions and events. In fact, the technology now exists to eliminate newspapers altogether. There are services that deliver the news through

TABLE 11-2

Public Use of Media to Follow Presidential Campaigns, 1952–1992 (percent)

MEDIA	1952	1956	1960	1964	1968	1972	1976	1980	1984	1988	1992
Read newspaper articles about the election											
Regularly			44	40	37	26	28				
Often[a]	39	69	12	14	12	14	17	27	24	—	—
From time to time[b]	40		16	18	19	16	24	29	34	—	—
Once in a great while[c]			7	6	7	4	10	17	19	—	—
No	21	31	21	22	25	40	22	27	23	—	—
Attention paid to newspaper articles about the presidential campaign											
Great deal									8	6	9
Quite a bit									14	12	15
Some									28	22	20
Very little									20	9	6
None									31	52	50
Listen to speeches or discussions on radio											
Good many[d]	34		15	12	12	8	12	14	10	5	7
Several[e]		45	17	23	16	21	20	22	20	10	11
One or two[f]	35		10	12	12	13	16	15	16	17	18
No	30	55	58	52	59	59	52	50	55	69	64
Watched programs about the campaign on television											
Good many[d]	32		47	41	42	33	37	28	25	—	31
Several[e]		74	29	34	34	41	38	37	37	—	39
One or two[f]	19		11	13	13	16	15	22	24	—	19
No	49	26	13	11	11	9	10	13	14	—	11
Attention paid to television news about the presidential campaign											
Great deal									17	15	20
Quite a bit									24	26	29
Some									28	29	28
Very little									11	13	11
None									20	17	13
Read about the campaign in magazines											
Good many[d]	15		12	10	9	7	12	7	7	—	—
Several[e]		31	15	16	12	15	24	19	16	—	—
One or two[f]	26		13	13	15	14	15	12	11	—	—
No	60	69	59	61	64	64	49	62	66	—	—
Attention paid to magazine articles about the presidential campaign											
Great deal									3	3	4
Quite a bit									4	6	7
Some									7	11	10
Very little									2	3	3
None									84	76	77

NOTE: "—" indicates question not asked.   [a] "Quite a lot, pretty much" in 1952; "yes" in 1956; "good many" in 1980–1984.   [b] "Not very much" in 1952; "several" in 1980–1984.   [c] "One or two" in 1980–1984.   [d] "Quite a lot, pretty much" in 1952.   [e] "Yes" in 1956.   [f] "Not very much" in 1952.

SOURCE: National Election Studies codebooks. Center for Political Studies. Institute for Social Research, University of Michigan, Ann Arbor, Mich. Reprinted from Harold W. Stanley and Richard G. Niemi, *Vital Statistics on American Politics* (Washington, D.C.: Congressional Quarterly, 1994), 72–73. Reprinted by permission of Congressional Quarterly, Inc.

Instantaneous news, world-wide, is now a reality. It provides alternate, often superior information to the government's, and it shortens the time for communication and action. (Left) CNN's Peter Arnett reported on the bombing of Iraq from Iraq, and his reports often differed from the "official" version (some accused Arnett of aiding the enemy). (Right) Ongoing C-SPAN coverage of the House of Representatives shows members addressing their constituents in speeches with little if any legislative impact. The camera does not pan the floor of the House, and thus does not reveal members' absence or inattention.

a fiber-optic cable directly to the home or office, allowing the user to read the news, editorials, and other features on a computer screen.

A major change for the general public has been the growth and accessibility of cable television. It began to operate in the early 1950s, largely to improve television reception in areas that had difficulty getting a clear picture. As cable technology became more sophisticated and as more of the country became wired for cable, its potential as a news and entertainment medium has expanded and improved. By the beginning of the 1990s, cable was available in most metropolitan areas and, increasingly, in rural areas as well. By 1992, more than 56 million households were subscribing to a basic cable service.[19] Cable's share of the total television market has grown from 9 percent in 1984 to 21 percent in 1991. Its revenues totaled $20 billion in 1991, compared to $25 billion for the television broadcast industry.[20]

The development of cable has more closely paralleled that of contemporary radio than that of television. Instead of appealing to the broadest possible audience, cable stations engage in what political scientist Austin Ranney describes as "narrowcasting," offering specialized programming designed for special audiences.[21] One cable network, CNN, is exclusively devoted to news. Another, Cable Satellite Public Affairs Network (C-SPAN), deals with public events and government. Both have had a significant impact on the breadth and depth of news coverage.

Cable News Network (CNN), with its 24-hour news service, worldwide news bureaus, and satellite hookups, challenged the near-monopoly on national and international news coverage that ABC, CBS, and NBC formerly enjoyed. With its exclusive focus on news and its capacity to report news as it happens almost anywhere in the world, CNN has become the network that the public and government both depend on for information about fast-breaking developments. Early in the Persian Gulf War, for example, CNN correspondent Peter Arnett in Baghdad reported the first air strikes from his hotel window, and he continued to report from Iraq even though he was censored by authorities.

C-Span regularly televises the official proceedings of Congress, important committee hearings, and news conferences held by the State and Defense Departments as well as the president. Approximately 6 million people watch these activities of government on a regular basis.

In the 1990s the expansion of cable news coverage, the high cost of maintaining foreign news bureaus and foreign correspondents, and shrinking profits prompted ABC, CBS, and NBC to cut back their news operations and reduce the amount of time they devoted to public affairs programming. This change was evident in the limited amount of prime-time coverage given by the three broadcast networks to the Democratic and Republican national conventions in 1992. In contrast, CNN and C-SPAN provided gavel-to-gavel coverage, and public television provided complete evening coverage.

Other developments in the electronic media include the improvement of satellite technology, which is particularly important for extending broad coverage to rural areas not serviced by cable. Low-powered stations that provide specialized programming to local audiences have also expanded.[22]

Not only has the diversity of programs increased, but so has the capacity of viewers to shift quickly from one channel to another by using remote controls. To hold their audiences, particularly during news programming, the networks have speeded up the action, shortened the statements they air by candidates and public officials, and emphasized argumentation and conflict in their on-the-air remarks.

All of these changes have had an impact on politics and government. In the next two sections we examine that impact, describing contemporary media coverage of elections and government and exploring how that coverage affects the events that are reported.

NEWS MEDIA AND POLITICS

Media coverage is not neutral. No coverage can be. What do the news media choose to emphasize and to whom are their stories directed? How do candidates for political office react, and how do they try to shape the news to their advantage? And, finally, what impact does all this have on voters?

The Media Slant

The key to media coverage of political events is **newsworthiness.** This complex concept includes timeliness, importance, conflict, drama, and surprise. To be considered news, an event must have the potential to capture the attention of the public—readers, listeners, and viewers. From the media's perspective, their job is to emphasize those events that have this potential.

What is reported as news is also influenced by factors such as access and convenience. With limited resources, the media have to decide what to cover and how much time to devote to it. The cost of coverage and the importance of the event figure in that decision.

How does the media slant affect coverage? Let's take an electoral campaign as an example. First and foremost, election news must be exciting. Thus, campaigns are reported as if they were sporting contests. Correspondents stress the "horserace" aspects: according to the polls, which of the candidates is winning and losing, who is doing better than expected, who is not doing as well as expected. And they do this at the expense of stories about substantive issues,

When allegations of marital infidelity threatened his presidential campaign, Bill Clinton appeared on "60 Minutes" with wife Hillary. Their appearance— right after the Superbowl and just weeks before the first primary in New Hampshire—let Clinton explain his side of the story to a huge television audience. Although the interview did not satisfy everyone (or even directly address the allegations), it did allow Clinton to get beyond side-issues and continue the campaign. It was damage control at its best.

particularly at the beginning of the primaries and caucuses when horserace stories tend to dominate the evening news (see Table 11-3). As a front-runner emerges, the focus shifts, often to character issues and to campaign controversies.

The media slant on the campaign makes it possible for a candidate who does not get the most votes to receive upbeat coverage anyway. This can happen, for example, if the candidate comes in second when a third- or fourth-place finish was anticipated. Conversely, candidates who do worse than expected suffer adverse publicity that could damage their quest for office. In the 1992 New Hampshire primary, President George Bush's closer-than-expected win over columnist Pat Buchanan captured media attention, as did Governor Bill Clinton's strong second-place finish among the Democratic candidates. Bush's showing hinted at the president's vulnerability in his quest for reelection. Clinton's showing hinted at his strength despite allegations about his character and past personal behavior.

Only the candidates' standings in the polls have greater newsworthiness than their personal characteristics. Stories on candidates' private lives and personalities quickly capture public attention. During the 1980 primaries, coverage of Senator Edward Kennedy often focused on his troubled marriage and his 1969 car accident at Chappaquiddick, in which a young woman died. Before the 1988 primaries, reporters observed Senator Gary Hart spending time with a woman who was not his wife and raised questions about his fidelity, his credibility, and his judgment. In the 1992 primaries, Bill Clinton faced a barrage of questions about his personal life after a supermarket tabloid published a report linking him romantically with a woman who had been a club singer and a local television personality in Little Rock. More than half of the network news stories about Clinton between January 1, 1992, and April 15, 1992, dealt with a character issue.[23]

Such stories, however, also raised questions about the media. In Hart's case, reporters from the *Miami Herald* had hidden themselves outside Hart's Washington townhouse to keep tabs on who entered and left, and when they did so. In Clinton's case, the accusations during the campaign had been made by a single individual who was paid for her story. Other such allegations against Clinton arose in December 1993. Again, they drove substantive issues off the front pages and television screens.

In general, personality issues have been receiving more attention in recent years, and policy issues seem to be receiving less. One reason for this shift has to do with the fact that personal questions are more interesting to more people than are complex and often abstract policy issues. Another reason has to do with the medium of television itself. The average length of a story on the evening news is 45 to 90 seconds, too short a time in which to provide in-depth analysis and barely long enough to hear candidates discuss the issues, much less state their position.[24] Policy issues accounted for less than one-third of all the campaign stories on the evening news programs broadcast by the three major networks in 1992, compared to 40 percent in 1988.[25] There were more stories on the horserace, campaign strategy, and candidate controversies than on policy issues (see Table 11-3). In the print media, however, policy questions received more attention and in-depth treatment.

Does the coverage of the campaign have an ideological bias in addition to its media slant? Many people allege that it does. Losing candidates ritually blame the media for their plight. The Bush campaign went so far as to issue a bumper sticker:

ANNOY THE MEDIA
RE-ELECT BUSH

The candidates had reason for their complaint. On the evening news, both Bush and Clinton received more negative than positive coverage during the nomination process. In the first ten weeks alone, one out of six television news stories on Clinton concerned his alleged marital infidelity, his draft dodging, or some personal conflict of interest.[26] Even during the Republican convention, a period of usually good news for the party's nominee, Bush got more bad

TABLE 11-3

Campaign Topics on the Evening News, 1992 Election Cycle

TOPIC	PRIMARIES (JAN. 1–JUNE 2)	POST-PRIMARY (JUNE 3–AUG. 21)	GENERAL ELECTION (SEPT. 1–NOV. 3)
Horserace standings	270	103	258
Campaign strategy	260	260	239
Candidate controversies	270	203	234
Policy issues	266	278	233

SOURCE: "Battle of the Sound Bites," *Media Monitor* (August/September 1992): 2; "Clinton's the One," *Media Monitor* (November 1992): 3. Published by the Center for Media and Public Affairs, a nonpartisan and nonprofit research organization. Copyright © 1993, CMPA.

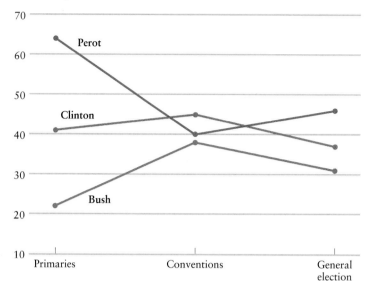

Percent positive

Figure 11-3 *Positive evaluations of the 1992 presidential candidates.* SOURCE: *"Clinton's the One," Media Monitor (November 1992): 5. Published by the Center for Media and Public Affairs, a nonpartisan and nonprofit research organization. Copyright © 1993, CMPA.*

news.[27] And during the 1992 election all three candidates received more negative than positive coverage with Bush getting the worst.[28] Figure 11-3 indicates the percentage of favorable coverage on the evening news that each of the candidates received over the course of the 1992 campaign.

In addition to the spin, the amount of coverage candidates receive during a campaign also varies. Although roughly equal time is given to the two major-party candidates, certain candidates, particularly during the nomination phase of the campaign, have an advantage. Those who are seen as likely winners get more coverage than those who are not. This puts lesser-known candidates in a quandary from which they have trouble escaping. They are not taken seriously and will have difficulty building an organization and raising money until they receive coverage; and they will not receive coverage because they are not seen as serious candidates. Candidates who, by virtue of their personalities, positions, or followers, are newsmakers tend to get the most coverage. The reverends Jesse Jackson and Pat Robertson fit into this category in 1988, as did columnist Pat Buchanan and H. Ross Perot in 1992. Jackson in fact received more coverage on the evening news than did his successful rival for the nomination, Michael Dukakis, before the Iowa caucus and after the first full week of primaries and caucuses in early March, 1988.[29]

Manipulation of the News by Candidates

The media report a campaign as it unfolds, but candidates try to affect the coverage they receive. They do this by scheduling and staging events, releasing information and granting access to reporters, and preparing speeches and responses.

Although face-to-face campaigning is decreasing in importance, the staging of public appearances is not. To accommodate television's need for good visual images, candidates often pose in unusual dress or do unusual things to dramatize their message or appeal. In 1984, for example, Gary Hart, dressed as a woodsman, threw an ax at a target and hit it. This scene was shown on television repeatedly and reinforced Hart's image as vigorous, young, and unorthodox. In a debate during the 1988 Democratic primaries, Governor Bruce Babbitt suddenly stood up to dramatize his call for higher taxes. He asked the other candidates to do the same. None did. Television showed his gesture repeatedly because it was "good video"; Babbitt therefore succeeded in getting his message across. The problem in this case was the message; few people want to pay higher taxes.

When candidates travel from state to state, they frequently get no farther than the airport. They hold a news conference on the tarmac and feel assured that they will appear in the local press and on the local television news that evening. Then they fly off to another staged event.

Campaign organizations control access to the candidate and, to a great extent, information about the candidate. Because of the media's constant need for new information and stories, reporters often turn to the candidates and their staffs for help. An analysis of twenty newspapers carried out by Doris Graber found that during the 1968 campaign the candidates were the main source of more than half of the election stories.[30] A good example of this phenomenon occurred in 1992, when staff from George Bush's campaign and the Republican National Committee provided the media with information about H. Ross Perot's dealings with the government and his investigations of public officials—information that discredited Perot.

In addition to providing information, the candidates influence coverage by what they say and how they say it. From the stump speech to the so-called spontaneous debate, candidates exercise some control over their own destinies. With an eye to the media's emphasis on the new, the unusual, the unpredictable, and even the flub, candidates carefully prepare their speeches, time their announcements, and try to restrain their off-the-cuff remarks. As a result, much of the campaign reads like a script.

Even the responses in debates are rehearsed. Candidates have begun to sound like their ads. They speak in sound bites—very short, catchy statements that are likely to attract media attention, such as George Bush's famous promise, "Read my lips: no new taxes." Ross Perot's much-quoted quip about Washington lobbyists in their $1,000 suits and alligator shoes buying and selling influence is another example of a verbal image enhancing a theme, in Perot's case, a back-to-the-people theme.

Long-winded and seemingly unresponsive answers can have the opposite effect. A case in point was Michael Dukakis's answer in the second presidential debate in 1988 to a reporter's question about whether he would oppose capital punishment for a man who had raped and murdered his wife. Instead of sounding outraged by the thought of such a crime, or even by the question, Dukakis gave a highly restrained and seemingly canned response that focused on the evils of drugs. His answer did nothing to overcome his image as a passionless technocrat who did not care about the real problems of real people.

One technique that candidates used in 1992 to circumvent tough questions by national news reporters was to exhibit themselves in a more friendly environment, a public forum, for example, or an entertainment talk show with audience or listener participation. The general public tends to ask candidates easier and generally more substantive policy questions than do reporters, who are often confrontational, tricky, and interested in the political issues of the

In 1992, to reach larger, less politically involved audiences, presidential candidates appeared on entertainment shows. Here Bill Clinton plays his saxophone for Arsenio Hall (left). This appearance, like one on MTV, contrasted the younger, "swinging" Clinton with the more aloof, stuffy George Bush—a contrast that helped Clinton capture the youth vote.

campaign—an opponent's charge, a character allegation, or a strategic tactical plan.[31] New venues, such as Arsenio Hall's show and MTV, also helped the candidates reach younger audiences that were less likely to tune in to the traditional Sunday news talk shows or view advertising on the commercial television networks.

Campaign Advertising

Candidates increasingly use paid media advertising to convey a message about themselves and their opponents. Since 1984, more than half of presidential campaign budgets have been spent on media advertising, with television receiving the bulk of the expenditures. The objectives of media advertising are (1) to gain recognition for a candidate and (2) to educate voters about why they should support one person against the others. To achieve these objectives, a desirable image must be established and reinforced. Essential to this image are such desirable traits as competence, experience, predictability, and empathy. The goal is to portray a person who knows what he or she believes and who stands up for those convictions.

Image creation cuts two ways. Television advertisements can be created to show that a candidate has positive traits or that an opponent lacks them. Advertising of the latter type is called **negative advertising**. One of the most famous negative ads was produced by the Democrats in 1964. Trying to paint Senator Barry Goldwater as trigger-happy and potentially irresponsible with nuclear weapons, the ad showed a young girl counting softly as she pulled the petals from a daisy in a field. While the camera focused on the girl, an ominous-sounding announcer began counting backward from ten. When he reached zero, a nuclear explosion caused the girl to disappear in a mushroom cloud. The implication was clear: Lyndon Johnson understood the need for peace; with Goldwater, there might be nuclear war.

With the increasing emphasis placed on personal factors, negative advertising has grown in quantity and importance in recent years—so much so that voters today find themselves trying to decide which candidate is the lesser of two evils. The Republicans ran notably negative advertising in the 1988 presidential election campaign (see the box on page 395). In 1992 George Bush's advertising again raised questions, this time about Bill Clinton's trustworthiness, his record in Arkansas, and his experience and qualifications for president. Clinton was quick to respond to these negative ads. Both he and Bush used 30- and 60-second advertisements to reinforce their campaign themes.

The most interesting innovation in the 1992 campaign was the 30-minute "infomercial" used by Ross Perot. Seated at a desk with a pointer and computer-made graphics, Perot talked in a no-nonsense manner about the economic and political problems facing the United States and his determination to do something about them. These commercials reinforced Perot's homespun image as a straight-talking country boy with none of the veneer and polish of slick politicians and Washington insiders. Perot also used a free 800 telephone number to solicit volunteers, a device pioneered by Jerry Brown during his quest for the Democratic nomination in the spring of 1992.

The Impact of the Media on Politics

With all the effort and energy that are put into news coverage and the candidates' media responses, one would think that the media have a significant impact on the outcome of elections. This is debatable, however. As we have seen, attitudes toward the parties and their candidates remain remarkably stable over a voter's lifetime. That stability limits but does not eliminate the media's effect on partisan voters.

Another limiting factor is the process of self-selection by readers and viewers. People tend to seek support for their own views in what they see or read. To maintain the consistency of their attitudes, they tend to filter out information that could challenge their views: they may deny its truthfulness, interpret it in a convenient way, or completely avoid exposure to it. In fact, many people are not exposed to media coverage of campaigns at all. As indicated in Table 11-2 (see page 386), approximately one-fourth of the voting-age population does not regularly read newspaper articles or watch television programs about presidential campaigns.

From the perspective of the candidates, one of the benefits of television and radio advertisements is that they are difficult to avoid. In addition, the more advertisements are repeated, the more likely they are to be recalled. The decline in partisanship, the emphasis on personality, and the importance of visual imagery have increased the impact of the media, particularly television, on candidates and voters.

In general, during a campaign the media affect voters' awareness and impressions of candidates more than they influence their political attitudes or change their opinions on major issues. They may, however, elevate the importance of certain issues through the attention they devote to them. In 1988, for example, the extensive coverage given to illegal drug use forced candidates to develop and publicize strategies to deal with this problem; in 1992, it was job layoffs in many industries that prompted the candidates to come up with plans to stimulate the economy and create new jobs. By setting the agenda for discussion, the media are able to influence the criteria that voters use to evaluate candidates and decide for whom they will vote.

In 1988 George Bush attacked Michael Dukakis for his positions on defense, the environment, and crime. One of his hardest-hitting commercials featured a Massachusetts prison furlough program that Dukakis had supported as governor. The ad showed tough-looking inmates in prison garb walking through a revolving door from prison to freedom and back to prison again. It suggested that Dukakis was soft on crime. An even more sensational spot with racial overtones, sponsored by a PAC that was supporting Bush, showed a picture of Willie Horton, an African-American male who had stabbed a man and raped his female companion, both Caucasian, while on a furlough from a Massachusetts prison. Amid gruesome commentary about Horton's criminal acts, the ad contrasted the positions of Dukakis and Bush on crime—much to Dukakis's disadvantage.

The extent of the negative advertising by the Bush campaign and by groups that supported Bush's candidacy led Dukakis to run antinegative ads about Bush's negative advertising. In one, the governor is seen sitting in front of a television showing a Bush commercial that accused Dukakis of being against virtually every new weapons system for the military. An angry Dukakis turns off the set and says: "I'm fed up with it. Haven't seen anything like it in twenty-five years of public life. George Bush's negative TV ads: distorting my record, full of lies, and he knows it."

To counteract Bush's charges in the wimp/warlord debate, Dukakis made another strategic mistake. His appearance in campaign commercials

Wide World Photos, Inc.

wearing a huge helmet and perched atop an enormous tank was more comical than commanding, as most voters noticed.

The negative advertising of the GOP 1988 presidential campaign, while effective in achieving its political objectives, touched off a storm of protest about negative campaigning in general and the Bush campaign in particular. This criticism tempered the political climate in the 1992 presidential election. Although the candidates criticized their opponents, their ads did not go for the same emotional impact that they had four years earlier.

SOURCE: George C. Edwards III and Stephen J. Wayne, *Presidential Leadership: Politics and Policy Making*, 2nd ed. (New York: St. Martin's Press, 1990), 70.

The media also affect what the candidates may do if elected. Clinton's adherence to his economic stimulus program at the beginning of his presidency in spite of economic recovery, the need for deficit reduction, and Republican opposition to his plan indicates how much the publicity given his campaign promise to generate new jobs had shaped his administration's policy agenda.

The media are more influential at the beginning of the electoral process, when people have relatively little knowledge about the candidates and their positions, than at the end. Especially in presidential elections, the disproportionate coverage given to the candidates in the first contests can be crucial to their success in winning the nomination. In 1988 two states, Iowa and New Hampshire, with just 3 percent of the population, received 34 percent of the coverage on the networks' evening news.[32] In 1992 there were even more stories on New Hampshire than in 1988, although there were fewer on Iowa because it was not closely contested in either party.[33]

The media seem to have a greater impact on public perceptions when the candidates are not well known. In 1992 the favorable coverage given to H. Ross Perot's independent candidacy helped propel Perot to national prominence and buoyed his political movement. Once he surged into the lead in national public opinion polls, however, negative stories about his past business dealings, his investigation of public officials, and his failure to address substantive policy issues raised questions about his presidential capabilities, undermined his public support, and led to his temporary withdrawal from the campaign. His return in October was not marked by as much negative press, in part because he was seen by the media as unelectable.

By directing attention to the contests and to the contestants, the media may affect voter turnout. By emphasizing certain policy issues and personal characteristics, they frame discussion and can influence voting. The media themselves become participants in the campaign by focusing attention on certain issues, evaluating the candidates and their campaigns, and reporting public opinion and forecasting the results. In this way they influence the events that they report on.

The media have also affected the political parties by becoming the principal vehicle through which campaigns are communicated. Voters no longer need to turn to their parties for information about candidates. Conversely, candidates gain independence from party organizations by mounting direct media appeals, although in the process they increase their dependence on fundraisers, media consultants, and political action committees.

Finally, the media shape the environment for governing. Candidates who emphasize their leadership capabilities and media that focus on these qualities create expectations that may be difficult to achieve. Telegenic candidates, those who look good on television, are expected to be telegenic leaders, to use the style of campaigning that got them into office to stay in office. Moreover, they are expected to perform their official duties in full public view. Behind-the-scenes negotiation, quiet diplomacy, confidential communications—all necessary for effective government—are more difficult to achieve today when the media see it as their responsibility to report on the politics and process of policy making as well as the policy itself.

Even the personal lives of government officials are subject to considerable scrutiny by the media, and the highest ethical standards are applied to those in the most powerful positions. All of this has made government more open and visible, and governing a much more public endeavor.

NEWS MEDIA AND GOVERNMENT

Coverage of government officials and policies by the news media does not end with the election. Often the news is an important factor in shaping debates over public policy. The media influence the national policy agenda by identifying substantive policy problems or concerns about how the government is functioning and how public officials are behaving. Reporting these problems generates pressure for public officials to deal with them.

As with election coverage, certain journalistic conventions shape what is reported and how it is presented. National news is usually brief and simple, dramatic and thematic, and it often has a human interest component. The focus on government activities centers on people rather than on institutions or policy, partly because the issues and operations of government are so complex that they are difficult to explain in a news story. Little background or contextual information is provided, particularly by the electronic media. Instead, the personal dimensions of the story are emphasized. The personalities and actions of those who were involved in the Iran-contra affair were more interesting to the American public than were the confusing and twisted financial and arms sale networks, the place of covert actions in the nation's history, or even the constitutional issues raised by the investigation and final report.

News coverage often stresses the style and strategy employed by government officials to pass or defeat a particular piece of legislation, rather than the effect the policy might have on the country. This variation of horserace journalism commonly appears in government coverage. Issues are shown as arguments between two sides: one side gives its view, the other gives its response. Congressional votes are portrayed as either wins or losses for the president; conflicts within agencies or committees are seen as pluses or minuses for the party in power. The media described the debate and division over President Clinton's health-care proposal as a tug of war among those affected—business, labor, health-care groups, members of Congress, and the administration.

In their watchdog role, the media also emphasize information and events that are critical of government and those who lead. Bad news is almost always reported; good news may not be.

Coverage of the President

In their coverage of the national government, the media focus on the presidency. One media watcher found that ABC, CBS, and NBC devoted an average of 7½ hours per month to the presidency, compared to an hour for Congress and a half-hour for the Supreme Court.[34] The presidency receives so much attention because the president is seen as the principal initiator and prime mover, as the head of the government and the state, and as a chieftain with multiple roles, all deserving attention. Moreover, the presidency provides a "handle" for evaluating the many facets of government. The president personifies the government, at least in the view of the media.

The amount of coverage of the rest of the executive branch varies. Certain cabinet secretaries and departments (State, Defense, Justice, Treasury) are given more attention than others because the problems they deal with and the policies they implement have more important national consequences. The bureaucracy that actually implements policies is given even less attention, except for instances of fraud, waste, and abuse. However, specialized media, such as trade journals and newsletters, concentrate on specific areas of policy and on the congressional committees and executive agencies that deal with them. Directed toward (and frequently published by) interest groups, these publications provide in-depth coverage for those who are most affected by these policies.

The media's focus on the president naturally produces incentives for an administration to try to shape the coverage it receives. Presidents want to place their administration in a favorable light and build support for their policies. They may also want to use the media to communicate with Congress and with foreign leaders without having to go through formal channels such as submitting a presidential message to Congress or calling in the ambassador of another country to deliver an official letter about the United States' position on an issue of mutual concern.

The president has many tools for "managing" the news. For example, the release of news may be timed to make the administration look good. If good

Before television, print reporters—almost all male—would meet with the president for an "off the record" give and take, as in this photo of President Truman meeting the press in Hawaii (top). The general rule was that reporters could quote the president only with his permission—which gave presidents more control and let them use press conferences to send up trial balloons. Television changed this. Beginning in the Eisenhower administration (bottom), transcripts of a press conference have been released to reporters; and, since the Kennedy administration, the conferences have been broadcast live.

U.S. Navy/Courtesy Harry S Truman Library

Courtesy Dwight D. Eisenhower Library

President Reagan points to his ear and indicates that he cannot hear the questions shouted by reporters as he walks to his helicopter. Reagan avoided questions that he did not wish to answer, which gave his administration more control over its media agenda. Presidents who reply to all inquiries often step on their administration's own stories.

news is released, it is likely to be the only information made available by the administration. If bad news must be released, other announcements may also be made in an attempt to smother it; and if possible, it is made public over the weekend, when less attention will be paid to it. The general rule is that good news is announced by the president and bad news by others, often the White House press secretary or a cabinet official. The White House can also affect what the media report. With limited resources to discover presidential news and limited time to air it, reporters tend to rely on the pictures and stories made available to them by the White House.

Presidents may use other tactics to avoid commenting on unpleasant topics. When Ronald Reagan left for a trip that was covered by the media, the helicopter that took him to his plane, Air Force One, would remain running while the president walked to and from it. Reporters would shout questions, and if the president did not wish to answer them, he would point to the helicopter and indicate that he could not hear what was being said. Facilities for press conferences were also arranged so that the president would not have to walk past reporters after a conference was over; he simply turned around and left out a back way, thus avoiding further questioning.

The White House also provides services for the press corps that may help shape the news. These include briefings, interviews, off-the-record background sessions, photo opportunities, travel arrangements, and handouts and other press releases. The Clinton administration has been particularly adept at feeding news to reporters. Their three press briefings a day not only present the president's perspective but give reporters stories, keep them busy, and limit their time to pursue other leads. The media depend heavily on these services, especially when the president is away from Washington and their access to other decision makers is extremely limited. One of the reasons that President Bush chose to meet Soviet president Mikhail S. Gorbachev at sea for their first summit meeting was that media coverage could be controlled more easily.

The media's dependence on government became a subject of some controversy during and after United States' military involvements in Grenada (1983), Panama (1989–1990), and the Persian Gulf (1991). In all three campaigns, the military operations were kept secret and the press was barred from combat areas. A press pool had limited access to the staging areas but only under military supervision. As a result, reporters had to rely on government briefings and supplied films, and some of this information turned out to be incorrect or misleading. Once the media could obtain greater access and more information, various foul-ups came to light, particularly the poor coordination of the Grenada invasion and the overblown success attributed to the Patriot missile defense system during the Gulf war.

In addition to the heavy coverage of presidential activities, the president can usually obtain airtime for speeches and events. As Doris Graber reports,

In August 1964 only 42 percent of the American public supported President Johnson's Vietnam policies. Many questioned his ability to continue to raise men and money for the war. After the president broadcast an explanation, however, these doubts were apparently dispelled; approval ratings of his Vietnam policies rose to a comfortable 72 percent. Similarly, President Nixon's dispatch of troops to Cambodia in April 1970 won a 50 percent approval rating after he explained it on television. Prior to the broadcast, only 7 percent of the public had approved. Favorable ratings for President Jimmy Carter's foreign policy jumped by 34 percentage points, from 22 to 56 percent, after the news media announced that the 1978 Camp David meeting had produced a peace settlement between Egypt and Israel.[35]

Most speeches and events, however, have much less public impact. More typical was the 8 percent increase in President Clinton's approval ratings reported by the Gallup poll following his first message to Congress in February 1993 and a much-publicized trip around the country garnering support for his legislative proposals. His health-care speech in September 1993 also improved his public standing, but failure to follow it with legislation dissipated the support he had gained.

Presidents, however, have to be careful not to appeal to the public too often. Overexposure may reduce the impact of their address, making it seem like an ordinary occurrence rather than a special event.

Another tactic available to the president is to curry favor with reporters. President Bush began his tenure in office by being extremely accessible to the press, in sharp contrast with his predecessor. He held impromptu news conferences, telephoned reporters, and even invited them to the White House for social occasions. Bush apparently believed that if reporters knew him personally they would be more understanding of his motives and actions. Nevertheless, the evaluation of Bush on the television's evening news was more negative than positive during his term in office.[36]

Coverage of Congress

Congress gets much less coverage on television than the president does, but it does receive coverage. Some of this is direct: some committee hearings and floor debates are so important that they are broadcast live on the major radio and television networks. The Senate confirmation hearings of Clarence Thomas for Supreme Court justice in October 1991 and the floor debate in the Senate over the authorization of force in the Persian Gulf in January 1991 are good examples. Other famous congressional hearings that have received live coverage include the investigations of the Iran-contra affair during the Reagan administration, Watergate and related scandals during the Nixon administration, and Senator Joseph McCarthy's hunt for communists in the government during the Eisenhower administration.

In addition to the commercial networks' coverage of major congressional events, cable television has provided gavel-to-gavel coverage of floor debate in the House of Representatives since 1979 and in the Senate since 1986. It has also provided live coverage of selected committee hearings in both houses. Many newspaper reporters as well as radio and television correspondents also have Congress as their "beat." They provide daily reports on the behavior of legislators, the enactment of legislation, and the operation of the legislative process.

The coverage of Congress emphasizes political conflicts between competing parties, philosophies, and personalities. The media tend to stress the divisions within Congress, the difficulties its members have in reaching agreement, and the obstacles to the president's legislative leadership. Because the internal policy-making processes of Congress are complex, slow moving, undramatic, and often unpredictable, the media describe Congress as constantly involved in struggles against itself or against the president.

There is much less emphasis on the substance of policy and its consequences for society. When substantive policy is discussed, it is frequently presented in simplified form and as a divisive political issue. Newspapers and news magazines provide more in-depth coverage of policy issues than the electronic media do, but the most in-depth coverage comes from the specialty press—journals that focus on Congress, such as *Congressional Quarterly* and *Roll Call*, and the newsletters of interest groups.

Within the legislature, coverage tends to focus on the final stages of the lawmaking process and frequently on the final vote that will determine a bill's fate. The formative processes of legislation—the introduction of a bill, subcommittee and committee hearings—are largely ignored, except for controversies over presidential initiatives and investigations by key committees. But even when Congress is inquiring into allegations of abuse and misconduct by public officials, it is likely to be pictured in an unfavorable light. The appearance of Colonel Oliver North before the joint congressional committee that was investigating the Iran-contra affair produced such an effect. North's commanding presence, well-articulated convictions, and persuasiveness in explaining his actions captured the attention and evoked the sympathies of many viewers. Similarly, Attorney General Janet Reno's testimony before the congressional committee investigating the tragedy in Waco, Texas, when federal agents stormed the Branch Davidian compound generated more public approbation for her than for her congressional critics.

In addition to being harsh on Congress as an institution, the media are tough on its members—when they get any coverage at all. The personal foibles and questionable behaviors of members of Congress—the abuse of banking and postal privileges by members of the House of Representatives, for example, the charges of sexual harassment and misconduct made against several sena-

*Media coverage of Congress often emphasizes the person-
alities of public officials, with most of the attention going
to investigations and hearings, presidential involvement in
legislation, and major policy conflicts. (Top) Lt. Col. Oliver North testifies before the committee investigating the
Iran-contra affair. His uniform and his confident, robust
defense made him a hero to many people, and by 1994 he
was a candidate for the Senate from Virginia. (Bottom)
Republican senators Alan Simpson and Orrin Hatch confer during the confirmation hearings of Clarence Thomas
for the Supreme Court. In defending Judge Thomas
against the charges of sexual harassment brought by Anita
Hill, the senators used the hearings to voice and build
support for Bush's nominee and for their own conservative judicial philosophy.*

tors, and the periodic investigations of members of Congress for fraudulent use
of public funds—command attention. The public service, policy positions, and
legislative work of most legislators do not. Only the policy positions of the
leaders of the House and Senate and their role on controversial issues receive
attention in the national media, but even this coverage pales in comparison to
that given to the president.

The local media, however, present a different picture. They report less on
Congress as a whole and more on local representatives, particularly when they
are back in their home districts. This coverage is important to the members
because it conveys to constituents the message that they are being well represented. Local coverage tends to be of the "soft," human interest variety—a

speech to the chamber of commerce, a tour of the state fair, a ceremony at a high school graduation, a ribbon cutting at a senior center financed by federal funds that the member helped obtain. Most of this coverage conveys a favorable image of the member, in sharp contrast to the generally harsh evaluation of Congress as an institution.

The coverage of Congress has affected the legislative process in several fundamental ways. It has made members of Congress more conscious of the media and more eager for media coverage in order to gain recognition, enhance their political influence, and improve their chances for reelection. This desire has changed their behavior. Members of Congress now position themselves to be newsmakers. They grant interviews to reporters, more regularly attend and participate in hearings that the media are likely to cover, use their staffs to issue press releases about their positions and legislative initiatives, and keep the media—particularly the local press back home—informed about their activities. Most of them take advantage of radio and television studios in Congress to record programs for the folks back home. This media-oriented behavior led one student of Congress to conclude that "making news has become a crucial component of making laws."[37]

Media coverage of Congress has affected the institution's behavior as well. It has influenced congressional deliberations by focusing attention on certain issues and events. It has also made the legislative process more difficult by making it more visible: it is hard to compromise in full public view, particularly when television cameras are rolling. Increased visibility may be one of the factors that has contributed to decreased legislative output. Since cable television began gavel-to-gavel congressional coverage, the number of bills enacted into law has declined.

Coverage of the Judiciary

The third branch of government, the judiciary, is often a stranger to the national media, except during controversial hearings such as the confirmation hearings for Clarence Thomas or major trials such as those connected with the Iran-contra affair. The Supreme Court receives only a fraction of the attention received by the president and Congress. Only a few news organizations assign reporters to the Supreme Court on a full-time basis.

There are several reasons for the lack of extensive coverage of the judiciary. The Supreme Court does not welcome attention. Justices rarely give interviews or discuss the decision-making process in which they have been involved. In addition to the problem of access, many judicial decisions are complex. To understand them, one must give them careful consideration, often applying specialized legal knowledge. Only a few major newspapers, networks, and magazines can afford to hire journalists who have this knowledge. Therefore, the initial reports of Supreme Court decisions are often brief descriptions of the majority and minority opinions, the justices who voted on each side, and the implications of the decision. This information is frequently presented in the context of whose interests were benefited or hurt by the Court's judgment.

Reporters who cover the lower courts tend not to be lawyers or students of the law. Their coverage often concentrates on sensational cases rather than on important legal issues and trends. For example, the use of a handgun by *Washington Post* columnist Carl Rowan, a gun control advocate, was front-page news in Washington and other parts of the country, but a speech by former Supreme Court justice Lewis Powell on the constitutionality of handgun bans was given only brief attention.

At the state level, coverage of the judiciary is more common because many judges are elected rather than appointed. And some state courts now permit radio and television coverage of trials, some of which appear on the cable court channel. Moreover, highly publicized events, often involving alleged criminal activity, such as the beating of Rodney King by several Los Angeles policemen or the use of illegal drugs by Mayor Marion Barry of Washington, D.C., gain coverage by virtue of the actions or the people involved.

THE IMPACT OF THE MEDIA ON PUBLIC POLICY

The media affect policy and government in three ways: they shape priorities, they shorten time frames, and they limit options. As noted previously, the media help set the agenda for government. For example, in 1979–1980, through their extensive daily coverage of the Iranian hostage crisis, when diplomats at the American embassy in Teheran were taken hostage by paramilitary guards loyal to the Iranian government, the media kept the problem before the public and thereby heightened the demand for a satisfactory solution. Similarly, the attention given to deficit spending, the economy, and various educational, environmental, and health-care issues during the early 1990s elevated those ongoing concerns to priorities that the Bush and Clinton administrations had to address.

The coverage of the hostage crisis in Iran also raised expectations for a quick solution, effectively shortening the response time available to the Carter administration. The daily television coverage began by noting the number of days the hostages had been in captivity and thus reminded the public not only of the problem but also of the administration's inability to deal with it. Similarly, television coverage of the Soviet Union's invasion of Afghanistan in 1979 created the need for President Carter to respond quickly. He did so, ordering an unpopular ban on American farm exports to the Soviet Union and prohibiting American athletes from competing in the Moscow Olympics. In short, by focusing attention on a problem, the media can force decisions and actions. The public has little patience for a seemingly inactive and uncaring president.[38]

The media may also limit the president's options by making disclosures that generate a hostile reaction. At the beginning of the Bush administration, for example, various plans for bailing out the failed and failing savings and loan associations were considered. When reports surfaced that the Treasury Department might require depositors to pay for insurance to protect their deposits, the idea was immediately criticized as a hidden tax imposed by an administration that had pledged no new taxes. The negative public response generated by the report doomed the proposal and even led the president to deny that his administration was seriously considering it.

The media provide a channel of continuous communication between the public and public officials. That channel enables citizens to be informed about public issues and to make judgments about how public policy affects society. By focusing on certain problems, the media help set the agenda and stimulate public pressure on officials to act, often providing them with broad policy guidelines and a time frame in which to respond. Such mediation between the public and policy makers helps to make democratic government possible.

Agence France Presse

Just after an election, interest in a new president and first family tends to be overwhelming, often bordering on the absurd. Here—desperate for a picture—photographers surround Socks, Chelsea Clinton's cat. President Bush's dog, Millie, also spent a good deal of time in the limelight.

SUMMARY

The news media function to inform and educate the public about policy issues and to sensitize the government to public opinion. To perform those functions, they need to be able to investigate and report without restrictions. The First Amendment guarantees freedom of the press, but the Supreme Court has ruled that this freedom must be balanced by the rights of others to privacy, truthfulness, and fairness.

Limits on freedom of the press include standards holding the press liable for falsehoods that cause a person harm—libel. To win a libel suit, however, a public figure must prove that the publisher or broadcaster knew that the statement in question was false and maliciously published or broadcast it anyway.

Another issue related to freedom of the press is the confidentiality of news sources. The Supreme Court has ruled that journalists must respond when subpoenaed for information, but many states have passed *shield laws* that give journalists some protection against the forced disclosure of sources. In ad-

dition, the Freedom of Information Act gives journalists access to classified documents unless the government can show that the documents must remain classified for reasons of national security. Occasionally the government has tried to prevent information from becoming public by obtaining a judicial order to prevent the publication or broadcasting of that information. This action is known as *prior restraint*, and the courts have been reluctant to approve it.

Regulation of the electronic media is more extensive than regulation of the print media. Broadcasters are required to operate in the public interest and were subject to several rules designed to ensure *fairness* in the discussion of important issues, *equal time* for candidates to present their views to the electorate, and the *right of rebuttal* when attacked on the air. The result of these rules, however, has been to discourage the electronic media from becoming a forum for debate because of the requirement to provide free time for opposing points of view.

Free time costs money, and the American media are predominantly private and profit making. Moreover, today, they are big business. Concentrated ownership reduces diversity in news coverage and exposes the media to charges of bias. Economic constraints affect the scope of news operations, the resources devoted to newsgathering, and the slant given the news. Because profit-making media must capture and hold the attention of as large an audience as possible, the news must be entertaining. Thus, the media emphasize competition, conflict, and human interest and deemphasize detailed discussion of policy issues. They may be tempted to avoid airing or printing information that could be harmful to their advertisers.

The history of the news media illustrates the tension between the media's democratic goals and economic needs. Mass journalism developed during the nineteenth century, spurred by the invention of the telegraph and later by sensational *yellow journalism*. The electronic media developed during the twentieth century. First radio and then television became the most important medium for reporting fast-breaking news stories and foreign news. Both initially sought large audiences by broadcasting national entertainment and news programs. Because of their potential for increasing name recognition and enhancing personal image, radio in the 1940s and television beginning in the 1950s became major vehicles for parties and candidates in election campaigns and for government officials who responded to public issues.

In the past two decades, communication satellites, fiber optics, and other new technologies have opened up additional channels for communicating news quickly. For television, the major change has been the growth of cable. The Cable News Network can report news as it happens almost anywhere in the world, and public service cable channels provide in-depth coverage of some of the official proceedings of government.

The mass media have had a major impact on politics and government. Their coverage is slanted toward material that has *newsworthiness*. The media tend to stress the controversies in campaigns and the personal characteristics of candidates rather than substantive policy issues. Moreover, candidates who are seen as likely winners receive more coverage than candidates who are not expected to win.

Candidates try to affect the coverage they receive by scheduling and staging events, releasing information and granting access to reporters, and preparing speeches and responses. They also use paid advertising to convey a message about themselves and their opponents. Much of that advertising is designed to create a favorable image of themselves, but in recent years *negative advertising*, which attacks an opposing candidate, has grown in quantity and importance.

The decline in partisanship, the emphasis on personality, and the importance of visual imagery have increased the impact of the media on candidates and elections. However, the influence of the media is limited by the stability of many voters' attitudes and by the fact that people tend to filter out information that challenges their views. In general, the media affect voters' awareness and impressions of candidates more than they influence voters' political attitudes or change their opinions on major issues within an election cycle.

In covering the operations of government, the media often stress the style and strategy used in enacting or defeating a proposed policy rather than the likely effect of that policy on the country. Issues are portrayed as arguments between two sides, congressional votes as victories or defeats for the president. The media also tend to emphasize issues and events that are critical of government and those who serve in it.

In their coverage of the national government, the media's focus on the president gives the presidential administration an incentive to try to shape the coverage it receives. The president can "manage" the news by timing the release of information to make the administration look good, avoiding commenting on unpleasant topics, and providing services for the press corps such as briefings, photo opportunities, and press releases. In addition, the president can usually obtain air time for speeches and events.

Congress receives less coverage than the president, and that coverage emphasizes politics between competing parties, philosophies, and personalities rather than the substance of policy and its consequences for society. The national media are often harsh on Congress as an institution and on individual legislators. Local media, however, report more favorably on their representatives, especially when they are back in their home districts.

In contrast to Congress and the president, the judiciary receives little media coverage except during controversial hearings or major trials. Supreme

Court justices rarely give interviews or discuss the Court's proceedings, and few journalists have the knowledge needed to evaluate judicial decisions and their impact.

The media affect public policy through the issues they choose to cover and the information they choose to disclose. Those choices affect the government's agenda and priorities, shorten time frames for policy decisions, and limit the options of government officials. The media thus provide a linkage between the public and its governing officials, a role that is essential in a democracy.

KEY TERMS AND CONCEPTS

shield laws
prior restraint
fairness doctrine

equal time rule
right of rebuttal
yellow journalism

newsworthiness
negative advertising

LEARNING MORE ABOUT THE MEDIA

Scholarly studies

Abramson, Jeffrey B., F. Christopher Arterton, and Gary R. Orren. *The Electronic Commonwealth: The Impact of New Media Technologies on Democratic Politics.* New York: Basic Books, 1990. An insightful analysis of how contemporary changes in the media have affected and may continue to affect democratic politics.

Graber, Doris A. *Mass Media and American Politics.* 4th ed. Washington, D.C.: Congressional Quarterly, 1993. A comprehensive discussion of media and government, from ownership patterns to press freedom to characteristics of coverage and its effects.

Iyengar, Shanto, and Donald R. Kinder. *News That Matters.* Chicago: University of Chicago Press, 1989. A study that clearly shows the ability of television news to set the agenda for the public.

McCubbins, Mathew D., with John H. Aldrich, F. Christopher Arterton, Samuel L. Popkin, and Larry J. Sabato. *Under the Watchful Eye.* Washington, D.C.: Congressional Quarterly, 1992. A brief but insightful series of essays on presidential campaigning.

Owen, Diana. *Media Messages in American Presidential Elections.* Westport, Conn.: Greenwood Press, 1991. A scholarly analysis of the influence of special types of media messages on political learning during recent presidential campaigns.

Ranney, Austin. *Channels of Power: The Impact of Television on American Politics.* New York: Basic Books, 1985. An interesting, broad discussion of the difference between reality and television coverage and television's effect on politicians, government, and the audience.

Robinson, Michael J., and Margaret A. Sheehan. *Over the Wire and on TV: CBS and UPI in Campaign '80.* New York: Russell Sage, 1984. A thorough examination of the differences and similarities between print and television during a presidential election campaign.

Leisure reading

Bernstein, Carl, and Bob Woodward. *All the President's Men.* New York: Simon and Schuster, 1987. A gripping account by the two *Washington Post* reporters who uncovered the truth behind the Watergate break-in.

Halberstam, David. *The Powers That Be.* New York: Knopf, 1979. A lengthy but highly readable account of the development, organization, and operation of media giants CBS, the *New York Times*, Time Inc., the *Los Angeles Times*, and the *Washington Post.*

Hertsgaard, Mark. *On Bended Knee: The Press and the Reagan Presidency.* New York: Farrar, Straus and Giroux, 1988. A journalist's description of how the Reagan administration successfully manipulated the media.

Ellerbee, Linda. *"And So It Goes": Adventures in Television.* New York: Berkley Publishing, 1987. The recollections of a woman who did not fit into television's strict mold but managed to put quality television on the air anyway.

Powell, Jody. *The Other Side of the Story.* New York: Morrow, 1984. The target of media coverage as White House press secretary under President Carter, Powell discusses the trials and tribulations of bad press coverage.

Primary sources

The New York Times Index. New York: New York Times Company, semimonthly with quarterly compilations. A subject index of articles appearing in the *New York Times* since it was founded in 1851. A "How to Use" section appears at the end of each volume.

Public Affairs Video Archives. West Lafayette, Ind.: Purdue University, annual. A chronological index of public affairs events and programs telecast by C-SPAN each year. Volumes began in 1987.

The Washington Post. Ann Arbor: University Microfilms, annual. A subject index of the articles appearing in the *Washington Post*.

Organizations

Accuracy in Media, 1275 K Street, N.W., Washington, DC 20005; (202) 371-6710. An organization with a conservative orientation that researches examples of liberal bias in the media.

Center for Media and Public Affairs, 2100 L Street, N.W., Suite 303, Washington, DC 20037; (202) 223-2942. An organization that conducts scientific studies of how the television news treats contemporary social and political issues.

Corporation for Public Broadcasting, 901 E Street, N.W., Washington, DC 20004; (202) 879-9600. A government corporation that funds public broadcasting.

Federal Communications Commission, 1919 M Street, N.W., Washington, DC 20554; (202) 632-6600. The government agency that regulates the use of the airwaves in the United States.

Reporters Committee for Freedom of the Press, 800 18th Street, N.W., Washington, DC 20006; (202) 466-6313. A group that examines First Amendment issues that pertain to freedom of the press.

PART **IV**

American

Political

Institutions

12

Congress

- The institution of Congress: members, work environment, staff, and support services

- The organization of Congress: congressional parties and the committee system

- The functions of Congress: legislation, representation, and administrative oversight

- Congressional reform and its impact

In 1928, the Democrats nominated New York's governor, Al Smith, who wore a brown derby, was "wet" (against Prohibition), and was Catholic. The Republicans countered with Herbert Hoover, a Protestant who showed talent for using a new advertising tool—the radio. Religion and Prohibition were major issues of the campaign. Hoover won, but within seven months of his smashing victory, the stock market crashed. Hoover was as decisively defeated by Franklin D. Roosevelt in 1932 as he had triumphed four years earlier.

One of a president-elect's first duties is to select a cabinet. Although the Senate has the authority to review and confirm presidential appointments, it has rarely interfered in the selection of cabinet officers. In fact, the Senate has a long-standing tradition of confirming appointments made by a newly elected president, as well as appointments of present and former senators to positions in the judicial and executive branches. Thus, it was a dramatic surprise when, on March 9, 1989, the Senate voted to reject President Bush's nomination of John Tower of Texas as secretary of defense. Tower had served in the Senate from 1962 to 1986, and for six years he had been chair of the Senate Armed Services Committee, which had jurisdiction over his nomination.

Even though he was a former senator, Tower had few friends in the Senate. Widely regarded as arrogant and egotistical, he had often engaged in bruising conflicts with his colleagues. One of those who had felt the brunt of Tower's "body contact" approach to politics was Senator Sam Nunn (D-Georgia), who succeeded Tower as chair of the Armed Services Committee and therefore presided

411

over his confirmation hearings. Nunn was further alienated when President Bush's staff held a briefing on the Tower nomination to which only Republicans were invited. A few days later the Armed Services Committee voted to recommend that the full Senate reject the Tower nomination.

Suddenly the nomination was in danger. President Bush and Republican leaders in the Senate began an aggressive effort to maintain Republican support and to secure some Democratic backing for the nomination. With a 55-to-45 Democratic majority, the Republicans needed at least five Democratic votes—if they could hold the support of all 45 Republicans. In the event of a tie, the Republican vice president, Dan Quayle, could cast the deciding vote in Tower's favor.

The Republicans appeared to be holding together, and a few Democrats crossed party lines to support Tower. However, as the debate wore into its second week, the Republican leaders became increasingly outspoken in their criticism of the Democrats, especially Nunn. The harshness of the Republican attack seemed to harden Democratic opposition.

The conflict over the Tower nomination unraveled the fabric of personal relations in the Senate. On the surface the debate focused on Tower's character and competence. Below the surface, however, the debate revolved around relations between Democrats and Republicans; it also revolved around the president's latitude in staffing the cabinet, loyalties within the Democratic party, and lingering resentment of those whose egos had been too often bruised by Tower during his own service in the Senate.

The unprecedented rejection of the Tower nomination reveals a good deal about relations between the president and Congress, about politics within Congress, and about qualifications for major cabinet appointments. The principal charges against Tower were that he occasionally used alcohol to excess, that he was a womanizer, and that he had earned substantial sums of money as a consultant to defense contractors after retiring from the Senate. Nonetheless, Tower might have survived all these and other charges if the nominating and confirmation process had unfolded differently.

POLITICS IS THE MOST PERSISTENT and most important element in the legislative process. Indeed, politics dominates day-to-day life in Congress. Members of Congress struggle constantly to build political coalitions for or against particular bills. They fight to change the institution's procedures and organization to gain leverage over legislative decisions. And they do constant battle with other political institutions, especially the president and the bureaucracy, to assert their institutional prerogatives and to influence the shape of public policy.

In this chapter we examine the central role of Congress in the American government. We view Congress first from a broad perspective. What sort of institution is Congress? Who are its members? What kind of environment do they work in? We next examine the organization and principal functions of Congress, especially its responsibilities for constituency representation, legislation, and administrative oversight. We explore the role of political parties and legislative committees in organizing and accomplishing the work of Congress, and the increasingly significant role that interest groups and political action

Texan John Tower served in the Senate from 1962 through 1986, but when President Bush nominated him to be secretary of defense in 1989, a bruising confirmation battle ensued. Concerns about Tower's personal life and his business dealings with defense contractors—along with lingering resentment among some former Senate colleagues—led to lengthy hearings and floor debate. In the end, his nomination was rejected.

committees play in the legislative process. Each of these topics reveals something about how politics determines what Congress does.

THE INSTITUTION OF CONGRESS

The United States Congress is a **bicameral legislature**—that is, it is composed of two legislative bodies. The larger is the House of Representatives, which has 435 voting members, plus 5 other delegates who represent the District of Columbia and the United States territories and possessions but do not vote on passage of bills in the full House. Each member of the House represents a congressional district with a population of about 575,000 (in accordance with the principle of *one person, one vote*). All House members serve terms of two years.

The smaller legislative chamber is the Senate. It has 100 members, two from each state. Senators serve six-year terms, but the terms are staggered so that approximately one-third of the seats in the Senate are up for election every two years.

Elections to Congress occur in November in even-numbered years. The new Congress convenes in the following January. Each Congress lasts two years and is numbered; thus, the First Congress convened in 1789, and the 103rd convened in 1993. The first year of a Congress is called the "first session," and the second year is called the "second session." The first session of the 103rd Congress met in 1993, and the second session in 1994.

The Members of Congress

The Constitution establishes minimum requirements for service in Congress. To serve in the House, one must have reached the age of 25, have been a United

TABLE 12-1		
Characteristics of Members of the 103rd Congress		
CHARACTERISTIC	HOUSE	SENATE
Average age	51.7	58.0
Females	48	6
African Americans	39	1
Hispanics	19	0
Principal occupations*		
Law	181	58
Business or banking	131	24
Politics/public service	87	10
Education	66	11
Real estate	26	5
Journalism	24	9
Agriculture	19	8
Engineering	5	0
Medicine	6	0
Aeronautics	2	1
Other	17	3
Religion		
Protestant	271	63
Roman Catholic	118	23
Jewish	32	10
Other	14	3

* Some members specified more than one principal occupation.

SOURCE: "New Members, New Districts," *Congressional Quarterly Weekly Report*, Special Report, November 7, 1992, 7–10.

States citizen for seven years, and be an inhabitant of the state (but not necessarily the district) from which one is elected. Senators must also be inhabitants of the states from which they are elected, but they must be at least 30 years old and have been United States citizens for nine years at the time they begin their service.

Although all members of Congress have those simple requirements in common, they differ widely in other ways.[1] In their speech, ideas, and values they mirror the regional and religious diversity of the American people. Table 12-1 provides some indication of how diverse the Congress is in terms of age, gender, ethnicity, occupation, and religion.

Despite the variety of their backgrounds, legislators cannot be accurately described as a cross-section of the American people. As a group they rank relatively high in socioeconomic status. Few blue-collar workers serve in Congress, and not one of its members is poor. The percentages of women and minority group members are also much smaller than their percentages in the population as a whole. Also notable is the preponderance of lawyers and the

The interior of the Capitol dome, viewed from the floor of the rotunda 180 feet beneath it, is a monumental painting entitled The Apotheosis of Washington, *by Constantino Brumidi (1805–1880). Arranged around the border are six groups of figures representing War, Science, Marine, Commerce, Manufacturing, and Agriculture. In the spring of 1865, as Brumidi worked with pigments and plaster to create this great fresco, the Civil War was ending with Lee's surrender to Grant, and President Lincoln was assassinated. In December, when the Thirty-ninth Congress convened, the artist barely finished his work amid demands that the scaffolding come down.*

dearth of members with scientific backgrounds. Lawyers have long been the dominant occupational group in Congress—not surprising given the importance of lawmaking as a legislative responsibility. The small number of members with scientific training is more problematic, however, because the agenda facing Congress includes many issues of technical complexity, such as space exploration, the survival of endangered species, and the establishment of standards for high-definition television. Members of Congress must often rely on the expertise of others—the executive branch, their own staffs, and special interest groups—to guide their decision making on issues that involve complex technology and groundbreaking science.

The Work Environment

In recent decades, service in Congress has become difficult and demanding. The demands on a member's time are enormous and constant. Hundreds of thousands of people view the member as their personal representative in the federal government. When they have problems such as a lost Social Security check or when they need help in getting a small-business loan or a passport, they expect their representative to assist them. They also expect their representative to be a source of information about what is going on in Washington and around the world.

Members are also legislators. Each year they must vote on hundreds of legislative issues, many of which are too complex to be grasped in the short time available before the vote. Members also serve on several congressional committees and subcommittees, where they are expected to involve themselves deeply in the development of new legislation and in reviewing the implementation of legislation passed by previous Congresses. They must also attend meetings of party caucuses and other specialized groups that members form to help advance their legislative priorities.

In addition, most members of Congress are candidates for reelection. The election campaign requires frequent meetings with the leaders of various interest groups in the home state or district, regular travel to meet with constituents, and contact with political action committees and other funding sources to ensure the availability of campaign funds.

Missing from this catalog of activities is adequate time for serious reading, reflection, and creative thought. Members of Congress spend so much time trying to get through their daily schedules that they have little or no free time to think about policy objectives and legislative priorities. One study found that in an average day a member of the House has only eleven minutes for uninterrupted reflection.[2] Most members lament this, but few have found a way to avoid it.

Staff and Support Services

Members of Congress are not the only people who work on Capitol Hill. Senators and representatives are surrounded by thousands of congressional employees whose jobs have been created to help them deal with the workload. The principal responsibility of these employees is to provide support for the elected members of Congress.

One form of support is provided by personal staffs. Each member has the authority to hire staff employees to work for him or her alone. In the House, staff allowances are the same for all members; in the Senate, they are based on the population of the state that a senator represents. In recent years House members have typically had about twenty people on their personal staffs. Senators have larger staffs; those from the largest states employ as many as sixty people. The personal staff is divided between the member's Washington office and the offices that most members maintain in their home districts or states.

Personal staff aides perform a variety of functions. They do routine clerical chores: typing, greeting visitors, answering the mail, photocopying. They write speeches and help the member develop policy initiatives. They meet with lobbyists and constituents. They handle **casework,** the individual problems that

Inside the typically crowded, busy office of Representative Dick Swett of New Hampshire, staff members endure over-crowding, long hours, and shared facilities. The growth of congressional staffs has been spurred both by workloads and by the desire to be reelected.

constituents bring to the member's attention for assistance or a solution.[3] They work closely on issues that come up in the committees on which their employers serve, and they monitor issues as they develop in other committees, especially legislation that may be of concern to constituents.

Committee staff members form another important group of congressional employees. Congress has hundreds of committees and subcommittees. Each has its own staff, which assists committee members in setting an agenda, scheduling hearings, developing legislation, and overseeing the work of the executive agencies that fall within its area of interest. Responsibilities for hiring committee staff employees differ in the House and Senate and even from one committee to another. The most common practice, however, is for each committee or subcommittee to have one group of staff employees who serve the committee members from the majority party and another group who serve the members from the minority party. The majority staff is usually hired by the committee chair (who is always a member of the majority party); the minority staff is usually hired by the ranking minority member of the committee.

Politics plays a large role in committee staffing. Staff members who work for the majority party are expected to share that party's views on relevant policy matters; the minority party imposes the same expectations. When control of the House or Senate changes from one party to the other, major changes occur in committee staffing.

A third important group of congressional employees includes those who work for the four specialized support agencies in the legislative branch:

1. The Congressional Research Service is part of the Library of Congress; its professional staff conducts studies on a wide range of topics at the request of members and subcommittees.

2. The Office of Technology Assessment is a small agency that supports Congress with specialized information on scientific and technical matters like toxic-waste cleanup and the validity of polygraph tests.

3. The Congressional Budget Office, established in 1974, provides Congress with its own source of economic information and analysis.

4. The General Accounting Office determines whether government programs have been cost-effective (it is described in detail later in this chapter).

TABLE 12-2

Congressional Staff, 1991

	NUMBER OF EMPLOYEES
House of Representatives	
Committee staff	2,321
Personal staff	7,278
Leadership staff*	149
Officers of the House staff**	1,293
Senate	
Committee staff	1,154
Personal staff	4,294
Leadership staff*	95
Officers of the Senate staff**	1,092
Joint committee staffs	145
Support agencies	
General Accounting Office	5,034
Congressional Research Service	831
Congressional Budget Office	226
Office of Technology Assessment	143

* Staff who work directly for the party leaders in each house on leadership matters.

** Includes doorkeepers, parliamentarians, sergeants-at-arms, clerk of the House, Senate majority and minority secretaries, and postmasters.

SOURCE: Norman J. Ornstein, Thomas E. Mann, and Michael J. Malbin, *Vital Statistics on Congress, 1993–1994* (Washington, D.C.: Congressional Quarterly, 1994), 126. Reprinted by permission of Congressional Quarterly, Inc.

The number of people employed in staff and support functions is indicated in Table 12-2. The rapid expansion of congressional staff and support services is directly related to a series of important changes in Congress itself and in the federal government as a whole. The federal budget has increased tenfold in two decades. Hundreds of new government programs have been initiated. Public dissatisfaction with the presidencies of Lyndon Johnson and Richard Nixon created a demand for greater congressional effectiveness and more vigilant oversight of executive actions. These changes produced incentives for increases in congressional capabilities and led directly to staff expansion. When serious abuses of authority were committed by federal intelligence agencies in the 1970s, for example, two new congressional committees were created to oversee those agencies. In 1990 those committees employed almost one hundred staff members.

An equally important factor in the expansion of congressional staff has been the widespread perception among members of Congress that staff aides help members do things that contribute directly to reelection. The more legislation members can be involved in, the more publicity their offices can generate, and the more efficiently and successfully they can respond to constituents' requests for help, the greater is the likelihood of success at election time. To the intensely political people who serve in Congress, the prospect of reelection has been a powerful motive for the steady enlargement of congressional staff and support agencies.

THE ORGANIZATION OF CONGRESS

How does Congress set its agenda and organize the flow of its business? In a sense, these are technical questions because they involve the mechanics of congressional operation. But they are much more than that. The way Congress organizes itself reveals a great deal about the allocation of legislative power, and that allocation of power tells us much about the politics of public policy making.

The internal structure of Congress has changed and grown over time, as each generation of legislators has shaped Congress to fit its needs. Parties emerged early in the nation's history to organize the business of the initial Congresses. Party caucuses hammered out important policy decisions. For a few decades after the Civil War, committees began to play a more dominant role in lawmaking. By the last decade of the nineteenth century, party leaders in Congress, particularly the Speaker of the House and the majority leader of the Senate, had become the principal powers.

(Left) *Speaker Joseph G. Cannon (R-Illinois) before the House of Representatives and* (right) *Speaker Thomas B. Reed (R-Maine). From 1890 to 1910, these two House speakers dominated the legislative process and are regarded as the most powerful leaders in congressional history. A "revolt" against Cannon in 1911 changed the House rules to reduce the Speaker's authority, and no congressional leader since has exercised such broad power.*

Library of Congress

Library of Congress

But the party leaders of the time, notably Speaker Joseph G. Cannon (R-Illinois) and Speaker Thomas Brackett Reed (R-Maine), became so dominant that a revolt occurred at the end of the first decade of the twentieth century. The authority of the party leaders was reduced, and for most of the next seventy years committees were again the power centers in Congress. A **seniority system** ensured that the member of the majority party with the longest consecutive service on each committee would automatically chair the committee for as long as he or she remained in Congress. Seniority permitted the committee chairs, many of whom were elderly men, to assume powerful roles in the legislative process. But another revolt (described on page 450), this time against the dominance of the committee chairs, unfolded in the 1970s and produced another restructuring of congressional power.[4]

Throughout these decades of change, two principles have remained at the core of congressional organization: (1) control of the legislative agenda and the legislative machinery ought to be in the hands of the majority party; (2) for purposes of efficiency and enhanced expertise, most day-to-day details of legislative work ought to be handled by small groups of legislators meeting as committees. Since the early decades of the nineteenth century, the party system and the committee system have been the dominant elements in every scheme of congressional organization.

Congressional Parties

The single most distinctive feature of political parties in Congress is their limited control over their own members, particularly over the way their members vote on legislative issues. In legislatures in other countries, **party discipline** is normal. Party leaders in Britain and France can count on the members of their party to support them on virtually every vote that occurs, and if they do not, the party can impose sanctions on them. Not so in the United States. Party leaders in Congress can neither expect nor coerce all the members of their party to support them on legislative votes. When the two parties take opposing positions on an issue, some members of each party will typically defect to the opposition, thus undermining party discipline (see Figure 12-1).

The absence of party discipline reflects, more than anything else, the limited authority of party leaders in Congress. In both the House and the Senate, leaders have very little direct control over the members of their own party and therefore have few ways to force them to vote for the party's position on a bill. They cannot prevent party members from running for reelection; they have little influence on the outcome of elections; and, without the support of the majority of their party, they cannot even affect committee assignments. To understand better the relationship between party leaders and rank-and-file party members, it is useful to look separately at party organization in the House and the Senate.

Parties in the House   Because the House is larger than the Senate, parties play a more important role in organizing the legislative agenda and building legislative majorities in the House. The majority party has the principal responsibility for both tasks. It controls the selection of the Speaker of the House, and its members compose a majority on each committee and subcommittee.

The **Speaker** is almost always the most important figure in the House.

Average party unity scores

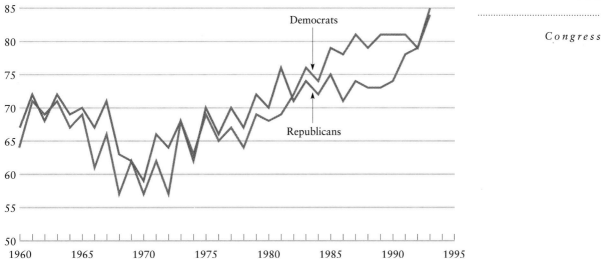

Figure 12-1 *Party unity scores in House and Senate combined, 1960–1993.*
SOURCE: Congressional Quarterly Weekly Report, *December 18, 1993, 3479.*

Technically, the Speaker is the presiding officer, although little of the Speaker's time is actually spent in the chair. Political leadership of the majority party is the Speaker's dominant concern. Working with other party leaders—especially those designated as **whips,** who perform leadership functions—the Speaker

In June 1993, House Democratic whips plot strategies for passing President Clinton's economic stimulus package. Whips are liaisons between a party's leaders and its rank-and-file members.

Jane Hosfros/NYT Pictures

helps determine the issues that will be given top priority in the House.[5] Among the Speaker's other duties are participating in scheduling debates; mediating among members who disagree on important legislation; working with the White House to coordinate measures that are important to the president; and assisting members of the majority party in such matters as getting the committee assignments they want and retaining their seats at election time.[6]

An astute Speaker has a substantial impact on the kinds of policy issues that come before the House and the way they are decided. The Speaker's leadership is based more on persuasion and political skill than on any real authority over individual House members, however. A successful Speaker commands the respect of other party members and is able to convince them to support his or her position on critical policy issues. Strong Speakers make full use of the tools of authority available to them: parliamentary direction of floor debate and assignment of bills to committee, control over the flow of information within the House, ability to determine the scheduling of legislative action, appointment powers, and personal prestige and influence with other political actors in Washington. A member who consistently supports the Speaker, for example, can expect assignment to preferred committees, assistance in securing campaign funds from political action committees, and help from the leadership in gaining passage of legislation introduced by that member.[7]

The Speaker does not act alone in attempting to guide the operations of the House. Figure 12-2 shows the elaborate structure of majority party organization when the Democrats are in the majority, as they have been since 1955. The Speaker is supported by, and works through, a variety of committees and networks that enhance internal communication in the party, aid in the formation of party positions on policy issues, and help improve the chances of the party's candidates for seats in the House.

The size and complexity of the majority party leadership in the House reflect the difficulty of maintaining unity among a group with several hundred members. This size and complexity also indicate the problem of building legislative majorities when leaders lack the authority to demand support. A less complex leadership structure would be sufficient if the majority party leaders had more authority.

The minority party in the House has its own elected leaders and a structure that mirrors, on a reduced scale, the organization of the majority party. There are, of course, fewer members to organize in the minority party, and the minority party has less responsibility for managing the House agenda. The leader of the minority party is the minority leader, who is assisted by the minority whip. Both are elected by the minority party caucus.

Parties in the Senate   Because the Senate is smaller, parties play a much less important role there than in the House. Individual senators are able to deal with each other directly on most matters. Senate parties do elect leaders. The majority party elects a majority leader and a majority whip; the minority party elects a minority leader and a minority whip. Each party also has a structure of leadership committees, but these have less influence on party operations than do their counterparts in the House. Most leadership functions in the Senate are concentrated in the hands of the elected party leaders.[8]

The primary job of the party leaders, especially the majority leader, is to organize the business of the Senate: to nudge legislation along through the legislative process, to schedule debate, and to oversee most aspects of day-to-

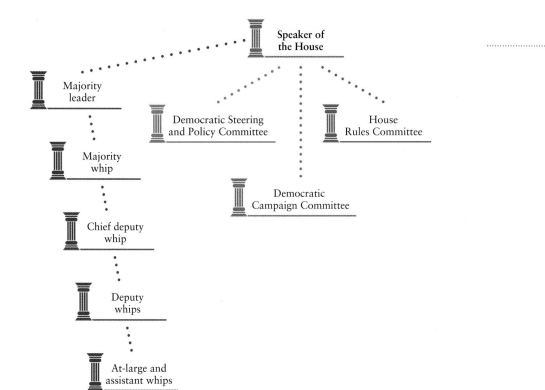

Figure 12-2 *Majority party leadership in the House of Representatives.*

day administration. Party leaders also help the proponents of legislation round up the votes necessary to make a majority, meet regularly with the president to discuss policy and legislative strategy, and serve as public spokespersons for their party on important policy matters. The spokesperson role is especially prominent for the leaders of the party of which the president is not a member. During the Republican administration of George Bush, for example, Senator George Mitchell (D-Maine), the majority leader, was an important spokesperson for the Democrats. When Bush was replaced by Bill Clinton, a Democrat, Senator Robert Dole (R-Kansas) became a leading articulator of the views of his party, particularly when those views clashed with the president's.

Despite the extent of their duties and their public visibility, party leaders in the Senate are severely constrained in their ability to influence the outcome of policy debates. Their control over the votes and activities of other members of their party is even weaker than that of their House counterparts. Party discipline is no stronger in the Senate than in the House, and leadership control over other levers of influence (election, removal, salaries, staff resources) is equally insignificant. In the Senate, therefore, leadership is even more dependent on persuasion and political sensitivities than it is in the House. Senator Mike Mansfield (D-Montana), who served as majority leader in the Senate longer than anyone else in this century, once said: "What power do the leaders have to force these committees, to twist their arms, to wheel and deal, and so forth

The character of congressional party leadership has evolved considerably during this century. In the first decade, Joseph G. Cannon (R-Illinois) in the House and Nelson W. Aldrich (R-Rhode Island) in the Senate dominated the legislative process. In the decades that followed, the seniority system became more rigid, and the chairs of the standing committees came to share legislative power with the party leaders. Since 1960, legislative power has decentralized even further, placing new demands and constraints on party leaders. In the statements that follow, some recent party leaders describe their work.

Thomas P. O'Neill (D-Massachusetts),
House Speaker (1977–1986)
[At a meeting with a handful of legislative leaders in 1942, President Franklin Roosevelt introduced Albert Einstein.] Einstein explained the theory of the atomic bomb, and told the group that Hitler also had scientists working on it, and that the first nation to get the bomb would win the war and control the world.

Einstein estimated that the project would cost two billion dollars. Not surprisingly, the president was concerned about how to allocate that kind of money without alerting the public or the press.

"Leave it to me," said Sam Rayburn [then Speaker of the House].

The next day Sam called all the committee and subcommittee chairmen and told them to put an extra hundred million dollars into their budgets.

"Yes, Mr. Rayburn," they all said. There were no questions asked and no meetings held. The Manhattan Project was one of the best-kept secrets in history. The money was allocated and nobody on the committees ever questioned why a chairman was setting aside a certain amount for reasons he didn't even know about.

But that's the way things worked in Sam's time. Today, of course, you'd have ninety-two guys wanting to know what was happening and where the money was going.[1]

John McCormack (D-Massachusetts),
House Speaker (1962–1970)
I have never asked a member to vote against his conscience. If he mentions his conscience—that's all. I don't press him any further.[2]

Charles Halleck (R-Illinois),
House Minority Leader (1959–1964)
You get pressure from guys who have come along with you on a tough vote about the fellows who went off the reservation. Some of them want to read these guys out of the party. But, hell, there may be a vote next week when you need a fellow who has strayed real bad and you can catch him on the rebound.[3]

Carl Albert (D-Oklahoma),
House Speaker (1971–1976)
If you can't win them by persuasion, you can't win them at all. If you whip them into line every time, by the time you reach the third vote you're through.[4]

Mike Mansfield (D-Montana),
Senate Majority Leader (1961–1976)
It's pretty hard to hold the leadership accountable, because we can't dictate to our associates how they should vote. I think that these people who are representing the various states have been sent here to exercise their own judgment, that they should not be pressured because that's a counterproductive tactic.

I watched Lyndon Johnson while I was assistant majority leader for four years, and our styles are diametrically different. He was a man who liked to keep power in his own hands. He would like to collect IOU's. . . . I don't collect any IOU's. I don't do any special favors. I try to treat all Senators alike, and I think that's the best way to operate in the long run, because that way you maintain their respect and confidence. And that's what the ball game is all about.[5]

[1] Tip O'Neill, *Man of the House* (New York: Random House, 1987), 129.

[2] Quoted in Donald G. Tacheron and Morris K. Udall, *The Job of the Congressman*, 2nd ed. (Indianapolis: Bobbs-Merrill, 1970), 18.

[3] Ibid., 19.

[4] Ibid.

[5] Quoted in Daniel Rapoport, "It's Not a Happy Time for House, Senate Leadership," *National Journal,* February 7, 1976, 173.

and so on, to get them to rush things up or to speed their procedure? The leaders in the Senate, at least, have no power delegated to them except on the basis of courtesy, accommodation, and a sense of responsibility."[9]

Leadership styles in the Senate are constantly changing. When Lyndon Johnson (D-Texas) was majority leader in the 1950s, he used his position to dominate his party and its policy agenda. Recent Senate majority leaders—Mike Mansfield (1961–1976), Robert Byrd (1977–1980, 1987–1988), Howard Baker (1981–1984), Robert Dole (1985–1986), and George Mitchell (1989–1994)—have defined their roles more in administrative than in policy terms. They have concentrated on organizing the business of the Senate to fit the needs of individual members and have spent less time trying to define positions on issues. Since 1961, when Johnson left the Senate to become vice president, the party system in the Senate has ceased to play a major role in the development of public policy. Most of its former activities in that regard have been absorbed by Senate committees and by individual senators.

UPI/Bettmann

(Top) *In June 1960, Chairman of the Foreign Relations Committee William Fulbright (D-Arkansas) found himself flanked by Majority Leader Lyndon Johnson (D-Texas) on the right and by Minority Leader Everett Dirksen (R-Illinois) on the left: Where could Fulbright turn? In the years after World War II, when the Senate was often described as a club, congressional leaders were personal and informal. But leadership styles have changed. Even in shirtsleeves* (bottom), *long-time Senate leaders like Bob Dole (R-Kansas) are more deferential and more distant.*

UPI/Bettmann

© Teresa Zabala/Gamma-Liaison

C-SPAN

Recent elections have brought more women to Congress, including senators Barbara Mikulski (D-Maryland) and Carol Moseley-Braun (D-Illinois), and their presence has changed the tone of some congressional debate. For example, as the first African American female in the Senate, Moseley-Braun successfully challenged ongoing funding for a group called the Dames of the Confederacy, because it used segregationist symbols.

Party politics in Congress The proponents of each bill introduced in Congress must form a coalition in support of that bill. These coalitions, which may include members of the opposition party, vanish as quickly as they appear; their composition changes from bill to bill and from day to day. Politics in Congress focuses on the task of building these shifting alliances. Bargaining and negotiation among individual members, rather than edicts from party leaders, are the principal techniques used in the formation of coalitions. Party leaders often play an important role, but the role is that of lead negotiator, not commanding officer.[10]

In recent years individual legislators, known as **issue entrepreneurs,** have tended to specialize in particular substantive matters and to seek support among their colleagues for policies dealing with those matters. In the House, issue entrepreneurs are often subcommittee chairs; in the Senate, entrepreneurship is widely dispersed and bears little relation to formal institutional roles. For six years in the 1980s, for example, Representative Romano Mazzoli (D-Kentucky) sought to build congressional support for a major new immigration law. This legislation held little interest for most of Mazzoli's constituents in Louisville but was part of his sphere of influence as chair of the House Judiciary Committee's subcommittee on immigration. In the Senate, Barbara Mikulski (D-Maryland) was a major architect of the coalition that passed the Child Abuse Act in 1984. Her interest in this issue bore no direct relationship to any of her committee assignments; instead, it stemmed from her experience as a former social worker and her leadership in the movement for women's rights. In the debate on tax policy at the beginning of the Clinton administration, Senator Bill Bradley (D-New Jersey) played an influential role, as he had on earlier tax policy debates in the 1980s. From the outset of his Senate career, Bradley had worked hard to educate himself on tax issues, and his knowledge commanded considerable respect among his colleagues.

Leadership is always necessary in the bargaining and negotiation that constitute legislative politics (see the profile on page 427). It often takes years to get a bill enacted, and someone has to persist in seeking the support that ultimately adds up to a legislative majority. But in the United States Congress

John Dingell: Congressional Strongman

John Dingell, Jr. (D-Michigan), was 29 years old when he was elected to Congress in 1955, succeeding his father who had held the same seat for the previous twenty-three years. The younger Dingell had grown up on Capitol Hill, and he understood the legislative process better than most of his senior colleagues. In the decades that followed, he became a master of legislative tactics and procedure.

One of the things that Dingell learned early and practiced often was that administrative oversight, if aggressively performed, can translate into significant political power. As his seniority accumulated, he became chair of the House Energy and Commerce Committee, an octopus with jurisdiction over such matters as laboratory regulation, insider trading, railroads, oil, and communications. Heading that committee gave Dingell the perfect platform for his incursions into a broad array of legislative issues. He retained for himself the chair of the committee's subcommittee on oversight and investigations. He built a staff of astute and aggressive investigators and technicians, and the subcommittee's annual budget of over $5 million for investigations and oversight is the largest in the House.

Dingell himself is both widely respected and widely feared within the government and the House. The grandson of a blacksmith, he is a large man with a forceful personality. He badgers witnesses and colleagues, pounding them with rapid-fire questions and often inserting his own abrasive comments. "Power," he has said, "is a tool, like a hammer or a saw or a wrench." Those upon whom he has used his tools have no trouble understanding the analogy.

Dingell has been most fervent in his oversight of the performance of federal agencies, particularly regulatory bodies. When regulators fail to enforce the law as diligently as Dingell believes they should, he calls them before his subcommittee to lambaste their work. Some critics contend that Dingell's efforts are meddlesome and intrusive, are driven by personal bias, and too often reach beyond the appropriate oversight role of Congress. Supporters, however, suggest that Dingell's kind of aggressive oversight is essential to keep the vast executive bureaucracy responsive to Congress and the public.

The power Dingell has accumulated is used for a number of purposes. He is the leading congressional defender of the automobile industry, which is the dominant economic force in his congressional district. For years, he has sought—often successfully—to weaken the provisions of clean-air legislation that apply to auto emissions. The intensity of his support for the auto industry has been matched by his attacks on other industries, especially pharmaceutical companies and the securities business.

John Dingell: widely respected, widely feared.

John Dingell is not all-powerful. He sometimes loses legislative battles with other committee chairs and on the House floor. But he has become an enduring force in the House of Representatives by combining a safe seat, broad jurisdiction, keen understanding of legislative procedure, talented staff, well-honed negotiating skills, and sheer aggressiveness into genuine political power.

Many members of Congress shy away from administrative oversight because they find it time-consuming and politically unproductive. John Dingell has taken the opposite approach. In so doing, he has built himself a base of political influence that inspires envy among many of his colleagues.

SOURCE: David Rogers, "John Dingell: Advocate and Arbiter," *Wall Street Journal*, March 5, 1990; and Congressional Quarterly, *Politics in America: 1990 The 101st Congress* (Washington, D.C.: Congressional Quarterly, 1989), 769–772.

that role is not the sole province of the party leaders. Because party discipline is weak, legislative leadership is decentralized and the construction of coalitions is a painstaking and time-consuming process of give-and-take among individual members.

The Committee System

Most of the work of Congress is done in committees. One function of committees is to delete from the legislative agenda matters that are not important, urgent, or politically viable. Committees prepare legislation for consideration on the floors of the House and Senate, but they also "kill" bills. Only a small percentage of the bills that are referred to a committee survive its scrutiny.

Committees also hold public hearings at which experts, leaders of interest groups, and other supporters and opponents of bills are permitted to express their views. In addition, they initiate studies, conduct investigations, and publish information. Each year, for example, the State Department is required by law to submit a report to Congress on the human rights policies of all the world's countries. The House Foreign Affairs Committee's subcommittee on human rights and international organizations holds hearings at which it reviews that report and receives comments on it from government officials, interest groups, and private citizens. The subcommittee publishes those hearings, which are used by other committees in their annual decisions on American foreign aid.

Another important function of committees is **administrative oversight.** Committees monitor the work of the executive agencies in their areas of jurisdiction, review budget requests, and pass judgment on the qualifications of presidential appointees. In fact, they are the principal contact points between the executive and legislative branches. (The oversight function is discussed in detail on page 445.)

Committees are the primary source of creativity and policy leadership in Congress. The most knowledgeable military specialists in Congress are members of the House and Senate Armed Services Committees. Those who are most familiar with farm issues are on the Agriculture Committees. The senior members of most congressional committees have been dealing for several decades with the policy issues that fall in their committee's area of jurisdiction. They are as well informed about those issues as anyone in the federal government. And they have the support of specialists on the committee staffs. Not surprisingly, therefore, committees initiate much of the legislation that makes its way to the floors of the House and Senate.[11]

There are several kinds of committees. The most common and most important are **standing committees.** These are permanent committees that have full authority to recommend legislation. A few of them, like the Rules Committee in the House, are responsible for organizing and regulating the operations of Congress. Most standing committees have jurisdictions defined along substantive policy lines: energy, agriculture, foreign relations, and so on. The standing committees are listed in Table 12-3.

Most of the standing committees are divided into subcommittees, which hold most of the hearings and conduct the initial review of most legislation. Full committees rarely convene to consider a piece of legislation until after it has been carefully reviewed by the appropriate subcommittee. As the legislative

TABLE 12-3

Standing Committees of the 103rd Congress, 1994

HOUSE COMMITTEES	NUMBER OF SUBCOMMITTEES	SENATE COMMITTEES	NUMBER OF SUBCOMMITTEES
Agriculture	8	Agriculture, Nutrition, Forestry	7
Appropriations	13	Appropriations	13
Armed Services	7	Armed Services	6
Banking, Finance, Urban Affairs	8	Banking, Housing, Urban Affairs	4
Budget	0	Budget	0
District of Columbia	3	Commerce, Science, Transportation	8
Education and Labor	8	Energy and Natural Resources	5
Energy and Commerce	6	Environment and Public Works	5
Foreign Affairs	9	Finance	8
Government Operations	7	Foreign Relations	7
House Administration	7	Governmental Affairs	5
Interior and Insular Affairs	6	Judiciary	7
Judiciary	6	Labor and Human Resources	6
Merchant Marine and Fisheries	5	Rules and Administration	0
Post Office and Civil Service	7	Small Business	6
Public Works and Transportation	6	Veterans' Affairs	0
Rules	2		
Science, Space and Technology	6		
Small Business	6		
Standards of Official Conduct	0		
Veterans' Affairs	5		
Ways and Means	6		
Total 22	131	Total 16	87

SOURCE: Congressional Quarterly, *Politics in America: 1994 The 103rd Congress* (Washington, D.C.: Congressional Quarterly, 1993). Reprinted by permission of Congressional Quarterly, Inc.

workload has grown in size and complexity, experience and specialized knowledge have made the subcommittees increasingly important.

The committee system also includes a variety of **select**, or **special, committees**. These are temporary committees created to deal with specific issues; they disappear when they have completed their work. Many select committees have clearly limited functions and authority. Most, for instance, are not authorized to recommend legislation. Among the best-known recent temporary committees were the Senate Select Committee on Presidential Campaign Activities, which uncovered much of the Watergate scandal in the 1970s, and the House Select Committee to Investigate Covert Arms Transactions with Iran, which joined its Senate counterpart in exploring the Iran-contra affair in the 1980s.

Joint committees are composed of members of both houses of Congress. They are permanent study committees with no authority to initiate legislation. The most important is the Joint Committee on the Economy, which receives

Chairman Sam Ervin (D-North Carolina) with members and counsel of the Senate Select Committee on Presidential Campaign Activities—better known as the Watergate committee. Their televised hearings into the Nixon administration's corruption held Americans spellbound.

J.P. Laffont/SYGMA

and reviews the president's annual Economic Report and conducts studies of the national economy. In addition to the standing joint committees, there are temporary joint committees known as **joint conference committees.** There are hundreds of joint conference committees during each Congress. Their principal function is to resolve the differences that occur when the two houses pass varying forms of the same bill. At the end of the 101st Congress, for example, House and Senate conferees wrangled over different versions of the Clean Air Act. The House bill had included tougher controls than the Senate bill on emissions from steel plants. A compromise in the joint conference committee retained the emissions standards but gave steelmakers a longer period in which to comply. Compromises of this sort are a frequent outcome of conference committee deliberations.

Some committees and subcommittees have especially powerful or effective chairs who are able to dominate the group's internal politics. Representative Jamie Whitten (D-Mississippi), for example, was long a potent force on the House Appropriations Committee, which he chaired through the 1980s and into the 1990s. But his influence was particularly strong in the Appropriations Committee's subcommittee on agriculture, which he also chaired through that period. Indeed, so profound was his impact on agricultural policy that he was often called the "permanent secretary of agriculture." In other House committees and more commonly in the Senate, committee chairs are not so dominant. Like party leaders, they have to engage in constant negotiation with the members of their committee or subcommittee to build support for legislation they favor. Their legislative success thus rests heavily on their political skills.

Because the framers of the Constitution viewed the legislative branch as the safest and most reliable arbiter of the disagreements that are likely to arise among a democratic people, they gave Congress a number of important functions. Those functions have expanded in number and complexity as the scope of the federal government's responsibilities has grown. Historically, the two most significant congressional functions were legislation and representation. In this century, the expansion of presidential power and the growth of a large federal bureaucracy have added a third major function—administrative oversight—to the legislature's responsibilities.

Legislation

People who are not very familiar with Congress tend to regard it as a kind of factory where laws are made. In reality, Congress makes very few public laws, a couple of hundred at most, even in its most productive years, and many of those laws are of very minor consequence—the laws passed in the 101st Congress to designate "State-Supported Homes for Veterans Week" (PL 101-307) and "Helsinki Human Rights Day" (PL 101-341), for example.

Legislation, or lawmaking, is accomplished through deliberation and partisan adjustment, a process that involves information gathering, prolonged discussion, complex and often tedious negotiation, bargaining, and compromise. Most of the time the result of this process is nothing. Most of the bills introduced in Congress do not survive. In fact, 90 percent of the bills introduced in a typical Congress never become law. Enactment of the few that survive may require years, even decades. A long gestation period is common for significant legislation. For example, Medicare, first introduced during the Truman administration, was not enacted until 1965. Congress debated tax reform for more than half a decade before it passed the Tax Reform Act of 1986. National health insurance, a top legislative priority for President Clinton, had been on and off the congressional agenda for decades.

In recent decades the impediments to legislation have been greatly increased by the proliferation and growing sophistication of political interest groups (see Chapter 8). Lawmaking is affected at every stage by special interests. They propose and help draft legislation. They testify at hearings. They lobby members in committee and during floor debate. They try to pressure the president to veto bills that they oppose. The influence of political interest groups has been magnified by the rapid growth in the campaign contributions made by political action committees. Many members of Congress feel indebted to groups that support their campaigns, or at least feel obligated to listen when representatives of those groups present their positions on legislation.[12]

The pervasiveness of politics means that most legislative decisions are compromises, and compromise usually weakens the impact of legislative proposals. Yet the openness of congressional lawmaking, which is one of its strengths, encourages politics. The legislative process provides many opportunities for individuals and groups to express the content and the intensity of their concerns. Politics flourishes in Congress because that setting provides a forum for a broad spectrum of voices and opinions.

This feature of the lawmaking process also has the advantage of legitimating public policy decisions. Everyone has opportunities to speak out about legislation and to try to influence its ultimate shape. Few laws are totally abhorrent to any group because all groups are able to achieve some protection at least for the interests they value most. And Americans can always try to enact new laws to undo the harm they perceive in existing ones.

In 1989, for example, Congress completely reversed itself in response to intense public pressure. In 1988 both houses had strongly supported a bill to improve insurance coverage for elderly citizens suffering a catastrophic illness. Funds were to come from a tax amounting to as much as $800 a year for some senior citizens. In passing this legislation, Congress believed that it was responding to genuine concerns of the elderly. Indeed, it was. But no one foresaw the anger that soon arose over the new tax created to fund this insurance coverage. Tens of thousands of elderly citizens and their interest groups pressured Congress to repeal the tax. As a result, the program was terminated before it ever went into effect. (This incident is described more fully in Chapter 17.)

The lawmaking process   It is no simple matter to enact a law in the United States. A bill becomes a law only after it has successfully passed a number of hurdles, traps, and pitfalls. It can die in subcommittee, in full committee, on the floor of either house, in conference committee, or by presidential veto. It must pass all of these obstacles to become law; defeat at any one of them will likely be a death knell. Figure 12-3 indicates the complexity of the congressional lawmaking process.

The process begins when an individual member of the House or Senate introduces a bill. A **bill** is a proposal, drafted in the form of a law, that a member would like his or her colleagues to consider. A bill may be introduced in either house of Congress by any member of that house. Often, to give the appearance of broad political support, members solicit their colleagues to cosponsor a bill. When a bill is introduced, it is assigned a number by the clerk and referred to a committee by the presiding officer. Many bills go no farther; they die because the committee lacks the time or interest to deal with them.

For bills that do not die, the next step is examination by the committee.[13] Most congressional committees have subcommittees that conduct the initial examination of legislative proposals. Subcommittees hold hearings at which they gather written and oral testimony from witnesses who have knowledge of, or interest in, the bill. Typically the list of witnesses includes the congressional proponents of the bill, officials from agencies with a direct interest in it, the leaders of concerned interest groups, state and local officials who may be affected if the bill becomes law, and individuals who are directly concerned because the bill will affect their taxes or benefits. At hearings in the early 1990s on the regulation of cable television, for example, members of Congress heard testimony from local cable company owners and from the National Cable Television Association in opposition to federal control. They also heard from local mayors, the National League of Cities, and the Consumer Federation of America about the need for more consistent and effective federal regulation.

At the conclusion of the hearings, the subcommittee votes on the bill. Usually the voting occurs after a **mark-up session**, in which all of the members of the subcommittee participate in revising the bill to put it into a form that is acceptable to a majority of them. If the subcommittee supports the bill, it is

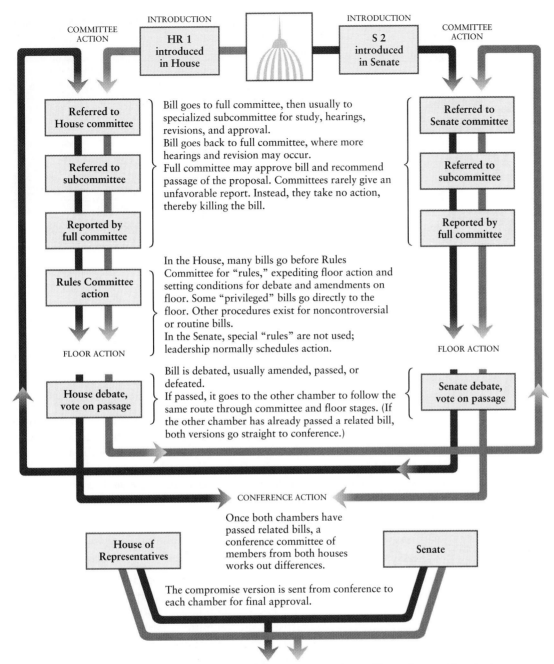

COMMITTEE ACTION   INTRODUCTION   INTRODUCTION   COMMITTEE ACTION

HR 1 introduced in House   **S 2** introduced in Senate

Referred to House committee

Referred to subcommittee

Reported by full committee

Bill goes to full committee, then usually to specialized subcommittee for study, hearings, revisions, and approval.
Bill goes back to full committee, where more hearings and revision may occur.
Full committee may approve bill and recommend passage of the proposal. Committees rarely give an unfavorable report. Instead, they take no action, thereby killing the bill.

Referred to Senate committee

Referred to subcommittee

Reported by full committee

Rules Committee action

In the House, many bills go before Rules Committee for "rules," expediting floor action and setting conditions for debate and amendments on floor. Some "privileged" bills go directly to the floor. Other procedures exist for noncontroversial or routine bills.
In the Senate, special "rules" are not used; leadership normally schedules action.

FLOOR ACTION   FLOOR ACTION

House debate, vote on passage

Bill is debated, usually amended, passed, or defeated.
If passed, it goes to the other chamber to follow the same route through committee and floor stages. (If the other chamber has already passed a related bill, both versions go straight to conference.)

Senate debate, vote on passage

CONFERENCE ACTION

Once both chambers have passed related bills, a conference committee of members from both houses works out differences.

House of Representatives   **Senate**

The compromise version is sent from conference to each chamber for final approval.

The compromise version approved by both houses is sent to the president, who can either sign it into law or veto it and return it to Congress.
Congress may override veto by a two-thirds majority vote in both houses. When this happens, the bill then becomes law without the president's signature.

HR 1 VETO   S 2 Signed

Figure 12-3 *How a bill becomes a law.* SOURCE: Guide to Congress *(Washington, D.C.: Congressional Quarterly, 1976), 345. Reprinted by permission of Congressional Quarterly, Inc.*

433

Members of the Senate (left) and the House (right) meeting as a joint conference committee to discuss disagreements over a bill passed by both houses of Congress. Conference committees are formed to resolve differences between House and Senate versions of a bill.

© Paul S. Conklin

returned to the full committee, where another mark-up may take place, followed by a vote of the full committee. Mark-up sessions are a key battleground for all the political forces that seek to shape the text—and thus the impact—of a bill.

If a majority of the full committee supports the bill, it is reported to the full House or Senate. The committee normally issues a written report in which it explains the contents of the bill, justifies committee support for it, and explains the arguments of dissenting committee members.

The House's procedure at this point differs from the Senate's. Bills reported out of committee in the Senate go directly to the floor, where debate is scheduled by the party leaders. The House, because of its larger size, has a Rules Committee that determines when a bill will be debated, how long the debate will last, and what kinds of amendments (if any) may be introduced during debate. Because the rule that governs a bill's consideration on the floor often has a significant impact on its final shape, the Rules Committee sometimes wields significant power in the House legislative process.

Once a bill has been reported to the floor, it is placed on a legislative calendar. In the House of Representatives debate is usually limited to a few hours or less, depending on how important or controversial a bill is. Senate floor rules are less rigid, and debate may last for several hours or days or, in some cases, weeks. In each house, debate is usually controlled by members who are designated as floor managers for the bill. The floor manager for the proponents (typically a committee or subcommittee chair who has worked for the bill) and the floor manager for the opposition (usually, but not always, a member of the minority party) will organize the debate and allot time to other members who share their views on the bill.[14]

During the debate individual members may introduce amendments that change the substance of the bill in some way. The House has much more rigid rules about amendments than the Senate. Unless specifically permitted by the rule on the bill, amendments offered in the House must be directly related, or germane, to the substance of the bill. In the Senate there are few restrictions on amendments, and senators are more prone to attaching nongermane amendments to any bill that happens to be under consideration. A common political tactic in the Senate, for example, is to attach a controversial provision to an essential or a popular piece of legislation. Such additions are called **riders** because they "ride" through the legislative process on the backs of other bills when they might not have survived on their own. In 1990, for example, proponents attached to a widely supported bill creating new federal judgeships a proposal that would permit the copyrighting of architectural designs of buildings. The amendment bore no relation to the content of the judgeship bill; the bill was simply a convenient vehicle for the amendment to "ride."

Amendments are voted on as they are introduced. Those that receive the support of a majority are integrated into the bill. When debate is completed and all amendments have been considered, a final vote on the bill occurs. Today this is almost always a recorded vote—that is, the position of each member is noted and recorded in the *Congressional Record,* the official journal of House and Senate proceedings. Senators vote orally when their names are called by the clerk. In the House, voting is done electronically. Members insert a plastic card in one of the teller machines on the House floor and push a button to indicate a vote of yea, nay, or present. Each member's vote is then indicated on a large tote board on the wall at the front of the chamber.

How do members decide their position on a bill or an amendment? For most members, the answer involves a complex personal calculus. Although the position taken by the party leaders often has a significant impact, Congress does not have the kind of party discipline that requires members to vote the party line on every issue. Some issues are highly relevant to members' constituents, and on such votes members are strongly inclined to take a position that best serves the interests of the people they represent. On other issues, members' personal views may determine how they vote. Some votes come in response to heavy lobbying by the president or by interest groups.[15]

On a great many legislative votes, most or all of these pressures are at

Cheryl Kemper–Starner Photography

Marjorie Margolies Mezvinsky, a first-term Democrat from Pennsylvania who cast the deciding vote approving President Clinton's 1993 budget proposal. The vote was potentially costly to this representative's chances for reelection, since her district had historically elected Republicans to the House. Back in her district after the vote, Mezvinsky had to explain her decision and restore the confidence of her constituents.

work, often tugging members in different directions. Most studies suggest that in such situations constituency interests and party loyalty weigh most heavily. But there is no simple, consistent explanation of individual voting behavior.

If a majority of the members present vote in favor of a bill, it is sent to the other house, where the process is repeated. It often happens that when a bill passes in the second house, it differs from the version passed in the first house. To resolve the differences, a joint conference committee is created. Its sole purpose is to construct from the differing versions a single bill that can win the approval of both houses. When the conference committee has completed its work, usually by forging a compromise, it reports back to each house. Another floor vote is taken in each house. If both houses agree to the conference committee's version of the bill, it is sent to the president for signature.

The president has several options. One is to sign the bill, at which point it becomes law. Another is to allow the bill to become law without a signature; this will occur ten working days after the bill is received, if Congress is still in session. The president may also veto the bill by declining to sign it and returning it to the house where it originated within ten days, accompanied by a message stating the reasons for the veto. Congress then has an opportunity to override the president's veto. An override, however, requires a two-thirds majority in each house and, as Table 12-4 indicates, rarely happens.

If the annual session of Congress ends within ten days of the passage of a bill, the president may exercise another option, the **pocket veto**, simply by declining to sign the bill. Because Congress is not in session, the president does not return the bill, nor is there any possibility of a congressional override. Because many bills are passed in the legislative rush that comes at the end of a congressional session, opportunities for pocket vetoes occur with some frequency.

The veto power is an important source of political leverage in the struggle between the president and Congress over the shape of legislation. For example, after the Chinese government's crackdown on dissident students in 1989, Congress passed a bill that would have allowed Chinese students to stay in the United States longer than their original visas permitted. This measure was intended to protect the students from prosecution when they returned to China. President Bush vetoed the bill. He was concerned with the effect it would have on his efforts to reestablish relations with China, and he believed that protection of the Chinese students could be accomplished by other means.

The veto angered many members of Congress, where the bill had passed overwhelmingly. The House overrode the veto by a vote of 390 to 25. But in the Senate President Bush lobbied heavily to retain support for his authority to lead the country in foreign affairs. The Senate voted 62 to 37 to override the bill, a few votes short of the two-thirds majority needed. The veto stood.

Rules, procedures, and precedents   The lawmaking process is governed by a highly developed set of rules and precedents. The first rules, written by Thomas Jefferson, still exist, although they have been altered considerably since Jefferson's time. Rules and precedents control such matters as parliamentary procedures in debate, the assignment of bills to committees, the operations of committees, and legislative recordkeeping. Because the rules shape political conflicts in Congress and play a large role in determining the strategies of political adversaries, some of their general effects on the operations and decisions of Congress are worth noting.[16]

TABLE 12-4

Presidential Vetoes of Congressional Bills, 1933–1993

PERIOD	PRESIDENT	REGULAR VETOES	POCKET VETOES	TOTAL VETOES	VETOES OVERRIDDEN
1933–1945	Roosevelt	372	363	735	9
1945–1953	Truman	180	70	250	12
1953–1961	Eisenhower	73	108	181	2
1961–1963	Kennedy	12	9	21	0
1963–1969	Johnson	16	14	30	0
1969–1974	Nixon	24	18	42	6
1974–1977	Ford	53	19	72	12
1977–1981	Carter	13	18	31	2
1981–1989	Reagan	39	39	78	9
1989–1993*	Bush	31[1]	15	46	1

* President Bush was president until January 20, 1993. As of April 1994, President Clinton had not issued any congressional vetoes.

[1] President Bush contended that four of his regular vetoes were pocket vetoes. Some members of Congress disagreed, noting that the president can exercise a pocket veto only after Congress has adjourned for the year, not during a recess. The dispute over terminology was not resolved, and all of those vetoes are listed here as regular vetoes.

SOURCE: Data from *Congressional Quarterly Weekly Report*, December 19, 1992, 3925–3926.

First, the rules enforce a decentralization of legislative power in both houses of Congress. They require that legislation be considered and acted on at a number of points (committee, subcommittee, floor, and joint conference) before final passage. In effect, each of these stages is a veto point, for defeat at any one of them usually kills a bill. There are procedures in the House and Senate rules for bypassing some of these steps, but they are unwieldy and rarely employed. Hence, members who control the veto points in the legislative process—an especially strong and obdurate committee chair, for instance—have significant power in determining what will or will not become law.

Second, the rules favor proponents of the status quo over proponents of change. The rules, in effect, bias the legislative process against change. The proponents of a new piece of legislation must succeed at every stage in the process. Their bill must win majorities in subcommittee, in full committee, on the floor, and so on. Opponents of a bill must win a majority at only one of these stages. They can defeat the bill in subcommittee, in full committee, or wherever they can construct a majority in opposition to the bill. The cards thus are stacked against new legislation. In recent Congresses only about 5 percent of all bills and joint resolutions introduced have been enacted.

Third, the rules work to slow the pace of legislative consideration. Congress has occasionally shown an ability to legislate quickly, particularly when confronted with a national security crisis. In September 1983, for instance, Congress was able in just a few days to work out a compromise with President Reagan permitting American peacekeeping forces to remain in Lebanon. In 1964, responding to reports of North Vietnamese attacks on American naval vessels, Congress passed in one day a resolution authorizing President Johnson

Senator Jesse Helms (R-North Carolina) is among the most conservative members of Congress and is often at odds even with his own party. But Helms is adept at using Senate rules to advance positions that have little support. He attaches riders to bills, delays confirmation of presidential nominations, and filibusters against legislation he opposes.

Robert Trippett/Sipa Press

to respond to the attacks. But quick action by Congress is the exception, not the norm. Most of the time the legislative process grinds away slowly because so many participants at so many stages have to study and deliberate.

Fourth, the rules provide several mechanisms by which determined minorities can thwart the will of congressional majorities. In the Senate, for instance, much is accomplished through a procedure called **unanimous consent.** Action can be taken without debate when all members consent to that procedure, but only one dissenting senator can prevent action under unanimous consent and thus slow the progress of the Senate. Senator Jesse Helms (R-North Carolina) has sometimes used this tactic to force the Senate to pay attention to issues that are important to him personally. His objections to unanimous-consent resolutions have earned him the title "Senator No."

Also in the Senate, which has a long tradition of unlimited debate, a small group of senators may delay or even prevent a vote on a bill by carrying out a **filibuster.** They do this by gaining recognition to speak in debate and then not relinquishing the floor. Some senators have held the floor for more than twenty-four consecutive hours, and a group of senators working together can hold the floor indefinitely. It now takes a vote by three-fifths of the entire Senate (sixty senators) to invoke **cloture** and thereby end a filibuster. This means that if 41 percent or more of the senators are intensely opposed to a bill that has majority support, final action on the bill can be slowed or prevented. Even after cloture, loopholes in the Senate rules permit a single senator to prolong debate.

In 1988, Senate sponsors of a bill requiring that workers be notified when they are exposed to toxic substances in the workplace failed on four occasions to gain cloture when opponents undertook a filibuster. This legislation was strongly supported by most labor unions; its principal advocates were liberal Democrats led by Senator Howard Metzenbaum (D-Ohio). The bill was strongly opposed by many business interests; conservative Republicans, led by Senator Orrin Hatch (R-Utah), participated in the filibuster. When only forty-two senators voted for cloture on the fourth cloture vote, proponents of the bill gave up their effort to end the filibuster. The bill was withdrawn from the calendar and effectively killed. The conservatives had succeeded in using the filibuster to accomplish their political goals. The successful Republican effort to kill President Clinton's economic stimulus proposal in the spring of 1993 is another example of the filibuster at work.

A bill can die in a committee or a subcommittee when a majority of its members opposes it, even though a majority of the members of the house in which it was introduced favors it. In these and other ways, the rules permit the will of a determined minority to supersede that of a majority.

The legislative process is decentralized, slow, and tedious, and crushes most bills. For members of Congress who have legislative goals, it is a demanding consumer of time and effort and an unrelenting source of frustration. But it does ensure that in most cases new laws are carefully considered and solidly supported before they are enacted.

Representation

In the United States, participation in the national government occurs through the process of **representation.** The framers of the Constitution were most concerned about the quality of representation. To help ensure that members of Congress would be sensitive to the interests of the people they represent, the Constitution requires that they reside in the state from which they are elected. This requirement does not exist in most other countries. To ensure that the people know what the government is doing, the Constitution requires both houses of Congress to keep and publish a journal of their activities in which the yea and nay votes are recorded so that individual members can be held accountable. And to ensure that members of Congress keep faith with their constituents, the Constitution provides for regular and frequent elections.

Every member of Congress represents two groups of citizens. In that every member has some responsibility to the national interest, he or she represents the nation as a whole. The member also represents a **constituency,** the state or congressional district that elects her or him to Congress.

The interests of these two groups may be in conflict. Sometimes what is best for the district may not be best for the nation. Higher farm prices benefit individual farmers but not the nation's consumers. Federal subsidies for the construction of a dam in a particular district will have local benefits but will cause an increase in everyone's taxes (a similar problem—the closing of military bases—is discussed in the Case Study on page 440). Members also confront conflicts between their own views and the views of their constituents. Some policies that a representative believes to be best for the nation may have little support in his or her own district.

Constituent relations How do members of Congress keep in touch with their constituents? How do they know their constituents' opinions? How do they deal with disagreements within their constituency? Each member develops his or her own ways of doing these things.

Constituencies are not monolithic, single-minded groups of voters. They tend instead to be composed of people with varying attitudes, levels of information, interests, and partisan preferences. Richard Fenno, a political scientist who has studied relationships between members of Congress and their constit-

Military Base Closings

Across the mouth of the James River from Norfolk, Virginia, sits Fort Monroe, constructed during the War of 1812. Though a relic of the early nineteenth century, Fort Monroe continued to be an active military base in the last decade of the twentieth. The Department of Defense had sought for years to close the fort, arguing that it was costly to operate and no longer served any needed military purpose. But the base remained open because Virginia's representatives in Congress consistently and effectively fought its closing.

For members of Congress few issues more fully provoke the conflict between national and constituent interests than the closing of military bases. There are hundreds of military installations scattered all over the United States. Each brings federal personnel and federal dollars into the state and congressional district where it is located and helps to support the local economy. But as military strategies change, some bases become obsolete or unnecessary, and to reduce defense costs, the Department of Defense seeks to close them. That's when the conflict sets in.

Members of Congress believe in tight budgets and the avoidance of wasteful spending. All other things being equal, most would willingly vote to close military bases that no longer serve any important purpose. A member's perceptions often change, however, when one of the bases recommended for closing is in his or her state or district.

© Katherine Lambert

Defense contractors have had to retool and downsize as military bases have closed and business opportunities have dwindled. Here a former defense worker monitors a computer terminal to track not missiles or airplanes but city buses. Companies like Westinghouse, Lockheed, Hughes Aircraft, and Martin Marietta are now marketing such products as safety equipment, airport and weather radar, mail-sorting and reservations systems, and satellites for cellular phone networks.

Members almost always oppose the closing of bases in order to protect the local economy from the harmful impact of lost federal funds. But they also do so for personal reasons. A base closing is often viewed as evidence that a member lacks clout in

uents, has indicated that most members of Congress view their constituencies in several different ways, or as what he calls a "nest of concentric circles"[17] (see Figure 12-4).

The outer and largest of these circles is the "geographic constituency," the whole district viewed from the standpoint of location and demographic characteristics. Is it a farm district or an inner-city district? What are its principal commercial products? What is the religious and ethnic composition of the people who live there? The largest circle represents the district in the broadest sense.

The next circle is the "reelection constituency." It represents a much more political constituency than does the first. Thus, the reelection constituency is more important than the geographic constituency in determining the member's

Washington. A future opponent will fix on a base closing as evidence of poor representation, in the same way that an incumbent will focus on the prevention of a base closing as evidence of effective representation.

Members help each other in the effort to forestall a base closing. A member whose district has an endangered base will join with other members whose districts also have such bases in a mutual effort to thwart any closings. Few members can single-handedly prevent a closing, but all the members from districts with proposed closings have enough collective clout to do so. These political coalitions often reach across party and ideological lines.

It has become extremely difficult for the Defense Department to close any bases. In 1976 Congress passed a bill requiring congressional approval of all base closings. President Gerald Ford vetoed the bill, but Congress later passed another measure requiring hazardous-waste studies to be conducted on any base that was proposed for closing. Not a single military base was closed in the fourteen years after this time-consuming requirement went into effect.

To undercut the political coalitions that had so often prevented closings, in 1988 some members of Congress proposed a new approach. Instead of recommendations coming from the Defense Department, a new law established an independent commission to identify bases no longer essential to national defense. The commission's recommendations go into effect unless both houses of Congress vote to overturn them. Under the law, Congress cannot remove individual bases from the list; it must vote to close all the bases or none.

Toward the end of 1988, the commission recommended the closing of eighty-six bases, for an eventual savings of $700 million a year. There was much opposition to the recommendations, especially in the House. The opposition was led by Representative George Brown (D-California). Norton Air Force Base, one of the bases recommended for closing, was in his district. A majority prevailed, however, and Congress did not overturn the commission's recommendations, despite the discomfort they created for many members. Base closings continued into the Clinton administration. With each round, the players change, but the politics remains the same. Those who represent districts with bases on the closure list fight to keep "their" bases open, even as they agree with the need to reduce overall military spending.

Discussion questions
1. How does the new procedure for closing bases alter the politics of congressional decision making on this matter? With what effect?
2. Are members of Congress being irresponsible when they oppose the closing of an obsolete military base in their district? Why or why not?
3. How might the base-closing process be improved?

positions on policy issues. The reelection constituency consists of the people who vote for the member in the general election. Members often perceive communities and special interests in their districts in terms of the political support they provide. They say things like "I never get many votes over on the west side" or "I can always count on the support of the Chamber of Commerce crowd." It is a common fact of political life that members of Congress are more responsive to those who vote for them than to those who do not.

Members of Congress are even more responsive to people in the inner circle, the "primary constituency." These are the people who provide loyal support in primary elections. They not only vote for members but also work and spend for them. They form the core of the member's political support.

The fourth circle is the "personal constituency." These are the people with

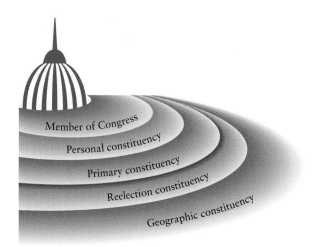

Figure 12-4 *House members' perceptions of their constituencies.* SOURCE: *Adapted from Richard F. Fenno, Jr.,* Homestyle: House Members in Their Districts *(Boston: Little, Brown, 1978), 1–27.*

whom the member has close personal ties. Some may be active in politics, others not. This group includes the people who are most likely to advise the member on political and policy matters. They provide funds and help during campaigns. The member trusts their political perceptions and leans heavily on them for advice.

Fenno's explanation of congressional constituencies sheds light on the politics of representation. Constituencies are quite complex, with overlapping and often conflicting interests. As a consequence, members must constantly interact with the "folks back home" to discern the direction and intensity of their constituents' opinions.

The representative at work   Conventional wisdom suggests that representation is a one-way process, that representatives are given "instructions" by their constituents and simply react to those instructions. That is a misperception. Members rarely receive anything resembling instructions from home. They do tend to hear a good deal from the people they represent, but studies of congressional mail suggest that this type of communication has a number of limitations.

First, although members may receive thousands of letters a week, most of their constituents never write or call. A flood of communications about some particular issue is likely to indicate a campaign "stimulated" by one or more interest group. The communications that members receive on such occasions often look or sound exactly the same, and this somewhat diminishes their impact. Public opinion polls indicate that only about 15 percent of all adults have ever communicated with their representatives in Congress.[18]

Second, many of the communications that members receive have little to do with legislative issues. They are requests for help with specific problems such as expediting a passport, assisting with a grant application, or getting a disabled veteran into a veterans' hospital. Much of a member's mail also includes form letters stimulated by political interest groups in an attempt to sway the member's vote on a bill.

Third, many of the communications that a member receives contradict each other. Some constituents may recommend a vote for a bill, others a vote against it. On clean-air legislation, for instance, environmentalists may want

The American Congress is one of the most accessible legislatures in the world. Debates and votes are open to the public and are reported in full. Anyone can phone, write, or visit the office of a member of Congress.

A good source of background information about a representative is *The Almanac of American Politics*, published biennially. To find out exactly what a representative has said on the floor of Congress and how he or she has voted on a bill, check the *Congressional Record*, the official journal of congressional proceedings. It is published every day that Congress is in session. To learn your representative's position on any issue, start with the *Congressional Quarterly Weekly Report*, a magazine known as *CQ*. At the end of each week's *CQ* is a list of each member's vote on every bill on which there is a recorded vote.

When writing to a member of Congress, address the letters as follows:

Honorable John A. Cruz
United States Senate
Washington, DC 20510

Honorable Sally S. Goodman
United States House of Representatives
Washington, DC 20515

Normally, the member's office will respond by mail within two or three weeks on a policy issue. A response may take longer if you write about a personal problem involving an agency of the government.

To contact a member's local office, look for the address and phone number in the government pages (blue pages) of the local phone book. A call to the local office will often provide the quickest solution to a problem or the most efficient (and least expensive) way to register your views on a policy issue. To contact your representative's Washington office, call the Capitol switchboard: (202) 224-3121.

If you wish to visit your representative's office to get help with a problem or to express your views while you are in Washington, D.C., call ahead. Members of Congress are always happy to see their constituents. Remember, though, that their schedules are hectic, and they are rarely available for unscheduled visits.

the member to vote for stringent regulations, but factory owners may want weaker regulations. Members hear a lot from constituents—veterans, farmers, schools, hospitals, and others—who want increases in the benefits they receive from the government. But they also hear frequently from people who want budget cuts and lower taxes.

Fourth, members hear nothing or next to nothing from their constituents about many issues, especially issues that have little direct bearing on the district. Members from inner-city districts hear little from their constituents about agricultural subsidies, for example. Nor do representatives from New England hear much from the folks at home about coal mine safety.

To overcome deficiencies in the communications received from constituents, many members of Congress work hard to interact with the people they represent. They try to improve their understanding of constituent opinion, especially on complex issues that are important to the district. But they also want to build constituent support for their own views. There are many issues on which the member's personal opinion is clearly formulated and constituents' opinions are ambiguous or contradictory. In these cases members have genuine

Speaker of the House Thomas Foley (D-Washington) visits citizens in his district. The complexity of contemporary issues requires all members of Congress—no matter how powerful—to stay in close touch with the people they represent.

Jeff Green/NYT Pictures

opportunities to become opinion leaders in their districts. Leadership of constituent opinion is an important, but often overlooked, component of the representative relationship.

In recent years members of Congress have developed a number of successful techniques for reaching out to their districts. A generous **franking privilege** enables them to mail newsletters and questionnaires to every postal box in their states or districts, free of charge. The congressional recording studios enable them to send video or audio tapes to television and radio stations back home. There are ample funds for travel between Washington and their districts. Many of those who live east of the Mississippi River try to get home every week. Most members spend at least part of every month in their home districts, aided by the typical monthly schedule of Congress: three weeks in session and one week for "district work periods." All members have one or more offices in their districts with full-time staffs. Members also keep in touch by reading local newspapers, telephoning district leaders, and meeting visitors from the district when they come to Washington.

But the relationship between members and their constituents is based on more than just the frequency and technology of communication. Most members have grown up in their districts. Their political socialization took place there. They entered politics and achieved their first political successes there. They tend to share the economic and social values of the people they represent, not simply because it is politically expedient to do so but because those are their personal values as well. In reality, much of the relationship between members and their districts is felt rather than communicated.

In Chapter 10 we noted the extraordinary success rate of members of Congress who run for reelection. Here we see an important part of the reason. In electoral decisions Americans seem to be expressing considerable satisfaction with the way they are represented by their own member of Congress. There is nothing easy or automatic about this satisfaction; it reflects the substantial effort that contemporary members of Congress apply to their responsibilities as representatives and the abundant array of resources available to them in carrying out those responsibilities. Recent studies of the House of Representatives, for example, show that average House members now have more than a quarter of their allotted staff working on specific constituent problems.[19] For members of Congress there is an electoral reward for responsive representation.[20] This gives them a powerful incentive to concentrate a substantial portion of their energies on this aspect of their job.

Administrative Oversight

The policy experts in the executive branch make the day-to-day decisions, and the people's representatives in the legislative branch review them. The legislative branch watches and, when necessary, attempts to alter the actions of the executive branch. Administrative oversight is an essential congressional function because Congress is ill equipped to make every important public policy decision. In many areas it delegates responsibility to bureaucratic agencies, charging them with making expert decisions but subjecting those decisions to legislative review. When this process works as intended, it combines bureaucratic expertise and popular control.

The importance of administrative oversight derives from the view, widely held among the framers of the Constitution, that the American people should be not only served by their government but protected from it as well. As public policy grows more complex, the opportunities for administrative error and abuse increase. Pentagon procurement scandals, flaws in the 1990 census count, and the *Challenger* shuttle disaster are examples of such errors. Vigilant oversight has become increasingly important.

Techniques Congress performs its oversight function in a great many ways.[21] Most of the standing committees of Congress conduct **oversight hearings** as a regular part of their responsibilities. Some have subcommittees to which they assign those hearings. (The performance of administrative oversight by one powerful representative is described on page 427.) During an oversight hearing the activities of an executive agency or the management of a specific program are reviewed in depth. Such hearings are often held when the authorized tenure of an agency or a program is nearing an end. The hearing is usually preceded by an investigation by the committee staff. At the hearing itself, executive-branch officials are called to explain their activities and to answer the committee's questions. The product of an oversight hearing may be a report suggesting changes in administrative procedures, remedial legislation, or reauthorization of the agency or program.

Political conflict over institutional powers often emerges in oversight hearings. In 1989, for example, the House Intelligence Committee sought at several such hearings to obtain copies of internal reports issued by the inspector general of the Central Intelligence Agency (CIA) examining the agency's activities and administration. William Webster, the director of the CIA, refused to release the reports. After months of wrangling, the committee finally voted to include in the 1990 authorization legislation for the CIA a provision that would broaden congressional access to the reports. In other words, having failed to obtain the reports through the oversight process, the committee turned to the legislative process, where its authority was more formal—and ultimately more effective.

In addition to oversight hearings, Congress conducts **special investigations**. Some special investigations are virtually indistinguishable from oversight hearings. They are conducted by permanent committees and subcommittees with no special appropriations of funds or additions to committee staffs. More commonly, however, investigations differ from routine oversight hearings in the depth of their examinations, the vigor with which they are conducted, and the amount of funds and staff resources committed to them.

Congress often establishes a temporary committee to conduct major investigations. The committee has its own staff (frequently headed by an attorney with a national reputation) and its own, often very ample, budget. For example, to conduct the investigation of the presidential campaign activities of 1972, which came to be known as the Watergate investigation, a separate committee headed by Senator Sam Ervin (D-North Carolina) was established. It lasted for a year and a half and had a budget of almost $2 million and a staff of more than sixty people. Similar investigations have been conducted in the past three decades on such matters as the assassination of President John F. Kennedy, the fate of soldiers missing in action in Vietnam, and the diversion of funds from Iranian arms sales to the contras in Nicaragua.

Special investigations are often a source of tension between the president and Congress. Presidents frequently claim that such investigations are inspired by the opposition party to embarrass or weaken the administration. In the late 1940s, President Harry Truman, a Democrat, made the claim of partisanship against a young Republican representative named Richard Nixon for his role in the aggressive investigation of communist influence in Truman's administration. A quarter of a century later, Nixon, then the Republican president, made the same claim against the Democrats who led the Watergate investigations.

Employees of the executive branch also fall under congressional oversight through **personnel control**. Those who serve at the top levels—cabinet secretaries, agency heads, regulatory commissioners—are presidential appointees whose appointments are subject to Senate confirmation. When the president nominates a candidate to fill one of these positions, the nomination must be reviewed and approved by majority vote in the Senate before it takes effect. The Senate can, and occasionally does, reject candidates proposed by the president, as it did in the case of John Tower.

Congress also has control over the salaries and employment conditions of all federal employees, both career civil servants and presidential appointees. It sets federal pay scales; establishes "personnel ceilings" that limit the number of people who can work in a specified agency or office; creates general hiring qualifications; and approves routine personnel policies regarding annual leave, sick pay, dismissals, retirements, and pensions. This range of control gives Congress some discretion in determining who will work where in the executive branch and under what conditions. Congress sought to enlarge its political control over the activities of the inspector general of the CIA, for example, by enacting legislation making that position a presidential appointment subject to Senate confirmation.

Financial control—the power of the purse—is the most important and effective of Congress's techniques for overseeing the work of the executive branch. The Constitution (Article I, Section 9) is quite specific on this point: "No money shall be drawn from the treasury, but in consequence of appropriations made by law." Before Congress appropriates funds to an agency or

UPI/Bettmann

As a young member of the House of Representatives in the 1940s, Richard Nixon (R-California) aggressively investigated activities of the executive branch, especially if they involved allegations of communist influence. This helped him gain a national reputation that propelled his political career and ultimately landed him in the White House.

program, it assesses the manner in which previous appropriations have been used, and it examines the stated plans for the use of the funds being requested. This work is usually conducted by the House and Senate Appropriations Committees, which hold annual hearings for virtually every program and agency in the government. At the hearings executive-branch officials must explain their past activities and defend their budget requests for the coming year.[22]

In a great many cases Congress appropriates less money than executive agencies request.[23] By shifting funds from one program to another, it may also change the priorities reflected in executive budget requests. Late in 1989, for example, Congress made significant alterations in President Bush's recommendations for weapons programs. It reduced by more than $1 billion the president's request for the Strategic Defense Initiative ("Star Wars"), but it also sought to fund continued production of the Navy's F-14D fighter plane and the Army's AHIP helicopter, programs that the president had sought to reduce.

The General Accounting Office (GAO), the federal government's accounting arm, is located in the legislative branch. The GAO conducts audits of government programs to determine whether they have been well managed and whether their benefits justify their costs. GAO audit reports are submitted to Congress, which sometimes uses them to target inefficiency or malfeasance in the management of federal programs or in the use of federal funds. Much of the information that led to intense congressional review of mismanagement in the Department of Housing and Urban Development (HUD) during the Reagan years came from GAO audits.

Impeachment is the legislature's weapon of last resort. It is the power to remove from office the president, the vice president, or any other civil officer of the United States who has been found guilty of (in the words of Article II, Section 4) "treason, bribery, or other high crimes and misdemeanors."

The impeachment process begins with the introduction of a bill of impeachment in the House of Representatives. This bill is referred to the Judiciary Committee, which may do nothing or may debate the bill and report it to the full House. The full House debates the charges and then determines by majority vote whether to impeach the person named in the bill. If a majority opposes the bill, the charges are dropped; if a majority supports the bill, the person is impeached. The process then moves to the Senate for trial with the members of the Senate serving, in effect, as the jury. When the impeached officer is the president, and only then, the Chief Justice of the United States presides over the Senate trial. Conviction by the Senate can occur only with the assent of two-thirds of the senators present and voting.

The framers of the Constitution devised an impeachment procedure that is unwieldy and difficult to use.[24] They did not intend impeachment to be routinely used, and it has not been. Over the course of American history, impeachment proceedings have been initiated in the House more than sixty times, but as of the end of 1992 only fifteen federal officials had ever been impeached and only seven had been convicted. Most of them were federal judges, including three who were impeached and removed from office in the 1980s.

Only one president, Andrew Johnson, the seventeenth president, has been impeached. His opponents in Congress accused him not of corruption but of personnel actions to which they were opposed. He was acquitted in 1868 and remained in office until the expiration of his term. Richard Nixon's timely resignation in 1974—he decided to resign when support from members of his own party in Congress collapsed—prevented his near-certain impeachment and conviction.

Performance Congress has been criticized for inconsistency in the performance of its oversight function and for failing to uncover or remedy inefficiencies in the management of executive agencies. Given the ample opportunities available for effective oversight, what accounts for these shortfalls?

The best way to answer this question is to look at oversight from the perspective of individual members of Congress. As Representative Norman Y. Mineta (D-California) once said, "Oversight is very tough. It's time-consuming, painstaking investigative work. And there's no political appeal in it. There's much more appeal in getting a bill passed and saying, 'Here's what my bill will do for senior citizens.' "[25]

There are numerous disincentives to effective administrative oversight. Oversight provides fewer rewards to individual members than other congressional activities provide. Except in a highly publicized episode like the Watergate investigation, oversight rarely wins acclaim or publicity for a member. It fuels institutional rivalry, often angering the target agency and the political interest groups that benefit from that agency's programs. Finally, oversight takes away from time that might be spent more profitably on legislation or constituent relations. For these reasons the incentive systems that govern the behavior of most individual members may not inspire the arduous and often unrewarding effort required for successful oversight.

The perennial "message":
Throwing the bums back in

WE GET IT!

CONGRESSIONAL REFORM AND ITS IMPACT

One way to understand the changes undergone by Congress after 1968 is to put yourself in the position of a new member who is trying to establish a legislative career. To establish a career, you need to accomplish two things: (1) get yourself reelected every time your term is over and (2) make your influence felt in legislative policy making and participate in the process by which the legislature makes policy. The former is essential to any legislative career at all; the latter is essential to achieving a measure of satisfaction and success.

In the 1950s and early 1960s a new legislator could not easily accomplish either goal. The internal operations of Congress were dominated by the chairs of the powerful committees and by the party leaders, such as Senate Majority Leader Lyndon Johnson and House Speaker Sam Rayburn, who worked with them. Junior members had small staffs, meager allowances, little access to committee and subcommittee influence, and minimal impact on the policy agenda.

That began to change in the late 1960s under the impetus of an organization called the Democratic Study Group (DSG), formed by Democrats recently elected to the House. The DSG sought to alter House rules so that members who lacked seniority could play a more significant role in legislative policy making. Beginning in 1968, its efforts succeeded. The turning point came in 1974, when the seventy-five Democrats newly elected to the House banded together to accelerate the reform movement.

These new members were different in important ways from members elected earlier in the twentieth century.[26] Many were younger and less politically experienced; fewer had served in state legislatures before coming to Congress; and as a group they were far less likely to possess long-standing connections to state or local political party organizations. They were, on the whole, more independent and more ideological and issue oriented than most of their predecessors. As a result, they were far less tolerant of the traditions and procedures of Congress that denied new members access to legislative power. The "Class of '74" stimulated revisions in House rules and Democratic party procedures to permit broader participation in decision making and more equitable access to resources and to positions of influence.

The first target of reform was the seniority system. For most of the twentieth century, committee chairs had automatically gone to the member of the majority party with the longest consecutive service on the committee. No meaningful provision existed for altering that selection process or for removing committee chairs who were unresponsive to their party leaders or colleagues. Safe from the threat of removal, some chairs acted arbitrarily: putting on the committee agenda only the bills that they personally supported, granting subcommittee chairs to their friends and not to their adversaries, tightly controlling staff and other committee resources. In the heyday of the seniority system, Congress operated very much like an oligarchy in which a score or so of committee chairs dominated.

In the 1970s the newer members of the House succeeded in loosening the hold of the seniority system. Most committee chairs continue to be the senior members of the majority party on the various committees, but the majority party caucus now elects committee chairs at the beginning of each Congress. Some senior members have been removed by this procedure, and those removals have had a chastening effect on the others. In addition, committee chairs have lost much of the control they once had over subcommittees and committee resources. Though still powerful figures in Congress, committee chairs are no longer unassailable oligarchs.

In the 1970s junior members also started to get seats on the most prestigious committees. The number of subcommittees grew so that virtually every member of the majority party could expect to chair a subcommittee after just a few years in Congress. The enlargement of subcommittee and personal staffs and the growth in support agencies like the Congressional Research Service made individual members less reliant on congressional leaders for information. The ability of new members to develop legislation and conduct their own inquiries was enhanced. Legislative initiatives succeeded that might previously have been quashed at the whim of a party leader or committee chair.

The most far-reaching reform took place in the House, but similar efforts were under way in the Senate. In both houses individual members achieved greater and more effective involvement in the legislative process, and they acquired more autonomy than their counterparts had at any time in this century.

For the performance of Congress as an institution, this change had both advantages and disadvantages.[27] Although the openness and representative quality of the legislative process expanded, Congress's capacity for coordination was weakened. The autonomy of members came at the expense of the authority of leaders. No individual or ruling elite could provide a clear sense of direction, set priorities, or coordinate legislative activities.

Mandatory Term Limits

In the early 1990s the combination of public dissatisfaction with the performance of Congress and remarkably high reelection rates for members of Congress led to calls for the imposition of mandatory limits on the number of terms a member could serve. The framers of the Constitution had debated this matter at some length, concluding that the decision was best left to the voters in individual states and districts. No term limits were included in the language of the Constitution.

In 1988 and 1992, however, the national Republican party platform called for mandatory term limits for members of Congress. The party's nominees, George Bush and Dan Quayle, strongly endorsed the proposal. In 1990, voters in California, Colorado, and Oklahoma imposed term limits on members of their state legislatures, and citizens in the state of Washington narrowly defeated a proposal to impose limits on the terms of their representatives in Congress. In 1992, a number of state ballots included referendum questions on legislative term limits. Public opinion polls suggested that term limits was an idea whose time had come.

Most of the proposals called for limits of twelve consecutive years on House or Senate service. Senators would be forced to retire after two six-year terms, House members after six two-year terms. Proponents of term limits argued that this limitation was the only effective way of ensuring significant turnover in Congress. Because of existing campaign finance procedures and the many other perquisites and resources available to incumbents, it had become nearly impossible for challengers to defeat a sitting member of Congress. As a result, it was argued, Congress had become increasingly insulated and self-serving and decreasingly responsive to the will of the American people.

Opponents of term limits argued that they are too blunt an instrument for solving the problems of Congress. They would force the retirement of good legislators as well as bad ones. They would produce, especially in the Senate, a sizable class of lame-duck representatives who would have little incentive to be responsive to the public after winning their last election before mandatory retirement. And, by removing from Congress its most experienced and powerful members, the imposition of term limits would inevitably enhance the influence of nonelected congressional staff and executive-branch bureaucrats. Many of the opponents of term limits admitted the magnitude of an incumbent's advantages in congressional elections but believed that the problem should be addressed by campaign finance reform rather than by term limits.

Unusually high congressional turnover in 1992 temporarily slowed the movement for term limits. But the proposal is likely to be a source of discussion and controversy throughout the 1990s.

In the early 1980s there was a reaction to this powerful wave of congressional reform. Some scholars have referred to the legislature in this period as the "postreform Congress."[28] It is characterized principally by a resurgence in partisanship. Party leaders, especially in the House, have regained a significant portion of the influence they lost during the previous two decades. In part, their success has resulted from internal efforts to reinvigorate and institutionalize the party caucuses. Party leadership committees like the Democratic Steering and Policy Committee in the House and the Democratic Policy Committee in the Senate have become important forums for the development of substantive party positions. The whip system in the House, an essential element of the party leadership structure, has grown so that now one-third of House Democrats have whip responsibilities.

Two other changes in the 1980s abetted the revitalization of congressional partisanship. One was the growing ideological homogeneity of the legislative parties. As politics in the South was changing, the southern Democrats in Congress came to resemble their northern colleagues more closely than at any time since World War II. At the same time, the liberal, or moderate, wing of the Republican party was shrinking almost to the vanishing point. Beginning in the late 1970s, therefore, party unity in floor voting began to grow. Although the congressional Democrats and Republicans can hardly be compared to the tightly disciplined parliamentary parties of western Europe, they did reach important new levels of internal unity and consistency in the postreform period.

The momentum of party revitalization in Congress was accelerated by a period of divided government that lasted from 1981 through 1992. With Republicans firmly in control of the White House and Democrats equally firmly in control of the House of Representatives, partisan disagreements between the executive and legislative branches reinforced party unity in Congress. Realizing that they had little chance for presidential support of their policy initiatives, Democrats in Congress turned increasingly to their own party leaders. They began to grant those party leaders the instruments of power and the deference they needed to construct and pursue a party program. Emboldened, successive Speakers of the House responded with increasingly vigorous leadership efforts.

The contemporary Congress thus is a product of two recent trends. One was driven by the needs of individual members for electoral security and internal influence, the other by institutional needs for centralized leadership. In an era marked by large budget deficits and critical shortages of funds for new programs, Congress often struggles to resolve conflicts between competing groups making demands on the same limited resources. Coping with policy issues that require painstaking compromises that impose sacrifices on specific segments of the population has always been difficult for Congress. Those, however, are precisely the kinds of issues that occupy the most prominent positions on the legislative agenda. President Clinton's initial proposals for deficit reduction in 1993, for example, quickly ran into opposition from a variety of interests: western ranchers who did not want to pay fees for the right to graze their cattle on public lands, oil producers who did not want their products burdened with new taxes, the elderly who held out against any decrease in annual cost-of-living adjustments to Social Security benefits. Everyone, it seemed, was for deficit reduction, but no one wanted to bear the cost.

Over the course of American history, the internal organization of Congress has swung back and forth between the desire for a legislative process that is truly democratic and participatory and the desire for legislative efficiency. These are contradictory goals. Efficiency requires centralization of authority; broad participation does not easily tolerate centralized authority. Unable to accomplish both objectives simultaneously, Congress periodically reforms itself to adjust the balance between them. The legislative upheaval of the 1960s and 1970s maximized procedural democracy and broad participation in decision making at the expense of legislative efficiency. The efforts of the recent postreform period swung the balance in the other direction by empowering central leadership mechanisms. If history is a reliable guide, neither change will be permanent.

Congress is a *bicameral legislature* composed of two legislative bodies: the House of Representatives and the Senate. Each member of the House represents a district with a population of about 575,000 and serves for a two-year term. Senators serve six-year terms; there are two senators from each state.

Members of Congress typically have large staffs of aides who do clerical chores, write speeches, meet with lobbyists, and handle *casework*—the individual problems of constituents. Congressional committees also have staffs, which assist them in setting an agenda, scheduling hearings, developing legislation, and overseeing the work of executive agencies. A third group of congressional employees includes those who work for specialized support agencies: the Congressional Research Service, the Office of Technology Assessment, the Congressional Budget Office, and the General Accounting Office. The number of congressional employees has grown rapidly in recent years.

In the initial Congresses, party caucuses hammered out important policy decisions. Committees began to play a more dominant role after the Civil War, but by the end of the nineteenth century party leaders in Congress had become the principal powers. Within a decade they had become so powerful that a revolt occurred and the committees again became the power centers. The *seniority system* ensured that the member of the majority party with the longest consecutive service on a committee would automatically be its chair.

Whereas tight *party discipline* is normal in legislatures in Britain and France, political parties in Congress have limited control over their own members. In the House, the majority party controls the selection of the *Speaker of the House*. Working with other party leaders, especially *whips*, the Speaker helps determine the issues that will be given top priority. The Speaker's leadership is based less on real power than on persuasion and political skill. In the Senate, the primary job of the party leaders is to organize the business of the Senate.

The proponents of each bill introduced in Congress must form a coalition in support of that bill. Politics in Congress focuses on the task of building these shifting alliances. In recent years individual legislators known as *issue entrepreneurs* have tended to specialize in particular substantive matters and to seek support among their colleagues for policies dealing with those matters.

Most of the work of Congress is done in committees. Committees hold public hearings at which supporters and opponents of bills may express their views. They also engage in *administrative oversight*—monitoring the work of the executive agencies in their areas of jurisdiction, reviewing budget requests, and passing judgment on the qualifications of presidential appointees. *Standing committees* are permanent committees that have full authority to recommend legislation; most are divided into subcommittees. *Select (special) committees* are created to deal with a specific set of issues and have limited functions and authority. *Joint committees* are composed of members of both houses of Congress; *joint conference committees* are formed to resolve the differences that occur when the two houses pass varying forms of the same bill.

Legislation is accomplished through deliberation and partisan adjustment. A long gestation period is common for significant legislation, and 90 percent of the bills introduced in a typical Congress never become law.

The lawmaking process begins when a member of the House or Senate introduces a *bill*, or proposal, for consideration. The bill is assigned to a committee, which may decide not to consider it. If the bill is considered, it is initially examined by a subcommittee, which may hold hearings on the subject of the bill. At the conclusion of the hearings, the subcommittee holds a *mark-up session*, in which the bill is revised and then voted on. If the subcommittee supports the bill, it is returned to the full committee, where another mark-up and vote take place.

If a majority of the full committee supports the bill, it is reported to the full House or Senate. It is then placed on a legislative calendar and sent to the floor for debate. During the debate individual members may introduce amendments. In the Senate, controversial provisions called *riders* are often attached to popular bills. When voting on a bill, senators vote orally in a roll-call vote; representatives vote electronically. If a majority of the members present vote in favor of the bill, it is sent to the other house, where the process is repeated. If the two houses pass different versions of the bill, it is sent to a conference committee. If both houses agree to the conference committee's version, the bill is sent to the president for signature.

The president may sign the bill or allow it to become law without a signature. He may also veto the bill by declining to sign it and returning it to Congress within ten days. Congress may override a veto, but an override requires a two-thirds majority in each house and hence is rare. If the annual session of Congress ends within ten days of the passage of a bill, the president may exercise a *pocket veto* by simply declining to sign the bill.

Congressional rules and procedures require that legislation be considered and acted on at a number of points; defeat at any of those points usually kills the bill. The rules thus favor proponents of the status quo, work to slow the pace of legislation, and enable determined minorities to thwart the will of majorities. In the Senate, a single senator can delay or prevent action by objecting to the procedure known as *unanimous consent*. Or a small group of senators may prevent a vote on a bill through a *filibuster*, in which they gain recognition to speak and then do not relinquish the floor. A vote by three-fifths of the entire Senate is required to invoke *cloture* and end a filibuster.

Many members of Congress work hard to interact with the people they represent. Their *franking privilege* enables them to mail newsletters and questionnaires to their constituents free of charge. They travel frequently between Washington and their home state or district, where they also maintain offices with full-time staffs.

Most of the permanent committees of Congress conduct *oversight hearings*, in which the activities of an executive agency or the management of a specific program are reviewed in depth. In addition, Congress often establishes a temporary committee to conduct *special investigations*. Employees and agencies of the executive branch fall under congressional oversight through *personnel control* and *financial control*. The legislature also has the power to remove a public official by means of *impeachment*.

During the 1970s a number of reforms were made in congressional rules and procedures. In the House, the majority party now elects committee chairs at the beginning of each Congress. Junior members may get seats on prestigious committees and may chair subcommittees. In both houses of Congress, individual members have more effective involvement in the legislative process and more autonomy than their counterparts of earlier decades had.

KEY TERMS AND CONCEPTS		
bicameral legislature	joint committee	cloture
casework	joint conference committee	representation
seniority system	legislation	constituency
party discipline	bill	franking privilege
Speaker of the House	mark-up session	oversight hearings
whip	rider	special investigation
issue entrepreneur	pocket veto	personnel control
administrative oversight	unanimous consent	financial control
standing committee	filibuster	impeachment
select (special) committee		

Scholarly studies

Davidson, Roger H. *The Postreform Congress*. New York: St. Martin's Press, 1992. A collection of readings exploring the readjustments that occurred in both houses of Congress after the dynamic reforms of the 1970s.

Fenno, Richard F., Jr. *Homestyle: House Members in Their Districts*. New York: HarperCollins, 1987. An examination of the relationship between members of Congress and their constituents. Identifies different ways in which members conceptualize the people and regions they represent.

Hibbing, John R. *Congressional Careers: Contours of Life in the U.S. House of Representatives*. Chapel Hill: University of North Carolina Press, 1991. An exploration of the career patterns and professional lifestyles of members of the House of Representatives.

Jacobson, Gary C. *The Electoral Origins of Divided Government: Competition in House Elections, 1946–1988*. Boulder, Colo.: Westview Press, 1990. A penetrating look at changing outcomes in House elections in the postwar period.

Light, Paul C. *Forging Legislation*. New York: Norton, 1991. A revealing case study of the legislative process; the author follows from inception to enactment a bill to create the Department of Veterans Affairs.

Rohde, David W. *Parties and Leaders in the Postreform House*. Chicago: University of Chicago Press, 1991. An empirical analysis of revitalized partisanship in the House of Representatives after 1980.

Leisure reading

Drew, Elizabeth. *Senator*. New York: Simon and Schuster, 1979. A close examination of the congressional routines of one United States senator, as observed by one of Washington's most perceptive reporters.

Drury, Allen. *Advise and Consent*. New York: Doubleday, 1959. A Pulitzer Prize–winning novel about the political intrigue over Senate confirmation of a presidential appointment.

O'Neill, Thomas P., Jr., and William Novak. *Man of the House*. New York: Random House, 1987. Reminiscences by former Speaker of the House "Tip" O'Neill,

with word portraits of many postwar American political leaders.

Wicker, Tom. *Facing the Lions*. New York: Viking Press, 1973. A novel about the career of a United States senator by a longtime political columnist for the *New York Times*.

Primary sources

Congressional Directory. Washington, D.C.: Government Printing Office, annual. An official compendium of information about congressional organizations and operations.

Congressional Quarterly. *Congress and the Nation*. Vols 1–8. Washington, D.C.: Congressional Quarterly, quadrennial. Extensive reviews of politics and policy for the previous four years. Published at the end of each presidential term.

Congressional Quarterly. *Guide to Congress*. 4th ed. Washington, D.C.: Congressional Quarterly, 1991. A comprehensive history and analysis of all phases of congressional operations.

Congressional Quarterly. *Politics in America*. Washington, D.C.: Congressional Quarterly, biennial. Backgrounds and voting records of all members of Congress and descriptions of each state and congressional district. Updated after each congressional election.

Organizations

Center for Democracy, 1101 15th Street, N.W., Washington, DC 20005; (202) 429-9141. Nonpartisan organization that works to strengthen democratic institutions. Monitors elections and provides democratizing governments with technical and informational assistance.

Center for Responsive Politics, 1320 19th Street, N.W., Washington, DC 20036; (202) 857-0444. Conducts research on Congress and related issues with particular interest in campaign finance and congressional operations.

U.S. Capitol Historical Society, 200 Maryland Avenue, N.E., Washington, DC 20002; (202) 543-8919. Conducts historical research and maintains information centers in the Capitol.

13

The

Presidency

- The authority of the presidency: its creation and evolution

- Presidential leadership: bargaining and going public

- Institutional resources: the cabinet; the executive office of the president; the president's spouse; the vice president

- The personal dimension: physical health, character, managerial style, and belief system

- The struggle for power: setting the agenda; influencing the legislature; building public support; implementing priorities in the executive branch

Democrat Franklin Delano Roosevelt, president from 1933 to 1945, has been considered the most predominant figure in twentieth-century American politics. Breaking the two-term tradition, Roosevelt won four consecutive elections. He had three running mates: John Nance Garner (1932 and 1936), Henry Wallace (1940), and Harry Truman (1944).

In his first campaign in 1932, Roosevelt pledged a "New Deal," promising to balance the budget, repeal Prohibition, support federal work projects, and aid agriculture and labor. His promises were much more appealing to the American electorate than was Republican Herbert Hoover's performance as president. Voters blamed Hoover for the Great Depression.

The central issue in 1936 *was* the New Deal, and particularly the Social Security Act. The electorate gave FDR's policies a massive vote of confidence, and Republican challenger "Alf" Landon did not "land on" Washington as predicted by his popular campaign pin *(bottom left)*.

In the "No Third Term" contest of 1940, FDR defeated Wendell Willkie by a huge popular margin, and he repeated this feat in 1944, against Thomas Dewey.

On October 1, 1989, representatives of the United States were contacted by Panamanian rebels attempting to remove military strongman Manuel Noriega from power. The rebels initially made two requests: sanctuary for the coup leaders' families and the establishment of roadblocks to prevent Panamanian troops, stationed outside the capital, from returning to put down the rebellion. The requests presented President George Bush with a leadership dilemma and his first major foreign-policy crisis: Should the United States support the coup, and, if so, should that support be active or passive?

Bush wanted Noriega out of power, but he was hesitant to involve United States troops directly. American public opinion was strongly opposed to the use of United States troops in the internal affairs of Central American countries. Moreover, the history of United States activities in Latin America generated fears that the president wished to avoid arousing. Finally, some presidential advisers feared a trap designed to embarrass the United States.

The day before the expected coup, President Bush met with his top aides to discuss the Pana-

manian situation. His initial decision was to go halfway—to use United States troops, but only in a manner that conformed to a treaty between the two countries, which required the United States to inform the Panamanians of all troop exercises. To avoid a possible confrontation with Panamanian forces, orders were given to block roads only where they cut through American bases.

The coup occurred a day later than expected, and there was much confusion. Rebel forces attacked Noriega's military headquarters and captured him, but they were divided over what to do next. While they debated, Noriega telephoned for help, and forces loyal to him recaptured the headquarters, freed Noriega, and killed the rebel leader.

Bush was heavily criticized in the American media. News stories suggested that United States intelligence was faulty, that coordination between various United States representatives in the field was poor, and that the president's lack of vision, cautious temperament, makeshift advisory system, and unwillingness to use military force contributed to the debacle.

Relations between the United States and Panama deteriorated after the coup. Noriega continued his hostile rhetoric and actions, persuading the Panamanian legislature to declare the existence of a state of war with the United States. Americans living in Panama were threatened. When an unarmed American marine was killed and a Navy lieutenant was beaten and his wife threatened with sexual abuse by Panamanian defense forces, the president decided to act.

Convening a meeting of his top national security advisers, Bush reviewed the options and contingency plans that had been developed and refined after the failed coup attempt. This time he chose a full-scale invasion to topple Noriega and establish a democratic government. In a carefully planned and well-executed operation, approximately twenty-four thousand American troops overwhelmed Panamanian forces, eventually captured Noriega, and allowed a new government—chosen in elections that Noriega had negated—to take over.

During the coup, then, a newly elected president, not wanting to alienate political leaders in the United States and abroad or to divide the American public, chose to let events run their course. The unsatisfactory outcome (from Bush's perspective), combined with criticism of his inaction by the media, set the stage for a much stronger response less than four months later. During the invasion, a more experienced president, not wanting to appear weak, unprepared, or uncertain, implemented a carefully planned and coordinated invasion by American troops that successfully removed Noriega but in the process alienated most Latin American governments.

THE PRESIDENT'S PREDICAMENT IN THE PANAMANIAN situation and his responses to it illustrate the dilemmas of presidential leadership, the capacity of presidents for dealing with such dilemmas, and the political forces that affect their decisions. Leadership is usually a response to unfavorable events over which the president has limited control but for which the president is expected to find a satisfactory solution. More often than not, this expectation exceeds the resources available to deal with the situation.

Sipa Press

Manuel Noriega was never deposed by Panamanians. Under indictment by a U.S. federal court, he was instead captured by agents from the U.S. Drug Enforcement Administration and brought by plane to Miami. There a jury convicted him of violating federal drug laws, and he is now serving his sentence in an American jail.

Presidents often face a "damned if they do, damned if they don't" dilemma. They are expected to make decisions on the basis of available information without necessarily knowing how complete, accurate, or up-to-date it is. They are expected to act in accordance with their previously stated goals and positions even though circumstances may have changed. They are expected to be sensitive to public opinion even though that opinion may be divided or ambiguous. And they are expected to solve problems even though they do not control all or even most of the factors that generated them. Moreover, if the problems persist, they will be criticized, and their capacity to lead in the future may be impaired.

Presidents have a persistent leadership problem.[1] The roots of the problem lie in the American system of government. To achieve their goals, presidents need the cooperation of many individuals over whom they may have little or no influence. Yet the Constitution divides authority, institutions share power, and political parties lack cohesion and long-term policy positions.

The pluralistic nature of American society is another source of the problem. Presidents are required to do what is best for the country. Yet assessments of their actions depend on how those actions affect individuals and groups within the society. The leadership problem has been aggravated in the last two decades by the proliferation of single-issue groups. The range of groups with an interest in most public policy issues has forced contemporary presidents to devote increasing amounts of time and energy to mobilizing support for their priorities.

How can presidents overcome their leadership problem? The key to presidential success is the skillful use of legal, institutional, and political powers:

1. *Legal powers.* Presidents can utilize the formal authority that is vested in the presidency. Here they command by virtue of constitutional and statutory powers as well as precedent.

2. *Institutional powers.* Presidents can utilize subordinates in the executive branch. Here they delegate to others the job of collecting information and assessing options while reserving the critical decisions for themselves.

3. *Political powers.* Presidents can utilize the informal powers of the presidency. Here they persuade on the basis of their elected position, political reputation, and public approval.

This chapter focuses on those powers and the environment in which they are exercised. We begin by exploring the legal basis of presidential authority, the creation of the executive at the Constitutional Convention, and the evolution of presidential powers through statute and precedent. Next we look at presidential leadership and the institutional and personal resources necessary to achieve it. We conclude by examining how presidents use their political powers to try to get things done—how they attempt to make, sell, and implement public policy.

THE AUTHORITY OF THE PRESIDENCY

Empowering the Institution

The formal powers of the presidency are stated in Article II of the Constitution, but even when it was created, the presidential office was not without controversy. There was a consensus among the framers that a strong executive was needed to balance the powers of the legislature, but differences arose over the structure of the institution, the powers invested in it, and the nature and operation of the selection process. Three controversial issues were involved:

> Should the executive branch be headed by a single person or by several people?
>
> Should the chief executive be chosen by those in government or by those outside of it?
>
> Should the traditional powers of the chief executive be subject to additional checks?

In resolving the first of these issues, the delegates to the Constitutional Convention decided to create a single executive, but one that would not be so strong as to threaten the other institutions of the national government.[2] They initially agreed to limit executive powers to ensuring that the laws would be faithfully executed and to making appointments that were not otherwise provided for. These powers were broadened when they were later enumerated in Article II of the Constitution.

Determining how the executive was to be chosen was harder. The delegates debated several options: election by the people, election by the legislature, or election by a group of specially chosen electors. Direct election by the people was viewed as undesirable and infeasible. It was undesirable because the framers believed that the masses could not make an informed, dispassionate, rational judgment. It was infeasible because they thought the country too large, its communications too primitive, and its sectional rivalries too great to permit an honest national election.

Selection by the legislature would solve those problems but would create others. How could an executive who was dependent on the legislature for election and reelection exercise power independently? One possible solution—a single, long term of office (seven years)—created another potential hazard: Who or what body would ensure that the executive acted responsibly? When this question was raised, the delegates voted against a single term, thereby making the option of election by the legislature much less desirable.

The third alternative, to have electors choose the president, was proposed toward the end of the Constitutional Convention. The Electoral College compromise was designed to meet the objections of two groups: (1) those who feared legislative selection but saw the benefits of having a small group make the decision and (2) those who desired to give the people a voice in the election but feared the judgment of the masses.

Empowering the executive proved to be the least controversial of the three issues that initially divided the delegates. A consensus emerged on the scope of executive authority. To prevent that authority from being exceeded, the framers created internal checks. They required the concurrence of one or both houses of Congress in the exercise of the powers that had been most abused during the colonial period: the power to make appointments, to enter into treaties, and to veto legislation. Congress was also given the right to declare war and to impeach an executive who violated the public trust by committing treason, bribery, or other high crimes and misdemeanors.[3]

Much was left for later generations to interpret, however. The president's authority was not defined with nearly the same precision as the authority of Congress. Having left constitutional authority vague, the framers ensured that their executive would be flexible enough to adjust to changing circumstances. They also ensured that controversy would persist (see the Constitutional Conflict on page 462).

The Evolution of Presidential Authority

Over the years Congress and the president have clashed repeatedly over their respective powers. If the framers were alive today, they would not be surprised. The constitutional structure they established was based on the assumption that this rivalry would limit the excesses and abuses of power by any one institution. This has indeed been the result, but the rivalry between the two branches has also made governing difficult.

What powers were initially given to the president and how have those powers changed over the years? Charged with faithfully executing the law, the president was given a broad grant of executive authority as well as more narrowly defined legislative and judicial powers.

Executive duties and powers   According to the Constitution, the president is to have primary responsibility for overseeing the execution of the law. The framers, however, did not believe that the president should perform this function alone. Subordinates would assist with this, but the issue was how to select them to ensure that they were properly qualified. The decision was to give the president the initiative to nominate subordinates but to involve the Senate in

The Item Veto

Can the president veto part of a law enacted by Congress, or must he negate the entire bill? The Constitution is not totally clear on this point. Article I, Section 7, says:

Every bill which shall have passed the House of Representatives and the Senate, shall, before it become a law, be presented to the President of the United States; if he approve he shall sign it, but if not he shall return it with his objections to that house in which it originated, who shall enter the objections at large on their journal, and proceed to reconsider it.

Those who argue that the president has the authority to veto part of a bill point to the president's oath to defend the Constitution as justification for his refusal to execute any provision of any law that he believes conflicts with the Constitution. President Bush argued this position in 1989, when he approved legislation that contained a provision that he said he could not enforce. One year later Bush identified thirty-one such provisions in nine bills; he approved the bills but declared those provisions to be without legal force.

Those who contend that the president does not have the authority to negate part of a bill defend their case by pointing to the constitutional language (the Constitution says "bill," not "part of a bill"). They also cite the intent of the provision (to protect executive authority from the legislature) and the practice that has developed since the government has been in operation (only entire bills have been vetoed).

Was President Bush's interpretation correct or incorrect? Can Congress force the president to enforce an entire law even if he believes part of it to be unconstitutional?

The answers to these questions are likely to be decided by the federal judiciary and perhaps by the Supreme Court if and when a member of Congress or a private individual or group, hurt by the president's failure to enforce part of a law, challenges his action in court. The stakes are high because the authority to veto part of a law, often referred to as a *line-item veto*, would shift considerable power from Congress to the president.

the confirmation process. Moreover, as part of the system of checks and balances, the Congress was to be responsible for the creation of the executive departments and agencies. Thus, the president was placed in the unenviable position of directing a branch of government without being able to exercise total control over the personnel in it and the structure of it.

Almost immediately members of the legislature challenged the president's discretion to choose people to work in the executive branch. In 1789, Georgia's two senators opposed George Washington's nomination of Benjamin Fishbourn to be naval officer of the port of Savannah and persuaded their colleagues to reject the nomination. To minimize the likelihood of other rejections, *before* placing a name in nomination, Washington began to consult with the senators from the same state as the prospective nominee. Presidents still follow this practice, which is known as **senatorial courtesy**.

Today a senator can delay or prevent a presidential nomination by simply stating his or her opposition. Other senators usually back up their colleague, and the resulting united front may force the president to withdraw the nomination. Senatorial courtesy—and opposition to formal nominations—limits the president's ability to choose subordinates, but it also enhances one's prospects of confirmation, given support from the relevant senators.

The Constitution specifically divides the responsibility for appointments, but it is far less clear about removal from office. Those who abuse their authority by committing treason, high crimes, or misdemeanors are subject to impeachment. But what about those who do not commit a crime but are undesirable because of incompetence, insubordination, or incompatibility with their superiors? The First Congress dealt with this issue when it established the executive departments in 1789. Four methods for removing department officials were discussed: by the president alone, by the president with the advice and consent of the Senate, by the statute that created the position, and by impeachment. In the end, a closely divided Congress vested removal power in the president alone.

By virtue of this decision, all political appointees who serve in executive positions do so at the pleasure of the president. A 1926 Supreme Court decision, *Myer v. United States* (written by Chief Justice and former president William Howard Taft), upheld this broad grant of executive authority. Subsequent Court decisions, however, have narrowed the president's discretion to remove executive-branch officials who serve on independent regulatory agencies, such as the Federal Trade Commission, the Federal Election Commission, or the Federal Reserve Board. Civil servants are also exempt from the president's removal power.

Thus, President Clinton could and did request the resignation of the ninety-three U.S. Attorneys, the chief federal prosecutors in each of the judicial districts across the country who were appointed by presidents Reagan and Bush, but he could not demand that the judges whom these presidents appointed also resign since they serve during good behavior for life. Nor could Clinton require Reagan or Bush appointees to federal regulatory agencies, such as the Federal Election Commission, to resign before their term expired.

Even though the president can remove political appointees, firing them may be politically disadvantageous, particularly if that president appointed them. It brings attention to an internal administration problem and points to the president's failure to deal with it effectively. Richard Nixon, Jimmy Carter, Ronald Reagan, and George Bush all had to ask for the resignations of at least one of their cabinet secretaries. Sometimes resignations are not forthcoming. When FBI Director William Sessions refused to step down, President Clinton had to fire him.

The power to hire and fire can foster but not guarantee cooperation and the effective execution of the laws. Executive officials exercise considerable discretion in their jobs, and the president's ability to oversee their performance is extremely limited. Congress exercises administrative oversight over the departments and agencies by defining their jurisdictions, authorizing their programs, appropriating their funds, and investigating their activities. Presidents do have some control over the information that their subordinates receive, their budgets, and the implementation of major legislation, but as chief executives they have relatively little influence on what goes on within the executive branch most of the time.

Presidents can require their subordinates to implement a policy in a particular way by issuing an **executive memorandum** or a formal **executive order**. These memoranda and orders are usually very specific. They apply to a partic-

Having refused to resign as director of the FBI, William Sessions reads to the press his letter of dismissal from President Clinton. Bush's attorney general, William Barr, had accused Sessions of using federal funds and transportation for personal gain. Sessions steadfastly denied the charges and accused the Justice Department of launching a personal vendetta against him. The Clinton administration finally decided that keeping him on was harmful to the FBI.

Reuters/Bettmann

ular agency and require its officials to perform a task in a particular way. But they can also have broad policy implications, for example, Kennedy's order declaring segregated housing off-limits to armed forces personnel, or Reagan's order requiring all executive departments and agencies to assess the costs of any new regulation before they promulgate it, or Clinton's memorandum on the "gag rule" (see box on page 465).

Although presidents have the authority to issue memoranda and orders to their subordinates, they often lack the time and expertise to do so, especially when technical information is involved. Thus it is difficult for a president to oversee the executive branch by executive order alone.

For all these reasons, presidents have tended to leave the business of administration to those in charge of the departments and agencies, sometimes with disastrous results. President Reagan is a case in point. Having little interest in administrative matters, Reagan did not exercise adequate oversight over department heads and others within his administration. Had he done so, problems involving conflicts of interest among political appointees in the Justice Department, political favoritism in the awarding of contracts in the Department of Housing and Urban Development, and irregularities in contracting in the Department of Defense might have been avoided. The Iran-contra affair is another situation in which Reagan's hands-off management style came back to haunt him.

In 1984 President Reagan approved a plan, prepared by his subordinates, in which the United States would sell arms to Iran in the hope that this sale would lead to the release of hostages held by terrorists sympathetic to Iran. He delegated the responsibility for implementing the plan to the staff of the National Security Council (NSC). Members of the NSC staff diverted funds from the arms sales to meet another administration objective: support of the contras, a group that opposed the Marxist government in Nicaragua. When the diver-

Memorandum on the Title X "Gag Rule"
January 22, 1993

Memorandum for the Secretary of Health and Human Services

Subject: The Title X "Gag Rule"

Title X of the Public Health Services Act provides Federal funding for family planning clinics to provide services for low-income patients. The Act specifies that Title X funds may not be used for the performance of abortions, but places no restrictions on the ability of clinics that receive Title X funds to provide abortion counseling and referrals or to perform abortions using non-Title X funds. During the first 18 years of the program, medical professionals at Title X clinics provided complete, uncensored information, including nondirective abortion counseling. In February 1988, the Department of Health and Human Services adopted regulations, which have become known as the "Gag Rule," prohibiting Title X recipients from providing their patients with information, counseling, or referrals concerning abortion. Subsequent attempts by the Bush Administration to modify the Gag Rule and ensuing litigation have created confusion and uncertainty about the current legal status of the regulations.

The Gag Rule endangers women's lives and health by preventing them from receiving complete and accurate medical information and interferes with the doctor-patient relationship by prohibiting information that medical professionals are otherwise ethically and legally required to provide to their patients. Furthermore, the Gag Rule contravenes the clear intent of a majority of the members of both the United States Senate and House of Representatives, which twice passed legislation to block the Gag Rule's enforcement but failed to override Presidential vetoes.

For these reasons, you have informed me that you will suspend the Gag Rule pending the promulgation of new regulations in accordance with the "notice and comment" procedures of the Administrative Procedure Act. I hereby direct you to take that action as soon as possible. I further direct that, within 30 days, you publish in the *Federal Register* new proposed regulations for public comment.

You are hereby authorized and directed to publish this memorandum in the *Federal Register*.

William J. Clinton

SOURCE: *Weekly Compilation of Presidential Documents*, January 25, 1993, 87–88.

---

sion became public, the president claimed that he was unaware of it. Two commissions, one appointed by Reagan and the other by Congress, criticized the actions of several national security aides and blamed the president for his failure to supervise them properly. The lesson of this affair and of the other managerial problems that beset the Reagan administration was clear: presidents cannot avoid their executive responsibilities without serious risk to themselves, their policies, and their political influence (see the Case Study on page 466).

Legislative duties and powers   Although shared responsibilities and dispersed powers have limited the president's ability and incentive to oversee the law, they have not prevented him from assuming greater responsibility in the lawmaking process. The framers of the Constitution anticipated only a modest policy-making role for the president, primarily in foreign affairs, but today presidents are expected to be active legislators.

The Iran-Contra Affair

Congress and the executive are engaged in a perpetual struggle. They differ over the scope of each other's powers, the wisdom of each other's policies, and the ways in which policies should be implemented if they become law. The Iran-contra affair illustrates all of these areas of conflict.

The Boland Amendment, a provision of an appropriations bill, prohibited executive agencies involved in intelligence activities from spending federal funds, either directly or indirectly, on military operations in Nicaragua. Colonel Oliver North, an official on the National Security Council (NSC) staff, diverted to the contras money generated by the sale of arms to Iran. NSC officials believed that they were pursuing presidential policy and were not bound by the Boland Amendment. Colonel North kept his actions secret even from Congress. For over nine months Congress was not informed about either the arms sales or the diversion of funds, in spite of a law that requires the president to fully inform the intelligence committees of Congress about such activities in a timely fashion.

Did the president violate the law by not telling Congress about these covert activities? Did the sale of arms to Iran and the diversion of profits to the contras fall within the purview of Congress's authority to make the law or the president's authority to conduct foreign policy? Despite the findings of a congressional committee that held the president responsible and his aides culpable, these issues remain the subject of considerable debate.

The Iran-contra affair was not the first confrontation between Congress and the presidency over the formulation and execution of policy, nor is it likely to be the last. A system in which separate institutions share power and operate within a framework of checks and balances practically ensures that political struggles like the Iran-contra affair will continue to plague American government.

UPI/Bettmann

When the diversion of funds from Iran was discovered, Congress appointed a special investigator, Lawrence Walsh, to determine whether the administration, or any accomplices, had violated federal laws. The principals in the inquiry were also forced to testify at public hearings.

The criminal trials were held after President Reagan left office. He refused to testify in person, but he did submit to questions by lawyers for both sides in the trial of his national security adviser, Admiral John Poindexter. Neither Reagan nor Bush was found to have violated the law, but the final report criticized both for their involvement and oversight.

Discussion questions

1. Is the United States Constitution outdated in terms of the making and executing of foreign policy?
2. Should Congress or the president exercise the power to make foreign policy, or should that power be shared?
3. How can institutional conflicts like the Iran-contra affair be avoided in the future?

A president's formal legislative powers are quite limited. Article II of the Constitution spells out only four duties and responsibilities: (1) to inform Congress from time to time about the state of the union; (2) to recommend necessary and expedient legislation; (3) to summon Congress into special session and adjourn it if the two houses cannot agree on adjournment; and (4) to negate an act of Congress by vetoing it. Congress can override a presidential veto by a two-thirds vote of both houses. With the exception of the veto, these responsibilities were designed to facilitate government in emergencies.

Over the years presidents have used their legislative duties and powers to enlarge their policy-making role and their influence in Congress. They have established and curtailed relations with other countries, as Jimmy Carter did when he recognized the People's Republic as the legitimate government of China and terminated official relations with the Chinese Nationalists on the island of Taiwan. They have entered into **executive agreements**, agreements with other heads of governments, as George Bush did when he renegotiated the rental agreements on American bases in Spain.[4] Such agreements have to be reported to Congress, but they do not require Senate ratification. Finally, presidents have used diplomacy and armed forces to protect American interests, as Bush did in the Persian Gulf War.

Although Congress has generally accepted presidential leadership in foreign and military affairs, it has not always approved what presidents have done. In some cases, Congress has criticized and formally condemned presidents, as it did after James K. Polk sent troops into territory claimed by Mexico in 1846. In other instances, it has used its appropriations power to thwart presidential policy, such as when it denied funding requested by Richard Nixon for bombing operations in Cambodia in the early 1970s. It has even tried to limit the president's power to involve American troops in hostile or potentially hostile situations. In 1973 Congress enacted the War Powers Resolution over President Nixon's veto. This statute requires the president to consult with Congress and gain its approval when ordering armed forces into hostile situations without a declaration of war. In 1991 Congress debated but eventually enacted resolutions authorizing the president to use force in the Persian Gulf. A similar debate occurred in October 1993, over use of United States naval forces to impose a United Nations blockade of Haiti.

Congressional involvement in foreign-policy decision making has been most evident in recent years. The absence of a public consensus on many foreign-policy matters, the growth of political interest groups concerned with international affairs, and the interdependence of the American economy with economies of other developed and underdeveloped countries have encouraged that involvement, as has public dissatisfaction with specific presidential actions and initiatives. In short, presidential leadership in foreign affairs is still expected, but congressional approval can no longer be taken for granted.

The president's role as domestic-policy maker and chief legislator developed more recently. Throughout most of the nineteenth century, Congress was seen as the principal architect of domestic policy. Not until the beginning of the twentieth century did presidents become more actively engaged in proposing legislation, and not until the end of Franklin Roosevelt's administration did formulating new domestic policy become an important activity of the executive.

Today the president is expected to be the nation's chief policy maker. He presents an annual legislative program to Congress, lobbies for that program, and oversees its implementation. The problem is that presidents frequently lack the political clout to achieve their policy goals, particularly in Congress.

One month into office, President Gerald Ford signs the document that pardoned his predecessor, Richard Nixon, for all federal crimes he "committed or may have committed or taken part in." Some said a deal had been struck, with Nixon agreeing to resign if his vice president would grant the pardon upon taking office. Both men have vehemently denied this.

Clinton's failure to achieve his economic stimulus plan at the beginning of his administration is a case in point. Citing the need to prod the economy and create jobs, the president proposed a $16-billion plan in the early days of his administration. The legislation passed the House of Representatives but was stalled in the Senate by a Republican-led filibuster. Unable to invoke cloture to stop the filibuster, Clinton was forced to abandon the package, although parts of the plan were subsequently enacted into law.

Judicial duties and powers Derived from the traditional position of the king as the court of last resort, the president's judicial powers include issuing pardons, granting clemency, and proclaiming amnesty. Although the scope of these powers has not been subject to much controversy, their exercise has. President Gerald Ford's pardon of his predecessor, Richard Nixon, in 1974 is a case in point. Issued before any judicial proceedings could determine Nixon's innocence or guilt in the Watergate affair, the pardon, which subverted the legal process, was criticized as ill timed and politically inspired. Ford's power to issue it, however, was not in question. Similarly, President Jimmy Carter's proclamation of amnesty for Vietnam draft resisters in 1977 was criticized by veterans' groups and members of Congress as harmful to national security. Yet there was little these critics could do to prevent it from taking effect.

Presidents can exercise judicial power in other ways. They can influence the composition of the federal judiciary through their nominations of judges—subject, of course, to Senate approval (for an extended discussion of judicial appointments, see Chapter 15). They and their political appointees in the Justice Department can determine the government's position on controversial legal matters, decide which cases the department will prosecute, and decide whether to appeal adverse decisions to a higher court. Similarly, in cases in which the government is not directly involved but has an interest, the Justice Department can file an amicus curiae brief. There is little that presidents can do, however, if the final judgment of the court goes against their position.

The independence of the judiciary in deciding matters of law limits the extent to which presidents can directly influence judicial decisions. For this reason, the relationship between the president and the federal judiciary tends to be more distant, less visible, and less conflicted than the relationship between the president and Congress. In general, there is less sharing of power and, as a consequence, less interaction between the president and the courts than between the president and Congress.

PRESIDENTIAL LEADERSHIP

The roles and responsibilities of the president have expanded, but the formal authority of the president has not kept pace. Thus, presidents need to exercise political leadership to close the gap between expectations and performance. They must try to persuade others to follow their lead by bargaining behind closed doors or making a public appeal.

Bargaining

Richard E. Neustadt, in his classic study on presidential power, points out that those who occupy the Oval Office must be persuasive; they must be able to convince others that it is in *their* interest to do what the president wants.[5] Being persuasive often involves bargaining behind closed doors.

In the give-and-take of bargaining, the president enjoys certain advantages. The presidency itself is respected. Others look to the president for guidance and leadership. Moreover, the president controls some valued commodities. Presidents can share publicity, make nominations, provide electoral support, offer social invitations, and use their discretion to propose and implement programs that benefit particular groups and constituencies. They can also impose a variety of sanctions, usually as a last resort. Sanctions range from not doing favors, not raising money, or not offering jobs to certain people, to campaigning against candidates or opposing policies.

Take the case of Democratic Senator Richard Shelby of Alabama, who embarrassed the administration by publicly criticizing the new taxes President Clinton proposed to reduce the federal budget deficit. To punish the senator and discourage other members of Congress from opposing the president's policy initiatives, the administration ordered the transfer of jobs from a NASA facility in Shelby's state to a facility in another state. To reinforce the point, Senator Shelby was given only one ticket to attend the president's reception for the University of Alabama football team at the White House while fellow Senator Howell Heflin received eleven.

Despite the rewards and sanctions, presidents cannot always get their way. Elective officials in Congress or the state governments, bureaucrats in the civil service, and even individuals appointed by the president can and do oppose the chief executive. Thus, presidents need to be persuasive to gain cooperation and build support.

Neustadt identifies two strategic imperatives that contribute to presidential success: reputation and prestige. Reputation is based on will and skill; prestige is related to popularity. Both are likely to affect those with whom the president must deal.

Of the two, reputation tends to be the more important. Presidents who say what they mean and do what they say are likely to gain more support than those who vacillate, whose priorities are unclear, and whose positions are subject to continual change. For example, in his first year of office George Bush reiterated his pledge not to raise taxes; in his second year he abandoned that pledge. Bill Clinton backed away from his campaign promises to cut middle-class taxes, allow homosexuals in the armed forces, and admit Haitian refugees seeking political asylum into the United States almost as soon as he took office. Ronald Reagan, in contrast, stuck to his promises to cut taxes, increase defense spending, and reduce the role of government in the domestic sphere. Bush's and Clinton's vacillation and Reagan's steadfastness helped shape their reputations as presidents. Once in place, such reputations are difficult to shake.

Reputation affects what the president can do, which in turn helps shape the public's perceptions of a presidency. These perceptions are closely linked to the president's prestige. In general, presidents who enjoy the broadest public support are likely to be most persuasive with Congress, with executive officials, with foreign leaders, and with others.

Political scientists have found some empirical evidence to support the proposition that a president's legislative influence increases as his popularity, measured in terms of public approval, increases. Political scientist George Edwards, who has analyzed the results of Gallup polls and congressional voting patterns from the Eisenhower administration through 1986, found that the more popular presidents were, the more congressional support they got.[6]

Public approval, however, cannot be easily converted into congressional votes. There must be a relationship between the basis of the president's popularity and the issue before Congress. George Bush found this out the hard way during the budget deficit debate of 1990. His plea to the American people and to members of Congress to support the compromise that his administration had negotiated with the Democratic leadership fell on deaf ears despite his high standing in the polls. In 1990 Americans approved of Bush's performance as president, particularly in foreign affairs, but did not support his budget policy. Similarly, despite Bush's popularity after the Persian Gulf War in 1991, the Congress did not rush to support his legislative initiatives.

Going Public

Going to the public augments presidential power in two fundamental ways.[7] First, it legitimizes the position of the president in the eyes of others. Public support enables the president to withstand criticism better, and it decreases the amount of criticism he is likely to receive. People are less likely to oppose a popular president than they are to oppose an unpopular one.

Going public also enables the president to apply pressure more effectively. Elected officials are usually very responsive to the beliefs and desires of organized groups and coalitions that may support or oppose them the next time they seek office. Political appointees and even civil servants are also sensitive to the needs of the groups affected by their decisions and policies.

There are dangers, however, to heavy reliance on public support. Public opinion tends to be volatile and inconsistent. Moreover, public approval is usually tied to visible results. For policies that take time to work, such as changes in tax law designed to stimulate the economy or encourage savings, the tide can turn against the president, forcing modifications before the program has been completed or the intended effect has occurred. Thus, during the 1981–1982 recession President Reagan had to plead with Congress and the public to give his economic program a chance to work after legislation for that program had been enacted into law.

Presidents face another problem when they go public. They raise expectations, sometimes to unrealistic heights. Failure to meet these expectations results in disappointment and damages the president's reputation, making it difficult to generate support for other proposals down the line. The high priority that President Bush gave to the drug problem and to educational reform at the beginning of his administration is a case in point. By emphasizing these issues and his plans for dealing with them, Bush heightened public awareness, created expectations, and even established criteria by which his effort could be judged. The persistence of those problems despite the president's public declaration to do something about them highlighted the gap between expectations and performance. Bill Clinton faced much the same problem of heightened expectations by his oft-repeated promises to stimulate the economy, reduce the federal deficit, and yet extend health-care benefits to millions of Americans.

The electoral process also tends to inflate public hopes. In his quest for the presidency, Jimmy Carter talked in unequivocal terms about the strong, honest, purposeful leadership he would provide as president. His inability to project that type of leadership or to make good on all of the 125 promises that he made during the campaign and reiterated after he took office contributed to the sharp decline in his popularity during his four years in office.

These examples illustrate the necessity and hazards of going public. In an age dominated by television, however, presidents often have little alternative to the public route for building and maintaining support. Public approval does contribute to presidential power, but it also raises the stakes and may ultimately work to mar a president's image and reduce his ability to lead.

INSTITUTIONAL RESOURCES

Presidents need help. Their job is too big, their tasks are too diverse, and their expectations are too great for them to operate alone. The Constitution anticipated that the president would have advisers, but it did not establish an advisory structure. Beyond the role of the Senate in providing advice and consent to appointments and treaties, the president was left to his own devices.

The Cabinet

In 1792 President Washington began to meet frequently with the heads of the three executive departments in existence at that time—State, War, and Treasury—plus the attorney general, who initially had no department. These meetings became more frequent and eventually evolved into an informal advisory system known as the **cabinet**. The cabinet assumed its partisan character in 1794 after Thomas Jefferson resigned as secretary of state in protest over the administration's economic and foreign policies. The cabinet was the first advisory body to which the president turned for information and advice, and eventually a presidential bureaucracy was created.

For more than 160 years, the cabinet, composed of the heads of the various executive departments plus the vice president, functioned as the president's principal advisory body. (Figure 13-1 depicts the growth of the cabinet over the years.) Administration positions on controversial proposals were often thrashed out at cabinet meetings. Cabinet secretaries lent their prestige to the president and helped his administration maintain its political support in the party, the Congress, and the country.

In the 1950s, the relationship between the president and the cabinet began to change. As presidents began to shape public opinion and exercise more legislative leadership on their own, their reliance on the cabinet declined. Not only have presidents become less dependent on cabinet members for external support, but they have also grown more reluctant to use the cabinet as their principal advisory body. Increasing size and diversity, plus the advocacy role that the heads of the executive departments have assumed, have made cabinet meetings more confrontational than they were in the past and reduced their usefulness as a consensus-building mechanism.[8]

Presidents have continued to consult with department heads individually or in small groups. In an effort to gain the benefits of a cabinet-oriented system without being saddled with a large, unwieldly advisory body, President Reagan and President Bush created "cabinet councils," organized on the basis of broad policy areas. The councils, composed of the department heads whose expertise and administrative responsibilities fell within certain areas, debated policy, developed recommendations, and helped in the implementation of key presidential priorities. Thus, it was the Council on Economic Affairs, consisting primarily of the heads of the Treasury, Commerce, and Labor Departments, the director of the Office of Management and Budget, and the chair of the Council of Economic Advisers, that fashioned the economic policy of the Reagan ad-

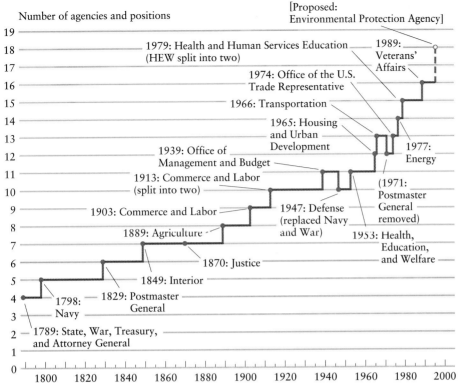

Number of agencies and positions

[Proposed: Environmental Protection Agency]

1979: Health and Human Services Education (HEW split into two)

1989: Veterans' Affairs

1974: Office of the U.S. Trade Representative

1966: Transportation

1965: Housing and Urban Development

1977: Energy

1939: Office of Management and Budget

1913: Commerce and Labor (split into two)

1903: Commerce and Labor

1947: Defense (replaced Navy and War)

(1971: Postmaster General removed)

1889: Agriculture

1953: Health, Education, and Welfare

1870: Justice

1849: Interior

1829: Postmaster General

1798: Navy

1789: State, War, Treasury, and Attorney General

Figure 13-1 *The development of the president's cabinet.*
SOURCE: Washington Post, *February 9, 1993, A15.* © *1993 The Washington Post. Reprinted with permission.*

ministration. The Clinton administration created a National Economic Council, headed by a senior presidential adviser, to coordinate economic policy while he continued to depend on the National Security Council and the Domestic Policy Council.

The Executive Office of the President

With the cabinet declining in importance, presidents have turned increasingly to their own staffs for advice, coordination, and public relations activities. Before 1939, presidents had very small staffs to help them with their day-to-day work. In fact, not until 1857 did Congress authorize the president to hire a secretary. What help presidents had, they paid for themselves.

Nor did presidential staffs grow rapidly. Throughout the nineteenth century the number of aides was small enough to be housed in the mansion where the president lived. In 1926, during Calvin Coolidge's administration, the total budget for staff support was $88,000. Coolidge's successor, Herbert Hoover, had four administrative assistants plus thirty-six clerks, typists, and messengers.

The lack of adequate staffs forced presidents to do office work themselves. George Washington maintained custody of the public papers; Abraham Lincoln wrote his own speeches; Grover Cleveland often answered the White House

Chief Justice William Rehnquist swears in the new Clinton cabinet. The cabinet as a body has declined in importance because of its size and diversity. The full cabinet meets less and less frequently over the course of an administration. It does meet for symbolic purposes, such as picture-taking, however.

phone; Woodrow Wilson typed the final drafts of his principal addresses. The inadequacy of this system became evident during the first term of Franklin Roosevelt's administration. In 1936, responding to criticism that the presidency was not being run efficiently, Roosevelt appointed a committee to study the problem. The committee proposed the establishment of a presidential office, and in 1939 Congress gave the president the authority to do so.

The first **Executive Office of the President (EOP)** consisted of five separate units: three wartime agencies, the Bureau of the Budget, and a White House Office. Over the years the EOP has grown in size, responsibility, and power. Today it consists of twelve offices (including the president's) and two executive residents with approximately sixteen hundred employees—far larger than the staffs of the British prime minister and the French president—and a budget of almost $185 million (see Figure 13-2). The largest and most powerful units are the Office of Management and Budget and the White House Office.

The Office of Management and Budget   The Budget and Accounting Act of 1921 created a Bureau of the Budget to help the president prepare an annual budget to be submitted to Congress. Initially housed in the Department of the Treasury, the bureau was moved into the newly created EOP in 1939. This move converted the Budget Bureau into an important presidential agency, extending the chief executive's reach and influence to the ongoing budgetary process. As the president's substantive policy-making responsibilities increased, the bureau was given an additional role—to coordinate legislative policy for the president. During the 1950s and 1960s, senior officials in the Budget Bureau also served as an institutional memory for those in the White House, providing information and expertise about how to get things done within the government. This source of knowledge by experienced and trustworthy civil servants facilitated the operation of government, particularly during presidential transitions.

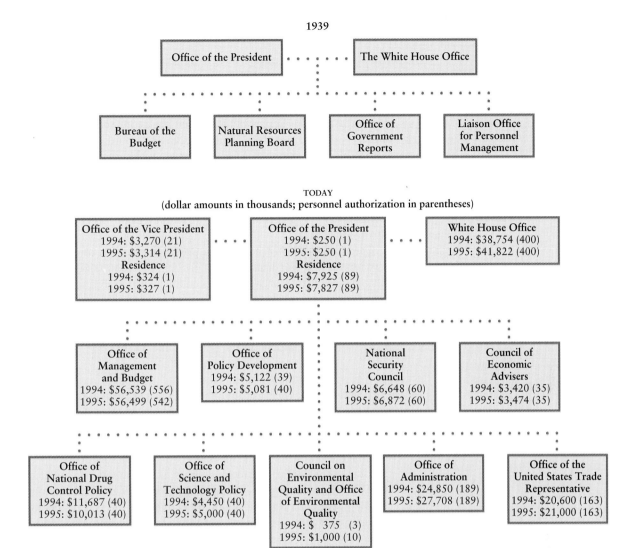

1939

Office of the President .... The White House Office

Bureau of the Budget | Natural Resources Planning Board | Office of Government Reports | Liaison Office for Personnel Management

TODAY
(dollar amounts in thousands; personnel authorization in parentheses)

Office of the Vice President
1994: $3,270 (21)
1995: $3,314 (21)
Residence
1994: $324 (1)
1995: $327 (1)

Office of the President
1994: $250 (1)
1995: $250 (1)
Residence
1994: $7,925 (89)
1995: $7,827 (89)

White House Office
1994: $38,754 (400)
1995: $41,822 (400)

Office of Management and Budget
1994: $56,539 (556)
1995: $56,499 (542)

Office of Policy Development
1994: $5,122 (39)
1995: $5,081 (40)

National Security Council
1994: $6,648 (60)
1995: $6,872 (60)

Council of Economic Advisers
1994: $3,420 (35)
1995: $3,474 (35)

Office of National Drug Control Policy
1994: $11,687 (40)
1995: $10,013 (40)

Office of Science and Technology Policy
1994: $4,450 (40)
1995: $5,000 (40)

Council on Environmental Quality and Office of Environmental Quality
1994: $ 375 (3)
1995: $1,000 (10)

Office of Administration
1994: $24,850 (189)
1995: $27,708 (189)

Office of the United States Trade Representative
1994: $20,600 (163)
1995: $21,000 (163)

Figure 13-2 *The Executive Office of the President—at its inception and today.*
SOURCE: *Budget of the United States Government, Fiscal Year 1995.*

The increasing importance of the budget office led President Nixon to rename and restructure it in 1970.[9] Calling it the **Office of Management and Budget (OMB)**, he gave it advisory responsibilities in addition to its budgetary review and legislative policy functions. Nixon also increased the number of political appointees to top positions in the budget office. The use of political appointees in the OMB to oversee policy making and implementation in the departments and agencies has continued under subsequent presidents and has reduced the role of senior civil servants during transitions and downgraded their influence in the budgetary and policy-making processes.

To the extent that presidents require executive departments to consult with the OMB and allow the OMB to have the last word, the budget office has become both feared and powerful. It has gained a reputation as the institution that says no. In the process it has generated considerable controversy, much of it stemming from its budgetary orientation and presidential perspective in contrast to the service orientation and more parochial view of the departments and agencies.

The OMB traditionally applies a budgetary calculus to its policy recommendations. It tries to save money by limiting spending. In an age of budget deficits, this power can be a potent weapon and a source of continuing tension within the administration. Moreover, the OMB is also concerned with setting precedents, in contrast to the departments, which are more sensitive to protecting the interests of their clientele. Thus, the OMB would be inclined to oppose a program likely to result in a large increase in budget expenditures, but a department whose clientele benefited from the program would probably support it. This type of conflict occurred during formulation of the Clinton budget for the Department of Defense for fiscal year 1995. Secretary Aspin had to go public to gain Clinton's support for more money than Budget Director Panetta had recommended.

Since its inception, the OMB has been a potent instrument of the American presidency. Nixon and Ford turned to it to improve the management of government. Carter used it to reorganize parts of the executive branch, including his own office. Reagan and Bush relied on it to achieve significant budget cuts and management reforms, including the oversight of regulations issued by departments and agencies. Clinton has also indicated that he will depend on the OMB to make government more efficient and to oversee regulatory activity.

In addition to its budgetary and management functions, the OMB performs another critical role for the president. It acts as a central clearance house, monitoring what the executive departments and agencies want to do and how they want to do it. All proposals for new legislation, positions on existing legislation, and testimony before congressional committees must first be cleared by the OMB to make certain that they are in accord with the president's program. This is known as the **central clearance process**. Departments and agencies cannot proceed with their proposals if the OMB determines that they are inconsistent with the president's programmatic objectives. At the end of the legislative process the OMB also coordinates executive branch recommendations to the president to approve or disapprove legislation enacted by Congress. This is known as the **enrolled bill process**. These two processes are illustrated in Figure 13-3.

The OMB performs still another clearance operation for pending regulations to be issued by the departments and agencies. In exercising this **regulatory review**, the OMB must determine if a regulation is necessary, consistent with administration policy and legislative intent, and cost effective.

The White House Office   Like the OMB, the **White House Office** has evolved into a large and powerful presidential staff. From its inception in 1939 until the mid 1960s, the office was relatively small and informal. A handful of administrative aides performed assignments dictated by specific presidential needs, such as writing a speech, planning a trip, or getting sufficient information for the president to make a decision. The president's assistants did not exercise exclusive domain over a policy or functional area; they did not rival cabinet secretaries for status and influence. Rather, they acted as the president's personal representatives, enhancing his information, extending his influence, and coordinating his activities with those of the rest of the government.

Gradually the presidential staff began to expand. During the 1950s, a

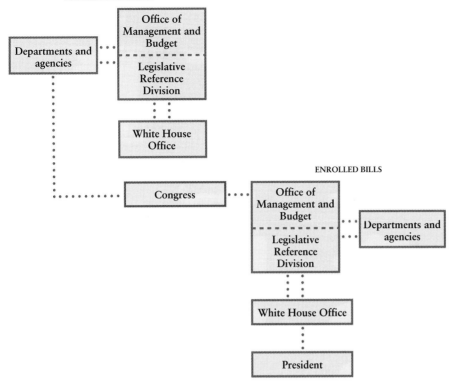

Figure 13-3 *The central clearance and enrolled bill processes.*

liaison with Congress was established. During the 1960s, a policy-making capacity in national security and domestic affairs was developed. During the 1970s and 1980s, regular links with the president's principal constituencies—interest groups, state and local governments, and the political parties—were created. In the 1990s, an economic coordinating unit was added.

As presidential responsibilities grew, so did the White House Office. In 1950, it numbered about 300 people; by 1960, it exceeded 400; by 1970, it was close to 500. After the Watergate controversy, the number of presidential aides on the White House payroll declined. Today the White House Office has an official staff size of approximately 400 plus another 100 people from the executive departments and agencies who are detailed to the White House for special assignments and a budget of almost $39 million.[10] Although President Clinton proposed that staff size be reduced, he increased its size during his first five months in office. Moreover, the budget of this office had to be increased by more than $3.5 million in 1993 to update its communications technology, and another $3.1 million was added for fiscal year 1995.

In theory the Clinton White House resembles its predecessors. There is a hierarchical structure with a chief of staff, policy assistants, a large public relations operation, and the traditional units that help the president meet his day-to-day responsibilities and link him to his principal political constituencies (see Figure 13-4). In practice, however, the operation is less structured. Particularly at the beginning of the administration, ad hoc assignments overlay and undercut traditional lines of authority and responsibility. And the president

THE FIRST LADY	THE PRESIDENT	THE VICE PRESIDENT
Chief of Staff Press Secretary Scheduling Advance Correspondence Social Secretary	Chief of Staff Deputy	Chief of Staff Press Secretary Scheduling Advance Policy advisers Legislative Affairs National Performance Review
Political offices	Support services	Policy offices

Counsellor
Communications
  Media Affairs
  Speechwriting
  Research
  Press Secretary
Legislative Affairs
Public Liaison
Intergovernmental
  Affairs
Political Affairs
	Staff Secretary
	Personnel
	Scheduling and
	  Advance
	Management and
	  Administration
	Operations
	  Military
	  Medical
	  Secret Service
		National Security Council
		National Economic Council
		Domestic Policy Council
		Environmental Policy
		Cabinet Affairs
		National Service
		Counsel

Figure 13-4 *The contemporary White House.*

himself is in the thick of his administration's political, policy, and personnel decisions.

The growth of the White House Office has presented presidents with their own internal management problems: how to supervise the operation of a large, diverse, and increasingly specialized staff. Presidents Ford and Carter tried unsuccessfully to do this supervision themselves. Inundated with decisions that could have been settled by others, both presidents eventually turned to a chief of staff to oversee these and other administrative tasks. Their successors have also depended on a chief of staff to run the White House.

The president's chief of staff has three important responsibilities: (1) to act as an honest broker, ensuring that the president has a wide range of information and advice; (2) to offer recommendations to the president about decisions he should make and actions he should take; and (3) to serve as a lightning rod for criticism directed at the president. The general rule of thumb in the White House is that the president should be credited with good news and favorable actions and the staff should be blamed for foul-ups and problems. Thus, when President Clinton found himself in difficulty after only four months in office, he appointed a man who had served in two previous White Houses, David Gergen, as counselor and moved other senior aides to new positions; when President Bush's popularity began to tumble at the end of his third year in office, he replaced top White House personnel, including his chief of staff, and added a new domestic-policy counselor; and when President Reagan was

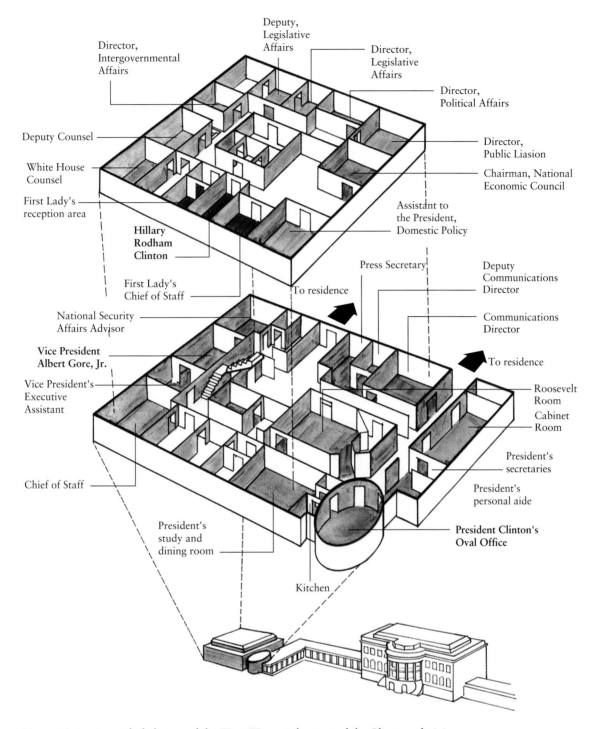

Figure 13-5 *An exploded view of the West Wing at the start of the Clinton administration. Who sits where is interesting in its own right. The Chief of Staff's corner office near the president's rooms is not surprising. But notice how the office of the Communications Director guards the entrance to the West Wing. Hillary Rodham Clinton's suite is on the second floor, but she sits very close to the other influential policy advisors.* SOURCE: Washington Post, *February 5, 1993, A23.* © *1993 The Washington Post. Reprinted with permission.*

479

criticized for the excesses of his national security staff during the Iran-contra affair, he fired his national security adviser, John Poindexter, accepted the resignation of staff aide Oliver North, and replaced his White House chief of staff, Donald Regan.[11]

As the White House Office has expanded in size and functions, power has shifted to it from the departments and agencies. This shift has enhanced the status, visibility, and influence of the president's principal aides and decreased those of most of the cabinet secretaries. Proximity to the president, growing policy-making responsibilities, and large support staffs have placed White House aides in a better position than other executive-branch officials to shape administration goals and coordinate strategies to achieve them.

The larger, more powerful White House Office has increased presidential discretion and extended presidential influence. It has provided a cadre of politically loyal strategists and technicians. No longer must the president depend solely or primarily on the executive departments and agencies. The White House provides a supportive environment, one tuned to the president's philosophy, policy objectives, and time frame. But tensions have also been created between the officials in the White House and those in the departments and agencies. Complaints that the White House is formulating more and more major policies, that presidents and their staffs are getting more directly involved in the implementation of policy, and that access to top decision makers is being impaired have been heard from cabinet secretaries and their deputies.

Tension has also increased between presidential appointees and civil servants within the departments. Suspicion of the loyalty of civil servants has led a series of presidents from Nixon to Reagan to create more political positions and to try to exert more influence over them. Since the Reagan administration, for example, the White House Office has exercised a veto over major political appointments in the departments and agencies.

Internal staff conflicts within the White House Office have also become evident. Increases in size and specialization have generated turf battles, policy disputes, and personality clashes. These conflicts are frequently reported in the media, making it harder for an administration to speak with a single voice. Leaks have become more frequent, along with "kiss-and-tell" books and articles by departing presidential aides. The White House has become a battleground in which personal and institutional politics *within* the administration influence decisions almost as much as political pressures outside of it.

The President's Spouse

The role of the president's spouse has also changed to include more than simply ceremonial and social responsibilities. A president's spouse is expected to campaign, to make speeches, and to attend events in the president's absence and on the president's behalf. Communicating public reactions and perspectives to the president is another important task, one which Eleanor Roosevelt pioneered as first lady. Mrs. Roosevelt traveled across the country for her husband, monitoring public opinion and reporting the country's mood to him, and writing a newspaper column entitled "My Day" (see box on page 481).

All too often personal aides are reluctant to tell a president bad news. A presidential spouse may be in a better position to do so. Nancy Reagan was instrumental in conveying which presidential aides and department secretaries adversely affected her husband's reputation and public standing. Her efforts

Eleanor Roosevelt: Premier First Lady

When President Clinton appointed his wife, Hillary Rodham Clinton, as coordinator for developing the administration's health-care program, he engendered considerable criticism. Was this a proper role for the nation's first lady? Should presidential spouses be engaged in matters of public policy, or should they merely be given ceremonial and social responsibilities? A similar controversy arose during the administration of Franklin Delano Roosevelt.

The president's wife, Eleanor, had been active in politics for some time before his election in 1932. When he had been stricken with polio in 1921, which left his legs paralyzed and for a while left him unable to participate in public affairs, she became his stand-in, partly to keep his name in the forefront of Democratic party politics and partly to fulfill her own interests.

By the time Franklin Roosevelt became president in 1933, Eleanor Roosevelt was an accomplished politician and a respected leader in her own right. Throughout the White House years, her influence on the president, and thus on the nation, was profound. Rexford Tugwell, who was a member of the president's "Brain Trust," recalled in later years,

No one who ever saw Eleanor Roosevelt sit down facing her husband and, holding his eyes firmly, say to him, "Franklin, I think you should . . ." or, "Franklin, surely you will not . . ." will ever forget the experience. . . . It would be impossible to say how often and to what extent American governmental processes have been turned in new directions because of her determination that people should be hurt as little as possible and that as much should be done for them as could be managed; the whole, if it could be totalled, would be formidable.[1]

Eleanor was particularly active in social issues, as her early civil rights efforts attest. In 1936 Marian Anderson sang at the White House, but three years later the Daughters of the American Revolution (DAR) refused to let her rent their auditorium, Constitution Hall, for a concert because she was an African American. Outraged, Eleanor Roosevelt promptly resigned her membership in the DAR and helped arrange for Anderson to perform at an open-air concert at the Lincoln Memorial attended by seventy-five thousand people. Later that year, Eleanor

UPI/Bettmann

Like her husband, Eleanor Roosevelt became a master of the mass media, chiefly radio in the 1940s. She also wrote a daily newspaper column called "My Day."

Roosevelt joined the NAACP (the National Association for the Advancement of Colored People).

The issue of racial discrimination in the military and defense industries became increasingly urgent to African Americans as the likelihood of United States participation in World War II grew in 1940. Working with the leaders of the NAACP, Eleanor pressed Franklin to use his executive authority to order the removal of racial barriers. Finally, her influence, and the NAACP's threat of a march on Washington, led Roosevelt to sign an executive order that mandated nondiscrimination in the defense industries and set up a Fair Employment Practices Committee to enforce the order.

[1] *Roosevelt Day Dinner Journal* of Americans for Democratic Action, January 31, 1963, quoted in Joseph Lash, *Eleanor and Franklin* (New York: W. W. Norton, 1971), 457–458.

The roles of a presidential spouse range far and wide. Dancing at one of twelve inaugural balls, Mrs. Clinton looks regal: hair swept up, wearing a gown destined for the Smithsonian Institution, and gazing happily at the new president. Testifying on Capitol Hill about health-care reform, Hillary Rodham Clinton is the picture of confidence and competence. Her command earned lavish praise.

culminated in the resignation of two senior officials, Chief of Staff Donald Regan and Attorney General Edwin Meese.

Presidential spouses have also involved themselves on issues of public policy. Betty Ford and Rosalynn Carter spoke out on health-care issues. Mrs. Carter was the first spouse to attend cabinet meetings regularly. Nancy Reagan promoted the Reagan administration's campaign against illegal drugs.

Hillary Rodham Clinton has been the most active spouse thus far in the formulation and coordination of policy. The first to be given an office in the west wing of the White House with the rest of the president's principal policy advisers, Mrs. Clinton took on the task of developing the new administration's health-care program and then mobilizing congressional support for it. In performing this task, she met with members of Congress, industry representatives, and policy experts. She also held town meetings in which many individuals and groups were invited to speak. She also participated in the cabinet and in the subcabinet appointment process, advising the president on the qualifications of candidates proposed for office, particularly those who were being considered for the Justice Department. Mrs. Clinton was a practicing attorney in Arkansas before her husband was elected president.

The Vice Presidency

Like the role of the OMB and the White House Office, the role of the vice president has been enhanced, and the stature of the position has been enhanced as well. Today the vice presidency is considered a prestigious office in its own right. That was not always the case. Throughout much of American history the position was not well regarded even by those who served in it. The nation's first vice president, John Adams, complained, "My country has in its wisdom contrived for me the most insignificant office that ever the invention of man contrived or his imagination conceived."[12] Thomas Jefferson, the second person to hold the office, was not quite as critical. Describing his job as "honorable and easy," he added, "I am unable to decide whether I would rather have it or not have it."[13]

Why was such a position created? The framers did not discuss a vice presidency until the end of the Constitutional Convention, and then it was almost an afterthought. They wanted to ensure an orderly succession if the presidency became vacant. However, there were other government positions from which a new president could have been designated. Moreover, the vice president's only constitutional function, to preside over the Senate and vote in case of a tie, could have been assumed by a senator.

The manner in which the vice president was to be selected, however, offers a clue as to why the framers established the position. Originally, the candidate with the second-highest number of Electoral College votes was to be the vice president. This placed the second-most-qualified person (in the judgment of the electors) in a position to take over if something happened to the president. In 1800, however, the presidential election ended in a tie in the Electoral College. Since the electors could not designate which position, president or vice president, they wished Jefferson and Burr to have, both Democratic-Republican candidates had received the same number of votes, and the House of Representatives had to determine the winner. To prevent this situation from recurring, Congress proposed and the states ratified the Twelfth Amendment, which requires separate Electoral College ballots for president and vice president. This modification in Electoral College voting upset the logic of the framers' reasoning, because the parties began to choose their vice presidential nominees for partisan political reasons rather than for their capacity to govern. It is probably no coincidence that the office declined in importance following this constitutional amendment.

Until the mid twentieth century, vice presidents performed very few roles other than their limited constitutional functions. But after Franklin Roosevelt's sudden death in April 1945, Eisenhower's illnesses in the 1950s, and Kennedy's assassination in 1963, the position of vice president became a subject of public concern. In response, Congress enacted the Twenty-fifth Amendment, which was ratified by the states in 1967. The amendment permits the president to fill the vice presidency if that position becomes vacant, subject to the approval of a majority in both houses of Congress.

Since the end of World War II, presidents have also done more to prepare the vice president for the nation's toughest job. Eisenhower invited Vice President Richard Nixon to attend cabinet, National Security Council, and legislative strategy meetings. During Eisenhower's illnesses Nixon presided over these sessions. He also represented the president on a number of well-publicized trips abroad. Lyndon Johnson, John Kennedy's vice president, also participated in a variety of administrative activities, including coordinating efforts to eliminate racial discrimination, promoting the exploration of outer space, and lobbying Congress.

Despite their own experiences, neither Johnson nor Nixon gave major

Not only have some vice presidents not had the most distinguished qualifications for office, but their behavior in office has been occasionally indiscreet or of dubious morality and legality. In the early nineteenth century the vice presidency was a hotbed of controversy. Aaron Burr, the nation's third vice president, killed Alexander Hamilton in a duel and was indicted for murder while serving in office. Richard M. Johnson, who served as vice president during the administration of Martin Van Buren, kept a series of slave mistresses and spent one summer during his tenure managing a tavern. In the 1870s both of Ulysses Grant's vice presidents, Schuyler Colfax and Henry Wilson, were implicated in the Crédit Mobilier stock scandal.

By the turn of the century, scandals involving the vice presidency had become less frequent. For several decades, vice presidents suffered from the necessity of combating a well-deserved reputation for mediocrity. Controversies resurfaced after World War II. While campaigning with Dwight Eisenhower in 1952, Richard Nixon was accused of maintaining a secret slush fund of campaign contributions. He defended himself in a nationally televised address that ended the controversy but failed to change his reputation as a cutthroat politician out to further his own interests. Twenty years later, Nixon's vice president, Spiro Agnew, was forced to resign for accepting kickbacks during his tenure as a Maryland public official and later as vice president.

Agnew was the second vice president to resign from office (the first was John C. Calhoun, who resigned in 1832 as Andrew Jackson's vice president over the issue of states' rights). Since then, no public scandals have marred the office, although questions about Dan Quayle's qualifications came up, particularly when he began his vice presidency in 1988.

SOURCE: Marie D. Natoli, *American Prince, American Pauper: The Contemporary Vice Presidency in Perspective* (Westport, Conn.: Greenwood Press, 1985); and Michael Dorman, *The Second Man* (New York: Delacorte Press, 1968).

Spiro T. Agnew leaves federal court in 1973. He pleaded "no contest" to one charge of tax evasion rather than face criminal charges of taking kickbacks. "It is in the best interests of the Nation that I relinquish the Vice Presidency," he wrote to Nixon.

UPI/Bettmann

Library of Congress

*Richard M. Nixon, then vice president, made quite a name for himself in 1959 when
he engaged Nikita Khrushchev, premier of the U.S.S.R., in the "kitchen debate."
The two men were standing in the kitchen appliances section of an American manufacturing exhibition in Moscow. Praising the superiority of the Communist system,
Khrushchev boasted, "We will bury you." Nixon replied that capitalism would win
out in the end.*

new responsibilities to their vice presidents. But Ford and Carter did. Nelson
Rockefeller and Walter Mondale were given more discretion in advising the
president on policy issues, particularly in the domestic sphere. Both saw the
president on a regular basis and acted as liaison for him with others in the
administration, Congress, interest groups, and the president's political party.
Symbolically, Jimmy Carter gave Walter Mondale an office in the West Wing
of the White House, close to the Oval Office, thereby indicating to others how
he regarded his vice president. Although vice presidents George Bush and Dan
Quayle did not exert as much clout as Mondale, they too participated in major
policy discussions, headed committees to examine interagency problems, and
represented the president on trips abroad.

Vice President Al Gore is the Clinton administration's chief "designated
hitter." He participated in the selection process for the entire cabinet and for
those subcabinet appointments that fell within the areas of science, environmental affairs, and advanced technology. He also has broad responsibilities to
improve the functioning of government, heading a National Performance Review commission to "reinvent government," and overseeing the regulatory policy of the administration. A key adviser to the president and lobbyist for the
administration's major legislative policy initiatives, Gore also does party fundraising and speech making, acts as the president's personal representative, and
participates in other outreach activities.

The changes in the contemporary vice presidency have made the office
more attractive. It is now regarded as a stepping-stone to the presidency. Increased visibility and political influence have made vice presidents front-runners

Before Al Gore was elected vice president, he had become an expert on the environment, and that is considered "his" area. President Clinton also charged him with heading an investigation into government waste and inefficiency. In the fall of 1993, he announced his conclusions, backed by forklifts loaded with tons of wasteful bureaucratic paperwork. Gore's report pinpointed duplicative agencies, outdated subsidies, and proliferating regulations.

in their party's nomination process. This, in turn, has increased the chances for a vice president to become president, as George Bush did in 1988. In the twentieth century, six vice presidents have succeeded to the presidency and one former vice president, Richard Nixon, was elected to it after having been out of office for eight years.

Unlike the relationship between the president and the cabinet or between presidential staff and executive departments and agencies, the relationship between the vice president and the president cannot tolerate much tension. The vice president cannot disagree publicly with the president, take attention away from him, or appear eager to have his job. Thus, after President Reagan was shot, Vice President Bush, who was in Texas at the time of the assassination attempt, had his helicopter land at the vice president's residence at the Naval Observatory in Washington, D.C., rather than at the White House, to avoid any appearance that he was eager to take over as president. (The box on page 484 highlights another aspect of the vice presidency.)

THE PERSONAL DIMENSION

Presidents need advice, but they also have discretion in making decisions and conditioning their relationships with others. How skilled and smart they are, what they believe, how quickly they absorb information and make decisions, how they view their roles and tasks, how they feel on a particular day, and how they feel about themselves in general will affect their perceptions, their evaluations, and ultimately their actions.

Physical Health

Despite the importance of health, public information about the diagnosis and treatment of presidential illnesses is usually vague and incomplete, particularly at the onset of a health problem. In an effort to prevent precipitous reactions and maintain continuity, White House spokespersons have tended to play down the president's medical problems and underinform the public about them. Thus, it was not until weeks after Ronald Reagan left the hospital following the attempt on his life that the public learned how close to death he actually had come. Similarly, Grover Cleveland's two cancer operations in 1893, Woodrow Wilson's incapacity after a stroke in 1919–1920, Franklin Roosevelt's worsening health during the mid 1940s, and John F. Kennedy's Addison's disease were not publicized during those presidents' tenure in office.

Contemporary presidents seem to have had more than their share of illnesses.[14] Eisenhower had three major illnesses: coronary thrombosis in 1955, acute ileitis in 1956, and a minor stroke in 1957. Kennedy had a back problem that was treated with special braces, exercises, and a chair designed to alleviate pressure. Lyndon Johnson had gall bladder and hernia operations as president and caught pneumonia on at least one occasion. Ronald Reagan had operations for the removal of malignant growths in his colon and on his face. George Bush was treated for an overactive thyroid (Graves' disease) and had precancerous skin growths removed. Clinton regularly gets shots for his allergies and his characteristic hoarseness. The burdens of Vietnam and Watergate put both Johnson and Nixon under severe mental strain.

The effects of illness and mental stress on presidential performance vary. Some presidents are better able than others to cope with illness or injury. In general, the more serious the medical problem and the longer the recovery period, the more removed the president becomes from the day-to-day functioning of the office. Under such conditions, critical decisions are likely to be delayed or delegated. What is more difficult to discern is how decision making is affected when the president is not feeling up to par or when his judgment is affected by medication or pain. Consider, for example, the incredible amount of activity that President Bush engaged in at the beginning of the Persian Gulf

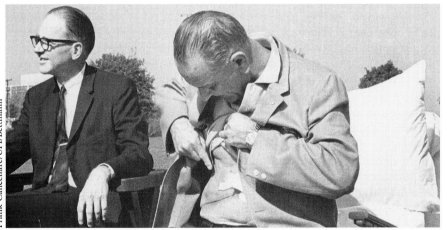

Frank Cancellare/UPI/Bettmann

Lyndon Johnson was hospitalized several times during his presidency. Leaving the hospital in 1965, he points to the spot where the doctors "messed around" in removing his gall bladder. The public got quite a few chances to see the incision. The scar resembled the shape of Vietnam, and Johnson often pulled up his shirt to show it and how the Vietnam War had scarred him.

crisis. Determined not to be a prisoner of the White House as Jimmy Carter had been during the early months of the Iranian hostage crisis in 1979, Bush frantically vacationed in Maine with "nonstop golf and horseshoes, iron-man jogs, marathon sets of tennis, relentless trolls for bluefish aboard his speedboat, *Fidelity*."[15] Was this activity a consequence of his overactive thyroid, frustration over his inability to prevent or thwart the Iraqi invasion, or simply normal for George Bush?

Character

Common sense suggests that personality also affects behavior, but the impact of personality is hard to measure. It must be inferred from words and actions.

How presidents conduct themselves in and out of office—how they organize the White House, make decisions, and interact with their aides—is undoubtedly affected by how they feel about themselves: their self-esteem, confidence, and feelings of being loved, attractive, and in control. Political scientist James David Barber has advanced a psychological model for explaining presidential behavior (see the box on page 489). Barber's model describes how presidents approach their job in terms of their level of activity (active or passive) and their ability to relate to others (positive or negative).[16]

Of the four character types in Barber's scheme, Barber considers the *active-positive* to be best suited to the presidency. Such a person brings to the office the high level of activity needed to sustain the multiple roles a president must assume. Moreover, a positive attitude toward work generates its own psychological and physical benefits. It contributes to a heightened energy level; it eases the inevitable conflicts that result from competing perspectives, interests, goals, and ambitions; and it increases tolerance. Presidents who enjoy their work tend to be eager and able to take on new and difficult challenges. *Active-negative* presidents, on the other hand, tend to be dangerous because they become rigid and unyielding when they are challenged.

Barber's model assumes that typecasting, or categorizing on the basis of certain dominant traits, can provide valuable clues to the problems that might develop during a presidency. Although the model cannot predict with certainty or anticipate particular reactions to particular events, it can indicate general tendencies and reactions to which certain personality types are prone.

However, there is a problem with this kind of analysis. Presidents who have been characterized as psychologically most qualified have not always turned out to be the most effective, and those who have been considered to be the most successful have not always had the most desirable psychological qualities (see the box at the right). Franklin Roosevelt is an example of an active-positive type who is generally regarded as a great president. James Polk and Woodrow Wilson, also well regarded by some presidential scholars, are examples of the active-negative types. Dwight Eisenhower and Ronald Reagan, both extremely popular presidents, are considered passive types—passive-negative in Eisenhower's case. Gerald Ford and Jimmy Carter—who were much less popular and, many would argue, less successful than Eisenhower and Reagan—are both active-positive types. Abraham Lincoln, categorized as active-negative by political scientist Jeffrey Tulis, is generally considered one of the nation's greatest presidents.[17]

Presidential Character Types

Active-Positive

An energetic president who enjoys his work and tends to be productive and capable of adjusting to new situations. Such a person generally feels confident and good about himself.

Active-Negative

A president who works hard but does not gain much pleasure from the work and who tends to be intense, compulsive, and aggressive. He may pursue his public actions in a self-interested manner. Such a person generally feels insecure and uses his position to overcome feelings of inadequacy and even impotence.

Passive-Positive

A relatively receptive, laid-back president who wants to gain agreement and to mute dissent at all costs. Such a person is likely to feel pessimistic and unloved on a deep psychological level. As president, the passive-positive individual attempts to compensate for these feelings by being overly optimistic and by continually trying to elicit agreement and support from others.

Passive-Negative

A president who abhors politics and withdraws from interpersonal relationships. Such an individual is ill suited for political office, much less for the nation's highest one. Suffering from low self-esteem and a sense of uselessness, a passive-negative president is likely to take refuge in generalized principles and standard procedures.

SOURCE: Adapted from James David Barber, *The Presidential Character*, 4th ed. (Englewood Cliffs, N.J.: Prentice-Hall, 1992), 9–10.

The Personality Types of Presidents

Active-Positive

Franklin D. Roosevelt
Harry S Truman
John F. Kennedy
Gerald Ford
Jimmy Carter
George Bush

Active-Negative

James Polk
Abraham Lincoln
Woodrow Wilson
Herbert Hoover
Lyndon B. Johnson
Richard M. Nixon

Passive-Positive

William Howard Taft
Warren G. Harding
Ronald Reagan

Passive-Negative

Calvin Coolidge
Dwight Eisenhower

SOURCE: James David Barber, *The Presidential Character*, 4th ed. (Englewood Cliffs, N.J.: Prentice-Hall, 1992); and Jeffrey Tulis, "On Presidential Character," in *The Presidency in the Constitutional Order*, ed. Joseph M. Bessette and Jeffrey Tulis (Baton Rouge: Louisiana State University Press, 1981), 293–301.

Although few would dispute the general conclusion that personality affects performance, isolating psychological influences from other influences is difficult. How much did George Bush's reaction to press stories that he was weak and indecisive in the failed Panamanian coup attempt influence his later decision to use overwhelming military force to invade Panama and remove Noriega from power? How much did conservative Republican opposition to Bush's support for increased taxes in 1990, media criticism of his handling of the budget deficit, and the public perception of him as inconsistent and weak contribute to his decision to use military force in the Persian Gulf in 1991? How much is Bill Clinton's moderate position on policy issues a consequence of his style and skill as a politician who seeks common ground as a means of building support?

Barber's model has been criticized on a number of grounds: (1) his categories are simplistic and too broad; (2) personalities do not fit neatly into them; and (3) the expectations and predictions that flow from them are too general to be useful as explanations, much less as predictions of specific events. Nevertheless, Barber's model continues to frame much of the debate on personality and the presidency. Although he has not succeeded in providing a comprehensive theory or an airtight explanation of why presidents behave as they do, he has focused attention on the obvious importance of personality and has identified certain facets of it that must be considered in discussions of presidential leadership.

Managerial Style

Presidents interact with their subordinates and make decisions in a variety of ways. Some presidents feel that they must dominate. Lyndon Johnson monopolized discussions with his aides and was unable to accept criticism. Kennedy and Bush treated their assistants more as equals.

Some presidents need to operate in a protective environment. Nixon saw only a few trusted aides and wanted all recommendations and advice to be presented to him in writing. Ford, Eisenhower, and Reagan were more open, saw more people, and were willing to make decisions on the basis of oral presentations.

Some presidents need to be involved in everything. Johnson, Carter, and Bush took a hands-on approach to decision making. Clinton falls into this category as well. On the other hand, Eisenhower and Reagan delegated considerable authority to their aides, waiting for issues to be brought to the Oval Office rather than reaching out for them.

The president's managerial style affects the way the White House works. Nixon's standoffish manner, his unwillingness to interact with many aides, and his all-business approach created an atmosphere in which aides had to prove how tough they were, how long they toiled, and how many sacrifices they made. In the Nixon administration there was little compassion and no patience for poor or late performance. Presidents Ford and Carter were more tolerant, more open, and less imposing than Nixon. In their administrations there were fewer penalties for poor performance, and senior aides who did not produce good work were circumvented rather than being asked to leave.

Ronald Reagan was perceived as benevolent but distant by his aides. A passive administrator, he delegated operational responsibility for the White

As George Bush's chief of staff, John Sununu embarrassed his president by using government transportation for personal trips. Here, at a press conference, Sununu, known for his abrasiveness, himself looks unusually contrite and embarrassed. At this press conference, the president announced that Sununu had apologized for any "mistakes he made." The mistakes continued, however, and Sununu was forced to resign.

UPI/Bettmann

House Office to his chief of staff. In theory presidential assistants reported to Reagan, but in practice they answered to his chief of staff. President Bush was a much more active manager. Although not nearly so dependent on his staff as Reagan was, Bush nonetheless delegated the day-to-day responsibility of running the White House Office to his chief of staff as well. With the exception of a few top aides, such as Brent Scowcroft, the national security adviser, those who worked in the Bush White House generally stayed out of the public spotlight, and certain cabinet members, primarily those who were personal friends of the president, were more visible and, presumably, more influential.

The Clinton White House is more collegial and free floating than the White House was during the Reagan and Bush administrations. It also operates in a more ad hoc manner. Clinton, who thrives on being involved on a range of policy and personnel issues, relies on his principal assistants in domestic, economic, and national security affairs for a wide range of information and expertise. Their failure to anticipate public reaction to certain presidential decisions and actions (from homosexuals in the military, to U.S. policy in Bosnia, to a $200 haircut the president received on an airport runway in Los Angeles) embarrassed Clinton and cast doubts about his judgment, leading him to restructure his White House just five months into office.

Belief System

Belief systems are shaped by how individuals view themselves and others. Beliefs about how the world works provide a frame of reference for presidents, who must filter information, evaluate options, and choose a course of action that is consistent with their policy goals.[18]

At the outset of the Cuban missile crisis, for example, President Kennedy ruled out diplomatic and nonmilitary responses and considered a fairly narrow range of military options. He believed that the presence of Soviet missiles in Cuba posed a major threat to national security and that the Soviet Union would remove the missiles only if forced to do so by the threat of American military sanctions. His decision to institute a blockade of Cuba rather than employ diplomatic means followed naturally from these premises. Similarly, President Reagan believed that the Soviet Union would negotiate an arms treaty with the United States only if America had a superior military force. His policy was to build up that force and to use it as a negotiating chip.

The president's world view is especially likely to limit consideration of alternatives in a crisis. The North Korean invasion of South Korea in 1950, the domestic strife in Nicaragua in the mid 1980s, and the Iraqi invasion of Kuwait in 1990 were seen by presidents Truman, Reagan, and Bush, respectively, as threats to the United States and its interests, and they decided that American armed forces might have to be employed. In contrast, President Carter did not view the hostage crisis in Iran as a grave threat to American security. Preoccupied with safeguarding the lives of those who had been taken prisoner, Carter spent a year trying to find an acceptable, peaceful diplomatic solution.

THE STRUGGLE FOR POWER

The increasing number of presidential decisions that have major national and international consequences has inflated the importance of the president's character, managerial style, and beliefs. It has also directed attention to the president's changing policy role. The framers of the Constitution intended for presidents to have an impact on public policy, but they did not expect them to dominate the policy process. Yet that is precisely what has happened; the president has become the nation's chief policy maker. Today the public expects the president to establish and achieve national goals, respond to policy emergencies, and propose solutions to major problems at home or abroad.

For various reasons, these expectations often exceed the president's abilities. The policy-making environment is hostile much of the time. A public consensus does not exist on most issues. People may agree about a problem but not about a solution. Moreover, the president's constitutional authority is extremely limited. Although presidents have considerable resources at their disposal—policy experts, political strategists, and support staff in the executive branch and the Executive Office—there is frequently disagreement about what to do and how to do it. These constraints make the formulation and management of public policy a time-consuming and difficult process. Presidents use diverse strategies and techniques to set an agenda, influence Congress, build public support, and implement priorities.

Setting the Agenda

Presidential agendas used to be laundry lists of proposals designed to appeal to as broad a segment of electoral supporters as possible. Franklin Roosevelt's New Deal, Truman's Fair Deal, Kennedy's New Frontier, Johnson's Great Society, and Nixon's New Federalism programs fit this description. Beginning in the 1980s, agendas have been more limited. Scarce resources and continuing budget deficits have forced presidents to reduce the number and costs of their programs.

By limiting their proposals and establishing clear priorities, presidents try to set the pace and tone of public debate and hope to give the impression that they are in command. Limiting priorities also enables presidents to concentrate the administration's resources. The disadvantage of focusing on a few policy proposals, however, is that the administration may appear to ignore issues that sizable portions of the public believe are important. President Bush was accused of neglecting domestic problems during his third and fourth years in office.

And if the few designated priorities are not converted into public policy, that may damage the president's reputation more than a mixed record with a larger number of proposals. President Clinton's loss of luster when he failed to obtain Senate approval of his economic stimulus package illustrates the danger of putting too much emphasis on a single legislative proposal.

A policy agenda cannot be determined solely by the president. Congress contributes to it, as do individuals and groups outside the government. It often takes several years for an idea to germinate, for policy to crystallize into a concrete proposal, and for sufficient support to be mobilized. Many of the ideas for Johnson's Great Society program originated during the Kennedy administration. Much of Reagan's legislative agenda was created during his 1976 and 1980 campaigns for the presidency.[19] Reducing the federal deficit has been an administration objective since the 1980s.

Timing is another strategic concern of presidents intent on achieving their legislative policy goals. Presidential influence tends to decrease over time. As members of Congress position themselves for the next election, as bureaucrats begin to press their claims on political appointees, and as the minority party begins to coalesce in opposition to the incumbent, achieving domestic-policy goals may become more difficult for the president. The problem becomes acute in the second term of an administration, particularly in the last two years of that term. During this period the president is often called a **lame duck**. Like a duck that cannot fly because its wings have been clipped, the president loses momentum and power as the administration draws to a close.

Presidential reputations are built early and tend to outlast the president's ability to achieve policy successes. Thus, presidents need to take advantage of their initial position of strength and move quickly after inauguration to achieve their most controversial programs. Carter found this out the hard way. He used his first six months in office to develop policies to implement his election promises. By the time those proposals were ready for Congress, he had lost the advantage that presidents have at the beginning of their term, when public expectations are high and media criticism is low.[20]

George Bush also moved slowly but, unlike Carter, did not overwhelm Congress with new legislation. Lacking a congressional majority and, initially, a strong popular following, he sought compromises on the most divisive issues to facilitate a "politics of accommodation" strategy, which he pursued during his first two years in office. Ronald Reagan and Bill Clinton, on the other hand, moved quickly with key components of their legislative agenda. Each wanted to take advantage of his victory, and specifically the momentum and the mandate that resulted from it. Each needed to establish a legislative reputation at the beginning of his administration that, he hoped, would augment his influence with Congress. And each used the budget as an instrument to encapsulate the tax and expenditure components of his economic program.

Influencing the Legislature

Presidents have to work hard at influencing Congress. Differing interests, constituencies, and even parties affect presidential and congressional perspectives and policy decisions. Key to the president's success is focusing and orchestrating the administration's efforts. This orchestration requires the mobilization of cabinet heads, other executive officials, party leaders, and representatives of sympathetic interest groups behind presidential priorities. During the Reagan administration the White House Office assembled a legislative strategy group to accomplish the president's goals. The Bush and Clinton administrations operated in a more ad hoc manner in dealing with Congress.

The congressional leadership must also be involved in the development of legislative proposals. The nature of that involvement depends on the policy in question as well as on the political environment and the president's preferences. Carter and Reagan relied on their party's congressional leaders, bringing in the opposition party leaders when necessary. Facing Democratic majorities in both houses of Congress, Bush adopted a bipartisan approach and dealt directly and regularly with the Democratic leadership. Clinton initially adopted a partisan legislative strategy with majorities in both houses. This approach worked well in the House of Representatives, where a cohesive majority can dominate, but in the Senate, Clinton's failure to consult with Republicans resulted in filibusters that killed or modified House-enacted legislation supported by the administration. Such setbacks forced the president to alter his approach. He began to consult with moderate Republicans who were sympathetic to the tenor of his policy objectives, and his administration expanded its contacts with rank-and-file Democrats in Congress.

Regardless of their strategic plans, presidents must be personally involved in lobbying for their legislative goals. The extent of this involvement is often taken as a sign of how much importance presidents attach to a particular issue. There are a variety of ways for presidents to get involved, ranging from requesting support to twisting arms to making deals. Lyndon Johnson was legendary for effective lobbying. He communicated constantly with members of Congress, attempting to persuade them of the merits of his proposals. Sometimes he accompanied his case with implicit promises or veiled threats. Clark Clifford, a cabinet secretary and adviser to Johnson, described the president's persuasive style in the following way:

President Johnson calls in a senator and he says, "Joe . . . Does that law partner of yours still want to be a federal judge?"

"Oh," he says, "he certainly does."

"Well," he says, "you know I've been thinking about that lately and we're going to talk about that. But in the process of talking about that, I want to talk with you about the fact that I think we've got to increase our Social Security program."

"Well, Mr. President, I've spoken against that."

"Well, I know, Joe. But times have changed. And you think about it awhile. . . . Let a week go by, you call me."

Reuters/Bettmann

Getting along with members of Congress, particularly the leadership, is critical for a president. Facing the wrath of the Republicans after neglecting them in developing his budget proposals, President Clinton attends a "fence-mending" dinner with Senate Minority Leader Robert Dole. Robert Strauss, a popular Democratic insider who was President Bush's ambassador to Russia, arranged it all. Hillary Clinton greets Mrs. Strauss. Elizabeth Dole, the Senator's wife and head of the Red Cross, was absent.

Joe calls him in a week and says, "Mr. President, I've been thinking about that and I think there's a lot of merit to your position. And I believe I can change on . . . Social Security. I want to come over and talk to you. And, incidentally, I talked to my partner, and he is just tickled to death."[21]

Despite such tactics, presidential influence is still limited. Most presidents cannot dictate to Congress, nor can they easily reverse overwhelming sentiment on an issue. In fact, congruity between what Congress and presidents desire is often critical in determining the outcome of an issue. According to Charles O. Jones, congruity is likely to be most influenced by the election results (such as those of 1964 and 1980, when the president's party did relatively well in the congressional elections) or by significant events (such as the Kennedy assassination or the Watergate affair). Thus, Johnson in 1964 and Reagan in 1980 benefited from a Congress that was responsive to their legislative agenda, but Ford in 1974 and Bush in 1988 suffered from a Congress that had a different political agenda.[22]

In recent times the Johnson and Reagan experiences have been the exception, not the rule. Since 1968, divided government, with different parties controlling the Congress and the White House, or divisions within the majority party in one or both houses, has been the norm. These partisan divisions have reduced the president's effectiveness with Congress.

How influential can presidents be? According to political scientist George Edwards, presidents can affect Congress only at the margins.[23] In a closely divided legislature, however, affecting the votes of a few members of Congress can be crucial. One indication of presidential influence in Congress is the extent

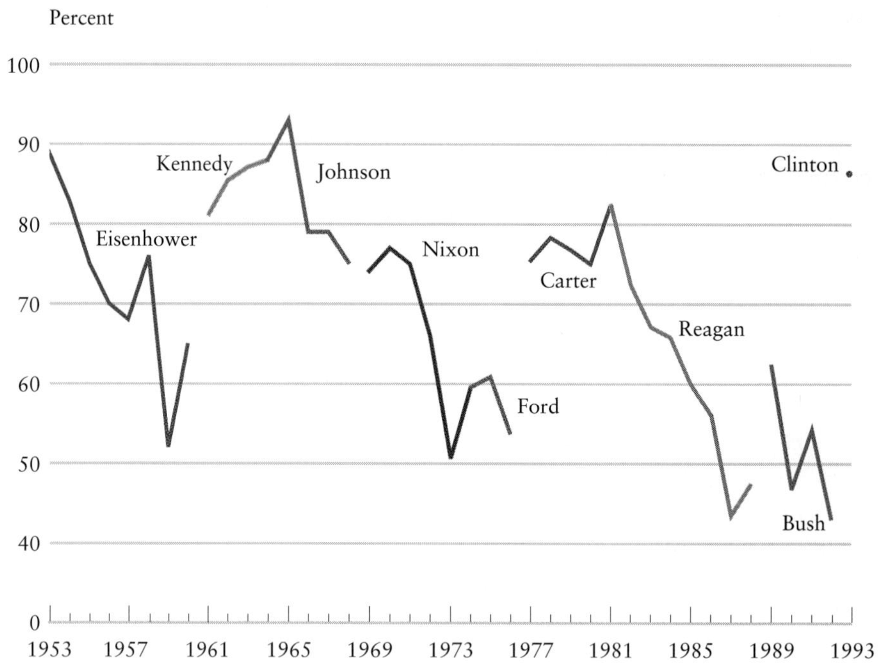

Percent

Figure 13-6 *Presidential success in Congress.* SOURCE: Congressional Quarterly Weekly Report, *December 18, 1993, 3428, 3473.*

of support presidents receive for positions they take on legislation. This support can be determined by calculating the proportion of times members of Congress vote in accordance with the stated position of the president. Figure 13-6 graphs the support scores of presidents since 1953.

Presidential support increases when the president's party controls both houses of Congress. But partisan control is no guarantee of success in Congress, as it is in parliamentary systems in which straight party voting is expected and prime ministers are selected because they control a partisan legislative majority. In the United States, presidents have to work to build and maintain majorities even within their own party.

Although presidential influence varies with the issue, presidents have had more success in Congress with foreign affairs than with domestic issues. This dominance, which was particularly evident in the period from the end of World War II to the Vietnam War, led some political scientists to conclude that there were actually two presidencies, one in foreign affairs and one in domestic policy.[24] Today the distinction between foreign and domestic policies is less clear. Foreign-policy issues have a greater impact on domestic policy than they did in earlier decades. For this reason, Congress has become more interested and involved in foreign-policy matters. As a consequence, presidents can no longer be assured that their foreign-policy initiatives will prevail. They must mobilize support for them much as they do in the domestic arena.

Although presidents cannot control Congress in normal times, they usually can prevent legislation that they do not like from becoming law by exercising a veto. The veto is not absolute, but it is a powerful instrument. Only about 4 percent of all presidential vetoes have been overridden (see Table 12-4). The threat of a veto is frequently sufficient to get Congress to modify a proposal. To make a veto threat stick, however, the president must be prepared to exercise the veto and must have reason to believe that it will be sustained.

George Bush used the veto effectively to supplement his strategy for dealing with Congress. In political discussions with the Democratic leadership, he indicated how far he was willing to go on major legislative proposals by suggesting what he was prepared to veto. He backed up his threat by sending back to Congress thirty-five bills of which he disapproved. All but one of these vetoes were sustained.

Building Public Support

Public support is thought to contribute to the president's legislative success. That is why presidents devote much time and effort to shaping public opinion.

The White House Office works hard to promote a favorable image of the administration by shaping the form, content, and timing of information that flows from the government. It provides a host of services for the media—from information packets to daily briefings to interviews and photo opportunities. White House efforts to shape news coverage of the president can succeed because the media are so dependent on material supplied by the White House.

The pomp and ceremony of the presidency also help the president. The public aspects of the institution receive extensive coverage and enhance the stature of the individual who occupies the Oval Office. Presidents go public more now than in the past (see Figure 13-7).

Figure 13-7 *Public appearances by presidents, 1929–1990.* SOURCE: *Samuel Kernell, "Going Public," 2nd ed.,* Congressional Quarterly, *1993, 102. Reprinted by permission of Congressional Quarterly, Inc.*

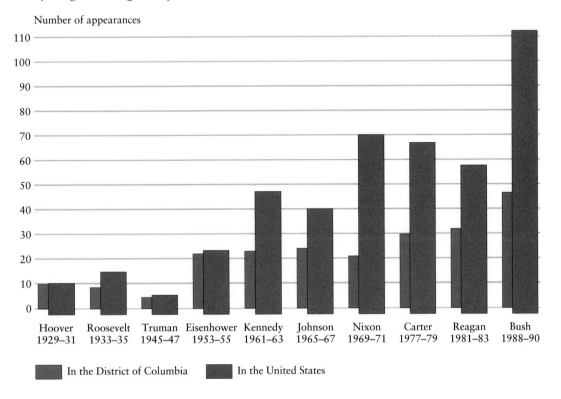

Peace negotiations between Israel and its Arab neighbors began under President Bush and continued under President Clinton. But the greatest progress was negotiated secretly in Norway. After reaching agreement, both sides wanted to sign the accords in Washington, with the president presiding (and lending moral, political, and economic support). Here Yitzhak Rabin and Yassir Arafat shake hands.

The White House

Jimmy Carter is a good example of a president who used symbolism to boost his popularity. In the aftermath of Watergate, he played down the grandeur of office. He walked down Pennsylvania Avenue following his inauguration, wore a sweater when he delivered his first address to the nation, and dispensed with the playing of "Hail to the Chief" at public ceremonies. But when his popularity declined, he dressed more formally and reinstated "Hail to the Chief." Other examples of presidents using ceremony to enhance their public image include Reagan's speech at Normandy fifty years after the D-Day invasion that was the turning point of World War II, Bush's Thanksgiving meal with the troops in the desert of Saudi Arabia in 1990, and Clinton's presiding over the signing of the agreement between Israel and the PLO in 1993.

Presidents can also be their own best boosters. By virtue of their position, they command attention. Presidents have often resorted to national addresses to build their public support. Franklin D. Roosevelt and Ronald Reagan were extremely successful at building and maintaining loyal followings through direct appeals to the public. Roosevelt's "fireside chats" calmed a jittery nation during the Great Depression and World War II. Reagan's White House addresses, particularly during his first term in office, buoyed the spirits of a people upset by a stagnant and inflated economy. Roosevelt's and Reagan's successes stemmed from their communicative skills. Roosevelt had a reassuring tone that was well suited to radio. Reagan, an experienced actor, talked in a soft but earnest voice to his television audience. John F. Kennedy's quick wit and pleasant appearance helped him project a favorable image. By contrast, Jimmy Carter's low, monotonous singsong, Gerald Ford's and George Bush's inarticulateness, and Lyndon Johnson's and Richard Nixon's unease, particularly with television, adversely affected their ability to persuade the public.

One device that some presidents have used successfully to demonstrate their mastery of the issues and to build support for their programs is the press conference. Roosevelt, Kennedy, Carter, and Bush did well in these forums.

Presidents have their own personal styles. Franklin Roosevelt grew to be almost larger than life during his 14 years as president. On the day of his third inaugural in 1941, he appeared regal sitting beside Eleanor and waving his top hat from an open car. Jimmy Carter showed a more down-to-earth style when he walked along Pennsylvania Avenue holding his wife Rosalynn's hand. With the Republican nomination assured in 1980, Ronald and Nancy Reagan invited photographers to their ranch for a glimpse of the "hero on horseback" at home. George Bush polished his image as family man and commander in chief when he and Barbara had Thanksgiving dinner with U.S. troops in Saudi Arabia in 1990.

Their extensive knowledge about policy and personnel stood them in good stead with the White House reporters. Ronald Reagan fared less well. Lacking detailed information about his administration, he was unable to answer questions as accurately and fully as the media demanded, and the need for extensive preparation and the fear of making embarrassing mistakes discouraged him from holding many press conferences. Bill Clinton has also not used the press conference as much as some others; he did not hold a live prime-time press conference until five months after taking office. Instead, Clinton tried to reach out and around the national news media at the beginning of his administration,

What the President Said

Everything the president officially says is a matter of public record. All the president's public speeches, remarks, proclamations, executive orders, letters, and so on are preserved and published by the National Archives and Records Administration. These documents are found in all federal depository libraries and in many other research libraries.

The *Federal Register* publishes a daily record of the president's words and official actions. A weekly record, along with a digest of the president's activities that week, is found in the *Weekly Compilation of Presidential Documents.* A complete record of the president's speeches appears annually in the *Public Papers of the Presidents. Codification of Presidential Proclamations and Executive Orders* contains these documents from 1945 to 1989 in one convenient, indexed volume. More recent executive orders and memoranda can be found in the *Federal Register* and in the *Weekly Compilation of Presidential Documents.*

The *New York Times* usually runs the full text of major presidential speeches and transcripts of most presidential press conferences the next day.

The president is also on-line with special data bases and bulletin boards, accessible through most of the popular on-line information services and through the Internet system. Users can access official White House documents and speeches through on-line libraries, leave e-mail for the president, and participate in bulletin board discussions of policy issues.

A recorded message for the press listing the president's schedule for the day can be heard by calling (202) 456-2343. A similar message for the first lady can be heard at (202) 456-6269.

preferring the more congenial format of a town meeting with average citizens to the more adversarial confrontation with the Washington press corps.

The extensive efforts by the White House to secure favorable media coverage are a direct response to the situation in which presidents often find themselves. The general public is often divided, uninterested, and uninvolved; but organized groups, political parties, and public officials are not shy about taking stands and promoting their positions. Thus, the president has to take his communicator-in-chief role seriously and try to build consensus both inside and outside the government.

Implementing Priorities in the Executive Branch

Implementation is the final stage in the policy process. Here the president must deal primarily with officials in the executive branch. Traditionally presidents have not gotten deeply involved in the details of implementation because of the size of the bureaucracy, time constraints, and their limited resources for affecting executive-branch decisions. However, with the increased attention given to management issues—bureaucratic red tape, federal contracting, and nonperformance of services, for example—by the media and the allegations of mismanagement within the executive branch that have plagued recent presidential administrations, the efficient operation of government has become a salient concern for the president.

The easiest and most direct way for presidents to exercise control over policy implementation is to have White House aides communicate their wishes to those in the departments and agencies who are responsible for implementing them. In most cases a telephone call or White House meeting will suffice. Occasionally an executive order may be necessary.

The president can also oversee the regulations that departments and agencies issue to implement legislation. President Carter standardized procedures for issuing these regulations, and President Reagan created the division in the Office of Management and Budget that reviews them. President Clinton has modified that review process.

The practice of having the OMB review and approve departmental regulations often creates tension between the OMB and the departments and agencies, because of their differing perspectives and goals. The OMB evaluates regulations on the basis of their anticipated cost, precedent, and conformity to presidential policy. The departments and agencies focus on the substance of the regulations, the procedures, the time frame, and the criteria for dispersing money or services.

Presidents also have indirect means of affecting executive-branch decision making. They have some discretion to reorganize the executive branch, subject to congressional approval, and can use the annual budget process as a means of establishing new priorities, reaffirming existing ones, and rewarding or sanctioning the departments and agencies. The contrast between the American president and the heads of other governments is dramatic. The British prime minister and the French president have complete discretion in filling executive appointments and making structural changes. To a lesser extent, the Italian and Japanese prime ministers exercise this power as well.

A significant part of the president's problem is rooted in the sharing of power. With Congress responsible for the creation of the executive-branch structure, the authorization of executive-branch programs, and the appropriation of executive-branch funds, not to mention Senate confirmation of appointments, ratification of treaties, and congressional oversight of bureaucratic operations, the president must contend with congressional involvement in all phases of the policy-making and implementation processes. This involvement, in turn, forces the executive-branch bureaucracy to be sensitive to the interests of Congress as well as the interests of the president. This dual allegiance becomes apparent when department and agency officials testify before congressional committees that consider their appropriations.

Part of the president's management difficulty also stems from a civil service system based on merit. Members of the civil service must be chosen for their knowledge, skills, and competence (demonstrated in competitive examinations) rather than for their political allegiance and affiliation (see Chapter 14). This system ensures that policies are implemented by skilled personnel, but it also requires presidents to contend with subordinates who do not necessarily share their views, goals, or time frame.

The development of an outside clientele for the departments and agencies has further eroded the president's influence on the executive branch. Even political appointees must be sensitive to the interests and needs of their department's constituency. When those interests and needs are at odds with the president's goals, political appointees face a dilemma. If they are to maintain credibility with the clients they serve, they must be advocates for their department's goals, but over time this advocacy may strain their relationship with the president. Thus, for example, officials of most departments will request more money for programs and operations than the president, who may wish to economize or change priorities. To counter the tendency of department heads to ask

Bush, Reagan, Carter, Ford, and Nixon pose for the one and only picture of five living ex-presidents, taken at the opening of Ronald Reagan's library. Critics pounced when it was learned that these five men apparently agreed to sign (and sell) a limited number of prints to raise money for their libraries and personal charities.

for more and more, presidents have relied on their budget directors to impose ceilings and set goals during the annual budgetary cycle.

Exercising Leadership

The difficulties that presidents encounter in their efforts to make and implement public policy expose the multiplicity of pressures that affect all aspects of presidential decision making. In a pluralistic society in which political actors and institutions are responsive to their clienteles, politics is likely to occur within and between each institution of government, making it hard for any one of them to dominate the policy-making process.

This situation is precisely what the framers desired and the Constitution intended. It places the burden on the advocates of change: they must form coalitions and gain the support of those who share power. This burden of consensus building often falls on the president's shoulders. There is no other position in the American government from which that leadership can regularly emanate.

The president's leadership dilemma stems from the gap between public expectations and constitutional and statutory limits on presidential authority. Sometimes the gap can be bridged by the exercise of political leadership. But even if the president does try to exercise that leadership, even if the president is sensitive to the politics of the presidency, success is not guaranteed. Presidents still must contend with factors beyond their personal and institutional control; they are still hostage to events. In the end, their reaction to events, what they say and do when conditions are not favorable, is the true test of their leadership skills. Lincoln during the Civil War crisis, Franklin Roosevelt during the Great Depression and World War II, and Ronald Reagan during a period of economic stagnation, declining international prestige, and loss of confidence at home all demonstrated their leadership. They had a vision, the ability to articulate it, and the skills to achieve it: that is the essence of presidential leadership. In good times presidents may preside over the government; in bad times they must prevail within it.

The creation of the American presidency was characterized by both conflict and consensus. After a short but pointed debate, the delegates agreed on a single executive but disagreed on the method of selection. In deciding on an electoral college, they rejected a direct popular vote as unwise and unfeasible, and legislative selection as antithetical to the maintenance of separate and independent institutions. Believing that electors who were not beholden to any government institution or outside group would be better able to decide on the most qualified persons for president and vice president, they devised an indirect electoral system in which the states determined how their electors would be chosen.

In contrast to the divisions over how the president should be selected, a consensus developed over the course of the Constitutional Convention on the scope and limits of the president's authority. That consensus, shaped by experiences during the colonial period and after independence, was to give the president enough discretion to meet the executive responsibilities of the office but not enough to dominate the government.

To exercise these responsibilities the president was given the power to nominate and, with the advice and consent of the Senate, to appoint subordinates. The president could also remove them, although civil servants and members of independent regulatory commissions are exempt from removal power. In addition to choosing personnel, presidents can tell their subordinates what to do. They do this formally by issuing an *executive memorandum* or an *executive order*. The issuance of an order, however, requires time and expertise which presidents may lack. The difficulty of exercising continuous oversight over the executive departments and agencies has encouraged presidents to leave the business of administration to their senior appointees in the executive branch.

The president has four formal legislative duties and powers: (1) to inform Congress from time to time about the state of the union; (2) to recommend necessary and expedient legislation; (3) to summon Congress into special session and adjourn it if the two houses cannot agree on adjournment; and (4) to negate an act of Congress by vetoing it. The executive's judicial powers include issuing pardons, granting clemency, and proclaiming amnesty. Presidents can also affect judicial decisions by influencing the composition of the federal judiciary through the nomination of judges and (with the Justice Department) by determining the government's position on controversial legal matters.

Despite these powers, the president is still faced with a dilemma. Public expectations of what the president should do often exceed the resources of the president for doing it. As a consequence, presidents are continually engaged in political struggles to achieve their policy objectives. In their efforts to prevail, they can bargain behind closed doors with government officials, and they can also go public. In bargaining, the president has several advantages. The office itself is respected, and the president also controls valued commodities such as nominations, electoral support, and social invitations, as well as sanctions such as directly opposing a candidate or policy. The president's reputation and prestige can also contribute to success in bargaining.

Going public can take several forms, including trying to control the news, magnifying the ceremonial aspects of the presidency, and engaging in public activities such as speeches and press conferences. Going public augments presidential power by legitimizing the president's position in the eyes of others and by enabling the president to apply pressure more effectively. However, public opinion tends to be volatile and inconsistent, and public approval is usually tied to visible results. In addition, by going public presidents raise expectations; failure to meet those expectations damages their reputations.

The president's institutional resources include the cabinet, the Executive Office of the President, and the vice presidency. The *cabinet* consists of the heads of the various executive departments. Until the 1960s it functioned as the president's principal advisory body. Because of its increasing size and diversity, however, it became cumbersome and less efficient. In addition, increasing pressure from outside groups forced cabinet members to become advocates for their respective departments. Presidents beginning with Reagan have depended on smaller advisory bodies organized on the basis of broad policy areas.

The *Executive Office of the President* consists of twelve units, of which the largest and most powerful are the Office of Management and Budget and the White House Office. The *Office of Management and Budget* acts as a central clearinghouse, coordinating recommendations to the president and making sure that the executive departments' legislative proposals and official positions are in accord with the president's program. The *White House Office* provides staff support for the president, makes priority policy, and builds support for that policy.

Until the mid twentieth century, vice presidents performed very few roles other than presiding over the Senate and voting in case of a tie. Recent presidents have given the vice president additional responsibilities, and the position has become more important politically as a stepping stone to the presidency. Similarly, the role of the president's spouse has also been enlarged.

How presidents use their vice president, how they interact with their staff, and how they approach their job depends to a large extent on their personality. In examining the impact of personality on performance in office, James David Barber has advanced a psychological model based on presidential character. In his model, Barber describes job performance in terms of level of activity (active or passive) and ability to relate to others (positive or negative). Barber considers the active-positive type best suited to the presidency. Critics claim that Barber's categories are simplistic and too general to be useful. Nevertheless, Barber has focused attention on the importance of presidential personality.

Presidents interact with their subordinates and make decisions in a variety of ways. Some presidents need to operate in a protected environment; others are more open. Some need to be involved in everything; others are more willing to delegate authority. In addition, the president's belief system provides a frame of reference for evaluating information and making decisions.

Key to the president's success in obtaining legislative support is mobilizing cabinet heads, other executive officials, party leaders, and interest group representatives to support the administration's pri-

orities. Congressional leadership must be involved in the development of legislative proposals. As time goes by, achieving domestic-policy goals may become increasingly difficult for presidents, especially if they are *lame ducks*—that is, in the last two years of their second term.

Presidents devote considerable time and effort to shaping public opinion. They do this by trying to control and disseminate information to the media about their administration. They also try to enhance their stature through public events such as speeches, town meetings, foreign travel, and other situations in which they interact with the public. Coverage of pomp and ceremony works to the president's advantage, as do the president's own communications skills.

In implementing policy, the president must deal primarily with the executive branch and with the various political forces that influence decision making. The tools they have to maintain coordination and extend their influence include the issuance of executive orders and the use of regulatory review and the budgetary review process, both run by the OMB.

Part of the president's difficulty in managing the executive branch is due to power sharing with Congress. The president's management problem also results from the civil service system, which fills some executive-branch positions with people who do not necessarily share the president's views, goals, and time frame. The development of an outside clientele for the departments and agencies further erodes the president's influence on the executive branch.

All these factors contribute to the dilemma all presidents face: how to meet ever-growing expectations of leadership in a political system that separates institutions and makes them responsible to different constituencies, yet forces them to work together to make and implement public policy.

KEY TERMS AND CONCEPTS

senatorial courtesy	cabinet	lame duck
executive memorandum	Executive Office of the President	central clearance process
executive order	Office of Management and Budget	enrolled bill process
executive agreement	White House Office	regulatory review
going public		

Scholarly studies

Barber, James David. *The Presidential Character*. 4th ed. Englewood Cliffs, N.J.: Prentice-Hall, 1992. A pioneering but controversial study of the impact of personality on performance in office. Short, psychologically oriented chapters on individual presidents make for interesting reading and speculative interpretations.

Cronin, Thomas E., ed. *Inventing the American Presidency*. Lawrence: University of Kansas Press, 1989. A collection of original essays that examine the creation of the presidency.

Edwards, George C., III. *At the Margins: Presidential Leadership of Congress*. New Haven: Yale University Press, 1990. A quantitative analysis of congressional roll call votes aimed at measuring presidential influence in Congress.

Edwards, George C., III, and Stephen J. Wayne. *Presidential Leadership*. 3rd ed. New York: St. Martin's Press, 1994. A comprehensive text that synthesizes the principal literature and knowledge on the presidency.

Kernell, Samuel. *Going Public*. 2nd ed. Washington, D.C.: Congressional Quarterly, 1993. A monograph that argues effectively that presidents need to adopt a public strategy to achieve their policy objectives.

Light, Paul C. *The President's Agenda: Domestic Policy Choice from Kennedy to Reagan*. Rev. ed. Baltimore: Johns Hopkins University Press, 1991. A comprehensive, well-written discussion of agenda building in the modern presidency, based on the experiences of presidents from Kennedy to Reagan.

Neustadt, Richard E. *Presidential Power and the Modern President*. New York: Free Press, 1990. The classic study, originally published in 1960, of the president's basic dilemma: how to exert influence within a highly decentralized political system in normal times.

Pfiffner, James P., ed. *The Managerial Presidency*. Belmont, Calif.: Brooks/Cole, 1991. An excellent compilation of readings about how contemporary presidents structure their office and make and implement decisions.

Leisure reading

Goodwin, Doris K. *Lyndon Johnson and the American Dream*. New York: St. Martin's Press, 1991. A psychologically oriented biography by a person who was very close to President Johnson during his last year in office.

Reedy, George. *The Twilight of the Presidency*. New York: New American Library, 1987. A discussion of the dangers that presidents should avoid: a swelled head, overzealous loyal assistants, and a rarefied and unreal atmosphere for decision making.

Shogan, Robert. *The Riddle of Power: Presidential Leadership from Truman to Bush*. New York: Plume, 1992. A leading political journalist reflects on the dilemma of presidential power and the exercise of presidential leadership in contemporary times.

Woodward, Bob, and Carl Bernstein. *The Final Days*. New York: Simon and Schuster, 1989. A gripping account of a damaged presidency—Richard Nixon's last days in office.

Primary sources

Levy, Leonard W., and Louis Fisher, eds. *Encyclopedia of the American Presidency*. New York: Simon and Schuster, 1994. An encyclopedia of short articles about the presidency written by the leading scholars.

Nelson, Michael, ed. *Guide to the Presidency*. Washington, D.C.: Congressional Quarterly, 1989. A collection of brief biographies and institutional histories, as well as descriptions of many facets of the contemporary presidency.

Weekly Compilation of Presidential Documents. Washington, D.C.: U.S. Government Printing Office. A selective compilation of the official presidency: schedules, speeches, news conferences, executive orders, presidential proclamations, nominations, appointments, and communiqués to foreign heads of state.

Organizations

Center for the Study of the Presidency, 208 East 75th Street, New York, NY 10021; (212) 249-1200. Publishes the journal *Presidential Studies Quarterly* and occasional books; organizes annual conferences on the presidency.

Office of Management and Budget, Executive Office of the President, Washington, DC 20501; (202) 395-3000. Distributes an annual budget for the U.S. government and other documents of interest to students of the presidency.

White Burkett Miller Center of Public Affairs, University of Virginia, Charlottesville, VA 22905; (804) 924-7236. Holds seminars and publishes monographs and articles on the contemporary presidency.

The White House, 1600 Pennsylvania Avenue, N.W., Washington, DC 20500; (202) 456-1414. Provides information and press releases on the president and his programs.

CHAPTER

14

The

Executive

Bureaucracy

- The organization of the federal bureaucracy: types of organizational structure; staffing the bureaucracy; the executive bureaucracy in perspective

- Functions of the executive bureaucracy: implementation; policy making; determinants of bureaucratic influence

- Problems of accountability: legal and legislative controls; popular participation; the adequacy of controls

In the election of 1940, as war loomed on the horizon, the primary issue was President Franklin Roosevelt's decision to seek a third term. Wendell L. Willkie was chosen as the Republican candidate after winning the nomination from Thomas Dewey and Robert Taft. FDR's running mate, Secretary of Agriculture Henry Wallace, was a New Deal proponent. While the Democrats sounded the theme of "no change in the pilot," the Republicans warned against crowning FDR king by making him the first three-time president. The turnout was huge, and FDR won decisively.

In November 1988 the Department of Energy announced its decision to build the world's largest atom smasher, a superconducting supercollider (SSC), in Waxahachie, Texas, about twenty-five miles south of Dallas. The selection of the Texas site, said Energy Secretary John Herrington, was "impartial [and] non-political." The choice, he noted, was made not by the political appointees in the department but by "the highest-ranking career and scientific personnel." Herrington's comment brought hoots of derision from others in Washington, especially those representing states that had sought unsuccessfully to land the SSC project.

Federal agencies award grants every day (see Chapter 3); doing so is part of the routine for government agencies. But this was no ordinary grant, and its sheer magnitude had generated one of the most intense and most political episodes in bureaucratic history. It was estimated that construction of the SSC would require about $600 million a year for six years and another $270 million annually for operation. The local economy of the state that won the project would receive approximately $11 billion over the following twenty-five years.

507

Many states sought the SSC; initially there were twenty-five applicants. Most of them did whatever they could to put pressure on the Reagan administration and the Department of Energy. That Texas won was an important measure of its clout in Washington during the last year of Reagan's term. The vice president at the time was George Bush, a Texan (he had been elected president two days before the announcement). Also from Texas were Treasury Secretary James Baker, Speaker of the House Jim Wright, and Senate Finance Committee Chair Lloyd Bentsen.

Members of Congress from states that lost out in the competition cried "Politics!" Senator Donald W. Reigle (D-Michigan) said, "The Texas decision has a strong smell of White House politics. That was our major concern all along. The Michigan application was clearly better than the Texas proposal. We and the other five finalist states got a raw deal." His colleague, Senator Alan J. Dixon (D-Illinois), said that the decision was "based on politics rather than merit." Representative Don Ritter (R-Pennsylvania) added, "If there was one state that they could have picked to optimize the political power base, they picked it. It was Texas."

Senator Phil Gramm (R-Texas) disagreed. "I think to try to inject politics into this thing because you're a sour loser does not serve the national interest well," he said. "It was not a political decision."[1]

THE PROJECT WAS UNUSUALLY LARGE, AND THE potential benefits were uncommonly great, but the pattern was familiar. Programs and projects must be placed somewhere. Proposals are invited, with the promise that the one with the greatest merit will be selected. But "merit" is often difficult to define, and the selection process is buffeted by the efforts of members of Congress and others to win the prize for the people they represent. Thus, politics is a major feature of decision making in the executive bureaucracy.

The bureaucracy is the part of government that implements decisions made by the president and Congress. Many people believe that bureaucracies are complex, apolitical, and controlled by stringent rules and procedures. That is only partially true. The federal bureaucracy is certainly complex, and its activities are guided by a mystifying array of rules, but it is anything but apolitical. The administrative offices and the people who staff them are important political actors. They have their own policy preferences and prejudices. They fight to protect and expand their own vision of what is best for the country. They are not merely neutral implementers of decisions made elsewhere in the political process; they are at the center of the political process, involved in the struggles among individuals, interest groups, and government institutions to affect decisions. One cannot understand the administration of public policy without acknowledging its fundamental political character. Politics is as common an occurrence and as profound a force in the halls and offices of federal agencies as it is anywhere else in government.

When you hear the word *bureaucrat*, what images come to mind? An overweight middle-aged man sitting at a desk shuffling papers from one pile to another, or an air traffic controller bringing planes in through an ice storm? A curt woman peering out through a barred window to announce that the deadline for your application was yesterday, or a young microbiologist doing AIDS

A large federal construction project that gets under way is nearly always completed. But this "supercollider" for nuclear research in Waxahachie, Texas, was an exception. After the state and federal governments had spent billions developing it, in 1993 Congress cut off funds—essentially killing the project. The long-term budgetary gains will be enormous for the federal government, but so will the short-term loss of jobs and tax revenues be for Texas.

research? An anonymous person with an ink pad and stamp who returns the wrong forms, or a diplomat held hostage in a small African nation?

The word *bureaucrat* is loosely used to describe career government employees. It often brings to mind a bored and rigid person interested only in collecting a paycheck and putting in the time to get a lucrative pension. But among the millions of career government employees, many have demanding jobs, and most enjoy their work and do it skillfully (see the profile of Ambassador Arnold Raphel on page 519).

In this chapter we look at American public servants, the work they do, and the political environment they do it in. We begin with the size and shape of the contemporary executive branch, how it is structured and staffed. Then we examine the roles that bureaucratic agencies play in the policy-making process. We conclude by probing the issue of bureaucratic accountability.

THE ORGANIZATION
OF THE FEDERAL BUREAUCRACY

Bureaucracy is a system in which the business of an organization is carried on by bureaus, agencies, and departments in which there is a clear hierarchy of authority and special emphasis on fixed routines. Bureaucracies have jurisdictions established by law or administrative rules. Their employees are specialists who are trained to perform the specific tasks assigned them and who maintain written records of their decisions and activities. The point of bureaucracies is to achieve objectivity, precision, efficiency, continuity, consistency, and fairness.

Bureaucracies have been around for most of the history of human civilization. The early Catholic church, ancient China, and the Roman Empire all

© Paul S. Conklin

Courtesy, Secret Service

© Jeff Henry

*Few federal jobs are glamorous. Govern-
ment employees maintain trails in national
parks, inspect mines, deliver mail, guard
presidents, and keep planes landing safely.*

relied on bureaucratic principles of organization. Not until the nineteenth century, however, as industrialization occurred and nations became more active
in social and economic affairs, did bureaucracy become a prominent organizational system.

Except for the Post Office Department, the administrative agencies of the
United States government were few in number and small in size until the second
half of the nineteenth century. Their growth began to accelerate after the Civil
War as the population and the range of federal activities expanded. Nevertheless, the federal government remained a relatively small enterprise until the
onset of the Great Depression and World War II. Today the executive branch
is the largest component of the federal government. Its civilian employees number 3 million; its military employees, 1.8 million. There are more than a hundred separate organizational units. Federal employees include not only clerks,
soldiers, and letter carriers but also physicians, attorneys, physicists, historians,
economists, accountants, and pharmacists. In size and complexity the federal
executive branch is an entity without peer in American society. Some landmarks
in the development of the executive bureaucracy are listed in Table 14-1.

TABLE 14-1
Landmarks in the Development of the Executive Bureaucracy

YEAR	APPROXIMATE FEDERAL CIVILIAN EMPLOYMENT	EVENTS
1789	Less than 2,000	First cabinet departments are created by law (State, War, Treasury); Office of Attorney General is created.
1800	2,800	Federal government moves to Washington, D.C.
1828	10,000	Andrew Jackson is elected president; many executive-branch officials are replaced under the "spoils system."
1849	25,000	Department of the Interior is created.
1862	37,000	Department of Agriculture is created.
1870	51,000	Department of Justice is created.
1872	52,000	Post Office, which began operation in 1775, becomes a cabinet department.
1883	100,000	Pendleton Act creates the civil service system, establishes Civil Service Commission.
1887	140,000	Interstate Commerce Act creates the first independent regulatory commission (ICC).
1903	250,000	Departments of Commerce and Labor are created.
1921	560,000	Budget and Accounting Act creates the Bureau of the Budget and the General Accounting Office.
1933	700,000	New Deal spawns many new agencies.
1939	1,200,000	Administrative Reorganization Act creates the Executive Office of the President; Hatch Act imposes restrictions on the political activities of federal employees.
1947	2,000,000	National Security Act merges War and Navy Departments into the Department of Defense and creates the National Security Council and the Central Intelligence Agency.
1953	2,400,000	Department of Health, Education, and Welfare is created (becomes the Department of Health and Human Services in 1979).
1966	2,700,000	Department of Transportation and Department of Housing and Urban Development (HUD) are created.
1970	2,900,000	Bureau of the Budget becomes Office of Management and Budget (OMB); Environmental Protection Agency (EPA) is created.
1971	2,900,000	Post Office Department is replaced by U.S. Postal Service and is removed from the president's cabinet.
1977	2,700,000	Department of Energy is created.
1978	2,700,000	Civil Service Reform Act replaces Civil Service Commission with Office of Personnel Management (OPM), establishes Merit Systems Protection Board, and creates Senior Executive Service (effective in 1979); Ethics in Government Act is enacted.
1979	2,700,000	Department of Education is created.
1988	3,000,000	Department of Veterans Affairs replaces the Veterans Administration.

Types of Organizational Structures

The federal bureaucracy is composed of many kinds of organizations. Its structure is a little difficult to comprehend at first because the labels attached to particular units do not always precisely define their functions or levels of authority. Sometimes an "agency," a "bureau," and an "office" are indistinguishable from one another. Some agencies are subunits of cabinet departments, and others are independent from those departments. A bureau may be a small, barely visible unit like the Bureau of Quality Control in the Health Care Financing Administration, or it may be relatively large and highly visible, like the Federal Bureau of Investigation (FBI).

Politics is responsible for this apparent confusion. The creation of bureaucratic organizations is itself a political process. What a unit is called, where it is placed in the executive branch, the degree of authority it is granted, and the qualifications established for its leaders are all political decisions. They reflect the balance of political forces existing at the time the unit was created. Because the balance of political forces changes over time, units created in one period often differ from units created in another.

Figure 14-1 shows the organizational structure of the entire federal government. Figure 14-2 shows the structure of a single cabinet department, the Department of Agriculture.

Departments   The major operating units of the federal government are **departments**. There are fourteen of them, and each is an aggregate of many related functions. The head of a department—the secretary or, in the case of the Justice Department, the attorney general—is a member of the president's cabinet. The number of departments is not fixed. In the late 1970s, two new ones were added: the Department of Education and the Department of Energy. In 1988, the Veterans Administration, an independent agency, was replaced with the Department of Veterans Affairs.

Agencies   In general, an **agency** is responsible for a narrower set of functions than a department. Some agencies exist within departments, and some are independent. The Social Security Administration, a very large agency, is part of the Department of Health and Human Services. The Coast Guard, another agency, is located in the Department of Transportation in peacetime and in the Department of Defense in wartime. (Notice that agencies do not necessarily have the word *agency* in their name.) The General Services Administration and the United States Information Agency are independent agencies; they are not components of any of the departments.

Although an agency's jurisdiction is likely to be narrower than a department's, some agencies spend more money and employ more people than some departments do. For example, the National Aeronautics and Space Administration is an independent agency that had an annual budget of more than $14 billion for fiscal year 1993. The State Department, a cabinet department, had an annual budget of $4 billion in the same year.

Bureaus, offices, administrations, services   The subunits of agencies and departments have a variety of names, none denoting a set of consistent, distinguishable characteristics. In the Department of Agriculture, for instance, the Food and Nutrition Service, the Packers and Stockyards Administration, and

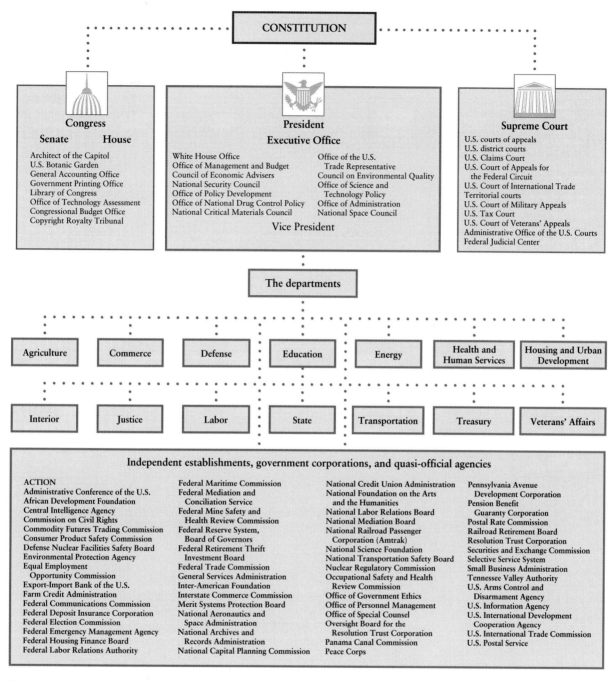

CONSTITUTION

Congress
Senate   House

Architect of the Capitol
U.S. Botanic Garden
General Accounting Office
Government Printing Office
Library of Congress
Office of Technology Assessment
Congressional Budget Office
Copyright Royalty Tribunal

President
Executive Office

White House Office
Office of Management and Budget
Council of Economic Advisers
National Security Council
Office of Policy Development
Office of National Drug Control Policy
National Critical Materials Council

Office of the U.S.
    Trade Representative
Council on Environmental Quality
Office of Science and
    Technology Policy
Office of Administration
National Space Council

Vice President

Supreme Court

U.S. courts of appeals
U.S. district courts
U.S. Claims Court
U.S. Court of Appeals for
    the Federal Circuit
U.S. Court of International Trade
Territorial courts
U.S. Court of Military Appeals
U.S. Tax Court
U.S. Court of Veterans' Appeals
Administrative Office of the U.S. Courts
Federal Judicial Center

The departments

Agriculture	Commerce	Defense	Education	Energy	Health and Human Services	Housing and Urban Development

Interior	Justice	Labor	State	Transportation	Treasury	Veterans' Affairs

Independent establishments, government corporations, and quasi-official agencies

ACTION
Administrative Conference of the U.S.
African Development Foundation
Central Intelligence Agency
Commission on Civil Rights
Commodity Futures Trading Commission
Consumer Product Safety Commission
Defense Nuclear Facilities Safety Board
Environmental Protection Agency
Equal Employment
    Opportunity Commission
Export-Import Bank of the U.S.
Farm Credit Administration
Federal Communications Commission
Federal Deposit Insurance Corporation
Federal Election Commission
Federal Emergency Management Agency
Federal Housing Finance Board
Federal Labor Relations Authority

Federal Maritime Commission
Federal Mediation and
    Conciliation Service
Federal Mine Safety and
    Health Review Commission
Federal Reserve System,
    Board of Governors
Federal Retirement Thrift
    Investment Board
Federal Trade Commission
General Services Administration
Inter-American Foundation
Interstate Commerce Commission
Merit Systems Protection Board
National Aeronautics and
    Space Administration
National Archives and
    Records Administration
National Capital Planning Commission

National Credit Union Administration
National Foundation on the Arts
    and the Humanities
National Labor Relations Board
National Mediation Board
National Railroad Passenger
    Corporation (Amtrak)
National Science Foundation
National Transportation Safety Board
Nuclear Regulatory Commission
Occupational Safety and Health
    Review Commission
Office of Government Ethics
Office of Personnel Management
Office of Special Counsel
Oversight Board for the
    Resolution Trust Corporation
Panama Canal Commission
Peace Corps

Pennsylvania Avenue
    Development Corporation
Pension Benefit
    Guaranty Corporation
Postal Rate Commission
Railroad Retirement Board
Resolution Trust Corporation
Securities and Exchange Commission
Selective Service System
Small Business Administration
Tennessee Valley Authority
U.S. Arms Control and
    Disarmament Agency
U.S. Information Agency
U.S. International Development
    Cooperation Agency
U.S. International Trade Commission
U.S. Postal Service

Figure 14-1 *The government of the United States.* SOURCE: Washington Information Directory, 1992–1993 *(Washington, D.C.: Congressional Quarterly, 1992), 4. Reprinted by permission of Congressional Quarterly, Inc.*

the World Agricultural Outlook Board are all located at roughly the same level in the hierarchy. The differences in their titles do not indicate significant differences in their authority or functions.

Bureaus and other subunits are the specialized operating units of the government. Their jurisdictions are defined by the programs Congress has assigned

DEPARTMENT OF AGRICULTURE

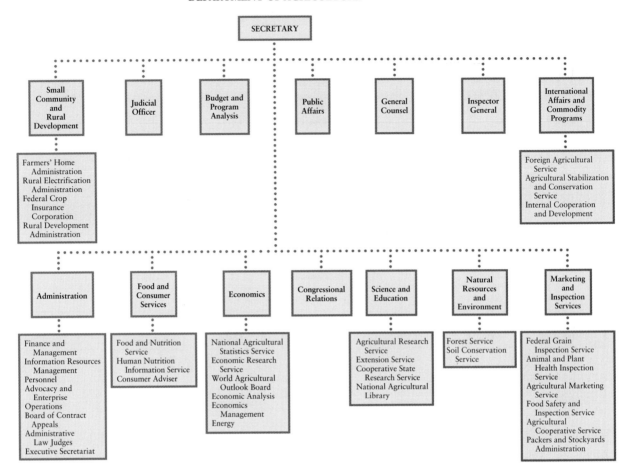

Figure 14-2   *The Department of Agriculture.* SOURCE: Washington Information Directory, 1992–1993 *(Washington, D.C.: Congressional Quarterly, 1992), 574. Reprinted by permission of Congressional Quarterly, Inc.*

to them and tend to be quite specific. Although many of these units may exist within the same department, they do not necessarily work closely together. Often, in fact, they engage in intense political competition for larger budgets and for a dominant role in determining policies that affect the groups they serve. For many years, for example, the Agriculture and Interior departments have disagreed about which of them ought to have jurisdiction over the national forests.

Independent regulatory commissions   Each **independent regulatory commission** is independent of any department and to some extent independent of presidential control. Each is run by a group of commissioners instead of by a single executive. Each commission has both quasi-legislative and quasi-judicial authority—that is, it can issue rules and regulations and can adjudicate disputes and issue rulings.

The principal purpose of the regulatory commissions is to regulate commerce and trade in an assigned area of jurisdiction. The Interstate Commerce Commission (ICC) regulates interstate trucking and railroads. The Federal Communications Commission (FCC) regulates telephones and the use of the public airwaves for radio and television broadcasting.

There are currently about a dozen independent regulatory commissions. Each has at least five members. The largest, the ICC, has eleven. Commission members serve for fixed terms, but the terms are staggered. The president is permitted to make appointments only as vacancies occur and thus does not have the same degree of control over personnel in these units as over employees in the agencies and departments.

Government corporations The federal government owns, in whole or in part, a variety of economic enterprises. Most of these are operated as **government corporations.**[2] This form of ownership is supposed to protect the organization against political meddling and encourage it to use businesslike and efficient methods of operation. Nevertheless, politics sometimes influences the decisions and activities of government corporations. President Reagan, for example, appointed several people with strong conservative views to the board of the Corporation for Public Broadcasting.

Most of the government corporations have boards of directors whose members are appointed by the president, usually for long and staggered terms that make it difficult for any single president to change the board's composition radically. Most of the corporations can operate their own personnel systems, borrow money, sell stock, even operate at a profit. Some, like the Federal Deposit Insurance Corporation (FDIC) and the Tennessee Valley Authority (TVA), are totally independent. Others, like the Commodity Credit Corporation in the Department of Agriculture, fall within a department's jurisdiction.

Boards, committees, commissions, advisory committees In addition to the major structural entities already identified, the federal government contains a great many units of lesser significance. Some, like the Committee for the Implementation of Textile Agreements, have very narrow functions; others, like the Federal Financing Bank Advisory Council, provide advice to other agencies. Few of these advisory committees have any significant impact on public policy. Many of them serve primarily as places where presidents can make appointments to reward individuals for their political support. Hundreds of advisory committees are located throughout the federal government. Most of the people who serve on them work for the federal government for only a few days each year and regard their appointments as honorific.[3]

Staffing the Bureaucracy

Despite the variations in the organizational units that make up the executive bureaucracy, and the efforts that have been made to limit political influence in some of them, no bureaucratic structure can be immune from or insensitive to the strong political forces at work in its environment. Administrative decisions have political consequences and hence are subject to political pressures and cross-pressures. The nature of democracy requires that government officials be responsive to the publics they serve. The extent to which that responsiveness is partisan in character, however, has long been the subject of controversy, especially in the selection of personnel to serve in the executive branch.

The "Typical" Federal Employee

What is the typical federal employee really like? There is no typical civil servant, but a composite portrait drawn from data about federal civilian, full-time, permanent, nonpostal employees would have these characteristics.

Age: 43.2 years
Length of government service: 14.2 years
Education: bachelor's degree or more, 36.5%
Gender: male, 56%; female, 44%
Race and national origin: 28.1% belong to minorities (16.8% African American; 5.6% Hispanic; 3.8% Asian/Pacific Islander; 1.9% Native American)
Handicapped status: 7% have handicaps
Annual base salary: $37,718
Average GS grade: 9.0

SOURCE: Data from U.S. Office of Personnel Management, Central Personnel Data File, March 31, 1993.

Before 1883, nonelective positions in the federal bureaucracy were filled by means of **patronage**—the distribution of jobs by winning candidates to those who had worked for their political campaign and supported their party. "To the victor go the spoils" was the rallying cry of the day, and the spoils of election victory were usually jobs in government. This use of patronage in federal employment was known as the **spoils system**.[4]

By the latter part of the nineteenth century the spoils system had fallen into disrepute. Administration was often in the hands of political hacks, corruption was common, and fending off job seekers was a major burden for successful politicians. In 1881 a disappointed applicant for a federal job shot and killed President James A. Garfield. The assassination strengthened cries for reform of the federal personnel system. In 1883 Congress responded by passing the Pendleton Act and establishing the **civil service system**, in which federal employment is based on merit.

The civil service system requires that two important criteria be met in hiring people for government jobs. First, hiring opportunities must be open to any citizen regardless of his or her political preference; everyone must have an opportunity to compete for government jobs. Second, civil servants must be chosen on the basis of some objective measure of their abilities—that is, on their merits. Historically the second criterion has meant qualification based on open, competitive examinations.

The civil service system   At first the civil service system covered only a small percentage of federal employees. Gradually its coverage grew, until today it includes more than 90 percent of all federal employees. (The box above highlights the characteristics of "typical" members of this group of workers.)

About two-thirds of the civil service employees are in what is known as the regular **civil service**. This group includes most of the career employees of the departments and the major agencies. Regardless of where they work, their salaries and fringe benefits are determined by Congress and implemented by the Office of Personnel Management, an independent agency in the executive branch. All civil service positions are graded according to the character of the work to be done. A pay range is assigned to each grade level (see Table 14-2).

In 1979 the **Senior Executive Service (SES)** was created to provide agencies with greater flexibility in deploying, compensating, and (if necessary) removing senior managers and technical specialists. There are now about eight thousand SES members, of whom at least 90 percent must always be career federal employees. They are entitled, and sometimes encouraged, to move from one agency to another where their skills and experience are needed, but most spend their entire careers in a single federal agency. SES members have their own pay grades (see Table 14-3), and they are eligible each year for merit pay raises and special performance and incentive bonuses.

About one-third of the federal government's career employees work in agencies that have their own merit systems, distinct from the regular civil service. These agencies include the TVA, the FBI, the Public Health Service, the Foreign Service, and the Postal Service. Most of the reasons for the existence of these separate merit systems have to do with politics and tradition. The agency merit systems work in much the same way as the regular civil service,

TABLE 14-2
Salary Schedule of the Regular Civil Service (effective January 1994)

JOB CHARACTERISTICS AND GRADE	PAY RANGE
Menial, clerical	
GS-1*	$12,406–15,521
GS-2	13,948–17,555
GS-3	15,221–19,789
GS-4	17,086–22,208
Management entry; low-level supervisory	
GS-5	19,116–24,847
GS-6	21,308–27,696
GS-7	23,678–30,779
GS-8	26,223–34,094
Technical; mid-level supervisory	
GS-9	28,964–37,651
GS-10	31,898–41,466
GS-11	35,045–45,561
GS-12	42,003–54,601
Highly technical; middle management	
GS-13	49,947–64,928
GS-14	59,022–76,733
GS-15	69,427–90,252

* *GS* stands for "general schedule."

SOURCE: U.S. Office of Personnel Management and *Washington Post*, January 3, 1994.

TABLE 14-3	
Salary Schedule of the Senior Executive Service (effective January 1994)	
"SUPERGRADES"; SENIOR EXECUTIVES	SALARY
ES-1*	$ 96,542
ES-2	101,218
ES-3	105,791
ES-4	111,506
ES-5	116,183
ES-6	120,594

* ES stands for "executive schedule." Salaries are for Washington, D.C., area.

SOURCE: U.S. Office of Personnel Management.

but they have different terminology and are run by the agencies themselves, not by the Office of Personnel Management.

Once federal employees are installed in one of the government's career personnel systems, they are relatively secure in their jobs. This security is intended to protect them from inappropriate political pressures and from removal when there is a change of administration. Career employees can be removed when there is a reduction in federal employment—a **reduction in force**—a tactic used aggressively at the beginning of the Reagan presidency but used rarely by Reagan's predecessors. Career employees can also be removed for inadequate performance. But proving that performance is inadequate is very difficult for managers to do, and an elaborate appeals procedure protects career employees from arbitrary removal. Firing a civil servant may take two years or more; as a consequence, it rarely happens.

Among the 10 percent of federal employees who are not part of the career merit system are a variety of people whose jobs are incompatible with systematic personnel procedures or competitive selection techniques. These include presidential appointees to the top positions in the government, some attorneys, faculty members at the military service academies, undercover drug enforcement agents, foreign nationals who work at American installations overseas, and temporary employees who hold short-term or summer jobs.

Political appointees Nearly all of the top-level positions in the executive branch are held by political appointees. Typically, they are individuals from the private sector who serve in the government for only a short time (about two years on average). Included in this group are cabinet secretaries and the senior officers in each of the cabinet departments, heads of the independent agencies, and members of the federal regulatory commissions, all of whom are appointed by the president and confirmed by the Senate.

Some appointees, like regulatory commissioners, have fixed terms of service. Most, however, serve at the pleasure of the president: they can be removed by a president who is unhappy with their performance or loyalty. In 1970, for example, Richard Nixon fired Secretary of the Interior Walter Hickel after Hickel released to the press a letter criticizing the invasion of Cambodia by American forces. Jimmy Carter sought the resignations of several of his cabinet

Arnold Raphel: Heroic Bureaucrat

The Ronald Reagan Library

An occasional perquisite of service is a photograph of a meeting with your president. Here Ronald Reagan greets Arnold Raphel.

Many bureaucrats play important national and international roles and do so with great skill and dedication. Arnold Raphel was one of those.

Raphel was a career Foreign Service officer, one of the millions of men and women who work for the United States government. In 1988, after almost two decades in public service, he was serving as ambassador to Pakistan. In August he was traveling with Pakistani president Mohammed Zia ul-Haq when a terrorist bomb blew their plane from the sky, killing them both. *Newsweek* contributing editor Gregg Easterbrook wrote this tribute:

Raphel was one of the true bright lights in the Foreign Service: smart, skilled, enviably successful, at 45 among the youngest American ambassadors ever assigned to a vital embassy. "Arnie was one of the top two or three officers of his generation, destined for the very top ranks," said Michael Armacost, Under Secretary of State for Political Affairs. . . .

But then the diplomatic world has lots of smart guys, many of them martinets with handshakes cold as fish fins. More impressive than formal credentials was that Raphel knew the joys of life. He wisecracked through high-level meetings, shunning all formalities of ambassadorial starch, saying he ran a "loosened-tie operation." Devoted to his own wife, Nancy, and his family, Raphel "took an interest in the careers and families of people in positions to do him *no good at all*," marvels one colleague.

No blue blood himself, Raphel made a special effort to encourage female officers, traditionally shut out of the old-boy Foreign Service network. His deputy, Elizabeth Jones, is believed to be the first woman ever chosen deputy chief of a "Class 1" embassy. When Raphel ran the Bureau of Near Eastern and South Asian Affairs, it had the highest percentage of female senior personnel. . . .

Raphel spent most of his State Department years in hot-spot countries. Nearly a decade ago he was the working-level negotiator who, jawboning in Persian, sealed the deal that released the hostages from Iran. Afghanistan and Pakistan were his other specialties. A simple testament to Raphel's diplomatic prowess is that he communicated with the factions of these three intensely Muslim countries despite being Jewish. He was equally effective in the bureaucratic thicket. . . . Raphel managed to be mentored by Henry Kissinger, Lawrence Eagleburger, Cyrus Vance, Warren Christopher and George Shultz. . . .

There are thousands of patriots like Arnie, who dedicate themselves to the American vision. Though their names won't make the papers, they are the blood plasma of the free, responsible nation we strive to be, and we never thank them till after it's too late. Countries like America are made possible by people like Arnold Raphel. Let that be his epitaph.

SOURCE: Gregg Easterbrook, "Epitaph for an Uncommon Diplomat," *Newsweek*, August 29, 1988, 34, Newsweek, Inc. All rights reserved. Reprinted by permission.

AP/Wide World Photos

Jocelyn Elders was appointed Surgeon General of the United States in 1993. Shown here making a point at her confirmation hearing before the Senate Labor and Human Resources Committee, Elders had been a senior official in Arkansas state government and was well known to President Clinton. He steadfastly supported her nomination, even though her views about abortion and sex education sparked controversy.

members—Joseph Califano (Health and Human Services), Michael Blumenthal (Treasury), and Brock Adams (Transportation)—after a review of their performance in 1979. In 1985 Ronald Reagan solved the problem of lackluster performance by one of his cabinet secretaries, Margaret Heckler (Health and Human Services), by appointing her ambassador to Ireland.

This system of drawing the highest-ranking executive-branch officials from the private sector is uniquely American. No other country relies so heavily on leaders who are not career government employees. The American approach has several advantages. It ensures a constant infusion of new creative energy. It fosters responsiveness to the popular will, and the dual tests of presidential nomination and Senate confirmation promote care and judiciousness in the choice of people to fill important government offices.[5]

But there are disadvantages as well. Leaders often lack training or experience in the complex policy areas over which they have jurisdiction. Many members of regulatory commissions, for example, receive their appointments as rewards for previous support of the president. Some appointees quickly discover that they lack the technical competence to comprehend the complex work of their agencies. The short tenure of most appointees also leads to inconsistency in administration and policy direction and creates the potential for ethical violations. Many appointees are more concerned with making an impact in a brief time than with management or program initiatives that may take a while to bear fruit.

The Executive Bureaucracy in Perspective

The personnel system of the federal government, like its organizational structure, is complex and confusing. Few logical principles or sets of decision-making rules exist to explain it. The federal government has been developing over two centuries of practice and experimentation; it is not the product of a single blueprint. Administrative units have been added and eliminated. Their structure and location reflect the political battles surrounding their origins rather than any consistent administrative theory. The personnel system shows the same inconsistencies. The head of one bureau is a career civil servant; the head of another is a presidential appointee. One must look to the political history of each bureau to explain such inconsistencies.

The process of constructing a government is no less political than the process of operating one. In 1979, for example, Congress created a new cabinet department, the Department of Education. Among the principal proponents of this change in the structure of government was the National Education Association (NEA), a powerful organization of elementary and secondary school teachers. Opponents of the new department included another teachers' organization, the American Federation of Teachers (AFT). The NEA sought to increase its political advantage by reshaping the administration of education programs; the AFT sought to retain relationships it had already developed within the existing educational bureaucracy. After Congress had approved the creation of the new department, both organizations lobbied President Carter to appoint a secretary who would be responsive to their individual interests. To prevent the appearance of favoring one group or one educational interest over another, Carter decided to appoint Shirley Hufstedler, a federal judge with no direct experience in educational matters, to head the new department.

When legislators create a new agency, their decisions about where to locate it, what to call it, and what to include in it are governed by the search for political advantage. When presidents appoint the leaders of such an agency, they too are deeply affected by the political situation of the moment. Legislators and presidents are politicians, and they are much less concerned with symmetry and consistency than with policy outcomes. As Harold Seidman has noted, "Economy and efficiency are demonstrably not the prime purposes of public administration. The basic issues of federal organization and administration relate to power: Who shall control it and to what ends?"[6]

FUNCTIONS OF THE EXECUTIVE BUREAUCRACY

Many people assume that the executive bureaucracy merely executes policy decisions made by Congress and the president. In fact, the administrative agencies of the federal government are themselves important participants in policy making. Almost every public policy is shaped in some ways by the characteristics and the actions of the agencies that oversee its implementation.

Implementation

The primary task of federal agencies is to interpret and implement the public policies that emerge from the legislative process. If a statute declares that the average fuel efficiency of automobiles must be 18 miles per gallon, an agency has to determine when and how to measure fuel efficiency, how to certify satisfaction of the standard, and how to bring companies that fail to meet the standard into compliance. Authority to perform these functions is delegated to the agency by Congress. In exercising such authority, however, the agency normally has a great deal of discretion.[7]

That discretion is a powerful invitation to political pressure. Political interests that fail to accomplish their goals in the legislative process often redouble their efforts to obtain satisfaction in the administrative process. Battles lost in the legislative branch are routinely refought in the executive branch. Often the two branches are simultaneous political battlegrounds, as in the supercollider case described at the beginning of the chapter.

The principal responsibility of most public agencies is action. They are the delivery end of the policy-making process, the government's agents in dealing directly with the people (hence the name "agency"). Their task is to translate the policy objectives determined in the legislative process into goods and services that will help accomplish those objectives. They do this in a number of ways, including regulation, rule making, adjudication, compliance enforcement, and allocation of funds.

Regulation In regulating economic and social activity, agencies are guided by two primary objectives: (1) to maintain the stability and accessibility of the free-market system and (2) to protect the health, safety, and welfare of the American people. The first agency designed solely to perform regulatory activities was the Interstate Commerce Commission, established in 1887. Many others have been added since. There are now few economic functions that do not fall under the regulatory jurisdiction of one or more federal agencies in what has become a heavily regulated American economy.[8]

Contemporary regulation takes two broad forms: economic regulation and social regulation. **Economic regulation** aims to control prices, market entry, and conditions of service in specific industries. The principal objective of economic regulation is to promote competition within a single industry while at the same time protecting the competitive position of individual companies. Economic regulation expanded significantly from 1887 into the 1960s.

Since the late 1960s, there has been a significant movement toward **deregulation**—freeing some industries from the broad government control of earlier years.[9] The effects of deregulation on commercial air travel are generally well known. For more than four decades the Civil Aeronautics Board (CAB) regulated domestic air travel. During that time no major national air carriers entered the marketplace, and CAB decisions tightly controlled airline fares and routes. In the 1970s the president and Congress moved to deregulate the airline industry in order to stimulate competition. The CAB went out of existence, price competition intensified, new airlines sprouted up, and several mergers occurred. All of this was a mixed blessing for consumers. Air travel opportunities improved for those in population centers where airline competition was strongest, but it became more difficult, more expensive, and less reliable for those in less populated areas served by fewer carriers. In the years that followed, many airlines experienced economic problems, the cost of air travel escalated, concern about air safety grew, and some people wished for reregulation by the federal government.

Social regulation, the second form of regulatory policy, aims to improve workplace operations and product safety across many industries. Government action in this area was sparked by the consumer movement of the 1960s. A series of books, articles, and television programs generated publicity about the threats to health and safety posed by everyday consumer goods. Public interest groups, spearheaded by the efforts of consumer activist Ralph Nader, put political pressure on Congress and the administrative agencies for greater protection of consumer welfare in such areas as automobile safety, truth in advertising, and truth in lending. At the same time, increasingly prominent civil rights groups demanded federal action to prevent discrimination against women and members of minority groups. Shortly thereafter, protection of the natural environment became a central issue on the policy agenda. Each of these initiatives found important support among the American people and yielded a stream of new regulatory legislation.

New regulatory commissions, such as the Equal Employment Opportunity Commission and the Consumer Product Safety Commission, were created. Most of them were placed under the jurisdiction of executive-branch agencies. Virtually all of the new regulatory policies focused not on competitive practices in specific industries but on the social impact of a wide range of economic activities. New policies required manufacturers to be truthful on product labels and in advertising, to provide safe and healthy working conditions, and to ensure equal employment opportunities for women, minorities, the elderly, and the handicapped. Expensive programs for the inspection and testing of food, drugs, and consumer products were established, and greater authority was delegated to federal agencies to ban the sale of products it found to be unsafe.

Broad policies were created to protect the natural environment and prevent air, water, and noise pollution. The Consumer Product Safety Commission required manufacturers of baby cribs to reduce the space between the slats to prevent injuries to infants. The Occupational Safety and Health Administration (OSHA) imposed rules limiting workers' exposure to disease-inducing cotton dust. The Food and Drug Administration accelerated the availability of experimental AIDS drugs in response to pressure from AIDS advocacy groups.

The emphasis on social regulation greatly expanded the scope of federal regulatory activity. By 1975 it was hard to find a business enterprise anywhere in the United States that was not subject to at least one regulatory program. Owners and managers began to complain about the regulatory burden. They were troubled by the costs they incurred in complying with regulatory policies, and they were uncomfortable with the uncertainty that resulted from constant changes in regulatory requirements, which made long-range planning both risky and difficult. They were unhappy about having to deal with powerful executive agencies that, in their view, were overly committed to the concerns of consumers and insufficiently sensitive to the needs of producers. By the mid 1970s opponents of social regulation were mustering their own political forces to influence the federal government to lessen the regulatory burden. Subsequent efforts to extend social regulation have generated intense political conflict.[10]

Rule making   Most agencies, operating within the jurisdiction granted them by Congress, have the authority to issue rules. Rules are best described as elaborations of the law. If the law says that you cannot fly an airplane without a pilot's license, rules will describe in detail the steps that you must take to get a license and the penalties you will incur if you fly without one. Rules have the force of law.

Rule making by federal agencies is subject to procedures laid down in the Administrative Procedures Act of 1946 and its amendments. A number of steps must be completed before a new rule can take effect.[11] For example, the draft of a new rule must be published in the *Federal Register* at least thirty days before the rule is to go into effect. When the draft of the rule is published, the agency must invite public comment on it. After the comments have been re-

Using the Federal Register

The *Federal Register* publishes government regulations and legal notices as they are issued by federal agencies. These include presidential proclamations and executive orders, federal agency documents having general applicability and legal effect, documents required to be published by act of Congress, and other federal agency documents of public interest.

Using the *Federal Register* can be a challenge. The documents it contains are organized by type— notices, proposed rules and regulations, rules and regulations, and presidential documents. In the notices section are found notices of hearings and investigations, committee meetings, agency decisions and rulings, and other administrative matters. The proposed and final rules and regulations sections contain regulatory documents having general applicability and legal effect. Presidential documents include executive orders, proclamations, and other documents from the president.

Within each type, the documents are organized alphabetically by agency. Each document is filed with the *Federal Register* by the agency; it is then assigned a *Federal Register* document number. For example, the Appalachian States Low-Level Radioactive Waste Commission notice of an open meeting, filed on May 15, 1992, was assigned the number FR Doc 92-11362. The 92 in the number indicates the year the document was filed; the rest of the number indicates that it was the 11,362nd document filed with the *Federal Register* that year. The notice appears on page 21057 of volume 57, number 96, dated May 18, 1992.

A specific document is relatively easy to find if you know its *Federal Register* document number. This number immediately narrows the search to a particular year and quickly narrows it to a specific

week. If you do not know the document number, you must search through the quarterly or cumulative indexes to find the document. The index entries are arranged first under the name of the agency that issued the document, then by the type of document (rule, notice, and so on). The number that appears at the end of each index entry identifies the page in the *Federal Register* on which the document begins.

Determining which agency might have issued a document is often the most difficult part of finding it. A helpful tool is the *United States Government Manual.* This volume, found in most libraries, lists and describes all the branches and departments of the government. Deciding into what category the document falls is a simpler step. Generally, if an issue is still in the decision-making process, documents relating to it (notices of hearings, for example) will be found in the notices section. Once a decision has been made, look in the rules and regulations section to see how it is being implemented. To find presidential documents, two other publications from the *Federal Register* are also useful: *Codification of Presidential Proclamations and Executive Orders* and *Weekly Compilation of Presidential Documents.*

Even experienced researchers sometimes have trouble finding documents in the *Federal Register.* Fortunately, helpful staff members in the Finding Aids Unit of the National Archives are readily available by telephone at (202) 523-5227.

The *Federal Register* is published daily, Monday through Friday, by the Office of the Federal Register, National Archives and Records Administration. Copies are found in most large libraries and in all federal depository libraries.

viewed (a task that may take months or even years), the rule is issued officially when it is published in final form in the *Federal Register* and codified in a volume called the *Code of Federal Regulations.*

As the scope of government activity has expanded in the twentieth century, so too has the number of administrative rules. In 1960 there were 14,479 pages in the *Federal Register*; by 1979 the number was up to 71,191.[12] As a result of deregulation during the Reagan administration, the number of *Federal Register* pages declined to 50,997 in 1984, but by 1991 it had crept back up to 67,715.

Rule making has become a very important part of policy making. The "law" made by executive agencies is often as important in determining the shape of public policies as the law made by Congress. Recognizing this, the Reagan administration made a determined attempt to gain full control over administrative rules. Beginning in 1981, it required that all major proposed rules be reviewed and approved by the Office of Management and Budget before publication. This requirement enabled the administration to exercise greater influence on these important instruments of public policy. In 1990, however, the Supreme Court limited the scope of the OMB's power to review administrative rules.

Adjudication   No matter how diligently executive agencies strive to remove ambiguity from the rules they issue, they are never completely successful. There are always some areas of uncertainty about the application of a specific law or rule to a particular circumstance. An agency may interpret a rule to mean one thing; a corporation may interpret it to mean another. When such differences of opinion occur, the agency is often asked to hold a hearing at which the affected party appeals what it perceives as an inappropriate or unfair interpretation.

Each year, for example, the National Highway Traffic Safety Administration (NHTSA) inspects automobiles for safety defects. If a defect is found, the NHTSA informs the manufacturer and holds a hearing to determine whether to order the automaker to recall all the affected vehicles and repair the defect. In 1984, following this procedure, the NHTSA required General Motors to recall more than a million vehicles that proved to have defective braking systems.

These hearings are often run like legal proceedings. Attorneys are usually present for both sides. Sometimes a hearing is presided over by an **administrative law judge**, an independent third party whose rulings are binding on both the agency and the complainant, although either side may appeal a ruling in the federal courts. Many of the rulings are published in the *Federal Register* so that other interested parties can get a clearer picture of the application of rules and laws to specific cases.[13]

Compliance enforcement   Ensuring that laws and rules are obeyed is one of the important tasks of executive agencies. For some—the FBI and the Bureau of Alcohol, Tobacco, and Firearms, for instance—it is the dominant concern. Virtually all agencies spend some of their efforts on compliance enforcement.

Some agencies conduct regular, scheduled inspections to ensure that agency guidelines are followed. For example, the Department of Agriculture routinely inspects food-processing facilities. The tag "USDA inspected" on food products indicates that they were processed under conditions that satisfied federal government standards. Other agencies prefer to make unscheduled inspections. The Coast Guard, for instance, follows the practice of stopping private boats without prior notice to inspect their life-saving equipment. Many government agencies employ accountants to examine the financial records of individuals, corporations, or groups to ensure that they are complying with applicable laws and rules. The Internal Revenue Service audits individual and corporate tax returns for this purpose, and the Comptroller of the Currency audits the financial records of national banks.

The imposition of reporting requirements is another way in which compliance enforcement is carried out. Institutions and corporations are required to file periodic reports on their activities. Employers, for instance, must file regular reports on the number of workers they employ, the amount of money they have withheld from paychecks for taxes and Social Security, and other matters relevant to specific businesses. Federal contractors must file reports indicating that their employment practices are nondiscriminatory. When businesspeople complain about the red tape they have to endure as a result of government regulation, they often identify these reports as the principal culprits.

One other important way in which agencies oversee compliance with laws and rules is by responding to complaints. Noncompliance often harms someone, and the harmed party may bring a complaint to the government agency that has jurisdiction. If a factory is dumping more pollutants into a stream than the law permits, people who enjoy fishing in that stream may bring a complaint

Many agencies intersect with the daily lives of ordinary citizens, usually in beneficial ways. The Coast Guard inspects boating gear and rescues boaters in distress, and the IRS manages massive routines to collect taxes.

During a 1993 raid on the Branch Davidian compound in Waco, Texas, the deaths of four federal officers and of some eighty people inside the compound led many to call for better coordination among law enforcement agencies.

Tom Pantages

Rod Aydelotte/SYGMA

© Bob Daemmrich/Stock, Boston

to the Environmental Protection Agency. If the EPA finds that the complaint is valid and that the factory is indeed violating the law, it can take steps to bring the factory into compliance.

Allocation of funds   In one way or another, almost all government agencies allocate funds to purchase the goods and services necessary to implement federal programs. The awarding of contracts is one of the principal ways they do this.[14] Federal contractors include construction companies that build veterans' hospitals, corporations that supply ships for the Navy, think tanks that do economic research for the Treasury Department, museums that mount exhibits sponsored by the National Endowment for the Arts, and a wide variety of other individuals and organizations.

Federal funds can also be allocated through intergovernmental transfers such as grants-in-aid (discussed in Chapter 3.) The competition over the location of the proposed superconducting supercollider (SSC), described at the beginning of this chapter, was such a case.

Policy Making

The activities of executive agencies are not confined solely to the implementation of public policy. The agencies also play an important role in policy initiation. This is not surprising, for agency employees are usually experts in a particular policy area. Their day-to-day activities provide a unique vantage point for observing the strengths and the weaknesses of particular programs. It is only natural for them to suggest policy changes. Soldiers who find that their rifles jam in wet weather may suggest changes in weapon design. Tax auditors who see that much revenue is being lost because citizens have discovered a loophole in the tax laws may recommend changes to close the loophole.

More important, agency employees have ideas of their own. Their training, their experience, and the values that prevail in their work environment shape their perceptions of the form policies should take. Agency staffs may care deeply about the policies for which they are responsible, and they play a very active role in trying to define and perfect them. Often they become vigorous advocates of their own views, negotiating with their superiors in the bureaucracy, with staff and members in Congress, and with their political constituencies to try to bring policies into line with their ideas.[15]

Admiral Hyman Rickover of the United States Navy is an example of the influence that members of the bureaucracy can sometimes have on public policy. For three decades, beginning in the 1950s and lasting into the 1980s, Rickover was the federal government's leading expert on nuclear-powered ships and the leading advocate of expanding the role of nuclear-powered vessels in American military strategy. He was also a formidable player in the political process, spending large segments of his time cultivating the congressional committees that reviewed naval policy and budgets and building support for his views in the White House and among powerful outside interests. Rickover's success in influencing policy resulted from a combination of expertise, reputation, and substantial political skills.[16]

Bureaucratic agencies share some of the characteristics of other institutions that participate in policy making. Despite efforts to isolate them from partisan politics, bureaucracies are intensely political organizations. They are concerned about their self-interest; they seek to enlarge their resources and

Rear Admiral Hyman Rickover (second from left) *was a major player in developing a nuclear navy. His grasp of issues and his persistence and skill in seeking support made him one of the century's most effective bureaucrats.*

protect their turf; they develop mutually beneficial long-term relationships with other political actors; and they engage in bargaining and negotiation to accomplish their objectives. The political character of the American policy-making process shapes the bureaucracy as thoroughly as it shapes the legislature, the courts, the White House, and interest group activity. But bureaucratic agencies are also distinct from other kinds of government decision makers in some important ways: hierarchical organization, character and culture, professionalization, and organizational pathology.

Hierarchy   Most bureaucratic decision making is hierarchical. Policy proposals typically emerge first at the lowest organizational levels, in the offices and bureaus that are most directly exposed to specific policy environments. Officials there make recommendations to their superiors, who in turn make recommendations to their superiors, and so on up the levels of hierarchy.

Two important things happen along the way. One is filtering, a process by which some proposals are eliminated as unnecessary, too costly, or untimely. Part of the responsibility of managers in the bureaucratic hierarchy is to filter out policy proposals that should not be recommended for further consideration higher up. Many proposals die this way, in the internal review process of the agencies in which they originate. Often they are rejected after political struggles that may involve people and interests from outside the agency.

The secretary of defense, for example, may receive a proposal from the Navy for a new carrier-based fighter airplane. Although the Navy may be enthusiastic about the new plane, the secretary may reject the proposal after determining that the new plane is not a significant enough improvement over current fighters to justify the cost of a new weapons system. This is a filtering decision. The secretary's decision will be complicated by heavy pressure from the Navy, the manufacturer of the new plane, and the members of Congress from the districts in which the planes would be built.

Another important activity of bureaucratic agencies is enforcing coordination. Every agency has many subunits that propose new policies and new expenditures of funds. Because the sum of these proposed expenditures always exceeds available resources, managers must set priorities: Which request should be approved as recommended, which should be modified, and which should be rejected? Priority setting occurs at every level in the hierarchy. Programs that survive initial review at the lowest levels may die at higher levels when they come into conflict with other proposals. A recommendation to improve dairy price supports may appear perfectly sensible when compared with a proposal to increase cotton price supports. But it may not fare so well when it is compared with a proposal for developing new soil conservation projects. The first comparison, between price supports for various agricultural commodities, is made at a low level in the hierarchy. The second comparison, involving two different kinds of policies, is made at a much higher level.

Character and culture Bureaucratic agencies are not empty vessels into which new programs are poured for implementation. Every agency has its own character and culture. Over time agencies acquire certain biases. These initially come from the kinds of programs an agency is asked to administer, but they are reinforced by the agency's contacts with the interest groups it serves, by the ways in which it recruits new employees, and by the operating procedures it employs.

The Labor Department is a case in point. Initially created to protect the health and safety of American workers, it quickly came to be perceived as an advocate for workers in the policy-making process. Its relationship with labor unions was symbiotic: organized labor and the Labor Department supported each other. People opposed to the labor movement found a hostile reception

An agency often reflects the philosophy and interests of its leader. James Watt (left), Secretary of the Interior from 1981 to 1983, had little patience with conservationists and let it be known. As secretary in 1993, Bruce Babbitt (right) showed a flair for listening and making compromises, as when he discussed President Clinton's forest plan with workers at a mill.

at the Labor Department and either did not seek or were not offered employment there. When the Reagan administration sought to sever the traditional relationship between the Labor Department and organized labor, it drew heavy criticism from union leaders and their friends in Congress.

One of the important ways in which agencies institutionalize their biases is by routinizing their work. They develop **standard operating procedures (SOPs)**—predetermined ways of responding to a particular problem or set of circumstances. The State Department has SOPs for dealing with foreign citizens who enter American embassies seeking political asylum. The Navy has SOPs for responding to contacts with foreign vessels in international waters. The IRS has SOPs for determining whether a tax return will be audited.

SOPs simplify bureaucratic decisions and contribute to their consistency. They also channel bureaucratic activity into rigid patterns and make agencies less adaptable to change, especially change that is initiated externally—by legislative oversight or presidential directive. (Presidents' expressions of frustration in dealing with the federal bureaucracy are quoted in the box on page 531.)

During the Cuban missile crisis in 1962, for example, Secretary of Defense Robert McNamara was worried about the way in which the Navy intended to carry out President John Kennedy's orders to blockade all shipping to and from Cuba. He posed a series of hard questions to Admiral George Anderson, the chief of naval operations, about procedures for managing a blockade at sea. Anderson waved the *Manual of Naval Regulations* in McNamara's face and said, "It's all in there."

McNamara replied, "I don't give a damn what John Paul Jones would have done. I want to know what you are going to do now."

Anderson ended the exchange by saying, "Mr. Secretary, if you and your Deputy will go back to your offices, the Navy will run the blockade."[17]

Professionalization In recent years decision making by the executive agencies has become increasingly professionalized because of the technical complexity of modern public policy. Agencies hire experts, and those experts, because of their command of complicated information, have steadily enlarged their role in bureaucratic policy making. The federal government employs 150,000 architects and engineers, 10,000 physicians, 14,000 scientists, and more than 30,000 attorneys.[18]

Experts add a new characteristic to bureaucratic decision making: reliance on professional as well as political criteria. As Francis E. Rourke has noted:

The framing of public policy in a bureaucratic setting can be seen to involve a constant interplay between two quite different sets of factors. It becomes in effect a mixed system of politics and professionalism. Clearly political considerations have to be taken into account in bureaucratic policy making in terms of the impact of decisions upon the outside community. At the same time, however, policy decisions certainly cannot fly in the face of professional advice when there is agreement among the experts as to the technically sound course of action.[19]

Striking a balance between professional advice and political realities is a constant struggle for executive-branch officials. When health policy officials in the Reagan administration planned a national survey of American sexual habits to assist in planning a program to combat the spread of AIDS, OMB leaders

Every modern president has experienced some frustration in dealing with the federal bureaucracy. Clearly, what is called the executive branch is not always the executive's branch.

Franklin D. Roosevelt
"The Treasury is so large and far-flung and ingrained in its practices that I find it almost impossible to get the actions and results I want. But the Treasury is not to be compared with the State Department. You should go through the experience of trying to get any changes in the thinking, policy, and action of the career diplomats and then you'd know what a real problem was. But the Treasury and State departments put together are nothing compared with the Navy. To change anything in the Navy is like punching a feather bed. You punch it with your right and you punch it with your left until you are finally exhausted, and then you find the damn bed just as it was before you started punching."

Harry S Truman
"I thought I was President, but when it comes to these bureaucracies, I can't make them do a damn thing."
"[After Eisenhower takes office, he] will sit here and he'll say, 'Do this! Do that!' And nothing will happen. Poor Ike—it won't be a bit like the Army. He'll find it very frustrating."

John F. Kennedy
"[National Security Adviser McGeorge] Bundy and I get more done in one day than they do in six months at State. The State Department is a bowl full of jelly."

Richard M. Nixon
"We have no discipline in this bureaucracy. We never fire anybody. We never reprimand anybody. We never demote anybody. We always promote the sons-of-bitches that kick us in the ass."

Jimmy Carter
"Before I became president, I realized and I was warned that dealing with the federal bureaucracy would be one of the worst problems I would have to face. It has been even worse than I had anticipated."

Ronald Reagan
"Once a program gets started, it's virtually impossible to reduce or stop it. Every one of these programs . . . develops a powerful constituency in Congress, and a bureaucracy that is dedicated to preserving it. . . . The tendency of government and its programs to grow are about the nearest thing to eternal life we'll ever see on this earth."

quashed the survey because they found some of its questions inappropriate. Those who intervened were responding to the moral qualms of congressional conservatives on whom the administration relied heavily for support.

Bureaucratic pathologies The natural characteristics of bureaucratic agencies often produce certain pathologies that adversely affect the way they approach policy decisions. These unhealthy conditions reduce the efficiency and effectiveness of some agencies and are a principal source of the criticism directed at the federal bureaucracy.

Persistence is a bureaucratic pathology. Agencies often endure long after their reason for existence has passed. Once created, they are hard to abolish.

General Billy Mitchell testifying in 1926 about the value of airplanes in combat. He was right, but bureaucrats made him pay for every word.

The National Screw Thread Commission, for instance, was established during World War I to standardize screw threads for military equipment. It had little to do after the war and did not hold a meeting or issue a report for a decade. Yet it continued to occupy a suite of offices and employ a staff until 1934.

Conservatism is a bureaucratic pathology. Agencies become set in their ways. As a result, they resist new ideas or new techniques that threaten to disrupt business as usual. For example, when General Billy Mitchell pushed for the creation of a permanent air force after World War I, he was resisted by the military establishment, which viewed airplanes as little more than glamorous gimmicks. Mitchell took his case to the public, arguing that air power would be critical in future wars. He was demoted, transferred, and ultimately court-martialed for his efforts. He died a frustrated man in 1936, just five years before the Japanese attack on the United States naval base at Pearl Harbor demonstrated convincingly how right he had been.[20]

Expansionism is a bureaucratic pathology. Growth is the one change that nearly all agencies seem to welcome. Expansion creates new opportunities for promotion, prestige, power, and policy impact—all matters of importance to bureaucrats. The desire to grow is based in large part on the perception that growth will make life in the agency more pleasant and meaningful. History provides few examples of agencies requesting smaller budgets, cutbacks in personnel, or reductions in the scope of their programs.

But agency growth is often driven by self-interest rather than public need. Even those agencies whose programs are outmoded or whose benefits are difficult to demonstrate seek to grow—not because the public interest requires growth, but because it benefits their own organizational interests. Expansionism is a strong and common tendency in bureaucratic life. Only the vigilance of executives and legislators can keep it in check.

Capture, the tendency of an agency to develop a symbiotic relationship with the special interests that it oversees and thus to protect rather than regulate those interests, is a bureaucratic pathology. The agency is "captured" by its clients. Capture is a special problem for regulatory commissions. The Civil Aeronautics Board, for example, during much of its existence protected commercial air carriers from the rigors of competition by refusing to certify new airlines. Similarly, the Interstate Commerce Commission and the Federal Communications Commission, at certain periods, were composed of commissioners who were very supportive of the industries regulated by those commissions. Many of the commissioners, in fact, were former employees of the regulated industries. Special interests put constant political pressure on presidents to nominate and on senators to confirm regulators who are sympathetic to the industries they will be regulating.[21]

The **territorial imperative**, the irresistible urge of an agency to jealously guard its own territory or turf, is a bureaucratic pathology. The most furious conflicts that agencies engage in are conflicts with other agencies that seem to be encroaching on their area of jurisdiction. Most turf battles center on control over programs. For decades, for instance, the Department of Agriculture has battled successfully to keep the Forest Service under its jurisdiction, despite the reasonable claim that the Forest Service more closely fits the mission of the Interior Department, which oversees the national parks. The relevant congressional committees and affected interest groups have been in the middle of this political struggle. In this case, as in all others, the interest groups look to Congress to help them with the bureaucracy, and they look to the bureaucracy to help them with Congress.

Every agency suffers, at least occasionally, from some of these pathologies. They are a common part of administrative life. They add new dimensions to the political struggles within the executive branch and between executive agencies and other political actors. And they help account not only for the difficulties in imposing a rational pattern of organization on the federal executive branch but also for the problems that presidents encounter in their efforts to use the executive branch for their own purposes.

© Paul S. Conklin

Debate rages in western states about the best way to harvest forests. Some claim that clear-cut logging—shown here in the Olympic peninsula of Washington—is most efficient and is also environmentally sound. Others say clear-cutting mortgages the future of our forests. Charged with both managing and protecting timber resources, the U.S. Forest Service is often caught in the middle.

Determinants of Bureaucratic Influence

Agencies vary in their ability to affect public policy. Some, like the FBI, are potent and respected. Others, like the Occupational Safety and Health Administration, are weak and maligned. Still others, like the Energy Department, are influential in some periods and less influential in others.

Many scholars have tried to identify factors that permit certain agencies to play a substantial role in shaping public policy. Francis E. Rourke has identified four determinants of bureaucratic influence: expertise, political support, organizational vitality, and leadership.[22]

The ways in which these variables combine significantly determine the extent of an agency's impact on public policy. They are not all easily controlled, however. Sometimes agencies are under presidential orders to pursue policies that are unpopular with their political constituencies. Leadership selection is an imperfect art. Old agencies are hard to shake out of their familiar habits. Thus, it is not surprising that agencies differ—often widely—in their ability to shape public policy.

Expertise Specialized knowledge has long been regarded as bureaucracy's principal contribution to the process of government. But some kinds of expertise are more valuable than others. The more technical and specialized an agency's expertise is, the greater will be the agency's opportunity to dominate policy making in its area of concern. If an agency has technical capabilities that few people possess or understand, challenges to its judgment will be rare. For many years the space program was in this position. Because most of the country's

J. Edgar Hoover (left), going to the fights in 1936 with friend Clyde Tolson. Hoover led the FBI for nearly five decades, and from the 1930s through the 1950s his handling of public relations gained strong support for the bureau. But Hoover sometimes used his authority and the FBI's resources to weaken or blackmail his enemies and those whose political views he disliked.

experts on space and rocketry worked for the government, there was little opportunity for serious technical criticism of the federal space program. Once the political decision to explore space was made, policy decisions on how to go about it were left largely to the National Aeronautics and Space Administration.

When expertise is not monopolized by an agency, it is a less significant source of influence. The more widely expertise is available outside an agency, the less valuable it is likely to be as a determinant of agency influence on public policy. The federal agencies that specialize in economic policy, for instance, have no corner on the market of economic expertise. Their recommendations are routinely challenged by other experts, both in and out of the government.

Political support   The more widespread and intense an agency's support is in Congress, in the White House, among interest groups, and in the public mind, the greater its ability to affect policy making in its area of jurisdiction. Agencies therefore work hard to cultivate external support. They cooperate closely with the congressional committees that oversee their programs and their budgets, doing everything in their power to curry the favor of committee members. They try to develop strongly supportive clienteles among the groups that benefit from their programs, hoping that those clienteles will generate political pressure for the continuation and growth of those programs.

During the forty-eight years that J. Edgar Hoover was FBI director, the FBI was remarkably successful in cultivating external support. It assisted in the production of radio programs and films that glorified its accomplishments, and it created the "Ten Most Wanted" list to dramatize its crime-busting efforts.

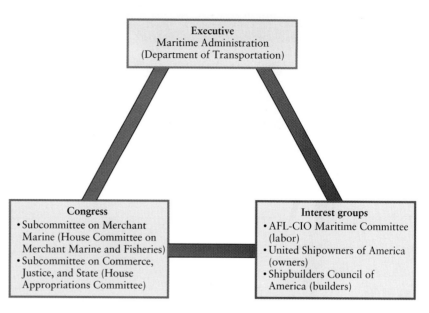

Figure 14-3   *The iron triangle of merchant shipping policy.*

Hoover himself devoted considerable attention to relations with his congressional overseers. As a result, FBI budget requests were rarely cut, and FBI recommendations regarding crime policies were usually heeded.

The close relationships that often develop among executive agencies, special interest groups, and congressional subcommittees are called **iron triangles**. All across the government, in almost every policy area, these mutually supportive relationships exist. Some of the most powerful participants in each triangle endure year after year: the subcommittee's ranking members and staff, the agency bureaucrats, and the leaders of the special interest groups (see Figure 14-3). They come to know each other well, and over time they develop understandings and procedures that allow all three points on the triangle to serve the interests of the affected constituents. (The Case Study on page 537 examines the survival of the United States Travel Service despite the efforts made by three presidents to eliminate it.)

Recent changes in American political life have caused some analysts to suggest a revision of the iron-triangle metaphor. Noting the growing prominence of experts in health, transportation, welfare, and many other areas of public policy, they argue that political power increasingly resides in issue networks. An **issue network** consists of specialists in a particular subject working in bureaucratic agencies at all levels of government, along with experts employed by legislative committee staffs, by interest groups, by think tanks, and by universities. Such networks play an important role in developing the national policy agenda, shaping consensus about preferred policies, and directing political leaders to develop and implement new proposals.

To take just one example, as government struggled to address the terrifying threat of the AIDS epidemic, an issue network quickly developed. As knowledge about AIDS developed, it was widely shared among experts in and

Saving the United States Travel Service: An Iron Triangle at Work

President Reagan, in his budget recommendations for fiscal year 1986, proposed the elimination of the United States Travel Service. To Washington veterans that was old news. Presidents had been trying to emasculate the Travel Service for more than a decade. The success of the Travel Service in surviving Reagan's attempt to eliminate it was also old news. Federal agencies—even little ones like the Travel Service—are hard to kill.

The Travel Service was established in the Department of Commerce in 1961 to encourage foreigners to take their vacations in the United States. Critics have contended that its functions could be performed better by hotels, airlines, and other industries that benefit from tourism and that there is no apparent need for the federal government to be involved in the tourism business. Supporters, however, have maintained that most other governments have an agency that promotes tourism and that the United States should also have one.

Over the years the Travel Service acquired two important Washington allies. The first ally emerged in 1969 with the merger of two trade associations into a group that is now called the Travel Industry Association of America. Its primary interest is the promotion of tourism in the United States, and it has become a staunch supporter of its "voice in government," the Travel Service. The other important ally of the Travel Service came on the scene in 1972, when the Senate Commerce Committee created a subcommittee on foreign commerce and tourism, chaired by Senator Daniel Inouye (D-Hawaii), whose state's economy is heavily dependent on tourism.

Inouye believed in the importance of the Travel Service and used his subcommittee position to see that it was protected from the budget cutters. When President Ford proposed significant cuts in the Travel Service budget in 1975, the Travel Industry Association and the subcommittee on foreign tourism and commerce were able to round up enough support to beat back the effort. Later, Inouye sponsored legislation to make the Travel Service an independent agency and thus free from the budget

constraints imposed on it by the Commerce Department. The bill passed both houses of Congress but was vetoed by President Carter. In 1979 President Carter proposed to eliminate the Travel Service, cutting most of its functions and assigning the rest to another part of the Commerce Department. Again the Travel Service's allies protected it. Carter tried once more the next year, and again the Travel Service survived. It still exists, and is now called the Travel and Tourism Administration.

What occurred in each of these instances is what typically occurs when an agency's existence is threatened. Agency leaders, interest groups, and the relevant congressional subcommittees join forces to protect the agency. The general goal of reducing federal spending, widely supported though it may be, rarely carries the same political impact as the desire of self-interested groups to save a program from which they benefit. Thus, the political energy generated by the defenders of programs usually exceeds the energy generated by the opponents. And when the defenders include potent elements from the executive branch, Congress, and the private sector— the traditional components of an iron triangle— they are hard to overcome.

Most Americans believe that the federal government spends more money than it should, but few believe that it spends enough on programs from which they benefit. And because the critical decisions on the survival of programs usually occur in the narrow confines of subcommittee rooms where the defending forces are strongest, the defenders often win. How else can one account for the failure of three successive presidents to eliminate one of the smallest agencies in the government?

Discussion questions
1. Why is the president of the United States unable to eliminate a small agency like the Travel Service?
2. On what principal sources of political power did the Travel Service depend?
3. What light does this case study shed on the federal government's persistent budget deficit?

Prominent public figures and celebrities have helped draw attention to the AIDS epidemic and have urged government to fund research. Here Elizabeth Taylor, national chair of the American Foundation for AIDS Research, testifies before a Senate subcommittee in 1986. Taylor has lost many friends to AIDS, as have most Americans, and she has tirelessly publicized the issues and solicited research funds.

out of government. They worked together in a variety of ways to develop a sense of direction for public policy and then to put pressure on public agencies to implement that agenda. Few issues have risen to prominence as quickly as AIDS did in the 1980s.

Organizational vitality   Like people, organizations have the capacity to stir the emotions. Such organizational vitality is most likely in an agency that is new and fresh. The agency bursts onto the scene, full of enthusiasm, staffed by bright, aggressive people carrying out a popular mission. Many of the New Deal agencies did this in the 1930s. The Peace Corps did it in the early 1960s and so did the Army's Green Berets a few years later. A high level of vitality facilitates the recruitment of talented people and opens the budget floodgates. The president is happy to be associated with such a popular enterprise, and people are more likely to defer to the agency's judgment.

Unfortunately, organizational vitality is difficult to sustain. The enthusiasm of an agency's youth rarely lasts. As an agency ages, it makes enemies. Its routines harden, slowing the decision-making process. The enthusiasts who ran the agency in its early days go on to other things, and the quality of performance declines. Before long the agency begins to drop back into the pack. As its vitality decreases, so too does its influence on policy making.

Leadership   The way an agency is run can make a difference in the way the agency is perceived and in the attention given to its recommendations. To improve an agency's effectiveness, leaders can boost internal morale. By providing a sense of excitement and improving the work environment, they can enhance performance. Good leaders can also be persuasive and effective in dealing with the agency's constituencies, especially with the interest groups and the congressional committees most concerned with the agency's programs. In a study of the congressional appropriations process, for example, political scientist Richard Fenno discovered that appropriations subcommittees were much more likely to support an agency's budget request when they had confidence in its leader.[23]

Toward the end of the Reagan administration, many of the members of Congress who dealt regularly with the Department of Housing and Urban Development (HUD) had lost confidence in the leadership of Secretary Samuel R. Pierce because of a pattern of weak management and favoritism in the awarding of grants and contracts. The failures of Pierce's leadership were later revealed in a series of hearings about what came to be known as the "HUD scandals." After his election in 1988, President Bush selected Jack Kemp to be the new HUD secretary. Kemp had served in Congress for eighteen years and was trusted and well regarded by most members. His vigorous early efforts to

Wide World Photos, Inc.

UPI/Bettmann

The Department of Housing and Urban Development was mired in scandal and mismanagement during the tenure of Secretary Samuel Pierce (above), from 1981 to 1989. His successor, Jack Kemp (below), helped to revitalize the agency and its public image. Here Kemp is shown in June 1990, as he testifies before the Senate Banking, Housing, and Urban Affairs Committee.

replace the top leadership at HUD and correct the lamentable legacy of his predecessor accelerated the restoration of congressional confidence in the department.

PROBLEMS OF ACCOUNTABILITY

Bureaucrats are not elected. Many of them spend their entire careers in government, often in the same agency. They make critical decisions about the economy, human welfare, the protection of the environment, war and peace. Only the most important, the most misguided, or the most blatantly corrupt of those decisions attract much public attention. Although bureaucrats operate in a political environment, they are often isolated from direct public scrutiny and public review.

That isolation is a significant concern in a democracy, where public policy is supposed to serve the public interest. What can be done to ensure that bureaucratic choices will give due priority to the public interest and that bureaucrats will be held accountable for their actions? How can the checks and balances that are so essential to curb the excesses of authority be imposed on agencies and individuals whose work is so often out of public view? In Chapter 13 we saw what efforts presidents undertake to control and direct the work of the executive branch. Several other approaches have been used to accomplish these objectives, including legal controls, legislative controls, and popular participation.

Legal Controls

Bureaucratic decisions are subject to judicial review—that is, they may be challenged in the federal courts. Most legal challenges are based on one of two grounds. The first is that the agency has acted outside its legal authority or jurisdiction. The second is that the agency's decision-making process has violated one or more of the legal rights and protections guaranteed by the Constitution.

The courts can respond to such suits in several ways. They can issue a declaratory judgment against the agency, restricting its actions in specified ways. They can grant an **injunction**—an order that usually prohibits the agency from taking further action against the aggrieved party until certain conditions, such as a rehearing, are satisfied. If the plaintiff has sued for damages, the courts may also order an agency to pay a sum of money as compensation for those damages.

At any given time, thousands of lawsuits are pending against federal agencies. Lawsuits are an important, but difficult and inconsistent, control technique. Lawsuits against federal agencies often take many years to wend their way through the federal courts. The high cost of litigation often deters the filing of lawsuits by people who have a genuine grievance. Even those who file suits rarely get satisfaction; federal agencies win most of the cases in which they are involved. Legal controls thus provide an imperfect guarantee of bureaucratic accountability.

Because administrative oversight is conducted by Congress, the popularly elected branch of the government, it is the most important guarantor of agency responsiveness to the public interest. In Chapter 12 we identified some of the ways in which Congress performs its oversight function. The most important of these are its review of personnel policy and presidential appointments and its ultimate control over agency budgets. It also exercises oversight through its central role in determining the organizational structure and location of administrative agencies.

Congress determines the maximum number of people an agency may employ. It also determines the qualifications that certain executive-branch officials must possess. Statutes require, for example, that the head of the Federal Aviation Administration be a civilian and that one of the members of the Federal Coal Mine Safety Board of Review be a "graduate engineer with experience in the coal mining industry."

Congress determines which positions shall be subject to Senate confirmation, and it has tended to expand that requirement when it has been in conflict with the executive branch. During the Nixon administration, for example, the Senate confirmation requirement was imposed on appointments of the director and deputy director of OMB and the director of the FBI. In the case of most senior, noncareer appointments in the executive branch, the Senate exercises direct oversight through the confirmation power.

Congress determines the location and level of new agencies and sometimes alters these aspects of existing agencies. When it approved the establishment of the EPA as an independent agency, for example, it did so to keep the EPA from falling under the control of one of the existing cabinet departments. Independent status was the structure preferred by most of the environmentalists who worked for the EPA's creation. Similarly, Congress responded to pressure from veterans' groups by elevating the existing Veterans Administration to cabinet status as the Department of Veterans Affairs. Organizational decisions of this sort are one of the ways in which Congress imposes its political preferences on the executive branch.

The General Accounting Office (GAO), an arm of Congress, plays a very important role in legislative efforts to control the bureaucracy. The GAO was first created in 1921 to perform financial audits of agency accounts. Over the years its functions have expanded, and now congressional committees often ask it to investigate agency management practices and the effectiveness of substantive programs. GAO reports cover a wide range of subjects and often lead to congressional oversight hearings and to changes in the way agencies do business.[24]

The most important form of legislative control is the power of the purse— the control that Congress exercises over agency budgets.[25] Agencies must appear before congressional appropriations subcommittees each year to present and defend their budgets. Those subcommittees then make recommendations that find their way into budget and appropriations bills.

Subcommittee decisions rarely follow the agency presentations precisely. Sometimes the subcommittees add funds for certain programs; more often they reduce funding. Frequently the subcommittees or the full Congress shift funds from one program to another, replacing agency and presidential preferences with those that have gained political support in the subcommittee or in Congress. One of Jimmy Carter's first initiatives on becoming president, for example, was to cut funding for nineteen dams, reservoirs, and other water development projects in different areas of the country. However, these projects were very important to the representatives from those areas, and they were able to build coalitions to support them. As a result, the projects were included in the budget that was finally enacted.[26]

Popular Participation

The ability of the American people to know about, participate in, and respond to bureaucratic decisions is greater than it has ever been. Part of the reason for this increase in popular participation is the constantly expanding access to em-

Seven astronauts died in a televised instant when the space shuttle Challenger *exploded on January 28, 1986. Millions of eyewitnesses, from schoolchildren to senators, wanted to know what happened, and President Reagan immediately appointed a commission. Astronaut Sally Ride (below) was among the members at the State Department hearing on February 26. The commission found that small components, called O-rings, were not designed to function at the temperatures which prevailed on the day the shuttle was launched. When an executive agency fails so visibly and tragically, a public investigation is almost certain.*

Wide World Photos, Inc.

AP/Wide World Photos

ployment in federal agencies. Most federal jobs are now filled through competitive examinations that open employment ranks to all citizens. Equal opportunity and affirmative action programs are designed to ensure the inclusion of female and minority employees in every agency. The dispersion of agency staffs into local and regional offices around the country has enhanced geographic representation among federal employees.

Agencies also take steps to encourage public comment on the issues they confront. They often hold hearings in Washington and elsewhere before making preliminary decisions on new rules or regulations. The Administrative Procedures Act requires that proposed rules be published before they take effect in order to permit public comment. So-called **sunshine laws** now require that important agency meetings and hearings be open to the public. And the Freedom of Information Act of 1967 permits public access to all but the most sensitive of government documents.[27] (And see pages 114–115 for more about this act and sample FOIA letters.)

When agencies take actions that threaten the public interest, they are often called to account by groups representing the public. There is a network of public interest groups, such as Common Cause, environmental groups, and the organizations founded by consumer advocate Ralph Nader, that monitor agency decisions and are quick to criticize those that seem to favor special interests at a high cost or real danger to the public. Other groups with special interests that may be adversely affected by bureaucratic actions also mount public relations campaigns aimed at increasing bureaucratic accountability and getting the bureaucracy to change its ways.

Another, perhaps more important, external source of pressure for accountability is investigative journalism. Print and broadcast reporters uncover and publicize stories that reveal the character of bureaucratic decisions and identify inadequacies or ineptitude in bureaucratic performance. Frequently they provide the leads that result in legislative investigations and legal action or remedial legislation. In 1975, for example, a series of articles in the *New York Times* by investigative reporter Seymour Hersh revealed domestic spying by the CIA, in violation of the agency's charter. Hersh's articles stimulated congressional hearings that resulted in new legislative restrictions on the CIA and the creation of more effective oversight procedures.

The Adequacy of Controls

As the United States government's reliance on bureaucracies increases and as the complexity and power of bureaucracies increase, the need for effective control mechanisms grows more acute. Bureaucracies are crucial to the efficient management of the national government, because of their expertise and their ability to simplify and routinize complex tasks. To get those benefits, however, Congress and the president have to delegate considerable authority and discretion to bureaucratic agencies. Delegation creates the problem of ensuring that authority and discretion are used in the public interest.

That is no easy task. Effective checks and balances, ever difficult to create and sustain, are especially elusive in the web of relationships that enmesh the bureaucratic agencies of the executive branch. The executive bureaucracy is huge, many of its functions are technically complex, and some of its functions must be conducted in secret.

Much of the work of government is routine and repetitive. This encourages the development and maintenance of enduring and mutually beneficial relationships between bureaucrats and other political actors. The desire to sustain these relationships and the shared rewards they produce often inhibits efforts to control bureaucratic activity.

The quest for accountability thus imposes a burden of vigilance on the political system and on the public. The media, special interest groups, and public opinion, however, are important but inconsistent monitors of bureaucratic activity. The record shows that oversight has been uneven and incomplete, and there is no reason to expect that it will improve significantly in the years ahead. It is hard to strike the proper balance between giving bureaucracies the freedom and encouragement they need to be effective while at the same time retaining sufficient control to redirect them when they go astray.

SUMMARY

Bureaucracy is a system in which the business of an organization is carried on by bureaus, agencies, and departments in which there is a clear hierarchy of authority and special emphasis on fixed routines. Bureaucracies have jurisdictions established by law, employ specialists trained to perform assigned tasks, and maintain written records of their decisions and activities. The federal bureaucracy—the executive branch—is the largest component of the federal government.

The federal bureaucracy includes several types of organizations. The fourteen *departments* are the government's major operating units. *Agencies* have responsibility for a narrower set of functions and may exist either within a department or independently. Bureaus, offices, administrations, and services are subunits of agencies.

Independent regulatory commissions are independent of any departmental affiliation and to some extent independent of presidential control. Commissions have quasi-legislative and quasi-judicial authority. Their purpose is to regulate commerce and trade in an assigned area of jurisdiction. Commission members serve for fixed terms, but the terms are staggered.

The federal government owns a variety of economic enterprises, most of which are operated as *government corporations*. Most government corporations have boards of directors whose members are appointed by the president, usually for long and staggered terms. Some corporations are totally independent; others fall within the jurisdiction of a department.

Before 1883, nonelective positions in the federal bureaucracy were filled by means of *patronage*. People who had supported winning candidates received government jobs as the spoils of victory. This use of patronage was known as the *spoils system*. Calls for reform led to the establishment of the *civil service system*, in which federal employment is based on merit rather than on political considerations. The regular civil service includes most of the career employees of the departments and the major agencies. All civil service positions are graded according to the character of the work to be done. A pay range is assigned to each grade level. The positions of senior managers and technical specialists are covered by the *Senior Executive Service*, which has its own pay grades. Federal employees are relatively secure in their jobs, although they can be removed when there is a *reduction in force*.

Nearly all of the top-level positions in the executive branch are held by political appointees. Most of them can be removed by a president who is unhappy with their performance or loyalty.

The primary task of federal agencies is to interpret and implement the public policies that emerge from the legislative process. They do this in a number of ways. One of these is regulation. *Economic regulation* aims to control prices, market entry, and conditions of service in specific industries. In recent decades there has been a movement toward *deregulation* of some industries. *Social regulation* is concerned with such matters as environmental protection, equal employment opportunity, and product safety. The emphasis on social regulation in recent decades has greatly expanded the scope of federal regulatory activity.

Most agencies have the authority to issue rules. The draft of a new rule must be published in the *Federal Register* at least thirty days before it is to go into effect. The agency invites and reviews public comment on the rule and then publishes the rule in its final form. In 1981 the Reagan administration required that all major proposed rules be reviewed and approved by the Office of Management and Budget. In 1990 the Supreme Court limited the scope of OMB's power.

Executive agencies perform quasi-judicial functions when they hold hearings to resolve conflicting interpretations of a rule. The hearings are often presided over by an *administrative law judge*, whose rulings are binding on both the agency and the complainant.

To ensure that laws and rules are obeyed, agencies make scheduled inspections, conduct audits, and impose reporting requirements. Agencies also oversee compliance by responding to complaints by parties that believe they have been harmed as a result of noncompliance.

Executive agencies play an important role in the initiation of policy. Agency employees usually are experts in a particular policy area. Their training, experience, and values shape their perceptions of the form policies should take.

Bureaucratic policy making is influenced by the distinctive characteristics of bureaucracy. Hierarchical decision making results in filtering, which eliminates some proposals because they are unnecessary, too costly, or untimely, and in the coordination of the proposals of various subunits. The character and culture of an agency affect the policies it generates. The biases of an agency may become institutionalized in its *standard operating procedures*. In recent years decision making by the executive agencies has become increasingly professionalized. As a result, striking a balance between professional advice and political realities is a constant struggle for executive-branch officials.

The natural characteristics of bureaucratic agencies often produce certain pathologies. Among these unhealthy characteristics are persistence, conservatism, expansionism, capture, and the territorial imperative. *Capture* is the tendency of agencies to develop symbiotic relationships with the special interests they oversee, becoming protectors rather than regulators of those interests. The *territorial imperative* is the common urge of an agency to jealously guard its own territory or turf.

Several factors determine an agency's ability to affect public policy; they include expertise, political support, organizational vitality, and leadership. The more technical and specialized an agency's expertise is, the greater will be the agency's opportunity to dominate policy making in its area of concern. Similarly, the more widespread and intense an agency's external political support is, the greater will be the agency's ability to affect policy making in its area of jurisdiction. Agencies try to develop supportive clienteles among the groups that benefit from their programs. The resulting close relationships among agencies, interest groups, and congressional committees are called *iron triangles*. Recent changes in American political life suggest that political power increasingly resides in *issue networks* consisting of specialists in a variety of public and private agencies.

Organizational vitality, another source of influence, is difficult to sustain. A good leader can increase an agency's influence by boosting internal morale and dealing persuasively with the agency's constituencies.

Several approaches have been used to make bureaucratic agencies more accountable to the public. Bureaucratic decisions are subject to judicial review. Courts can issue a declaratory judgment against an agency, grant an *injunction* that prevents the agency from taking certain actions, or order an agency to compensate a plaintiff for damages. Legislative controls on the bureaucracy include congressional review of personnel policy and presidential appointments, control of the structure of administrative agencies, and control over agency budgets. *Sunshine laws* require that important agency meetings and hearings be open to the public. Other sources of pressure for accountability are the activities of public interest groups and investigative journalism.

bureaucracy

department

agency

independent regulatory commission

government corporation

patronage

spoils system

civil service system

Senior Executive Service

reduction in force

economic regulation

deregulation

social regulation

administrative law judge

standard operating procedures

capture

territorial imperative

iron triangle

issue network

injunction

sunshine laws

LEARNING MORE ABOUT THE EXECUTIVE BUREAUCRACY

Scholarly studies

Fesler, James W., and Donald F. Kettl. *The Politics of the Administrative Process*. Chatham, N.J.: Chatham House, 1990. An excellent overview of public administration in the United States, with emphasis on the political forces that affect bureaucratic decisions.

Heclo, Hugh. *A Government of Strangers*. Washington, D.C.: Brookings Institution, 1977. An important analysis of the cultures and work environments of senior federal officials. Indicates that government leaders come from such a variety of backgrounds, are selected for such widely differing reasons, and are motivated by so broad an array of incentives that they often have little in common.

Kaufman, Herbert. *The Forest Ranger: A Study in Administrative Behavior*. Baltimore: Johns Hopkins University Press, 1967. A classic study of bureaucratic culture. Focuses on the development of the United States Forest Service and the highly refined set of values and perceptions that govern the behavior of its employees.

Lynn, Naomi B., and Aaron Wildavsky, eds. *Public Administration: The State of the Discipline*. Chatham, N.J.: Chatham House, 1990. An exploration of the approaches that are currently used to study and explain the actions of public agencies.

Rourke, Francis E. *Bureaucracy, Politics, and Public Policy*. 3rd ed. New York: HarperCollins, 1987. A clear and comprehensive exploration of the way politics shapes the organization, operation, and policy products of the federal executive branch.

Seidman, Harold, and Robert Gilmour. *Politics, Position, and Power*. 4th ed. New York: Oxford University Press, 1986. A study of the creation and management of political influence within the federal bureaucracy. Provides a good feel for how the bureaucratic universe appears from the inside.

Shafritz, Jay M., and Albert C. Hyde, eds. *Classics of Public Administration*. 3rd ed. Belmont, Calif.: Wadsworth Publishing Co., 1992. A book of readings that includes most of the seminal articles in the literature of public administration and bureaucratic operation. A good place to identify the principles and theories that have guided the scholarly study of the executive branch.

Leisure reading

Acheson, Dean. *Present at the Creation*. New York: Norton, 1987. An insider's account of the development of American foreign policy after World War II, with special emphasis on the role of the State Department.

Dickson, Paul. *The Official Rules*. New York: Dell, 1981. A sometimes tongue-in-cheek compilation of the "rules" and proverbs that determine outcomes in the bureaucratic world.

Halberstam, David. *The Best and the Brightest*. New York: Random House, 1993. A reporter's account of the backgrounds, motivations, and mindsets of the leading figures in the development of American policy in Vietnam.

Lowi, Theodore, and Benjamin Ginsberg. *Poliscide*. Lanham, Md.: University Press of America, 1990. An ingenious case study in which the decision to place an atom smasher in Illinois becomes an opportunity for political actors at every level to accomplish political objectives, with grave consequences for the residents of the community in which the project is to be located.

Primary sources

The Budget of the United States Government. Washington, D.C.: U.S. Government Printing Office, annual. A detailed account for each year's federal budget proposal with explanations of programs and contemporary and historical data on government spending.

Statistical Abstract of the United States. Washington, D.C.: Bureau of the Census, annual. A compendium of data on every aspect of American life and government, collected and updated by the Census Bureau and the Department of Commerce.

The United States Government Manual. Washington, D.C.: U.S. Government Printing Office, biennial. A volume describing the functions, authority, and structure of every agency of the federal government, including those that no longer exist.

Organizations

American Society for Public Administration, 1120 G Street, N.W., Washington, DC 20005; (202) 393-7878. Sponsors workshops and conferences, disseminates information about public administration. The society's mission is to promote high ethical standards for public service.

Council for Excellence in Government, 1775 Pennsylvania Avenue, N.W., Washington, DC 20006; (202) 728-0418. Works to broaden understanding of public service and management in the government; conducts outreach activities that encourage public and media discussion of public service.

National Academy of Public Administration, 1120 G Street, N.W., Washington, DC 20005; (202) 347-3190. Conducts studies and offers assistance to federal, state, and local government agencies and public officials on problems of public administration and public policy implementation.

- Judicial federalism: federal and state courts

- The power of judicial review: the political question doctrine; judicial review and political influence; activism versus self-restraint

- The cult of the robe: judges and justices; appointment of federal and Supreme Court justices; packing the Court

- The Supreme Court: caseload; deciding what to decide; oral argument; discussing cases and voting in conference; writing opinions; opinion days; Supreme Court decision making as a political process

- The politics of judicial policy making

In 1948, Republican Thomas E. Dewey and his choice of running mate, California governor Earl Warren, were considered unbeatable. Dewey, having lost to FDR in 1944, was "due" to win the presidency. And Democrat Harry Truman—who became president when FDR died in 1945—was a likely loser because of defections from the party by Progressives and Dixiecrats. But Truman campaigned more vigorously than Dewey and drew large crowds on his "whistlestop" train trips. He ran effectively against the Republican-controlled Congress of 1947-1948 and surprised the pollsters by coming from behind to win the election.

Beginning in the 1940s, questions were raised about the constitutionality of a late-nineteenth-century Connecticut law that prohibited virtually all individuals, whether married or single, from using contraceptives and barred physicians from giving advice about their use. In 1943 a doctor brought a suit in state court charging that the statute prevented him from giving information to patients. The state court upheld the law, and the doctor appealed that decision to the United States Supreme Court. But the Supreme Court ruled that he had failed to meet its tests for bringing such a lawsuit. The Court said that he lacked standing—*the basis for bringing a lawsuit—because he had not been arrested and had failed to show that he had suffered any personal injury as a result of the statute.*

Over a decade later, Dr. C. Lee Buxton and a patient were likewise denied standing on the ground that the law had not been enforced for eighty years, even though the state had begun to close birth control clinics. In this case, Poe v. Ullman *(1961), Justice Felix Frankfurter argued that since Connecticut's 1879 law prohibiting the* use of contraceptives was largely unenforced, Dr. Buxton lacked standing and the Court should exercise judicial self-restraint by not declaring the law unconstitutional.

Finally, after Dr. Buxton and Estelle Griswold, executive director of the Planned Parenthood League of Connecticut, were found guilty of prescribing contraceptives to a married couple, the Court struck down what Justice Potter Stewart called Connecticut's "uncommonly silly law." In announcing the Court's ruling in the case, Griswold v. Connecticut (1965), Justice William O. Douglas explained why Griswold and Buxton were now being granted standing. Buxton and Griswold had given medical advice to a married couple on how to prevent conception. They therefore had a professional relationship with the couple, which gave them standing to challenge the constitutionality of Connecticut's law as a violation of a married couple's right to privacy.

No less important for the Court's ruling in its Griswold decision was the fact that in 1962, the year after Poe v. Ullman, justices Frankfurter and Charles Whittaker resigned from the Court. They were replaced by President John F. Kennedy's two appointees, justices Byron White and Arthur Goldberg. With that change in the Court's composition came major changes in the Court's view of individuals' standing to sue and the kinds of rights they could claim in the courts. The Court's recognition of a constitutional right of privacy in Griswold, in turn, provided a basis for extending that right to include a woman's right to decide whether to have an abortion in Roe v. Wade (1973).

THE CONTROVERSY THAT BEGAN WITH CHALLENGES to the constitutionality of Connecticut's birth control law illustrates the importance of the Supreme Court's power to decide what cases it will review as well as how the Court responds to social forces. Individuals must have standing to bring cases and controversies to the courts, but whether they are granted standing may also depend on the composition of the court. Both public attitudes toward contraception and the composition of the Supreme Court were much different in the 1960s than they were in the 1940s.

The shift in the Court's position in the Connecticut birth control cases also indicates the political dynamics of judicial decision making and how changes in the composition of the bench may significantly alter the Court's role in larger controversies. The judiciary can decide only cases and controversies that are properly brought to it. Nevertheless, it is a political institution. Judges and justices are political actors who exercise great power in the United States, far more than judges and justices in other democracies. Their decisions, based on interpretations of law, sometimes have enormous political consequences. They may affect millions of people and involve billions of dollars. They may settle conflicts between special interest groups, alter the relationship between the president and Congress or that between the federal and state governments, and defend the rights of individuals and businesses against the coercive powers of government.

We begin this chapter by focusing on the organization and operation of courts and the politics of judicial federalism. We look at the power of judicial review, the politics of selecting and appointing judges, the judicial process itself, and the Supreme Court. Finally, we examine the politics of judicial decision making and explore the interaction between courts and other political insti-

tutions. In all of these areas, courts and judges are integral players in the politics of American government.

JUDICIAL FEDERALISM

In most countries there is a single, unitary system of courts. But in the United States judicial power is divided and decentralized. The United States has two separate judicial systems. Alongside the federal judiciary, each of the fifty states has its own independent judicial system. Within both the federal and the state systems, judicial power is further rationed between trial courts—and other lesser courts such as traffic courts—and one or two appellate courts, which hear appeals from the lower courts. (The organization of the federal judicial system is shown in Figure 15-1; the box on page 553 presents the basic types of law.)

The importance of this dual judicial system, termed **judicial federalism,** is that federal courts largely consider disputes over national law and state courts consider only disputes arising under state law. If there is a conflict between national and state law, the matter is settled by the federal courts and ultimately by the Supreme Court. This is so because (as discussed in Chapter 2) the Constitution and federal law are supreme over state law. Judicial federalism and the decentralized structure of federal and state courts have a number of important consequences for judicial policy making, as we will see in this chapter.

The U.S. Supreme Court in 1994. The chief justice always sits in the middle, with associate justices alternating out to his right and left, in descending order of years of service. (Seated) Sandra Day O'Connor (appointed by Reagan in 1981); Harry Blackmun (Nixon, 1970); Chief Justice William Rehnquist (associate justice, Nixon, 1972; chief justice, Reagan, 1986); John Paul Stevens (Ford, 1975); Antonin Scalia (Reagan, 1986). (Standing) Clarence Thomas (Bush, 1991); Anthony M. Kennedy (Reagan, 1988); David H. Souter (Bush, 1990); Ruth Bader Ginsburg (Clinton, 1993).

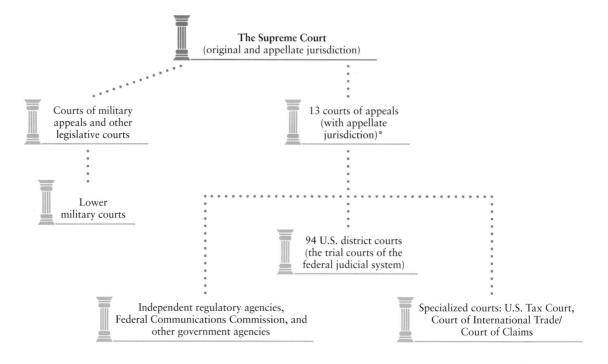

The Supreme Court
(original and appellate jurisdiction)

Courts of military
appeals and other
legislative courts

13 courts of appeals
(with appellate
jurisdiction)*

Lower
military courts

94 U.S. district courts
(the trial courts of the
federal judicial system)

Independent regulatory agencies,
Federal Communications Commission, and
other government agencies

Specialized courts: U.S. Tax Court,
Court of International Trade/
Court of Claims

*This includes eleven regional courts of appeals, one Court of Appeals for the District of Columbia Circuit, and one Court of Appeals for the Federal Circuit.

Figure 15-1   *The organization of the federal judicial system.*

Federal Courts

Article III of the Constitution vests judicial power "in one Supreme Court, and in such inferior courts as Congress may from time to time ordain and establish." Courts created under Article III are **constitutional courts**. Congress has the power to create another kind of court as well. Under Article I it may create **legislative courts** to carry out its own powers. The United States Court of Military Appeals, which applies military law, is one such court; federal bankruptcy courts are another type of legislative court. These courts have more specialized jurisdiction than those created under Article III, and their judges do not hold lifetime appointments.

Congress has established a number of courts under Article III. In 1789 it divided the country into thirteen districts (one in each state) and created a federal district court for each. **District courts** are the trial courts of the federal system. In addition, the Judiciary Act of 1789 created three federal **courts of appeals** to hear appeals from decisions of the district courts or from state courts. But Congress did not provide for any appellate court judges. Instead, these courts were staffed by two Supreme Court justices who twice a year sat with a district court judge to hear cases. The federal courts of appeals were not staffed by full-time appellate judges for another hundred years.

As the country grew, so did the number of district courts, along with the

Types of Law

Admiralty and Maritime Law: Law governing shipping and commerce on the high seas and on the navigable waters of the United States.

Administrative Law: Law governing the decision-making procedures and decisions of public agencies and public administrators.

Civil Law: Law dealing with the private rights and relations of individuals, though the government may become a party to civil actions when it seeks to prevent violations of law, as under the Sherman Anti-Trust Act.

Common Law: Judge-made law, originating in England in the twelfth century and based on the principle of *stare decisis* ("let the decision stand"), or precedent.

Constitutional Law: Rulings by the Supreme Court interpreting the United States Constitution.

Criminal Law: Law that defines crimes against the public order and specifies punishment for those crimes.

Statutory Law: Laws passed by legislatures and judges' interpretations of legislative enactments.

number of appeals of their rulings to the Supreme Court. Eventually the workload of the Supreme Court became too large for the justices to handle. Congress responded in 1891 by creating the circuit courts of appeals, which now hear most of the appeals coming from district courts or from state courts. Today the federal judiciary consists of ninety-four district courts, thirteen courts of appeals, and the Supreme Court.

Jim Wilson/NYT Pictures

Federal district court judge Terry J. Hatter, Jr., gained national attention when he issued an injunction forbidding the military from discriminating against homosexuals. He did this just one day before President Clinton announced his revised "Don't ask, Don't tell" policy about homosexuals serving in the armed forces.

District courts There is at least one federal district court in each state, depending on the population. Each court has at least one judge, though the number of judges changes with the size of the workload. In 1992 there were 637 district judges in all. Every judge has the assistance of one law clerk, one or two secretaries, and additional staff research and clerical support if needed. They may also employ *grand juries* (juries consisting of more than twelve jurors) for indicting individuals for crimes and *petit juries* (twelve-member juries) for trying individuals charged with violating federal laws.

District judges sit alone when hearing oral arguments at trial, deciding cases (if a jury is not involved) and imposing sentences and making judgments on the law (if there is a jury). They handle the bulk of all litigation in the federal system. Over 200,000 civil cases and over 45,000 criminal cases are filed each year in federal district courts.[1] The cases generally involve federal law, but district judges may also decide disputes between citizens of different states and, when authorized by legislation, apply state law.

In most cases trial courts are courts of first and last resort in the federal judicial system. This means that they are the place where the trial begins and ends. Only a small fraction of district court decisions are appealed and reviewed by appellate courts. A substantial number of federal criminal defendants, moreover, do not go to trial because they plead guilty, often as a result of plea bargaining. (A *plea bargain* is a deal struck between a prosecutor and a defendant whereby the latter agrees to plead guilty to a lesser offense in exchange for a lesser sentence or probation. See Chapter 4.)

Less than 15 percent of the criminal cases that do go to trial are later appealed. Thus, much of what district judges do is never reviewed by a higher court. As one federal judge puts it: "Justice stops in the district. They either get it here or they can't get it at all."[2]

Because district judges preside over trials, they experience the drama of the adversary process to a greater degree than do appellate judges, who rarely hear arguments in cases on appeal. As we saw in Chapter 4, the adversary process is based on the idea that two sides of a dispute should argue their cases before a neutral third party—a judge or a jury—that ensures procedural fairness and, after hearing the evidence from both sides, decides the dispute. Each side argues as hard as it can, and trial judges themselves often feel embattled, rather than like impartial and detached arbitrators.

Appellate courts In contrast with the individual decision making of trial judges, appellate court judges decide cases in a collegial manner. Judges on the thirteen federal courts of appeals sit in rotating panels of three and decide most cases solely on the basis of written **briefs** submitted by the litigants. Briefs filed by attorneys for both sides of a dispute discuss the facts of the case and relevant laws and precedents (prior rulings by the Supreme Court or federal circuit courts). Occasionally the entire appellate court sits as a panel, or **en banc**. The dynamics of decision making in federal courts of appeals therefore vary with the rotation of judges and the number of judges sitting *en banc*. Indeed, as the number of judges on appellate courts has increased from three or fifteen to twenty or more, some judges complain that they function more like a legislative body, dividing into groups and being forced to seek compromises with each other when deciding cases.

Although appellate judges share responsibility for decisions, their mounting caseloads present special problems. Federal courts of appeals face more than

Jury Duty

Trial by jury is guaranteed in four different places in the Constitution: in Article III, Section 2, and in the Fifth, Sixth, and Seventh Amendments. The purpose of a jury trial is to protect the accused from government oppression by demanding that members of the community—not a single judge or prosecutor—determine guilt or innocence.

The average citizen can expect to be called for service as a trial juror for a civil or criminal trial every three to five years or so. When calling individuals for jury duty, the courts seek to select at random a fair cross-section of the community. To do this, names are usually randomly drawn from lists of voters and holders of driver's licenses. This method arguably excludes younger, poorer, and minority citizens, who are less likely to register to vote.

Although serving on a jury is an obligation of citizenship, jury duty is often considered a nuisance or a burden. In many ways, it is. Jurors in federal courts receive about $30 a day, which works out to about the minimum wage. Jurors in state courts receive a token daily payment that is even less. In addition, jury service can be very time-consuming.

Many prospective jurors ask to be excused or to have their service postponed. The requests are usually granted to those who would find jury duty particularly burdensome (an elderly person in poor health, for example) or temporarily inconvenient (conflicting with a planned vacation or business trip). In some states, members of certain occupations such as lawyers and police officers are automatically excused; housewives are also automatically excused in some states. Many other states, however, have sharply curtailed automatic excuses. Many states have also moved to streamlined systems that put jurors "on call" and have them report to the courthouse only when they are actually needed.

Relatively few jurors actually participate in a full trial. In the *voir dire*, or selection process, judges and attorneys can challenge prospective jurors in one of two ways. Peremptory challenges remove a juror, usually a person who appears unsympathetic to one side or the other, without giving a specific reason. Challenges "for cause" remove people who express under questioning a specific bias that could keep them from being impartial.

Once a jury of twelve has been selected, the trial proceeds. In most cases, trials are over in a day or so (many are settled after the jury is selected but before the actual trial begins). The jurors listen to the evidence and then begin their deliberations. Generally a decision is reached quickly and unanimously. Reaching a decision in a complex case can take longer, sometimes several days. Often jurors in these cases are sequestered to keep them from outside influences during the deliberations. In some notorious criminal cases, the jurors serve anonymously and are sequestered during the entire trial.

A petit jury listens to attorneys argue in a courtroom.

Tom Pantages

forty thousand cases a year. The Ninth Circuit, which includes the Pacific Coast states, Alaska, and the islands of Hawaii and Guam, alone now issues over four thousand opinions a year. As the number of appeals rose in the last decade, Congress increased the number of judges. But more cases, more judges, and more opinions place greater strain on working relationships and threaten the stability and continuity of the law. Judges have had to delegate more of their work to law clerks. The number of law clerks assigned to an appellate judge has risen from one or two to three or four (at the Supreme Court). Some judges now warn of the bureaucratization of the federal courts and the advent of "bureaucratic justice."[3]

State Courts

State courts are by no means inferior to the federal judiciary, even though their decisions may be appealed to the federal courts and to the Supreme Court if they involve the application of federal law or issues guaranteed by the federal Constitution. State courts play a crucial role in the administration of justice. When interpreting state constitutions and bills of rights, state courts have great freedom to pursue their own directions in policy making rather than simply following the direction of the Supreme Court.

State courts handle by far the greatest volume of litigation. Well over 90 percent of all lawsuits filed each year are in state courts. The business of state courts also tends to diverge from that in federal courts. Apart from criminal cases, the largest portion of state supreme court litigation involves economic issues. State courts face, for instance, a large number of cases involving government regulation of public utilities, zoning ordinances, and small business disputes, as well as controversies over labor relations and the use of natural resources. The nature of such litigation varies from one state to another, depending on factors such as population size, urbanization, and socioeconomic conditions.[4] In the large, populous state of New York, with New York City the home of many large corporations, a higher percentage of the litigation involves disputes over economic regulations, antitrust laws, and commercial transactions, as well as criminal cases.

The Supreme Court intrudes on state-court policy making only in a very narrow class of litigation: cases in which state courts deal with **federal questions**. A federal question may involve disagreements over the interpretation of the Constitution, the Bill of Rights, or other federal laws. A federal question rarely emerges from the cases that normally come to the state courts. If a case is decided on **independent state grounds**—such as a state constitution or a state bill of rights—the Court declines review, respecting the **principle of comity** between federal and state courts. In other words, the Court out of courtesy defers to the decisions of state supreme courts that are based on a state, not the federal, constitution.

It would be wrong to conclude that there are no tensions in relations between state and federal courts. The tensions reflect the politics of a changing federal judiciary. In the 1950s and 1960s, for example, the Supreme Court applied the guarantees of the federal Bill of Rights to the states. Many state judges opposed the Court's liberal rulings and attacked it for intruding on the autonomy of state courts. By contrast, in the 1970s, 1980s, and 1990s, under more conservative chief justices, the Court cut back on the "liberal jurisprudence" of earlier decades. The justices now tend to take a more limited view of the role of the federal judiciary in protecting and expanding civil liberties and civil rights. As a result, some liberal state-court judges are now going in the opposite direction from the Supreme Court and are extending greater protection for civil rights and liberties under their state constitutions. Since 1969, in over six hundred cases state supreme courts have interpreted their state constitutions and bills of rights to provide greater protection and to afford rights that the United States Supreme Court has refused to recognize under the federal Constitution and Bill of Rights.[5]

THE POWER OF JUDICIAL REVIEW

Unlike other political institutions, courts are passive and reactive. They are not, as Justice Benjamin Cardozo observed, "knights-errant" and "roving commissions." They are not self-starters; they must await disputes in the form of a lawsuit—that is, an actual "case or controversy."

Article III of the Constitution, along with congressional legislation, specifies the **jurisdiction** of federal courts, the kinds of cases and controversies that courts may decide. Under Article III the Supreme Court has **original jurisdiction** in all cases involving disputes between two or more states and in cases brought against the United States by ambassadors of foreign countries. Original jurisdiction means that the case originates in the Supreme Court. Only two or three cases out of the more than six thousand that come to the Court each year involve matters of original jurisdiction. The overwhelming majority of cases coming to the Court arrive under its **appellate jurisdiction,** as established by congressional legislation. Under its appellate jurisdiction the Court hears appeals from lower federal courts and state courts. Federal legislation also defines the jurisdiction of the lower federal courts; state constitutions and legislation define the jurisdiction of state courts.

Courts have jurisdiction only over disputes involving adverse interests and a real controversy. They will not take "friendly lawsuits" brought by two parties who simply want to have some question settled. The parties must have **standing to sue;** they must show that they are suffering or are in danger of suffering an immediate and substantial personal injury (see box on page 558). Traditionally individuals could challenge government action only if they could demonstrate a personal and monetary injury. But since the 1960s Congress and the courts have expanded the law of standing in cases like *Griswold v. Connecticut.* As a result, today lawsuits may also involve nonmonetary interests like aesthetic and environmental well-being. For example, in *United States v. Students Challenging Regulatory Agency Procedures (SCRAP)* (1973), the Court granted standing to a group of law students attacking a proposed surcharge on railroad freight. The students contended that the surcharge would discourage the recycling of bottles and cans and thus contribute to environmental pollution. When granting SCRAP standing to bring its suit, the Court observed that "Aesthetic and environmental well-being, like economic well-being, are important ingredients of the quality of life in our society, and the fact that particular environmental interests are shared by the many rather than the few does not make them less deserving of legal protection through the judicial process."[6]

Requirements for Gaining Standing

1. *A personal injury must be claimed.* For example, an individual must have been denied some right under federal or state law.

2. *The dispute must not be hypothetical.* Real adverse interests must be at stake.

3. *A case must be brought before a court authorized to hear such disputes.* Cases must be within a court's jurisdiction.

4. *Other remedies must have been exhausted.* For example, litigants must have exhausted administrative appeals and appeals in other lower courts.

5. *The dispute must not be moot.* Circumstances since filing the lawsuit must not have changed so as to end the dispute or make it hypothetical.

6. *A case must be ripe for judicial resolution.* The dispute must not be hypothetical, and other opportunities for resolving it must have been exhausted.

7. *The dispute must be capable of judicial resolution.* The dispute must not involve a political question that should be decided by other branches of government.

More individuals and interest groups may now gain access to the courts, and they may raise a wider range of disputes. They may bring test cases and controversies in which they have a stake in the outcome but which also represent a conflict over the public interest. In the 1940s and 1950s, the National Association for the Advancement of Colored People brought a series of test cases challenging the constitutionality of racially segregated public schools. These cases led to the Supreme Court's landmark ruling, in *Brown v. Board of Education of Topeka, Kansas* (1954), striking down the doctrine of "separate but equal" facilities. More recently, environmental groups like the Natural Resources Defense Council and the Sierra Club have brought suits against polluters in order to protect the environment, and the U.S. Chamber of Commerce, business groups, and conservative legal foundations have used litigation to challenge the enforcement of health, safety, and environmental regulations.[7]

The Political Question Doctrine

After a lawsuit has been filed, judges may still refuse to decide a dispute. For example, they will not decide hypothetical disputes or give "advisory opinions" on possible future conflicts. Courts also avoid deciding **political questions**. A political question is one that judges think should be resolved by other branches of government, either because of the separation of powers or because the judiciary is not in a position to provide a remedy. Thus, courts generally avoid disputes involving foreign policy and international relations. But this does not make them less political. Deciding what is a "political question" is itself a political decision and an exercise of judicial review.

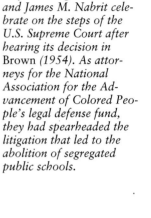

Attorneys George E. C. Hayes, Thurgood Marshall, and James M. Nabrit celebrate on the steps of the U.S. Supreme Court after hearing its decision in Brown (1954). As attorneys for the National Association for the Advancement of Colored People's legal defense fund, they had spearheaded the litigation that led to the abolition of segregated public schools.

The Constitution and legislation stipulate the kinds of cases and controversies that courts may consider. Yet, as Chief Justice Charles Evans Hughes once remarked, "We are under the Constitution, but the Constitution is what the judges say it is."[8] Legal doctrines governing access to the courts mean what judges and justices say they mean. Courts change, and judges change their minds. For many decades, for instance, courts applied the political question doctrine to avoid entering the "political thicket" of state elections and representation.[9] But under these conditions urban voters were often denied equal voting rights. The Court finally responded to this injustice in *Baker v. Carr* (1962), holding that such disputes were within its jurisdiction and were **justiciable disputes**—that is, open to judicial resolution and a judicial remedy. After abandoning the political question doctrine in this area, the Court forced state and local governments to provide equal voting rights and established the principle of one person, one vote.

Charles Evans Hughes served twice on the Supreme Court—from 1910 to 1916 as an associate justice, and from 1930 to 1941 as chief justice. He left the Court in 1916 to run as the Republican party's candidate for president. Although his bid failed, his work for the party was rewarded when President Hoover named him chief justice.

Judicial Review and Political Influence

In the United States the judiciary, particularly the Supreme Court, exercises great political power because its members have the authority to interpret the Constitution and the laws of the nation. This power of *judicial review* (see Chapter 2) gives the courts the power to strike down any law enacted by Congress or by the states and to declare official government actions unconstitutional.

Judicial review has been controversial ever since Chief Justice John Marshall asserted that power in the landmark case of *Marbury v. Madison* (1803). It remains controversial because by striking down acts of Congress or state legislatures the Court thwarts the democratic process and majority rule as expressed by elected representatives. This is so even when the Court uses its power to promote the democratic process, as it does when it enforces the First Amendment guarantees of freedom of speech and press and when it strikes down barriers to the electoral process.

The political influence of the judiciary has grown dramatically since the nation's founding. The judiciary is no longer, as Alexander Hamilton claimed in *The Federalist, No. 78,* "the least dangerous branch." Instead, it has become truly a coequal branch of the government. The Supreme Court increasingly asserts its power in striking down congressional legislation, state laws, and municipal ordinances. Lower courts likewise no longer serve simply as tribunals for private dispute resolution but more often serve as problem solvers and policy makers.

Courts have also increasingly become, as Judge Irving Kaufman points out, "an accelerator of government rather than a brake." In some instances, judges have taken over the management of schools, hospitals, and prisons when ordering remedial changes to make up for past discrimination or substandard facilities.[10] More often, though, Congress has given the courts a role in the implementation of public policies by extending their jurisdiction and giving them the power to hear lawsuits brought under legislation. The National Environmental Protection Act, for example, provides that citizens may file lawsuits in federal courts to challenge the decisions of the Environmental Protection Agency and even to force that agency to promulgate regulations under the act to protect the environment.

Activism Versus Self-Restraint

Do courts exercise too much power? Have they usurped the power of other branches of the government? The power of judicial review has been criticized, at different times, by both liberals and conservatives. In the 1920s and 1930s liberals attacked the Supreme Court for its **judicial activism** in striking down progressive economic legislation such as minimum-wage laws. (Judicial activism is the use of judicial review to invalidate state and federal laws.) The liberals criticized the Court for substituting its conservative economic views for the more progressive views of Congress and state legislatures. They urged the Court to exercise **judicial self-restraint** and defer to Congress and state legislatures. (Judicial self-restraint is the practice of deferring to the political branches, rather than asserting what the Court perceives to be in the public's interest.) By contrast, the Court's activism in defending civil liberties and civil rights in the 1960s and 1970s led conservatives to charge that the Court was usurping the power of other political institutions and thwarting the will of the majority. Presidents Nixon, Reagan, and Bush all called for the appointment of judges who would exercise judicial self-restraint.

But the political role of contemporary courts is only partially explained by judges' exercise of judicial review. Courts respond (more or less slowly) to the problems created by technological advances and political and social changes. The expansion of judicial power is also related to changes in government policies for dealing with illegal activities. The federal judiciary, for instance, played a minor role in environmental protection until the 1970s, when Congress passed legislation such as the Clean Air and Clean Water Acts and the National Environmental Protection Act. Then the courts had to resolve conflicts over the implementation of that legislation by federal agencies.

Other social trends are no less significant for increasing and changing the business of courts. In the late nineteenth century, railroads and businesses relied on the judiciary to protect property rights and to strike down progressive economic legislation. The civil rights movement of the 1950s and 1960s brought lawsuits, challenging racial discrimination in schools, in employment, and in public accommodations. The pace of litigation is also influenced by economic cycles. This is so because increased economic activity gives rise to new issues involving property rights and disputes over government regulations affecting labor-management relations; health, safety, and environmental matters; and other economic issues.

No less important is the fact that American society is exceedingly litigious—so much so that the United States is sometimes called an adversarial democracy. In the early 1990s, for instance, over 300,000 cases a year were filed in the federal courts, more than twice the number in the preceding decade. Moreover, the federal judiciary handles but a small percentage of all litigation that occurs in the United States. State courts face over 25 million cases a year. Another measure of the increasing litigiousness of the United States is the rather dramatic increase in the number of lawyers and judges. In 1990 it was estimated that there was one lawyer for every 298 American citizens.

Even more fundamental to the role of the judiciary are cultural factors that condition the way democratic politics works in pluralistic and litigious American society. The competition for power among diverse interest groups in other political arenas inexorably finds its way into the courts. As the astute French commentator Alexis de Tocqueville observed in the 1830s: "Scarcely any political question arises in the United States that is not resolved, sooner or later, into a judicial question."[11] This situation results from a distinguishing feature of democracy in America: the peculiar "legal habit" that accompanies Americans' devotion to civil rights and to the idea of the rule of law.

THE CULT OF THE ROBE: JUDGES AND JUSTICES

A hallmark of the federal judiciary is the virtual isolation of judges from direct political pressures such as the lobbying faced by senators, representatives, and other elected officials. Under the Constitution federal judges are appointed by the president (subject to confirmation by the Senate) and given lifetime appointments; the Constitution also bars Congress from decreasing their salaries. Still, judges are appointed largely for political reasons, get involved in political controversies, and make judgments that affect the rules that govern politics.

In contrast with the system for appointing federal judges, the selection of state court judges varies from one state to another and among different courts within the states. In states on the Atlantic seaboard, judges have historically been appointed either by the governor or by the state legislature. In other states, particularly in the South, judges are elected on either a partisan or a nonpartisan basis. In the Midwest and West, as well as in a growing number of other states, judges are appointed by some combination of both methods—that is, under so-called merit systems. Under a **merit system** a nonpartisan commission usually provides a list of possible nominees from which the governor or legislature makes appointments. Then, after one or two years of service, the judges' names are placed unopposed on a ballot, and voters decide whether they should be retained.

Politics ultimately determines the appointment of state court judges. Regardless of the method of selection, the same kinds of individuals tend to be appointed. White male lawyers from upper-middle-class Protestant backgrounds who have been politically active have historically predominated. Since the late 1970s, however, an increasing number of women and members of minority groups have been appointed or elected to state judgeships.

Appointment of Federal Judges

Politics also determines who is appointed to the federal bench. Article II of the Constitution gives the president the power to nominate and appoint, with the advice and consent of the Senate, all federal judges. Since federal judges enjoy lifetime tenure, appointments to federal judgeships are a prized form of political patronage. Presidents try to "pack" the federal courts in the hope of influencing the direction of public law and policy long after they have left the Oval Office. In the 1980s and early 1990s, for instance, Republican presidents Ronald Reagan and George Bush promised to appoint judges who were opposed to abortion. Political scientists studying the voting behavior of federal judges appointed by Reagan and by Democratic presidents Lyndon Johnson and Jimmy Carter found that "Reagan appointees were much more resistant to abortion rights than were the appointees of his predecessors, including the appointees of fellow Republican Richard Nixon. Likewise President Carter's appointees were much more supportive of abortion claims than were the appointees of other presidents."[12] President Clinton was slow to fill lower-court vacancies, but he made it clear that he favored those who support abortion rights and appointing more women and minorities to the federal bench. Table 15-1 shows the number of judicial appointments made by each of the last ten presidents and those made, thus far, by President Clinton; Table 15-2 presents some characteristics of appointees to the federal courts.

In appointing federal judges, however, presidents often must compete with the Senate and other political bodies. In addition to the president, the Senate, and judicial candidates themselves, other key actors include the Department of Justice, the Standing Committee on the Federal Judiciary of the American Bar Association, and leading political party officials. The practice of

TABLE 15-1										
Number of Judicial Appointments from Roosevelt through Bush										
	FDR	TRUMAN	EISENHOWER	KENNEDY	JOHNSON	NIXON	FORD	CARTER	REAGAN	BUSH	CLINTON*
Supreme Court	9	4	5	2	2	4	1		4	2	1
Circuit Court	52	27	45	20	41	45	12	56	78	37	3
District Court	137	102	127	102	125	182	52	206	290	148	24
Special Courts[1]	14	9	10	2	13	7	1	3	10		
Total	212	142	187	126	181	238	66	265	382	187	28

* Appointments made through April 1994.

[1] Includes Customs, Patent Appeals, and Court of International Trade.

A Profile of Presidential Appointees to the Lower Federal Courts

	JOHNSON	NIXON	FORD	CARTER	REAGAN	BUSH	CLINTON*
				NUMBER			
Gender							
Male	159	223	63	218	340	149	17
Female	3	1	1	40	28	36	10
Ethnicity or race							
White	152	215	58	203	344	165	21
Black	7	6	3	37	7	12	6
Hispanic	3	2	1	16	15	8	1
Asian		1	2	2	2		
ABA ratings							
Exceptionally/well qualified	89	114	31	145	203	109	22
Qualified	68	110	32	110	165	76	6
Not qualified	4		1	3			
Religious affiliation							
Protestant	95	165	45	156	218	117	
Catholic	48	40	13	69	111	51	
Jewish	19	19	6	33	38	17	
Total number of appointees	162	224	64	258	368	185	

* Appointments made through April 1994.

NOTE: One Johnson appointee did not receive an ABA rating, and one Reagan appointee was self-classified as nondenominational.

SOURCE: Sheldon Goldman, "Bush's Judicial Legacy: The Final Imprint," *Judicature* 282 (1993); Alliance for Justice, "Judicial Selection Project Annual Report, 1993."

senatorial courtesy developed in part to achieve this accommodation. The president consults with senators from his party and from the nominee's home state prior to making a formal nomination.

The appointment process encourages the Senate and the president to bargain with each other to achieve their political objectives. The president may trade lower-court judgeships for legislation and good relations. That is to say, the president may agree to nominate a senator's preferred candidate for a district court judgeship in exchange for the senator's vote on crucial legislation and support of the administration's policy goals. Federal judgeships are opportunities for the Senate, no less than for the president, to influence national policy and confer political patronage. As Griffin Bell, a former court of appeals judge and attorney general in the Carter administration, put it, "Becoming a federal judge wasn't very difficult. I managed John F. Kennedy's presidential campaign in Georgia. Two of my oldest friends were the senators from Georgia. And I was campaign manager and special unpaid counsel for the governor."[13]

At the lowest level of the federal judicial structure, the district courts, "it's senatorial appointment with the advice and consent of the President," in the words of former attorney general Robert Kennedy.[14] The president has greater discretion at the circuit court level. Since the jurisdiction of these courts spans several states, the president may play senators off against each other by claiming the need for representation of different political parties, geographic regions, religions, races, and so forth within a given circuit.

Appointment of Supreme Court Justices

Unlike other federal judgeships, appointments to the Supreme Court are usually considered a prerogative of the president. As President Herbert Hoover's attorney general, William Mitchell, observed, "with the whole country to choose from, the Senators from one state or another are in no position, even if they were so inclined, to attempt a controlling influence."[15] Although the Senate as a whole has the power to defeat a nominee, in this century only seven have been blocked: four were defeated, and three were withdrawn.

The principal obstacle that the president must overcome is the Senate's power to reject his nominees (see Table 15-3). This was vividly illustrated by the Senate's rejection of the nomination of Robert H. Bork to the Supreme Court in 1987 (see the Case Study on page 566).

The fate of the Bork nomination testifies to the political nature of the appointment process. It indicates the range of forces that can affect judicial appointments and the difficulty the president can encounter if he does not take these forces into account. It also demonstrates the need for cooperation in a process that requires agreement between two government institutions.

All presidents try to fill vacancies on the Supreme Court with political associates and individuals who share their ideological views. They make little or no effort to balance the Court by crossing party lines. Of the 107 individuals who have served on the Supreme Court, there have been 13 Federalists, 1 Whig, 8 Democratic-Republicans, 42 Republicans, and 43 Democrats.

In earlier eras presidents sought geographic balance on the Court as well as ideological compatibility. In the early nineteenth century, representation of different geographic regions was considered crucial to establishing the legitimacy of the Court. As the country expanded westward, presidents were inclined to give representation to new states and regions. But in this century appointments have rarely turned on geography. President Nixon, for instance, named two justices from Minnesota, and three of President Reagan's four appointees came from the West.

Most presidents delegate the responsibility for selecting candidates and getting them through the Senate to their attorney general and other close advisers. The assistant attorney general in charge of the Office of Legal Policy in the Department of Justice usually compiles a list of candidates from recommendations by White House staff, members of Congress, governors, and state and local bar associations. A committee of the president's top advisers narrows the number of candidates for each position down to two or three on the basis of a political evaluation and (until the Reagan administration) informal approval by the Standing Committee on the Federal Judiciary of the American Bar Association. The ABA committee ranks candidates as "well qualified," "qualified," or "not qualified." An exhaustive FBI investigation is then initiated, and a formal evaluation by the ABA is requested. Once these reports have been reviewed by the attorney general and White House counsel, a recommendation is sent to the president. If he approves, it is formally submitted to the

TABLE 15-3

Supreme Court Nominations Rejected, Postponed,
or Withdrawn Because of Senate Opposition

NOMINEE	YEAR NOMINATED	NOMINATED BY	ACTIONS[1]
William Paterson[2]	1793	Washington	Withdrawn (for technical reasons)
John Rutledge[3]	1795	Washington	Rejected
Alexander Wolcott	1811	Madison	Rejected
John J. Crittenden	1828	J. Q. Adams	Postponed, 1829
Roger B. Taney[4]	1835	Jackson	Postponed
John C. Spencer	1844	Tyler	Rejected
Reuben H. Walworth	1844	Tyler	Withdrawn
Edward King	1844	Tyler	Postponed
Edward King[5]	1844	Tyler	Withdrawn, 1845
John M. Read	1845	Tyler	No action
George W. Woodward	1845	Polk	Rejected, 1846
Edward A. Bradford	1852	Fillmore	No action
George E. Badger	1853	Fillmore	Postponed
William C. Micou	1853	Fillmore	No action
Jeremiah S. Black	1861	Buchanan	Rejected
Henry Stanbery	1866	Johnson	No action
Ebenezer R. Hoar	1869	Grant	Rejected, 1870
George H. Williams[3]	1873	Grant	Withdrawn, 1874
Caleb Cushing[3]	1874	Grant	Withdrawn
Stanley Matthews[2]	1881	Hayes	No action
William B. Hornblower	1893	Cleveland	Rejected, 1894
Wheeler H. Peckham	1894	Cleveland	Rejected
John J. Parker	1930	Hoover	Rejected
Abe Fortas[6]	1968	Johnson	Withdrawn
Homer Thornberry	1968	Johnson	No action
Clement F. Haynsworth, Jr.	1969	Nixon	Rejected
G. Harrold Carswell	1970	Nixon	Rejected
Robert H. Bork	1987	Reagan	Rejected
Douglas H. Ginsburg	1987	Reagan	Withdrawn

[1] A year is given if different from the year of nomination.

[2] Reappointed and confirmed.

[3] Nominated for chief justice.

[4] Taney was reappointed and confirmed as chief justice.

[5] Second appointment.

[6] Associate justice nominated for chief justice.

SOURCE: David M. O'Brien, *Storm Center: The Supreme Court in American Politics*, 3rd ed. (New York: Norton, 1993), 75. Reprinted by permission of W. W. Norton & Company, Inc.

The Battle over Judge Robert H. Bork

In 1987 a political battle erupted over President Ronald Reagan's nomination of Judge Robert H. Bork to fill the seat of Supreme Court justice Lewis F. Powell, Jr. Instead of becoming the 104th justice, Bork became the 28th Supreme Court nominee to be rejected or forced to withdraw because of opposition in the Senate. This confirmation battle underscored the Reagan administration's effort to make the Court a symbol and an instrument of the Reagan presidency, as well as the power of the Senate to defeat a nominee.

In nominating Bork, the president chose, over more moderate Republicans and conservative jurists, one of the most outspoken critics of the Warren and Burger courts. He did so despite the fact that Democrats had regained control of the Senate in 1986 and were prepared to oppose any nominee who was closely aligned with the right wing of the Republican party. Reagan underestimated the extent of this opposition, which was heightened by the pivotal nature of the appointment. The retiring justice, Lewis Powell, had often cast the crucial fifth vote in cases upholding such controversial issues as abortion and affirmative action programs.

The president's nomination of Bork was immediately denounced by Democratic senator Edward Kennedy of Massachusetts and by the chair of the Senate Judiciary Committee, Democratic senator Joseph Biden of Delaware. More than eighty-three organizations followed. Calling Bork "unfit" to serve on the high court, the American Civil Liberties Union abandoned its practice of not opposing nominees. The AFL-CIO also came out in opposition to Bork.

Right-wing organizations were no less active in support of Bork, though they were initially encouraged to downplay their support by White House chief of staff Howard Baker. Over the objections of the Justice Department, the White House adopted a strategy of recasting Bork's conservative record in order to make his opponents appear shrill and partisan. A 70-page White House briefing book was prepared, followed by a 240-page report released by the Justice Department; both attempted to portray Bork as a "mainstream" jurist.

The publicity was extraordinary. Numerous reports analyzing Bork's record were distributed to editorial boards around the country by both sides in the struggle. The People for the American Way, a liberal group, launched a $2-million media campaign opposing the nomination, and the National Conservative Political Action Committee committed over $1 million to lobbying for Bork's confirmation.

What had far greater impact, however, was Bork's own role in the preconfirmation fray and the confirmation proceedings. Even before the hearings began, Bork took the unusual step of granting newspaper interviews to explain, clarify, and amend his twenty-five-year record as a Yale Law School law professor, solicitor general, and judge. These actions broke with tradition and gave the appearance of a public relations campaign.

During his five days of nationally televised testimony before the Judiciary Committee, Bork continued to give the appearance of refashioning himself into a moderate, even "centrist," jurist. A key consideration thus became, in the words of Senator Patrick Leahy (D-Vermont), one of "confirmation conversion."

By the time Bork finished his thirty hours of testimony, he had contradicted much of what he had stood for in the past. Noting the "considerable difference between what Judge Bork has written and what he has testified he will do if confirmed," Arlen Specter, a Republican senator from Pennsylvania, observed, "I think that what many of us are looking for is some assurance of where you are." Even Bork seemed troubled, and at the end of his testimony he sought to assure the Senate that "It really would be preposterous to say things I said to you and then get on the Court and do the opposite. I would be disgraced in history."

Bork's testimony weighed far more than that of the 110 witnesses assembled for and against him in the following two weeks. To be sure, they contributed to the atmosphere of campaign politics that

Judge Robert H. Bork before the Senate Judiciary Committee on September 16, 1987, one day before the bicentennial of the U.S. Constitution.

surrounded the hearings. For the first time, a former president, Gerald Ford, introduced a nominee to the committee. And former president Jimmy Carter sent a letter expressing his opposition to the nomination. Nor had justices ever before come out as allies of a president or his nominee. Yet retired chief justice Warren Burger testified and justices John Paul Stevens and Byron White publicly endorsed Bork.

In spite of the publicity and pressure group activities, the hearings were illuminating. They focused on the nature of the Constitution. Is the Constitution defined by the intent of the framers, as the supporters of Bork maintained? Or is the Constitution a living document, one that has become more democratic through amendments and interpretations? In the end, this debate turned the tide against Bork in the Senate. Conservative southern Democrats and moderate Republicans joined liberal Democrats to oppose the nomination. The politics in their states, the position of their parties, and the opinion of a majority of the public would not have supported a return to an era in which civil rights and liberties were not protected as they are today.

Discussion questions

1. What role does and should the Senate play in the appointment of federal judges?
2. Has the appointment of Supreme Court justices become too politicized?
3. What standards should apply in the selection and confirmation of nominees to the federal bench?

Senate. The Senate Judiciary Committee then holds a **confirmation hearing** and recommends approval or rejection of nominees by a vote of the entire Senate.

The role of the ABA in the judicial appointment process has been important but also controversial. Since the ABA began reviewing the records of judicial nominees in 1955, the quality of the federal judiciary has generally improved. But the ABA has not altered the basic politics of judicial appointments. A former member of the ABA committee, Leon Jaworski, points out that the ABA typically functions as a "buffer" between the White House and the Senate. Senators may be told, "Well, the American Bar Association has turned [your candidate] down, who can we agree on now?"[16] However, at different times both liberals and conservatives have attacked the ABA's role in the judicial selection process. In the 1960s and 1970s liberals often criticized the ABA for having too many corporate lawyers on its judicial screening committee and not enough women, minorities, and lawyers with trial-court experience. By contrast, during the 1980s conservative groups and many Justice Department officials attacked the ABA for being too liberal and for its low ratings of potential judicial nominees. The conservative Washington Legal Foundation even sued to have the ABA's confidential process of evaluating potential nominees opened to the public under the Federal Advisory Committee Act. But in *Public Citizen v. U.S. Department of Justice* (1988) the Supreme Court held that the ABA was not covered by the act and that its participation in the judicial selection process did not violate the president's power to appoint federal judges.[17]

Some observers believe that religion, race, and gender have become more important considerations in judicial selection in recent years. But historically they have been barriers to appointment to the Court. The overwhelming majority (93) of the 107 justices have come from established Protestant religions. Of the remaining 14, 8 were Catholics and 6 were Jews. Justice Thurgood Marshall, who was appointed by President Lyndon Johnson in 1967, was the first African American to serve on the Court. When he retired in 1991, President George Bush named another African American, Judge Clarence Thomas, to fill his seat. In 1981 President Reagan fulfilled a campaign pledge to appoint the first woman to the Supreme Court, nominating Sandra Day O'Connor (see the profile of O'Connor on page 569). In 1986 Justice Antonin Scalia, Reagan's second appointee, became the first Italian American to serve on the Court.

The 1991 confirmation hearings into the nomination of Judge Clarence Thomas to the U.S. Supreme Court. Chairman Joseph Biden is seated at center; to his right is the then-ranking Republican senator, Strom Thurmond, and to his left is Senator Edward Kennedy.

© F. Lee Corkran/SYGMA

Sandra Day O'Connor: Centrist on the Court

When Sandra Day O'Connor received a law degree with distinction from Stanford University in 1952, she applied for jobs at a number of law firms. A woman in a field dominated by men, she was turned down everywhere. The firm in which William French Smith (later to become United States attorney general) was a partner offered her a secretarial job. O'Connor eventually went to work as deputy county attorney for San Mateo County in California. She and her husband later settled in Phoenix, Arizona, where they raised their children and she practiced law privately.

In 1965 O'Connor became an assistant attorney general in Arizona—the first woman appointed to the position. In 1969 she was appointed to the Arizona State Senate and won election on her own the next year. O'Connor served as a state senator for six years. For two of those years she was majority leader—the first woman in the country to hold this position of state legislative leadership. In 1974 O'Connor was elected a county judge, and in 1979 she was appointed to the Arizona Court of Appeals.

President Ronald Reagan nominated O'Connor to the Supreme Court of the United States in 1981 to replace the retiring Potter Stewart. She was confirmed by a 99-to-0 vote in the Senate on September 21, 1981, becoming the first woman justice.

In her first few years on the Court, Justice O'Connor was considered a conservative, usually voting along with Justice William Rehnquist. Within a few years, however, she established a center role for herself on many Court decisions. She has often provided the critical fifth vote needed to swing the outcome in one direction or another. In the areas of affirmative action and gender discrimination, for ex-

© Steve Northupa/Black Star

Justice O'Connor speaking in July, 1987.

ample, Justice O'Connor has been particularly important. It was she who wrote for a bare majority in setting new guidelines for affirmative action in *City of Richmond v. J.A. Croson* (1989). Her middle-of-the-road interpretation of the Fourteenth Amendment allows the states and localities to mandate affirmative action programs only as a remedy for their past discriminatory practices, and forbids them from adopting such programs simply because of prior discrimination by society in general.

Justice O'Connor's influence on gender discrimination cases has led to the Court's declaration that sexual harassment and sexual stereotyping are forms of gender discrimination and thus illegal. She has also lent her weight to decisions supporting government attempts to mandate equal opportunity for women in the workplace. Although Justice O'Connor has generally voted in support of restrictions on abortion, she continues to support the basic principle of *Roe v. Wade*.

Considerations such as religion, race, and gender are politically symbolic and largely reflect changes in the electorate. In the future such considerations are likely to compete with expectations for more ethnic representation, particularly from among Hispanics and Asians. Still, they are likely to remain less important than personal and ideological compatibility in presidents' attempts to "pack" the Court with justices who share their political views.

Packing the Court

How successful are presidents in packing the Court? Most succeed to some degree. Others fail, and some completely misjudge their appointees.

Democratic president Franklin Roosevelt succeeded more than most. He made eight new appointments and elevated Justice Harlan Stone to the position of chief justice. Roosevelt had bitterly attacked the Court for invalidating most of his early New Deal program. In 1937 he went so far as to propose expanding the size of the Court from nine to fifteen so that he could appoint justices who supported his economic policies. The Senate defeated this Court-packing plan. Later, however, when vacancies occurred on the Court, Roosevelt succeeded in appointing his supporters and thereby turning a conservative Court into a more moderately liberal one.

Almost thirty years later, Republican president Richard Nixon achieved some success in remolding the Court in his image. Whereas FDR had attacked the conservative Court in the 1930s, Nixon vehemently opposed the "liberal jurisprudence" of the Court as expressed in its rulings on school desegregation and criminal procedures. However, Nixon's appointments of Chief Justice Warren Burger and justices Harry Blackmun, Lewis Powell, and William Rehnquist failed to turn the Court completely around. Under Chief Justice Burger the Court was increasingly fragmented, with votes often divided 6 to 3 or 5 to 4, and it was pulled in different directions by either its most liberal or its most conservative members.

In the 1980 and 1984 presidential campaigns, Ronald Reagan promised to appoint only justices who were opposed to abortion and to the judicial activism that had characterized the Court under chief justices Earl Warren and Warren Burger. No other president since Roosevelt has had as great an impact on the federal judiciary. Before leaving the Oval Office in 1989, Reagan appointed close to half of all lower-court judges and elevated William H. Rehnquist to chief justice, as well as three other justices to the Supreme Court.

Although he was hugely successful in appointing lower-court judges, Reagan failed to win over a majority of the Court to his positions on abortion, affirmative action, and other hotly contested issues until Justice Lewis Powell stepped down in June 1987. Powell held the pivotal vote; during his last two terms the justices split 5 to 4 in eighty-one cases, with Powell having the deciding vote over 75 percent of the time. Powell also cast the crucial fifth vote in cases rejecting the Reagan administration's positions on abortion, affirmative action, and some other social policy issues.

With Powell's departure, Reagan had a chance to move the Court in a more conservative direction. His first nominee for Powell's seat, Judge Robert Bork, was defeated after a bitter confirmation battle. His second, Judge Douglas H. Ginsburg, was forced to withdraw after revelations about his personal affairs turned Republican senators against him. Fortunately for Reagan, his third nominee, Judge Anthony M. Kennedy, won easy confirmation. Although Kennedy was not the kind of justice that officials in the Justice Department hoped would "lock in the Reagan Revolution," there is no doubt that he and Reagan's other appointees brought a new conservatism to the Court. George Bush in turn appointed two more conservative justices, David H. Souter and Clarence Thomas. In 1993, when Justice Byron White retired, Bill Clinton became the first Democratic president in over twenty-five years to fill a vacancy on the

1789: CONGRESS DECIDED AT FIRST TO FIX THE NUMBER OF JUSTICES AT SIX.

1801: CONGRESS PLANNED ON A CHANGE TO FIVE, BUT THE SIX REMAINED VERY MUCH ALIVE.

1807: SIX HIGH JUDGES, SUPREME AS HEAVEN — AND JEFFERSON ADDED NUMBER SEVEN.

1837: SEVEN HIGH JUDGES, ALL IN A LINE — TWO MORE ADDED, AND THAT MADE NINE.

1863: NINE HIGH JUDGES WERE SITTING WHEN LINCOLN MADE THEM AN EVEN TEN.

1866: TEN HIGH JUDGES, VERY SEDATE; WHEN CONGRESS GOT THROUGH THERE WERE ONLY EIGHT.

1869: EIGHT HIGH JUDGES WHO WOULDN'T RESIGN; GRANT BROUGHT THE FIGURE BACK TO NINE.

1937: WOULD A JUSTICE FEEL LIKE A PACKED SARDINE IF THE NUMBER WAS RAISED TO — SAY — FIFTEEN?

HERBLOCK

"Historical Figures" © 1937 Herblock Cartoon

A famous cartoon by Herblock that appeared in 1937, when Democratic President Franklin D. Roosevelt wanted to expand the Court to secure a majority of justices favorable to the New Deal. The Court's size has changed a number of times because of presidential and congressional attempts to alter its direction.

Court. He elevated Judge Ruth Bader Ginsburg from the federal appellate bench to that position. At age sixty, the former law professor was at the forefront of the women's movement in the 1970s. Appointed to the federal bench by President Jimmy Carter in 1980, she established a reputation as a moderate jurist and a consensus builder. Justice Ginsburg became the second female and the sixth Jewish justice, bringing the total number of justices to sit on the Court to 107.

Through their appointments, presidents may influence the direction of future Supreme Court policy making, but there is no guarantee that they will succeed. Prior to his elevation to chief justice in 1986, Justice Rehnquist gave

In 1991, Justice Byron White (right) *administered the "Judicial Oath" to Justice Clarence Thomas. Standing behind them are Barbara and President George Bush and Justice Thomas's wife, Virginia Lamp.*

a speech at the University of Minnesota in which he indicated some of the reasons why:

Neither the President nor his appointees can foresee what issues will come before the Court during the tenure of the appointees, and it may be that none had thought very much about these issues. Even though they agree as to the proper resolution of current cases, they may well disagree as to future cases involving other questions when, as judges, they study briefs and hear arguments. Longevity of the appointees, or untimely deaths such as those of Justice [Frank] Murphy and Justice [Wiley B.] Rutledge [both died in 1949], may also frustrate a President's expectations; so also may the personal antagonisms developed between strong willed appointees of the same President.[18]

Judges and justices are independent and sometimes disappoint the presidents who appointed them. Republican president Dwight D. Eisenhower, for one, was profoundly disappointed by his selection of Chief Justice Earl Warren and Justice William J. Brennan, Jr., because of their liberal rulings. And Justice Oliver Wendell Holmes drew the ire of President Theodore Roosevelt by voting against the administration's antitrust policies. As the president put it, he "could carve out of a banana a Judge with more backbone than that!"[19] In 1992 many former Reagan-Bush administration officials and supporters were surprised and disappointed when justices O'Connor, Kennedy, and Souter formed a bare majority with justices Blackmun and Stevens to uphold "the essence" of *Roe v. Wade,* the controversial ruling on a woman's right to have an abortion, in *Planned Parenthood of Southeastern Pennsylvania v. Casey.*

THE SUPREME COURT

The Supreme Court is perhaps the least understood government institution in the United States. Although the public may attend oral arguments and the

Court's rulings are handed down in the form of published opinions, a tradition of secrecy surrounds the justices' decision making. The Court stands as a temple of law—an arbitrator of political disputes and an expression of the ideal of "a government of laws, not men." But it remains a fundamentally political institution. Behind the marble façade, the justices compete for influence.

The Court's annual term (or work year) begins on the first Monday in October and runs until the end of June. For most of this time, the justices are hidden from public view. They hear oral arguments only fourteen weeks a year—on Monday, Tuesday, and Wednesday—every two weeks from October through April. On Wednesday afternoons and again on most Fridays, they hold private conferences to decide which cases they will review and to make decisions on cases for which they have heard oral arguments. The rest of the time they work alone in their chambers with their law clerks, writing opinions and studying drafts of opinions circulated by other justices.

The Court's Caseload

The public learns about only a few of the Court's rulings each term. Usually only the most controversial decisions are given media coverage. The Court actually reviews and decides by written opinion between 120 and 140 cases each year. Still, that is less than 2 percent of the more than 7,000 cases filed and placed on the Court's **docket** each year. The vast majority of cases are denied review, leaving the lower-court rulings untouched.

The Court's caseload has grown (see Figure 15-2) and changed throughout its history. In the nineteenth century almost all cases came to the Court as mandatory appeals, which the justices had to decide. But as the caseload grew, Congress gave the Court the power to deny review. Congress eliminated most provisions granting rights of appeal and substituted **petitions for a writ of certiorari** (a petition requesting a court to order a review of the ruling of a lower

Chief Justice William H. Rehnquist with the Supreme Court's second female justice, Ruth Bader Ginsburg, just before the Court began its 1993 term on the first Monday in October.

© F. Lee Corkran/SYGMA

President George Bush reinforced the conservatism of the Reagan/Rehnquist Court when he nominated Judge David Souter to the high bench, three days after one of the most liberal justices, William Brennan, retired in July 1990. NOW and the Planned Parenthood Federation, among other groups, opposed the nomination, but the Senate confirmed it by a vote of 90 to 9.

Bush's nominee to replace Thurgood Marshall when he left the Court in 1991, however, caused an uproar. Clarence Thomas was a well-known black conservative judge whom the president had named a year earlier to the Court of Appeals for the District of Columbia Circuit in anticipation of Marshall's retirement.

Robert Trippett/Sipa Press

Women's groups, including NOW and the National Abortion Rights Action League (NARAL), immediately opposed Thomas. The civil rights community immediately split, the Congressional Black Caucus, the NAACP, the Leadership Conference on Civil Rights, and the AFL-CIO ultimately opposing him, and the National Urban League and the American Civil Liberties Union staying uncommitted. The American Bar Association rated Judge Thomas "qualified," though two committee members dissented and one abstained.

During his testimony before the Senate Judiciary Committee, Thomas sought to deflect criticism by emphasizing his "up-by-the-boot-straps" philosophy and personal struggle in overcoming the poverty of his youth. When asked about his prior writings, he gave closely guarded answers. He distanced himself from previous statements advocating a "natural law" approach to constitutional interpretation. And he steadfastly maintained, more than seventy times, that he had never seriously thought about the legitimacy of the controversial ruling in *Roe v. Wade* on a woman's right to choose an abortion. When Senator Howell Heflin (D-Alabama) noted a certain "conflict between what you've said in the past and what you've told us here," Republican senators Orrin Hatch, Alan Simpson, and Arlen Specter sprang aggressively to Thomas's defense. After two weeks of hearings, the judicial committee was deadlocked seven to seven. Finally it voted thirteen to one to send Thomas's nomination to the Senate without a recommendation.

Then several new allegations surfaced, including one that Thomas had sexually harassed a female assistant a decade earlier when he chaired the Equal Employment Opportunity Commission. Senator Joseph Biden had told several senators of these charges but had not fully investigated them, and then an FBI report was leaked to the press. Finally, law professor Anita Hill—Thomas's assistant at the EEOC—was forced to explain her charges.

Amid rising public anger over the accusations and counter-charges that Hill was part of a conspiracy to derail Thomas's confirmation, the all-white, all-male judiciary committee held hearings that pitted Hill against Thomas on national television. Hill cooly and confidently charged that in the early 1980s Thomas had harassed her, repeatedly pressed for dates, talked explicitly about pornographic movies, and created a hostile work environment. Thomas categorically denied the accusations and angrily protested that the confirmation process had become "a circus" and "a high-tech lynching for uppity blacks." "No job is worth it," he said. Thomas's supporters attacked Hill's motives. Senator Specter went so far as to charge her with "flat-out perjury."

The nasty drama of "she said, he said" raised larger issues of racism and sexism, but it failed to resolve the immediate questions about the veracity of either Hill or Thomas. The Senate voted 52 to 48 to confirm Thomas as the 106th justice.

SOURCE: Adapted from David O'Brien, *Storm Center: The Supreme Court in American Politics*, 3rd ed. (New York: Norton, 1993), 117–121. Reprinted by permission.

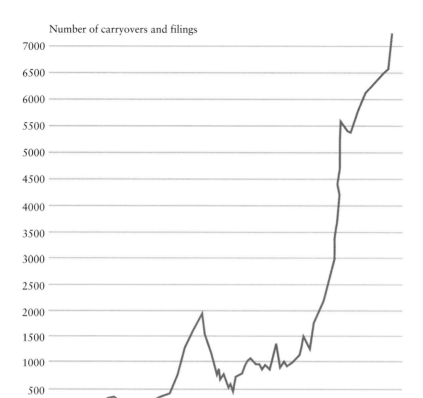

Figure 15-2 *Docket of and filings in the Supreme Court, 1800–1993.* SOURCE: *David M. O'Brien,* Storm Center: The Supreme Court in American Politics, *3rd ed. (New York: Norton, 1993), 190. Reprinted by permission of W. W. Norton & Company, Inc.*

court), which the Court may simply deny. Congress thus permitted the justices to determine which cases they would review. Figure 15-3 presents the main avenues of appeal to the Supreme Court. The box on page 577 describes the ways in which cases may be appealed to the Court.

The Court now exercises virtually absolute control over its caseload. The power to turn away cases enables it to limit the number of cases it reviews. The Court's discretionary power, moreover, enables it to pick what issues it wants to decide and when. In this sense the modern Supreme Court functions like a legislative body, setting its own agenda for adjudication and policy making.

When appeals or certiorari petitions arrive at the Court, they immediately go to the office of the clerk of the Court. There staff determines whether the petitions or appeals satisfy requirements for form and length and whether a filing fee of $300 has been paid. Over half of the petitions come from indigents. They must file with their briefs an *in forma pauperis* ("in the manner of a pauper") petition stating that they are too poor to pay the filing fee. The clerk of the Court then notifies the other party in the case that they must file a brief in response within thirty days. After receiving the briefs, the clerk circulates to the justices a list of cases that are ready for consideration and a set of briefs for each case.

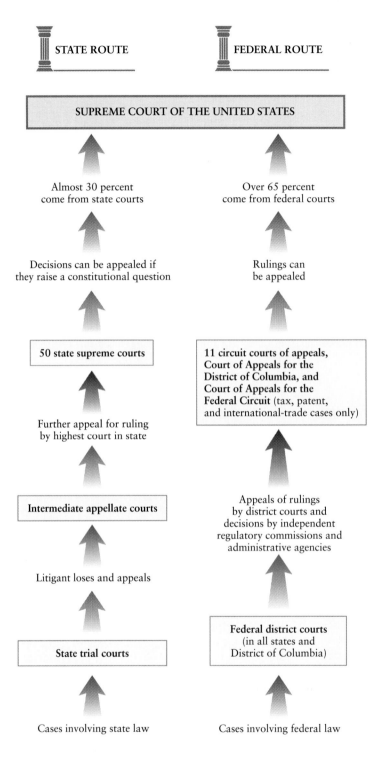

Figure 15-3   *Avenues of appeal to the Supreme Court.* SOURCE: *David M. O'Brien, Storm Center: The Supreme Court in American Politics, 3rd ed. (New York: Norton, 1993), 209. Reprinted by permission of W. W. Norton & Company, Inc.*

Ways of Appealing to the Supreme Court

Mandatory Appeal: A formal appeal for review, granted by congressional legislation. The Supreme Court must review and decide all appeals, but only a small fraction of all cases coming to the Court are on appeal.

Writ of Certiorari: A petition to the Supreme Court to order a lower court to send the record of a case to the Supreme Court for review. The Court has discretion to deny or grant petitions for certiorari. Over 90 percent of all cases coming to the Supreme Court are on certiorari.

Writ of Certification: A petition to the Supreme Court from a lower court asking that some question or interpretation of law be clarified, certified, and made more certain.

Writ of Habeas Corpus: A petition asking the Supreme Court to order officials holding a prisoner to justify the detention or release the person. Cases that assert a violation of constitutional rights and are appealed from state courts to the federal judiciary often come on writs of habeas corpus (Latin for "you have the body").

For much of the Court's history, each justice was responsible for reviewing every case; the justices did not delegate to others the responsibility for screening cases. That is no longer true. The justices now have their law clerks do virtually all the screening of cases. The law clerks write one- to two-page memos on each case, summarizing the facts and issues and recommending that the case be granted or denied. To further cut down the workload, eight members of the Court—all except Justice John Paul Stevens—have pooled their law clerks in what is called the "cert pool." These clerks divide up all the cases and write memos on each; the memos then circulate to the participating justices for their consideration.

Many observers question the propriety of delegating so much responsibility to law clerks, who are recent law school graduates and will serve for only one year before going on to teach at leading law schools or to join prestigious law firms. The justices counter that most cases are frivolous and that there is no other way to process the heavy caseload.

In the 1990s the Court signaled that it would no longer allow indigents to file petitions in cases that it deemed frivolous, denying several *in forma pauperis* petitions and amending its rules for granting cases. In one case, Michael Sindram was denied the right to file a petition requesting an order directing a state court to expedite his request to expunge a $35 speeding ticket from his record. Sindram was no stranger to the Court. In previous years he had filed forty-two separate petitions and motions on various matters. In denying Sindram's petition, the Court observed that "The goal of fairly dispensing justice . . . is compromised when the Court is forced to devote its limited resources to the processing of repetitious and frivolous requests."[20]

Deciding What to Decide

When the justices meet in conference, they vote on which cases to review. Prior to the conference the chief justice circulates two lists of cases. On the first—the Discuss List—are all the cases he thinks are worth considering, based on a review of the clerks' recommendations. Any justice may add other cases, but the list typically includes only forty to fifty cases. Attached is a second list—the Dead List—containing cases that are considered unworthy of discussion. Over 80 percent of all cases are unanimously denied without discussion, and most of those that make the Discuss List are denied as well. The conference lists are an important technique for saving time and focusing attention on the few cases deemed worthy of consideration.

The chief justice presides over conferences, as he does over oral arguments and all the Court's other public functions. At a conference he usually begins by summarizing each case and indicating why he thinks it should be accepted or denied. Discussion then passes from one justice to another in order of their seniority on the bench.

Although the Court decides all other matters by majority rule, the grant of review is based on the vote of four justices—the informal **rule of four**. Only a small number of the cases granted review, however, are actually accepted on this basis. For well over 70 percent of the cases accepted for review, a majority or more of the justices agree on the importance of the issues presented. The rule of four was adopted by the Supreme Court when Congress expanded the Court's discretionary power to pick the cases it accepts. The purpose was to assure Congress that important cases would be granted review even if less than a majority of the justices deemed them to present substantial questions of federal law. In addition, because less than a majority of the Court may grant review, the denial of a particular case is not considered a precedent that would be binding on lower courts.

Because of the Court's heavy docket, it does not grant cases in order to decide questions of fact, such as a person's guilt or innocence, or to correct mistakes made in lower courts. Instead, it takes cases that involve questions of law on which lower courts have disagreed. The Court thus tends to decide only cases that have national scope and involve significant controversies over public law and policy.

After a conference, the clerk of the Court is told which cases have been accepted or denied. The justices do not explain why they deny review of a case. This policy saves them time and enhances their flexibility. The Court may take up an issue in a later case without feeling bound by an earlier denial.

For the few cases that are granted review, the clerk notifies the litigants that they have thirty days to submit briefs on the **merits**—the questions to be decided. The clerk then sets a date for oral argument, usually about four months later.

Oral Argument

Oral argument is heard in fewer than 140 of the more than 7,000 cases on the Court's docket. Counsel once had unlimited time to present arguments; but as the caseload increased, the justices cut back on the time. Each case now gets only one hour—thirty minutes for each side. The Court hears four cases on oral argument days.

Oral argument days are virtually the only time that the public may see the justices. In a crowded courtroom, the marshal of the Court announces the sitting of the justices with the traditional introduction:

Oyez! Oyez! Oyez! All persons having business before the Honorable, the Supreme Court of the United States, are admonished to draw near and give their attention, for the Court is now sitting. God save the United States, and this Honorable Court.

The chief justice proceeds into the courtroom from behind the velvet curtains in back of the bench. The other justices follow and take their seats in order of seniority. Seating in the courtroom is limited to about 250 spectators. Visitors hear only three to four minutes of oral arguments before they are ushered out. Only by special request may members of the public hear entire arguments in a case. The press may hear all arguments, but no cameras are allowed in the courtroom when the Court is in session.

Oral arguments are the only opportunity attorneys have to communicate directly with the justices. The justices want crisp, concise, and conversational presentations. They do not want attorneys to read their briefs, and the time limit is strictly enforced. Chief Justice Charles Evans Hughes reportedly called time on a lawyer in the middle of the word *if*. The Court, however, is more tolerant now. As former chief justice Warren Burger once explained: "We allow a lawyer to finish a sentence that is unfolding when the red light goes on, provided, of course, the sentence is not too long."[21]

UPI/Bettmann

Chief Justice Warren Earl Burger resigned from the Court in 1986 to head the Commission on the Bicentennial of the U.S. Constitution. A principal aim of the commission was to educate Americans about the history of the Constitution, and here Burger accepts some books from Lynne Cheney, chair of the Reagan administration's National Endowment for the Humanities.

Supreme Court justices pursue many off-the-bench activities—giving speeches, attending meetings of the American Bar Association, and appearing before congressional committees. Here justices Byron White (center) and Antonin Scalia explain the federal judiciary's budget requests to the Senate Budget Committee in 1989.

Justices differ in their own preparation for oral arguments. Justice William O. Douglas insisted that "oral arguments win or lose a case," but Chief Justice Earl Warren found them "not highly persuasive." Most come prepared with **bench memos** drafted by their law clerks. The memos identify central facts, issues, and possible questions. Chief Justice Rehnquist and justices O'Connor, Scalia, and Stevens aggressively ask questions; the other justices usually say very little.

Discussing Cases and Voting in Conference

Within a day or two after oral arguments, the justices meet in secret conference to discuss and vote on the cases. The chief justice opens the discussion, which moves to each of the other justices in order of their seniority. For much of the Court's history the justices would vote in reverse order, the junior justice voting first so as not to be swayed by the votes of senior colleagues. But that practice has been abandoned. The heavier the caseload, the less time is available for conference discussions. Justices have only about three minutes to express their views and vote on each case. As a result, conferences involve less collective deliberation than was generally true in the past.

The justices' votes at conference are always tentative. Until the day the final decision comes down, justices may use their votes in strategic ways to influence the disposition of a case. They may threaten to switch their votes and refuse to join the Court's decision. Before, during, and after conference, justices thus bargain and negotiate the treatment of issues and the language of opinions. Justice Harlan F. Stone, for example, once candidly told Justice Frankfurter: "If you wish to write [the opinion] placing the case on the ground which I think tenable and desirable, I shall cheerfully join you. If not, I will add a few observations for myself."[22] On another occasion Justice James McReynolds gently appealed to Justice Stone: "All of us get into a fog now and then, as I know so well from my own experience. Won't you 'Stop, Look, and Listen'?"[23]

Opinion assignment is the first step in the process of opinion writing. After every two-week oral argument session, the chief justice assigns himself or one of the other justices to write an **opinion** for the Court on each case, provided that the justice selected voted with the majority during conference. By tradition, if the chief justice did not vote with the majority, the senior associate justice who was in the majority either writes the opinion or assigns it to another justice.

The power of opinion assignment presents significant opportunities for the chief justice to influence the final outcome of cases. In unanimous and landmark cases, chief justices often write opinions themselves. Chief Justice Earl Warren wrote the opinion striking down segregated schools in *Brown v. Board of Education* (1954). Chief Justice Warren Burger likewise delivered the opinion in *United States v. Nixon* (1974), rejecting President Nixon's claim of executive privilege to withhold tape recordings made in the Oval Office during the Watergate crisis.[24]

Chief justices usually try to see that all of the justices are assigned about the same number of opinions (thirteen to fifteen per year), both because of the workload and so as not to anger their colleagues. They may also make assignments on the basis of a justice's background and particular expertise or in anticipation of public reactions to a ruling. In addition, they sometimes ask the justice who is closest to the dissenters to write an opinion in the hope that other justices will switch their votes. Not surprisingly, the power of assigning opinions invites resentment and lobbying by other members of the Court.

Writing and circulating opinions is the justice's most difficult and time-consuming task. Although the justices differ in their styles and approaches to writing opinions, most delegate the preliminary drafting of opinions to their law clerks. Only after a justice is satisfied with an initial draft does it go to other justices for their reactions.

How long does opinion writing take? In the average case, Justice Tom Clark observed, about three weeks of work is required before an opinion is ready to circulate; "then the fur begins to fly."[25] It is not uncommon for a draft opinion to be revised three or four times and to circulate for three or four months before it becomes final. Justices may suggest minor editorial alterations or major substantive changes. Sometimes they will go to war over an opinion; at other times they may feel that a case is not worth fighting over. A few cases are so controversial that the justices reschedule them for oral argument and decision the next year. This was done with *Brown v. Board of Education* (1954) and *Roe v. Wade* (1973).

Opinions announcing the decision of the Court are not statements of the author's particular views of jurisprudence. Rather, they are negotiated documents forged from ideological divisions within the Court. The justice writing the Court's opinion must avoid pride of authorship and attempt to reach a compromise that will secure a majority and an **institutional opinion** for the Court's decision. If a justice fails to achieve this goal, the opinion is reassigned. For this reason, Justice Oliver Wendell Holmes often complained that the task of writing the Court's opinion was especially difficult; as he put it, "The boys generally cut one of the genitals out of mine, in the form of some expression that they think too free."[26]

What makes writing an opinion for the Court so difficult is that all of the

In 1993, when Justice Thurgood Marshall's working papers—including memos and draft opinions circulated by other justices—became available to the public, a majority of the Rehnquist Court created a minor controversy by pushing to curtail access to the papers, which they deemed a breach of confidentiality. Following retirement in 1991, Marshall donated his papers to the Library of Congress with the stipulation that, upon his death and "at the discretion of the Library," the collection be opened to "researchers or scholars engaged in serious research." Less than two years later Marshall died, and the Library opened his papers to the public.

At first, without controversy, only a few scholars studied the collection. But within a few months the *Washington Post* ran a three-part series of articles based on Marshall's memos. The articles portrayed the conservative shift of the Rehnquist Court and detailed how close the justices had come to overruling *Roe v. Wade* in *Webster v. Reproductive Health Services* (1989).

Chief Justice Rehnquist promptly protested the Library's "release [of] Justice Marshall's papers dealing with deliberations which occurred as recently as two terms ago," and he asked that the collection be closed. Claiming to "speak for a majority of the active Justices of the Court," he also threatened that "future donors of judicial papers will be inclined to look elsewhere for a repository." Congress held hearings on the matter, but the Library refused to yield, and Marshall's papers remain open.

Even more unprecedented was Justice William J. Brennan's making some of his papers available while still sitting on the bench. This angered several other sitting justices, because his collection also contains memos written by them and reveals their tentative thinking about cases, their attempts to influence each other, and the Court's inner workings.

Justices' papers also show that the Court as an institution has become more bureaucratic over recent decades, as seen in the increased number of law clerks, secretaries, and other personnel as well as in the addition of word-processing technology. The papers of justices Felix Frankfurter, Hugo Black, and William O. Douglas—who served thirty or fifty years ago—include many handwritten or typewritten letters and notes about pending cases and drafts of opinions circulated among the justices. But the collections of justices Brennan and Marshall provide fewer such correspondence. Instead, there are more memos from law clerks and communications from other justices that are often short and to the point, such as "Please join me in your opinion" or "I await the circulation of the dissent."

In 1990, as revealed in a memo from Marshall's papers, Justice Brennan defended his decision to allow scholars access to his papers. He did change his policies in response to colleagues' criticism and concerns about the Court's confidentiality; now he requires researchers to write in advance about their projects and to obtain his permission to use the papers. Moreover, a researcher's access to his papers is now limited to six months.

Justices, of course, differ about whether and when to make their papers available, and no rules or common practice govern what justices may do with their papers. About 40 percent of justices have destroyed their papers, particularly during the nineteenth century, but in this century justices have tended to give their papers to the Library of Congress or to the law school from which they graduated. Usually, their papers may not be made available for a period of time after their death, or until all the justices with whom they served have left the bench. In addition, Justice Hugo Black burned his docket books and conference notes before giving his files to the Library of Congress. Others, like Justice Douglas, also purged their collections of papers they deemed too sensitive, and they inserted personal notes for "posterity."

other justices are free to write their own individual opinions. They may write **concurring opinions**—opinions agreeing with the result reached by a majority but disagreeing with its reasons or legal analysis. Justices differ on the propriety of such opinions, which reflect failure or unwillingness to compromise. Some think that they are a sign of "institutional disobedience"; others believe that they are a valuable record of the justices' differing views. In any event, every justice now writes several concurring opinions each term.

Justices who disagree with the majority opinion usually write **dissenting opinions**. Dissenting opinions, in the words of Chief Justice Hughes, appeal "to the brooding spirit of the law, to the intelligence of a future day, when a later decision may possibly correct the error into which the dissenting judge believes the Court to have been betrayed."[27] Dissenting opinions undercut the Court's decision, and justices may use them as threats when trying to persuade the majority to narrow its holding or tone down its language. Some justices write more dissents than others, but all average about ten each term.

Opinion Days

Opinion days are the days when the Court hands down its final published opinions. On these days lawyers, the media, and the public finally learn the outcome of the justices' votes. The Court once announced opinions only on "Decision Mondays," but now it may do so on any day of the week. By tradition, there is no prior announcement as to when cases will be handed down. Instead of reading their opinions from the bench, as was once done, the justices simply announce their opinions in two to four minutes, merely stating the result in each case. Copies of opinions may be obtained from the offices of the clerk of the Court and the public information officer at the Court.

Supreme Court Decision Making as a Political Process

Decision making by the Supreme Court is a political process. The justices often follow their own political agendas when granting and deciding cases. Because the Court decides what cases to review on the basis of the vote of only four justices, the justices may form voting blocs to determine which cases will be granted review. But the justices decide the merits of those few cases by majority vote. In deciding those cases, the process of opinion writing is crucial to the final outcome and affords the justices opportunities to bargain and compromise with each other, as well as to write concurring or dissenting opinions.

The political struggles within the Court come to an end on opinion days, though the justices will continue to compete for influence and try to persuade each other to reconsider their views in other cases. Opinion days, however, may also mark the beginning of larger struggles for influence between the Court and rival political forces.

THE POLITICS OF JUDICIAL POLICY MAKING

The Court is an independent arbitrator of political conflicts. Through its decisions it legitimates one set of government policies or another, and in so doing it invites political controversy. But in most areas of public law and policy the fact that the Court makes decisions is more important than the decisions themselves. Much of the Court's work involves disputes over the interpretation and enforcement of statutes, and it is essential that those disputes be settled one way or another. Moreover, relatively few of the many controversies over domestic and foreign policy that arise in government actually reach the Court. Yet those few cases are almost always hard cases and politically controversial.

The Court decides conflicts over public law and policy by bringing them within the language, structure, and spirit of the Constitution. In this way the Court determines public policy. The struggles that follow are central to American politics. The key actors in that competition are the lower courts, Congress, the president, political interest groups, and ultimately the general public. Their reactions may enhance or thwart the implementation of the Court's rulings and determine the extent of compliance with judicial policy making.

Although the Court depends on lower courts to enforce its rulings, compliance is invariably uneven. The ambiguity of judicial opinions allows lower courts to pursue their own policy goals. Crucial language in an opinion may be treated like *dicta*—language that is not binding in other cases. Differences between the facts on which the Court ruled and the circumstances of another case may be emphasized so as to reach a result opposite to that reached by the Court. Lower courts, for example, interpreted *Abington School District v. Schempp* (1963), which struck down a law requiring the reciting of the Lord's Prayer in public schools, to permit voluntary and nondenominational prayer in public schools.[28] Likewise, state courts in Texas refused to extend the Court's ruling in *Norris v. Alabama* (1935) forbidding racial discrimination against blacks in the selection of juries.[29] They continued to allow the exclusion of Mexican Americans from juries until the Court finally ruled, in *Hernandez v. Texas* (1954), that all kinds of racial discrimination in jury selection violate the Fourteenth Amendment's equal protection clause.[30] In sum, open defiance is infrequent but not unprecedented. When it occurs, it reflects the differing policy preferences of state and federal judges.

On major issues of public policy Congress is likely to prevail or, at least, to temper the impact of the Court's rulings. Congress may pressure the Court in a number of ways. The Senate may try to influence future judicial appointments and may even try to impeach the justices. More often, Congress uses institutional and jurisdictional changes as weapons against the Court.

Congress has the power under Article III to "make exceptions" to the appellate jurisdiction of the federal courts. That authorization has been viewed as a way of denying courts the power to review certain kinds of cases. During the Reagan administration, for instance, there were numerous unsuccessful proposals to deny courts the power to decide cases involving school prayer and abortion. But Congress has succeeded only once in cutting back on the Court's jurisdiction; this occurred in 1868 with the repeal of the Court's jurisdiction over writs of habeas corpus (see the Constitutional Conflict on page 585).

Congress has somewhat greater success in reversing the Court by means of a constitutional amendment, which three-fourths of the states must ratify. The process is cumbersome, and thousands of amendments designed to overrule the Court have failed. But four Court decisions (see the box on page 586) have been overturned by constitutional amendments.

More successful are congressional enactments and the rewriting of legislation in response to the Court's rulings. In *Zurcher v. The Stanford Daily*

Does and should Congress have the power to deny the Supreme Court and lower federal courts the authority to decide cases that raise controversial issues such as abortion or prayer in public schools? The Constitution, in Article III, Section 2, says that "the Supreme Court shall have appellate jurisdiction, both as to law and fact, with such exceptions, and under such regulations, as the Congress shall make," and from time to time members of Congress claim that this "exceptions" clause gives Congress the power to curb the federal judiciary's jurisdiction over certain kinds of cases.

During the 1950s, a number of senators proposed legislation forbidding the Court to review cases challenging congressional investigations of un-American activities. A decade later, in response to the Supreme Court's rulings protecting the rights of the accused, other proposals were made that would have deprived the Court of the power to review certain state criminal cases. In 1979, the Senate passed by a vote of 51 to 40 an amendment eliminating federal court jurisdiction over school prayer cases, but the House of Representatives never considered the bill. And in the early 1980s several Republican senators unsuccessfully sought to deny federal courts jurisdiction over abortion controversies.

In fact, Congress has succeeded only once in limiting the Supreme Court's jurisdiction. In 1868 it repealed the Court's jurisdiction over writs of habeas corpus, and the Court upheld that restriction on its power in *Ex parte MacCardle* (1869). Because of the overwhelming failure of congressional attempts to strip the Court of jurisdiction, political scientists and legal scholars disagree about whether Congress may still claim the authority granted it in Article III. Some contend that Congress should continue to try to curb the Court in this way. Others counter that the Court could strike down a repeal of jurisdiction if it deprived the Court of the power to protect constitutional rights.

(1978), for example, the Court held that there is no constitutional prohibition against police searching newsrooms without a warrant for "mere evidence" of a crime, such as photographs.[31] Two years later, however, Congress basically reversed that ruling by passing the Privacy Protection Act of 1980, which prohibits unannounced searches of newsrooms and requires that police obtain a subpoena ordering writers to turn over desired evidence. So, too, Congress overrode more than a dozen rulings of the conservative Rehnquist Court when it enacted the Civil Rights Act of 1991. But Congress is not always successful in reversing the Court's decisions through legislation. In response to the Court's ruling in *Texas v. Johnson* (1989), which held that a state law prohibiting desecration of the American flag violated the First Amendment's guarantee of freedom of speech, Congress enacted the Flag Protection Act of 1989, which also forbade desecration of the flag.[32] But when that law was immediately challenged, the Court again defended the First Amendment and struck down that act in *United States v. Eichman* (1990).[33]

Congress cannot overturn the Court's interpretations of the Constitution through legislation, as the ruling in *United States v. Eichman* illustrates. But it can enhance or thwart the implementation of the Court's rulings. For example, Congress delayed implementation of the school desegregation decision in *Brown v. Board of Education* (1954) by not authorizing the executive branch to enforce the ruling until the passage of the Civil Rights Act of 1964. Later,

Chisholm v. Georgia (1793), holding that citizens of one state could sue another state in federal court, was reversed by the Eleventh Amendment, guaranteeing sovereign immunity for states from suits by citizens of another state.

Dred Scott v. Sanford (1857), ruling that blacks were not citizens under the Constitution, was technically overturned by the Thirteenth and Fourteenth Amendments, abolishing slavery and making blacks citizens of the United States.

Pollock v. Farmer's Loan and Trust Co. (1895), invalidating a federal income tax, was reversed in 1913 with the ratification of the Sixteenth Amendment.

Oregon v. Mitchell (1970), in which a bare majority of the Court held that Congress could not lower the voting age for state and local elections, was reversed in less than a year by the Twenty-sixth Amendment, extending the franchise to 18-year-olds in all elections.

by cutting back on appropriations for the Department of Justice and the Department of Health, Education, and Welfare during the Nixon and Ford administrations, Congress registered opposition to busing and further attempts to achieve integrated public schools.

Presidents may undercut the Court's policy making as well. By issuing contradictory directives to federal agencies and assigning low priority to enforcement by the Department of Justice, they may limit the impact of the Court's decisions. Presidents may also make broad moral appeals in response to the Court's rulings, and those appeals may transcend a president's limited time in office. For example, the Court put school desegregation and abortion on the national agenda, but it was President Kennedy's appeal for civil rights that captivated a generation and encouraged public acceptance of the Court's rulings. Similarly, President Reagan's opposition to abortion served to legitimate resistance to the Court's decisions in this area.

When it threatens to go too far or too fast in its policy making, the Court is ultimately curbed by public opinion. Except during transitional periods or critical elections, however, the Court has usually been in step with major political and social movements.[34] Moreover, the public tends to perceive the Court as a temple of law rather than of politics—as impartial and removed from the pressures of special or partisan interests. But the public also tends to understand little about the operation of the Court, and for this reason only about 30 percent of Americans express "great confidence" in the Court.

Public opinion about the Supreme Court also tends to fluctuate with public reactions to government as a whole. Issues like school desegregation, school prayer, and abortion focus public attention and mobilize political interest groups in support of or in opposition to the Court. But those issues are also the most likely to sharply divide public opinion while fueling political struggles at all levels of government. Thus, in the late 1960s, public confidence in the Court declined when the Court was widely criticized for handing down rulings guaranteeing the rights of the accused. In the early 1970s, the Court's standing improved, largely because a "crisis in confidence" in the presidency resulted from the Nixon administration's involvement in the Watergate episode and attempts to cover up other illegal activities. In the 1980s, public confidence in the Court increased further as confidence in government grew owing to the influence of highly popular President Reagan.

Some Court watchers warn of an "imperial judiciary" and a "government by the judiciary."[35] They point out that judicial review is antidemocratic because it enables the Court to overturn laws enacted by the popularly elected legislatures. But the Court's duty is to interpret the Constitution, and compliance with and enforcement of the Court's rulings depend on the cooperation of other political institutions as well as on public acceptance. Major confrontations over public policy are determined as much by what is possible in a pluralistic society with a system of free government as by what the Court says about the meaning of the Constitution.[36] That is the essence of politics in a constitutional democracy.

SUMMARY

The United States has two separate judicial systems, federal and state; this dual system is termed *judicial federalism*. If there is a conflict between national and state law, the matter is settled by the federal courts and ultimately by the Supreme Court.

Article III of the Constitution vests judicial power in the Supreme Court and any other courts created by Congress. Courts created under Article III are *constitutional courts*. Under Article I Congress may also create specialized courts like the United States Court of Military Appeals. Courts created under Article I are *legislative courts*.

In 1789 Congress divided the country into thirteen districts and created a federal *district court* for each; these are the trial courts of the federal system. Congress also created federal *courts of appeals* to hear appeals from decisions of the district courts. Today the federal judiciary consists of ninety-four district courts, thirteen courts of appeals, and the Supreme Court.

There is at least one federal district court in each state, and each district court has at least one judge. These courts may also employ grand juries to indict individuals for crimes and petit juries to try those individuals. A substantial number of federal criminal defendants do not go to trial because they plead guilty, often as a result of plea bargaining.

Those who do go to trial are tried in an adversary process in which the two sides argue the case and the jury determines which side has done so more convincingly.

Judges on the federal courts of appeals sit in rotating panels of three and decide most cases on the basis of written *briefs* submitted by the litigants. Occasionally the entire court sits as a panel, or *en banc*.

The Supreme Court hears cases from state courts only if the cases deal with *federal questions*, or issues involving the interpretation of the Constitution or other federal laws. Under the *principle of comity* the Court does not review cases decided on *independent state grounds* such as a state constitution.

The *jurisdiction* of a court determines the kinds of cases and controversies it may decide. The Supreme Court has *original jurisdiction* in cases involving disputes between two or more states and cases brought against the United States by foreign ambassadors; such cases originate in the Supreme Court. The majority of the cases that come to the Court arrive under its *appellate jurisdiction*: they are appealed from lower federal courts and state courts.

Courts have jurisdiction only over disputes involving adverse interests and a real controversy. The parties must have *standing to sue*; they must show that they are suffering or are in danger of suffering an immediate and substantial personal injury. Courts avoid deciding *political questions* that the judges think should be resolved by other branches of government. Disputes that are open to judicial resolution are referred to as *justiciable disputes.*

The power of judicial review gives the courts the ability to strike down any law enacted by Congress or by the states and to declare official government actions unconstitutional. Judicial review is controversial because it enables the Supreme Court to thwart the democratic process. Nevertheless, the Court has increasingly asserted this power. It has been criticized for its *judicial activism* and urged to exercise *judicial self-restraint*—to defer to Congress and state legislatures.

The selection of state court judges varies from one state to another. Some judges are elected. Others are appointed under a *merit system* in which a nonpartisan commission provides a list of possible nominees. Appointments of federal judges are made by the president with the advice and consent of the Senate. The president often encounters considerable senatorial opposition to his nominations of Supreme Court justices, who are usually political associates and individuals who share his political views.

Candidates for federal judgeships are investigated by the FBI and evaluated by the American Bar Association. The Senate Judiciary Committee then holds a *confirmation hearing* and recommends approval or rejection of nominees by a vote of the entire Senate. The overwhelming majority of the justices appointed to the Supreme Court have been white Protestant men.

Some presidents have been more successful in "packing" the Court than others. Franklin Roosevelt was unable to change the size of the Court, but he succeeded in appointing enough of his supporters to turn a conservative Court into a liberal one. Presidents Nixon and Reagan appointed several conservative justices, thereby shifting the Court away from the "liberal jurisprudence" of earlier decades.

The Supreme Court decides less than 3 percent of the cases placed on its *docket* each year. Most cases come to the Supreme Court through petitions for *certiorari*, which request the Court to review the ruling of a lower court; it may deny such a petition. The grant of review is based on the vote of four justices (the *rule of four*), but usually a majority of the justices vote for the grant. The Court takes only cases that involve questions of law on which lower courts have disagreed. Litigants then submit briefs on the *merits*—the questions to be decided.

The Court hears oral arguments in fewer than 150 cases a year. Each side has thirty minutes to present its arguments. Most justices use *bench memos* to prepare for oral arguments. Within a day or two after oral arguments, the justices meet in secret conference to discuss and vote on the case. The chief justice then assigns one of the justices to write an *opinion* for the Court on the case. The justice writing the opinion must attempt to reach a compromise that will serve as an *institutional opinion* stating the reasons for the Court's decision. The other justices are free to write *concurring opinions*, which agree with the decision but for different reasons, or *dissenting opinions.*

The Court decides conflicts by bringing them within the language, structure, and spirit of the Constitution. In this way it determines public policy. The reactions of other institutions of government and the public may enhance or thwart the implementation of the Court's rulings. Congress can temper the impact of a ruling by means of jurisdictional changes, through a constitutional amendment, or by rewriting legislation. The president can undercut the Court by issuing contradictory directives to federal agencies or assigning low priority to enforcement. Ultimately, however, the Court is curbed by public opinion.

judicial federalism
constitutional courts
legislative courts
district courts
courts of appeals
brief
en banc
federal question
independent state grounds
principle of comity

jurisdiction
original jurisdiction
appellate jurisdiction
standing to sue
political question
justiciable dispute
judicial activism
judicial self-restraint
merit system
confirmation hearing

docket
certiorari
rule of four
merits
bench memo
opinion
institutional opinion
concurring opinion
dissenting opinion

Scholarly studies

Abraham, Henry. *The Judicial Process.* 6th ed. New York: Oxford University Press, 1993. A standard and widely read introduction to the judicial process from a comparative perspective.

Cannon, Mark, and David M. O'Brien, eds. *Views from the Bench: The Judiciary and Constitutional Politics.* Chatham, N.J.: Chatham House, 1985. A collection of writings by justices and judges on the role and function of courts as well as theories of constitutional interpretation.

Gates, John, and Charles Johnson, eds. *The American Courts: A Critical Assessment.* Washington, D.C.: Congressional Quarterly, 1991. A good overview of the social science literature on judicial policy making.

O'Brien, David. *Storm Center: The Supreme Court in American Politics.* 3rd ed. New York: Norton, 1993. A detailed institutional history of Supreme Court politics.

Rosenberg, Gerald. *The Hollow Hope: Can Courts Bring About Social Change?* Chicago: University of Chicago Press, 1991. A well-written, provocative study that argues that courts cannot bring about massive social change.

Leisure reading

Craig, Barbara, and David M. O'Brien. *Abortion and American Politics.* Chatham, N.J.: Chatham House, 1993. A balanced examination of how the abortion controversy has played out in interest group politics, public opinion polls, the states, Congress, the presidency, and the Courts from *Roe v. Wade* (1973) to *Planned Parenthood of Southeastern Pennsylvania v. Casey* (1992).

Lewis, Anthony. *Gideon's Trumpet.* New York: Random House, 1989. A classic discussion of the watershed ruling on the right to counsel and an excellent introduction to the judicial process.

Primary sources

Congressional Quarterly. *Guide to the United States Supreme Court.* 2nd ed. Washington, D.C.: Congressional Quarterly, 1989. A comprehensive reference work on the Supreme Court and its processes and history.

Organizations

Administrative Office of the United States Courts, Thurgood Marshall Federal Judiciary Building, One Columbus Circle, N.E., Washington, DC 20544; (202) 273-3000. Conducts some research and collects data on federal caseloads; is responsible for the administration of the federal courts.

Federal Judicial Center, Thurgood Marshall Federal Judiciary Building, One Columbus Circle, N.E., Washington, DC 20002; (202) 273-4000. Conducts research and training programs for the federal judiciary and publishes a newsletter, *The Third Branch.*

Public Information Office, Supreme Court of the United States, One 1st Street, Washington, DC 20543; (202) 223-2584. Distributes opinions of the Court and occasional speeches by the justices.

Supreme Court Historical Society, 111 2nd Street, N.E., Washington, DC 20002; (202) 543-0400. Collects materials related to the history of the Supreme Court and funds research projects. Publishes newsletters and *The Yearbook of the Supreme Court Historical Society.*

Politics and

Public Policy

16

The Policy-Making Process

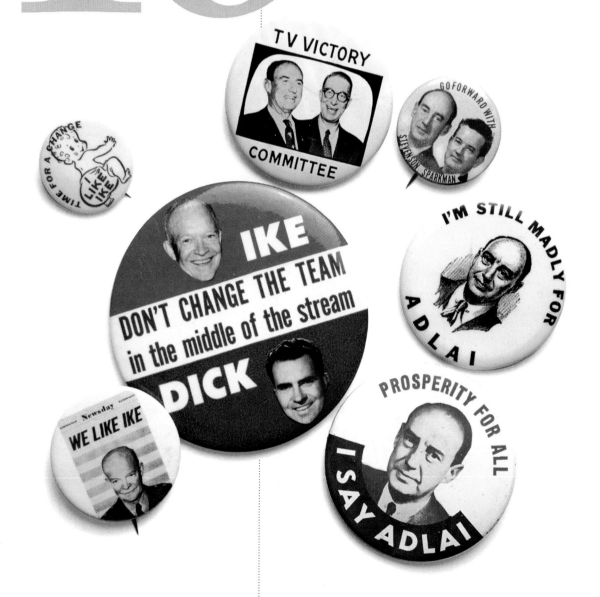

- Types of policy: issue-based and impact-based classification

- Stages in the policy-making process: problem recognition; policy formulation, adoption, implementation, evaluation, and termination

- Politics and the policy process: incrementalism; major policy shifts; mixed results

In both 1952 and 1956, Governor Adlai E. Stevenson of Illinois took aim at Republican Dwight David Eisenhower, whose choice of running mate in 1952 was Richard M. Nixon. Although these campaigns embraced many issues, including the Korean War and racial segregation, the results were not in doubt, because Americans did "Like Ike." Peace with prosperity was one Republican theme in 1956, along with "Don't change the team." As shown by the pin at top center, television was coming into its own in the 1950s, but it was not until the 1960s that TV became a significant campaign medium.

In June 1989 President George Bush declared that the 1990s would be "the era for clean air" and submitted to Congress major amendments to the country's clean-air policies. The president's proposals were designed to reduce acid rain, smog, and toxic pollution. "A sound ecology and a strong economy" are not mutually exclusive, the president said. "[Now is the time] when environmental issues move out of the courts, beyond conflict, into a new era of cooperation."

In spite of Bush's pleas for cooperation, almost a year and a half of intense wrangling among White House officials, congressional leaders, industry representatives, and environmentalists elapsed before the new clean-air bill finally was passed. When Congress began seriously considering the clean-air proposal in the spring of 1990, it found advocates for and against stronger clean-air regulations prepared to wage war. Industry groups spent millions of dollars on lobbying designed to persuade members of Congress to ease the bill's regulations and on public relations designed to convince the American public of the dangers of the legislation. A report prepared by the Business

Roundtable, a group representing two hundred corporations, concluded that industry would have to pay annual pollution control costs of as much as $104 billion under the proposals being considered. Phillip Maseiantonio, a spokesperson for USX Corporation, called the clean-air amendment proposals "a multimillion-dollar millstone around the neck of industry which would have serious side effects, namely reduced industrial production, job losses, employment dislocations, and possibly even shutdowns of industry."

Environmental groups countered by urging Congress to approve even stricter clean-air provisions than Bush had called for. A report distributed to Congress by the American Lung Association concluded that unless strong measures were passed, Americans would face additional medical costs of from $40 to $50 billion a year. A consultant for environmental groups stated, "We're talking here of lives cut short" by pollution-related illnesses.

Within Congress there was rancorous debate. Representative John Dingell (D-Michigan), widely seen as a strong defender of the automobile industry, declared that "the motor vehicle industry is under siege." But Senator George Mitchell (D-Maine), a strong supporter of strict clean-air laws, stated that "cheap solutions will only increase the pricetag for those adversely affected by pollution and those who later have to pay to clean it up."

As Senate majority leader, Mitchell was particularly important in forging a compromise bill that was stronger in some respects than the one President Bush had proposed but weaker than the one environmentalists wanted. Senator Mitchell's influence was made clear when Senator Christopher Dodd (D-Connecticut) refused to lend his support to an amendment opposed by Mitchell. When asked to explain his position, Dodd responded, "I'll tell you in one word: child care." By this

Senator Dodd was saying that Majority Leader Mitchell might threaten to use his powerful position to block a child-care bill that Senator Dodd considered very important unless he fully supported Senator Mitchell's proposal. Mitchell "used every ounce of his energy to cajole senators and come up with imaginative solutions," commented Senator Thomas Daschle (D-South Dakota).

A compromise bill was hammered out in a month of closed-door negotiations between White House and Senate leaders, and in April 1990 the Senate passed the Clean Air Act by a vote of 89 to 11. The compromise bill drew criticism from industry spokespersons (who argued that the costs to business were too high and would result in the loss of jobs) and from environmentalists (who complained that the bill was not tough enough). Senator Mitchell himself admitted that the process of guiding clean-air legislation through the Senate was "the most difficult and demanding thing I have ever been involved in."

Even as President Bush signed the new clean-air bill into law (in November 1990), saying that every American "deserves to breathe clean air," sharp criticism continued from industry and environmental groups. Industry spokespeople pointed to the high costs of implementing the bill. "The costs to American consumers and workers [of this act] cannot be sugarcoated. The American consumer and ratepayer better brace themselves for the cost of this bill," declared William Fay, representative of a coalition of two thousand business and trade associations. Environmentalists were particularly critical of what they believed to be the legislation's soft stand on automobile pollution. Albert F. Appleton, New York City's environmental protection commissioner, seemed to sum up the feeling of many environmentalists when he declared, "Automobiles, one; clean air, nothing."

THE STRUGGLE FOR CLEAN-AIR LEGISLATION illustrates several aspects of policy making in America. First, policy making is almost never "beyond conflict," to use President Bush's words. Policy making is a struggle between groups advocating one side or another. This struggle is especially intense when the stakes are high, and it does not always end with the passage of legislation. Second, private interest groups are critical in the policy-making process. They play important roles in formulating and adopting various policy positions and in shaping public opinion. The example of environmental legislation also shows that although the policy-making process rarely leaves everyone completely satisfied, compromise is essential if the process is to succeed. Finally, this example shows the importance of politics in the policy-making process. A certain amount of bargaining, negotiating, and old-fashioned arm twisting is often critical to the adoption of new policy initiatives.[1]

How do issues like air pollution become part of the national political agenda? How do they come to be viewed as important enough to warrant attention and consideration by the political system? How is government persuaded to act on public issues? These are the questions examined in this chapter.

TYPES OF POLICY

Public policy is action by government designed to address public problems. Simply stated, public policy is what government does (or does not do). In a more formal sense, public policy can be said to be "a goal-directed or purposive course of action [taken by government] in an attempt to deal with a public problem."[2] This definition focuses on the actual *accomplishments* of government.

Legislators, presidents, bureaucrats, and judges all may express an idea or a hope that some goals will be accomplished. Decision makers often express a commitment to eliminate poverty or provide equal educational opportunities,

© Ted Spiegel/Black Star

The quality of the nation's air has improved somewhat since passage of the 1990 Clean Air Act, the most aggressive and comprehensive attack on urban pollution. Shown here is Denver, in 1987. The 1991 Transportation Law provided $6 billion for mass transit and other programs designed to reduce automobile emissions in cities.

Homeless in St. Louis, 1993. While homelessness seems to be increasing, policy makers disagree about causes and solutions. Some see an improving economy as the cure; others want to provide more affordable public housing. Housing Secretary Henry Cisneros has presented a plan to convert many HUD-subsidized housing units into shelters for the homeless.

to protect American interests abroad or make adequate health care available for all Americans. Broad statements like these may be significant for the development and understanding of public policy; however, the study of public policy is about actual accomplishments. What is government *actually doing* to reduce poverty, provide equal educational opportunities, or expand health care?

Public policies may be classified in a number of ways. Some experts classify them in terms of who pays the cost of the program. Some classify them in terms of who benefits. Others focus on issues or on social impacts.

Issue-Based Classification

Charles O. Jones offers a classification based on "bundles of controversial public problems."[3] Jones's classification focuses on issues and therefore is consistent with how Americans ordinarily think of policy problems. If asked to name the most important problems facing the country, Americans would come up with a list of concerns similar to Jones's (although, of course, they might vary in how they ranked the importance of each concern). An examination of the federal budget also would indicate expenditures in areas similar to those on Jones's list.

Jones's classification makes it clear that the significance of various policy areas changes over time. During the 1960s and early 1970s, civil rights and foreign and defense issues (particularly the Vietnam War) were dominant policy concerns. During the 1970s, energy was a major concern, and in the 1980s—especially during the Reagan presidency—government organization and economic recovery issues received much attention. Today, health care, environmental degradation, illegal drug sales and use, and homelessness are considered major problem areas.

Impact-Based Classification

Classification of policies in terms of their impacts on society sheds light on the political strategies associated with different policies. An example of this approach is Theodore Lowi's classification of policies as distributive, regulatory, or redistributive.[4]

Distributive policies are those that distribute goods and services to citizens. Policies that provide recreational, public safety, transportation, and educational services are examples of distributive policies. Distributive policies also include subsidies to farmers, the Social Security program, the interstate highway system, grants for scientific research, grants-in-aid to cities and states, tax deductions for interest on home mortgage loans, and the construction of harbors, reservoirs, and dams. The important point about distributive policies is that although some group or groups may gain something, the costs associated with the policy are viewed as minimal because they are shared by the public as a whole. Even national defense is sometimes regarded as a distributive policy, because lucrative defense contracts are distributed among the districts of many members of Congress.

In distributive policy making everyone seems to win; no one appears to lose, or at least no one appears to lose very much. The politics of distributive policy making is generally described as "pork-barrel politics"—there is something for everyone, and individual legislators will support each other's particular programs. Although such programs may cost billions of dollars, they generate surprisingly little controversy.

Regulatory policies are those through which the government establishes

Courtesy of the State Historical Society of North Dakota

The Ludwig Welk homestead in Strasburg, North Dakota—including a life-sized figure of bandleader Lawrence Welk—was the focus of congressional wrangling in 1991. Representative Jim Slattery of Kansas led the House in repealing $500,000 of rural development grants for this project, which was viewed as "pork-barrel politics." But Welk's sod-block home had been restored with private funds, and the grant was to be used for a visitors' center and educational exhibits, which would bring jobs to the area.

rules and standards and thereby regulates or controls behavior. Regulatory policies often are developed in response to practices that are deemed harmful or destructive. Examples of regulatory policies include laws that regulate child labor, automobile emissions, minimum wages, harmful additives in food, and the dumping of industrial wastes in streams and rivers. Regulatory policy making generally is associated with intense lobbying as groups attempt to influence the passage of legislation advantageous to them. Regulatory politics may be described as "compromise politics": in order to get any legislation passed, legislators often must compromise on some of the most extreme measures.

Redistributive policies are those that are clearly perceived to take benefits (wealth, property, or other values) from some groups and give them to others. Some wealthy people view welfare programs as taking resources from them in order to fund programs that benefit poorer people. Some Anglos view policies designed to enhance the voting strength and participation of minorities as taking power from them. Policy making on such questions can be seen as a zero-sum game—one group will win, and another will lose. Redistributive policies are therefore least amenable to compromise. Usually there are two consistent and clearly identifiable sides. Liberals and conservatives line up on opposite sides of the issue, and rhetoric is intense on both sides. The politics of redistributive policy making often is described as "class politics." Those with many resources are battling those with few.

STAGES IN THE POLICY-MAKING PROCESS

Policy making can best be thought of as a *process*. Although it is not possible to describe in detail the elements of every policy, it is possible to discuss five general stages by which most policies are formulated: problem recognition, policy formulation and adoption, policy implementation, policy evaluation, and policy termination. (These stages are evident in the Case Study on page 590.)

Problem Recognition

Problem recognition is probably the most important stage in the policy-making process. Before Congress considers an issue, before an agency of the executive branch administers a program, and before the courts consider any disputes that may arise, the issue must first be recognized as a problem requiring government attention. Not every problem, however, requires public attention, particularly at the national level. Many disputes are resolved privately without government intervention. Many more are dealt with by local and state governments. Moreover, only a small portion of the problems that might warrant government attention and intervention are actually given serious consideration. Only after problem recognition can an issue be placed on the policy agenda, where it will compete with other issues for consideration.

Public awareness is critical for an issue to receive serious consideration. Dramatic social and economic events often trigger the realization that a problem requires public attention. The Great Depression of the 1930s is a classic example of an event that forced the country to pay attention to the need for significant public action in welfare, housing, and social policy. The Iraqi in-

*Public awareness of an issue can lead to public support for poli-
cies that address it. During the Depression, the image of an apple
seller on a Chicago street* (left) *focused attention on the plight of
the unemployed. Similarly, late in 1992, the image of an American soldier giving candy to a Somali boy* (right) *also helped shape
public attitudes.*

vasion of Kuwait in 1990 was an attention-getting event in international affairs
and precipitated American involvement in the Persian Gulf War.

Generally, people are likely to recognize a problem and believe that it
requires public action if the matter is critical, if the consequences of inaction
are likely to be serious, and if the situation affects large numbers of people.
Such conditions as significant and widespread declines in student scores on
standardized achievement tests, high and persistent levels of unemployment, an
upward surge in the cost of imported oil, dramatic and negative declines in the
nation's indicators of economic health, or sudden and long-lasting increases in
levels of crime, poverty, or serious illness could be expected to elicit widespread
public awareness of social problems requiring public action.

But sometimes, seemingly small, unexpected events provide the spark that
leads to significant public recognition of a problem and perhaps eventually to
new or modified policy solutions. In the early 1970s, for example, a rare three-
inch fish, the snail darter, was discovered living in an area where the Tennessee
Valley Authority planned to build a dam. Environmentalists argued that construction of the dam would lead to the extinction of this fish, which had been
declared an endangered species. The little fish and its plight captured the public's attention and came to symbolize the struggle between environmentalists
and groups promoting the development of new and expanded energy projects.
Environmentalists succeeded in halting construction of the dam for a number

The Elementary and Secondary Education Act

First passed in 1965, the Elementary and Secondary Education Act continues to be the centerpiece of the national government's response to education policy. The act, renewed and modified numerous times over the years, is a good illustration of the politics of policy formation and implementation.

Throughout the 1950s and 1960s various groups lined up in support of or in opposition to major federal assistance for education. Groups that generally supported federal aid included the National Education Association and the American Federation of Teachers (organizations supporting classroom teachers and administrators), the AFL-CIO, and various minority and liberal organizations. Typically opposed were such groups as the U.S. Chamber of Commerce, the National Association of Manufacturers, and various religious groups. Protestant organizations tended to oppose federal aid to education as a violation of the constitutional principle of separation of church and state. Catholic groups—such as the U.S. Catholic Conference—opposed federal aid to education that would serve to benefit public schools and neglect parochial schools.

Though a Catholic, President John F. Kennedy was a strong supporter of increased federal aid for education. Kennedy proposed a measure that would have provided major new federal assistance to public education but would also have denied such aid to parochial schools. The Catholic church was strongly opposed to the bill and encouraged its members to barrage Congress with hundreds of thousands of messages from constituents. Kennedy's proposal was also opposed by conservative groups fearful of expanded federal control over education policy and by many southern Democrats opposed to racial integration. In the end the Kennedy-supported bill died in committee, but the fact that a bill supporting significant federal aid to education had proceeded so far in the policy process meant that this issue would not soon fade from the policy agenda.

The huge Democratic victory in 1964 gave a major boost to supporters of increased aid to education. Not only were many new members of Congress elected who were sympathetic to such aid, but many observers interpreted Lyndon Johnson's landslide win as a public mandate for a larger role by the federal government in a variety of social programs, including education.

President Johnson made federal aid to education one of the top priorities of his administration, arguing that "poverty has many roots, but the taproot is ignorance." As in the past, the primary obstacle to increased federal aid to education came from various religious organizations. This deadlock was overcome through a series of negotiations involving the principal groups and forces that had clashed over federal aid in the past. The major participants in these meetings were representatives of the U.S. Catholic Conference and the National Education Association.

of years, and in the end Congress was forced to alter existing public policy to permit exceptions to the Endangered Species Act.

More recently, environmentalists have succeeded in bringing to the public's attention the plight of the northern spotted owl. This two-pound bird, whose habitat is the fir and spruce forests in Washington, Oregon, and California, is threatened by logging. In the late 1980s environmentalists succeeded in having the bird placed on the endangered-species list and forcing at least a temporary reduction of logging activities.

The resulting battle between environmentalists and the timber industry over the plight of the spotted owl was the most intense ever generated by the Endangered Species Act. Environmentalists argued that the ecosystem was in

Involving key congressional leaders, these negotiations forged the basis of the legislation that was to follow. The key understanding was the adoption of the "child benefit" program—the notion that federal aid would focus on disadvantaged children in both public and parochial schools. Aid was seen as benefiting children themselves, not the school system. In signing the 1965 Elementary and Secondary Education Act (ESEA) into law, President Johnson—in the one-room schoolhouse where he had once taught—proclaimed the act "the greatest breakthrough in the advance of education since the Constitution was written."

The education act also provides a good illustration of the role of politics in the implementation of public policy. As an artful blend of several opposing forces, the ESEA bill was ambiguous on many key points. The bill contained five separate "titles" (or parts), each very complicated in design, funding, and implementation. The act's vague language providing funds to meet the "special needs of educationally deprived children" meant that the range of services that could be funded was virtually endless. Administrators in the Office of Education, the agency charged with implementing the act, were divided over the legislation's intent. Veteran employees of the office favored a limited approach. Newer employees—many of whom had been appointed by presidents Kennedy and Johnson—favored a much more active role.

Federal aid to education eventually became linked with the desegregation issue, a development that was not anticipated when ESEA was enacted. The Civil Rights Act of 1964 prohibited discrimination in any federally assisted program, and the threat to withhold ESEA funds became a major tool in the enforcement of antidiscrimination measures. The original education act targeted federal funds for disadvantaged children. It has been amended several times to include funds for the gifted and talented, the non-English speaking, and other categories of children.

Discussion questions

1. How does passage of the Elementary and Secondary Education Act illustrate the role of presidential support in the initiation of public policy?
2. How does this case illustrate the role of interest groups in policy formulation and implementation?
3. What lessons can be learned from this case about the unintended consequences of public policy?

SOURCE: James Sundquist, *Politics and Policy* (Washington, D.C.: Brookings Institution, 1968), 187; Congressional Quarterly, *Congress and the Nation, Vol. 2: 1965–68* (Washington, D.C.: Congressional Quarterly Service, 1969), 720; Eugene Eidenberg and Roy Morey, *An Act of Congress* (New York: Norton, 1969), 80; and Jerome T. Murphy, "The Education Bureaucracies Implement Novel Policy: The Politics of Title I of ESEA, 1965–72," in *Policy and Politics in America*, ed. Allan P. Sindler (Boston: Little, Brown, 1973), 161.

decline and that more than one hundred species of plants and animals—including the spotted owl—were threatened with extinction. The timber industry countered that the forest provided employment for thousands of families as well as lumber for millions of American homes. Environmentalists filed a number of lawsuits claiming that the Interior Department and the United States Forest Service, the two federal agencies managing the forests, were not protecting the owl or its habitat and were breaking the law.

After more than a decade of struggle between the timber industry and environmental groups, in May of 1992 President Bush grudgingly approved a plan designed to restrict logging on 5.4 million acres of Pacific northwest forest where the spotted owl lives.

The spotted owl controversy continued to be a catalyst for policy change into the Clinton administration. One of the early actions of President Clinton's Secretary of the Interior, Bruce Babbitt, was the announcement of a major policy shift in the department's method of wildlife protection. Babbitt's plan, as he described it in congressional testimony in February of 1993, was to focus on entire ecosystems, rather than on individual plants and animals. Babbitt's proposal would provide for intervention before any crises arose and individual species were endangered, thus avoiding lengthy and contentious legal battles like those over the spotted owl.

Another issue that burst into public awareness in an unusual way came up early in the Clinton administration. With the withdrawal of the president's first two choices for attorney general, Zoe E. Baird and Judge Kimba M. Wood, because both women had used illegal aliens as nannies, the nation was forced to confront head-on the issue of *child care*. Whether this will lead finally to the adoption of comprehensive child-care legislation in the United States, as currently exists in many European countries, remains to be seen. But the issue has unquestionably now been recognized as a problem that requires government attention.

Public awareness of an issue is not enough to guarantee that the issue will successfully make its way to the policy agenda. Skillful advocacy by interest groups is also critical. As noted in Chapter 8, political interest groups see to it that issues that are of concern to them are brought to the public's attention and make their way to the agenda-setting stage of the policy process. In the case of the snail darter and the spotted owl, environmental groups like the Wilderness Society and the Environmental Defense Fund were instrumental in bringing the issue to the public's attention. Other groups, such as political parties, the media, academics, and even influential public and private individuals, may also serve as important advocates of particular policy issues.

The "Timber Summit" in Portland, Oregon, in April, 1993, brought together President Clinton, Vice-President Gore, and Interior Secretary Bruce Babbitt to discuss the conflicts between environmentalists and the timber industry. The Clinton administration proposed to reduce logging on federal lands and to provide more than $1 billion to retrain loggers and assist their communities.

Policy Formulation and Adoption

Once a problem has been placed on the government's agenda, an effective and feasible solution to the problem must be found. This stage is called **policy formulation**. Usually there are many possible courses of action for resolving a problem. The perceived problem of declining test scores among college-bound high school seniors, for example, might be addressed by policies to encourage better teachers, smaller classes, curriculum modification, or some combination of these. From the variety of options that exist, policy makers must identify a solution or set of solutions that will be effective in addressing the problem, acceptable to the parties concerned, and affordable.

Policy formulation does not always result in a new law or administrative action. Frequently policy makers may decide not to act at all. The fact that an issue has made it to the agenda-setting stage does not mean that action will automatically be taken.[5]

Marshaling the support needed to win official approval of a specific course of action is called **policy adoption**. At this stage, lobbying, bargaining, negotiating, and compromise may be needed. Seldom does any policy emerge from the process in the form in which it was initially proposed. To be adopted, to gain sufficient political support, policies often must be modified significantly.

Often the activities that take place during the formulation and adoption stages occur within a cluster of actors and institutions. The special relationship that sometimes develops among executive agencies, interest groups, and congressional committees has been called an "iron triangle" (see Chapter 14). Almost three decades ago Douglas Cater described this phenomenon as a **subgovernment**:

In one important area of policy after another, substantial efforts to exercise power are waged by alliances cutting across the [executive and congressional] branches of government and including key operatives from outside. In effect, they constitute *subgovernments* of Washington comprising the expert, the interested, and the engaged.[6]

In many issue areas, participants from the executive branch, Congress, *and* the groups affected work in close cooperation to formulate and adopt acceptable policy. "Policy making," says Robert Lineberry, "is thus a function of close cooperation and interaction among these triads of power. . . . When a group becomes strong enough, it gets a part of the government, its own piece of the action."[7]

Figure 16-1 shows the energy subgovernment. When energy policy is formulated, the most active and influential participants will come from the executive departments and agencies, congressional committees, and interest groups listed in the figure. Subgovernments also exist in education, employment and labor, health, urban affairs, agriculture, transportation, national security, and other issue areas (Figures 17-1, 17-4, 17-7, and 17-8 show, respectively, the education, welfare, housing, and environment subgovernments). "Revolving doors" allow individuals to move back and forth freely among the various institutions in a given subgovernment.

Time and again, agencies that regulate a particular sector of society are staffed by people who formerly served in leadership positions or as lobbyists in the area being regulated. For example, Alfred Sikes, whom President Bush appointed to serve as chairperson of the Federal Communications Commission, previously served as an officer in a number of companies that owned radio stations in Texas, Louisiana, and New Mexico. President Clinton picked Robert Sussman, an attorney who had formerly represented a number of chemical industry clients, to serve as deputy administrator of the Environmental Protection Agency. He also selected to serve in the EPA David Gardiner, a longtime lobbyist for the environmental interest group the Sierra Club.

Figure 16-1 *The energy subgovernment.* SOURCE: Washington Information Directory, 1993–94 *(Washington, D.C.: Congressional Quarterly, Inc., 1993); and* The Capital Source *(Washington, D.C.: National Journal, Fall, 1993).*

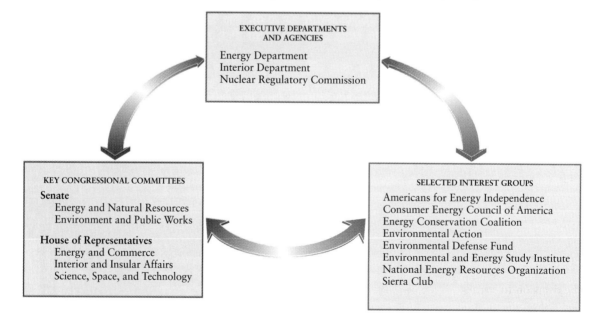

EXECUTIVE DEPARTMENTS
AND AGENCIES

Energy Department
Interior Department
Nuclear Regulatory Commission

KEY CONGRESSIONAL COMMITTEES

Senate
Energy and Natural Resources
Environment and Public Works

House of Representatives
Energy and Commerce
Interior and Insular Affairs
Science, Space, and Technology

SELECTED INTEREST GROUPS

Americans for Energy Independence
Consumer Energy Council of America
Energy Conservation Coalition
Environmental Action
Environmental Defense Fund
Environmental and Energy Study Institute
National Energy Resources Organization
Sierra Club

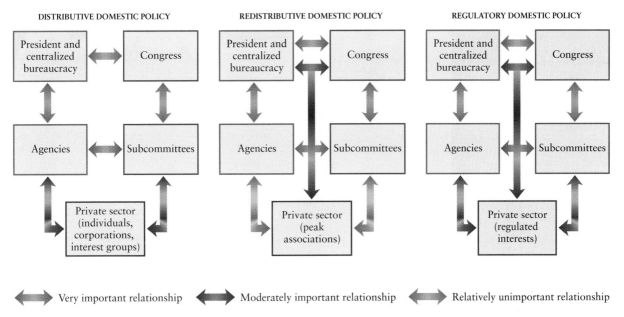

| DISTRIBUTIVE DOMESTIC POLICY | REDISTRIBUTIVE DOMESTIC POLICY | REGULATORY DOMESTIC POLICY |

Figure 16-2   *The relative importance of institutional relationships for determining policy actions.* SOURCE: *Randall B. Ripley and Grace A. Franklin,* Congress, the Bureaucracy, and Public Policy *(Homewood, Ill.: Dorsey Press, 1976). Copyright © 1976. Reprinted with permission of the publisher.*

Likewise, officials of regulatory agencies and even members of Congress often end up working as lobbyists in areas they once regulated. As an example, when Representative Tom Tauke (R-Iowa) lost his 1990 race for the Senate, he became chief lobbyist for the regional Bell telephone companies. As a member of the telecommunications and finance subcommittee of the House Energy and Commerce Committee, Tauke had frequently dealt with issues affecting these companies. A study conducted by Common Cause found that 20 percent of the members of Congress who left Congress during the 1980s took positions as lobbyists.[8] Some even became lobbyists for foreign governments.

Figure 16-2 brings together Theodore Lowi's impact-based classification of policies and the concept of subgovernments. As the figure shows, the relative importance of the relationships among the various actors in a subgovernment depends on whether the policy is distributive, regulatory, or redistributive. For example, when a policy is distributive, the most important relationship in the subgovernment is between agencies in the executive branch and congressional subcommittees; but when the policy is redistributive, that relationship is relatively unimportant.

Policy Implementation

Policies that have been adopted must be administered. Putting policy into place is called **policy implementation**. A few policy decisions may be self-executing. The decision to formally recognize a new foreign government, for example, is a policy that is essentially in place as soon as it is adopted. However, the vast

Politics and

Public Policy

Public concern about chemical contamination at Love Canal in upstate New York and at other sites, like this one in Saco, Maine, led Congress to pass the Superfund law in 1980. Although $15 billion was spent by 1993 to clean up polluted sites, only 180 of 1,200 designated sites had been completed. Each cleanup requires, on average, more than $30 million and ten years to complete. At first, communities were eager to participate in the program, but more recently some fear that designation as a Superfund site could hamper development and reduce property values.

UPI/Bettmann

majority of laws and policy decisions are not implemented automatically. Many may require a complex implementation structure, perhaps involving hundreds or thousands of people and the expenditure of millions or billions of dollars.

Policy implementation is not a simple, routine process. The administration of policy can be highly political, sometimes involving struggles as intense as those occurring during the policy adoption process. For example, in recent years the Environmental Protection Agency (EPA) and its administrators have been constantly embroiled in debates with environmentalists and certain members of Congress over the implementation of environmental legislation. Environmental groups frequently charge that EPA is too slow in implementing environmental legislation, and some members of Congress believe EPA has ignored or significantly modified congressional intent in certain areas. As Senator Frank Lautenberg (D-New Jersey) bluntly stated to EPA officials in hearings held before his subcommittee in 1987, "It is this Senator's belief that . . . you are violating the law, or if not the law, certainly the spirit of the law."

Administrators and bureaucrats in any agency frequently have wide latitude in the implementation and administration of policy. Such latitude is desirable when they need to modify policy to fit changing times and conditions. It can be detrimental, however, if administrators actively change the direction of policy. By choosing to apply laws rigorously or leniently, bureaucrats may actually shape the impact of policies and thus incur the wrath of Congress, the president, and outside groups. Speaking of the frustrating cycle of policy making and policy implementation in the area of environmental protection, one report stated, "In air pollution control, solid waste disposal, and other environmental protection programs, Congress passes laws, EPA implements them in ways displeasing to Congress, Congress passes more specific laws, EPA again carries them out to the dissatisfaction of Congress, and Congress threatens to enact even more specific legislation."[9] (See the Constitutional Conflict on page 608.)

The courts too may be important in shaping policy during the implementation phase. Judicial rulings often establish the precise direction a policy will take. In public education, for example, court decisions have required busing of schoolchildren to achieve racial balance, limited the power of local school boards to set student dress codes, forced local authorities to provide more educational options for handicapped and disadvantaged children, and altered the methods of state school financing to achieve greater equity among local school districts.

Policy Evaluation

A policy that has been formulated, adopted, and implemented is ready to be evaluated. **Policy evaluation** is the set of activities designed to determine whether a policy is working as intended. Does an energy policy actually reduce the wasteful use of energy? Did the Patriot missile perform effectively under combat conditions? Does an environmental policy result in a less polluted environment? Does a child nutrition policy result in healthier children? Does an educational program for disadvantaged children result in more years of education for those children? Does an antipoverty policy result in the reduction of poverty? And what is the cost of each of these programs? Cost can be measured in two ways: (1) *directly* in terms of federal dollars expended on a program and (2) *indirectly* in terms of the cost to state and local governments, as well as to private firms and individuals, of compliance.

Not only *intended* consequences, but also unanticipated consequences need to be evaluated. A highway construction program, for example, may relieve traffic congestion as hoped but may also stimulate growth and development in areas that are unprepared for such growth. A successful highway construction program may also generate unexpectedly higher levels of pollution or reduce ridership on mass transit.

Policy evaluation may be conducted in two ways. The first is informal or "seat of the pants" evaluation.[10] This kind of evaluation is impressionistic and often judgmental. If residents and administrators of a housing program express

To what extent may a president and his administration modify laws of Congress to change public policy? The Constitution (in Article I, Section 1) grants "all legislative powers" to Congress and (in Article II, Section 1) gives to the president the duty to "faithfully execute" the laws passed by Congress. The extent to which an administration may reinterpret laws of Congress to more nearly reflect the president's own policy agenda was part of a bundle of constitutional issues brought to the Supreme Court in the 1991 case of *Rust v. Sullivan*.

In 1970 Congress passed the Family Planning and Population Research Act creating Title X of the Public Health Service Act, providing federal support for family-planning clinics. When creating the program, Congress stipulated that "None of the funds appropriated under this title shall be used in programs where abortion is a method of family planning." Early on, this provision was interpreted to ban the use of federal funds to *perform* abortions. In 1988, however, under direction and support of President Reagan, the Department of Health and Human Services, which administered the program, issued new Title X guidelines: no clinic receiving Title X funds could provide abortion *advice* or *counseling*, nor could any Title X clinic *discuss* abortion as a method of birth control.

Planned Parenthood, along with the State and City of New York, sued the Department of Health and Human Services, claiming that the department's 1988 guidelines were not consistent with congressional intent and that the regulations violated First Amendment speech rights of doctors and other health providers and also interfered with a woman's rights of privacy.

In the 1991 *Rust v. Sullivan* case, the Supreme Court ruled that the Reagan administration had *not* overstepped its authority in changing its interpretations of the conditions under which Title X funds would be distributed. The Court in its decision stated, "Substantial deference is accorded to the interpretation of the authorizing statute by the agency authorized with administering it. When we find, as we do here, that the legislative history is ambiguous and unenlightening on the matters with respect to which the regulations deal, we customarily defer to the expertise of the agency."[1] Similarly, the Court rejected the First and Fifth Amendment challenges to the act.

This decision grants to a president wide discretion in interpreting laws of Congress, even to the point of changing historical interpretation of those laws to conform to his own policy agenda. Congress must be very explicit in dictating how the administration is to carry out enacted laws. Otherwise, "plausible" administrative interpretations of the law will be upheld.

[1] *Rust v. Sullivan*, 111 S.Ct. 1759 (1991).

satisfaction with the program, for example, there is at least an informal indication that the program is working. The problem with impressionistic evaluations is that the evaluators may not be disinterested parties. They may have been advocates of the program, have a stake in its success, or depend for their information on those who do. This can affect their judgments.

To avoid this problem, evaluators try to measure the impact of policy in more rigorous ways. They do so by collecting information from a variety of sources, by using sophisticated statistical analyses, and by following accepted methods of social-scientific research. This way, others can check their results and analysts can determine whether the policy is having the desired impact. This brings us to the last stage in the policy process.

Programs that are not meeting their objectives or have outlived the problem for which they were created may be overhauled or **terminated**. As one team of policy analysts has noted, "policies get old, they wear out, or they keep solving problems that have long since been resolved or replaced by more pressing social priorities. . . . Releasing dollars and other resources invested in outdated programs makes them available for deployment against new problems."[11]

One example of a program that was terminated is the general revenue sharing program, which allocated over $80 billion to local governments between 1972 and 1986. In the fall of 1986, in the wake of strong political and economic pressure to reduce the national budget, general revenue sharing was not renewed. Also in 1986, Congress abolished the federally supported Synthetic Fuels Corporation, which had been established a few years earlier to encourage the production of fuels from sources other than petroleum. President Clinton, as part of his deficit-reduction plan announced in February of 1993, called for the phasing down and eventual termination of the $4-billion program of grants to state and local governments for construction of waste-water treatment plants—a program which had begun in 1972. Also in 1993, Congress—bowing to pressure to cut spending—terminated support for the $11 billion Superconducting Supercollider (SSC) project being built in Texas.

There are many obstacles to program termination, and halting an ongoing project often is very difficult. As California Representative George Brown commented during debates on the SSC, "Something you learn quickly around here is that nothing ever dies."[12] Obviously, employees of the agency that was created to administer a program will fight to hold on to their jobs. Agency employees typically seek ways to demonstrate their value and to publicize the severe negative consequences of terminating the program. The agency's clients—those who are served by the program—will rally around a continuation of the program. Legislators, responding to pressure from potential voters or government contractors, also may side with groups seeking to preserve a program or an agency. Despite such difficulties, however, program terminations and modifications do occur—they are part of the policy-making process.

POLITICS AND THE POLICY PROCESS

The making of public policy is a process that moves through several identifiable stages and is never complete. What, then, are the implications of the continually changing and incomplete nature of domestic policy?

Incrementalism

Policy making is often extremely slow; and even when policy changes are made, the changes are likely to be very small departures from the status quo. Decades passed, for example, before Congress enacted significant environmental protection legislation; and the early laws were weak responses given the seriousness of the problems. Similarly, in housing, welfare, and education, the typical span of years separating problem recognition from the adoption of meaningful policy

The path that an issue follows through Congress is long and tortuous. Many bills are proposed at every session, but relatively few survive the legislative process to become law. There are several ways to track an issue at it moves along.

The first step is to get a copy of the bill itself. When a senator or representative introduces a bill, it is given a number or title by the clerk of the House. If you don't know the number of the bill, call the clerk of the House at (202) 225-7000 and ask. Once you have the number, you can request a free copy of a House bill from the House Document Room, U.S. Capitol, Washington, DC 20515; phone (202) 225-3456. Senate bills are available from the Senate Document Room, U.S. Capitol, Washington, DC 20510; phone (202) 224-7860. You can also find the bill in the *Congressional Record* for the day it was entered.

A bill is assigned to the committee of the House or Senate that is concerned with the topic the bill covers. The committee discusses the bill and holds hearings so that interested individuals can express their opinions. Most committee meetings and hearings are open to the public. The "Daily Digest" section of the *Congressional Record* lists the next day's schedule of committee meetings. Committees and subcommittees also generally issue their own calendars. Call the Capitol switchboard at (202) 224-3121, and ask for the relevant committee; a staff member will send you the calendar.

Another way to track a bill is to use the *Calendar of the House of Representatives and History of Legislation.* Published weekly when Congress is in session, this document contains, among other things, a list of bills in conference, a list of bills out of conference, histories of all the bills before the House, and the House calendar. It can be requested from the House Document Room.

The LEGIS computerized database system provides detailed information on bills in Congress for a small fee. For more information contact LEGIS, Ford House Office Building, Washington, DC 20515; phone (202) 225-1772.

You can also speak to staff members or listen to taped telephone messages on the status of bills and other activities in Congress. For a daily digest of the Senate portion of the *Congressional Record,* call (202) 224-2658; for the House, call (202) 225-2868. For a daily update on the status of bills in the House or Senate, call (202) 225-1772.

Both parties in Congress provide staff members and taped telephone messages that monitor the progress of legislation—so-called cloakroom messages. For daily legislative activity in the House of Representatives, call the Democrats at (202) 225-7400 and the Republicans at (202) 225-7430. For the next day's House legislative schedule, call the Republicans at (202) 225-2020 and the Democrats at (202) 225-7330. For daily legislative activity in the Senate, call the Democrats at (202) 224-8541 and the Republicans at (202) 224-8601. For the Senate legislative schedule, call the Republicans at (202) 224-5456 and the Democrats at (202) 224-4691.

Congressional debates, votes, committee meetings, and hearings are regularly televised on C-SPAN and C-SPAN 2, noncommercial cable channels supported by the cable television industry.

You can observe floor debates and votes in the Senate and House chambers from the visitors' galleries. Write to or call the Washington office of your state senator or representative to arrange for a free pass.

is wide. In national defense policy, a decade or more is usually needed to develop a new weapons system.

Incrementalism is a salient characteristic of policy making in the United States. Policy is made in slow, halting steps, or increments. Often policy makers seem to take two steps forward and one back. Many factors account for the slow pace. Social problems often are complex, simple solutions are rarely possible, and funds are almost always limited. The most important factor, however, is the fragmentation of political power.

Responsibility for any policy area is shared by a host of congressional committees and subcommittees, by numerous executive departments, commissions, and agencies, and by the already overloaded and overburdened court system. Moreover, the fragmentation found at the national level is magnified many times over at the state and local levels. Fragmented power means that interested groups and individuals have numerous opportunities to block or alter suggested policy changes and that an extraordinary amount of coalition building is necessary to bring about any significant change. Coalition building not only takes time but also necessitates a considerable amount of bargaining and compromise. Most policies that are adopted have been modified to satisfy the concerns of numerous groups and organizations.

Major Policy Shifts

Major changes in policy sometimes do occur. Examples include the passage of the Elementary and Secondary Education Act of 1965, the welfare program initiated in the 1930s, and the welfare reform measure of 1988. The Clinton administration has identified health care as a policy area where major changes will occur in the 1990s. In the American system, large-scale, fundamental policy shifts are often associated with major social, economic, or international upheavals like the Great Depression or the emergence of the Soviet Union as a superpower after World War II. Such events create a sense of urgency. Suddenly everyone agrees that something must be done, and it is possible to overcome some of the moderating forces of American politics.

Major policy changes are often associated with strong and persistent pressure from the White House. President Johnson's extraordinary interest in education played a major role in the passage of the 1965 education act. President Nixon's strong support of the general revenue-sharing program was largely responsible for its passage in 1972, and President Reagan's philosophy of New Federalism was the catalyst for passage of the large grant consolidation programs early in his administration. By making affordable and universal health care the centerpiece of his domestic program, President Clinton shaped the national debate for health-care reform in the 1990s.

The chances for major policy shifts are also enhanced when the same political party controls Congress and the presidency. President Johnson was greatly assisted in his campaign for passage of education reform, as well as other parts of his Great Society program, by the presence of large numbers of Democrats in the House and Senate who were sympathetic to his proposals. President Reagan was aided by a Republican majority in the Senate and strong Republican unity in the House during the first years of his administration. Throughout his term, President Bush's housing proposals were frustrated by Democratic control of key committees in both the House and the Senate.

Mixed Results

Does public policy have much impact on the problems it is designed to solve? Successful policy initiatives include the Social Security system, the Peace Corps,

Dramatic events can focus the public eye on a particular problem, such as the plight of illegal aliens. This group is escaping from a train's grain-hopper car in an effort to elude INS agents in Laredo, Texas. President Clinton has asked Congress for more money and new laws to combat illegal immigration while restating "support for keeping the rainbow and the melting pot of America going. . . ."

the Head Start program for preschool children, the school lunch program for those who cannot afford to purchase adequate meals, and the federal job training program, which has provided numerous people with the education and skills necessary for steady employment. Technical problems (such as whether an energy bill should require cars to average 35 to 40 miles per gallon or whether automakers should be required to place catalytic converters and electronic emission control systems under warranty for 50,000 or 80,000 miles) usually are easier to overcome than problems of a more political nature.

Some problems persist in spite of massive efforts to wipe them out. Billions of dollars have been spent to combat poverty, but there still are poor people in the United States. Billions of dollars have been spent to clean up the environment, but there still are polluted lakes, streams, and air. Billions of dollars have been spent on housing, but there still are homeless people.

Problems persist for a variety of reasons. One is the complexity of the problems themselves. Poverty, for example, has multiple causes, and experts often disagree about which causes are most important. Another reason why problems endure is that the costs of a proposed solution may be more than society is willing to pay. Cleaning up the environment at a level that satisfies the most ardent environmentalists might consume funds needed for other programs.

The high cost of solving, or even significantly affecting, complex problems is a particularly important issue—one that frequently brings its own set of policy questions. Proposals for solving a particular problem almost always raise the question of how to cover the costs of the proposed solution. Should funds for a new policy initiative be generated by raising taxes, or should they be taken from funds currently being applied in another area? Politicians, of course, want to avoid answering this question as long as possible. Consider, for instance, President Bush's response to a reporter's question about how he intended to finance his "war on drugs":

LaDonna Harris: Activist for Change

Government policy is not made only by government. Individuals and the organizations they lead can have a significant role. A good example is LaDonna Harris, founder and president of Americans for Indian Opportunity (AIO).

In the 1960s, LaDonna Harris, a member of the Comanche nation, started an organization called Oklahomans for Indian Opportunity (OIO). The founding premise of OIO was that strong tribal communities and governments could help reverse the stifling poverty and lack of opportunity that faced Native Americans in Oklahoma.

Today OIO remains an important institution to more than thirty tribes in the state. LaDonna Harris went on to form Americans for Indian Opportunity, a nationwide organization, in 1970. In 1971 AIO won its first important legislative victory when it helped secure the return of Taos Blue Lake, a sacred site that was scheduled for development, to the Taos Pueblo in New Mexico. Another important victory occurred in 1973, when Ms. Harris assisted the Menominee of Wisconsin in regaining their tribal recognition from the federal government.

Americans for Indian Opportunity is particularly strong in the area of developing tribal leadership for the future. For example, AIO was instrumental in establishing the Council of Energy Resource Tribes. The forty-five member tribes of the council work in concert to increase tribal control over their natural resources. Another environmental program brings together federal regulatory agencies, tribal governments, and environmental advocacy organizations to help ensure that tribal concerns and issues are incorporated into broader environmental agendas.

The personal leadership of LaDonna Harris has been a significant factor in the success of AIO. As a national Native American leader she has also influenced the agendas of the feminist and environmental movements. She was a founder of the National Women's Political Caucus. In 1980, she ran for vice president on the Citizens' Party ticket with environmentalist Barry Commoner. Through service on the boards of such national organizations as the Girl Scouts, Common Cause, and the National Organization of Women, through service on presidential commissions under four presidents, and international service as the United States representative to the United Nations Educational, Scientific, and Cultural Organization (UNESCO), and through ongoing service as head of AIO, LaDonna Harris continues to influence the policy-making process.

LaDonna Harris, a significant factor in the success of AIO.

Courtesy of LaDonna Harris/Americans for Indian Opportunity

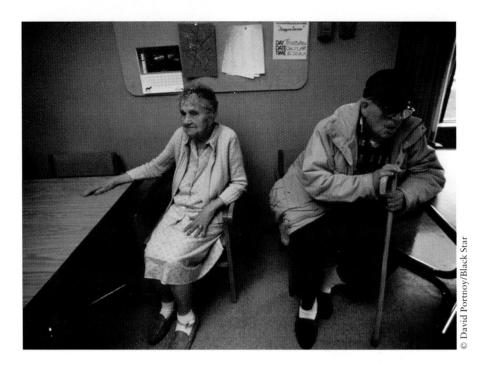

A state-run facility for the elderly, whose problems have gone unsolved despite efforts to help. In 1988, Congress and President Reagan amended Medicare to protect the elderly against the costs of catastrophic illness. But within eighteen months Congress repealed the new law because of pressure from older Americans. Many did not understand the program's funding, which required wealthier enrollees to pay for expanded benefits.

Q: Mr. President, you've told us you're going to expand vastly the fight against drugs. Are you willing to raise taxes to pay for that?

A: We're not going to have to, but we are going to expand Federal expenditures.

Q: Follow up on that. Mr. President, if you're not going to raise revenues to fight the drug war, where are you going to get this money? Could you be specific?

A: Stay tuned, and we will show you [later] how we're going to allocate the resources for this.[13]

President Bush used almost the same words again when discussing a new health-care plan announced in February 1992 that would cost an estimated $100 billion over a five-year period. When asked by reporters how he planned to fund the new program the president responded, "We'll figure that out [later]."[14]

Some problems are not solved because of disagreement about what the problems really are. In the area of housing, for example, public policy has had a split focus. At some times, the emphasis has been on the construction of large public housing projects. At other times, the goal has been to clean up urban blight. At still other times, policies have been designed to provide subsidies for homeowners and renters.

What exactly is the problem? How are programs going to be paid for? Which groups are going to benefit, which are going to lose? These are the sorts of political questions that policy makers must resolve. When the groups that are most directly involved in making policy decisions—Congress and its various committees, the president, agency administrators, interest groups, and the political parties—can reach agreement about the nature of the problem, and about the measures required to resolve the problem, solutions tend to be reached fairly quickly. At the core of policy making in the United States lies politics—the struggle among people with differing goals, objectives, and resources. Politics both defines the problems to be addressed by policy makers and shapes the solutions.

SUMMARY

Public policy is action by government designed to address public problems; it is what government actually does or accomplishes. Policies may be classified in a number of ways. One approach is to focus on issues. This approach makes it clear that the significance of policy areas changes over time.

Another way to classify policies is in terms of their impacts on society. *Distributive policies* are those that distribute goods and services to citizens. Certain groups gain something from such policies, but their costs are shared by the public as a whole. *Regulatory policies* are those through which the government establishes rules and standards and thereby regulates or controls behavior. Regulatory policies are often developed in response to practices that are deemed harmful or destructive. *Redistributive policies* are those that are perceived to take benefits from some groups and give them to others.

Policy making can be seen as a process that unfolds in five stages. The first and most important stage is *problem recognition*. An issue must be recognized as a problem requiring government attention in order to be placed on the policy agenda. Public awareness of a problem is critical for an issue to receive serious consideration; skillful advocacy by interest groups is also critical.

Once a problem has been recognized as requiring national attention, a feasible solution must be found. This is the stage of *policy formulation*. Usually there are many potential courses of action, and a choice must be made to pursue one of them (or not to act at all). *Policy adoption* involves marshaling the support needed to win approval of a course of action. Lobbying, bargaining, negotiating, and compromise may be needed. Often these processes occur within a cluster of actors and institutions that has been described as a *subgovernment*. Members of a given subgovernment work in close coop-

eration to formulate and adopt acceptable policies in a particular issue area. Individuals frequently move back and forth among the institutions in a given subgovernment.

Policies that have been adopted must be administered; putting policy into place is known as *policy implementation*. Very few policy decisions are self-implementing. Many may require a complex implementation structure. Officials in executive agencies frequently have wide latitude in the implementation of policy and can sometimes shape the impact of a policy. Judicial rulings may also establish the precise direction a policy will take.

Policy evaluation consists of activities designed to determine whether a policy is working as intended. Not only intended consequences but also unanticipated consequences need to be evaluated. Evaluation may be conducted by informal, impressionistic means or in more rigorous ways using accepted methods of social scientific research.

The final stage of the policy-making process is *policy termination*. There are many political obstacles to program termination. Agency employees want to keep their jobs; clients served by a program want it to continue; voters place pressure on legislators to preserve the program. Nevertheless, programs frequently are terminated or overhauled.

Policy making is often extremely slow; and even when policy changes are made, the changes are likely to be very small departures from the status quo. Among the reasons for the *incrementalism* of policy making in America are the complexity of social problems and the fragmentation of political power. Nevertheless, major policy shifts sometimes occur. They are often associated with strong and persistent pressure from the White House. Such shifts have a better chance when the same political party controls Congress and the White House.

The policy-making process has mixed results. Some policies succeed in achieving their goals; others fail. It is usually easier to identify and overcome technical problems than to solve problems that are more political. Complex social problems are not easily solved, and the costs of a proposed solution may be more than society is willing to pay. In addition, it is sometimes difficult to reach an agreement about what the problems really are and about the measures required to solve them.

KEY TERMS AND CONCEPTS

public policy
distributive policy
regulatory policy
redistributive policy

problem recognition
policy formulation
policy adoption
subgovernment

policy implementation
policy evaluation
policy termination
incrementalism

LEARNING MORE ABOUT THE POLICY-MACKING PROCESS

Scholarly studies

Anderson, James E. *Public Policymaking: An Introduction.* Boston: Houghton Mifflin, 1990. An excellent, brief overview that emphasizes formulation, adoption, implementation, impact, and evaluation.

Brewer, Garry D., and Peter deLeon. *The Foundations of Policy Analysis.* Homewood, Ill.: Dorsey Press, 1983. A thorough examination of all phases of the policy process, with an especially good analysis of the political aspects of the earliest phases of policy making: recognition of the problem and selection of alternatives.

Nakamura, Robert, and Frank Smallwood. *The Politics of Policy Implementation.* New York: St. Martin's Press, 1980. A look at the political aspects of implementing policy *after* legislative adoption of a particular course of action. An especially good examination of the politics of bureaucracies.

Stone, Deborah A. *Policy Paradox and Political Reason.* New York: HarperCollins, 1988. A study of public policy and policy analysis that places "politics" at the center of policy making. A thorough examination of the political struggles related to policy adoption.

Leisure reading

Heineman, Robert A., William T. Bluhum, Steven A. Peterson, and Edward N. Kearny. *The World of the Policy Analyst.* Chatham, N.J.: Chatham House, 1990. An interesting look at the vocation of policy analyst. Provides insight into how to become an effective policy analyst and examines the difficult political and social contexts in which analysts must work.

McCollough, Thomas E. *The Moral Imagination and Public Life: Raising the Ethical Question.* Chatham, N.J.: Chatham House, 1991. An examination of the role of ethics in policy making. Drawing on numerous examples from contemporary policy debates, the author raises fundamental questions about the role of the individual and the community in raising and resolving public issues.

Polsby, Nelson W. *Political Innovation in America: The Politics of Policy Initiation.* New Haven, Conn.: Yale University Press, 1985. A readable review of policy initiation. Asking "How does it happen that new policies are initiated in the American political system?" Polsby looks at innovation in the making of science, foreign, and domestic policy.

Primary sources

Policy Review. Published by the Heritage Foundation; contains reviews of various policy issues from a conservative perspective. Often includes articles by journalists, public officials, and party leaders as well as academics.

Policy Studies Journal. Published by the Policy Studies Organization; presents a scholarly examination of all policy issues in the United States.

Publius: The Journal of Federalism. Published by the Center for the Study of Federalism; presents scholarly articles dealing with various policy issues from an intergovernmental perspective.

Organizations

Brookings Institution. 1775 Massachusetts Avenue, N.W., Washington, DC 20036; (202) 797-6000. Founded in 1919, the Brookings Institution conducts research and publishes scholarly studies in many policy areas, including education, economics, government, and foreign policy.

Cato Institute. 1000 Massachusetts Avenue, N.W., Washington, DC 20001; (202) 842-0200. Founded in 1977, this policy research organization advocates limited government and individual liberty. Policy issues of prime concern include deregulation, privatization, limited taxation, and reduced government spending.

Heritage Foundation. 214 Massachusetts Avenue, N.W., Washington, DC 20002; (202) 546-4400. Founded in 1973, the Heritage Foundation conducts research, analysis, and policy forums on a variety of policy issues; it generally advocates individual freedoms, limited government, a free market, and strong national defense.

People for the American Way. 2000 M Street, N.W., Washington, DC 20036; (202) 467-4999. Founded in 1980, this organization examines policy issues primarily in light of First Amendment rights and issues. It also conducts extensive public education programs on constitutional issues through radio, television, and various print media.

17

Domestic
Policy

- Education policy: overview; education policy in the Reagan and Bush administrations

- Welfare policy: welfare programs; overview; social insurance and public assistance; the politics of welfare

- Housing policy: overview; the politics of housing; housing policy in the 1980s and 1990s

- Environment and energy policy: clean water and air; energy policy

The 1960 election was an enormous contrast to the Eisenhower landslides of the 1950s. Catholic John F. Kennedy ran on the Democratic ticket with Lyndon B. Johnson of Texas. Protestant Richard Nixon succeeded Ike as the Republican nominee. Although Kennedy's religion was a factor, even more important was his party's partisan advantage. Kennedy's campaign theme was building a "New Frontier," including the exploration of outer space, while Nixon and Henry Cabot Lodge used the slogan "Experience counts" to contrast themselves with their 43-year-old opponent.

The adoption of public policy, we noted in Chapter 16, is often a very slow process. We also made the point that the process is frequently complex and that it involves a considerable amount of bargaining, negotiating, and compromise. Those who seek changes in public policy—especially major changes—can rarely take a position on the extreme left or the extreme right. In order to capture the support of all the individuals and groups needed to pass and implement a new policy, the initiators often must stake out and defend a position in the center.

President Clinton's proposed package for health-care reform, announced in September of 1993, illustrates just such an effort to stake out the middle ground. In the president's own words, his proposal was designed to reflect the "vital center" of the debate about health-care reform.[1]

Health care is an especially complex area of public policy. A great many interest groups— and most voters—have a personal stake in the $900 billion spent each year on health care. Groups representing hospitals, doctors, nurses, patients, *pharmaceutical companies, medical insurers, insurance agents, employers, labor unions, and even state and local governments all care strongly about health-care reform. Any and all such groups can be expected to wage all-out war to oppose any proposal that limits or restricts their options. Given such a diverse and powerful array of interests, it is especially challenging for policy makers to find the "vital center."*

The proposal advanced by the Clinton administration sought to find the middle ground in several significant ways. First, it ruled out a model of centralized control (like the Canadian system) in favor of one that would blend free-market and government regulatory forces (an approach which the president called "managed competition"). Second, the proposal ruled out broad-based taxation to finance health-care reform, proposing instead a system in which employers and employees would pay premiums and the government would subsidize low-income families and small businesses. Additionally, under the Clinton proposal, state governments would play a role in appointing the boards of new administrative bodies, called regional alliances, that would have vast responsibilities for negotiating with health-care plans—compiling and distributing performance measures, responding to complaints, collecting premiums from employers, managing subsidies for low-income clients and small businesses, negotiating fees with doctors who choose to work outside health maintenance organizations, and many other tasks. President Clinton called for a National Health Board (which he would appoint) to oversee all this.

As President Clinton soon discovered, staking out the "vital center" carries a number of special risks. For one thing, the "middle-ground" option is sometimes the most complex policy alternative, simply because decision makers must merge many conflicting objectives and strategies into a unified

policy statement. Such proposals sometimes end up satisfying no one: conservatives and liberals will be equally disappointed that the proposed policy does not adequately represent their positions. For example, in responding to President Clinton's proposal, Louisiana's Republican representative, Robert L. Livingston, called the plan "another Big Government bureaucratic nightmare."[2] And California's Democratic representative, Pete Stark, decided that the proposal was "so complex and convoluted, we'll have to go through it a section at a time and just redo it."[3]

President Clinton also discovered that a middle-of-the-road policy sometimes complicates the process of bargaining and compromise. Deviating even slightly from the middle to appease one faction can raise the risk of alienating another. Even before the president's proposal reached Congress, dozens of changes were made—all designed to win the support of one faction or another. Thus, Clinton appeased those who feared increased budget deficits by agreeing to put a cap on government assistance for the poor and for small businesses. But this angered some liberal Democrats, such as Representative Stark, who stated, "That ain't the kind of Democratic bill I expect."[4] It was soon clear that the president would have to make many additional modifications in order to achieve congressional approval of a viable health reform bill.

Searching for the middle ground is an appropriate—even necessary—strategy in shaping public policy in any area. The translation of intentions into successful policies involves adaptation, which, in President Clinton's words, is intended to achieve the "vital center" of interest as that is defined by conflicting groups and organizations. The process demands extraordinary political skill, as we will see as we examine the politics of policy making in four major areas: education, health and welfare, housing, and the environment and energy.

THE MAKING OF AMERICAN PUBLIC POLICY in any area can be described in terms very similar to those we have used to describe health-care reform. The translation of intentions into successful policy involves adaptation, adaptation which, to use President Clinton's term, achieves the "vital center" of interest as that is defined by conflicting groups and organizations. This becomes clear as we examine the politics of policy making in four major areas: education, health and welfare, housing, and the environment and energy.

EDUCATION POLICY

The federal government annually spends about $9 billion on elementary and secondary education and about $9 billion on higher education. This money represents only about 6 percent of all spending on public education in the United States. The amount is so small because education has historically been left largely to state and local governments. As recently as 1974 the United States Supreme Court stated that "no single tradition in public education is more deeply rooted [in the United States] than local control over the operations of schools."[5] Nevertheless, federal involvement in education policy is growing. Indeed, back in the 1988 presidential election campaign George Bush declared that he would like to be known as the "education president."

Education in America: An Overview

National education policy is partly distributive and partly redistributive. Throughout the years, and especially since the 1950s and 1960s, the federal government's major policy concern in the educational arena has been to ensure equal access to educational opportunities. Federal courts have invalidated laws

In 1954, in the historic case of Brown v. Board of Education of Topeka, the Supreme Court ruled that racial segregation in public schools violated the Fourteenth Amendment. But desegregation came slowly, and the federal government used many means to advance it. The busing of students was one remedy tried—in this case, at South Boston High School in 1974.

UPI/Bettmann

Following World War II, the "G.I. Bill" helped millions of veterans seeking higher education. But colleges and universities were hard pressed to house their new students.

that denied equal access to educational facilities, and Congress has designed legislation to reduce racial and income disparities in educational opportunity.

Until the mid 1960s the major federal programs in education were the school lunch and milk program, the "impact" aid program (which made federal aid available to areas affected by federal activities), and programs providing funds for vocational rehabilitation education. The National Defense Education Act, passed in 1958, was designed to upgrade science, math, and foreign-language facilities in the public schools. Prior to 1965, the federal program with the greatest impact on education was the Serviceman's Readjustment Act of 1944 (the so-called G.I. Bill), which provided assistance to millions of veterans who wished to complete their education.

The level of federal involvement in education changed significantly with the passage of the Elementary and Secondary Education Act (ESEA) in 1965. This legislation—designed to distribute federal aid to school districts on the basis of the proportion of low-income children in those districts—virtually doubled the amount of federal aid allocated to public education. In 1979 Congress created a cabinet-level Department of Education, which was given responsibility for the implementation of federal education policy (the education subgovernment is illustrated in Figure 17-1).

Education Policy in the Reagan Administration

Ronald Reagan, in his campaign for the presidency, opposed the new Department of Education and called for its abolition. As president, however, he did not dismantle the department. Early in his administration President Reagan attempted to persuade Congress to fold many of the federal government's education programs into a single large block grant. Such a measure, he argued, would give state and local officials more control over the allocation of federal education funds. Although the president also proposed significant reductions

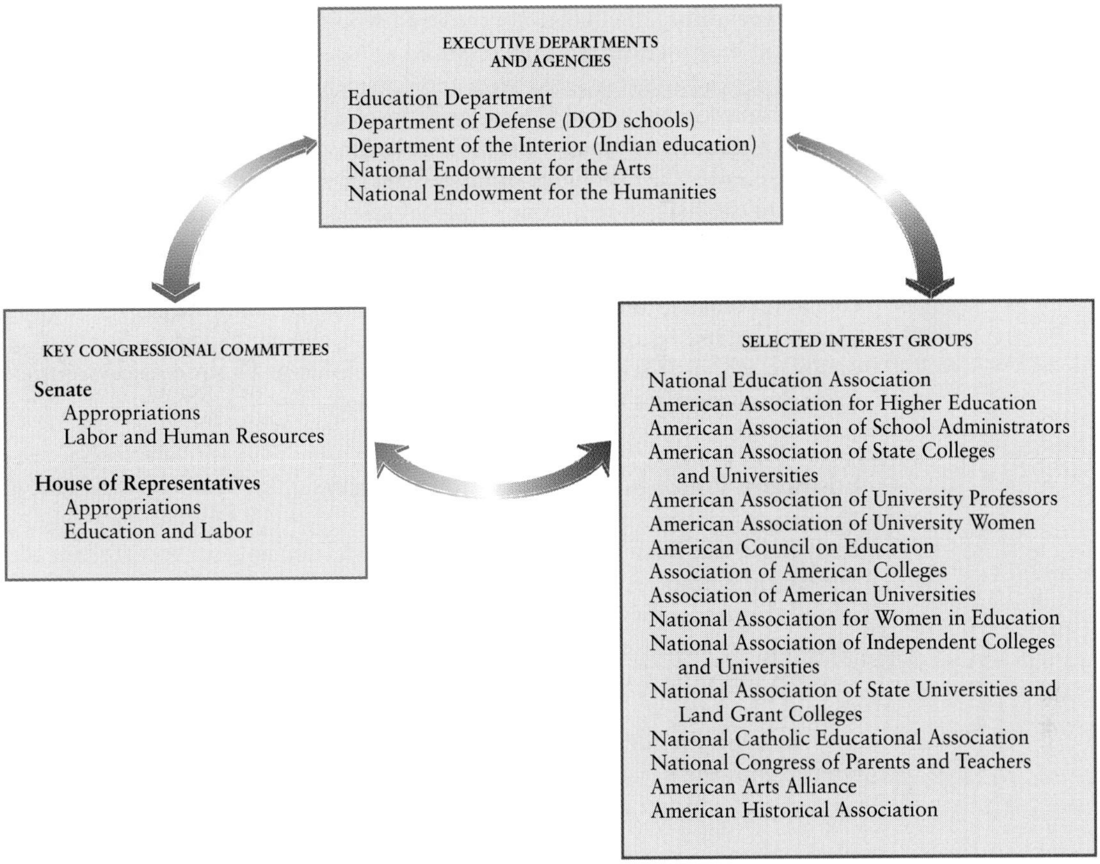

```
┌─────────────────────────────────────┐
│         EXECUTIVE DEPARTMENTS         │
│              AND AGENCIES             │
│                                       │
│   Education Department                │
│   Department of Defense (DOD schools) │
│   Department of the Interior (Indian education) │
│   National Endowment for the Arts     │
│   National Endowment for the Humanities │
└─────────────────────────────────────┘
```

KEY CONGRESSIONAL COMMITTEES

Senate
   Appropriations
   Labor and Human Resources

House of Representatives
   Appropriations
   Education and Labor

SELECTED INTEREST GROUPS

National Education Association
American Association for Higher Education
American Association of School Administrators
American Association of State Colleges
   and Universities
American Association of University Professors
American Association of University Women
American Council on Education
Association of American Colleges
Association of American Universities
National Association for Women in Education
National Association of Independent Colleges
   and Universities
National Association of State Universities and
   Land Grant Colleges
National Catholic Educational Association
National Congress of Parents and Teachers
American Arts Alliance
American Historical Association

Figure 17-1 *The education subgovernment.*

in levels of federal aid to education, he argued that the savings achieved through the use of a block grant would offset any losses to particular school districts.

Opposed to Reagan's proposal were civil rights groups and groups representing handicapped children and the poor. These organizations feared that without federal restrictions on how education funds were spent, the groups they represented would not fare as well under the block grant philosophy. A spokesperson for the Children's Defense Fund, for example, testified before the Senate education subcommittee that her organization was "deeply concerned about the possible effects of a block grant on education services and civil rights for disadvantaged, racial minorities, and handicapped children."[6]

Key members of the House and Senate committees with jurisdiction over education programs also voiced reservations about the president's proposal. Carl Perkins (D-Kentucky), chair of the House Education and Labor Committee, stated in hearings that because federal funds under the block grant program "could be used for local tax relief [rather than for education programs], I'm going to find it very difficult to support a no-strings, Brinks truck delivery of money to states."[7]

On the other hand, many state officials and educators supported the block grant proposal. Although they opposed reductions in education funding, these groups believed that the president's proposal would provide greater flexibility in the expenditure of education funds and would reduce the amount of paper-work and bureaucratic red tape required of local school officials.

In 1981 Congress sided with the president and approved an education block grant, known as the Education Consolidation and Improvement Act. It merged a number of small education programs into a single program. Funds allocated under the new block grant go to state education agencies, which then distribute the bulk of the money to local school districts. The school districts may use the money for such programs as skills development, education improvement, support services, and special projects. However, not included in the education block grant approved by Congress in 1981 was the provision of the Elementary and Secondary Education Act that allocated over $3.5 billion annually to school districts with disadvantaged children. This provision continues to be the centerpiece of federal education policy.

Education Policy in the Bush Administration

Early in George Bush's presidency the administration issued a report that called the nation's schools "merely average" and pointed to the large number of school dropouts, disappointing test scores, and low levels of state and local spending on education. In presenting the report, Education Secretary Lauro Cavazos called the nation's educational situation "a disaster that we must turn around."[8]

In 1989 President Bush held a widely publicized education summit conference with the nation's fifty governors. The result was the announcement of six national education goals to be achieved by the year 2000:

1. All children will start school ready to learn.
2. Ninety percent of all high school students will graduate.
3. Students will achieve competence in core subjects.
4. The United States will be "first in the world" in math and science.
5. Every adult American will be literate.
6. All schools will be free of drugs and violence.

In April 1991 President Bush outlined his education proposals in a report titled *America 2000*. The report called for additional spending of $670 million in 1992, most of it to enable parents to choose the schools their children would attend and to provide seed money for the establishment of 535 innovative schools, at least one in each congressional district. The report also called for a system of national testing and challenged business leaders to raise about $200 million to help fund the innovative schools.

Reactions to the president's proposals were mixed. Albert Shanker, president of the American Federation of Teachers, called the plan "a turning point in the federal role. This is the very first time the President of the United States has said the federal government [has] a major role in improving elementary and secondary education."[9]

Many educators, however, criticized the president for not supporting significant new federal funding to meet his goals and for paying scant regard to social conditions related to educational problems. Marc Tucker, president of the National Center for Education and the Economy, said, "The math and science goal is critical but reaching it with 20 percent of our kids living in poverty is ludicrous." Similarly, Bill Honig, California's state superintendent for public instruction, said that to achieve these goals "President Bush has to commit the resources." Sharon Morgan, a kindergarten teacher from New Mexico, seemed to express the views of many teachers when she said, "There's no way we can expect kids to perform well on standardized tests if we haven't met their basic [food, shelter, and safety] needs."[10]

Through some highly publicized activities—such as calling for the 1989 education summit conference and the appointment of a National Education Goals Panel—President Bush attempted to use the persuasive powers of the presidency to shape national educational priorities and goals. But his statement that "dollar bills don't educate students"[11] demonstrated his reluctance to commit much new federal spending to educational goals.

In April of 1993, President Bill Clinton proposed a "national service program" that was designed to make a college education available to all students, regardless of their financial situation. Under his proposal students could receive college loans and pay them off through automatic deductions from their future earnings or by performing community service jobs—as teachers, police officers, or social workers, for example—after graduation. The nation's banking industry, which would be cut out of the student loan process under the president's proposal, immediately began its lobbying campaign against the measure. In September of 1993 Congress passed and sent to the White House the National Service Bill, providing up to $9,450 in education grants to volunteers when they complete their community service. This was the first of President Cinton's new program proposals made ready for his signature.

HEALTH AND WELFARE POLICY

Poverty in America presents many paradoxes. Americans value individual responsibility and initiative and like to think they live in a land of abundance and opportunity. Yet many people do not share equally in that abundance.

In the past several decades the federal government has spent billions of dollars on programs designed to combat poverty. In 1965 federal spending on poverty programs totaled about $8 billion. This amount increased to over $100 billion by 1990. Nevertheless, large numbers of Americans continue to live in poverty. The government classifies as "poor" a family of four living on an annual cash income of less than $14,335. According to this standard, in 1993 almost 37 million Americans—the highest number since 1964, the year President Lyndon B. Johnson declared "war" on poverty—were defined as poor. Since 1965 the *percentage* of Americans living in poverty has fluctuated annually from about 11 to 17 percent. In addition, the *proportion* of Americans living below the poverty line varies greatly by race, ethnicity, age, and geographic region (see Figure 17-2).

Since 1965 the income gap between poor and rich Americans has increased; so too has the poverty rate among children and among households headed by women. Today it is estimated that about 22 percent of all children in America under the age of eighteen live in poor households (see Figure 17-3).[12]

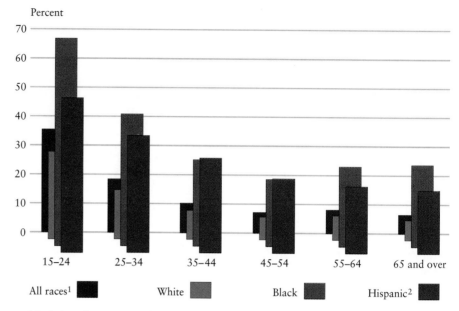

Percent

Figure 17-2   *Percentage of people living below the poverty level, by age and race, March 1992.* SOURCE: *U.S. Department of Commerce, Bureau of the Census,* Statistical Abstract of the United States, 1993.

All races[1]   White   Black   Hispanic[2]

[1] Includes other races not shown separately.
[2] Hispanic persons may be of any race.

Welfare Programs: An Overview

Although welfare policy is commonly thought of as redistributive, many of the nation's welfare programs are distributive. Nationally funded retirement, health, housing support, and college loan programs provide benefits to the public at large and enjoy widespread public support.

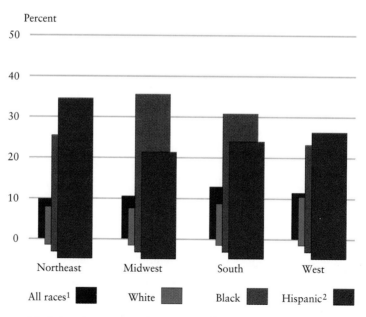

Percent

Figure 17-3   *Percentage of people living below the poverty level, by region and race, March 1992.* SOURCE: *U.S. Department of Commerce, Bureau of the Census,* Statistical Abstract of the United States, 1993.

All races[1]   White   Black   Hispanic[2]

[1] Includes other races not shown separately.
[2] Hispanic persons may be of any race.

(Left) In 1936, in the depths of the Depression, photographer Walker Evans revealed the architecture of poverty in a shantytown in Atlanta, Georgia. (Right) In 1993, poverty and its architecture have changed little for those who live in the shanties of Robinsonville, Mississippi. For them, the revolutions in social welfare and civil rights are still beyond the horizon.

Before the 1930s the United States had virtually no national policy in the area of public welfare or social insurance. Problems of hunger, unemployment, poverty, old age, and disability were handled by families, private charity, and state and local governments. The Great Depression of the 1930s dramatically revealed the inadequacies of the old system and the need for federal assistance for people affected by harsh economic and social conditions. The Social Security Act of 1935 established the framework for federally funded welfare and social insurance in the United States.

Broadly speaking, there are two types of social welfare programs. **Social insurance** is a "pay-as-you-go" program that requires employees and employers to contribute to a national insurance fund. **Public assistance** is a program that provides money and other forms of support to needy people. Public assistance programs are means-tested—that is, they require a certain level of poverty for eligibility. They are paid for out of general revenues and are commonly called welfare programs. The subgovernment of these entitlement programs is pictured in Figure 17-4.

Social Insurance

The basic social insurance programs in operation in the United States are old-age, survivors, and disability insurance (OASDI, commonly known as Social Security), Medicare, and unemployment insurance.

Social Security **Social Security** provides monthly payments to retired men and women, to disabled workers, and to survivors of workers who were covered by the program. Contributions to the program are made through a Social Security tax levied on employees and employers. As of 1993, employees paid 7.65 percent and employers 7.65 percent of employees' income, up to an annual income level of $57,600, into the Social Security trust fund. Incomes between

627

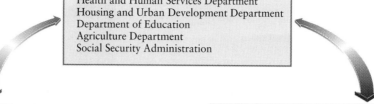

EXECUTIVE DEPARTMENTS
AND AGENCIES

Health and Human Services Department
Housing and Urban Development Department
Department of Education
Agriculture Department
Social Security Administration

KEY CONGRESSIONAL COMMITTEES

Senate
    Agriculture, Nutrition, and Forestry
    Appropriations
    Finance
    Labor and Human Resources
    Special Committee on Aging
House of Representatives
    Agriculture
    Appropriations
    Banking, Finance, and Urban Affairs
    Education and Labor
    Select Committee – Aging
    Select Committee on Children, Youth,
        and Families
    Select Committee on Hunger
    Ways and Means

SELECTED INTEREST GROUPS

American Association of Retired Persons
AFL–CIO
American Family Society
American Hospital Association
American Medical Association
American Public Welfare Association
Catholic Charities USA
Child Welfare League of America
Children's Defense Fund
The Children's Foundation
Center on Budget and Policy Priorities
Coalition for the Homeless
Coalition on Human Needs
Families USA
National Alliance of Senior Citizens
National Association of Chambers of Commerce
National Association of Social Workers
National Association for the Advancement of
    Colored People
National Community Action Foundation
National Council of Senior Citizens

Figure 17-4 *The welfare subgovernment.*

$57,600 and $135,000 were taxed at the rate of 1.45 percent for both employees and employers.

As the program is currently operated, workers qualify for partial Social Security payments at age 62 if they have worked about ten years. Workers may receive full benefits beginning at age 65, but over the next few years this age requirement will rise to 67. The actual amount that an individual receives depends on a number of factors, including age of retirement, category of recipient (employee or survivor), and average income over a period of years. In 1993 almost 42 million Americans received Social Security benefits, with an average monthly payment of $653 for retired workers.

Medicare In 1965 **Medicare** was added to the Social Security package as a health insurance program as part of President Johnson's Great Society proposals. Medicare pays partial costs of hospital bills and (for those selecting higher coverage) part of physicians' fees for retired people age 65 and over. As of 1990, approximately 35 million people were enrolled in the Medicare program, at an annual cost of more than $100 billion.

The 1988 amendments to the Medicare program present an interesting case study in the politics of policy making. In that year Congress, with much fanfare, amended the Medicare program to provide protection against the costs of catastrophic illness. These amendments represented the greatest expansion

Unemployment came home for many Americans as the jobless rate rose from about 5.5 percent in 1990 to almost 7.5 percent in 1992. Even the threat of unemployment can become a potent political argument, as was seen in 1993, when it was raised by opponents of the North American Free Trade Agreement (NAFTA).

of Medicare benefits since the program's inception in 1965. In signing the 1988 act, President Reagan proudly proclaimed that it "will remove a terrible threat from the lives of elderly and disabled Americans."[13]

Less than eighteen months later, Congress repealed the new law as a result of a tremendous lobbying effort by older Americans and organizations representing them, who objected to the way the act was funded. Under the law Medicare enrollees themselves paid for the cost of expanded benefits. But *only some* older Americans—those who owed more than $150 in federal income taxes (about 40 percent of all enrollees)—had to pay the surtax for the program. Thus, the wealthiest enrollees were footing the bill for the entire program. Congress was bombarded with complaints, and by wide margins both the House and the Senate voted to repeal the law. In the end, explained Representative Pete Starke of California, "[House members] just said, 'The hell with it. I don't want to deal with [opposition by senior Americans] anymore.' "[14]

Health-care reform   President Clinton made health care a primary issue of the 1992 election and a central issue of his domestic policy. Soon after the election, he appointed a task force, headed by Hillary Rodham Clinton, to prepare proposals. In September of 1993, the president presented a reform package to Congress that was the most dramatic new venture in social policy since the New Deal. It called for guaranteed universal health-care coverage. Costs were to be shared by businesses and employees; poor individuals and small businesses would be subsidized by the federal government.

Unemployment insurance   Set up as a result of the 1935 Social Security Act, **unemployment insurance** is a program designed to pay benefits to people who are unemployed. It is financed jointly by the federal government and the states through taxes paid by employers and in some cases by employees. States have considerable discretion in determining the size of benefits and the length of coverage. As a result, there is considerable variance among the states in monthly average payments.

629

Percent

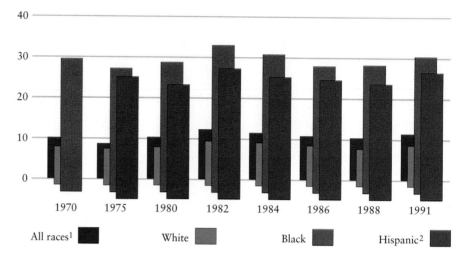

¹ Includes other races not shown separately.
² Hispanic persons may be of any race.

Figure 17-5 *Percentage of people living below the poverty level, by year,*
1970–1991. SOURCE: *U.S. Department of Commerce, Bureau of the Census,* Statistical Abstract of the United States, 1993.

Public Assistance

The 1935 Social Security Act established three public assistance programs: old-age assistance, aid to the blind, and a program that is now called Aid to Families with Dependent Children. Over time this package of programs has been supplemented with other legislation designed to provide assistance for various categories of needy people. In 1950, aid to the permanently and totally disabled was enacted. In 1964, Congress established the food stamp program. In 1965, Medicaid was approved. In 1974, Congress passed the Supplemental Security Income program, which was designed to establish uniform federal benefits for people receiving assistance under the aged, blind, and disabled programs.

Many public assistance programs are jointly funded by the federal government and the states, and in some areas local governments contribute to the programs as well. In most cases state and local governments are responsible for administering the programs.

Aid to Families with Dependent Children The most controversial public assistance program is **Aid to Families with Dependent Children (AFDC).** Originally the program was seen as a way to provide some income assistance to widows while their children were maturing. Over the years, however, because of increases in divorce rates, desertions, and teenage pregnancies, both the number of recipients and the costs of the program have risen substantially (see Figure 17-6). In 1988, Congress undertook a major overhaul of the program. Legislation passed at that time required states to establish job training programs for most AFDC recipients and also to guarantee child care, transportation, and medical coverage to participants. But well into the 1990s about half of AFDC recipients were long-term recipients; about 25 percent had been receiving benefits for ten years or more. Welfare had become the major source of family support—the way of life—for many.

Critics have charged that the AFDC program encourages people to have children in order to obtain AFDC payments and that the rules of some states that in past years barred payments to families in which there was a man in the house encouraged male desertion. Under recent federal court rulings, states may not restrict payments just because there is a man in the house unless it is shown that he is contributing financially to the support of the children.[15]

Food stamps   **Food stamps** are government-issued coupons that are redeemable for food. The food stamp program, designed to boost the food budget of low-income families, was established in 1964. Under the program as initially passed, low-income families could purchase food stamps at some fraction of their actual value and then redeem them for food. In 1977 Congress eliminated the provision that recipients must pay a portion of the value. The value of food stamps received is determined by a family's size and income level. Currently, almost 27 million Americans (10.4 percent of the population) are receiving food stamp benefits at an annual cost of over $23 billion.

Medicaid   In 1965 Congress established **Medicaid,** a program that is designed to help low-income people pay hospital, doctor, and medical bills. Today approximately 25 million people receive Medicaid benefits at a total cost of over $45 billion.

Each year more than a million teenagers become mothers. Many of them are poor and under age fifteen, and too many see no choice other than dropping out of school and beginning a life on welfare. But these girls are in a program that lets them continue to attend classes while learning to raise their babies in the school's full-time daycare center.

© B. Daemmrich/The Image Works

Political parties, interest groups, the president, and numerous departments and agencies of the states and federal government all have a significant interest in the welfare agenda (see Figure 17-4). However, much of the policy formation and agenda setting in the welfare arena takes place directly on the floor of Congress or in its various committees. Indeed, Congress probably is a more significant actor in welfare policy than in almost any other domestic social issue. Its significance stems from the high public visibility of welfare issues, the degree of organization and legislative skills of interest groups in the welfare arena, and the large amount of money appropriated to welfare programs each year. Legislators see welfare policy as an opportunity for significant resource distribution: most want to obtain as large a share of benefits for their districts and their constituents as possible.

Key actors　A host of committees and subcommittees in Congress are responsible for the various aspects of the welfare program. The Finance Committee in the Senate and the Ways and Means Committee in the House are important because they are responsible for raising the money to pay for federal programs. The health and the social security and income maintenance programs subcommittees of the Finance Committee are key actors in the Senate, and the health and social security subcommittees of the Ways and Means Committee are key actors in the House. Within the Senate, also, the labor and human resources subcommittees on aging, alcoholism, and drug abuse, education, family and human services, and the handicapped are concerned with various aspects of the welfare program; and the agriculture subcommittee of the Agriculture, Nutrition, and Forestry Committee is responsible for oversight of the food stamp program. In the House, the health and safety and human resources subcommittees of the Education and Labor Committee are key actors in welfare policy; the agriculture subcommittee on domestic marketing, consumer relations, and nutrition is concerned with the food stamp program.

Numerous interest groups also are active in the welfare arena. The AFL-CIO, the National Association of Chambers of Commerce, the NAACP, and others usually want to testify before any congressional committee or subcommittee that is considering alterations in the welfare system. Groups of state and local officials such as the National Governors' Association, the National League of Cities, and the American Public Welfare Association (representing state welfare officials) are also active on almost any welfare issue. In addition, academics, religious groups, and think tanks such as the American Enterprise Institute and the Brookings Institution may play an active role in the problem recognition and policy formulation stages of welfare policy.

Some interest groups focus on certain aspects of welfare policy. The American Association of Retired Persons and the National Council of Senior Citizens are most concerned with the problems of the aged. The American Hospital Association and the American Medical Association are concerned about health-care costs. The Children's Defense Fund and the Child Welfare League of America are concerned with programs dealing with children, youth, and families.

The political parties also tend to take stands on welfare issues. The Democratic party has tended to advocate an active role for government in establishing welfare programs and expanding benefits. The Republican party gen-

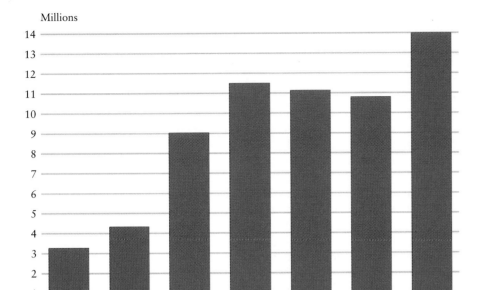

Figure 17-6 *Numbers of recipients of AFDC payments.* SOURCE: *U.S. Department of Commerce, Bureau of the Census,* Statistical Abstract of the United States, *for the years shown; and Robert Pear, "Poverty in U.S. Grew Faster Than Population Last Year,"* New York Times, *October 5, 1993.*

erally opposes expansion of welfare programs and, at times, favors a ceiling on costs and rollbacks in program activities. It emphasizes work incentives and private sector action to help those who are unable to work.

Welfare reform   In recent years there has been agreement on the need to contain, if not reduce, welfare costs; to crack down on "welfare cheats"; to focus efforts on people who are unable to break out of the poverty cycle; and to consider more work or work training requirements for welfare recipients.[16] This consensus led to the passage of a major welfare reform bill in the fall of 1988. The Family Support Act of 1988 (which authorized a five-year appropriation of $3.34 billion) emphasizes jobs and job training. It requires each state to create a job training program (with support services such as child care, medical care, and transportation) for all able-bodied recipients except those who are needed at home to care for ill dependents, are working thirty hours a week, are in the late stages of pregnancy, or are attending school. The law requires all states to enroll a minimum of 20 percent of their eligible population by 1995, but it gives the states significant flexibility in developing their programs.

The new approach embodied in the 1988 legislation views welfare as temporary: recipients are to be trained for work in the public or private sector. The new approach "redefines the whole question of [welfare] dependency," stated New York senator Daniel Moynihan, a major architect of the legislation. Welfare, he added, "is no longer to be a permanent or even extended circumstance. It is to be a transition to employment."[17] This approach establishes a principle of mutual obligation: welfare recipients are expected to participate in education or job training programs; states are expected to provide educational opportunities and necessary services to recipients as they seek jobs and job training.

The passage of the 1988 welfare reform bill is a classic illustration of American politics in action. After struggling with reform proposals for almost twenty years, Congress finally forged a compromise in which all sides got much of what they wanted and had to accept some things that they did not like. In this case the White House and the Senate were pressing for a strong work program for welfare recipients. The House, organized labor, and many anti-poverty groups wanted extended benefits and increased welfare coverage. The resulting bill took into consideration the charge that Republicans are not compassionate and understanding of the problems of the poor, and it took into consideration the criticism that Democrats are "soft" on welfare and oppose work and job training for welfare recipients.

Flaws in the 1988 legislation soon were evident. In particular, some welfare recipients were finding it difficult to receive enough money from their jobs to pay for child care. An unanticipated consequence of the new welfare program was that some states were forced to take money from other social service programs to meet their obligations under the 1988 act. The resulting loss of benefits forced some working people to quit their jobs, causing a net increase in the welfare rolls in some states. Also, as of 1992 only about 25 percent of welfare recipients participating in the program actually were working or looking for work. The remainder had elected to seek additional education, prompting some critics to argue that they were returning to the same classroom situation in which they had previously failed. President Clinton made imposing a two-year limit on benefits the centerpiece of his welfare reform proposals.

Despite its flaws, the 1988 welfare reform bill represents the most fundamental change in the nation's welfare system since its creation during the Depression years. It also illustrates the role of politics in the process of policy making. Major change is difficult, but it is not impossible to achieve. Convincing enough people that their interests are best served by a particular change remains the most effective political tool in the American policy process.

HOUSING POLICY

The recognition of housing as a problem requiring serious public attention can be traced to the Great Depression of the 1930s. President Franklin Roosevelt focused the nation's attention on housing problems with his second Inaugural Address, in January 1937, in which he declared, "I see one-third of the nation ill housed."

The various housing acts adopted by Congress since the Depression have generally adopted an *intergovernmental* approach to policy implementation— that is, the federal government has been largely responsible for establishing, funding, and evaluating programs; and state and local governments have been responsible for implementation. Housing policy has been characterized by shifting and frequently conflicting goals and objectives, intense and prolonged political conflicts, and continued debates over the appropriate role of the public and private sectors in meeting the nation's housing needs.

The results are reflected in the structure of the current housing subgovernment, shown in Figure 17-7.

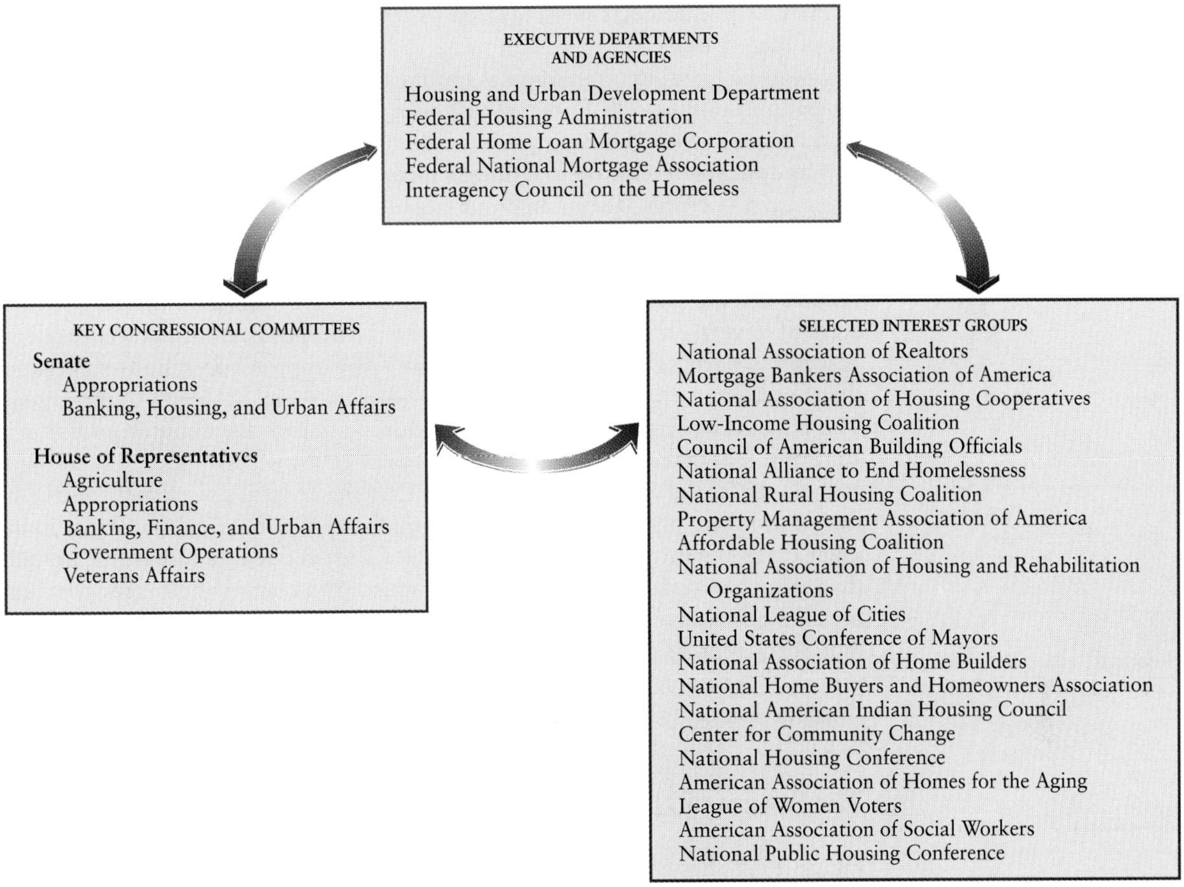

EXECUTIVE DEPARTMENTS AND AGENCIES
Housing and Urban Development Department
Federal Housing Administration
Federal Home Loan Mortgage Corporation
Federal National Mortgage Association
Interagency Council on the Homeless

KEY CONGRESSIONAL COMMITTEES

Senate
  Appropriations
  Banking, Housing, and Urban Affairs

House of Representatives
  Agriculture
  Appropriations
  Banking, Finance, and Urban Affairs
  Government Operations
  Veterans Affairs

SELECTED INTEREST GROUPS

National Association of Realtors
Mortgage Bankers Association of America
National Association of Housing Cooperatives
Low-Income Housing Coalition
Council of American Building Officials
National Alliance to End Homelessness
National Rural Housing Coalition
Property Management Association of America
Affordable Housing Coalition
National Association of Housing and Rehabilitation
    Organizations
National League of Cities
United States Conference of Mayors
National Association of Home Builders
National Home Buyers and Homeowners Association
National American Indian Housing Council
Center for Community Change
National Housing Conference
American Association of Homes for the Aging
League of Women Voters
American Association of Social Workers
National Public Housing Conference

Figure 17-7 *The housing subgovernment.*

Housing Policy: An Overview

When President Roosevelt took office in 1933, mortgages were being foreclosed at the rate of over a thousand per day, and housing construction was at a standstill. The nation's first significant housing act, passed in 1937, was designed to provide housing assistance for people who had been displaced by the harsh economic conditions of the Depression. Under the 1937 act, the federal government assumed most of the cost of constructing public housing, and local governments were responsible for developing and managing project sites.

The original program was not aimed at the poorest of Americans, nor was it intended to provide permanent shelter for homeless families. Rather, it was designed to assist the working poor, people who could pay enough rent to cover the units' operating costs and would leave public housing when their economic situation improved. But over the years public housing increasingly served people who were permanently trapped in poverty, many of whom were minority families. By 1974, when the public housing program was significantly overhauled, over 5 million families were living in public housing projects.[18]

Many of these projects were located in severely depressed sections of the nation's largest cities.

Public housing often attracts families—such as new immigrants and single-parent families—that are not just poor but have other social needs as well. And because public housing projects often are located in isolated, segregated, and undesirable areas, their residents face all of the problems associated with inner cities—crime, drugs, and vandalism—in addition to inadequate health care and education and other problems associated with poverty.

The location of public housing has long been a controversial issue. Advocates for the poor argue that the inner-city environment contributes to the cycle of poverty, crime, and drugs associated with public housing. Yet residents of wealthy parts of cities and suburbs frequently oppose public housing because they fear that it will bring crime, drugs, and other social problems to their areas. The issue has been fought out in city councils across the country and also in state and federal courts.

In 1976 the Supreme Court ruled that the federal government might be forced to locate public housing in predominantly white suburbs, not just in the inner cities.[19] However, the next year the Court refined its judgment, holding that suburban communities could not be forced to change their zoning laws to provide affordable housing for low-income families unless it could be shown that the intent of the existing zoning laws was to keep out certain minority groups.[20] As a result, suburbs continue to have considerable power to limit the construction of public housing.

The Politics of Housing

Figure 17-6 shows the important groups and agencies involved in the formulation of housing policy. Over the years, working through the political process, these organizations have forged a variety of policy responses to the nation's housing needs.

Urban renewal In 1949 a new approach to housing policy was initiated. In contrast with previous efforts in the area of public housing, **urban renewal** was designed to clear blighted and deteriorating areas of inner cities and replace them with new commercial and residential establishments. Under this program cities were to create local agencies that would identify and purchase the land to be cleared, relocate residents and commercial establishments, tear down structures, reinstall public facilities such as water and sewer services, and sell the land to developers at very favorable prices. Through the urban-renewal program the federal government would pay much of the cost of land acquisition, demolition, and new construction.

Urban renewal provides an excellent illustration of the politics of policy formulation and adoption. The basic concept of urban renewal was introduced as early as 1941. The struggle to formulate a policy that finally could be approved by Congress took eight years. The policy that was ultimately adopted represented a compromise between conservative groups concerned with deteriorating economic conditions in the inner cities and liberal groups concerned with deteriorating social conditions in slum areas.

The primary spokespeople for the conservative groups were the National Association of Real Estate Boards, the United States Savings and Loan League,

AP/Wide World Photos

Residents of Chicago's Cabrini-Green housing project, shortly after a seven-year-old boy was shot by a sniper in October 1992. The city closed this housing and revamped its security arrangements—at a cost of some $4 million—and tenants returned in 1993, pleased that the crime rate had fallen.

and the National Association of Home Builders. These groups, and others supporting them, pressed for a program whose features would include strong control by local governments, sufficient federal funds to keep the cost of land acquisition below market values, and reliance on private builders and developers for land redevelopment. To varying degrees, all of these features were written into the final legislation.

The liberal coalition was represented by various religious groups (such as the National Conference of Catholic Charities), civic organizations (such as the League of Women Voters), welfare and public housing advocates (such as the American Association of Social Workers and the National Public Housing Conference), organized labor, and various representatives of state and local officials (such as the National League of Cities and the United States Conference of Mayors). These groups wanted the legislation to deal with the housing needs of low-income families. They were successful in that the legislation that was enacted stipulated that redevelopment must be "predominantly residential" and that displaced residents must be provided with "decent, safe, and sanitary" housing options. The legislation authorized the construction of over 800,000 government-subsidized "low-rent" housing units during the next six years.[21]

Urban renewal remained controversial for the next quarter of a century. One of the primary issues was the displacement of residents and merchants in the renewal areas. Many of those who were displaced were forced to pay higher rents in their new locations—if they were able to find new accommodations at all. A 1954 amendment required local agencies to provide assistance in relo-

Although some critics object to the demolition of inner-city properties under urban renewal, and others lament the inability of such programs to reverse urban decay, these "Before" and "After" photographs are a strong argument for rehabilitation.

cation, but to those being displaced such assistance often seemed inadequate.[22] Community activists and minority groups frequently viewed the program as an attempt to remove blacks and other minority groups from inner-city business districts. Liberals often saw it as a "federally financed gimmick" to provide cheap land for local developers.[23] Conservatives were disappointed with the program's inability to reverse, or even slow, the decline of inner cities.

In the first fourteen years of operation, urban renewal demolished the homes of over 240,000 families and individuals and replaced less than one-fourth of those units.[24] Perhaps the main criticism of the program was that "despite the billions of dollars spent between 1949 and 1974, the central cities were not renovated."[25] At its conclusion, inner cities were still in decline, slums had not been eliminated, housing opportunities for the poor had not improved, and political support for the program's continuation had vanished.

Community development   Urban renewal was terminated in 1974, when Congress passed the Housing and Community Development Act. This act established the Community Development Block Grant (CDBG) program, which consolidated money that had previously been allocated through urban renewal and several other federal housing programs. Although cities must submit plans for the use of CDBG funds, local governments are given much greater discretion than they were under previous housing programs. Cities may use **Community Development Block Grants** for urban renewal, public housing, street paving, lighting, attracting commercial development, industrial parks, and numerous related activities. During the Reagan administration the amount of money allocated through the CDBG program was reduced significantly, but the flexibility given to local governments in spending the funds was increased.

The 1974 housing act also established an assistance program for poor families. Section 8, as it is called, has two major components. The first is a rent supplement program: eligible tenants pay up to 30 percent of their income for rent, and the program pays the remainder up to a maximum amount set by the Department of Housing and Urban Development (HUD). The subsidy goes directly to tenants in the form of a certificate that can be used to locate housing. This arrangement offers some freedom of choice to low-income families, and it also gives landlords an incentive to rehabilitate and repair rental units.[26]

The second component of the 1974 act encourages construction of new housing units by committing the federal government to subsidizing tenants in new units for long periods, from twenty to thirty years. This protects developers against the risk of having unoccupied units. To stimulate construction of low-cost apartment complexes, HUD also acts as insurer for many construction loans. Under this program, the Federal Housing Administration (FHA) insures mortgages for private developers. If a developer defaults and the property is foreclosed, HUD becomes its owner. By 1993 more than 2,400 of 15,000 complexes that HUD had insured had defaulted, making HUD the owner of thousands of foreclosed apartments. But HUD had neither the personnel nor the experience to manage the units, many of which became slums. HUD Secretary Henry Cisneros stated it bluntly in testimony to Congress: "HUD's management of its inventory has been abysmal. The physical conditions of many properties are deteriorating; others have been overrun by drug trafficking and crime. The truth is stark: HUD has in many cases exacerbated the declining quality of life in America."[27] As a remedy, Cisneros asked Congress to lessen restrictions required of HUD prior to reselling foreclosed properties.

Housing Policy in the 1980s and 1990s

Throughout the 1980s and into the 1990s, the major controversy in the area of public housing continued to be whether the nation's policy should be designed to increase the supply of public housing (supported by liberals, Democrats, and some urban Republicans) or to provide vouchers or rent subsidies to poor families (supported by conservatives and many Republicans). Put simply, was the nation's housing problem one of availability or affordability?

President Reagan argued that there was an adequate supply of rental housing units across the nation. His administration favored a housing voucher plan in which eligible families would receive vouchers to pay for rent on units of their choosing. Critics, however, pointed out that available vacant units were too expensive or were not located in urban markets. One staff member of the Senate Banking, Housing, and Urban Affairs Committee's housing and urban affairs subcommittee said of the Reagan philosophy, "Luxury apartments do not help large families, minority groups, or people who are very poor, and vacancies in Houston don't help people in Boston, Washington, D.C., or San Francisco."[28] As a result of the Reagan approach, the production of new subsidized housing units declined sharply in the 1980s.

President Bush early in his administration announced his housing proposal, Home Ownership and Opportunity for People Everywhere (HOPE). The Bush plan focused on homeownership by enabling tenants in housing projects to purchase their units. "The true measure of success," Bush said, "isn't how many families we add to the housing-assistance rolls, it's how many families move up and out and into the ranks of homeowners."[29]

Typical of Democrats responding to the president's proposal was Representative Charles Schumer of New York, who said, "Our problem is a shortage of units of low-income housing, and there still is a need for a well-thought-out, cost-efficient, low-income production program."[30] Another Democrat, Representative Barney Frank of Massachusetts, stated that "George Bush and [HUD Secretary] Jack Kemp think they are going to buy every poor person a house. But their proposal denies the reality that most poor people, most of the time, have to rent."[31]

The fate of Bush's housing proposals is an example of the sort of policy deadlock that can occur when a president and cabinet member from one party (Republican in this case) propose legislation unacceptable to a Congress dominated by the other party. HUD Secretary Kemp and President Bush strongly supported the idea of selling public housing to housing tenants, but the key housing subcommittee chairs in the House and Senate (Representative Bob Traxler of Michigan and Senator Barbara Mikulski of Maryland, both Democrats) were just as committed to preserving, expanding, and improving conventional public housing. So frustrated was Secretary Kemp with the lengthy stalemate over passage of the administration's proposals that in 1990 and again in 1991 he recommended that President Bush veto the entire appropriation for the Department of Housing and Urban Development.

One of President Clinton's earliest housing proposals was to transfer about $600 million from public housing programs to a flexible grant program known as HOME. While local governments must share HOME grants with a 30-percent match, this program permits greater flexibility in using the funds. Among those concerned that these funds would not be used for housing for the poor was Frank Shafroth of the National League of Cities, who commented that the Clinton plan "provides an excuse for those who wish to discriminate against minorities or low-income people."[32]

Housing is an area where the lines of division are sharply drawn, where partisan politics rules, and where a national consensus concerning a solution

Henry Cisneros, President Clinton's Secretary of Housing and Urban Development, has described his task as "reinventing HUD." His goal is to increase the supply of affordable housing and "move people along a ladder of [housing] opportunity." Here he spends the night in a homeless shelter in Queens, New York.

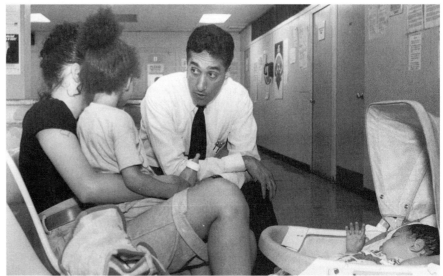

NYT Pictures

to the problem, or even a definition of what the problem is, has yet to emerge. The debate over the best approach to housing the nation's poor and low-income families is sure to be one of the major domestic policy issues in coming years.

ENVIRONMENT AND ENERGY POLICY

The policy areas discussed so far—education, housing, and welfare—are all matters of long-standing concern in the United States. Public concern with environmental issues is of more recent origin. In the early to mid 1960s, polls indicated that only about 10 percent of the American population believed pollution to be a very serious issue. Over the next few years this percentage rose significantly. By 1970 over half of the population mentioned environmental pollution as a serious public problem.[33] (The profile of Lois Gibbs on page 642 describes the early efforts of one woman to increase her neighbors' awareness of the chemical pollution of their neighborhood, the Love Canal section of Niagara Falls, New York.)

It is not surprising that the public was slow to perceive environmental degradation as a major concern. For most of the nation's history Americans have thought of the nation's natural resources as almost inexhaustible free goods. But dramatic events of recent years—including severe energy shortages, electric blackouts, nuclear-plant disasters, oil spills, toxic chemical leaks, and significant increases in environmentally related diseases and deaths—have directed the public's attention to environmental issues. (The politics of toxic waste and its disposal is described further in the Case Study on page 644.)

Today it is widely recognized that the nation's resources are not inexhaustible and that serious, even life-threatening consequences result from unwise use of the earth's resources. Americans also realize that human activities can cause fundamental changes in the earth's ecosystem. Increasingly scientists warn of the potentially catastrophic consequences of the greenhouse effect— the trend toward global warming—that results from the unchecked emission of carbon dioxide, methane, nitrous oxides, and various industrial chemicals into the earth's atmosphere. And Americans are increasingly aware of their special role in addressing this problem. The United States emits more carbon dioxide than any other nation—and more than all of western Europe.[34]

Responding to increased public concern, Congress has passed a number of environmental laws. In 1970 it created the Environmental Protection Agency (EPA), which is charged with enforcing those laws. In 1993 President Clinton proposed elevating the EPA to cabinet-level status. (The environment subgovernment is illustrated in Figure 17-8.) While significant legislative actions have been taken in recent years to improve the quality of water and air and to reduce pollution from and dependence on fossil fuels, environmental policy is largely an example of regulatory policy.

Clean Water

Modern congressional action to limit water pollution dates from 1956, when Congress approved significant amendments to the Water Pollution Control Act

Lois Gibbs: A Voice from the People

The first toxic dump site to be identified as a serious health hazard was the Love Canal area in the town of Niagara Falls in northern New York. The unfinished canal was originally built in 1892. In the 1920s, the Hooker Chemical Company began using the site as a dump for chemical waste. In 1953, Hooker filled in the canal and sold the land for a nominal dollar to the Niagara Falls Board of Education. An elementary school and houses were soon built on the site.

From the start, residents of the area complained about odors and unidentified corrosive substances in the soil. State health officials took notice of the problem only in the late 1970s—and then only as a result of community pressure. Several residents of the Love Canal area helped mobilize their neighbors. One of them, Lois Gibbs, tells how she became involved and what she learned:

Love Canal actually began for me in June 1978 with Mike Brown's articles in the Niagara Falls *Gazette*. At first, I didn't realize where the canal was. . . . I didn't think he meant the place where my children went to school or where I took them to play on the jungle gyms and swings. . . . Then when I found out the 99th Street School was indeed on top of it, I was alarmed. My son attended that school. . . . I decided to go door-to-door with a petition. . . . I had never done anything like this, however, and I was frightened. I was afraid a lot of doors would be slammed in my face, that people would think I was some crazy fanatic. But I decided to do it anyway.

I shouldn't have been too surprised when I discovered later that emergencies like this bring out the best and worst in people. Sometimes people have honest differences about the best way to solve a problem. Sometimes, however, people have big egos; it's more important for them to be up front and draw attention to themselves than cooperate with others in working for a cause. I really did have a lot to learn.

Michael J. Philippot/SYGMA

Gibbs and neighbors celebrate President Carter's promise of another $3.8 million for medical exams and health studies in the Love Canal.

The community pressure brought to bear by Lois Gibbs and her neighbors finally began to tell on unresponsive officials. Relocation of residents living on the canal site began in August 1978. In October 1980, President Jimmy Carter signed a bill evacuating all families from the site permanently.

SOURCE: Lois Marie Gibbs, as told to Murray Levine, *Love Canal, My Story* (Albany: State University of New York Press, 1982). Reprinted by permission of the author, Lois Gibbs.

of 1948. The 1956 amendments authorized the federal government to convene conferences to study the problems of streams and lakes. The conferences were to be open to all interested individuals and groups. Conference findings were to be forwarded to appropriate state officials. If the states did not take corrective action within six months, public hearings could be called to focus attention

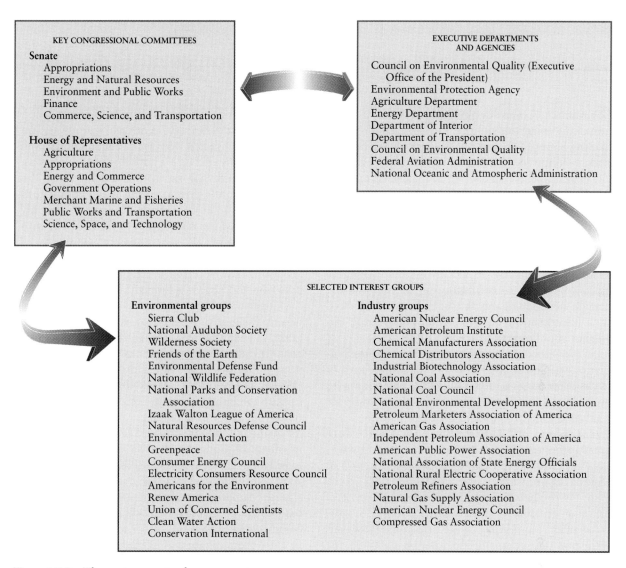

KEY CONGRESSIONAL COMMITTEES

Senate
  Appropriations
  Energy and Natural Resources
  Environment and Public Works
  Finance
  Commerce, Science, and Transportation

House of Representatives
  Agriculture
  Appropriations
  Energy and Commerce
  Government Operations
  Merchant Marine and Fisheries
  Public Works and Transportation
  Science, Space, and Technology

EXECUTIVE DEPARTMENTS
AND AGENCIES

Council on Environmental Quality (Executive
    Office of the President)
Environmental Protection Agency
Agriculture Department
Energy Department
Department of Interior
Department of Transportation
Council on Environmental Quality
Federal Aviation Administration
National Oceanic and Atmospheric Administration

SELECTED INTEREST GROUPS

Environmental groups
  Sierra Club
  National Audubon Society
  Wilderness Society
  Friends of the Earth
  Environmental Defense Fund
  National Wildlife Federation
  National Parks and Conservation
    Association
  Izaak Walton League of America
  Natural Resources Defense Council
  Environmental Action
  Greenpeace
  Consumer Energy Council
  Electricity Consumers Resource Council
  Americans for the Environment
  Renew America
  Union of Concerned Scientists
  Clean Water Action
  Conservation International

Industry groups
  American Nuclear Energy Council
  American Petroleum Institute
  Chemical Manufacturers Association
  Chemical Distributors Association
  Industrial Biotechnology Association
  National Coal Association
  National Coal Council
  National Environmental Development Association
  Petroleum Marketers Association of America
  American Gas Association
  Independent Petroleum Association of America
  American Public Power Association
  National Association of State Energy Officials
  National Rural Electric Cooperative Association
  Petroleum Refiners Association
  Natural Gas Supply Association
  American Nuclear Energy Council
  Compressed Gas Association

Figure 17-8   *The environment subgovernment.*

on particular problems and polluters. If the problem was not addressed in another six months, the United States attorney general could be asked to file suit
against the offending polluter. Between 1956 and 1972 only once was an injunction sought against a polluter.[35]

The Water Quality Act of 1965 represented the first attempt to establish
standards for water quality. That act permitted each state to develop its own
water quality standards and submit them to the federal government for approval. Because many state officials were reluctant to set standards that might

The Politics of Toxic Waste

Environmental regulation provides a classic illustration of interest group politics. Environmental groups like the Sierra Club and the Wilderness Society frequently lobby for new legislation to protect the environment and for stricter enforcement of existing legislation. Other groups—including those representing business, trade associations, and land developers—frequently claim that the demands of the environmental groups are unreasonable and that implementing their goals would create financial hardship. Members of Congress often disagree among themselves and with the administration. Caught in the middle is the federal agency charged with implementing environmental policy—the Environmental Protection Agency (EPA).

Nowhere has the politics of environmental regulation been more clearly evident than in the area of toxic-waste management. In 1980, responding to growing public concern over toxic-waste dumps—such as the highly publicized situation in the Love Canal section of Niagara Falls, New York—Congress approved a $1.6-billion expenditure, known as the "superfund," to clean up such sites. The job of identifying and supervising the cleanups fell to the EPA. As the law was written, much of the cost of cleaning up toxic dumps was to be borne by the companies responsible for the pollution. However, if the polluting company could not be identified, the cleanup was to be paid for by the superfund.

From the outset, the EPA was embroiled in controversy over its administration of the superfund legislation. EPA Director Anne Burford prepared a list of approximately four hundred dangerous toxic-waste dumps, but environmentalists charged that the EPA moved much too slowly in forcing cleanups and that its standards were not as rigorous as Congress had intended. A number of congressional committees investigated EPA's handling of the superfund and discovered that the former employer of Rita Lavelle, Burford's chief assistant, was dumping toxic wastes at a site in California. These and other revelations forced the resignation of Burford and most other upper-level EPA appointees in 1983.

The enforcement and funding of the superfund program never received more than lukewarm support from the Reagan administration. In 1985, when the superfund legislation was considered for renewal, Reagan threatened to veto the entire program. Attempting to persuade the president to accept the measure, eighty-one senators signed a letter urging him to sign the bill. House Speaker Thomas O'Neill and Majority Leader Jim Wright promised to keep the House in session to override a presidential veto if that was necessary. Applying pressures of its own, EPA administrator Lee Thomas informed members of Congress that he would have to dismantle much of the EPA if a bill was not approved soon. On October 17, 1986, President Reagan did sign the superfund reauthorization bill, which extended the program for another five years with a commitment of $8.5 billion for toxic-waste cleanup. In 1990 the program was extended to December 31, 1995.

Interest groups representing both environmentalists and business associations have maintained a close watch over the EPA's handling of the superfund, noting inconsistencies and irregularities in its application of the law. For example, in 1987 a

deter business from locating in their states, the standards established in response to this legislation were minimal.[36]

In 1972 Congress enacted the Clean Water Act, designed to establish more uniform and rigorous standards. As a result, Congress—not the states—set national objectives. The goal was the complete elimination of the discharge of pollutants in the nation's waterways by 1985. The EPA was authorized to

Homeowners were forced to abandon this house near the Love Canal.

spokesperson for the Sierra Club noted in congressional testimony that the EPA's plan for a site cleanup in Kentucky was considerably more stringent than its plan for a site cleanup in Louisiana. As the Sierra Club's representative told Congress, "The unlucky citizens of Louisiana can envy their counterparts in Kentucky for being the inexplicable beneficiaries of a bureaucratic roll of the dice." Environmental groups have frequently taken the EPA to federal court to require the enforcement of standards that environmentalists believe are being handled too slowly or too laxly by the EPA.

Discussion questions
1. How does this case illustrate the role of interest groups in the formulation, implementation, and oversight of regulatory policies like the superfund?
2. How does the case illustrate the strategies that various groups—including members of Congress—might employ in support of policies when presidential approval is lacking?
3. Can regulatory agencies like the EPA remain "nonpolitical" in the administration of programs like the superfund? What does this case say about the role of regulatory agencies in the administration of controversial programs?

set quality standards for interstate streams as well as for intrastate waters if states refused to do so. An expenditure of $18 billion was authorized to help states pay for the construction of sewage treatment facilities.

In 1977 the 1965 and 1972 clean-water acts were amended to extend some of the deadlines set in 1972 and strengthen the EPA's control over the discharge of certain toxic substances. In 1987, overriding President Reagan's veto, Congress reauthorized the 1972 Clean Water Act, pledging $18 billion over the next ten years for continued assistance to states and localities for the construction of sewage plants.

Clean Air

The Clean Air Act of 1963 was intended to develop for the federal government a role in the area of air pollution much like the role envisioned in the area of water pollution. Under the provisions of the act, the federal government was to serve as a convener of conferences and hearings dealing with air pollution, and suits were to be pressed after polluters had been given ample opportunity to correct offending situations. Only eleven conferences were held in the first seven years of the act's existence, and only once did the federal government actively attempt to stop the actions of a polluting firm.

The 1970 amendments to the Clean Air Act set strict national air quality standards for local governments and industry, including controls on automobile emissions, and provided heavy fines for violators. Subsequent amendments extended the deadlines for compliance. In 1982 President Reagan supported amendments that would have weakened the Clean Air Act, which business leaders claimed cost them billions of dollars. Those amendments were never passed, but the Reagan administration managed to block any serious attempt to strengthen existing laws. As one businessperson put it, "It was nice [during the Reagan years] for us to know that if an extreme bill were to pass Congress, it would be vetoed by Ronald Reagan."[37]

President Bush early in his administration voiced a strong commitment to clean air. In his February 1989 budget message to Congress he declared, "We must protect the air we breathe. I will send you legislation for a new, more effective Clean Air Act. It will include a plan to reduce . . . the emissions which cause acid rain, because the time for study alone has passed, and the time for action is now."[38]

New amendments to the Clean Air Act were passed by Congress and signed into law by President Bush in 1990. The new legislation set strict federal standards for automobile exhaust, urban smog, toxic air pollution, and acid rain. When signing the bill, the president stated, "This bill means cleaner cars, cleaner power plants, cleaner factories, and cleaner fuels."[39] Indeed, from 1990 to 1993 air quality did improve. Then, in April 1993, President Clinton proposed "reducing our emissions of greenhouse gases to their 1990 levels by the year 2000."[40] This proposal featured voluntary goals and incentives and avoided new industrial mandates and regulations.

Energy Policy

Before World War II virtually all the oil consumed in the United States was domestically produced. By the 1960s, almost one-third of the country's oil was imported, and Americans were becoming increasingly dependent on foreign oil. In 1990 almost 60 percent of the imports came from nations belonging to the Organization of Petroleum Exporting Countries (OPEC).[41] By the early 1990s

Dairy cows graze near the cooling towers of Three Mile Island's nuclear-power plant. No meltdown occurred when a valve failed in 1979, but some radioactivity did escape.

the United States, with only about 5 percent of the world's population, was consuming almost 25 percent of the world's energy supplies.[42]

America's heavy and precarious dependence on foreign sources of energy was driven home in 1973 and 1974, when OPEC imposed an embargo on shipments of oil to the United States and gasoline shortages forced drivers across the country to wait in long lines for a turn at the gas pump. Throughout the rest of the 1970s and into the 1980s, the escalating cost of fuel to heat and cool homes, drive cars, and run factories was a constant reminder of the importance of energy as a political issue.

Perhaps no single event more dramatically focused the public's attention on energy-related issues than the March 1979 incident at the Three Mile Island nuclear-power plant in Pennsylvania: a valve failure in the cooling system precipitated the worst nuclear accident in the nation's history. A meltdown—in which the nuclear core melts through its steel-and-concrete casing, releasing lethal radioactivity—did not occur, but some radioactivity did escape. This incident, along with a nuclear accident in 1986 at a nuclear plant at Chernobyl in the Soviet Union, which resulted in more than a dozen deaths, greatly intensified the debate between proponents and opponents of nuclear energy.

The debate extended to alternative energy sources as well. In 1977 President Carter described the nation's energy crisis as "the moral equivalent of war" and proposed new programs designed both to conserve energy and to develop new energy sources. He recommended, and Congress enacted, laws creating a Department of Energy and a Synthetic Fuels Corporation. The latter was to provide subsidies for the production of fuels from sources other than oil, such as coal, wind, garbage, and plants. However, the corporation received only token support from the Reagan administration and was abolished in 1986.

Early in 1991 President Bush submitted energy-related legislation to Congress. Emphasizing production over conservation, Bush's proposal called for opening new oil fields in the Alaskan National Wildlife Refuge and on the outer continental shelf, and speeding federal licensing of nuclear-power plants. The president's proposals were not accepted enthusiastically in Congress. Demo-

Attention came to Alaska's beautiful southern coastline when the oil tanker Exxon Valdez *ran aground in March 1989, spilling 11 million gallons of crude oil. (Left) Black crude coats the rocks on the shore of Greene Island in Prince William Sound. (Right) Dead sea otters on the beach figured into the $2-billion cleanup cost.*

crats opposed easing restrictions on the nuclear-energy industry and on opening the Alaskan National Wildlife Refuge to oil and gas exploration. Many Republicans also opposed aspects of the legislation, especially those requiring an increase in gas mileage for new cars. Environmentalists opposed virtually the whole package. "There is nothing in there that we want," declared David Alberswerth, of the National Wildlife Federation.[43] In 1992 Congress passed and President Bush signed the Energy Policy Act of 1992, a bill that aimed to decrease United States dependency on foreign oil by promoting conservation and supporting domestic production. The bill as passed did *not,* however, include references to drilling in the Alaskan National Wildlife Refuge, nor did it attempt to force United States automakers to build more fuel-efficient automobiles.

The return to more "normal" and affordable fuel prices in the 1990s lessened the public's interest in the pursuit of a comprehensive energy policy. To many Americans, President Carter's call for a "war" on energy problems seemed distant and largely irrelevant. In 1993 President Clinton proposed an energy tax (specifically, a tax on BTU output of oil, gas, coal, and other fuels) as part of his deficit-reduction plan. In the president's view, the tax—if adopted—would serve to both raise revenue and promote energy conservation. But facing great opposition from energy-intensive industries (petrochemicals, steel, cement) and from House and Senate members in states with many such employers, Clinton backed off his program for a tax based on the heat content of fuels. He settled, instead, for an increase in the federal excise tax on gasoline as well as other sources of revenue.

Since the 1950s and 1960s the major policy concern of the federal government in the educational arena has been to ensure equal access to educational opportunities. The Elementary and Secondary Education Act of 1965 was designed to distribute federal aid to school districts on the basis of the proportion of low-income children in those districts. In 1979 Congress created the Department of Education, and in 1981 it approved the block grant known as the Education Consolidation and Improvement Act, which merged a number of small education programs into a single program.

The Bush administration made several proposals for improving American education, including allowing parents to choose the schools their children attend and establishing a system of national testing. These proposals were criticized for giving little consideration to social conditions related to educational problems. Nevertheless, the administration remained reluctant to commit much new federal spending to education.

In contrast, in the past several decades the federal government has spent billions of dollars on programs to combat poverty. Those programs are of two basic types. *Social insurance* is a program that requires employees and employers to contribute to a national insurance fund to be used to provide assistance when needed. *Public assistance* is a program that provides money and other forms of support to needy people.

The basic social insurance programs are Social Security (formally called old-age, survivors, and disability insurance), Medicare, and unemployment insurance. *Social Security* provides monthly payments to retired people, disabled workers, and survivors of workers who were covered by the program. *Medicare* pays partial costs of hospital bills and physicians' fees for retired persons age 65 and over. *Unemployment insurance* is a program that pays benefits to people who are unemployed.

Public assistance programs include *Aid to Families with Dependent Children (AFDC)*, *food stamps* (designed to boost the food budget of low-income families), *Medicaid* (designed to help low-income people pay medical bills), and the Supplemental Security Income program (which provides assistance to the aged, blind, and disabled). Many public assistance programs are jointly funded by the federal government and the states.

AFDC was originally seen as a way to assist widows while their children were maturing. Because of increases in divorce rates, desertions, and teenage pregnancies, the number of recipients and the costs of the program have risen substantially. Critics claim that the program encourages men to desert their wives and also encourages women to have children in order to receive AFDC payments.

The politics of welfare takes place primarily in Congress. A number of committees and subcommittees are responsible for various aspects of the program, and legislators see welfare policy as an opportunity for significant resource distribution. Numerous interest groups also are active in the welfare arena, and the political parties also tend to take stands on welfare issues.

In 1988, responding to pressure for welfare reform, Congress passed the Family Support Act. The act requires each state to create job training programs for able-bodied welfare recipients. Recipients are expected to participate in the programs, and states are expected to provide educational opportunities and necessary services to recipients.

Housing was first recognized as a problem requiring public attention during the Great Depression of the 1930s. Under the nation's first significant housing act, passed in 1937, the federal government was to assume most of the cost of constructing public housing, and local governments were to develop and manage project sites. Public housing was originally designed to assist the working poor, but over the years it increasingly served people who were permanently trapped in poverty. The location of public housing is a controversial issue. Advocates for the poor argue that the inner-city environment contributes to the drug and crime problems associated with public housing. Suburban residents oppose public housing in their communities because they fear that it will bring those problems with it.

In 1949 a new approach known as *urban renewal* was initiated. It was designed to clear blighted areas of inner cities and replace them with new commercial and residential establishments. The federal government paid much of the cost of land acquisition, demolition, and new construction. Urban renewal was controversial because it displaced residents and merchants, who often were forced to pay higher rents elsewhere. It was terminated in 1974.

The 1974 Housing and Community Development Act established the Community Development Block Grant program. Local governments may use federal funds in the form of *Community Development Block Grants* for urban renewal, public housing, street paving, lighting, industrial parks, and related activities. The act also established a program of housing assistance for poor families.

During the 1980s and early 1990s there was continued controversy over whether the nation should attempt to increase the supply of public housing or provide vouchers or rent subsidies to poor families. The production of new subsidized housing units declined sharply during the Reagan administration, and the Bush administration's housing proposal focused on homeownership, providing little assistance to poor people who could not afford to buy even the cheapest of homes.

In recent decades Congress has passed a number of environmental laws in response to increased concern about environmental issues. The Environmental Protection Agency was created in 1970 to enforce those laws. The major environmental laws in the area of water pollution are the Water Quality Act of 1965 and the Clean Water Act of 1972 and the 1977 amendments to those acts. The Clean Air Act was passed in 1963 and amended in 1970 and 1990. All of this legislation attempts to establish and enforce uniform national standards for the reduction or elimination of air and water pollution.

In energy policy, there has been little consistent or concerted action at the national level. Some attempts have been made to encourage energy conservation and to develop new energy sources, but these policies have received little support. Recent proposals to open new oil fields and speed federal licensing of nuclear-power plants have also met with opposition. The nation therefore lacks a comprehensive energy policy.

KEY TERMS AND CONCEPTS

social insurance
public assistance
Social Security
Medicare

unemployment insurance
Aid to Families with Dependent
    Children
food stamps
Medicaid

urban renewal
Community Development Block
    Grant

LEARNING MORE ABOUT DOMESTIC POLICY

Scholarly studies

Campbell, Colin, and Bert A. Rockman. *The Bush Presidency: First Appraisals.* Chatham, N.J.: Chatham House, 1991. An examination of policy issues in the early Bush presidency, focusing on the political and policy context, President Bush's style of administration within that context, and the implications of this interaction for policy making.

Cochran, Clarke E., Lawrence C. Mayer, T. R. Carr, and N. Joseph Cayer. *American Public Policy: An Introduction.* 4th ed. New York: St. Martin's Press, 1993. An excellent overview of contemporary policy problems, with chapters devoted to energy, crime, welfare, health, and education.

Conlan, Timothy. *New Federalism: Intergovernmental Reform from Nixon to Reagan.* Washington, D.C.: Brookings Institution, 1988. A look at changing domestic policy issues in the Nixon and Reagan presidencies, focusing on revenue sharing and block grant policies during those years.

Heidenheimer, Arnold J., Hugh Heclo, and Carolyn Teich Adams. *Comparative Public Policy.* New York: St. Martin's Press, 1990. An excellent examination of policy choices, comparing options and outcomes in a number of major industrialized nations.

Sundquist, James L. *Politics and Policy: The Eisenhower, Kennedy, and Johnson Years.* Washington, D.C.: Brookings Institution, 1968. A good review of domestic policies in those presidencies, with special focus on the battles each president faced in Congress.

Leisure reading

Harrington, Michael. *The Other America*. New York: Macmillan, 1994. Perhaps the most widely read essay about poverty in the United States.

Nivola, Pietro S. *The Politics of Energy Conservation*. Washington, D.C.: Brookings Institution, 1986. A readable overview of energy problems in the United States, with emphasis on conservation as a solution, focusing on interest groups and public opinion.

Ravitch, Diane. *The Schools We Deserve*. New York: Basic Books, 1987. An interesting collection of essays from a political perspective, dealing with tax credits, the use of standard testing procedures, financing, bilingual programs, and other education policy issues.

Rose, Mark H. *Interstate: Express Highway Politics, 1939–1989*. Knoxville: University of Tennessee Press, 1990. A thorough examination of highway policy in the United States, with special attention to congressional politics and interest group pressures in developing the interstate highway system.

Rosenbaum, Walter A. *Environmental Politics and Policy*. 2nd ed. Washington, D.C.: Congressional Quarterly, 1990. An overview of environmental policy in the United States, with emphasis on politics.

Primary sources

Both the *New York Times* and the *Washington Post* have national news sections that provide excellent analysis of all major policy issues.

Statistical Abstract of the United States. Washington, D.C.: Bureau of the Census, annual. An excellent source of data and statistics on all aspects of domestic policy issues, with chapters on health and nutrition, education, law enforcement, and social insurance and human services.

Organizations

National Wildlife Federation. 1400 16th Street, N.W., Washington, DC 20036; (202) 797-6800. This organization provides information about the environment (including air, water, solid-waste pollution, and toxins) and also is involved in environmental litigation.

American Public Welfare Association. 810 First Street, N.W., Washington, DC 20002; (202) 682-0100. Founded in 1930, this organization comprises state and local human services agencies and individuals who work in or are interested in public welfare. The organization develops national positions about social policy and promotes the professional development of members.

Sierra Club. 408 C Street, N.E., Washington, DC 20002; (202) 547-1141. Founded in 1892, the Sierra Club promotes the protection of natural resources, with special interest in such topics as air quality, national forests and parks, wilderness lands, toxins, and global warming.

American Federation of Teachers. 555 New Jersey Avenue, N.W., Washington, DC 20001; (202) 879-4440. Besides working to advance and bargain for teachers' issues, this organization conducts research and publishes extensively about public education and its reform.

CHAPTER

18

Economic Policy

- The emergence of the modern American economy

- Economic policy objectives: promotion of economic growth; full employment; price stability; preserving the free-enterprise system

- Monetary policy

- Fiscal policy: history of the federal budget; the budget process; revenue policy; the budget as a policy instrument

- Direct government intervention in the economy: regulation; subsidies; antitrust policy; government contracts; allocation of scarce resources; wage and price controls

- The politics of economic policy making: presidential leadership; compartmentalization; uncertainty; incrementalism

Richard Nixon finally won the presidency in 1968, defeating Democrat Hubert Humphrey in a campaign that centered on the war in Vietnam and protests at home. During that year both Martin Luther King and Robert Kennedy were assassinated, and the Democratic party convention in Chicago was the site of demonstrations and violence. Nixon won by focusing his campaign on law and order, while Humphrey could not overcome the repudiated policies of the Johnson administration, of which he was a part as vice president. Third-party candidate George Wallace, who garnered almost ten million votes on the American Independent Party ticket, probably hurt Nixon more than Humphrey.

In 1972, Nixon easily won reelection over Democrat George McGovern, who supported withdrawal from Vietnam. During the campaign McGovern replaced running mate Thomas Eagleton, who had suffered severe emotional depressions. He turned to R. Sargent Shriver, former director of the Peace Corps, but the campaign was damaged by McGovern's indecision in handling the Eagleton matter.

Throughout his campaign for president in 1992, Bill Clinton had promised to get the national economy working again by putting people to work. After his election, economic stimulus was his highest priority. Speaking to a joint session of Congress on February 17, 1993, he said, "Our task as Americans is to make our economy thrive again."

Clinton soon introduced a $16.3-billion economic stimulus package. In the House, Democrats had a 256 to 175 advantage over Republicans, and the plan passed easily. In the Senate, with 57 Democrats and 43 Republicans, passage would be more difficult. Many Democrats were uncomfortable with some items in the stimulus package, but most were reluctant to oppose their party's first president in twelve years. For Republicans this was a crucial first chance to deal forcefully with a president of the opposition party.

For the previous twelve years the Senate had been the pivot of American policy making. Republicans had held a majority of seats in the Senate from 1981 through 1986, the only years since 1955 when they controlled either house of Congress. Even after they lost control of the Senate in the 1986 election, Republicans continued to hold a sizable minority of the seats in a closely divided body. With Republican presidents Reagan and Bush in the White House, Senate Republicans could almost always muster the one-third plus one of the votes needed to sustain a presidential veto of programs sponsored by Democrats.

Now, without one of their own in the White House, what leverage could Republicans find? The answer, many of them hoped, was the filibuster. Under Senate rules, debate on legislation may go on for as long as senators wish to speak. Debate can be brought to a close only by a vote of cloture, which requires the approval of three-fifths of the Senate membership—sixty senators. That means, of course, that as long as forty-one senators refuse to vote for cloture, endless debate can be used as a tactic to prevent voting on a bill under consideration, thus killing that bill.

So the test for Republicans who opposed President Clinton's stimulus plan—and particularly for their leader, Senator Robert Dole (Kansas)— was to see if they could hold enough of their members together to sustain a filibuster.

Four times in April, the Democrats sought to end the Republican filibuster with motions for cloture. Each time the motion failed to get the needed sixty votes, and no motion attracted a single Republican vote. Republican leader Dole and his colleagues held together, using their unity— and the leverage provided by Senate rules—to compensate for their minority status. When it became clear that the stimulus package could not be forced through the Senate as it had been through the House, President Clinton had to compromise by offering a substantially scaled-down version of his initial proposal.

If President Clinton had a honeymoon at all, it ended on these Senate cloture votes. Republicans had shown that they were not impressed by Clinton's narrow victory in the 1992 election and that they would take full advantage of congressional rules to stand in the way of Clinton and Democratic initiatives with which they disagreed. The 1992 election might have changed the political equation in Congress, but it had not changed an enduring congressional reality. Policy making remained an intensely political exercise.

THE AMERICAN CONSTITUTION WAS CONCEIVED IN a dispute over the relationship between government and the economy. The Constitution addresses a number of economic issues, but it leaves unanswered a host of fundamental questions about the proper role of government in the economy and the extent of government authority to influence economic decisions. Debates about those matters continue.

Much has changed in the two centuries since the Constitutional Convention. The American economy has become a remarkable engine of progress. It has produced a degree of collective wealth and a standard of living that are beyond the imagination of most people. The energy of economic competition has yielded creative new products to cure disease, speed transportation, and make homes warm, comfortable, and easy to manage. But debate still rages about the proper relationship between government and the economy. Some argue that government deserves a good deal of the credit for the growth of the economy. Others say that economic progress has occurred in spite of government interference and, in fact, would have occurred more rapidly and more fully with fewer government-imposed restrictions.

C-SPAN recorded the final House vote on President Clinton's budget proposal in 1993. Note how close the vote was as members gathered in the well of the House, watching the tally and trying to influence the last few votes. In the 1990s congressional votes on economic policy often have had very close outcomes.

This chapter is about national economic policy: activities of the federal government aimed at influencing economic behavior. It is also about the debates that shape the government's economic policy decisions. We examine the changing relationship between the government and the economy during the twentieth century. Then we explore the principal instruments of government involvement in the economy: monetary policy, fiscal policy, and direct government intervention. Finally, we describe the essential political character of economic policy making.

THE EMERGENCE OF THE MODERN AMERICAN ECONOMY

Government has always had a role to play in encouraging the economic development of the United States and providing services to commerce and industry. From the very beginning of the Republic, the government delivered mail, built roads and canals, managed the currency, established customs duties to protect domestic industry, and, for a time, operated a national bank. But for most of the nation's early history the operations of the economy were regarded as outside the authority of government. **Laissez faire**, or noninterference, was the dominant characteristic of relations between the government and the economy. The government left the economy alone to respond to the forces of a free market.[1]

A free-market economy, however, operates inconsistently. Periods of prosperity and growth are followed by periods of stagnation and depression, which often lead to economic crises, which generate demands for some form of government intervention. Each intervention is likely to continue after the crisis has passed. Thus, the government's role in the economy grows, not because the nation adopts an economic theory calling for a larger government

Library of Congress

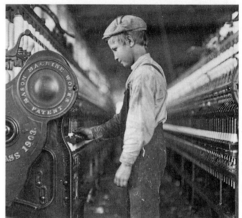

Lewis Hine/Library of Congress

(Top) *Children picking cotton in the South in 1912 and* (right) *milling thread in the North at about the same time. Until the federal and state governments passed child-protection laws early in this century, children often worked fourteen-hour days on farms or in factories, and they received little or no schooling.*

role, but because those who suffer in the economy seek from the government the relief that they cannot get in the marketplace.

In the early part of the twentieth century, following vigorous political debate, the government took a series of steps to regulate at least some economic practices. The development of mass markets, the national distribution of goods, industrialization, unionization, tragedies like the death of more than a hundred women in the Triangle Shirtwaist factory fire in New York, and Upton Sinclair's muckraking accounts of unsanitary practices in the meat-packing industry all led to demands for government action.[2] And the government began to act. The national banking system was brought under federal regulation. Restrictions were placed on companies known as trusts, which had grown so large that they dominated their industries. Standards were set for the production of potentially dangerous products, for safety in the workplace, and for the employment of women and children. The economy was changing, and so was the government's role in its development.

The shift in the relationship between the government and the economy was dramatically accelerated by the onset of the Great Depression after the stock market crash in October 1929. As the economy was thrown into a tailspin, demands began to grow both for temporary relief from the financial ag-

Franklin Roosevelt's first inauguration in 1933 marked the beginning of a new relationship between government and the economy. The New Deal also heralded a new relationship between the president and the American people, who looked increasingly to the White House for economic leadership.

onies of the Depression and for permanent reform of the economy to prevent them from recurring. These demands drove a widening wedge between the political parties, as the Democrats proposed fundamental changes that the Republicans thought were unnecessary and dangerous.

The principal thrust of the reform proposals was a call for more active government participation in setting and enforcing the rules of the marketplace. Thus, when union leaders visited President Herbert Hoover in 1932, they said, "We have come to tell you that unless something is done to provide employment and relieve distress among the families of the unemployed ... we will refuse to take responsibility for the disorder which is sure to arise. There is a growing demand that the entire business and social structure be changed because of the general dissatisfaction with the present system."[3] Hoover counseled patience, but a growing number of Americans could not wait, and the long-standing allegiances that had produced a generation of Republican dominance in American politics began to deteriorate. The Depression led to the emergence of a new political majority, the New Deal coalition, which controlled national politics for the following three decades.[4]

The years following Franklin Roosevelt's election to the presidency in 1933 mark a turning point in the relationship between the federal government and the American economy. In his first inaugural address, Franklin Roosevelt made clear his intention to use the power of government to fight the effects of the Depression. He indicated that he would ask Congress for "broad executive power to wage a war against the emergency as great as the power that would be given me if we were in fact invaded by a foreign foe."[5] The actions that followed deeply and permanently changed the character of the relationship between the government and the economy.

Roosevelt's New Deal proceeded on many fronts. The Civilian Conservation Corps and the Works Progress Administration created jobs for the unemployed. The Securities and Exchange Commission and the National Labor Relations Board expanded the government's role in regulating the marketplace and in protecting the rights of organized labor. The Agricultural Adjustment Administration and the National Recovery Administration attempted to stabilize production and pricing. And the federal budget was used to "prime the pump" of the private economy. Government spent more than it took in; the unbalanced federal budget was a conscious effort to stimulate production and consumption and thereby speed recovery from the Depression.

These changes were not carried out without controversy. The Democrats who dominated Congress in the 1930s supported them, but Republicans grew increasingly bitter in their opposition. Franklin Roosevelt was simultaneously one of the most-loved and most-hated politicians of the twentieth century. And

(Top) *The New Deal experimented with countless programs to remedy the nation's economic ills and put people back to work.* (Bottom) *When farmers, like these in South Dakota, lost their farms to the great drought of the 1930s, they were hired by the Works Progress Administration and went to work on a nearby water conservation project.*

Library of Congress

UPI/Bettmann

Economically depressed artists also found work with the WPA—painting and sculpting, designing buildings and parks, and writing books and plays. Art often reflects life, of course, and during the Depression it often celebrated work and glorified workers. In this mural, entitled Artists on W.P.A. *(1935), Moses Soyer celebrated the work of creative artists.*

by the middle of the 1930s the Supreme Court had entered the political fray, often in opposition to New Deal policies—at least until several of Roosevelt's appointments to the Court began to change the Court's political leanings.

Many of the New Deal agencies and programs were short-lived, but collectively they produced deep and lasting changes in the political economy. Perhaps the most important was the emergence of a new concept: government bears ultimate responsibility for the health of the economy. This concept permitted and encouraged the government to play a more active role than ever before in regulating and influencing the economy. Since the early days of the New Deal, the federal government has been a key participant in national economic activity.

It is important to note, however, what the New Deal did *not* yield. Government did *not* take ownership of the means of production. The government's regulatory role grew steadily, but economic enterprises remained in private hands. Nor was there any effort to bring about central planning of the economy. Economic decisions remained the province of the owners of private businesses. Although the government sought to stimulate production and consumption, it did not seek to impose a central plan.

The changes in the government's role in economic policy and the change in public attitudes that supported it were certified after World War II with the passage of the Employment Act of 1946. The preamble to the act declared it "the continuing policy and responsibility of the Federal Government to . . . afford useful employment opportunities . . . for those able, seeking and willing to work." The act also required the president to monitor national economic policy and to submit an annual report to the Congress with policy recommendations. The Council of Economic Advisers was created to assist the president in performing these new duties.

Two important and lasting philosophical changes were reflected in the Employment Act.[6] One was the idea that government bears the ultimate responsibility for the health of the economy and hence is obligated to use all of its instruments of authority toward that end. The other was the notion that the formulation of economic policy is an activity in which the president should be the principal actor. Both of these ideas remain very much with us today. Even Ronald Reagan, a conservative Republican president who believed passionately in free enterprise, private ownership, and limited government, used his executive powers aggressively to stimulate economic growth, control inflation, and reorient budget priorities.

ECONOMIC POLICY OBJECTIVES

Several implicit objectives have guided the federal government's participation in economic matters during the second half of the twentieth century. Among the most important of these are economic growth, full employment, price stability, and the protection of the free-enterprise system.

Promotion of Economic Growth

Economic growth occurs when there is an increase in real income per person—that is, when individuals earn, on the average, more money this year than they earned last year, even after inflation is taken into account. When economic growth occurs, it brings about a rise in the standard of living. With more money, people can acquire more goods, eat better food, live in nicer homes, and so on. Government policy aims to stimulate growth across the economy. When there is aggregate growth in the value of all the goods and services sold in the economy, and when that growth is widely distributed, there is a national increase in the standard of living.

Economists now use a statistical indicator, the **gross domestic product (GDP)**, to monitor economic growth. GDP represents the value of goods and services produced by factors of production—land, labor, and capital—located in the United States, whether the factors are provided by U.S. residents or nonresidents. Figures 18-1 and 18-2 indicate the patterns of change in GDP in recent years. When economists say that government pursues the objective of economic growth, they usually mean that it seeks to bring about real (not merely inflationary) per person increases in GDP.

There is virtually no debate about the desirability of economic growth. Almost everyone wants the economy to grow so that individual and aggregate standards of living can improve. There is intense debate, however, about the best way of accomplishing this objective.

Some people (usually categorized as *liberals*) think the best way to stimulate growth is for the government actively to invest, or encourage others to invest, in the private sector—in education, job training, and public health and safety programs—to increase the productivity of society. They believe that the

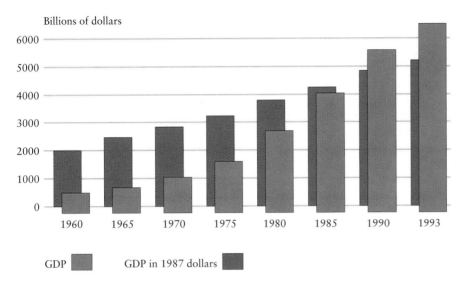

Billions of dollars

GDP ▮ GDP in 1987 dollars ▮

Figure 18-1 *Changes in the gross domestic product, 1960–1993.* SOURCE: Economic Report of the President, 1994 *(Washington, D.C.: U.S. Government Printing Office, 1994), 268, 270.*

government should lead the way in building the foundations of a strong and growing economy.

Some people (generally regarded as *moderates*) think the best way to ensure economic growth is for the government to invest in public works projects to create jobs and stimulate and facilitate commerce. They support government expenditures on such things as highways, dams, atom smashers, weapons systems, and space exploration. They believe that such activities will transfer large amounts of money from the federal treasury to the private economy and thereby

Figure 18-2 *Changes in the gross domestic product per person, 1960–1993 (in constant 1987 dollars).* SOURCE: Economic Report of the President, 1994 *(Washington, D.C.: U.S. Government Printing Office, 1994), 277.*

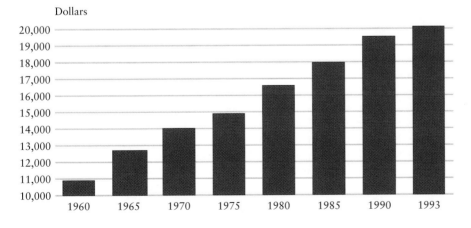

Dollars

encourage subsidiary economic activities that can dramatically multiply the impact of government spending.

Some people (usually considered *conservatives*) hold that government should interfere as little as possible in the operations of the free-enterprise system. Proponents of this view believe that the government should set the economy free by reducing corporate taxes and minimizing regulations so that the free-market system can operate efficiently. President Reagan emphasized this theme in his first inaugural address:

These United States are confronted with an economic affliction of great proportions.

. . . In this present crisis, government is not the solution to our problems. Government is the problem.

. . . I will propose removing the roadblocks that have slowed our economy and reduced productivity. Steps will be taken aimed at restoring the balance between the various levels of government. . . . It is time to reawaken this industrial giant, to get government back within its means, and to lighten our punitive tax burden. And these will be our first priorities, and on these principles, there will be no compromise.[7]

Every debate over national economic policy places the liberal, moderate, and conservative approaches in conflict, despite widespread commitment to economic growth as a valid national goal. But there is nothing unusual about that conflict. It is common for agreement about economic objectives to be accompanied by disagreement, often intense, about the appropriate means of accomplishing those objectives.

Full Employment

Few politicians go through a day without expressing the view that every American is entitled to a decent job. Presidential campaigns often focus on jobs: how to create them and how to preserve them. Republicans and Democrats agree about the desirability of full employment; both seek to convince voters that they know best how to bring it about.

Full employment is distinct from economic growth. In fact, reasonably high levels of economic growth can be maintained with almost any degree of employment. The mechanization of a production line, for example, can simultaneously improve productivity and put people out of work. Full employment is desirable for other reasons: to reduce the human suffering caused by poverty; to help cure social problems, such as crime and disease, that are often rooted in joblessness; and to reduce the costs to society of supporting people who cannot or will not support themselves. Increases in employment reduce the costs of unemployment insurance, housing subsidies, Medicaid, and Aid to Families with Dependent Children.

Full employment does not mean literally that everyone has a job. There is always some **structural unemployment**.[8] At any given time there is a sizable number of people who are just entering the work force, are leaving one job to look for another, or are having difficulty finding a job because they lack valuable skills. Some economists believe that approximately 4 percent unemployment is as close to full employment as the American economy can ever come at any given time; this percentage is referred to as the "natural" rate of unemployment. Table 18-1 indicates the growth in new jobs and fluctuations in national unemployment levels in recent years.

	CIVILIAN EMPLOYMENT (IN MILLIONS)	CIVILIAN UNEMPLOYMENT (IN MILLIONS)	CIVILIAN UNEMPLOYMENT RATE
TABLE 18-1			
Levels of Employment and Unemployment in the United States Economy, 1950–1993			
YEAR			
1950	58.9	3.3	5.3%
1955	62.1	2.6	4.4
1960	65.7	3.9	5.5
1965	71.1	3.4	4.5
1970	78.7	4.1	4.9
1975	85.8	7.9	8.5
1980	99.3	7.6	7.1
1985	107.2	8.3	7.2
1990	117.9	6.9	5.5
1993	119.3	8.7	6.8

SOURCE: *Economic Report of the President, 1994* (Washington, D.C.: U.S. Government Printing Office, 1994), 306.

Although there is broad agreement about the desirability of full employment, there is no consensus about the best way to accomplish it. One view, held by liberal Democrats, labor union leaders, and most minority group leaders, is that the economy has become much too complex to meet the objective of full employment without regular government intervention. They believe that ultimately government has to take the responsibility to find or create jobs for those whose needs are not served by the free-enterprise system. In other words, the government must be, if necessary, an employer of last resort. The Works Progress Administration served this purpose during the Depression, and in more recent decades the CETA program (established by the Comprehensive Employment and Training Act of 1973) served the same purpose.

That approach has plenty of critics. Conservative Republicans and many business leaders contend that government-created make-work jobs provide only temporary relief. In their view, the best way to accomplish full employment is to avoid excessive government intervention, to free the economy from heavy taxes and unnecessary regulations. They tend to regard the free-enterprise system as the best job creation mechanism ever devised, if it is left to work without government interference.

Price Stability

Inflation, an increase in the general price level, is a constant and troublesome threat to the health of any economy. The United States experienced a significant increase in inflation in the 1970s. The **Consumer Price Index (CPI),** a measure of the costs of some goods that are commonly purchased by American consumers, grew from 116.3 in 1970 to 246.8 in 1980.[9] This means that the same "market basket" of goods cost more than twice as much in 1980 as it had cost a decade earlier.

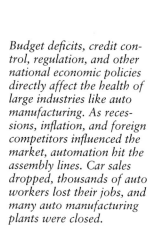

Budget deficits, credit control, regulation, and other national economic policies directly affect the health of large industries like auto manufacturing. As recessions, inflation, and foreign competitors influenced the market, automation hit the assembly lines. Car sales dropped, thousands of auto workers lost their jobs, and many auto manufacturing plants were closed.

SYGMA

Inflation is harmful in several ways. It creates uncertainty for investors.[10] They can never be sure whether the benefits of a particular investment will be diminished or perhaps even superseded by inflation. Earnings may grow, but not fast enough to match declines in the purchasing power of the dollar. Assume, for example, that an investor purchases a painting, expecting its value to increase by 5 percent a year and intending to sell it for a profit ten years later. If the rate of inflation during that period exceeds 5 percent a year, the investment will not be a good one because the real value of the piece of art (corrected for inflation) will be lower after ten years than it was at the time of purchase. In periods of high inflation potential profits can turn into real losses in value.

Inflation is especially hard on certain groups within the population. Americans who are not wealthy or knowledgeable enough to put their savings in investments that keep pace with inflation suffer disproportionately. Their needs may remain unchanged, but the cost of satisfying those needs grows as inflation drives up prices throughout the economy. Retired people and others who live on fixed incomes are hurt because they are no longer working and cannot rely on promotions and pay increases to keep their purchasing power in line with their expenses. To compensate, some government programs make annual **cost-of-living adjustments (COLAs)** in benefits to keep pace with inflation.

No group is more concerned about inflation than people who depend on Social Security benefits as a principal source of income. If those benefits fail to keep pace with inflation, the recipients' ability to purchase needed goods and services diminishes. In 1972 Congress voted to index Social Security benefits— that is, to provide for automatic cost-of-living adjustments when inflation drives the Consumer Price Index upward. Prior to that time, Congress had responded to pressure to increase benefits by voting for those increases; not coincidentally, those votes always occurred in election years.[11] The 1972 change made the increase automatic when triggered by an increase in the CPI.

(As we note later in this chapter, the indexing of Social Security benefits led to the so-called uncontrollable spending increases that contributed to the enormous budget deficits of the 1980s and 1990s.)

Price stability, then, is an important objective of government policy. However, intense political conflict complicates the government's efforts to maintain price stability. There is widespread disagreement about the fundamental causes of inflation and hence little consensus about how to combat it.

One view is that inflation results essentially from greed, from industries charging exorbitant prices and making huge profits and from workers demanding excessive wage increases. The combination of these pressures is sometimes called the *wage-price spiral*. People who see this as the principal cause of inflation sometimes conclude that government has to intervene in the economy by establishing controls on wage and price increases, as it has done in wartime and as it did during the Nixon administration in the face of growing inflation and budget deficits.

Another view holds that inflation results from deficit spending by the federal government, which spends more money each year than it takes in. Proponents of this view believe that the government covers its debts by printing more money, thereby increasing the money supply and reducing the value of each dollar. To them, the solution is apparent: the government should balance its budget and stop spending more than it collects.

There are other perspectives as well. Some people believe that inflation may be beyond the direct control of the federal government. It may result from such things as an acceleration in consumer demand or an unprecedented increase in the price of imported oil. This view produces other kinds of policy proposals: higher interest rates to chill consumer demand or a reduction in dependence on imported oil.

Preserving the Free-Enterprise System

Ordinary citizens and politicians generally agree on the desirability of maintaining the free-enterprise system. The disagreement arises over how to achieve this objective.

UPI/Bettmann

In 1973 the Organization of Petroleum Exporting Countries (OPEC) interrupted sales to the United States. The oil embargo sent shockwaves throughout the economy and led to policies aimed at conserving oil and developing other sources of energy— but only until oil prices leveled off in the 1980s.

Many liberal Americans believe that the government needs to intervene actively and regularly in the economy to ensure the maintenance of competition, the equitable treatment of disadvantaged groups, and a wide distribution of economic benefits. To preserve genuine free enterprise, they contend, the government has to protect the economy against its worst potential excesses.

Conservatives take a different approach. They believe that there are occasions when government intervention may be needed but the less intervention that occurs the better off the economy will be. The free-enterprise system, they believe, works most efficiently when it is left alone.

Democrats and Republicans tend to line up on different sides of this debate. Typically, Democrats are more likely than Republicans to find reasons to encourage government intervention in the economy. Republicans prefer to keep government out. But even within each party there is a broad range of views on economic policy, and some economic issues do not divide along party lines at all. Recent debates and opposing views about trade legislation, for example, have tended not to adhere strictly to party lines. More often, legislators from districts that contain industries which are challenged by foreign competitors are on one side of the issue, while representatives of districts in which foreign competition has had little impact are on the other. In 1993, for example, President Clinton had to work hard to obtain congressional approval for the North American Free Trade Agreement (NAFTA). Among those opposing the agreement were important members of the president's own party, including the House majority leader and majority whip.

Realizing These Objectives

Americans want economic growth, good jobs for everyone, and stable prices. By and large, they do not want the government to own or manage the economy. But these are goals, not policies.

Government has a number of instruments, or tools, it can use to develop economic policy. In fact, one of the great challenges for political leaders is to coordinate these instruments so that they encourage the economy in the same direction at the same time. Yet because the president, the committees of Congress, the members of regulatory commissions, the Federal Reserve Board, and other participants in economic policy making have different objectives and different political constituencies, such coordination is rarely achieved for any length of time.

The instruments of federal economic policy fall into three broad categories: monetary policy, fiscal policy, and direct intervention. Although they occasionally overlap, each has its own characteristics and its own set of actors.

MONETARY POLICY

The principal focus of **monetary policy** is the availability and flow of money in the economy. Its central concern is the terms on which money can be borrowed—that is, interest rates and repayment requirements.[12] When interest rates are lowered and repayment terms are eased, the flow of money through the economy speeds up. In general, this flow serves as a stimulus to economic activity. For example, when interest rates go down, mortgages are cheaper, more people decide to build new houses, more construction workers are employed, more lumber is sold, and so on. When interest rates go up and repayment terms become more difficult, the reverse is likely to occur: the flow of money slows, and economic activity cools off.

Most economists believe that monetary policy is an important instrument of economic policy, especially for maintaining price stability. Indeed, those economists known as **monetarists** believe that it is the only effective instrument for doing that.

Monetary policy is the responsibility of the **Federal Reserve Board of Governors** (usually called **the Fed**).[13] Created by Congress in 1913, the Fed is an independent agency of the government, not part of the executive or legislative branch. It is composed of seven members, all of whom are appointed by the president with the advice and consent of the Senate. The members are appointed to fourteen-year terms and may serve only one full term. Because the terms of members are longer than the term of the president, the Fed has considerable independence from the president. It was designed by Congress to be as independent as possible in order to insulate monetary policy from contemporary politics.

The Fed has several important functions. One is to regulate the national banking system. The **Federal Reserve System** is composed of twelve Federal Reserve Banks, their twenty-five branches throughout the country, and many of the nation's commercial financial institutions. The Fed makes general credit, monetary, and operating policy for the system as a whole. In this way, it operates very much like a central bank for the United States, setting standards and rules that constrain the actions of many of the country's banks.

Members of the Federal Reserve Board of Governors meeting at the board's headquarters in Washington. The Fed is less open to public view than most federal agencies. When board members deliberate about national monetary policy, they meet in private, and their individual votes are not reported.

© Paul S. Conklin

For example, the Fed is the United States Treasury's fiscal agent—in essence, the government's banker. When the government issues Social Security checks or income tax refunds, those checks are drawn on and cleared through accounts that the Treasury Department has with the Fed. The Fed also oversees the functioning of the payments system for all of the national banking system, managing check processing and providing adequate amounts of currency and coin for individual transactions.

The Fed regulates the nation's money supply. It does this in a number of ways, of which the most important is the purchase and sale of Treasury bills, notes, and bonds. Such purchases put more money into circulation, usually causing interest rates to drop (because money is more available and, in effect, "cheaper"). When interest rates drop, more money is borrowed and spent, and economic activity increases. In addition, Federal Reserve Banks must keep a percentage of their deposits as reserves. This percentage is determined by the Fed and is called the **required reserve ratio**. As the reserve rate goes up, the amount of money available for banks to lend goes down. Credit is therefore harder to come by, interest rates increase, and the economy is "cooled down."

The Fed controls the **discount rate**, which is the interest rate that Federal Reserve Banks charge when they lend money to member banks. When the Fed lowers the discount rate, it is cheaper for member banks to get money from the Fed, and they can pass the savings on to their own customers in the form of lower interest rates. These banks, in turn, can then lower their own **prime rate**, the percentage they charge their best customers to borrow money. Lower rates encourage economic activity throughout the country by reducing the cost of borrowing.

Historically the Fed has been independent in its actions as well as in its organizational structure, often denying requests that it pursue some specific policy direction. In fact, the president often finds himself forced to negotiate with the chair of the Federal Reserve Board, even if he appointed that person. In 1971, for example, Richard Nixon was unable to get his own appointee, Arthur Burns, to accede to his request for a reduction in interest rates. Finally, after considerable negotiation in which Nixon promised some cuts in spending by his administration, Burns agreed to initiate policies aimed at lowering interest rates.

Most of the time, however, the members of the Fed try to align monetary policy with other aspects of national economic policy. Disagreements with other policy makers occur, but as Herbert Stein, a former chair of the Council of Economic Advisers, has noted, "the Federal Reserve is an independent duchy but shouldn't be confused with such foreign powers as the House Ways and Means Committee or the Kremlin. The Fed keeps in touch and wants to get along."[14]

Other government agencies also play a role in monetary policy. The Treasury Department sells government securities at periodic auctions; these sales have a direct effect on interest rates. Other agencies supervise national credit markets and undertake programs that have some impact on monetary policy. These include the Federal Home Loan Bank Board, the Federal National Mortgage Association, and the Farm Credit Administration. All of these agencies pay attention to what the others are doing, to what the Fed is doing, and to the president's economic policy initiatives. But none of them is required by law to coordinate its policies with those of the others, nor has an effective mechanism ever been created to achieve such coordination.

Alan Greenspan: Eminence at the Fed

Ted Thai/SYGMA

The Federal Reserve Bank, the Fed, for short, is the central bank of the United States. The chief duty of the Fed's governors is to control inflation by controlling the money supply. By raising the discount rate—the interest rate that banks pay to borrow money from the twelve regional Federal Reserve banks—the Fed signals that it wants to slow inflation by making other interest rates rise. By lowering the discount rate, the Fed signals that it wants to stimulate a recessionary economy, in spite of the inflationary risk, by causing other rates to fall.

The Fed chairman's job is to achieve a consensus among the Bank's governors, at meetings held behind tightly closed doors, about what the Fed's, and thus the nation's, monetary policy should be. (The Fed makes its decisions in private, free of political pressures from Treasury and the president.) He or she also acts as an "economic ambassador" from the Fed to the country and the world.

The current chairman of the seven-member Board of Governors of the Federal Reserve Bank is Alan Greenspan. Appointed to his first fourteen-year term by Ronald Reagan in 1987, he was reappointed in 1992 by George Bush. His tenure on the Board does not expire until 2006.

Born in New York City in 1926, Greenspan was greatly influenced in graduate school by Arthur Burns, an economist who later served as Fed chairman under presidents Nixon, Ford, and Carter.

Greenspan has also been influenced by "objectivism," a philosophy propounded by his friend, the novelist Ayn Rand, that idealizes laissez-faire capitalism and individual self-interest.

Greenspan first advised Richard Nixon's presidential campaign in 1967 and later served in several appointive posts including stints as chair of the Council of Economic Advisers under both Nixon and Ford. Greenspan left government during the Carter years, but was returned to government as chair of the National Commission on Social Security Reform under Ronald Reagan. His recommendations adopted, the then-near-bankrupt system now appears to be solvent for many years to come. Greenspan succeeded Paul Volcker as chairman of the Fed in July of 1987. When the stock market crashed three months later, he quickly assured investors that the Fed would provide liquidity to any major financial institutions that needed it.

Since the late 1980s, Greenspan has called for a major reduction in the federal budget deficit. But inflation is his passion. Although he has led the Fed in a policy of lowering interest rates in an effort to stimulate the recessionary American economy, preventing and controlling inflation remain his chief concerns. Thus Greenspan continues to view (and use when necessary) the Fed's power to raise interest rates as the weapon of choice against inflation in the Fed's monetary arsenal.

FISCAL POLICY

Fiscal policy deals with federal expenditures and revenues, such as taxes, customs duties, and fines. Fiscal policy involves the amounts of annual expenditures and revenues, the purposes for which money is spent and the sources from which it comes, and the relationship of expenditures to revenues. The principal instrument of fiscal policy is the annual federal budget.[15]

The Federal Budget: A Brief History

In some basic ways, the federal budget is like a family budget. One part of it reflects the amount of money to be spent; another part is the amount of money to be received in income. The difference between the two is a surplus (more income than expenditure) or a deficit (more expenditure than income). In federal budget terminology, the spending side is called *expenditures* or *outlays*, and the income side is called *revenues*.

The federal budget covers a period called a *fiscal year*. The federal fiscal year runs from October 1 to September 30. Fiscal years take the number of the calendar year in which they end. Fiscal year 1993, for example, began on October 1, 1992, and ended on September 30, 1993.

There has always been a federal budget, but it has not always been considered a tool of economic policy. For most of American history, the budget was regarded as little more than an accounting device. That view began to change early in the twentieth century, after the government experienced several years of budget deficits. Deficits were especially troublesome to presidents Theodore Roosevelt and William Howard Taft because they were unanticipated and there was no mechanism for getting them under control. At the time, there was no central clearinghouse for budget decisions. Cabinet departments sent their requests directly to Congress without necessarily getting the approval of the president. Revenues were calculated and raised by the Treasury Department with little effort or ability to relate them to changes in federal expenditures.

In 1911 President Taft appointed a commission to study the budget problem. The commission concluded that the country needed a centralized and coordinated federal budget and that the president should be the centralizing agent. It recommended that all spending requests and revenue estimates for each year should be sent to the president and put into balance before they went to Congress. The commission did not suggest that the president usurp Congress's traditional responsibility for budget decisions. Rather, it recommended that he assist Congress by presenting it with a unified, fiscally responsible budget recommendation for its consideration.

No action occurred on this recommendation until almost a decade later, when Congress passed the Budget and Accounting Act of 1921.[16] Among the act's provisions were three important changes in the budgetary process. First, Congress established the president's responsibility for presenting a unified budget recommendation in January of each year. Second, it created the Bureau of the Budget, a new agency to assist the president in the formulation of that annual budget (in 1970 this agency's functions were expanded, and its name was changed to the Office of Management and Budget). Third, the act established a General Accounting Office (GAO) in the legislative branch. The GAO is the government's auditing agency; its principal role is to make sure that the government spends its money for the purposes for which it has been budgeted.

The Budget and Accounting Act was the first step toward the modern management of federal economic responsibilities. One of its primary effects was to present the president with previously unavailable opportunities to use the federal budget not simply as an accounting device but as an instrument for making economic policy. Franklin Roosevelt was the first president to consciously manipulate budget totals to encourage desired kinds of economic activity. Roosevelt submitted unbalanced budgets to Congress in the early years of the Depression. By recommending that the government spend more money than it took in, he hoped to stimulate consumer spending and capital investment. He argued that this policy would "prime the pump" and get the national economy started again.

As the Depression continued, a number of economists began to see budget manipulation as a permanent rather than a temporary component of economic policy making. In the 1930s economists became increasingly interested in the theories of a British economist named John Maynard Keynes.[17] Central to Keynes's views was the notion that government ought to pursue a *compensatory* fiscal policy. If private spending declined, public spending should increase or taxes should be reduced. Or, if private spending increased too rapidly, public spending should diminish or taxes should be raised. Fundamental to Keynesian economics is the assumption that government must play a central role in encouraging certain kinds of economic behavior. That assumption was stated explicitly in the Employment Act of 1946, and it has pervaded the economic policies of all presidents in the years since its enactment.

After World War II a burgeoning national economy, and the ample tax revenues it provided, permitted the federal government to expand into many new policy areas—health insurance for the elderly, aid to education, interstate highway and hospital construction, to name just a few. The United States also maintained large standing armed forces and stationed troops and ships all over the world. By the late 1960s, largely because of the combined costs of these expanded domestic programs and the Vietnam War, the federal government was regularly spending more money each year than it collected in revenues. Large budget deficits became a fact of life, and concern over the impacts of those deficits began to grow.

Concern also began to grow in Congress about its inability to match the analytical resources and political power of the president in the competition for influence on the annual budget. In 1974 Congress passed the Congressional Budget and Impoundment Control Act. One of the objectives of this law was to focus congressional attention on budget totals and thereby bring revenues and expenditures into closer balance.

In fact, however, quite the opposite occurred. The demand for increased benefits and new programs, combined with the ferocious inflation of the late 1970s, drove federal expenditures to unprecedented heights. In 1980 Ronald Reagan campaigned heavily against what he termed excessive spending and fiscal irresponsibility by the Carter administration and Democratic-controlled Congresses. But the Reagan years brought larger deficits than ever before, a consequence of the president's inability to overcome the political support for most domestic programs and his own initiatives to reduce income taxes and substantially increase defense spending.[18] The pattern of deficit growth is indicated in Figure 18-3.

British economist John Maynard Keynes (1883–1946), who argued that government should intervene in economic matters to stimulate employment and prosperity. Keynesian thinking greatly influenced American economic policies during and after the Great Depression. By the 1970s, even conservatives like Richard Nixon were announcing that they were Keynesians.

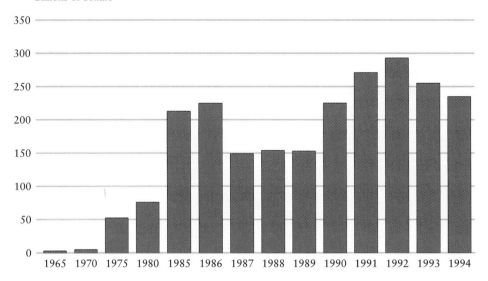

Billions of dollars

Figure 18-3   *Federal budget deficits, 1965–1994.* SOURCE: Economic Report of the President, 1993 *(Washington, D.C.: U.S. Government Printing Office, 1993), 435. 1994 deficit is an estimate.*

In 1985 Congress sought to regain control over the budget by passing the Balanced Budget and Emergency Deficit Control Act, better known as the Gramm-Rudman-Hollings Act (GRH).[19] GRH created several mechanisms designed to force deficit reduction automatically over a five-year period. But most of this law's intended effects were undermined by continued political impetus for increased spending on particular programs and widespread opposition to tax increases. (The Constitutional Conflict on page 674 describes the movement to amend the Constitution to make a balanced budget mandatory.)

The Budget Process

Political demands and constraints have a major influence on the budget process. The principal lesson of recent decades is that the budget process, no matter how it is shaped and reshaped, is more likely to reflect those influences than to control them. The federal budget process is summarized in the box on page 676.

The great value—and the great appeal—of the federal budget as an instrument of economic policy is its size. For fiscal year 1993, Congress approved a budget with $1.475 trillion in total expenditures, $1.148 trillion in total revenues, and a consequent deficit of $327 billion. Figures 18-4 and 18-5 indicate the major sources of revenue and the major categories of spending. If we compare expenditures with the gross domestic product, we find that in recent years nearly one dollar in every four dollars spent in the United States was spent by the federal government.

Clearly, the federal budget is by far the largest single factor in national economic activity. As a consequence, even subtle adjustments in federal expenditures or taxes can have significant effects on other kinds of economic activity.

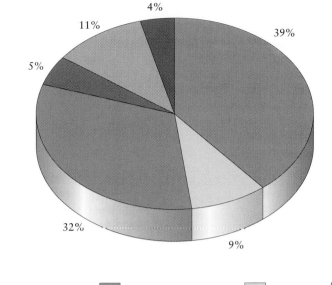

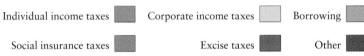

Figure 18-4   *Major sources of federal revenue in fiscal year 1995.* SOURCE: *Estimates from* Budget of the United States Government, Fiscal Year 1995 *(Washington, D.C.: U.S. Government Printing Office, 1994), 12.*

Figure 18-5   *Major categories of federal expenditure in fiscal year 1995.* SOURCE: *Estimates from* Budget of the United States Government, Fiscal Year 1995 *(Washington, D.C.: U.S. Government Printing Office, 1994), 12.*

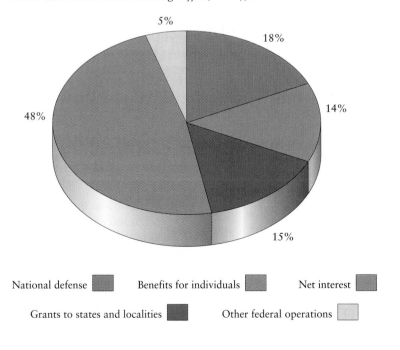

In 1992 Congress deliberated on a proposed constitutional amendment that would require the federal government to operate with a balanced budget.

The Constitution says little about the federal budget. Section 7 of Article I stipulates that "All bills for raising revenue shall originate in the House of Representatives; but the Senate may propose or concur with amendments as on other bills." Section 9 of Article I further requires that "No money shall be drawn from the treasury, but in consequence of appropriations made by law; and a regular statement and account of the receipts and expenditures of all public money shall be published from time to time." There has never been a constitutional requirement for a balanced federal budget.

For most of the past three decades the federal budget has been in deficit: expenditures have exceeded revenues. Despite a significant reform of the congressional budget process in 1974 and the self-disciplining procedures of the Gramm-Rudman-Hollings Act in 1985, the budget deficit has continued to grow. The failure to produce a balanced budget inspired several members of Congress to propose a constitutional amendment. In fact, a balanced-budget amendment has been proposed often in recent years. Presidents Reagan and Bush both advocated it.

But opponents charge that a balanced-budget amendment will not relieve Congress of the burden of tough political choices that a balanced budget requires. A constitutional mandate will force Congress to undertake deep cuts in federal spending or painful increases in federal taxes. These are precisely the kinds of politically agonizing choices that members have been avoiding over the years in which budget deficits have been growing. Opponents of the amendment also fear that, if it is ratified, it will shift the locus of budget decision making away from Congress and toward the federal courts. If Congress continues to fail to make the hard choices necessary to balance the federal budget, citizens will sue in court in order to try to persuade judges to make those choices.

When the measure came to a vote on the floor of the House of Representatives in June of 1992, it fell nine votes short of the two-thirds majority necessary to pass a constitutional amendment. In the days before the vote, Democratic leaders lobbied hard to defeat the amendment. Some members who had originally sponsored the amendment even voted against it in response to their leaders' requests for support.

The Constitution is difficult to amend. Even though significant majorities in both the Senate and the House supported a balanced-budget amendment in 1992, they could not muster the two-thirds majority they needed to send the measure on to the states for ratification. For the time being, at least, other techniques will be necessary to bring the federal budget into balance.

For example, President John Kennedy sought to stimulate economic activity. Early in his administration he ordered a speedup in federal spending for insurance dividends to veterans: $258 million in funds that normally would have been spent over a twelve-month period were to be spent in the first quarter of the fiscal year.[20] For much the same reason, in 1992 President Bush ordered a reduction in withholding-tax rates. The objective was to put money into private hands more quickly so as to encourage increased spending and investment in the economy. The federal budget, because of its size, invites those kinds of adjustments by economic policy makers.

Economic policy decisions, however, go much deeper than the annual consideration of budget totals. The budget contains thousands of other decisions about specific spending and taxing programs. Each decision involves its own set of political interests and political actors. Almost every group of Americans, from defense contractors to scholarship students, is affected by federal taxing and spending decisions.

Because so many people are directly affected by budget decisions, the budget process is pervaded by conflict. Government agencies fight for more money for their programs. Individuals and interest groups fight for more government benefits and lower taxes, at least for themselves. Presidents fight for more funds for their favorite programs and for budgets that fit their fiscal objectives. Members of Congress fight, some for more spending, some for less, depending on their committee assignments and on the particular programs under consideration.

Given all this conflict, one would expect the budget process to be sheer anarchy, and at times it does resemble that. But two important characteristics of the budget process help keep the fighting under control. The first is that the budget process is action-forcing. The federal government does most of its budgeting on an annual basis. Each year it makes decisions on budget totals and subtotals only for the year ahead. If a new budget is not enacted by the beginning of the fiscal year, one of two things will happen, both of them undesirable. One possibility is that no money will be available, for the Constitution specifically says that "No money shall be drawn from the treasury, but in consequence of appropriations made by law." Spending for existing programs will stop and government employees will not get paid.

The other, more likely, possibility is that Congress will pass a stopgap measure called a **continuing appropriations resolution**. Continuing resolutions take a variety of forms, but typically they continue spending in the new fiscal year at the same level as in the preceding year. That means that no new program initiatives can be undertaken and, because of inflation, that the value of the funds available for a program is actually diminished. Government agencies don't like continuing resolutions, and neither do the people who benefit from government programs. The only people who like them are those whose programs are threatened with elimination or substantial reduction.

The unattractiveness of the two alternatives creates strong incentives for participants in the budget process to overcome their disagreements and get the budget enacted. Thus, when the deadline approaches, decision makers are under pressure to compromise.

The second way in which conflict has been controlled is through the development of a set of fixed procedures and norms aimed at conflict avoidance and conflict resolution. The budget cycle includes a multitude of decision points that provide ample opportunities for almost any group to get a hearing and, if it has a good case, to influence budget decisions. Defeat in one place is rarely more than a temporary setback; it is almost never a knockout. There are usually other places to carry on the fight. A group that feels that the OMB, for example, has treated it unfairly can take its case to a congressional appropriations committee or to a budget committee. The budget process and budget politics are, in a sense, continuous.

Even more important in holding down the level of conflict is an implicit set of decision rules governing the budget process. By far the most important is that the budget will change incrementally rather than radically. If the budget

The Federal Budget Process

First year

BUDGET POLICY DEVELOPMENT

March
Senior economic advisers review the forecasts for current and future fiscal years; they predict effects on revenue and spending programs and report to the president.

April–June
OMB conducts spring planning review sessions, exploring funding implications of major issues or programs that will be considered in the fall budget review. OMB sets overall guidelines for the executive agency budget submissions and sends these, along with instructions on preparing their proposed budgets, to the agencies.

AGENCIES PREPARE PROPOSED BUDGETS

July–August
Agencies develop their proposed budgets.

September
Agencies send OMB their proposed budgets for the fiscal year that begins 13 months later.

OMB REVIEW

September–October
OMB staff analyzes proposed budgets and holds hearings with agencies.

October–November
Economic advisers again review the outlook for the fiscal year that begins in October a year later. The OMB director holds agency-by-agency reviews at which are considered agency requests and staff recommendations. The director decides on recommendations to the president. These recommendations are communicated to the agencies.

PRESIDENTIAL DECISION

December
The president reviews OMB recommendations and decides on totals for agencies and programs. Agencies may choose to make appeals to the president. OMB prepares budget documents for presentation to Congress.

for a program gets cut, the cut tends to be small. The budgets for most programs grow from year to year, however, even if only by a small amount.

A typical example might go something like this. Scores of appropriations hearings are held on Capitol Hill each year. In those hearings, an executive agency will come before a House or Senate appropriations subcommittee to defend its annual budget request. Almost invariably the agency representative

Second year

January–February	The president delivers proposed budget to Congress. OMB sends an "allowance letter" to each agency giving its total within the president's budget and also transmitting "planning numbers" for the next two fiscal years.

CONGRESSIONAL REVIEW

January	Congress receives the president's budget.
February	The Congressional Budget Office (CBO) reports to the House and Senate Budget Committees on the president's budget. The Budget Committees hold hearings as background for a concurrent resolution.
March	Each standing committee sends its budget estimates to the House and Senate Budget Committees.
April 15 (target date; Congress often misses the target)	Congress passes a concurrent resolution in which the House and Senate agree on budget targets for overall revenues, budget authority, and outlays. The resolution includes "reconciliation instructions" to guide committees in cutting spending and raising revenue to meet the projected deficit.
May–September (and often later)	House and Senate Appropriations Committees establish allocations or ceilings on discretionary spending for each of their 13 subcommittees. Subcommittees conduct a detailed review of agency budget proposals. (The president's budget recommendations are often altered in this process.) Appropriations bills are reported to the House and Senate floor.
July	OMB sends Congress an update of the president's January budget.
August	CBO and OMB provide a "snapshot" of the projected budget deficit. By August 20, CBO issues its initial report on the projected deficit. By August 25, OMB issues its initial report on the projected deficit.
October 1	New fiscal year begins. If Congress has not enacted appropriations bills by this time, it must enact a continuing appropriations resolution to permit spending at the current rate or at some other specified rate.

will be asked by a member of the subcommittee where funds would be cut if the subcommittee reduced the agency's request by 5 percent. The typical answer is, "We couldn't live with that. This is a bare-bones budget. There isn't an ounce of fat in it. Any cuts you make will negatively affect our ability to carry out the programs Congress has assigned us."

When the hearing is over, the subcommittee will cut the budget request

Leon Panetta (right), *director of the Office of Management and Budget, introduces President Clinton's $1.5 trillion budget proposal for fiscal year 1994. With him are Laura D'Andrea Tyson, chair of the Council of Economic Advisers, and Lloyd Bentsen, secretary of the Treasury.*

by something like 5 percent. The agency head doesn't commit suicide. In fact, he or she is not surprised at all. The same subcommittee has been consistently cutting the budget request of that agency by 5 percent for years. Knowing that, the agency probably made sure that its budget request was 5 percent higher than the amount actually needed. If the agency really needed a 5 percent increase to do its job next year, it probably would have sought a 10 percent increase in anticipation of the 5 percent cut.

The budget process is often criticized for being irrational and inefficient. There is much to sustain both of those charges. But the size of the federal budget, the complexity of the activities it pays for, and the extent of its impact on individual pocketbooks and on the national economy make it remarkable that the process works at all. There is much to be said for rationality and efficiency, and much to applaud in the efforts of reformers who have tried to impose higher standards of both on the budget process. But other objectives are at least as valuable in a democratic society: openness, broad participation, compromise, and stability. The contemporary American budget process takes its shape as much from the intensely political arena in which it unfolds as from the economic objectives it serves.

Revenue Policy

Revenues are the monies that government collects to pay its bills. Federal revenues currently come from three primary sources: income taxes on individuals and corporations, payroll taxes withheld from employees' paychecks for a specific purpose like Social Security or other "social insurance," and excise taxes charged at the time of purchase of automobiles, firearms, and other items. Figure 18-4 indicates the proportion of revenues provided by each of these sources.

Although taxes have a direct impact on the federal budget, tax policy is the province of a set of officials different from those directly responsible for appropriations.[21] And, unlike appropriations, tax policy decisions are not made anew every year. Two powerful congressional committees—the House Ways and Means Committee and the Senate Finance Committee—play a central role in tax policy deliberations. (Representative Dan Rostenkowski's chairing of the Ways and Means Committee is the subject of the Case Study on page 680.) Tax initiatives and changes are often suggested by the members of these committees, but the president and executive-branch officials play important roles as well. Through the first half of the 1980s, for example, several members of Congress, notably Senator Bill Bradley (D-New Jersey) and Representative Richard Gephardt (D-Missouri) pushed for a significant reform of federal tax policy. But only when President Reagan and the Treasury Department offered their own proposals and began to participate in the political coalition building did the Tax Reform Act of 1986 become law.

The Internal Revenue Service (IRS) is responsible for the collection of taxes and enforcement of the federal tax code. After the Postal Service, IRS is the federal agency with which Americans have the most direct contact. In 1991 the IRS processed 112 million tax returns and collected $1.09 trillion in revenues. The agency examined 1,124,000 of those returns.[22]

The percentage of American incomes that are subject to some form of taxation has grown steadily through the twentieth century. Income taxes were rarely imposed until after the ratification of the Sixteenth Amendment to the Constitution in 1913, and before World War II the marginal tax rate on even the highest incomes was quite low. Even with the growth in the tax burden, however, Americans pay a small percentage of their incomes to government relative to people in many other industrial democracies. In 1990, total tax revenues in the United States were 30 percent of the gross domestic product. As Figure 18-6 indicates, that was a smaller figure than in most other Western democracies.

Figure 18-6 *Tax revenues as a percentage of gross domestic product, 1990.* SOURCE: *U.S. Department of Commerce, Bureau of the Census,* Statistical Abstract of the United States *(Washington, D.C., 1991), 846.*

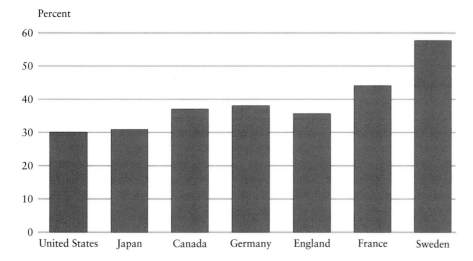

Dan Rostenkowski and the Politics of Tax Policy

In the House of Representatives tax policy is the province of the Committee on Ways and Means. Since 1981 the chairman of that powerful committee has been Representative Dan Rostenkowski, a Democrat from Chicago.

Rostenkowski represents the heavily ethnic 8th District of Illinois. His father was a Chicago alderman, and young Danny took to politics as the family business. At 24, he was the youngest member of the Illinois House of Representatives. Two years later, he became the youngest member of the Illinois Senate. At age 30, in 1958, he was elected to Congress.

Since then he has rarely had any significant opposition in his races for reelection, generally winning with 75 percent or more of the vote. His senior position on Ways and Means has made him a favored recipient of campaign funds from the political action committees of economic interests affected by tax policy decisions. In 1986, Rostenkowski spent $240,208 in his reelection bid; he raised $199,124 from PACs. In 1988, he spent $428,607 and raised $444,698 from PACs. In 1992, Rostenkowski spent $1,455,455 on his reelection campaign. He raised $962,937 from PACs.

Throughout his time in Congress Rostenkowski has operated much as he does at home in Chicago: compromising, persuading, bargaining,

Dan Rostenkowski, chair of the House Ways and Means Committee, which has jurisdiction over tax policy.

UPI/Bettmann Newsphotos

sometimes even bullying to accumulate political power. Until he became chairman of Ways and Means, he showed no great interest in issues. He focused instead on politicking—on building coalitions and arranging deals. As chair, he tends to run

Tax policy decisions are highly charged politically, for several reasons. Tax policy imposes burdens on citizens, and the politicians who make tax policy are under constant pressure from individuals and interest groups that want to maintain or reduce their own tax levels. Political conflict also results from the mixture of purposes for which tax policy is used. The primary purpose of taxation is to raise revenue to meet budgetary needs. But there is no single way to do that, and policy makers must choose among a broad array of options, including higher or lower income tax rates, more or fewer tax deductions, and increases or decreases in capital gains taxes. Each choice produces winners and losers. Some people's taxes are raised; others' taxes are reduced. The benefits and costs are easily quantified and detected. Those who are likely to be affected fight hard to protect their economic interests.

Tax policy is also conflictual because these decisions are guided by purposes other than merely raising revenues. Some tax policies, like luxury taxes the committee as he runs his ward back home. He expects loyalty of other committee members, and he returns it in kind. He does favors and expects that others will do favors for him. He gives his word and keeps it, and he remembers the names of those who don't do the same for him.

In 1986 Rostenkowski became the most important figure in the House debate over tax reform. Sensing little grassroots interest in tax reform but recognizing the heated passions of those who might suffer from its enactment, Rostenkowski became the major-domo of a complex, intense political process. When other members made demands, Rostenkowski would agree to them only if the member would promise to support the final bill, saying at one point, "You might as well kick a guy's brains out if he's not for you."[1] He carefully selected only committee members who were loyal to him to serve on the joint conference committee that would iron out differences in the House and Senate versions of tax reform. And he did much of the negotiating himself with Robert Packwood, then chairman of the Senate Finance Committee.

On tax reform, Rostenkowski never articulated any dominant or coherent economic objectives. But he was very clear about his political objectives: to produce a bill that reflected the priorities and concerns of members of the House and not to be steamrollered by a president or a Senate controlled by the opposition party. That is his style, and it dominated House decision making from the beginning of the tax reform debate to the end.

In 1992, Rostenkowski faced a grand jury investigation into possible abuses of House office accounting practices. He denied the charges, but they weakened his impact in the debate on the 1993 tax reform initiated by President Clinton. The charges did not, however, prevent his district from reelecting him in 1994.

Discussion questions
1. How are the political skills that Dan Rostenkowski and other members of Congress use to get elected in their districts different from the skills they use to build legislative coalitions in Congress?
2. Some people are critical of politicians like Rostenkowski for compromising rather than sticking to principle. How do you feel about that?
3. What, if anything, should be done to change the financing of congressional elections in order to improve the electoral chances of challengers running against incumbents?

[1] Quoted in Alan Ehrenhalt, ed., *Politics in America: The 100th Congress* (Washington, D.C.: Congressional Quarterly, 1987), 436.

on expensive yachts, are aimed at redistributing wealth among the American people. Others, like the excise taxes charged on gasoline and airplane tickets, aim to treat all people equally, regardless of income. Many tax policies are designed to encourage certain kinds of economic activities. Traditionally, for example, Americans have been able to deduct from their taxable income the interest they pay on their home mortgages. This deduction reduces the cost of borrowing for that purpose and encourages private homeownership. In the same fashion, the ability to deduct charitable contributions encourages gifts to charity.

At any given moment, tax policy represents a set of standing decisions about how much money the government will collect, through what devices, from which sources. Each such "snapshot" in time is also a balance sheet of political winners and losers. For example, if the capital gains earned from appreciation in the value of a stock are taxed at half of the rate of interest earned on investments in a certificate of deposit, tax policy is treating people who invest in stocks more favorably than people who invest in CDs. The former will employ whatever political clout they have to maintain their advantage; the latter will seek to alter the tax laws to reduce their current disadvantage.

There is constant momentum for change in tax policy as those who feel penalized by the status quo seek change and those who benefit seek to prevent change. Periodically, as in the significant tax reforms of 1981, 1986, and 1993, the proponents of change are able to build a political coalition of sufficient force to alter tax policies and change the alignment of winners and losers.

The Budget as a Policy Instrument

The political nature of the budget process explains why the budget has become a less accessible and less manipulable instrument for economic policy making. Since World War II a common practice has been to enact programs that create mandatory entitlements for certain groups. A **mandatory entitlement program** is a program that confers benefits, usually in the form of payments or loan guarantees, to any citizen who meets certain stipulated qualifications. Anyone who has made the minimum required contributions to the Social Security program is entitled to Social Security benefits at retirement age. Anyone who served on active duty in the armed forces for more than 180 days is entitled to veterans' benefits. Anyone whose income falls below a specified level is entitled to food stamps, Aid to Families with Dependent Children, and other welfare benefits. Full-time students whose families meet certain income tests are entitled to government-guaranteed education loans. Although government can eliminate or cut back these programs, doing so is nearly impossible—for political reasons.[23]

Also reducing the manipulability of the budget is the growing percentage of the budget that goes to pay interest on the national debt. When the government spends more in a particular year than it takes in—that is, when it runs a deficit—it covers the shortfall by borrowing. The government pays interest, called **debt service**, on the money it borrows. Over many years of budget deficits the federal government's debt has increased rapidly; so too has the annual cost of servicing the debt. In 1970, the federal debt was $383 billion, and the federal budget for that year included $14.4 billion in debt service, or 7.4 percent of federal expenditures. In 1993, the federal debt totaled more than $4.4 trillion, and the amount budgeted for debt service in fiscal year 1993 was $230 billion— 15.6 percent of federal spending.

The federal budget deficit raises several concerns.[24] First, expenditures to pay interest on the national debt reduce the amount of money available for other programs. As a result, there is more fighting over scarcer resources. Second, an increasing proportion of the national debt is owed to foreign investors. Payments to them leave the United States and do not circulate through the American economy. Third, the government has to compete for investors that are willing to finance the debt by buying government securities (such as bonds and Treasury bills). When interest rates rise, the government has to increase the interest it is willing to pay to investors in order to ensure that there are sufficient funds to finance the national debt. But raising interest rates to attract investors increases the cost of servicing the debt and thus puts even more pressure on the annual budget.

TABLE 18-2	
Nondiscretionary Expenditures, Fiscal Year 1995	
EXPENDITURE	BILLIONS OF DOLLARS
Nondiscretionary outlays	
Payments for individuals:	
Federal retirement	65.2
Means-tested entitlements	96.7
Medicaid	96.4
Medicare	153.3
Social Security	334.5
Unemployment insurance	23.0
Other	− 5.4
Net interest	212.8
Total: Nondiscretionary	976.5
Discretionary outlays	
Defense	271.1
Nondefense	271.3
Total: Discretionary	542.4

SOURCE: Estimated from *Budget of the United States Government, Fiscal Year 1995* (Washington, D.C.: U.S. Government Printing Office, 1994), 235.

The combination of mandatory entitlement programs and the cost of servicing the federal debt is often called the nondiscretionary or "uncontrollable" part of the budget. Because the government has to pay interest on the debt and because reducing expenditures on popular entitlement programs is nearly impossible, economic policy makers have little latitude to alter that part of the budget—and it is very substantial. In fiscal year 1993 the uncontrollable portion of the budget accounted for 64 percent of all federal spending. Table 18-2 indicates the major categories of uncontrollable expenditures. With so much of the budget tied up in expenditures that policy makers can neither significantly reduce nor easily manipulate, there are not many items left that can be tinkered with to affect economic behavior.

DIRECT GOVERNMENT INTERVENTION IN THE ECONOMY

The federal government may intervene directly in certain industries. It tests and approves consumer products, establishes standards for safety and health in the workplace, and prevents some companies from dominating their industries. It does all this—and more—to prevent the free-enterprise system from undermining competition, fairness, or safety. Such intervention takes several forms.

Regulation

Regulation is a fact of daily life in the United States. The regulators who work in government agencies inspect food, test the safety of appliances, award licenses to radio stations, set emissions standards for automobiles, and so on, through a long and comprehensive list of regulatory activities (see Chapter 14). Although most people rarely give government regulatory policies much thought, they directly and significantly affect people's health, safety, financial status, and quality of life.

Why does the federal government regulate? **Economic regulation** is aimed at correcting what economists term "market failures." An unregulated economic market may fail to give consumers the information they need to make wise choices. It may produce a natural monopoly, as in the provision of electricity or telephone service, where the economics of large-scale production make

Officials from the Federal Aviation Administration and the National Transportation Safety Board investigate air collisions to detect their causes and prevent future disasters. These inspectors are examining debris from a 1991 midair collision between a helicopter and a small plane. Among the seven who died in the crash was Senator John Heinz of Pennsylvania.

TABLE 18-3

Major Federal Regulatory Commissions and Their Jurisdictions

REGULATORY AGENCY	ABBREVIATION	JURISDICTION
Commodity Futures Trading Commission	CFTC	Trading on U.S. futures exchanges
Consumer Product Safety Commission	CPSC	Safety of consumer products
Environmental Protection Agency	EPA	Air and water pollution, solid waste, pesticides, toxic substances
Equal Employment Opportunity Commission	EEOC	Discrimination in employment practices
Federal Communications Commission	FCC	Radio, television, and telephone industries
Federal Maritime Commission	FMC	Commercial shipping industry
Federal Trade Commission	FTC	Prevention of restraints on trade and unfair or deceptive trade practices
Interstate Commerce Commission	ICC	Trains, trucks, buses, and other surface transportation
Nuclear Regulatory Commission	NRC	Nuclear power industry
Occupational Safety and Health Administration	OSHA	Safety and health of workers in the workplace
Securities and Exchange Commission	SEC	Securities and financial markets

it reasonable for one company to be the single provider of a service. Requiring a manufacturer to identify the chemicals used to treat children's pajamas or reviewing proposals for increases in interstate phone rates are regulatory actions designed to correct market failures.

Protection of health and safety is another justification for regulation. The testing and approval of new drugs, automobile bumpers, food additives, and consumer products are part of the extensive effort by the federal government to protect the health and promote the safety of citizens. Regulatory policies are also established to help root out discrimination against women and minorities in employment and education.

The federal government directly regulates some industries by vesting authority in independent regulatory commissions. Table 18-3 identifies the major regulatory agencies and the industries or activities they regulate. The broadcasting industry, for example, is closely supervised by the Federal Communications Commission (FCC). No one can get a radio or television station on the air without an operating license from the FCC. The five members of the FCC are appointed for five-year terms by the president with the advice and consent of the Senate. No more than three of them may be members of the same political party. The commission is independent of the executive branch, and its decisions do not require the president's approval.

Independent regulatory commissions are designed to be neutral bodies performing quasi-judicial and quasi-legislative functions. Their principal responsibilities are to maintain competition in the industries they regulate and to balance the needs of consumers against those of the industry. In practice, the reality may be quite different from what was intended. Regulatory commissions may be "captured" by the industries they are supposed to regulate. (*Capture* is one of the bureaucratic pathologies described in Chapter 14). They may develop chummy and protective relations with those industries. Their dominant concern may be to maintain the prosperity of existing companies, not to assist new competitors trying to enter the marketplace or to balance consumer interests against industry needs.

By using political influence to secure the appointment of friendly commissioners and by hiring the best lawyers in Washington to argue their cases before those commissioners, the major companies in an industry are sometimes able to use regulatory bodies to perpetuate their own dominance.[25] For much of its history, for example, the Interstate Commerce Commission (ICC) was heavily influenced by the railroads. The ICC was created in 1887 and for several decades distributed routes and established rate scales designed to protect the railroads from cutthroat competition and to preserve their economic health. Members of the ICC were generally sympathetic to the interests of the railroads; many of those members, in fact, came to government from the railroad industry.

Government regulation also occurs in a broader form. The federal government regulates certain economic functions to ensure that specified objectives are pursued. This is sometimes called **social regulation**. For example, the government regulates occupational safety and health to protect workers from unsafe working conditions; it regulates fairness in hiring and personnel practices to prevent discrimination; and it regulates the environmental impact of industrial activity to limit the pollution of water and air. In each of these areas, the government is concerned with particular functions that are common to most industries. Typically, the process involves setting standards in the national interest, applying those standards to all industries, and enforcing them.

By the early 1970s it was hard to find a business anywhere in the United States that was not subject to significant regulation by the federal government. Owners and managers began to chafe under their regulatory burdens. And they began to demand reforms of the regulatory process, an effort that came to be known as **deregulation**.[26]

The movement to deregulate found proponents in both political parties. Republicans tended to favor it because of their traditional belief in free enterprise with minimal restriction. Their efforts at deregulation tended to focus on antitrust laws and social regulation, especially equal employment opportunity laws, environmental protection, and occupational safety and health restrictions. During Ronald Reagan's presidency, for example, there was a significant cutback in the enforcement of civil rights legislation and antitrust policy. In contrast, Democrats focused on the failures of regulatory policy, especially the tendency of some regulatory agencies to limit competition and protect the industries they were supposed to be regulating. The Carter administration concentrated its deregulation efforts on some of the traditional regulatory agencies. One of those, the Civil Aeronautics Board, was actually shut down.

Regulatory policy remains an area of constant political combat. The same political forces that lead to the creation of regulatory policy continue to influ-

Bank regulators follow routine procedures in most of their inspections. Although the idea of deregulation and a smaller government is appealing, regulatory agencies do protect citizens and ensure compliance with standards.

ence efforts to implement that policy. Those who win battles in Congress for more aggressive regulation know that they must keep up the pressure on the executive agencies that implement those policies. And those who lose battles in Congress over regulation know that all is not lost if they can get regulatory agencies to minimize the vigor with which they implement new policies.

Subsidies

Government may intervene in the economy by providing **subsidies**, financial support, to individuals or companies. The most common subsidies are cash grants, loan guarantees, and tax advantages.

Since the creation of the Commodity Credit Corporation (CCC) during the Great Depression, American farm policy has aimed to stabilize the supply of agricultural products and the incomes of farmers by intervening in the agricultural marketplace. At various times, the government has paid farmers a cash grant to reduce their output, required farmers to take acreage out of production, purchased and stockpiled nonperishable agricultural commodities, and guaranteed prices at artificially high levels. The CCC continues to exist, and in fiscal year 1993 more than $10 billion was spent by the federal government to support its operations. The objective has been to regulate agricultural production and demand in order to maintain price levels that will make it profitable for farmers to continue to produce certain products.

A **loan guarantee** is a government obligation that allows a financially troubled company (or, in some programs, an individual) to borrow from banks the money needed to get back on solid ground. The government does not provide the money, but it does guarantee that if the debtor is ultimately unable to pay back the loan, the government will do so. This eliminates the risk to banks and other creditors because they have the government guarantee to fall back on if the debtor fails to meet the loan obligations.

Loan guarantees are sometimes used to help large companies that are experiencing economic hardship. In recent years they have been provided to the Lockheed Corporation and the Chrysler Corporation. Lockheed is a major defense contractor, and Congress was convinced that if it went bankrupt American national security would suffer. Chrysler is one of the country's largest employers. During the 1970s its economic difficulties threatened to put thousands of people out of work. It received loan guarantees to help it through a period of stabilization and restructuring.[27]

Political factors determine which companies get loan guarantees. Large companies like Chrysler and Lockheed, with employees and manufacturing facilities in many congressional districts, are able to build political support for government assistance in ways that smaller, more localized businesses cannot match. Size and influence, when strategically applied, can translate into political power, which can then be used to preserve economic size and influence. Companies that decry government intervention in the economy when it means regulation and corporate taxes do not mind such intervention when it takes the form of loan guarantees.

Tax advantages, or "tax expenditures" as some economists call them, are another form of government subsidy to private economic enterprises. Tax advantages are a mechanism for encouraging certain kinds of economic activities (for example, purchasing a home, investing in new manufacturing equipment, contributing to charity) by reducing the tax liabilities of particular industries, companies, or individuals.[28] The theory is that a reduction in taxes is just as valuable a subsidy to a company or an individual as a cash grant: it leaves the company and person with more money to use for their own purposes.

For example, from 1926 until 1974, an oil depletion allowance permitted oil-producing companies to avoid taxes on 27.5 percent of their income, to compensate for the depletion (or depreciation) of oil supplies as a well was pumped dry. The 27.5 percent figure was arbitrary and bore no relation to costs; as a consequence, it often provided the oil companies with tax advantages that significantly exceeded the amount they had invested in a property. It also cost the federal treasury large amounts of potential revenue. One estimate projected the potential loss at $2.6 billion in fiscal year 1975.[29]

Tax subsidies of this sort are an important form of direct intervention in the economy. In a report published in 1987, the House Budget Committee estimated that the cost to the federal treasury of all the tax subsidies available to individuals and corporations would total $378 billion by fiscal year 1992.[30] Much of this amount represents money that the government would collect if it did not grant tax breaks to particular companies or industries or for particular kinds of economic activities.

It is important to note that politics plays a very large role in government decisions about intervention in the economy. Cash grants, loan guarantees, and tax subsidies usually go to groups with enough political influence to shape public policy. The most aggressive supporters of loan guarantees for Chrysler were members of Congress who represented Chrysler employees whose jobs were in jeopardy. Representatives from farm states have always led the way in trying to protect farmers against price declines in the marketplace. The oil depletion allowance survived as long as it did because the tax-writing committees in Congress were dominated by representatives from oil-producing states. In short, it is usually the needs of special economic interests, not concern for the general welfare, that inspire government intervention in the economy.

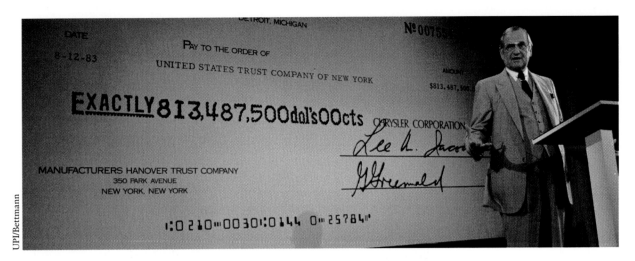

In 1983, when Chrysler Corporation had regained financial health after receiving federal loan guarantees, Chairman Lee Iacocca symbolically repaid the loan to demonstrate the worthiness of the government's intervention.

The extent of government regulation and subsidy is highlighted in the box on page 690.

Antitrust Policy

Through the Antitrust Division of the Department of Justice and the Federal Trade Commission, the federal government has the responsibility for preventing concentrations of economic power that restrain trade and undermine competition. When one company so outgrows all of its competitors that it is able to set prices artificially high, or when several large companies collude to fix prices or wages, the freedom of the marketplace is jeopardized. In such cases, federal policy may require the government to intervene.

When the industrialization of the American economy accelerated at the end of the nineteenth century, Congress became increasingly concerned about the emergence of a few dominant corporations, or trusts, in such critical industries as steel, oil, railroads, and meat packing. By the end of the last century, for example, the American Sugar Refining Company controlled 98 percent of the sugar industry in the United States, and the Standard Oil Company controlled 91 percent of the oil business. These companies were driving out or buying up their competitors and becoming so powerful that they could set prices or manufacture products as they chose, regardless of supply and demand. An important consequence was that farmers, small manufacturers, and consumers often were charged exorbitant prices because they had nowhere else to go to purchase needed goods and services.

In 1890 Congress passed the Sherman Act, the first of several important pieces of antitrust legislation. The Sherman Act was simple and straightforward; it prohibited "every contract, combination in the form of trust or otherwise, or conspiracy, in restraint of trade or commerce." In practice, however, the officials responsible for enforcing and interpreting the Sherman Act often limited its impact. Some large trusts were broken up. In 1911, both the Standard Oil Company and the American Tobacco Company were required to break

You are about to call it a night. As you review the events of the day, it never occurs to you that you had any contact at all with government. But you did—in more ways than you could have imagined.

You did not get food poisoning when you ate your eggs for breakfast. Those eggs were inspected by the U.S. Department of Agriculture. Your coffee pot did not give you an electric shock when you had your mid-morning coffee break. When you blew your hair dry, no cancer-causing asbestos fibers blew out at you with the forced air. Both the coffee pot and the hair dryer were inspected and approved by the U.S. Consumer Product Safety Commission.

The building where you attended classes did not catch fire; but if it had, the fire probably would not have spread quickly enough to endanger your life. The exit signs were clearly marked, and there were fire extinguishers on each floor. Local building codes require both.

The lecture in your physics course was given by a professor who spent the summer doing research paid for by a grant from the National Aeronautics and Space Administration. The library in which you worked during the afternoon was recently remodeled with the help of a large grant from the National Endowment for the Humanities, a federal agency. The touring exhibit you went to view at the college museum was mounted with funds provided by the National Endowment for the Arts, also a federal agency. The museum itself was recently able to stay open later because of a grant from another federal agency, the Institute of Museum Services.

When you went for your late afternoon swim,

you did not contract polio at the public swimming pool. In 1952, fifty-nine thousand Americans died from polio—that was before Dr. Jonas Salk, with generous federal support for his research, discovered the polio vaccine.

The microwave oven in which you prepared your dinner did not endanger your health by emitting intolerable levels of radiation. It was approved by the Consumer Product Safety Commission. When you drove your car to the movies, the exhaust did not send unhealthy levels of lead into the atmosphere, and the seat belt enhanced your safety in case of an accident. The Environmental Protection Agency and the National Highway Safety Board made sure of that.

You attend a public university. The cost of your education there is directly subsidized by the state government. Nevertheless, the cost is more than your family can afford. So you receive financial aid, principally in the form of student loans guaranteed by the federal government. But the loans don't cover all of your expenses, so you contribute to your own education with the money you earn from a federally subsidized work-study job on campus.

You didn't think much about government today. But government was with you in almost everything you did. Like most college students, you are the direct beneficiary of a wide range of government regulatory and subsidy policies. Many colleges would have trouble surviving without government support. And without government support, many students would be unable to attend college at all.

up into several entirely separate units. But other large companies were allowed to remain intact.

Presidential administrations differ in their approach to antitrust activity. In the years from 1890 through the New Deal, Democratic presidencies and the Progressive administration of Theodore Roosevelt tended to be more vigorous in bringing suit against activities in restraint of trade. Republican administrations tended to be less aggressive, preferring to leave the marketplace

" YES, WILLIE, PAPA LIKES TO HAVE THOSE LITTLE BOYS COME IN TO PLAY WITH YOU. THEY ARE BEING BROUGHT UP EXACTLY ACCORDING TO PAPA'S IDEAS; AND, SEE! SANTA CLAUS HAS GIVEN THEM ALL THE RAILROADS IN THE MARKET. ALWAYS ACT ACCORDING TO PAPA'S IDEAS, WILLIE, AND YOU'LL GET EVERYTHING IN SIGHT!"

San Francisco Academy of Comic Arts

Early in this century, before federal antitrust legislation and polices took hold, a few large companies dominated many national markets. Cartoonists often pictured such trusts as here: comfy, complacent, and in control.

as free as possible from government interference. But even these distinctions are often blurred.[31] The Eisenhower, Nixon, and Ford administrations, all Republican, often demonstrated more vigor in pursuing antitrust action than recent Democratic administrations have shown. Some commentators suggest that they did so in order to counter their perceived pro-business bias. The Reagan administration, however, took what many characterized as a hands-off approach to antitrust matters, giving rise to one of the most extensive series of corporate mergers in American history.

Government Contracts

One of the federal government's most powerful tools for shaping economic behavior is its own enormous role as a purchaser of goods and services. In fiscal year 1992, the federal government purchased $460 billion worth of goods and services.[32] In some important industries, such as aerospace and highway construction, companies are heavily dependent on federal contracts for their survival. Because the federal government is the country's single largest buyer, it has powerful leverage in attaching conditions to its contracts. All government contracts impose requirements about health and safety standards, environmental and civil rights laws, and accounting procedures. Contractors complain that such specifications add to costs, but by law officials have to serve broad social and economic purposes in contracts they negotiate.

There are a number of ways in which government can use its contracting authority to affect the marketplace. Its size gives it advantages in negotiating prices for goods and services—advantages that reverberate throughout an industry. By placing large orders for certain goods, government can spur the development of new product lines that create economies of scale that are passed on to consumers. For example, if the government orders fifty thousand units of a particular kind of personal computer, the cost of those computers for other consumers will probably decrease because of the cost savings of mass production.

Government negotiators can also attach to contracts conditions that affect economic behavior. In 1979, for example, as part of an anti-inflation plan, President Carter announced that the government would not award a contract to any company that refused to abide by the administration's wage and price guidelines. Similarly, government agencies have sometimes refused to award contracts to companies that failed to meet certain standards for minority hiring.

Allocation of Scarce Resources

The federal government not only has several ways of affecting the demand for goods and services; it also has some influence on the supply. Government agencies—particularly the Department of Defense—stockpile certain critical resources (such as chrome, steel, and oil) to guard against the interruption of supply in case of war. The government thus has the ability to flood a market by selling from its stockpiles. The result of such sales is a substantial and sudden increase in supply that drives down prices. The government rarely does this but sometimes threatens to do so in order to get concessions from companies that would be harmed by a sudden price drop. In 1965, for example, President Lyndon Johnson threatened to release aluminum from the government stockpile in order to flood the market and drive down aluminum prices. The threat was intended to persuade leaders of the aluminum industry to rescind an announced price increase that the administration deemed inflationary.

In wartime, the government may set up programs to ration goods that are essential to the war effort. During World War II, meat, gasoline, rubber, and metal were all rationed to domestic consumers so that adequate supplies would be available for military needs. Americans at home were supplied with ration books that limited the amounts of gasoline or meat they could buy.

Even in peacetime, the government occasionally feels compelled to participate in allocation decisions. After the Arab oil embargo of 1973, Congress passed legislation directing the president to issue regulations for the allocation and pricing of crude oil and oil products. When shortages became widespread, the government intervened to influence the national energy market—for example, by establishing a national 55-miles-per-hour speed limit, requiring greater fuel efficiency in automobiles, developing a standby gas-rationing plan, and diverting highway taxes to mass transit.

UPI/Bettmann

During World War II, to preserve crucial resources for military use, the government limited the availability of many goods. Rationing books were a common sight in grocery markets as people did their bit for the war effort.

Wage and Price Controls

On some occasions Congress has granted the president the authority to establish controls on wages and prices as a way to harness inflation or prevent profiteering. This is the most direct and potent form of government intervention in the economy. It means, in effect, that the government has taken pricing decisions and wage determinations out of the hands of businesses and other economic actors in the private sector.

Congress has been reluctant to delegate the power to control wages and prices to presidents, and presidents have been reluctant to exercise this power. Such decisions have potentially harmful consequences for presidents: businesses do not like to be told what prices to charge; workers do not like to have ceilings placed on their wages. Implementing wage and price controls in a large and diversified economy is a bureaucratic nightmare, and that too causes political leaders to shy away from this form of intervention. Reluctance also stems from the lack of evidence that wage and price controls are an effective way to curb inflation over an extended period.

Historically, government leaders have been far more likely to try to accomplish wage and price controls informally. Through persuasion, sometimes called "jawboning," they seek voluntary compliance from industry and union leaders in adhering to certain wage and price guidelines. They participate in major labor negotiations to bring about contracts that suit the needs of the national economy as well as the parties directly involved. In 1982, for example, a four-day nationwide railroad strike ended when President Reagan recommended, and Congress passed, legislation ordering twenty-six thousand members of the Brotherhood of Locomotive Engineers to go back to work.

When policy makers feel that the economy is out of balance and not serving national purposes, they have a variety of instruments that they can use to intervene directly in economic decisions. The patterns of government intervention are shaped by the pulling and tugging of politics more often than by economic theory. The federal government intervenes when there is political pressure to do so. It generally intervenes to provide special benefits to a particular industry or company when there is a perceived political advantage in doing so.

Economic policy making is unique in several respects: in the relation between the public and private sector, in the array of actors who participate, in the kinds of decisions that are required, and in the directness of its effects on American citizens. It bears the imprint of presidential leadership, compartmentalization, uncertainty, and incrementalism.

Presidential Leadership

The American people look to the president to lead the economy and to initiate necessary changes in economic policy. They are supportive of presidents when the economy is healthy and critical of them when it is not. Depression and inflation were contributing factors in the defeats of Herbert Hoover in 1932 and Jimmy Carter in 1980. Ronald Reagan's reelection in 1984 and the election of George Bush in 1988 were aided by the economic prosperity of those years. Bill Clinton's election in 1992 was a response, in part, to the recession that occurred during Bush's term.

The contemporary importance of the president as an economic leader represents a significant shifting of government responsibility for economic policy. Through the early years of American history and well into the twentieth century, Congress was the forum in which most national economic policy—particularly fiscal policy—was hammered out. As the size and complexity of the economy grew, so did the extent of government involvement in it. Management of all the instruments of economic policy making became a more and more difficult task, requiring a kind of leadership that Congress was unable to generate internally. Congress began to look to the president for help and, in so doing, began to grant authority to presidents and to provide them with staff support to take the initiative in economic policy development. Congress still challenges presidential recommendations on the budget, taxes, antitrust actions, and a host of other economic matters, but it also recognizes the need for vigorous presidential leadership.

Leadership does not always produce action, however, at least not the sort of action presidents may seek. So many forces affect the health of the national economy, and so many of them are beyond presidential control, that presidents must struggle mightily—using a broad array of limited instruments—to exert their influence.[33] Sometimes they succeed, but often they do not. Sometimes they receive credit for economic prosperity that they do not deserve; sometimes they receive blame for economic suffering they have not caused. A president is a powerful economic actor, but there are many other economic actors both within the government and outside of it, each with strength and independence of its own.

When President Bush signed the North American Free Trade Agreement (NAFTA) in December of 1992, it culminated three years of negotiations with Mexico. Along with a 1989 agreement with Canada, NAFTA would create the world's largest free trade zone, covering the entire North American continent.

The printed agreement weighed fifteen pounds. Its goals were to lower tariffs and taxes that inhibited trade among the three countries, clarify immigration policies, protect corporate investments, ensure consumer safety, and improve the consistency of environmental standards. But there was a catch. NAFTA had to be approved by both houses of Congress, where many members considered it poison.

No one knew exactly what the economic effects of NAFTA would be. Most business leaders thought NAFTA would be beneficial, that it would create new and freer markets for their products. Professional economists leaned toward NAFTA, because most of them believe that national economies work most efficiently with the least government intervention. But for many in the United States, especially for labor union members and other advocates like Ross Perot, NAFTA seemed to threaten wages and jobs.

Opponents of NAFTA pointed to the huge differential in wages between the two countries and argued that United States businesses would move their factories south of the border, where cheaper labor would reduce production costs. As the NAFTA vote approached in November of 1993, members of Congress were buffeted by some of the most frantic lobbying in years. The normal difficulty of coalition building was made worse by how this issue cut across party lines. The Speaker of the House and the majority leader of the Senate, both Democrats, supported NAFTA; so did the Republican minority leaders in both houses. But in the House, Majority Leader Richard Gephardt and Majority Whip David Bonior led the opposition. Just weeks before the vote, NAFTA seemed to be in big trouble.

So, too, did President Bill Clinton, who was its chief promoter. Clinton went to work, cajoling and bargaining with members of Congress in ways reminiscent of Lyndon Johnson. He retained the support of a few southern members by promising to keep existing protections against imported orange juice. He gained some votes from western members by promising to protect beef prices from Australian imports. He promised representatives of peanut-farming states that shipments from Canada would not be allowed to accelerate rapidly. The store was open, and the president was dealing.

A week before the vote, the tide turned. Members who had been undecided began to announce their support for NAFTA—often after lengthy discussions with the president. When the final ballot occurred on November 17, 1993, the House supported NAFTA with a vote of 234 to 200. The winning coalition included 102 Democrats and 132 Republicans. President Clinton had won in the House, even though a majority of his own party voted against him. Senate endorsement of NAFTA followed a week later.

Compartmentalization

The president's ability to lead the economic policy-making process is diminished by the compartmentalization of that process. One set of actors engages in making monetary policy, another in making fiscal policy, another in the formulation of tax policy, and yet another in the implementation of regulatory policy. There is some overlap among these actors, but each policy area has its own routines and traditions, its own powerful political forces, and its own dominant participants.

An activist president may be successful in redirecting economic policy in one area but unsuccessful in others. Recent presidents have sought to develop formal and informal mechanisms to coordinate economic policy development, but they have encountered difficulty in weaving together the strands of activity and authority that complicate economic policy making.

As a result, economic policy is not cohesive; there is not a single economic policy but a variety of economic programs, often working at cross-purposes. With ingenuity and extraordinary political effort it is sometimes possible to bring these programs into alignment. But that alignment is never permanent. The president and other political leaders must constantly struggle to bring coordination to national economic policy.

Uncertainty

Despite advances in recent decades, economics remains an imperfect science. That is especially true of **macroeconomics**, which deals with the behavior of the economy as a whole. Economists often do not know with any certainty what consequences will result from particular government actions. Indeed, the performance of the American economy frequently contradicts the predictions of economic experts.

Because uncertainty is so pervasive, politics often dominates economic policy making. With no real consensus among economists about the proper course to follow and no great confidence that any particular course will lead to a desired result, policy makers have little to protect them from the political forces that pervade economic policy making. Each competing side hires its own economists and sets them to work producing a rationale for supporting its interests.

When major pieces of economic legislation come before Congress, testimony is offered by economics experts who work for labor unions, economics experts who work for the U.S. Chamber of Commerce, and economics experts who work for interest groups. The experts offer different views and different economic predictions, all based on seemingly valid interpretations of available evidence.

In the early 1970s, Congress often felt overwhelmed by the budget projections it received from the Office of Management and Budget, so it created its own economics advisory agency, the Congressional Budget Office, to do independent projections. The two agencies often come up with widely divergent views of the state of the economy, the size of the annual deficit, and other measures of economic performance. Thus, instead of crystallizing consensus, the effect has been to inspire and legitimize disagreement. In this context politics, not convincing evidence, has become the principal shaper of national economic policy.

Incrementalism

The main consequence of the compartmentalization and uncertainty that characterize economic policy making is that change is slow, not radical. When the government alters the annual budget or undertakes tax reform or manipulates interest rates, it tends to do so in small steps. Because there is rarely consensus about what the effects of a policy change will be, the government hedges its bets by making gradual changes.

Economic statistics are compiled by most agencies of government. Many benchmark statistics such as the gross domestic product (GDP) and leading indicators are provided by the Bureau of Economic Analysis of the Department of Commerce. Unemployment figures are provided by the Department of Labor. Industrial production figures are compiled by the Federal Reserve. In a few cases, important statistics are provided by private industry or nonprofit organizations such as the Conference Board, which compiles the influential Consumer Confidence Index every month. Interpreting these complex and sometimes contradictory statistics is not always easy, and economists often disagree about what the figures mean.

The gross domestic product (GDP) is the dollar (market) value of the nation's output of goods and services over a specified period. This figure is arrived at monthly by adding up consumer spending on goods and services, business spending on investments, consumer spending on new housing, all government spending on goods and services, and net exports. The GDP is a standard measurement of the growth of the economy. One period's GDP (adjusted for inflation) can be compared to an earlier GDP to determine how much or how rapidly the American economy grew in the period in between.

Unemployment figures are compiled by the Bureau of Labor Statistics of the Department of Labor. The unemployment numbers are based on information provided by state unemployment insurance offices and by the Department of Labor's Current Population Survey. The unemployment figures are used to determine the eligibility of states and localities for federal economic assistance programs.

Beyond the basic monthly unemployment rate,

the Department of Labor tabulates and analyzes employment statistics in general. For example, the department looks at employment structures and trends and provides detailed data on wages, hours, and earnings; employment estimates by state and locality; employment estimates within various industries; employment by age, sex, race, and education status; and much more. These statistics are a key indicator of local economic conditions.

The Department of Labor also provides monthly reports of the Consumer Price Index (CPI). The CPI basically compares the current cost of living (including housing, food, clothing, and more than 350 other items) to a cost-of-living base index; the result is presented as the percentage by which prices have changed in comparison with the base figure.

Economic statistics compiled by the Bureau of Economic Analysis are published in the monthly *Survey of Current Business*, published by the Department of Commerce. This publication of comprehensive statistical information is the journal of record for United States economic statistics, including GDP, balance of payments, consumer spending, and foreign trade.

Another useful publication is *Monthly Labor Review*, published by the Department of Labor. In addition to articles on such labor issues as occupational safety and health, this magazine contains a monthly summary of labor statistics, including comparative indicators (national and international) and data on the labor force, compensation and collective bargaining, prices and productivity, and injury and illness. *Survey of Current Business* and *Monthly Labor Review* are found in most business and research libraries.

The primary cause of incrementalism, however, is the political intensity of economic policy making. So many political interests have a stake in economic policies, and there is so much disagreement among them, that developing a policy initiative that commands broad political support is virtually impossible. The government thus avoids bold policy initiatives, except in times of crisis, and moves in small ways at the margins of current policy. Small changes may be possible where larger changes are not because it takes less effort to build the necessary political support for small changes.

Incremental policy responses frustrate many Americans. Most people have an agenda of things they would like the government to do—especially things that would benefit them directly—and are disappointed when government does less than they would like. But these agendas are often conflicting. People want higher benefits but lower taxes. They want more support for programs from which they gain but less for programs from which others gain. And they want low interest rates, low unemployment, *and* a balanced budget.

With no way to accomplish these objectives simultaneously and without any neutral or objective indicator of the right path to pursue, policy makers constantly feel the force of political winds. Those winds blow from many points on the compass, and action begets reaction almost endlessly. The incremental nature of policy making is no surprise, nor is the frustration it often creates. And in a policy area as complex, as compartmentalized, and as intensely political as economics, it also comes as no surprise that policy is difficult to make and slow to change.

SUMMARY

Before 1933 the dominant characteristic of relations between the government and the economy was *laissez faire*. The government left the economy alone to respond to the forces of a free market. The Depression led to the emergence of a new political majority determined to use the power of government to stimulate economic recovery. Franklin Roosevelt's New Deal policies attempted to create jobs, regulate the marketplace, and stabilize production and pricing. Collectively these policies produced deep and lasting changes in the political economy and gave rise to the principle that government bears ultimate responsibility for the health of the economy.

Economic growth is measured in terms of the *gross domestic product (GDP)*, or total expenditures for goods and services by consumers, businesses, and government. Although there is little disagreement about the desirability of economic growth, there is intense debate over how to achieve it. Some believe the government should actively invest in the private sector. Others believe it should invest in public works projects. Still others believe it should interfere as little as possible in the operations of the free-enterprise system.

Another economic policy goal of the federal government is full employment, which does not mean that everyone has a job. There is always some *structural unemployment* created by workers entering the work force or changing jobs. The government's efforts to maintain employment at high levels may take the form of job creation or stimulation of the private sector through incentives such as lower taxes.

Efforts to maintain price stability focus on controlling *inflation* (an increase in the general price level). Inflation, which is measured in terms of the *Consumer Price Index (CPI)*, is especially hard on people who live on fixed incomes. Some government programs make annual *cost-of-living adjustments (COLAs)* in benefits to keep pace with inflation.

The government may use a variety of policy instruments to manipulate economic conditions.

The principal focus of *monetary policy* is the availability and flow of money in the economy. Economists known as *monetarists* believe that monetary policy is the only effective means of maintaining price stability. Monetary policy is carried out by the *Federal Reserve Board of Governors (the Fed)*, an independent agency that regulates the national banking system (the *Federal Reserve System*) and the nation's money supply. The main tools used in regulating the money supply are the purchase and sale of Treasury bills, notes, and bonds and manipulation of the *required reserve ratio* (the percentage of deposits kept as reserves by the Federal Reserve Banks). The Fed also controls the *discount rate*, the interest rate charged by Federal Reserve Banks to member banks, and (indirectly) the *prime rate*, the rate banks charge their best customers to borrow money.

Fiscal policy deals with federal expenditures and revenues. The Budget and Accounting Act of 1921 directed the president to present a unified budget recommendation in January of each year and created the Bureau of the Budget (now the Office of Management and Budget). Franklin Roosevelt was the first president to use compensatory fiscal policy—that is, efforts to offset declines or increases in private spending with compensatory changes in public spending.

After World War II federal spending increased dramatically and by the 1980s appeared to be out of control. Efforts to bring the federal budget process under control have had little success because almost every group of Americans is affected by federal taxing and spending decisions. Some measure of control is achieved by the fact that a new budget must be enacted by the beginning of the fiscal year (October 1) if spending for existing programs is to continue. If a budget is not enacted, Congress may pass a stopgap measure called a *continuing appropriations resolution.*

Revenue policy focuses on the monies collected by the federal government from income, payroll, and excise taxes. Tax policies are guided by other purposes in addition to raising revenue. Some are aimed at redistributing wealth, whereas others aim to treat all people equally. Many are designed to encourage certain kinds of economic activities. Tax policies are under constant pressure as those who feel that they are penalized seek change and those who benefit from the status quo seek to prevent change.

The flexibility of the budget as a policy instrument is hampered by the large percentage of federal funds tied up in *mandatory entitlement programs*, which confer benefits to any citizen who meets certain stipulated qualifications. Also reducing the manipulability of the budget is the growing percentage of the budget required for *debt service*—that is, payment of interest on the national debt.

Direct government intervention in the economy may take the form of *economic regulation* aimed at correcting "market failures" and *social regulation* aimed at protecting health and safety and preventing discrimination. The major companies in an industry sometimes "capture" regulatory agencies and perpetuate their own dominance. In many industries there is considerable pressure for *deregulation.*

Government *subsidies* include cash grants, which have long been used in efforts to stabilize the supply of agricultural products and the incomes of farmers. Subsidies may also take the form of *loan guarantees*, which obligate the government to repay a loan if a company is unable to do so.

Antitrust legislation such as the Sherman Act of 1890 authorizes the federal government to attempt to prevent concentrations of economic power that restrain trade and undermine competition. The government also shapes economic behavior through the size of government contracts and the conditions attached to them and through its power to allocate scarce resources by such means as stockpiling and rationing. The most direct and potent form of government intervention in the economy is the imposition of wage and price controls.

Economic policy is shaped by the pulling and tugging of politics more often than by economic theory. The American people look to the president to initiate necessary changes in economic policy. The president's influence, however, is diminished by the compartmentalization of economic policy making: different sets of actors are involved in monetary, fiscal, tax, and regulatory policy. Another factor that complicates policy making is the uncertainty of the imperfect science of economics, especially *macroeconomics*, which deals with the behavior of the economy as a whole. The main consequence of compartmentalization and uncertainty is incrementalism. Small changes may be achievable because it takes less effort to build the necessary political support for them.

laissez faire
gross domestic product (GDP)
structural unemployment
inflation
Consumer Price Index
cost-of-living adjustment
monetary policy
monetarists

Federal Reserve Board of Governors
Federal Reserve System
required reserve ratio
discount rate
prime rate
fiscal policy
continuing appropriations resolution
mandatory entitlement program

debt service
economic regulation
social regulation
deregulation
subsidy
loan guarantee
macroeconomics

LEARNING MORE ABOUT ECONOMIC POLICY

Scholarly studies

Fenno, Richard F., Jr. *The Power of the Purse.* Boston: Little, Brown, 1966. A comprehensive, classic study of the motivations of members of Congress in their roles as budget makers.

Krugman, Paul R. *The Age of Diminished Expectations: U.S. Economic Policy in the 1990s.* Cambridge, Mass.: MIT Press, 1992. A clearly written analysis of current economic policy issues such as the savings and loan crisis, the productivity slowdown, corporate mergers, and trade relations.

Porter, Michael E. *The Competitive Advantage of Nations and Their Firms.* New York: Free Press, 1990. A comprehensive discussion of the impact of government policy on the competitive position of the United States in the global economy.

Shuman, Howard E. *Politics and the Budget.* 3rd ed. Englewood Cliffs, N.J.: Prentice-Hall, 1992. An overview of economic policy making, focusing on the interaction between the president and Congress. Written with abundant personal insights by a long-time congressional employee.

Stein, Herbert. *Presidential Economics: The Making of Economic Policy from Roosevelt to Reagan and Beyond.* 2nd ed. Washington, D.C.: American Enterprise Institute, 1988. An examination of presidential leadership of economic policy written by a former chair of the Council of Economic Advisers.

Wildavsky, Aaron. *The New Politics of the Budgetary Process.* 2nd ed. New York; HarperCollins, 1991. A major revision of Wildavsky's pathbreaking inside view of the complexities of budgetary politics. Espe-

cially revealing in its descriptions of the interplay of executive agencies and congressional appropriations subcommittees.

Leisure reading

Birnbaum, Jeffrey H., and Alan S. Murray. *Showdown at Gucci Gulch.* New York: Random House, 1987. An interesting journalistic description of the political struggle to produce the Tax Reform Act of 1986.

Galbraith, John Kenneth. *Economics in Perspective: A Critical History.* Boston: Houghton Mifflin, 1988. A sweeping and readable history of economics from the ancients through the 1980s.

Light, Paul H. *Artful Work: The Politics of Social Security Reform.* New York: Random House, 1985. A detailed case study of economic policy making, enlightened by a penetrating picture of the pressures and constraints under which decision makers labor.

Primary sources

The Budget of the United States Government. Washington, D.C.: U.S. Government Printing Office, annual. The president's budget message to Congress, proposing federal revenues and expenditures for the next fiscal year.

Economic Report of the President. Washington, D.C.: U.S. Government Printing Office, annual. A report in which the president outlines economic policy goals for the coming year and assesses the state of the economy. Includes a lengthy appendix of data on private economic conditions and government finances.

Organizations

Americans for Tax Reform, 1301 Connecticut Avenue, N.W., Washington, DC 20036; (202) 785-0266. Advocates reduction of federal and state taxes.

Citizens for a Sound Economy, 470 L'Enfant Plaza East, S.W., Washington, DC 20024; (202) 488-8200. Promotes reduced taxes, free trade, and deregulation. Sponsors the Legal and Regulatory Reform Project which monitors legislation and regulation.

OMB Watch, 1731 Connecticut Avenue, N.W., Washington, DC 20009; (202) 234-8494. Monitors and interprets the policies and activities of the Office of Management and Budget.

U.S. Chamber of Commerce, 1615 H Street, N.W., Washington, DC 20062; (202) 463-5300. Advocates business's position on government and regulatory affairs. Monitors legislation and regulation.

19

Foreign

and

Defense

Policy

- Foreign and defense policy makers: the president; Congress; diplomacy; intelligence, spying, and covert operations; armed forces and national security

- The roots of foreign and defense policy: political culture, historical experience, and public opinion

- The recent evolution of foreign and defense policy: nuclear deterrence; foreign trade; foreign economic and military aid; alliances; military force

- Contemporary challenges: the fading of communism; the fracturing of nation-states; economic interdependence; terrorism; conflict between the legislative and executive branches

Republican former governor of California Ronald Reagan and his vice-presidential choice, George Bush, defeated President Jimmy Carter in 1980 and Walter Mondale in 1984. In 1980, a stagnant, inflated economy, combined with the Iran hostage crisis, hurt Carter and doomed his chances for reelection.

In 1984, a popular Ronald Reagan was reelected. To try to take advantage of an emerging gender gap between male and female voters, Walter Mondale chose Geraldine Ferraro as his running mate, making her the first woman to receive a major party's nomination. Campaign issues that year included a huge budget deficit as well as President Reagan's age—he was seventy-three at the time of the election. But, in a sweeping triumph, Reagan won every state except Minnesota.

Throughout the administration of Ronald Reagan, Congress and the president were engaged in a struggle over American policy toward Nicaragua, a country about the size of Iowa located in Central America twelve hundred miles from the United States border. Since the overthrow of the American-backed regime of Anastasio Somoza in 1979, Nicaragua had been governed by a leftist group called the Sandinistas. Opposition came from a small band of rebels called the contras.

President Reagan was a strong supporter of the contras, calling them "freedom fighters" and the "moral equivalent of the Founding Fathers." Throughout his two terms, he sought to provide them with financial and military aid in their efforts to regain control of Nicaragua. But most Democrats in Congress opposed military aid to the contras, believing that it would encourage hostility in Central America.

After his inauguration in 1989, George Bush moved quickly to end the conflict on this issue. Secretary of State James Baker negotiated a compromise with the Democratic leaders of Congress in which the contras would receive $4.5 million a month in "nonlethal aid" (food, shelter, clothing, and medical supplies) until the Nicaraguan elections scheduled for February 1990. In exchange for their support, the Democrats elicited a promise that no money would be sent to the contras after November 1989 unless the president received letters of approval from each of four committees of Congress with jurisdiction in this policy area.

In announcing the agreement, the president said that "the executive and the Congress, Republicans and Democrats, will be speaking with one voice on an extremely important foreign policy issue."[1] But critics saw the agreement as a significant concession to Congress. First, President Bush seemed to recognize that no policy could be successful in Central America without congressional support, and congressional support could not be obtained for the policy of military aid for the contras that the Reagan administration had pushed so vigorously. So Bush had agreed to a program that was much closer to the congressional position than to the position pursued by Reagan. Second, to get any agreement at all, the president had to go along with a procedure that seemed to undermine presidential prerogatives in the conduct of foreign policy. The Nicaragua agreement, in essence, allowed a single congressional committee to terminate financial aid to the contras. Bush's own legal counsel, C. Boyden Gray, publicly protested the agreement's harmful effect on presidential authority.

What made all of this unusual was its context. The American president usually plays a powerful leadership role in foreign policy making. Here, however, the president faced a peculiar set of circumstances. Both houses of Congress were controlled by the opposition party, and congressional leaders were united in their opposition to military aid to the contras. Public opinion polls showed that a large majority of the American people shared this view. And the embarrassment of the Iran-contra scandal, in which President Reagan's aides had used the proceeds from arms sales to aid the contras—in violation of specific congressional prohibitions—had heightened tensions and mistrust between the two branches.

If the president had sought further military aid, he would have been defeated because most political forces were aligned against him. So he pursued the only course available to him: a compromise that forced him to surrender some measure of presidential authority to get part of what he wanted. In so doing, he recognized that even in foreign policy, where the president traditionally plays a dominant role, a policy cannot survive long without broad political support.

FOREIGN AND DEFENSE POLICY IS COMPOSED OF many elements: diplomacy, foreign trade and aid, espionage, dissemination of information, and the use of military force. Knitting these strands together into a coherent policy that serves the nation's interests is a difficult task that is made all the more difficult by disagreements about the nature and extent of apparent threats to American security and the level and kind of response they require.

Policy making is further complicated by electoral and interest group politics. Often foreign and defense policies reflect domestic political pressures and calculations. One cannot begin to understand these policies without constant reference to the political combat from which they emerge.

Although the struggle to influence foreign and defense policy is a constant of American politics, it is a political arena with unique dimensions. Most notable is the enhanced role of the president. Persuasion, coordination, and compromise remain the keys to effective presidential leadership. But with more information, fewer domestic constraints, and higher public expectations, the president has opportunities to affect foreign and defense policy that are larger than his opportunities in other policy domains.

This chapter focuses on the politics of foreign and defense policy making. We look first at who participates in these decisions, with special attention to the role of the president. We then turn to the substance of recent American foreign and defense policies.

FOREIGN AND DEFENSE POLICY MAKERS

The United States ranks fourth among the world's countries in size, and third in population. It has the world's most productive economy and is the world's largest producer of food. It is a military superpower. There is little that happens in the United States that does not affect other parts of the world. The election of a new president, changes in the value of the dollar, a severe drought in the Midwest, the development of new commercial products—all of these have international consequences. But this relationship is a two-way street. What happens abroad has significance for the United States as well. No country is an island in the modern world.

International relations proceed through many different channels—eco-

A.K.G./Sipa Press

The most dramatic symbol of the Cold War was the Berlin Wall dividing communist East Berlin from democratic West Berlin. Built by the communists to prevent citizens of East Berlin from defecting to the West, the wall is shown here under construction in November, 1961, when tensions between the superpowers were especially high.

nomic, diplomatic, and military. The primary task for foreign and defense policy planners is to make those channels flow in the same direction toward a coherent purpose. This is no simple task. Many groups participate in making foreign policy, each of which sees the world quite differently. Each has its own sources of information and internal ways of making decisions. Each also spins in its own political orbit, drawing support from distinctly different quarters and interacting routinely with its own set of special interest groups and congressional committees. Most important of all, each has its own special—and constantly changing—relationship with the president.

The President

Throughout the nation's history, the president has been the dominant participant in foreign policy making. Although presidential authority in this area is not unlimited, the American political system has afforded great advantages to presidents in their efforts to shape foreign and defense policy.

Little in the language of the Constitution suggests that the framers intended the executive to dominate foreign policy.[2] In fact, the Constitution is relatively silent on foreign policy. It gives the president the authority to receive ambassadors, to appoint (with the advice and consent of the Senate) American ambassadors abroad, to serve as commander-in-chief of the armed forces, and to negotiate treaties with foreign nations (subject to the consent of two-thirds of the Senate). But these threads of authority do not in themselves constitute "the power to conduct foreign affairs."

Presidential dominance in foreign policy has not been based on the formal language of the Constitution alone. It has also relied on its peripheral language, and especially its silences—that is, on implied and inherent powers. Wherever authority to conduct foreign affairs is not specifically granted to some other branch of the government, presidents have claimed it for themselves. Although their attempts to do that in domestic affairs have often failed, in foreign affairs they have usually succeeded.

For example, the Constitution states that the president will be commander-in-chief of the armed forces.[3] Presidents have successfully argued that this position gives them broad authority to move American troops around the globe whenever they think American lives are endangered or American security is jeopardized. Thomas Jefferson sent the Navy to protect American shipping from the Barbary pirates, and Ronald Reagan sent the Marines to help keep peace in Lebanon. Both men acted under the implied power of the commander-in-chief clause.

Because of the imprecision of the Constitution, presidential authority to conduct foreign affairs has often been subject to legal challenges. With very few exceptions, the federal courts have sided with the president. In 1799, in a debate on the House floor, then-representative John Marshall said, "The president is the sole organ of the nation in its external relations, and its sole representative with foreign nations. Of consequence, the demand of a foreign nation can only be made on him."[4]

In 1803 Marshall became chief justice of the United States. For the next thirty-four years he remained in that post; the view he had expressed in the House—that the president is the sole organ of the nation in matters of foreign

In 1972, Richard Nixon became the first American president to travel to China, symbolizing a new direction in Sino-American relations after more than two decades of Cold War hostility. On Nixon's left are Chinese premier Chou-En-Lai and his aide; on his right are Secretary of State William P. Rogers and (at left in the photo) National Security Adviser Henry Kissinger, whose secret negotiations paved the way for this historic trip.

affairs—became the dominant view of the federal courts. In subsequent years, the courts have repeatedly upheld broad interpretations of presidential authority for the conduct of foreign affairs and the protection of national security.[5]

In recent decades the expansion of the presidency (see Chapter 13) has strengthened the president's role in foreign affairs. Contemporary presidents draw on many sources for information and advice. As a result, the most influential insider in contemporary administrations has often been the staff of the **National Security Council (NSC)**. The NSC was created in 1947 to assist the president in coordinating foreign and defense policy. Its formal membership includes the president, the vice president, the secretary of state, and the secretary of defense. The director of central intelligence and the chair of the Joint Chiefs of Staff are statutory advisers to the council. The NSC also has its own staff in the Executive Office of the President. The head of that staff, the assistant to the president for national security affairs, has direct access to the president on a daily basis and thus frequently becomes the president's principal adviser on national security issues.[6]

Indeed, some recent presidents have sought a national security adviser well equipped to play that role because they feared that the secretaries of defense and state and the heads of other important agencies would be "captives" of the biased viewpoints of their own agencies. The national security adviser, in contrast, is beholden only to the president and therefore is likely to offer more balanced judgments. McGeorge Bundy (Kennedy, Johnson), Walt Rostow (Johnson), Henry Kissinger (Nixon), and Zbigniew Brzezinski (Carter) were national security advisers who played a leading role in formulating the foreign and defense policies of the administrations in which they served.[7]

But no pattern of presidential advising is truly "normal." Some presidents have relied heavily on a single adviser in shaping national security policy.

Dwight Eisenhower did this with his secretary of state, John Foster Dulles; so did Gerald Ford with Henry Kissinger. Other presidents prefer a more collective approach. During the Cuban missile crisis, for instance, John Kennedy brought together a group of advisers that included not only the secretaries of defense and state but also some "old Washington hands" who held no formal position in the government. The main criterion for their selection was Kennedy's trust in their judgment.[8]

In the Reagan administration, Secretary of State George Shultz and Defense Secretary Caspar Weinberger often took different positions on major issues, especially how to deal with the Soviet Union. The two departments and their secretaries engaged in regular political conflict—sometimes in the Oval Office, sometimes at meetings of the National Security Council, sometimes in "leaks" reported in the news media. No single person dominated foreign-policy decisions during the Reagan administration.[9] President Bush, however, relied very heavily on the judgment and advice of Secretary of State James Baker, a close personal friend and long-term political ally.

In foreign and defense policy making, everyday decisions are handled routinely through formal foreign-policy agencies and procedures. More important decisions usually follow different channels. Former Secretary of State Dean Rusk was referring to this difference when he said: "The real organization of government at higher echelons is not what you find in textbooks or organization charts. It is how confidence flows down from the president. Besides it fluctuates. People go up—and people go down."[10]

One other factor contributing to the president's enlarged role in foreign affairs is public expectations. The American people look to the president for a sense of direction on broad foreign-policy questions, and they expect the president to take command in time of threat or crisis.

All of these factors—the opportunities contained in the Constitution, the support of federal courts, the enlargement of the institutionalized presidency and the executive branch, and public expectations—put the president in the vanguard of foreign policy making. Every president enjoys these inherent advantages to some degree. What a president makes of those advantages, how-

Shortly after UN forces drove the Iraqi army from Kuwait early in 1991, Secretary of State James Baker (right) *began shuttling between Israeli and Palestinian representatives in an effort to resolve longstanding hostilities in the Middle East. Here he meets with Palestinian leaders Hanan Ashrawi* (left) *and Faisal Husseini* (middle).

SYGMA

ever, depends heavily on his political skills. Truly effective leadership in foreign affairs can result only from the political arts of persuasion, coordination, and compromise.

Congress

Congress is a potent but inconsistent participant in foreign and defense policy decisions. Its members are often overmatched and outmaneuvered by the president when they disagree with the president's initiatives. Although Congress often plays a significant role in shaping the details of policy implementation, it rarely demonstrates much aptitude for defining broad foreign-policy directions. Its impact is more often felt when it reacts to or alters presidential proposals.

Some exceptions to this general pattern have occurred, especially in the period after 1968, when Congress and the presidency were often controlled by different political parties. In 1986, Congress initiated much more severe sanctions against the government of South Africa than President Reagan wanted. And in 1989 it responded to violence against student protesters in China by moving more assertively than President Bush to extend the visas of Chinese students studying in the United States.

Congressional participation in foreign and defense policy making is usually led by members of the Foreign Relations Committee in the Senate, the Foreign Affairs Committee in the House, the House and Senate Armed Services Committees, and the appropriations subcommittees in each house that oversee the military and foreign-aid budgets. A determined committee majority or a powerful chair can occasionally affect the shape of foreign and defense policy, but most of the time Congress reacts to presidential initiatives. It reviews presidential proposals, perhaps altering them somewhat but usually acquiescing to presidential leadership.

This congressional deference to the president results in part from the recognition that if foreign affairs are to be conducted rationally, the president must serve as an authoritative point of contact with other nations. In addition, the foreign-policy actions initiated by the president usually enjoy widespread popular support, at least initially, and Congress is rarely willing to tangle with a president who commands such support.

When Congress does oppose the president, it has great difficulty thwarting presidential initiatives because it has only limited "handles" for controlling foreign-policy decisions. Many important actions in this sphere are nonstatutory and thus do not depend on congressional action. The president can recognize the legitimacy of a foreign government, negotiate with foreign leaders, enter into executive agreements, issue communiqués, and even blockade a foreign country's ports without asking Congress for permission to do so.

In addition, the president can initiate many foreign-policy actions without special appropriations. The power of the purse has long been Congress's most effective control over presidential behavior. But when the president negotiates a grain sale with the Soviet Union or recognizes the new state of Israel or cuts off purchases of oil from Iran, no appropriations are needed, and Congress cannot use that "handle" to control executive action.

During and after the Vietnam War Congress took a number of steps designed to strengthen its role in foreign and defense policy making. It enacted new laws and resolutions to ensure that commitments of troops, agreements with foreign countries, sales of weapons, and covert operations would receive closer scrutiny and prior approval by Congress. It established new committees and subcommittees to expand congressional participation in foreign and defense policy decisions. Those committees in turn became more aggressive in questioning executive-branch officials and more assertive and creative in developing their own policy alternatives.

These efforts were driven in part by intensified pressures from special interest groups—farmers selling grain in overseas markets, for example, or Greek Americans, or human rights activists—whose numbers and interest in foreign affairs were growing. Bipartisanship, a guiding principle in foreign policy making in the immediate aftermath of World War II, deteriorated. And congressional deference to the president declined.

Yet even as these changes in the political environment and the organization of the legislature strengthened Congress's hand, they did so by improving its ability to react to presidential initiatives, not to substitute its own. The president is still the leader on most foreign and defense policy matters, and Congress follows that lead, though less obediently than it did in the past.

Diplomacy

Governments talk to each other. Sometimes they do so in public, in the forums provided by the United Nations and other international organizations. Sometimes they communicate through public statements to the news media. Sometimes they talk in private, in face-to-face meetings or in direct correspondence between national leaders or ministers of foreign affairs. Sometimes they exchange views in secret, in contacts between designated emissaries. All of these activities constitute **diplomacy**, the conduct of relations between nations. The key elements of American diplomacy are the State Department, bilateral relations, treaties and executive agreements, and participation in international organizations.

The State Department   One of the original cabinet offices created by the First Congress in 1789, the State Department is the principal diplomatic agency of the United States. It manages much of the day-to-day activity involved in conducting relations with foreign governments and is the primary channel for routine communications between the United States and foreign governments. The secretary of state heads the department and is normally regarded as the country's principal foreign minister. The secretary of state is usually the government's most visible foreign-policy spokesperson. As Figure 19-1 indicates, the top levels of the department are composed of many bureaus and offices that manage specific aspects of American foreign policy.

The State Department maintains and manages American embassies in virtually all foreign countries. The American **embassy** is usually located in the capital city of the country. In some larger countries there may also be American **consulates** in cities outside the capital. The embassy and the consulates are offices staffed by State Department employees. In most countries the leader of the entire entourage from the United States is the American ambassador, and he or she also heads the staff at the embassy.

In Washington, the State Department is organized into a series of regional

DEPARTMENT OF STATE

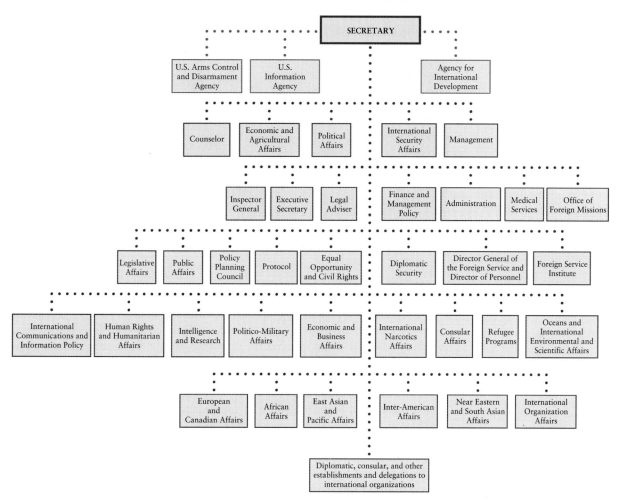

Figure 19-1 *The Department of State (January 1993).*

and country "desks," which interpret information and make policy recommendations. Each desk is staffed by people who are knowledgeable about, and usually have served in, the countries for which they have responsibility. Although the State Department has always had a central role in foreign policy making, presidents and their White House aides have often criticized it for lack of creativity in its policy recommendations and for tardiness in carrying out presidential directives.

Within the State Department, conflict over policy matters is a way of life. On no matter of national concern is there a monolithic view. In recent years, for example, some political appointees in senior State Department positions have often been more supportive of Israel's actions in the Middle East than career Foreign Service officers. The State Department's position on any issue is the result of a complex juggling act among competing political factions within the department; the slow unfolding of its policy positions often outlasts presidential patience.[11]

The public affairs office of the State Department holds daily briefings for the press. Here the briefer is Mike McCurry, one of several designated spokespeople. The briefings allow the government to speak with one voice about its foreign policies and its responses to crises and other events abroad.

© Paul S. Conklin

Bilateral relations One-to-one dealings between the United States and a foreign government are **bilateral relations**. Routine interactions between American diplomats and foreign officials are the most common form of bilateral relations. Much of this interaction involves the mundane details of processing visas, passports, and customs claims. The United States government is represented in most foreign countries by an American ambassador. Exceptions are countries whose governments the United States does not officially recognize and countries with which the United States has severed diplomatic relations. For example, from 1949 until 1979, no American ambassador served in the People's Republic of China. At first, the United States government declined to give formal recognition to the revolutionary regime of Mao Zedung; later, the Chinese were reluctant to reestablish full diplomatic relations as long as the United States continued to grant recognition to the government of Taiwan. Similarly, in 1979 diplomatic relations between the United States and Iran were severed after the overthrow of the shah of Iran and the seizure of American hostages by a new regime headed by the ayatollah Ruhollah Khomeini.

Ambassadors are members of the State Department, but all of them are appointed by the president with the approval of a majority of the Senate. Normally about 75 percent of the ambassadors are members of the Foreign Service, the professional diplomatic corps; the other 25 percent are private citizens, most likely personal or political allies of the president.[12] Some of America's most effective and most esteemed ambassadors have come from the latter group, but so too have some who turned out to be embarrassments because they lacked the knowledge, skills, or sensitivity needed to operate effectively in a foreign country.

Other departments of the federal government also have overseas representatives, and they often work at American embassies and consulates. Most embassies have military attachés from the United States armed forces, and many have trade, cultural, scientific, and agricultural representatives as well. Embassies and consulates may also be part—usually a covert and unacknowledged part—of American intelligence operations in a foreign country. In addition, some United States government employees overseas, such as members of the

The Bettmann Archive

Dalmas/Sipa Press

*Since the beginning of World War II, summit
meetings have played an important role in American diplomacy. (Top) In 1945, at Yalta, in the
Soviet Union, Franklin Roosevelt met with Winston Churchill (left) and Joseph Stalin (right).
(Middle) In 1961, in Vienna, John Kennedy met
with Soviet leader Nikita Khrushchev. And (bottom) in 1993, in Vancouver, British Columbia
(Canada), Bill Clinton met with Russian president Boris Yeltsin.*

Reuters/Bettmann

Peace Corps and the Agency for International Development, are scattered about
the countryside and not attached to embassies or consulates.

Bilateral relations also occur at a higher level. On some occasions a nation's foreign minister or head of state meets directly with the president, the
secretary of state, or some other high-ranking federal government official.
These may be ceremonial or courtesy visits or official discussions of matters of
high importance to both countries. Frequently these meetings are as valuable

for allowing national leaders to develop personal relationships as for their substantive diplomatic accomplishments.

On the grandest scale, bilateral relations might take the form of a **summit meeting** between the American president and an important foreign leader. Between World War II and the demise of the Soviet Union in 1991, every American president met with his Soviet counterpart at least once. Summit meetings serve several purposes. They allow leaders of the most powerful and dangerous countries in the world to get to know each other in a personal way. Richard Nixon noted that his two summit meetings with Soviet premier Leonid Brezhnev

gave me an opportunity to get to know Brezhnev better and to try to take his measure as a leader and as a man. I had spent forty-two hours with him in 1972, and now thirty-five hours with him in 1973. However superficial this kind of personal contact may be, it can still provide important insights. . . .

Despite the shortness of Brezhnev's visit, I felt that he had seen a diversity of American life for which no briefing books and studies could possibly have prepared him. I know that he returned home with a far better understanding of America and Americans than he had before he came.[13]

Jet travel helped to make summit meetings an important part of diplomacy. Here President and Mrs. Nixon welcome Soviet premier Leonid Brezhnev to the United States for a summit in 1973. Nixon often hosted foreign leaders, and he himself traveled widely during his time in office.

© Ruelas L.A. Daily News/SYGMA

As *national leaders, Ronald Reagan and Mikhail Gorbachev met on official business several times during the 1980s. Here, after leaving office, they and their wives met informally at the Reagans' ranch in California, in 1992.*

Ronald Reagan's and George Bush's meetings with Soviet leader Mikhail Gorbachev allowed the participants to overcome their ideological biases and get to know each other better. When Bill Clinton met with Russian president Boris Yeltsin in April of 1993, the American leader hoped to form a personal relationship with Yeltsin that would strengthen the improving relations between their countries.

Some summit meetings have been the last stage in a long series of negotiations between representatives of the two countries, a stage at which painstakingly negotiated agreements are finalized and signed. In 1961, for example, President John Kennedy and Soviet premier Nikita Khrushchev met in Vienna to discuss differences over the future of Berlin. In 1975, President Gerald Ford and Soviet premier Leonid Brezhnev met in Helsinki to sign an agreement supporting human rights and the freer movement of citizens between nations.

Summit meetings can also be risky, generating unrealistic expectations or jeopardizing the reputations of one or both of the leaders involved. President Ronald Reagan and Soviet premier Mikhail Gorbachev failed to reach an agreement on the limitation of nuclear missiles at their summit in Reykjavik in 1986, and Reagan was criticized in the American press for being poorly prepared for the meeting.[14] In 1992, George Bush's economic summit in Japan produced few beneficial accomplishments, and news coverage at home was dominated by pictures of Bush's sudden illness at a state dinner.

Most summit meetings do not produce major agreements. Instead, they provide opportunities for wide-ranging, often preliminary discussions of important matters of mutual interest, discussions that may give the leaders a clearer sense of the range within which they can negotiate their differences.

The character of high-level communication between national leaders has begun to change in recent years as a partial consequence of advances in technology. President Bush, for example, often communicated by telephone with his counterparts in other countries. This form of "Rolodex diplomacy" was especially notable as Bush sought to construct a coalition of countries to oppose the Iraqi invasion of Kuwait in 1990. In addition, television satellites and international networks like CNN permit leaders to communicate by means of television. Thus, after the coup against Mikhail Gorbachev in 1991, American leaders acquired important information about the status of authority in the Soviet Union by watching television coverage of the coup and its aftermath. Employing a combination of these new technologies, President Bush held a press conference to inform the world that he had talked with Boris Yeltsin by telephone and Yeltsin had informed him that the coup was unraveling.

Treaties and executive agreements A frequent result of bilateral relations is the establishment of formal agreements between nations. These may take the form of treaties or executive agreements.

A **treaty** is an official, written set of accords in which the parties agree to certain specific actions. When the United States enters into a treaty with a foreign government, the treaty is negotiated by American diplomatic officials, sometimes including the president. It must then be approved by two-thirds of the members of the Senate. The Senate's role can be very important, for the votes of only one-third plus one of the members of the Senate can defeat a treaty. Thus, in treaty making, the political negotiations between the president and the opposition in the Senate are often as telling as the diplomatic negotiations between the United States and a foreign government.

The Panama Canal Treaty of 1978 is a case in point. In the summer of 1977 President Jimmy Carter completed lengthy negotiations with the government of Panama. Carter and General Omar Torrijos Herrera of Panama signed two treaties, one returning control of the canal to the Panamanian government after 1999 and the other guaranteeing the political neutrality and accessibility of the canal to all nations.

The Senate discussed and debated the treaties for six months. Opponents used every available political and legislative means to prevent ratification: a massive public opinion and mail campaign, heavy pressure on senators who were undecided or uncommitted, threats to make the treaties the dominant issue in the upcoming congressional campaigns, and proposed amendments acceptable to the Senate as a whole but unacceptable to Panama. Ultimately the Senate discussed and voted on 145 amendments, 26 "reservations," 18 "understandings," and 3 "declarations." Discussions between the Senate and the administration were as intricate as the original negotiations between the United States and Panama. The two treaties were finally ratified in March and April of 1978 by identical votes of 68 to 32.[15]

Executive agreements often have much the same legal effect as treaties but differ from treaties in an important respect: they do not have to be approved by the Senate. Executive agreements can be negotiated and finalized by the president (or his deputies) and representatives of foreign countries. Because they do not necessarily require congressional approval, they are a favored instrument for presidential initiatives abroad. As Table 19-1 indicates, since World War II executive agreements have accounted for the vast majority—almost 95

TABLE 19-1		
Treaties and Executive Agreements, 1789–1992		
YEAR	TREATIES	EXECUTIVE AGREEMENTS
1789–1839	60	27
1839–1889	215	238
1889–1929	382	763
1930–1932	49	41
1933–1944 (F. Roosevelt)	131	369
1945–1952 (Truman)	132	1,324
1953–1960 (Eisenhower)	89	1,834
1961–1963 (Kennedy)	36	813
1964–1968 (L. Johnson)	67	1,083
1969–1974 (Nixon)	93	1,317
1975–1976 (Ford)	26	666
1977–1980 (Carter)	79	1,476
1981–1988 (Reagan)	125	2,840
1989–1992 (Bush)	67	1,371
Total	1,551	14,162

SOURCE: Harold W. Stanley and Richard G. Niemi, *Vital Statistics on American Politics,* 4th ed. (Washington, D.C.: Congressional Quarterly, 1994), 280.

percent—of the understandings reached between the United States and other countries, often on matters of significance like the end of the Vietnam War, the establishment of military bases abroad, and the Truman Plan for providing foreign aid to Greece and Turkey.

Executive agreements are binding. They have the force of law. Not only can presidents conclude such agreements on their own, but prior to 1972 there was no requirement that they be made public. When Congress discovered secret agreements that presidents Johnson and Nixon had made during the Vietnam War, it enacted the Case Act, named after its sponsor, Senator Clifford Case (R-New Jersey). The act requires the executive branch to reveal all international agreements to Congress within sixty days of their execution. A provision of the Case Act, however, permits the administration to submit any such agreement to the Senate Foreign Relations and House Foreign Affairs Committees in secret if it determines that disclosure of the agreement would jeopardize national security.

Participation in international organizations Relations between the United States and other countries unfold in a variety of international organizations. These are formal institutions that have been established to provide member nations with a place and a set of procedures for resolving differences and for working together on problems of mutual concern.

The best known of these international organizations is the United Nations (UN), which was created in 1945 and is currently headquartered in New York

Courtesy, Jimmy Carter Library

Jimmy Carter (left) *and General Omar Torrijos Herrera* (right) *signed the Panama Canal Treaty in 1977. But Carter still needed to secure Senate ratification, which was won by a narrow margin, after a long battle, in 1978.*

City. Nearly 160 nations are represented in the membership of the UN—all but a few of the countries of the world. Many other international organizations are part of the UN, including the International Labor Organization (ILO), the United Nations Educational, Scientific and Cultural Organization (UNESCO), the World Health Organization (WHO), the United Nations Children's Fund (UNICEF), and the International Court of Justice.

Most international organizations are federations: they provide forums in which nations may meet and discuss international issues, but they have little real authority to direct or constrain the actions of member nations. In 1980, for example, the International Court of Justice declared that Iran had acted unlawfully in seizing American hostages and ordered their release. However, the Court was powerless to force Iran to free those hostages. In 1984, the Court held that the government of the United States had violated international law by providing military support to rebels opposing the Sandinista government in Nicaragua—including mining the harbors of that country. The United States argued that the Court was not an appropriate forum for the resolution of complex political issues in Central America and refused to abide by the Court's findings.

International organizations have been especially helpful in organizing international efforts in matters of world health, agricultural development, and commerce. However, those organizations have been unable to substitute for direct discussions among nations, particularly on matters on which the countries disagree deeply. In 1991, for example, a conference of Middle Eastern nations convened in Madrid for direct discussions of contentious issues that could not be resolved at the UN. As a general rule, the more important an international dispute is and the wider the gap between the contesting nations, the greater is the likelihood that critical negotiations will *not* be relegated to the formal procedures of an international organization.

On October 14, 1962, these photographs from a United States spy plane showed the construction of a nuclear-missile launch site in San Cristobal, Cuba. The resulting confrontation between the United States and the Soviet Union came to be known as the Cuban missile crisis.

Intelligence, Spying, and Covert Operations

In the uncertainties of contemporary world politics, foreign and defense policy makers hunger for accurate information. Such information is critical to wise decisions, but it is often difficult to collect and verify. Thus, all large governments have their own intelligence agencies, charged with using every available means to find out about real and potential adversaries and often about allies as well.

The Cuban missile crisis of 1962 demonstrated the importance of such information. The discovery of nuclear-missile installations under construction in Cuba resulted from aerial photographs taken during routine intelligence overflights. The interpretation of these photos by intelligence agencies revealed that the missile bases were being constructed by the Soviet Union, that the missiles had long-range nuclear capability, and that construction was nearing completion. President Kennedy thus was given relatively reliable information about the nature and imminence of the threat.

Espionage (the use of spies to obtain secret information about foreign governments) and intelligence gathering have long been part of foreign and defense policy making in the United States. However, the modern intelligence establishment took its current form in 1947, when, as part of a broad reorganization of the national security apparatus, the Central Intelligence Agency (CIA) was created. Forty other agencies of the government also collect and analyze intelligence information. They include the State Department's Bureau of Intelligence and Research, the Defense Intelligence Agency, the National Security Agency, and the Federal Bureau of Investigation. But the CIA is the most important of these, and the director of central intelligence is the president's principal intelligence adviser.

The techniques of modern intelligence gathering are amazingly sophisticated. In some areas of activity—determining troop strength, monitoring military movements, and detecting nuclear tests, for example—the United States can use satellite and other aerial reconnaissance to find out a great deal about what its allies and adversaries are up to. Other areas are more difficult to penetrate, especially those involving the development of new weapons technologies and strategies for negotiation and military activity. Information about the latter areas is often best derived through espionage or through the purchase of information from foreign nationals who reveal secrets about their own governments. Despite the growing importance of sophisticated technology, human espionage remains a critical ingredient of the intelligence operations of every large country. The 1987 court-martial of Marine guards at the American embassy in Moscow revealed that their amorous relationships with Soviet female agents had compromised embassy security through the oldest of all spying techniques.

Within the executive branch, tensions often arise between those responsible for making national security policy and those on whom the policy makers depend for intelligence. The intelligence community constantly laments that it is never given clear guidance about the specific information that policy makers need. Policy makers often complain that they lack the specific information they need for making critical decisions. Intelligence agencies often react by roaming far and wide in their search for information. Without adequate direction from policy makers, the agencies develop their own agendas and priorities. Examples abound in which intelligence agencies have been accused of running their own foreign policies, sometimes without the knowledge or support of their political superiors in the executive branch. In 1987, for instance, Congress held lengthy hearings to review the Iran-contra affair, in which Reagan administration officials—in direct reversal of stated administration policy—carried out a covert effort to sell arms to Iran in exchange for the release of American hostages.

Gathering and properly using intelligence is not a simple matter in any country. It is an especially difficult task in a democracy. Intelligence activities, by their inherent secrecy and dependence on stealth, violate important democratic principles.[16] Congress, for example, has long had difficulty overseeing the intelligence agencies. Administrative oversight sometimes involves reviewing and approving programs that would become ineffective if their existence became known. In the 1970s, after several intelligence agencies abused the freedom of action they had traditionally been accorded, Congress sought to tighten its control. Both the Senate and the House created select committees on intelligence and developed new procedures to permit more thorough review of intelligence budgets and programs.

Despite these measures, there remains considerable tension between the legislative and executive branches with regard to the conduct of intelligence gathering and analysis. Congress often feels that it has been denied the information it needs to carry out its constitutional responsibilities. The president and his advisers often worry about congressional meddling in intelligence activities and the consequent risk of secrecy violations that will jeopardize programs and endanger intelligence agents. Among those who participate in these debates, there is little doubt about the need for an effective intelligence establishment. Struggles occur, however, over the details of intelligence policies and their implementation.

Armed Forces and National Security

Military strategist Karl von Clausewitz (1780–1831) once noted that "War is diplomacy carried on by other means." It is an important point, but one that may be an oversimplification for the present time. Not simply war itself but the *threat* of war extends the range and character of potential interaction among nations. Contemporary world powers spend trillions of dollars developing weapons and maintaining armed forces. Those weapons systems and the potential for destruction that they present are a central component of modern foreign and defense policy. The ability to use massive military force—whether or not it is ever used—is the principal characteristic of power in international relations today. It is not surprising, therefore, that programs for building and positioning armed forces consume a good deal of the attention of foreign and defense policy makers. The primary responsibility for this activity in the United States falls to the Department of Defense.

The Department of Defense was created by the National Security Act of 1947, which joined two very old American agencies, the War Department and the Navy Department. The modern Defense Department includes all of the service branches: Army, Navy (including the Marine Corps), and Air Force. The Coast Guard is part of the Transportation Department in peacetime but shifts to the Defense Department in time of war. The tradition of civilian control of the armed forces was maintained in the creation of the department, which is led by the secretary of defense with the support of a number of deputy and assistant secretaries who are responsible for specific national security functions such as logistics, mapping, communications, and contracting (see Figure 19-2, page 723).

The highest-ranking uniformed officer in each of the military services serves as a member of a body called the **Joint Chiefs of Staff**. The chair of the Joint Chiefs is an officer from one of the services and is appointed by the president for a two-year term. The Joint Chiefs are important advisers to the president on military matters, and American involvement in armed conflict is rarely undertaken without consultation with them. (A profile of General Colin L. Powell, chair of the Joint Chiefs from 1989 to 1993, appears on page 722.)

The Department of Defense is one of the world's largest organizations. It has a budget of more than $250 billion a year; it awards $140 billion a year in contracts to American businesses; and it employs more than 3 million people. Because it is so large and complex, the department is difficult to manage, and the coordination of military policy is an enormous administrative challenge. Political infighting is common. The Army, Navy, and Air Force have their own traditions and cultures and are often at odds about military strategy and the choice of new weapons systems. A new airplane design that might be entirely suitable for the Air Force, which launches planes from the ground, may not be suitable at all for the Navy, which often launches planes from aircraft carriers

Colin L. Powell: Cool Commander

The National Security Council (NSC) is advised by the director of the Central Intelligence Agency and by the chair of the Joint Chiefs of Staff. The head of the NSC staff serves as national security adviser to the president. General Colin L. Powell had the distinction of holding two of those three NSC advisory posts. From 1987 to 1989 he was President Reagan's national security adviser. In 1989 President Bush appointed him chair of the Joint Chiefs of Staff, the most prestigious position in the American military. In 1991 he was reappointed for a second two-year term.

At the time of the initial appointment, General Powell was, at age 52, the youngest chair of the Joint Chiefs ever. He was the first African American to lead the Joint Chiefs and to be national security adviser.

As chair of the Joint Chiefs in 1989, Powell oversaw Operation Just Cause, the military invasion of Panama that captured Manuel Noriega and extradited the former Panamanian president to the United States to face drug charges. In August 1990, Powell was again in the spotlight as Operation Desert Shield began. This massive military mobilization in response to the Iraqi invasion of Kuwait brought some 500,000 troops to Saudi Arabia within six months. The second phase of the mobilization, Operation Desert Storm, lasted from January to March 1991 and forced Iraqi troops from Kuwait with minimal loss of American lives. During the Persian Gulf War, General Powell was a highly visible figure, appearing beside President Bush and testifying before Congress. His calm demeanor and articulate explanation of military goals did much to help build a positive national consensus about the military operations in the Gulf.

Despite the headlines, much of the real work of the chair of the Joint Chiefs of Staff involves the

© J.L. Atlan/SYGMA

General Colin Powell gives the press a briefing on air strikes in Iraq during preparations for the Persian Gulf War.

restructuring of the American military for a post–Cold War world. Major reductions in the size and cost of the military services are planned, yet these plans must be balanced against the need for a strong and effective military. As head of the Joint Chiefs, Powell advised the president and the secretary of defense about the strategic direction of the armed forces and about the programs, requirements, and budgets needed to achieve those goals.

When General Powell retired from the Army in September 1993, he was one of the most popular American leaders. Many commentators speculated that he would be a strong candidate for high political office, including the presidency, in the future.

DEPARTMENT OF DEFENSE

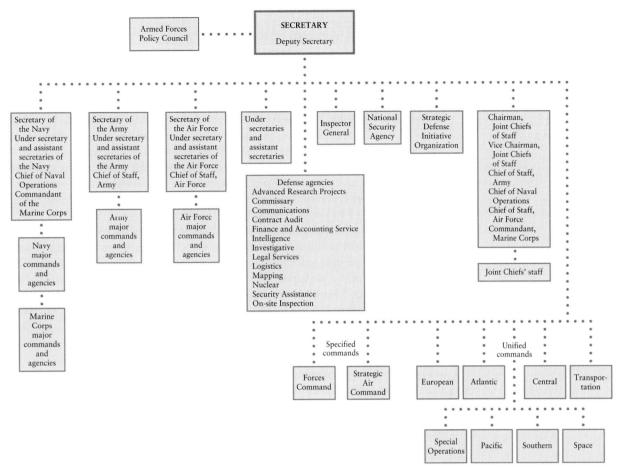

Figure 19-2 *The Department of Defense (January 1993).*

at sea. A strategy that calls for heavy artillery support from Navy ships may please the Navy but displease the Army, whose own artillery units would be underutilized and whose infantry units would be forced to rely on support from a service branch outside the Army chain of command. Interservice rivalries and tensions are constant, and civilian leaders—the president and the secretary of defense—must often resolve them.

In foreign affairs, diplomatic and military initiatives usually occur simultaneously. Diplomacy, however, may drag on for long periods without producing satisfactory results. Diplomatic undertakings depend on persuasion and mutual accommodation and may not succeed in getting foreign nations to agree with each other or to act in accordance with American national interests. Thus, military initiatives often seem more promising. In Nicaragua in the mid 1980s, for instance, the United States was unable through negotiation to alter the policies of the Sandinista regime (which the Reagan administration believed would increase communist influence in Central America), nor was it able to bring about an accommodation between the Sandinistas and the contra opposition. The administration therefore sought to provide military aid to the contras (and continued to do so through covert means even after Congress prohibited such assistance). Its objective was to succeed through the use of military force where it had failed diplomatically. Similarly, in 1993 President Clinton deployed American military forces in Somalia and sought to convince the United Nations to undertake expanded military activity in Bosnia.

Part of the appeal of military over diplomatic approaches is the common perception among American presidents that the Defense Department is more responsive to presidential wishes than is the State Department or other diplomatic agencies. John F. Kennedy once called the State Department a "bowl of jelly."[17] This perception may be misleading, for there are many examples of military resistance to presidential leadership, but most presidents have felt that military approaches promise quicker and surer responses than diplomacy and that they often generate greater public support at home. George Bush's rejection of diplomacy in favor of military action to force the removal of Iraqi forces from Kuwait in 1991 was an example of this tendency.

On national security issues, as in all aspects of policy making, the president is engaged in political struggles even with his highest-ranking and closest advisers. For example, after American hostages were seized in Iran in 1979, intense debate occurred within the top levels of the Carter administration over how to respond.[18] Some of Carter's advisers, especially National Security Adviser Zbigniew Brzezinski and Defense Secretary Harold Brown, felt that bold action, perhaps even military intervention, was necessary. Others, including Secretary of State Cyrus Vance, believed that the military risks were too high and that the best hope for avoiding injury to the hostages lay in patient diplomacy. When public support for Carter's handling of the hostage crisis diminished—and with the presidential election of 1980 looming on the horizon—Carter began to side with those who urged bolder action. Against the strong counsel of Secretary of State Vance, Carter ordered a military rescue mission. The mission failed when a helicopter and an airplane collided before reaching

In 1980, President Carter's effort to rescue fifty-three American hostages in Iran failed when a military helicopter and a plane collided in the desert as they approached Teheran. The inability to secure the release of the hostages after more than a year in captivity frustrated Carter and the nation as a whole.

© J.L. Atlan/SYGMA

Television and press photos often shape public opinion about foreign policy. In 1993, support for intervention in Somalia diminished significantly after publication of pictures like this one, showing Somalis dancing around a downed United Nations helicopter carrying a crew of American soldiers.

© P. Watson/SYGMA

their objective. Vance, feeling that his effectiveness as an adviser to the president had been compromised, resigned in protest.

A decision by the president to pursue a particular policy course is no guarantee that all the other participants will agree with the policy or comply fully in carrying it out. The president not only must struggle with the legislative branch in defining foreign and defense policy but must struggle with elements of the executive branch for the same purpose. This internal strife is an enduring feature of foreign and defense policy making.

THE ROOTS OF FOREIGN AND DEFENSE POLICY

A nation's relations with the rest of the world are rooted in its perspectives and objectives, in the way it views events and opportunities and in the way it defines its own interests. All nations are a product of their history, their geography, and the ideas of their great political thinkers. Contemporary public opinion sets broad parameters, but foreign policy is also guided by patterns and predispositions that draw deeply on past experiences.

Political Culture

In every country, foreign and defense policy makers take important cues from the political culture. To international policy makers the American political culture (see Chapter 1) is both a source of clarity and a source of confusion. It provides them with important points of reference for gauging American public opinion and defining the boundaries of policy decisions. And it offers them a set of ideas that they can use to give their decisions the appearance of moral propriety and to mobilize public support for their actions. Political culture, however, is a broad concept and is difficult to apply to specific situations.

Throughout the 1980s, for example, United States policy in Central America suffered from a lack of national consensus, a result of the difficulty of applying American values to countries in which competing parties claimed adherence to democratic ideals. In El Salvador, the Reagan administration supported the official regime against guerrilla forces that it believed were bent on establishing a communist dictatorship. In Nicaragua, the Reagan administration supported guerrilla forces against the official regime, which it believed was a communist dictatorship. As a result, the Reagan administration simultaneously undertook actions designed to protect the regime in El Salvador and to defeat the regime in Nicaragua. Many Americans, including prominent members of Congress, took the opposite view in each case and opposed the administration's Central American policies. Both sides, however, based their actions on the argument that political power is legitimate only when it is based on the consent of the governed.

The imperatives of political culture tend to operate in the background of policy making. They define fundamental values that may limit the range of choices available to decision makers, and they provide a broad and sometimes crude sense of right and wrong. Yet despite the existence of a dominant American culture, it is a vast and misleading oversimplification to assume that all Americans respond to all government policies in the same way. In fact, the United States is a nation of subcultures, each with its own history, world view, and prevailing attitudes. A midwestern, working-class community of second- and third-generation descendants of central Europeans may have different values and expectations than an eastern college town or a wealthy suburb on the West Coast or a rural southern county. What "plays" in Peoria may not "play" in San Diego or Knoxville or Cambridge. In deciding whether to support American policy initiatives abroad, each subculture employs a set of filters that color its perception of those initiatives and shape its reaction to them. This filtering further complicates international policy making by guaranteeing that American leaders will have to deal with political disagreement about every major decision they make.

Historical Experience

A country's historical experience meshes with public opinion and political culture to affect the perceptions and predispositions of its political leaders. Each generation learns certain lessons from the events that occur during its lifetime, and each inherits a set of historical legacies that have accumulated over time. Like the notions inherent in political culture, these provide guidance to policy makers and place constraints on their freedom of action.

For many contemporary policy makers, the most important sources of historical experience are World War II and the spread of communism in the following decade. The war was a prominent part of the personal experiences of most of the individuals who became national leaders in the postwar period. All the presidents from Truman through Bush had roles in World War II: Truman chaired a Senate committee that investigated war policies, and he later served as commander-in-chief; Eisenhower was a general of the Army; Kennedy was a naval officer in the Pacific; Johnson was a representative in the House

Recent ethnic tensions in Bosnia are a tragic reminder of the outbreak of World War I. (Top) In Sarajevo in 1914, Serbian student Gavrillo Prinzzip is taken into custody after assassinating Archduke Franz Ferdinand. (Bottom) Nearly eighty years later, Ruza Glavas is wounded by mortar fire aimed at the cemetery where she was attending the funeral of her grandchild—who had been killed by a sniper while being evacuated from Sarajevo.

who served briefly in uniform; Nixon and Ford were naval officers; Carter was a midshipman at the Naval Academy; Reagan held a commission in an Army public affairs unit; and Bush was a naval aviator. The primary lesson that these leaders and others of their generation drew from World War II is that peace is not a natural condition; it must be aggressively pursued. And the war and its aftermath suggested to them that vigilance and strength are the best assurances of peace. None of them believed that America could contribute to peace by minding its own business. Indeed, for most of them World War II was the price that America had paid for minding its own business during the 1930s while Germany, Japan, and Italy prepared for war.

In justifying American involvement in Vietnam, presidents Eisenhower, Kennedy, and Johnson sometimes spoke of the "Munich analogy," a reference to the 1938 conference in Munich at which British prime minister Neville Chamberlain attempted to satisfy the expansionist objectives of Hitler's government by sacrificing the independence of Czechoslovakia to German control. The Munich analogy impelled American leaders to argue that unless communism was stopped in Vietnam it would soon spread to all of Southeast Asia and begin to move across the Pacific toward the United States. As Vice President

Lyndon Johnson noted after returning from a fact-finding tour in 1961, "The basic decision in Southeast Asia is [in Vietnam]. We must decide whether to help these countries to the best of our ability or throw in the towel and pull back our defenses to San Francisco."[19]

In more recent justifications of American involvement in Central America, defenders of Reagan administration policy cited the need to prevent "another Cuba," referring to their concern that inaction in Nicaragua and El Salvador would lead to the development of another communist government in the Western Hemisphere like the one that emerged in Cuba in the early 1960s. Their opponents, however, drew a different lesson from a different experience. Alluding to the problems experienced by the United States in withdrawing from the long and costly war in Vietnam, they argued that American involvement in Central America would become "another Vietnam." Some commentators on the intense conflict in Bosnia in the 1990s noted its resemblance to ethnic tensions that led to World War I and feared a similar outcome.

The difficult task for any policy maker is to separate the appropriate historical lessons from the inappropriate ones. Although Munich may tell something important about the world a half-century later, it does not tell everything that is important. And although the costs of involvement in Vietnam may have been a painful lesson for the American people, it does not necessarily follow that Americans should never again intervene in the affairs of other countries. Historical experience shapes the actions of contemporary policy makers in many ways. But the range of that experience is broad, and one can never be entirely sure that any of the varied lessons it provides is best applied to a particular decision.

Public Opinion

Conflict over foreign policy has an important public dimension. Public pressures, exerted through public opinion and interest group politics, sometimes play a significant role in foreign and defense policy decisions. In general, however, public opinion is a looser constraint on day-to-day matters of foreign policy than it is in domestic affairs. Public opinion establishes the range within which policy makers can operate, but it also gives them considerable latitude. As Table 19-2 indicates, most Americans support an active American role in foreign affairs. The particulars of that role are not clearly defined, however.

The principal reason for the freedom that public opinion affords foreign and defense policy makers is that most Americans do not feel directly affected by, and are therefore not well informed about, international issues. They are usually willing to leave decisions on such matters to the president and other political leaders and to support them when they appear to be acting in the national interest. Public opinion on foreign and defense matters is also highly responsive to action. When a president acts—to blockade Cuba, to visit China, to invade Panama, to bomb Iraq—the immediate public response is normally supportive.[20]

Public opinion may become a liability, however, when the president confronts an international situation that he seems unable to resolve. Harry Truman and Lyndon Johnson saw their public support steadily drain away in the face

TABLE 19-2

American Attitudes on United States Involvement in International Affairs, 1945–1991

QUESTION: "Do you think it would be best for the future of this country if we take an active part in world affairs, or if we stay out of world affairs?" (Answers reported as a percentage of respondents.)

DATE	ACTIVE PART	STAY OUT	NO OPINION
October 1945	70	19	11
December 1950	66	25	9
March 1955	72	21	7
June 1965	79	16	5
March 1973	66	31	3
March 1978	64	32	4
November 1982	53	35	12
March 1986	65	32	4
March 1991	73	24	2

SOURCE: Adapted from Harold W. Stanley and Richard G. Niemi, *Vital Statistics on American Politics*, 4th ed. (Washington, D.C.: Congressional Quarterly, 1994), 346.

of Asian wars that dragged on for years without victory. Jimmy Carter, though his actions were prudent in the eyes of most analysts, suffered in public opinion because of his inability to secure the return of the Americans who were held hostage in Iran for more than a year.

Interest groups often seek to influence foreign and defense policy decisions when their own interests are likely to be affected. Some such groups exist to provide a voice for ethnic concerns. American Jewish organizations, for instance, have long been active in trying to influence policy toward Israel. In the mid 1970s, Americans of Greek descent undertook an aggressive effort to stop American arms sales to Turkey, which was using those arms against Greek citizens of the island of Cyprus. The "China lobby," composed of supporters of Chiang Kai-shek, actively sought to prevent American recognition of the revolutionary government of Mao Zedung on the mainland of China after World War II.

Other groups seek to influence foreign policy primarily for economic reasons. They wish to improve their opportunities to trade with foreign nations, or they seek to protect certain products from foreign competition. In recent decades, for example, the national organizations that represent American farmers have taken a new interest in foreign trade as Russia and many other countries in Eastern Europe and Asia have become important markets for agricultural products, especially grain.

Among the most prominent of the interest groups that influence defense policy making are those representing the **military-industrial complex**. The Defense Department spends tens of billions of dollars each year to purchase weapons from American corporations. It does this by awarding contracts to companies to develop and produce individual weapons systems like the B-2 bomber, the M-16 rifle, and the Aegis cruiser. Some of these contracts are worth more than $10 billion and can have a life-or-death impact on the health of the companies that get or fail to get them.

Confronting that reality, companies and industries actively engage in the politics of defense policy. They mount comprehensive public relations campaigns, make large contributions to congressional and presidential candidates, and hire some of the most expensive lobbyists in Washington. They work closely with the congressional representatives of the states and districts where defense plants are located—and where local economies may be heavily dependent on the jobs and dollars that defense contracts provide. Defense contractors seek to get supporters of particular weapons systems elected and re-elected and then to persuade them and their counterparts in the Defense Department to grant them contracts to produce expensive weapons.

Every international policy decision attracts its own large and energetic cluster of special interest groups seeking to affect the outcomes. Even foreign governments have their own lobbyists. Special interest groups have become important and often influential participants in foreign and defense policy choices.

THE RECENT EVOLUTION OF FOREIGN AND DEFENSE POLICY

The two atomic bombs that American planes dropped on Japanese cities in 1945 marked the beginning of contemporary American international policy. Rarely has a historical turning point been more clearly—and more dramatically—marked. On those two August days a new era in world affairs began, one dominated by the availability and the fear of a single terrifying weapon.

Before World War II the history of American foreign policy had been characterized by almost continual **isolationism**—disengagement from the affairs of foreign countries except when they intersected directly with United States interests. The isolation was occasionally broken by wars—wars with Britain and Spain and, later, World War I. But each of those wars was followed by rapid demobilization and a return to isolationism.

After World War II, however, the historical pattern of American isolationism was broken, probably irrevocably. The postwar world was markedly different from the prewar world. Two superpowers loomed over it, "super" in terms of both natural resources and military might. The two superpowers had very different concepts of the proper economic and political organization of a society and very different visions of the future. Their differences bred suspicion and distrust. Each was anxious to prevent the other's influence from spreading over a defeated Europe and into the new nations of Asia and Africa. They quickly came to focus on each other as adversaries, and the result was what came to be called the **Cold War**, a period of intense and often hostile competition between the United States and the Soviet Union. All of this required—and caused—some critical changes in American foreign policy.

In the years following World War II, American policy makers began to develop responses to the changes that had taken place in the international environment. By the end of the 1940s, several new and fundamental principles of American national security policy had emerged.[21]

The first principle was that the United States must play an active and continuing role in world affairs. Isolationism was rejected. American interests

Even as Axis aggression was raging in Europe and the Far East, many Americans—like these members of the America First Committee—clung to isolationist views. Here Charles Lindbergh addresses a "No Foreign Wars" rally in Philadelphia in May of 1941, six months before the attack on Pearl Harbor.

were not limited to the continental United States but extended all over the globe. The lesson drawn from the two world wars was that America could never again afford to withdraw from world affairs. As a superpower it had a responsibility to deter aggression and to prevent local hostilities from ballooning into worldwide conflicts.

Second, American policy strategists identified communism as the greatest danger confronting the United States. In the early postwar years, communism was widely regarded as a monolithic movement based on Marxist ideology and directed insidiously from the Soviet Union. That view dominated American policy making for almost two decades. By the late 1960s a more sophisticated view, one that recognized distinctions among communist governments, had begun to emerge.

Third, the ultimate objective of American foreign and defense policy would be **containment** of the influence of the Soviet Union. The Soviet Union was regarded as the driving force in the world communist movement, and it therefore became the principal concern of American policy makers. They developed not a policy of active military engagement with the Soviet Union but a policy designed to prevent the spread of Soviet influence into noncommunist countries. (The origins of the policy of containment are described in the box on page 732.)

Containment of Soviet expansionism remained the dominant goal of American foreign and defense policy, but it inspired plenty of political debate. There was strong consensus about the existence of a communist threat, but there was broad disagreement about the degree of danger posed by that threat and about the programs that ought to be pursued in dealing with it.

Some political and opinion leaders thought the communist threat was imminent and could be effectively opposed only by military force. Members of this group, which included both Republicans and Democrats, were often referred to as "cold warriors" or, later, as "hawks." They supported large peace-

Few writings have so influenced the thinking of a generation as the article "The Sources of Soviet Conduct," published under the pseudonym "Mr. X" in the journal *Foreign Affairs*. In 1947, George F. Kennan, then a Foreign Service officer, laid out the strategy that came to be called containment. Here are some excerpts from the article.

"The men in the Kremlin have continued to be predominantly absorbed with the struggle to secure and make absolute the power which they seized in November 1917. They have endeavored to secure it primarily against forces at home, within Soviet society itself. But they have also endeavored to secure it against the outside world. For ideology, as we have seen, taught them that the outside world was hostile and that it was their duty eventually to overthrow the political forces beyond their borders. . . .

Since capitalism no longer existed in Russia and since it could not be admitted that there could be serious or widespread opposition to the Kremlin springing simultaneously from the liberated masses under its authority, it became necessary to justify the retention of the dictatorship by stressing the menace of capitalism abroad. . . .

There is ample evidence that the stress laid in Moscow on the menace confronting Soviet society from the world outside its borders is founded not in the realities of foreign antagonism but in the necessity of explaining away the maintenance of dictatorial authority at home. . . .

It is clear that the main element of any United States policy toward the Soviet Union must be that of a long-term, patient but firm and vigilant containment of Russian expansive tendencies. . . .

The Soviet pressure against the free institutions of the Western world is something that can be contained by the adroit and vigilant application of counterforce at a series of constantly shifting geographical and political points, corresponding to the shifts and maneuvers of Soviet policy, but which cannot be charmed or talked out of existence. . . .

It is clear that the United States cannot expect in the foreseeable future to enjoy political intimacy with the Soviet regime. It must continue to regard the Soviet Union as a rival, not a partner, in the political arena. It must continue to expect that Soviet policies will reflect no abstract love of peace and stability, no real faith in the possibility of a permanent happy coexistence of the Socialist and capitalist worlds. . . .

This would itself warrant the United States entering with reasonable confidence upon a policy of firm containment, designed to confront the Russians with unalterable counterforce at every point where they show signs of encroaching upon the interests of a peaceful and stable world."

SOURCE: X [George F. Kennan], "The Sources of Soviet Conduct," Reprinted by permission of *Foreign Affairs* 25 (July 1947), 566–582. Copyright 1947 by the Council on Foreign Relations, Inc.

time military expenditures and military responses to acts of communist aggression. This policy prevailed in 1950, when the communist government of North Korea invaded South Korea. American troops were sent in force to repel the threat and remained there for three years in a war in which over thirty thousand Americans died. That was the first of many American military interventions during the Cold War period.

Other Americans, some of whom came to be known as "doves," disagreed with this approach. They believed that the communist threat was most likely to be felt in the smaller industrialized nations and in the less developed countries. The best response to the spread of communism, in their view, was to use America's wealth and its ideological commitment to freedom and human rights—not its armed forces—to win support in those countries. They believed that there was little to gain and much to lose by military intervention in the affairs of foreign countries. A better approach, they thought, was to encourage foreign trade, to increase foreign aid, and to support foreign political leaders who were most likely to pursue democratic goals.

What came out of the post–World War II debate over foreign policy was a mixture of initiatives. The United States did indeed expand its foreign-aid program and increase its foreign trade. But it also maintained, for the first time in its history, a large standing armed force, which it positioned around the world in an effort to deter communist expansionism. Those postwar policies had several major components, the most awesome of which was nuclear deterrence.

Nuclear Deterrence

For most of the postwar period American policy strategists have regarded nuclear weapons as primarily defensive in purpose. According to this view, their highest value lies in preventing wars, especially wars among the superpowers. For nuclear deterrence to be an effective strategy, the United States had to convince its adversaries that the costs of aggressive action would be too large to risk incurring and that the United States could and would use nuclear arms to punish aggression. In the 1980 presidential campaign Ronald Reagan reiterated what had been a constant refrain in American policy for decades: "Our best hope of persuading [adversaries] to live in peace is to convince them that they cannot win a war."[22]

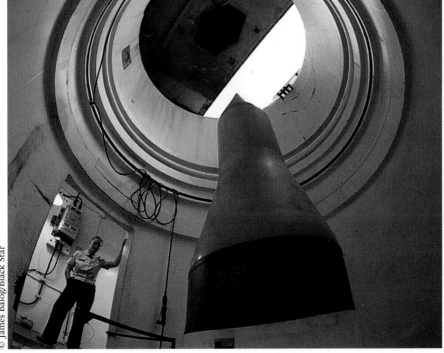

© James Balog/Black Star

During the Cold War, both offensive and defensive missiles were deployed at missile sites all over the United States and on Trident submarines beneath the oceans. Here is a Minuteman II missile silo in the mid 1980s. The end of Cold War tensions initiated the dismantling of some sites as the superpowers sought to "build down" their nuclear arsenals.

Nuclear deterrence worked because the United States spent hundreds of billions of dollars to build and maintain a nuclear arsenal so that it would present a credible nuclear threat to the Soviet Union and other potential adversaries. Other nations believed that the United States possessed the capability to inflict significant damage in a nuclear attack—even if the American attack was a retaliatory response. In the jargon of nuclear-policy makers, this capability was labeled **mutual assured destruction** (its acronym, MAD, became a convenient "handle" for the policy's opponents). It implied that a nuclear attack on the United States would be suicidal for the country that launched it.

Foreign Trade

In recent decades, the American economy has become increasingly entwined with the world economy. In constant dollars, Americans sold $36 billion worth of goods and services abroad in 1939; in 1990, they sold sixteen times as much.[23] The sale of goods, the purchase of raw materials, the search for fuel sources and labor and credit, all now routinely cross national boundaries. As a consequence, economic issues have come to play a more central role in American foreign policy, and agencies of the federal government that were once concerned solely with the domestic economy are now deeply involved in foreign policy making. (The Case Study on page 735 examines American trade with Japan.)

Foreign trade is a major concern of private economic enterprises. American corporations seek broad markets, inexpensive labor and materials, and protection against alleged unfair foreign competition. In each of these areas they look to the federal government for assistance. The government responds by establishing trade policies to encourage the sale of American goods overseas and, in some cases, to control the flow of foreign goods into American markets. These complex issues often pit American manufacturers against American consumers.

American diplomatic relations are closely tied to economic decisions. In recent decades increased trade has often been used as a wedge to open and strengthen relations between the United States and its foreign adversaries. Sales of grain and technology to the Soviet Union, which began in earnest in the 1970s, helped provide food for Soviet citizens and cash for American farmers. They also added to the interdependence of the two nations. Similarly, a significant expansion of trade with the People's Republic of China has been an important part of improved American relations with that country.

The complexities of the world economy make foreign trade a difficult area of international policy making. That difficulty is compounded by the American tradition of a free-market economy in which the highest priority of individual corporations, labor unions, farmers, and banks is their own economic interests, not the national interest. The character and success of international economic policy thus is determined to a substantial extent by the ability of political leaders to create consensus from an exceedingly diverse set of economic interests.

In recent decades, Japan has flooded the American market with attractive and relatively low-priced automobiles, electronics, cameras, and other consumer products. In 1992 Americans spent $94 billion to purchase those Japanese goods. The Japanese, in contrast, spent only $47 billion to purchase American goods. The result for the United States was a $47-billion deficit in its trading partnership with Japan—nearly half the total deficit for 1992.

Restoring the balance is no simple matter. International economic policies in both countries reflect domestic politics. Recent administrations in the United States have sought to reduce the trade deficit without imposing duties and tariffs to restrict the inflow of Japanese goods. They have tried to negotiate a set of agreements aimed at getting Japan to restrict its exports voluntarily and to increase its imports from the United States.

Presidential initiatives have been complicated by pressure from Congress, particularly from members whose districts include industries that suffer from Japanese competition. Some of those members have argued that Japanese economic policies are different from American policies in ways that have the same effect as a tariff—that is, they increase the price of American goods to Japanese consumers and thus make them less attractive. Some pricing mechanisms in Japan force consumers there to pay as much as 70 percent more for American goods than consumers in the United States pay. In the minds of some members of Congress, retaliatory American policies that diminish the appeal of Japanese goods for American consumers are justified.

The Japanese government, and especially the long-dominant Liberal Democratic party, has walked a tightrope between its desire to maintain access to American markets and its need to be responsive to its own constituents. One of those constituent groups is the owners of small stores, traditionally loyal to the Liberal Democratic party. At the urging of the small-store owners, the government has supported a policy of requiring large retail stores to get the permission of nearby small competitors before opening an outlet. This requirement has forced some retailers to wait a decade or more before opening a large store, and it is the large stores that are most likely to stock goods imported from the United States.

The Japanese government has attempted to shift the blame for the bilateral trade imbalance. The claim is that the United States has poor international trade relations because of its large budget deficits, the low savings rate of its citizens, and the need to train its workers to produce higher-quality goods at lower cost. Japan has sought agreements with the United States to make progress on those fronts in return for Japanese concessions about changes in the economy of Japan.

In March 1990 President George Bush and Prime Minister Toshiki Kaifu of Japan met in California for two days of talks. The meeting was part of an effort to persuade the Japanese to open up Japanese markets to more American goods in exchange for the United States' agreement to back down from its threat to tighten restrictions on imports of Japanese goods. The talks produced no significant policy change because both administrations had to maintain delicate political balances at home. The Japanese, perhaps recognizing the fact that the American president shares power with a potent legislature, also spent large amounts to hire lobbyists to deal directly with Congress. In 1993, President Clinton demonstrated the high priority he placed on improving trade relations with Japan by appointing Walter Mondale—a former vice president and presidential candidate—as ambassador to Japan.

Discussion questions
1. How is the American president constrained by domestic politics in dealing with the Japanese on trade matters?
2. Should foreign countries be permitted to hire lobbyists to influence votes in Congress? Why or why not?
3. What influence or pressure can an American president bring to bear on a friendly foreign government like that of Japan?

SOURCE: Coverage of United States–Japanese trade discussions in *Congressional Quarterly Weekly Report* during 1990.

Foreign Economic and Military Aid

One of America's great resources in international relations is its wealth and industrial capacity. As the world's richest nation, the United States has the ability to give money and weapons to other countries to help them develop economically and protect their own interests.

Many of the European nations that were devastated by World War II experienced great difficulty in reestablishing their economies after the war. As a consequence, many experienced periods of political instability that made them vulnerable to external threats and internal revolt. In 1947 the United States responded with an emergency program to provide economic aid to many war-torn countries of Europe. The Marshall Plan (named for George C. Marshall, the secretary of state who announced it) established a pattern and a precedent for a major new component of American national security policy: the annual distribution of American economic assistance and, later, other forms of assistance to countries all over the world (see Table 19-3).

Today most foreign economic-aid programs are administered by the United States Agency for International Development. Increasingly in recent years, however, foreign-aid programs have taken the form of military rather than simply economic aid. Instead of giving cash and subsidies to foreign countries, the United States has given or sold them arms or has provided direct military assistance in the form of American advisers or training.

The strong bipartisan congressional support for the foreign-aid program that existed at the time of its establishment has dissipated over the years. Con-

---

TABLE 19-3

United States Foreign Grants and Credits by Area, 1945–1991

AREA	TOTAL NET EXPENDITURES (IN MILLIONS OF DOLLARS)					
	1945–55	1956–65	1966–75	1976–85	1986–91	TOTAL
Financial institutions	635	655	2,719	10,432	8,108	22,549
Western Europe	33,067	6,752	1,004	1,526	−6,408	35,941
Eastern Europe	823	501	226	1,028	2,620	5,198
Near East and South Asia	4,944	16,828	17,196	50,817	13,854	103,639
Africa	147	2,272	3,610	11,062	26,179	43,270
Far East and Pacific	9,678	16,199	34,778	9,566	−11,080	59,141
Western Hemisphere	1,248	5,181	6,816	9,861	12,395	35,501
Others	969	1,335	4,018	9,761	12,516	28,599
Totals	51,511	49,723	70,367	104,053	58,184	333,838

SOURCE: U.S. Department of Commerce, Bureau of the Census, *Statistical Abstract of the United States* (Washington, D.C., 1987), 785–786; and *Statistical Abstract of the United States* (Washington, D.C., 1993), 803–805.

NOTE: Negative figures occur when the total of grant returns, principal repayments, and/or foreign currencies disbursed by the United States government exceeds new grants and new credits utilized and/or acquisitions of foreign currencies through new sales of farm products.

gress has routinely cut presidents' foreign-aid budget requests and has sought to link the provision of aid to requirements that recipient countries improve their human rights policies, use the money for specified humanitarian purposes, or loosen emigration restrictions. Many members of Congress question the benefits produced by the billions of dollars spent on foreign aid every year. Some criticize the practice of giving American money to foreign dictators for no other real purpose than to purchase their continuing friendship. Others criticize government priorities that provide more money to aid other countries than to meet pressing domestic needs. As a consequence, the American foreign-aid program is controversial, and passage of the foreign-aid bill each year has grown politically more complex and difficult—a constant source of tension between the president and Congress.[24]

Alliances

The policy of containment produced a flurry of American alliance building in the years following World War II. The North Atlantic Treaty Organization (NATO), the Central Treaty Organization (CENTO), the Southeast Asian Treaty Organization (SEATO), and the Organization of American States (OAS) were all formed during that period. What is remarkable about this spate of alliance building is how profoundly it reversed America's historical aversion to such activity. In his Farewell Address, President George Washington had declared it "our true policy to steer clear of permanent alliances with any portion of the foreign world."[25] Avoidance of permanent alliances was a characteristic of American foreign policy through the 1930s. But the changed environment of the postwar world brought about a significant shift in American strategy.

In reality, these alliances were employed to define the frontiers of American influence and to draw the lines behind which Soviet expansion was to be contained. The borders of the nations to which the United States had pledged

P. Piel/Gamma-Liaison

Just as construction of the Berlin Wall symbolized the tensions of the Cold War (see page 705), so did its dismantling, pictured here, become a powerful symbol of the crumbling of communism and the end of the Cold War.

its protection marked the boundaries between the communist and noncommunist worlds. In essence, the treaties were a statement to the Soviet Union that crossing any of these lines would be regarded as a direct affront to American national interests and would invoke a forceful response.

With the profound changes in European communism that began in the late 1980s, the role and future of NATO, the most important of the American alliances, was thrown into question. The potential for broad military conflict in Europe seemed to decline rapidly, and the loyalties of countries like Poland and Hungary, which had been Soviet allies for decades, were no longer certain. Indeed, several of them applied for membership in NATO in the early 1990s. Newly independent republics of the former Soviet Union began to make similar inquiries. The search for a proper response to these changes provoked significant political debate in the United States.

Military Force

After World War II the United States maintained much larger armed forces than it had after previous wars. Several million Americans remained in uniform and were stationed at posts around the world (see Table 19-4). Their principal role was to indicate to the Soviet Union that the United States was prepared and willing to respond to communist aggression.

This was not an idle threat. Twice since 1945—in Korea and in Vietnam—American forces have engaged in lengthy "frontier wars" to defend United States allies against the perceived threat of communist aggression. On several other occasions—in the Dominican Republic, Grenada, Panama, and the Persian Gulf, for example—American troops have intervened to protect American interests in foreign countries or to ensure the stability or control of regimes friendly to the United States.

The deterioration of Soviet alliances in eastern Europe and the disintegration of the Soviet Union itself in the early 1990s forced the United States to

TABLE 19-4		
Military Expenditures and Personnel Levels, 1955–1993		
YEAR	ACTIVE DUTY PERSONNEL (IN THOUSANDS)	DEFENSE AND VETERANS EXPENDITURES (IN BILLIONS OF DOLLARS)
1955	2,935	$ 47.4
1960	2,476	53.5
1965	2,655	56.3
1970	2,066	90.4
1975	2,128	103.1
1980	2,051	155.2
1985	2,151	279.1
1993	2,039 (1991)	326.1

SOURCE: U.S. Department of Commerce, Bureau of the Census, *Statistical Abstract of the United States* (Washington, D.C., 1987), 317, 326; and *Statistical Abstract of the United States* (Washington, D.C., 1993), 349, 355.

begin a broad review of its military strategies and expenditures. This review generated widespread political debate about America's military needs and objectives in a rapidly changing world. President Bush began to talk in general terms about a "new world order" in which the United States would seek to encourage peaceful diplomatic resolution of world tensions but would maintain potent mobile armed forces to deter aggression.

Some elements of this new approach emerged in the aftermath of Iraq's invasion of Kuwait in 1990. The Bush administration undertook unprecedented efforts to engage the Soviet Union and the United Nations in condemning and imposing economic sanctions against Iraq. At the same time, however, the president initiated the placement of a large, multinational force in Saudi Arabia, and in January 1991 he launched a formidable military assault that quickly evicted the occupying Iraqi troops from Kuwait.

CONTEMPORARY CHALLENGES

The past two decades have seen significant changes in the interests and capabilities of many nations and equally significant changes in the way American foreign and defense policy is made. It is too early to tell what the long-term impact of these changes will be, but it is clear that many of the traditional "realities" of America's relations with the rest of the world are being strongly challenged.

The doctrine of containment was based on the assumption that world politics was dominated by two superpowers and that the security of the United States depended on its ability to control the perceived aggressiveness of the Soviet Union. The perception of a world divided into two camps—one communist and dominated by the Soviet Union, the other capitalist and dominated by the United States—bears little resemblance to contemporary reality. The modern world is populated by many countries, nearly three times the number that existed at the end of World War II. Instead of being clearly capitalist or clearly communist, the relationships between the state and the economy within these countries vary greatly. Their internal political structures and their policies toward individual freedoms and human rights are even more varied.

In this complex environment international relations have a dynamic quality. Change is constant as countries seek to serve their own interests by establishing more favorable economic, political, and military relationships with other nations. Among the most significant recent global changes are the fading of communism, the emergence of nationalism and movements for cultural independence, growing economic interdependence among all nations, and worldwide terrorism. The vying for power between the president and Congress over who controls foreign policy is another ongoing challenge at home.

The Fading of Communism

The major premise of the policy of containment was that communism posed a direct and significant threat to the political and economic values of the United States. However, events in the 1980s and 1990s challenged this premise. Many of the world's communist governments initiated significant changes that moved them away from the collectivist economic policies and repressive political pol-

SYGMA

Lenin was the first powerful leader of the Soviet
Union and the saint of the
communist revolution.
When communist leaders
were ousted in many east-
ern European countries, including Russia, the statues
of Lenin fell.

icies that characterized communism after World War II. Racked by powerful
centrifugal forces, the government of the Soviet Union and the Communist
party finally came apart. And the Soviet military threat—the central impetus
of American foreign policy for forty-five years—no longer seemed imminent.

These changes in the former communist world vary from one country to
another, and there is still debate among Western strategists about their depth
and duration. But there is no denying that reform is in the air and that it has
profound—but still uncertain—implications for American foreign policy.

In the Soviet Union the 1985 ascension of Mikhail Gorbachev to the
leadership of the Communist party was quickly followed by new policies labeled *perestroika* (the pursuit of economic growth by shifting emphasis away
from a centrally planned, collectivist economy) and *glasnost* (expanded individual freedom and a more open political process). Gorbachev introduced the
first truly competitive elections since the Russian Revolution and began the
slow process of rebuilding the Soviet economy by introducing elements of competition and decentralization. He entered into arms reduction agreements with
the United States that marked the first major steps away from an arms race that
had been escalating for decades. He also traveled widely and became a media
hero, one of the world's most popular political figures and a symbol of a pur-
ported new age of enlightenment in the Soviet Union.

But then the communist bloc of nations in eastern Europe and the Soviet
Union itself began to unravel. In the former Soviet "satellite" states, especially
Hungary and Poland, major political and economic reforms were under way.
The Hungarian economy, relying on a relatively free market, was the healthiest
in the eastern bloc. In Poland, the trade union Solidarity, after years of protest
against a political system from which it was excluded, was formally recognized
by the communist government and allowed to compete in open elections. Many
of its candidates, some of whom had previously been jailed as political prisoners, were elected to the Polish parliament, where they took seats next to

members of the Communist party. Throughout eastern Europe national communist parties were reeling from the pace and extent of change.

As the first tentative steps toward democratization moved forward in the Soviet Union, opposition to Gorbachev and his policies emerged. Some factions wanted the pace of change accelerated; others wanted to return to centralized rule. A Gorbachev opponent and leader of the liberalizing forces, Boris Yeltsin, was elected president of Russia, the largest of the Soviet republics. In 1991 a brief coup by military leaders appeared to oust Gorbachev from power. But the coup failed quickly, in part because of Yeltsin's heroic resistance. Gorbachev returned, but to a significantly weakened position. He could not hold his country together. Soon Gorbachev was gone from power, and the Soviet Union disintegrated into more than a dozen independent republics. Yeltsin himself faced a serious crisis of authority in Russia in 1993 that led him to shut down the parliament and to arrest many of its members.

In China, the other great communist power of the twentieth century, a broad government effort to bring about economic growth by introducing some elements of private ownership and market competition led to a growing popular movement for political democracy spearheaded by intellectuals and students. In 1989 a major protest against the government captured world attention when hundreds of thousands of young Chinese occupied Tiananmen Square in Beijing. But hopes for major political reform were dashed when divisions of the Chinese army moved into the square and brutally suppressed the protesters.

Within the United States, the search for an appropriate response to these changes quickly became part of the national political debate. Uncertain about the ability of the former Soviet and other eastern European governments to sustain the changes they were initiating, some political leaders counseled patience and caution. Others called for bold action to take advantage of the opportunities these changes presented for altering the world balance of power.

AP/Wide World Photos

In this picture, transmitted around the world, a lone man faced down Chinese tanks in Tiananmen Square in Beijing on June 5, 1989. This brave individual survived the encounter, but the student revolt in China was crushed.

The Fracturing of Nation-States

The geopolitical character of the world has changed remarkably over the course of the twentieth century. In the last decade of that century it is changing faster than ever. The edifice of relatively large, heterogeneous nation-states that existed at mid century is breaking down through a process that some analysts call "ethnolinguistic fractionalization."

The colonial empires that were in place at the beginning of the century—in India, Africa, the Far East, and elsewhere—broke up under the force of nationalism. Now even those newly independent nations (and many older nations as well) are struggling to hold together in the face of internal conflicts between different ethnic, religious, and language groups. Tibetans seek their independence in China; Quebec pursues its own French-language identity in Canada; Kurds struggle for freedom in Iraq and Turkey; Serbs and Croats fight a bloody battle for control in the former country of Yugoslavia. No part of the globe is free from these vigorous efforts by groups of people seeking to govern themselves in their own language and in the tradition of their own culture.[26]

For American policy makers, weaned on notions of superpower competition and the threat of communist expansionism, the growing influence of ethnic, linguistic, and other cultural movements is another factor complicating the policy-making process. The foreign-policy agenda is in constant flux; defense priorities are increasingly difficult to calculate. The value of foreign aid in general, and the apportionment of it in particular, are debated more intensely than ever.

In sum, the self-destruction of communism may have reduced the threat of worldwide nuclear calamity, but it did not simplify the strategic task facing American foreign and defense policy makers. A reconception of American policy is under way, a reconception as sweeping as the development of the containment policy after World War II. That reconception is based on a broader and more realistic vision than the simple idea that the United States is locked in a life-and-death struggle with the Soviet Union.

Economic Interdependence

In recent decades politics in many countries has been influenced by a growing scarcity of critical resources. Many nations must search beyond their own borders for essential products like food, minerals, technology, and energy. Even the United States, long blessed with an abundance of natural resources and enormous productive capacity, has found itself deeply entrenched in the world marketplace as both a buyer and a seller.[27] The United States buys from foreign countries a considerable portion of the energy it consumes. It also buys coffee from Colombia, automobiles from Japan, and shoes from Italy. Since the mid 1970s, as Figure 19-3 indicates, the United States has spent more to purchase foreign goods than it has earned from the sale of its own goods abroad. This difference between imports and exports is called the **balance of trade**.

America's economic hegemony has been especially undermined in two areas: energy and technology. The United States has long been the world's major consumer of energy. Although its citizens make up only 5 percent of the world's population, they account for about 30 percent of the world's annual energy consumption. In the 1970s the international oil cartel, OPEC, initiated

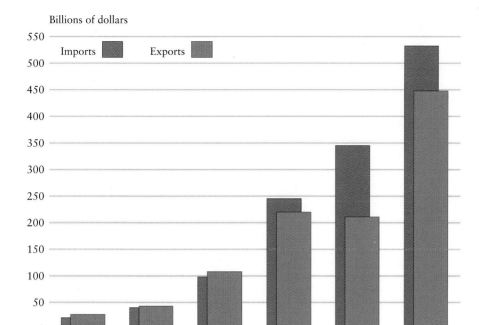

Figure 19-3   *American exports and imports, 1965–1992.* SOURCE: *U.S. Department of Commerce, Bureau of the Census,* Statistical Abstract of the United States *(Washington, D.C., 1989), 789; and* Statistical Abstract of the United States *(Washington, D.C., 1993), 808.*

a steady increase in the price of oil, from less than $2 a barrel to more than $30 a barrel at its peak. During the same period American oil imports almost doubled (though they subsequently declined). These shifts resulted in a substantial transfer of wealth from the United States to the oil-exporting countries.

Control over technology also dispersed broadly in this period. America stayed on the cutting edge in the development of many new technologies. But other countries, especially in East Asia, made significant advances in their ability to convert those new technologies into industrial and consumer products that could compete aggressively and effectively with American products, and the American market share has diminished as a result.

The trend toward interdependence accelerated in the 1990s. The European Community (EC) formed its own cooperative economic unit. The former communist nations of eastern Europe turned to capitalism and sought to become partners in the world market. Japan, Korea, Singapore, Taiwan, and other nations on the Pacific Rim were industrializing rapidly and became increasingly aware of the common marketplace in which they competed.

A consequence of these changes is that the lines between American domestic and foreign policy are increasingly blurred. The failure of a steel company in Pittsburgh is as likely to result from competition in Korea as from competition in Alabama. The market price of a commercial product at Wal-Mart may be determined in Singapore, not in New York. Welders on an automobile assembly line in Tennessee may get their paychecks from a company with headquarters in Tokyo, not in Detroit.

Reuters/Bettmann

In the 1980s, China did not experience a change of regimes, as occurred in most other communist countries. But it did dramatically turn away from communist economic policies and began to move steadily toward capitalism and entrepreneurship. Now its economy is one of the most robust in the world.

International economics has helped to create several new world powers whose international role is not based on military strength. Japan and Germany are the most notable of these, but the oil-rich members of OPEC and the high-capacity manufacturing countries of East Asia have also risen to prominence on the strength of their economic advantages. American foreign policy can no longer rest on economic superiority any more than on military dominance. The world's wealth is no longer concentrated in a very few countries, and successful trade relations have become an increasingly critical component of effective foreign policy.

Terrorism

The diversity and decentralization of the modern world have had many impacts on international relations. None is more troublesome, however, nor more resistant to solution than the spread of **terrorism,** the use of violence to disrupt the routines of international activity and to demoralize and frighten a country's population or regime. Assassinations of political leaders, kidnappings of diplomats, and bombings of government buildings are all examples of terrorism.

Human Rights Organizations

The progress of human rights worldwide is monitored in North America by several private, nonprofit organizations. Amnesty International, one of the best known, was founded in 1966 and now has 400,000 members, five regional groups, and 1,500 local groups. Amnesty International works impartially for the release of people detained anywhere because of their beliefs, race, ethnic origin, sex, religion, or language. The organization has consulting relationships with the United Nations, the Council of Europe, the Inter-American Commission on Human Rights, and the Organization of African Unity. Amnesty International received the Nobel Peace Prize in 1977.

Also well known is Human Rights Watch, founded in 1987 to be the umbrella organization for Americas Watch, the U.S. Helsinki Watch Committee, and several other groups. Human Rights Watch and its member organizations compare the human rights practices of governments against standards recognized by international accords and agreements such as the United Nations Declaration of Human Rights and the Helsinki Accords of 1975. The primary goal is to identify and publicize government abuses of human rights wherever they occur and to press for constructive change wherever possible.

Taking a somewhat different approach is Oxfam America, the United States branch of the worldwide network of Oxfam. Founded in 1942 in England as the Oxford Committee for Famine Relief, Oxfam today is a development and disaster assistance organization that funds small-scale development projects in the poorest countries of Asia, Africa, and Latin America. Oxfam also provides emergency relief for the victims of political and natural disasters by providing food, water, and medical programs.

Numerous other human rights organizations, some with very specific focuses, are active in the United States. Human Rights Internet at the University of Ottawa, an organization of scholars, activists, and policy makers concerned with the promotion and protection of internationally recognized standards of human rights, publishes regional human rights directories. They can be generally found in research libraries.

To contact these organizations, write or call:

Amnesty International of the U.S.A.
322 Eighth Avenue
New York, NY 10001
(212) 807-8400

Human Rights Internet
Human Rights Center
University of Ottawa
57 Louis Pasteur
Ottawa, Ontario K1N 6N5
(613) 564-3492

Human Rights Watch
485 Fifth Avenue
New York, NY 10017
(212) 972-8400

Oxfam America
115 Broadway
Boston, MA 02116
(800) 225-5800
(617) 482-1211

Terrorists have the advantage of stealth and surprise, and their actions are difficult to prevent. Their activities have become an increasingly common factor in world politics.[28]

Contributing to the spread of terrorism has been the emergence of non-government political organizations like the Palestine Liberation Organization (PLO), the Irish Republican Army (IRA), the Islamic Jihad, and the Armed

Reuters/Bettmann

The 1993 bombing of the World Trade Center in New York City was dramatic evidence that all societies are vulnerable to contemporary terrorists. Five people were killed, three hundred were injured, and property damage mounted to millions of dollars.

Forces of National Liberation (FALN) of Puerto Rico. These organizations have been unable to achieve their objectives by attaining political power. Failing to succeed by going through legitimate political channels, they have turned to guns and explosives to prey on the governments they oppose. There is little evidence that this tactic has helped any terrorists gain their political objectives, but their activities have become a significant source of concern for the governments that have been their targets.

Even the most powerful nations encounter great difficulty in defending themselves against terrorist attacks. In 1979 fifty-four American citizens and diplomats were seized by Iranian terrorists and held hostage for fourteen months despite constant efforts by President Carter and many international organizations to secure their release. In 1993, terrorists, some of whom had entered the country illegally, set off a bomb that killed five, injured hundreds, and did considerable damage to the World Trade Center in New York.

Stable relations between modern nations depend on their ability to maintain a civilized discourse based on mutual respect and some measure of trust. Terrorism is a constant threat to that stability and, therefore, a major concern to foreign and defense policy makers in the United States and elsewhere.

When the United States emerged from the Cold War as the world's only military superpower, pressures began to build—at home and abroad—for it to play a new role: peace keeper. Wherever democratic flames were snuffed by rebellion, as in Haiti; or ethnic strife resulted in genocide, as in Bosnia; or government failure caused intense human suffering, as in Somalia; or one country invaded another, as Iraq did to Kuwait—those in trouble looked to the United States for help. In many of these cases, the United Nations became the forum for multinational action. But the UN rarely acted militarily without the acquiescence of the United States. UN peace-keeping missions were usually dominated by American military forces and equipment.

During the Cold War, American public opinion and majorities in Congress often supported intervention abroad because such intervention was viewed as part of a larger effort to contain communist expansion. When the Cold War ended, the containment justification evaporated. The rationale for American intervention became less clear, and popular and congressional support for the use of American forces abroad diminished. In 1993, for example, when American soldiers began to die in what had been described as a humanitarian engagement in Somalia, a growing chorus in Congress and the country called for withdrawal. When a military dictator in Haiti expelled a democratically elected president and Haitians began to pour into the United States illegally, America participated in a naval blockade as part of a UN economic embargo. But there was little support at home for the use of American ground troops in Haiti.

Policing the world's hot spots is a new assignment for America in the post–Cold War period, an assignment full of uncertainty. The American people and Congress have not yet decided whether to support or reject this new call to arms.

Conflict Between the Legislative and Executive Branches

In 1964 President Lyndon Johnson sought congressional support for the use of armed force in retaliation for a North Vietnamese strike on American naval vessels. With only two dissenting votes, both houses moved quickly to pass the Tonkin Gulf Resolution. In many ways that was the high-water mark of postwar bipartisanship in foreign affairs. In the years that followed, Congress and the president found themselves increasingly at odds over the Vietnam War and many other matters of foreign and defense policy.

Congressional distrust of the presidency produced many changes in the traditional relationship between the two branches in the conduct of foreign policy. Newer, younger members who entered Congress in the late 1960s questioned the existing authority structures in the legislature and had little commitment to bipartisanship or deference to the president in foreign affairs. This "new Congress," as some came to call it, began to seek ways to define a more active and influential role for the legislature in foreign and defense policy making.

In 1973, near the end of the Vietnam War, after several years of trying and after overriding a presidential veto, Congress enacted the War Powers Resolution.[29] The resolution required the president to report to Congress within

In early 1991 the United States prepared for war. The goal was to eject the invading army of Iraq from its neighbor Kuwait. As so often in American history, the constitutional process for entering a war was in dispute. At the heart of the dispute was the ambiguity of the language of the Constitution. On its face, Section 8 of Article I seems to clarify the war power. It says that Congress has these powers:

To declare war, grant letters of marque and reprisal, and make rules concerning captures on land and water;

To raise and support armies, but no appropriation of money to that use shall be for a longer term than two years;

To provide and maintain a navy;

To make rules for the government and regulation of the land and naval forces;

To provide for calling forth the militia to execute the laws of the Union, suppress insurrections, and repel invasions.

But in Section 2 of Article II there is a clause that confuses the issue:

The President shall be commander in chief of the army and navy of the United States, and of the militia of the several states, when called into the actual service of the United States.

Does a commander-in-chief have authority to send troops wherever necessary? What is a "war"? Must a war always be declared before any hostilities can begin? For over two centuries, these and many related questions have befuddled presidents, members of Congress, and constitutional scholars.

In 1973 Congress sought to clarify the issue with the War Powers Resolution. But the resolution itself is riddled with uncertainties. Some of them were brought to the fore in the weeks preceding the engagement of American forces against Iraq. Iraq invaded Kuwait in August 1990, during a congressional recess. President Bush ordered American troops to go to the Persian Gulf region in a show of strength intended initially to prevent an Iraqi invasion of Saudi Arabia. By early 1991 almost a half-million Americans had taken up stations in and around the Persian Gulf. The force was almost as large as the peak number of American troops in Vietnam in the 1960s, but there had been no formal congressional acquiescence in these deployments.

Most presidents since 1973 have doubted the constitutionality of the War Powers Resolution. President Bush, in any case, did not believe that the deployment of American forces to the Persian Gulf triggered the provision of the resolution that requires congressional action for troops to stay beyond 60 days. Congress, however, sought to participate in this action, and on January 12, 1991, after intense debate, both houses voted to authorize the president to use force if necessary to eject the Iraqi army from Kuwait. The vote was 250 to 183 in the House and 52 to 47 in the Senate. These votes were not a formal declaration of war (Congress has formally declared war on only five occasions). But this was the first time since World War II that Congress had directly voted on sending large numbers of American troops into combat.

The congressional vote was an ad hoc procedure, outside the stipulations of the War Powers Resolution. It left the status of the resolution in a state of uncertainty. And it did little to resolve the long-term dispute about the allocation of the war-making authority between the legislative and executive branches.

SOURCE: "Constitution's Conflicting Clause Underscored by Iraq Crisis," a review of the constitutional dispute about the war-making power in *Congressional Quarterly Weekly Report*, January 5, 1991, 33–36.

48 hours of committing American armed forces to hostilities overseas. It also gave the president a maximum of 60 days for the continuation of hostilities without congressional approval. If, at the end of 60 days, both houses of Con-

gress had not approved the commitment of American forces, those forces would have to be withdrawn in the next 30 days. Congress could require the withdrawal of troops before the end of the 60-day period if it so voted by simple majorities in both houses.[30] (See the Constitutional Conflict on page 748.)

In 1975 Congress passed a law requiring the president to submit for its review any intended sale to foreign governments of weapons with a value of $25 million or more. If Congress, by a concurrent resolution of both houses, voted against the sale, it could not be carried out. Congress has never voted to prevent an arms sale through these provisions, but in 1984, in the face of strong congressional opposition to the proposed sale of Stinger missiles to Jordan and Saudi Arabia, President Reagan withdrew the proposal.

From 1947 until the mid 1970s Congress provided little meaningful oversight of intelligence activities. Only after a series of startling revelations of abuses by the intelligence agencies did Congress begin to assert a more active role in reviewing intelligence programs and budgets. The House in 1976 and the Senate in 1977 created new committees to oversee the intelligence agencies. Their principal influence comes through their authority to authorize expenditures for intelligence activities. These committees played an important role in the early stages of the Iran-contra investigation.

As Congress became a more assertive participant in foreign and defense policy making, it grew increasingly bold in its willingness to cut off funds for overseas activities that it did not support. In 1971, it prohibited the use of funds for any ground combat in Cambodia. In 1975, it proscribed the use of funds for American activities in the African nation of Angola. And in 1985 it cut off funds for military aid to the contra rebels in Nicaragua. In each of these cases Congress went against the expressed wishes of the president.

Historically, Congress rarely intervened in presidential appointments of foreign and defense policy makers. In recent years, however, it has been much more aggressive. Strong Senate opposition forced President Jimmy Carter to withdraw his first nominee to the post of director of the CIA. Through the late 1970s and 1980s conservative senators, particularly Jesse Helms (R-North Carolina), often delayed the confirmation of State Department nominees whose policy views they disliked. In 1981, the Senate Foreign Relations Committee voted to reject the appointment of Ernest W. Lefever as assistant secretary of state for human rights and humanitarian affairs. In 1989, the Senate rejected President Bush's nomination of John Tower to be secretary of defense. On many other appointments in this period, confirmation came only after lengthy questioning and vigorously expressed opposition in the Senate.

In each of these ways Congress has sought to enlarge its participation in foreign and defense policy making. The interaction of the two branches has been fitful, awkward, and inconsistent. A major challenge in the years ahead will be the development of more effective and constructive working relations between the president and Congress in the pursuit of a coherent American foreign policy.

The new realities of the past two decades have created an international environment in which American influence depends as much on wise strategy and careful diplomacy as on political and military power. As the communist threat dissipated, the underlying consensus that shaped American policy for much of the period after World War II dissipated as well. The political debates that have always characterized the search for the appropriate *means* to pursue American foreign policy now increasingly affect the debate over *ends* as well.

The president has the constitutional authority to receive ambassadors from other countries, appoint American ambassadors, serve as commander-in-chief of the armed forces, and negotiate treaties with foreign nations. However, the traditional presidential dominance in foreign policy is based more on implied and inherent powers than on the formal language of the Constitution. The expansion of the presidency in recent decades has strengthened the president's role in foreign affairs. Especially influential is the *National Security Council (NSC)*, which consists of the president, vice president, secretary of state, and secretary of defense.

Congress rarely takes the lead in defining broad foreign-policy directions, although it often plays a significant role in shaping the details of policy implementation. Congressional participation in foreign and defense policy making is usually led by the Senate Foreign Relations Committee, the House Foreign Affairs Committee, and the House and Senate Armed Services Committees. During and after the Vietnam War, Congress attempted to strengthen its role by enacting laws and resolutions governing such matters as commitments of troops, agreements with foreign countries, sales of weapons, and covert operations. Nevertheless, Congress still usually reacts to presidential initiatives in these areas.

The conduct of relations between nations is termed *diplomacy*. It is carried out primarily by the Department of State. The secretary of state is usually the government's most visible foreign-policy spokesperson, but other diplomats also participate in *bilateral relations* between the United States and a foreign government. The American *embassy* is usually located in the capital city of a country with which the United States maintains diplomatic relations; there may also be *consulates* in other cities. Sometimes bilateral relations occur on a higher level—between foreign ministers or national leaders and the president, secretary of state, or other high-ranking federal government officials. Meetings between the American president and the leader of a foreign country are known as *summit meetings*.

Bilateral relations often lead to formal agreements between nations. A *treaty* is an official, written set of accords in which the parties agree to certain specific actions. A treaty negotiated by American diplomats must be approved by two-thirds of the members of the Senate. *Executive agreements* are similar to treaties in their legal effects but do not have to be approved by the Senate.

Relations between the United States and foreign countries also take place within international organizations like the United Nations. Most such organizations are federations that provide forums for discussing international issues but have little authority to direct or constrain the actions of member nations.

To supply foreign and defense policy makers with information, large governments have agencies that collect and analyze intelligence—information about the military and defense-related activities of other nations. Such information may be obtained by means of *espionage*, or spying. Considerable tension exists between the legislative and executive branches with regard to the conduct of intelligence gathering and analysis.

War and the threat of war have a major influence on the interactions among nations. Defense and military preparedness therefore are a central component of modern national security policy. The Department of Defense is responsible for building and positioning the nation's armed forces. The *Joint Chiefs of Staff* (the highest-ranking officers from each of the military services) advise the president on military matters. Because diplomacy is a difficult process that may take a long time to produce satisfactory results, policy makers may be tempted to undertake military initiatives. This temptation is reinforced by the fact that military approaches often generate greater public support than diplomatic efforts generate.

Public pressures establish the range within which national security policy makers can operate but also give them considerable latitude. Most Americans are willing to leave national security decisions to the president and other political leaders. Interest groups seek to influence policy only when their own interests are likely to be affected. Among the most prominent groups affecting defense policy are those that represent the *military-industrial complex*.

A nation's historical experience affects the perceptions and predispositions of its political leaders. Before World War II American foreign policy was characterized by *isolationism*, or disengagement from the affairs of foreign countries. After the war this pattern was broken as two superpowers—the

United States and the Soviet Union—faced off in what came to be known as the *Cold War*. The ultimate objective of American foreign policy was *containment* of communism. For most of the postwar period containment was accomplished primarily through nuclear deterrence and the policy of *mutual assured destruction*, treaties with noncommunist countries, direct military confrontation, and the allocation of foreign-aid funds.

In recent decades economic issues, especially issues related to trade, have come to play a more central role in American foreign policy. Foreign aid has been part of United States foreign policy since the end of World War II, when the United States began providing economic aid to wartorn countries under the Marshall Plan. Today foreign-aid programs often include military as well as economic aid.

After World War II the United States entered into several alliances, including the North Atlantic Treaty Organization (NATO), the Central Treaty Organization (CENTO), the Southeast Asian Treaty Organization (SEATO), and the Organization of American States (OAS). These alliances were backed up by vastly increased armed forces stationed at posts around the world.

Today international relations take place within a much more complex and dynamic environment. Among the recent changes that have contributed to this new environment is the fading of communism, which no longer seems to pose a direct or significant threat. The emergence of nationalism and of movements for cultural and ethnic independence has also affected foreign and defense policy. The growing economic interdependence of nations has resulted in increasing emphasis on issues related to foreign trade—especially the *balance of trade*, or the difference between imports and exports. Economic competition has decreased the United States' control over energy sources and technology. Still another factor influencing international relations is an increase in *terrorism*, the use of violence to disrupt international activity and frighten a population or regime. And at home, Congress and the president continue to wrangle over what influence each should have in the development of American foreign and defense policy. These conditions have created an environment in which American influence depends as much on wise strategy and careful diplomacy as on political and military power.

KEY TERMS AND CONCEPTS

National Security Council
diplomacy
embassy
consulate
bilateral relations
summit meeting

treaty
executive agreement
espionage
Joint Chiefs of Staff
military-industrial complex
isolationism

Cold War
containment
mutual assured destruction
balance of trade
terrorism

LEARNING MORE ABOUT FOREIGN AND DEFENSE POLICY

Scholarly studies

Allison, Graham T. *Essence of Decision: Explaining the Cuban Missile Crisis.* New York: HarperCollins, 1987. A classic study of the Cuban missile crisis employing the perspectives of several analytical models.

Brzezinski, Zbigniew. *The Grand Failure: The Birth and Death of Communism in the Twentieth Century.* New York: Atheneum, Macmillan, 1990. A former national security adviser explains the demise of European communism.

Crabb, Cecil V., Jr., and Pat M. Holt. *Invitation to Struggle: Congress, the President and Foreign Policy.* 3rd ed. Washington, D.C.: Congressional Quarterly, 1989. A comprehensive assessment of the history of legislative-executive conflict over foreign affairs.

Kegley, Charles W., Jr., and Eugene R. Wittkopf. *American Foreign Policy: Pattern and Process.* 4th ed. New York: St. Martin's Press, 1991. A text that provides a broad introduction to foreign affairs and foreign policy making.

Keohane, Robert O., and Joseph S. Nye, Jr. *Power and Interdependence: World Politics in Transition.* Glenview, Ill.: Scott, Foresman/Little, Brown, 1989. An overview of the changing dynamics of contemporary international relations.

Lord, Carnes. *Presidential Management of National Security.* New York: Free Press, 1988. A study of the president's unique role in the direction of foreign and defense policy.

Leisure reading

Kissinger, Henry. *White House Years.* Boston: Little, Brown, 1979. A richly detailed insider's account of the ending of the Vietnam War, the development of détente with the Soviet Union, the reopening of relations with China, and other initiatives in the Nixon years.

Le Carré, John. *The Russia House.* New York: Bantam, 1990. A master storyteller spins a tale of espionage in Russia in the early days of *perestroika.*

Sheehan, Neil. *A Bright Shining Lie: John Paul Vann and America in Vietnam.* New York: Random House, 1988. The unfolding of the war in Vietnam as seen in the personal history of one of its leading supporters.

Tuchman, Barbara W. *The March of Folly: From Troy to Vietnam.* New York: Ballantine, 1985. A popular history of how and why countries get into wars.

Primary sources

U.S. Arms Control and Disarmament Agency. *World Military Expenditures and Arms Transfers.* Washington, D.C.: U.S. Government Printing Office, annual. A compendium of data on arms and military expenditures for most of the world's countries.

U.S. Department of State. *Annual Report.* Washington, D.C.: U.S. Government Printing Office, annual.

World Armaments and Disarmament: SIPRI Yearbook. New York: Oxford University Press, annual. Data on the world arms race and military spending compiled by the Stockholm International Peace Research Institute and information on efforts to promote disarmament.

Organizations

Arms Control Association, 11 Dupont Circle, N.W., Washington, DC 20036; (202) 797-4626. Nonpartisan organization interested in arms control. Seeks to broaden public interest in arms control and national security policies.

Center for Defense Information, 1500 Massachusetts Avenue, N.W., Washington, DC 20005; (202) 862-0700. Advocates a strong defense without increases in defense spending. Interests include weapons systems, troop levels, and defense budget.

Center for National Security Studies, 122 Maryland Avenue, N.E., Washington, DC 20002; (202) 544-5380. Specializes in Freedom of Information Act as it relates to national security matters.

National Security Archive, 1755 Massachusetts Avenue, N.W., Washington, DC 20036; (202) 797-0882. Research institute and library that provides information on U.S. foreign policy and national security affairs.

Appendixes

The Declaration

of Independence

When in the Course of human events, it becomes necessary for one people to dissolve the political bands which have connected them with another, and to assume among the Powers of the earth, the separate and equal station to which the Laws of Nature and of Nature's God entitle them, a decent respect to the opinions of mankind requires that they should declare the causes which impel them to the separation.

We hold these truths to be self-evident, that all men are created equal, that they are endowed by their Creator with certain unalienable Rights, that among these are Life, Liberty and the pursuit of Happiness. That to secure these rights, Governments are instituted among Men, deriving their just powers from the consent of the governed. That whenever any Form of Government becomes destructive of these ends, it is the Right of the People to alter or to abolish it, and to institute new Government, laying its foundation on such principles and organizing its powers in such form, as to them shall seem most likely to effect their Safety and Happiness. Prudence, indeed, will dictate that Governments long established should not be changed for light and transient causes; and accordingly all experience hath shown, that mankind are more disposed to suffer, while evils are sufferable, than to right themselves by abolishing the forms to which they are accustomed. But when a long train of abuses and usurpations, pursuing invariably the same Object evinces a design to reduce them under absolute Depotism, it is their right, it is their duty, to throw off such Government, and to provide new Guards for their future security. — Such has been the patient sufferance of these Colonies; and such is now the necessity which constrains them to alter their former Systems of Government. The history of the present King of Great Britain is a history of repeated injuries and usurpations, all having in direct object the establishment of an absolute Tyranny over these States. To prove this, let Facts be submitted to a candid world.

He has refused his Assent to Laws, the most wholesome and necessary for the public good.

He has forbidden his Governors to pass Laws of immediate and pressing importance, unless suspended in their operation till his Assent should be obtained; and when so suspended, he has utterly neglected to attend to them.

He has refused to pass other Laws for the accommodation of large districts of people, unless those people would relinquish the right of Representation in the Legislature, a right inestimable to them and formidable to tyrants only.

He has called together legislative bodies at places unusual, uncomfortable, and distant from the depository of their public Records, for the sole purpose of fatiguing them into compliance with his measures.

He has dissolved Representative Houses repeatedly for opposing with manly firmness his invasions on the rights of the people.

He has refused for a long time, after such dissolutions, to cause others to be elected; whereby the Legislative Powers, incapable of Annihilation, have returned to the People at large for their exercise; the State remaining in the mean time exposed to all the dangers of invasion from without, and convulsions within.

He has endeavoured to prevent the population of these States; for that purpose obstructing the Laws of Naturalization of Foreigners; refusing to pass others to encourage their migration higher, and raising the conditions of new Appropriations of Lands.

He has obstructed the Administration of Justice, by refusing his Assent to Laws for establishing Judiciary powers.

He has made Judges dependent on his Will alone, for the tenure of their offices, and the amount and payment of their salaries.

He has erected a multitude of New Offices, and sent hither swarms of Officers to harass our People, and eat out their substance.

He has kept among us in times of peace, Standing Armies without the Consent of our legislature.

He has affected to render the Military independent of and superior to the Civil power.

He has combined with others to subject us to a jurisdiction foreign to our constitution, and unacknowledged by our laws; giving his Assent to their acts of pretended Legislation.

For quartering large bodies of armed troops among us:

For protecting them, by a mock Trial, from punishment for any Murders which they should commit on the inhabitants of these States:

For cutting off our Trade with all parts of the world.

For imposing taxes on us without our Consent:

For depriving us in many cases, of the benefits of Trial by Jury:

For transporting us beyond Seas to be tried for pretended offences:

For abolishing the free System of English Laws in a neighbouring Province, establishing therein an Arbitrary government, and enlarging its Boundaries so as to render it at once an example and fit instrument for introducing the same absolute rule into these Colonies.

For taking away our Charters, abolishing our most valuable Laws, and altering fundamentally the Forms of our Governments:

For suspending our own Legislature, and declaring themselves invested with Power to legislate for us in all cases whatsoever.

He has abdicated Government here, by declaring us out of his Protection and waging War against us.

He has plundered our seas, ravaged our Coasts, burnt our towns, and destroyed the lives of our people.

He is at this time transporting large Armies of foreign Mercenaries to compleat the works of death, desolation and tyranny, already begun with circumstances of Cruelty & perfidy scarcely paralleled in the most barbarous ages, and totally unworthy the Head of a civilized nation.

He has constrained our fellow Citizens taken Captive on the high Seas to bear Arms against their Country, to become the executioners of their friends and Brethren, or to fall themselves by their Hands.

He has excited domestic insurrections amongst us, and has endeavoured to bring on the inhabitants of our frontiers, the merciless Indian Savages, whose known rule of warfare, is an undistinguished destruction of all ages, sexes and conditions.

In every stage of these Oppressions We have Petitioned for Redress in the most humble terms: Our repeated Petitions have been answered only by repeated injury. A Prince, whose character is thus marked by every act which may define a Tyrant, is unfit to be the ruler of a free People.

Nor have We been wanting in attention to our British brethren. We have warned them from time to time of attempts by their legislature to extend an unwarrantable jurisdiction over us. We have reminded them of the circumstances of our emigration and settlement here. We have appealed to their native justice and magnanimity, and we have conjured them by the ties of our common kindred to disavow these usurpations, which, would inevitably interrupt our connections and correspondence. They too have been deaf to the voice of justice and of consanguinity. We must, therefore, acquiesce in the necessity, which denounces our Separation, and hold them, as we hold the rest of mankind, Enemies in War, in Peace Friends.

We, therefore, the Representatives of the United States of America, in General Congress, Assembled, appealing to the Supreme Judge of the world for the rectitude of our intentions, do, in the Name, and by Authority of the good People of these Colonies, solemnly publish and declare, That these United Colonies are, and of right ought to be Free and Independent States; that they are Absolved from all Allegiance to the British Crown, and that all political connection between them and the State of Great Britain, is and ought to be totally dissolved; and that as Free and Independent States, they have full Power to levy War, conclude Peace, contract Alliances, establish Commerce, and to do all other Acts and Things which Independent States may of right do. And for the support of this Declaration, with a firm reliance on the protection of divine Providence, we mutually pledge to each other our Lives, our Fortunes and our sacred Honor.

The Constitution of the United States of America

We the People of the United States, in Order to form a more perfect Union, establish Justice, insure domestic Tranquility, provide for the common defence, promote the general Welfare, and secure the Blessings of Liberty to ourselves and our Posterity, do ordain and establish this Constitution for the United States of America.

[THREE BRANCHES OF GOVERNMENT]

[The legislative branch]

ARTICLE I

[Powers vested]

SECTION 1 All legislative Powers herein granted shall be vested in a Congress of the United States, which shall consist of a Senate and House of Representatives.

[House of Representatives]

SECTION 2 The House of Representatives shall be composed of Members chosen every second Year by the People of the several States, and the Electors in each State shall have the Qualifications requisite for Electors of the most numerous Branch of the State Legislature.

No Person shall be a Representative who shall not have attained to the Age of twenty-five Years, and been seven Years a Citizen of the United States, and who shall not, when elected, be an Inhabitant of that State in which he shall be chosen.

[Representatives and direct Taxes shall be apportioned among the several States which may be included within this Union, according to their respective Numbers, which shall be determined by adding to the whole Number of free Persons, including those bound to Service for a Term of Years, and excluding Indians not taxed, three fifths of all other Persons.][1] The actual Enumeration shall be made within three Years after the first Meeting of the Congress of the United States, and within every subsequent Term of ten Years, in such Manner as they shall by Law direct. The Number of Representatives shall not exceed one for every thirty Thousand, but each State shall have at Least one Representative; and until such enumeration shall be made, the State of New Hampshire shall be entitled to chuse three, Massachusetts eight, Rhode-Island and Providence Plantations one, Connecticut five, New York six, New Jersey four, Pennsylvania eight, Delaware one, Maryland six, Virginia ten, North Carolina five, South Carolina five, and Georgia three.

When vacancies happen in the Representation from any State, the Executive Authority thereof shall issue Writs of Election to fill such Vacancies.

The House of Representatives shall chuse their Speaker and other Officers; and shall have the sole Power of Impeachment.

[The Senate]

SECTION 3 The Senate of the United States shall be composed of two Senators from each State, [chosen by the Legislature thereof],[2] for six Years; and each Senator shall have one Vote.

Immediately after they shall be assembled in Consequence of the first Election, they shall be divided as equally as may be into three Classes. The Seats of the Senators of the first Class shall be vacated at the Expiration

---

[1]Changed by Section 2 of Amendment XIV.

[2]Changed by Amendment XVII.

of the Second Year, of the second Class at the Expiration of the fourth Year, and of the third Class at the Expiration of the sixth Year, so that one-third may be chosen every second Year; [and if Vacancies happen by Resignation, or otherwise, during the Recess of the Legislature of any State, the Executive thereof may make temporary Appointments until the next Meeting of the Legislature, which shall then fill such Vacancies].[3]

No person shall be a Senator who shall not have attained to the Age of thirty Years, and been nine Years a Citizen of the United States, and who shall not, when elected, be an Inhabitant of that State for which he shall be chosen.

The Vice President of the United States shall be President of the Senate, but shall have no Vote, unless they be equally divided.

The Senate shall chuse their other Officers, and also a President pro tempore, in the absence of the Vice President, or when he shall exercise the Office of President of the United States.

The Senate shall have the sole Power to try all Impeachments. When sitting for that Purpose, they shall be on Oath or Affirmation. When the President of the United States is tried, the Chief Justice shall preside: And no Person shall be convicted without the Concurrence of two-thirds of the Members present.

Judgment in Cases of Impeachment shall not extend further than to removal from Office, and disqualification to hold and enjoy any Office of honor, Trust, or Profit under the United States: but the Party convicted shall nevertheless be liable and subject to Indictment, Trial, Judgment, and Punishment, according to Law.

[Elections]

SECTION 4 The Times, Places and Manner of holding Elections for Senators and Representatives, shall be prescribed in each State by the Legislature thereof; but the Congress may at any time by Law make or alter such Regulations, except as to the Places of chusing Senators.

The Congress shall assemble at least once in every Year, and such Meeting shall be on the first Monday in December, [unless they shall by Law appoint a different Day].[4]

[Powers, duties, procedures of both bodies]

SECTION 5 Each House shall be the Judge of the Elections, Returns, and Qualifications of its own Members, and a Majority of each shall constitute a Quorum to do Business; but a smaller Number may adjourn from day to day, and may be authorized to compel the Attendance of absent Members, in such Manner, and under such Penalties as each House may provide.

Each House may determine the Rules of its Proceedings, punish its Members for disorderly Behavior, and, with the Concurrence of two thirds, expel a Member.

Each House shall keep a Journal of its Proceedings, and from time to time publish the same, excepting such Parts as may in their Judgment require Secrecy; and the Yeas and Nays of the Members of either House on any question shall, at the Desire of one fifth of those Present, be entered on the Journal.

Neither House, during the Session of Congress, shall, without the Consent of the other, adjourn for more than three days, nor to any other Place than that in which the two Houses shall be sitting.

[Compensation, privileges, limits on other government service]

SECTION 6 The Senators and Representatives shall receive a Compensation for their Services, to be ascertained by Law, and paid out of the Treasury of the United States. They shall in all Cases, except Treason, Felony and Breach of the Peace, be privileged from Arrest during their Attendance at the Session of their respective Houses, and in going to and returning from the same; and for any Speech or Debate in either House, they shall not be questioned in any other Place.

No Senator or Representative shall, during the Time for which he was elected, be appointed to any civil Office under the Authority of the United States, which shall have been created, or the Emoluments whereof shall have been encreased during such time; and no Person holding any Office under the United States, shall be a Member of either House during his Continuance in Office.

[Origin of revenue bills; presidential approval or disapproval of legislation; overriding the veto]

SECTION 7 All Bills for raising Revenue shall originate in the House of Representatives; but the Senate may propose or concur with Amendments as on other Bills.

Every Bill which shall have passed the House of Representatives and the Senate, shall, before it become a Law, be presented to the President of the United States; if he approve he shall sign it, but if not he shall return it, with his Objections to that House in which it shall have originated, who shall enter the Objections at large on their Journal, and proceed to reconsider it. If after such Reconsideration two thirds of that House shall agree to pass the Bill, it shall be sent, together with the Objections, to the other House, by which it shall likewise be reconsidered, and if approved by two thirds of that House, it shall become a Law. But in all such Cases the Votes of both Houses shall be determined by Yeas and Nays, and the Names of the Persons voting for and against the Bill shall be entered on the Journal of each House respectively. If any Bill shall not be returned by the President within ten Days (Sundays excepted) after it shall have been presented

---

[3]Changed by Amendment XVII.
[4]Changed by Section 2 of Amendment XX.

to him, the Same shall be a Law, in like Manner as if he had signed it, unless the Congress by their Adjournment prevent its Return, in which Case it shall not be a Law.

Every Order, Resolution, or Vote to which the Concurrence of the Senate and House of Representatives may be necessary (except on a question of Adjournment) shall be presented to the President of the United States; and before the Same shall take Effect, shall be approved by him, or being disapproved by him, shall be repassed to two thirds of the Senate and House of Representatives, according to the Rules and Limitations prescribed in the Case of a Bill.

[*Powers granted to Congress*]
SECTION 8 The Congress shall have power
To lay and collect Taxes, Duties, Imposts and Excises, to pay the Debts and provide for the common Defence and general Welfare of the United States; but all Duties, Imposts and Excises shall be uniform throughout the United States;

To borrow money on the credit of the United States;

To regulate Commerce with foreign Nations, and among the several States, and with the Indian Tribes;

To establish an uniform Rule of Naturalization, and uniform Laws on the subject of Bankruptcies throughout the United States;

To coin Money, regulate the Value thereof, and of foreign Coin, and fix the Standard of Weights and Measures;

To provide for the Punishment of counterfeiting the Securities and current Coin of the United States;

To Establish Post Offices and post Roads;

To promote the Progress of Science and useful Arts, by securing for limited Times to Authors and Inventors the exclusive Right to their respective Writings and Discoveries;

To constitute Tribunals inferior to the Supreme Court;

To define and punish Piracies and Felonies committed on the high Seas, and Offences against the Law of Nations;

To declare War, grant Letters of Marque and Reprisal, and make Rules concerning Captures on Land and Water;

To raise and support Armies, but no Appropriation of Money to that Use shall be for a longer Term than two Years;

To provide and maintain a Navy;

To make Rules for the Government and Regulation of the land and naval Forces;

To provide for calling forth the Militia to execute the Laws of the Union, suppress Insurrections and repel Invasions;

To provide for organizing, arming, and disciplining the Militia, and for governing such Part of them as may be employed in the Service of the United States, reserving to the States respectively, the Appointment of the Officers, and the Authority of training the Militia according to the discipline prescribed by Congress;

To exercise exclusive Legislation in all Cases whatsoever, over such District (not exceeding ten Miles square) as may, by Cession of particular States, and the acceptance of Congress, become the Seat of the Government of the United States, and to exercise like Authority over all Places purchased by the Consent of the Legislature of the State in which the Same shall be, for the Erection of Forts, Magazines, Arsenals, dock-Yards, and other needful Buildings;—And

[*Elastic clause*]
To make all Laws which shall be necessary and proper for carrying into Execution the foregoing Powers, and all other Powers vested by this Constitution in the Government of the United States, or in any Department or Officer thereof.

[*Powers denied to Congress*]
SECTION 9 The Migration or Importation of Such Persons as any of the States now existing shall think proper to admit, shall not be prohibited by the Congress prior to the Year one thousand eight hundred and eight, but a tax or duty may be imposed on such Importation, not exceeding ten dollars for each Person.

The privilege of the Writ of Habeas Corpus shall not be suspended, unless when in Cases of Rebellion or Invasion the public Safety may require it.

No Bill of Attainder or ex post facto Law shall be passed.

[No capitation, or other direct, Tax shall be laid, unless in Proportion to the Census or Enumeration herein before directed to be taken.][5]

No Tax or Duty shall be laid on Articles exported from any State.

No preference shall be given by any Regulation of Commerce or Revenue to the Ports of one State over those of another: nor shall Vessels bound to, or from, one State be obliged to enter, clear, or pay Duties in another.

No money shall be drawn from the Treasury, but in Consequence of Appropriations made by Law; and a regular Statement and Account of the Receipts and Expenditures of all public Money shall be published from time to time.

No Title of Nobility shall be granted by the United States: And no Person holding any Office of Profit or Trust under them, shall, without the Consent of the Congress, accept of any present, Emolument, Office, or Title, of any kind whatever, from any King, Prince, or foreign State.

[5]Changed by Amendment XVI.

SECTION 10 No State shall enter into any Treaty, Alliance, or Confederation; grant Letters of Marque and Reprisal; coin Money; emit Bills of Credit; make any Thing but gold and silver Coin a Tender in Payment of Debts; pass any Bill of Attainder, ex post facto Law, or Law impairing the Obligation of Contracts, or grant any Title of Nobility.

No State shall, without the Consent of the Congress, lay any Imposts or Duties on Imports or Exports, except what may be absolutely necessary for executing its inspection Laws: and the net Produce of all Duties and Imposts, laid by any State on Imports or Exports, shall be for the Use of the Treasury of the United States; and all such Laws shall be subject to the Revision and Control of the Congress.

No State shall, without the Consent of Congress, lay any duty of Tonnage, keep Troops, or Ships of War in time of Peace, enter into any Agreement or Compact with another State, or with a foreign Power, or engage in War, unless actually invaded, or in such imminent Danger as will not admit of delay.

[*The executive branch*]

A R T I C L E   I I

[*Presidential term, choice by electors, qualifications, payment, succession, oath of office*]

SECTION 1 The executive Power shall be vested in a President of the United States of America. He shall hold his Office during the Term of four Years, and, together with the Vice President, chosen for the same Term, be elected, as follows:

Each State shall appoint, in such Manner as the Legislature thereof may direct, a Number of Electors, equal to the whole Number of Senators and Representatives to which the State may be entitled in the Congress: but no Senator or Representative, or Person holding an Office of Trust or Profit under the United States, shall be appointed an Elector.

[The Electors shall meet in their respective States, and vote by Ballot for two persons, of whom one at least shall not be an Inhabitant of the same State with themselves. And they shall make a List of all the Persons voted for, and of the Number of Votes for each; which List they shall sign and certify, and transmit sealed to the Seat of the Government of the United States, directed to the President of the Senate. The President of the Senate shall, in the Presence of the Senate and House of Representatives, open all the Certificates, and the Votes shall then be counted. The Person having the greatest Number of Votes shall be the President, if such Number be a Majority of the whole Number of Electors appointed; and if there be more than one who have such Majority, and have an equal Number of Votes, then the House of Representatives shall immediately chuse by Ballot one of them for President; and if no Person have a Majority, then from the five highest on the List the said House shall in like Manner chuse the President. But in chusing the President, the Votes shall be taken by States, the Representation from each State having one Vote; A quorum for this Purpose shall consist of a Member or Members from two-thirds of the States, and a Majority of all the States shall be necessary to a Choice. In every Case, after the Choice of the President, the Person having the greatest Number of Votes of the Electors shall be the Vice President. But if there should remain two or more who have equal Votes, the Senate shall chuse from them by Ballot the Vice President.][6]

The Congress may determine the Time of chusing the Electors, and the Day on which they shall give their Votes; which Day shall be the same throughout the United States.

No person except a natural born Citizen, or a Citizen of the United States, at the time of the Adoption of this Constitution, shall be eligible to the Office of President; neither shall any Person be eligible to that Office who shall not have attained to the Age of thirty-five Years, and been fourteen Years a Resident within the United States.

[In case of the removal of the President from Office, or of his Death, Resignation, or Inability to discharge the Powers and Duties of the said Office, the same shall devolve on the Vice President, and the Congress may by Law provide for the Case of Removal, Death, Resignation or Inability, both of the President and Vice President, declaring what Officer shall then act as President, and such Officer shall act accordingly, until the Disability be removed, or a President shall be elected.][7]

The President shall, at stated Times, receive for his Services, a Compensation, which shall neither be encreased nor diminished during the Period for which he shall have been elected, and he shall not receive within that Period any other Emolument from the United States, or any of them.

Before he enter on the Execution of his Office, he shall take the following Oath or Affirmation:—"I do solemnly swear (or affirm) that I will faithfully execute the Office of President of the United States, and will to the best of my Ability, preserve, protect and defend the Constitution of the United States."

[*Powers to command the military and executive departments, to grant pardons, to make treaties, to appoint government officers*]

SECTION 2 The President shall be Commander in Chief of the Army and Navy of the United States, and of

---

[6]Changed by Amendment XII.
[7]Changed by Amendment XXV.

the Militia of the several States, when called into the actual Service of the United States; he may require the Opinion, in writing, of the principal Officer in each of the executive Departments, upon any subject relating to the Duties of their respective Offices, and he shall have Power to grant Reprieves and Pardons for Offenses against the United States, except in Cases of Impeachment.

He shall have Power, by and with the Advice and Consent of the Senate, to make Treaties, provided two-thirds of the Senators present concur; and he shall nominate, and by and with the Advice and Consent of the Senate, shall appoint Ambassadors, other public Ministers and Consuls, Judges of the Supreme Court, and all other Officers of the United States, whose Appointments are not herein otherwise provided for, and which shall be established by Law; but the Congress may by Law vest the Appointment of such inferior Officers, as they think proper, in the President alone, in the Courts of Law, or in the Heads of Departments.

The President shall have Power to fill up all Vacancies that may happen during the Recess of the Senate, by granting Commissions which shall expire at the End of their next Session.

[Formal duties]
SECTION 3 He shall from time to time give to the Congress Information of the State of the Union, and recommend to their Consideration such Measures as he shall judge necessary and expedient; he may, on extraordinary Occasions, convene both Houses, or either of them, and in Case of Disagreement between them, with Respect to the Time of Adjournment, he may adjourn them to such Time as he shall think proper; he shall receive Ambassadors and other public Ministers; he shall take Care that the Laws be faithfully executed, and shall Commission all the Officers of the United States.

[Conditions for removal]
SECTION 4 The President, Vice President and all civil Officers of the United States, shall be removed from Office on Impeachment for, and Conviction of, Treason, Bribery, or other high Crimes and Misdemeanors.

[The judicial branch]

A R T I C L E   I I I

[Courts and judges]
SECTION 1 The judicial Power of the United States, shall be vested in one supreme Court, and in such inferior Courts as the Congress may from time to time ordain and establish. The Judges, both of the supreme and inferior Courts, shall hold their Offices during good Behaviour, and shall, at stated Times, receive for their Services a Com-

pensation which shall not be diminished during their Continuance in Office.

[Jurisdictions and jury trials]
SECTION 2 The judicial Power shall extend to all Cases, in Law and Equity, arising under this Constitution, the Laws of the United States, and Treaties made, or which shall be made, under their Authority;—to all Cases affecting Ambassadors, other public Ministers and Consuls;—to all Cases of admiralty and maritime Jurisdiction;—to Controversies to which the United States shall be a Party;—to Controversies between two or more States;—[between a State and Citizens of another State;—][8] between Citizens of different States;—between Citizens of the same State claiming Lands under Grants of different States, [and between a State, or the Citizens thereof, and foreign States, Citizens or Subjects].[9]

In all Cases affecting Ambassadors, other public Ministers and Consuls, and those in which a State shall be Party, the supreme Court shall have original Jurisdiction. In all the other Cases before mentioned, the supreme Court shall have appellate Jurisdiction, both as to Law and Fact, with such Exceptions, and under such Regulations as the Congress shall make.

The trial of all Crimes, except in Cases of Impeachment, shall be by Jury; and such Trial shall be held in the State where the said Crimes shall have been committed; but when not committed within any State, the Trial shall be at such Place or Places as the Congress may by Law have directed.

[Treason and its punishment]
SECTION 3 Treason against the United States, shall consist only in levying War against them, or, in adhering to their Enemies, giving them Aid and Comfort. No Person shall be convicted of Treason unless on the Testimony of two Witnesses to the same overt Act, or on Confession in open Court.

The Congress shall have power to declare the Punishment of Treason, but no Attainder of Treason shall work Corruption of Blood, or Forfeiture except during the Life of the Person attainted.

[THE REST OF THE FEDERAL SYSTEM]

A R T I C L E   I V

[Relationships among and with states]
SECTION 1 Full Faith and Credit shall be given in each State to the public Acts, Records, and judicial Proceedings of every other State. And the Congress may by

[8]Changed by Amendment XI.
[9]Changed by Amendment XI.

general Laws prescribe the Manner in which such Acts, Records and Proceedings shall be proved, and the Effect thereof.

[*Privileges and immunities, extradition*]
SECTION 2 The Citizens of each State shall be entitled to all Privileges and Immunities of Citizens in the several States.

A Person charged in any State with Treason, Felony, or other Crime, who shall flee from Justice, and be found in another State, shall on demand of the executive Authority of the State from which he fled, be delivered up, to be removed to the State having Jurisdiction of the Crime.

[No Person held to Service or Labour in one State, under the Laws thereof, escaping into another, shall, in Consequence of any Law or Regulation therein, be discharged from such Service or Labour, but shall be delivered up on Claim of the Party to whom such Service or Labour may be due.][10]

[*New states*]
SECTION 3 New States may be admitted by the Congress into this Union; but no new State shall be formed or erected within the Jurisdiction of any other State; nor any State be formed by the Junction of two or more States, or parts of States, without the Consent of the Legislatures of the States concerned as well as of the Congress.

The Congress shall have Power to dispose of and make all needful Rules and Regulations respecting the Territory or other Property belonging to the United States; and nothing in this Constitution shall be so construed as to Prejudice any Claims of the United States, or of any particular State.

[*Obligations to states*]
SECTION 4 The United States shall guarantee to every State in this Union a Republican Form of Government, and shall protect each of them against Invasion; and on Application of the Legislature, or of the Executive (when the Legislature cannot be convened) against domestic Violence.

[MECHANISM FOR CHANGE]

A R T I C L E V

[*Amending the Constitution*]
The Congress, whenever two-thirds of both Houses shall deem it necessary, shall propose Amendments to this Constitution, or, on the Application of the Legislatures of two-thirds of the several States, shall call a Convention for proposing Amendments, which, in either Case, shall

[10]Changed by Amendment XIII.

be valid to all Intents and Purposes, as part of this Constitution, when ratified by the Legislatures of three-fourths of the several States, or by Conventions in three-fourths thereof, as the one or the other Mode of Ratification may be proposed by the Congress; Provided that no Amendment which may be made prior to the Year One thousand eight hundred and eight shall in any Manner affect the first and fourth Clauses in the Ninth Section of the first Article; and that no State, without its Consent, shall be deprived of its equal Suffrage in the Senate.

[FEDERAL SUPREMACY]

A R T I C L E V I

All Debts contracted and Engagements entered into, before the Adoption of this Constitution shall be as valid against the United States under this Constitution, as under the Confederation.

This Constitution, and the Laws of the United States which shall be made in Pursuance thereof; and all Treaties made, or which shall be made, under the Authority of the United States, shall be the supreme Law of the Land; and the Judges in every State shall be bound thereby, any Thing in the Constitution or Laws of any State to the Contrary notwithstanding.

The Senators and Representatives before mentioned, and the Members of the several State Legislatures, and all executive and judicial Officers, both of the United States and of the several States, shall be bound by Oath or Affirmation, to support this Constitution; but no religious Test shall ever be required as a Qualification to any Office or public Trust under the United States.

[RATIFICATION]

A R T I C L E V I I

The Ratification of the Conventions of nine States shall be sufficient for the Establishment of this Constitution between the States so ratifying the Same.

Done in Convention by the Unanimous Consent of the States present the Seventeenth Day of September in the year of our Lord one thousand seven hundred and eighty seven and of the Independence of the United States of America the twelfth. In witness whereof We have hereunto subscribed our Names.

[BILL OF RIGHTS AND OTHER AMENDMENTS]

Articles in addition to, and amendment of, the Constitution of the United States of America, proposed by Congress, and ratified by the several States, pursuant to the fifth Article of the original Constitution.

AMENDMENT I [1791]

[*Freedoms of religion, speech, press, assembly*]
Congress shall make no law respecting an establishment of religion, or prohibiting the free exercise thereof; or abridging the freedom of speech, or of the press; or the right of the people peaceably to assemble and to petition the Government for a redress of grievances.

AMENDMENT II [1791]

[*Right to bear arms*]
A well regulated Militia, being necessary to the security of a free State, the right of the people to keep and bear Arms, shall not be infringed.

AMENDMENT III [1791]

[*Quartering of soldiers*]
No Soldier shall, in time of peace be quartered in any house, without the consent of the Owner, nor in time of war, but in a manner to be prescribed by Law.

AMENDMENT IV [1791]

[*Protection against search and seizure*]
The right of the people to be secure in their persons, houses, papers, and effects, against unreasonable searches and seizures, shall not be violated, and no Warrants shall issue, but upon probable cause, supported by Oath or affirmation, and particularly describing the place to be searched, and the persons or things to be seized.

AMENDMENT V [1791]

[*Protection of citizens before the law*]
No person shall be held to answer for a capital, or otherwise infamous crime, unless on a presentment or indictment of a Grand Jury, except in cases arising in the land or naval forces, or in the Militia, when in actual service in time of War or public danger; nor shall any person be subject for the same offence to be twice put in jeopardy of life or limb; nor shall be compelled in any criminal case to be a witness against himself, nor be deprived of life, liberty, or property, without due process of law; nor shall private property be taken for public use, without just compensation.

AMENDMENT VI [1791]

[*Rights of the accused in criminal cases*]
In all criminal prosecutions, the accused shall enjoy the right to a speedy and public trial, by an impartial jury of the State and district wherein the crime shall have been committed, which district shall have been previously ascertained by law, and to be informed of the nature and cause of the accusation; to be confronted with the witnesses against him; to have compulsory process for obtaining witnesses in his favor, and to have the Assistance of Counsel for his defence.

AMENDMENT VII [1791]

[*Rights of complainants in civil cases*]
In suits at common law, where the value in controversy shall exceed twenty dollars, the right of trial by jury shall be preserved, and no fact tried by jury, shall be otherwise reexamined in any Court of the United States, than according to the rules of the common law.

AMENDMENT VIII [1791]

[*Constraints on punishments*]
Excessive bail shall not be required, nor excessive fines imposed, nor cruel and unusual punishments inflicted.

AMENDMENT IX [1791]

[*Rights retained by the people*]
The enumeration in the Constitution, of certain rights, shall not be construed to deny or disparage others retained by the people.

AMENDMENT X [1791]

[*Rights reserved to states*]
The powers not delegated to the United States by the Constitution, nor prohibited by it to the States, are reserved to the States respectively, or to the people.

AMENDMENT XI [1798]

[*Restraints on judicial power*]
The Judicial power of the United States shall not be construed to extend to any suit in law or equity, commenced or prosecuted against one of the United States by Citizens of another State, or by Citizens or Subjects of any Foreign State.

AMENDMENT XII [1804]

[*Mechanism for presidential elections*]
The electors shall meet in their respective states and vote by ballot for President and Vice-President, one of whom, at least, shall not be an inhabitant of the same state with themselves; they shall name in their ballots the person voted for as President, and in distinct ballots the person voted for as Vice-President, and they shall make distinct

lists of all persons voted for as President, and of all persons voted for as Vice-President, and of the number of votes for each, which lists they shall sign and certify, and transmit sealed to the seat of the government of the United States, directed to the President of the Senate;—The President of the Senate shall, in presence of the Senate and House of Representatives, open all the certificates and the votes shall then be counted;—The person having the greatest number of votes for President, shall be the President, if such number be a majority of the whole number of Electors appointed; and if no person have such majority, then from the persons having the highest numbers not exceeding three on the list of those voted for as President, the House of Representatives shall choose immediately, by ballot, the President. But in choosing the President, the votes shall be taken by states, the representation from each state having one vote; a quorum for this purpose shall consist of a member or members from two-thirds of the states, and a majority of all the states shall be necessary to a choice. [And if the House of Representatives shall not choose a President whenever the right of choice shall devolve upon them, before the fourth day of March next following, then the Vice-President shall act as President, as in the case of the death or other constitutional disability of the President.—][11] The person having the greatest number of votes as Vice-President, shall be the Vice-President, if such number be a majority of the whole number of Electors appointed, and if no person have a majority, then from the two highest numbers on the list, the Senate shall choose the Vice-President; a quorum for the purpose shall consist of two-thirds of the whole number of Senators, and a majority of the whole number shall be necessary to a choice. But no person constitutionally ineligible to the office of President shall be eligible to that of Vice-President of the United States.

AMENDMENT XIII [1865]

[*Abolishment of slavery*]

SECTION 1 Neither slavery nor involuntary servitude, except as a punishment for crime whereof the party shall have been duly convicted, shall exist within the United States, or any place subject to their jurisdiction.

SECTION 2 Congress shall have power to enforce this article by appropriate legislation.

AMENDMENT XIV [1868]

[*Citizens' rights and immunities, due process, equal protection*]

SECTION 1 All persons born or naturalized in the United States, and subject to the jurisdiction thereof, are citizens of the United States and of the State wherein they reside. No State shall make or enforce any law which shall abridge the privileges or immunities of citizens of the United States; nor shall any State deprive any person of life, liberty, or property, without due process of law; nor deny to any person within its jurisdiction the equal protection of the laws.

[*Basis of representation*]

SECTION 2 Representatives shall be appointed among the several States according to their respective numbers, counting the whole number of persons in each State, excluding Indians not taxed. But when the right to vote at any election for the choice of electors for President and Vice-President of the United States, Representatives in Congress, the Executive and Judicial officers of a State, or the members of the Legislature thereof, is denied to any of the male inhabitants of such State, being twenty-one years of age, and citizens of the United States, or in any way abridged, except for participation in rebellion, or other crime, the basis of representation therein shall be reduced in the proportion which the number of such male citizens shall bear to the whole number of male citizens twenty-one years of age in such State.

[*Disqualification of Confederates for office*]

SECTION 3 No person shall be a Senator or Representative in Congress, or elector of President and Vice-President, or hold any office, civil or military, under the United States, or under any State, who, having previously taken an oath, as a member of Congress, or as an officer of the United States, or as a member of any State legislature, or as an executive or judicial officer of any State, to support the Constitution of the United States, shall have engaged in insurrection or rebellion against the same, or given aid or comfort to the enemies thereof. But Congress may by a vote of two-thirds of each House, remove such disability.

[*Public debt arising from insurrection or rebellion*]

SECTION 4 The validity of the public debt of the United States, authorized by law, including debts incurred for payment of pensions and bounties for services in suppressing insurrection or rebellion, shall not be questioned. But neither the United States nor any State shall assume or pay any debt or obligation incurred in aid of insurrection or rebellion against the United States, or any claim for the loss or emancipation of any slave; but all such debts, obligations and claims shall be held illegal and void.

SECTION 5 The Congress shall have power to enforce, by appropriate legislation, the provisions of this article.

[11]Superceded by Section 3 of Amendment XX.

AMENDMENT XV [1870]

[Explicit extension of right to vote]
SECTION 1 The right of citizens of the United States to vote shall not be denied or abridged by the United States or by any State on account of race, color, or previous condition of servitude.

SECTION 2 The Congress shall have power to enforce this article by appropriate legislation.

AMENDMENT XVI [1913]

[Creation of income tax]
The Congress shall have power to lay and collect taxes on incomes, from whatever source derived, without apportionment among the several States, and without regard to any census or enumeration.

AMENDMENT XVII [1913]

[Election of senators]
The Senate of the United States shall be composed of two Senators from each State, elected by the people thereof, for six years; and each Senator shall have one vote. The electors in each State shall have the qualifications requisite for electors of the most numerous branch of the State legislatures.

When vacancies happen in the representation of any State in the Senate, the executive authority of such State shall issue writs of election to fill such vacancies: *Provided*, That the legislature of any State may empower the executive thereof to make temporary appointments until the people fill the vacancies by election as the legislature may direct.

This amendment shall not be so construed as to affect the election or term of any Senator chosen before it becomes valid as part of the Constitution.

AMENDMENT XVIII [1919]

[Prohibition of alcohol]
[SECTION 1 After one year from the ratification of this article the manufacture, sale, or transportation of intoxicating liquors within, the importation thereof into, or the exportation thereof from the United States and all territory subject to the jurisdiction thereof for beverage purposes is hereby prohibited.

SECTION 2 The Congress and the several States shall have concurrent power to enforce this article by appropriate legislation.

SECTION 3 This article shall be inoperative unless it shall have been ratified as an amendment to the Constitution by the legislatures of the several States, as provided in the Constitution, within seven years from the date of the submission hereof to the States by the Congress.][12]

AMENDMENT XIX [1920]

[Voting rights and gender]
The right of citizens of the United States to vote shall not be denied or abridged by the United States or by any State on account of sex.

Congress shall have the power to enforce this article by appropriate legislation.

AMENDMENT XX [1933]

[Terms of executives, assembly of Congress, presidential succession]
SECTION 1 The terms of the President and Vice President shall end at noon on the 20th day of January, and the terms of Senators and Representatives at noon on the 3d day of January, of the years in which such terms would have ended if this article had not been ratified; and the terms of their successors shall then begin.

SECTION 2 The Congress shall assemble at least once in every year, and such meeting shall begin at noon on the 3d day of January, unless they shall by law appoint a different day.

SECTION 3 If, at the time fixed for the beginning of the term of the President, the President elect shall have died, the Vice President elect shall become President. If a President shall not have been chosen before the time fixed for the beginning of his term, or if the President elect shall have failed to qualify, then the Vice President elect shall act as President until a President shall have qualified; and the Congress may by law provide for the case wherein neither a President elect nor a Vice President elect shall have qualified, declaring who shall then act as President, or the manner in which one who is to act shall be selected, and such person shall act accordingly until a President or Vice President shall have qualified.

SECTION 4 The Congress may by law provide for the case of the death of any of the persons from whom the House of Representatives may choose a President whenever the right of choice shall have devolved upon them, and for the case of the death of any of the persons from whom the Senate may choose a Vice President whenever the right of choice shall have devolved upon them.

SECTION 5 Sections 1 and 2 shall take effect on the 15th day of October following the ratification of this article.

[12]Repealed by Amendment XXI.

SECTION 6 This article shall be inoperative unless it shall have been ratified as an amendment to the Constitution by the legislatures of three-fourths of the several States within seven years from the date of its submission.

AMENDMENT XXI [1933]

[*Repealing of prohibition*]
SECTION 1 The eighteenth article of amendment to the Constitution of the United States is hereby repealed.

SECTION 2 The transportation or importation into any State, Territory, or possession of the United States for delivery or use therein of intoxicating liquors, in violation of the laws thereof, is hereby prohibited.

SECTION 3 This article shall be inoperative unless it shall have been ratified as an amendment to the Constitution by conventions in the several States, as provided in the Constitution, within seven years from the date of the submission hereof to the States by the Congress.

AMENDMENT XXII [1951]

[*Limits on presidential term*]
SECTION 1 No person shall be elected to the office of the President more than twice, and no person who has held the office of President, or acted as President, for more than two years of a term to which some other person was elected President shall be elected to the office of the President more than once. But this Article shall not apply to any person holding the office of President when this Article was proposed by the Congress, and shall not prevent any person who may be holding the office of President, or acting as President, during the term within which the Article becomes operative from holding the office of President or acting as President during the remainder of such term.

SECTION 2 This article shall be inoperative unless it shall have been ratified as an amendment to the Constitution by the legislatures of three-fourths of the several States within seven years from the date of its submission to the States by the Congress.

AMENDMENT XXIII [1961]

[*Voting rights of District of Columbia*]
SECTION 1 The District constituting the seat of Government of the United States shall appoint in such manner as the Congress may direct:
A number of electors of President and Vice President equal to the whole number of Senators and Representatives in Congress to which the District would be entitled if it were a State; but in no event more than the least

populous State; they shall be in addition to those appointed by the States, but they shall be considered, for the purposes of the election of President and Vice President, to be electors appointed by a State; and they shall meet in the District and perform such duties as provided by the twelfth article of amendment.

SECTION 2 The Congress shall have power to enforce this article by appropriate legislation.

AMENDMENT XXIV [1964]

[*Prohibition of poll tax*]
SECTION 1 The right of citizens of the United States to vote in any primary or other election for President or Vice President, for electors for President or Vice President, or for Senator or Representative in Congress, shall not be denied or abridged by the United States or any State by reason of failure to pay any poll tax or other tax.

SECTION 2 The Congress shall have power to enforce this article by appropriate legislation.

AMENDMENT XXV [1967]

[*Presidential disability and succession*]
SECTION 1 In case of the removal of the President from office or his death or resignation, the Vice President shall become President.

SECTION 2 Whenever there is a vacancy in the office of the Vice President, the President shall nominate a Vice President who shall take the Office upon confirmation by a majority vote of both houses of Congress.

SECTION 3 Whenever the President transmits to the President pro tempore of the Senate and the Speaker of the House of Representatives his written declaration that he is unable to discharge the powers and duties of his office, and until he transmits to them a written declaration to the contrary, such powers and duties shall be discharged by the Vice President as Acting President.

SECTION 4 Whenever the Vice President and a majority of either the principal officers of the executive departments, or of such other body as Congress may by law provide, transmit to the President pro tempore of the Senate and the Speaker of the House of Representatives their written declaration that the President is unable to discharge the powers and duties of his office, the Vice President shall immediately assume the powers and duties of the office as Acting President.

Thereafter, when the President transmits to the President pro tempore of the Senate and the Speaker of the House of Representatives his written declaration that no inability exists, he shall resume the powers and duties of his office unless the Vice President and a majority of either the principal officers of the executive department, or of such other body as Congress may by law provide, transmit within four days to the President pro tempore of the Senate and the Speaker of the House of Representatives their written declaration that the President is unable to discharge the powers and duties of his office. Thereupon Congress shall decide the issue, assembling within 48 hours for that purpose if not in session. If the Congress, within 21 days after receipt of the latter written declaration, or, if Congress is not in session, within 21 days after Congress is required to assemble, determines by two-thirds vote of both houses that the President is unable to discharge the powers and duties of his office, the Vice President shall continue to discharge the same as Acting President; otherwise, the President shall resume the powers and duties of his office.

AMENDMENT XXVI [1971]

[*Voting rights and age*]

SECTION 1 The right of citizens of the United States, who are eighteen years of age, or older, to vote shall not be denied or abridged by the United States or by any state on account of age.

SECTION 2 The Congress shall have the power to enforce this article by appropriate legislation.

FEDERALIST NO. 10 [1787]

To the People of the State of New York: Among the numerous advantages promised by a well-constructed union, none deserves to be more accurately developed than its tendency to break and control the violence of faction. The friend of popular governments, never finds himself so much alarmed for their character and fate, as when he contemplates their propensity to this dangerous vice. He will not fail, therefore, to set a due value on any plan which, without violating the principles to which he is attached, provides a proper cure for it. The instability, injustice, and confusion introduced into the public councils, have, in truth, been the mortal diseases under which popular governments have everywhere perished; as they continue to be the favourite and fruitful topics from which the adversaries to liberty derive their most specious declamations. The valuable improvements made by the American constitutions on the popular models, both ancient and modern, cannot certainly be too much admired; but it would be an unwarrantable partiality, to contend that they have as effectually obviated the danger on this side, as was wished and expected. Complaints are everywhere heard from our most considerate and virtuous citizens, equally the friends of public and private faith, and of public and personal liberty, that our governments are too unstable; that the public good is disregarded in the conflicts of rival parties; and that measures are too often decided, not according to the rules of justice, and the rights of the minor party, but by the superior force of an interested and overbearing majority. However anxiously we may wish that these complaints had no foundation, the evidence of known facts will not permit us to deny that they are in some degree true. It will be found, indeed, on a candid review of our situation, that some of the distresses under which we labour have been erroneously charged on the operation of our governments; but it will be found, at the same time, that other causes will not alone account for many of our heaviest misfortunes; and, particularly, for that prevailing and increasing distrust of public engagements, and alarm for private rights, which are echoed from one end of the continent to the other. These must be chiefly, if not wholly, effects of the unsteadiness and injustice, with which a factious spirit has tainted our public administrations.

By a faction, I understand a number of citizens, whether amounting to a majority or minority of the whole, who are united and actuated by some common impulse of passion, or of interest, adverse to the rights of other citizens, or to the permanent and aggregate interests of the community.

There are two methods of curing the mischiefs of faction: The one, by removing its causes; the other, by controlling its effects.

There are again two methods of removing the causes of faction: The one, by destroying the liberty which is essential to its existence; the other, by giving to every citizen the same opinions, the same passions, and the same interests.

It could never be more truly said, than of the first remedy, that it was worse than the disease. Liberty is to faction what air is to fire, an ailment without which it instantly expires. But it could not be a less folly to abolish liberty, which is essential to political life, because it nourishes faction, than it would be to wish the annihilation of air, which is essential to animal life, because it imparts to fire its destructive agency.

The second expedient is as impracticable, as the first would be unwise. As long as the reason of man continues fallible, and he is at liberty to exercise it, different opinions will be formed. As long as the connection subsists between his reason and his self-love, his opinions and his passions will have a reciprocal influence on each other; and the former will be objects to which the latter will attach themselves. The diversity in the faculties of men, from which the rights of property originate, is not less an insuperable obstacle to an uniformity of interests. The protection of these faculties is the first object of government. From the protection of different and unequal faculties of acquiring property, the possession of different degrees and kinds of property immediately results; and from the influence of these on the sentiments and views of the respective proprietors, ensues a division of the society into different interests and parties.

The latent causes of action are thus sown in the nature of man; and we see them everywhere brought into different degrees of activity, according to the different circumstances of civil society. A zeal for different opinions concerning religion, concerning government, and many other points, as well as of speculation as of practice; an attachment to different leaders ambitiously contending for preeminence and power; or to persons of other descriptions whose fortunes have been interesting to the human passions, have, in turn, divided mankind into parties, inflamed them with mutual animosity, and rendered them much more disposed to vex and oppress each other, than to cooperate for their common good. So strong is this propensity of mankind, to fall into mutual animosities, that where no substantial occasion presents itself, the most frivolous and fanciful distinctions have been sufficient to kindle their unfriendly passions and excite their most violent conflicts. But the most common and durable source of factions, has been the various and unequal distribution of property. Those who hold, and those who are without property, have ever formed distinct interests in society. Those who are creditors, and those who are debtors, fall under alike discrimination. A landed interest, a manufacturing interest, a mercantile interest, a moneyed interest, with many lesser interests, grow up of necessity in civilized nations, and divide them into different classes, actuated by different sentiments and views. The regulation of these various and interfering interests forms the principal task of modern legislation, and involves the spirit of the party and faction in the necessary and ordinary operations of the government.

No man is allowed to be a judge in his own cause; because his interest will certainly bias his judgment, and, not improbably, corrupt his integrity. With equal, nay, with greater reason, a body of men are unfit to be both judges and parties at the same time; yet what are many of the most important acts of legislation, but so many judicial determinations, not indeed concerning the right of single persons, but concerning the rights of large bodies of citizens? And what are the different classes of legislators, but advocates and parties to the causes which they determine? Is a law proposed concerning private debts? It is a question to which the creditors are parties on one side, and the debtors on the other. Justice ought to hold the balance between them. Yet the parties are, and must be, themselves the judges; and the most numerous party, or, in other words, the most powerful faction, must be expected to prevail. Shall domestic manufactures be encouraged, and in what degree, by restrictions on foreign manufactures? are questions which would be differently decided by the landed and the manufacturing classes; and probably by neither with a sole regard to justice and the public good. The apportionment of taxes, on the various descriptions of property, is an act which seems to require the most exact impartiality; yet there is, perhaps, no legislative act, in which greater opportunity and temptation are given to a predominant party to trample on the rules of justice. Every shilling, with which they overburden the inferior number, is a shilling saved to their own pockets.

It is in vain to say, that enlightened statesmen will be able to adjust these clashing interests, and render them all subservient to the public good. Enlightened statesmen will not always be at the helm: nor, in many cases, can such an adjustment be made at all, without taking into view indirect and remote considerations, which will rarely prevail over the immediate interest which one party may find in disregarding the rights of another, or the good of the whole.

The inference to which we are brought is, that the *causes* of faction cannot be removed; and that relief is only to be sought in the means of controlling its *effects*.

If a faction consists of less than a majority, relief is supplied by the republican principle, which enables the majority to defeat its sinister views, by regular vote. It may clog the administration, it may convulse the society; but it will be unable to execute and mask its violence under the forms of the constitution. When a majority is included in a faction, the form of popular government, on the other hand, enables it to sacrifice to its ruling passion or interest, both the public good and the rights of other citizens. To secure the public good, and private rights, against the danger of such a faction, and at the same time to preserve the spirit and the form of popular government, is then the great object to which our inquiries are directed. Let me add, that it is the great desideratum, by which alone this form of government can be rescued from the opprobrium under which it has so long laboured, and be recommended to the esteem and adoption of mankind.

By what means is this object attainable? Evidently by one of two only. Either the existence of the same passion or interest in a majority, at the same time, must be prevented; or the majority, having such coexistent passion or interest, must be rendered, by their number and local situation, unable to concert and carry into effect schemes of oppression. If the impulse and the opportunity be suffered to coincide, we well know that neither moral nor religious motives can be relied on as an adequate control. They are not found to be such on the injustice and violence of individuals, and lose their efficacy in proportion to the number combined together; that is, in proportion as their efficacy becomes needful.

From this view of the subject, it may be concluded, that a pure democracy, by which I mean a society consisting of a small number of citizens, who assemble and administer the government in person, can admit of no cure for the mischiefs of faction. A common passion or interest will, in almost every case, be felt by a majority of the whole; a communication and concert, results from the form of government itself; and there is nothing to check the inducements to sacrifice the weaker party, or an obnoxious individual. Hence, it is, that such democracies have ever been spectacles of turbulence and contention; have ever been found incompatible with personal security, or the rights of property; and have in general been as short in their lives, as they have been violent in their deaths. Theoretic politicians, who have patronized this species of government, have erroneously supposed, that by reducing mankind to a perfect equality in their political rights, they would, at the same time, be perfectly equalized and assimilated in their possessions, their opinions, and their passions.

A republic, by which I mean a government in which the scheme of representation takes place, opens a different prospect, and promises the cure for which we are seeking. Let us examine the points in which it varies from pure democracy, and we shall comprehend both the nature of the cure and the efficacy which it must derive from the union.

The two great points of difference, between a democracy and a republic, are, first, the delegation of the government, in the latter, to a small number of citizens, elected by the rest; secondly, the greatest number of citizens, and greater sphere of country, over which the latter may be extended.

The effect of the first difference is, on the one hand, to refine and enlarge the public views, by passing them through the medium of a chosen body of citizens, whose wisdom may best discern the true interest of their country, and whose patriotism and love of justice, will be least likely to sacrifice it to temporary or partial considerations. Under such a regulation, it may well happen, that the public voice, pronounced by the representatives of the people, will be more consonant to the public good, than if pronounced by the people themselves, convened for the purpose. On the other hand the effect may be inverted. Men of factious tempers, of local prejudices, or of sinister designs, may by intrigue, by corruption, or by other means, first obtain the suffrages, and then betray the interest of the people. The question resulting is, whether small or extensive republics are most favourable to the election of proper guardians of the public weal; and it is clearly decided in favour of the latter by two obvious considerations.

In the first place, it is to be remarked that, however small the republic may be, the representatives must be raised to a certain number, in order to guard against the cabals of a few; and that however large it may be, they must be limited to a certain number, in order to guard against the confusion of a multitude. Hence, the number of representatives in the two cases not being in proportion to that of the constituents, and being proportionally greatest in the small republic, it follows, that if the proportion of fit characters be not less in the large than in the small republic, the former will present a greater option, and consequently a greater probability of a fit choice.

In the next place, as each representative will be chosen by a greater number of citizens in the large than in the small republic, it will be more difficult for unworthy candidates to practise with success the vicious arts, by which elections are too often carried; and the suffrages of the people being more free, will be more likely to centre in men who possess the most attractive merit, and the most diffusive and established characters.

It must be confessed, that in this, as in most other cases, there is a mean, on both sides of which inconveniences will be found to lie. By enlarging too much the number of electors, you render the representatives too little acquainted with all their local circumstances and lesser interests; as by reducing it too much, you render him unduly attached to these, and too little fit to comprehend and pursue great and national objects. The federal constitution forms a happy combination being referred to the national, the local and particular, to the state legislatures.

The other point of difference is, the greater number of citizens, and extent of territory, which may be brought within the compass of republican, than of democratic government; and it is this circumstance principally which renders factious combinations less to be dreaded in the former, than in the latter. The smaller the society, the fewer probably will be the distinct parties and interests composing it; the fewer the distinct parties and interests, the more frequently will a majority be found of the same party; and the smaller the number of individuals composing a majority, and the smaller the compass within which they are placed, the more easily will they concert and execute their plans of oppression. Extend the sphere, and you take in a greater variety of parties and interests; you make it less probable that a majority of the whole will have a common motive to invade the rights of other citizens; or if such a common motive exists, it will be more difficult for all who feel it to discover their own strength, and to act in unison with each other. Besides other impediments, it may be remarked, that where there is a consciousness of unjust or dishonourable purposes, communication is always checked by distrust, in proportion to the number whose concurrence is necessary.

Hence, it clearly appears, that the same advantage, which a republic has over a democracy, in controlling the effects of faction, is enjoyed by a large over a small republic,—is enjoyed by the union over the states composing it. Does this advantage consist in the substitution of representatives, whose enlightened views and virtuous sentiments render them superior to local prejudices, and to schemes of injustice? It will not be denied that the representation of the union will be most likely to possess these requisite endowments. Does it consist in the greater security afforded by a greater variety of parties, against the event of any one party being able to outnumber and oppress the rest? In an equal degree does the increased variety of parties, comprised within the union, increase the security? Does it, in fine, consist in the greater obstacles opposed to the concert and accomplishment of the secret wishes of an unjust and interested majority? Here, again, the extent of the union gives it the most palpable advantage.

The influence of factious leaders may kindle a flame within their particular states, but will be unable to spread a general conflagration through the other states; a religious sect may degenerate into a political faction in a part of the confederacy; but the variety of sects dispersed over the entire face of it, must secure the national councils against any danger from that source: a rage for paper money, for an abolition of debts, for an equal division of property, or for any other improper or wicked project, will be less apt to pervade the whole body of the union than a particular member of it; in the same proportion as such a malady is more likely to taint a particular county or district, than an entire state.

In the extent and proper structure of the union, therefore, we behold a republican remedy for the diseases most incident to republican government. And according to the degree of pleasure and pride we feel in being republicans, ought to be our zeal in cherishing the spirit, and supporting the character of federalists.

JAMES MADISON

FEDERALIST NO. 51 [1788]

To the People of the State of New York: To what expedient then shall we finally resort for maintaining in practice the necessary partition of power among the several departments, as laid down in the constitution? The only answer that can be given is, that as all these exterior provisions are found to be inadequate, the defect must be supplied, by so contriving the interior structure of the government, as that its several constituent parts may, by their mutual relations, be the means of keeping each other in their proper places. Without presuming to undertake a full development of this important idea, I will hazard a few general observations, which may perhaps place it in a clearer light, and enable us to form a more correct judgment of the principles and structure of the government planned by the convention.

In order to lay a due foundation for that separate and distinct exercise of the different powers of government, which to a certain extent, is admitted on all hands to be essential to the preservation of liberty, it is evident that each department should have a will of its own; and consequently should be so constituted, that the members of each should have as little agency as possible in the appointment of the members of the others. Were this principle rigorously adhered to, it would require that all the appointments for the supreme executive, legislative, and judiciary magistracies, should be drawn from the same fountain of authority, the people, through channels, having no communication whatever with one another. Perhaps such a plan of constructing the several departments would be less difficult in practice than it may in contemplation appear. Some difficulties however, and some additional expense, would attend the execution of it. Some deviations therefore from the principle must be admitted. In the constitution of the judiciary department in particular, it might be inexpedient to insist rigorously on the principle; first, because peculiar qualifications being essential in the members, the primary consideration ought to be to select that mode of choice, which best secures these qualifications; secondly, because the permanent tenure by which the appointments are held in that department, must soon destroy all sense of dependence on the authority conferring them.

It is equally evident that the members of each department should be as little dependent as possible on those of the others, for the emoluments annexed to their offices. Were the executive magistrate, or the judges, not independent of the legislature in this particular, their independence in every other would be merely nominal.

But the great security against a gradual concentration of the several powers in the same department, consists in giving to those who administer each department, the necessary constitutional means, and personal motives, to resist encroachments of the others. The provision for defense must in this, as in all other cases, be made commensurate to the danger of attack. Ambition must be made to counteract ambition. The interest of the man must be connected with the constitutional rights of the place. It may be a reflection on human nature, that such devices should be necessary to control the abuses of government: But what is government itself but the greatest of all reflections on human nature? If men were angels, no government would be necessary. If angels were to govern men, neither external nor internal controls on government would be necessary. In framing a government which is to be administered by men over men, the great difficulty lies in this: You must first enable the government to control the governed; and in the next place, oblige it to control itself. A dependence on the people is no doubt the primary control on the government; but experience has taught mankind the necessity of auxiliary precautions.

This policy of supplying by opposite and rival interests, the defect of better motives, might be traced through the whole system of human affairs, private as well as public. We see it particularly displayed in all the subordinate distributions of power; where the constant aim is to divide and arrange the several offices in such a manner as that each may be a check on the other; that the private interest of every individual, may be a sentinel over the public rights. These inventions of prudence cannot be less requisite in the distribution of the supreme powers of the state.

But it is not possible to give to each department an equal power of self defense. In republican government the legislative authority, necessarily, predominates. The remedy for this inconveniency is, to divide the legislature into different branches; and to render them by different modes of election, and different principles of action, as little connected with each other, as the nature of their common functions, and their common dependence on the society, will admit. It may even be necessary to guard against dangerous encroachments by still further precautions. As the weight of the legislative authority requires that it should be thus divided, the weakness of the executive may require, on the other hand, that it should be fortified. An absolute negative, on the legislature, appears at first view to be the natural defense with which the executive magistrate should be armed. But perhaps it would be neither altogether safe, nor alone sufficient. On ordinary occasions, it might not be exerted with the requisite firmness; and on extraordinary occasions, it might be perfidiously abused. May not this defect of an absolute negative be supplied, by some qualified connection between this weaker department, and the weaker branch of the stronger department, by which the latter may be led to support the constitutional rights of the former, without being too much detached from the rights of its own department?

If the principles on which these observations are founded be just, as I persuade myself they are, and they be applied as a criterion, to the several state constitutions, and to the federal constitution, it will be found, that if the latter does not perfectly correspond with them, the former are infinitely less able to bear such a test.

There are moreover two considerations particularly applicable to the federal system of America, which place that system in a very interesting point of view.

First. In a single republic, all the power surrendered by the people, is submitted to the administration of a single government; and usurpations are guarded against by a division of the government into distinct and separate departments. In the compound republic of America, the power surrendered by the people, is first divided between two distinct governments, and then the portion allotted to each, subdivided among distinct and separate departments. Hence a double security arises to the rights of the people. The different governments will control each other; at the same time that each will be controlled by itself.

Second. It is of great importance in a republic, not only to guard the society against the oppression of its rulers; but to guard one part of the society against the injustice of the other part. Different interests necessarily exist in different classes of citizens. If a majority be united by a common interest, the rights of the minority will be insecure. There are but two methods of providing against this evil: The one by creating a will in the community independent of the majority, that is, of the society itself; the other by comprehending in the society so many separate descriptions of citizens, as will render an unjust combination of a majority of the whole, very improbable, if not impracticable. The first method prevails in all governments possessing an hereditary or self appointed authority. This at best is but a precarious security; because a power independent of the society may as well espouse the unjust views of the major, as the rightful interests, of the minor party, and may possibly be turned against both parties. The second method will be exemplified in the federal republic of the United States. While all authority in it will be derived from and dependent on the society, the society itself will be broken into so many parts, interests and classes of citizens, that the rights of individuals or of the minority, will be in little danger from interested combinations of the majority. In a free government, the security for civil rights must be the same as for religious rights. It consists in the one case in the multiplicity of sects. The degree of security in both cases will depend on the number of interests and sects; and this may be presumed to depend on the extent of country and number of people comprehended under the same government. This view of the subject must particularly recommend a proper federal system to all the sincere and considerate friends of republican government: Since it shows that in exact proportion as the territory of the union may be formed into more circumscribed confederacies or states, oppressive combinations of a majority will be facilitated; the best security under the republican form, for the rights of every class of citizens, will be diminished; and consequently, the stability and independence of some member of the government, the only other security, must be proportionally increased. Justice is the end of government. It is the end of civil society. It ever has been, and ever will be pursued, until it be obtained, or until liberty be lost in the pursuit. In a society under the forms of which the stronger faction can readily unite and oppress the weaker, anarchy may as truly be said to reign, as in a state of nature where the weaker individual is not secured against the violence of the stronger: And as in the latter state even the stronger individuals are prompted by the uncertainty of their condition, to submit to a government which may protect the weak as well as themselves: So in the former state, will the more powerful factions or parties be gradually induced by alike motives, to wish for a government which will protect all parties, the weaker as well as the more powerful. It can be little doubted, that if the state of Rhode Island was separated from the confederacy, and left to itself, the insecurity of rights under the popular form of government within such narrow limits, would be displayed by such reiterated oppressions of factious majorities, that some power altogether independent of the people would soon be called for by the voice of the very factions whose misrule had proved the necessity of it. In the extended republic of the United States, and among the great variety of interests, parties and sects which it embraces, a coalition of a majority of the whole society could seldom take place on any other principles than those of justice and the general good; and there being thus less danger to a minor from the will of the major party, there must be less pretext also, to provide for the security of the former, by introducing into the government a will not dependent on the latter; or in other words, a will independent of the society itself. It is no less certain than it is important, notwithstanding the contrary opinions which have been entertained, that the larger the society, provided it lie within a practicable sphere, the more duly capable it will be of self government. And happily for the *republican cause,* the practicable sphere may be carried to a very great extent, by a judicious modification and mixture of the *federal principle.*

JAMES MADISON

Presidential

Elections

CANDIDATES	PARTY	ELECTORAL VOTE
1789		
George Washington	Federalist	69
John Adams	Federalist	34
Others		35
1792		
George Washington	Federalist	132
John Adams	Federalist	77
George Clinton		50
Others		5
1796		
John Adams	Federalist	71
Thomas Jefferson	Democratic-Republican	68
Thomas Pinckney	Federalist	59
Aaron Burr	Democratic-Republican	30
Others		48
1800		
Thomas Jefferson[1]	Democratic-Republican	73
Aaron Burr	Democratic-Republican	73
John Adams	Federalist	65
Charles C. Pinckney		64
1804		
Thomas Jefferson	Democratic-Republican	162
Charles C. Pinckney	Federalist	14
1808		
James Madison	Democratic-Republican	122
Charles C. Pinckney	Federalist	47
George Clinton	Independent-Republican	6
1812		
James Madison	Democratic-Republican	122
DeWitt Clinton	Federalist	89

CANDIDATES	PARTY	ELECTORAL VOTE
1816		
James Monroe	Democratic-Republican	183
Rufus King	Federalist	34
1820		
James Monroe	Democratic-Republican	231
John Quincy Adams	Independent-Republican	1
1824		
John Quincy Adams[1]	Democratic-Republican	84
Andrew Jackson	Democratic-Republican	99
Henry Clay	Democratic-Republican	37
William H. Crawford	Democratic-Republican	41
1828		
Andrew Jackson	Democratic	178
John Quincy Adams	National-Republican	83
1832		
Andrew Jackson	Democratic	219
Henry Clay	National-Republican	49
William Wirt	Anti-Masonic	7
John Floyd	National-Republican	11
1836		
Martin Van Buren	Democratic	170
William H. Harrison	Whig	73
Hugh L. White	Whig	26
Daniel Webster	Whig	14
1840		
William H. Harrison[2]	Whig	234
(John Tyler)	Whig	
Martin Van Buren	Democratic	60

CANDIDATES	PARTY	ELECTORAL VOTE
1844		
James K. Polk	Democratic	170
Henry Clay	Whig	105
James G. Birney	Liberty	
1848		
Zachary Taylor[2]	Whig	163
(Millard Fillmore)	Whig	
Lewis Cass	Democratic	127
Martin Van Buren	Free Soil	
1852		
Franklin Pierce	Democratic	254
Winfield Scott	Whig	42
1856		
James Buchanan	Democratic	174
John C. Fremont	Republican	114
Millard Fillmore	American	8
1860		
Abraham Lincoln	Republican	180
Stephen A. Douglas	Democratic	12
John C. Breckinridge	Democratic	72
John Bell	Constitutional Union	39
1864		
Abraham Lincoln[2]	Republican	212
(Andrew Johnson)	Republican	
George B. McClellan	Democratic	21
1868		
Ulysses S. Grant	Republican	214
Horatio Seymour	Democratic	80
1872		
Ulysses S. Grant	Republican	286
Horace Greeley	Democratic	66
1876		
Rutherford B. Hayes	Republican	185
Samuel J. Tilden	Democratic	184
1880		
James A. Garfield[2]	Republican	214
(Chester A. Arthur)	Republican	
Winfield S. Hancock	Democratic	155
James B. Weaver	Greenback-Labor	
1884		
Grover Cleveland	Democratic	219
James G. Blaine	Republican	182
Benjamin F. Butler	Greenback-Labor	

CANDIDATES	PARTY	ELECTORAL VOTE
1888		
Benjamin Harrison	Republican	233
Grover Cleveland	Democratic	168
1892		
Grover Cleveland	Democratic	277
Benjamin Harrison	Republican	145
James R. Weaver	People's	22
1896		
William McKinley	Republican	271
William J. Bryan	Democratic, Populist	176
1900		
William McKinley[2]	Republican	292
(Theodore Roosevelt)	Republican	
William J. Bryan	Democratic, Populist	155
1904		
Theodore Roosevelt	Republican	336
Alton B. Parker	Democratic	140
Eugene V. Debs	Socialist	
1908		
William H. Taft	Republican	321
William J. Bryan	Democratic	162
Eugene V. Debs	Socialist	
1912		
Woodrow Wilson	Democratic	435
Theodore Roosevelt	Progressive	88
William H. Taft	Republican	8
Eugene V. Debs	Socialist	
1916		
Woodrow Wilson	Democratic	277
Charles E. Hughes	Republican	254
1920		
Warren G. Harding[2]	Republican	404
(Calvin Coolidge)	Republican	
James M. Cox	Democratic	127
Eugene V. Debs	Socialist	
1924		
Calvin Coolidge	Republican	382
John W. Davis	Democratic	136
Robert M. LaFollette	Progressive	13
1928		
Herbert C. Hoover	Republican	444
Alfred E. Smith	Democratic	87

CANDIDATES	PARTY	ELECTORAL VOTE
1932		
Franklin D. Roosevelt	Democratic	472
Herbert C. Hoover	Republican	59
Norman Thomas	Socialist	
1936		
Franklin D. Roosevelt	Democratic	523
Alfred M. Landon	Republican	8
William Lemke	Union	
1940		
Franklin D. Roosevelt	Democratic	449
Wendell L. Wilkie	Republican	82
1944		
Franklin D. Roosevelt[2]	Democratic	432
(Harry S Truman)	Democratic	
Thomas E. Dewey	Republican	99
1948		
Harry S Truman	Democratic	303
Thomas E. Dewey	Republican	189
J. Strom Thurmond	States' Rights	39
Henry A. Wallace	Progressive	
1952		
Dwight D. Eisenhower	Republican	442
Adlai E. Stevenson	Democratic	89
1956		
Dwight D. Eisenhower	Republican	457
Adlai E. Stevenson	Democratic	73
1960		
John F. Kennedy[2]	Democratic	303
(Lyndon B. Johnson)	Democratic	
Richard M. Nixon	Republican	219

CANDIDATES	PARTY	ELECTORAL VOTE
1964		
Lyndon B. Johnson	Democratic	486
Barry M. Goldwater	Republican	52
1968		
Richard M. Nixon	Republican	301
Hubert H. Humphrey	Democratic	191
George C. Wallace	American Independent	46
1972		
Richard M. Nixon[3]	Republican	520
(Gerald R. Ford)	Republican	
George S. McGovern	Democratic	17
1976		
Jimmy Carter	Democratic	297
Gerald R. Ford	Republican	240
1980		
Ronald Reagan	Republican	489
Jimmy Carter	Democratic	49
John Anderson	Independent	
1984		
Ronald Reagan	Republican	525
Walter Mondale	Democratic	13
1988		
George Bush	Republican	426
Michael Dukakis	Democratic	111
1992		
Bill Clinton	Democratic	370
George Bush	Republican	168
Ross Perot	Independent	

[1]Elected by the House of Representatives.
[2]Died while in office.
[3]Resigned from office.

Party Control of
Congress, 1901–1995

	SENATE			HOUSE			
	DEM.	REP.	OTHER	DEM.	REP.	OTHER	PRESIDENT
57th Congress, 1901–1903	31	55	4	151	197	9	McKinley
							T. Roosevelt
58th Congress, 1903–1905	33	57	—	178	208	—	T. Roosevelt
59th Congress, 1905–1907	33	57	—	136	250	—	T. Roosevelt
60th Congress, 1907–1909	31	61	—	164	222	—	T. Roosevelt
61st Congress, 1909–1911	32	61	—	172	219	—	Taft
62nd Congress, 1911–1913	41	51	—	228	161	1	Taft
63rd Congress, 1913–1915	51	44	1	291	127	17	Wilson
64th Congress, 1915–1917	56	40	—	230	196	9	Wilson
65th Congress, 1917–1919	53	42	—	216	210	6	Wilson
66th Congress, 1919–1921	47	49	—	190	240	3	Wilson
67th Congress, 1921–1923	37	59	—	131	301	1	Harding
68th Congress, 1923–1925	43	51	2	205	225	5	Coolidge
69th Congress, 1925–1927	39	56	1	183	247	4	Coolidge
70th Congress, 1927–1929	46	49	1	195	237	3	Coolidge
71st Congress, 1929–1931	39	56	1	167	267	1	Hoover
72nd Congress, 1931–1933	47	48	1	220	214	1	Hoover
73rd Congress, 1933–1935	60	35	1	319	117	5	F. Roosevelt
74th Congress, 1935–1937	69	25	2	319	103	10	F. Roosevelt
75th Congress, 1937–1939	76	16	4	331	89	13	F. Roosevelt
76th Congress, 1939–1941	69	23	4	261	164	4	F. Roosevelt
77th Congress, 1941–1943	66	28	2	268	162	5	F. Roosevelt
78th Congress, 1943–1945	58	37	1	218	208	4	F. Roosevelt
79th Congress, 1945–1947	56	38	1	242	190	2	Truman
80th Congress, 1947–1949	45	51	—	188	245	1	Truman
81st Congress, 1949–1951	54	42	—	263	171	1	Truman
82nd Congress, 1951–1953	49	47	—	234	199	1	Truman
83rd Congress, 1953–1955	47	48	1	211	221	—	Eisenhower
84th Congress, 1955–1957	48	47	1	232	203	—	Eisenhower
85th Congress, 1957–1959	49	47	—	233	200	—	Eisenhower

	SENATE			HOUSE			
	DEM.	REP.	OTHER	DEM.	REP.	OTHER	PRESIDENT
86th Congress, 1959–1961	65	35	—	284	153	—	Eisenhower
87th Congress, 1961–1963	65	35	—	263	174	—	Kennedy
88th Congress, 1963–1965	67	33	—	258	177	—	Kennedy
							Johnson
89th Congress, 1965–1967	68	32	—	295	140	—	Johnson
90th Congress, 1967–1969	64	36	—	247	187	—	Johnson
91st Congress, 1969–1971	57	43	—	243	192	—	Nixon
92nd Congress, 1971–1973	54	44	2	254	180	—	Nixon
93rd Congress, 1973–1975	56	42	2	239	192	1	Nixon
							Ford
94th Congress, 1975–1977	60	37	2	291	144	—	Ford
95th Congress, 1977–1979	61	38	1	292	143	—	Carter
96th Congress, 1979–1981	58	41	1	276	157	—	Carter
97th Congress, 1981–1983	46	53	1	243	192	—	Reagan
98th Congress, 1983–1985	45	55	—	267	168	—	Reagan
99th Congress, 1985–1987	47	53	—	252	183	—	Reagan
100th Congress, 1987–1989	54	46	—	257	178	—	Reagan
101st Congress, 1989–1991	55	45	—	262	173	—	Bush
102nd Congress, 1991–1993	56	44	—	276	167	—	Bush
103rd Congress, 1993–1995*	57	43	—	258	176	1	Clinton

* Numbers indicate initial composition of the Congress.

SOURCES: Department of Commerce, Bureau of the Census, *Statistical Abstract of the United States* (Washington, D.C.: U.S. Government Printing Office); and *Members of Congress Since 1789*, 2nd ed. (Washington, D.C.: Congressional Quarterly Press, 1981), 176–177.

United States

Supreme Court

Justices, 1789–1994

Justice	President	Years of Service
John Jay	Washington	1789–1795
John Rutledge	Washington	(1789–1791)*
William Cushing	Washington	1789–1810
James Wilson	Washington	1789–1798
John Blair, Jr.	Washington	1789–1796
James Iredell	Washington	1790–1799
Thomas Johnson	Washington	1791–1793
William Paterson	Washington	1793–1806
John Rutledge	Washington	(1795)*
Samuel Chase	Washington	1796–1811
Oliver Elsworth	Washington	1796–1800
Bushrod Washington	J. Adams	1798–1829
Alfred Moore	J. Adams	1799–1804
John Marshall	J. Adams	1801–1835
William Johnson	Jefferson	1804–1834
Henry B. Livingston	Jefferson	1806–1823
Thomas Todd	Jefferson	1807–1826
Gabriel Duval	Madison	1811–1835
Joseph Story	Madison	1811–1845
Smith Thompson	Monroe	1823–1843
Robert Trimble	J. Q. Adams	1826–1828
John McLean	Jackson	1829–1861
Henry Baldwin	Jackson	1830–1844
James M. Wayne	Jackson	1835–1867
Roger B. Taney	Jackson	1836–1864
Philip P. Barbour	Jackson	1836–1841
John Catron	Jackson	1837–1865
John McKinley	Van Buren	1837–1852
Peter V. Daniel	Van Buren	1841–1860
Samuel Nelson	Tyler	1845–1872
Levi Woodbury	Polk	1846–1851
Robert C. Grier	Polk	1846–1870

Justice	President	Years of Service
Benjamin R. Curtis	Fillmore	1851–1857
John A. Campbell	Pierce	1853–1861
Nathan Clifford	Buchanan	1858–1881
Noah H. Swayne	Lincoln	1862–1881
Samuel F. Miller	Lincoln	1862–1890
David Davis	Lincoln	1862–1877
Stephen J. Field	Lincoln	1863–1897
Salmon P. Chase	Lincoln	1864–1873
William Strong	Grant	1870–1880
Joseph P. Bradley	Grant	1870–1892
Ward Hunt	Grant	1872–1882
Morrison R. Waite	Grant	1874–1888
John M. Harlan	Hayes	1877–1911
William B. Woods	Hayes	1880–1887
Stanley Matthews	Garfield	1881–1889
Horace Gray	Arthur	1881–1902
Samuel Blatchford	Arthur	1882–1893
Lucius Q. C. Lamar	Cleveland	1888–1893
Melville W. Fuller	Cleveland	1888–1910
David J. Brewer	Harrison	1889–1910
Henry B. Brown	Harrison	1890–1906
George Shiras, Jr.	Harrison	1892–1903
Howell E. Jackson	Harrison	1893–1895
Edward D. White	Cleveland	1894–1910
Rufus W. Peckham	Cleveland	1895–1909
Joseph McKenna	McKinley	1898–1925
Oliver W. Holmes, Jr.	T. Roosevelt	1902–1932
William R. Day	T. Roosevelt	1903–1922
William H. Moody	T. Roosevelt	1906–1910
Horace H. Lurton	Taft	1909–1914
Charles E. Hughes	Taft	1910–1916
Edward D. White	Taft	1910–1921
Willis Van Devanter	Taft	1910–1937
Joseph R. Lamar	Taft	1910–1916
Mahlon Pitney	Taft	1912–1922
James C. McReynolds	Wilson	1914–1941
Louis D. Brandeis	Wilson	1916–1939
John H. Clarke	Wilson	1916–1922
William H. Taft	Harding	1921–1930
George Sutherland	Harding	1922–1938
Pierce Butler	Harding	1922–1939
Edward T. Sanford	Harding	1923–1930
Harlan F. Stone	Coolidge	1925–1941
Charles E. Hughes	Hoover	1930–1941
Owen J. Roberts	Hoover	1930–1945
Benjamin N. Cardozo	Hoover	1932–1938
Hugo Black	F. Roosevelt	1937–1971

Justice	President	Years of service
Stanley F. Reed	F. Roosevelt	1938–1957
Felix Frankfurter	F. Roosevelt	1939–1962
William O. Douglas	F. Roosevelt	1939–1975
Frank Murphy	F. Roosevelt	1940–1949
James F. Byrnes	F. Roosevelt	1941–1942
Harlan F. Stone	F. Roosevelt	1941–1946
Robert H. Jackson	F. Roosevelt	1941–1954
Wiley B. Rutledge	F. Roosevelt	1943–1949
Harold H. Burton	Truman	1945–1958
Fred M. Vinson	Truman	1946–1953
Tom C. Clark	Truman	1949–1967
Sherman Minton	Truman	1949–1956
Earl Warren	Eisenhower	1953–1969
John M. Harlan	Eisenhower	1955–1971
William J. Brennan, Jr.	Eisenhower	1956–1990
Charles E. Whittaker	Eisenhower	1957–1962
Potter Stewart	Eisenhower	1958–1981
Byron R. White	Kennedy	1962–
Arthur J. Goldberg	Johnson	1962–1965
Abe Fortas	Johnson	1965–1969
Thurgood Marshall	Johnson	1967–1991
Warren E. Burger	Nixon	1969–1986
Harry A. Blackmun	Nixon	1970–
Lewis F. Powell, Jr.	Nixon	1972–1988
William H. Rehnquist	Nixon	1972–1986
John Paul Stevens	Ford	1975–
Sandra Day O'Connor	Reagan	1981–
William H. Rehnquist	Reagan	1986–
Antonin Scalia	Reagan	1986–
Anthony M. Kennedy	Reagan	1988–
David H. Souter	Bush	1990–
Clarence Thomas	Bush	1991–
Ruth Bader Ginsburg	Clinton	1993–

Bold type indicates chief justice.
*Rutledge resigned after his confirmation to become chief justice of South Carolina; in 1795 he served during a Court recess.

Glossary

administrative law judge a quasi-independent employee of a federal agency who supervises hearings at which disputes between the agency and a regulated party are resolved. The judge's rulings are binding on both the agency and the complainant, although either side may appeal a ruling in the federal courts.

administrative oversight the review and control by congressional committees of the work conducted by the executive branch of the federal government.

adversary system a system of criminal justice in which a neutral judge presides over the introduction of evidence by a prosecutor and a defense attorney. The defendant is presumed to be innocent until proven guilty and cannot be forced to testify.

affirmative action government and private policies or programs designed to help women and minorities advance in areas in which they have historically been discriminated against or disadvantaged.

agency a unit of the federal government with responsibility for a set of functions that are generally less broad than those of a department. Some agencies are independent; others exist within departments.

agents of political socialization groups and individuals, such as parents, peers, and churches, from whom citizens acquire political information and learn political attitudes and values.

America 2000 a report issued during the presidency of George Bush that established six national educational goals to be attained by the year 2000.

American ethos what Americans believe; the attitudes, values, and traditions of American society. At its core, the American ethos consists of a commitment to a democratic political system and a capitalistic economic system.

amicus curiae brief a written opinion on a judicial case submitted to the court by a party who is not directly involved in the litigation but has an interest in the outcome. Such a brief is also known as a "friend of the court" brief.

Anti-Federalists the group of people who opposed adoption of the Constitution following its drafting in 1787.

appellate jurisdiction the authority of courts to review decisions of lower courts and administrative agencies. Under Article III of the U.S. Constitution, Congress has the power to provide for the appellate jurisdiction of the Supreme Court and courts of appeals.

Articles of Confederation the first constitution of the United States, approved by the Second Continental Congress in 1777 but not ratified by all thirteen former colonies until 1781. It provided for a unicameral legislature, the Continental Congress, which had extremely limited powers.

attentive public the people in a society who follow political issues and politically relevant events but do not usually participate in political activities other than voting. The attentive public constitutes about 15 to 20 percent of the population.

attitudes broad orientations people have toward areas of public policy. Attitudes consist of a number of interrelated opinions that provide a basis for interpreting events and making judgments on issues.

authoritarian personality a personality type that requires a highly structured environment with precise rules and guidelines in order to function. People with such a personality tend to be most willing to adopt doctrinaire beliefs and to follow strong and inflexible political leaders.

authority lawful power. In a democracy, authority is derived directly or indirectly from the people. It is embodied in the rule of law—the Constitution, statutes, treaties, executive orders, and judicial opinions.

balance of trade the difference in value between a country's imports and its exports.

bandwagon effect a shift in support to a front-running candidate. At a presidential nominating convention the front-runner tries to create such an effect by demonstrating the ability to win crucial votes that occur before the nomination and thus removing any doubt about who the nominee will be.

belief system a set of related ideas, such as a religion or a political ideology, that helps people understand and cope with the world around them. People use belief systems as guides for thought and action.

bench memos notes written by law clerks that Supreme Court justices take with them to the bench when hearing oral arguments in a case. They typically summarize the questions presented by the case, the lower court's decision, and the arguments presented by both sides.

bicameral legislature a legislature composed of two houses, such as the U.S. Congress.

bilateral relations one-to-one dealings between the United States and a foreign government. The most common such relations involve routine interactions among diplomats and officials, as in the processing of visas, passports, and customs claims.

bill a proposal, drafted in the form of a law, that a member of Congress would like the other members to consider. A bill may be introduced into either house of Congress by any member of that house.

bill of information a document specifying the charges and evidence against a criminal defendant, which in some states prosecutors may obtain from a judge instead of seeking a grand jury indictment.

Bill of Rights the first ten amendments to the U.S. Constitution, which guarantee specific civil rights and liberties. Introduced in the First Congress, the amendments were ratified by the states in 1791.

Bill of Rights, nationalization of the Supreme Court's application to the states of guarantees in the Bill of Rights, made on the basis of the guarantee of "due process of law" in the Fourteenth Amendment to the Constitution. As a result, the First Amendment, for example, limits the power of both the national government and the states.

block grants grants-in-aid that state and local governments can spend as they wish within specified broad policy areas, such as housing, transportation, or job training.

briefs written legal arguments filed by each side in cases or controversies before a court.

bureaucracy an organization of activity based on hierarchies of authority and fixed routines. Bureaucracies have jurisdictions established by law or administrative rules. Their employees are specialists, and they maintain written records of their decisions and activities. Bureaucracies are created to achieve objectivity, precision, efficiency, continuity, consistency, and fairness.

cabinet a body consisting of the heads of the executive departments of the federal government, plus the vice pres-
ident. Presidents have used the cabinet to counsel them on policy issues, to build support for their programs and positions, and to gain legitimacy for their administrations.

capitalism a system of private ownership and control of the means of economic production and distribution that operates within a free market. It is often contrasted with socialism and communism, systems in which government controls some or all of the means of production and distribution.

capture the tendency of federal agencies to develop symbiotic relationships with the special interests that they oversee and thus to become protectors rather than regulators of those interests. This has been a special problem with regulatory commissions.

casework the individual problems that constituents bring to the attention of a member of Congress for assistance or solution.

categorical grants grants-in-aid that can be used only for narrowly defined purposes, such as education for homeless children or prevention of drug abuse.

caucus a meeting of partisans. Both major political parties permit the use of caucuses at the precinct level as the first stage in a process by which delegates may be chosen for the parties' national nominating conventions. The Democratic party requires that the number of delegates awarded to each candidate be proportional to the support the candidate receives in the caucus; the Republican party does not impose this requirement.

central clearance process a procedure by which all legislative proposals, positions, and testimony of the executive departments and agencies are cleared beforehand by the Office of Management and Budget to ensure that they are in accord with the president's program.

citizen a member of a political society, with rights and obligations that structure political participation.

civil liberties freedoms that the government must respect, such as the freedom of speech, press, and assembly, that are guaranteed under the U.S. Constitution or legislation or through judicial interpretation of laws.

civil rights rights that the government may not deny or infringe on because of an individual's race, gender, national origin, age, or ethnicity.

civil service system the career employees of the federal departments and major agencies whose salaries and fringe benefits are determined by Congress and implemented by the Office of Personnel Management.

Clean Air Act, 1963 the first major federal law attempting to set standards of air quality and to regulate air pollution.

Clean Water Act, 1972 the law by which the federal government took over from the states the establishment of minimum water quality standards.

clear and present danger test a test created by Supreme

Court justice Oliver Wendell Holmes for determining the scope of freedom of speech under the First Amendment to the U.S. Constitution. Under this test, only speech that poses a "clear and present danger" to the country may be punished.

closed-ended question a question on a public opinion poll that forces respondents to choose from a designated list of answers. Most polls consist of closed-ended questions because they are easier to categorize and analyze than open-ended questions.

cloture the limitation of debate on a measure before the Senate. It takes a vote by three-fifths of the entire Senate (sixty senators) to invoke cloture and thereby end a filibuster.

Cold War the period of intense and often hostile competition between the United States and the Soviet Union from 1945 through the late 1980s.

comity the principle by which federal courts respect and leave undisturbed rulings of state courts that are based solely on independent state grounds.

commercial speech advertising, which for many years was interpreted by the Supreme Court as lacking socially redeeming value and thus falling outside the scope of protection for free speech under the First Amendment. But recent rulings of the Court have extended First Amendment protection to many kinds of commercial speech, so long as it is truthful and not deceptive.

concurrent powers powers shared by both the national government and the state governments, such as the power to tax.

concurring opinion a document submitted by one or more justices or judges of a court that agrees with the decision reached in a case but not with all of the reasoning or explanations offered in the institutional opinion. It explains how the same result would have been reached by different reasoning.

confirmation hearings hearings held by a legislative body before approving the appointment of a government official. Under the U.S. Constitution, the president nominates federal judges and other high officials in the executive branch, but they must be confirmed by the Senate.

confront witnesses, right to a criminal defendant's right, guaranteed by the Sixth Amendment to the U.S. Constitution, to call and question witnesses who testify as to the defendant's guilt.

conservatism a political ideology that emphasizes economic rights and liberties for individuals with a minimum of government restraint. Compared with liberals, conservatives favor a more active role for government in promoting national and personal security and tend to be more satisfied with the status quo.

constituency the residents of the state or district that elect a particular member of Congress.

constitutional courts the U.S. Supreme Court and other federal courts created under Article III of the U.S. Constitution, which gives Congress the power to establish "inferior courts" below the Supreme Court. Federal district courts and courts of appeals are constitutional courts and have general jurisdiction over virtually all matters of federal law.

consulate an office outside a country's capital at which a foreign country is represented.

Consumer Price Index (CPI) a measure of inflation based on the costs of certain goods commonly purchased by American consumers.

containment a policy designed to prevent the spread of Soviet influence into noncommunist countries, which formed the central thrust of post–World War II American foreign policy.

continuing appropriations resolution stopgap legislation passed when Congress has failed to pass an agency's budget before the beginning of a new fiscal year. Such a resolution typically continues spending in the new fiscal year at the same level as in the preceding year.

cooperative federalism a view of federalism held between the mid 1930s and the 1960s that stressed a partnership and sharing of government functions between the states and the national government.

courts of appeals the courts within the federal judicial system that hear appeals of decisions of lower courts, state courts, or administrative agencies. There are thirteen courts of appeals.

crosscutting requirements conditions imposed on almost all grants-in-aid to further various social and economic objectives, such as nondiscrimination or environmental protection.

crossover sanctions conditions imposed on grants-in-aid in one program area that are designed to influence state and local government policy in another area.

dealignment a weakening of the attachment people feel toward political parties. A dealignment of the American electorate has been occurring since the 1960s, with the result that increasing numbers of voters consider themselves independent and vote on the basis of candidates' qualifications rather than party affiliation.

debt service the amount of each year's budget that the government pays as interest on the federal debt. It has been growing steadily as a proportion of federal expenditures.

de facto segregation racial segregation due to housing patterns rather than laws or official government policies.

de jure segregation racial segregation due to laws or government policies. The Fourteenth Amendment to the U.S.

Constitution has been interpreted by the Supreme Court as forbidding de jure segregation.

democracy a political system in which the people as a whole have the ultimate authority; citizens make public policy themselves or choose people to make it for them. In an ideal democracy, all citizens have the same opportunity to affect policy; this goal is accomplished by having equal representation and by having electoral and governing decisions made on the basis of majority rule.

democratic elitists scholars who believe that as long as people in leadership positions support the principles and practices of democracy, the apathy and intolerance of the masses do not in and of themselves threaten the democratic character of the political system.

Democratic-Republicans (Republicans) the principal opponents of George Washington's administration. Backers of Thomas Jefferson, they favored policies that would benefit their primary support groups, farmers and laborers, and are considered the forerunners of the contemporary Democratic party.

Democrats the faction of the Democratic-Republican party that supported Andrew Jackson. The Democrats consisted primarily of small farmers, new immigrants, and other recently enfranchised voters in the West and the South.

department one of the major operating units of the federal government and of the president's cabinet.

deregulation an effort begun in the late 1960s to reform the federal regulatory process by reducing or eliminating regulations that seemed to stifle competition. The most notable effort was in commercial air travel.

determinate sentencing a system of sentencing criminals in which mandatory sentences are specified for particular offenses, leaving judges and juries little discretion in individual cases.

diplomacy the conduct of relations between nations, usually through negotiation and consultation between foreign ministers and ambassadors.

direct orders legal measures adopted by the national government, and enforced by civil or criminal penalties, that require certain actions by state and local governments.

discount rate the interest rate that Federal Reserve Banks charge when they lend money to member banks. When the Federal Reserve lowers the discount rate, it is cheaper for member banks to get money from the Fed, and they can pass the savings on to their own customers in the form of lower interest rates.

dissenting opinion a document submitted by one or more justices or judges of a court that disagrees with the majority's reasoning and decision in a case.

distributive policies public policies that distribute goods and services to citizens. Examples are policies that provide recreational, public safety, transportation, and educational programs.

district courts the trial courts of the federal judicial system. There are ninety-four federal district courts, at least one in each state.

disturbance theory a theory that explains why political interest groups develop and flourish. It holds that changes within the political environment encourage people to organize to protect or promote their interests and that the organization and activity of these groups spur others to organize and become active.

docket the list of filings or cases that come before a court. The U.S. Supreme Court, for example, has an annual docket of over seven thousand cases.

double jeopardy trying a person in court more than once for the same crime, a practice forbidden by the Fifth Amendment to the U.S. Constitution.

dual federalism a view of federalism held between the time of the Civil War and the mid 1930s that attempted to recognize and maintain separate spheres of authority for the national and state governments.

due process fair and regular or usual procedures. The Fifth and Fourteenth Amendments to the U.S. Constitution provide that no one shall be deprived of life, liberty, or property by the government "without due process of law."

economic regulation government regulation of particular industries to correct what economists call market failures, such as natural monopolies, inadequate consumer information, or the dangerous side effects of manufacturing processes.

Education Consolidation and Improvement Act, 1981 a federal education program consolidating a number of small categorical grants into one major block grant.

elector a person chosen to vote for candidates to office. In presidential elections, the voters of each state select electors to vote for president. Initially these electors were expected to exercise independent judgment in their choice; today they are expected to ratify the choice of the majority or plurality of the state's voters.

Electoral College the body that selects the president and vice president, consisting of the 538 electors chosen in the fifty states and the District of Columbia. A majority of the college's votes is required for election.

Elementary and Secondary Education Act, 1965 one of the most significant federal education programs, which distributes aid to school districts on the basis of the proportion of low-income-family children in those districts.

elites people in leadership positions. Elites tend to be more tolerant than the average citizen of beliefs and behavior that deviate from social and political norms.

embassy the headquarters of a country's diplomatic corps in a foreign country.

en banc as a panel; with all judges participating. Cases in federal courts of appeals are usually heard and decided by three-judge panels, but in especially important cases the entire court will sit en banc.

enrolled bill process a procedure by which the Office of Management and Budget coordinates executive branch recommendations on legislation that has been passed by Congress and is awaiting presidential action.

Environmental Protection Agency the federal agency, created in 1970, that is charged with enforcing the nation's environmental laws.

equal time provision the requirement that broadcasters who allow political candidates to appear or advertise on their station permit other candidates equal opportunities. The rule, from which news reports and public debates are excluded, has actually discouraged broadcasters from providing free time to any candidate.

equality of opportunity a situation in which members of historically disadvantaged or discriminated-against groups, such as women or ethnic minorities, have a chance to obtain an education or employment that is equal to that of other individuals in a society.

equality of result a situation in which groups unequal in terms of such factors as educational background and historical socioeconomic advantages enjoy the same benefits or status in income or employment.

espionage the deployment of operatives who spy on foreign governments or pay foreign nationals to reveal secrets about their own governments.

establishment clause the part of the First Amendment to the U.S. Constitution that forbids Congress from establishing a national religion or favoring particular religions. As a result of the Supreme Court's interpretation of the amendment, state governments are subject to the same prohibitions.

exacting scrutiny test the test generally used by federal courts when reviewing whether laws and regulations involving nonracial discrimination violate the equal protection clause of the Fourteenth Amendment to the U.S. Constitution. Under this test, discrimination on the basis of gender, age, or wealth is unconstitutional unless it furthers some legitimate government interest in a reasonable way. This test is more rigorous than the minimal scrutiny test but less rigorous than the strict scrutiny test.

exclusionary rule the rule that evidence obtained illegally by police cannot be used against a defendant at trial.

executive agreement an agreement between heads of governments on a matter of mutual concern. Presidents often enter into executive agreements to avoid the more rigorous requirements involved in making a treaty. Executive agreements must be reported to Congress, but they do not require Senate ratification.

executive memorandum a formal statement of official policy or procedure, issued by the president to inform his subordinates of what he wishes them to do.

Executive Office of the President a bureaucracy created in 1939 to provide institutional staff support for the president.

executive order a presidential order to subordinates to perform a particular task in a particular way.

executive privilege the power claimed by the president to keep certain communications within the White House confidential from the U.S. Congress and the courts.

express powers powers that are enumerated in a constitution. Article I, Section 8, of the U.S. Constitution, for example, enumerates seventeen specific powers of Congress, including the power to tax, coin money, regulate commerce, and provide for the national defense.

fairness doctrine a requirement that broadcasters provide time for the discussion of issues of public concern and that conflicting sides of the issue be presented. The doctrine, which encouraged the media to avoid airing controversial issues because of the demand for time to reply, was suspended by the Federal Communications Commission in 1987.

Family Support Act, 1988 a major welfare reform law emphasizing jobs and job training.

federal questions issues concerning the interpretation and application of federal as opposed to state law.

Federal Reserve Board of Governors (the Fed) an independent agency of the federal government outside the executive and legislative branches that makes general credit, monetary, and operating policy for the Federal Reserve System as a whole.

Federal Reserve System the system that serves as the central bank for the United States, setting standards and rules that constrain the actions of other banks. It is composed of twelve Federal Reserve Banks, their twenty-five branches throughout the country, and many of the nation's commercial financial institutions. The system is managed by the Federal Reserve Board of Governors.

federalism a system of government in which powers are shared between a central or national government and state or regional governments. The U.S. Constitution establishes a federal system.

Federalists the name given to the people who supported ratification of the U.S. Constitution following its drafting in 1787 and also to the principal supporters of George Washington's administration (many of whom were the same people). The Federalists of the Washington administration, men of property and social standing, favored policies that benefited commercial and manufacturing interests—policies that the administration pursued.

fighting words words that may incite violence or a breach of the peace and public order. Historically, they have not been considered protected speech under the First Amendment to the U.S. Constitution, but in recent years the Supreme Court has overturned all convictions on these grounds.

filibuster a technique for preventing a vote in the Senate, in which senators gain recognition to speak in debate and then do not relinquish the floor. A filibuster can be ended only by a vote of cloture, and even then, loopholes in the Senate rules permit a single senator to prolong debate.

financial controls the most important and effective of Congress's techniques for overseeing the work of the executive branch. Before it appropriates funds to an agency or a program, Congress assesses the manner in which previous appropriations have been used and examines the stated plans for use of the funds currently being requested.

fiscal policy government economic policy dealing with the amounts of annual government expenditures and revenues, the purposes for which money is spent and the sources from which it comes, and the relationship of expenditures to revenues. The primary instrument of fiscal policy is the annual federal budget.

fluidity changeableness; instability. When public opinion is fluid, it shifts quickly from one judgment or set of judgments to another.

formula grants grants-in-aid distributed on the basis of a formula applied to all eligible recipients.

franking privilege the right of members of Congress to mail newsletters and questionnaires free of charge to every mailbox in their states or districts.

free exercise clause the part of the First Amendment to the U.S. Constitution that guarantees individuals the freedom of religious belief. As a result of the Supreme Court's interpretations of the amendment, state governments are barred from coercing individuals' religious beliefs.

freedom of association a right that the First Amendment to the U.S. Constitution has been interpreted as guaranteeing to individuals, including the right to organize and to belong to political parties and religious, economic, and other kinds of social organizations.

free-enterprise system a competitive economic system in which people are encouraged to pursue their own financial interests and the market determines their success or failure. Such a system rewards individual initiative and discourages government involvement.

general revenue sharing a federal program existing between 1972 and 1986 in which grants-in-aid were distributed to state and local governments with few strings attached.

general ticket system a winner-take-all method of selecting presidential and vice presidential electors that is used in all states but two, Maine and Nebraska. Under this system, the entire slate of electors pledged to the candidate who receives the most votes in the state is elected.

gerrymandering the practice of drawing legislative districts in such a way as to give one party an advantage.

going public making an appeal to the people for support for presidential policies. Presidents go public to obtain the backing they need from other public officials, particularly members of Congress.

government the formal institutions within which decisions about public policy are formulated, implemented, and adjudicated.

government corporation an economic enterprise owned in whole or in part by the federal government; examples are the Tennessee Valley Authority and the Federal Deposit Insurance Corporation.

grand jury a group of twelve to twenty-three persons who meet in private to determine, on the basis of evidence presented by prosecutors, whether to approve an indictment against an individual.

grant of immunity a judicial order giving an individual who testifies in court or before a congressional committee legal protection from subsequent prosecution on the basis of incriminating testimony.

grants-in-aid federal payments to state and local governments.

grantsmanship efforts by state and local governments to maximize the federal aid they receive.

Great Compromise the compromise reached at the Constitutional Convention in 1787 between the Virginia and New Jersey plans. It provided that each state would be equally represented in the Senate and that representation in the House of Representatives would be based on population.

gross domestic product (GDP) a statistical indicator of economic growth that measures the value of goods and services produced by factors of production—land, labor, and capital—located in the United States.

Housing and Community Development Act, 1974 the legislation that established the Community Development Block Grant program, which provided cities with money for a wide variety of housing and development needs such as public housing, street paving, lighting, and attracting commercial development.

ideological party a political party whose members share a belief system distinct from those of other parties. Ideological parties in the United States, such as the Socialists and the Libertarians, have been minor parties with a limited membership base.

impeachment the power of Congress to remove any civil officer of the United States who has been found guilty of "treason, bribery, or other high crimes and misdemeanors." The impeachment process begins with the introduction of a bill of impeachment in the House of Representatives. If the House approves the bill by majority vote, the impeached person is then tried in the Senate. Conviction requires the votes of two-thirds of the senators present and voting.

implied powers government powers that are inferred from the powers expressly enumerated in a written constitution. The "necessary and proper" clause of Article I, Section 8, of the U.S. Constitution has been interpreted to give Congress broad implied powers.

incrementalism the tendency for public policy to be made in slow, halting steps, a characteristic of policy making in the United States.

independent regulatory commission a unit of the federal government whose principal purpose is to regulate commerce and trade in an assigned area of jurisdiction. Commissions are independent of any department and, to some extent, of presidential control. All are run by a group of commissioners rather than a single executive.

independent state grounds a state constitution or state law used as the basis for a decision by a state court instead of federal law or federal courts' interpretation of the U.S. Constitution and Bill of Rights.

indictment the formal statement of charges against a criminal defendant, based on evidence presented by a prosecutor to a grand jury.

inflation an increase in the general price level in an economy.

in forma pauperis "in the manner of a pauper." When appealing a decision to the U.S. Supreme Court, indigents may file an *in forma pauperis* petition, stating that they are too poor to pay the Court's $300 fee for filing an appeal and asking that it be waived.

inherent powers powers possessed by a national government not enumerated in a constitution. In the conduct of foreign affairs, presidents have often claimed that they possess inherent powers.

injunction a prohibitory court order, such as one that prevents a federal agency from taking further action against an aggrieved party until certain conditions—a rehearing, for example—have been met.

inquisitorial system a system of criminal justice used in some countries, such as France, in which the accused person is presumed guilty, interrogated by magistrates, and denied other rights afforded in adversary systems.

institutional opinion an official explanation or justification of a decision by a court with multiple judges or justices.

intensity depth of feeling. The greater the intensity of public opinion, the more likely people are to act.

intergovernmental lobby the group of state and local government organizations, such as the National League of Cities and the National Governors' Association, that lobby the national government for legislation and decisions favorable to state and local governments.

iron triangle the close, mutually supportive relationship that often develops among executive agencies, special interest groups, and congressional subcommittees.

isolationism disengagement from the affairs of foreign countries except when they intersect directly with those of the United States. This approach characterized American foreign policy almost continuously until World War II.

issue entrepreneurs individual members of Congress who tend to specialize in particular substantive matters and to seek support among their colleagues for policies dealing with those matters. In the House, these are often subcommittee chairs; in the Senate, entrepreneurship is widely dispersed and bears little relation to formal institutional roles.

issue network an interconnected group of specialists in a particular subject area working in bureaucratic agencies at all levels of government, along with experts employed by legislative committee staffs, interest groups, think tanks, and universities. Issue networks play an important role in developing the national policy agenda, shaping consensus about preferred policies, and directing political leaders to develop and implement new policy proposals.

issue party a splinter party.

Jim Crow laws laws passed in the late nineteenth century that required racial separation in public transportation, restaurants, and other places of accommodation and discriminated against African Americans in various other ways.

Joint Chiefs of Staff (JCS) a body that advises the president on military matters, made up of the highest-ranking uniformed officer in each of the military services. It is chaired by an officer from one of the services who is appointed by the president to a two-year term.

joint committees committees composed of members of both houses of Congress. They are permanent study committees with no authority to initiate legislation.

joint conference committees temporary joint committees whose principal function is to resolve the differences between forms of the same bill passed by the House and the Senate, respectively.

judicial activism the use of judicial review to invalidate a law or other official action.

judicial double standard the Supreme Court's tendency since 1937 to uphold virtually all economic regulations under the Fifth and Fourteenth Amendments' guarantees of due process but to give heightened scrutiny to laws and regulations that affect individuals' noneconomic civil rights and liberties.

judicial federalism the dual judicial system in the United States, consisting of a system of federal courts and separate judicial systems in each of the fifty states.

judicial review, power of the power and authority of a court to determine whether acts of a legislature or an executive violate a constitution. The U.S. Supreme Court, for instance, has the power to strike down any congressional or state legislation, as well as any other official government action, that it deems to violate the U.S. Constitution.

judicial self-restraint deference by courts to the decisions of other branches of government.

jurisdiction the authority of a court to decide particular cases. The jurisdiction of federal courts is provided for in Article III of the U.S. Constitution and by Congress in statutes.

justiciable disputes disputes that are within a court's jurisdiction and do not present a political question.

laissez faire the absence of government involvement in the economy.

lame duck label often applied to a president in the last two years of a second term because the president is ineligible to run for reelection and may thus have difficulty building and maintaining political support.

legislation the making of laws, one of the major functions of Congress.

legislative courts courts created by Congress under Article I of the U.S. Constitution and having jurisdiction or authority over particular areas of law. The U.S. Court of Military Appeals, which applies military law, is one such court.

level of confidence the degree of certainty that the results of a public opinion poll (within the range of sampling error) are accurate for the population as a whole. Most national surveys are based on a level of confidence of about 95 percent, meaning that nineteen times out of twenty, the results will be accurate.

libel false statement of fact or defamation of character in print or by portrayal on television. Libel falls outside the scope of protection for free speech under the First Amendment to the U.S. Constitution.

liberalism a political ideology that emphasizes political rights and liberties for individuals and equal opportunity for all. Liberals oppose government restraints on the exercise of political freedoms but favor government programs that help the less fortunate.

limited government the idea that government powers are limited and specified or are traceable to enumerated powers in a written constitution.

loan guarantee a government guarantee that if a company or an individual is unable to pay back a loan, the government will do so.

lobbying the art of persuading public officials to support a particular policy position. The term alludes to legislators' being accosted by interest group representatives in the lobby outside the legislative chamber.

macroeconomics the study of the behavior of the economy as a whole.

mandatory entitlement program a federal program that confers benefits, usually in the form of payments or loan guarantees, to any citizen who meets certain stipulated qualifications. Examples include Social Security, veterans' benefits, and student loan guarantees.

mark-up session a meeting at which all of the members of a congressional subcommittee or committee participate in revising a bill to put it into a form that is acceptable to a majority of them.

mass public the people in a society who do not follow political issues closely, whose mood and opinions change the most rapidly, and who may thus be the easiest to manipulate by others who wish to affect public policy outcomes. The mass public is the largest group (75 to 80 percent) within the general population.

masses people who are not in leadership positions. They are less tolerant than elites of beliefs and behavior that deviate from social and political norms.

meaningful choice the opportunity for voters to select among different options—candidates, parties, and policies. Meaningful choice requires at least two candidates whose views are dissimilar and who have sufficient resources to present their views to the public.

merit system a system of appointing judges or other government officials on the basis of ability, competitive examinations, or comparisons with other qualified candidates. Some states have so-called merit systems for the selection of state judges, in which a nonpartisan commission recommends a list of possible nominees from which the governor or legislature makes appointments.

military-industrial complex the link between the Defense Department and the companies that manufacture weapons for the armed services; a term first used in the 1950s.

minimal scrutiny test the test used by federal courts when reviewing whether laws and regulations dealing with economic matters violate the equal protection clause of the Fourteenth Amendment to the U.S. Constitution. On this test, laws and regulations will be upheld if they have a rational basis.

Miranda warnings a set of reminders about constitutional rights that police must give before interrogating criminal suspects. Suspects must be told that they have the right to remain silent and to consult an attorney and that an attorney can be provided if they cannot afford to hire one. This requirement was the result of the Supreme Court's ruling in *Miranda v. Arizona* (1966).

monetarists economists who believe that monetary policy is the most important instrument of government economic policy, especially for maintaining price stability.

monetary policy government control of the availability and flow of money in the economy. Its central concern is the terms on which money can be borrowed—that is, interest rates and repayment requirements.

multimember district an electoral district in which more than one of the candidates for a particular office is elected. The winners are determined on the basis of the proportion of votes that they or their party receive. Some states and cities in the United States have multimember legislative districts.

mutual assured destruction an element of containment policy holding that for nuclear deterrence to be effective, the United States had to convince the Soviet Union and other potential adversaries that it possessed the capability to inflict significant damage in a nuclear attack, even if that attack came as a retaliatory response to a nuclear attack on the United States. This capability implied that nuclear attack on the United States would be suicidal for the country that launched it.

National Defense Education Act, 1958 a federal program designed to upgrade the science, math, and foreign-language skills of schoolchildren.

National Security Council (NSC) a component of the Executive Office of the President that is intended to facilitate the coordination of foreign and defense policy. It consists of the president, the vice president, the secretary of state, and the secretary of defense, advised by the director of central intelligence and the chairman of the Joint Chiefs of Staff. The head of NSC staff, the assistant to the president for national security affairs, is often the principal presidential adviser on national security issues.

National Service Act, 1993 a federal program providing college loans that can be paid off by working at community service jobs.

nation-centered federalism a view of federalism held in the pre–Civil War era that advocated an active and expanded role for the national government.

negative advertising commercials that seek to discredit a political candidate. First used in 1964, such advertising has come to characterize modern media campaigns.

new federalism the view of federalism associated with presidents Nixon and Reagan, which stressed greater flexibility in the use of grants-in-aid by the recipients and, in the Reagan years, reductions in the total amount of grants.

New Jersey Plan one of the main proposals for the overall structure of government that was presented at the Constitutional Convention in 1787. It was proposed by William Paterson and called for a unicameral legislature in which all states would be represented equally, a multi-member executive with no power to veto legislation, and a supreme court. This plan was favored by smaller states.

newsworthiness the characteristic of stories and events that merit attention by the news media because they capture public interest. Frequently they involve conflict, drama, and surprise in addition to timeliness and importance.

nullification, doctrine of the claim, associated most closely with South Carolina senator John C. Calhoun, that states could declare acts of Congress null and void within their borders.

Office of Management and Budget (OMB) the president's principal office for preparing a budget, coordinating legislative and regulatory activities, and improving management in the executive branch.

one person, one vote the principle that all legislative districts within the same state must be approximately equal in population in order to ensure that all citizens have equal representation in government. This principle was enunciated by the Supreme Court in *Westberry v. Sanders* (1964).

open-ended question a question on a public opinion poll that allows respondents to frame their own answers in their own words. Responses to open-ended questions may reflect personal opinions more accurately than answers to closed-ended questions, but they are very difficult to categorize and subsequently to analyze.

opinion (1) a judgment made about current issues, including feelings people have, positions they take, and conclusions they reach. (2) the written explanation or justification of a court's or an individual judge's decision.

opinion makers the people in a society who shape the opinions of others. The opinion makers, who constitute less than 5 percent of the population, are well informed about political issues and are often directly involved in political activities and in positions to affect public debate.

original jurisdiction the authority of a court to have a case originate in it. Article III of the U.S. Constitution specifies the "cases or controversies" over which the Supreme Court has original jurisdiction.

oversight hearings regular in-depth reviews by congressional committees of the activities of executive agencies or the management of specific programs. Such a hearing is usually preceded by an investigation by the committee staff. At the hearing itself, executive branch officials are called to explain their activities and to answer the committee's questions. The product of an oversight hearing may be a report suggesting changes in administrative procedures, remedial legislation, or reauthorization of the agency or program.

partial preemption the national government's establishment of minimum standards in a policy area and its requiring state and local governments to meet those standards or lose their authority in that area.

partisan a person who identifies with a political party.

party caucus a meeting of all members of a party in a legislative body to set legislative strategy or seek to determine a party position on important policy decisions.

party discipline the ability of party leaders in a legislature to count on the members of their party to support them on votes and to impose sanctions on members who do not. It is normal in legislatures in other countries but rare in the U.S. Congress.

patronage the distribution of government jobs as a reward for working on a winning candidate's campaign or providing other service to a party or political machine.

personnel control congressional control over presidential appointments and over the number, qualifications, salaries, and employment conditions of all federal employees.

petit jury a trial jury, made up traditionally of twelve persons but in some states now as few as six, that hears evidence and decides whether the defendant is guilty or innocent of the charges.

plea bargaining an arrangement whereby a criminal defendant pleads guilty to lesser charges than those originally brought in exchange for a reduced sentence. As a result, both the prosecution and the defense are saved the time and expense of a trial.

pocket veto a presidential veto of a bill that occurs when a congressional session concludes within ten days of the bill's passage and without the president having signed it. Because Congress is not in session, the president does not return the bill, nor is there any possibility of a congressional override.

policy adoption marshaling the support needed to win official approval of a specific public policy. This stage of the policy-making process is typically characterized by bargaining, negotiating, and compromise.

policy evaluation determination of whether a particular public policy is working as intended.

policy formulation the stage in the process of making public policy during which an effective and feasible solution to a problem is developed.

policy implementation the stage in the process of making public policy during which the policy is actually put into action.

policy termination the process of halting public policies that are not meeting their objectives or have outlived the problem for which they were created.

political action committee (PAC) a nonparty group that solicits contributions from its members and uses the money to influence the outcome of elections.

political correctness the avoidance or prohibition of language and behavior that are offensive to certain segments of the population, such as women or minority groups. Opponents claim that such a prohibition violates individuals' rights protected by the First Amendment to the U.S. Constitution.

political culture the dominant values, beliefs, and attitudes of members of a society about their governance, their history, and their rights and responsibilities as citizens. A political culture conditions the structure of the society's political system, the rules by which it operates, and the bounds of acceptable behavior within it.

political efficacy an individual's sense of his or her own ability to influence political outcomes and to participate in politics in ways that make a difference.

political equality the principle that the vote of each citizen in a democracy counts equally. Two conditions apply: the majority rules, and the candidate with the most votes wins.

political ideology a set of interrelated attitudes that shape judgments about and reactions to political issues. Political ideologies, such as liberalism and conservatism, provide people with a general orientation toward government that helps them form opinions and react to events.

political interest group an organization that attempts to influence the staffing and policies of government.

political party a group organized to win elections in order to influence the policies of government. American political parties are broad-based, decentralized, pragmatic political organizations.

political questions issues presented to courts that judges decide would more appropriately be resolved by other branches of government.

political socialization the ongoing process whereby individuals acquire the information, beliefs, attitudes, and values that help them comprehend the workings of a political system and orient themselves within it.

politics the process by which people pursue their own needs and preferences within a society. Politics frequently involves a struggle to achieve power in order to attain individual and group goals.

popular sovereignty the idea that government is based on the consent of the people and is accountable to the people for its actions.

power the influence that some individuals, groups, or institutions have over others; the ability to get people to do something they might not otherwise do. It may be exercised through the use of persuasive skills, legal authority, force or the threat of force, or the promise of rewards.

preemption the national government's removal of an area of authority from state and local governments.

prime rate the interest rate that banks charge their best customers to borrow money. A lower prime rate encourages economic activity by reducing the cost of borrowing.

prior restraint issuing a judicial restraining order to prevent the publication or broadcasting of information that might be harmful to the nation's security. The U.S. Supreme Court has upheld the principle of prior restraint but has been reluctant to approve it in practice.

privacy, right of a constitutional right not enumerated in the Bill of Rights but construed by the U.S. Supreme Court to be in the "penumbras," or shadows, of the First, Third, Fourth, and Fifth Amendments and enforceable against the states under the Fourteenth Amendment.

probable cause reasonable justification; specifically, sufficient evidence for an arrest or a police search, a requirement of the Fourth Amendment to the U.S. Constitution.

problem recognition the stage in the process of making public policy during which decision makers and the public become aware of the existence of a problem possibly requiring public attention.

procedural due process the application of laws and regulations according to fair and regular procedures. It imposes limits on how government may carry out its activities.

project grants grants-in-aid for which potential recipients must apply to a federal agency; such grants are usually awarded on a competitive basis.

proportional voting the principle by which delegates chosen in the Democratic party's presidential nominating primaries and caucuses are awarded to candidates in proportion to the number of popular votes that they receive.

prospective voting judgments about how to vote that anticipate candidates' future decisions and actions. According to this model of voting behavior, voters compare their own values and positions on issues with those of the candidates and parties in an effort to determine which party and which candidates are likely to benefit them the most.

public assistance a welfare program providing money and other forms of support to needy people. Examples in the United States are Aid to Families with Dependent Children, Medicaid, and food stamps.

public opinion the opinions, attitudes, and values of the public as they relate to the issues of the day.

public opinion poll a survey of the beliefs, attitudes, and/or opinions of the general population. Public opinion polls have been conducted regularly since the 1940s to gauge opinion on a wide range of contemporary issues.

public policy government decisions designed to address public problems. Public policy is established by the Constitution, law, and precedent; it constitutes the rules by which a society lives.

random selection the process of choosing a representative sample for a public opinion poll. In random selection, every element of the population must have an equal chance of being included in the sample, and the choice of any one element should not preclude the choice of any other.

realignment a shifting of partisan attitudes among the electorate. Realignment occurs over a period of years when the dominant party loses the allegiance of some of its supporters and the other party gains the allegiance of some of these voters as well as a majority of newer ones coming into the electorate. The last realignment in American politics occurred during the 1930s when the Democrats became the dominant party.

reapportionment the reallocation of legislative seats on the basis of population, geography, or some combination of the two. Seats in the U.S. House of Representatives, for example, are reapportioned among the states every ten years, after the national census, on the basis of population changes since the previous census.

rebuttal, right of the requirement that broadcasters give people who are criticized on the air or political candidates whose opponents are endorsed by a station the opportunity to reply free of charge. This right, upheld by the U.S. Supreme Court in 1969, has discouraged broadcasters from airing controversial issues or endorsing candidates.

redistributive policies public policies, such as welfare programs, that are perceived to take benefits from one group and give them to others.

redistricting redrawing the boundaries of legislative districts, especially as required of states that gain or lose congressional seats as a result of reapportionment.

reduction in force an overall reduction in employment within a federal agency or the federal bureaucracy as a whole, which permits the removal of career employees from their jobs.

regulatory policies public policies that establish rules and standards and thereby control behavior. Examples include laws that regulate child labor, minimum wages, and industrial pollution.

regulatory review a procedure by which the Office of Management and Budget oversees regulations that executive agencies wish to issue to implement legislation. In assessing regulations, the OMB examines their necessity, cost-effectiveness, and consistency with administration policy and congressional intent.

representation the processes through which members of

Congress seek to determine, articulate, and act on the interests of residents of their state or district.

republic a government whose powers are exercised by elected representatives, who are directly or indirectly accountable to the people governed.

Republicans the party formed in the 1850s by disillusioned Whigs and supporters of other minor parties who opposed the expansion of slavery and new immigration. Comprised primarily of laborers, small farmers, and entrepreneurs, it was the forerunner of the contemporary Republican party.

required reserve ratio the percentage of their deposits that Federal Reserve Banks must keep as reserves, as determined by the Fed. As the reserve ratio goes up, the amount of money available for banks to lend goes down; this makes credit harder to obtain, causes interest rates to rise, and cools economic activity.

reserved powers powers that have not been delegated to a government body. The Tenth Amendment to the U.S. Constitution provides that powers not delegated to the national government are reserved to state governments or the people of the states.

restrictive covenants contracts in which it is stipulated that property may not be sold or leased to members of certain racial or religious groups. In *Shelley v. Kraemer* (1948), the Supreme Court held that such covenants were unconstitutional under the Fourteenth Amendment.

retrospective voting judgments about how to vote that are based on the past performance of the parties and their elected officials in light of the promises they made and the conditions that resulted from their actions. According to this theory of voting behavior, voters look back and decide whether they (and society) are better or worse off as a result of the performance of the people in power.

reverse discrimination discrimination against whites and/or men, the basis of which affirmative action programs have been challenged under the equal protection clause of the Fourteenth Amendment to the U.S. Constitution.

rider one or more controversial provisions attached to a piece of legislation. Proposals that might have difficulty surviving on their own are thereby permitted to "ride through" the legislative process on the backs of other bills.

rule of four the informal rule that for a case to be accepted for review by the U.S. Supreme Court, at least four of the justices must vote to take it.

salience importance. The most salient public policy issues are those that arouse the most attention and interest.

sample the portion of the general population that is selected for a public opinion poll. A sample must be representative of the entire population if pollsters are to make generalizations from it.

sampling error the degree to which the opinions of people questioned in a public opinion poll could diverge from the opinions of the population as a whole. Sampling error depends on the size of the sample. For a sample of about one thousand, the error will be in the range of plus or minus 3 percent.

secondary group a group, such as a labor union, church congregation, or bridge club, that individuals choose to join and may help shape or reinforce their political views and values.

Section 8 a provision of the 1974 Housing and Community Development Act that established a rental subsidy program for needy families and encouraged the construction of subsidized rental housing units.

secular regulation rule a rule used by the U.S. Supreme Court in applying the First Amendment's guarantee of the free exercise of religion. It requires that national and state laws have a secular (nonreligious) purpose and not discriminate on the basis of religion.

seditious libel libel or slander that defames or criticizes the government or its officials. The First Amendment to the U.S. Constitution has been interpreted as forbidding governments from punishing seditious libel.

select committees (special committees) temporary congressional committees created to deal with a specific set of issues. They usually disappear once they have completed their work. Many such committees have explicitly limited functions and authority, and most are not authorized to recommend legislation.

selective benefits, theory of a theory that explains why people join political interest groups. It holds that the primary incentives for joining a group are the selective benefits that its members receive.

selective perception the tendency of most people to use their reading and television watching to acquire information and opinions that support their existing political views and party preferences.

self-incrimination confessing to a crime or testifying in a court in a way that implicates oneself in a crime. The Fifth Amendment to the U.S. Constitution provides a guarantee against forced self-incrimination.

senatorial courtesy consultation by the president with senators prior to making a formal nomination that requires Senate confirmation. Begun during the Washington administration, this practice gives senators influence over potential presidential nominations, but it also enhances the prospects of nominees who have received prior clearance.

Senior Executive Service (SES) the highest-ranking group of federal civil service employees, created in 1979 to provide agencies with greater flexibility in deploying, compensating, and, if necessary, removing their senior managers and technical specialists. There are now about eight thousand SES members, of whom at least 90 percent must always be career federal employees.

seniority system the former system under which the member of the majority party with the longest consecutive service on each congressional committee was automatically its chair for as long as he or she remained in Congress.

separate but equal doctrine the principle that laws requiring separate facilities for white and black citizens were permissible under the U.S. Constitution's Fourteenth Amendment guarantee of equal protection. The doctrine was upheld by the Supreme Court in *Plessy v. Ferguson* (1896) but abandoned in the mid twentieth century.

separation of powers the division of power and authority within a government among three branches, typically the legislature, the executive, and the judiciary.

Servicemen's Readjustment Act, 1944 a federal program, also known as the *GI Bill*, that provided financial assistance to military veterans for completing their education.

shield laws laws in many states that protect journalists from being forced to reveal their sources. The protection of shield laws is similar to that enjoyed by doctors, lawyers, and clergy but does not extend to information subpoenaed by courts of law.

single-member district an electoral district in which only one of the candidates for a particular office can be elected. Districts for members of Congress are of this type.

slander defamation of character by speech, for which individuals may be subject to prosecution.

social insurance a "pay as you go" welfare program in which employees and employers contribute to a national insurance fund. Examples in the United States are Social Security, Medicare, and unemployment insurance.

social regulation government regulation of certain economic functions that are common to most industries to ensure that specific objectives are pursued. Typically, the process involves setting standards that are deemed to be in the national interest, applying those standards to all industries, and enforcing them.

socially redeeming value the criterion used by the Supreme Court in determining whether speech is protected under the First Amendment. Only the categories of libel and slander, obscenity, fighting words, and commercial speech have been deemed to lack socially redeeming value and to receive less protection under the First Amendment.

socioeconomic status (SES) an analytic measure of relative social and economic standing.

Speaker the elected leader of the majority party in the House of Representatives, who serves as the presiding officer of the House.

special committees select committees.

special investigations special examinations by Congress

of executive branch or presidential activities. Some are conducted by permanent committees and subcommittees with no special appropriations of funds or additions to committee staffs. More commonly, however, investigations differ from routine oversight hearings in the depth of their examinations, the vigor with which they are conducted, and the amount of funds and staff resources committed to them.

speech-plus-conduct the communication of ideas through marching, picketing, and sit-in demonstrations. Under the Supreme Court's interpretation of the First Amendment, such forms of expression are protected speech so long as they are not disruptive or destructive of public or private property.

speedy and public trial a right guaranteed to criminal defendants by the Sixth Amendment to the U.S. Constitution. As a result, secret trials are forbidden, and an arrested person must be tried within a period specified by Congress.

splinter party a party created out of dissatisfaction with one or both of the major parties when they ignore an important issue, take an unpopular stand, or nominate an unattractive candidate. A splinter party exercises power by threatening the major parties with loss of electoral support until they change their ways.

split-ticket voting the practice of voting for candidates of different parties on the same ballot. Split-ticket voting has increased in recent decades with the weakening of partisan allegiances.

spoils system the distribution of federal jobs to supporters of the victorious presidential candidate. It was the primary way of staffing the federal bureaucracy prior to the creation of the civil service system.

stability permanence; persistence. When public opinion is stable, it persists with little or no change.

standard operating procedures (SOPs) predetermined ways of responding to a particular problem or set of circumstances. SOPs simplify bureaucratic decisions and contribute to their consistency, but they also channel bureaucratic activity into rigid patterns and make agencies less adaptable to change.

standing committees permanent congressional committees that have full authority to recommend legislation. A few, like the Rules Committee in the House, are responsible for organizing and regulating the operations of Congress; most have jurisdictions defined along substantive policy lines.

standing to sue the right or legal status to initiate a lawsuit or judicial proceedings. To have standing to sue, parties must show that they are suffering or in danger of suffering an immediate and substantial personal injury.

state-centered federalism a view of federalism held in the pre–Civil War era that opposed increasing national power at the expense of the states.

strict construction the idea that the U.S. Constitution can and should be interpreted in a narrowly literal sense, as it was written and understood by its framers.

strict scrutiny test the test used by federal courts when reviewing whether the equal protection clause of the Fourteenth Amendment to the U.S. Constitution is violated by laws or regulations that limit or deny individuals' "fundamental rights" or that discriminate on the basis of race, national origin, or religion. Under this test, government must have a "compelling interest" that justifies the law or regulation.

structural unemployment the "natural" or lowest possible rate of unemployment, reflecting the number of people who at any given time are just entering the work force, leaving one job to look for another, or having difficulty finding a job because they lack valuable skills.

subgovernment an alliance that develops among executive agencies, interest groups, and congressional committees in a particular policy area. (Also called an *iron triangle*.)

subsidy direct government intervention in the economy in the form of cash grants, loan guarantees, and tax advantages extended to particular industries or economic areas.

substantive due process conformity of the subject matter of laws and regulations to a standard of reasonableness. It imposes limits on what government may do.

subversive speech speech that is considered likely to undermine the government. Until the mid twentieth century, the Supreme Court allowed the national and state governments to punish subversive speech, but more recently the Court has interpreted the First Amendment as protecting even subversive speech.

suffrage the right to vote.

summit meeting a meeting between the American president and an important foreign leader.

sunshine laws laws requiring that important meetings and hearings of federal agencies be open to the public.

superdelegates delegates to the Democratic party's national nominating convention who are chosen from among the party's elected and appointed leaders. Unpledged to any candidate, they constitute approximately 15 percent of the convention's delegates.

supremacy clause a clause of Article IV of the U.S. Constitution providing that the Constitution and other national laws are "the supreme law of the land." National laws thus supersede state and local laws when there is a conflict between them.

symbolic speech nonverbal communication through the use of symbols that the U.S. Supreme Court has ruled to

be protected speech under the First Amendment, such as the wearing of black armbands as a sign of protest.

Synthetic Fuels Corporation a program passed during the Carter presidency that provided subsidies for the production of fuel from sources other than oil, such as wind, garbage, and plants. It was abolished during the Reagan presidency.

territorial imperative the tendency of federal agencies to guard their own area of jurisdiction against other agencies that seem to be trespassing on it.

terrorism the use of violence to disrupt the routines of international activity and to demoralize and frighten a country's population or regime.

three-fifths compromise the decision made at the Constitutional Convention in 1787 to count three-fifths of slaves as persons for the purposes of determining taxation and representation in the U.S. House of Representatives.

Three Mile Island a nuclear power plant in Pennsylvania that in 1979 experienced the worst nuclear accident in United States history. That event dramatically focused the public's attention on energy issues in general and nuclear dangers in particular.

travel, right to a right not enumerated in the Bill of Rights but construed by the U.S. Supreme Court to be a basic guarantee of the Fourteenth Amendment. As a result, states are forbidden from infringing on individuals' right to travel from one state to another.

treaty an official, written set of accords between nations in which the parties agree to certain specific actions. When the United States enters into a treaty with a foreign government, it is negotiated by American diplomatic officials, sometimes including the president. It must then be approved by two-thirds of the members of the Senate.

unalienable rights in the social theory of John Locke, certain natural rights of individuals that are believed to precede the creation of government and that government may not deny. The Declaration of Independence proclaimed that individuals have the unalienable right to "Life, Liberty, and the Pursuit of Happiness."

unanimous consent a common device used for procedural efficiency in the Senate, in which action is taken without debate when all members consent to it.

unconventional participation efforts to influence public policy, such as street demonstrations, boycotts, and sit-ins, that fall outside the normal channels of political participation.

universal suffrage the right of all citizens who have reached maturity to vote. It reflects the democratic principle that if government is to based on the consent of the governed, all citizens should be able to participate in the selection of their public officials.

urban renewal an approach to federal housing policy, established in 1949 and terminated in 1974, that was designed to clear blighted and deteriorating areas of inner cities and replace them with new commercial and residential establishments.

values the most important attitudes and beliefs people have; the ideas, principles, and opinions that are most intensely felt and rank as the most significant for an individual.

Virginia Plan one of the main proposals for the overall structure of government that was presented at the Constitutional Convention in 1787. It was drafted by James Madison and called for a strong central government, including a bicameral legislature with representation of states based on their wealth and population, a chief executive chosen by the legislature, and a powerful judiciary. This plan was favored by larger states.

void for vagueness a judicial standard used to strike down laws that are overly broad or so vague that it is uncertain what they apply to or whether they infringe on freedoms such as those protected under the First Amendment to the U.S. Constitution.

Water Quality Act, 1965 the first major federal law attempting to establish standards for water quality.

Whigs the opponents of Andrew Jackson. The Whigs were a diverse, decentralized group that stayed unified in elections by nominating military heroes as candidates.

whip the member of each party's leadership structure in the House and the Senate who works closely with rank-and-file members to determine party positions and to seek to form legislative coalitions.

White House Office the president's principal political aides, who provide staff support for formulating presidential policy, communicating it to the public, and helping the president meet the day-to-day responsibilities of the office.

winner-take-all voting the principle by which the candidate who receives the most votes in an electoral district or state wins all of the delegates or electors at stake. The Republicans permit this method of voting in their presidential nominating primaries and caucuses; the Democrats do not.

writ of certiorari a formal order issued by the U.S. Supreme Court to a lower federal court or state court requesting the record of the decision in a case that the Supreme Court has accepted for review. Four of the Court's nine justices must agree to grant a writ of certiorari in order for a case to be reviewed.

writ of mandamus an order issued by a superior court that directs a lower court or other government authority to perform a particular act.

yellow journalism reporting that emphasizes sensationalism—crime, sex, and other issues that grab readers' attention. The term had its origin in the fight between publishers Joseph Pulitzer and William Randolph Hearst over rights to the comic strip "The Yellow Kid."

References

Chapter 1   The American Political Environment

1. Survey by Mellman and Lazarus and Public Opinion Strategies for the Health Insurance Association of America, conducted January 4–5, 1992, as reported in *American Enterprise* III (March-April 1992), 85.
2. Barnaby J. Feder, "Medical Group Battles to Be Heard Over Others on Health-Care Changes," *New York Times,* June 11, 1993, A22; and Dana Priest, "Health Plan Worries Spur PACs: Industry Group Donations Up 20%," *Washington Post,* July 14, 1993, A19.
3. Ceci Connolly, "Developing the Sales Pitch for the Overhaul Plan," *Congressional Quarterly* 51 (July 10, 1993), 1806.
4. Clinton Rossiter, *Conservatism in America* (New York: Vintage Books, 1962), 72.
5. Law Day address by Sen. J. William Fulbright, University of Arkansas, 1974.
6. Herbert McClosky and John Zaller, *The American Ethos: Public Attitudes Toward Capitalism and Democracy* (Cambridge, Mass.: Harvard University Press, 1984).

Chapter 2   The Constitutional Basis of American Politics

1. See Max Farrand, *The Framing of the Constitution* (1913); and John P. Roche, "The Founding Fathers: A Reform Caucus in Action," *American Political Science Review* (December 1961): 799.
2. For further discussion, see Gordon S. Wood, *The Creation of the American Republic, 1776–1787* (Chapel Hill: University of North Carolina Press, 1969).
3. "Resolution of Federal Convention (May 30, 1787)," in *The Records of the Federal Convention of 1787,* ed. Max Farrand (New Haven, Conn.: Yale University Press, 1911), vol. 1, 30.
4. "James Madison," in *The Federalist Papers,* ed. Clinton Rossiter (New York: New American Library, 1961), no. 39, 240–246.
5. See Forrest McDonald, *Novus Ordo Seclorum: The Intellectual Origins of the Constitution* (Lawrence: University of Kansas Press, 1985).
6. "James Madison," in Farrand, *The Records of the Federal Convention of 1787,* vol. 1, 122–123.
7. "Patrick Henry," in *The Complete Anti-Federalist,* ed. Herbert J. Storing (Chicago, Ill.: University of Chicago Press, 1981), vol. 5, 211.
8. For studies of the debates in the various state ratification conventions, see *Ratifying the Constitution,* ed. Michael Gillespie and Michael Lienesch (Lawrence: University of Kansas Press, 1989).
9. Quoted and discussed in David O'Brien, "The Framers' Muse on Republicanism, the Supreme Court, and Pragmatic Constitutional Interpretivism," *The Review of Politics* 53 (1991): 251.
10. See Charles A. Beard, *An Economic Interpretation of the Constitution* (New York: Macmillan, 1913).
11. See Bernard Bailyn, *The Ideological Origins of the American Revolution* (Cambridge, Mass.: Harvard University Press, 1967); Forrest McDonald, *We the People: The Economic Origins of the Constitution* (Chicago, Ill.: University of Chicago Press, 1958); Gordon S. Wood, *The Creation of the American Republic, 1776–1787;* and Gordon S. Wood, *The Radicalism of the American Revolution* (New York: Knopf, 1992).
12. Martin Diamond, "The Declaration and the Constitution: Liberty, Democracy, and the Founders," *The Public Interest* 41 (Fall 1975): 40.
13. "James Wilson," in *The Debates in the Several State Conventions on the Adoption of the Federal Constitution,* ed. Jonathan Elliot, 2nd ed. (Washington, D.C., 1836), vol. 2, 524.
14. Thomas Paine, *Common Sense* (1776), excerpts reprinted in *Free Government in the Making,* ed. Alpheus T. Mason and Gordon E. Baker, 4th ed. (New York: Oxford University Press, 1985).
15. See Peter Onuf, "State Sovereignty and the Making of the Constitution," in *Conceptual Change and the Constitution,* ed. Terence Ball and J. G. A. Pocock (Lawrence: University of Kansas Press, 1988).
16. See John Reid, *The Concept of Liberty in the Age of the American Revolution* (Chicago: University of Chicago Press, 1988).
17. *McCulloch v. Maryland,* 17 U.S. 316 (1819).

18. See Ellis Sandoz, *A Government of Laws: Political Theory, Religion, and the American Founding* (Baton Rouge: Louisiana State University Press, 1990).

19. *Meyers v. United States,* 272 U.S. 52 (1926).

20. This discussion draws on David O'Brien, "Federalism as a Metaphor in the Constitutional Politics of Public Administration," *Public Administration Review* 49 (1989): 411.

21. For two studies of judicial review and the founding, see Robert Clinton, *Marbury v. Madison and Judicial Review* (Lawrence: University of Kansas Press, 1989); and Sylvia Snowiss, *Judicial Review and the Law of the Constitution* (New Haven, Conn.: Yale University Press, 1990).

22. James Madison, speech in the House of Representatives, in *Annals of the First Congress* (Washington, D.C.: Gales and Seaton, 1834), vol. 1, 532.

23. Charles Evans Hughes, *Addresses of Charles Evans Hughes* (New York: Putnam's 1916), 185–186.

24. See Howard Ball, *"We Have a Duty": The Supreme Court and the Watergate Tapes Litigation* (Westport, Conn.: Greenwood, 1990).

25. Felix Frankfurter, "The Zeitgeist and the Judiciary," in *Law and Politics,* ed. A. MacLeish and E. Prichard (New York: Capricorn, 1939), 6.

26. Edward White, "The Supreme Court of the United States," 7 *American Bar Association Journal* (1921), 341.

Chapter 3   Federalism in Theory and Practice

1. Quotes from Secretary Riley and Representative Gunderson are found in Rochelle L. Stanfield, "New Ways of Sizing Up the Schools," *National Journal* 18 (May 1, 1993): 1052–1053. Quoted in Susan Chira, "Clinton to Offer Plan for Change in U.S. Schools," *New York Times,* April 21, 1993. The letter from Roy Romer and Carrol Campbell to Richard Riley is dated May 6, 1993.

2. Remarks to the National Governors' Association meeting in Washington, D.C., February 2, 1993; published in *Weekly Compilation of Presidential Documents* 29, no. 5 (Washington, D.C.: Office of the Federal Register, National Archives and Records Administration, February 2, 1993), 125–128.

3. *McCulloch v. Maryland,* 17 U.S. 316 (1819).

4. Quoted in Alfred H. Kelly and Winfred A. Harbison, *The American Constitution* (New York: Norton, 1955), 180.

5. The laws known as the Alien and Sedition Act were four separate acts. The Naturalization Act raised from five to fourteen years the period an alien had to wait to acquire citizenship. The Alien Act empowered the president to order out of the country all aliens judged dangerous to the peace and safety of the nation. The Alien Enemies Act empowered the president in case of war to remove or detain as enemy aliens all male subjects of a hostile power. The Sedition Act provided for fines against or imprisonment of any persons conspiring against the United States government.

6. It should be noted that the Virginia and Kentucky resolutions were drawn to address specific political issues of the time and that neither Madison nor Jefferson governed as president in a way that was congruent with the resolutions. Further, neither accepted Calhoun's extended nullification theories. For further discussion, see Andrew C. McLaughlin, *A Constitutional History of the United States* (New York: Appleton-Century, 1935).

7. See Edward S. Corwin, *The Twilight of the Supreme Court* (New Haven, Conn.: Yale University Press, 1934), ch. 1.

8. *Texas v. White,* 74 U.S. 700 (1869).

9. *United States v. E. C. Knight Company,* 156 U.S. 1 (1895).

10. *Hammer v. Dagenhart,* 247 U.S. 251 (1918).

11. *Schechter Poultry Corporation v. United States,* 295 U.S. 495 (1935).

12. For elaboration, see David B. Walker, *Toward a Functioning Federalism* (Cambridge, Mass.: Winthrop, 1981), 54–65.

13. *National League of Cities v. Usery,* 426 U.S. 833 (1976).

14. See *Hodel v. Virginia Surface Mining & Reclamation, Inc.,* 452 U.S. 264 (1981); and *EEOC v. Wyoming,* 460 U.S. 226 (1983).

15. *Intergovernmental Perspective* 11, no. 2/3 (Spring-Summer 1985): 23. In response to this "Garcia update," it should be noted that Congress in 1986 amended the Fair Labor Standards Act to allow states and localities to use compensatory time in lieu of overtime pay for their workers. See John J. Harrigan, *Politics and Policy in States and Communities* (New York: HarperCollins, 1991), 58.

16. *Garcia v. San Antonio Metropolitan Transit Authority,* 469 U.S. 528 (1985).

17. *Missouri v. Jenkins,* 495 U.S. 33 (1990).

18. For a review of some of these, see Michael A. Pagano, Ann M. Bowman, and John Kincaid, "The State of American Federalism— 1990–1991," *Publius: The Journal of Federalism* 21 (Summer 1991): 1–26.

19. See Michael D. Reagan and John G. Sanzone, *The New Federalism* (New York: Oxford University Press, 1981), 175–179.

20. President Ronald Reagan, Executive Order 12612, 1987. Cited in *National Journal,* July 21, 1990, 1760.

21. Edward I. Koch, "The Mandate Millstone," *The Public Interest* 61 (Fall 1980): 42–57.

22. Ibid.

23. Presidential Task Force, *Reagan Administration Regulatory Achievements* (Washington, D.C., August, 1983), 1.

24. U.S. Congress, House Committee on Ways and Means, Hearings *On the Subject of General Revenue Sharing,* 92nd Cong., 1st sess., June 28, 1971, 1305–1306.

25. Quoted in W. John Moore, "Anything Goes in Grants Fight," *National Journal,* April 2, 1988, 900–901.

26. For background on this controversy, see Ann Markusen and Jerry Fastrup, "The Regional War for Federal Aid," *The Public Interest* 53 (Fall 1978): 87–99.

27. For an interesting look at these regional debates, see Dick Kirschten, "Formula Friction," *National Journal,* February 2, 1991, 272–273. The quotations from senators

Gramm, Dixon, and Moynihan are taken from that piece.

28. Quoted in John Rehfuss, *The Job of the Public Manager* (Chicago: Dorsey, 1989), 154.

29. For an excellent discussion of this issue, see Sarah F. Liebschutz, "The National Minimum Drinking-Age Law," Publius: *The Journal of Federalism* 15 (Summer 1985): 39–51.

30. Quoted in *Congressional Quarterly Weekly Reports*, June 30, 1984, 1557.

31. *Congressional Record*, 98th Cong., 2nd sess., 1984.

32. Ibid.

33. President Ronald Reagan, "Remarks on Signing H.R. 4614 into Law," July 17, 1984.

34. Charles Corker, "Water Rights and Federalism: The Western Water Rights Settlement Bill of 1957," *California Law Review* 45 (December, 1957), 604.

35. Quoted in Daniel McCool, *Command of the Waters* (Berkeley: University of California Press, 1987), 19.

36. Quoted ibid., 22.

37. Quoted in Richard D. Lamm and Michael McCarthy, *The Angry West* (Boston: Houghton Mifflin, 1982), 192.

38. Quoted in *Congressional Quarterly Weekly Reports*, March 29, 1986, 713.

39. McCool, *Command of the Waters*, 218.

Chapter 4   Civil Rights and Liberties

1. *Roe v. Wade*, 410 U.S. 113 (1973). For further discussion of the abortion controversy, see Barbara Craig and David M. O'Brien, *Abortion and American Politics* (Chatham, N.J.: Chatham House, 1993).

2. *Barron v. Baltimore*, 32 U.S. 243 (1833).

3. On the debate over whether the Fourteenth Amendment was intended to apply to the states, see Horace E. Flack, *The Adoption of the Fourteenth Amendment* (Baltimore, Md.: Johns Hopkins University Press, Baltimore, Md.: 1908); Charles Fairman, *Reconstruction and Reunion, 1864–88* (New York: Macmillan, 1971); and Raoul Berger, *Government by Judiciary*

(Cambridge, Mass.: Harvard University Press, 1977).

4. *Gitlow v. New York*, 268 U.S. 652 (1925).

5. For an excellent history of the nationalization of the Bill of Rights, see Richard C. Cortner, *The Supreme Court and the Second Bill of Rights: The Fourteenth Amendment and the Nationalization of Civil Liberties* (Madison: University of Wisconsin Press, 1981).

6. "Text of 96 Congressmen's Declaration on Integration," *New York Times,* March 12, 1956, A19. (Five Congressmen later joined the manifesto as well.)

7. *Joint Anti-Fascist Refugee Committee v. McGrath*, 341 U.S. 123 (1951).

8. *Rochin v. California*, 341 U.S. 165 (1952).

9. *Connolly v. General Construction Co.*, 269 U.S. 385 (1976).

10. See, for example, *Goldberg v. Kelly*, 397 U.S. 254 (1970); *In re Ruffalo*, 390 U.S. 544 (1968); *Goss v. Lopez*, 419 U.S. 565 (1975); and *Memphis Light, Gas & Water Division v. Craft*, 436 U.S. 1 (1978).

11. See *Gray v. Mississippi*, 107 S.Ct. 2045 (1987); and *Rose v. Clark*, 106 S.Ct. 3101 (1986).

12. *Griswold v. Connecticut*, 391 U.S. 145 (1965).

13. *DeShaney v. Winnebago County Department of Social Services*, 109 S.Ct. 998 (1989).

14. Quoted in *Frank v. Maryland*, 359 U.S. 360, 378 (1959).

15. *California v. Hodari D.*, 111 S.Ct. 1547 (1991).

16. *National Treasury Employees Union v. Von Raab*, 489 U.S. 656 (1989).

17. *Skinner v. Railway Labor Executives' Association*, 489 U.S. 602 (1989).

18. *Olmstead v. United States*, 277 U.S. 438 (1928).

19. *Katz v. United States*, 389 U.S. 347 (1967).

20. *Escobedo v. Illinois*, 378 U.S. 478 (1964).

21. *Gideon v. Wainwright*, 372 U.S. 335 (1963).

22. *Miranda v. Arizona*, 384 U.S. 436 (1966).

23. For further discussion of rulings that have cut back or refused to extend the *Miranda* ruling, see David

M. O'Brien, *Constitutional Law and Politics*, vol. 2, *Civil Rights and Civil Liberties* (New York: Norton, 1991), 937–969.

24. Jerome Frank, *Courts on Trial* (Princeton, N.J.: Princeton University Press, 1949), 80 (quoting Macaulay, a legal scholar).

25. *Michigan v. Lucas*, 111 S.Ct. 1743 (1991).

26. *White v. Illinois*, 112 S.Ct. 736 (1992).

27. *Chandler v. Florida*, 449 U.S. 560 (1981).

28. *Nebraska Press Association v. Stuart*, 427 U.S. 539 (1976); and *Seattle Times Co. v. Rhinehart*, 104 S.Ct. 2199 (1984).

29. See, for example, *Georgia v. McCollum*, 112 S.Ct. 2348 (1992).

30. *Williams v. Florida*, 399 U.S. 78 (1970) (criminal cases); and *Colegrove v. Batten*, 413 U.S. 149 (1973) (civil cases).

31. *Burch v. Louisiana*, 441 U.S. 130 (1979) (unanimity required in six-member juries in criminal cases); and *Johnson v. Louisiana*, 406 U.S. 356 (1972) (approval of nonunanimous verdicts).

32. *Rummel v. Estelle*, 445 U.S. 263 (1980).

33. *Solem v. Helm*, 463 U.S. 277 (1983).

34. *Furman v. Georgia*, 408 U.S. 238 (1972).

35. See *Gregg v. Georgia*, 428 U.S. 153 (1976); and cases discussed in O'Brien, supra note 23, 1074–1145.

36. *Griffin v. Illinois*, 360 U.S. 252 (1959).

37. *Ake v. Oklahoma*, 105 S.Ct. 1087 (1985).

38. *Bounds v. Smith*, 430 U.S. 817 (1977).

39. See *Tate v. Short*, 401 U.S. 395 (1971); and *Williams v. Illinois*, 399 U.S. 235 (1970).

40. *Olmstead v. United States*, 277 U.S. 438, 478 (1928) (Brandeis, J. dis. op.).

41. See *National Association for the Advancement of Colored People v. Alabama*, 357 U.S. 449 (1958).

42. *Bowers v. Hardwick*, 478 U.S. 186 (1986).

43. See *Pacific Mutual Life Insurance Company v. Haslip*, 111 S.Ct. 1032 (1991).

44. *Nollan v. California Coastal Com-*

mission, 483 U.S. 825 (1987); also see *Lucas v. South Carolina Coastal Commission*, 112 S.Ct. 2886 (1992).

45. *West Virginia State Board of Education v. Barnette*, 319 U.S. 624 (1943).

46. Edward White, "The Supreme Court of the United States," 7 *American Bar Association Journal* (1921), 341.

Chapter 5   Issues of Freedom and Equality

1. *Texas v. Johnson*, 491 U.S. 397 (1989).

2. Quoted in David M. O'Brien, *Storm Center: The Supreme Court in American Politics*, 3rd ed. (New York: Norton, 1993), 124.

3. *United States v. Eichman*, 110 S.Ct. 2404 (1990).

4. *Everson v. Board of Education of Ewing Township*, 330 U.S. 1 (1947).

5. See Walter Berns, *The First Amendment and the Future of American Democracy* (New York: Basic Books, 1976), ch. 1.

6. *Engel v. Vitale*, 370 U.S. 421 (1962); and *Abington School District v. Schempp*, 374 U.S. 203 (1963).

7. *Wallace v. Jaffree*, 472 U.S. 38 (1985).

8. *Lynch v. Donnelly*, 465 U.S. 668 (1984).

9. *County of Allegheny v. American Civil Liberties Union Greater Pittsburgh Chapter*, 109 S.Ct. 3086 (1989).

10. *Lee v. Weisman*, 112 S.Ct. 2649 (1992).

11. *Witters v. Washington Department of Services for the Blind*, 474 U.S. 481 (1986).

12. *Reynolds v. United States*, 98 U.S. 145 (1879).

13. *Wisconsin v. Yoder*, 406 U.S. 208 (1972).

14. *Employment Division, Department of Human Resources of Oregon v. Smith*, 110 S.Ct. 1595 (1990).

15. *West Virginia State Board of Education v. Barnette*, 319 U.S. 624 (1943).

16. *New York Times v. Sullivan*, 376 U.S. 254 (1964).

17. *Gitlow v. New York*, 268 U.S. 652 (1925).

18. *Schenck v. United States*, 249 U.S. 47 (1919).

19. *Dennis v. United States*, 341 U.S. 494 (1951).

20. *Smith v. California*, 361 U.S. 147 (1959).

21. See, for example, *Yates v. United States*, 356 U.S. 363 (1957) (overturning the convictions of six functionaries of the American Communist party under the Smith Act); and *Scales v. United States*, 367 U.S. 203 (1961) (limiting prosecutions under the Smith Act to only those who are shown to have "a specific intent to bring about violent overthrow" of the government).

22. *Brandenburg v. Ohio*, 395 U.S. 444 (1969).

23. *New York Times Company v. United States*, 403 U.S. 670 (1971).

24. *R.A.V. v. City of St. Paul, Minnesota*, 112 S.Ct. 2538 (1992).

25. *Chaplinsky v. New Hampshire*, 315 U.S. 568 (1942).

26. *Roth v. United States*, 354 U.S. 476 (1957).

27. *Miller v. California*, 413 U.S. 15 (1973).

28. See *Cohen v. California*, 403 U.S. 15 (1971).

29. *Bethel School District No. 403 v. Fraser*, 106 S.Ct. 3159 (1986).

30. *New York v. Ferber*, 458 U.S. 747 (1982).

31. *California v. LaRue*. 409 U.S. 109 (1972).; and *City of Newport, Kentucky v. Iacobucci*, 107 U.S. 383 (1986).

32. *Renton v. Playtime Theatres*, 475 U.S. 41 (1986).

33. *Federal Communications Commission v. Pacifica Foundation*, 438 U.S. 726 (1978).

34. *New York Times v. Sullivan*, 376 U.S. 254 (1964).

35. *Hustler Magazine v. Falwell*, 485 U.S. 46 (1988).

36. See *Pacific Gas & Electric v. Public Utilities Commission of California*, 475 U.S. 1 (1986).

37. *Tinker v. Des Moines Independent Community School District*, 393 U.S. 503 (1969).

38. *Stromberg v. California*, 283 U.S. 359 (1931).

39. *Spence v. Washington*, 418 U.S. 405 (1974).

40. *Brown v. Socialist Worker '74 Campaign Committee*, 459 U.S. 87 (1982).

41. *Gibson v. Florida Legislative Investigating Committee*, 371 U.S. 539 (1963).

42. *Elfbrandt v. Russell*, 384 U.S. 11 (1966).

43. *Application of Stolar*, 401 U.S. 23 (1971).

44. *United States v. Harris*, 347 U.S. 612 (1954).

45. *Minor v. Happersett*, 88 U.S. 162 (1875).

46. *Baker v. Carr*, 369 U.S. 186 (1962).

47. *Plessy v. Ferguson*, 163 U.S. 537 (1896).

48. *Brown v. Board of Education of Topeka*, 347 U.S. 483 (1954).

49. *Brown v. Board of Education of Topeka*, 349 U.S. 294 (1955).

50. *Alexander v. Holmes County Board of Education*, 396 U.S. 19 (1969).

51. *Milliken v. Bradley*, 418 U.S. 717 (1974).

52. *Freeman v. Pitts*, 112 S.Ct. 1430 (1992). Also see *Board of Education of Oklahoma City Public Schools v. Dowell*, 111 S.Ct. 630 (1991).

53. *United States v. Fordice*, 112 S.Ct. 2727 (1992).

54. *Rostker v. Goldberg*, 453 U.S. 57 (1981).

55. *Michael M. v. Superior Court*, 450 U.S. 464 (1981).

56. *Dothard v. Rawlinson*, 433 U.S. 321 (1977).

57. *Geduldig v. Aiello*, 417 U.S. 484 (1974).

58. *Frontiero v. Richardson*, 411 U.S. 677 (1973).

59. *Craig v. Boren*, 429 U.S. 190 (1976).

60. *Nashville Gas Co. v. Satty*, 434 U.S. 136 (1977).

61. *International Union, Automobile Workers, Aerospace, Agricultural Implement Workers of America, UAW v. Johnson Controls, Inc.*, 111 S.Ct. 1196 (1991).

62. *Gregory v. Ashcroft*, 111 S.Ct. 2395 (1991).

63. *Plessy v. Ferguson*, 163 U.S. 537 (1896).

64. *Regents of the University of California v. Bakke*, 438 U.S. 265 (1978).

65. *City of Richmond v. J. A. Croson*, 488 U.S. 469 (1989).

66. *Metro Broadcasting, Inc v. Federal Communications Commission*, 110 S.Ct. 2997 (1990).

67. Overturning *Wards Cove Packing Co. v. Atonio*, 490 U.S. 642 (1989),

which had reversed an earlier ruling and had shifted to employees the burden of proving that an employer's hiring practices had a discriminatory impact.

68. Overturning *Patterson v. McLean Credit Union,* 491 U.S. 164 (1989).

69. Overturning *Equal Employment Opportunity Commission v. Arabian American Oil,* 11 S.Ct. 1227 (1991).

70. Overturning *Price Waterhouse v. Hopkins,* 490 U.S. 228 (1989); and *West Virginia University Hospitals v. Casey,* 111 S.Ct. 1138 (1991).

71. Overturning *Lorance v. AT&T,* 490 U.S. 900 (1989); and Martin v. Wilks, 490 U.S. 755 (1989).

Chapter 6   Political Socialization and Participation

1. Doris Kearns, *Lyndon Johnson and the American Dream* (New York: New American Library, 1976), 38–39.

2. On research in political socialization, see *Handbook of Political Socialization,* ed. Stanley Allen Renshon (New York: Free Press, 1977).

3. David O. Sears, "Political Socialization," in *Handbook of Political Science,* ed. Fred I. Greenstein and Nelson Polsby (Reading, Mass.: Addison-Wesley, 1975), 102.

4. Roberta S. Sigel, "The Case for Educating for Gender Equality," in *Political Socialization, Citizenship Education, and Democracy,* ed. Orit Ichilov (New York: Teachers College Press, 1990), 243–265.

5. M. Kent Jennings and Richard G. Niemi, "Patterns of Political Learning," in *Political Opinion and Behavior,* ed. Edward C. Dreyer and Walter A. Rosenbaum (North Scituate, Mass.: Duxbury, 1976), 80–97; and Martin P. Wattenberg, *The Decline of American Political Parties* (Cambridge, Mass.: Harvard University Press, 1984).

6. Fred I. Greenstein, *Children and Politics* (New Haven, Conn.: Yale University Press, 1984).

7. Jennings and Niemi, "Patterns of Political Learning."

8. See Michael X. Delli Carpini, *Stability and Change in American Politics* (New York: New York University Press, 1986).

9. Stephen Earl Bennett, *Apathy in America, 1960–1984: Causes and Consequences of Citizen Political Indifference* (Dobbs Ferry, N.Y.: Transnational, 1986).

10. For a discussion of different explanations of the socialization process, see David O. Sears, "Whither Political Socialization Research? The Question of Persistence," in *Political Socialization, Citizenship Education, and Democracy,* 69–97.

11. R. W. Connell, "Political Socialization in the American Family: The Evidence Re-Examined:" *Public Opinion Quarterly* 36 (1972): 330.

12. Bryant Robey, *The American People: A Timely Exploration of a Changing America and the Important New Demographic Trends Around Us* (New York: Dutton, 1985), 55.

13. M. Kent Jennings, Kenneth P. Langton, and Richard G. Niemi, "Effects of the High School Civics Curriculum" in *The Political Character of Adolescence,* ed. M. Kent Jennings and Richard G. Niemi (Princeton, N.J.: Princeton University Press, 1974), 181–206.

14. M. Kent Jennings, Lee H. Ehman, and Richard G. Niemi, "Social Studies Teachers and Their Pupils," in *The Political Character of Adolescence,* 207–228.

15. Frank P. Scioli and Thomas J. Cook, "Political Socialization Research in the United States: A Review," in *Political Attitudes and Public Opinion,* ed. Dan D. Nimmo and Charles M. Bonjean (New York: McKay, 1972), 154–174.

16. Bennett, *Apathy in America,* 78.

17. Theodore M. Newcomb, *Persistence and Change: Bennington College and Its Students After Twenty-five Years* (New York: Wiley, 1967).

18. Renshon, *Handbook of Political Socialization,* 133; and Kenneth B. Clark, *Dark Ghetto* (New York: Harper & Row, 1965), 63–64.

19. W. Russell Newman, "Television and the American Culture: The Mass Medium and the Pluralist Audience," *Public Opinion Quarterly* 46 (1982): 471.

20. Virginia Mansfield, "Issues: A Look at Television's Non-Viewers," *Washington Post,* March 15, 1983, 65.

21. "Who Gets News from TV—And Who Does Not," *U.S. News and World Report,* February 21, 1983, 52.

22. See, for example, Douglas Kellner, *Television and the Crisis of Democracy* (Boulder, Colo.: Westview, 1990).

23. Paul C. Light, *Baby Boomers* (New York: Norton, 1988), 125.

24. E. J. Dionne, *Why Americans Hate Politics* (New York: Simon and Schuster, 1991), 17.

25. See Jane Dick, *Volunteers and the Making of Presidents* (New York: Dodd, Mead, 1980).

26. See, for example, Bennett, *Apathy in America,* 63–70.

27. See Samuel L. Popkin, *The Reasoning Voter: Communication and Persuasion in Presidential Campaigns* (Chicago: University of Chicago Press, 1991).

28. Norman H. Nie and Sidney Verba, "Political Participation," in *Handbook of Political Science,* 24–25.

29. Ibid., 27.

30. Sidney Verba and Norman H. Nie, *Participation in America: Political Democracy and Social Equality* (New York: Harper & Row, 1972).

31. M. Kent Jennings, "Gender Roles and Inequalities in Political Participation: Results from an Eight-Nation Study," *Western Political Quarterly* 36 (September 1983): 367.

32. See, for example, Verba and Nie, *Participation in America,* 284–285.

Chapter 7   Public Opinion

1. Gallup poll of 5,000 adults conducted for *Newsweek* on June 23, 1989, as reported in *Newsweek* July 3, 1989, 18.

2. James N. Rosenau, ed., *Public Opinion and Foreign Policy* (New York: Random House, 1961), 34–35.

3. Herbert McClosky, "Consensus and Ideology in American Politics," *American Political Science Review* 58 (June 1964): 363; and Herbert McClosky and Alida Brill, *Dimensions of Tolerance* (New York: Russell Sage, 1983), 239.

4. The discussion that follows on the history and mechanics of polling is drawn primarily from Stephen J. Wayne, *The Road to the White*

House, 1992, 4th ed. (New York: St. Martin's 1992), 246–250

5. Steven J. Rosenstone, *Forecasting Presidential Elections* (New Haven, Conn.: Yale University Press, 1983), 24.

6. Ibid., 27–28.

7. The Gallup Poll, November 1992, unnumbered cover.

8. Angus Campbell, Philip E. Converse, Warren E. Miller, and Donald E. Stokes, *The American Voter* (New York: Wiley, 1960), 249.

9. Norman H. Nie and Kristi Anderson, "Mass Belief Systems Revisited: Political Change and Attitude Structure," *Journal of Politics* 36 (September 1974), 541–591.

10. In 1988, approximately 80 percent of people who identified themselves as conservative supported Bush, and a similar percentage of self-identified liberals supported Dukakis. In 1992, although the candidacy of independent H. Ross Perot reduced these percentages, 68 percent of the liberals voted for Clinton, while 64 percent of the conservatives cast their ballots for Bush, according to the large exit poll conducted for the major news networks on election day.

11. Kathleen Knight, "Ideology in the 1980 Election: Political Sophistication Matters," *Journal of Politics* 47 (August 1985): 828–853.

12. Political scientists have found a strong association between political efficacy and political participation. Naturally, people who believe that they can make a difference have more incentive to get involved than those who feel powerless. See Sidney Verba and Norman H. Nie, *Participation in America* (New York: Harper & Row, 1972).

13. Martin B. Abravnel and Ronald J. Busch, "Political Competence, Political Trust, and the Action Orientation of University Students," *Journal of Politics* 37 (February 1975), 57–82; and Joel Aberbach and Jack L. Walker, "Political Trust and Racial Ideology," *American Political Science Review* 64 (December 1970): 1199–1219.

14. James W. Prothro and Charles M. Gregg, "Fundamental Principles of Democracy: Bases of Agreement and Disagreement," *Journal of Politics* 22 (May 1960): 276–294. Also

see McClosky, "Consensus and Ideology"; and McClosky and Brill, *Dimensions of Tolerance.*

15. John Muller, "Trends in Political Tolerance," *Public Opinion Quarterly* 52 (Spring 1988): 1–25; and Paul R. Abramson, *Political Attitudes in America* (San Francisco: Freeman, 1983). For a summary of this literature, see Robert Erikson, Norman Luttbeg, and Kent L. Tedin, *American Public Opinion: Its Origins, Content, and Impact* (New York: Macmillan, 1991), 109–112.

16. McClosky, "Consensus and Ideology"; McClosky and Brill, *Dimensions of Tolerance;* Clyde Z. Nunn, Harry J. Crockett, Jr., and J. Allen Williams, Jr., *Tolerance for Nonconformity* (San Francisco: Jossey-Bass, 1978); and James L. Gibson and Richard D. Bingham, *Civil Liberties and the Nazis: The Skokie Free-Speech Controversy* (New York: Praeger, 1985).

17. This position is well stated in Stephen Earl Bennett, "'Know-Nothings' Revisited: The Meaning of Political Ignorance Today," *Social Science Quarterly* 69 (June 1988): 476–490.

18. The seminal work on the authoritarian personality is Theodore Adorno, E. Frankel-Brunswik, D. J. Levinson, and R. N. Sanford, *The Authoritarian Personality* (New York: Harper, 1950). For a more contemporary discussion of this topic, see Fred I. Greenstein, Personality and Politics (Chicago: Markham, 1969).

19. Benjamin I. Page and Robert Y. Shapiro, "Effects of Public Opinion on Policy," *American Political Science Review* 77 (March 1983): 175–190; and Gerald C. Wright, Jr., Robert S. Erikson, and John P. McIver, "Public Opinion and Policy Liberalism in the American States," *American Journal of Political Science* 31 (November 1987): 980–1001.

20. Erikson, Luttbeg, and Tedin, *American Public Opinion,* 332.

Chapter 8   Political Interest Groups

1. Jimmy Carter, *Why Not the Best?* (New York: Bantam, 1975), 4.

2. Truman's theory was built on the writings of another student of social

and political movements, Arthur F. Bentley, who in *The Process of Government* (1908) was the first to study group behavior systematically.

3. David B. Truman, *The Governmental Process* (New York: Knopf, 1960).

4. Ibid., 97.

5. Mancur Olson, Jr., *The Logic of Collective Action* (New York: Schocken, 1968).

6. Robert H. Salisbury, "An Exchange Theory of Interest Groups," *Midwest Journal of Political Science* 13 (February 1969): 1–32.

7. Jack L. Walker, "The Origins and Maintenance of Interest Groups in America," *American Political Science Review* 77 (June 1983): 390–406.

8. Ibid., 403.

9. Ibid., 394.

10. Mark P. Petracca, "The Rediscovery of Interest Group Politics," in *The Politics of Interests,* ed. Mark P. Petracca (Boulder, Colo.: Westview, 1992), 14.

11. *The Washington Representatives* (Washington, D.C.: Columbia Books, 1992), 3.

12. *The Washington Representatives,* 3–4.

13. Jonathan Rauch, "The Parasite Economy," *National Journal,* April 25, 1992), 982.

14. For an excellent discussion of the increasing importance of the monitoring function, see Robert H. Salisbury, "The Paradox of Interest Groups in Washington—More Groups, Less Clout," in *The New American Political System,* 2nd ed., ed. Anthony King (Washington, D.C. AEI Press, 1990), 203–230.

15. Edward O. Laumann and David Knoke, *The Organizational State: Social Choice in National Policy Domains* (Madison: University of Wisconsin Press, 1987), 3.

16. *Encyclopedia of Associations* (Detroit: Gale Research, 1991).

17. Federal law limits PAC contributions to $5,000 per candidate per election. This means that a PAC can give a congressional candidate up to $5,000 in a primary and up to another $5,000 in a general election.

18. This is known as independent spending. Federal law prohibits PACs from coordinating this spend-

ing with a candidate's campaign committee.

19. Common Cause, "News Release," March 12, 1993.

20. James A. Barnes, "Sticky Wicket," *National Journal* 25 (May 8, 1993), 1109.

21. Charles R. Babcock, "Buying Access to Congress: How a Company Pays to 'Tell Our Story,'" *Washington Post,* June 8, 1992, A17.

22. Frank J. Sorauf, *Money in American Elections* (Glenview, Ill.: Scott, Foresman, 1988), 314.

23. Richard L. Hall and Frank W. Wayman, "Buying Time: Moneyed Interests and the Mobilization of Bias in Congressional Committees," *American Political Science Review* 84 (September 1990): 814.

24. This statement was made to one of the authors (Stephen J. Wayne) by Tom Korologus, president of Timmons and Company, one of the most powerful legislative lobbying firms in Washington. Korologus has also worked in the White House as a lobbyist for the president.

25. Hedrick Smith, *The Power Game* (New York: Ballantine Books, 1988), 242–244.

26. Richard Viguerie, as quoted in Burdett A. Loomis, "A New Era: Groups and the Grass Roots," in *Interest Group Politics,* ed. Allan J. Cigler and Burdett A. Loomis (Washington, D.C.: Congressional Quarterly, 1983), 172.

27. John T. Tierney, "Organized Interests and the Nation's Capitol," in *The Politics of Interests,* 207.

28. Members of Congress must now donate their honoraria to charity.

29. Gary Lee, "Trade, National Security and the Revolving door," *Washington Post,* April 13, 1992, A19.

30. Stephen Engelberg and Martin Tolchin, "Foreigners Find New Ally in U.S. Industry," *New York Times,* November 2, 1993, B8.

31. E. E. Schattschneider, *The Semisovereign People: A Realist's View of Democracy* (Hinsdale, Ill.: Dryden, 1960), 34–35.

32. Ibid., 30–35.

Chapter 9 Political Parties

1. Jefferson's Republicans were not the forerunners of the modern Republican party, which was organized in 1854 and nominated its first presidential candidate in 1856. Democrats, however, claim Jefferson as their first president and trace their party's origins to the Democratic-Republican party at the end of the eighteenth century.

2. This is the only time a tie occurred. Upon taking office, Jefferson and his supporters proposed a constitutional amendment that required electors to cast separate ballots for president and vice president. The Twelfth Amendment was ratified in 1804.

3. For a more extended discussion of the creation of the American party system, see William Nisbet Chambers, *Political Parties in a New Nation: The American Experience, 1776–1809.* (New York: Oxford University Press, 1963). Another helpful interpretation of the beginning of parties in the United States can be found in Wilbred E. Binkley, *American Political Parties: Their National History* (New York: Knopf, 1959).

4. Richard P. McCormick, *The Second American Party System: Party Formation in the Jacksonian Era* (Chapel Hill: University of North Carolina Press, 1966).

5. For an extended discussion of voter turnout during this and subsequent periods, see Walter Dean Burnham, "The Turnout Problem," in *Elections American Style,* ed. A. James Reichley (Washington, D.C.: Brookings Institution, 1987), 112–133.

6. Contemporary trends are discussed in Martin P. Wattenberg, "From a Partisan to Candidate-centered Electorate," in *The New American Political System,* 2nd version, ed. Anthony King (Washington, D.C.: American Enterprise Institute, 1990), 139–174; also see Thomas E. Cavanagh and James L. Sundquist, "The New Two Party System," in *The New Directions in American Politics,* ed. John E. Chubb and Paul E. Peterson (Washington, D.C.: Brookings Institution, 1985), 33–68.

7. In *An Economic Theory of Democracy* (New York: HarperCollins, 1957), Anthony Downs provides a logical explanation for the "mainstream" phenomenon.

8. For a history of the Republican and Democratic national committees, see Ralph M. Goldman, *The National Party Chairmen and Committees* (Armonk, N.Y.: Sharpe, 1990).

9. Federal Election Commission, "Press Release," December 14, 1992, 2–3.

10. Ibid.

11. For an excellent discussion of the strengthening of national party organizations in their campaign activities, see Paul S. Herrnson, *Party Campaigning in the 1980s* (Cambridge, Mass.: Harvard University Press, 1988).

12. See John F. Bibby, Cornelius P. Cotter, James L. Gibson, and Robert J. Huckshorn, "Parties in State Politics," in *Politics in the American States: A Comparative Analysis,* ed. Virginia Gray, Herbert Jacob, and Robert B. Albritton (Glenview, Ill.: Scott, Foresman/Little, Brown, 1990), 108–111.

13. James L. Gibson, Cornelius Cotter, John F. Bibby, and Robert J. Huckshorn, "Assessing Party Organizational Strength," *American Journal of Political Science* 17 (May 1983): 193–222.

14. John F. Bibby, *Politics, Parties, and Elections in America,* 2nd ed. (Chicago: Nelson-Hall, 1992), 104.

15. Ibid., 98.

16. For a good study of trends in state parties, see Robert J. Huckshorn and John F. Bibby, "State Parties in an Era of Political Change," in *The Future of American Political Parties,* ed. Joel L. Fleishman (Englewood Cliffs, N.J.: Prentice-Hall, 1982), 70–100.

17. The most comprehensive study of local parties, primarily at the county level, was conducted in 1979–1980 and reported in James L. Gibson, Cornelius P. Cotter, John F. Bibby, and Robert J. Huckshorn, "Whither the Local Parties? A Cross-sectional and Longitudinal Analysis of the Strength of Party Organizations," *American Journal of Political Science* 29 (February 1985): 139–160.

18. V. O. Key, Jr., *American State Politics: An Introduction* (New York: Knopf, 1956), 107–111; and Sarah M. Morehouse, *State Politics, Parties and Policy* (New York: Holt,

Rinehart and Winston, 1981), 180–183.

19. This discussion is based on Stephen J. Wayne, *The Road to the White House, 1992* (New York: St. Martin's, 1992), 72–80.

20. Paul R. Abramson, John H. Aldrich, and David W. Rohde, *Change and Continuity in the 1988 Elections* (Washington, D.C.: Congressional Quarterly, 1990), 123–126.

21. Gerald M. Pomper with Susan S. Lederman, *Elections in America* (White Plains, N.Y.: Longman, 1980), 161.

22. Jeff Fishel, *President and Promises* (Washington, D.C.: Congressional Quarterly, 1985), 38.

23. Ibid., 42–43.

24. For a discussion of the concept of responsible party government, see Committee on Political Parties of the American Political Science Association, *Toward a More Responsible Two-Party System* (New York: Holt, Rinehart and Winston, 1950); and Austin Ranney, *The Doctrine of Responsible Party Government* (Urbana: University of Illinois Press, 1962).

25. Parties tend to divide most sharply on the issues that underlie recent election campaigns and their platform positions. Jerome M. Clubb and Santa A. Traugott, "Partisan Cleavage and Cohesion in the House of Representatives," *Journal of Interdisciplinary History* 7 (Winter 1977): 374–401.

26. David W. Rohde, "'The Reports of My Death Are Greatly Exaggerated': Parties and Party Voting in the House of Representatives," in *Changing Perspectives on Congress*, ed. Glenn R. Parker (Knoxville: University of Tennessee Press, 1990); and Malcolm E. Jewell and David M. Olson, *Political Parties and Elections in American States* (Chicago: Dorsey, 1988), 246–249.

27. "Proportion of Partisan Roll Calls," *Congressional Quarterly,* December 19, 1992, 3906.

28. Ibid., "Party-Unity Average Scores," 3905.

29. Randall L. Calvert and John A. Ferejohn, "Coattail Voting in Recent Presidential Elections," *American Political Science Review* 77 (June 1983): 407–419; and John A. Ferejohn and Randall L. Calvert,

"Perspective," *American Journal of Political Science* 28 (February 1984): 164–183.

30. Paul Allen Beck and Frank J. Sorauf, *Party Politics in America,* 7th ed. (New York: HarperCollins, 1992), 423.

31. This subject is discussed for federal judges in Robert A. Carp and Ronald Stidham, *The Federal Courts* (Washington, D.C.: Congressional Quarterly, 1985), 142–148; also see Craig Ducat and Robert L. Dudley, "Federal District Judges and Presidential Power During the Postwar Era," *Journal of Politics* 51 (February 1989): 98–118. An examination of the influence of party on state judges can be found in Stuart Nagel, "Political Party Affiliation and Judges' Decision," *American Political Science Review* 55 (December 1961): 843–850; and David W. Adamany, "The Party Variable in Judges' Voting: Conceptual Notes and a Case Study," *American Political Science Review* 63 (March 1969): 57–83.

Chapter 10   Elections

1. For all practical purposes, people are deemed to be responsible for their own actions if they are 18 years of age or older and are mentally competent. In some states, individuals who have been convicted of a felony or dishonorably discharged from the military may not vote.

2. If the percentage of eligible voters who actually vote in the United States is compared with that of twenty-one other democratic countries, the United States ranks twentieth; if, however, the percentage of *registered voters* who actually vote is the basis of comparison, the United States ranks eleventh out of twenty-four. See David P. Glass, Peverill Squire, and Raymond E. Wolfinger, "Voter Turnout: An International Comparison," *Public Opinion* 6 (December–January 1984): 49–55.

3. Raymond E. Wolfinger and Steven J. Rosenstone, *Who Votes?* (New

Haven, Conn.: Yale University Press, 1980), 73.

4. For an extended discussion of the history of campaign finance, see Herbert E. Alexander, *Financing Politics: Money, Elections, and Political Reform* (Washington, D.C.: Congressional Quarterly, 1984), 1–54.

5. Presidential candidates who accept federal funds are limited to a $5,000 personal contribution or loan to their own campaign.

6. Federal Election Commission, "Record," vol. 19, no. 2 (February 1993), 4–5.

7. Angus Campbell, Philip E. Converse, Warren E. Miller, and Donald E. Stokes, *The American Voter* (New York: Wiley, 1960), 101–107.

8. Ibid., 96–101.

9. Wolfinger and Rosenstone, *Who Votes?* 13–26.

10. Ibid., 18–20, 35–36.

11. Paul R. Abramson, John H. Aldrich, and David W. Rohde, *Change and Continuity in the 1988 Elections* (Washington, D.C.: Congressional Quarterly, 1990), 105.

12. James A. Barnes, "Tainted Triumph?" *National Journal,* November 7, 1992, 2539.

13. Besides, Teixeira notes, "it is a great deal easier to change an election by switching the preferences of existing voters than by adding new voters." Ruy A. Teixeira, "What If We Had an Election and Everybody Came?" *The American Enterprise* 3 (July-August 1992): 55.

14. This theory was first postulated in the classic study by Campbell et al., *The American Voter.*

15. William H. Flanagan and Nancy H. Zingale, *Political Behavior of the American Electorate,* 7th ed. (Washington, D.C.: Congressional Quarterly, 1991), 49–54.

16. Campbell et al., *The American Voter,* 133–136. Party identification is determined by asking the following question: "Generally speaking, do you usually think of yourself as a Republican, a Democrat, an Independent, or what?"

17. The theory of cross pressures was first advanced by Paul Lazarsfeld, Bernard Berelson, and Hazel Gaudet in *The People Choice* (New York: Columbia University Press,

1944). Also see Bernard Berelson, Paul Lazarsfeld, and William McPhee, *Voting* (Chicago: University of Chicago Press, 1954).

18. Of the Democrats who supported Ronald Reagan in 1984, 56 percent voted for Bill Clinton in 1992, compared with 23 percent for George Bush and 21 percent for H. Ross Perot. "Exit Poll," *USA Today,* November 4, 1992, 6A.

19. Flanagan and Zingale, *Political Behavior of the American Electorate,* 124.

20. Morris Fiorina, *Retrospective Voting in American National Elections* (New Haven, Conn.: Yale University Press, 1981), 65–83.

21. "Primary Turnout: Ups and Downs," *Congressional Quarterly,* July 4, 1992, 71; and "1992 Republican Primary Turnout," *Congressional Quarterly,* August 8, 1992, 67.

22. John S. Jackson, Barbara Brown, and David Bositis, "Herbert McClosky and Friends Revisited: 1980 Democratic and Republican Party Elites Compared to the Mass Public," *American Politics Quarterly* 10 (1982): 158–180; and Martin Plissner and Warren J. Mitofsky, "The Making of the Delegates, 1968–1988," *Public Opinion* 3 (September-October 1988): 46.

23. The Equal Rights Amendment prohibited all discrimination on the basis of gender. It failed to achieve ratification. In the 1980s, Republican platforms opposed the amendment, and Democratic platforms supported it.

24. A few caucuses and primaries in the smaller states are held in February. Officially, the nominations begin on the first Tuesday in March and end on the first Tuesday in June.

25. Buchanan's speech backfired on the Republicans. Although it was well received by most of those attending the convention, the public perceived the speech as too shrill, too ideological, and too negative. Its right-wing rhetoric and policy views enabled critics to assert that the Republican party had been taken over by conservative extremists.

26. For an excellent study of the impact of media on modern conventions, see Byron E. Shafer, *Bifurcated Politics: Evolution and Reform in the National Party Convention* (Cambridge, Mass.: Harvard University Press, 1988).

27. Thomas E. Patterson, *The Mass Media Election* (New York: Praeger, 1980), 72–74.

28. Ibid., 103.

29. In Maine and Nebraska, one elector is chosen in each state congressional district, and two electors are selected at large; thus, in these states a divided electoral vote is possible.

30. There is a substantial literature on the impact of inter- and intra-party competition on the electoral system. See, for example, John F. Bibby, Cornelius P. Cotter, James L. Gibson, and Robert J. Huckshorn, "Parties in State Politics," in *Politics in the American States,* 5th ed., ed. Virginia Gray, Herbert Jacob, and Robert B. Albritton (Glenview, Ill.: Scott, Foresman, 1990); Samuel J. Eldersveld, *Political Parties in American Society* (New York: Basic Books, 1982). 35–36; and James D. King, "Interparty Competition in the American States: An Examination of Index Components," *Western Political Quarterly* 42 (1989): 83–92.

31. Flanagan and Zingale, *Political Behavior of the American Electorate,* 14.

32. Phil Duncan, "Majority Minority Mandate Will Reshape the House," *Congressional Quarterly,* December 21, 1991, 3689.

33. There is a wealth of literature on reapportionment and redistricting. For the political ramifications, see Robert S. Erikson, "The Partisan Impact of State Legislative Reapportionment," *Midwest Journal of Political Science* 15 (1971): 57–71; Timothy G. O'Rourke, *The Impact of Reapportionment* (New Brunswick, N.J.: Transaction, 1980); Amihai Glazer, Bernard Grofman, and Marc Robbins, "Partisan and Incumbency Effects of 1970s Congressional Redistricting," *American Journal of Political Science* 31 (1987): 680–707; and Richard Born, "Partisan Intentions and Election Day Realities in the Congressional Redistricting Process," *American Political Science Association* 79 (1985): 305–319.

34. For a discussion of redistricting in the 1990s, see Beth Donovan, "Political Dance Played Out Through Legal Wrangling," *Congressional Quarterly,* December 21, 1991, 3690–3695.

Chapter 11   Politics and the News Media

1. Walter Pincus, "Neutron Killer Warhead Buried in ERDA Budget," *Washington Post,* June 6, 1977, 1.

2. Ibid.

3. John Milton, *Areopagitica, in Complete Poems and Major Prose,* ed. Merritt Y. Hughes (New York: Odyssey, 1957), 746.

4. John Stuart Mill, *On Liberty* (New York: Norton, 1975), 18.

5. Thomas Jefferson, "Letter to Colonel Edward Carrington, January 16, 1787, " in *The Papers of Thomas Jefferson,* vol. 11, ed. Julian Boyd (Princeton, N.J.: Princeton University Press, 1955), 49.

6. For an extended discussion of how media reflect and affect society, see Fred S. Siebert, *Four Theories of the Press* (Urbana: University of Illinois Press, 1956).

7. The conviction of Iran-contra defendant Oliver North was overturned by a federal appeals court on the grounds that the testimony of witnesses against North might have been influenced by the public congressional hearings in which North was promised immunity from prosecution. The special investigator who prosecuted North could not prove that the witnesses had not been influenced by the hearings, and so their testimony could not be used against North in the trial.

8. Public television and radio stations in the United States depend primarily on contributions from viewers and listeners and from corporate sponsors. They may receive government grants for specific programs, but their operating costs are not paid by the government.

9. According to the 1993 edition of *Editor and Publisher's International Yearbook,* an annual that lists all publications in the United States, there were 1,570 daily newspapers in February 1993. Of these, 24 published in cities with populations of

more than 1 million; 28 served populations between 500,000 and 1 million; and 843 reached populations of less than 25,000.

10. Doris Graber, *Mass Media and American Politics*, 3rd ed. (Washington, D.C.: Congressional Quarterly, 1989), 45.

11. Times Mirror Company, "The People and the Press" (November 1989), 13.

12. See, for example, Ben H. Bagdikian, *The Media Monopoly* (Boston: Beacon, 1987); and W. Lance Bennett, *News: The Politics of Illusion* (New York: Longman, 1988).

13. Michael Parenti, *Inventing Reality: The Politics of the Mass Media* (New York: St. Martin's, 1986).

14. Austin Ranney, "Broadcasting, Narrowcasting, and Politics," in *The New American Political System*, 2nd version, ed. Anthony King (Washington, D.C.: American Enterprise Institute, 1990), 195.

15. Thomas R. Dye, Harmon Zeigler, and S. Robert Lichter, *American Politics in the Media Age*, 4th ed. (Pacific Grove, Calif.: Brooks/Cole, 1992), 85.

16. S. Robert Lichter, Stanley Rothman, and Linda S. Lichter, *The Media Elite* (Bethesda, Md.: Adler and Adler, 1986), 294.

17. Ibid.

18. Times Mirror Company, "The People and the Press," 13–15.

19. U.S. Bureau of the Census, *Statistical Abstract of the United States 1993* (Washington, D.C., 1993), 561.

20. Mike Mills, "Senate Action on Cable Bill Provokes Clash of Titans," *Congressional Quarterly,* January 11, 1992, 49.

21. Ranney, "Broadcasting, Narrowcasting, and Politics," 190–191.

22. Ibid., 192.

23. "Questions of Character," *Media Monitor* (April 1992), 6.

24. "Clinton's the One," *Media Monitor* (November 1992), 2. The average length of a statement by the candidate, known as a sound bite, that appeared on the evening news in 1988 was 9.8 seconds; in 1992 it was 8.4 seconds.

25. Ibid.

26. "The Parties Pick Their Candidates," *Media Monitor* (March 1992), 2.

27. "Battle of the Sound Bites," *Media Monitor* (August-September 1992), 5.

28. "Clinton's the One," 3.

29. S. Robert Lichter, Daniel Amundson, and Richard Noyes, *The Video Campaign: Network Coverage of the 1988 Primaries* (Washington, D.C.: American Enterprise Institute, 1989), 111.

30. Doris Graber, "Presidential Images in the 1968 Campaign" (Paper delivered at the annual meeting of the Midwest Political Science Association, Chicago, April 30–May 2, 1980), 3.

31. Richard L. Berke, "Why Candidates Like Public's Questions," *New York Times*, August 15, 1992, 7.

32. Lichter, Amundson, and Noyes, *The Video Campaign*, 12.

33. "The Parties Pick Their Candidates," *Media Monitor* (March 1992), 2.

34. Graber, *Mass Media and American Politics*, 236.

35. Ibid., 261.

36. "The Postwar President: TV News Coverage of the Bush Administration, 1989–1991," *Media Monitor* (November 1991), 2; and "Election Update: The Fall Campaign," *Media Monitor* (October 1992), 5.

37. Timothy E. Cook, *Making News and Making Laws* (Washington, D.C.: Brookings Institution, 1989), 7.

38. For an extended discussion of the impact of the media on policy making, see Martin Linsky, *Impact: How the Press Affects Federal Policymaking* (New York: Norton, 1986), 87–147.

Chapter 12   Congress

1. The members of each Congress and their districts are described in detail in Congressional Quarterly's *Politics in America* series, which is updated after each congressional election.

2. House of Representatives, Commission on Administrative Review, *Administrative Reorganization and Legislative Management,* vol. 2, 95th Cong., 1st sess. (1977), 38.

3. See John R. Johannes, *To Serve the People: Congress and Constituency Service* (Lincoln: University of Nebraska Press, 1984).

4. For an overview of congressional reform, see David W. Brady, Joseph Cooper, and Patricia A. Hurley, "The Decline of Party in the U.S. House of Representatives, 1887–1968," *Legislative Studies Quarterly* 4 (1979): 381–407.

5. The term *whip* derives from a participant in English fox hunts, the "whipper-in," whose task was to keep the hounds from leaving the pack.

6. See Barbara Sinclair, "House Majority Party Leadership in the Late 1980s," in *Congress Reconsidered,* ed. Lawrence C. Dodd and Bruce I. Oppenheimer (Washington, D.C.: Congressional Quarterly, 1989).

7. For a former Speaker's view, see Thomas P. O'Neill, Jr., and William Novak, *Man of the House* (New York: Random House, 1987).

8. See Frank H. Mackaman, ed., *Understanding Congressional Leadership,* (Washington, D.C.: Congressional Quarterly, 1981).

9. Quoted in Robert L. Peabody, *Leadership in Congress* (Boston: Little, Brown, 1976), 339–340.

10. See Samuel C. Patterson and Gregory A. Caldeira, "Party Voting in the United States Congress," *British Journal of Political Science* 18 (1988): 111–131.

11. See Richard L. Hall, "Participation and Purpose in Committee Decision Making," *American Political Science Review* 81 (1987): 105–127.

12. See Gary C. Jacobson, *The Politics of Congressional Elections,* 2nd ed. (Boston: Little, Brown, 1987).

13. See Steven S. Smith and Christopher J. Deering, *Committees in Congress* (Washington, D.C.: Congressional Quarterly, 1984).

14. See Steven S. Smith, *Call to Order: Floor Politics in the House and Senate* (Washington, D.C.: Brookings Institution, 1989).

15. See John W. Kingdom, *Congressmen's Voting Decisions,* 3rd ed. (Ann Arbor: University of Michigan Press, 1989).

16. See Walter J. Oleszek, *Congressional Procedures and Policy Process,* 3rd ed. (Washington, D.C.: Congressional Quarterly, 1989).

17. See Roger Davidson, *The Role of*

the Congressman (New York: Pegasus, 1969).

18. Richard F. Fenno, Jr., *Homestyle: House Members in Their Districts* (Boston: Little, Brown, 1978), 1.

19. House of Representatives, Commission on Administrative Review, *Final Report*, 95th Cong., 1st sess. (1977), 830.

20. See Johannes, *To Serve the People*, 64.

21. See, for example, Morris S. Ogul, *Congress Oversees the Bureaucracy* (Pittsburgh, Penn.: University of Pittsburgh Press, 1976).

22. A dated but rich analysis is Richard F. Fenno, Jr., *The Power of the Purse* (Boston: Little, Brown, 1966). A more recent study is D. Roderick Kiewiet and Mathew D. McCubbins, *The Spending Power* (Chicago: University of Chicago Press, 1990).

23. On the actions of congressional appropriations committees, see Aaron Wildavsky, *The New Politics of the Budgetary Process* (Glenview, Ill.: Scott, Foresman, 1988).

24. See Raoul Berger, *Impeachment* (Cambridge, Mass.: Harvard University Press, 1973).

25. Quoted in "Oversight Congress," *Congressional Quarterly Weekly Report*, December 22, 1979, 2880.

26. See Burdett Loomis, *The New American Politician* (New York: Basic Books, 1988).

27. See Burton D. Sheppard, *Rethinking Congressional Reform* (Cambridge, Mass.: Schenkman, 1985).

28. See, for example, David W. Rohde, *Parties and Leaders in the Postreform House* (Chicago: University of Chicago Press, 1991).

Chapter 13   The Presidency

1. For an excellent discussion of the leadership dilemma that contemporary presidents face, see Bert A. Rockman, *The Leadership Question* (New York: Praeger, 1984).

2. Our knowledge of the debates in the Constitutional Convention comes from the diaries of the delegates, the most comprehensive of which was written by James Madison. A historian interested in this period, Max Farrand, compiled these diaries in a comprehensive collection of original sources on the Constitutional Convention. See Max Farrand, ed., *Records of the Federal Convention* (New Haven, Conn.: Yale University Press, 1937). For a more recent analysis, see Sidney M. Milkis and Michael Nelson, *The American Presidency: Origins and Development, 1776–1990* (Washington, D.C.: Congressional Quarterly, 1990), 1–68.

3. Thomas E. Cronin, ed., *Inventing the American Presidency* (Lawrence: University of Kansas Press, 1989).

4. Presidents have used executive agreements to circumvent the treaty-making provision of the Constitution. Treaties require ratification by two-thirds of the Senate; executive agreements do not. In fact, executive agreements may not require any congressional concurrence if no new authorization or appropriations are required.

5. Richard E. Neustadt, *Presidential Power and the Modern Presidents* (New York: Free Press, 1990).

6. George C. Edwards III, *At the Margins* (New Haven, Conn.: Yale University Press, 1989), 124.

7 Samuel Kernell, *Going Public* (Washington, D.C.: Congressional Quarterly, 1986).

8. When new departments are created by act of Congress, the heads of those departments are automatically invited to cabinet meetings. The increasingly technical nature of policy making and the need for highly specialized information also makes it difficult for department heads to be familiar enough with issues outside their own areas to carry on an intelligent discussion.

9. For an excellent institutional history of this presidential agency, see Larry Berman, *The Office of Management and Budget and the Presidency, 1921–1979* (Princeton, N.J.: Princeton University Press, 1979).

10. The White House budget is supplemented by other executive departments that provide services for the president and his staff. These include units of the Defense Department, such as White House Communications (secure communications), the Air Force (air transportation for the president and vice president), the Army (explosives detection and ground transportation), and the Navy (helicopter transportation, Marine guards, food and medical facilities). They also include the General Services Administration (buildings and grounds), National Park Service (visitors and the fine-arts collection), National Archives (custody of official documents), Secret Service (protection of president, vice president, and their families), and the State Department (state visits and receptions).

11. John Sununu, Bush's first chief of staff, had become an embarrassment to the administration because of his personal use of White House cars and airplanes. Moreover, he had become a political liability because he had antagonized many members of Congress and executive-branch officials by his brusque and abrasive manner. Bush replaced him with his transportation secretary, Samuel Skinner, a person whose style was more low-key and conciliatory.

12. John Adams, *The Works of John Adams*, vol. 1, ed. C. F. Adams (Boston: Little, Brown, 1850), 289.

13. Thomas Jefferson, *The Writings of Thomas Jefferson*, vol. 1, ed. P. L. Ford (New York: Putnam, 1896), 98–99.

14. For a discussion of presidential illnesses, see Michael P. Riccards, "The Presidency: In Sickness and Health," *Presidential Studies Quarterly* 7 (Fall 1977): 215–231.

15. Tom Mathews, "The Road to War," *Newsweek*, January 28, 1991, 60.

16. James David Barber, *The Presidential Character*, 4th ed. (Englewood Cliffs, N.J.: Prentice-Hall, 1992).

17. Jeffrey Tulis, "On Presidential Character," in *The Presidency in the Constitutional Order*, ed. Joseph M. Bessette and Jeffrey Tulis (Baton Rouge: Louisiana State University Press, 1981), 293–301.

18. John P. Burke and Fred I. Greenstein, *How Presidents Test Reality* (New York: Russell Sage, 1989).

19. Charles O. Jones, "Presidents and Agendas: Who Defines What for Whom?" in *The Managerial Presidency*, ed. James P. Pfiffner (Pacific Grove, Calif.: Brooks/Cole, 1991), 197–213.

20. Charles O. Jones, *The Trusteeship*

Presidency (Baton Rouge: Louisiana State University Press, 1988).

21. Quoted in Barbara Kellerman, *The Political Presidency* (New York: Oxford University Press, 1984), 25.

22. Jones, "Presidents and Agendas," 199.

23. Edwards, *At the Margins,* 213–234.

24. This theory of the two presidencies was first postulated by Aaron Wildavsky in "The Two Presidencies," *Trans-Action* 4 (December 1966): 7–11. It has subsequently engendered considerable debate. Much of that debate appears in Steven A. Shull, ed., *The Two Presidencies: A Quarter Century Assessment* (Chicago: Nelson-Hall, 1991).

Chapter 14   The Executive Bureaucracy

1. The source of the preceding quotations is *Congressional Quarterly Weekly Report,* November 12, 1988, 3315.

2. See Francis J. Leazes, *Accountability and the Business State: The Structure of Federal Corporations* (New York: Praeger, 1987.

3. See Thomas R. Wolanin, *Presidential Advisory Commissions: Truman to Nixon* (Madison: University of Wisconsin Press, 1975).

4. See Martin Tolchin and Susan Tolchin, *To the Victor: Political Patronage from the Clubhouse to the White House* (New York: Random House, 1971).

5. See G. Calvin Mackenzie, ed., *The In and Outers* (Baltimore, Md.: Johns Hopkins University Press, 1987).

6. Harold Seidman, *Politics, Position, and Power,* 3rd ed. (New York: Oxford University Press, 1980), 29.

7. Randall B. Ripley and Grace A. Franklin, *Policy Implementation and Bureaucracy* (Chicago: Dorsey, 1986).

8. Faith Hawkins and John M. Thomas, *Making Regulatory Policy* (Pittsburgh, Penn.: University of Pittsburgh Press, 1989).

9. See Susan J. Tolchin and Martin Tolchin, *Dismantling America: The Rush to Deregulate* (New York: Oxford University Press, 1985).

10. See Susan Rose-Ackerman, *Rethinking the Progressive Agenda: The Reform of the American Regulatory State* (New York: Free Press, 1992).

11. See Jerry L. Mashaw, *Due Process in the Administrative State* (New Haven, Conn.: Yale University Press, 1985).

12. George J. Gordon, *Public Administration in America,* 2nd ed. (New York: St. Martin's, 1982), 494. New requirements that most rules must be published twice have accounted for some of the growth in the *Federal Register.*

13. See Philip J. Cooper, *Public Law and Public Administration* (Englewood Cliffs, N.J.: Prentice-Hall, 1988).

14. See John Hanrahan, *Government by Contract* (New York: Norton, 1983).

15. A classic study of such bureaucratic cultures is Herbert Kaufman, *The Forest Ranger: A Study in Administrative Behavior* (Baltimore, Md.: Johns Hopkins University Press, 1967).

16. See Eugene Lewis, *Public Entrepreneurship: Toward a Theory of Bureaucratic Political Power* (Bloomington: Indiana University Press, 1980).

17. Reported in Graham T. Allison, *Essence of Decision: Explaining the Cuban Missile Crisis* (Boston: Little, Brown, 1971), 131–132.

18. Kenneth J. Meier, *Politics and the Bureaucracy: Policymaking in the Fourth Branch of Government,* 2nd ed. (Monterey, Calif.: Brooks/Cole, 1987), 65.

19. Francis E. Rourke, *Bureaucracy, Politics, and Public Policy,* 2nd ed. (Boston: Little, Brown, 1976), 134–135.

20. See Alfred F. Hurley, *Billy Mitchell: Crusader for Air Power* (New York: Franklin Watts, 1964).

21. See Arthur Belonzi, *The Weary Watchdogs: Governmental Regulators in the Political Process* (Wayne, N.J.: Avery 1977).

22. Francis E. Rourke, *Bureaucracy, Politics, and Public Policy,* 3rd ed. (Boston: Little, Brown, 1976), 91–122.

23. Richard F. Fenno, Jr., *The Power of the Purse: Appropriations Politics in Congress* (Boston: Little, Brown, 1966), 288, 337.

24. See Wallace E. Walker, *Changing Organizational Culture: Strategy, Structure, and Professionalization in the U.S. General Accounting Office* (Knoxville: University of Tennessee Press, 1986).

25. The classic and still-valuable study is Fenno, *The Power of the Purse.* Also see Aaron Wildavsky, *The New Politics of the Budgetary Process* (New York: HarperCollins, 1992).

26. See the description of this in Charles O. Jones, *The Trusteeship Presidency: Jimmy Carter and the United States Congress* (Baton Rouge: Louisiana State University Press, 1988), 143–149.

27. For a description of the procedures developed under the Freedom of Information Act, see *How to Use the Freedom of Information Act* (Washington, D.C.: Washington Researchers Publishing, 1986).

Chapter 15   The Judiciary

1. Report of the Director, *Administrative Office of the United States Courts* (Washington, D.C.: Administrative Office of the United States Courts, 1991).

2. Quoted by Rowland Carp and Russell Wheeler, "Sink or Swim: The Socialization of a Federal District Judge," *Journal of Politics* 21 (1972): 359, 361.

3. See Wade McCree, Jr., "Bureaucratic Justice: An Early Warning," *University of Pennsylvania Law Review* 129 (1981): 777.

4. See Henry Glick and Kenneth Vines, *State Court Systems* (Englewood Cliffs, N.J.: Prentice-Hall, 1973).

5. For further discussion, see Ronald Collins and Peter Galie, "Models of Post-Incorporation Judicial Review," *University of Cincinnati Law Review* 55 (1986): 317.

6. *United States v. Students Challenging Regulatory Agency Procedures,* 412 U.S. 669 (1973).

7. See, for example, Lee Epstein, *Conservatives in Court* (Knoxville: University of Tennessee Press, 1985); Nan Aron, *Liberty and Justice for All: Public Interest Law in the 1980s and Beyond* (Boulder, Colo.: Westview, 1989); and Clement Vose, *Caucasians Only* (Berkeley: University of California Press, 1959).

8. Charles E. Hughes, *Addresses of Charles Evans Hughes,* (New York: Putnam, 1916), 185.

9. *Colegrove v. Green,* 328 U.S. 549 (1946).

10. Irving Kaufman, "Chilling Judicial Independence," *Yale Law Journal* 88 (1979): 681, 685. Also see Abraham Chayes, "The Role of the Judge in Public Law Litigation," *Harvard Law Review* 89 (1976): 1281.

11. Alexis de Tocqueville, *Democracy in America,* ed. Philip Bradley (New York: Doubleday, 1945), 151.

12. Steve Alumbaugh and C. K. Rowland, "The Links Between Platform-based Appointment Criteria and Trial Judges' Abortion Judgments," *Judicature* 74 (1990): 153.

13. Quoted in David M. O'Brien, *Storm Center: The Supreme Court in American Politics,* 3rd ed. (New York: Norton, 1993), 73.

14. Ibid., 74; Kennedy oral history interview.

15. Ibid.

16. Ibid., 78.

17. *Public Citizen v. U.S. Department of Justice,* 491 U.S. 440 (1989).

18. William H. Rehnquist, "Presidential Appointments to the Supreme Court" (lecture at the University of Minnesota, 1984), reprinted in *Constitutional Commentary* 2 (1985), 319.

19. Quoted by Henry J. Abraham, *Justices & Presidents,* 3rd ed. (New York: Oxford University Press, 1991), 72.

20. *In re Sindram,* 111 S.Ct. 596 (1991).

21. Quoted in O'Brien, *Storm Center,* 290.

22. Quoted by Alpheus T. Mason, *Harlan Fiske Stone: Pillar of the Law* (New York: Viking, 1956), 222.

23. Quoted by Alpheus T. Mason, *The Supreme Court from Taft to Burger,* 3rd ed. (Baton Rouge: Louisiana State University Press, 1979), 65.

24. *United States v. Nixon,* 418 U.S. 683 (1974).

25. Tom Clark, "Internal Operation of the United States Supreme Court," *Judicature* 43 (1959): 45, 51.

26. Letter (January 24, 1918), reprinted in *Pollock-Holmes Letters,* vol. 1, ed. Mark DeWolfe Howe (Cambridge, Mass.: Harvard University Press, 1942), 258.

27. Charles E. Hughes, *The Supreme Court of the United States* (New York: Columbia University Press, 1928), 68.

28. *Abington School District v. Schempp,* 374 U.S. 203 (1963).

29. *Norris v. Alabama,* 294 U.S. 587 (1935).

30. *Hernandez v. Texas,* 347 U.S. 475 (1954).

31. *Zurcher v. The Stanford Daily,* 436 U.S. 547 (1978).

32. *Texas v. Johnson,* 491 U.S. 397 (1989).

33. *United States v. Eichman,* 496 U.S. 310 (1990).

34. See Robert Dahl, "Decision-Making in a Democracy: The Supreme Court as a National Policy-Maker," *Journal of Public Law* 6 (1957): 279; and Richard Funston, "The Supreme Court and Critical Elections," *American Political Science Review* 69 (1975): 795.

35. See Donald Horowitz, *The Courts and Social Policy* (Washington, D.C.: Brookings Institution, 1977); and Raoul Berger, *Government by the Judiciary* (Cambridge, Mass.: Harvard University Press, 1977).

36. For further discussion of the Court's role as a policy maker, see Gerald Rosenberg, *The Hollow Hope: Can Courts Bring About Social Change?* (Chicago: University of Chicago Press, 1991).

Chapter 16 The Policy-Making Process

1. Sources for the preceding discussion include *Weekly Compilation of Presidential Documents,* June 13, 1989; *National Journal,* May 6, 1989, July 8, 1989, September 23, 1989, January 27, 1990, March 31, 1990; and *New York Times,* June 13, 1988, March 16, 1990, April 4, 1990, November 16, 1990, October 30, 1990.

2. James E. Anderson, David W. Brady, and Charles Bullock, *Public Policy and Politics in America* (North Scituate, Mass.: Duxbury, 1978), 5.

3. Charles O. Jones, *An Introduction to the Study of Public Policy,* 3rd ed. (Monterey, Calif.: Brooks/Cole, 1984), 43.

4. Theodore J. Lowi, "American Business, Public Policy Case Studies, and Political Theory," *World Politics* 16 (July 1964): 677–715. In later works Lowi added a fourth policy type, "constituent policies," which are administrative in nature and are of little concern to the public in general. For a critique of the Lowi scheme, see Hugh H. Heclo, "Review Article: Policy Analysis," *British Journal of Political Science* 2 (1972): 83–108.

5. See James E. Anderson, *Public Policy-Making* (New York: Praeger, 1975), 66–75, for a discussion of this point.

6. Douglas Cater, *Power in Washington* (New York: Random House, 1964), 17 (emphasis added).

7. Robert L. Lineberry, *American Public Policy* (New York: Harper & Row, 1978), 55.

8. Carol Matlack, "Moving from Capitol Hill to K Street," *National Journal,* April 20, 1991, 941. It should be noted that the congressional ethics bill passed in 1990 bars any member of Congress who left Congress after January 1, 1991, from lobbying activities for at least one year after leaving.

9. Rochelle L. Stanfield, "Stewing over Superfund," *National Journal,* August 8, 1987, 2031.

10. "Seat of the pants" is a term used by Anderson, Brady, and Bullock in *Public Policy and Politics in America,* 11.

11. Gary D. Brewer and Peter deLeon, *The Foundations of Policy Analysis* (Homewood, Ill.: Dorsey, 1983), 387.

12. Quoted in *New York Times,* October 20, 1993.

13. President Bush's news conference, August 15, 1989; *Weekly Compilation of Presidential Documents,* Office of the Federal Register, National Archives and Records Administration, Washington, D.C., vol. 25, no. 26, 1241–1248.

14. Quoted in *New York Times,* February 7, 1992.

Chapter 17 Domestic Policy

1. Speech to National Governor's Association, August 16, 1993, reprinted in *New York Times,* August 17, 1993.

2. Quoted in Robin Toner, "Complexities of the Middle of the Road,"

New York Times, November 9, 1993.

3. Quoted in Alissa J. Rubin and Ceci Connolly, "Clinton Delivers Health Bill, All 1,342 Pages of It," *Congressional Quarterly Weekly Report,* October 30, 1993, 2969.

4. Ibid.

5. Quoted in Advisory Commission on Intergovernmental Relations, *Intergovernmentalizing the Classroom: Federal Involvement in Elementary and Secondary Education* (Washington, D.C.: ACIR, 1981), 1.

6. Quoted in *Congressional Quarterly Weekly Report,* June 6, 1981, 1006.

7. Quoted ibid.

8. Quoted in *New York Times,* May 4, 1989.

9. Quoted in William Schneider, "Bush Is Reshaping the Schools Debate," *National Journal,* April 27, 1991, 1026.

10. Quoted in *New York Times,* July 5, 1991.

11. Quoted in *New York Times,* May 4, 1991.

12. Robert Pear, "Poverty in U.S. Grew Faster Than Population Last Year," *New York Times,* October 5, 1993.

13. Quoted in Julie Rovner, "The Catastrophic-Costs Law: A Massive Miscalculation," *Congressional Quarterly Weekly Report,* October 14, 1989, 2712.

14. Ibid., 2715.

15. *King v. Smith,* 392 U.S. 309 (1968); and *Lewis v. Martin,* 397 U.S. 552 (1970).

16. Similar points are made by Julie Kosterlitz, "Reexamining Welfare," *National Journal,* December 6, 1986, 2926–2931.

17. Quoted in *New York Times,* September 27, 1988, 1.

18. John J. Harrigan, *Politics and Policy in States and Communities,* 3rd ed. (Glenview, Ill.: Scott, Foresman, 1988), 429.

19. *Hills v. Gautreaux,* 425 U.S. 284 (1976).

20. *Village of Arlington Heights v. Metropolitan Development Corporation,* 429 U.S. 252 (1977).

21. The preceding discussion relies on the excellent account of urban renewal struggle presented by Dennis R. Judd, *The Politics of American Cities* (Glenview, Ill.: Scott, Foresman, 1988), 263–268.

22. See Herbert Gans, "The Failure of Urban Renewal: A Critique and Some Proposals," *Commentary,* vol. 39, no. 4 (April 1965): 29–37.

23. National Commission on Urban Problems, *Building the American City* (New York: Praeger, 1969), 153.

24. Martin Anderson, *The Federal Bulldozer: A Critical Analysis of Urban Renewal, 1949–1962* (Cambridge, Mass.: MIT Press, 1964), 65–66.

25. Harrigan, *Politics and Policy in States and Communities,* 432.

26. Jeffrey R. Henig, *Public Policy and Federalism: Issues in State and Local Politics* (New York: St. Martin's, 1985), 187–190.

27. Cited in Stephen Engleberg, "Leader of HUD Assesses It Harshly," *New York Times,* June 23, 1993.

28. Cited in Carol F. Steinbach, "Kemp's Crusade," *National Journal,* December 9, 1989, 2997.

29. For an excellent review of housing policy in the Bush years, see Carol F. Steinbach, "The Hour-Glass Market," *National Journal,* March 10, 1990, 568–577.

30. Quoted in Phil Kuntz, "Bush Plan Echos Reaganism," *Congressional Quarterly Weekly Report,* November 18, 1989, 3157.

31. Ibid.

32. Rochelle L. Stanfield, "Fewer Strings and Dollars," *National Journal,* February 27, 1993, 523.

33. For a presentation and discussion of these data, see J. Clarence Davis and Barbara S. Davis, *The Politics of Pollution,* 2nd ed. (Indianapolis: Pegasus, 1975).

34. "Major 'Greenhouse' Impact Is Unavoidable, Experts Say," *New York Times,* July 19, 1988.

35. James E. Anderson, David W. Brady, and Charles Bullock, *Public Policy and Politics in America* (North Scituate, Mass.: Duxbury, 1978), 76.

36. Ibid.

37. For background, see "Clean Air Act Rewritten, Tightened," *Congressional Quarterly Almanac,* 1990, 229–247.

38. Quoted in *New York Times,* June 13, 1989.

39. Quoted in *New York Times,* November 16, 1990.

40. Cited in Richard L. Berke, "Clinton Supports Two Major Steps for Environment," *New York Times,* April 22, 1993.

41. U.S. Department of Commerce, Bureau of the Census, *Statistical Abstract of the United States* (Washington, D.C.: 1992), 514.

42. Ibid., 515.

43. Quoted in Margaret E. Kriz, "A Bill Too Big for Its Britches?" *National Journal,* June 1, 1991, 1312.

Chapter 18   Economic Policy

1. The classic treatment of laissez faire is Adam Smith, *An Inquiry into the Nature and Causes of the Wealth of Nations* (1776; reprint, Oxford, England: Clarendon, 1976).

2. See Upton Sinclair, *The Jungle* (1906; reprint, Urbana: University of Illinois Press, 1988).

3. Quoted in Arthur M. Schlesinger, Jr., *The Crisis of the Old Order* (Cambridge, Mass.: Houghton Mifflin, 1957), 185.

4. See Herbert S. Parmet, The Democrats: *The Years After FDR* (New York: Macmillan, 1976).

5. *Inaugural Addresses of the Presidents of the United States* (Washington, D.C.: Government Printing Office, 1989), 273.

6. See Stephen K. Bailey, *Congress Makes a Law: The Story Behind the Employment Act of 1946* (New York: Columbia University Press, 1950).

7. *Inaugural Addresses of the Presidents of the United States* (Washington, D.C.: Government Printing Office, 1989), 332–335.

8. See Paul G. Schervish, *The Structural Determinants of Unemployment: Vulnerability and Power in Market Relations* (New York: Academic Press, 1983).

9. *Economic Report of the President, 1987* (Washington, D.C.: U.S. Government Printing Office, 1987), 307.

10. See Paul Peretz, *The Political Economy of Inflation in the United States* (Chicago: University of Chicago Press, 1983).

11. See Paul H. Light, *Artful Work: The Politics of Social Security Reform* (New York: Random House, 1985).

12. See Milton Friedman, *Monetarist Economics* (Cambridge, Mass.: Blackwell, 1991).

13. See John T. Wooley, *Monetary Politics: The Federal Reserve and the Politics of Monetary Policy* (New York: Cambridge University Press, 1984).

14. Quoted in James P. Pfiffner, ed., *The President and Economic Policy* (Philadelphia: Institute for the Study of Human Issues, 1986), 17.

15. See Herbert Stein, *The Fiscal Revolution in America* (Washington, D.C.: AEI Press, 1990).

16. For an interesting historical perspective, see Charles G. Dawes, *The First Year of the Budget of the United States* (New York: HarperCollins, 1923).

17. See John Maynard Keynes, *The General Theory of Employment, Interest, and Money* (Fort Worth, Tex.: Harcourt Brace Jovanovich, 1936).

18. See Benjamin M. Friedman, *Day of Reckoning: The Consequences of American Economic Policy Under Reagan and After* (New York: Random House, 1988).

19. See John B. Gilmour, *Reconcilable Differences: Congress, the Budget Process, and the Deficit* (Berkeley: University of California Press, 1990).

20. See Louis Fisher, *Presidential Spending Power* (Princeton, N.J.: Princeton University Press, 1975), 139.

21. See Joseph A. Pechman, *Federal Tax Policy*, 5th ed. (Washington, D.C.: Brookings Institution, 1987).

22. U.S. Department of Commerce, Bureau of the Census, *Statistical Abstract of the United States* (Washington, D.C., 1993), 338.

23. See Peter G. Peterson and Neil Howe, *On Borrowed Time: How the Growth in Entitlement Spending Threatens America's Future* (San Francisco: ICS Press, 1988).

24. See Richard J. Cebula, *The Deficit Problem in Perspective* (Lexington, Mass.: Lexington Books, 1987).

25. See Paul J. Quirk, *Industry Influence in Federal Regulatory Agencies* (Princeton, N.J.: Princeton University Press, 1981).

26. See Susan J. Tolchin and Martin Tolchin, *Dismantling America: The Rush to Deregulate* (New York: Oxford University Press, 1985).

27. See Robert B. Reich and John D. Donahue, *New Deals: The Chrysler Revival and the American System* (New York: Penguin, 1986).

28. See Stanley S. Surrey, *Tax Incentives* (Lexington, Mass.: Lexington Books, 1971).

29. *Congress and the Nation, Vol. 4, 1973–1976* (Washington, D.C.: Congressional Quarterly, 1977), 88.

30. Cited in Howard E. Shuman, *Politics and the Budget*, 2nd ed. (Englewood Cliffs, N.J.: Prentice-Hall, 1988), 102.

31. See Donald Dewey, *The Antitrust Experiment in America* (New York: Columbia University Press, 1990).

32. U.S. Department of Commerce, Bureau of the Census, *Statistical Abstract of the United States* (Washington, D.C., 1991), 431.

33. See Herbert Stein, *Governing the $5 Trillion Economy* (New York: Oxford University Press, 1989).

Chapter 19 Foreign and Defense Policy

1. Bernard Weinraub, "Bush and Congress Sign Policy Accord on Aid to Contras," *New York Times,* March 25, 1989, A1.

2. See Edward S. Corwin, *The President: Office and Powers, 1787–1984,* 5th ed. (New York: New York University Press, 1984).

3. For an example of presidential use of this power, see Eric Larrabee, *Commander in Chief: Franklin Delano Roosevelt, His Lieutenants and Their War* (New York: HarperCollins, 1987).

4. Quoted in Corwin, *The President,* 178.

5. See, for example, *Ware v. Hylton,* 3 U.S. 199 (1976); *Williams v. Suffolk Insurance Company* 13 Pet. 414 (1839); and *U.S. v. Curtiss-Wright Export Corporation,* 299 U.S. 304 (1936).

6. On the operation and procedures of the National Security Council, see Karl F. Inderfurth and Loch K. Johnson, eds., *Decisions of the Highest Order: Perspectives on the National Security Council* (Pacific Grove, Calif.: Brooks/Cole, 1988).

7. On presidential interaction with the National Security Council, see Carnes Lord, *The Presidency and the Management of National Security* (New York: Free Press, 1988).

8. The process is described in Robert F. Kennedy, *Thirteen Days: A Memoir of the Cuban Missile Crisis* (New York: Norton, 1969).

9. For a description of the interplay between the State and Defense departments during the Reagan years, see Lou Cannon, *President Reagan: The Role of a Lifetime* (New York: Simon and Schuster, 1991), 402ff.

10. Quoted in I. M. Destler, *Presidents, Bureaucrats, and Foreign Policy,* 2nd ed. (Princeton, N.J.: Princeton University Press, 1974), vi.

11. See Barry M. Rubin, *Secrets of State: The State Department and the Struggle Over U.S. Foreign Policy* (New York: Oxford University Press, 1985).

12. See Martin F. Herz, *The Modern Ambassador: The Challenge and the Search* (Washington, D.C.: Institute for the Study of Diplomacy, 1983).

13. Richard M. Nixon, *RN: The Memoirs of Richard Nixon,* vol. 2 (New York: Warner Books, 1978), 432–433.

14. Subsequently, however, the two countries agreed to a treaty to limit intermediate-range ballistic missiles.

15. For more on the Panama Canal treaties, see George D. Moffett, *The Limits of Victory: The Ratification of the Panama Canal Treaties* (Ithaca, N.Y.: Cornell University Press, 1989).

16. See Loch K. Johnson, *America's Secret Power: The CIA in a Democratic Society* (New York: Oxford University Press, 1989).

17. Quoted in Arthur M. Schlesinger, Jr., *A Thousand Days* (New York: Fawcett, 1965), 377.

18. For a discussion of these debates, see Hamilton Jordan, *Crisis: The Last Year of the Carter Presidency* (New York: Putnam, 1982).

19. Quoted in Arthur M. Schlesinger, Jr., *The Bitter Heritage: Vietnam and American Democracy, 1941–1966* (New York: Fawcett, 1967), 38.

20. See John E. Mueller, *War, Presidents and Public Opinion* (New York: Wiley, 1973).

21. For a more detailed discussion of postwar changes, see Charles W. Kegley and Eugene R. Wittkopf, *American Foreign Policy: Pattern and Process,* 3rd ed. (New York: St. Martin's, 1987), 35ff.

22. Quoted ibid., 85.
23. *Economic Report of the President, 1992* (Washington, D.C.: U.S. Government Printing Office, 1992), 318.
24. See Raymond Vernon, *Beyond Globalism: Remaking American Foreign Economic Policy* (New York: Free Press, 1989).
25. George Washington, "Farewell Address," in Robert A. Goldwin and Harry M. Clor, *Readings in American Foreign Policy,* 2nd ed. (New York: Oxford University Press, 1971), 127.
26. See James Mayall, *Nationalism and International Society* (New York: Cambridge University Press, 1990).
27. See Martin Feldstein, ed., *The United States in the World Economy* (Cambridge, Mass.: National Bureau of Economic Research, 1987).
28. See Walter Laqueur, *The Age of Terrorism* (Boston: Little, Brown, 1987).
29. A recent update on the status of the war power may be found in Marc E. Smyrl, *Conflict or Codetermination? Congress, the President, and the Power to Make War* (Cambridge, Mass.: Ballinger, 1988).
30. This provision was later changed to employ a joint resolution, which requires the president's signature, as the mechanism for withdrawing troops before the end of the sixty-day period.

Index to References

Index

Throughout this index, the lowercase letters *c*, *t*, and *f* indicate *captions*, *tables*, and *figures* respectively.

King, Martin Luther, Jr., 153, 154, 155*c*, 382
King, Rodney, 124*c*
Kinsley, Michael, 188
Kirkland, Lane, 189
Kissinger, Henry, 707
Kitchen debate, 485
Klopfer v. North Carolina, 107
Knights of Labor, 247
Knoke, David, 252
Know-Nothing Party, 247, 293*t*
Knox, Henry, 39
Koch, Edward, 81
Korean War, 732
Krueger, Bob, 348
Ku Klux Klan, 8, 145*c*, 145, 173, 218

Labor, government intervention, 693
Labor unions, formation of, 247
Laissez faire, 655
Lame duck, 493
Lamp, Virginia, 572*c*
Landfills
    federal standards for, 78
    Freshkill landfill, 78*c*
Landon, Alf, 213, 214
La Raza, 247
LaRouche, Lyndon, 293–294
Laumann, Edward, 251
Lautenberg, Frank, 607
Law
    administrative law, 553
    admiralty/marine law, 553
    civil law, 553
    common law, 553
    Constitutional law, 553
    criminal law, 553
    and functioning of government, 11–12
    statutory law, 553
Lawmaking process, 431–439
    amendments to bill, 434–435
    bill, introduction of, 432, 434
    filibuster, 438
    impediments in, 431–432
    killing of bill, 439
    mark-up session, 432, 434
    riders, 435
    rules and precedents related to, 436–439
    unanimous consent, 438
    veto, 436
    voting on bill, 435–436
Lawsuits
    requirements for gaining standing, 558
    standing to sue, 557
Lawyer's Edition, 166
Lead Contamination Control Act of 1988, purpose of, 79
Leahy, Patrick, 566
Lee v. Weisman, 138
Lefever, Ernest W., 749
LEGIS, 610
Legislation
    interpretation by president, 608
    and lobbying, 265–266
    See also Lawmaking process

Legislative branch
    bicameral structure, 39–40
    political party influences on, 309–310, 420
    powers of, 50
    presidential powers and duties, 465–468
    See also Congress; House of Representatives; Senate
Legislative courts, 552
Lenin, Joseph, 740*c*
Lescher, Richard, 253*c*
Lewis, John, 195–196
Libel, 148, 368–369
    definition of, 148
    and press, 368–369
    seditious libel, 143, 148
Liberalism/liberals, 224
    characteristics of, 224
    economic policy of, 660–661, 666
    of population, 225*f*
Libertarian Party, 286, 291*t*
Liberty
    American beliefs about, 15–16
    versus equality, 16, 19
Liberty Party, 286
Library of Congress, functions of, 56
Lichter, Linda, 384
Lichter, S. Robert, 384
Liddy, G. Gordon, 301
Light, Paul, 182, 188
Limited government, 46–48
Lincoln, Abraham, 71*c*, 286, 287*c*, 473, 488
Lincoln Savings and Loan Bank of California, 269, 270
Lindberg, Charles, 731*c*
Lineberry, Robert, 604
Line-item veto, 462
Literacy tests, and voting, 155, 156
Literary Digest poll, 213, 216
Livingston, Robert L., 620
Loan guarantees, 687–688
Lobbying, 260–273
    changes related to, 269
    and computer technology, 264
    direct and indirect, 261–262*f*
    direct mail approach, 263–264
    functions of, 261
    influence on judiciary, 266–267, 269
    influence on president, 266
    intergovernmental lobby, 89–91
    and legislation, 265–266
    regulation of, 272–273
    targeted membership campaigns, 263–264
Local political parties
    as machines, 298–299
    organization of, 298–300
Locke, John, 48
Lockheed Corporation, 688
Los Angeles Times, 378
Love Canal, 606*c*, 642, 645
Lower, Ann, 87
Lowi, Theodore, 597, 605
Lynch v. Donnelly, 139*c*

McCain, John, 270, 271*c*

McCarthy, Eugene, 339
McCarthy, Joseph, 381, 401
McCormack, John, 424
McCormick v. United States, 326
McCorvey, Norma (Jane Roe), 205
McCulloch v. Maryland, 48, 69, 70, 76, 166
McCurry, Mike, 712*c*
McDonald, Forrest, 45
McGovern, George, 291, 339
McGrory, Mary, 188
Machines, local parties, 298–299
McNamara, Robert, 530
Macroeconomics, definition of, 696
Madison, James, 9, 38, 39, 41, 48, 53, 54, 70, 104, 135, 143, 244, 320
    accomplishments of, 41
Magna Carta, 104, 110
Majority rule, 9, 104
Malloy v. Hogan, 107
Manatt, Charles, 265
Mandatory appeal, 577
Mandatory entitlement program, 682
Manifest destiny, 7*c*
Mansfield, Mike, 423, 424, 425
Mapp v. Ohio, 107, 108
Marbury v. Madison, 53–54, 59, 69, 559
Marbury, William, 54
Marine Corps, 721
Marine law, 553
Marine Protection Research and Sanctuaries Act of 1977, 76
Mark-up session, 432, 434
Marshall, George C., 736
Marshall, John, 48, 49, 54, 59, 68, 105, 139, 559, 706–707
    accomplishments of, 53*c*, 69
Marshall Plan, 736
Marshall, Thurgood, 559*c*, 568, 582
    accomplishments of, 116
Maryland v. Craig, 123
Maseiantonio, Phillip, 594
Mason, George, 41
Massachusetts v. Sheppard, 108, 109
Masses, definition of, 231
Mass media
    Congress, coverage of, 400–403
    and democracy, 366–368
    economic trends related to, 372–373
    and elections, 302
    judiciary, coverage of, 403–404
    media elite concept, 384–385
    newspapers, 373–378
    and political socialization, 187–188
    presidency, coverage of, 397–400
    and public policy, 404
    radio, 378–380
    regulation of, 371–372
    technological changes related to, 385, 387–388
    television, 380–385
    trustworthiness of, 383*t*
Mass media and presidential elections, 381–382, 386*t*
    campaign advertising, 393–394
    candidates manipulation of news, 391–393